ALL-ROMANIZED
ENGLISH-JAPANESE
DICTIONARY

ALL-ROMANIZED

ENGLISH-JAPANESE DICTIONARY

by Hyōjun Rōmaji Kai

This reprint edition is published with the kind permission
of Mr. Taizo Ishizaka, Chairman of the Hyōjun Rōmaji Kai
and Mr. Masajikadono
Managing Director of the same organization.

Published by the Charles E. Tuttle Company, Inc.
of Rutland, Vermont & Tokyo, Japan
with editorial offices at
Suido 1-chome, 2-6, Bunkyo-ku, Tokyo, Japan

Library of Congress Catalog Card No. 73-90212

International Standard Book No. 0-8048-1118-0

First edition, 1961 by Hyōjun Rōmaji Kai, Tokyo
First Tuttle edition, 1973
Seventh printing, 1979

CHARLES E. TUTTLE COMPANY
Rutland, Vermont & Tokyo, Japan

PRINTED IN JAPAN

Representatives
Continental Europe: BOXERBOOKS, INC., *Zurich*
British Isles: PRENTICE-HALL INTERNATIONAL, INC., *London*
Australasia: BOOK WISE (AUSTRALIA) PTY. LTD.
104-108 Sussex Street, Sydney 2000

This reprint edition is published with the kind permission
of Mr. Taizo Ishizaka, Chairman of the Hyōjun Rōmaji Kai,
and Mr. Masaji Kadono,
Managing Director of the same organization.

Published by the Charles E. Tuttle Company, Inc.
of Rutland, Vermont & Tokyo, Japan
with editorial offices at
Suido 1-chome, 2–6, Bunkyo-ku, Tokyo, Japan

© 1973 by Charles E. Tuttle Co., Inc.

Library of Congress Catalog Card No. 73-90232

International Standard Book No. 0-8048-1118-0

First edition, 1961 by Hyōjun Rōmaji Kai, Tokyo
First Tuttle edition, 1974
Seventh printing, 1979

0082-000363-4615
PRINTED IN JAPAN

PREFACE

When we are on a trip in a foreign country, it may happen sometimes that we might have a sort of intellectual curiosity aroused of the language of the country, to say nothing of the business which is the chief purpose of our travel. As some experienced tourists remarked, it is a sort of recreation—a recreation of mind, if I might say.

Well, the same thing may be said in the case of foreign visitors to Japan. For instance, some foreigners may be curious and eager to know what word or expression in Japanese will correspond to such and such an English word. Thus I have long cherished an idea : What, if a dictionary which will answer all the questions of this kind were published? And the desirable dictionary should be a handy one of convenient pocket size.

Several years ago, when I was chosen president of the *Hyōjun Rōmaji Kai*, I had occasion to lay the above-mentioned idea before the members, who then unanimously approved of my plan. Thereupon we decided to carry out the plan at the earliest possible time.

At first, the present work was intended solely for foreign tourists and those people who desire to study the Japanese language, but later the aim was turned to the young Japanese students as well. Consequently the scope of the readers of this dictionary has become much wider and complex than was first expected.

Now, the Japanese language is a language which has developed in the form of writing with the aid of both Chinese characters and the Japanese syllabary, " kana "; and in compiling this dictionary not a Chinese character nor even a letter of " kana " has been used. So I think that the compilers have, perhaps, experienced almost the same difficulty in some respects, as did Dr. Hepburn, who a century or so ago compiled the Japanese and English Dictionary, laboring under the great difficulty of having had little to assist him from the works of predecessors in the same field.

Now that the work is completed, I find, to my regret, that there are not a few weak points and undesirable features in unity of forms and unpolished words in Japanese equivalents. It is my intention, however, to make a thorough revision some day and lay it before the public in an improved form.

Be that as it may, the Romanized Japanese Dictionary in which no Chinese character nor " kana " is used, so far as the Japanese language is concerned, is the very first that has ever been published in the world. Being interested in this cultural sense, I ardently wish such a kind of work will come out in a perfect form in the near future. With this desire, I will introduce this work into the public.

Now allow me to introduce Mr. Haruji Sato, Mr. Kozo Nishimura, Mr. Nobuya Ishigami, Miss Yuriko Tamemitsu, and Miss Junko Shimada, who were kind enough to write the manuscripts; they are all teachers of senior high schools in Tokyo.

My gratitude is due to Mr. Masaji Kadono, president of the Okura Shoji K. K., Mr. Fujio Mamiya, lecturer of the Toyo University, Mr. Haruji Sato, ex-professor of the Okura Higher Commercial School, and Mr. Shin'ichi Miyazaki, a chief of a section in the Tokyo High Public Prosecutor's Office, who have given us unstinted assistance in reading the proofs.

iii

Again I must express my deep sense of gratitude to Dr. Sanki Ichikawa, who gave me valuable advice and suggestions, and Prof. Ryoichi Inui, professor of the Tokyo Foreign Language University and lecturer of Tokyo University, who have assisted me in carefully reading the proofs and Mr. Edmund C. Wilkes of USAFI, who was so kind as to give some valuable suggestions of the gramatical notes.

Lastly, in publishing this dictionary, I wish to express my deep sense of gratitude to Mr. Ichiro Yano, president of the Yano Zaidan Hojin and Mr. Kiyoshi Ichimura, president of the Riken Kogaku Kogyo K. K. both of whom were kind and generous enough to afford us no small amount of financial assistance.

Taizo Ichizaka

1961   President of
              Zaidan Hojin Hyojun Romaji Kai

Pronunciation Guide of Japanese

a is like English **a** in *father*.

b is like English **b** in *bed*.

d is like English **d** in *dog*.

e is like English **e** in *egg*.

f is a bi-labial voiceless fricative, not labio-dental.

g is like English **g** in *get*; but even before **e,i** and **y** it is always hard.

h is like English **h** in *hen*. As in English, this is also used in digraph, **ch** and **sh**.

i is like English **i** in *in*; but the front of tongue is pressed a little upwords.

j is like English **j** in *joy*.

k is like English **k** in *kit*.

m is like English **m** in *man*.

n is like English **n** in *neck*; but when it is used as syllabic, standing at the end of a word, it is pronounced with the tip of tongue hanging loosely; a peculiar nasal in Japanese.

o is like English **o** in initial vowel of diphthong **o** [ou].

p is like English **p** in *pen*.

r is pronounced with the tip of tongue moving midway of English l and r.

s is like English **s** in *sit*, but never voiced.

t is like English **t** in *top*.

u is like English **u** in *full*.

w is the vowel **u** consonantized; so it is going to be left out quite easily.

y is the vowel **i** consonantized as in the case of **w**. Being put into a syllable, between consonant and vowel, this makes up a palatilised syllables, as : **kya, pyu, myo**. etc.

z is like English **z** in *zinc*.

ch is like English **ch** in *chin*.

sh is like English **sh** unstressed.

ts is like an English affricate caused in the plural form of *cats*. Besides these 24 cardinal speech sounds there are five long vowels and seven long consonants.

Long vowels are put a macron over each the letter, except **i** that is two letters juxtaposed as **ii.**

Long consonants are called **sokuon** among the Japanese who are taught to think that they are each two consonants. In pronunciation, however, these **sokuons** are one consonant prolonged during double the time .

The long consonants are :—

-pp-; -tt-; -kk-; -ss-; -shsh- (written -ssh-); -ttsh- (written tch) -tts-.

Abbreviations Used in This Dictionary

a/djective	conjug/ation, -ive	mil/itary
ad/verb	conj/unction	min/eralogy
agric/ulture	elect/ricity	mus/ic
airp/lane	facet/ious	n/oun
Am/erica	fig/urative	onomat/opoea
anat/omy	flow/er	photo/graphy
Anc/ient	Fr/ance, -ench	philol/ogy, -cal
anim/al	geog/raphy, -ical	philos/ophy
arch/aic	geol/ogy	phys/ics
archi/tecture	Ger/man	physiol/ogy
arith/metic	G(ree)k	pl/ural
art/icle	gram/mar	poet/ry
astr/onomy	ins/ect	pref/ix
attr/ibute	inter/jection	prep/osition
base/ball	It/aly, -ian	pron/oun
biog/raphy	lang/uage	rel/igion
biol/ogy	leg/al	sing/ular
bot/any	ling/uistic	sl/ang
box/ing	liter/ature	suf/fix
Brit/ain, -ish	log/ic	surg/ery
Cath/olic	math/ematics	v/erb
cf. compare	med/icine, -al	
col/loquial	meteo/rology	

To Foreign Readers

Contents

Conjugative

Foreign readers who are not well versed in the Japanese language are advised to read the following suggestions; there are not a few peculiarities in the wording of Japanese sentences. For instance, one may think it very strange that a verbal phrase is used as an adjective in the very same word arrangement as it was a verbal phrase; or reversely, an adjective can, as a rule, stand in the predicate of a sentence without the help of any word as a copula.

Consequently there need be no use of relative pronouns or relative adverbs in Japanese. All such parts can be played by what are here named " **conjugative** ". By " **conjugative** " the author means,

> " a pattern of arrangement of words that have a common stem and significance, each holding its own special ending and usage."

In this sense, learning and studying the conjugatives is grasping the heart and core of the Japanese language. So we will see the conjugatives first, and then some other forms helpful to understanding this language.

Conjugatives

There are three large groups of conjugatives:
    I. Verb-Conjugatives
    II. Adjective-Conjugatives
    III. Auxiliary-Conjugatives

Conjugation

All these three conjugatives have each two kinds of conjugations; one is the Cardinal Conjugation and the other, the Perfect Conjugation.

I. Verb-Conjugative

There are two large branches of Verb-Conjugatives, as:
A. Aiueo-Branch
B. Rureyō-Branch

A. Aiueo-Branch

Aiueo-Branch is sub-divided into 9 sub-groups, which conjugate as follows:

1st. From	2nd F.	3rd F.	4th F.	5th F.	6th F.	
(a) kaka	kaki	kaku	kake	kakō	kaite	(to write)
(b) kaga	kagi	kagu	kage	kagō	kaide	(to smell)
(c) shina	shini	shinu	shine	shinō	shinde	(to die)
(d) toba	tobi	tobu	tobe	tobō	tonde	(to fly)
(e) yoma	yomi	yomu	yome	yomō	yonde	(to read)
(f) ura	uri	uru	ure	urō	utte	(to sell)
(g) osa	oshi	osu	ose	osō	oshite	(to push)
(h) uta	uchi	utsu	ute	utō	utte	(to strike)
(i) kawa	kai	kau	kae	kaō	katte	(to buy)

The endings are common to all the sub-groups of A. branch conjugatives. They are: -a, -i, -u, -e, -ō, -te, (or -de).

The Function

The function of these six forms of conjugation is common through all the A, B, branches of verb-conjugatives with but a very few exceptions which will be seen later. (Let us take (f) **uru** for the example of sentences.)

1. **The 1st Form. (ura)** This form is to be suffixed with (i) **-nai** (*negation*), (ii) **-seru** (*causation*), (iii) **-reru** (a, *passivity*; b, *ableness*; c, *politeness*).

(i) **-nai** (*negation*) Watashi wa **ura***nai*. (I do not sell (it)).

(ii) **-seru** (*causation*)

Yoroshii, watashi ga **ura***seru* kara.

(*Never mind; All right; Well. I will make him sell (it); or I will allow him to sell it*).

(iii) **-reru** (a. *passivity*)

Ura*reru* mi nimo natte miro. (*Suppose you are to be sold yourself; Let you be one who is to be sold.*)

-reru (b. *ableness*) Kyō ichinichi de minna **ura***reru* ka na? (*Do you think they (you) can sell them all in the course of today?*)

Note 1. In this suffixion, the ending " *-a* " of " *ra* " and the the initial " *-r* " of " *re* " (-r[a+r]e-) are often (rather commonly) left out and there is made up a new verb-conjugative form as :

kak[ar]eru   kag[ar]eru   shin[ar]eru
tob[ar]eru   yom[ar]eru   ur[ar]eru
os[ar]eru   ut[ar]eru   kaw[ar]eru=
                                       ka(w)eru

Note 2. These new verbs (kakeru ; kageru ; shineru ; toberu ; yomeru ; ureru ; oseru ; uteru ; kaeru) are used in the sense of " ableness ", and sometimes " natural effect ".

-reru (c. *politeness*) Ano kata mo tōtō ie o **ura***reru*. (*He also sells (will sell) his own house at last*) politer than " Kare mo tōtō ie o uru ".

2. **The 2nd Form. (uri)** This form is used in the following function, as :

(i) to make a polite remark with the auxiliary " **masu** ".

(ii) to express wishes with the auxiliary " **tai** ".

(iii) to express eager desire with the auxiliary " **tagaru** ".

(iv) to be used as a noun by itself.

(v) to make an adverb phrase by standing at the end of the phrase.

(vi) To be used as a noun-element in a compound word.

Examples :

(i) Watashi ga **uri** *masu*. (*I will sell it*). (Politer than " Ore ga **uru** ").

(ii) **Uri** *tai* nara o-**uri** nasai. (*If you would sell it, do as you like; Sell it if you would*).

(iii) Sonna ni **uri** *tagaru* nara urashite (**ura-seru**) yaru sa. (*If he is so eager to sell, let him do as he would*).

(iv) Tōtō ano ie mo **uri** ni deta. (*That house is put for sale at last*).

(v) Ie o **uri**, hatake o **uri**, tōtō kyōri o dete shimatta. (*Selling the house, and then the farm, he left his native village at last*).

(vi) hana**uri** (*a flower seller*); **uri**isogi (*selling in a hurry*); **uri**kire (*being sold out*); **uri**dashi (*opening sale; bargain sale*); yobi**uri** (*hawking*), etc.

3. **The 3rd Form. (uru)** This form is used,

(i)   to show likelihood with the auxiliary, "**rashii**".

(ii) to state negative supposition with "**mai**".

(iii) to modify a noun.

(iv) to predicate a sentence.

(v) the representative form of the conjugative.

Examples:

(i) Ano ie o **uru** *rashii*.
     (*He seems to (be going to) sell that house*).

(ii) Iya, ano ei wa **uru** *mai*.
     (*Really? I think he won't sell that house*).

(iii) Hoka ni **uru** *mono* ga nai. (*I have nothing else to sell*).

(iv) Watashi no mono o **uru**. (*I'll sell my own things*).

(v) **Uru** to iu dōshi wa aiueo-branch no go desu.
     (*The verb "**uru**" belongs to the "aiueo-branch"*).

4. **The 4th. From (ure)** This form is used:

(i) as a conditional adverb with "**-ba**" suffixed:
     Ano hon o **ure**ba mō uru mono wa nai.
     (*If I sell that book, I'll have nothing else to sell*).

(ii) as imperative
     Kimi, sono hon o watashi ni **ure** yo.
     (*You sell me that book, I ask you*).

Note: In this use "**yo**" is usually added to make the statement mild. (*How about selling me that book?*)

5. **The 5th. Form. (urō)** Remark of one's determination is chiefly expressed in this form, as:

(i) **Urō** to iu nara watashi ga kaō.
    (*If he would* (*sell*), *I would buy it*).
    Literary : *If he says he will sell, I will buy it*.

(ii) **Urō.** Anna mono motte ite mo shiyōga nai.
    (*I'll sell it. Such a thing is no worth keeping*).

(iii) **Urō** to uru mai to sore wa nanata no kangae da.
    (*To sell it or not, that depends upon your own will*).

6. The 6th Form. (utte)

(i) Here is another adverbial phrasing ;
(ii) used in entreaty ;
(iii) the nucleus to the Perfect Conjungation.

Examples :

(i) Kore o **utte** atarashii no o kaō.
    (*Selling this* (it) *I'd buy a new one*).

(ii) Sore o **utte** yo. (*Please sell it*).

Note : This pattern of remark is mostly used by young women, though sometimes a man may use it as :

    Omae kaettara sō **itte** yo ne. (*Tell him so when you go home*).

(iii) English perfect tenses are to be compared with our **"Perfect Conjugation"**, for they both treat an action or an event as done and finished. English perfect tenses are expressed with the auxiliary verb " have " while Japanese Perfect Conjugations are formed by suffixing the following endings in place of -e of this 6th form **utte**, as :

1st F.	2nd F.	3rd F.	4th F.	5th F.	6th F.
—	utt-ari	utt-a	utt-ara	utt-arō	—

These endings of the Perfect Conjugation are thoroughly universal throughout all the conjugatives.

The Function

1. **The 1st Form.** Does not exist.
2. **The 2nd Form.** (uttari) (Juxtaposing adverbial)
    Uttari, kattari, shite kurashi o tatete iru.
    (*He supports his family by buying and selling things* —literary meaning).
3. **The 3rd Form.** (utta) This form is used,

(i) to show likelihood with the auxiliary "*rashii*".
(ii) as an adjective (something like English pp. of the verb).
(iii) as a predicate of a sentence.
Examples :
(i) Ano ie o **utta** rashii. (*He seems to have sold that house*).
(ii) Kinō **utta** hon wa minna de 30-satsu datta.
    (*The books I sold yesterday were thirty volumes in all*).
(iii) Sayō, kinō **utta**. (*Yes, I sold (them) yesterday*).
4. The 4th Form. (uttara) Supposing a remark to be an action perfected; that is, Subjunctive Future.
    Kono hon o **uttara** dore kurai neuchi ga aru darō ka?
    (*How much do you think these books are worth if I should sell?*)
5. The 5th Form. (uttarō) This form states a supposition, relying on a fact already recongized, as :
    Sore jā ano ie mo mō **uttarō**. (*If so, he must have sold that house now*).
6. The 6th Form. Does not exist.

These ten forms (6 cardinals and 4 perfects) of conjugation are all that one conjugative can make out to express the thoughts and feelings in the Japanese language.

B. Rureyō-Branch

Besides the Aiueo-Branch there is one more important branch of verb-conjugative, as before-mentioned. It is the **Rureyō-Branch**. The conjugation of this branch is as follows :

    1st F. 2nd F. 3rd F. 4th F. 5th F. 6th F.
(j) ori   ori   oriru orire oriyō orite (to get down)
(k) uke   uke   ukeru ukere ukeyō ukete (to receive)
    The endings are : —, —, -ru, -re, -yō, -te.
Note 1. Because of the endings this branch is called **Rureyō-Branch**.
Note 2. The two verb-conjug. here adopted, (j) and (k), are of quite the same kind, as it is the case with A.-branch. After Kana grammar, however, these are classified as (a) i-rureyō, (b) u-rureyō, owing to the stem vowel.

The Function

The functions of **B. branch** are quite the same as those of

A.-branch, except for some trivial differences that will be found as :

1. **The 1st Form. (ori)** " -saseru " and " -rareru " are used as auxiliaries instead of " -seru " and " -reru " respectively. The examples are as follows :

(i) " Oriro yo? Abunai kara." " Iya, ori*nai*."
    (" *Come down, I say. It is dangerous.*" " *No, I won't* ").

(ii) Are o ori*sashite* kudasai. (*Make him come down, please*).

(iii) (a) Chotto mate. Sonna koto shite **orirarete** wa abunakute tamaranai. (*Wait a bit. I cannot bear (to see) to have you get down in that way*).

Note These " -reru " and " -rareru " are used as auxiliaries to remark *passivity* which correspond to the English passive voice. In this example, however, the boy's " dangerous way of coming down " is an action quite independent of the people thereabout, though some lookers-on may tremble for fear of the probability of the boy's receiving a serious injury by falling down. The boy on the tree does nothing to them nor they to him. But the auxiliary " -rareru " shows that the lookers-on are caused to feel uneasiness by the boy's reckless way. In the Japanese language this kind of passivity is quite commonly used. This also might be counted among one of Japanese peculiarities.

(iii) (b) Soko kara **orirareru** kai? (*ableness*)
    (*Can you get down from there?*)

(iii) (c) Ano kata ga orirarereba…(*politeness*)
    (*If he (deign to) get down…*)
    This expression is possible in Japanese, but the use is now decreasing.

2. **The 2nd Form. (ori)** (cf. A.-branch 2nd F.) Besides " masu ", " tai ", " tagaru ", the auxiliary " mai " is used in the 2nd Form in Rureyō-Branch, while in the Aiueo-Branch " mai " is used in the 3rd Form only. This is only difference in the 2nd F.

3. **The 3rd Form. (oriru)** This is quite the same as Aiueo-Branch with only exception of the foresaid " mai ".

4. **The 4th Form. (orire)**
    (i) The conditional use is similarly made with " -ba " suf-

fixed as in the case of Aiueo-Branch verb-conjugatives

(ii) As to the imperative use, a little change is necessary.
The last vowel " -e " of " -re " (orire; ukere etc.) must
be replaced with " -o "; that is, " oriro; ukero " are the
imperative remarks. (orire; ukere are dialectally used in
some districts).

5. **The 5th Form.** (oriyō) Quite the same as that of A.-
Branch.

6. **The 6th Form.** (orite) Quite the same as the form of
A-Branch conjugatives.

Irregurarity

The following two verb-conjug. which are only (remark-
able) irregular ones, must be noticed here in the Rureyō-
Branch. (n) is suffixing, as : ōzuru.

	1st F.	2nd F.	3rd F.	4th F.	5th F.	6th F.	
(l)	ko	ki	kuru	kure	koyō	kite	(to come)
(m)	shi	shi	suru	sure	shiyō	shite	(to do)
(n)	-ji	-ji	-zuru	-zure	-jiyō	-jite	(to do)

II. Adjective-Conjugatives

In most languages, the adjective does not conjugate, but
declines. In Japanese, however, there are something more
than declention. As formerly defined, this group of words
positively fulfil the conditions to be a conjugative; they have
as many forms and functions as the verb-conjugatives have.
The following is what the adjective-conjugatives conjugate :

	1st F.	2nd F.	3rd F.	4th F.	5th F.	6th F.	
	—	aka(k)u	akai	akakere	akakarō	akaku(t)te	(red)
	—	akakatt-ari -a		-ara	-arō	—	(Perf. Conjug.)

Card. Ending is   —, -(k)u, -i, -kere, -karō, -kut(t)e.

The Function (akai, for the example)

1. **The 1st Form.** Does not exist.
2. **The 2nd Form.** (akaku) This form is used

(i) to modify verb-conjugatives (Adverb-use).

(ii) sometimes as a noun by itself.

Examples

(i) **akaku** someru (*to dye red*); **akaku** nutta (*painted red*); etc. Most of Japanese adverbs are found here.

(ii) "**tōku**", "**chikaku**" and some such are used as nouns, as :

Tōku no shinrui yori **chikaku** no tanin.

(*A good neighbour living near is better than a brother far off*).

tōku ni; **chikaku** ni; **tōku** kara; **chikaku** kara etc.

Note: Some others are used in the same way, but they are not so many as those of verb-conjugatives.

3. **The 3rd Form.** (akai) This form is used:

(i) as predicate.

(ii) as the attribute of noun.

(iii) with "**rashii**" remarks a supposition.

Examples

(i) Nishi no sora wa yūhi de **akai**.

(*The western sky is aglow with the setting sun*). Sore wa **omoshiroi**. (*That is interesting; will be a fine fun*). The 3rd form of every adjective-conjugative can be used as predicate of a sentence.

(ii) Sono **akai hana** ga hoshii. (*I'd like to have that red flower*)).

(iii) Ano shōnen wa sukoshi **akai rashii.**

(*That boy seems affected red*).

4. **The 4th Form.** (akakere) This form is the conditional use about quality, with the **-ba** suffixed, as :

Sonna ni **akakereba** (**akakerya**) hoka no ni shiyō.

(*If you think it so red I'll take another color*).

5. **The 5th Form.** (akakarō) This form is used to remark one's opinion or supposition.

Sore wa sukoshi **takakarō**. (*That may be a little too red*).

6. **The 6th Form.** (akakutte)

(i) Used adverbial, as :

Sono kimono wa **akakutte** boku iya da nā.

(*The red color of the clothes is not to my taste; The clothes, being red, are not to my taste*).

Note "**Akakutte wa**" is usually contracted into **-cha,** (<**tya** <**tea**), in colloquial.

(ii) Nucleus of Perfect Conjugation

1 The 1st Form. Does not exist.

2 The 2nd Form. (**akakattari**) Used as "Juxtaposing Adverbial":

Akakattari, aokattari iroiro desu.

(*Some being red and others blue, they are various in color.*)

3 The 3rd Form. (**akakatta**) This form is

  (i) used as predicate:

    Sono hana wa minna **akakatta.** (*Those flowers were all red*).

  (ii) as attributive to a noun:

    Ima made **akakatta** hana ga atto iu ma ni kuroku natta. (*Those flowers that had been red to that very moment, turned black in the twinkling of an eye*).

4 The 4th Form. (**akakattara**) Conditionally used:

  Sonna ni **akakattara** sorya nisemono da yo.

  (*If it was so red it must be (have been) an imitation*).

5 The 5th Form. (**akakattarō**) Used for assurance of past fact, as

  Sono hon no hyōshi wa **akakattarō**

  (*The cover of that book was red, wasn't it?*)

6) Does not exist.

III. Auxiliary-Conjugatives

(As to the meaning, or significance, of these auxiliaries, refer to the examples of the respective forms of Aiueo-Branch). They conjugate, as:

1. tagaru	-ra	-ri	-ru	-re	-rō	-tte (A-Branch(f))
2. reru	—	—	-ru	-re	-yō	-te (B-Branch(k))
rareru	—	—	"	"	"	"
seru	—	—	"	"	"	" (")
saseru	—	—	"	"	"	"
3. tai	—	-ku	-i	-kere	-karō	-kutte (Adj.)
rashii	—	"	"	"	"	"

Note 1 "**Mai**" is defective, and has lost all other forms.

Note 2 The Perfect Conjugations can be inferred.

4. Two copulas, "**da**" and "**desu**" are defective, as:

	1st F.	2nd F.	3rd F.	4th F.	5th F.	6th F.
da	—	—	da	—	darō	datte
desu	—	—	desu	—	deshō	deshite
P.C.	—	-ari	-a	-ara	-arō	—

5. One more irregular auxiliary is "**masu**", which conjugates as: mase(n) mashi masu mase mashō mashite
masu (mase)

P.C. — -(t)ari -(t)a -(t)ara -(t)arō —

Note The 2nd form was used to say "mase" as the imperative, but at present "mashi" being used in its place, the imperative remark "mase" is thought classical.

IV. On Transitive Verb

Strictly speaking Japanese has no transitive verb, such as those defined in English grammar; for the word order of the two languages are fundamentally different.

(i) In English sentences the predicate verb comes, as a rule, next to the subject while Japanese one stands at the very end of the sentence. For example the sentence " I (1) taught (2) him (3) English (4)," is in Japanese, " Watashi ga (1) kare ni (3) Eigo o (4) oshieta (2) ", or " Watashi ga (1) Eigo o (4) kare ni (3) oshieta (2)." The objects **him** and **English** follow the predicate verb **taught** and complete the verbal sense by showing " What? " and " Whom? " In Japanese, however, they do not stand behind as objects but come before in position and naturally modify the action that the verb conveys, as phrases showing " When? " " Where? " " How? " " Whom? " or " What? " Their grammatical categories are quite different. They are adverbial phrases, but cannot be objects.

(ii) As to the passive voice Japanese depends upon auxiliary suffixes as before-mentioned. (cf. B. Rureyō-Branch Function: The 1st Form (iii) Note)

V. Adjectives as Modifiers

Japanese adjectives, modifiers of nouns, come from the following functions:
1. (a) The 3rd Form of all the verb-conjugatives (A, B branches).
   (b) The 3rd Form of the adjective-conjugative.
   (c) The 3rd Form of all the auxiliary-conjugatives, and the perfect conjugation of all the conjugatives. In other words, all the third forms of conjugations are used as the modifiers of following nouns.
2. Some nouns representing quality, when suffixed with "-na" (remnant of classical auxiliary "nari, naru, etc." *to be*) becomes adjectives as: **kirei-na** (*beautiful*) hana; **rippa-na** (*very good*) house; **shizuka-na** (*quiet; still*); **kyū-na** (*urgent; pressing; precipitous*); etc.

VI. Adverbs

Japanese adverbs come from
1. by repeating same syllables into one word, as: **daradara** (*in a sloven way*); **pikapika** (*sparkling; shining*) etc. (Sometimes the repeated initial consonant vocalized as: **komagoma,** minutely; in details.).
2. the 2nd form of the adjective-conjug., for its inherent function to modify a verb as adverb. For ex. **akaku nutta** (*painted red*); **hayaku hashiru** (*run fast*) etc. (cf. II. Adjective-Conjug.; the 2nd Form (i)).
3. the 6th form of all the conjugatives, as: **yonde** (*read* [red]); **tonde** (*flown*); **orite** (*got down*); **ukete** (*received*); **akakutte** (*being red*) etc.
4. a noun expressing **time** or **distance** etc., as **kinō** sore o yomi mashita. (*I read it yesterday*). **ima** i*ki* masu. (*I'll be there now*). **100-metoru** hashitta. ((He) ran 100-metres).
5. the 2nd form of perfect conjugation, as Kare to wa kono 4-nen **ittari, kitari** *shite iru*.

(I have enjoyed mutual visits with him these four years).

6. the 4th form of verb-conjugative (conditional) which is also used as sentence-modifier, as

Asuko e **ikeba,** wakaru yo.

(Go there, and (If you go there) you will see the fact).

7. the adjective suffixed " **-na** ", by replacing the " **-na** " with " **-ni** " (etymologically the same word—cf. IV. adjective 2). In this case, these **-na, -ni** with **-nara** may be arranged as an irregular and defective adjective-conjugative. The conjugation will be as:

1st F.   2nd F.   3rd F.   4th F.   5th F.   6th F.
  —   -ni   -na   —   -nara   —

Note ;   This conjugative is not yet approved among linguists, but practically its usage is firmly established.

VII.   On Particles

Though the particles are the smallest elements in sentence-building and are apt to be sometimes neglected, they are equally important to other parts of speech for the exact expression of the thoughts. They are to show the logical relations of sentences ; so we should recommend foreign readers to be as well informed of the usage as that of the aforementioned conjugatives, the backbone of the Japanese language. The following arbitrary allotment of the particles to the Latin cases may suggest the function of these small words.

Nominative	ga ; wa
Accusative	o (formerly *wo*)
Genitive	no
Dative	e ; ni ; made
Ablative	de ; to ; kara

Nominative

When there is a subject-noun (or noun equivalent) of a sentence there is necessarily **ga** or **wa** following to show the case relation. As these particles have each its proper significance it determines the exact meaning of the sentence. The following will show how their case relations are determined by the so-called inherent significance.

a) Hana **ga** saita (*Flowers bloomed*)—choice.
b) Hana **wa** saita(*"*)—contrast.
c) Watashi **ga** kaki mashita (*I wrote it*)
d) Watashi **wa** kaki mashita(*"*)

These two pairs of sentences have each a delicate difference in the meaning as the results of these two particles, as:

a) Hana **ga** saita, means "*Flowers bloomed*, (1) *which we have long awaited.* (2) *I am so glad to have flowers in full bloom* etc.

b) Hana **wa** saita, means "*But there is or are unsatisfied things left…*"

c) Watashi **ga** kaki mashita, means, "*It is I who wrote* (*it*), *for there was no one to do so etc.*"

d) Watashi **wa** kaki mashita, means, "*But others have not finished yet*", or "*I have done my duty, but do not know of others,*" etc.

Besides these nominative uses their proper meanings are also found in the following objective function in English, as,

Watashi (wa) pan ga tabe tai; gohan wa mō aki mashita. (*I'd like to eat bread; I grew tired of gohan-rice now.*)

In this sentence the subject is "I", gohan (*rice*) and pan (*bread*) are objects of the verb, "to eat".

So we see here that the two particles are used in their proper, inherent significance only to stand for nominative case.

Accusative

O. Owing to the syntactical word order Japanese cannot have, as above-mentioned, any object that the English grammar has. In sense, however, we can find the corresponding transitive verbs and the object-like phrase relating to the verb. This is an adverbial phrase modifying the following verb, but not object. So we should say that the **noun+o**-phrase stands for the object in English, as:

gohan **o** (*meal; rice*) taberu (*eat*).
Tegami **o** (*a letter*) kaku (*write*).
enzetsu **o** (*a speech*) suru (*deliver*).

Genitive

No. This particle corresponds to the English preposition

" of " that makes up an adjective phrase. The word-order is reverse as it is the case with the object just mentioned, as :

> tsukue (*table*) no (*of*) ashi (*legs*)
> **the legs of a table**
> hon (*book*) no (*of*) hyōshi (*cover*)
> **the cover of the book**

Dative

E. is a Japanese postposition meaning the direction of movement toward somewhere or something, as :

> Tōkyō e iku—go **to** Tokyo.
> mae e deru—to move forward
> sono naka e ireru—put (a thing) **into** it
> ita e ana o akeru—*bore a hole* **in** *a board*

Ni. corresponds to English *at, in, into*, etc.

> **at** : *I get up* **at** *seven every morning*—Watashi wa maiasa 7-ji ni okiru.
> *He was standing at the gate*—Kare wa toguchi **ni** (de) tatte ita.
> **in** : *He made a long stay* **in** *London*—Kare wa London *ni* nagatōryū o shita.
> *The sun rises* **in** *the east and sets* **in** *the west*—Hi wa higashi **ni** dete nishi **ni** iru.
> **into** : *He plunged* **into** *the depth*—Kare wa fuchi **ni** tobikonda.
> **to** : *I gave the book* **to** *Tom*—Watashi wa rei no hon o Tom **ni** yatta.

Made correlates with **kara** and corresponds with English preposition *before, till, until, to, up to* :

> **before** *We waited a long time* **before** *the train arrived* — —Watashi-tachi wa kisha ga tsuku **made** nagaku machi mashita.
> **till** : *from morning till night*—asa kara ban **made**.
> **until** : *until I come back*—Watashi ga kaeru **made**.
> **up to** : *Let us walk* **up to** *the castle*—Shiro **made** aruki mashō.

Ablative

De. English prepositions, *at, by, in, on, with*, etc. correspond with this particle as :

> **at** *The cab is waiting for you* **at** *the gate*—Okuruma ga mon

no tokoro **de (ni)** matte ori masu.

He died **at** *thirty*—Kare wa 30 **de** shinda.

Frank and I first met **at** *a dance*—F. to watashi wa butōkai **de** hajimete atta.

by: *I shall start* **by** *the eleven o'clock train*—watashi wa 11 ji no kisha **de** tatsu tsumori desu.

Many goods are bought and sold **by** *weight*—Ōku no shina ga mekata **de** urikai sareru.

in: *Speak to me* **in** *Japanese, please.*—Nippongo **de** ohanashi kudasai.

Don't write your answer **in** *pencil, but* **in** *pen and ink*—anata no tōan wa empitsu **de** kakanai **de,** pen **de** kaite kudasai.

I saw it **in** *the school*—W. wa sore o gakkō **de** mita.

on: *She brought up the child* **on** *milk.* kare wa milk **de** sono ko o sodateta.

from: *Wine is made* **from** *grape*—Budōshu wa budō **de** tsukuri masu.

To corresponds to English conjunctions **and, if,** etc.; and prepositions **for, with** etc.

and: *You and I*—Kimi **to** Boku

if: *He will be angry,* **if** *you do such a thing*—Sonna koto o suru **to (**sureba) kare wa okoru zo.

Whatever may happen...Nani goto ga okorō **to**...

for: *Will you please exchange this* **for** *that.*—Kore o sore **to** kaete kure masen ka?

with: *I will go* **with** *my father*—Watashi wa chichi **to** iki masu.

Kara is used in *place* (**from**), *time* (**since**), etc.

from: *How far is it* **from** *here to your school?*—Koko **kara** kimi no gakkō **made** dono kurai aru?

since: *It is five years* **since** *we saw you last.*—Watashi-tachi owakare shite **kara** mō 5 nen ni nari masu ne.

VIII How to Read Figures

Japanese has two ways of numerical appellation, as:

1. Influenced (by Chinese Characters).
2. Original.

1. "Influenced" has been established by reading those

Chinese numerical characters in Japanese way and is now nationally adopted.

2. " Original " seems to have been used since great antiquity. Though its enumeration can only be done from 1 to 10, some numbers are used hydridly with the influenced, and others as poetic diction. Foreigners are advised to learn **the influenced** first. They are as follow :

Figure	Influenced	Original
1	ichi	hito(tsu)
2	ni	futa(tsu)
3	san	mi(t)(tsu)
4	shi	yo(t)(tsu)
5	go	itsu(tsu)
6	roku	mu(t)(tsu)
7	shichi	nana(tsu)
8	hachi	ya(t)(tsu)
9	ku(kyū)	ko(ko)no(tsu)
10	jū	to(w)o or (so)
11	jūichi	
12	jūni	
13	jūsan	
14	jūshi ....jūyon	
15	jūgo	
16	jūroku	
17	jūshichi ....jūnana	
18	jūhachi	
19	jūku(jūkyū)	
20	nijū	hatachi (futajū)
21	nijūichi	
29	nijūku (-kyū)	
30	sanjū	miso-
40	shijū	yoso- ; yonjū
50	gojū	iso-
60	rokujū	muso-
70	shichijū	nanajū (nanaso-)
80	hachijū	yaso-
90	kujū (kyūjū)	

99	kujūku (kyūjūkyū)	tsukumo
100	hyaku	momo
200	nihyaku	futahyaku
300	sambyaku	
400	shihyaku	yonhyaku
900	kuhyaku (kyūhyaku)	
999	kuhyaku-kujū-ku (kyūhayku-kyūjūkyū)	
1000	sen	chi-
2000	nisen	futasen
3000	sanzen	michi-
4000	shisen	yonsen
7000	shichisen	nanasen
9000	kyūsen	
10000	ichiman	yorozu

Note 1   Parenthesized syllables are to be left out when combined or in enumeration, as : futa-mata (**forked**).

  2:　" Kyū (9) " is widely adopted for auditory convenience's sake, though school education sticks to " ku ".

  3:　" Shi " is of the same sound as " death ". So they choose " yonjū " for " shijū ", etc.

A

A, a [ei], *n.* (*pl.* A's *a's.* as [eiz]) Eigo *alphabet* no dai-1-bamme no moji.

a [ei/ə] *a., prep.* hitotsu no; aru: *a person*, aru hito. ...ni: *three times a week*, isshū *ni* sando.

A 1 [eiwʌn] dai ikkyū no; saijō no; tobikiri no.

A. B. [ei biː] shūshi; **Bachelor of Arts** no ryaku.

aback [əbǽk] *ad.* ushiro e: *be taken* ~, bikkuri suru.

abacus [ǽbəkəs] *n.* soroban.

abandon [əbǽndən] *v.* misuteru. ~ *oneself to*, ... ni fukeru. ~ed *a.* suterareta; jibōjiki no.

abase [əbéis] *v.* sageru. ~ment *n.* (hin'i, mibun nado o.) sageru koto.

abash [əbǽʃ] *v.* hazukashigaraseru; sekimen saseru: *to be*~ed, mojimoji suru.

abate [əbéit] *v.* hesu; genzuru; (chikara ga) heru; (kaze ga) yawaragu. ~ment *n.* genshō.

abatis [ǽbətis] *n.* rokusai; sakamogi.

abattoir [ǽbətwɑː] *n.* tosatsujō.

abbacy [ǽbəsi] *n.* sōinchō no shoku.

abbatial [əbéiʃəl] *a.* sōinchō no.

abbé [ǽbei] *n.* sōinchō; shimpu.

abbess [ǽbis] *n.* joshi shūdōinchō.

abbey [ǽbi] *n.* shūdōin; sōin.

abbot [ǽbət] *n.* shūdōinchō; sōinchō.

abbreviate [əbríːvieit] *v.* ryaku suru; tanshiku suru.

abbreviation [əbrìːviéiʃən] *n.* habuku koto; shōryaku.

abdicate [ǽbdikeit] *v.* (kokuō ga kurai nado o) yuzuru.

abdication [ǽbdikéiʃən] *n.* taii.

abdomen [ǽbdəmən / əbdóu-] *n.* fukubu; hara.

abdominal [æbdɔ́minəl] *a.* fukubu no.

abduct [æbdʌ́kt] *v.* yūkai suru; kadowakasu. ~or *n.* yūkaisha.

abduction [æbdʌ́kʃən] *n.* yūkai; kadowakasu koto.

abed [əbéd] *ad.* nedoko ni.

aberration [æbəréiʃən] *n.* jōki o issuru koto ; seishin ijō.

abet [əbét] *v.* keshikakeru. **aid and ～,** (*leg.*) hankō josei. **～ment** *n.*

abettor, abetter [əbétə] *n.* kyōsasha ; keshikakeru hito.

abeyance [əbéiəns] *n.* chūshi ; tochū de yameru koto.

abhor [əbhɔ́:] *v.* hidoku kirau. **～rence** *n.* dai-kirai. **～rent** *a.* daikirai no : *It is ～ent to me,* sore wa watakushi niwa awanai ; ki ni iranai.

abide [əbáid] *v.* **abode** *or* **abided ; abiding.** taizai suru ; matsu ; gaman suru, mochikotaeru. *He ～s by his promise,* kare wa yakusoku o mamoru.

abiding [əbáidiŋ] *a.* eizokutekina ; jōjū no.

ability [əbíliti] *n.* nōryoku ; sainō ; *man of ～,* binwanka.

abject [ǽbdʒekt] *a.* iyashimu beki ; hiretsuna ; mijimena.

abjection [æbdʒékʃən] *n.* gesen ; hiretsu.

abjuration [æbdʒuréiʃən] *n.* chikatte yameru koto.

abjure [əbdʒúə] *v.* chikai o tatete yameru.

ablative [ǽblətiv] *a.* (*gram.*) dakkaku no. *n.* dakkaku. "...kara" to iu kaku.

ablaut [ǽblaut] *n.* (*philol.*) boin no kisoku teki tenkan.

ablaze [əbléiz] *a. ad.* moeagatte ; hageshiku.

able [éibl] *a.* ...suru koto ga dekiru ; yarite no ; yūnōna. **～bodied** [-bɔ́did] karada no jōbuna. **-able** [-əbl] *suffix.*

ablution [əblú:ʃən] *n.* mokuyoku (shūkyō no) ; araikiyome (no shiki).

ably [éibli] *ad.* takumini ; jōzuni.

abnegation [æbnigéiʃən] *n.* kyozetsu ; hōki ; jibun kara yameru koto ; jisei.

abnormal [æbnɔ́:məl] *a.* futsū de nai ; hentai no.

abnormality [æbnə:mǽliti] *n.* ijō ; hentai.

aboard [əbɔ́:d] *ad. prep.* fune, kisha ni notte.

abode [əbóud] *n.* jūsho. *v. see:* **abide.**

abolish [əbɔ́liʃ] *v.* haishi suru. **～ment** *n.* haishi.

abolition [æbəlíʃən] *n.* haishi. **～ism** *n.* (doreiseido) haishi shugi ; -ron. **～ist** *n.* (doreiseido) haishi ronsha.

A-bomb [éibɔ́m], =*atomic bomb,* *n.* genshi bakudan.

abominable [əbóminəbl] *a.* iyana ; imawashii. ~**ly** *ad.* imawashiku ; hidoku.

abominate [əbómineit] *v.* hidoku kirau ; imikirau.

abomination [əbòminéiʃən] *n.* daikirai na mono.

aboriginal [æbərídʒinəl] *a.* hajime kara no ; dochaku no.

aborigines [æbərídʒini:z] *n.* (*pl.*) genjūmin ; dojin.

abort [əbó:t] *v.* ryūzan suru ; datai suru.

aborticide [əbó:tisaid] *n.* datai.

abortion [əbó:ʃən] *n.* ryūzan (datai ; shippai) suru koto.

abortive [əbó:tiv] *a.* ryūzan no ; shippai ni owatta ; onagare ni natta.

abound [əbáund] *v.* tomu ; takusan aru (iru) : *America* ~*s in oil*, Beikoku wa sekiyu ni tonde iru.

about [əbáut] *prep.* mawari ni ; no atari ni ; ni tsuite. *ad.* mawari ni ; achikochi ni ; hobo ; yaku : ~ *ten miles* (yaku jū mairu). *be* ~ *to* (*do*), .. shiyō to shite iru.

about-face [əbáutfeis] *n.* maware migi o suru koto. *v.* [əbautféis] maware migi o suru ; tenkō suru.

above [əbʌ́v] *ad.* ue ni. *prep.* ...no ue ni ; ...yori masatte (*better than*) ; no oyobanai (*out of reach of*). *above all*, toriwake. ~ **board** [-bɔ:d] *ad.* kōzen to ; kōmei-seidaini.

abracadabra [æbrəkədǽbrə] *n.* jumon ; byōki yoke no omamori ; tawagoto (*nonsense*).

abrasion [əbréiʒən] *n.* surimuki ; surikizu ; mametsu.

abreast [əbrést] *ad.* narande ; heikō shite.

abridge [əbrídʒ] *v.* shōryaku suru ; tanshuku suru.

abridgment [əbrídʒmənt] *n.* shōryaku ; tanshuku.

abroach [əbróutʃ] *ad.* (taru nado no) nomikuchi o akete.

abroad [əbró:d] *ad.* gaikoku e ; kaigai ni ; hiroku.

abrogate [æbrəgeit] *v.* torikesu ; haishi suru.

abrogation [æbrəgéiʃən] *n.* haishi ; teppai.

abrupt [əbrʌ́pt] *a.* fui no ; bukkirabōna. ~**ly** *ad.* fuini ; totsuzenni. ~**ness** *n.*

abscess [æbses] *n.* haremono.

abscond [æbskónd] *v.* tōbō suru ; nigeru. ~**ence** *n.* tōbō.

absence [æbsəns] *n.* fuzai ; rusu ; ketsubō ; nai koto.

absent [æbsənt] *a.* fuzai no ; rusu no. [æbsént] *v.* ~ *oneself* *from*, ...ni(o) kesseki suru.

absentee [æbsənti:] *n.* kessekisha; fuzaisha.

absent-minded [æbsəntmáindid] *a.* ukkari shite; bon'yari shite (iru); uwanosora no. ～**ly** *ad.* ukkari shite. ～**ness** *n.* uwa-nosora.

absinth [æbsinθ] *n.* abusan-zake; nigayomogi.

absolute [æbsəlu:t] *a.* zettai(teki) no; mattaku no; sensei no. *the A.*, Jōtei, Kami. ～**ly** *ad.* zettaitekini.

absolution [æbsəlú:ʃən] *n.* hōmen; shamen; menjo.

absolutism [æbsəlu:tizm] *n.* sensei shugi. ～**tist** *n.* sensei seiji ronja.

absolve [əbsɔ́lv] *v.* (tsumi o) yurusu; toku; kaijo suru.

absorb [əbsɔ́:b] *v.* hikitsukeru (chūi nado o); *be* ～*ed in*, ni koru. ～**edly** [-idli] *ad.* yonen naku. ～**ing** *a.* kyūshū suru; kokoro o ubau.

absorbent [əbsɔ́:bənt] *a.* kyūshūsei no. ～ *cotton*, dasshimen.

absorption [əbsɔ́:pʃən] *n.* muchū; kyūshū; senshin.

abstain [əbstéin] *v.* yameru (from); kinshu suru.

abstemious [æbstí:miəs] *a.* sessei suru.

abstention [æbsténʃən] *n.* jisei; sessei; kaihi; kiken: ～ *from voting*, tōhyō o kiken suru.

abstinence [æbstinəns] *n.* kin'yoku; kinshu: *total* ～, zettai kinshu.

abstract [æbstrækt] *a.* chūshōtekina; rirontekina. *n.* (rombun nado no) bassui. *v.* [æbstrækt] chūshō suru; hikiwakeru.

abstracted [æbstræktid] *a.* bon'yari shite iru; uwanosora no. ～**ly** *ad.* bon'yari suru.

abstraction [æbstrækʃən] *n.* nukidasu koto; chūshō; hō-shin; uwanosora.

abstruse [æbstrú:s] *a.* muzukashii; nankaina; shin'enna.

absurd [əbsɔ́:d] *a.* fugōrina; (giron nadoga) rikutsu ni awa-nai.

absurdity [əbsɔ́:diti] *n.* fugōri; rikutsu ni awanai koto.

abundance [əbándəns] *n.* takusan; hōfu.

abundant [əbándənt] *a.* takusan no; hōfuna.

abuse [əbjú:z] *v.* akuyō suru; gyakutai suru; nonoshiru; warukuchi o iu.

abusive [əbjú:siv] *a.* nonoshiru.

abut [əbʌ́t] *v.* sakai o sessuru. **~ment** *n.* rinsetsu.

abyss [əbís], **abysm** [əbízm] *n.* shin'en ; fukai fuchi.

A/C., a/c *account.* kanjō to iu imi.

acacia [əkéiʃə] *n.* akashia.

academic [ækədémik] *a. Platon* gakuha no ; daigaku no ; kū-ron ni hashiru.

academical [ækədémikl] *a.*=**academic**. **~s** *n.* (*pl.*) daigaku no shikifuku.

academy [əkǽdəmi] *n.* gakuen ; gakushiin ; gakkai.

accede [æks:íd] *v.* dōi suru ; (kurai ni) noboru ; (shoku ni) tsuku.

accelerate [ækséləreit] *v.* hayameru ; sokuryoku o masu ; soku-shin suru.

acceleration [ækseləréiʃən] *n.* kasokudo.

accelerator [ækséləreitə] *n.* sokudo o hayameru kikai ; kasoku-sōchi ; (*photo.*) genshō sokushinzai.

accent [ǽksent] *n.* aksento ; *ac.* no fugō. *v.* [æksént] *ac.* o tsu-keru ; on o tsuyomeru ; *ac.* no fugō o tsukeru.

accentuate [ækséntjueit] *v.* kyōchō (rikisetsu) suru.

accentuation [æksəntjuéiʃən] *n. ac.* o tsukeru koto.

accept [əksépt] *v.* ukeru ; shōdaku suru. **~able** *a.* ki ni itta ; ukeirerareru. **~ance** *n.* shōdaku ; tegata no hikiuke. **~er**, **~or** *n.* juryōsha ; judakusha ; tegata no hikiukenin.

acceptation [ǽkseptéiʃən] *n.* aru go ya ku ga, ippan ni uketo rarete iru imi.

access [ǽkses] *n.* chikazuki ; sekkin : *to have ~ to*, ...ni sekkin dekiru ;...

accessibility [æksesəbíliti] *n.* chikazuki yasui koto.

accessible [æksésəbl] *a.* chikazukiyasui ; te ni ire yasui.

accession [ækséʃən] *n.* kurai ni noboru koto ; shūshoku , tō-tatsu ; tassuru koto.

accessory [æksésəri] *a.* fuzoku no ; hojo no. *n.* fuzokuhin ; hanzai no tesaki ; ak(u)sessari.

accidence [ǽksidəns] *n.* (*gram.*) gokeiron ; keitairon.

accident [ǽksidənt] *n.* dekigoto ; jiko : *by ~*, gūzen ni.

accidental [ǽksidéntl] *a.* gūzen no. **~ly** *ad.* gūzen ni.

acclaim [əkléim] *n.* kassai. *v.* kassai suru.

acclamation [æ̀kləméiʃən] *n.* kassai ; kanko.

acclimate [əkláimeit] *v.* fūdo (*climate*) ni narasu (nareru) ; kyōgū ni junnō saseru (suru).

acclimation [æ̀klaiméiʃən] *n.* fūdo (*climate*) junka ; fūdo ni narasu (nareru) koto.

acclimatize [əkláimətaiz] *v.* fūdo ni narasu (nareru).

acclivity [əklíviti] *n.* noborizaka.

accolade [æ̀kəléid] *n.* knight-shakui juyoshiki.

accommodate [əkɔ́mədeit] *v.* junnō saseru. chōtei suru. shikuhaku saseru. wakai saseru. ～ *oneself to*, (kyōgū ni) junnō suru.　　　　　　　　　　　┌yūzū no kiku.

accommodating [əkɔ́mədeitiŋ] *a.* shinsetsuna ; sewazukina.

accommodation [əkɔ́mədéiʃən] *n.* tekiō suru koto ; setsubi : *This hotel has ～ for 100 persons*, kono hotel wa 100 nin no shūyōryoku ga aru. ～ *ladder*, fune no waki no hashigo. ～ *train*, futsū ressha.

accompaniment [əkʌ́mpənimənt] *n.* otomo ; fuzokubutsu ; bansō (ongaku de).

accompany [əkʌ́mpəni] *v.* tomo o suru ; bansō suru.

accomplice [əkʌ́mplis] *n.* kyōhansha ; dōrui.

accomplish [əkɔ́mpliʃ] *v.* shitogeru ; kansei suru. ～**ed** [-t] *a.* shitogeta ; dekiagatta (hito). ～**ment** *n.* jōju ; (*pl.*) geinō ; saigei.

accord [əkɔ́:d] *v.* itchi suru ; ataeru. *n.* itchi ; chōwa ; jibun no ishi de : *of one's own ～*, jihatsutekini.

accordance [əkɔ́:dəns] *n.* itchi : *in ～ with*, …ni shitagatte.

accordant [əkɔ́:dənt] *a.* itchi shite.

according [əkɔ́:diŋ] *ad.* ni shitagai (shitagatte) : ～ *as*, ni shitagatte. ～ *to*, no iu tokoro ni yoreba. ～**ly** *ad.* sore yue ni ;

accordion [əkɔ́:diən] *n.* tefūkin. (jijō ni ōjite) tekitō ni.

accost [əkɔ́st] *v.* hanashikakeru.

account [əkáunt] *n.* kanjō(gaki) ; hōkoku(sho) : *give an ～ of*, no hanashi o suru. *keep ～s*, chōmen o tsukeru. *lay one's ～ with B*, B o ate ni suru. *to be much* (*little*) *～ed*, …omoku (karuku) mirareru. *of no ～*, toru ni tarinai. ～**ant** *n.* kaikeishi.

accouter, -tre [əkúːtə] *v.* gunsō nado o suru ; sōbi suru. ~
ment *n.* gunsō ; sōbi.

accredit [əkrédit] *v.* shinnin suru ; (shinninjō o sazukete) haken suru. ...to (ni) suru : *He was* ~*ed with the remark,* kare
ga sō itta to sarete ita.

accretion [əkríːʃən] *n.* kuttsuite (fueru), ōkiku naru koto.

accrue [əkrúː] *v.* shōzuru ; kuwawaru.

accumulate [əkjúːmjuleit] *v.* tsumu ; tameru ; tamaru.

accumulation [əkjúːmjuléiʃən] *n.* taiseki ; chochiku.

accumulative [əkjúːmjulətiv] *a.* tsumikasaneru : ~ *fund,* ta-
mete oite shakkin nado o kaesu kane.

accumulator [əkjúːmjuleitə] *n.* chikudenchi.

accuracy [ǽkjurəsi] *n.* seikakusa.

accurate [ǽkjurit] *a.* seikakuna ; seimitsuna.

accursed [əkɔ́ːsid] *a.* norowareta ; nikumubeki.

accusation [ǽkjuzéiʃən] *n.* kokuhatsu ; hinan.

accuse [əkjúːz] *v.* kokuhatsu suru ; hinan suru. *the* ~*ed,* hikoku. ~*r n.* kokusosha ; hinansha.

accustom [əkʌ́stəm] *v.* narasu. ~ed [-d] *a.* nareta : *be*~ *ed to,*
ni nareru.

ace [eis] *a.* ichiryū no ; sai-yūshūna. *n.* (karuta, sai-no-me no)
ichi ; ichi no fuda ; saijō no mono ; yūshū senshu.

acerbity [əsɔ́ːbiti] *n.* shibumi (*astringence*), nigami (*bitterness*),
sammi (*sourness*), karami (*hotness*) nado no aji. (*taste*) ; shinratsuna (*sharp, cutting*) kotoba.

acetic [əsíːtik] *a.* su no : ~ *aid,* sakusan.

acetylene [əsétiliːn] *n.* asechiren.

ache [eik] *n.* itami : *toothache,* ha no itami.

achieve [ətʃíːv] *v.* shitogeru. ~ment *n.* rippana shigoto : ~
test, seiseki kōsa.

Achillean [ǽkilíːən] *a. Achilles* no.

Achilles [əkíliːz] *n.* Akires. Girisha Shinwa no yūshi (*brave
warrior*).

aching [éikiŋ] *a.* itamu ; kokoro o itameru.

achromatic [ǽkrəmǽtik] *a.* irokeshi no : ~ *vision,* zenshikimō.

acid [ǽsid] *a.* san(se)i no.

acidity [əsíditi] *n.* sammi ; sansei.

acidulous [əsídjuləs] *a.* sansei no.

ack-ack [ǽk-ǽk] *n.* kōshahō (**anti-aircraft gun**).

acknowledge [əknólidʒ] *v.* mitomeru; kansha suru.

acknowledgement [əknólidʒmənt] *n.* shōnin; kansha.

acme [ǽkmi:] *n.* chōjō; teppen (*the highest point*).

acolyte [ǽkəlait] *n.* jisō (*altar boy*).

aconite [ǽkənait] *n.* (*bot.*) torikabuto

acorn [éikɔ:n] *n.* donguri; kashi no mi.

acoumeter [əkú:mitə] *n.* chōryokukei.

acoustic [əkú:stik] *a.* onkyōgaku no; chōryoku no. ~**s** *n.* onkyōgaku.

acquaint [əkwéint] *v.* shiraseru: ~ *him with* (*the fact*), jijitsu o kare ni shiraseru. *I am* ~*ed with him*, watashi wa kare to shiriai da.

acquaintance [əkwéintəns] *n.* shiriai: *make his acquaintance*, kare to chikazuki ni naru.

acquiesce [ækwiés] *v.* damatte shitagau.

acquire [əkwáiə] *v.* narai-oboeru. ~**ment** narai-oboeru koto; (*pl.*) gakushiki; geinō.

acquisition [ækwizíʃən] *n.* shūtoku (*thing acquired*).

acquit [əkwít] *v.* menjo suru: *He* ~ *himself* (*well, ill*) *of his duty*, kare wa sono gimu o (yoku; waruku) hatasu.

acre [éikə] *n.* eikā. **acreage** [éikəridʒ] *n.* tsubosū.

acrid [ǽkrid] *a.* karai; nigai. ~**ity** [ækríditi] *n.* shinratsusa.

acrimonious [ækrimóuniəs] *a.* kibishii; dokudokushii.

acrimony [ǽkriməni] *n.* dokudokushisa; shinratsusa.

acrobat [ǽkrobæt] *n.* karuwazashi. ~**ic** [ækrobǽtik] *a.* karuwaza no. ~**ics** [ækrobǽtiks] *n.* karuwaza; kyokugei.

Acropolis [əkrópolis] *n. Athens* no toride no oka.

across [əkrós] *ad.* yokogitte: *come* ~, deau. *go* ~, mukō e wataru.

act [ækt] *n.* kōi; okonai: ~ *of God*, fukakōryoku. *in the very* ~ *of doing*, genni shite iru saichū ni; genkōhan o.

acting [ǽktiŋ] *a.* dairi no: *an* ~ *principal*, kōchō jimu tori-atsukai. *an* ~ *manager*, shihainin dairi.

action [kǽʃən] *n.* okonai; dōsa: *put into* (*in*) ~, jikkō suru.

activate [ǽktiveit] *v.* katsudōteki ni suru.

active [ǽktiv] *a.* kappatsuna : ～ *list*, gen'eki meibo. ～ *voice*, (*gram.*) nōdōtai.

activity [æktíviti] *n.* katsudō. (*pl.*) katsudō han'i ; shigoto.

actor [ǽktə] *n.* haiyū ; yakusha.

acress [ǽktris] *n.* onna no haiyū.

actual [ǽktʃuəl] *a.* genjitsu no. ～ly *ad.* genjitsu ni.

actuality [æktʃuǽliti] *n.* ima no hontō no sugata.

actuary [ǽktʃəəri] *n.* hokengishi ; hoken tōkeigakari.

actuate [ǽktjueit] *v.* ugokasu ; hito ni...saseru.

acumen [əkjú:men / ǽkju-] *n.* eibin ; meibin.

acute [əkjú:t] *a.* surudoi ; kireru ; (byōki) kyūsei no. ～ly *ad.* surudoku. ～ness *n.* surudosa.

ad [æd] *n.* kōkoku : *ad column*, shimbun no kōkoku-ran.

A.D. *Anno Domini*, Seireki (*in the year of our Lord*).

adage [ǽdidʒ] *n.* kakugen.

Adam [ǽdem] *n.* hajimete no ningen : *A～'s apple*, nodobo-toke.

adamant [ǽdəmənt] *n.* tesseki ; kongōseki.

adamantine [ǽdəmənti:n] *a.* hijōni katai ; tesseki no yōna.

adapt [ədǽpt] *v.* tekiō saseru. ～able *a.* yūzū no kiku.

adaptability [ədæptəbíliti] *n.* tekiōsei.

adaptation [ædæptéiʃən] *n.* tekigō ; tekiō.

add [æd] *v.* kuwaeru ; tasu : ～ *to*, ni tasu. ～ *up*, gōkei suru.

addendum [ədéndəm] *n.* furoku.

adder [ǽdə] *n.* dokuhebi ; mamushi (*viper*) no rui.

addict [ədíkt] *v.* ni fukeraseru : ～ *oneself to*, ni fukeru. *be ～ed to*, ni fukette iru. [ǽdikt] *n.* opium jōyōsha nadono.

addiction [ədíkʃən] *n.* tandeki (*giving oneself up to*).

addition [ədíʃən] *n.* kahō ; (*arith.*) tashizan.

additional [ədíʃənəl] *a.* fuka no ; issō no. ～ly *ad.* sarani.

addle [ǽdl] *a.* kusatte iru. **-brained** [bréind] = **-headed.** [-hedid] *a.* bakana.

address [ədrés] *n.* tegami nado no atena ; ōzei no hito ni suru enzetsu. *v.* hanashikakeru ; enzetsu suru ; tegami no atena nado o kaku ～ee [ædresí:] *n.* jushinsha ; naate no hito. ～ing machine [ədrésiŋməʃí:n] *n.* atena-insatsuki.

adduce [ədjú:s] *v.* (shōko to shite—*as proof*) in'yō suru.

adenoid [ǽdənoid] *n.* (*med.*) adenoido (tsūjō *pl.*).

adept [ədépt] *a.* jōzuna. *n.* jukurensha.

adequacy [ǽdikwəsi] *n.* tekitō de aru koto.

adhere [ədhíə] *v.* fuchaku suru ; kuttsuku (*stick to*).

adherence [ədhíərəns] *n.* fuchaku ; koshu ; shūchaku.

adherent [ədhíərənt] *a.* fuchakusei no aru. *n.* mikata ; shinja.

adhesion [ədhí:zən] *n.* fuchaku ; nenchaku.   ⌈sei

adhesive [ədhí:siv] *a.* nenchakusei no. ～**ness** *n.* nenchaku-

ad hoc [ǽdhók] (*L.*) *ad. a.* tokubetsuna. (tokuni) sono tame ni.

adieu [ədjú:] *inter.* sayōnara. *n.* owakare ; kokubetsu.

adjacent [ədʒéisənt] *a.* fukin no ; kinjo no.

adjective [ǽdʒiktiv] *n.* (*gram.*) keiyōshi. *a.* keiyōshi no.

adjoin [ədʒóin] *v.* tonariau ; heigō suru.

adjourn [ədʒə̀:n] *v.* enki ; kyūkai ; heikai suru. ～**ment** *n.* enki ; heikai ; kyūkai.

adjudge [ədʒádʒ] *v.* hanketsu suru.

adjudicate [ədʒú:dikeit] *v.* hanketsu ; saiketsu suru.

adjudication [ədʒù:dikéiʃən] *n.* hanketsu ; senkoku.

adjunct [ǽdʒáŋkt] *n.* fuzokubutsu ; (*gram.*) shūshokugo.

adjuration [ǽdʒuəréiʃən] *n.* gemmei ; kongan.

adjure [ədʒúə] *v.* gemmei (kongan) suru.

adjust [ədʒást] *v.* chōsetsu suru. ～**ment** *n.* chōsetsu.

adjutant [ǽdʒutənt] *a.* hojo no. *n.* fukkan.

ad-lib [ǽdlib] *v.* sokuseki ni (serifu nado o) iu ; buttsuke hom-ban o suru. (*L.* **ad libitum**)

administer [ədmínistə] *v.* kanri (shukkō) suru.

administration [ədmìnistréiʃən] *n.* gyōseibu ; seifu ; kanri ; (*leg.*) isan-kanri.

administrative [ədmínistrətiv] *a.* gyōsei (kanri) no.

administrator [ədmínistreitə] *n.* kanrisha ; gyōseikan.

admirable [ǽdmirəbl] *a.* shōsan subeki ; rippana.

admiral [ǽdmirəl] *n.* kaigun taishō ; teitoku. ～**ty** [ǽdmirəlti] *n.* kaigun taishō (*admiral*) no shokken (*authority*). *Ad*～*ty* (*Brit.*) Kaigunshō : *Board of A.* (*A* ～,) kaigunhombu.

admiration [ǽdməréiʃən] *n.* kantan (*wonder*), **s**ambi (*glorify*).

admire [ədmáiə] *v.* homeru ; kampuku suru. ～**r** *n.* [-rə] sam-

admiringly [ədmáiəriŋli] *ad.* kanshin shite.   ⌊bisha.

admissible [ədmísəbl] *a.* hairu shikaku ga aru ; zenin dekiru.

admission [ədmíʃən] *n.* hairu no o yurusu koto ; nyūjō (nyūgaku) kyoka.

admit [ədmít] *v.* ireru ; yurusu ; mitomeru. ~**tance** *n.* nyūjō (kyoka). ~**tedly** [-tidli] *ad.* akirakani.

admixture [ədmíkstʃə] *n.* kongō ; mazemono.

admonish [ədmóniʃ] *v.* satosu ; kunkai suru. ~**ment** *n.* kunkai.

admonition [ædməníʃən] *n.* kunkai.

admonitory [ədmónitəri] *a.* kunkai no.

ado [ədú:] *n.* sawagi : *much* ~, ōsawagi.   ⌈sun).

adobe [ədóubi] *n.* hiyaki (tempi de yaita) renga (*dried up by*

adolescence [ædoulésns] *n.* seinenki ; shishunki.

adolescent [ædəlésnt] *a.* seinen no ; shishunki no.

adopt [ədópt] *v.* saiyō suru ; yōshi ni suru.

adoption [ədópʃən] *n.* saiyō ; yōshi-engumi.

adoptive [ədóptiv] *a.* saiyō suru ; yōshi-kankei ni yotta. ~ *son* (*daughter*), yōshi (yōjo).

adorable [ədó:rəbl] *a.* sūhai-subeki.

adoration [ædəréiʃən] *n.* sūhai ; keibo ; akogare.

adore [ədóə] *v.* sūhai (keibo) suru ; akogareru.

adorn [ədó:n] *v.* kazaru. ~**ment** *n.* sōshoku.

adrift [ədríft] *ad.* tadayotte ; hyōryū shite. tohō ni kurete (*at a loss*).

adroit [ədróit] *a.* tokuina ; kōmyōna. ~**ly** *ad.* tokuini.

adsorb [ədsó:b] *v.* kyūchaku saseru ; suitsukete katamaraseru.

adulation [ædjuléiʃən] *n.* hetsurai ; obekka.

adult [ədʌlt] *n.* otona ; seijin. *a.* otona no ; seijin shita.

adulterate [ədʌltəreit] *v.* mazemono o suru ; hinshitsu o waruku suru. **adulteration** [ədʌltəréiʃən] *n.* mazemono o suru koto ; hinshitsu o otosu koto.

adulterous [ədʌltərəs] *a.* kantsū no ; fugi no ; fujunna.

adultery [ədʌltəri] *n.* kantsū ; fugi.

ad valorem [æd vəló:rəm] *a.* (*L.*) jūkazei no : ~ *duty*, jūkazei (shōhin no urine ni yotte kakeru zei).

advance [ədvá:ns] *v.* susumeru ; susumu ; ageru ; agaru.

nedan ga tōki suru. *n.* zenshin; shōshin; maegashi. *in*~, mae motte maebarai de. ~**guard** *n.* zen'ei.

advantage [ədvá:ntidʒ] *n.* rieki: *take* ~ *of*, ...o riyō suru. ~**ous** [ӕdvəntéidʒəs] *a.* yūrina. ~**ly** *ad.* yūrini.

advent [ӕdvent] *n.* tōrai (*coming, arrived*); (*the A* ~,) Kirisuto no kōrin; Kōrinsetsu.

adventure [ədvéntʃə] *n.* bōken; (*col.*) yama.

adventurer [ədvéntʃərə] *n.* bōkensha; yamashi.

adventurous [ədvéntʃərəs] *a.* bōken no. ~**ly** *ad.* bōkenteki ni.

adverb [ӕdvəb] *n.* (*gram.*) fukushi. ~**ial** [ədvə:biəl] *a.* fukushi no.

adversary [ӕdvəsəri] *n.* tekishu; aite.

adverse [ӕdvə:s] *a.* gyaku no; hantai no; fuunna.

adversity [ədvə́:siti] *n.* fukō; gyakkyō.

advert [ədvə́:t] *v.* kokoro o tomeru.

advertise, tize [ӕdvətaiz] *v.* kōkoku suru. ~**ment** [ədvə́:tizmənt/ӕdvətáizmənt] *n.* kōkoku. ~**r** [ӕdvətaizə] *n.* kōkokusha; kōkokushimbun.

advice [ədváis] *n.* chūkoku; iken; (*pl.*) hōdō; hōkoku.

advisability [ədvàizəbíliti] *n.* susumeuru koto; tokusaku.

advisable [ədváizəbl] *a.* susume uru; tokusaku no.

advise [ədváiz] *v.* chūkoku suru, jogen suru. ~**ment** *n.* jūbun kangaeru koto, jukuryo. ~**r** *n.* sōdan'yaku; komon.

advisary [ədváizəri] *a.* chūkoku suru; komon no.

advocacy [ӕdvəkəsi] *n.* bengo; shiji.

advocate [ӕdvəkit] *n.* bengosha; yōgosha; shuchōsha. ~ *v.* [-keit] bengo suru.

adz(e) [ӕdz] *n.* chōna; teono.

AEC *n.* genshiryoku iinkai (*Atomic Energy Commission*).

aerate [éiəreit] *v.* kūki ni ateru; tansangasu nado o ireru. ~**ed** [id] **water** tansansui.

aerial [éəriəl/éri-] *a.* kūki no, kōkū no: ~ *current*, kiryū. ~ *defense*, bōkū. ~ *ladder*, kuridashi-hashigo (shōbōyō). ~ *mail* (*post*), kōkū yūbin.

aerie, aery, eyrie, eyry [éəri/íəri] *n.* (taka, washi nado no) su.

aeriform [éərifɔ:m] *a.* kitai no; mukei no.

aerobe [έəroub] *n.* sansochū ni sumu saikin.

aerobus [έərəbʌs] *n.* ōgata-hikōki.

aerodrome [έərədroum] *n.* kūkō ; hikōjō.

aerogram [έərəgræm] *n.* musen-denshin ; kōkūbin.

aerolite [έərəlait] *n.* inseki ; ten kara ochita ishi.

aeronaut [έərənɔ:t] *n.* hikōsha ; kōkūshi.

aeronautic [èərənɔ́:tik] *a.* kōkūjutsu no. ~s *n.* kōkūgaku.

aeroneurosis [èərənjuróusis] *n.* kōkūbyō.

aeroplane [έərəplein] *n.* hikōki ; kōkūki (*airplane*).

aerostat [έərəstæt] *n.* hikōsen.

aerostatics [èərəstǽtiks] *n.* kikyū-kōkūgaku.

aerostation [èərəstéiʃən] *n.* kikyū sōjū jutsu.

aesthete [í:sθi:t és-] *n.* shimbika ; bigakusha.

aesthetic [esθétik/esθ-/í:sθ-] *a.* biteki no ; bi o aisuru. ~al *a.* ~s *n.* bigaku.

A F *n.* kūgun (*Air Force*).

afar [əfá:] *ad.* tōku : *from* ~, tōku kara.

affability [æfəbíliti] *n.* teinei ; aiso no yoi koto.

affable [ǽfəbl] *a.* aiso no yoi ; yasashii. ~bly *ad.* aiso yoku.

affair [əféə] *n.* jiken. (*pl.*) shigoto ; jimu.

affect [əfékt] *v.* furi o suru ; eikyō suru ; konomu.

affectation [ǽfektéiʃən] *n.* kidori.

affected [əféktid] *a.* kidotta ; kizana. ~ly *ad.*

affecting [əféktiŋ] *a.* itamashii ; kandō saseru yōna.

affection [əfékʃən] *n.* aijō ; byōki ; kanjō.

affectionate [əfékʃənit] *a.* aijō no fukai. ~ly *ad.*

affiance [əfáiəns] *n.* kon'yaku ; seiyaku. *v.* kon'yaku suru.

affidavit [ǽfidéivit] *n.* senseisho.

affiliate [əfílieit] *v.* kanyū saseru ; yōshi to suru ; gappei suru : ~ *oneself with*, ni kanyū suru ; kyōryoku suru ; shimmitsu ni suru.

affiliation [əfiliéiʃən] *n.* nyūkai ; yōshi-engumi.

affinity [əfíniti] *n.* enko ; shinwaryoku.

affirm [əfá:m] *v.* dangen suru ; kōtei suru.

affirmation [ǽfə:méiʃnə] *n.* dangen ; kōtei.

affirmative [əfá:mətiv] *a.* kōteiteki no. ~ly *ad.* sansei (kōtei) shite.

affix [əfíks] *v.* kuttsukeru. *n.* kuttsuketa mono.

afflict [əflíkt] *v.* kurushimeru; nayamasu. ~**ing** *a.* kurushii.

affliction [əflíkʃən] *n.* fukō; sainan; kurushimi.

affluence [ǽfluəns] *n.* yutakasa; yūfuku. (*wealth*).

affluent [ǽfluənt] *a.* hōfuna; yūfukuna. *n.* shiryū (*river*).

afford [əfɔ́:d] *v.* (**can** ~,) ...suru koto ga dekiru; suru yoyū ga aru: *can not* ~, dekinai; yoyū ga nai (sore hodo no kane ⌊ga nai.).

affray [əfréi] *n.* kenka; sōdō.

affright [əfráit] *v.* odorokasu; odokasu.

affront [əfrónt] *n.* bujoku; (*insult to the face*). *v.* (men to mukatte) bujoku suru (*treat with contemat*).

afield [əfí:ld] *ad.* nohara ni; uchi kara, tōku hanarete.

afire [əfáiə] *ad.* moete (*burning*).

AFL *n.* Amerika-Rōdō-Sōdōmei (*American Federation of Labor*).

aflame [əfléim] *a.* (en'en to) moete iru (*on fire*).

afloat [əflóut] *ad.* tadayotte; ukande; fune no ue de.

afoot [əfút] *ad.* aruite (*on foot*); shinkōchū de. *set* ~, hajimeru.

aforesaid [əfɔ́:sed] *a.* mae ni nobeta.

aforethought [əfɔ́:θɔ:t] *a.* maemotte kangaeta; keikakuteki.

AFP *n.* Furansu tsūshinsha (*Agence France Presse*).

afraid [əfréid] *a.* osorete. *be afraid of*, dewa nai ka to omou.

afresh [əfréʃ] *ad.* aratani; shinkini.

African [ǽfrikən] *a.* Afurika no. Afurikajin.

AFRS *n.* Amerika Rikugun Hōsō Kyoku. (*American Forces Radio Service*).

aft [ɑ:ft] *ad.* sembi ni.

after [ɑ́:ftə] *ad.* nochi ni(no); okurete. *prep.* ni okurete(ta); o motomeru. *conj.* (...shita) ato de. *a.* ato no; kōhō no. ~**care** [ɑ́ftəkéə] *n.* byōgo no sewa. ~**crop** *n.* nibansaku. ~ **dinner** *a.* shokugo no. ~**glow** [-glou] *n.* yūyake. ~**image** [ɑ́:ftə ímidʒ] *n.* zanzō. ~**math** [ɑ́:ftəmæθ] *n.* yoha; nibangari. ~**most** *a.* saigo no. ~**noon** [-nú:n] *n.* gogo. ~ **piece** [-pì:s] *n.* kirikyōgen. ~**shock** *n.* yoshin. ~**taste** *n.* ato-aji; yoin. ~**thought** *n.* atojian; atojie. ~**ward(s)** [-wɔd(z)] *ad.* ato de.

again [əgén] *ad.* futatabi. *now and* ~, tokidoki.

against [əgénst] *prep.* taishite; sonaete; haikei to shite.

agar-agar [éigəʔéigə] *n.* kanten (tokoroten).

agate [ǽgət] *n.* menō.

age [eidʒ] *n.* nenrei ; nendai ; jidai : *come of* ~, seinen ni naru. ~**d** [éidʒid] *a.* toshi o totta : *an aged* [éidʒid] *man*, kōrei no rōjin. ~**ed** [eidʒd] 10, jissai no : *a man* ~ *seventy years*, 70-sai no hito.

agency [éidʒensi] *n.* hataraki ; dairi ; dairiten.

agenda [ədʒéndə] *n.* gijinittei ; kyōgijikō.

agent [éidʒent] *n.* dairisha ; dairishō.

agglomeration [əglɔməréiʃən] *n.* atsumaru (-meru) koto.

agglutinate [əglú:tineit] *v.* nenchaku suru ; setsugō suru. ~ **language** (*ling.*) kōchakugo.

aggrandize [ǽgrəndaiz] *v.* ōkiku suru ; zōdai suru. ~**ment** [-mənt] *n.* zōdai ; kakuchō.

aggravate [ǽgrəveit] *v.* issō waruku suru. ~**ing** [ǽgrəveitiŋ] *a.* mondai o ōkiku suru. ~**tion** *n.* akka ; jūdaika.

aggregate [ǽgrigit] *a.* shūgō no ; gōkei no. *n.* gōkei ; sōsū. *v.* [ǽgrigeit] atsumeru ; sōkei... ni naru. ~**tion** [ægrigéiʃən] *n.* shūgō ; shūdan.

aggression [ægréʃən] *n.* kōgeki ; shinryaku.

aggressive [ægrésiv] *a.* shinryakuteki no ; kōgekiteki no.

aggressor [ægrésə] *n.* kōgekisha ; shinryakusha.

aggrieve [ægri:v] *v.* kurushimeru ; shingai suru ; appaku suru.

aghast [əgá:st] *a.* *be* ~ *at*, akirete iru.

agile [ǽdʒil] *a.* keikaina ; subashikkoi.

agility [ədʒíliti] *n.* keikai ; kibin ; binshō.

agitate [ǽdʒiteit] *v.* yuri ugokasu ; sendō suru. ~**tion** [ædʒitéiʃən] *n.* sendō. ~**tor** [-tə] *n.* sendōsha.

aglow [əglóu] *ad.*, *a.* moete ; akakunatte.

agnail [ǽgnéil] *n.* sakamuke ; sasakure.

agnostic [ægnóstik] *a.* fukachiron no. *n.* fukachironsha. ~**ism** *n.* fukachiron.

ago [əgóu] *ad.* izenni. *long* ~, zutto mae ni ; mukashi.

agog [əgɔ́g] *a.*, *ad.* muchū de.

agoing [əgóuiŋ] *ad.* ugoite : *set* ~, ugokasu ; hatarakasu.

agonize [ǽgənaiz] *v.* modaeru ; nayamasu.

agony [ǽgəni] *n.* kumon : ~ *column*, (shimbun) tazunebito-ran.

agrarian [əgréəriən] *a.* kōsakuchi kankei no (onaji yōni wa-keru—*equally divide*). *n.* tochikimbunronsha.

agree [əgrí:] *v.* itchi suru; dōi suru. ~**able** *a.* kokoroyoi. ~**ably** *ad.* itchishite; kokoroyoku. ~**ment** *n.* dōi; kyōyaku.

agricultural [æ̀grikʌltʃurəl] *a.* nōgyō no.

agriculture [æ̀grikʌltʃə] *n.* nōgyō. ~**ist** [æ̀grikʌltʃurist] *n.* nōgyōka.

aground [əgráund] *ad.* zashōshite: *run* ~, (fune ga) zashō suru.

ague [éigju] *n.* (*med.*) okori (byōki).

aguish [éigju(:)iʃ] *a.* zokuzoku suru; miburui suru; okori ni kakatta.

ah [á:] *inter.* ā! (tsuyoi kanjō o arawasu koe.)

aha [a(:)há:] *inter.* haha! (yorokobi, keibetsu, odoroki nado o arawasu koe.)

ahead [əhéd] *ad.* zemmen ni; zento ni.

aide-de-camp [éidəkā:ŋ] *n.* shōkantsuki bukan; fukkan.

aigrette [éigret] *n.* (*bird*) shirasagi; (bōshi no) kazarige.

ail [éil] *v.* nayamasu; nayamu. ~**ment** *n.* [éilmənt] (karui) byōki; fukai.

aileron [éilərɔn] *n.* hojoyoku (hikōki no).

aim [eim] *v.* nerau; mezasu. *n.* nerai : *take* ~, nerai o sadame-ru. ~**less** [-lis] *a.* meate nashi no. ~**lessly** [-lisli] *ad.* meate nashi ni.

ain't [éint] *are not* ; *am not* nado no tanshukukei.

air [ɛə] *n.* kūki : *My plan is still in the air*, watashi no kei-kaku wa mada kimaranai. *castle in the air*, kūchū no rōkaku ; yume. rajio : *on the air*, rajio de. ongaku no kyoku. furi : *He has an air of importance*, erai furi o suru. *put on airs*, furi o suru. *v.* kūki o tōsu. ~ **attack** [ɛ́ərətæk] *n.* kūshū. ~**base** [ɛ́əbeis] *n.* kūgun kichi. ~**bladder** [ɛ́əblæ̀də] *n.* uo no ukibukuro. ~**castle** [ɛ́əka:sl], yume *n.* ~**craft** [ɛ́əkra:ft] *n.* hikōki, hikōsen no sōshō. ~**craft-carrier** [ɛ́əkra:ftkæriə] *n.* kōkūbokan. ~**drome** [ɛ́ədroum] *n.* hikōjō. ~**gun** [ɛ́əgʌn] *n.* kūkijū. ~**ily** [ɛ́ərili] *ad.* kigaruni; kaikatsuni. ~**ing** [ɛ́əriŋ] *n.* mushiboshi; sampo. ~**less** *a.* kūki no nigotta : *an airless room*, kūki no nigotta heya. ~**line** [ɛ́əlain] *n.* teiki kōkūro.

~ **mail,** kōkūbin. ~**man** [ɛ́əmən] *n.* hikōka. ~**manship**
n. hikōjutsu. ~**plane** [ɛ́əplein] *n.* hikōki. ~**port** [ɛ́əpɔːt] *n.*
kūkō. ~**raid** [ɛ́əreid] *n.* kūshū. ~**ship** [ɛ́ʃip] *n.* hikōsen:
nonrigid ~, nanshiki hikōsen; **rigid** ~, kōshiki hikōsen. ~
tight [ɛ́ətait] *a.* kūki o shadanshita. ~**way** [ɛ́əwei] *n.* kōkūro.
~**y** [ɛ́əri] *a.* kūki no yoku tōru : **an** ~**room,** kūki no ryūtsū
suru heya.

aisle [áil] *n.* (zaseki no aida no) tsūro ; rōka.

ajar [ədʒáː] *ad.* fuchōwa de ; sukoshi hiraite.

akimbo [əkímbou] *ad.* te o koshi ni ate hiji o hatte.

akin [əkín] *a.* ketsuzoku no ; nita (*to*).

à la [áːlá(ː)] *prep.* (*Fr.*) ...fūni. *à la carte,* okonomi de ; teishoku (*table d'hôte*) no hantai. *à la mode,* ryūkō no.

alabaster [ǽləbæ̀stə] *n.* sekkasekkō.

alacrity [əlǽkriti] *n.* binkatsu ; binshō : *with* ~, tekipaki to ;
binkatsuni.

alarm [əláːm] *n.* keihō ; keihōki. *v.* keikai suru ; odorokasu.
~ **bell,** *n.* keishō, keirin. ~ **clock,** mezamashidokei. ~**ing**
a. odorokubeki. ~**ingly** *ad.* bikkuri suru hodo.

alarmist [əláːmist] *n.* shimpaishō no hito ; hitosawagasena
hito.

alas [əláːs] *inter.* kanashii kana !, ā !

alb [ǽlb] *n.* shiroasa no sōfuku ; byakue.

albatross [ǽlbətrous] *n.* ahōdori.

albeit [ɔːlbíːit] *conj.* ...to wa ie ; demo (...*although*).

albino [ælbíːnou] *n.* shirako.

Albion [ǽlbiən] *n.* Igirisu no mukashi no namae (*poet.*).

album [ǽlbəm] *n.* arubamu. shashinchō ; kittechō.

albumen [ælbjúːmən] *n.* tamago no shiromi ; tampakushitsu.

albuminous [ælbjúːminəs] *a.* tampakushitsu no.

alchemist [ǽlkəmist] *n.* renkinjutsushi.

alchemy [ǽlkəmi] *n.* renkinjutsu.

alcohol [ǽlkəhəl] *n.* arukōru. ~**ic** [æ̀lkəhɔ́lik] *a.* arukōru
chūdoku no ; arukōru no. ~**ism** [æ̀lkəhɔ́lizm] *n.* arukōru-
chūdoku.

Alcoran [æ̀lkəráːn] *n.* Kōran ; Kaikyō no keiten.

alcove [ǽlkouv] *n.* kabe no irikomi; kobeya.

alder [ɔ́:ldə] *n.* (*bot.*) hannoki.

alderman [ɔ́:ldəmən] *n.* shisanjikaiin.

ale [eil] *n.* biiru; tsuyoi biiru. ~**house** [éilhaus] *n.* biahōru.

alee [əlí:] *ad.* kazashimo ni.

algebra [ǽldʒibrə] *n.* daisūgaku. ~**ic** [ǽldʒibréiik] *a.* daisū-gaku(jō)no. ~**ical** [-kəl] *a.* daisūgaku no.

Alhambra [ælhǽmbrə] *n.* Aruhambra Kyūden (Spein ni aru).

alias [éiliəs] *n.* betsumei; hemmei. *ad.* betsumei wa.

alibi [ǽlibai] *n.* aribai; gemba fuzai shōmei (*proof of absence*).

alien [éiliən] *a.* gaikoku no; tachi no chigau *n.* gaikokujin.

alienate [éiljəneit] *v.* tōzakeru; soen ni suru. ~**tion** [eiliə-néiʃən] *n.* soen; fuwa; rikan (*separation*).

alight [əláit] *v.* (uma nado kara) oriru. **alight** [əláit] *a.* moete; terasarete.

align [əláin] *v.* ichiretsu ni naraberu. ~**ment** *n.* seiton; sei-retsu.

alike [əláik] *a.* hitoshii; onaji no. *ad.* dōyōni; onajiyōni.

aliment [ǽlimənt] *n.* eiyōbutsu; shokumotsu.

alimentary [æ̀liméntəri] *a.* shokumotsu no; eiyō no. ~ **canal** shōka-kikan.

alimony [ǽliməni] *n.* fuyōryō; rikonteate.

alive [əláiv] *a.* ikite iru; ikiiki shite iru; binkan de.

alkali [ǽlkəlai] *n.* arukari.

alkaline [ǽlkəlain] *a.* arukari no; arukarisei no.

alkaloid [ǽlkəloid] *n.*, *a.* arukaroido (no).

aline [əláin] *v.* ichiretsu ni naraberu (*align*).

all [ɔ:l] *a.* subete no. *n.* mina; issai : *after* ~, kekkyoku. *at* ~, iyashikumo; sukoshimo *ad.* mattaku : ~ *along*, zutto; hajime kara. ~ *but*, hotondo. ~ *over*, owatte; karadajū. ~ *up*, kyū-shite; dame ni natte. ~**-important** [ɔ́:límpɔ:tənt] *a.* mottomo jūyōna. ~**out** [-áut] *a.*, *ad.* sōryoku o ageta(-te). ~**round** [-ráund] *a.* tageina; bannōna.

Allah [ǽlə/ǽlɑ:] *n.* Ara (Kaikyō no kami).

allay [əléi] *v.* shizumeru; yawarageru.

allegation [æ̀ligéiʃən] *n.* shuchō; mōshitate (shōko no nai).

allege [əlédʒ] *v.* shuchō suru; mōshitateru. ~**dly** [əlédʒdli]

ad. shuchō ni yoreba.
allegiance [əlí:ʒəns] *n.* chūsei; chūsetsu (*loyalty*).
allegory [ǽligəri] *n.* gūwa; hiyu. ~**rical** [æligórikəl] *a.* hiyuteki. ~**rically** *ad.* hiyutekini.
allegro [əléigrou] (*mus.*) *a.* keikaina. *ad.* keikaini. *n.* aregurochō
alleluia [æ̀lilú:jə] *inter.* harerūya (=hallelujah).
allergy [ǽlədʒi] *n.* arerugii; ijōbinkanshō.
alleviate [əlí:vieit] *v.* yawarageru; yurumeru.
alleviation [əlì:viéiʃən] *n.* kanwa; nadame.
alley [ǽli] *n.* komichi; roji.
All Fools' Day [ɔ́:lfú:lzdei] 4gt. 1ch. Shigatsu Baka no Hi
All Hallows [ɔ́:lhǽlouz] *n.* Banseisetsu (11gt. 1ch).
alliance [əláiəns] *n.* dōmeikoku.
allied [əláid] *a.* dōmei shite iru; ruiji no. *A*~ *Forces* Rengōgun.
allies [əláiz] *n.* dōmeikoku. *the A*~, rengōkoku.
alligator [ǽligeitə] *n.* wani (Amerika san no); suiriku ryōyō sensha.
alliteration [əlìtəréiʃən] *n.* tōin (gyō no atama ga in o fumu).
allocate [ǽləkeit] *v.* wariateru. ~**tion** [æ̀ləkéiʃən] *n.* wariate.
allopathic [æ̀lo(u)pǽθik] *a.* taishō ryōhō no.
allopathy [əlópəθi] *n.* taishō ryōhō.
allot [əlɔ́t] *v.* wariateru. ~**ment** *n.* wariate, wakemae; un.
allow [əláu] *v.* yurusu; ataeru. ~**able** *a.* yurusareru; seitōna. ~**ance** *n.* kyoka; teate.
alloy [əlɔ́i/ǽ-] *n.* gōkin; mazemono. *v.* gōkin ni suru.
All Saints' Day [ɔ́:lséintsdei] Banseisetsu (*All Hallows*).
All Souls' Day [ɔ́:lsóulzdei] Banreisetsu (11gt. 2k.).
allspice [ɔ́:lspáis] *n.* kōryō; (no ki) (Nishi Indo san).
allude [əlú:d] *v.* honomekasu.
allure [əljúə] sosonokasu; yūwaku suru. ~**ment** *n.* yūwaku.
alluvium [əljúviəm] *n.* chūsekido(sō).
ally [əlái] *v.* dōmei suru. (*L.*) *n.* [ǽlai] dōmeisha; dōmeikoku.
alma mater [ǽlmə méitə] *n.* bokō; shusshin gakkō.
almanac [ɔ́:lmənǽk] *n.* koyomi.

almighty [ɔ́:lmaiti] *a.* zennō no. *n.* (the A~) Kami.

almond [ɑ́:mənd] *n.* āmondō.

almoner [ǽlmənə] *n.* hodokoshimono bumpai gakari (mukashi

almost [ɔ́:lmoust] *ad.* hotondo ; **taitei**. Lōshitsu no.

alms [ɑ:mz] *n.* (*sing. pl.*) hodokoshi ; ofuse. ~**giving** [ɑ́:mz-gíviŋ] *n.* hodokoshi. ~**house** [-haus] *n.* yōrōin.

aloft [əlɔ́ft] *ad.* takaku.

alone [əlóun] *a.*, *ad.* hitori no (de) ; dokuryoku de. *ad.* tanni, tada...dake. *let* ~, sonomama ni shite oku.

along [əlɔ́ŋ] *ad.*, *prep.* (...ni) sotte ; (to) tomo ni. *all* ~ zūtto. ~ *with*, to tomo ni. *get* ~, kurasu ; seikō suru. ~**side** [-said] *ad. prep.* (...no) katawara no (de).

aloof [əlú:f] *ad.* hanarete. ~**ness** *n.* mukanshin ; reitan.

aloud [əlaud] *ad.* koe o dashite ; ōgoe de. *think* ~, hitorigoto

alp [ǽlp] *n.* kōzan. the **Alps**, Arupusu Sammmyaku. Lo iu.

alpaca [ælpǽkə] *n.* arupaka (Nambei no kachiku) ; arupaka

alpenstock [ǽlpinstɔk] *n.* tozanzue. Lno ke.

alpha [ǽlfə] *n.* Girisha moji no daiichiji. ~ *and omega*, hajime to owari ; zentai. ~**bet** [ǽlfəbet] monji zentai. ~**betical** [æ̀lfəbétikəl] alfabet no.

alpine [ǽlpain] *a.* kōzan no ; *Alps* no.

already [ɔ:lrédi] *ad.* sudeni, mō, mohaya.

also [ɔ́:lsou] *ad.* mata ; yahari ; sonoue.

alt [ǽlt] *n.* (*mus.*) kōon ; aruto.

altar [ɔ́:ltə] *n.* saidan.

alter [ɔ́:ltə] *v.* kaeru ; kawaru. ~**able** *a.* kaerareru.

alteration [ɔ̀:ltəréiʃən] *n.* henkō ; kaizō.

altercation [ɔ̀:ltəkéiʃən] *n.* kuchigenka ; kōron.

alternate [ɔ:ltɔ́:nit] *a.* kawarugawaru ; kōgo no. ~**ly** *ad.* kōgo. ni ~**ing current** [ɔ́:ltənèitiŋ kə:rənt] denki no kōryū.

alternation [ɔ̀:ltənéiʃən] *n.* kōgo ; kōtai.

alternative [ɔ:ltɔ́:nətiv] *a.*, *n.* dotchika hitotsu ; are ka kore ka. *n.* sentaku.

although [ɔ:lðóu] *conj.*..., tatoe...tomo ; ...dakeredo.

altitude [ǽltitju:d] *n.* kōdo ; takasa. Fteion.

alto [ǽltou] *n.* (*mus.*) chūombu ; dansei saikōon ; josei sai-

altogether [ɔ̀:ltəgéðə] *ad.* mattaku ; issho ni.

altruism [ǽltruizm] *n.* ritashugi; hito o aisuru kokoro.
altruist [ǽltruist] *n.* ritashugisha. **~ic** [æltruístik] *a.* ritashugi
alum [ǽləm] *n.* myōban. ⌐no.
alumina [əlú:minə] *n.* arumina; aruminium no sankabutsu.
aluminum [əlú:minəm] (*Am.*) **aluminium** [æljumínəm]
(*Brit.*) *n.* aruminyūmu.
alumnus [əlʌ́mnəs] *n.* (*pl.* **-ni**) sotsugyōsei; kōyū.
always [ɔ́:lwiz] *ad.* tsuneni; itsumo.
A.M., a.m. gozen (*L. ante meridiem*).
amah [á:mə] *n.* uba (Tōyō de); jochū.
amain [əméin] *ad.* chikara ippai ni; ōisogi de.
amalgam [əmǽlgəm] *n.* amarugam. **~ate** [əmǽlgəmeit] *v.*
gōkin ni suru; gappei suru. **~ation** [əmæ̀lgəméiʃən] *n.*
gōkin o tsukuru koto.
amanuensis [əmæ̀njuénsis] (*pl.* **-ses** [-si:z]) *n.* hikkō-sha; sho-
amaranth [ǽmərænθ] *n.* shibomanai hana (densetsu no). ⌐ki.
amaryllis [æ̀mərílis] *n.* (*bot.*) amaririsu (higambana ka no ha-
amass [əmǽs] *v.* tsumu; tameru. ⌐na).
amateur [ǽmətʃə] *n.* shirōto; amachua.
amatory [ǽmətəri] *a.* ren'ai no; koigokoro o okosu.
amaze [əméiz] *v.* odorokasu. **~dly** [əméizidli] *ad.* odoroite.
~ment *n.* (*poet.*) odoroki.
amazing [əméiziŋ] *a* odoroku beki; bikkuri suru hodo no.
~ly *ad.* odoroku hodo; hijōni.
Amazon [ǽməzən] *n.* onna musha (densetsu no), (*the A~*)
ambassador [æmbǽsədə] *n.* taishi. ⌐Amazon Gawa.
amber [ǽmbə] *n.* kohaku; kohakuiro.
ambergris [ǽmbəgri(:)s] *n.* (*bot.*) ryūzenkō.
ambidextrous [æ̀mbidékstrəs] *a.* ryōtegiki no; zurui.
ambiguity [æ̀mbigjú:iti] *n.* aimai; fumeiryō.
ambiguous [æmbígjuəs] *a.* aimaina; magirawashii. **~ly** *ad.*
aimaini.
ambition [æmbíʃən] *n.* yashin; ōkina kokorozashi.
ambitious [æmbíʃəs] *a.* yashinteki; taimō no aru. **~ly** *ad.*
taimō o idaite.
amble [ǽmbl] *n.* chōshi (uma no yurui aruki kata).
ambrosia [æmbróuzjə] *n.* kamisama no shokumotsu; hijōni

umai mono.

ambulance [ǽmbjuləns] *n.* yasen byōin ; kyūkyūsha.

ambulatory [ǽmbjulətəri] *a.* aruku ni tekishita. *n.* yūhojō.

ambuscade [æ̀mbəskéid] *n.* machibuse (basho). *v.* machibuse suru.

ambush [ǽmbuʃ] *n.*, *v.* machibuse (suru).

ameba [əmí:bə] *n.* amiiba (*amoeba*).

ameliorate [əmí:ljəreit] *v.* kairyō suru ; yoku suru (naru). **~tion** [əmì:ljəréiʃən] *n.* kairyō ; kaizen.

amen [éimén] *inter.* Amen !

amenable [əmí:nəbl] *a.* jūjunna ; shitagau gimu no aru.

amend [əménd] *v.* aratameru ; kaizen suru. **~ment** *n.* kaizen ; shūsei. **~s** [əméndz] *n.* baishō ; tsugunoi.

amenity [əmí:niti] *n.* kokochiyosa ; (*pl.*) kanji no yoi taido.

amerce [əmə́:s] *v.* bakkin o kasuru ; bassuru. **~ment** *n.* bakkin.

amerciable, ~cea- [əmə́:siəbl] *a.* bakkin o kashiuru.

American [əmérikən] *a.* Amerika no (-fūno). **~ism** *n.* Beikoku gohō ; Beikokushiki (A~ ryū) no iikata. **~ization** [-naizeiʃən] *n.* Amerikafūni suru koto.

Americanize [əmérikənaiz] *v* U.S.A. ni kika suru ; Amerikafū ni suru (naru).

amethyst [ǽməθist] *n.* (*min.*) murasakisuishō.

amiability [èimiəbíliti] *n.* airashii koto ; shinsetsu.

amiable [éimiəbl] *a.* airashii ; yasashii. **~bly** [éimiəbli] *ad.* aisoyoku.

amicable [ǽmikəbl] *a.* heiwatekina ; **~ settlement**, naka naori. **~bly** [ǽmikəbli] *ad.* heiwa ni. *adj.* shitashii.

amidst [əmídst] *prep.* ...no naka ni.

amino acid [əmí:nou ǽsid] *n.* amino-san.

amiss [əmís] *ad.*, *a.* ayamatte -ta ; waruku.

amity [ǽmiti] *n.* shimboku : in ~ with, to naka yoku. *treaty of ~*, shūkō jōyaku.

ammonia [əmóunjə] *n.* ammoniya.

ammunition [æ̀mjuníʃən] *n.* dan'yaku.

amnesia [æmní:ziə] *n.* kembōshō.

amnesty [ǽmnesti] *n.* taisha ; tokusha ; zainin o yurusu koto.

amoeba [əmí:bə] *n.* (*pl.* **-bae** [-bi:] ; **-s** [-bəz]). amiiba.

among [əmʌ́ŋ], **amongst** [əmʌ́ŋkst] *prep.* ...no naka ni.

amoral [æmɔ́rəl] *a.* dōtoku mushi no.

amorist [ǽmərist] *n.* iro ni fukeru hito.

amorous [ǽmərəs] *a.* kōshoku no.

amorphous [əmɔ́:fəs] *a.* ittei no katachi no nai.

amortize [əmɔ́:taiz] *v.* nashikuzushi ni shōkyaku suru.

amount [əmáunt] *v.* sōkei ga ... to naru. *n.* sōkei; gōkei.

ampère [ǽmpɛə] *n.* (denryū no) ampea. ～**meter** [-mí:tə] den-ryokukei.

amphibian [æmfíbian] *a.* suiriku ryōsei no.

amphibious [æmfíbiəs] *a.* suiriku ryōsei no.

amphitheater, -tre [ǽmfiθi(:)ətə] *n.* enkei tōgijō (gekijō).

ample [ǽmpl] *a.* hiroi; ōkina.

amplification [æ̀mplifikéiʃən] *n.* motto ōkiku, tsuyoku suru koto.

amplifier [ǽmplifaiə] *n.* rajio no dempa kakuseiki.

amplify [ǽmplifai] *v.* kakudai suru; hiroku naru.

amplitude [ǽmplitju:d] *n.* hirosa; ōkisa.

amply [ǽmpli] *ad.* hiroku; jūbunni.

amp(o)ule [ǽmpú:l/ǽm-] *n.* chūshayaku (ikkai-bun iri no kobin).

amputate [ǽmpjuteit] *v.* setsudan suru (geka shujutsu de).

amputation [æ̀mpjutéiʃən] *n.* setsudan; kiritori.

amuck [əmʌ́k] *ad.* chi ni uete: *run* ～, abaremawaru.

amulet [ǽmjulit] *n.* omamori; gofu.

amuse [əmjú:z] *v.* tanoshimaseru: ～ *onself with*, ... shite ta-noshimu. ～**ment** *n.* goraku.

amusing [əmjú:ziŋ] *a.* omoshiroi.

an [æn, ən] *a.* (*gram.*) futei kanshi.

anachronism [ənǽkrənizm] *n.* jidaisakugo.

anaconda [æ̀nəkɔ́ndə] *n.* isshu no daija.

anaemia [əní:miə] *n.* hinketsushō.

anaesthesia, anes- [æ̀nəsθí:ʒiə] *n.* masui.

anagram [ǽnəgræm] *n.* moji o okikaete, atarashii, go ya ku o tsukuru asobi.

anal [éinəl] *a.* kōmon no.

analects [ǽnəlekts] *n.* bassuishū.

analogical [ænəlɔ́dʒikl] *a.* ruisui no.

analogous [ənǽləgəs] *a.* ruiji no ; niyori no.

analogy [ənǽlədʒi] *n.* ruiji ; ruisui.

analyse [ǽnəlaiz] *v.* bunkai (bunseki) suru.

analysis [ənǽləsis] *n.* (*pl.* ~ses [-si:z]). bunkai.

analytic(al) [ænəlítikəl] *a.* bunkaiteki ; bunseki no. ~**ally** *ad.*

anarchical [æná:kikəl] *a.* museifu no ; museifu-(shugi) no.

anarchy [ǽnəki] *n.* museifu ; konran-jōtai. ~**ism** *n.* museifu-shugi. ~**ist** *n.* museifu-shugisha.

anathema [ənǽθimə] *n.* kinzei ; noroi ; kyōkai kara no tsui-hō (*explusion from church*).

anatomical [ænətɔ́mikl] *a.* kaibōgakujō no.

anatomy [ənǽtəmi] *n.* kaibōgaku. ~**ist** *n.* -gakusha.

ancestor [ǽnsestə] *n.* sosen.

ancestral [ænséstrəl] *a.* sosen no ; sosen denrai no.

ancestry [ǽnsestri] *n.* keizu ; iegara.

anchor [ǽŋkə] *n.* ikari : *at* ~ teihaku shite. *cast* ~, tōbyō suru. *lie at* ~, teihaku suru. *weigh* ~, ikari o ageru. ~**age** [ǽŋkəridʒ] *n.* fune no teihaku basho. *n.* (fune no) teihaku ; sono tame no zei.

anchoret [ǽŋkərit], anchorite [ǽŋkərait] *n.* inja (yo o saketa hito).

anchoress [ǽŋkəris] *n.* onna no inja. (*cf. anchoret.*)

ancient [éinʃənt] *a.* mukashi no : *the* ~*s*, kojin. ~**ly** *ad.* mukashi wa.

and [ǽnd, ən(d)] *conj.* to ; oyobi.

Andes [ǽndi:z] *n.* (*pl.*) Andes Sammyaku.

andiron [ǽndaiən] *n.* uma (irori no).

androgen [ǽndrədʒən] *n.* dansei horumonzai.

anecdote [ǽnikdout] *n.* itsuwa (mijikai omoshiroi hanashi). ~(e)al [ænikdóutl] *a.* itsuwa no.

anemia [əní:miə] *n.* (*med.*) hinketsushō (byōki).

anemic [əní:mik] *a.* hinketsushō no.

anemometer [ænimɔ́mitə] *n.* fūsokukei.

anemone [ənéməni] *n.* anemone : *sea* ~ isoginchaku.

anemophilous [ænimɔ́filəs] *a.* (*bot.*) fūbai no (kaze ga kafun (*pollen*) o hakobu.

aneroid [ǽnərɔid] *a*. ekitai (*liquid*) o tsukawanai : ～**barometer**, aneroid seiukei.

anesthesia, anaesthesia [æ̀nəsθí:ziə] *n*. masui.

anesthetic [æ̀nəsθétik] *a*. masui no. *n*. masuiyaku. ～**tist** [æní:sθitist] masui no kakari.

anesthetize [ənésθətaiz] *v*. masui o kakeru.

anew [ənjú:] *ad*. aratani.

angel [éindʒəl] *n*. tenshi; kami no tsukai. ～**ic(al)** [ændʒélik(l)] *a*. enjel no ; tenshi no yōna.

angelus [ǽndʒələs] *n*. mitsuge no inori.

anger [ǽŋgə] *n*. ikari. *v*. ikaru; okoraseru.

angle [ǽŋgl] *n*. kaku ; kakudo ; tsuribari. *v*. uo o tsuru. ～**r** [ǽŋglə] *n*. tsurishi; anko (*fish*). ～**ling** *n*. uo tsuri.

Angles [ǽŋglz] *n*. (*pl*) Angljin.

Anglican [ǽŋglikən] *a*. Eikoku no ; Eikoku-kokkyō no. ～**ism** *n*. Eikoku kokkyō.

Anglicize [ǽŋglisaiz] *v*. Eikokufū ni suru.

Anglo-American [ǽŋglouəmérikən] *a*. Ei-Bei no.

Anglo-Japanese [ǽŋgloudʒæ̀pəní:z] *a*. Ei-Wa no, Igilis to Nippon no.

Anglomania [æ̀ŋgləméiniə] *n*. Eikoku-biiki.

Anglophobia [æ̀ŋgləfóubiə] *n*. kyō-Eibyō (*excessive fear of England*).

Anglo-Saxon [ǽŋglousǽksn] *a*. *Anglo-Saxon* no.

Angola [æŋgóulə], **Angora** [æŋgó:rə] *n*. Angora-ori. *A*～ *wool* ; Angora yagi no ke.

angry [ǽŋgri] *a*. okotta ; hara o tateta. ～**ily** *ad*. okotte.

anguish [ǽŋgwiʃ] *n*. hammon ; kumon ; kurushimi.

angular [ǽŋgjulə] *a*. kado no aru.

angularity [æ̀ŋgjulǽriti] *n*. kado no aru koto.

anile [éinail] *a*. rōbajimita ; toshiyori no onna no yōna.

aniline [ǽnili(:)n] *n*. anirin.

anility [əníliti] *n*. mōroku ; rōmō.

animadversion [æ̀nimædvɔ́:ʃən] *n*. hinan ; warukuchi.

animadvert [æ̀nimædvɔ́:t] *v*. hinan suru.

animal [ǽniməl] *n*. dōbutsu. ～**ism** *n*. jūyokushugi. ～**cule**

[-kju:l] *n.* kyokubi (*microscopic*) dōbutsu.

animate [ǽnimeit] *v.* kakkizukeru. *a.* [ǽnimit] kakki no aru. ～**d** [-id] *a.* kiryoku sakanna.

animation [æ̀niméiʃən] *n.* kakki ; seiki.

animosity [æ̀nimɔ́siti] *n.* enkon ; urami.

animus [ǽniməs] *n.* nikushimi ; tekii.

anise [ǽnis] *n.* (*bot.*) anisu. ～**ed** [ǽnisi:d] (*bot.*) anisu no mi.

ankle [ǽŋkl] *n.* kurubushi. ～**t** [ǽŋklit] *n.* kurubushi kazari.

annalist [ǽnəlist] *n.* nendaiki henshūsha.

annals [ǽnləz] *n.* (*pl.*) nendaiki.

anneal [əní:l] *v.* yaki-namasu ; (*temper metal*).

annex [ənéks] *v.* tsuketasu ; gappei suru. *n.* tsuketashi ; tatemashi ; gappei.

annexation [æ̀nekséiʃən] *n.* tsuketasu koto ; gappei.

annihilate [ənáihileit] *v.* zemmetsu saseru ; zembu horobosu.

anniversary [æ̀nivɔ́:səri] *n.* kinembi ; kinensai.

Anno Domini [ǽnou dɔ́minai] =**A.D.**

annotate [ǽnouteit] *v.* chūshaku o tsukeru. ～**tion** [æ̀noutéiʃən] *n.* chūshaku. ～(**e**)**or** *n.* chūshakusha.

announce [ənáuns] *v.* happyō suru. ～**ment** *n.* tsūkoku ; happyō. ～**r** *n.* happyōsha ; anaunsā.

annoy [ənɔ́i] *v.* komaraseru. ～**ance** *n.* meiwaku. ～**ing** *a.* meiwaku suru. ～**ingly** *ad.* meiwaku shite.

annual [ǽnjuəl] *a.* maitoshi no ; nen-nen no. ～**ly** *ad.* maitoshi.

annuitant [ənjú:itənt] *n.* nenkin juryōsha.

annuity [ənjú:iti] *n.* nenkin.

annul [ənʌ́l] *v.* mukō ni suru ; torikesu. ～**ment** *n.* torikeshi.

annular [ǽnjulə] *a.* wa no katachi no ; wagata no.

annum [ǽnəm] *n.* nen ; toshi : *per* ～, maitoshi.

annunciate [ənʌ́nʃieit] *v.* kokuchi suru. ～**ion** *n.* tsūkoku. A～ Kami no otsuge. ～(**t**)**or** *n.* yobirin ; hyōjiki.

anode [ǽnoud] *n.* yōkyoku ; (+) no hō (*electricity*).

anodyne [ǽnədain] *a.* itami o shizumeru. *n.* chintsūzai ; itamidome no kusuri.

anoint [ənɔ́int] *v.* abura (*oil*) o nuru.

anomalous [ənómələs] *a.* namihazure no ; hensoku no.

anomaly [ənóməli] *n.* futsū to chigau.

anon [ənón] *ad.* jiki ni ; yagate. *ever and* ~ tokidoki ; oriori.

anonymous [ənóniməs] *a.* tokumei no. ~**ly** *ad.* namae o iwazu ni.

another [ənʌ́ðə] *a.* mōhitotsu no : *one* ~, otagai ni.

answer [ǽnsə] *n.* kotae. henji. *v.* kotaeru ; yaku ni tatsu ; seme o ou.

ant [ǽnt] *n.* ari. ~**eater** *n.* arikui.

an't [ɑ:nt/ænt/eint] = *ain't*.

antagonism [æntǽgənizm] *n.* tekitai ; hankō. ~**ist** *n.* teki ; hantaisha. ~**istic** [æntǽgənistik / æntægənístik] *a.* hantai no.

antagonize [æntǽgənaiz] *v.* tekitai suru ; tekii o idakaseru.

antarctic [æntá:ktik] *a.* Nankyoku no : *the A- Ocean*, Nan-pyō-yō.

ante-bellum [ǽntibéləm] *a.* senzen no.

antecedence [æ̀ntisí:dns] *n.* sakidachi.

antecedent [æ̀ntisí:dnt] *a.* sakidatsu. *n.* zenrei. (*pl.*) keireki. (*gram.*) senkōshi.

antechamber [ǽntitʃèimbə] *n.* hikae-shitsu ; tsugi no ma.

antedate [ǽntidéit] *v.* hizuke (*date*) o maeni suru.

antediluvian [æ̀ntidilú:viən] *a. Noah* no Kōzui izen no.

antelope [ǽntiloup] *n.* kamoshika.

ante meridiem [ǽntimərídiəm] = A.M. a.m.

ante mortem [ǽntimó:təm] *a.* seizen no ; shinanu mae no.

antenna [ænténə] *n.* (*pl.* -**nae** [-ni:]) shokkaku ; antena.

anterior [æntíəriə] *a.* mae no ; saki no.

anteroom [ǽntirù:m] *n.* hikae-shitsu ; tsugi no ma.

anthem [ǽnθəm] *n.* sambika : **national** ~, kokka.

anther [ǽnθə] *n.* (*bot.*) yaku (oshibe no atama ni aru). ~**dust**, kafun.

anthology [ænθólədʒi] *n.* meishishū, senshū (sugureta shi (*poems*) o atsumeta hon).

anthracite [ǽnθrəsait] *n.* muentan ; sekitan (kemuri no denai).

anthropoid [ǽnθrəpoid] *a.* hito ni nita. ruijin-en (*ape*).

anthropology [æ̀nθrəpólədʒi] *n.* jinruigaku. ~**ist** n. jinrui-gakusha.

anthropomorphic [æ̀nθrəpəmɔ́:fik] *a.* Shinjin-dōkeiron no (kami to ningen to ga onaji da to iu.)

anthropomorphize [æ̀nθrəpəmɔ́:faiz] *v.* kami o jinkakuka suru.

antiaircraft [æ̀ntiέəkrɑːft] *a.* kōkūki shageki-yō no hō: ～ *gun*, kōsha-hō.

antibiotic [æ̀ntibaiɔ́tik] *a.* bakuteria taikōsei no.

antic [ǽntik] *a.* kokkeina; fūgawari no. *n.* (*pl.*) kokkei.

anticipate [æntísipeit] *v.* saki o mikosu.

anticipation [æntìsipéiʃən] *n.* yosō; mikoshi.

anticipatory [æntísipeitəri / -tísipətori] *a.* yosō no; mikoshite no.

anticlimax [æ̀ntikláimæks] *n.* (*rhetoric*) bunsei-zenraku.

antidotal [ǽntidòutəl] *a.* doku o kudasu; gedoku no.

antidote [ǽntidòut] *n.* gedokuzai.

antifreeze [æ̀ntifríːz] *n.* (*Am.*) tōketsu-bōshizai.

antimony [ǽntiməni] *n.* anchimon.

antipathy [æntípəθi] *n.* hankan; daikirai.

antipodal [æntípədl] *a.* taishōteki no; ma-hantai no.

antipodes [æntípədìːz] *n.* (*pl.*) ma-hantaina basho (Nippon to Argentine no yōni).

antipyrin [æ̀ntipáiərin] *n.* anchipirin(e) (genetsuzai).

antiquarian [æ̀ntikwέəriən] *a.* kodai-kenkyū no.

antiquary [ǽntikwəri] *n.* kōkogakusha; kodai no kenkyūsha.

antiquated [ǽntikweitid] *a.* furuku natta; sutareta.

antique [æntíːk] *n.* kodai no ibutsu.

antiquity [æntíkwiti] *n.* ippan ni kodai no (fūshū; mono; seido etc.); (*pl.*) furui utsuwa nado.

antiseptic [æ̀ntiséptik] *a.* bōfuzai (no).

antitank [æ̀ntitǽŋk] *a.* tai-sensha no: ～ *gun*, taisensha-hō.

antithesis [æntíθisis] *n.* taishō; (*rhetoric*) tsuiku; taishōhō.

antithetic [æ̀ntiθétik] *a.* seihantai no; taishōhō no.

antitoxin [æ̀ntitɔ́ksin] *n.* kō-dokuso.

antitrades [ǽntitréidz] *n.* (*pl.*) hantai-bōeki-fū.

antler [ǽntlə] *n.* mata ni natta tsuno; matazuno.

antonym [ǽntənim] *n.* imi ga hantai no kotoba.

asnus [éinəs] *n.* kōmon.

anvil [ǽnvil] *n*. kanatoko (kajiya no) : *on the* ∼, jumbichū.

anxiety [æŋzáiəti] *n*. shimpai ;

anxious [ǽŋkʃəs] *a*. shimpaina ; shimpai shite ; setsubō shite. ∼**ly.** *ad* shimpaisōni.

any [éni] *a., pron*. dare ka ; ikura ka. ∼ **time** itsu demo. *not* ∼ *longer*, mō shinai.

anybody [énibɔ̀di], **anyone** [éniwən] *pron*. dare ka ; dare demo. *n*. bonjin.

anyhow [énihau] *ad*. tomokaku.

anyone [éniwən] *pron*. dare demo ; dore demo ; dare ka.

anything [éniθiŋ] *pron*. nan demo ; nani ka. ∼ *like*, nani demo...no yōna....

anyway [éniwei] *ad*. tomokaku ; dō demo (*anyhow*).

anywhere [énihwɛə] *ad*. doko ni (e) demo ; doko ni ka.

anywise [éniwaiz] *ad*. dō shite mo ; kesshite.

aorta [éiɔ:tə] *n*. (*pl.* **-tae** [-ti:]) daidōmyaku.

A.P. AP tsūshin-sha (*Associated Press*).

apace [əpéis] *ad*. isoide ; sassato.

apart [əpá:t] *ad*. wakarete ; hanarete ; wa betsu to shite.

apartment [əpá:tmənt] *n*. apāto. ∼ *house*, apāto jūtaku.

apathetic [ӕpəθétik] *a*. kanji nai ; reitanna.

apathy [ǽpəθi] *n*. reitan ; mukankaku (*indifference*).

ape [éip] *n*. saru. *v*. maneru.

aperient [əpíəriənt] *a*, tsūji o tsukeru. *n*. gezai.

apéritif [æperiti:f] *n*. shokuyoku zōshinzai.

aperture [ǽpətʃuə] *n*. ana ; wareme.

apex [éipeks] *n*. (*pl.* **-es** *or* **apices** [ǽpisi:z]) chōten.

aphasia [əféiʒiə] *n*. shitsugoshō.

aphelion [əfí:liən] *n*. (*pl.* **-lia** [-liə]) enjitsuten.

aphorism [ǽfərizm] *n*. kingen ; kakugen.

aphrodisiac [ӕfrədíziæk] *a*. saiin-zai no. *n*. saiin-zai.

apiary [éipjəri] *n*. yōhōjo.

apiculture [éipikəltʃə] *n*. yōhō.

apiece [əpí:s] *a*. hitori (ikko) ni tsuki ; meimei ni.

apocalypse [əpɔ́kəlips] *n*. mokushi ; Kami no osatoshi (*instruction*). A∼ Mokushiroku.

apish [éipiʃ] *a*. saru ni nita ; hito mane suru.

Apocrypha [əpɔ́krifə] *n.* (*sing.* & *pl.*) Seishoigai no Seisho.
apogee [ǽpədʒi:] *n.* enchiten; chikyū kara ichiban tōi tokoro.
Apollo [əpɔ́lou] *n.* Aporo Gami.
apologetic [əpɔ̀lədʒétik] *a.* benkaiteki. ～s *n.* (*pl.*) Kirisuto-kyō benshōron. ～ally *ad.* benkai shite; benkaitekini.
apologize [əpɔ́lədʒaiz] *v.* ayamaru; wabiru.
apologue [ǽpəloug] *n.* gūwa; kyōkun monogatari.
apology [əpɔ́lədʒi] *n.* benkai; owabi.
apoplexy [ǽpəpleksi] *n.* sotchū.
apostasy [əpɔ́stəsi] *n.* haikyō; oshie ni somuku (*violate*).
apostate [əpɔ́steit] *n., a.* hai-kyōsha (no); hensetsu no.
aposteriori [éipɔstəriɔ́:rai] *a., ad.* kōtenteki no; kinōteki no
apostle [əpɔ́sl] *n.* shito; dendōsha.
apostolic [ǽpəstɔ́lik] *a.* shito (*apostle*) no.
apostrophe [əpɔ́strəfi] *n.* apostrofii; ji o habuita shirushi (').
apothecary [əpɔ́θikəri] *n.* kusuriya.
apotheosis [əpɔ̀θióusis] (*pl.* **-ses** [-si:z]) *n.* kami to shite aga-meru koto.
appal [əpɔ́:l] *v.* **-palled**; **-palling.** gyōten (bikkuri) saseru. ～ling *a.* osoroshii.
apparatus [ǽpəréitəs] *n.* kigu; kikai.
apparel [əpǽrəl] *n., v.* ifuku; (ifuku o) kiseru.
apparent [əpǽrənt] *a.* meihakuna; uwabe no : *heir* ～, chaku-shi; yotsugi. ～ly *ad.* gaiken-jō.
apparition [ǽpəríʃən] *n.* shutsugen; yōkai; yūrei (nado).
appeal [əpí:l] *v.* kōso suru; kōkan o idakaseru. *n.* kōso; uttae.
appear [əpíə] *v.* arawareru. ～ance *n.* shutsugen; gaikan.
appease [əpí:z] *v.* shizumeru; yawarageru. ～ment *n.* yūwa. ～policies, yūwa seisaku.
appellant [əpélənt] *n.* kōso-nin.
appellate [əpélit] *a.* kōso no; jōkoku no.
appellation [ǽpəléiʃən] *n.* meishō; namae.
appellative [əpélətiv] *a.* meishō no. *n.* sono kaikyū (*class*) ip-pan ni tsūjiru yōna namae.
append [əpénd] *v.* kakeru (ito nado de); tsuika suru. ～age [-idʒ] *n.* furoku.
appendices [əpéndisi:z] *n. see* : **appendix**

appendicitis [əpèndisáitis] *n.* mōchōen.

appendix [əpéndiks] *n.* (*pl.* -ces [-si:z]) furoku.

appertain [æpətéin] *v.* zoku suru.

appetite [ǽpitait] *n.* shokuyoku.

appetize [ǽpitaiz] *v.* shokuyoku o sosoru. ⌐o sosoru mono. ～r *n.* shokuyoku

appetizing [ǽpitaiziŋ] *a.* umasōna.

applaud [əplɔ́:d] *v.* hakushu-kassai suru.

applause [əplɔ́:z] *n.* kassai.

apple [ǽpl] *n.* ringo. ～pie, ringo iri no pai.

appliance [əpláiəns] *n.* dōgu ; utsuwa.

applicable [ǽplikəbl] *a.* tsukaeru ; yaku ni tatsu.

applicant [ǽplikənt] *n.* shutsugansha ; ōbosha.

application [æplikéiʃən] *n.* tekiyō ; ōyō ; mōshikomi.

appliqué [ǽplikéi] (*Fr.*) *a., n.* nuitsuketa (kazari). *v.* moyō nado o tsukeru.

apply [əplái] *v.* ōyō suru ; ateru : ～ *oneself to* ..., ni sennen suru ; mōshikomu. ～ *for a position*, shūshoku o mōshikomu. ～ied [əpláid] ōyō no.

appoint [əpɔ́int] *v.* nimmei suru. ～ed [-id] *a.* shitei no. ～ment *n.* nimmei. ～ee [əpɔ̀inti:] *n.* nimmeisareta hito.

apportion [əpɔ́:ʃən] *v.* wariateru. ～ment *n.* wariate.

apposite [ǽpəzit] *a.* tekitōna. ～ly *ad.* tekitōni. ～ness *n.* tekitō.

apposition [æpəzíʃən] *n.* (*gram.*) dōkaku. ～al *a.* dōkaku no.

appraisal [əpréizl] *n.* hyōka ; kantei.

appraise [əpréiz] *v.* hyōka suru ; kantei suru. ～ment *n.* hyōka ; kantei. ～r *n.* hyōkasha ; kanteisha.

appreciable [əpríːʃiəbl] *a.* hyōka no neuchi ga aru.

appreciate [əpríːʃieit] *v.* hyōka suru ; kansha suru. ～(t)ion *n.* [əprìːʃiéiʃən] hyōka ; kanshō. ～(t)ive [əpríːʃiətiv] *a.* kanshōsuru ; manzoku shita.

apprehend [æprihénd] *v.* toraeru ; rikai suru ; kizukau.

apprehensible [æprihénsəbl] *a.* rikai sare uru.

apprehension [æprihénʃən] *n.* rikai ; rikai suru chikara ; fuanshin ; taiho (*arrest*).

apprehensive [æprihénsiv] *a.* etoku (wakari no hayai) ; kizukatte (iru). ～ *of one's safety*, mi no anzen o osoreru (kizukau).

apprentice [əpréntis] *n.* totei ; deshi. ~**ship** *n.* totei no nenki.

apprise [əpráiz] *v.* shiraseru.

approach [əpróutʃ] *v.* chikazuku ; …ni chikazuku. *n.* sekkin. ~**able** *a.* chikazuki yasui.

approbation [æ̀prəbéiʃən] *n.* zenin ; sansei ; kyoka.

appropriate [əpróuprieit] *v.* wagamono ni suru. — *a.* tekitōna. ~**ly** *ad.* tekitō ni. ~**(t)ion** *n.* tekitōni ryūyō suru koto.

approval [əprú:vəl] *n.* zenin ; sansei.

approve [əprú:v] *v.* zenin suru ; sansei suru.

approximate [əpróksimeit] *v.* chikazukeru ; chikazuku. [əpróksimit] *a.* ōyoso no ; chikai. ~**ly** *ad.* ōyoso, hobo. ~**(t)ion** *n.* sekkin ; chikai koto.

appurtenance [əpə́:tinəns] *n.* fuzokuhin.

appurtenant [əpə́:tinənt] *a.* fuzoku no.

apricot [éiprikɔt] *n.* anzu.

April [éiprəl/-ril] *n.* shigatsu : ~ *fool*, shigatsu-baka.

apriori [éipraió:rai] (*L.*) sententeki ; gen'in kara kekka ni iku.

apron [éiprən] *n.* epron ; maekake. ~**string** *n.* maekake no himo.

apropos [æ̀prəpóu] *ad.* tekitōni ; tsuide ni : ~ *of*, ni tsuite wa.

apt [æpt] *a.* tekisetsuna ; …shi yasui. ~**ly** tekisetsu ni. ~**ness**

aptitude [ǽptitju:d] *n.* keikō ; tachi ; soshitsu. [tekisetsu.

aquamarine [æ̀kwəmərí:n] *n.* aidama ishi (rangyokuishi) ; akamarin.

aquaplane [ǽkwəpléin] *n.* kassō-ita (*motor-boat* ga hipparu).

aquarium [əkwéəriəm] *n.* suizokkan.

aquatic [əkwǽtik] *a.* mizu no ; suichū (suijō) no. *n.* suichū ni ikiru mono ; (*pl.*) suijō kyōgi.

aqua vitae [ǽkwə váiti(:)] (*L.*) *n.* jōryū shita arukōru inryō.

aqueduct [ǽkwidʌkt] *n.* suidō ; (no kuda).

aqueous [éikwiəs/ǽ] *a.* mizu no.

aquiline [ǽkwil(a)in] *a.* washi (no kuchibashi) no yōna.

Arab [ǽrəb] *n.* Arabiyajin (uma).

arabesque [æ̀rəbésk] *n.* karakusa-moyō.

Arabian [əréibiən] *a., n.* Arabiya (jin) no ; Arabiyajin.

Arabic [ǽrəbik] *a., n.* Arabiya no. Arabiyago.

arable [ǽrəbl] *a.* kōsaku ni tekishita : ~ *land*, kōchi.

arbiter [á:bitə] *n*. chūsainin; saiketsusha.
arbitral [á:bitrəl] *a*. chūsai (nin) no.
arbitrament [ɑ:bítrəmənt] *n*. chūsai; saiketsu.
arbitrary [á:bitrəri] *a*. kimamana; sen'ōna. ∼**ly** *ad*. kimamani. ∼**iness** *n*. sen'ō.
arbitrate [á:bitreit] *v*. chūsai suru.
arbitration [à:bitréiʃən] *n*. chūsai: ∼ *of exchange*, gaikoku kawase saitei.
arbitrator [á:bitreitə] *n*. chūsainin; saiketsusha.
arbor [á:bə] *n*. ki; takai ki: ∼ *day*, (*Am*.) ki o ueru· hi.
arbo(u)r [á:bə] *n*. azumaya; chin.
arc [á:k] *n*. ko; yumigata. ∼**-lamp**, āku-tō.
arcade [ɑ:kéid] *n*. yanetsuki gairo; nakamise. 「stery).
arcanum [ɑ:kéinəm] *n*. (*pl*. ∼**na** [-nə]) himitsu; shimpi (*my*-
arch [ɑ:tʃ] *n*. āchi; ryokumon; han'enkei: *triumphal* ∼, gaisen mon. *a*. kashira no. ∼**ed** [-d] *a*. yumigata no.
archaeologic [à:kiɔ́lədʒik] *a*. kōkogaku no.
archaeologist [à:kiɔ́ləbʒist] *n*. kōkogakusha.
archaeology [à:kiɔ́lədʒi] *n*. kōkogaku.
archaic [ɑ:kéiik] *a*. kodai no; furui, sutareta jidai no.
archaism [á:keiizm] *n*. kodai no go (buntai, kenchiku, bijitsu
archangel [á:kɔ̀indʒəl] *n*. dai-tenshi; tenshichō. 「nado).
archbishop [á:tʃbíʃəp] *n*. dai-kantoku; dai-shikyō.
archdeacon [á:tʃdí:kən] *n*. fukukantoku.
archduchess [á:tʃdátʃis] *n*. taikōhi.
archduchy [á:tʃdatʃi] *n*. taikōkoku.
archduke [á:tʃdjú:k] *n*. taikō (kyū Ōstriya no kōtaishi).
archer [á:tʃə] *n*. (yumi o) iru hito; ite. ∼**y** [-ri] *n*. kyūjutsu.
archetype [á:kitaip] *n*. genkei (*prototype*).
archfiend [á:tʃfí:nd] *n*. akuma no ō, Satan.
archipelago [à:kipélɔgou] *n*. guntō; Tatōkai. *The A*∼, Ēge-
architect [á:kitekt] *n*. kenchikuka. 「kai.
architectural [à:kitéktjurəl] *a*. kenchikujutsu (∼*gaku*) no.
architecture [á:kitektjuə] *n*. kenchikujutsu; kenchikugaku (yōshiki).
archives [á:kaivz] *n*. kiroku-hosonjo; kiroku; kōmonjo.
Arctic [á:ktik] *a*. Hokkyoku no: *the A. Ocean*, Hoppyōyō.

ardency [á:dənsi] *n.* nesshin ; netsuretsu.
ardent [á:dənt] *a.* nesshinna ; netsuretsuna : ~*spirit*, tsuyoi sake. ~**ly** *ad.* ~**ni**.
ardo(u)r [á:də] *n.* nesshin.
arduous [á:djuəs] *a.* hone no oreru ; konnanna.
are [ɑ:] *v.* 'you', 'we', 'they' nado ni tsukau "be" no
area [éəriə] *n.* hirosa ; menseki ; han'i. ⌊genzaikei.
arena [ərí:nə] *n.* dōjō ; kyōgijō.
argent [á:dʒənt] *a.* gin no (yōna) ; gin'iro no.
Argentine [á:dʒəntain] *n., a.* Aruzenchin Kyōwakoku (no).
argon [á:gən] *n.* arugon.
Argonaut [á:gənɔ:t] *n.* Arugosen norikumiin.
argosy [á:gəsi] *n,* dai-shōsen (-tai).
argot [á:gou] *n.* ingo ; kakushi kotoba (toku ni tōzoku nado no).
argue [á:gju:] *v.* giron suru. ~**ment** [á:gjumənt] *n.* giron.
argumentation [à:gjumentéiʃən] *n.* giron (tōron) suru koto.
argumentative [à:gjuméntətiv] *a.* giron-zukina ; rikutsuppoi.
Argus [á:gəs] *n.* Arugos (me o 100 motta kyojin -*giant*).
aria [á:riə/éə-] *n.* (*mus.*) aria chō no uta.
arid [ǽrid] *a.* kawaita ; kansō shita. ~**ity** [əríditi] kansō ; bosshumi (*prosaic*).
aright [əráit] *ad.* tadashiku
arise [əráiz] *v.* **arose, arisen; arising.** okiru ; noboru shōzuru.
arisen [ərízn] *see :* arise.
aristocracy [æ̀ristɔ́krəsi] *n.* kizoku-seitai ; kizoku-shakai.
aristocrat [ərístəkræt] *n.* kizoku (kaikyū).
aristocratic [ərìstəkrǽtik] *a.* kizoku no ; kizokuteki. ~**ally**, kizokuteki ni.
arithmetic [əríθmetik] *n.* sanjutsu. ~**al** [æ̀riθmétikl] *a.* sanjutsu no. ~**ian** [əriθmətíʃən] *n.* sanjutsuka.
ark [ɑ:k] *n.* hakobune (*Noah* ga daikōzui no toki notta fune)
arm [ɑ:m] *n.* (1) ude : *keep at* ~'s *length*, tōzakeru ; keien suru. (1) heiki ; buki. *v.* busō saseru (suru). ~**chair** *n.* hijikake-isu. ~**ful** *a.* hitokakae. ~**hole** *n.* (fuku no) sodetsuke. ~**less** *a.* ude no nai ; buki o motte inai. ~**pit** *n.* wakinoshita.
armada [ɑ:má:də] *n.* kantai ; hikōtai : *the Invincible A-.*, Muteki

Kantai (16 c. Spein no).

armadillo [à:mədílou] *n.* yoroi nezumi.

armament [á:məmənt] *n.* heiki ; gumbi ; busō.

armature [á:mətjuə] *n.* buki ; busō (dōbutsu ippan no).

armed [á:md] *a.* busō shita : ~ **neutrality**, busō chūritsu.

Armenian [ɑ:mí:niən] *n.* Arumeniya (jin ; go) no.

armistice [á:mistis/-mís-] *n.* kyūsen : A~*Day*. Daiichiji Sekaitaisen Kyūsen Kinembi.

armlet [á:mlit] *n.* udekazari.

armorial [ɑ:mɔ́:riəl] *a.* monshō no : ~ *bearings*, monshō.

armo(u)r [á:mə] *n.* katchū ; yoroi kabuto : ~ **plate**, kōtetsu ban. **coat** ~, monshō. ~**er** [-rə] *n.* heikikō.

armo(u)red [á:məd] *a.* busō no ; busō shita : ~ **car**, sōkō-jidōsha. ~**cruiser** sōkō-junyōkan.

armo(u)ry [á:məri] *n.* heikishō.

arms [ɑ:mz] *n.* buki ; monshō.

army [á:mi] *n.* rikugun ; guntai. ~ **corps**, gundan. ~ **list**, rikugun meibo.

aroma [əróumə] *n.* kaori ; nioi.

aromatic [ærəmætik] *a.* kōki (nioi) no aru. *n.* kōryō.

arose [əróuz] *v. see* : **arise**.

around [əráund] *ad., prep.* (...no) mawari ni ; (*Am.*) ...koro (goro) : ~ *5 o'clock*, goji goro.

arouse [əráuz] *v.* okosu ; samasu ; yobiokosu.

arpeggio [ɑ:pédʒiou] *n.* arupejio ; waon no renkyūdansō.

arraign [əréin] *v.* shōkan suru ; yobidasu. ~**ment** *n.* shōkan ; yobidashi.

arrange [əréindʒ] *v.* (arasoi o) matomeru ; torikime o suru ; ~**ment** *n.* seiri ; kyōtei (*agreement*).

arrant [ærənt] *a.* kyokutanni warui ; gokuaku no.

arras [ærəs] *n.* arasu-ori (utsukushii tsuzureori).

array [əréi] *n.* chinretsu ; gunzei ; ishō. *v.* naraberu ; yosou.

arrear [əríə] *n.* okureru koto ; todokōri (shiharai nado no). ~**age** [əríəridʒ] *n.* todokōri ; miharaikin.

arrest [ərést] *v., u.* taiho (suru) ; (kokoro o) ubau (ko to).

arrive [əráiv] *v.* tōchaku suru. **arrival** [-əl] *n.* tōchaku.

arrogance [ærəgəns] *n.* sondai ; ōhei.

arrogant [ǽrəgənt] *a.* sondaina ; ōheina.

arrogate [ǽrəgeit] *v.* yokodori suru ; watakushi suru.

arrogation [ærəgéiʃən] *n.* yokodori suru koto ; sen'etsu.

arrow [ǽrou] *n.* (yumi no) ya. ~**head,** *n,* yajiri ; kuwai. ~ **-headed** [-hédid] *a.* yajiri gata no. ~**root** *n.* kuzuko.

arrowy [ǽroui] *a.* ya no yōna.

arsenal [á:sənəl] *n.* heikishō : **naval** ~, kaigun kōshō.

arsenic [á:sənik] *n.* hiso.

arson [á:sn] *n.* hōka ; hitsuke ; hōkazai.

art [ɑ:t] (1) *v.* 'thou' (2-ninshō, tansū) no 'be' no genzai. (2) (2) *n.* gigei ; geijutsu : *fine arts*, bijutsu. *Master of Arts*, bungakushūshi.

arterial [ɑ:tíəriəl] *a.* dōmyaku (kekkan) no.

artery [á:təri] *n.* dōmyaku.

artesian well [ɑ:tí:zjiən wel] *n.* horinuki ido.

artful [á:tful] *a.* takumina ; kōkatsuna. ~**ly** *ad.* kōmyōni. ~**ness** *n.* takurami-no aru koto ; kōkatsu.

artichoke [á:titʃouk] *n.* (*bot.*) chōsen-azami ; kikuimo.

article [á:tikl] *n.* shinamono ; kajō ; ronsetsu ; (*gram.*) kanshi (*a, an, the*).

articular [ɑ:tíkjulə] *a.* kansetsu no ; fushi no aru.

articulate [ɑ:tíkjulit] *a.* fushi no aru (' o-ka-shi-mi', nado wa 3 no fushi ga aru to iu). [ɑ:tíkjuleit] *v.* fushi o tsukeru.

articulation [ɑ:tìkjuléiʃən] *n.* kotoba no on ni fushi o tsukeru koto.

artifice [á:tifis] *n.* sakuryaku ; tekuda. ~**r** *n.* shokunin ; gijutsusha.

artificial [à:tifíʃiəl] *a.* jinkō no ; fushizenna. ~**ly** *ad.* jinkōtekini.

artillery [à:tíləri] *n.* taihō ; hōhei ; hōheitai : ~ **train,** hōheijūretsu. ~**man** *n.* hōhei.

artisan [á:tizæn] *n.* shokunin.

artist [á:tist] *n.* bijutsuka ; geijutsuka.

artiste [ɑ:tí:st] (*Fr.*) *n.* geijutsuka (haiyū, kashu ; dansā nado no yōna).

artistic [ɑ:tístik] *a.* geijutsu no ; bijutsuteki no. ~**ally** *ad.* bijutsutekini.

artless [ά:tlis] *a.* kazari no nai ; hetana. **～ly** *ad.* **～ness** *n.* heta ; busaiku.

Aryan [έəriən/ά:-] *a.* Arian shuzoku no. *n.* Arianjin ; Arias [æz] *ad., conj.* no yōni ; dake ; toki ni ; ...nagara ; toshite : ～ (or *so*) ...to onaji hodo ni. **～for** (or *to*) ...wa to ieba ; ni kanshite wa. ～ *if* (or *though*) atakamo ...ka no yōni. **～it is**, sono mama. ～ *it were*, iwaba.

asbestos [æzbéstəs] *n.* sekimen ; ishiwata.

ascend [əsénd] *v.* noboru. **～ancy** ; **～ency** *n.* yūetsu ; kensei. **～ant**, **～ent** *a.* sugureta ; seiryoku aru ; nobotte iku.

ascension [əsénʃən] *n.* jōshō ; (*the A*～) (Kirisuto no) shōten.

ascent [əsént] *n.* jōshō ; noborizaka ; noborimichi.

ascertain [æsətéin] *v.* tashikameru.

ascetic [əsétik] *a.* kin'yokuteki no ; kugyōsha no. *n.* kugyōsha.

asceticism [əsétisizm] *n.* kin'yokushugi ; nangyō-kugyō.

ascribable [əskráibəbl] *a.* kiserareru.

ascribe [əskráib] *v.* ni kisuru ; no sei ni suru.

aseptic [əséptik] *a.* bōfusei (kusaridome) no.

asexual [əséksuəl/æ-] *a.* sei (*sex*) no nai ; musei seishoku no.

ash [æʃ] *n.* (*bot.*) toneriko. **～es** [æʃiz] *n.* (*pl.*) hai. **～pan** *n.* haiuke. **～en** [æʃn] *n.* toneriko no ; haiiro no. **～y** [æʃi] *a.* haidarake no ; haiiro no. **～-tray** *n.* haizara.

ashamed [əʃéimd] *a.* hajite ; sekimenshite.

ashore [əʃɔ́:] *ad.* hama ni ; rikujō ni : *run*～, zashō suru. (funega)

Ash Wednesday [æʃwénzdi] *n.* *Easter* no mae no Dai 7 kai no Suiyō, *Lent* Sai no Dai 1-nichi.

Asiatic [eiʃiǽtik] *a.* Ajia no. *n.* Ajiajin.

aside [əsáid] *ad.* soba ni ; katawara ni. *n.* wakiserifu (*aside*).

asinine [ǽsinain] *a.* roba no yōna ; gudonna.

ask [ɑ:sk/æsk] *v.* kiku ; tazuneru ; tanomu.

askance [əská:ns], **askant** [əská:nt] *ad.* yokome de (niramu).

askew [ǽskju:] *ad.* naname ni ; yokome de.

aslant [əslá:nt] *ad.* naname ni.

asleep [əslí:p] *ad.* nemutte ; shinde : *fall* ～ nekomu ; netsuku.

assimilation [əsìmiléiʃən] *n.* dōka (*cf. dissimilation*).

asparagus [əspǽrəgəs] *n.* asparagas.

aspect [ǽspekt] *n.* kōkei ; kyokumen ; arisama.

aspen [ǽspn] *n.* hakoyanagi. *a.* hakoyanagi no ; furueru.

asperity [æspériti] *n.* araarashisa ; buaisō ; (tenkō no) ken'aku.

asperse [əspɔ́:s] *v.* soshiru ; chūshō suru.

asperson [əspɔ́:sən/æs-] *n.* chūshō ; warukuchi.

asphalt [ǽsfælt/æsfǽlt] *n.* asfaruto.

asphodel [ǽsfədel] *n.* Gokuraku ni saku yuri.

asphyxia [æsfíksiə] *n.* (*med.*) chissoku ; kashi (*apparent death*).

asphyxiate [æsfíksieit] *v.* chissoku saseru.

aspirant [əspáirənt] *a.* akugarete *n.* netsubōsha.

aspirate [ǽspirit] (*phon.*) *n., a.* [h]-on noyōni ; iki dake no.

aspiration [æspiréiʃən] *n.* taibō ; iki no hitosui ; kion hassei ; " h " -on no hassei.

aspire [əspáiə] *v.* netsubō suru.

aspirin [ǽspirin] *n.* aspirin.

aspiring [əspáiəriŋ] taimō o idaku ; kōjōshin no aru.

asquint [əskwínt] *ad.* yokome de.

ass [æs] *n.* roba ; baka : *make an* ~*of,* o chōrō suru.

assail [əséil] *v.* kōgeki suru. ~**able** *a.* kōgeki dekiru. ~**ant** *a.* kōgeki suru. *n.* kōgekisha ; kagaisha.

assassin [əsǽsin] *n.* ansatsusha. ~**ate** [-eit] *v.* ansatsu suru. ~**ation** [əsæsinéiʃən] *n.* ansatsu.

assault [əsɔ́:lt] *n., v.* shūgeki, bōkō (suru). ~**er** *n.* shūgeki-sha.

assay [əséi] *n.* kōseki (*ocher*) no junsuido (*pureness*) no kensa. *v.* kensa o suru.

assemblage [əsémblidʒ] *n.* shūgō ; shūgō shita gunshū.

assemble [əsémbl] *v.* atsumeru (-aru) ; kumitateru.

assembly [əsémbli] *n.* shūkai ; kaigi : ~ *line,* nagare-sagyō (hō). ~**man** *n.* (*Am.*) shū-gikai-giin.

assent [əsént] *n., v.* dōi, kyōsan (suru).

assert [əsɔ́:t] *v.* iiharu ; shuchō suru. ~**ive** *a.* dangenteki. ~**tion** [-ʃən] *n.* shuchō ; gemmei ; dangen.

assess [əsés] *v.* satei suru (zaisan nado o) ; kazei suru. *n.* zeikin (*tax*) no wariate. ~**ment** *n.* sono zeigaku. ~**or** *n,* kazei hyōka o suru hito.

assets [ǽsets] *n.* (*pl.*) shisan (*property*) ; zaisan : ~ *and liabilities,* shisan to fusai.

asseverate [əsévəreit] v. dangen suru; iiharu. **~tion** [əsèvəréiʃən] n. dangen.

assiduity [æsidjú:iti] n. kimben. (*pl.*) konsetsu; hairyo. ┌de.

assiduous [əsídjuəs] a. kimbenna; shinsetsuna.**~ly** ad. hagen-

assign [əsáin] v. wariateru; nimmei suru. n. yuzuri-ukenin. **~ee** [əsainí:] n. yuzuri-ukenin. **~er**, **~or** n. jōto-nin; yuzuri-watasu hito. **~ment** n. wariate; shitei.

assignation [æsignéiʃən] n. wariate; seishiki jōto (yuzuri watashi); (jikan, basho no) shitei.

assimilate [əsímileit] v. dōka suru.

assimilation [əsìmiléiʃən] n. dōka; onajiyō ni naru koto.

assist [əsíst] v. tasukeru; nakamairi suru. **~ance** n. joryoku. **~ant** a. tasukeru. n. joshu. ┌dan.

assize [əsáiz] n. junkai saiban; pan ya *ale*-shu no hōtei ne-

associate [əsóuʃieit] v. rensō suru; majiwaru: **~oneself with** ...ni kanyū suru. n. [**~it**] nakama; kumiai-chō (*president*).

association [əsòsiéiʃən] n. rengō; kyōkai; rensō.

assort [əsɔ́:t] v. bunrui suru; nakama ni naru: **~ with**, nakama ni naru. **~ment** n. bunrui. ┌kanwa.

assuage [əswéidʒ] v. yawarageru; shizumeru. **~ment** n.

assume [əsjú:m] v. furi o suru: He **~ed a look of innocence**, kare wa nani kuwanu kao o shite ita. ...to uketoru: let us **~that this is true**, kore o hontō to shiyō. toru: He **~ed the rein of government**, kare wa seiken o totta.

assuming [əsjú:miŋ] a. ōheina; sen'etsuna. n. ōhei; gōman.

assumption [əsʌ́mpʃən] n. furi; sen'etsu; katei, (suitei).

assurance [əʃúərəns] n. hoshō; kakushin.

assure [əʃúə] v. hoshō suru; tashikameru. **~d** [-d] a. tashi-kana; jishin no aru. **~dly** [-idli] ad. tashikani.

Assyrian [əsíriən] a. Asshiriya no. n. Asshiriyajin; Asshiriya-go.

Assyriology [æsiriɔ́ləgi] n. Ashiriagaku; A**~** no gengo, bun-ken (*document*) nado no kenkyū.

aster [ǽstə] n. (*bot.*) shion; ezogiku.

asterisk [ǽstərisk] n. hoshijirushi.

astern [əstɔ́:n] ad. sembi ni; sembi no hō e.

asteroid [ǽstərɔid] *n.* Kasei to Mokusei no aida ni atte taiyō o mawaru shōyūsei.

asthma [ǽsmə] *n.* (*med.*) zensoku. ～**tic** *a.* zensoku no.

astigmatism [əstígmətizm] *n.* ranshi (*focus* no midare).

astir [əstə́:] *a.* ugoite ; sawaide.

astonish [əstɔ́niʃ] *v.* odorokasu. ～**ment** *n.* odoroki.

astound [əstáund] *v.* bikkuri (gyōten) saseru.

astrakhan [ǽstrəkən] *n.* Astrakan-gawa (*leather*).

astral [ǽstrəl] *a.* hoshi (*star*) no.

astray [əstréi] *ad* mayotte : *go* ～,mayou ; tadashii michi o fumihazusu.

astride [əstráid] *a.*, *ad.* mataide. *prep.* ...ni matagatte.

astringency [əstríndʒənsi] *n.* shūrensei ; kibishisa, hikishimeru koto.　⎰ru (*austere, binding*).

astringent [əstríndʒənt] *a.* shūrensei no ; kibishi ; hikishime-

astrologer [əstrɔ́lədʒə] *n.* hoshiuranaisha.

astrology [əstrɔ́lədʒi] *n.* sensei gaku ; hoshiuranai. ～**ical** *a.* hoshiuranai no.

astronomer [əstrɔ́nəmə] *n.* temmongakusha.

astronomy [əstrɔ́nəmi] *n.* temmongaku. ～**ic(al)** [æstrənɔ́mik(l)] *a.* temmongakujō no.

astute [əstjú:t] *a.* nukeme no nai ; surudoi.

asunder [əsʌ́ndə] *ad.* futatsu ni warete ; betsubetsu ni

asylum [əsáiləm] *n.* hinanjo ; yōikuin.

at [æt, ət] *prep.* ...no tokoro ni ; ...ni oite. ; itten ni ; jūji shite.

atavism [ǽtəvizm] *n.* kakusei-iden (sofu kara mago ni iden suru) ; senzogaeri.

ate [eit/et] *v. see* : **eat.**

atelier [ǽtəljei] (*Fr.*) *n.* atorie.

atheism [éiθiizm] *n.* mushinron. ～**ist** *n.* mushinronsha.

atheistic(al) [èiθiístik(l)] *a.* mushinron (teki) no.

Athena [əθí:nə], **Athene** [əθí:ni(:)] *n.* Atene, (*Anc. Greece* no megami (*Goddess*)).

Athenaeum [æ̀θiní:əm] *n.* Atene no shinden ; bungaku-kagaku-sha no kurabu.

Athenian [əθí:niən] *a.* Atene (*Athens*) no. *n.* Atenejin.

athirst [əθə́:st] *a* mizu ga nomi takute ; katsubō shite (iru).

athlete [ǽθli:t] *n.* kyōgisha ; undōka ;.

athletic [æθlétik] *a.* kyōgi no. ~s [æθlétiks] *n.* kyōgi.

at-home [əthóum] *n.* menkai no tame ni uchi ni iru koto : ~ *day*, menkaibi.

athwart [əθwɔ́:t] *prep.* yokogitte ; *ad.* ni aitaishite.

Atlantic [ətlǽntik] *a.* Taiseiyō no : *the* ~ *Ocean*, Taisei-yō.

atlas [ǽtləs] *n.* chizu sho.

atmosphere [ǽtməsfiə] *n.* taiki. (*air*) fun'iki (*general tendency*).

atmospheric(al) [ætməsférik(l)] *a.* taiki no. ~ **depression**, teikiatsu. ~ **pressure**, kiatsu.

atoll [ætɔ́l/ǽ-] *n.* kanjō sangotō ; kanshō.

atom [ǽtəm] *n.* genshi.

atomic(al) [ətɔ́mik(l)] *a.* genshi no : ~ *bomb*, genshi baku-dan. ~ *energy*, genshi ryoku. ⌈nyūki.

atomize [ǽtəmaiz] *v.* genshi ni suru. ~**r** *n.* fummuki ; kyū-

atone [ətóun] *v.* tsugunau. ~**ment** *n.* tsugunai.

atrocious [ətróuʃəs] *a.* mōakuna ; gongo-dōdan no. ~**ly** ; *ad.* gongo-dōdan ni.

atrocity [ətrɔ́siti] *n.* gokuaku ; mōaku.

atrophy [ǽtrəfi] *n.* (*med.*) ishukushō (byōki).

attach [ətǽtʃ] *v.* kuttsuku ; kuttsukeru : *I advise you not to* ~ *yourself to the Party*, boku wa kimi ga Tō ni hairanai yōni chūkoku suru yo. fuchaku suru : *be* ~*ed to*. *He is deeply* ~ *ed to her*, kare wa kanojo ni kubittake da. ~**ment** *n.* fuchaku ; aijaku.

attaché [ætəʃéi] *n.* (*Fr.*) zuikōin ; fukkan. *military* (*naval*) ~, kōshikan (mata wa taishikanzuki no rikugun (kaigun) bu- ⌊kan.

attack [ətǽk] *v.* kōgeki (suru).

attain [ətéin] *v.* tassuru ; togeru. ~**able** *a* tasshiuru ; erareru. ~**ment** *n.* jōtatsu ; (*pl.*) gakushiki.

attainder [ətéində] *n.* (*Brit. leg.*) kōken (*citizenship*) sōshitsu.

attaint [ətéint] *v.* yogosu ; kansen suru.

attar [ǽta:] *n.* bara-yu (abura). ⌈shūgeki.

attempt [ətémpt] *v.* kokoromiru ; nerau ; osou. *n.* kokoromi.

attend [əténd] *v.* tsukisou ; shusseki suru ; tomonau. chūi suru ; haberu ; tomonau. *n.* tsukisoi ; zuikō. ~**ant** *a.* tsukisou ; tomonau. *n.* jisha, zuikō-in ; shussekisha.

attention [əténʃən] *n.* chūi ; hairyo.

attentive [əténtiv] *a.* chūi-bukai ; teineina. ~ly *ad.* chūibukaku ; teineini.

attenuate [əténjueit] *v.* kihaku ni suru ; hosoku (usuku) naru. kihakuna.

attenuation [ətènjuéiʃən] *n.* kihakuni suru koto.

attest [ətést] *v.* shōmei suru. ~ation [ətestéiʃən] shōmei ; shōgen

attic [ǽtik] *n.* yaneurabeya. okuyane.

Attic [ǽtik] *a* Atene (*Athens*) no ; Atenefū no.

attire [ətáiə] *n.* fukusō. *v.* kiru ; yosoou.

attitude [ǽtitjuːd] *n.* taido : *strike an* ~, kidoru.

attorney [ətɔ́ːni] *n.* bengonin. *power of* ~, ininjō. ~ *generai* kenji-sōchō.

attract [ətrǽkt] *v.* (hitome, kokoro o) hiku ; ~ing *a.* hikitsukeru ; hito me o hiku. ~tion [ətrǽkʃən] *n.* hikitsukeru koto ; inryoku. ~ive *a.* me ni tsuku ; hikitsukeru. ~ively *ad.* hikitsukete. ~ness *n.* hiku chikara ; aikyō.

attributable [ətríbjutəbl] *a.* ...ga gen'in no ; ...no sei de.

attribute [ətríbjut] *v.* kisuru ; ...no sei ni suru. [ǽtri-] *n.* zokusei. aru mono no seishitsu.

attributive [ətríbjutiv] *a.* zokusei no ; keiyō suru. *n.* keiyō-go. ~ly *ad.* zokushitè.

attrition [ətríʃən] *n.* mametsu (surete tsubureru koto).

attune [ətjúːn] *v.* chōshi o awaseru ; chōsetsu suru.

auburn [ɔ́ːbəːn] *a.* akatobiiro no.

auction [ɔ́ːkʃən] *v.* kyōbai suru. *n.* kyōbai (seri uri) : *Dutch* ~, seri sage kyōbai hō. *public* ~, kyōbai. ~eer [ɔ́ːkʃníːə] *n.* kyōbainin.

audacious [ɔːdéiʃəs] *a.* zubutoi ; bōjaku-bujin no. ~ly *ad.* zubutoku.

audacity [ɔːdǽsiti] *n.* daitan-futeki ; zūzūshisa.

audibility [ɔːdibíliti] *n.* kikoeru koto.

audible [ɔ́ːdəbl] *a.* kikoeru ; kikiuru. ~bly *ad.* kikitoreru yōni.

audience [ɔ́ːdiəns] *n.* chōshū ; kokuō nado ni au koto.

audio [ɔ́ːdiou] *a.* rajio de kikoeru shūhasū (*cycling*).

audit [ɔ́ːdit] *n. v.* kaikei kensa. (o suru)

audition [ɔːdíʃən] *n.* kiku koto ; chōkaku ; (*Am.*) shikentekini kiku koto. *v.* shikenteki ni kiku.

auditor [ɔ́:ditə] *n.* kiku hito; kikite; kansa yaku. ~**ium** [ɔ:-ditɔ́:riəm] *n.* (*pl.* -s [-əmz]; **ria** [-riə]) kōdō; chōshūseki. ~**y** *a.* mimi no; chōkaku no. *n.* =~**ium**; chōshū.

auger [ɔ́:gə] *n.* ōgiri (ōkina kiri).

aught [ɔ:t] *n.* nani ka; nan demo: *help came too late to avail* ~, enjo ga okurete chotto mo yaku ni tatanakatta. *for* ~ *I know*, watakushi no shiru (*know*) kagiri dewa. ⌊fueru koto.

augment [ɔ:gmént] *v.* fueru. ~**ation** [ɔ̀:gmentéiʃən] *n.* zōka;

augur [ɔ́:gə] *n.* uranaiyaku (*Anc. Rome* no). ~**y** [ɔ́:gjuri] *n.* ⌊uranai.

August [ɔ́:gəst] *n.* Hachigatsu.

august [ɔ:gʌ́st] *a.* sōgonna; dōdō to shita. ~**ly** *ad.* sōgonni. ~**ness** *n.* sōgon.

aunt [ɑ́:nt] *n.* oba; obasan.

auntie, aunty [ɑ́:nti/æn-] *n.* obasan; obachan.

aura [ɔ́:rə] *n.* nioi; (hana nado no) kōki (*fragrance*).

aural [ɔ́:rəl] *a.* mimi no; chōkaku no.

aureole [ɔ́:rioul] *n.* kōrin; (taiyo nado no) gokō.

auricle [ɔ́:rikl] *n.* mimitabu. shinji (*upper cavity of heart*).

auricular [ɔ:ríkjulə] *a.* mimi no; chōkaku no.

auriferous [ɔ:rífərəs] *ad.* kin (*gold*) o fukunda; ...o sansuru.

aurist [ɔ́:rist] *n.* jika-i; mimi no isha.

aurora [ɔ:rɔ́:rə] *n.* kyokkō (nankyoku, hokkyoku no jikyoku kara deru hikari): ~ *borealis* [bɔ̀:riǽlis], kita no kyokkō; ~ *australis* [ɔ:stréilis], minami no k yokkō.

auspice [ɔ́:spis] *n.* zenchō; mae kara no yōsu. (*pl.*) hogo: *under the* ~*s of*, no hogo no moto ni.

auspicious [ɔ:spíʃəs] *a.* yoi zenchō (*good omen*) no; kitchō no; engi no yoi. ~**ly** *ad.* engiyoku. ⌊genshukuni.

austere [ɔ:stíə] *a.* kibishii; genshukuna. ~**ly** *ad.* kibishiku.

austerity [ɔ:stériti] *n.* shungen; genkaku. (*pl.*) taibō-seikatsu.

Australasian [ɔ̀:strəléiʒjən] *a.* Ōstoraria oyobi sokora (*there-about*) no shimajima (*islands*). *n.* sokora no jūmin (*natives*).

Australian [ɔ:stréiljən] *a.* Ōstoraria (Gōshū) no. *n.* Ōstoraria-

Austrian [ɔ́:striən] *a.* Ōstoriya no. *n.* Ōstoriajin. ⌊jin.

Austro-Hungarian [ɔ̀:strouhʌ̀ŋgéəriən] *a.* Ōsutoria-Hanga-

autarchy [ɔ́:tɑ:ki] *n.* zettai shuken; senseiseiji. ⌊riya no.

autarky [ɔ́ːtɑːki] *n.* jisoku-jikyū no keizai soshiki no seiji.

authentic(al) [ɔːθéntik(əl)] *a.* shinzubeki; kakujitsuna. ~**ally** *ad.* shinjite; kakujitsuni.

authenticate [ɔːθéntikeit] *v.* kakujitsu ni suru; kakushō suru.

authentication [ɔːθéntikéiʃən] *n.* kakunin; kakushō.

authenticity [ɔ̀ːθentísiti] *n.* kakujitsusei; shinjitsusei.

author [ɔ́ːθə] *n.* chosha; sakka; hottōnin. ~**ess** [-rès] *n.* joryū sakka. ~**ship** *n.* chosakugyō.

authoritarian [ɔːθɔ̀ritéəriən] *n.* kanken-dokusaishugisha.

authoritative [ɔːθɔ́ritətiv/-tei-] *a.* ken'i aru; genzen taru; sono suji no.

authority [əθɔ́riti] *n.* ken'i; taika. (*pl.*) tōkyoku; sonosuji.

authorization [ɔ̀ːθərizéiʃən] *n.* inin; ninka; kōnin.

authorize [ɔ́ːθəraiz] *v.* ken'i o ataeru; ninka suru.

authorized [ɔ́ːθəraizd] *a.* ken'i o ataerareta; ninka sareta.

auto [ɔ́ːtou] *v.* jidōsha de norimawasu. *n.* jidōsha.

autobiographer [ɔ̀ːtəbaióɡrəfə] *n.* jijoden sakusha.

autobiography [ɔ̀ːtəbaióɡrəfi] *n.* jijoden.

auto-car [ɔ́ːtoukɑ̀ː] *n.* jidōsha.

autocracy [ɔːtɔ́krəsi] *n.* dokusai seiji.

autocrat [ɔ́ːtəkræt] *n.* dokusai kunshu. ~**ic(al)** *a.* dokusai no.

autocycle [ɔ́ːtousàikl] *n.* jidō jitensha.

auto-da-fe [ɔ̀ːtoudəféi] (*port.*) *n.* (*pl.* **autos-** [ɔ̀ːtouz-]) *n.* (*Spein*) shūkyō saibansho no hanketsu senkokushiki.

autogiro, autogyro [ɔ̀ːtoudʒáirou] *n.* ōtojairo.

autograph [ɔ́ːtəɡrɑːf] *n.* jihitsu; shimpitsu; jibunde kaita moji. *a.* jihitsu no. ~**ic** [ɔ́ːtəɡrǽfik] *a.* jihitsu no.

autointoxication [ɔ́ːtouintɔ̀ksikéiʃən] *n.* jika-chūdoku.

automat [ɔ́ːtəmæt] *n.* jidō hambaiki. [ɔ̀ːtəmǽtik] ~**ic** *a.* jidō no; jidō shiki no. ~**ically** *ad.* jidōtekini.

automation [ɔ̀ːtəméiʃən] *n.* ōtomeishon.

automaton [ɔːtɔ́mətən] *n.* (*pl.* **-s**; **-ta** [-tə]) jidō kikai; kikaiteki ni ugoku hito.

automobile [ɔːtǽmóubiːl] *n.* jidōsha (*motor-car*).

automobilist [ɔ̀ːtəmóubilist/-bíː] *n.* jidōsha o norimawasu hito; jidōsha no shoyūsha.

automotive [ɔ̀ːtəmóutiv] *a.* jidō no; jidōsha no.

autonomous [ɔːtónəməs] *a.* jichi(teki) no.

autonomy [ɔːtónəmi] *n.* jichiken ; jichitai.

autopolo [ɔ̀toupóulou] *n.* jidōsha dakyūgi (*polo*).

autopsy [ɔ́ːtəpsi] *n.* shitai-kensa ; kenshi.

autosuggestion [ɔ̀ːousədʒéstʃəs] *n.* jikoanji ; jikakannō.

autotruck [ɔ́ːtətrʌ̀k] *n.* kamotsu (*freight* ; *goods*) jidōsha.

autotype [ɔ́ːtətaip] *n.* ōto-taipu ; tanshoku shashin-ban. *v.*, *a.* *autotype* de fukusha suru. ⌐na.

autumn [ɔ́ːtəm] *n.* aki. ~al [ɔːtʌ́mnl] aki no ; aki ni saku ha

auxiliary [ɔːgzíljəri] *a.* hojo no : ~ *verb*, (*gram.*) jodōshi. ~ *coin*, hojokahei. *n.* joryokusha ; kōenkai.

avail [əvéil] *v.* risuru ; yakudateru : ~ *oneself of*, jōzuru ; riyō suru ; yaku ni tateru. *n.* rieki ; kōyō ; (*pl.*) ritoku. ~able yaku ⌐ni tatsu.

avalanche [ǽvəlɑ:n(t)ʃ] *n.* nadare.

avarice [ǽvəris] *n.* don'yoku.

avaricious [ævəríʃəs] *a.* yoku no fukai. ~ly *ad.* yoku fukaku ~ness *n.* don'yoku ; yokubuka.

avast [əvǽst] *inter.* (*naut.*) Yame l.

avatar [ævətáː] *n.* keshin ; gonge.

avaunt [əvɔ́ːnt] *inter.* Atchi ike !

avenge [əvéndʒ] *v.* fukushū suru : ~ *oneself*, ada o kaesu ; fukushū suru. ~r [əvéndʒə] *n.* fukushūsha.

avenue [ǽvənju:] *n.* ōdōri ; namiki michi.

aver [əvɔ́ː] *v.* dangen suru.

average [ǽvəridʒ] *n.*, *a.* heikin no. *v.* heikin suru.

averse [əvɔ́ːs] *a.* kirai no. ~ness *n.* kirai.

aversion [əvɔ́ːʃən] *n.* kirai ; iyana mono (hito).

avert [əvɔ́ːt] *v.* sakeru ; somukeru (me, kao nado o).

aviary [éivieri] *n.* tori-goya ; yōkin-jo.

aviate [éivieit] *v.* hikō suru ; tobu (hikōki de).

aviation [èivééiʃen] *n.* hikō : ~ **corps** [-kɔː] (*pl.* [-kɔːz]), hikō-tai. ~ **garment**, hikō-fuku. ~ **ground**, hikōjō. ~ **hood**, hikōbō. ~ **meet**, hikō-kyōgi (kai).

aviator [éivieitə] *n.* hikōshi ; hikōka : ~'s *ear*, isshu no chūjien (*owing to flying high in the air*). **civil** ~, minkan hikōka.

aviatress [éivieitris], **aviatrix** [èivéétriks] *n.* joryū hikōka.

avid [ǽvid] *a.* musaboru ; yokubaru.

avidity [əvíditi] *n.* yoku no fukai koto ; nesshin.

aviette [èviét] *n.* hatsudōki no nai hikōki.

avion [ǽviòːŋ] (*Fr.*) *n.* gun'yō hikōki.

avocation [æ̀vəkéiʃən] *n.* naishoku ; fukugyō ; nagusami goto.

avoid [əvɔ́id] *v.* sakeru. ~**able** *a.* sakerareru. ~**ance** *n.* sakeru koto.

avoirdupois [ǽvədəpɔ́iz] *n.* jōkō (futsū no hakari) (16 onsu o 1-pondo to suru) ; (*Am. col.*) taijū.

avouch [əváutʃ] *v.* dangen suru ; jihaku suru. ~**ment** *n.* dangen ; jihaku.

avow [əváu] *v.* mitomeru ; jihaku suru. ~**al** *n.* hakujō. ~**ed** [-d] *a.* mitometa. ~**edly** [-idli] *ad.* meihakuni.

await [əwéit] *v.* matsu.

awake [əwéik] *v.* **awoke** or **awaked : awaking.** me o samasu ; okosu ; satoru. *a.* kizuite ; me ga samete (iru) ; yoku shitte (iru).

awaken [əwéikən] *v.* me o samasu ; yobiokosu ; funki suru.

award [əwɔ́ːd] *v.* shinsa shite ataeru ; *n.* shimpan ; shōyo.

aware [əwéə] *a.* shitte (iru).

awash [əwɔ́ʃ] *a., ad.* suimen ni arawarete ; nami ni utarete (iru).

away [əwéi] *ad.* hanarete ; tōku (achira) ni ; ~ *with him* ! kare o oiharae ! *right* ~, sugu ; tatta ima ! rusu ; shite shimau.

awe [ɔː] *n.* erasa ni taisuru osore. *v.* osore saseru. (*inspiring*), osore o idakaseru. *a.* igen no aru. ~**struck** ; ~**stricken** *a.* kashikomi osorete ; erasa ni utarete.

awful [ɔ́ːful] *a.* osoroshii ; i ni utareta. (*col*) hidoi ; sugoi. ~**ly** osoroshiku ; (*col.*) hijōni ; hidoku. ~**ness** *n.* osoroshisa ; sōgon.

awhile [əbwáil] *ad.* shibaraku.

awkward [ɔ́ːkwəd] *a.* hetana ; bukiyōna. ~**ly** *ad.* ~**ness** *n.*

awl [ɔːl] *n.* tsukigiri (kutsuya nado no tsukau isshu no kiri).

awn [ɔːn] *n.* nogi (mugi nado no saki no suru doi ke).

awning [ɔ́ːniŋ] *n.* hi-yoke ; ama-yoke.

awoke [əwóuk] *v. see* : **awake.**

A.W.O.L., a.w.o.l. [éiwɔːl] *a.* (*Am.*) mudan gaishutsu no ; mudan kesseki no (*absent without leave*).

awry [ərái] *a., ad.* nejirete ; nanameni ; machigatte ; mazuku.

ax, axe [æks] *n.* (*pl.* **axes** [ǽksiz]) ono.

axial [ǽksiəl] *a.* jiku no ; jiku ni sotta.

axiom [ǽksiəm] *n.* genri ; kōri ; jimei no ri. ～atic(al) [ǽksiə-mǽtik(l)] *a.* hakkiri wakaru ; jimei no.

axis [ǽksis] *n.* (*pl.* axes [ǽksi:z]) jiku ; sūjiku koku (remmei shite iru kuni).

axle [ǽksl] =～tree *n.* shimbō ; shajiku ; ～ed [-d] *a.* jiku no aru.

ay [ei] *inter. a.* odoroki ; kuyashisa nado o arawasu toki no koe).

ay, aye [ai] *inter.* sayō ; sansei. *n.* (*pl.* ayes) sanseisha.

aye [ei] *ad.* itsumo. *for* ～, eikyūni.

azalea [əzéiljə] *n.* tsutsuji.

azimuth [ǽzimǝθ] *n.* (*astr.*) hōi ; hōi kaku.

azure [ǽʒ] *n., a.* sorairo (no), aoku sunda. aozora.

B

B, b [biː] *n.* (*pl.* B's; Bs [biːz]) Eigo *alphabet* no dai-2-bamme no moji.

baa [bɑː] *v.*, *n.* (hitsuji nado ga) naku. nakigoe.

babble [bǽbl] *v.* becha becha shaberu. *n.* katakoto; (mizu no) seseragi. ~**r** *n.* mudaguchi o kiku hito.

babe [béib] *n.* (*poet.*) akago; akambo; ubuna hito.

Babel [béibəl] *n.* Baberu no tō; takai tatemono; sawagashisa.

baboon [bəbúːn/bæ-] *n.* hihi.

baby [béibi] *n.* akambo; chinomigo. *v.* amayakasu. ~**hood** *n.* osanaikoro. ~**ish** *a.* akago no yōna.

Babylonian [bæbilóuniən] *a.* Babiron no; Babirōniya Ōkoku no. *n.* Babironiyajin

baccalaureate [bækəlɔ́ːriit] *bachelor* no gakui.

bacchanal [bǽkənəl] *a.* Bakkasu no. *n.* nonde sawagu hito.

bacchanalia [bækənéiljə] *n.* (*pl.*) Bakkasusai; ranchiki-sawagi.

bacchanalian [bækənéiljən] *a.* Bakkasu no; yotte sawagu.

Bacchus [bǽkəs] *n.* Bakkasu (*Anc. Rome* no sake no kami).

bachelor [bǽtʃələ] *n.* (otoko no) dokushin-sha; gakushi. ~**hood** *n.* dokushin.

bacillus [bəsíləs] *n.* (*pl.* **-li** [-lai]) bachirusu; kanjō saikin.

back [bæk] *n.* senaka; ushiro; ura; (isu no) yokkakari. *behind one's* ~, hisokani. *turn the* ~ *on...* o misuteru. *a.* ushiro no; (*Am.*) kigen o sugita: ~*number*; (zasshi nado) tsuki-okure. *ad.* ushiro ni. *v.* ato e sagaru. enjo suru. ~**door** [bǽkdɔː] *n.* ura guchi. ~**ground,** *n.* haikei (butai, kaiga nado no). kako no keireki. ~**side,** (dōbutsu no) shiri. ~**slide** *v.* daraku suru. ~**stairs** *n.* urabashigo. ~**street** *n.* uradōri. ~**water** *n.* gyakuryū; modori mizu. ~**woods** [-wúdz] *n.* (*pl*) (*Am.*) mikaihatsu shinrinchi; okuchi. ~**yard** *n.* [jɑːd] ura niwa.

backbite [bǽkbait] **-bit, -bitten: biting.** *v.* kageguchi o kiku.

backbone [bǽkbòun] *n.* sebone: *to the* ~, mattaku; jūbun ni. *a.* hone no aru; kikotsu no aru.

backer [bǽkə] *n.* enjosha; ushirodate; kōensha.

backgammon [bǽkgæmən] *n.* seiyō sugoroku.

backhand [bǽkhænd] *n.* gyakuteuchi. ~**ed** [-id] *a.* te no kō de suru ; gyakute no ; bukiyōna.

backing [bǽkiŋ] *n.* shiji(sha) ; kōen(sha).

backstop [bǽkstɔp] *n.* (*baseball*) bakku netto ; (*criket*) hoshu (*catcher*). 　　　　　　　　　　　　　　　　　　　　⌈yogi.

backstroke [bǽkstròuk] *n.* uchikaeshi ; gyakuteuchi ; seo-

backward [bǽkwəd] *a.* kōhō no ; shirigomi shite (suru). *ad.* ushiro ni. ~**ly** *ad.* ~**ness,,** *n.*

backwards [bǽkwədz] *ad.* =**backward**.

bacon [béikən] *n.* bēkon.

bacteria [bæktíəriə] *n.* bakuteria (*pl. of bacterium*).

bactericide [bæktíərisaid] *n.* sakkinzai.

bacteriology [bæktiəriólədʒi] *n.* saikingaku.

bacterium [bæktíətiəm] *n.* (*sing. of bacteria*) bakuteria ; saikin.

bad [bæd] *a.* warui ; hidoi. ~**ly** *ad.* hidoku. ~**ness** *n.* warui koto ; aku.

bade [bæd] *v. see :* **bid**.

badge [bædʒ] *n.* kishō ; shirushi.

badger [bǽdʒə] *n.* anaguma ; tanuki. *v.* ijimeru ; nayamasu.

Baedeker [béidikə] *n.* (Doitsu no shuppansha Bedeka no) ryo-kō annaisho.

baffle [bǽfl] *v.* massugu iku no o samatageru ; komarasu. *n.* hōkō no kimaranai kaze.

bag [bæg] *n.* tesage bukuro ; kaban ; (ryō no) emono. ~ *of bones,* yasekoketa hito. *v.* fukuramu (-masu) ; fukuro ni ireru ; tsukamaeru. ~**ging** [bǽgiŋ] *n.* fukuro no zairyō. ~**gy** *a.* fukuro no yōna ; dabudabu no.

bagatelle [bægətél] (*Fr.*) *n.* tsumaranai mono ; isshu no tama-tsuki asobi.

baggage [bǽgidʒ] *n.* konimotsu ; yakuza onna ; otemba. ~ **master** [-mástə] *n.* nimotsu gakari.

bagpipe(s) [bǽgpaip(s)] *n.* fūkin (*Scotland* nado de tsukau). ~**r** *n.* *bagpipe* o fuku hito.

bah [bɑ:] *inter.* nan da! ; bakana !

bail [béil] *n.* (funazoko no) akatori. hoshaku ; hoshaku (ho-shōkin). mombashira no ue no yokogi. *v.* (funazoko no mizu kumidasu; hoshaku suru. ~ out (*Am*) rakkasan de oriru.

bailiff [béilif] *n.* shittatsuri; kanshunin.

bairn [bɛən] *n.* (*N-Eng. Scot.*) kodomo.

bait [beit] *n.* esa. *v.* esa o tsukeru; nayamasu; ijimeru.

baize [beiz] *n.* isshu no me no arai rasha (tēburu nado ni ka-keru).

bake [beik] *v.* (pan nado o) yaku; yakeru. ~r [béike] *n.* pan'-ya; tempi. ~ry [-əri] *n.* pan-seizōjō; pan'ya.

bakelite [béikəlait] *n.* bēkuraito.

baking [béikiŋ] *n.* (pan nado o) yaku koto; pan yaki. ~ powder *n.* [páudə] fukurashi-ko.

balalaika [bæləláikə] *n.* bararaika (gitā ni nita Roshiya no gakki)

balance [bæləns] *n.* hakari; heikin; tsuriai; zandaka. *v.* (hakari de)hakaru; hikaku suru; seisan suru; tsuriau; tamerau. ~-sheet, taishaku taishō hyō.

balcony [bǽlkəni] *n.* barukonii, (gekijō no) nīkai-sajiki.

bald [bɔːld] *n.* hage; kazari no nai; ~head [bɔ́ːldhed] *n.* hage-atama. ~ly *ad.* kazarike nashi ni; mukidashi ni. ~ness *n.* hage-(atama); rokotsu; mukidashi.

baldric [bɔ́ːldrik] *n.* kazari-obi (kata kara mune ni kakete katana ya rappa nado o tsurusu mono).

bale [beil] *n.* tsutsumi; tawara; kōri. *v.* tsutsumi ni suru; ta-wara (kōri) ni ireru.

baleful [béilfəl] *a.* gai no aru; iji no warui.

balk, baulk [bɔːk] *n.* shippai; bōku. *v.* samatageru; shitsubō saseru: *to be* ~*ed of one's hopes*, kibō o kujikareru.

ball [bɔːl] *n.* tama; marui mono. butōkai. *v.* tama ni suru. *three golden* (or *blass*) ~*s*, shichiya (*pawn-broker's*) no kam-ban. *catch the* ~ *before the bound*, kisen o seisuru. *The* ~ *is with you*, anata no ban da. *have the* ~ *at one's feet*, seikō e no shokō ga mieru. ~**proof** [bɔ́ːlprúːf] *a.* tamayoke no. ~**room** [-rum] butōkaijō.

ballad [bǽləd] *n.* kouta; min'yō. ~**-monger** [-máŋgə] *n.* min'yō sakusha; hebo-shijin.

ballast [bǽləst] *n.* fune no soko-ni; ashini; (dōro no) barasu; (kikyū no) suna-bukuro; jari.

ballerina [bæ̀lerí:nə] *n.* bareriina ; barē-no odorite.

ballet [bǽlei] *n.* barē ; barēdan ; dantai-buyō.

balloon [bəlú:n] *n.* fūsen ; keikikyū. *a.* maruku fukureta. ~**ist** *n.* fūsen-nori.

ballot [bǽlət] *n.* tōhyō-yōshi ; tōhyō-sōsū. *v.* tōhyō suru.

balm [bá:m] *n.* kōyu ; itamidome. ~**y** *a.* [bá:mij] kaori no yoi ; chintsū no ; sawayakana.

balsam [bɔ́:lsəm] *n.* barusam ; kōyu ; nagusameru mono. ~**ic** [bɔ:lsǽmik] *a.* barusam no yōna ; nagusame ni naru.

Baltic [bɔ́:ltik] *a.* Baruto (Barutikku) Kai no.

baluster [bǽləstə] *n.* rankan no kobashira.

balustrade [bæ̀ləstréid] *n.* rankan ; tesuri.

bamboo [bæmbú:] *n.* take : ~ *shoot*, takenoko.

bamboozle [bæmbú:zl] *v.* (*col.*) damasu ; mayowasu.

ban [bǽn] *n.* kinshi ; noroi : *lift the* ~, kinshi o toku. *v.* kinzuru ; norou ; hamon suru.

banal [béinl] *n.* heibonna ; chimpuna. ~**ity** [bənǽliti] *n.* heibon ; chimpu.

banana [bənú:nə] *n.* banana.

band [bǽnd] *n.* (1) obi ; himo ; (*pl.*) (te) kase. (2) shūdan ; gakutai : *military* ~, gungakutai. *v.* (1) (himo de) shibaru. (2) rengō-suru. ~**box** [bǽnd̃bɔ̀ks] *n.* (bōshi, karā nado o ireru) kamibako. ~**master** [~-mà:stə] *n.* gakutai no taichō. ~**sman** [bǽnd̃zmen] *n.* gakudan no ichiin ; gakushu. ~**stand** [bǽnd̃stænd] *n.* (kōen nado ni aru) ongaku-dō.

bandage [bǽndidʒ] *n.* hōtai. *v.* hōtai de shibaru.

bandan(n)a [bændǽnə] *n.* somemoyō no aru ōgata no hankachi ; shibori-zome.

bandit [bǽndit] (*pl.* -**s** [-s] ; -**ditti** [-díti]) *n.* akkan ; tōzoku ; sanzoku. **mounted** ~**s** bazoku.

bandoleer, bandlier [bæ̀ndəlíə] *n.* (kata kara kakeru) dan'yaku tai (obi) ; oi-kawa.

bandy [bǽndi] *n.* hokkē ; hokkē no batto. *v.* nageau ; tama o uchi au ; kōkan suru. ~**legged** [-légid] *n.* ganimata no.

bane [béin] *n.* doku ; gai. ~**ful** *a.* gai (doku) no aru.

bang [bæŋ] *n.* (don, batan, to iu) hidoi oto ; kirisage-maegami. hidoi oto o tateru ; kirisage-maegami ni suru. *ad.* batan to araku (rambō ni) oto o tatete aruku (to nado ga).

bangle [bǽŋgl] *n.* kazariwa; ude, kurubushi nado no kazari.

banian [bǽnjən] *n.* (1) shōnin (*merchants*); (issai nikushoku o shinai). (2) Indo, no banyan.

banish [bǽniʃ] *v.* tsuihō suru; oiharau. ∼**ment** *n.* tsuihō.

banister [bǽnistə] *n.* tesuri. (*pl.*) rankan no kobashira.

banjo [bǽndʒou] *n.* banjō (isshu no gengakki).

bank [bæŋk] *n.* teibō; tsutsumi. ginkō. (*Am.*) yobi chozōsho. kobune no kogite no zaseki. *v.* tsutsumi (teibō) o kizuku; keisha saseru (hikōki nado o); ginkō ni azukeru. ∼**account** [bǽŋkəkáunt] ginkō kanjō; yokin. ∼ **bill** (*Am.*) ginkōken; shihei; (*Brit.*) ginkō tegata. ∼ **book** [bǽŋkbuk] ginkō yokin tsūchō. ∼**er** ginkō gyōsha. ∼ **holiday** *n.* ginkō kyūjitsu. ∼**ing** *n.* ginkō-gyō. ∼ **note,** ginkōken; shihei. ∼ **rate** ginkō riritsu.

bankrupt [bǽŋkrəpt] *a., n.* hasan shita. ∼**cy** *n.* hasan.

banner [bǽnə] *n.* hata; gunki.

bannock [bǽnək] *n.* (*Scot.*) kashi-pan no isshu.

banns [bænz] *n.* (*pl.*) (kekkon mae ni kyōkai de okonau) kekkon yokoku: *forbid the* ∼, igi (*objection*) o mōshitateru. *publish the* ∼, yokoku suru.

banquet [bǽŋkwit] *n.* enkai. *v.* kyōō suru.

bantam [bǽntəm] *n.* chabo; kogara de genkina hito. ∼**weight** [-wèit] *n.* taijū 118 pondo ika no kentōka.

banter [bǽntə] *n.* hiyakashi; jōdan. *v.* hiyakasu; jōdan o iu.

bantling [bǽntliŋ] *n.* kozōkko; aonisai.

banyan, baniyan [bǽnjən] *n.* banian no ki.

baptism [bǽptizm] *n.* senrei. ∼**al** *a.* senrei no.

Baptist [bǽptist] *n.* zenshin mizu ni haitte senrei o ukeru kiristokyōha no kyōto. ∼**(e)ry** [-əri] *n.* senrei o ukeru basho (suisō); senrei-shitsu.

baptize [bæptáiz] *v.* senrei o okonau; nazukeru, meimei ⌐suru.

bar [ba:] *n.* bā; yokogi; kannuki; (saibansho no) hikokuseki; bengoshi-dan. sakaba. ∼**maid** *n.* bā no jokyū. ∼**room** *n.* sakaba, bā. ∼**tender** *n.* (*Am.*) bāten. *v.* kannukio suru; samatageru. *prep.* ...o nozoite: *He is the best boy in town, bar none*, kare wa danzen machi ichiban no shōnen da. ～ **iron,** tetsu-bō.

barb [bɑ:b] *n.* sakatoge. ～**ed wire,** toge tsuki tessen.

barbarian [bɑ:béəriən] *a.* yabanna *n.* yabanjin.

barbaric [bɑ:bǽrik] *a.* soyana ; yabanna.

barbarism [bɑ́:bærizm] *n.* yaban. soyana kotoba-zukai ya dōsa.

barbarity [bɑ:bǽriti] *n.* zannin, yabanna okonai.

barbarize [bɑ́:bəraiz] *v.* yabanni furumau ; soyani suru (kotoba nado). ⌈mugakuna. ～**ly** *ad.* ～**ness** *n.*

barbarous [bɑ́:bərəs] *a.* yabanna ; hibummei no ; gehinna.

barbecue [bɑ́:bikju:] *n.* (buta nado no) maru-yaki. (*Am.*) maruyaki no deru daienkai yagairyōri. *v.* maru-yaki ni suru.

barber [bɑ́:bə] *n.* rihatsushi. ～'s **shop,** rihatsuten ; tokoya.

bard [bɑ:d] *n.* henreki shijin. hōrō shijin.

bare [bɛə] *a.* hadaka no ; mukidashi no ; tannaru. *v.* hadaka ni suru ; bakuro suru (*disclose*). ～**back,** *a. ad.* hadaka uma ni notte. ～**backed** [-bὲkt] *a.* hadaka-uma no. ～**faced** [-féist] *a.* mukidashi no. ～**footed** *a., ad.* hadashi no (de). ～**headed** *a., ad.* bōshi nashi de. ～**ly** *ad.* mukidashi ni ; wazukani ; karōjite. ～**ness** *n.* sekirara.

bargain [bɑ́:gin] *n.* keiyaku ; torihiki ; mikiri-mono : ～ **day,** tokubai-bi. *buy at a* ～, yasuku kau. *into the* ～, sono ue ni. *v.* dampan suru ; baibai o torikimeru.

barge [bɑ:dʒ] *n.* temma-sen ; yūran-sen. *v.* (*Am. col.*) deshabaritone [bǽritoun] *n., a.* dansei chūon (no). ⌊baru.

bark [bɑ:k] *n.* (1) ki no kawa. (2) (inu ga) hoeru koe. (3) sambon masuto no fune. (1) *v.* ki no kawa o hagu. (2) kawa o namesu. hoeru.

barley [bɑ́:li] *n.* ōmugi. ～**corn** [-kɔ:n] *n.* ōmugi no tsubu. *John Barley corn,* biiru, wisukii (gijin hō, *personfied use*).

barm [bɑ:m] *n.* kōji ; kōbo (ōyakeni tsunoru.)

barn [bɑ:n] *n.* naya ; kokumotsu-gura.

barnacle [bɑ́:nəkl] *n.* (*zoo.*) fujitsubo ; eboshigai.

barnyard [bɑ́:njɑ:d] *n.* naya no niwa ; ura niwa.

barometer [bərɔ́mitə] *n.* seiuki ; kiatsukei.

barometric(al) [bὲrəmétrik(l)] *a.* seiuki no : *barometric maximum,* saikō kiatsu.

baron [bǽrən] *n.* danshaku ; (*Am. col.*) yūryokusha, (zaikai no) ōdatemono. ~age [bǽrɔnidʒ] *n.* danshaku-tachi; kizokukaikyū. ~ess [-is] *n.* danshaku fujin no.

baronet [bǽrɔnit] *n.* (*Brit.*) danshaku no shita, naito (*knight*) no ue no kurai. ~cy [-si] *n. baronet* no kurai.

barony [bǽrɔni] *n. baron* no ryōchi (kurai).

barouche [bɔrúːʃ] (*Fr.*) *n.* nitō-date, yonin-nori no yonrim-basha.

barque, bark [bɑːk] *n.* sambon-masto no hansen.

barrack [bǽkɔk] *n.* (*pl.*) heiei; barakku.

barrage [bɔrúːʒ] *n.* kawa no naka no seki. hōdan no maku.

barrel [bǽrɔl] *n.* taru; bāreru-daru (hito taru no bunryō). *v.* taru ni ireru.

barren [bǽrɔn] *a.* ninshin shinai; kusaki no haenai; fumō no *n.* fumō chi. ~ness *n.* fumō.

barret [bǽret], **biretta** [birétɔ] *n.* hirabettai bōshi (*stiff, spuare cap*).

barrette [bɑːrét] *n.* isshu no kurippu (*clip*); *hair pin.*

barricade [bǽrikéid] *n.* barikēdo; shōheki. *v.* barikēdo o tsu-kuru.

barrier [bǽriɔ] *n.* saku; sekisho; yarai.

barring [bɑ́ːriŋ] *prep.* ...no hoka; ...o nozoite: *B~ accidents, the train will reach Chicago at twelve o'clock,* jiko no nai ka giri kisha wa 12 ji ni Shikago ni tsuki masu.

barrister [bǽristɔ] *n.* (*Brit.*) bengoshi.

barrow [bǽrou] *n.* teoshi guruma; kofun; furui tsuka.

barter [bɑ́ːtɔ] *n., v.* butsu-butsu-kōkan (o suru).

barytone, baritone [bǽlitoun] *n., a.* dansei chūon (no).

basal [béisl] *a.* kiso no; kihon no.

basalt [bǽsɔlt/bɔsɔ́lt] *n.* (*min.*) gembugan.

base [béis] *n.* soko; kiso; dodai; shuppatsuten. *a.* iyashii; hikui; gehinna. *v.* kiso o oku. ~ball *n.* yakyū. ~born *a.* iyashii umare no. ~less *a.* konkyo no nai. ~ly *ad.* iyashiku. ~ment *n.* chikashitsu. ~ness *n.* hiretsu; akushitsu. ~steal-ing *n.* tōrui (*baseball*).

bashful [bǽʃfɔl] *a.* uchikina. ~ly *ad.* hazukashisōni. ~ness *n.* hanikami, uchiki.

basic [béisik] *a.* kiso no: *B~ English,* kihon Eigo.

basilica [bəsílikə] *n.* (*Anc. Rome*) chōhōkei no kōkaidō. (kata-chi no sore ni nita) kyōkai dō.

basilisk [bǽzilisk/-sə-] *n.* hitome de hito o koroshita to iu densetsu no hebi ; tokage no isshu. ~ *glance*, akui no me.

basin [béisn] *n.* semmenki ; tarai ; ike ; bonchi.

basis [béisis] *n.* (*pl.* -ses [si:z]) kiso ; konkyo.

bask [bɑ:sk/æ:] *v.* hinatabokko suru ; atatamaru.

basket [bá:skit] *n.* kago ; basuketto. ~**ball** basuketto-bōru. ~**ful** *n.* kago ippai. ~**work** *n.* kago zaiku.

bas-relief [bǽsrili:f/bɑ:rili:f] *n.* usu-ukibori ; usu-nikubori.

bass [beis] *n.* teiombu ; teion-kashu. *a.* teion no.

bassinet [bǽsinet] *n.* yurikago ; yōran.

basso [bǽsou] *n.* teion-kashu.

bassoon [bæsú:n] *n.* basūn (gakki. —*musical instrument*).

basswood [bǽswud] *n.* (*bot.*) shinanoki.

bast [bæst] *n.* shokubutsu-sen'i (*bast fiber*).

bastard [bǽstəd] *n.* shiseiji ; magaimono. *a.* fujunna ; itsuwari, magai no. ⌈nado o nuru.

baste [beist] *v.* (1) karinui suru ; kukeru. (2) (yakiniku ni) batā

Bastille [bæstí:l] *n.* (*B.* ~) rōgoku. *Paris* no kangoku.

bastion [bǽstiən] *n.* (*mil*) (shiro *castle*) no ryōhō (*projecting part*).

bat [bæt] *n.* (1) kōmori. (2) tama o utsu bō ; dasha (*batter*). *v.* utsu. ⌈ba

batch [bætʃ] *n.* (pan no) hito-yakibun ; ichido-bun ; hito-ta-bate [beit] *v.* herasu, geniuru.

bath [bɑ:θ] *n.* mizuabi, nyūyoku ; furoba. ~**house** [bá:θhaus] *n.* yuya ; yokujō. ~**robe** [-roub] *n.* yukata. ~**tab** *n.* yubune.

bathe [beið] *v.* arau ; yu ni iru ; mizu o abiru.

bathing [béiðiŋ] *n.* mizuabi ; nyūyoku.

baton [bǽtən] *n.* baton (*staff of office*) ; keibō ; shikibō.

batrachian [bətréikiən] *n.*, *a.* (*zoo.*) ryōseirui (no) (*amphibian*).

batsman [bǽtsmən] *n.* (yakyū no) dasha.

battalion [bətǽliən] *n.* daitai ; guntai ; (*pl.*) daibutai.

batten [bǽtn] *v.* koyasu ; futoru ; koeru ; kowari-ita o haru. *n.* kowariita ; nuki.

batter [bǽtə] *v.* koneru. *n.* konetamono (*cooking*). dasha (*base.*).

battery [bǽtəri] *n.* hōdai ; hōhei-chūtai ; denchi ; (*base.*) hitokumi (*pitcher & catcher*).

batting [bǽtiŋ] *n.* dakyū ; dakyūhō.

battle [bǽtl] *n.* tatakai. ～ **array** [-əréi] *n.* jin ; jindate. ～ **cruiser** [-krú:zə] *n.* sentō-jun'yōkan. ～**field** [-fíl:d] *n.* senjō. ～**front** [frʌntt] *n.* = ～ **line** *n.* sensen. ～**plane** *n.* sentōki. ～ ; **battledore** [bǽtldɔ:] *n.* hagoita. ⌊**ship** *n.* senkan.

battlement [bǽtlmənt] *n.* hazama ; kyōheki ; dekobokokabe.

bauble [bɔ́:bl] *n.* yasupikamono ; yasuppoi mono.

bauxite [bɔ́:ksait] *n.* bōkisaito.

bawdy [bɔ́:di] *a.* gehinna ; midarana.   ⌈bigoe ; donarigoe.

bawl [bɔ:l] *v.* sakebu ; donaru ; ～ *out,* shikaritsukeru. *n.* sake-

bay [bei] *n.* (1) irie, wan. (2) gekkeiju (*laurel tree*) ; (*pl.*) gek-keikan. (3) kurige-no-uma. (4) (inu no) tō boe. oitsumererata jōtai : *stand at* ～, oitsumerarete. ～ **window,** haridashimado. ～**rum** isshu no kōsui. *v.* hoetsuku. *a.* kurige no.

bayonet [béiənit] *n.*, *v.* jūken (de sasu).

bazaar [bəzú:] *n.* bazā ; ichi (*market*) ; jizen-ichi (*charity* ～).

bazooka [bəzú:ka] *n.* bazūka-hō ; keitai roketto hasshaki.

B.B.C., BBC *British Broadcasting Corporation,* Eikoku Hōsō

B.C., b.c. *Before Christ.* Seiyō kigen zen.   ⌊Kyōkai.

B/D *Bank Draft,* ginkō tegata.

B.E., B/E, b.e. *n. bill of exchange.* kawase tegata.

be [bii] *v.* aru, iru ; (...de) aru ; *am, are, is* nado no genkei, ka-tsuyō wa : **be** (*am* ; *are* ; *is*) ; **were** (**was**) : **been** : **being**.

beach [bi:tʃ] *n.* hama ; iso ; kaigan. *v.* hama ni hikiageru ; hama ni noriageru. ～**head** [-hed] *n.* jōriku-kyoten.

beacon [bí:kən] *n.* kōrohyōshiki ; shingōtō ; noroshi (*signal*

bead [bí:d] *n.* juzudama. ⌊*fire*).

beadle [bí:dl] *n.* kyōku no yakuin ; zokkan (*minor official*).

beagle [bí:gl] *n.* isshu no ryōken ; kanchō (*spy*).

beak [bí:k] *n.* kuchibashi.

beaker [bí:kə] *n.* (dai-tsuki no) hirokuchi koppu ; biikā.

beam [bí:m] *n.* hari ; (hakari no) sao (*a steelyard*) ; kōsen. *v.* (hikari o) hanatsu ; kagayaku. ～**ing** *n.* uruwashii ; kagayaku.

bean [bí:n] *n.* mame. ～ **cake** mamekasu. ～ **curd** tōfu.

bear [beə] *n.* kuma ; sobōna hito ; (kabushiki shijō no) uri-kata, yowaki. ～**ish** soyana ; yowaki no.

bear [bɛə] *v.* **bore, born**(a) *or* **borne**(b); **bearing.** (a) ko o umu; (b) omoni o hakobu. sasaeru (*support*); hakobu (*carry*); koraeru (*endure*); (mi ni) tsukeru; furumau; ko o umu; (mi ga) naru. ~ *down,* osaetsukeru. ~ *out,* shiji suru. ~**able** [bɛ́ərəbl] *a.* sasaerareru; taerareru. ~**er** [bɛ́ərə] *n.* katsugite; umpansha; shojisha (*possessor*).

beard [biəd] *n.* hige; agohige. ~**ed** [bíədid] *a.* hige no aru. ~**less** *a.* hige no nai; aonisai no.

bearing [bɛ́əriŋ] *n.* nintai; taido (*behaviour*); kankei; igi (*meaning*); hōi (*aspect*); monshō (*emblem*); (kikai no) jiku-uke.

beast [bi:st] *n.* kemono; nimpinin (*brute in human shape*). ~**ly** *a.* kedamono no yōna; iyana. ~**liness** *n.* zannin.

beat [bí:t] **beat, beat** *or* **beaten; beating** *v.* (tsuzukezama ni) utsu; (uchi) makasu; ~ *about the bush,* tōmawashi ni saguru. ~ *down,* uchiyaburu; negiru. ~ *off,* oiharau. ~ *out,* uchinobasu. ~ *up,* kakimazeru; kōgeki suru. *n.* tataku oto; (ongaku) hyōshi. junkai-kuiki. ~**ing** *n.* utsu koto; kodō (shinzō no). ~**er** [bí:tə] *n.* utsu hito; kari no seko.

beaten [bí:tn] *see* : **beat.**

beatific(al) [biətífik(əl)] *a.* shukufuku o ataeru. ~**ation** [biætifikéiʃən] *n.* shikufuku.

beatify [biǽtifai] *v.* fuku o ukesaseru.

beatitude [biǽtitju:d] *n.* mujō no kōfuku.

beau [bou] *a.* (*pl.* ~**s**; ~**x** [bouz]) yoi. ~ *ideal* [bouaidiəl] risōtekina emman. ~ *monde,* ryūkō-shakai. *n.* sharemono; irootoko; aijin.

beauteous [bjú:tiəs] *a.* utsukushii; kireina.

beautiful [bjú:tiful] *a.* utsukushii; bireina. ~**ly** *ad.* utsukushiku; kireina.

beautify [bjú:tifai] *v.* utsukushiku suru.

beauty [bjú:ti] *n.* utsukushisa; bi; bijin; utsukushii mono.

beaver [bí:və] *n.* kairi. (umi-danuki)

becalm [biká:m] *v.* shizumeru; kaze ga naide fune ga susumanaku naru.

became [bikéim] *v. see* : **become.**

because [bikɔ́:z] *conj.* ...dakara; nazenara...kara. ~ *of,* no yue ni; no tame ni. ...dakaratote: *Don't be vain b~ you are good looking*, otokoburi ga ii karatte ii ki ni naru na.

beck [bék] *n*. unazuki; temanegi(-ki).

beckon [békən] *v*. temanegi suru.

becloud [bikláud] *v*. kumoraseru.

become [bikʌ́m] *v*. **became, become: becoming.** (...ni) naru; (...ni) niau; tekisuru: ~ *a singer*, kashu ni naru. ~ *wise*, kashikoku naru. *What has ~ of him?* kare wa dō natta ka? *a white dress becomes her*, shiroi kimono ga(wa) kanojo niwa niau. ~**ing** *a*. niau. ~**ingly** *ad*. niatte.

bed [béd] *n*. nedoko. shindai; naedoko (*seedbed*); kawadoko (*riverbed*). *v*. nekaseru; nemuri ni tsuku. ~**chamber** [béd-ʃèimbə] *n*. shinshitsu. ~**ding** [bédiŋ] *n*. shingu. ~**pan** [-pæn] *n*. benki; nedoko atatame-ki. ~**ridden** [-rídn] *a*. toko ni tsuitakkiri no. ~**room** [-rum] *n*. shinshitsu.

bedabble [bidǽbl] *v*. (mizu nado o) hanekakeru; yogosu.

bedaub [bidɔ́:b] *v*. nuritateru; akudoku (*tawdrily*) kazaru.

bedeck [bidék] *v*. kazaru.

bedew [bidjú:] *v*. uruosu; nurasu.

bedim [bidím] *v*. kumoraseru.

bedizen [bidáizn] *v*. akudoku kazaru.

bedlam [bédləm] *n*. seishin-byōin; konran-jōtai.

bedraggle [bidrǽgl] *v*. zuruzuru hikizutte yogosu.

bee [bi:] *n*. mitsubachi. ~ **culture** *n*. yōhō. ~**hive** [bí:haiv] *n*. mitsubachi no subako. ~**line** [-lain] *n*. saitanro. ~**'swax** [-wæks] *n*. mitsurō.

beech [bi:tʃ] *n*. buna. ~**en** [bí:tʃən] *a*. buna no.

beef [bi:f] *n*. gyūniku. (*pl. beeves; beefs in Am.*) nikuushi. ~ **tea** gyūniku ekisu. ~**eater** *n. London*-tō (*Tower*) no eji (keibeen [bín] *v. see :* **be**.   ⌊shí).

beer [biə] *n*. biiru. ~**house** *n*. biyahōru.

beet [bi:t] *n*. tensai; satō-daikon.

beetle [bí:tl] *n*. kabutomushi; kizuchi. *a*. tsukideta. *v*. tsukideru. ~**-browed** [--brʌud] *a*. odeko no.   ⌈furikakaru.

befall [bifɔ́:l] *v*. **befell, befallen; befalling.** okoru; (mi ni)

befit [bifít] *v*. teki suru; niau. ~**ting** *a*. tekitōna.

befog [bifɔ́g] *v*. kiri de kakusu; madowasu.

befool [bifúːl] *v.* baka ni suru.

before [bifɔ́ɔ] *prep.*, *ad.*, *con.*, (...no) mae ni ; ...senu uchi ni ; yori wa (mushiro) (*rather than*). ~**hand** *with ad.* arakajime ; maemotte. ~-**mentioned** *a.* zenki no.

befriend [bifrénd] *v.* tasukeru ; ...no mikata ni naru.

beg [beg] *v.* negau ; motomeru ; kou ; kojiki o suru.

began [bigǽn] *see* : **begin.**

beget [bigét] *v.* **begot, begot** *or* **begotten; begetting.** umu ; shōzuru. ⌈kechina.

beggar [bégə] *n.* kojiki. ~**ly** *a.* kojiki no yōna ; mazushii ;

beggary [bégəri] *n.* kojiki no kyōgū ; sekihin (*the abject poverty*) ; kojiki-nakama.

begin [bigín] *v.* **began, begun; beginning.** hajimaru (-meru). *to* ~ *with*, mazu daiichi ni.

beginner [bigínə] *n.* shoshinsha (*novice*) ; kaishisha (*originat-*

beginning [bigíniŋ] *n.* hajime ; hajimari. ⌊*or*).

begone [bigɔ́n] *inter.* yuke !, sare !, dero !, itte shimae !

begonia [bigóunjə] *n.* shūkaidō.

begrime [bigráim] *v.* yogosu.

begrudge [bigrʌ́dʒ] *v.* (mono o) oshimu ; netamu (*be envious*).

beguile [bigáil] *v.* damasu ; magirasu. ~**ment** *n.* damasu koto ; magirasu koto.

begun [bigʌ́n] *v. see* : **begin.** ⌈hyō shite.

behalf [bihɑ́ːf] *n.* rieki : *in* (or *on*) ~ *of*, no tame ni ; o dai-

behave [bihéiv] *v.* furumau ; gyōgi o yokusuru.

behavio(u)r [bihéiviə] *n.*, *v.* gyōgi ; hinkō ; furumai ; okonai.

behead [bihéd] *v.* kubi o kiru.

beheld [bihéld] *see* : **behold.**

behest [bihést] *n.* meirei ; kunrei.

behind [biháind] *ad.* ushiro ni (o) ; ato ni (o) ; okurete : *look* ~ *ushiro o miru. prep.* no ushiro ni ; no kage ni : ~ *the times*, jisei ni okurete. ~ *time*, chikoku shite. ~ **hand**, *ad. a.* okurete ; (...ga) todokōtte (*be in arrears with*).

behold [bihóuld] *v.* **beheld; beholding.** *hebooving* miru. ~**er** **beholden** [bihóuldn] *a.* on o ukete (iru). ⌊*n.* miru-hito.

behoof [bihúːf] *n.* rieki ; ben'eki.

behoove [bihúːv], (*Brit.*) **behove** [bihóuv] *v.* gimu ga aru ;

hitsuyō de aru.

being [bí:ŋ] *see :* **be.** *n.* sonzai ; seison ; seibutsu ; jinrui.

belabo(u)r [biléibə] *v.* hidoku utsu ; naguru.

belated [biléitid] *a.* okureta ; osomaki no.

belay [biléi] *v.* nawa nado o kui ya tsunadome ni makitsukeru.

belch [beltʃ] *n.* okubi. *v.* okubi o suru.

beleaguer [bilí:gə] *v.* hōi-kōgeki suru ; hittsutsunde kōgeki

belfry [bélfri] *n.* shōrō ; kanetsukidō.   ⌊suru.

Belgian [béldʒiən] *a.* Berugii no. *n.* Berugii-jin.

belie [bilái] *v.* itsuwaru ; somuku.

belief [bilí:f] *n.* shinnen ; shinkō ; kangae.

believable [bilí:vəbl] *a.* shinjirareru ; shin'yō dekiru.

believe [bili:v] *v.* shinzuru ; shinkō suru. **~r** *n.* shinzuru hito ; shinto ; shinja.

belittle [bilítl] *v.* kenasu ; kusasu.

bell [bel] *n.* kane ; suzu ; denrei (*electric* ~). *v.* suzu o tsukeru :
~ *the cat,* daitanna koto o suru. ~ **clapper,** kane no shita
(*tongue*). ~ **flower** *n.* tsuriganesō. ~ **rope** *n.* kane no hiki-
himo. ~ **tower** *n.* shōrō ; kane-tsukidō.

belle [bel] *n.* bijin.

belles-letters [béllétr] *n.* (*pl.*) bibungaku ; jun-bungaku.

bellicose [bélikous] *a.* ikusazukino ; kōsentekina.

belligerency [bilídʒəreənsi] *n.* kōsenjōtai.   ⌈sazuki.

belligerent [bilídʒərənt] *a.* kōsentekina. *n.* kōsenkoku (iku-

bellow [bélou] *n.* (oushi no) nakigoe. *v.* (ushi ga) ōgoe de
naku ; ōgoe de iu ; donaru.

bellows [bélouz] *n.* fuigo.

belly [béli] *n., v.* hara ; fukureru. **~ache** [-eik] fukutsū. ~
band *n.* uma no haraobi. **~ful** *n.* hara ippai (no bunryō).

belong [bilɔ́:ŋ] *v.* zoku suru ; (...no) umare de aru : *That book
belongs to me,* sono hon wa watakushi no desu. *I* ~ *to Alabama,* watakushi wa Alabama no jūmin desu. **~ings** *n.* (*pl.*)
shoyūbutsu ; zaisan.

beloved [bilʌ́vid] *a.* saiai no ; itoshii. *n.* saiai no (itoshii) hito.

below [bilóu] *prep.* no shita ni ; ika ; ...yori ototte. *ad.* shita-
ni.

belt [belt] *n.* obi ; (kikai no) shirabegawa. *v.* obi o maku ;

kawaobi de utsu. ~**ed cruiser,** sōkō jun'yōkan (*iron-clad*).
bemoan [bimóun] *v.* naku ; kanashimu.
bench [bentʃ] *n.* nagakoshikake, benchi ; saibansho, saibankan (no seki).
bend [bend] *v.* bent *or* **bended, ; bending.** mageru ; magaru ; katamuku. *n.* magari. ~**ed** *a.* magatta. ⌐ni.
beneath [biní:θ] *prep.* (...no) shita ni ; (...ni) ototte. *ad.* shita
benediction [bènədíkʃən] *n.* shukufuku (no inori).
benefaction [benəfǽkʃən] *n.* megunde yaru koto ; hodokoshi-
benefactor [benəfǽktə] *n.* onjin ; hogosha. ⌊mono.
benefice [bénəfis] *n.* bokushi no chii ; tera no teate (*allow-*
beneficence [binéfisns] *n.* jizen ; zenkō. ⌊*ance*).
beneficent [binéfisnt] *a.* jizen no ; nasakebukai.
beneficial [bènəfíʃəl] *a.* yūekina. *sunshine and moisture are* ~ *to plants,* nikkō to shikki wa shokubutsu niwa arigatai mono da. ~**ly** *ad.* ⌐ru hito.
beneficiary [bènəfíʃəri] *n.* megumi o ukeru hito ; rieki o uke-
benefit [bénəfit] *n.* rieki ; onkei. *v.* eki suru ; rieki o eru (ata-
benevolence [bənévələns] *n.* jin ; jin'ai. ⌊eru).
benevolent [bənévələnt] *a.* nasakebukai. ~**ly** *ad.* nasake-
bukaku. ⌐Bengarugo.
Bengali [bengá:li] *a.* Bengaru (*Bengal*) no. *n.* Bengarujin ;
benighted [bináitid] *a.* yukikureta ; yoru ni natta ; orokana.
benign [bináin] *a.* (kokoro ga) odayakana ; teineina.
benignancy [binígnənsi] *n.* jihi ; shinsetsusa ; onwa.
benignant [binígnənt] *a.* jihibukai (meshita ni) ; onwana. ~-
benignity [binígniti] *n.* jinji ; onwa. ⌊**ly** *ad.*
benison [bénizn] *n.* shukufuku.
bent [bent] *see* : **bend.** *a.* magatta ; nesshinni. *n.* keikō.
Benthamism [bénθəmizm] *n.* Bentham no tonaeta kōrishugi.
bentonite [béntənait] *n.* (isshu no) nendo.
benumb [binʌ́m] *v.* shibiresaseru ; kujikesaseru.
benzene, benzine [bénzin] *n.* benjin.
bequeath [bikwíθ] *v.* isan to shite ataeru ; yuzuru.
bequest [bikwést] *n.* isan ; katami.
bereave [birí:v] *v.* **bereft** *or* **bereaved ; bereaving.** ubau : *be* ~*d of,* ni shiniwakareru. ~**ment** *n.* shiniwakare.

bereft [biréft] *see* : **bereave**.
beret [bérei] *n*. bereibō.
berg [bəːg] *n*. hyōzan.
bergamot [bə́ːgəmɔt] *n*. kankitsurui no isshu.
beriberi [béribéri] *n*. kakke.
Berlin [bəːlíːn] *n*. Berurin. ~er [-ə] Berurin-jin.
berry [béri] *n*. (ichigo nado no) mi.
berth [bəːθ] *n*. (kisha, kisen no) shindai ; (fune no) teihakujo.
beseech [bisíːtʃ] *v*. **besought ; beseeching**. kongan suru. ~
   ingly *ad*. kongan suru yōni.
beseem [bisíːm] *v*. mieru. niau. ~**ingly** *ad*. niawashiku.
beset [bisét] *v*. **beset ; besetting**. kakomu ; fusagu ; kazaru.
   ~**ting** [bisétiŋ] *a*. tsukimatou.
beshrew [biʃrúː] *v*. norou ; B~ *me !* chikushō !
beside [bisáid] *ad*., *prep*. soba ni ; katawara ni.
besides [bisáidz] *ad*. sono ue ni. *prep*. no hoka ni.
besiege [bisíːdʒ] *v*. torikakomu ; hōi suru.
besieger [bisíːdʒə] *n*. hōi suru hito ; (*pl*.) semeyoseru guntai.
besmear [bismíə] *v*. betatsuku mono o nuru ; yogosu.
besom [bíːzəm] *n*. (nagai e no tsuita) hōki.
besot [bisɔ́t] *v*. yopparawaseru. ~**ted** [-tid] *a*. yoitsubureta.
besought [bisɔ́ːt] *v*. *see* : **beseech**.
bespatter [bispǽtə] *v*. (doromizu nado o) hanekakeru.
bespeak [bispiːk] *v*. **bespoke, bespoken ; bespeaking**. (*arch*.)
   bespake, bespoken. *v*. maemotte yakusoku suru ; yoyaku
   suru.
best [best] *a*. ichiban ii. *n*. sairyō : *at* ~, saizen : *do one's* ~, zenryoku o tsukusu. *get the* ~ *of*, ni katsu. *make the* ~ *of*, o dekiru dake riyō suru. *ad*. mottomo yoku. *v*. uchikatsu ; aite o
   makasu.
bestial [béstjəl] *a*. chikushō no yōna. ~**ly** *ad*. chikushō no
   yōni. ~**ity** [bestiǽliti] *n*. jūyoku ; dōbutsusei.
bestir [bistə́ː] *v*. funki saseru : ~ *oneself*, funki suru.
bestow [bistóu] *v*. ataeru ; ~ *a thing on someone*, mono o aru
   hito ni ataeru. ~**al** *n*. zōyo (*presentation*).
bestrew [bistrúː] *v*. **bestrewed, bestrewed** or **bestrewn** ;
   bestrewing. makichirasu ; furikakeru.

bestride [bistráid] *v.* **bestrode, bestridden**; **rare bestrid, bestrid** or **bestrode**; **bestriding.** ni matagaru.

bestrode [bistróud] *v. see*: **bestride.**

bet [bet] *v.* **bet** or **betted**; **betting.** kakeru. *n.* kake; kaketa kane (*money bet*).

betake [bitéik] *v.* **betook, betaken, betaking.** makaseru (karada o) : ~ *oneself to the mountain*, yama e iku.

bethink [biθíŋk] *v.* **-thought**; **-thinking**, yokukangaete miru : *I* ~ *myself of a good plan*, ii kangae ga(o) omoitsuita. omoiukaberu (*think of*).

betide [betáid] *v.* okoru (*happen*); mi ni furikakaru (*befall*).

betimes [bitáimz] *ad.* yoi toki ni ; hayaku.

betoken [bitóukən] *v.* ...no zenchō o (miseru) shimesu.

betray [bitréi] *v.* (nakama o) uragiru. (himitsu nado o) morasu. ~**al** [-əl] *n.* uragiri ; himitsu-roei. ~**er** [-ə] uragiri-mono.

betroth [bitróθ] *v.* kon'yaku suru. ~**al** [bitróuðəl] *n.* konyaku.

better [bétə] *a., ad. see*: **good.** *a.* yori yoi. *n.* issō yoi (mono) ; sempai : *get the* ~ *of*, ni katsu (masaru). *ad.* yori yoku : *be* ~ *off*, kurashi muki ga issō yoi. *know* ~, motto yoku shitte iru. ~**ment** *n.* kaizen ; yokunaru koto.

better, better [bétə] *n.* kakegoto o suru hito.

between [bitwí:n], (*arch.*) **betwixt** [bitwíkst] *prep. ad.* aida ni : ~ *ourselves*, naisho da ga ne.

bevel [bévəl] *n.* shakaku ; nanamena (chokkaku de nai) kaku ; shamen. *v.* naname ni (hasuni) kiru ; hasu ni naru.

beverage [bévəredʒ] *n.* nomimono.

bevy [bévi] *n.* (kotori nado no) mure ; atsumari.

bewail [biwéil] *v.* kanashimu ; nageku.

beware [biwéə] *v.* yōjin suru.

bewilder [biwíldə] *v.* magotsukaseru. ~**ing**, *a.* magotsukaseru ; bikkurisaseru. ~**ment** tōwaku.

bewitch [biwítʃ] *v.* uttori saseru ; mahō ni kakeru. ~**ing** miwakutekina ; uttori sasete iru.

beyond [bijónd] *prep., ad.* (o...) koete (mukō ni) ; ...ijō ni : ~ *measure*, hijō ni. ~ *one's power*, no chikara ijō ni. ~ *seas*, kaigai ni. *ad.* mukō ni. *n. the* ~, ano yo.

B/F, b.f. kuri koshi (*brought forward*).

⌈nial.)

biannual [baiǽnjuəl] *a.* (ichi-nen ni-kai no.) **~ly** *ad.* (*cf.* bien-

bias [báiəs] *n.* yugami; naname; nanamegire. **~ed** [báiəst]

bib [bib] *n.* yodarekake. ⌊kata yotta.

Bible [báibl] *n.* Seisho. **Biblical** [bíblikəl] *a.* Seisho no.

bibliofilm [bíbliəfilm] *n.* daijina hon (*books*) o shashin ni totta firumu (*film*).

bibliographer [bìbliógrəfə] *n.* shoshigakusha.

bibliography [bìbliógrəfi] *n.* shoshigaku; shomotsu ni kansuru gakumon.

bibulous [bíbjuləs] *a.* sake no sukina; yoku suikomu.

bicameral [baikǽmərəl] *a.* Shū- San- niinseido no.

biceps [báiseps] *n.* nitōkin (tokuni uwaude ya momo no kinniku); kinryoku.

bichloride [baiklóraid] *n.* (*chem.*) nienka butsu.

bicker [bíkə] *v.* kuchiarasoi **s**uru; sazameki nagareru; honō ga yurameku. kuchiarasoi suru. **~ing** *n.* kuchigenka; arasoi.

bicycle [báisikl]*n.* jitensha. *v.* jitensaha ni noru. **~clist** [báisiklist] *n.* jitensha nori.

bid [bid] *v.* **bid, bade** *or* **bad, bid** *or* **bidden; bidding.** meizuru: *He bade me sit down,* kare wa boku ni suware to (itta). *I bad him fairwell,* botu wa kare ni wakare o nobeta. (*arch.*) *He was bidden to the feast,* kare wa enkai ni manekareta. *The plan bids fair to succeed,* keikaku wa seikō shisō da. **~ing** [bídiŋ] *n.* nyūsatsu; meirei (*command*); shōtai (*invitation*). **~**

der [bídə] *n.* nedan o tsukeru hito.

bidden [bídn] *v. see* : **bid.**

bide [baid]*v.* **bided** *or* **bode; bided; biding.** matsu: **~** *one's time,* toki no kuru no o matsu.

biennial [baiéniəl] *a., n.* ninen ni ichido no; ninensei no (shokubutsu); (*cf. biannual*).

bier [báiə] *n.* hitsugi (*coffin*) no dai.

big [big] *a.* ōkii; erai; **~** *shot* (*Am.*), yūryokusha. *talk* **~** ōkina koto o iu. **~ness** *n.* ōkii koto; ōkisa.

bigamy [báigəmi] *n.* nijū kekkon. **~ist** *n.* nijūkekkonsha.

bight [bait] *n.* irie ;wan (*bay*); nawa no wa.

bigot [bígət] *n.* gankona meishinka; henkutsuna hito. ~**ed** [-id] *a.* gankona; kori katamatta. ~**ry** *n.* ganko.

bigwig [bígwig]*n.* erai hito; yūryokusha.

bijou [bi:ʒ:] *n.* (*pl.* -**joux** [-ʒu:z]) hōseki, chiisakute migotona bike [baik] *n.* (*Am. col.*) jitensha. ⌊mono.

bilateral [bailǽtərəl[*a.* ryōgawa no.

bile [bail] *n.* tanjū; fukigen; kanshaku. ~**stone** *n.* tanseki.

bilge [bildʒ] *n.* fune no soko; soko ni tamatta mizu. *v.* fune ni ana ga aku. ~**water,** fune no soko no tamari mizu

biliary [bíljəeri] *a.* tanjū no. ⌊aqua).

bilingual [bailíŋgwəl] *a.* nikakoku no go o hanasu.

bilious [bíljəs] *a.* tanjū no; kanshaku mochi no.

bill [bil] *n.* (1) kanjōgaki; bira; tegata; (gikai no) gian. (2) shihei. ~ *of exchange,* kawase tegata. ~ *of health,* kenkō no shōmeisho (fune no naka de no). ~ *of lading,* nimotsu no azukari shō. (torino) kuchibashi; *v.* (1) chōmen nado ni kinyūsuru; bira de kōkoku suru. (2) kuchibashi o awaseru (aijō o shimesᴜ): ~ **and coo,** ichatsuku. ~ **broker** [bróukə] (*Brit.*) tegata nakagainin. ~ **collector,** shūkinnin. ~**-sticker,** [bílstikə] biraharinin. ⌈haku saseru.

billet [bílet] *n.* (heitai no) shukusha; shigoto (*job*). *v.* shuku-**billet-doux** [bilidú] *n.* (*Fr.*) *love-letter* ; (koibumi.)

bill-fold [bílfould] *n.* (*Am.*) shihei (satsu=*banknote*) ire.

billiard marker [bíliədmà:kə] (tama tsuki no) gēmutori.

billiards [bíljədz] *n.* tamatsuki. ~ **table,** tamatsuki no dai.

Billiken [bílikən] *n.* Biriken; kōfuku no kami.

billion *n.* (*Am., Fr.*) 10-(ju)oku; (*Brit., Germ.*) 1-chō (itchō).

billow [bílou] *n.* ōkina nami. *v.* ōnami o tateru. ~**y** *a.* ōnami no; ōnami (yama no yōna).

billycock [bílikɔk] *n.* yamataka bōshi. **billy goat** *n.* osu no yagi.

bimetallic [baimǽtælik] *a.* kin-gin nihondate kaheiseido (o kiso to suru kahei seido).

bimetallism [baimétəlizm] *n.* fukuhon'isei. (cf. *monometall-***bimonthly** [baimʌ́nθli] *a.* nikagetsu ichido no. ⌊*ism*).

bin [bin] *n.* ire mono; hako; kura.

bind [baind] *v.* **bound; binding.** shibaru; sokubaku suru;

gimu o owaseru. seihon suru. **~ing** *a.* sokubaku suru; gimutekina (*obligatory*). *n.* sokubaku; hon no sōtei.

binder [báində] *n.* shibaru hito; seihonshi; (nawa; himo nado) shibaru mono. **~y** *n.* seihon o suru tokoro; seihonsho.

binnacle [bínəkl] *n.* rashingi compasu no haitteiru hako.

binocular [bainókjulə] *n.* sōgankyō; sōgankembikyō.

binominal [bainóminəl] *n.* (*math.*) nikōshiki.

biographer [baiógrəfə] *n.* denki no chosha.

biographic(al) [bàiəgráefik(l)] *a.* denki no.

biography [baiógrəfi] *n.* denki.

biological [baiəlódʒikl] *a.* seibutsu gaku no.

biology [baiólədʒi] *n.* seibutsu gaku. **~ist** seibutsugakusha.

bipartisan [baipá:tizən] *a.* futatsu no tōha no; kyōryoku shita.

bipartite [baipá:tait] *a.* futatsu no bubun kara dekite iru.

biped [báipid] *a.* futatsu no ashi no aru. *n.* ryōsoku dōbutsu.

biplane [báiplein] *n.* fukuyō hikōki.

birch [bə:tiʃ] *n.* kaba no ki. *v.* muchi utsu.

birchen [bó:tʃən] *a.* kaba no ki no; kaba no ki de tsukutta.

bird [bə:d] *n.* tori; (*Am. sl.*) yatsu; (azakeri no sh—sh— iu koe). **~ call** tori no koe; tori o yobu koe. **~ fancier**, [fǽnsiə], *n.* tori no suki na hito. **~lime** [laim] *n.* tori-mochi. **~ man** [mən] *n.* hikōka.

birdie [bó:di] *n.* kotori (kotori no aishō).

bird's-eye [bó:dzai] *a.* tori no me no yōni (hanten no aru); uekara mioroshita. *n.* (*bot.*) yukiwarisō.

biretta [birétə] *n.* R. *Catholic* no bōsan no kaburu bōshi.

birth [bə:θ] *n.* tanjō; **~ control**, [kóntroul] sanji seigen. **~day** tanjōbi. **~mark** [-mɑ:k] *n.* umaretsuki no aza. **~place** [pleis] *n.* umare kokyō. **~right** [rait] *n.* umaretsuki no kenri.

B.I.S. Kokusai Kessai Ginko (*Bank for International Settlement*).

biscuit [bískit] *n.* bisketto; (*Am.*) isshu no kashipan.

bisect [baisékt] *v.* nitōbun suru.

bisector [baisékte] *n.* nitōbun-sen.

bishop [bíʃəp] *n.* kantoku; sōjō. **~ric** [-rik] kantoku no shoku; kantoku kanku.

bismuth [bízməθ] *n.* (*chem.*) sōen.

bison [báisn] *n.* yagyū. (*Am.*)=**bnffalo** usi. ⌈kuriim.
bisque [bisk] *n.* suyaki no tōki (jiki); (isshu no) sūpu; aisu-
bit [bit] *v.* see: (1) **bite**. *n.* (kutsuwa no) kami. (2) kiri no
saki; sukoshi (*Am. col.*) (3); kozeni 12½ cents. *v.* kami o
hamaseru; kōsoku (*birdle*) suru.
bitch [bitʃ] *n.* mesu (inu, ōkami, kitsune nado).
bite [bait] *v.* **bit, bit** *or* **bitten**; **biting**. kamu; kuwaeru;
kamitsuku; ~ *in*, fushoku suru (*corrode*). ~ *the dust* (or *the
ground*) taoreru. ~ kamu koto; fushoku.
biting [báitiŋ] *a.* sasu yōna; fushoku-sei no. ~**ly** *ad.* shin-
bitten [bítn] *v. see:* **bite**. ⌊ratsuni.
bitter [bítə] *a.* nigai; tsurai: *to the* ~ *end*, saigo made. *n.*
nigai mono. ~**ly** *ad.* kanashiku; hidoku. ~**ness** *n.* nigami; (*fig.* nimo). ~**s** [-z] *n. pl.* nigai kusuri.
bittern [bílə:n] *n.* (*bird*) sankanogoi (isshu no sagi). nigari.
bitumen [bítjumen/-tjú:-] *n.* (*min.*). chan; rekisei.
bituminous [bítjuminəs] *a.* rekisei no; ~ *coal* rekisei tan.
bivalent [baivéilənt] *a.* (*chem.*) nika no.
bivalve [báivælv] *a.* ryōben no. *n.* nimai-gai.
bivouac [bívuæk] *n.* roei, nojiku. *v.* roei suru.
biweekly [bàiwí:li] *a., n.* nishūkan ni ikkai; shū nikai no.
nishū kan ni ikkai, mata wa shū nikai no shuppan butsu.
bizarre [bizá:] *a.* (*Fr.*) kimyōna; henna.
B/L funa ni shōken (*bill of lading*).
blab [blæb] *v.* bechakucha shaberu. ~**ber** *n.* bechabecha shaberu hito.
black [blæk] *a.* kuroi; kokujin no; yūutsuna; fukigenna. ~
art. [ɑ:t] *n.* majutsu. ~ **death**, kokushibyō. **B. Hand.** (*Am.*),
himitsu-kessha no namae (kyōhaku, bōkō o suru). ~**list**
[list] *n.* chūijimbutsu meibo. ~**Maria**. *n.* shūjin gosō basha;
keisatsu no *patrolcar*. ~**market(eer)** [mɑ:kit(iə)]*n.* yamiichiba
(shōnin). ~**sheep** *n.* yakkai mono; kawaridane. ~**tea**
kōcha. *n.* kuro (kuroi mono) senryō; e no gu; kokujin;
mofuku nado *etc.* *v.* kuroku suru: ~**out**, makkuro ni suru:
~**ball** *v.* kurodama (hantai hyō) o tō zuru; nakama hazure
ni suru. ~**en** *v.* kuroku suru. **blackguard** [-gɑ:d] *n.* gesu;
v. gesu no furumai o suru. kuchigitanaku nonoshiru. ~**lead**

n. kokuen. ~ **letter** (goshikku) katsuji. ~**ness** *n.* kuro

Black Friar blǽkfráiə] *n.* dominika-ha (*Dominican*) no sōryo.

bladder [blǽdə] *n.* bōkō.

blade [bleid] *n.* hiratai usui mono.

blamable [bléiməbl] *a.* hinan subeki. ~**bly** *ad.* hinan subeku.

blame [bleim] *n.* kashitsu no sekinin ; hinan. *v.* ...no seme o owasu. ~**less** [bléimlis] *a.* ayamachi no nai ; keppakuna ; ~**worthy** [bléimwə̀:ði] hinanni atai suru.

blanch [blæntʃ] *v.* shiroku suru ; shiroku naru. ⌐onwa

bland [blænd] *a.* odayakana. ~**ly** *ad.* odayakani. ~**ness**

blandish [blǽndiʃ] *v.* oseji o iu ; kobiru. ~**ment** *n.* hetsurai.

blank [blæŋk] *a.* kūhaku no ; karappo no. ~ **cartridge** kūhō. ~ **verse**, in o fumanai shi. ~**ly** *ad.* bon'yari to. ~**ness** *n.* bōzen.

blanket [blǽŋkit] *n.* mōfu. *a.* hōkatsuteki. *v.* de tsutsumu.

blare [blɛə] *v.* rappa ga nari hibiku ; koe takaku narasu. *n.* rappa no hibiki.

blarney [blɑ́:ni] *n.* oseji. *v.* odateru ; umaku damasu.

blaspheme [blæsfí:m] *v.* kami o kegasu ; kitanai kuchi o kiku ; nonoshiru.

blasphemous [blǽsfiməs] *a.* kami o nonoshiru.

blasphemy [blǽsfim] *n.* kami o nonoshiru koto.

blast [blɑ:st] *n.* ichijin no kaze. *at one* ~, ikki ni. *v.* bakuha suru. ~**ed** *a.* bachiatari no. ~ **furnace** *n.* yōkōro.

blatant [bléitənt] *a.* sōzōshii ; hadena.

blaze [bleiz] *n.* honō ; kattonaru koto ; jōnetsu. *v.* moetatsu ; akirakani suru.

blazer [bléizə] *n.* burezā (undō senshu no kiru uwagi).

blazing [bléiziŋ] *a.* moesakaru ; hanahadashii.

blazon [bléizən] *n.* monshō (*coat of arm*). *v.* monshō o kaku ; ōgesani suru. ~**ry** *n.* monshō kaisetsu.

bleach [bli:tʃ] *v* shiroku naru ; sarasu (suru).

bleachers [bli:tʃəz] *n. pl.* (*Am.*) gaiya kanranseki.

bleak [bli:k] *a.* arehateta ; fuki sarashi no.

blear [bliə] *a.* kasunda. *v.* (me o) urumaseru. ~**-eyed** [-aid] *a.* tadare me no ; mesaki no kikanai.

bleat [bli:t] *v., n.* (hitsuji nado ga) naku. sono nakigoe.

bleb [bleb] *n.* mizu-bukure ; awa.

bled [bled] *see* : **bleed.**

bleed [bli:d] *v.* **bled ; bleeding.** chi ga deru ; shukketsu sa seru ; kane o dasaseru. ~ *for,* dōjō suru : *My heart* ~s *for him,* kare ga fubin de naranai. ~**ing** *n.* shukketsu.

blemish [blémiʃ] *n.* shimi ; kizu ; ketten. *v.* yogosu ; shimi o tsukeru.

blench [blentʃ] *v.* shirigomi suru.

blend [blend] *v.* **blended** or **blent ; blending.** mazeru ; mazaru. *n.* kongō.

blent [blent] *v. see* : **blend.**

bless [bles] *v.* **blessed** *or* **blest ; blessing.** megumu ; shikufuku suru. *B*~ *me ;* (or *my soul*)*!* are ma !

blessed [blésid] *a.* megumareta ; kōfukuna. ~**ness** *n.* kōfuku. *single blessedness,* (*facet.*) dokushin.

blessing [blésiŋ] *n.* shikufuku ; ten no megumi : *ask* (*say*) *a* ~, shokuji mae ni inori o suru.

blest [blest] *v. see* : **bless.**

blew [blu:] *v. see* : **blow.**

blight [blait] *n.* shokubutsu o karasu byōki ; nani ka kurai kage. *v.* karasu ; sokonau.

blimp [blimp] *n.* kogata hikōsen.

blind [blaind] *a.* mekura no : ~ **alley** ikidomari. ~ *v.* mekura ni suru ; azamuku. *n.* mekakushi ita ; hiyoke. ~**door** [dɔ:] yoroido. ~ **shell** fuhatsu dan. ~ **spot** mōten. ~ **wall** mado no nai kabe. ~**window** keshi mado. ~**ly** *ad.* keisotsuni ~**ness** *n.*mōmoku ; muchi. ~**er** *n.* mekakushi. ~**fold** [bláindfould] *v.* mekakushi suru ; me o kuramasu. *a.* mekakushi shita ; muchana.

blindman's buff [blindmən's bʌf] mekakushi asobi ; mekura oni. [kirameki.

blink [blink] *v.* mabataki suru ; chiratto miru. *n.* mabataki;

blinker [blíŋkə] *n.*(uma no) mekakushi ; mei metsu shingō.

bliss [blis] *n.* kōfuku ; kono ue nai yorokobi. ~**ful** *a.* [blísfʌl] kono ue naku ureshii. ~**fully** *ad.* michi tarite. ~**fulness** [fulnis] *n.* mujō no kōfuku.

blister [blístə] *n.* mizu-bukure ; hibukure ; mame. *v.* mame ga dekiru ; hibukure ni naru blithe [blaið] *a.* tanoshisōna; kaikatsuna. ~**ly** *ad.* yōkini. ~**ness** *n.* tanoshimi. ~**some** *a.* tanoshisōna.

blitzkrieg [blítskrì:g] (*Ger.*) *n.* dengeki sakusen.

blizzard [blízəd] *n.* mōfubuki; hageshii fubuki.

bloat [blout] *v.* (1) fukuramasu; fukureru (*swell*); manshin-saseru. (2) (nishin o) kunsei ni suru. ~**ed** [blóutid] *a.* fuku-reta, mukunda; kōmanna. kunsei no. ~**er** *n.* kunsei nishin.

bloc [blɔk] *n.* burokku (seiji, keizai no teikei dantai).

block [blɔk] *n.* mono no katamari; kugitta ikkaku; bōgai. *v.* samatageru; fusagu. ~**ing expedition** [blɔ́kiŋekspedíʃən] heisokutai. ~**ade** [blɔkéid] *n.*, *v.* fūsa; heisa (suru). *v.* fūsa suru; samatageru. ~**head** [blɔ́khed] *n.* ishiatama; baka. ~**house** [-blɔ́khaus] *n.* marutagoya. ~ **printing** mokuhan insatsu.

blond [blɔnd] *a.* kimpatsu no. *n.* kimpatsu; aoi me no hito.

blonde [blɔnd] *a.* =blond. *n.* burondo no josei.

blood [blʌd] *n.* chi; kettō; iegara (*birth*). *in* ~ yūsōna. *in cold* ~, heiki de; reizen to. *in hot* ~, geki shite. *prince of the* ~, kōzoku. *Blood is thicker than water*, chi wa mizu yori koi. **bad** ~ naka no yokunai koto. **half** ~ kata oya chigai. ~ **bank** kétsueki ginkō. ~**ed** [blʌ́did] *a.* ketto no yoi. ~**guilty** [blʌ́dgilti] *a.* satsujin no. ~ **heat** [kétsueki ondo. ~**horse** jun-ketsushu no uma. ~**hound** [-haund] *n.* keisatsu inu; tantei (*detective*). ~**less** *a.* reitanna. ~**letting** [-létiŋ] *n.* chi o toru ~ **poisoning** [pɔizniŋ] *n.* haiketsushō. ~**red** *a.* chi iro no. ~ **relation** [reléiʃən] *n.* ketsuzoku. ~**shed** *n.* chi o nagasu. ~**shot** *a.* chibashitte iru. ~**stained** [steind] *a.* chimamire no. ~**sucker** [sʌ́kə] hito no chi o suu dōbutsu; hiru (*leech*). ~**thirsty** [θə́:sti] *a.* chi ni ueta (*cruel*). ~ **vessel** kekkan. ~**y** *a.* chi no; zangyakuna. ~~**ily** chimamire ni. ~**iness** *n.* chi-mamire.

bloom [blu:m] *n.* hana; hanazakari. *v.* hana ga saku; sakaeru. ~**ing** *a.* sakiniou.

blomer [blú:mə] *n.* (*sl.*) shippai. (*pl.*) burūma (fujinfuku).

blossom [blɔ́səm] *n.* hana; kaika. *v.* hana ga saku.   [toru.

blot [blɔt] *n.* shimi; fumeiyo. *v.* yogosu; massatsu suru; sui-

blotch [blɔtʃ] *n.* dekimono; shimi. ~**y** *a.* shimidarake no;

odekidarake no.

blotter [blɔ́tə] *n.* suitori-gami ; kiroku ; hikaechō.

blotting paper [blɔ́tiŋ peipə]. suitori gami. ⌈kushiki uwagi.

blouse [blauz/-s] *n.* brausu ; shigotogi. (*Am.*) gunjin no rya-

blow [blou] *v.* **blew, blown; blowing.** fuku (kaze ga) ; (oru-gan, fue nado) narasu ; (kujira ga shio o) fuku. (hana ga) saku. ～ *one's nose,* hana o kamu. ～ *out* fuite kesu. ～ *up* fuite fukuramasu. (shashin o) hikinobasu. *n.* shibaraku tsu-zuku kaze. ～**er** [-blóuə] *n.* sōfūki. ～**fly** [flai] *n.* aobai. (= aobae). ～**gun** [gʌn] *n.* fukiya. *blow great guns,* kaze ga hido-ku fuku. ～**-hole** *n.* kujira (*whale*) ga shio o fuku ana. ～**pipe** [-paip] *n.* hifukidake ; fuku kuda. ～ **up** [ʌp] *n.* bakuhatsu.

blown [bloun] *see :* **blow.**

blowzy bláuzi *a.* akaragao no ; darashinai.

blubber [blʌ́bə] *v.* kao o naite yogosu ; watto naku. *n.* watto naku koto. kujira no shibō.

bluchers [blú:tʃəz] *n.* (*pl.*) (mukashifū no) hannagagutsu.

bludgeon [blʌ́dʒən] *n.* mijikai kombō. *v.* kombō de naguru.

blue [blu:] *a.* aoiro no ; genki no nai. ～**book** aobyōshi no hon ; (*Brit.*) seifu ya gikai no hōkoku sho. (*Am.*) shinshiro-ku. ～ **devils,** yūutsu. *n.* aoiro ; aozora ; umi. (*pl.*) ki no fusa-gi. ～ **ribbon** (ichiban ii shōyo). ～**beard** [blú:biəd] mugoi otto. ～ **bell** (*bot.*) hotaru bukuro no isshu. ～**bird** aoi tori. (*Am.*) komadri no isshu. ～**bottle** aobae (*meat fly*). ～**jacket** [-dʒǽkit] suihei. ～ **print** aojashin. ～**stocking** [stɔkiŋ] *n.* on-na no gakusha ; gakusha buru onna.

bluff [blʌf] *a.* zeppeki no ; yamanote no ; sotchokuna. *n.*, *v.* zeppeki ; hattari. *v.* odosu. ～**ly** bukkirabōni.

bluish [blú:iʃ] *a.* aomi o obita.

blunder [blʌ́ndə] *n.* daishippai ; hema. *v.* yarisokonau. ～ *out* ukkari morasu. ～**buss** [-bʌs] *n.* hema o yaru hito.

blunt [blʌnt] *a.* kirenai ; nibui ; namakura ; sugenai. *v.* ni-buku suru. niburu. ～**ly** bukkirabōni.

blur [bləː] *n.* yogore ; shimi. *v.* shimi o tsukeru. ～ *out* kesu.

blurt [bləːt] *v.* shaberichirasu. ～ *out* ukkari shaberu.

blush [blʌʃ] *v.* kao o akaku suru ; hajiiru ; sekimen suru.

bluster [blʌ́stə] *v.* nami kaze ga areru. donaru ; donaritsukeru. *n.* ōare; karaibari.

boa [bóuə] *n.*, *boa constrictor* [kɔnstriktə] uwabami. ⌈shishi.

boar [bɔ:] *n* osu no buta; inoshishi. **wild ~** [wáildbɔə] ino-
board [bɔ:d] *n.* ita; bōrugami. makanai; iinkai; jūyakukaigi,
(*pl.*) butai: **~ of director**, jūyaku kai; rijikai. **~ of trade**
(*Am.*) shōkō-kaigi-sho; (*Brit.*) shōmushō. *v.* (1) ita o mochiiru. (2) geshuku saseru (suru). (3) (fune, kisha nado ni) norikomu. **~er** *n.* geshukunin; teki no fune ni norikomu heitai.
~wages shokuji teate. *tread the* **~** haiyū ni naru.

boarding [bɔ́:diŋ] *n.* ita-gakoi; ita-bari; geshuku. **~ house**
n. kishikusha; geshukuya. **~ school** *n.* kishiku gakko; jiku.

boast [boust] *v.* hokoru; jiman suru. **~er** *n.* jiman suru hito.
~ful *a.* jiman no. **~fully** *ad.* jiman(ge)ni

boat [bout] *n.* bōto; kogata no fune, kisen. *v.* kobune o tsukau. bōto o kogu. **~ hook** [bóuthuk] *n.* kagizao. **~ house**
n. bōtogoya. **~ing** *n.* funaasobi. **~man** [-mən] sendō; bōto
o kogu hito. **~ race**, bōtoreis. **~swain** [bóusn] *n.* kampan-
chō; dashu.

bob [bɔb] *n.* (furiko, hakari nado no) omori; (tsuri ito no)
uki; dampatsu. (*Brit.*) *shilling* kahei. *ten bob* (10 *shillings*). *sing.*
pl. v. hyoi to ojigi suru. kami o mijikaku karu. **~ bed** *hair*;
dampatsu. **~ up like a cork**, morikaesu. **~tail** [bɔ́bteil] *n.*
(umanado) mijikaku kitta o (*tail*).

bobbin [bɔ́bin] *n.* itomaki; hosohimo.

bobby [bɔ́bi] *n.* (*Brit.*) junsa. **~soxers** [-sɔksəz] **sockers**
[-sɔkəz] *n.* (*pl.*) (*Am. col.*) yūkō ni netsu o ageru 10 dai no
shōjo-tachi.

bobsled [bɔ́bslid], **bobsleigh** [bɔ́bslei] *n.* (*Am.*) tsunagi sori.
Boche [bouʃ] *n.* Doitsujin (keibetsu go).

bode [boud] *v. see* : **bide**. **~ful** *a.* fukitsuna.

bodice [bɔ́dis] *n.* fujin no kyōi (mune no mawari); dō ni pittari tsuku bubun.

bodiless [bɔ́dilis] *a.* mukei no; katachi no nai.

bodily [bɔ́dili] *a.* karada no. *ad.* karada gurumi; sokkuri.

boding [bóudiŋ] *a.* engi no warui. *n.* zenchō; fukitsuna maebure. *in a* **~**, ichidan to natte. gutaika suru.

bodkin [bɔ́dkin] *n.* himo-tōshi; kiri; semmai-dōshi.

body [bɔ́di] *n.* karada ; (fune no) sentai ; (kuruma shatai) ; dan-tai. ～ **corporate** [kɔ́:pərit] hōjin dantai. ～ **politic** [pəlítik] kokka (=**state**). ～**guard** *n.* goei (hei).

Boer [bóuə/buə] *n.* Boerjin (*Transvaal* nado no Doitsu, Oran-da, Oranda-kei hakujin).

bog [bɔg] *n.* numachi ; shitchi. *v.* (numa nado ni) shizume-ru ; shizumu. ～**gy** [bɔ́gi] *a.* numa no ōi ; numachi no.

bogey, bogie [bóugi] *n.* obake ; yōkai. *golf* (pā yori hitotsu dake ōi dasū.

boggle [bɔ́gl] *v.* (uma nado ga) osorete tachidomaru ; mago-tsuku ; gomakasu.

bogie [bóugi] *bogie car.*, *n.* (*Brit.*) bōgii sha.

bogus [bóugəs] *a.* (*Am.*) nise no ; ikasama mono no.

Bohemian [bouhí:miən] *a.* Bohemia no ; kattena seikatsu o suru hito.. yogorete kitanai nado ikkōni ki ni shinai seikatsu.

boil [bɔil] *v.* nietatsu ; niru. *n.* futtō. dekimono. **blind** ～ nebuto. ～**ed** *a.* nita ; tagitta. ～**er** *n.* kikan ; boira.

boiling point [bɔ́iliŋpɔ̀int] *n.* futtō-ten. ⌐rutte.

boisterous [bɔ́istərəs] *a.* arekuruu ; sōzōshii. ～**ly** *ad.* areku-

bold [bould] *a.* daitanna ; sen no futoi. ～**ly** *ad.* daitanni. fude buto ni (*written in bold type*). ～**ness** *n.* daitan ; zubutosa ;

bole [boul] *n.* ki no miki (*trunk*). ⌐hompō.

bolero [boulérou] *n.* borero (Spein buyō no isshu) ; fujinyō borero fuku.

boll [boul] *n.* mi (wata ya mame nado, saya (*pod*) no marui mono) ; maruzaya.

Bolshevik [bɔ́lʃəvik] *n.* hageshii kakumei shugisha ; kageki-shugi-sha. *a.* kageki shugi no. ⌐*Mensheviki*)

Bolsheviki [bɔ́lʃəviki] *n.* (*pl.*) (Roshiya no) kagekiha. (*cf.*

Bolshevism [bɔ́lʃəvizəm] *n.* kagekishugi. ～**ist** *n.* kagekishu-gisha. (*cf. Mensheviki*)

Bolshevize [bɔ́lʃəvaiz] *v.* kagekishugika saseru ; sekka suru.

bolster [bóulstə] *n.* nagamakura. *v.* makura de sasaeru.

bolt [boult] *n.* kannuki ; ōkugi ; bōruto. nigedasu koto. (nunoji nado no) hitomaki. denkō : *a* ～ *from the blue*, sei-ten no hekireki. *v.* kakedasu ; tōbō suru ; (*Am.*) totsuzen dat-tai suru. kannuki (*bolt*) de shimeru ; yə o iru (*discharge an* *arrow*) ; furui wakeru ; komakaku shiraberu. *ad.* ~ upright, massuguni.

bomb [bɔm] *n., v.* bakudan. bakugeki suru. ~proof [bómpru:f] *a.* bakudan ni taeru. ~shell [-ʃel] *n.* bakudan ; toppatsu jinji. ~sight [-sait] *n.* (hikōki no) bakugeki shōjunki.

bombard [bómbəd] *v.* (mōretsuni) hōgeki suru. ~ment *n.* hōgeki. ⌜kochō shita.

bombast [bómbæst] *n.* taigen sōgo. ~ic [-bǽstik] *a.* ōgesana ;

bona fide [bóunə fáidi] (L.) *ad., a.* zen'i de (no) ; seijitsu o motte ; shinjitsu ni (no).

bonanza [bonǽnzə] *n.* (*Am.*) hōfuna kōmyaku hakken ; ōatari ; kane mōke no tane. ~gram [bounǽnzəgræm] *n.* bonanzagram ; otakarakakiate.

bonbon [bɔnbɔn] *n.* (*Fr.*) bonbon gashi.

bond [bɔnd] *n.* shibaru himo ; saiken ; shōsho ; keiyaku ; kizuna ; sokubaku. *v.* shōken o ataete shiharai o yakusoku suru ; musubi tsukeru. ~age [bóndidʒ] *n.* sokubaku. ~holder [bóndidʒ houldə] *n.* saiken shojinin. ~man [bóndmən] *n.* dorei. ~sman [bóndzmən] *n.* hoshōnin ; dorei.

bone [boun] *n.* hone. ~ *of contention*, arasoi no tane. *v.* ~ china, isshu no tōki. (uo nado no) hone o nozoku ; (kasa nado ni) hone o ireru. ~setter [bóunsétə] *n.* hone tsugi isha.

bonfire [bónfáiə] *n.* ōkina kagaribi (oiwai (*fête*) ya aizu (*signal*)

bonito [bóni:tou] *n.* katsuo. ⌞ni taku.

bon mot [bón mou] (*Fr.*) meigen ; ki no kiita share.

bonnet [bónit] *n.* fuchi nashi bōshi ; bonnet.

bonny, bonnie [bóni] *a.* kireina ; kenkōsōna.

bonus [bóunəs] *n.* tokubetsu haitōkin ; shōyokin nado.

bony [bóuni] *a.* hone no ; hone-batta.

booby [bú:bi] *n.* baka ; noroma. ~ prize, saigo shō ; noromashō. ⌜isshu.

boogiewoogie [búgiwúgi/bú:giwú:gi] *n.* bugiugi (jazu no

book [bʌk] *n.* shomotsu : *speak like a* ~, seimitsu nihanasu. *v.* kinyū suru ; yoyaku suru. ~binder *n.* [búkbàində] seihonya. ~binding [bàindiŋ] *n.* seihon. ~case [-keis] *n.* honbako ; hondana. ~ing clerk, shussatsu gakari ; kippu uri. ~ing office shussatsujo. kippu uriba. ~ish *a.* hon-zuki no.

katakurushii. ~**-keeper** [-kí:pə] *n*. chōbo-gakari. ~**keeping** [kí:piŋ] *n*. boki. ~ **learning** [lə̀:niŋ] *n*. hon kara mananda chishiki. ~**let** *n*. shōsasshi; panfuretto. ~**maker** [-mə̀ikə] *n*. chosakusha. ~**mark** [mɑːk] *n*. shiori. ~**seller** [sèlə] *n*. hon'-ya. ~**stall** [-stɔ:l] *n*. hon'ya; furu hon'ya. ~**-store** [stɔ:] *n*. (*Am.*) shoten; hon'ya. ~**worm** [-wɔ:m] *n*. shimi; hon no mushi (*fig.*)·

boom [bu:m] *n*. hogeta; niwaka kōkeiki. *v*. taihō no dōn; hachi no bumbum nado no oto o tateru; keiki ga deru. *a*. keiki no yoi; sakanna.

boomerang [bú:məræŋ] *n*. būmeran (nageru to modotte kuru *Austraria* dojin no tobidōgu).

boon [bu:n] *n*. tanomi; onkei. *a*. tanoshii; yukaina.

boor [bu:ə] *n*. gehinna busahōmono; soyana otoko. ~**ish** [búəriʃ] yabona.

boost [bu:st] *n*. atooshi; tedasuke. *v*. atooshi suru; hagemasu (*cheer*) ~**er** *n*. tedasuke suru.

boot [bu:t] *n*. (1) (*Am.*) nagagutsu; (*Brit.*) fukagutsu. (2) (*arch.*) rieki (*profit*). to ~, sono ue (*in addition*) *v*. (1) keru. (2) rieki o ataeru. ~**black** [bút:blæk] *n*. kutsu migakinin. ~**jack** [-dʒæk] *n*. kutsu nugiki. ~ **last, ~ tree** kutsu gata. ~**booth** [bu:θ] *n*. roten; karigoya. ⎰**less** *a*. muekina.

bootleg [bu:tleg] *v*. (*Am*) yamitorihiki suru. *a*. yami no.

booty [bu:ti] *n*. bundorihin; senrihin.

bopeep [boupí:p] *n*. inai-inai bā!

borax [bɔːræks] *n*. (*chem.*) hōsha.

Bordeaux [bɔ:dóu] *n*. Bourdō-san no budōshu.

border [bɔ́:də] *n*. sakai; (*boundary*); fuchi (*edge*); henkyō (*frontier*); kadan. *v*. sessuru; (...ni) chikai; fuchidoru. ~**ed** *a*. fuchi o totta. ⎱-**land** [-lænd] *n*. kokkyō.

bore [bɔː] *v*. (1) *see* : **bear**. (2) **bored**; **boring**. ana o akeru; unzarisaseru; jirijiri susumu. *n*. ana. urusai hito. ~**dom** [bɔ́:dəm] *n*. taikutsu; urusai koto. —**r** [bɔ́:rə] *n*. ana o akeru **Boreas** [bɔ́:riəs] *n*. kitakaze (no kami). ⎰dōgu; kiri.

boric [bɔ́:rik] *a*. hōsa (*borax*) no. ~ **acid**, hōsan.

boring *n*. bōringu; tameshi ni ana o horu koto.

born [bɔːn] *see* : **bear**.

borne [bɔːn] *see* : **bear.**

borough [bárə] *n.* (*Brit.*) jichi toshi. (*Am*) jichi chōson.

borrow [bórou] *v.* kariru ; hyōsetsu suru (*crib*). ～**er** *n.* shaku-yōnin ; kariru hito.

bosh [bɔʃ] *n.* tawakoto. *inter.* (*el.*) Bosh !, baka o ie !

bosom [búzəm] *n.* mune ; kokoro : ～ *friend,* shin'yū.

boss [bɔs] *n.* (1) tokkibutsu ; ibo ; tsumami. (2) *n.* oyakata ; (*Am.*) seitō no ryōshu. *v.* shiki suru.

botanic(al) [bətǽni(kl)] *a.* shokubutsugaku no. ～ *garden.,* shokubutsuen.

botanist [bótənist] *n.* shokubutsugakusha.

botanize [bótənaiz] *v.* shokubutsu o saishū suru ; shokubutsu o kenkyū suru.

botany [bótəni] *n.* shokubutsugaku.

botch [bɔtʃ] *n.* fudekina tokoro ; futegiwa. *v.* migurushiku tsukurou. ～**er.** bukiyōmono.

both [bóuθ] *a., pron.* ryōhō no ; dochira mo. ～ *A and B, A mo B mo.*

bother [bóðə] *v.* jama suru. B. *it* ! urusai ! Iya da na ! *n.* mendō ; urusai hito. ～**some** [-səm] *a.* mendokusai. ～**ation** [bəðəréiʃən] *n.* mendō. *inter.* urusai !

bottle [bótl] *n.* bin. *v.* bin ni tsumeru ; (ikari nado o osaeru). ～**d** *a.* bin zume no. ～**neck** [nek] *n.* airo.

bottom [bótəm] *n.* soko ; fumoto (*foot*) ; kiso (*base*) : *be at the* ～ *of,* no shudōsha de aru. ～**less** *a.* soko no nai.

boudoir [búːdwɑː] *n.* fujin shitsu.

bough [báu] *n.* ōeda.

bought [bɔːt] *v. see* : **buy.**

bouillabaisse [búːljəbeis] *n.* (*Fr.*) gyoniku no shichū ryōri.

boulder [bóuldə] *n.* mizu ni arawareta marui ishi ; hyōseki.

boulevard [búːlvɑː] *n.* hirokōji ; namiki michi.

bounce [bauns] *v.* hazumu. haneru ; okotte donaru ; ōbora o fuku,. **bouncer** [báunsə] *n.* tobu hito (mono) ; ōbora fuki (*big talker*). **bouncing** [báunsiŋ] *a.* genkina ; hōgaina (*unreasonable*) ; hora o fuku. ～**girl** hanekkaeri.

bound [baund] *v. see* : **bind.** *n.* genkai (*boundary*) ; kagirareta jimen ; tobi haneru koto. *a.* tojita ; seihon shita ; sokubaku sareta.

bounteous [báuntiəs] *a.* kimae no yoi. ～**ly** *ad.* kimae yoku.

bountiful [báuntiful] *a.* monooshimi shinai. ～**ly** *ad.* oshimi

bounty [báunti] *n.* kandai ; megumi ; shōrei-kin ; ⌐naku.

bouquet [búkei/bukéi] *n.* (*Fr.*) hanataba ; (budōshu nado no) yoi kaori.

bourgeois [búɔʒwɑ:] *n.* (*Fr.*) chūsan-kaikyū no hito ; (*middle class citizen*) yūsan kaikyū. (*propertied class*) *a* chūryū no.

bourgeoisie [búɔʒwazi] *n.* (*Fr.*) chūsan-kaikyū ; burujoa kai-kyū.

bourn(e) [buən] *n.* ogawa ; kyōkai (*limit*) ; mokuteki (ten).

bourse [buəs] *n.* (*Fr.*) torihikijo (Pari no).

bout [baut] *n.* hitoshōbu ; ichi-ban (*trial*) ; hitoshikiri (*spell*).

bovine [bóuvain] *a.* ushi no yōna ; nibui (*dull*).

bow [bau] *v.* kagameru ; reihai (ojigi) suru.

bow [bou] *n.* yumi (no yōni magatta mono) ; *violin* no yumi (*gakkyū*) ; chōnektai. *draw the* (*a*) *long bow*, hora (*big talk*) o fuku. *v.* yumigata (*bow shape*) ni magaru. ～ **legged.** [-báulegd] ganimata. ～ **man,** *n.* kyūjutsuka (*archery expert*).

bowels [báuelz] *n.* chō ; jihi (*mercy*) no kokoro ; (*pl.*) naizō : jihishin (*bowels of mercy*).

bower [báuə] *n,* azumaya ; kokage no tokoro ; fujin no shi-shitsu.

bowl [boul] *n.* hachi ; taihai (*big cup*). *v.* (tama o) nageru (korogasu).

bowlder, boulder [bóuldə] *n.* maruishi ; hyōseki.

bowler [bóulə] *n.* tama o korogasu hito. (*cricket*) tōshu.

bowler [bóulə] *n.* yamatakabō.

bowling [bóuliŋ] *n.* (*cricket* no) tama no nagekata. ～ **green** [-grí:n] tama korogashi o suru shibafu. ～**-alley** tama korogashi no basho.

bowwow [báuwáu] *n.* inu no nakigoe ; wan wan.

box [bóks] *n.* hako ; (gekijō, hōtei no) tokubetsu seki ; (baishin-in (*jury*) nado no) seki ; bangoya (*sentry-box*) ; gyosha dai. *v.* hako ni ireru ; genkotsu matawa hirate de naguru (*strike*). kentō (*box*) suru : ～ *a person's ears*, tare sore no yokottsura o haru. ～ **calf,** bokkusu gawa.

boxer [bóksə] *n.* kentōka. *the Boxers*, Kempi (*Chinese history*).
boxing [bóksiŋ] *n.* kentō (jutsu).
Boxing Day [bóksiŋ dèi] (*Brit.*) Xmas no yokujitsu *postman* nado ni okurimono o suru hi.
boy [bɔi] *n.* otoko no ko ; shōnen ; kozō (*shop-boy*) ~ **scouts** shōnendan. ~**hood** [bɔ́ihud] *n.* shōnen jidai. ~**ish** *a.* kodomoppoi. ~**ishly** *ad.* kodomoppoku.
boycott [bɔ́ikɔt] *n.*, *v.* (kawanai) hibai-dōmei (o suru), boikotto
B/P (bills payable) shiharai tegata. ⌊(suru)
B/R (bills receivable) uketori tegata.
brace [breis] *n.* sujikai, (ie no kabe nado ni tsukau X-gata) ; shimeita no kakkō. (*pl.*) (*Brit.*) zubontsuri. *v.* shimekukuru : ~ *up*, yūki o dasu : ~ *onself up for a task*, kinchō shite shigoto ni kakaru. ~**let** [bréislit] udewa.
bracer [bréisə] *n.* tekubi ya ude o mamoru mono ; genkizukeru mono (*tonic*).
bracing [bréisiŋ] *a.* ikioi o tsukeru.
bracken [bræk(ə)n] *n.* shida (*fern*) ; warabi.
bracket [brǽkit] *n.* mochiokuri ; (*pl.*) insatsu (*printing*) de
brackish [brǽkiʃ] *a.* shioke (*salty*) no aru. ⌊([ ]).
bract [brǽkt] *n.* (*bot.*) hō ; hana no ukeba (gaku no shita no).
brad [bræd] *n.* bōzu kugi.
brae [brei] *n.* (*Scot.*) kyūna saka ; sampuku (*hillside*).
brag [bræg] *n.* jiman ; jiman mono. jiman suru hito. (*boaster*). *v.* jiman suru.
braggadocio [brægədóuʃiou] *n.* horafuki.
braggart [brǽgət] *n.* horafuki.
Brahma [brá:mə] *n.* (*Skt.*) Bonten.
Brahman [brá:mən], **Brahmin** [brá:min] *n.* Baramon Indo saikō-i no sōryo (*priest*) kaikyū.
braid [breid] *n.* uchihimo ; bempatsu (*tress*). *v.* amu ; uchihimo de kazaru. ~**ed** [bréidid] *a.* anda.
Braille [bréil] *n.* *Braille* shiki tenji hō.
brain [brein] *n.* zunō ; (*pl.*) rikairyoku. *v.* nōmiso o tataki tsubusu. ~**less** [bréinlis] *a.* orokana. ~**pan** [-pǽn] zugai. ~**sick** *a.* ki no henna. ~**work** [-wɔ:k] *n.* zunō rōdō. ~**y** *a.* (*Am.*) sōmeina ; atama no yoi.

braise [breiz] *v*. (niku o) mushi-ni ni suru.

brake [bréik] *n*. (1) hadome. (2) warabi (*bracken*). *v*. bureiki o kakeru. ~**sman** (*Brit.*) [bréik(s)mən] *n*. seidōshu. (*Am.*) **brakeman**.

bramble [brǽmbl[*n*. ki-ichigo ; ibara. ~**bly** *a*. ibara no ōi.

bran [brǽn] *n*. nuka ; fusuma.

branch [brɑːntʃ] *n*. eda ; shiten ; shutchōjo. *v*., *a*. wakeru. wa-

branchia [brǽŋkiə] *n*. (*pl*.) era (*gills*). ⌊kareru. *a*. wakareta.

brand [brǽnd] *n*. moesashi ; yaki-in ; omei (*stigma*). *v*. yaki-in o osu ; omei o kiseru. ~**ing iron,** yakigote.

brandish [brǽndiʃ] *v*. furi-mawasu ; furuu.

bran(d)-new [brǽn(d)njuː] *a*. maatarashii ; dekitate no.

brandy [brǽndi] *n*. burande.

brass [brɑːs] *n*. shinchū. ~ **band** [bǽnd], suisō gakudan. ~ **ware** [brɑ́ːswɛə] shinchū seihin.

brassiere [brǽsjɛə] *n*. (*Fr.*) fujin (*woman*) no chichi-ate.

brassy [brɑ́ːsi] *a*. shinchū o kiseta ; atsukamashii. ~**ly** *ad*.

brat [brǽt] *n*. kodomo ; gaki. ⌊zūzūshiku.

bravado [brəvɑ́ːdou] *n*. karaibari. kyosei o haru.

brave [breiv] *a*. yūkanna ; *n*. (*Am.*) *American Indian* no senshi (*fighters*). *v*. kiken o okasu. ~**ly** *ad*. yūkanni. ~**ry** [bréivəri] *n*. yukan ; buyū. ⌈zō ! Iyō ! Umai ! Dekashita !

bravo [brɑ́ːvou] *n*. sekkaku ; shikyaku (*hired killer*). *inter*. Erai-

brawl [brɔːl] *v*. kenka suru (mizu nado) gōgō to nagareru. *n*. kenka (*quarrel*). ⌈ii karada no.

brawn [brɔːn] *n*. kinniku (*muscle*) ; wanryoku. ~**y** [brɔ́ːni] *a*.

bray [brei] *n*. roba no inanaki ; rappa no oto. *v*. roba dado no nakigoe o tateru.

braze [breiz] *v*. shinchū de tsukuru ; handa-zuke suru (*solder*).

brazen [bréizn] *a*. shinchūsei no. zūzūshii (*audacious*) ; ~ **faced** [-fèist] *a*. tetsumempi no. ~**ly** *ad*. zūzūshiku.

brazier [bréiziə] *n*. shinchū-saikushi ; hibachi (*a charcoal* ~).

Brazilian [brəzíljən] *n*. Brazirujin. *a*. Braziru no. ⌈yaburu.

breach [briːtʃ] *n*. ihan (*violation*) ; nakatagai ; wareme (*gap*) ; *v*.

bread [bred] *n*. pan. *v*. panko (~*crumbs*) o mabusu. ~**crumb** [brédkrʌm] pan-kuzu. ~**fruit** *n*. pan-no-ki no mi. ~**stuffs** *n*. pan no genryō.

breadth [bredθ] *n.* haba.

break [breik] *v.* **broke, broken,** *or* **brake, broke; breaking.** *n.* hakai; wareme (*crevice*); yoake. *v.* kowasu. (kowareru). hasansaseru (-suru). kudaku, kudakeru; ∼ *down,* kowasu. ∼ *forth,* totsuzen patto deru. ∼ *into,* oshiiru; rannyū suru. ∼ *short,* pokkiri oreru. ∼ *through,* chikarazuku de tōru. ∼ *with,* zekkō suru. ∼**able** kowashi yasui. ∼**age** hason; hason daka. ∼**-down** [-daun] *n.* kikai nado no koshō.

breaker [briékə] *n.* kowasu hito; iwa ni atatte kudakeru shiranami.

breakfast [brékfəst] *n.* asameshi.

bream [bri:m] *n.* koi no rui no tansui-gyo.

breast [brest] *n.* mune; chibusa; kokoro (*heart*): *make a clean* ∼ *of,* ...o sukkari hakujō suru. *v.* daitanni teikō suru. ∼**pin** [bréstʃpin] *n.* burōchi (*brooch*). ∼**plate** [-pleit] *n.* muneate.

breath [breθ] *n.* iki, kokyū; *at a* ∼, ikki ni. *hold the* ∼, iki o korasu. *out of* ∼ ikigire shite. *take* ∼ ikiotsugu, yasumu.

breathe [bri:ð] *v.* kokyū suru: ∼ *one's last,* saigo no iki o hikitoru.

breathing [brí:ðiŋ] *n.* kokyū; soyokaze (*breeze*).

bred [bred] *see* : **breed.**

breech [bri:tʃ] *n.* hashi; jūbi. (∼ *of gun, cannon*). *v.* jūbi (hōbi) o tsukeru. ∼**ing** [brí:tʃiŋ] *n.* uma no shiriobi; ∼**-loader** [-lòudə] *n.* motogome-jū. ∼**loading** *a.* motogome no.

breeches [brítʃiz] *n.* (*pl.*) momohiki; zubon, *wear the* ∼, teishu o shiri ni shiku.

breed [bri:d] *v.* **bred; breeding.** ko o umu; sodateru. *n.* hinshu. ∼**er** [brí:də] *n.* sodateru hito. ∼**ing** *n.* sodate; shitsuke (*training*).

breeze [bri:z] *n.* (1) soyokaze (*soft wind*). (2) abu (*horse-fly*).

breezy [brí:zi] *a.* soyokaze no fuku; kaikatsuna (*lively*).

brethren [bréðrin] *n.* (*pl. of* **brother.**) dōhō; kōjū (*friendly society*).

Breton [brét(ə)n] *a.* (*Fr.*) Buritanii no. *n.* Buritaniijin.

breve [bri:v] *n.* tan'ompu (∼) hatsuon fugō. (*cf.* · *macron*).

brevet [brévit] *n.* meiyo shōshin (jirei). *a* ∼ *colonel,* meiyo-shōshin taisa.

brevity [bréviti] *n.* mijikasa ; kanketsu (*conciseness*).

brew [bru:] *v.* jōzō suru ; sake o tsukuru. ~**age** [brú:idʒ] *n.* jōzōshu (biiru nado). jōzōhō. ~**er** [brú:ə] *n.* jōzōgyōsha ; sake o tsukuru hito. ~**ery** [brú:əri] *n.* jōzōsho.

briar, brier [bráiə] *n.* ibara.

bribe [braib] *n.* wairo. *v.* wairo de baishū suru ; wairo o tsukau. ~**r** [bráibə] *n.* zōwaisha. ~**ry** [bráibəri] zōwai.

brick [brik] *n.* renga. (*col.*) kaidanshi (*good fellow*). *v.* renga de kakou (o shiku). ~**field** [bríkfi:ld] ; ~**yard** [-jɑ:d] renga seizōjo. ~**kiln** [-kiln] *n.* renga yakigama. ~**layer** [-leijə] *n.* renga shokunin.

bridal [braid(ə)l] *a.* hanayome no ; konrei no. *n.* kekkonshiki.

bride [braid] *n.* hanayome. ~**groom** [bráidgrum] hanamuko. ~**smaid** [-dzmeid] hanayome-zuki no musume.

bridge [bridʒ] *n.* hashi ; hanabashira ; *tramp* asobi. *v.* hashi o kakeru (*build*). ~**head** [brídʒhed] kyōtōho.

bridle [bráidl] *n.* uma no omogai (*headstall*). *v.* jiyū o seisuru.

brief [bri:f] *a.* mijikai ; kantanna. *in* ~, *to be* ~, yōsuru ni. *n.* jijitsu no yōryō(sho). *v.* yōyaku suru. ~**case** [brí:fkeis] shorui kaban. ~**ly** *ad.* kantan ni. ~**ness** *n.* kantan.

brier [bráiə] *n.* nobara no isshu.

brig [brig] *n.* nihon masuto (*mast*) no hokakebune.

brigade [brigéid] *n.* ryodan ; tai (*corps* [kɔ:]).

brigadier [brigədíə] *n.* ryodan. ~ **general** [dʒén(ə)rəl] ryodanchō. (ryodanchō zaininchū no kammei). ⌈datsu.

brigand [brígənd] *n.* sanzoku ; tōzoku (*robber*). ~**age** *n.* gō-

brigantine [brígənti:n] *n.* nihon masto no hansen.

bright [brait] *a.* kagayaku ; hareta (*clear*) ; kaikatsuna (*cheery*) ~**ly** *ad.* kagayaite. ~**ness** *n.* hikarikagayaku koto ; kaikatsu.

brighten [bráitn] *v.* hikaraseru ; hikaru ; migaku.

Bright's disease [bráits dizí:z] *n.* (*med.*) Buraito-shibyō (jinzō (*kidney*) byō).

brilliance [bríljəns] *n.* kōmyō ; kōtaku.

brilliant [bríljənt] *a.* kagayaku ; rippana. ~**ly** *ad.* kagayaite ; rippani. ⌈abura.

brilliantine [brìljəntí:n] *n.* tōhatsu (*hair*) no tsuya dashi

brim [brim] *n.* fuchi ; heri. *v.* fuchi made mitasu (michiru).

~**ful** [brímful] *a.* fuchi made no. ~**fully** *ad.* afureru hodo.
less *a.* fuchi nashi no.

brimstone [brímstən] *n.* iwō. *a.* iwo iro no.

brinded [bríndid] *a.* buchi (madara) no. (*arch.*).

brindle [bríndl] *n.* buchi ; madara. ~**d** *a.* buchi no.

brine [brain] *n.* shio mizu ; nigari ; namida (*tears*).

bring [briŋ] **brought ; bringing.** *v.* mottekuru ; ~ *about*, ...
okosu. ~ *back*, ...o omoidasu. ~ *down the house*, manjō no
kassai o hakusuru. ~ *forward*, ōyake ni suru. ~ *home*, nattoku saseru. ~ *on*, hikiokosu. ~ *over*, ...o watasu ; mikata
ni suru. ~ *round*, tokifuseru. ~ *up*, o sodateru. ~ *to pass*,
brink [briŋk] *n.* kiwa ; fuchi ; gake. [okosu ; hatasu.

briny [bráini] *a.* shiomizu no.

briquette [brikét] *n.* rentan.

brisk [brisk] *a.* sokudo no hayai ; kappatsuna. *v.* kappatsu ni
suru (naru). ~ *up*, kappatsuni suru. ~**ly** *ad.* kappatsuni. ~
ness *n.* kappatsu.

brisket [brískit] *n.* (kemono nado no) mune.

bristle [brísl] *n.* gōmō (arai ke, *tough hair*) *v.* ke o sakadateru.
ke ga sakadatsu. ~**d** [-d] *a.* kowai ke no aru.

bristly [brísli] *a.* gōmō (kowage) no aru.

Britain [brít(ə)n] *n.* Dai Briten (*England, Scotland, & Wales*).

Britannic [britǽnik] *a.* Dai Buriten no ; Eikoku no.

British [brítiʃ] *a.* Dai Briten no ; Dai Eikoku no.

Briton [brít(ə)n] *n.* Buritonjin ; *Celt-(kelt)*-jin.

brittle [brítl] *a.* koware yasui. ~**ness** *n.* morosa.

broach [broutʃ] *n.* tetsugushi (*iron spit*) ; kiri. *v.* (taru (*barrel*)
no) kuchi o akeru.

broad [brɔ:d] *a.* hiroi : ~ **cast** [brɔ́:dka:st] *a.* hōsōsareta. *v.*
hōsō suru. *n.* hōsō. ~**cloth** *n.* isshu no haba no hiroi rasha.
~**guage** *a.* kōki no. ~**ly** *ad.* hiroku ; hakkiri. ~**minded**
[-máindid] *a.* kokoro no hiroi. ~**ness** *n.* hirosa ~**side** *n.*
hangen issei shageki. ~**sword** [-sɔ:d] *n.* dambira ; hababiro
no katana. ~**wise** *a.* yoko ni. ~**en** *v.* [brɔ́:dn] hirogaru ;
hirogeru.

brocade [broukéid] *n.* nishiki ; kin-ran. ~**ed** *a.* kinran no.

brochure [bróuʃjuəl/brɔʃúə] *n.* (*Fr.*) shōsasshi ; karitoji no hon.

brogue [broug] *n.* chihō namari; isshu no kutsu (*shoes.*).

broil [brɔil] *n., v.* (1) kenka. (2) yaitaniku. *v.* kenka suru. niku o yaku. ～ing *a.* yaketsuku yōna.

broke [brouk] *v. see :* **break.**

broken [bróukn] *v. see :* **break.** *a.* yabureta; kudakareta. hasanshita. ～ *English,* katakoto majiri no Eigo. ～hearted [-hɑ́:tid] *a.* kiochi shita; uchinomesareta. ～ly [-hɑ:tidly] *ad.* gakkari shite. ┌no tesūryō.

broker [bróukə] *n.* nakagainin. ～age [-kəridʒ] *n.* nakagai; so-**bromide** [bróumaid] (*chem.*) shūkabutsu; (*Am. col.*) chimpuna kangae (hanashi, hito).

bromine [bróumi(:)n] *n.* (*chem.*) shūso.

bronchia [brɔ́ŋkiə] *n.* (*pl.*) kikanshi.

bronchial [brɔ́ŋkiəl] *a.* kikanshi no. ～ **tubes,** kikanshi.

bronchitis [brɔŋkáitis] *n.* kikanshi-en.

bronze [brɔnz] *v. n.* seidō; karakane. *the* ～ *age,* seidōki jidai.

brooch [broutʃ] *n.* brōchi; eridome. ┌*v.* seidō iro ni suru.

brood [bru:d] *n.* hito hara no hina : *sit on* ～, tamago o daku; chinshi suru; kuyokuyo omou (*fret*). ～er *n.* shian suru hito; fukaki (hina o kaesu kikai).

brook [bruk] *v.* shinobu; taeru. *n.* ogawa.

brooklet [brúklit] *n.* sairyū; chiisai kawa (nagare). ┌e.

broom [bru:m] *n.* hōki; enishida. ～stick [-stik] *n.* hōki no **broth** [brɔ:θ] *n.* niku (*meat*) no sūpu; usui yasai sūpu.

brothel [brɔ́ð(ə)l] *n.* jorōya; (**ill-fame house**). baishun yado.

brother [brʌ́ðə] *n.* (*pl.* **brethren** [bréðrin] **brothers**) kyōdai; dōgyōsha. ～ **officer** [ɔ́fisə] nakama no yakunin. ～hood [-hud] *n.*k yōdai taru koto; ～in-law [brʌ́ðərinlɔ:] *u.* gikyōdai. ～liness *n.* yūəi; shinsetsu. ～ly *a.* kyōdai no; kyōdai dōyōna.

brougham [brú:əm] *n.* isshu no shirin-basha.

brought [brɔ:t] *see :* **bring.**

brow [brau] *n.* mayu(ge); hitai; kengai; ～ *of clif.*

browbeat [bráubi:t] *v.* odokashi tsukeru.

brown [braun] *n.* chairo. *a.* chairo no : ～ *study,* bon'yari kangae komu. ～ chairo ni suru (naru). ～ *out* (*Am.*) keikai kansei (*warning control*) o shiku. ┌(*fairies*).

brownie [bráuni] *n.* yukaina shō-yō-sei; chiisai yōsei-tachi

browse [brauz] *n.* wakaba. *v.* shimme o taberu.

Bruin [brú:in] *n.* kuma (*bear*).   「bokushō.

bruise [bru:z] *v.* tsukikudaku; genko (*fist*) de uchiau. *n.* da-

brunet(te) [bru:nét] *a. n.* kami (*hair*) to me (*eye*) to ga kokkas-shoku (*dark brown*) de hada wa asaguroi (*dark*) hito.

brunt [brʌnt] *n.* ichiban konnanna tokoro : *bear the* ～ *of,* ... no yaomote ni tatsu.

brush [brʌʃ] *n.* (1) hake ; mōhitsu ; yabu. (2) kozeriai (*brief encounter*). (3) soda yabu. *v.* hake de harau : ～ *up* migaki o kakeru. ～**wood** [brʌʃwud] *n.* yabu. ～**y** [brʌʃi] *a.* (1) hake no yōna. (2) ya bu no shigetta.

brusque [brusk] *a.* bukkirabōna.

Brussels sprouts [brʌs(ə)lz sprúts] *n.* mekyabetsu.

brutal [brú:t(ə)l] *a.* yajūtekina ; zanninna (*cruel*). ～**ity** [bru:-tǽriti] *n.* zannin ; yabanna okonai.   「yabanna (*barbarous*).

brute [bru:t] *n.* kedamono ; chikushō. *a.* risei (*reason*) no nai ;

brutish [brú:tiʃ] *a.* yaban no yōna ; yabanna.

b.s., B/S taishaku (kashi, kari) taishōhyō (*balance-sheet*).

bubble [bʌbl] *n.* mizu no awa ; minawa (o tateru, ga tatsu). ～**company** [kʌmpəni] hōmatsugaisha. *v.* awa o tateru ; awa ga tatsu.   「sen pesto (*pest*).

bubonic [bju:bónik] *a.* yokone no. ～**plague** [pleig plæg]

buccaneer *n.* [bʌkəníə] kaizoku (*sea robber*).

buck [bʌk] *n.* shika nado no osu ; sharemono (*dandy*) ; (Ameri-can Indian ya kokujin no otoko). (*Am. col.*) *v.* uma ga hane-agaru ; (*Am. football*). tama o motte tekigawa ni tobikomu. ～**wheat** [bʌk(h)wi:t] *n.* soba. ～**shot** [-ʃot] *n.* shika o utsu tama. ～**skin** [-skin] *n.* shika no kawa : (*pl.*) *buckskin* no zu-bon (o haite iru heishi.

bucket [bʌkit] *n.* baketsu ～**ful** *n.* baketsu ippaibun.

buckle [bʌkl] *n.* shimegane. *v.* shimegane de shimeru. ～ *one-self to,* ...ni sennen suru.

buckler [bʌklə] *n.* maruitate. *v.* fusegu ; mamoru.

buckram [bʌkrəm] *n.* bakuramu ; (gomunori nado de kataku-shita asanuno).   「(*pastroral poem*).

bucolic [bju(:)kólik] *a.* bokkatekina. *n.* (*pl.*) bokka ; den'enshi

bud [bʌd] *n.* mebae ; tsubomi. *v.* me o dasu ; metsugi suru.

~**ding** *n.* mebae, hatsuga.
Buddha [búdə] *n.* Butsuda ; Hotoke.
Buddhism [búdizm] *n.* Bukkyō. **Buddhist** *n.* Bukkyōto.
buddy [bádi] *n.* (*Am. col.*) nakama ; aibō (*pal.*).
budge [bʌdʒ] *v.* ugoku ; ugokasu : *He wouldn't ~ an inch*, ichi-ichi datte ugokō to shinai.   ⌈kumu.
budget [bádʒit] *n.* yosan (an) ; fukuro no nakami. *v.* yosan o
buff [bʌf] *n.* (suigyū nado kara totta) yawarakai kawa ; kusun-da kiiro. *v. buff* de migaku.   ⌈odasu (*threaten*).
buffalo [báfəlou] *n.* suigyū *v.* (*Am. col.*) damasu ; ikaku suru
buffer [báfə] *n.* kanshōki ; shōgeki (*shock*) o yowameru kikai.
~ **state**, kanshō-koku.
buffet [báfit] *n.* (*Fr.*) shokki-dana ; bāryū no shō-inshokuten.
buffet [báfit] *n.* hirateuchi ; dageki (*blow*). *v.* uchi nomesu.
buffoon [bʌfúːn] *n.* dōkemono. ~**ery** [-fúːnəri] *n.* dōke-mono ; odokemono.
bug [bʌg] *n.* mushi ; nankin mushi (*bed-bug*).
bugaboo [bágəbuː], **bugbear** [bágbeə] *n.* obake.
buggy [bági] *n.* (*Brit.*) isshu no nirimbasha ; (*Am.*) horotsuki yonrimbasha.   ⌈shu.
bugle [bjúːgl] *n.* rappa. ~ **horn** rappa. ~**r** [bjúːglə] *n.* rappa-
build [bild] *v.* **built ; building.** tateru ; kenchiku suru. ~ *in*, tatemono de kakomu. ~ *on* (*upon*), ...ni kibō o kakeru. ~ *up*, kizuki ageru. *n.* kōzō ; taikaku. ~**er** [bíldə] *n.* kenchiku gyōsha. ~**ing** tatemono.   ⌈ʌp] *a.* tatetateta.
built [bilt] *see :* **build.** *a.* kenchiku shita ; tateta. ~**up** [bílt-
bulb [bʌlb] *n.* kyūkon ; (dentō no) marui *lamp.* ~**ous** [bálbəs] *a.* kyūkei no ; kyūkon no.   ⌈Burugariyago (no).
Bulgarian [bʌlbéəriən] *a., n.* Burugariya no ; Burugariyajin ;
bulge [bʌldʒ] *n.* (oke, taru nado no) dō ; fukurami (*swelling*). (*col.*) *have* (*get*) *the ~ on*, (...yori) yūsei da ; ...ni masaru. *v.* fu kureru.
bulk [bʌlk] *n.* ōkisa, zūtai ; daitasū ; funani (*cargo*). ~**head** [bálkhed] (fune no naka) shikiri kabe. ~**y** [bálki] *a.* kasa-batta, ōkina.
bull [bul] *n.* (1) oushi : *take the ~ by the horns,* konnan ni tachi mukau. (2) Rōma Hōō no kunrei. (*Am. sl.*) yota, baka-banachi

John ~ Eikokujin. **~dog** [búldɔg] *n.* burudoggu. mŏken. **~doze** [buldouz] *v.* odosu : (*Am. col.*) jinarashi suru. ~ **dozer** [búldouzə] *n.* kyŏhakusha ; burudōza. **~fight** *n.* tōgyū. **~finch** (*bird*) uso. ⌈no.

bullet [búlit] *n.* dangan ; tama. **~proof** [-pru:f] *a.* tamayoke **bulletin** [búlitin] *n.* kokuji ; kaihō (*report*). **~board** [-bɔːd] *n.* keijiban.

bullion [búljən] *n.* (kahei (*coin*) no) jigane ; junkin (-gin).

bullock [búlək] *n.* (yonsai ijō no) oushi ; kyosei gyū (*ox*).

bull's-eye [búlzai] *n.* mato no mannaka ; akari tori marumado.

bully [búli] *n.* bōkan ; gorotsuki. **~beef** kanzume gyūniku. *a.* sutekina. *v.* ijimeru.

bulrush [búlrʌʃ] *n.* ashi ; gama no ho.

bulwark [búlwək] *n.* hōdai ; toride (*rampart*) ; bōgo butsu.

bumblebee [bámblbi:] *n.* maru-hana-bachi (*bee*).

bump [bʌmp] *n.* shōtotsu ; kobu (*swelling*). *ad.* dosun to, batan to, tsuki ataru. ⌈(*buffer*).

bumper [bámpə] *n.* ōkina sakazuki. (jidōsha no) kanshōki.

bumpkin [bám(p)kin] *n.* bukotsu mono ; inaka mono.

bumptious [bám(p)ʃəs] *a.* ōheina ; namaikina.

bumpy [bámpi] *a.* kobu no aru ; dekoboko no.

bun [bʌn] *n.* isshu no ama-pan.

buna [bjú:nə] *n.* jinzō gomu.

bunch [bʌntʃ] *n.* fusa ; taba ; dantai. (*Am.*) gun ; mure : *a* ~ *of cattle,* kachiku no gun. *v.* atsumaru (-meru) ; tabaneru.

bunco [báŋkou] *v.* (*Am. col.*) peten ni kakeru (*swindle*).

buncombe ; bunkum [báŋkəm] *n.* ninki tori enzetsu ; baka-banashi.

bundle [bándl] *n.* taba ; tsutsumi. *v.* tsutsumu ; tabaneru.

bung [bʌŋ] *n.* sen (*stopper*) ; taru (*barrel*) no kuchi. *v.* sen o **bungalow** [báŋgəlou] *n.* bangarō ; hiraya date. ⌊suru.

bungle [báŋgl] *v.* busaikuni tsukurou ; heta o suru. n. bu-**bungling** [báŋgliŋ] *a.* (*med.*) bukiyōna. ⌊saiku.

bunion [bánjən] *n.* ashi ga harete (*swelled*) netsu (*inflammation*) o motsu byōki. ⌈goto. (*Am.*) *v.* neru (*sleep*).

bunk [bʌŋk] *n.* (1) nedana (*sleeping berth*) ; (2) (*Am. col.*) tawa-**bunker** [báŋkə] *n.* (fune no) sekitangura ; sekitan guruma ;

jamamono. ～**capacity** sumi o tsumu chikara ; saitan ryoku.

bunny [bʌ́ni] *n.* usagi no aishō (*pet name*) ; usachan.

Bunsen burner [bʌ́nsn bə́:nə] *n.* Bunzentō (kagaku jikken ni tsukau).

bunt [bʌnt] *n.* koushi, yagi nado ga atama de osu koto ; yakyū no " banto ". *v.* banto suru ; osu ; tsuku.

bunting [bʌ́ntiŋ] *n.* (1) (*bird*) hōjiro-rui no kotori. (2) hatanuno (*cloth for flag*).

buoy [bɔi/bui] *n.* fuhyō ; uki. *v.* ukasu ; uki o tsukeru. ～**ancy** [bɔ́iənsi] *n.* ukuchikara ; furyoku. ～**ant** [-ənt] *a.* yoku uku ; kigaruna. ～**ant force** *n.* ukuchikara. ～**ant mine** [bɔ́iəntmain] fuyūkirai.

bur [bə:] *n.* (kuri (*chestnut*) nado no) iga ; yakkai mono.

burden [bə́:dn] *n.* futan ; omoi nimotsu. uta no kurikaeshi ; kōras ; hanashi no shushi (*gist*). *v.* omoni o owaseru. ～**some** [-sʌm] *a.* wazurawashii.

burdock [bə́:dək] *n.* gobō (*vegetable*).

bureau [bjuəróu/bjúərou] *n.* (pl. Fr. **-eaux**, **-eaus** [ouz]) shō ; kyoku ; bu ; ka. hikidashi tsuki no tsukue ; kore o tsukau yakusho. (*Am.*) kagami tsuki no tansu. ～**cracy** [-krəsi] *n.* kanryō seiji. ⌈kanryōseiji no.

bureaucrat [bjúərəkræt] *n.* kanryō-seijika. ～**ic** [-krǽtik] *a.*

burg [bə:g] *n.* (*Brit.*), **borough** [bʌrə] ; (*Am.*) toshi ; machi.

burgess [bə́:dʒis] (*Brit*) *n.* shimin ; kōminken o motsu hito.

burgh [bʌ́rə] *n.* (*Scotland* no) jichi toshi ; ＝**borough**.

burglar [bə́:glə] *n.* yoru oshiiru gōtō. ～**alarm** *n.* tōnan keihōki. ～**y** [bə́:gləri] *n.* (*leg.*) oshiiri-gōtō-zai.

burgle [bə́:gl] *v.* yatō o suru.

burgomaster [bə́:gomà:stə] *n.* (Oranda, Berugii no) shichō.

burgundy [bə́:gəndi] *n.* (*Burgandy* san no) budōshu.

burial [bériəl] *n.* maisō. ～ **ground,** maisō-chi. ～ **service** maisō-shiki.

burl [bə:l] *n.* (ito, nuno nado no) fushi ; kobu *v.* fushi o toru.

burlap [bə́:læp] *n.* isshu no arai asanuno (*for packing*).

burlesque [bə:lésk] *a.* odoketa geki. *v.* chakasu.

burly [bə́:li] *a.* ganjōna ; deppuri shita (*plump*).

Burmese [bə:mí:z] *a.* Biruma no. *n.* Birumajin (～**go**).

burn [bə:n] *v.* **burned** *or* **burnt; burning.** yaku; moeru; (hi ni) yakeru. *n.* yakedo. **~ing** *a.* moeru; netsuretsuna. **~er** [bə́:nə] *n.* higuchi.

burnish [bə́:niʃ] *v.* migaku; tsuya (*gloss*) ga deru (o dasu). *n.* kōtaku; tsuya.

burnoose, burnous [bə:nú:s] *n.* (*Arabia* no) zukin (*hood*)

burnt [bə:nt] *v. see* : **burn.**

burr [bə:] *n.* gasagasa nodo ni kakaru koe; kono koe de hanasu.

burrow [bárou] *n.* (usagi no) ana. *v.* ana o horu; ana ni sumu.

bursar [bə́:sə] *n.* (daigaku nado no) kaikei-gakari; (*Scot.*) tokutaisei.

burst [bə:st] *v.* **burst; bursting.** toppastsu suru; haretsu suru.

bury [béri] *v.* umeru; hōmuru. **~ing** *n.* maisō.

bus [bʌs] *n.* noriai basha, (jidōsha, nado). *v.* noriai de iku.

bush [buʃ] *n.* yabu; shigemi. **~whacker** [hwǽkə] (*Am.*) kaitakusha; gerira tai-in. **~y** *a.* kamboku; (yabu) no shigetta.

bushel [búʃ(ə)l] *n.* bussheru (hobo 36.4 rittoru), bussheru masu.

business [bíznis] *n.* jimu; shōbai : *Mind your own ~* ! yokeina osewa da. *on ~*, shōyō de. *~ hours* eigyō jikan; shitsumu jikan. *~ man* [-mən] *n.* jitsugyōka. **~like** [-laik] *a.* jimutekina.

buskin [báskin] *n.* (*Greece, Rome*) han-nagagutsu; higeki.

bust [bʌst] *n.* kyōzō (jōhanshin-zō).

bustle [básl] *v.* isogashiku kakemawaru. *n.* ōsawagi.

busy [bízi] *a.* isogashii. *v.* isogashiku suru : *~ oneself about...* ni honsō suru. *~ oneself with...* ni jūji suru. **~body** [-bódi] *n.* sewa-zuki; osekkai-mono. **~ily** [bízili] *ad.* sesseto; isogashiku.

but [bʌt] *conj.* shikashi; da ga. (*only*.) ...de nakereba. *ad.* tada; tan ni. *prep.* nohoka wa. *all ~*, hotondo mattaku (*almost*). *~ for,* ..., ga nakattara.

butcher [bútʃə] *n.* nikuya. *v.* tosatsu suru. **~bird** [-bə:d] *n.* mozu. **~y** [bútʃəri] *n.* tosatsujō.

butler [bátlə] *n.* shitsuji; shiyōnin gashira.

butt [bʌt] *n.* (buki nado no) futoi hō no hashi (=haji); mato (*target*); nerai no meate. *v.* atama de tsuku.

butte [bjuːt] *n.* oka; koritsu shite tatte iru yama.

butter [bʌ́tə] *n.* bata. *v.* bata o nuru; obekka o iu (*flatter*).
~ **boat** bataire. ~**cup** [-kəp] *n.* kimpōge. ~**fly** [-flai] *n.*
chōchō. ~**milk** [-milk] *n.* bata o totta ato no (*milk*) gyūnyū.
~**nut** [-nʌt] *n.* kurumi no isshu. ~**y** *a.* bata no yōna.

buttock [bʌ́tək] *n.* shiri; dembu.

button [bʌ́tn] *n.* botan o tsukeru; de tomeru. ~**hole** *n.* bo-
tan-ana. ⌈sasaeru.

buttress [bʌ́tris] *n.* tsukkai-kabe; tsukkaibō. (*buttress* de) *v.*

buxom [bʌ́ksəm] *a.* marupocha no; nikuzuki no yoi.

buy [bai] *v.* **bought; buying.** kau; dakikomu. ~ *off*, kane o
yatte oiharau. ~ *up*, kaishimeru. ~**er** *n.* kaite; kau hito.

buzz [bʌz] *n.*, *v.* bun-bun (iu), ~**ing** *a.* bunbun iu.

buzzard [bʌ́zəd] *n.* (*bird*) nosuri (taka no rui).

by [bai] *prep.* ...no soba ni; ...ni yotte: *He was kissed by them*,
karera ni *kiss* sareta. made ni: *Finish it by tomorrow evening*,
asu no yūgata made ni shiage nasai. ~ *the by(e)* (*way*), tsuide
ni; toki ni. *ad.* soba ni. *near by* sugu soba ni. *by and by*, sono
uchi ni.

by, bye [bai] *n.* amatta hito; fusenshō; aite nashi.

bye-bye [báibai] *inter.* sayōnara; aba yo.

by-election [baiilékʃən] *n.* hoketsusenkyo.

bygone [báigɔːn] *n.*, *a.* kako (no koto): *Let bygones be bygones*,
sugita koto wa sugita koto da.

bylaw [báilɔ́ː] *n.* (moto no kisoku no) fusoku; naiki; saisoku.

byname [báinèim] *n.* adana; betsumei. ⌈suru.

bypass [báipɑːs] *n.* uramichi. *v.* uramichi o tsukuru; mushi

bypath [báipɑ̀ːθ], **byroad** [báiròud] *n.* uramichi; kandō.

by-product [báiprɔ̀dəkt] *n.* fuku sambutsu.

bystander [báistæ̀ndə] *n.* bōkansha; kembutsunin.

bystreet [báistrìːt] *n.* yokochō; uradōri.

byway [báiwei] *n.* uramichi; nukemichi.

byword [báiwə̀ːd] *n.* kotowaza; waraigusa.

bywork [báiwèːk] *n.* naishoku.

C

C, c [si:] *n.* (*pl.* C's; cs, [si:z]) Eigo *alphabet* no dai-3-bamme no moji.

c [si:] Sesshi (kandankei). sento (*cent*); santiimu (*centime*).

c [si:] *prep.* (*L.*) *circa* [sə́:kə]; *circiter* [sə́:sitə] hobo.; (*about, round*). **circa., ca. c.** no yōni kaku : *born c. 1550*, hobo 1550 nen goro umareta.

cab [kæb] *n.* (ittō-biki no) tsujibasha; takushii. *v.* takushii de iku. **~man** [kǽbmən] *n.* gyosha; untenshu.

cabal [kəbǽl] *n.* himitsukessha; imbō. *v.* imbō o kuwadateru; totō o kumu.

cabalistic [kæ̀bəlístik] *a.* Heburai shimpi-tetsugaku no; shimpiteki.   ⌈aru resutoran).

cabaret [kǽbərei] *n.* (*Fr.*) kyabarē (ongaku ya dansu nado

cabbage [kǽbidʒ] *n.* kyabetsu; kanran.

cabin [kǽbin] *n.* koya; senshitsu; kebin. **~ boy** senshitsu-zuki bōi.

cabinet [kǽbinit] *n.* chiisai jibun no heya; kabine-ban shashin. (*C~*) naikaku. **~maker** *n.* kagushi; tategushi.

cable [kéibl] *n.* futoi tsuna; kaitei denshinsen; kaitei dempō. *by ~*, kaitei denshin de. **~address** [-ədres] *n.* gaiden ryakugō. **~car** *n.* kēburukā. **~gram** [-græm] *n., v.* kaigai dempō (o hassnru)

cabriolet [kæ̀brɪəléi] *n.* ittō-biki no basha no isshu.

cacao [kəkéiou] *n.* kakao no mi (ki). (kokoa no genryō) to sono ki.

cache [kæʃ] *n.* kakushi basho; (naisho no) chozōbutsu.

cackle [kǽkl] *n.* tamago o unda mendori no nakigoe; kudaranu oshaberi. *v.* geragera warau; oshaberi suru.

cactus [kǽktəs] *n.* saboten.   ⌈na.

cad [kæd] *n.* geretsuna otoko; gesu. **~dish** [kǽdiʃ] *a.* gehin-

cadaverous [kədǽvərəs] *a.* shinda hito no yōna; monosugo-ku aozameta.

caddie [kǽdi] *n.* gorufujō no tama-hiroi.

caddy [kǽdi] *n.* (1) =caddle. (2) cha o ireru kan; hako. cha-zutsu.

cadence [kǝidǝns] *n.* chōshi; yokuyō; gakushō no musubi.

cadet [kǝdét] *n.* shikangakkōseito; otōto; minaraisei

cadmium [kǽdmiǝm] *n.* (*chem.*) kadomiumu genso.

caecum [síkǝm] *n.* (*pl.* -ca [-kǝ]) mōchō.

Caesar [sí:zǝ] *n.* Rōma Kōtei; sensei kunshu (*dictator*).

caesura [siʒúǝrǝ] *n.* (shi ya ongaku de) gyō no tochū de totsu-zen chūchi suru.

cafe [kǽfe] *n.* (*Fr.*) kōhii-ten; kissaten; restoran.

cafeteria [kæfitiǝriǝ] *n.* (*Am.*) kafeteria; jikyū shokudō (*self-caffein(e)* [kǽfi:n] *n.* kafein.   Lservice no kan'i shokudō).

cage [keidʒ] *n.* torikago; ori. *v.* ori ni ireru.

cairn [kéǝn] *n.* tozammichi no kerun; ishizuka.

caisson [kéisn] *n.* dan'yakubako; dan'yaku guruma; kēson.

caitiff [kéitif] *a.*, *n.* hiretsuna (hito).

cajole [kǝdʒóul] *v.* odateru. *n.* kuchiguruma ni noseru.

cake [keik] *n.* kēki, kashi; katai katamari. *v.* katameru; (-ma-calabash [kǽrǝbǽʃ] *n.* hyōtan.   Lru).

calamitous [kǝlǽmitǝs] *a.* sainan no; fukōna; itamashii. ~ly *ad.* fukōni; hisanni.

calamity [kǝlǽmiti] *n.* sainan; fukō.

calcareous [kælkéǝriǝs] *a.* sekkai(shitsu) no.

calcimine [kǽlsimain] *n.*, *v.* isshu no ekitai toryō (o nuru).

calcine [kǽlsin] *v.* yaite sekkai ni suru.

calcite [kǽlsait] *n.* hōkaiseki.

calcium [kǽlsiǝm] *n.* (*chem.*) karushiumu.

calculable [kǽlkjulǝbl] *a.* keisan (yosō) no dekiru.

calculate [kǽlkjuleit] *v.* keisan (keikaku) suru; ~ *on*, ...o ate ni suru. calculating *a.* keisan suru; dasantekina; nukeme no nai (*shrewd*).

calculation [kælkjuléiʃǝn] *n.* keisan; dasan; yosō; suitei.

calculator [kǽlkjuleitǝ] *n.* keisansha; keisanki.

calculus [kǽlkjulǝs] *n.* (*pl.* -li [-lai]) (*med.*) kesseki. (*math.*) keisanhō; bisekibungaku: *differential* ~, *n.* bibungaku. *integral* ~, *n.* sekibungaku.

caldron [kó:ldrǝn] *n.* ōgama; ōnabe.

calendar [kǽləndə] *n.* koyomi; gyōjiichiran(hyō). *lunar* ～, taiinreki. *solar* ～, taiyōreki.

calender [kǽləndə] *n.* tsuyadashiki.

calf [kɑːf] *n.* (*pl.* **calves**). (1) koushi; (kujira, azarashi nado no) ko. (2) (*sl.*) manuke. (3) fukurahagi. ～**bound** [káːʃbaund] *a. calf* no nameshigawa toji no (hon *-book*). ～**skin** [-skin] *n. calf* no nameshigawa.

caliber, calibre [kǽlibə] *n.* (jū-hō no) kōkei; dangan (*shot*) no ōkisa; kokoro no ōkisa. kiryō. saikan : *a man of excellent* ～, shuwan no aru hito.

calibrate [kǽlibreit] *v.* (taihō nado no) kōkei o shiraberu; memori o suru.

calico [kǽlikou] *n.* kyarako; (*Am.*) sarasa.

calif, caliph [kéilif] *n. Halifa* (Mohame to no atotsugi; Kai-kyō-koku no kokuō).

calipers, callipers [kǽlipəːs] *n.* (*pl.*) wankyokuki (*compas.*)

calk [kɔːk] *n., v.* togari gane; suberi dome (o suru).

call [kɔːl] *v.* yobu. ～*at* ...ni tachiyoru. ～ *down* (megumi o) motomeru. ～ *for*, motomeru, yōkyūsuru; tori ni kuru (iku). ～ (*a persson*) *names*, warukuchi o iu. ～ *on*, o hōmon suru. *n.* sakebi; yobidashi. shōshū; hōmon. ～**ing** [kɔːliŋ] *n.* ten ko; shōshū; shokugyō (*occupation*). ～**loan** [-loun] *n.* tōza-kashikin. ～**money** [-mʌnə] tōzagari. ～**er** [kɔːlə] hōmonsha.

calligraphy [kəlígrəfi] *n.* jōzu ni kaita moji; kaku koto.

cal(l)isthenics [kælisθéniks] *n.* jūnan (biyō) taisō.

callosity [kælɔsiti] *n.* tako; mukankaku (*insensibility*).

callous [kǽləs] *a.* (hifu no) kataku natta; tako ni natta. ninjō no nai. ～**ly** *ad.* reitanni. ～**ness** *n.* funinjō.

callow [kǽlou] *a.* ubuna; aonisai no. ⌐nai koto.; nagi.

calm [kɑːm] *a.* odayakana; *v.* shizumeru (maru). *n.* kaze no

calomel [kǽləmel] *n.* (*chem.*) kankō (enka daiichi suigin).

caloric [kəlɔrik] *n., a.* netsu (*heat*) (no).

calorimeter [kælərímitə] *n.* netsuryōkei.

calory [kǽləri] *n.* karorii (netsuryō no tan'i (*unit*)).

calumet [kǽljumit] *n.* (Hoku Bei genjiumin no) kazari-giseru (*pipe*).

calumniate [kəlʌ́mnieit] *v.* chūshō suru (*slander*).

calumniaion [kəlʌmniéiʃən] *n.* soshiri; chūshō.

calumniator [kəlʌmniéitə] *n.* chūshō suru hito.

calumniatory [kəlʌmniéitəri]̰ **calumnious** [kəlʌmniəs] *a.* soshiru; chūshōtekina.

calumny [kǽləmni] *n.* hibō ;chūshō (*slander*).

calve [kɑːv/kæv] *v.* (ushi, shika, kujira nado ga) ko o umu.

calx [kælks] *n.* (*pl.* -ces [-siz]) kinzoku no hai (*ashes*).

calyx [kéiliks] *n.* (*pl.* -ces [-siz]) hana (*flowers*) no gaku ; (utena).

camaraderie [kæmərɑ́ːdri/kɑː-] *n.* (Fr.) yūjō ; (*comradeship*) dōshi-ai.

camber [kǽmbə] *n.* dōro nado no naka ga takaku natte iru koto. *v.* uwa-zori ni suru ; (naru).

cambric [kéimbrik] *n.* shiroasa no hankachi.

came [keim] *v. see* : **come**.

camel [kǽməl] *n.* rakuda. ～**eer** [kæmíliə] *n.* rakuda-tsukai

camellia [kəmɛ́liə] *n.* (*flower*) tsubaki.

camelopard [kæmɛ́ləpɑː d/kǽ-] *n.* kirin ; jirafu.

cameo [kǽmiou] *n.* ukibori (*relief work*) o shita hōseki (*gem*) mata wa kaigara.

camera [kǽmərə] *n.* kamera ; shashinki ; hanji (*judge*) no heya. ～**man** *n.* kameraman ; satsueigishi(-tachi).

camlet [kǽmlit] *n.* orimono no isshu. (kinu to ke no) utsukushii mazeori ; tsuyoi bōsui nunoji.

camouflage [kǽməflɑːdʒ] *n.* kamufurāji ; meisai ; gisō (*deception*) *v.* kamofurāji suru.

camp [kæmp] *n.* yaei ; jinchi ; yokuryūjo. *v.* yaei suru. ～**chair** [-tʃɛə] *n.* oritatami isu. ～**fire** [⊥faiə] *n.* kagaribi ; sono mawari no madoi. ～**ing** [kǽmpiŋ] *n.* yaei ; kyampu seikatsu. ～**meeting** [mí:tiŋ] (*Am.*) yagai shūkai. ～ **stool** [stuːl] *n.* keitai koshikake.

campaign [kæmpéin] *n.* tatakai ; (soshikitekina) undō. *v.* shussei suru ; yūzei o suru. ～**er** *n.* jūgunsha : *an old* ～, rōrenka. ⌈*tower*⌉

campanile [kæmpəníːli] *n.* (*pl.* -s ; -li [-liː]) kanetsukidō (*bell*

camphol [kǽmfɔl] *n.* ryūnō.

camphor [kǽmfə] *n.* shōnō. ～ *ball*, tama shōnō (mushiyoke). ～**ate** [-reit] *v.* shōnō to kagō saseru.

campus [kǽmpəs] *n.* (*Am.*) gakkō (daigaku) kōnai, kōtei.

can¹ [kæn/kən] *aux. v.* **could.** dekiru; ...shite yoi; (ari-)eru: C~ I *go now?* ima itte mo ii ka? *It ~ not be so,* sonna hazu wa nai.

can³ [kæn] *n.* (*Am.*) (buriki no) kan. *v.* (*Am.*) kanzume ni suru; (*sl.*) kaiko suru (*dismiss*). **~ned** [kænd] *a.* (*Am.*) kanzume ni shita. **~goods** [kændgudz]*n.* (*Am.*) kanzume. **~ner** [kǽnə] *n.* (*Am.*) kanzume-gyōsha. **~nery** [kǽnəri] *n.* kanzume kōjō.

Canadian [kənéidiən] *a.* Kanada (*Canada*) no. *n.* Kanadajin.

canal [kənǽl] *n.* unga; mizo. **~ize** [kǽnəlaiz] *v.* unga o tōsu.

canard [kəná:d] *n.* (*Fr.*) ryūgen; kyohō (*false rumor*).

canary [kənéəri] *n.* (*bird*) kanariya. budōshu no isshu.

cancel [kǽnsəl] *v.* torikesu; yameru. (*math.*) yakubun suru. **~ation** [kænsəléijən] *n.* torikeshi; sakujo.   [*a.* gan no.

cancer [kǽnsə] *n.* gan; (*astr.*) (C-) Kaniza. **~ous** [kǽnsərəs] **candelabrum** [kændiléibrəm] (*pl.* **-s**; **-ra** [rə]) *n.* eda no katachi no (*branchlike*) kazari shokudai.

candid [kǽndid] *a.* kōheina (*fair*); kakushidate shinai. (*frank*): *to be ~ with you,* uchiakete eiba. **~ camera,** kogata sokusha shashinki. **~ly** *ad.* kōheini. **~ness** *n.* kōhei; shōjiki, sotchokusa.

candidate [kǽndidit] *n.* kōhosha; shigansha.

candied [kǽndid] *a.* satōzuke ni shita; kuchisaki no umai (*honeyed*). (*cf.* **candy.**)

candle [kǽndl] *n.* rōsoku. *can't hold a ~ to,* ...towa kurabemono ni naranai. **~light** [-lait] *n.* rōsoku no hi. **~mas** [-məs] *n. Catholic* no Seishokusetsu (2gt. 2k.). **~power** [-pʌ́wə] *n,* denki no shokkō no tan'i. **~stick** [-stik] *n.* shokudai.

cando(u)r [kǽndə] *n.* sotchokuna; kōhei (*fairness*).   [suru.

candy [kǽndi] *n.* kyandii; satō-gashi. *v.* satōzuke ni **cane** [kein] *n.* tsue; satōkibi; tō. *v.* tsue de utsu; tō de tsukuru. **~ chair** [tʃeə] *n.* tōisu. **~brake** [-breik] *n.* tōyabu, takeyabu. **~sugar** [ʃúgə] *n.* tōkibi satō.

canine [kéinain] *a.* inu no yōna; **~tooth**, kenshi (inuba).

Canis [kéinis] *n.* inu no shuzoku: **~** *major* (*minor*) (*astro.*) Ōinuza (Koinuza).

canister [kǽnistə] *n.* kan (ironna mono o ireru).

canker [kǽŋkə] *n.* kuchi no naka no gan (*cancer*); jumoku
(*tree*) no gan. *v.* gan ni naru. ～ous [kǽŋkərəs] *a.* yō (gan) ni
kakatta. ～worm [-wə:m] *n.* shakutori mushi.

canna [kǽnə] *n.* (*flower*) kanna (no hana). ⌈sekitan].

cannel [kǽnəl] *n.* shokutaⁱ (abura ya gasu o takusan fukumu

cannibal [kǽnibəl] *n.* hitokuijin; tomogui suru dōbutsu. *a.*
hitokui (tomogui) no. ～ism [-izm] *n.* hito o kuu fūshū;
zannin. ～istic [kæ̀nibəlístik] *a.* hitokui (tomogui) no.

cannikin [kǽnikin] *n.* chiisana kan; sakazuki.

cannon [kǽnən] *n.* taihō; kyanonhō. ～ade [kæ̀nənéid] *n., v.*
hōgeki (suru). ～ball [-bo:l] taihō no tama; hōdan. ～eer
cannot [kǽnət] =**can not**. *see* : **can**. ⌊[kæ̀nəníə] *n.* hōshu

canny [kǽni] *a.* nukeme nai (*shrewd*); yōjimbukai.

canoe [kənú:] *n.* kanū (kai de kogu) *v.* kanū ni noru.

canon [kǽnən] *n.* seiten; (shūkyōjō no kimari o kaita hon).

canon, canyon [kǽnjən] *n.* (1) *canon.* (2) kyōkoku (semaku
fukai tani). ⌈na. ～s *n.* (*pl.*) sōryo no reifuku.

canonical [kənónikl] *a.* shūkyōjō no kimari no; hyōjunteki-
canonicity [kæ̀nənísiti] *n.* kyōkaihō ni kanau koto.

canonist [kǽnənist] *n. canon* no gakusha; ～ic [-ik] shūkyō
kai no hōgakutekina. ⌈kuwaeru.

canonize [kǽnənaiz] *v.* seito (*saint*, junkyōsha) no uchi ni

canopy [kǽnəpi] *n.* tengai; ōzora *v.* tengai de ou. ⌈tekina.

canorous [kənó:rəs] *a.* ne (=oto) no yoi (*melodieous*); ongaku-

cant [kænt] *n.* (1) soranembutsu; nakama no aikotoba.
phrase ; tōri kotoba. (2) keisha; shamen. *v.* soranemuntsu o
thieves ～ tōzoku no ingo. ⌊suru. katamukeru(-ku).

can't [kɑ:nt/kænt] *aux. v.* =**cannot.**

cantaloup [kǽntəlu:p] *n.* (*bot.*) meron no isshu.

cantankerous [kæ̀ntǽŋkərəs] *a.* iji no warui; kenka zuki no.

cantata [kæntá:tə] *n.* (*It. mus.*) kantata; (gasshō, dokushō no
aru) seika.

canteen [kæntí:n] *n.* suitō (*water bottle*); suiji dōgu bako.

canter [kǽntə] *n.* (uma no) kakeashi. *v.* kakeashi saseru (suru).

canticle [kǽntikl] *n.* sambika (*hymn*); (C～) (*pl.*) soromon
no tataeuta.

canto [kǽntou] *n.* (shi ya uta no) hen (ippen, nihen....).

canton [kǽntən] *n.* *Switzerland* no shū (*state*). *v.* shū ni wakeru ; [kəntú:n] *canton* ni wakeru. ～ment [kæntú:mənt] *n.* (*Brit.*) *soldiers* no shukueisho.

cantor [kǽntə:] *n.* (*mus.*) gasshō no shikisha (*conductor.*)

canvas [kǽnvəs] *n.* honuno ; zukku ; gafu, aburae. ～*shoes* zukku-gutsu. ⌈er *n.* kan'yūsha ; yūzeisha.

canvass [kǽnvəs] *v.* jūbun rongi suru ; *n.* tenken ; kan'yū ～

caoutchouc [káutʃuk/kaú:tʃuk] *n.* dansei gomu (*India rubber*).

cap [kæp] *n.* (fuchinashi) bōshi ; *v.* bōshi o kabuseru. ～ *in hand* datsubō shite (*humbly*).

capability [kèipəbíliti] *n.* nōryoku ; sainō.

capable [kéipəbl] *a.* dekiru ; nōryoku ga aru. ⌈(*generous*).

capacious [kəpéiʃəs] *a.* hirobiro to shita ; kokoro no ōkii.

capacitate [kəpǽsiteit] *v.* (aru koto o) suru shikaku o ataeru.

capacity [kəpǽsiti] *n.* hōyōryoku ; (hito o ireru) nōryoku.

caparison [kəpǽrisn] *n.* (uma no) seisō ; utsukushii fuku. *v.* (uma o) seisō saseru.

cape [keip] *n.* (1) misaki (umi ni tsukideta). (2) kata-manto.

caper [kéipə] *v.* hanemawaru ; fuzakeru. *n.* hanemawari ; fuzake.

capillarity [kæpilǽriti] *n.* (*phys.*) mōkan genshō. ⌊ke.

capillary [kəpílri] *a.* mōsaikan (no).

capital [kǽpitl] *a.* omona ; subarashii. *n.* shufu ; ōmoji ; shihon. ～ization [kæpitəl(ə)izéiʃən] *n.* shihon o tōzuru koto. ～ist *n.* shihonka. ～ize *v.* shihon o tōzuru.

capitation [kæpiteiʃən] *n.* atama wari ; nintōzei (*poll tax*).

capitol [kǽpitl] *n.* (*Anc. Rome*) Jupitā no shinden. (*Am.*) kokkai gijidō. ～ine [-ain] *n.* Jupitā no shinden no.

capitular [kəpítjulə] *a.* sōkai no. (sōryo no dantai) *n.* sōkaiin (*member of a chapter*) ; sōkai no hōki.

capitulary [kəpítjuləri] *a.* sōkai no ; n. sōkaiin.

capitulate [kəpítjuteit] *v.* jōkentsuki de kōfuku suru.

capitulation [kəpìtjuléiʃən] *n.* jōkentsuki kōfuku.

capon [kéipən] *n.* kyosei shita (*castrated* ondori). ～ize [kéipənaiz] *v.* kyosei suru.

capric [kǽprik] *a.* osuyagi no. ⌈kyōsōkyoku.

capriccio [kəprítʃiou] (*It.*) *n.* (*pl.*) itazura ; kimagure. (*mus.*)

caprice [kəpri:s] *n.* kimagure; kimama.
capricious [kəpriʃəs] *a.* kimagurena. ~ness *n.* kimagure.
Capricorn [kǽprikɔ:n] *n.* (*astr.*) Yagiza.
caprine [kǽprain] *a.* yagi no yōna.　　　　　　　 ⌈suru.
capriole [kǽprioul] *n.* chōyaku; tobiagari (-ru). *v.* chōyaku
capsize [kæpsáiz] *v.* hikkurikaesu (-kaeru) *n.* tempuku saseru
　(suru).
capstan [kǽpstən] *n.* makiage-ki.　　　　　　　　　 ⌈ishi.
capstone [kǽpstoun] *n.* (sekichū (*stone pillar*) nado no) kasa-
capsule [kǽpsju:l] *n.* kapuseru; tane o tsutsumu saya.
captain [kǽptin] *n.* shushō; senchō; rikugun taii; kaigun
　taisa. *v. captain* ni naru; shiki suru. ~cy *n. captain* no chii;
　yakume. ~ship *n. captain* to shite no sainō.　　　　 ⌈jimaku.
caption [kǽpʃən[*n.* daimoku (*title*); midashi (*heading*); eiga no
captious [kǽpʃəs] *a.* arasagashi no; koyakamashii.
captivate [kǽptiveit] *v.* kokoro o toraeru; miwaku suru. ~-
　tion [kæptivéiʃən] *n.* miwaku suru koto.
captive [kǽptiv] *n.* toriko; horyo. *a.* horyo no. ~ balloon
　[bəlú:n] *n.* keiryū kikyū (*ad-balloon* nado).
captivity [kæptívíti] *n.* ikedori; toraware no mi; kankin.
captor [kǽptə] *n.* tsukamaeru hito. captress [kǽptris] *n.* onna
　no *captor*.　　　　　　　　　　　　　　　　　 ⌈bundoru.
capture [kǽptʃə] *n.* ikedori; bundori (hin) *v.* hokaku suru,
car [kɑ:] *n.* kuruma; jidōsha : *take a* ~, kuruma ni noru. ~-
　man [-mən] *n.* densha no jūgyōin; nibasha no gyosha.
caracole [kǽrəkoul] *n.* rasen kaidan.
carafe [kərá:f] *n.* garasu no mizusashi.
caramel [kǽrəmél] *n.* yakizatō; kyarameru; karumera.
carapace [kǽrəpeis] *n.* (kame, kani nado no) senaka no kōra,
　kō.　　　　　　　　　　　　　　　　　　　　　 ⌈tan'i.
carat [kǽrət] *n.* karatto (hōseki no mekata, kin (*gold*) jundo no
caravan [kǽrəvǽn] *n.* taishō; ~sary [kæ̀rəvǽnsəri] *n.* taishō
carbarn [ká:bɑ:n] *n.* (*Am.*) kuruma o ireru kura. ⌊no yado.
carbide [ká:baid] *n.* (*chem.*) tanso kagōbutsu; kābaido.
carbine [ká:bain] *n.* kiheijū; kābinjū.
carbohydrate [ká:bouháidreit] *n.* (*chem.*) tansuikabutsu.
carbolic [kɑ:bólik] *a.* tanso no. ~ acid, sekitan-san.

carbolize [ká:bəlaiz] *v.* sekitansan o kuwaeru; sekitansan de shori suru.

carbon [ká:bən] *n.* tanso. ~ **paper** tanso fukushashi. ~**acious** [kà:bənéiʃəs] *a.* tanso no; tanso o fukumu. ~**ado** [kà:bənéidou] *n.* (*pl.* -es), *v.* aburiyaki ni suru.

carbonate [ká:bəneit] *n.* tansan'en *v.* tansan'en ni kaeru. ~**ation** [kà:bənéiʃən] *n.* (*chem.*) tansan'enka (ni suru) sayō.

carbonic [ka:bánik] *a.* tanso no; tansan no. ~ **acid** tansan. ~ **acid gas,** *n.* tansan gasu.

carboniferous [kà:bəníferəs] *a.* (*geol.*) sekitan o fukumu.

carbonization [kæ̀:bənizéiʃən] *n.* tanka; tankahō.

carbonize [ká:bənaiz] *v.* tanso to kagōsaseru; tanka suru.

carborundum [ka:bərándəm] *n.* kongōsha.

carboy [ká:bɔi] *n.* hako (kago) iri no ōgata garasu bin.

carbuncle [ká:bʌŋkl] *n.* (*med.*) yō; odeki. (*gem*) kōgyoku. ~**d** [ká:bʌŋkld] *a.* kōgyoku o mochiita. ~**uar** [ka:bʌ́ŋkjulə] =**carbancled.**

curburet [ká:bjurət] *v.* (*chem.*) tanso to kagō saseru; tanso o mazeru.

carburet(t)or [ká:bjuretə] *n.* kūki (*air*) to *gasoline* to o mazete bakuhatsu saseru sōchi.

carcase, carcass [ká:kəs] *n.* (kedamono (*beast*) no) shitai.

card [ka:d] *n.* kādo; (*pl.*) karuta asobi : *throw up one's* ~*s,* keikaku o suteru. ~**board** [-bɔ́:d] *n.* atsugami.

cardiac [ká:diək] *a.* shinzō no (kusuri) no. *n.* kyōshinzai.

cardigan [ká:digən] *n.* kādigan (mae o botan de tomeru).

cardinal [ká:dinəl] *a.* kihontekina (*fundamental*) : ~ *number,* kihonsū. ~ *points,* kihon hōi. (*R. Catholic*) wa *pope* no daijina sōdan'yaku. ~ *flower* benibana-sawagikyō. ~**ate** [ká:dinəleit] *n. Cardinal* no shoku.

care [kɛə] *n.* chūi shimpai ; sewa (sur). ~ *of* (*c/o*), ...kizuke (tegami no uwafu no monku). *take* ~ *of,* sewa o suru. ~ *for,* ...o hoshigaru. *do not* ~ *about,* ...niwa kamawanai ; ...wa konomanai. ~**less,** *a.* fuchūina. ⌐nado no tame).

careen [kərí:n] *n.* keisha ; fune o katamukeru koto (shūri

career [kərí:ə] *n.* rireki ; shokugyō. *v.* shissō suru.

carefree [kéəfri:] *n.* shimpai no nai ; nonkina ; tanoshii.

careful [kéəful] *a.* chūibukai; teineina. **~ly** [kéəfuli] *ad.* chūibukaku; teineini. **~ness** [-nis] *n.* shinchō; nyūnen.

caress [kərés] *n.* aibu. *v.* aibu suru. **~ing** [kéərisiŋ] *a.* aibu suru; kawaigaru. **~ingly** [kéərisiŋli] *ad.* kawaigatte; aibu shite.

caret [kǽrət] *n.* (kōsei no) ji no nuketa kigō (∧).

cargo [ká:gou] *n.* funani; fune no tsumini.

caribou [kǽribu:] *n.* (*sing. & pl.*) Hokubei-san no tonakai.

caricature [kǽrikətʃə] *n.* fūshitekina e (*picture*); manga.

caricaturist [kǽrikətʃùrist] *n.* fūshigaka; mangaka.

caries [kéəriiz] *n.* (*med.*) kariesu.

carillon [kǽrilən] *n.* hitokumi no kane (*bell*); kane no shirabe.

carminative [ká:minətiv] *a., n.* (*med.*) i-chō kara *gas* o haisetsu suru (kusuri).

carmine [ká:main] *n.* (*col.*) murasakigakatta shinku.

carnage [ká:nidʒ] *n.* gyakusatsu; satsuriku.

carnal [ká:nəl] *a.* nikutai no; nikuyoku no.

carnation [ká:néiʃən] *n.* niku-iro; (*flower*) kāneishon (no hana).

carnival [ká:nivəl] *n.* shanikusai; bakasawagi.

carnivora [ká:nivərə] *n.* (*pl.*) nikushoku-rui; nikushoku dōbutsu.

carnivorous [ka:nívərəs] *a.* nikushoku no (*cf. herbivorous*).

carol [kǽrəl] *n.* yorokobi no uta; *Xmas* no iwai uta. *v.* yorokobi utau.

car(r)om [kǽrəm] *v.* (*Am.*) tamatsuki de *canon* ni naru, (*Brit.*) *carrom* o suru; tsuita tama ga hoka no futatsu ni ataru.

carousal [kəráuzl] *n.* tanoshiku nomi sawagu enkai (*jovial feast*).

carouse [kəráuz] *n.* shuen; bōin. *v.* bōin suru; baka sawagi (suru).

carp [ka:p] *v.* arasagashi o suru (*at*). *n.* koi (*a fresh water fish*).

carpenter [ká:pintə] *n.* daiku.

carpentry [kápintri] *n.* daikushoku; daiku no shigoto.

carpet [ka:pət] *n.* jūtan: *v.* jūtan o shiku. *on the* **~**, tōgichū de. **~bag** [-bæg] *n.* (jūtanji no) ryokō kaban. **~bagger** [-bægə] *n.* (*Am.*) watarimono. **~ing** *n.* shikimono (zairyō).

carriage [kǽridʒ] *n.* (basha, kuruma, shōhin no) umpan; unchin. **~ forward,** unchin sakibarai de. **~ free** unchin muryō de; haraizumi (de). **~ porch** kurumayose.

carrier [kǽriə] *n.* unsōya; umpannin; kōkūbokan.

carrion [kǽiən] *n., a.* kusatta niku (no); obutsu (no).

carrot [kǽrət] *n.* ninjin.

carry [kǽri] *v.* **carried; carrying.** hakobu; tsutaeru; ~ *all-before one*, mukō tokoro teki nashi; ~ *away*, hakobi saru. muchū ni saseru. ~ *coals to Newcastle*, mudabone o oru. ~ *off*, yūkai suru; hōbi (shō) o uru. ~ *on*, keizoku suru; (jigyō o) itonamu. ~ *out*, yaritogeru. ~ *over* kurikosu; tsugi no peiji e okuru. ~ *the house*, manjō no kassai o hakusuru.

cart [kɑːt] *n.* nirin-basha. *v.* niguruma de hakobu. *put the ~ before the horse*, hommatsu tentō suru. ~**age** [-idʒ] *n.* niguruma; unchin. ~**er** *n.* unsō-nimbu. ~**load** [-loud] *n.* kuruma ichi-daibun no kamotsu.

carte blanche [kɑːt blãnʃ] (*Fr.*) hakushi (*white card*); hakushi inin (jō). ⌐jōyakusho.

cartel [káːtəl] *n.* karuteru; (*econ.*) kigyō-rengō. horyokōkan

cartilage [káːtilidʒ] *n.* nankotsu (*gristle*).

carton [káːtən] *n.* bōru-bako.

cartoon [kɑːtúːn] *n.* fūshi manga; jitsubutsudai no shitae *v.* manga o kaku.

cartridge [káːtridʒ] *n.* yakkyō; dan'yakutō. ~ **belt** [-belt] *n.* dan'yakutai. ~ **box** [-bɔks] *n.* yakkyōire. ~ **case** [-keis] *n.* yakkyō. ~ **paper** [péips] *n.* gayōshi; hatoronshi.

carve [kɑːv] *v.* (niku nado o) usuku kiru; chōkoku suru. ~**er** [káːvə] *n.* chōkokushi; niku o kiru hito; naifu.

cascade [kæskiéd *n.* chiisai taki no kugiri (*cf. cataract*); cascade ni natte ochiru.

case [keis] *n* hako; saya; jiken, soshō. kanja (*patient*); (*gram.*) kaku. *v.* hako ni ireru. ~ **bottle**, kakubin. (hako ni hairu). ~ **harden** [-háːden] *v.* (tetsu ni) yaki o irete kataku suru. ~ **hardened** [-háːdnd] *a.* mujōna; reikokuna. ~**ment** *n.* hira-kimado. ~**mate** [kéismeit] *n.* hōdai; hōshitsu.

casein [kéisiin] *n.* kasein.

cash [kæʃ] *n., v.* shōkin; genkin (de shiharau). ~ *on delivery*, daikin hikikaebarai. (*c.o.d.*). ~ **account**, genkin kanjō. ~**book** [kǽʃbúk] *n.* genkin suitōchō. ~**register** [redʒístə] *n.* kin sen tōrokuki.

cashier [kǽʃiə] *n.* suitō-gakari. *v.* menshoku suru (*dismiss*).

cashmere [kǽʃmiə] *n.* kashimiya ori.

casing [kéisiŋ] *n.* nizukuri ; iremono ; waku.

casino [kəsí:nou] *n.* kashino ; gorakujō (dansu, tobaku nado o suru). ⌈tsugi.

cask [ka:sk] *n.* oke ; taru. ～et [ká:skit] *n.* kobako. (*Am.*) hi-casque [kæsk] *n.* kabuto (*helmet*).

cassation [kɔséiʃən] *n.* suteru koto ; haiki. *Court of* ～ (Furan-su de) saikō saibansho.

casserole [kǽsəroul] *n.* donabe ; tsuchi no nabe.

cassia [kǽsiə] *n.* kei (no ki) ; (nikkei no isshu)

cassock [kǽsək] *n.* (sōryo no) hōi ; koromo ; kesa.

cassowary [kǽsəweəri] *n.* (*bird*) hikuidori.

cast [ka:st/kæst] cast ; casting. *v.* nageru ; senkyo de tōhyō su-ru. kara o nugu ; chūzō suru (*mold*). kaiko suru (*dismiss*). *n.* nageru koto. undameshi. imono. yakuwari. ～ *down*, o raku-tan saseru. ～ *out*, oidasu. ～ *up*, keisan suru. ～away [ká:-stəwei] *n.* nampasen de hōridasareta hito ; yotamono. ～ iron [aiən] *n.* chūtetsu. ～ steel, *n.* chūkō.

castanets [kǽstənets] *n.* kasutaneto (*dancer's chinking instru-*

caste [ka:st] *n.* kaikyū ; mibun (Indo no fūshū). ⌊*ment*.

castellated [kǽstəleitid] *a.* shiro-zukuri no ; shiro-gamae no.

caster, castor [kǽstə] *n.* nageru-hito (mono) ; yakumibin ; (isu nado no) ashiwa.

castigate [kǽstigeit] *v.* muchiutsu ; sekkan suru ; shūsei suru.

castigation [kæstigéiʃən] *n.* sekkan ; shūsei.

casting [kǽstiŋ] *n.* chūzō ; imono. ～ net, toami ; nageami. ～ vote, kettei tōhyō.

castle [ká:sl] *n.* shiro ; ～*in the air*, kūchū no rōkaku ; kūsō.

castor [kǽstə] *n.* kairi (*beaver*) ; (kairi no kawa no) bōshi. ～ oil, himashiyu. ⌈sei.

castrate [kǽstreit] *v.* kyosei suru. ～tion [kæstréiʃən] *n.* kyo-casual [kǽʒuəl] *a.* gūzen no ; rinji no. ～ly [-li] *ad.* gūzenni. ～ty [-əlti] *n.* gūzen ; jihen ; (*pl.*) shishōshasū.

casuist [kǽʒjuist] *n.* dōgakusha ; kibenka. (*phil.*) ～ry [-tri] *n* ketsugiron ; kiben.

cat [kæt] *n.* neko : *a* ～ *has nine lives*, neko wa inochi ga kokonotsu aru. ～**fish** [kǽtfiȝ] *n.* namazu. ～**foot** [-fut] *v.* (neko no yōni) kossori susumu. ～**gut** [-gʌt] *n.* neko no chō (hara-wata).

catabolism [kətǽbəlizm] *n.* bunkai shite chigatta mononi suru hataraki.

catachresis [kætəkrí:sis] *n.* tatoe o ran'yō suru koto.

cataclysm [kǽtəklizm] *n.* kōzui ; daihendō.

catacomb [kǽtəkoum] *n.* hakaana.

catalepsy [kǽtəlepsi] *n.* (*med.*) (zenshin) kōchokushō.

catalogue [kǽtəloug] *n.* mokuroku *v.* mokuroku (o tsukuru).

catamaran [kæ̀təmərǽn] *n.* ikada ; gamigami onna.

catapult [kǽtəpʌlt] *n.* ishiyumi ; pachinko ; hikōki hasshasōchi.

cataract [kǽtərækt] *n.* ōdaki ; bakufu. (*med.*) sokohi (me no byōki).

catarrh [kətú:] *n.* kataru. nemmaku no enshō.

catastrophe [kətǽstrəfi] *n.* geki no daidan'en ; dai-saigai.

catch *v.* [kætʃ] **caught; catching.** toraeru ; (byōki ni) kakaru ; (...ni) hikkakaru (*on, in*) ; hi (*fire*) ga tsuku. *n.* toraeru koto, gyokaku-daka. ～ *it*, omedama o kuu. ～ *on*, ninki o hakusuru. ～ *up with*, ...ni oitsuku. *A drowning man will* ～ *at straws*, oboreru mono wa wara o mo tsukamu. ～**er** *n.* [kætʃə] hokakusha ; kyatcha. ～**ing** *a.* densen suru ; kokoro o ubau. ～**penny** [kǽtʃpeni] *a.* yasu-pika no ; zenitorishugi no. ～ *phrase*, ～**word** [-wə:d] *n.* midashigo ; hyōgo.

catchup [kǽtʃəp] *n.* kechappu.

catechism [kǽtəkizm] *n.* kyōgimondōsho.

catechize [kǽtəkaiz] *v.* mondō de oshieru.

catechumen [kætəkjú:mən] *n.* senrei-shigansha ; nyūmonsha.

categorical [kæ̀təgɔ́rikəl] *a.* mujōken no ; dangentekina ; hanchū no : ～ *imperative,* (*phil.*) mujō-meirei.

category [kǽtəgɔri] *n.* (*log.*) hanchū, kategori.

cater [kéitə] *v.* makanau ; tanoshimaseru ; ni manzoku o ataeru. ～**er** [kéitərə] *n.* makanaikata.

caterpillar [kǽtəpilə] *n.* kemushi ; imomushi ; mugenkidō.

caterwaul [kǽtəwɔ:l] *v.* (neko ga sakatte) unaru.

cathartic [kəθá:tik] *a.* gezai no ; geri no. *n.* gezai.

cathedral [kəθí:drəl] *n.* (Kirisuto-kyō no) daikaidō ; daijiin.

catheter [kǽθitə] *n.* (*med.*) dōnyōkan ; nyō no deru kuda.

cathode [kǽθoud] *n.* (*elect.*) inkyoku. (opp. *anode*).

catholic [kǽθəlik] *a.* ippan no ; fuhentekina ; kandaina ; (*C~*) katorikkukyō no. *n.* (*C~*) Katorikkukyōto.

Catholicism [kǽθəlisizm] *n.* Katorikkukyō ; Tenshukyō.

catkin [kǽtkin] *n.* (yanagi, kuri nado no) neko ; o no katachi o shita hana no keba (*ament*).

cat-o'-nine-tails [kǽtənáinteils] *n.* kuhon no nawa no muchi.

cat's-cradle [kǽtskreidl] *n.* ayatori asobi.

cat's-pow [kǽtspɔː] *n.* tesaki ni tsukawareru mono.

catsup [kǽtsəp] *n.* kechap (sauce no isshu).

cattle [kǽtl] *n.* kachiku ; ushi. **~ plague** [-pleig] *n.* gyūeki.

Caucasian [kɔːkéizən] *a.* Kōkasasujinshu no. *n.* kōkasasujin ; hakujinshu.

caucus [kɔ́ːkəs] *n.* (seitō no) kambukai.

caudal [kɔ́ːdəl] *n.* shippo (*tail*) no.

caught [kɔːt] *v. see :* **catch.**

caul [kɔːl] *n.* daimōmaku (taiji no atama o ōu maku).

caudron [kɔ́ːdrən] *n.* ōgama.

cauliflower [kɔ́ːliflauə] *n.* hanakyabetsu ; hanayasai.

ca(u)lk [kɔːk] *v.* maihada (*oakum*) o tsumeru.

causal [kɔ́ːzəl] *a.* gen'in no ; ingaritsu no.

  causality [kɔːzǽliti] *n.* ingakankei : *the principle of ~,* ingaritsu. (*causal relation*).

causation [kɔːzéiʃən] *n.* gen'in (to naru koto) ; ingakankei : *the law of ~,* ingaritsu. ᚦeki no.

causative [kɔ́ːzətiv] *a.* gen'in to naru ; okosaseru. (*gram.*) shi-

cause [kɔːz] *n.* gen'in ; (*leg.*) soshō ; hongi, mokuteki. *v.* ... saseru, gen'in to naru. *make common ~ with,* ni kumisuru. **~less** [kɔ́ːzlis] *a.* gen'in no nai ; riyū no nai.

causeway [kɔ́ːzwèi] *n.* dotemichi.

caustic [kɔ́ːztik] *a.* fushokusei no ; shinratsuna. *n.* fushoku-zai ; hiniku.

cauterize [kɔ́ːtəraiz] *v.* yakigane de yaku ; fushoku saseru.

cautery [kɔ́ːtəri] *n.* fushoku ; yakigote.

caution [kɔ́ːʃən] *n.* yōjin, keikoku ; (*col.*) henna yatsu. *v.* kei-koku suru. **~ money** (*Brit.*) (gakusei no) hoshōkin. **~ary** [-əri] *a.* keikai suru.

cautious [kɔ́:ʃəs] *a.* yōjimbukai. ～**ly** *ad.* yojimbukaku. ～**ness** *n.* yōjimbukasa.

cavalcade [kæ̀vəlkéid] *n.* kibagyōretsu.

cavalier [kæ̀vəlíə] *n.* kishi; (kifujin no) odori-aite; tsukisoi-otoko. *a.* kōmanna.

cavalry [kǽvəlri] *n.* kiheitai. ～**man** [-mən] *n.* kihei.

cave [keiv] *n., v.* horaana (o horu.) ～ *in,* kambotsu suru (saseru); kuppuku suru. ～**man** [kéivmən] *n.* kekkyojin.

cavern [kǽvən] *n.* dai-dōkutsu; iwaya.

cavernous [kǽvənəs] *a.* dōkutsu no yona.

caviar(e) [kǽviɑ:/kæviá:] *n.* shiozuke no chōzame no hararago.

cavil [kǽvil] *v.* ara o sagasu. *n.* togamedate.

cavity [kǽviti] *n.* ana; utsuro.

caw [kɔ:] *v.* kā to naku. *n.* karasu no nakigoe

cayenne [keién] *n.* tōgarashi (*cayenne pepper*).

cease [si:s] *v.* yamaru; taeru. ～**less** [sí:slis] *a.* taema no nai.

cedar [sí:də] *n.* seiyōsugi.

cede [si:d] *v.* yuzuru; hikiwatasu.   ⌈mesu fugō (ç).

cedilla [sídilə] *n.* " C " no ji no shita ni tsukete [s]-on o shi-

ceil [si:l] *v.* tenjō o haru. ～**ing** [sí:liŋ] *n.* tenjō.

celebrant [séləbrənt] *n.* saishi; shiki o ageru sōryo.

celebrate [séləbreit] *v.* iwau; sambi suru. ～**ed** [-tid] *a.* yū-meina.

celebration [sèləbréiʃən] *n.* shukuga; saiten; shiki o ageru

celebrity [səlébriti] *n.* meisei; nadakai hito.   ⌊koto.

celerity [səlériti] *n.* jinsoku; kibin.

celery [séləri] *n.* serori; orandamitsuba.

celestial [səléstʃəl] *a.* ten no; kōgōshii. *n* . (*C-*) Chūkajin.

celibacy [sélibəsi] *n.* (otoko yamome) dokushin-seikatsu.

celibate [sélibit] *n.* dokushinsha. *a.* dokushin no.

cell [sel] *n.* chiisai heya; dokubō; saibō (*protoplasm*); denchi.

cellar [sélə] *n.* anagura; chikashitsu. ～**age** [séləridʒ] *n.* ana-gura (shiyōryō).

cello [tʃélou] *n.* chero.

cellophane [séləfein] *n.* serofan.

cellular [séljulə] *a.* saibō kara naru.

celluloid [séljuləid] *n.* seruroid.

cellulose [séljulous] *n.* serurōzu ; sen'iso. ⌈Kerutogo.

Celt [selt] *n.* Kerutojin. ~**ic** [séltik/kel-], *a.* Kerutojin no. *n.*

cement [səmént] *n.* semento. *v.* semento de katameru.

cemetery [séməteri] *n.* bochi.

cenotaph [sénətæf] *n.* kinenhi.

censer [sénsə] *n.* kōro (*incense burner*).

censor [sénsə] *n.* (shuppambutsu no) ken'etsukan *v.* ken'etsu suru. ~**ship** [sénsəʃip] *n.* ken'etsukan no shoku ; ken'etsu.

censorious [sensó:riəs] *a.* hihanzukina ; arasagashi o suru.

censure [sénʃə] *v.* hinan suru ; togameru *n.* hinan.

census [sénsəs] *n.* kokusei-chōsa ; jinkō-chōsa.

cent [sent] *n.* sent (1/100 doru) ; *per* ~, hyaku ni tsuki (%)

centaur [séntəə] (*Gk. myth.*) atama wa ningen, karada wa uma to iu kaibutsu.

centenarian [sentinéəriən] *n.*, *a.* hyakusai no hito.

centenary [séntinəri] *n.* hyakunensai.

centennial [sénténiəl] *a.* 100-nen no ; 100-nen goto no *n.* hyakunensai.

center, ~tre [séntə] *n.* chūshin ; chūken. *v.* itten ni atsumaru. (meru). ⌈zanda.

centigrade [séntigreid] *a.* Sesshi kandankei no ; 100-do ni ki-**centigram(me)** [séntigræm] *n.* senchigram (ichi-gram no hyakubun no ichi).

centiliter, centilitre [séntiliitə] *n.* senchirittoru (ichi-rittoru no hyakubun no ichi).

centime [sánti:m] *n.* France no sanchiimu kahei, 1/100 *franc.*

centimeter [séntimit:ə] *n.* senchimētoru (ichi-mētoru no **centiped(e)** [séntipi:d] *n.* mukade. ⌊1/100).

central [séntrəl] *a.* chūshin no ; chūō no. *n.* (*Am.*) denwa-kōkan-kyoku.

centralization [səntrəlizéiʃən] *n.* shūchū ; chūōshūken.

centralize [séntrəlaiz] *v.* chūshin ni atsumaru ; shūchū suru.

centrifugal [sentrífjugəl] *a.* enshin (sei) no.

centrifuge [séntrifju:dʒ] *n.* enshin-bunriki.

centripetal [séntripitl] *a.* kyūshin (sei) no.

centurion [sentjúriən] *n.* (*Anc. Rome*) hyakunin no taichō.

century [séntʃəri] *n.* hyakunen ; isseiki.

ceramic [sərǽmik] *a.* tōki no. ～s *n.* seitōhō ; tōki-rui.

cereal [síəriəl] *a.* kokurui no. *n.* (*pl.*) kokumotsu.

cerebellum [sèlibéləm] *n.* (*anat.*) shōnō.

cerebral [séribrəl] *a.* (*anat.*) dainō no.

cerebrate [séribreit] *v.* atama o hatarakasu ; kangaeru.

cerebrum [séribrəm] *n.* (*anat.*) dainō ; nō.

cerement [síəmənt] *n.* kyōkatabira.

ceremonial [serimóuniəl] *a.* gishiki no. *n.* gishiki. ～ly [-li] *ad.* gishikibatte.

ceremonious [serimóuniəs] *a.* gishiki no ; gishikibatta. ～ly *ad.* gishikibatte.

ceremony [sériməni] *n.* gishiki : *stand on* ～, enryo suru.

cerise [sərí:z] *n., a.* sakurairo (no).

certain [sé:tin] *a.* tashikana ; aru. *for* ～, tashika ni. ～ly, [sə́:-tinli] *ad.* tashikani ; ii tomo. ～ty *n.* kakujitsu ; kakujitsusei.

certificate [sətífikeit] *v.* shōmei suru. *n.* shōmei (sho). ～tion

certify [sə́:tifai] *v.* ukeau ; hoshō suru.   ⌊*n.* shōmei.

certitude [sə́:titju:d] *n.* kakujitsu(sei).

cerulean [sirú:liən] *a.* sorairo no.

cessation [seséiʃən] *n.* teishi ; kyūshi.

cession [séʃən] *n.* katsujō ; yuzuriwatasu.

cesspool [séspù:l] *n.* osuidame (kitanai mizu no tamariba).

Ceylonese [sì:ləní:z] *a., n.* Seirontō no (hito).

cf. (*confere*) sanshō seyo.

C.G.S., c.g.s. *centimeter-gram-second.*

Ch., ch, *Chapter* ; *chief.*

chafe [tʃeif] *v.* kosutte atatameru ; okoraseru ; okoru. *n.* suri-kizu ; iradachi.   ⌈no yōna.

chaff [tʃæf] *n.* momigara. karakai. *v.* karakau. *a.* momigara

chaffer [tʃǽfə] *v.* nedan o kakeau ; negiru. *n.* negiru koto.

chaffinch [tʃǽfintʃ] *n.* hiwa no rui (no kotori).

chagrin [ʃəgrín] *n.* zannen ; munen. *v.* kuyashi (garaseru) : *be* ～*ed,* kuyashigaru.

chain [tʃein] *n.* kusari. (*pl.*) kase ; *v.* kusari de tsunagu.

chair [tʃεə] *n.* isu ; kōza ; gichō ; kyōju no shoku. *take* (*leave*) *the* ～, kaikai (heikai) suru.

chairman [tʃέəmən] *n.* gichō ; zacho, iinchō.

chaise [ʃeiz] *n.* (nirin mata wa yonrin no) keikaina basha.

chalet [ʃǽléi] *n.* sharē (*Switzerland* no yama no naka no boku-jingoya); sharēfū no bessō.

chalice [tʃǽlis] *n.* seisan no sakazuki.

chalk [tʃɔːk] *n.* chōku; hakua. *v.* hakuboku de kaku.

chalky [tʃɔ́ːki] *a.* hakua-shitsu no.

challenge [tʃǽlindʒ] *n.* chōsen; chōsenjō; *v.* chōsen suru; idomu. ～**er** [tʃǽlindʒə] *n.* chōsensha.

challis, challie [ʃǽli] *n.* merinsu no rui.

chamber [tʃéimbə] *n.* (*archi*) shinshitsu; hiroi heya; (*pl.*) bengoshi jimushitsu. ～ *of commerce*, shōgyō kaigisho. ～**maid** *n.* shinshitsugakari no jochū ～**pot** *n.* benki.

chamberlain [tʃéimbəlin] *n.* jijū; karei; *Lord C* ～, naidaijin.

chameleon [kəmíːliən] *n.* kamerion; utsurigi na hito.

chamois [ʃǽmwaː] *n.* kamoshika no rui; semikawa.

champ [tʃæmp] *v.* oto o tatete kamu.

champagne [ʃæmpéin] *n.* shampan.

champaign [ʃæmpéin] *n.* heigen; heiya.

champion [tʃǽmpiən] *n.* tōshi, yūshōsha, senshu. *v.* ...no tame ni tatakau; yōgo suru. ～**ship** *n.* senshuken.

chance [tʃɑːns] *n.* gūzen; kikai; *a.* gūzen no. *v.* gūzen...suru.

chancel [tʃɑːnsl] *n.* (kyōkaidō no) naijin; seidansho.

chancellor [tʃǽnsilə] *n.* kōkan; saishō; meiyo-sōchō. ～ *of the Exchequer*, ōkura daijin. *Lord High* ～, daihōkan.

chancery [tʃǽnsəri] *n.* (*Brit.*) daihōkanchō; (*Am.*) kōheihō-saibansho.

chandelier [ʃændəliə] *n.* shanderiya.

chandler [tʃǽndlə] *n.* zakkashō; rōsokushō.

change [tʃeindʒ] *v.* kaeru, kawaru. *n.* henkō. kozeni. ～ *of air* tenchi (suru). ～**ability** [tʃeindʒəbíliti] *n.* kawariyasusa. ～**able** [tʃéindʒəbl] *a.* henka shiyasui.

channel [tʃǽnəl] *n.* kaikyō; suiro; mizo (*groove*). *v.* suiro o hiraku mizo o horu.

chanson [ʃǽnsən] *n.* uta; kouta.

chant [tʃænt] *v.* utau; (shi o) ginzuru. *n.* uta; seika.

chanticleer [tʃǽntiklíə] *n.* ondori,

chaos [kéiɔs] *n.* konton; konran.

chaotic [keiɔ́tik] *a.* konton to shite iru; konran shite iru.

chap [tʃæp] v. chapped; chapping. hibi ga kireku. n. hibi;
akagire. yatsu (*fellow*).

chapel [tʃǽpl] n. reihaidō.   ⌈tsukisou.

chaperon [ʃǽpəloun] n. (wakai fujin no) tsukisou fujin. v.

chaplain [tʃǽplin] n. reihaidō bokushi; kyōkaishi.

chaplet [tʃǽplit] (*bot.*) n. atama ni maku kazariwa (hanataba
... nado no). hanakazura; juzu (*string of beads*).

chapman [tʃǽpmən] n. gyōshōnin.

chapter [-tʃǽptə] n. (hon no) isshō; shibu; (*cathedral*, shozo-
ku no) sōryo no dantai. a ～ of accidents, uchitsuzuku fukō.
～ house, sō-tachi no shūkaijo.

char [tʃɑ:] v. sumi ni yaku; kogasu. n. sumi.

character [kǽrəktə] n. jinkaku; mibun; jimbutsu; (geki no)
yaku; moji.   ⌈kutoku no.

characteristic [kæ̀rəktərístik] n. tokushitsu. a. tokuyū no; do-

characterize [kǽriktəraiz] v. seishitsu o shimesu; tokusei o
arawasu.   ⌈*of guessing a word*).

charade [ʃəréid] n. nazo no rui. kotoba o ateru asobi (*a game*

charcoal [tʃɑ́:koul] n. mokutan. ～ burner, sumiyaki (nin).

charge [tʃɑ:dʒ] v. sekinin o motaseru; tama nado o komeru.
a. hogo; sekinin; tamakome; sozei. ～able [tʃɑ́:dʒəbl] n. sekinin o owasu koto ga dekiru.

charger [tʃɑ́:dʒə] n. itakusha, kokusosha; gumba.

chariot [tʃǽriət] n. (mukashi no) sensha; nitōdate no basha.

charioteer [tʃæ̀riətíə] a. sensha no gyosha.   ⌈bukaku.

charitable [tʃǽritəbl] a. jihibukai; jizen no. ～bly ad. jihi-

charity [tʃǽriti] n. jizen; hodokoshi; jikeiin; yōikuin.

charlatan [ʃɑ́:lətən] n. yamashi; yabuisha.

charm [tʃɑ:m] n. miryoku, aikyō; majinai. v. miwaku suru.
～ing a. horebore suru.

charmer [tʃɑ́:mə] n. mahōtsukai; hebitsukai; sutekina bijin.

charnel house [tʃɑ́:nəl haus] n. nōkotsudō (hone o osameru
tokoro).

chart [tʃɑ:t] n. kaizu; zu(hyō), ～ v. zu de shimesu.

charter [tʃɑ́:tə] n. tokkyojō; kenshō. v. menkyo suru; keiyaku ni yotte) fune o yatou. ～ party yōsen-keiyakusho (fune
o kariru yakusoku).

charwoman [tʃá:wùmən] *n.* hiyatoi-onna ; hashutsufu.

chary [tʃéəri] *a.* ki o tsukeru ; sashihikaeru ; saishin no.

chase [tʃeis] *v.* oikakeru ; ryō o suru. *n.* tsuiseki ; kari.

chasm [kæzm] *n.* wareme.

chassis [ʃǽsi:] *n.* (*sing. & pl.*) (hōsha, jidōsha nado no) shadai.

chaste [tʃeist] *a.* teisetsuna ; junketsuna. ~**ly** *ad.* misao tadashiku. ~**ness** *n.* teisetsu.

chasten [tʃéisn] *v.* sekkan suru ; senren suru.

chastise [tʃǽstaiz] *v.* korasu. ~**ment** [tʃǽstaizmənt] *n.* korashime.

chastity [tʃǽstiti] *n.* teisetsu ; junketsu.

chat [tʃæt] *n., v.* oshaberi(suru) ; zatsudan(suru).

château [ʃætóu/ʃǽtou] *n.* shiro ; yakata ; dai-bessō.

chatelaine [ʃǽtəlein] *n.* (fujin-yō no) koshigusari ; jōshu (gotaike) no okugata.

chattel [tʃǽtəl] *n.* dōsan (*movables*).

chatter [tʃǽtə] *v.* (pechakucha to) shaberu ; (tori ga urusaku) saezuru. ~ *n.* oshaberi ; saezuri. ~**box** [tʃǽtəbɔks] *n.* oshaberi (no kodomo).

chatty [tʃǽti] *a.* oshaberi no.

chauffeur [ʃóufə] *n.* (jidōsha no) untenshu.

chauvinism [ʃóuvinizm] *n.* mōmokuteki aikokushugi.

chauvinist [ʃóuvinist] *n.* mōmokuteki aikokusha.

cheap [tʃi:p] *a.* yasui. ~**ly** [tʃí:pli], *ad.* yasuku. ~**ness** [tʃí:pnis], *n.* anka ; yasune.

cheapen [tʃí:pn] *v.* yasuku suru (naru).

cheat [tʃi:t] *n.* sagi(shi). *v.* damasu ; fusei o suru (hataraku).

check [tʃek] *n.* (1) soshi ; jama. (2) kogitte (*cheque*). (3) (*chess* no) ōte. (4) kōshijima (kimono). *v.* tomeru ; jama suru. chikki de azukeru. ~**book** [tʃékbuk] *a.* kogittechō. ~**ed** [tʃekt] *n.* kōshijima no.

checker, chequer [tʃékə] (1) Seiyō shōgi. (2) ~**board** [tʃékəbɔːd] *n.* *chess*-goban. ichimatsu moyō. ~**ed** [tʃékəd], ichimatsu moyō no ; gobanjima no.

checkmate [tʃékmeit] *n.* (*chess*) ōtezumi. *v.* ōtezume ni suru.

cheek [tʃi:k] *n.* (1) hō. ~**by jowl**, shimmitsu de. ~**bone** [tʃí:kboun] *n.* hōbone. ~**y** [tʃí:ki] *a.* namaikina. ~**ily** [tʃí:kili] *ad.* namaikini.

cheep [tʃi:p] *v.* (hina ga) piyo-piyo naku. *n.* hina no nakigoe.

cheer [tʃiə] *n.* kassai ; seien ; jōkigen. *v.* kassai suru. seien suru. ～ **up**, genki o dase. ～**y** [tʃíəri] *a.* jōkigen no. ～**ily**
[tʃíərili] *ad.* yukaini.

cheerful [tʃíəful] *a.* kigen (genki) no yoi. ～**ly** *ad.* genkiyoku.
～**ness** *n.* jōkigen ; yōki.

cheese [tʃi:z] *n.* chiizu.

cheetah, chetah [tʃí:tə] *n.* hyō (*panther*) no isshu.

chef [ʃef] *n.* ryōrinin-gashira.

chef-d'oeuvre [ʃədó:vr] *n.* kessaku.

chemical [kémikəl] *a.* kagaku no. *n.* kagakuseihin ; yakuhin.

chemise [ʃəmí:z] *n.* shimiizu ; fujin no hadagi.   ⌈kagaku.

chemist [kémist] *n.* kagakusha ; kusuriya. ～**ry** [kémistri] *n.*

cheque [tʃek] *n.* kogitte. ～**book** [tʃékbuk] *n.* kogittechō.

cherish [tʃériʃ] *v.* kawaigaru ; daijini suru.

cheroot [ʃerú:t] *n.* ryōgiri-hamaki-tabako.   ⌈rambo no tane.

cherry [tʃéri] *n.* sakura ; sakurambo. ～**stone** [-stoun] *n.* saku-

cherub [tʃérəb] *n.* (*pl.* -**bim**) kerubimu (dai 2 kyū no tenshi
angel) ; kawaii kodomo. ～**ic** [tʃerú:bik] *a.* tendō no yōna.

chess [tʃes] *n.* seiyō-shōgi. ～**board** [tʃésbɔ:d] *n.* chesu(go)ban.
～**man.** *n. chess* no koma.

chest [tʃest] *n.* hako ; mune : ～ *of drawers*, tansu.

chestnut [tʃésnət] *n.* kuri. *a.* kuriiro no ; kurige no.

chevalier [ʃóvəlíə] *n.* kishi.   ⌈shō.

chevron [ʃévrən] *n.* (kashikan, junsa no), yamagata no sode-

chew [tʃu:] *v.* kamu ; chinshi suru (*upon* or *over*). *n.* soshaku. ～
the cud, hansū (jukkō) suru.

chewing gum *n.* chūin-gamu.

chic [ʃi(:)k] *n.* iki. *a.* ikina.

Chicago [ʃiká:gou] *n.* Shikagō (Beikoku chūbu no toshi).

chicane [ʃikéin] *n.* gomakashi. *v.* gomakasu. ～**ry** [ʃikéinəri]
n. gomakashi, iinuke.

chick [tʃik] *n.* hiyoko. ～**en** [tʃíkn] *n.* hiyoko ; keiniku. ～
hearted [hɑ:tid] *a.* okubyōna. ～**pox** [-pɔks] *n.* mizubōsō.
～**yard** [-jɑ:d] *n.* yōkeijō. ～**weed** *n.* (*bot.*) hakobe no rui.

chicory [tʃíkəri] *n.* (*bot.*) kikujisa.

chid [tʃid] *v. see* : **chide.**

chidden [tʃídn] *v. see* : **chide.**

chide [tʃaid] *v.* (*Brit.*) **chid, chiden**; **chiding**; (*Am.*) **chid** ro **chided**; *or pp.* **chidden**; **chiding**. shikaru, kogoto o iu.

chief [tʃi:f] *n.* chō. *a.* shuyō no. ~**ly** [tʃí:fli] *ad.* shu to shite. ~**tain** [tʃí:ftein] *n.* shuzoku no chō.

chiffon [ʃifən] *n.* usui kempu; kinumosurin.

chiffonier [ʃifəníə] *n.* chadansu.

chilblain [tʃílblein] *n.* shimoyake.

child [tʃaild] *n.* (*pl.* **-ren** [tʃíldren]) kodomo. *with*~, ninshin shite. ~**birth** [tʃáildbə:θ] *n.* bumben. ~**hood** *n.* shōnen (yō-nen) jidai. ~**like** [-laik] *a.* mujakina.

childish [tʃáildiʃ] *a.* kodomoppoi. ~**ly** *ad.* kodomoppoku. ~**ness** *n.* kodomopposa.

Chilian [tʃílian] *a.* Chili no; Chilijin no. *n.* Chilijin.

chill [tʃil] *n.* samuke. *a.* tsumetai; reitanna. *v.* hiyasu (hieru); kyō o samasu. ~**ed** *a.* tsumetaku natta.

chilly [tʃíli] *a.* samui, tsumetai; reitanna.

chime [tʃaim] *n.* hitokumi no kane; (*pl.*) sono kane no oto. *v.* kane ga naru (o narasu); chōwa suru. ~ *in*, aizuchi o utsu. ~ *in with*, to chōshi o awaseru.

Chimera [kaimíərə] *n.* (*Gk. myth.*) atama wa *lion*, karada wa hitsuji, shippo wa ryū, kuchi kara hi o haku to iu kaibutsu.

chimeric(al) [kaimérik(əl)] *a.* kūsō no.

chimney [tʃímni] *n.* entotsu; ~ **corner** [-kó:nə] *n.* robata, ~ **piece** *n.* danro no maekazari. ~**sweep**(er) *n.* entotsu-sōji-(nin). ~**swallow** [-swólou] *n.* (*zoo.*) tsubame.

chimpanzee [tʃìmpænzíi] *n.* kuro-shōjō.

chin [tʃin] *n.* ago.

china [tʃáinə] *n.* jiki; setomono. ~**ware.** *n.* jiki; setomono.

Chinaman [tʃáinəmən] *n.* Chūgokujin; Shinajin.

chinchilla [tʃíntʃilə] *n.* chinchira; chinchira-usagi no kawa

chine [tʃain] *n.* sebone; niku no tsuita sebone. ⌐go.

Chinese [tʃainíːz] *a.* Chūgoku no. *n.* Chūgokujin; Chūgoku-chink [tʃiŋk] *n.* chinchin (oto); wareme. *v.* chinchin naru (na-rasu); wareru (waru).

chintz [tʃints] *n.* sarasamomen.

chip [tʃip] *v.* kezuru; koppa ni suru. *n.* hahen; koppa. ~**s,** jagaimo chippu (*fried potatoes*).

chipmunk [tʃípmənk] *n.* risu no isshu.

chipper [tʃípə] *a.* kaikatsuna.

chirp [tʃə:p], **chirrup**, **chirrup** [tʃírəp] *n.* (tori nado no) nakigoe. *v.* chūchū (chiichii) naku.

chisel [tʃízl] *n.* nomi. *v.* nomi de horu; chōkoku suru.

chit [tʃit] *n.* kodomo; shōjo. dempyō; (mijikai) tegami.

chitchat [tʃít:ʃæt] *n.* zatsudan.

chivalric [ʃívəlrik] *a.* kishidō no; chūsei bushidō no.

chivalrous [ʃívəlrəs] *a.* bukyō no. ~**ly** [ʃívəlrəsli] *ad.* kishidō tekini. ~**ness** [-nís] *n.* bushidō no seishin.

chivalry [ʃívəlri] *n.* kishidō; (bushidō); kishidan (*group of knights*); fujinsūhai (*lady worship*).

chloride [klɔ́:raid] *n.* (*chem.*) enkabutsu (enso to kagō shita mono).

chlorine [klɔ:ri(:)n] *n.* (*chem.*) enso. [mono).

chloroform [klɔ́:rəfɔ:m] *n.* kuroroforumu.

chlorophyl(l) [klɔ́:rəfil] *n.* (*bot.*) yōryokuso; yōryokutai.

chock [tʃɔk] *v.* (kusabi nado de) tomeru. *n.* kusabi. fune no [chokku.

chocolate [tʃɔ́kəlit] *n.*, *a.* chokoreito (no).

choice [tʃɔis] *n.* sentaku; yūryōhin (*the pick*). *a.* yorinuki no ~**ly** [tʃɔ́isli] yorinuite.

choir [kwáiə] *n.* (kyōkaidō no) shōkatai.

choke [tʃouk] *v.* iki o tomeru; fusagu (*fill up*); chissoku suru; musebu. *n.* chissoku. ~**damp** [tʃóukdæmp] *n.* chissoku suru hodo no tansangasu.

choler [kɔ́lə] *n.* kanshaku; kampeki.

cholera [kɔ́lərə] *n.* (*med.*) korera.

choleric [kɔ́lərik/kəlé-] *a.* okorippoi; kanshaku mochi no.

choose [tʃu:z] *v.* **chose, chosen; choosing.** erabu; sentaku suru.

chop [tʃɔp] *v.* komakaku kiru : ~ *down*, kiritaosu. ~ *n.* setsudan. *off*, kiriotosu. ~ *in*, sashideguchi suru. ~ *about* (*round*), kaze nado ga kyūni hōkō o kaeru. ~**sticks** [tʃɔ́pstiks] *n.* hashi. ~**suey** [tʃɔ́psú:i]. Amerika-shiki chapusui.

chopping [tʃípíŋ] *a.* kawari yasui; nami ga sakadatsu. ~ **block** [⊥blɔk] ~ **board** [⊥bɔ:d]. *n.* mana-ita.

choral [kɔ́:rəl] *n.*, *a.* gasshōtai (no); gasshōkyoku (no). ~ **chorale** [kəlá:l] *n.* =choral.

chord [kɔːd] *n.* (gakki no) gen. **vocal** ∼s [vóuklkɔ́ːdz] seitai.

choreograph [kɔ́rɔɔgrɑːf] *n. ballet* (barē) no furitsuke-shi (*designer*).

chorister [kɔ́ristə] *n.* gasshōtaiin ; (tokuni) shōnentaiin.

chorus [kɔ́ːrəs] *n.* gasshōtai (*choir*). *v.* gasshō suru.

chose [tʃouz] *v. see* : **choose**.

chosen [tʃóuzn] *v. see* : **choose**. *v.*, *a.* erabareta.

chouse [tʃaus] *v.* damasu. *n.*, *v*, peten (ni kakeru).

chowder [tʃáudə] *n.* isshu no yosenabe ryōri.

chrism [krizm] *n.* kasorikku (*Catholic*) kyō de mochiiru shinseina (*holy*) abura.

Christ [kraist] *n.* Kirisuto ; Kyūseishu.

christen [krísn] *v.* senrei o hodokoshi namae o tsukeru. ∼**ing** [krísniŋ], *n.* senreishiki.

Christendom [krís(ə)ndəm] *n.* Kirisutokyōkoku.

Christian [krístʃən] *n.* Kirisutokyō shinja. *a.* Kirisutokyō no. (*col.*) jōhinna. *the C*∼ *era* [-íərə] seireki kigen. *C*∼ *name*, senrei namae. ∼**ity** [kristʃǽniti] *n.* Kirisutokyō. ∼**ize** *v.* Kirisuto kyōto ni suru.

Christmas [krísməs] *n.* Kiristo Kōtansai (12 gt. 25 ch.). **Xmas box** (yūbin'ya ; meshitsukai ni okuru *Xmas* no okurimono). **Christmas Day** (12 gt 25 ch.). **Christmas Eve**, Kurisumasu zen'ya (24 k.). **Xmas tide**, *Christmas Eve* kara 1-shūkan gurai, mata wa 1 gt. 6. k. made tomo iu.

chromatic [kromǽtik] *a.* iro no ; (*mus.*) han-onkai no (*semitone*). ∼**s** *n.* shikisairon.

chrome [kroum] *n.* (*chem.*) kurōmu ; kuromu ōshoku.

chromium [króumiəm] *n.* (*chem.*) kuromiumu.

chromolithograph [króumoulíθəgrɑːf] *n.* chakushoku seki-chromosome [króumosoum] *n.* senshokutai.   ⌊ban-zuri.

chronic [krɔ́nik] *a.* mansei no.

chronicle [krɔ́nikl] *n.* nendaiki.

chrologic(al) [krɔnɔ́ldʒik(əl)] *a.* nendai-gaku no ; nendaijun no : *in* ∼ *order*, nendaijun ni ; *a* ∼ *table*, nempyō.

chronology [krɔnɔ́lədʒi] *n.* nendaigaku ; nendaiki.

chronometer [krɔnɔ́mitə] *n.* kuronometā ; seimitsudokei

chrysalis [krísəlis] *n.* sanagi.

chrysanthemum [krisǽnθiməm] *n.* (*bot.*) kiku.
chrysolite [krísəlait] *n.* (*min.*) kanranseki.
chub [tʃəb] *n.* (*fish*) ugui no isshu.
chubby [tʃʌ́bi] *a.* maru-maru shita ; marubocha no.
chuck [tʃʌk] *v.*, *n.* hyoito nageru ; karuku tataku (koto).
chuckle [tʃʌ́kl] *n.* mendori ga "kuk, kuk, kuk" to hina o
yobu ; hina o yonde naku koe. *v.* kusukusu warau ; manzoku
no hitori-warai o suru. ⌈kon'i ni naru.
chum [tʃʌm] *n.* shin'yū. *v.* dōshitsu ni iru. ～ *up with*, …to
chump [tʃʌmp] *n.* ōkina mokuhen (kigire) ; (*col.*) manuke
(*stupid person*).
chunk [tʃʌŋk] *n.* katamari ; kire. ～y [tʃʌ́ŋki] *a.* zunguri shita.
church [tʃə́:tʃ] *n.* kyōkai ; reihai. *as poor as a* ～ *mouse*, sekihin
arau ga gotoku. *go to* ～, kyōkai e reihai ni iku. ～**man**
[-'mən] *n.* (*Brit.*) (*Anglican* kyōkai) kokkyō no shinto. ～
warden [tʃə́:tʃwɔ́:dn] *n.* (zokujin no) kyōkai-iin. ～**yard**
[tʃə́:tʃjɑ:d] *n.* ji-in keidai ; ohaka.
churl [tʃə:l] *n.* inakappe(i) ; yahina hito. ～**ish** [tʃə́:riʃ] *a.* ge-
suna (*vulgar*).
churn [tʃə:n] *n.* (bata o tsukuru) kakunyūki. *v.* gyūnyū o kakimawasu ; kakimawasu.
chute [ʃu:t] *n.* ikioi yoku ochiru taki no rakka.
cicada [sikéidə] (*pl.* **-s**; **-ae** [i:]), **cicala** [siká:lə] (*pl.* **-ls**; **-le**
[-le]) *n.* *It.* semi.
cicatrix [síkətriks] (*pl.* **-trices** [-trisi:z]) *n.* kizuato.
cicerone [tʃitʃəróun] *n.* meisho, kyūseki (nado no) annainin.
cider [sáidə] *n.* ringo-shu ; saidā.
C. I. F. (okiwatashi) nedan. (*cost, insurance, freight*)
cigar [sigá:] *n.* hamaki tabako. ～ **case** [si:á:keis] hamaki ire.
cigaret(te) [sigrét] *n.* kami-maki-tabako. ～ **case** [-keis] kami
tabako ire. ～ **holder** [houldə] maki-tabako-yō paipu (*pipe*).
cinch [sintʃ] *n.* (*Am.*) (uma no) haraobi ; (*Am. sl.*) tashikana
koto.
cinchona [siŋkóunə] *n.* (*bot.*) kina no ki ; kina no kawa.
cincture [síŋktʃə] *n.* obi ; kakoi. *v.* torimaku.
cinder [síndə] *n.* moegara ; (*pl.*) hai (*ashes*).
cinema [sínəmə] *n.* eiga ; eiga-kan.

cinematograph [sinimǽtəgrɑ:f] *n.* eishaki ; (*Am.*) satsueiki.
cineraria [sinərɛ́əriə] *n.* (*bot.*) shineraria.
Cingalese [singəlí:z] *a.* Seiron (*Ceylon*) no ; Seirontōjin no. ~ *n.* (*sing & pl.*) Seironjin ; Seirongo.
cinnabar [sínəbɑ:] *n.* (*min.*) shinsha ; shu (*vermilion*).
cinnamon [sínəmən] *n.* nikkei. ⌐chigata.
cinquefoil [síŋkfoil] *n.* (*bot.*) kijimushiro zoku. (*archi.*) umeba-
C. I. O. (Beikoku) Sangyōbetsu Rōdōkumiai Kaigi (*Congress of Industrial Organization*).
cipher [sáifə] *n.* zero ; tsumaranu hito (-mono) ; angō ~ angō-kay). *v.* angō de kaku ; (angō o) yomitoku.
circle [sɔ́:kl] *n.* maru ; wa ; han'i (*sphere*) ; shakai. *v.* torimaku ; mawaru.
circlet [sɔ́:klit] *n.* chiisai maru ; (kin, hōseki nado no) kazariwa.
circuit [sɔ́:kit] *n.* junkai ; junkai-saiban. (*elec.*) kaisen ; kōgyō keitō. *closed* (*open*) ~ (*elec.*) hei(kai)ro. *go on* ~, junkai saiban ni mawaru. *make a* ~, mawarimichi o suru. *short* ~, chikamichi ; (*elec.*) shōto.
circuitous [sə:kjúitəs] *a.* tōmawari no. ~**ly** *ad.* tōmawari shite. mawari kudoku.
circular [sə:kjulə] *a.* marui ; junkai suru. *n.* kaijō (kairan). ~**ly** *ad.* junkantekini ; kairantekini. ~ **railway,** junkai tetsudo. ~ **ticket** [-tíkit] *n.* junkai kippu. ~ **tour** [-tuə] *n.* shūyū ryokō.
circulate [sɔ́:kjuleit] *v.* yo no naka ni hiromeru (hiromaru) ; junkan suru. **circulating capital,** ryūdō shihon. **circulating library,** junkai bunko.
circulation [sə:kjuléiʃən] *n.* junkan ; ryūtsū ; hakkō.
circulatory [sɔ́:kjulətəri] *a.* junkan suru.
circumcise [sɔ́:kəmsaiz] *v.* katsurei o okonau. **circumcision** *n.* katsurei (Yudayakyō no).
circumference [səkámfərəns] *n.* shūi ; mawari.
circumflex [sɔ́:kəmfleks] *a.* ∧ ⌒ ~ nado no yōni magatta. ~ **accent** *n. Fr., Port.* nado ni aru *accent* (∧).
circumlocution [sɔ́:kəmlokjú:ʃən] *n.* enkyoku ; mawarikudoi iikata. ⌐kudoi.
circumlocutory [sə:kəmlɔ́kjutəri] *a.* tōmawashi no ; mawari

circumnavigate [sə:kəmnǽvigeit] *v.* mawarimichi no kōkai (*navigation*) o suru.

circumscribe [sə́:kəmskraib] *v.* seigen suru.

circumspect [sə́:kəmspekt] *a.* shinchōna ; yōjin-bukai. ~**tion** [sə̀:kəmspékʃən] *n.* ironna hōmen kara miru koto.

circumstance [sə́:kəmstəns] *n.* aru dekigoto o meguru shūi no issai no koto.

circumstantial [sə̀:kəmstǽnʃəl] *a.* gūzen no ; kuwashii. ~**ly** *ad.* fuzuitekini ; gūzenni.

circumvent [sə̀:kəmvént] *v.* dashinuku ; keiryaku no ura o kaku.

circus [sə́:kəs] *n.* kyokuba(kōgyō)-jō ; kyokuba(kōgyō)-dan.

cirrus [sírəs] (*pl. cirri* [sírai]) *n.* (*meteo.*) ken'un.

cistern [sístən] *n.* mizutame ; ike (*pond*).

citadel [sítədl] *n.* toride ; nejiro.

citation [saitéiʃən] *n.* nukigaki no monku ; in'yōbun ; kanjō (*public commendation*).

cite [sait] *v.* in'yō suru ; shōkan suru. kanjō o ataeru.

citizen [sítizn] *n.* shimin ; kōmin. ~**ship** [sítiznʃip] *n.* kōminken ; shiminken.

citric [sítrik] *a.* shitoron (*lemon*) no ; ~*acid*, kuensan.

citron [sítrən] *n.* (*bot.*) shitoron (ōgata remon).

city [síti] *n.* shi ; toshi. ~ **assembly** [sítiəsémbli] shikai. ~ **council(l)or** [sítikáunsilə] *n.* shikaigiin. ~ **hall** [sítihɔ:l] shiyakusho ; shikaigijidō.

civet [sívit] *n.* jakō-neko ; sore kara toru kōryō (*aromatic*).

civic [sívik] *a.* shimin no. ~**s** *n.* kōmingaku.

civil [sívil] *a.* shimin no ; kokunai no ; reigi tadashii (*urbane*). ~ **law** [sivil lɔ:] *n.* mimpō. ~**ly** *ad.* mimpō ni shitagatte. ~ **rights** [sivil raits] *n.* jinken. ~ **service** [sívilsə́:vis] *n.* bunkan. ~ **war** [sívil wɔ:] *n.* nairan. ~**ian** [-jən] *n.* ippanjin. ~**ity** [sivíliti] *n.* teichō ; ingin. ~**ization** [sivil(a)izéiʃən] *n.* bummei ; kyōka (*education*) ga hattatsu shite iru koto.

civilize [sívilaiz] *v.* kyōka suru. ~**d** [-d] bummei no susunda.

clack [klæk] *v.* pachit to oto o tateru ; bechakucha shaberu.

clad [klæd] *v.* see : **clothe** (*Old English, arch.*).

claim [kleim] *n., v.* yōkyū (suru). ~**able** [kléiməbl] *a.* seikyū dekiru. ∼ant [-ənt] *n.* yōkyūsha ; seikyū suru hito. ∼er = **claimant.**

clairvoyance [klɛəvɔ́iəns] *n.* tōshi ; senrigan.

clairvoyant [klɛəvɔ́iənt] *a.* tōshi no. *n.* senrigan no hito.

clam [klɔm] *n., v.* (*zoo.*) hamaguri (o asaru).

clamber [klǽmbə] *v.* yojinoboru.

clammy [klǽmi] *a.* shittori to tsumetai.

clamorous [klǽmərəs] *a.* sōzōshii ; yakamashii. ∼**ly** *ad.* sōzō-shiku ; yakamashiku.

clamo(u)r [klǽmə] *n.* sawagi ; kensō. *v.* donaru ; sawagu.

clamp [klǽmp] *n.* kasugai. *v. clamp* de tomeru.

clan [klæn] *n.* ichizoku.

clandestine [klændéstin] *a.* himitsu no. ∼**ly** [klændéstinli] *ad.* himitsuni.

clang [klæŋ] *v.* garan, garan narasu (naru). *n.* sono oto.

clango(u)r [klǽŋgə] *v., n.* narihibiku (oto). ∼**ous** [-rəs], *a.* garan, garan to naru.

clank [klǽŋk] *n., v.* kachan, gatan (to oto o tateru.)

clannish [klǽniʃ] *a.* shizoku no ; danketsu shite iru.

clansman [klǽnzmən] *n.* dōshuzoku no hito.

clap [klǽp] *v.* hakushu suru. ∼*a person in prison,* sugu rōya ni ireru. ∼*a person on the back,* senaka o karuku tataku, (aisatsu, shitashimi). ∼*spurs to a horse,* uma ni kyūni hakusha o ireru. ∼*up,* isoide torikimeru. ∼**board** [klǽpbɔːd] *n.* shitami-ita. ∼**trap** [klǽptræp] ninki-tori. ∼**per** [klǽpə] *n.* kane (*bell*) no shita. **wooden** ∼ *n.* hyōshigi.

claque [klæk] *n.* (*Fr.*), yatowarete kassai suru renjū ; sakura

claret [klǽrət] *n.* aka-budōshu.

clarification [klærifikéiʃən] *n.* kiyomeru koto ; meirōka.

clarify [klǽrifai] *v.* kireini (mizu o) sumaseru ; kireini (mizu ga) sumu.

clarinet [klærinét], **clarionet** [klæriənét] *n.* kurarinetto (gakki).

clarion [klǽriən] *n.* (surudoion, sukkiri shita on o dasu) isshu no rappa.

clarity [klǽriti] *n.* kireini sumikitta arisama ; seichō.

clash [klǽʃ] *v.* kachiau ; shōtotsu suru. ⌈tami naifu.

clasp [klǽsp] *v., n.* nigiri ; shikkari daku (koto). ∼ *knife,* orida

class [klɑ:s] *n.* tōkyū ; kaikyū ; kumi ; gakkyū.

classic [klǽsik] *n.* koten ; daiikkyū no sakuhin. (*pl.*) koten-bungaku ; kotengo. *a.* daiikkyū no ; koten no. ～**al** [-kəl] *a.* koten no : ～*education*, kotengo kyōiku. ～**ism** [klǽsisizm] *n.* kotenfū no geng(y)o, bunka.

classification [klæsifikéiʃən] *n.* bunrui

classify [klǽsifai] *v.* bunrui suru.

clatter [klǽtə] *n.*, *v.* gara gara, kachi kachi (naru) ; becha becha (shaberu).

clause [klɔ:z] *n.* hōritsu kiyaku nado no ikkajō ; (*gram.*) setsu (meishi), keiyoshi, fukushi no yakume o suru bun.

clavicle [klǽvikl] *n.* sakotsu (*collar-bone*).

claw [klɔ:] *n.* tsume (washi, taka nado no). *v.* tsume de hikkaku. ～**ed** *a.* tsume no aru.

clay [klei] *n.* nendo (*porcelain clay*). ～**ey** [kléii:] nendo no ōi.

clean [kli:n] *a.* seiketsuna ; sukkiri shita. *ad.* kireini ; takumini. *v.* kireini suru ; sōji suru. ～*bill of health*, kenkō shōmeishō. ～**cut** [klí:nkʌt] *a.* me-hana-dachi no hakkiri shita. **dry cleaning** *n.* kansō sentakuhō.

cleanly [klénli] (1) *a.* kogireina. (2) *ad.* [klí:nli] kireini. ～**iness** [klénlinis] *n.* kireizuki ; seiketsu.

cleanse [klenz] *v.* seiketsu ni suru.

clear [kliə] *a.* akarui ; akirakana. *v.* kireini (suru). *ad.* akirakani ; ～ *the track* ; jama o dokeru. harasu ; hareru. ～ *up*. kibun o harasu ; heya (*room*) no sōji o suru ; ～**cut** [-kʌt] meikaina ; hakkiri shita ; ～ *cut pronounciation*, meikaina hatsuon. ～**headed** [-hèdid] *a.* sōmeina (atama no). ～**ly** *ad.* akirakani ; hakkiri to. ～**ness** [klíənis] *n.* meihaku.

clearance [klíərəns] *n.* sōji ; tegatakōkan. ～**fee**, shukkō tesūryō. ～**notice** shukkō tsūchi. ～**permit** [-pə̀:mit] shukkō ninkashō. ～**sale**, mikiriuri ; kurabarai.

clearing [klíəriŋ] *n.* sōji ; tegata kōkan ; seisan (*liquidation*) ～**house,** tegata (nado no) kōkanjo.

clear-sighted [klíəsáitid] *a.* sōmeina ; mesaki no kiku.

cleat [kli:t] *n.* tomerukane ; tsunadome. *v. cleat* de tomeru

cleavage [klí:vidʒ] *n.* sakeme.

cleave [kli:v] *v.* (**cleft** or **cleaved** or **clove, cleft** or **cleaved,**

or **cloven; cleaving**. waru ; hikisaku. ~**r** [klí:və] *n.* niku-
clef [klef] *n.* (*mus.*) ombu-kigō. ⌊kiribōchō.
cleft [kleft], *u. see :* **cleave**.
clematis [klémətis] *n.* (*bot.*) botan-zuru, sennin-sō
clemency [klémənsi] *n.* nasakebukai koto ; jinji.
clement [klémənt] *a.* kandaina ; onwana (*mild*). ~**ly** *ad.* kan-
daini ; odayakani.
clench [klentʃ] *v.* (kobushi o) gyutto nigirikatameru : ~*one's
fist in anger*, okotte kobushi o nigirishimeru.
clergy [klɔ́:dʒi] *n.* bokushi ; seishoku (*holy orders*). ~**man**
[-mən] *n.* bokushi : ~*s sore throat*, mansei (*chronic*) kōtōen
(*laryngitis*).
cleric(al) [klérik(əl)] *a.* sōryo no ; bokushi no ; shoki (*clerk*)
no. *n.* bokushi. ⌈shoki.
clerk [klɑ:k] (*Brit.*) shoki ; (*Am.*) ten'in (*shop-girl*) ; jimuin ;
clever [klévə] *a.* kiyōna ; rikōna (*intelligent*). ~**ly** *ad.* rikōni ;
umaku. ~**ness** *n.* kashikosa ; rikō.
clew [klu:] *n.* ito no tama ; tegakari ; itoguchi.
click [klik] *n., v.* kachit (to naru ; narasu).
client [kláiənt] *n.* soshō irainin ; bengo irainin ; otoku.
clientele [kláiəntèil] *n.* (*pl.*) soshō irainintachi ; otokui-tachi.
cliff [klif] *n.* gake ; zeppeki. ~**y** [klífi] *a.* kewashii ; zeppeki
climate [kláimit] *n.* kikō ; fūdo. ⌊no ōi.
climatic(al) [klaimǽtk(l)] *a.* kikō no.
climax [kláimæks] *n.* zetchō ; chōten ; (hanashi nado no) ichiban daijina tokoro.
climb [klaim] *v.* yojinoboru (te to ashi de). ~**er** *n.* tozansha ;
(*bot.*) tsurukusa (asagao no yōna). ~**ing** [kláimiŋ] *n.* yojinoboru koto. **climbing irons**, kanjiki ; tozangutsu no soko
nado no kanagu.
clime [klaim] *n.* (*poet.*) kuni ; chihō.
clinch [klintʃ] *v.* kotei saseru ; (giron ni) keri o tsukeru. *n.*
kochaku (saseru mono) ; nawa no musubime.
cling [kliŋ] *v.* **clung ; clinging.** kuttsuku, kajiritsuku (*to*) ;
koshu suru (*keep to*).
clinic [klínik] *n.* shinsatsushitsu ; shinryōsho ; rinshō-kōgi.
~**al** [-əl] *a.* rinshō no.

clink [klínk] *n.*, *v.* chirin, kachin (to oto o tateru).
clinker [klíŋkə] *n.* shitsu no katai renga ; kanakuso (*slag*) ; (*Brit. col*) subarashii mono (ippin).
clip [klip] *n.* karikomi (hasami kiru koto). kirinuki. kamibasami. *v.* karikomu ; habuku. *at a* ~, (*col.*) ippenni· ~**per** [klípə] *n.* hasamite ; karite. (*pl.*) hasami
clique [kl:k] *n.* totō, habatsu.
cloak [klouk] *n.* manto ; *v.* gaitō (de ōu) ; kakusu. *under the* ~ *of*, ni kakotsukete. ~**room** [-rum] *n.* keitai-hin azukari-sho.
clock [klɔk] *n.* tokei. ~ **tower,** tokei-dai. ~**wise** *ad.* [klɔ́kwaib] migi (*right*) mawari ni. ~**work** [-wə:k] *n.* zemmai-jikake. *like* ~, tokei no yōni seikakuni.
clod [klɔd] *n.* tsuchikure ; baka (*fool*). ~**hopper** [klɔ́dhɔpə] *n.* inakamono ; (*pl.*) dotagutsu.
clog [klɔg] *n.* jama ; kizoko-gutsu ; geta (*Japanese* geta). *v.* jama suru ; fusagu (-garu).
cloisonne [klɔ̀izɔnéi] *a.* (*Fr.*) shippō-sei no. ~*n.* shippō-yaki.
cloister [klɔ́istə] *n.* shūdōin ; kairō (*passage*). *v.* tonsei saseru
cloistral [klɔ́istrəl] *a.* shūdōin no ; tonsei shita.   ⌊(suru).
close [klous] *a.* tojita ; shimmitsuna ; chikai. *n.* owari, shūketsu. [klouz] *v.* tojiru ; chikayoru ; ~ *a gap*, wareme o fusagu ~ *the debate*, tōron o owaru.
closet [klɔ́zit] *n.* chiisai jibun no heya ; oshiire.
closure [klóuʒə] *n.* heisa ; shūketsu (*end*).
clot [klɔt] *n.* (chi no) katamari. *v.* (chi o) katamaraseru.
cloth [klɔθ] *n.* (*pl.* **-s** [klɔθs]) nuno, kireji ; orimono. *lay the* ~, shokuji no shitaku o suru.
clothe [klouð] *v.* **clothed** *or* **clad** (*arch.*), **clothing** ifuku o ataeru ; kiseru.
clothes [klouðz] *n.* (*pl.*) kimono. ~**horse** [klóuðzhɔ:s] *n.* emonkake, (hosu tame no). ~**line** [-lain] *n.* monohoshi (tsuna).
clothier [klóuðiə] *n.* rashashō ; hifukushō.
clothing *n.* kimono ; hifukurui.
cloud [klaud] *n.* kumo (sora no). ~*of sand*, suna-kemuri. ~**burst** [kláudbə:st] *n.* doshaburi. ~**capped** [klaudkæpt] *a.* kumo o itadaita. ~**less,** kumo no nai. ~ **rack,** ukigumo. *in the* ~*s,* sora takaku. *under a* ~, utagai no kumo no moto ;

kurushimi nayande. ~y [kláudi] *a.* kumotta ; mōrō to shite iru (*dim*). **cloudiness** *n.* kumori, donten.

clout [klaut] *n., v.* borogire de tsukurou.

clove [klouv] *v. see* : **cleave.**

cloven [klóuvn] *see* : **cleave.** *show the* ~ *hoof,* honshō o arawasu. ~**footed** [-fùtid] (ushi no yōni) tsume no wareta.

clover [klóuvə] *n.* (*bot.*) kuróba ; Óranda genge. *in* ~, yutaka ni.

clown [klaun] *n.* dōke-yakusha. ~**ish** [kláuniʃ] *a.* dōketa.

cloy [klɔi] *v.* haraippai ni tabesaseru.

club [klʌb] *n.* kombō ; (*golf no*) bō ; shūkaijo ; kurabu. *v.* kombō de utsu.~ **foot** [klʌbfut] *n.* ebiashi. ~**house** [-haus] *n. club* kaikan. ~**law** *n.* bōryoku. ~**moss** *n.* (*bot.*) hikage no kazura.

cluck [klʌk] *n.* (tamago o unda ato no) mendori no nakigoe.

clue [klu:] *n.* itoguchi ; tegakari.

clump [klʌmp] *n.* kodachi. *v.* bikko no yōni aruku. *a.* ~ *of trees,* yabu (*bush*).

clumsy [klámzi] *a.* bukiyōna. **clumsily** [-ili] *ad.* bukiyōni. ~**iness** [klámzinis] *n.* bukiyōsa.

clung [klʌŋ] *v. see* : **cling.**

cluster [klʌ́stə] *n.* mure, ichidan. *v.* muragaru.

clutch [klʌtʃ] *v., n.* shikkari nigiru (koto) ; tsukami kakaru (koto) ; *n.* (*pl.*) akuma no tsume.

clutter [klʌtə] *n.* konran. *v.* torimidasu ; chirakasu.

Co. kaisha (*Company*).

c/o ...kizuke (*care of*).

coach [koutʃ] *n.* yonrin-ōbasha. kyōgi no shidō o suru hito.

coachman [-mən] *n.* gyosha. ⌈ku hojo.

coadjutor [ko(u)ædʒutə] *n.* kyōryokusha (*Roman Cath.*) kanto-

coagulate [ko(u)ǽgjuleit] katamaraseru. ~**tion** [kouæ̀gjuléiʃən] *n.* gyōketsu ; katamaru koto.

coal [koul] *n.* sekitan. *v.* sekitan o kyōkyū suru (...sekitan ireru). ~**bed** [kóulbed] *n.* sekitan no sō (*strata*). ~**bunker** *n.* sekitansha. ~**field** [fi:ld] *n.* tanden. ~**gas** *n.* sekitan gas. ~**heaver** [-hí:və] *n.* sekitan tsumi-oroshi nimpu. ~ **mine** *n.* tanzan ; tankō. ~**oil** *n.* sekiyū. ~**pit** *n.* tankō. ~**tar** [-tá] *n.*

kōrutā. **~ing station** [kóuliŋ stéiʃən] *n.* kisha, kisen ni sekitan o tsumikomu tokoro.

coalesce [kò(u)əlés] *v.* gōdō suru ; rengō suru. **~nce** [ko(u)-əlés(ə)ns] *n.* gōitsu ; rengō.

coalition [ko(u)əlíʃən] *n.* rengō ; teikei. **~ cabinet** *n.* renritsu naikaku.

coarse [kɔːs] *a.* arai ; somatsuna ; gehinna. **~ly** *ad.* araku ; somatsuni ; gehinni. **~ness** *n.* ara-arashisa ; gehin.

coast [koust] *n.* kaigan ; suberi kudari. **~defence ship**, kaibōkan. *the ~ is clear*, Atari ni jamamono wa nai. *v.* sakamichi (*slope*) o suberi oriru. **~al** [kóustəl] *a.* kaigan no. **~er** *n.* enkai bōeki-sen. **~er brake**, *n.* jitensha no *brake*. **~ guard** [kóustgɑːd] *n.* engan keibitai (in). **~line** *n.* kaigansen. **~ing** [kóustiŋ] *a.* engan no. **~ing trade**, engan bōeki. **~ing vessel** [vésl] *n.* engan bōekisen.

coat [kout] *n.* uwagi ; kōto. *v.* nuru ; haru (*cover*). **~ of arms**, monshō. **~ of mail**, kusari katabira. **~ing** *n.* kabusemono (*cover*) ; toryō (*paints*).

coax [kouks] *v.* nadameru ; kagi nado o umaku hamekomu.

cob [kɔb] *n.* tōmorokoshi no hojiku ; ashi no mijikai jōbuna uma.

cobalt [kóubɔːlt] *n.* (*min.*) kobaruto ; kobaruto-iro (*color*).

cobble [kɔ́bl] *n.* marui ishi (shikiishiyō no). *v.* kutsu o naosu. **~stone** *n.* maruishi. **~er** [kɔ́blə] *n.* kutsu naoshi ; (*Am.*) yaita pai.

cobra [kóubrə] *n.* (*zoo.*) kobura (Indo no dokuja).

cobweb [kɔ́bweb] *n.* kumo (*spider*) no su : **~s of superstition**, furukusai meishin.

coca [kóukə] *n.* (*bot.*) koka (ha kara kokain o tsukuru Bolivia san no kamboku).

coca cola [koukə kóulə] *n.* isshu no seiryō inryō.

cocain(ə) [ko(u)kéin] *n.* kokain (masui zai *anæsthetic*).

cochineal [kɔ́tʃiniːl] *n.* saboten ni kisei suru mushi.

cock [kɔk] *n.* niwatori no osu ; suidō no mizuguchi. **~and bull story**, usorashii hanashi. **~-a-doodle-doo** [-ədúːdldu:] *n.* kokkekōkō. **~ade** [kɔkéid] *n.* bōshi no maedate. **~crow** *n.* yoake. **~eyed** *a.* yabunirami no. **~fighting** *n.* niwatori no keai. ～**horse** *n.* kodomoyō no mokuba. ～**loft** *n.* yaneura no heya. ～**pit** *n.* tōkeijō ; gekijō no doma. ～**roach** *n.* abura-mushi. ～**sure** *a.* kakushin shite ; unuborete (*self-conceited*). ～**robin** *n.* komadori noosu. ～**scomb** *n.* (*bot.*) keitō.

cockatoo [kɔkətú:] *n.* (*bird*) isshu no inko.

cockatrice [kɔ́kətris] *n.* dokuhebi (hitonirami de hito o koro-su to iu) (*basilisk*).

cockerel [kɔ́k(ə)rəl] *n.* osu no hinadori.

cockle [kɔkl] *n.* torigai (no kara). ～**shell** *n.* kobune.

cockney [kɔ́kni] *n.* London shimin (tokini keibetsu no imi). ～**accent** *n.* Kokkunii Eigo.

cocktail [kɔ́kteil] *n.* shippo (*tail*) o kitta uma (*horse*) ; kaku-cocky [kɔ́ki] *a.* (*col.*) namaikina. ⌊teru.

coco [kóukou] *n.* yashi no ki. ～**palm** *n.* yashi no ki. ～**nut** *n.* yashi no mi.

cocoa [kóukou] *n.* kakao no tane no kona (*powder*) ; sore kara tsukutta nomimono.

cocoon [kɔkú:n] *n.* mayu.

cod [kɔd] *n.* (*fish*) tara (*codfish*). ～**ling** [kɔ́dliŋ] *n.* kodara. ～**liver** [-livə] *n.* tara no kimo. ～ *liver oil*, kan'yu.

C.O.D., c.o.d. daikin hikikae-barai (*cash on delivery*).

coddle [kɔ́dl] *v.* amayakashite sodateru.

code [koud] *n.* hōten : *civil* ～, mimpōten. ～**book** [kóudbuk] *n.* denshin ryakugochō. ～**telegram** *n.* angō dempō. ～**word** *n.* denshin ryakugō moji. **intenational** ～, bankoku tsūshinfugō.

codex [kóudex] *n.* (*pl.* **-dices** [kóudisi:z]) shahon ; kakiutsu-shita hon.

codger [kɔ́dʒə] *n.* (*col.*) kawarimono ; henkutsu.

codicil [kɔ́disil] *n.* yuigonjō hosoku-sho (*addition to a will*).

codificaton [kɔdifikéiʃən] *n.* hōten (*code of laws*) hensan (*editing*).

codify [kɔ́difai] *v.* sho-hōritsu o hōten (*code*) ni atsumeru.

coed [kouéd] *n.* (*Am. col.*) jogakusei (kyōgaku, daigaku no).

coeducation [kóu-edju(:)kéiʃən] *n.* danjo kyōgaku.

coefficient [ko(u)ifíʃənt] *a.* kyōdō sagyō suru. (*math.*) keisū.

coerce [ko(u)ə́:s] *v.* shiiru ; kyōsei suru.

coercion [ko(u)ɔ́:ʃən] *n.* kyōsei ; kyōhaku.
coercive [ko(u)ɔ́:siv] *a.* kyōsei no.
coeval [ko(u)i:vəl] *a.* dōjidai no. 〔kyōson.
coexist [kó(u)igzíst] *v.* kyōson suru. ～**ence** [kóuigzístəns] *n.*
coffee [kɔ́fi] *n.* kōhii. ～**beans** [-bí:nz] *n.* kōhii no mi. ～
house [-haus] *n.* kōhii-ten.
coffer [kɔ́fə] *n.* kichōhimbako ; (*pl.*) shisan ; zaigen. ～**dam**
[-dæm] suichū-kōji de, mizu no hairanai yōni kakou hako.
kakoizeki.
coffin [kɔ́fin] *n.* kan ; hitsugi.
cog [kɔg] *n.* haguruma no ha. ～**wheel** [kɔ́g(h)wi:l] *n.* ha no
tsuita haguruma.
cogency [kóudʒənsi] *n.* hito o kampuku saseru chikara ; settokuryoku. (*convineing power*).
cogent [kóudʒənt] *a.* chikarazuyoi ; settokuryoku aru. ～**ly** *ad.*
cogitate [kɔ́dʒiteit] *v.* yoku kangaeru ; jukuryo suru.
cogitation [kɔdʒitéiʃən] *n.* jukkō.
cogitative [kɔ́dʒitətiv] *a.* kangaeru nōryoku no aru.
cognac [kóunjæk] *n.* konyaku. *France*-san no burandii.
cognate [kɔ́gneit] *a.,* *n.* dōzoku (no), shinrui (no). ～**object**
(*gram.*) dōshu mokutekigo.
cognition [kɔgníʃən] *n.* ninshiki ; ninshiki-ryoku ; myōji.
cognizable [kɔ́gnizəbl] *a.* ninshiki sareru. 〔ki suru.
cognizance [kɔ́gnizəns] *n.* ninshiki ; nintei. *take* ～ *of*, ninshi-
cognizant [kɔ́gnizənt] *a.* ninshiki shita ; jurishita.
cognomen [kɔgnóumen] *n.* kamei (*family name*).
cohabit [kouhǽbit] *v.* dōsei suru ; issho ni sumu.
cohabitation [kouhæbitéiʃən] *n.* dōsei ; kyōdō seikatsu.
coheir [kóuéə] *n.* kyōdō sōzokunin.
cohere [kouhíə] *v.* kuttsuku ; shubi ikkan suru. ～**nce,** ～
ncy [-híərəns, -si] *n.* ketsugōryoku (*union*).
coherent [ko(u)híərənt] *a.* shikkari kuttsuita ; shubi ikkan
shita (*consistent*).
coherer [ko(u)híərə] *n.* kohiira (muden-yō no kempaki).
cohesion [ko(u)hí:ʒən] *n.* nenchaku ; ketsugō-ryoku.
cohesive [ko(u)hí:ziv] *a.* kuttsuku ; fuchaku-ryoku no aru.
cohort [kó(u)hɔ:t] *n.* hohei-tai ; (*pl.*) guntai, gurūpu.

coiffeur [kwɑ:fɔ́:] *n.* (*Fr.*) rihatsushi (*hair-dresser*).

coiffure [kwɑ:fjúə] *n.* (*Fr*) kami no yuikata ; kamikazari.

coign [kɔin] *n.* sumi-ishi ; ～ of vantage, yūrina chii.

coil [kɔil] *v.* toguro o maku ; uzu o maku. *n.* toguro ; uzu maki ; koiru.

coin [kɔin] *n.* kahei ; kōka. *v.* (kahei o) chūzō suru (*mint*) ; shingo (*new word*) o tsukuridasu. ～**age** [kɔ́inidʒ] *n.* kahei chūzō.

coincide [kɔinsáid] *v.* itchi suru ; fugō suru. ～**nce** [ko(u)ínsidəns] *n.* fugō ; itchi. ～**nt** [ko(u)ínsidənt] *a.* itchi(fugō) suru.

coiner [kɔ́inə] *n.* kahei chūzōsha ; nisegane tsukuri ; shingo o tsukuru hito.

coition [kɔ́iʃən] *n.* kōsetsu ; seikō

coke [kouk] *n.* kōkusu.

cola [kóulə] *n.* kōra ; Afurika-san no ki (matawa sono mi).

colander [kɔ́ləndə] *n.* rokaki ; mizukoshi ; mizu o kosu mono.

colatitude [ko(u)lǽtitju:d] *n.* yoido (aru ido to 90° to no sa).

colchicum [kɔ́ltʃikəm] *n.* (*bot.*, *med.*) inu safuran ; sorekara tsukutta mayaku.

cold [kould] *a.* samui ; reitanna (*indifferent*). *n.* samusa ; kazehiki. *catch* (*or take*) *a*) *cold,* kaze o hiku. ～ **meat** reiniku. ～ **shoulder**, (*Am.*) reitanna furumai. ～ **storage**, reizō (kō). ～ **war**, tsumetai sensō. ～ **wave**, kampa. ～**blooded** [-blʌ́did] *a.* reiketsu no. ～ **chisel** [-tʃízl], tagane. ～**hearted** [-hɑ́:tid] *a.* mujōna. ～**ly** *ad.* hiyayakani. ～**ness** *n.* samusa ; tsumetasa ; reitan. ⌐

cole [koul] *n.* aburana, yasai.

colic [kɔ́lik] *n.* senki ; fukutsū. *a.* ketchō no ; sentsū no.

collaborate [kəlǽbəreit] *v.* tomo ni hataraku ; gassaku suru

collaboration [kəlǽbəréiʃən] *n.* kyōryoku ; gassaku. ⌐(*with*)

collaborator [kolǽbəreitə] *n.* gassakusha ; kyōdōkenkyūsha.

collapse [kəlǽps] *v.* tsubureru ; kuzureru. *n.* kaimetsu ; hametsu.

collapsible [kəlǽpsəbl] *a.* oritatami dekiru ; tsubureru : ～ **boat,** kumitate bōto. ⌐sakotsu.

collar [kɔ́lə] *n.* karā. *v.* eri mata wa kubi o tsukamu. ～**bone** *n.*

collate [kəléit] *v.* terashi awaseru ; taishō suru. (*rel.*) sōshoku (kurai) o sazukeru. ～**ed telegram** *n.* shōgō dempō.

collateral [ko(u)lǽtərəl] *a.* dainijiteki no ; heikō suru. *n.* bōkei shinzoku ; mikaeri busshi. **~ly** *ad.* heikō shite ; kansetsu ni ; fuzuitekini.

collation [kəléiʃən] *n.* shoseki no taishō chōsa.

colleague [kɔ́li:g] *n.* dōryō ; dōgyōsha.

collect [kəlékt] *v.* atsumeru ; atsumaru. ~ *oneself*, ki o torinaosu ; kokoro o ochitsukeru. *n.* [kɔ́lekt] mijikai inori. **~ed** [kəléktid] *a.* atsumeta. **~ly** *ad.* ochitsuite. **~ness** *n.* ochitsuki. **~ive** [kəléktiv] *a.* atsumatta ; kyōdō no ; shūgō no **~noun** (*gram.*) shūgō-meishi. **~ively** *ad.* zentai o shite.

collection [kəlékʃən] *n.* saishū ; shūshū(hin), korekushon.

collectivism [kəléktivizm] *n.* shūsanshugi. **~ist** *n.* shūsan-shugisha.

collector [kəléktə] *n.* shūshūka ; shūkinnin.

college [kɔ́lidʒ] *n.* semmon gakkō ; (tanka) daigaku.

collegian [kəlí:dʒiən] *n.* *college* no gakusei.

collegiate [kəli:dʒiit] *a.* daigaku(sei) no.

collide [kəláid] *v.* shōtotsu suru (*with*).

collie [kɔ́li] *n.* korii ; hitsuji no banken.

collier [kɔ́liə] *n.* tankōfu ; sekitan-umpansen ; sono sen'in. **~ry** [kɔ́liəri] tankō (*coal mine*).

collimate [kɔ́limeit] *v.* shōjun suru (bōenkyō nado o).

collimation [kɔləméiʃən] *n.* shōjun.

collision [kəlídʒən] *n.* shōtotsu ; atsureki.

collocate [kɔ́ləkeit] *v.* naraberu ; haichi suru.

collocation [kɔləkéiʃən] *n.* haichi ; go no haichi.

collodion [kəlóudiən] *n.* korōjion (shashin gemban nado ni nuru eki).

colloid [kɔ́lɔid] *n.* koroido ; nikawa-shitsu no.

colloquial [kəlóukwiəl] *a.* kōgo (hanashi-kotoba) no. **~ism** *n.* kōgotai ; kaiwatai. **~ly** *ad.* kōgo de.

colloquy [kɔ́ləkwi] *n.* kaiwa ; taiwa.

collotype [kɔ́lətaip] *n. a.* korotaipu ban (shashin no).

collusion [kəlu:dʒən] *n.* nareai ; kyōbō (*conspiracy*).

cologne [kəlóun] *n.* koron (keshō) sui.

colon [kóulən] *n.* koron (:), (*anat.*) ketchō.

colonel [kɔ́:nəl] *n.* rikugun taisa, **lieutenant** ~ *n.* rikugun chū-sa.

colonial [kəlóuniəl] *a.* shokumin(chi) no. ~ **militia** [-mílíʃə] *n.* tonden-hei.

colonist [kɔ́lənist] *n.* shokuminchijin ; ijūmin.

colonization [kɔ̀lənizéiʃən] *n.* shokumin. ⌐(saseru).
colonize [kɔ́lənaiz] *v.* shokuminchi ni suru ; shokumin suru,
colonnade [kɔ̀lənéid] *n.* onaji kyori ni tateta hashira.
colony [kɔ́ləni] *n.* shokumin ; shokuminchi.
colo(u)r [kʌ́lə] *n.* iro ; senryō ; (*pl.*) hata. *v.* irodoru ; someru
(*dye*). ~**able** *a.* chakushoku dekiru. ~**-blind** *a.* shikimō no.
~**-blindness** *n.* shikimō. ~ **box,** enogu-bako. ~**ed** *a.* iro
dotta. ~**filter** [-filtə] rokōban ; filutā. ~**ful** *a.* shikisai ni
tonda ; hadena. ~**ing** [-ləriŋ] *n.* enogu ; iroai. ~**less** *a.*
mushoku no. ~ **printing,** *n.* irozuri. **protective** ~ [prɔtéktiv
kʌ́lə] *n.* hogoshoku.
colo(u)ration [kàlɔréiʃən], **colo(u)ring** *n.* [kʌ́ləriŋ] shikisai
colorific [kɔ̀lərífik] *a.* iro o dasu ; hanayakana.
colossal [kəlɔ́səl] *a.* kyodaina (*huge*) ; zunukete ōkii.
Colosseum [kɔ̀lɔsí:əm] *n.* (*Anc. Rome*) dai enkei engijō.
colossus [kəlɔ́səs] *n.* (*pl.* **-si** [-sai], **-suses**) *Rhode* [roud]-tō
no *Apollo* no kyozō (*giantic statue*).
colt [koult] *n.* komma ; shoshinsha (*inexperienced*) ; (*C*~) Ko-
rutoshiki kenjū. ~**ish** [kóultiʃ] *a.* komma no yōna.
Columbia [kəlʌ́mbiə] *n.* Amerika, Minami Karoraina Shū no
columbine [kɔ́ləmbain] *n.* (*bot.*) odamaki.
column [kɔ́ləm] *n.* marui hashira ; tate no ran. ~**ar** [kɔlʌ́mnə]
a. enchū no. ~**ist** *n.* shimbun nado de tokubetsuran no tan-
tōsha. ⌐konsui (*stupor*).
coma [kóumə] (*pl.* **-mae** [-mi:]) *n.* suisei no mawari no seiun.
comatose [kóumətous] *a.* konsui shite iru.
comb [koum] *n.* kushi ; tosaka ; namigashira ; hachi no su. *v*
kushi de suku. namidatsu.
combat [kɔ́mbæt] *n. v.* kakutō (*fight*) (suru). ~**ant** [-ənt] *a.* tatakau. *n.* sentōin (*fighter*). ~**ive** *a.* tatakaizuki no. ⌐kagō.
combination [kɔ̀mbinéiʃən] *n.* ketsugō ; danketsu ; (*chem.*)
combine [kəmbáin] *v.* ketsugō (danketsu) suru. (*chem.*) kagō
suru. *n.* rengō kumiai ; karitori dakkoku suru kikai.
combustibility [kə̀mbəstibíliti] *n.* moeyasui seishitsu.
combustible [kəmbʌ́stibl] *a., n.* moeyasui (mono). kanenshō ;
moeyasui (mono).
combustion [kəmbʌ́stʃən] *n.* nenshō ; moeru koto

come [kám] *v.* **came, come; coming.** kuru; iku; naru. *come* !
sā !, kore ! ~ *about*, okoru; shōjiru. ~ *across*, deau. ~
away, dete iku; hanareru. ~ *back*, kaette kuru. ~ *down*, geraku
suru. ~ *down in the world*, ochibureru. ~ *down on* (or *upon*),
osoikakaru. ~ *in*, hairu; hayatte kuru. ~ *in for*, o seikyū
suru; o uketoru. ~ *off*, nukeru; kekka suru. ~ *on*, susumu.
~ *on* ! sā koi ! ~ *out*, dete kuru; (…ni) naru. ~ *out with*, o
ōyake ni suru. ~ *over*, watatte kuru; osou. ~ *round*, mawatte
kuru; kaifuku suru (*recover*). ~ *to*, shōki-zuku; todomaru.
~ *up*, noboru. ~ *up to*, ni tassuru. ~ *up with*, oitsuku. ~
upon, deau; osou.

comedian [kəmí:diən] *n.* kigeki haiyū; kigeki sakusha

comedienne [kəmè:dién:] *n.* kigeki joyū.

comedy [kómədi] *n.* kigeki (*cf. tragedy*).

comer [kámə] *n.* kuru hito.

comely [kámli] *a.* kaodachi no yoi (*handsome*); tekitōna. **come-
liness** [kámlinis] *n.* yōsu no yoi koto; fusawashisa.

comet [kómit] *n.* suisei.

comfit [kámfit] *n.* satōgashi; bombon.

comfort [kámfət] *n.*, *v.* nagusame(ru). anraku (ni suru). ~**able**
a. kimochi no ii. ~**ably** *ad.* anrakuni; nani fusoku naku.
~**er** *n.* nagusame o ataeru hito; (*Am.*) hanebuton, (*C-*) seirei
(Holy Spirit). ~**less** *a.* fujiyūna; wabishii.

comic(al) [kómik(əl)] *a.* kigeki no; odoketa. ~**ally** *ad.* kok-
coming [kámiŋ] *a.* kondo no; tsugi no. ⌊keini.

Cominform [kóminfɔ:m] *n.* Kyōsantō Jōhōkyoku (*information
bureau*). ⌈*national*) (1943n. haishi.)

Comintern [kómintə:n] *n.* Kokusai Kyōsantō (*Third Inter-
comity [kómiti] *n.* kokusai kan no yūkō-kankei.

comma [kómə] *n.* kuten (,); komma.

command [kəmǽnd] *v.* shiki suru (*lead*). *n.* meirei; shiki; shihai. ~ *of the sea*, seikaiken. ~**ing** [-iŋ] *a.* shiki suru; miharashi no yoi. ~**ment** [-mənt] *n.* meirei. *the Ten Commandments*, Mōze no Jukkai.

commandant [kòməndǽnt] *n.* shikikan.

commandeer [kòməndíə] *v.* chōhatsu suru (*press horses and
others to service*).

commander [kəmǽndə] *n.* shikikan ; kaigun-chūsa. **lieutenant** ~ (*Am.*) kaigun shōsa.

commander in chief [kəmǽndərintʃí:f] *n.* saikō shikikan ; shirei chōkan.

commemorate [kəméməreit] *v.* iwau (*celebrate*) ; kinen suru.

commemoration [kəmèməréiʃən] *n.* kinen (sai) ; shikuten : *in* ~ *of*, ...o kinen shite.

commemorative [kəmémərətiv] *a.* kinen no.

commence [kəméns] *v.* hajimeru (maru) ; gakui o ukeru. ~ **ment** *n.* kaishi (*start*) ; sotsugyō shiki ; gakui juyoshiki.

commend [kəménd] *v.* suisen suru ; homeru. ~**able** [-əbl] *a.* suisen dekiru ; rippana. ~**ation** [kɔ̀mendéiʃən] *n.* suisen ; shōsan. ~**atory** [kəméndətəri] *a.* suisen no ; shōsan no.

commensurable [kəménʃərəbl] *a.* tsuriai no toreta (*to*) ; dōitsu tan'i de hakareru.

commensurate [kəménʃərit] *a.* onaji ryō no ; tsuriai no toreta.

comment [kɔ́ment] *v.* chūkai suru ; hihyō suru. *n.* chūkai ; rompyō ; (jiken no) setsumei (o suru).

commentary [kɔ́məntəri] *n.* chūshaku ; rompyō (*remark*).

commentator [kɔ́məntèitə] *n.* chūshakusha ; (rajio no) jiji kai-setsusha.

commerce [kɔ́mə:s] *n.* tsūshō ; bōeki ; kōsai (*intercourse*) : **Chamber of** ~, shōgyō kaigisho.

commercial [kəmə́:ʃəl] *a.* tsūshō no ; bōeki no. ~ **agent** [-éidʒənt] *n.* bōeki jimukan. ~ **law** [-lɔ:] *n.* (*leg.*) shōhō. ~**ism** [-izm] *n.* eiri-shugi. ~**ly** *ad.* shōgyōjō ; tsūshōjō.

commingle [kəmíŋgl] *v.* kongō suru ; issho ni mazaru.

commiserate [kəmízəreit] *v.* awaremu (*pity*) ; fubingaru.

commiseration [kəmizəreiʃən] *n.* awaremi.

commissar [kɔ̀misá:] *n.* (Soren no) jimmin-iin.

commissariat [kɔ̀miséəriət] *n.* ryōshoku keiribu ; heitambu. **People's** ~ *n.* (Soren no) jimmin-iinkai.

commissary [kɔ́misəri] *n.* daihyōsha (*deputy*) ; iin ; heitan gakari shōkō. *Cb*~ **general** [-dʒénərəl] *n.* heitan sōkan. ~ **line**, heitansen.

commission [kəmíʃən] *n.* meirei ; inin (jō) ; nimmu (*charge*), iinkai, tesūryō. *in* (*out of*) ~, gen'eki no (taieki no). *v.* inin

suru ; nimmei suru (*appoint*). ~ **merchant,** nakagainin. ~
ed officer, shōkō ; shikan. ~**ed ship,** gen'eki kan. ~**er** *n.*
iin ; jimukan.

commit [kəmít] *v.* (warui koto o) suru ; yudaneru (*entrust*).
~ *oneself to,* ni mi o yudaneru ; genshitsu o ataeru (*pledge*).
~ *to memory,* anki suru. ~ *to prison,* rō ni ireru. ~**ment,**
~**tal** *n.* suikō ; futaku ; yakusoku ; kōsoku.

committee [kəmíti] *n.* iin, iinkai. ~ *of the whole house,* (gikai
no) zen'in (ryōin) iinkai.

commode [kəmóud] *n.* tansu ; shitsunai semmendai nado.

commodious [kəmóudiəs] *a.* hirokute benrina ; (sumiyoi). ~
ly *ad.* hirokute sumiyoku. ~**ness** *n.*

commodity [kəmóditi] *n.* nichiyōhin ; shōhin.

commodore [kómədə:] *n.* kaigun (daishō) ; kantai shireichō- ⌈kan.

common [kómən] *a.* futsū no (*ordinary*) ; kyōtsūna : ~ **Bench**
[-bentʃ] *n.* (*Brit.*) minji saibansho. ~ **law,** kanshū-hō. ~**pleas**
(*Brit.*) minji kōtō saibansho. (*Am.*) min-keiji kōtō-saibansho.
~ **Prayer,** kōshiki kitōbun. ~ **sense,** *n.* jōshiki ; kyōyūchi.
~**er** [kómənə] *n.* heimin. (*Brit.*) Kain giin ; tochi kyōyūsha.
~**ly** *ad.* futsūni. ~**ness** *n.* futsū. ~**place** [kómənpleis] *a.,*
n. arifureta ; futsū no (koto, mono). ~**s** [kómənz] *n.* (*pl.*)
heimin ; shomin kyōdōsho kudō. **House of** ~**s ; the** ~*, n.*
(*Brit.*) Kain.

commonalty [kómənəlti] *n.* ippan jimmin ; minshū (*common
people*). ⌈fukushi.

commonweal [kómóuʃən] *n.* kōan (*general welfare*) ; kōkyō no

commonwealth [kómenwèlθ] *n.* kokka ; kyōwakoku (*republic*).
the ~, Eikoku kyōwa seiji (1649~1660). *the* ~ *of Australia,*
Osutoraria Rempō.

commotion [kəmóuʃən] *n.* sōdō ; dōyō (*disturbance*).

communal [kómjunəl] *a.* jichitai no ; kōkyō no.

commune [kómju:n] *n.* (*Fr.*) saishō gyōseiku ; gun ; chihō jichitai. *v.* sōdan suru. (*Am*) Seisan (*Holy Communion*) o ukeru.

communicable [kəmjú:nikəbl] *a.* tsutaerareru ; densen suru.

communicant [kəmjú:nikənt] *n.* seisan o ukeru mono ; hōdō
ni kankeisuru mono ; hōdōsha.

communicate [kəmjú:nikeit] *v.* tsutaeru ; tsūshin suru ; kōtsū suru (*with*) ; seisan o ukeru.

communication [kəmjùnikéiʃən] *n.* dentatsu ; tsūshin ; kōtsū-(kikan) : *in* ～ *with*, to kōtsū (tsūshin) shite.   ⌈(*talkative*).

communicative [kəmjúnikətiv] *a.* uchitoketa ; oshaberi no

communion [kəmjú:njən] *n.* shitashii majiwari ; Seisan(shiki) ; shūkyōdantai. ～**ist** [kəmjú:niənist] *n.* seisan haijusha.

communique [kəmjú:nikei] *n.* (*Fr.*) komyūnike ; kōhō.

communism [kəmjú:nizm] *n.* kyōsan-shugi. ～**ist** [kəmjúnist] *n.* kyōsan-shugisha.

communistic [kɔ̀mju:nístik] *a.* kyōsanshugi no.

community [kəmjú:niti] *n.* shakai ; dantai. ～ **chest** shakai jigyō kyōdō bokin.

commutable [kəmjú:təbl] *a.* torikaerareru.

commutation [kɔ̀mjutéiʃən] *n.* kōkan (*exchange*). ～ **ticket** *n.* (*Am.*) kaisūken.

commutator [kɔ́mjuteitə] *n.* denryū tenkanki ; seiryūshi.

commute [kəmjú:t] *v.* torikaeru (*exchange*). (kane de) daishō suru ; denryū o kaeru ; teikiken de kayou.   ⌈kau hito.

commuter [kəmjú:tə] *n.* kōkansha ; kaisūken (teikiken) o tsu-

compact [kɔ́mpækt] *n.* keiyaku ; kompakuto. [kəmpǽkt] *v.* keiyaku suru.

compact [kəmpǽkt] *a.* chimitsuna ; kanketsuna (*concise*). *v.* chimitsuni suru ; kanketsuni suru. ～**ly** *ad.* gisshiri to ; kojimmarito.

companion [kəmpǽniən] *n.* nakama. ～ **hatch,** (*navy*) shōkō guchi-ōi. ～**able** [-nəbl] *a.* hitozuki no suru (*sociable*). ～**ladder** [-lǽdə] *n.* kampan shōkōguchi no hashigo. ～**ship** *n.* nakama taru koto. ～**way** *n.* kampan shōkōguchi.

company [kʌ́mpəni] *n.* nakama ; kaisha ; hohei chūtai (cf. *battalion*), fune no norikumi-in.

comparable [kɔ́mpéərəbl] *a.* hikaku dekiru ; kuraberareru. ～**bly** *ad.* hikaku kanōni ; dōtōni.

comparative [kəmpǽrətiv] *a.* hikaku no. *n.* (*gram.*) hikakukyū. ～**ly** *ad.* hikakutekini ; wariaini.

compare [kəmpéə] *v.* hikaku suru ; tatoeru (*liken*).

comparison [kəmpǽrisn] *n.* hikaku.

compartment [kəmpá:tmənt] *n.* shikitta heya.

compass [kámpəs] *n.* rashimban ; mawari (*circuit*) ; han'i, genkai. (*pl.*) kompasu ; *v.* keikaku suru (*plot*).

compassion [kəmpǽʃən] *n.* awaremi. ～ate [-it] *a.* awaremi-

compatibility [kəmpὰtibíliti] *n.* tekigō ; ryōritsu. ⌊bukai.

compatible [kəmpǽtibl] *a.* ai-ireru ; ryōritsu dekiru.

compatriot [kəmpǽtriət] *n.* dōkoku (dōkyō) jin.

compeer [kəmpíə] *n.* dōhai ; nakama.

compel [kəmpél] *v.* shiiru ; muri ni...saseru.

compendious [kəmpéndiəs] *n.* kanryakuna.

compendium [kəmpéndiəm] (*pl.* -dia or -ums) *n.* tekiyō ; yōryō (*summary*).

compensate [kǽmpenseit] *v.* tsugunau ; (*Am*) kyūryō o harau.

compensation [kὸmpenséiʃən] *n.* baishō ; umeawase ; (*Am.*)

compensator [kámpenseitə] *n.* baishō suru hito. ⌊kyūryō.

compensatory [kəmpénsətəri] *a.* tsugunai no ; baishō no.

compete [kəmpíːt] *v.* kyōsō suru (*with*) ; taikō suru.

competence [kɔ́mpətəns] *n.* tekitō ; tekinin ; sōtō no zaisan (shiryoku). ～cy [-si] =competence.

competent [kɔ́mpətənt] *a.* yūnōna ; shikaku no aru ; tekitōna. ～ly *ad.* tekitōni.

competition [kɔ̀mpetíʃən] *n.* kyōsō ; kyōgi (kai).

competitive [kəmpétitiv] *a.* kyōsō no. ～ exhibition *n.* kyō-

competitor [kəmpétitə] *n.* kyōsōsha. ⌊shinkai.

compilation [kɔ̀mpiléiʃən] *n.* henshū ; henshūbutsu.

compile [kəmpáil] *v.* henshū suru. ～r *n.* henshūsha.

complacence [kəmpléisens] *n.* manzoku ; anshin.

complacent [kəmpléisənt] *a.* manzoku shite iru ; anshin shita. ～ly *ad.* manzoku shite.

complain [kəmpléin] *v.* nageku ; fuhei (kujō) o iu ; kokuso suru. *n.* fuhei ; kokuso ; byōki (*ailment*). ～ant *n.* kujō o iu hito ; kokusonin (*plantiff*).

complaisance [kəmpléizəns] *n.* ingin (*courtesy*), jūjun.

complaisant [kəmpléizənt] *a.* teineina, jūjunna.

complement [kɔ́mpliment] *n.* oginai ; zensū (*full number*) ; zenryō (*full amount*) ; teiin. (*math.*) yokaku. (*gram.*) hogo. ～ary *a.* hoketsu no.

complete [kəmplíːt] *a.* jūbunna. *v.* kansei suru. ～ly *ad.* mattaku. ~ness *n.* jūbun ; kanzen.

completion [kəmplí:ʃən] *n.* kansei ; manryō.

complex [kómpleks] *a.* fukuzatsuna (*complicated*) ; gōsei no. ~ sentence ; (*gram.*) fukubun.

complexion [kəmplékʃən] *s.* kaoiro ; yōsu ; kyokumen.

complexity [kəmpléksiti] *n.* fukuzatsusa. ⌈...ni ōji.

compliance [kəmplíəns] *n.* fukujū : *in* ~ *with*, ...ni shitagai,

compliant [kəmpláiənt] *a.* ōzuru ; shitagau ; jūjunna (*yielding*).

complicacy [kómplikəsi] *n.* fukuzatsu ; sakuso.

complicate [kómplikeit] *v.* fukuzatsu ni suru ; sakusō saseru. ~d [-tid] *a.* fukuzatsuna. ⌈te iru koto.

complication [kòmplikéiʃən] *n.* sakusō ; funkyū ; kongarakat-

complicity [kəmplísiti] *n.* kyōbō ; akuji o issho ni suru koto.

compliment [kómpliment] *n. v.* oseji (o iu) ; sanji (o teisuru). aisatsu (*greeting*) (o suru). ~ary [kòmpliméntəri] *a.* aisatsu no ; shukuga no. ~ letter, gajō. ~ ticket, shōtai-ken.

comply [kəmplái] *v.* ōzuru ; shitagau (*with*).

component [kəmpóunənt] *n.* seibun. *a.* gōsei suru seibun no.

comport [kəmpó:t] *v.* itchi suru (*agree with*). furumau (*behave*) ; mi o shosuru (*comport oneself*).

compose [kəmpóuz] *v.* kumitateru ; (shi ya, bun o) tsukuru katsuji o kumu. ~d *a.* ochitsuita. ~dly *ad.* ochitsuite. taizen to.

composite [kəmpózit] *a.* kongō no ; ~ *carriage* kongōsha (o-naji ressha ni chigatta tōkyū ie aru). *n.* gōseibutsu.

composition [kòmpəzíʃən] *n.* kumitate ; sakubun ; sakkyoku.

compositor [kəmpózitə] *n.* shokujikō ; shokujiki.

compost [kómpoust] *n.* taihi ; shikkui.

composure [kəmpóuʒə] *n.* ochitsuki ; chinchaku (*calmness*).

compote [kómpout] *n.* kudamono no satō-ni.

compound [kómpaund] *n.* kongōbutsu ; kagōbutsu ; (*gram.*) fukugō-gō. [kəmpáund] *a.* gōsei no. ~ interest, *n.* fukuri. ~ ratio *n.* (*math.*) fukuhi.

comprehend [kòmprehénd] *v.* rikai suru (*understand*) ; fukumu (*include*).

comprehensible [kòmprəhénsibl] *a.* wakariyasui. ~bly *ad.* wakariyasuku.

comprehension [kɔ̀mprehénʃən] *n.* rikai ; rikairyoku.

comprehensive [kɔ̀mprihénsiv] *a.* rikairyoku aru ; hiroi imi no. ~**ly** *ad.* hiroku.

compress [kəmprés] *v.* oshitsukeru ; assaku suru. ~**ible** [-présibl] *a.* asshuku dekiru. ~**ion** *n.* asshiku. ~**ive** *a.* asshiku suru.

comprise, comprize [kəmpráiz] *v.* fukumu ; …kara naru (*consist of*).

compromise [kómprəmaiz] *n.* dakyō. *v.* dakyō suru. *make* ~ *with*, to dakyō suru.　　　　　　　　　　　　　⌈sagakari.

comptroller, controller [kəntróulə], *n.* kaikei kensa kan ; kan-

compulsion [kəmpálʃən] *n.* kyōsei ; muri-jii.

compulsory [kəmpálsəri] *a.* kyōseitekina (*compelling*). ~ **education** [èdjukéiʃən] *n.* gimu kyōiku. ~**service system** *n.* chōhei seido. ~**ily** *ad.* kyōseitekini.

compunction [kəmpáŋkʃən] *n.* kōkai (*regret*).

computation [kɔ̀mpjutéiʃən] *n.* keisan.

compute [kəmpjú:t] *v.* keisan suru.

comrade [kámrid] *n.* nakama ; tomo (*companion*). ~**ship** [ʃip] *n.* nakama no yoshimi ; yūjō.

con [kɔn] *r.* (1) anshō suru. (2) fune no hōkō o sashizu suru. *n.* hantai (*cf. pro.*).

concatenate [kɔnkǽtineit] *v.* renkei (renzoku) suru. ~**ation** [kɔnkætinéiʃən] *n.* renzoku.

concave [kɔnkéiv] *a.* ōmen no ; nakabiku no (*cf. convex*).

concavity [kɔnkǽviti] *n.* nakabiku ; ōmen ; hekomi.

conceal [kənsi:l] *v.* kakusu. ~**ment** *n.* intoku ; kakurebasho.

concede [kənsi:d] *v.* jōho suru (*yield*) ; mitomeru (*admit*).

conceit [kənsí:t] *n.* unubore ; kimagure (*whim*). ~**ed** unubore-te iru ; namaikina.

conceivable [kənsí:vəbl] *a.* sōzō no dekiru. *every* ~ *means*, kangaerareru kagiri no shudan.　　　　　　　　　⌈itsuku.

conceive [kənsí:v] *v.* ninshin suru ; sōzō suru (*imagine*) ; omo-

concentrate [kónsentreit] *v.* shūchū (shūketsu) suru (saseru) ; sennen suru : ~**d** [-id] *a.* shūchū shita.

concentration [kónsentréiʃən] *n.* shūchū ; senshin. ~ **camp,** (horyo nado no) shūyōjo.

concentric [kənséntrik] *a.* onaji ten o chūshin to suru ; shū-
concept [kónsept] *n.* gainen. ⌐chū shita.

conception [kənsépʃən] *n.* ninshin ; gainen ; kangae : *have no*
~ *of*, ...o ikkō shiranai.

concern [kənsə́:n] *n.* kankei ; rigai kankei (*interest*). *v.* kakawaru ; kankei suru : ~ *oneself*, kankei suru. *so far as it* ~*s*,
sore ga kansuru kagiri dewa. ~**ing** *prep.* ...ni kanshite. ~
ment *n.* kankei (jikō).

concerned [kənsə́:nd] *a.* shimpaina ; kankei no aru : *the au-
thorities* ~, kankei tōkyoku. *the* ~, rigai kankeinin. ~**ly**
[-nidli] *ad.* shimpai shite.

concert [kónsə:t] *n.* ensōkai : sōdō : itchi. [kənsə́:t] *v.* kyōtei
concertina [kənsə:tínə] *n.* tefūkin. ⌐suru ; kufū suru.

concerto [kontʃɔ́:tou/-tʃɛə́-] *n.* kyōsōkyoku ; koncheruto.

concession [kənséʃən] *n.* jōho ; kyoka ; kyoryūchi.

conch [kɔntʃ] *n.* kai ; horagai.

conchology [kɔŋkɔ́lədʒi] *n.* kairuigaku.

conciliate [kənsílieit] *v.* nadameru ; chōtei suru (*reconcile*).

conciliation [kənsìliéiʃən] *n.* nadameru koto ; wakai.

conciliator [kənsílieitə] *n.* nadameru mono. ~**y** [-təri] *a.* nadameru yōna.

concise [kənsáiz] *a.* kanketsuna (*cf. diffuse*). ~**ly** *ad.* kanketsu
ni. ~**ness** *n.* kanketsu.

conclave [kónkleiv] *n.* himitsu-kaigi ; mitsugi shitsu.

conclude [kənklú:d] *v.* kettei suru ; suidan suru (*infer*). owaru.

conclusion [kənklú:ʒən] *n.* ketsumatsu ; ketsuron.

conclusive [kənklú:siv] *a.* ketteitekina ; saigotekina (*final*). ~
ly *ad.* ketteitekini. ~**ness** *n.* saigoteki kettei.

concoct [kənkɔ́kt] *v.* chōsei suru ; iroiro mazete tsukuri
concoction [kənkɔ́kʃən] *n.* chōsei ; chōgōbutsu. ⌐tateru.

concomitant [kənkɔ́mitənt] *a.* fuzui suru. *n.* fukusambutsu.

concord [kónkɔ:d] *n.* wagō ; itchi (*agreement*) ; (*mus.*) kyōwa on
(*cf. discord*).

concordance [kənkɔ́:dəns] *n.* itchi (*agreement*) ; yōgo sakuin.

concordant [kənkɔ́:dənt] *a.* itchi (wagō) suru.

concordat [kənkɔ́:dæt] *n.* keiyaku.

concourse [kónkɔ:s] *n.* shūgō ; gunshū (*crowd*) ; kaigōsha.

concrete [kɔ́ŋkriːt] *a.* gutaitekina (*cf. abstract*). *n.* konkuriito. *in the* ~, gutaitekini. ~**noun** [-naun] *n.* (*gram.*) gutai meishi. ~ **number** [-námbə] *n.* meisū. *v.* [kɔnkríːt] giketsu saseru ; katamaru ; konkuriito de katameru. **steel** ~, tekkin konkuriito. ~**ly** *ad.* gutaitekini.

concretion [kɔnkríːʃən] *n.* gyōketsu ; katamari.

concubine [kɔ́ŋkjubain] *n.* mekake.   ┌*al disire*).

concupiscence [kɔŋkjúːpisns] *n.* tsuyoi yokubō ; jōyoku (*sexu-*

concur [kɔnkə́ː] *v.* dōji ni okoru ; fugō suru ; dōi suru. ~**rence** [kɔnkárəns] *n.* dōji ni okoru koto ; kyōryoku. ~**rent** [-rənt] *a.* dōji no ; kyōryoku suru. ~**rently** [-rəntli] *ad.* issho-ni natte.

concussion [kɔnkáʃən] *n.* shindō ; shōgeki (*shock*).

condemn [kəndém] *v.* tsumi o senkoku suru (*sentence*) ; toga-meru. bosshū o iiwatasu. ~**ed** *a.* yūzai to senkoku sareta. ~**ation** [kɔndemnéiʃən] *n.* tsumi no senkoku. ~**atory** [-ətəri] *a.* no senkoku no.

condensable [kəndénsəbl] *a.* asshuku dekiru ; tanshuku shi-

condensation [kɔ̀ndenséiʃən] *n.* tanshiku ; gyōshiku.

condense [kəndéns] *v.* gyōshiku (tanshiku) suru ; nōkō ni suru. ~**d** [-t] *a.* nōshiku sareta (shita) ; tanshiku shita. ~ **milk** [kəndénstmilk] *n.* rennyū. ~**r** [-ə] *n.* gyōshikuki ; chiku-denki ; shūkōrenzu.

condescend [kɔ̀ndisénd] *v.* meshita ni teineini suru. ~**ing** *a.* kensonna. ~**ingly** *ad.* teineini.

condescension [kɔ̀ndisénʃən] *n.* teinei (meshita ni).

condign [kəndáin] *a.* sōtō no.

condiment [kɔ́ndimənt] *n.* chōmiryō ; yakumi.

condition [kəndíʃən] *n.* jōken. (*pl.*) jōkyō. (*Am.*) saishiken. *v.* jōken o tsukuru ; kitei suru. ~**al** [-əl] *a.* jōken tsuki no. ~**ally** [-əli] *ad.* jōken tsuki de.

condolatory [kəndóulətəri] *a.* mimai no ; nagusame no.

condole [kəndóul] *v.* kuyami o iu ; imon suru.

condolence [kɔ́ndouləns] *n.* chōmon ; kuyami.

condone [kəndóun] *v.* yurusu ; ōme ni miru (*overlook*).

condor [kɔ́ndə] *n.* kondoru ; hagewashi.

conduce [kəndjúːs] *v.* tame ni naru ; kōken suru (*to*). **con-**

ducive [-siv] *a.* tame ni naru. ⌈nai suru.
conduct [kɔ́ndəkt] *n.* okonai ; sashizu. [-dʌ́kt] *v.* okonau ; an-
conduction [kəndʌ́kʃən] *n.* michibiki. (*phys.*) dendō.
conductive [kəndʌ́ktiv] *n.* dendōsei no.
conductivity [kɔ̀ndʌktíviti] *n.* dendōsei (ryoku). ⌈tai.
conductor [kəndʌ́ktə] *n.* annaisha ; shikisha ; shashō ; dendō-
conduit [kɔ́ndjuit] *n.* mizo (*channel*) ; suikan (*-pipe*).
cone [koun] *n.* matsu-kasa (*pine-*) ; ensui-kei (no mono).
confabulate [kənfǽbjuleit] *v.* danshō suru (*with*). ⌊(*-shape*).
confection [kənfékʃən] *n.* kashi. ~**er** *n.* kashiya. ~**ery** *n.*
kashi seizōsho.
confederacy [kənfédərəsi] *n.* dōmei ; rempō (*united countries*) ;
kyōbō (*conspiracy*)
confederate [kənfédəreit] *v.* dōmei (rengō) suru (saseru). *a.*
dōmei shita. *n.* dōmeikoku ; kyōbōshita mono.
confederation [kənfèdəréiʃən] *n.* dōmei ; dōmei-koku.
confer [kənfə́:] *v.* ataeru ; sōdan suru. ~**ence** [kɔ́nf(ə)rəns] *n.*
sōdan ; (*Methodist* de wa) nenkai.
confess [kənfés] *v.* hakujō suru. ~**ed** [-t] *a.* jihaku shita. ~
edly [-idli] *ad* meihakuni. ~**ion** [-ʃən] *n.* jihaku ; hakujō. ~
ional [-ənəl] *n.* zange suru heya. ~**or** [-ə] *n.* confess suru hito.
confettio [kənfétiou] *n.* (*pl.* -**ti**) kompeitō ; shikishi kamigire
confidant [kɔ́nfidənt] *n.* shin'yū. ⌊(*-paper*).
confide [kənfáid] *v.* uchiakete hanasu (*tell one's sceret*).
confidence [kɔ́nfidəns] *n.* shinrai ; himitsu (*secret*). ~ **game**
(*or trick*), pombiki. ~**man** *n.* ikasamashi. ⌊motte.
confident [kɔ́nfidənt] *a.* kakushin shiteiru. ~**ly** *ad.* jishin o
confidential [kɔ̀nfidénʃ(ə)l] *a.* fukushin no ; anshin shite *confide* dekiru. ~**ly** *ad.* hisokani (*secretly*).
configuration [kənfìgjuréiʃən] *n.* gaikei ; rinkaku.
confine [kɔ́nfain] *n.* sakai ; kyōkai. [kənfáin] *v.* seigen suru ;
kankin suru : *be* ~**d**, hikikomotte iru. ~**ment** [-mənt] *n*
kankin.
confirm [kənfə́:m] *v.* tashikani suru ; nen o osu. ~**ed** *a.* katai ; gankona. ⌈shin-rei.
confirmation [kɔ̀nfəméiʃən] *n.* tashikame ; kakunin ; (*rel.*) ken-
confirmative [kənfə́:mətiv] *a.* tashikameru ; kakuteiteki no.

confirmatory [kənfɔ́:mətəri], **confirmative** [kənfɔ́:mətiv] *a.* ka-kunin suru ; tashikameru.

confiscate [kɔ́nfiskeit] *v.* bosshū suru ; chōhatsu suru.

confiscation [kɔ̀nfiskéiʃən] *n.* bosshū ; chōhatsu.

confiscatory [kənfískətəri] *a.* bosshū suru.

conflagration [kɔ̀nfləgréiʃən] *n.* taika ; ōkaji.

conflict [kɔ́nflikt] *n.* shōtotsu (*collision*). *v.* [kənflíkt] shōtotsu suru. ~**ing** [kənflíktiŋ] *a.* ai-arasou ; ai-ireru.

confluence [kɔ́nfluəns] *n.* gōryū ; gōryū-chi (~*place*) ; shūgō.

confluent [kɔ́nfluənt] *a.* gōryū suru.

conform [kənfɔ́:m] *v.* itchi saseru (suru) ; shitagau (-waseru). ~**able** [-əbl] *a.* itchi shite iru. ~**ably** [-əbli] *ad.* itchi shite. ~**ist** *n.* Eikoku kokkyō kaiin. ~**ation** [-éiʃən] *n.* kōzō ; hai-chi. ~**ity** [-iti] *n.* itchi ; onaji katachi.

confound [kənfáund] *v.* kondō suru. *be* ~**ed**, tōwaku suru. ~**ed** [-id] *a.* imaimashii. ~**edly** *ad.* imaimashiku.

confront [kənfrʌ́nt] *v.* chokumen saseru ; taikō suru (*face bravely*). ~**ation** [-éiʃən] *n.* chokumen ; taikō.

Confucian [kənfjú:ʃən] *n* Kōshi no. ~**ism** *n.* Jukyō.

confuse [kənfjú:z] *v.* konran saseru ; rōbai saseru (*disconcert*). ~**dly** *ad.* [-idli] ranzatsuni ; urotaete. ~**ing** *a.* magirawashii. ~**ion** [-zən] *n.* konzatsu ; rōbai.

confutation [kɔnfju(:)téiʃən] *n.* rombaku.

confute [kənfjú:t] *v.* yarikomeru ; rombaku suru.

congeal [kəndʒí:l] *v.* kōru ; gyōketsu suru (saseru).

congenial [kəndʒí:njəl] *a.* kigokoro no atta (*agreeable*).

congeniality [kəndʒi:niǽliti] *n.* shumi ya kigokoro ga shik-kuri au koto.

congenital [kəndʒénit(ə)l] *a.* umaretsuki no (*inborn*).

conger [kɔ́ŋgə], **conger eel** [kɔ́ŋgəri:l] *n.* (*fish*) anago.

congest [kəndʒést] *v.* (hijōni takusan) atsumaru. ~**ed** [-tid] *a.* kajōjinkō no (*too crowded*) ; jūketsu shita (*bloodshot*).

congestion [kəndʒéstʃən] *n.* ikkasho ni ijōni (chi nado ga) atsumaru koto.

conglomerate [kəngló̃mərit] *a.* misshū shita. *n.* shūdan. [kəŋgló̃məreit] *v.* marume katameru.

conglomeration [kəŋglòməréiʃən] *n.* katamari. shūdan.

congratulate [kəngrǽtjuleit] v. iwau ; shiku suru. ~ *oneself on* o yorokobu. ~**tion** [-ʃən] n. iwai.

congratulatory [kəngrǽtjulətəri] a. oiwai no.

congregate [kɔ́ŋgrigeit] v. atsumeru ; atsumaru. ~**ion** [kɔ̀ŋ-grigéiʃən] n. shūkai.

Congregational [kɔ̀ŋgrigéiʃ(ə)nəl] a. Kumiai Kyōkai no ; (c ~) kaishū no. ~**ism** n. (*relig.*) Kumiai Kyōkai shugi. ~**ist** n. Kumiai Kyōkai kai-in.

congress [kɔ́ŋgres] n. kaigi ; iin-kai. (C~) (*Am.*) Kokkai.

congressional [kəngréʃ(ə)nəl] a. kaigi no ; (C~) (*Am.*) Kokkai Congressman [kɔ́ŋgresmən] n. (*Am.*) kokkai giin. └no.

congruence [kɔ́ŋgruəns], **congruity** [kɔŋgrú(:)iti] n. tekigō ; itchi. ┌shite.

congruous [kɔ́ŋgruəs] a. tekigō suru ; itchi suru. ~**ly** ad. itchi

conic(al) [kɔ́nik(əl)] a. ensui-kei no. ~**ally** ad. ensui-jō ni.

conifer [kóunifə] n. (*bot.*) shin'yō-ju (matsu no yōna).

coniferous [ko(u)nífərəs] a. kyūka ga naru. (kuri, matsu, **conjectural** [kəndʒéktʃ(ə)rəl] a. suisoku no. └nado)

conjecture [kəndʒéktʃə] n., v. suisoku (suru).

conjoin [kəndʒɔ́in] v. ketsugō suru.

conjoint [kɔ́ndʒɔint] a. ketsugō shita. ~**ly** ad. ketsugō shite.

conjugal [kɔ́ndʒug(ə)l] a. kon'in no ; fūfu no (*connubial*).

conjugate [kɔ́ndʒugeit] v. (dōshi (*verb*) o) katsuyō suru. ~**tion** [kɔ̀ndʒəgéiʃən] n. (dōshi no) katsuyō.

conjunction [kəndʒʌ́ŋkʃən] n. ketsugō ; (*gram.*) setsuzokushi.

conjunctive [kəndʒʌ́ŋ(k)tiv] a. renketsu suru. n. (*gram.*) setsu-zokuhō. ~**ly** ad. renketsu shite.

conjuncture [kəndʒʌ́ŋ(k)tʃə] n. kotogara no musubitsuki ; ko-togara no jōtai.

conjuration [kɔ̀ndʒu(ə)réiʃən] n. kigan (*prayer*) ; jumon (*spell*) ; mahō (*magic*) no kotoba.

conjure [kʌ́ndʒə] v. mahō (*charm*) de yobu ; mahō o tsukau ; tejina o tsukau (*juggle*) ; ~ *up*, tsukuri dasu (*make*). [kəndʒúə] v. kongan suru (*entreat*).

conjuring [kʌ́ndʒəriŋ] n. tejina. ┌gler).

conjurer [kʌ́ndʒərə] n. mahō-tsukai (*magician*) ; tejina-shi (*jug-*

connate [kɔ́neit] a. umaretsuki no ; issho ni umareta.

connect [kənékt] *v.* tsunagu ; tsunagaru ; renraku suru. ~**ed** *a.* tsunagatte (iru). ~**edly** *ad.* renraku shite.

connection, connexion [kənékʃən] *n.* musubitsuki ; kankei.

connective [kənéktiv] *a.* renzoku suru ; (*gram.*) renketsushi.

conning tower [kóniŋ táuə] (gunkan no) shireitō.

connivance [kənáivəns] *n.* mokkyo (*tacit consent* ; *conniving*).

connive [kənáiv] *v.* minogasu ; minai furi o suru (*pretend not to see*).

connoisseur [kɔnisə́:] *n.* kanteika ; aru koto ni kuwashii hito.

connotation [kɔno(u)téiʃən] *n.* (*log.*) naihō ganchiku (*intension*) ; (*being full of significance*).

connote [kɔnóut] ganchiku o motsu (*suggestive*).

connubial [kɔnjú:biəl] *a.* kon'in no ; fūfu no.

conquer [kóŋkə] *v.* uchikatsu ; seifuku suru. ~**ed** *a.* maketa (*beaten*). ~**or** *n.* seifukusha.

conquest [kóŋkwest] *n.* shōri ; seifuku.

consanguineous [kɔ̀nsæŋgwíniəs] *a.* ketsuzoku no.

consanguinity [kɔ̀nsæŋgwíniti] *n.* ketsuzoku ; dōzoku.

conscience [kónʃ(ə)ns] *n.* ryōshin.

conscientious [kɔnʃiénʃəs] *a.* ryōshintekina ; seijitsuna. ~**ly** *ad.* ryōshintekini ; seijitsuni. ~**ness** *n.* ryōshintekina koto.

conscious [kónʃəs] *a.* jikaku shite iru ; ishiki shita. ~**ly** *ad.* jikaku shite. ~**ness** *n.* jikaku.

conscript [kónskript] *a.* heitai ni tōroku sareta ; chōhei no. *n.* chōhei. *v.* chōhei ni toru.

conscription [kənskrípʃən] *n.* chōhei ; heishi o tsunoru koto.

consecrate [kónsikreit] *v.* hōnō suru ; kiyomeru (*hallow*). ~**d** [-id] *a.* kiyoi ; shinseina. ⎡o naku suru koto.

consecration [kɔ̀nsikréiʃən] *n.* kami ni sasageru koto ; kegare

consecutive [kənsékjutiv] *a.* hikitsuzuku. *for three* ~ *weeks*, renzoku san-shūkan. ~**ly** *ad.*

consensus [kənsénsəs] *n.* itchi ; dōi.

consent [kənsént] *v.*, *n.* dōi, itchi (suru).

consequence [kónsikwəns] *n.* kekka. *in* ~ *of*, ...no tame ni.

consequent [kónsikwent] *a.* kekka to shite (*on, upon*). *n.* kekka. ~**ly** *ad.* soreyue ni.

consequential [kɔ̀nsikwénʃ(ə)l] *a.* kekka to shite. ~**ly** [-li] *ad.*

shitagatte (*as a result of*).

conservation [kɔnsə(:)véiʃən] *n.* hozon.

conservatism [kɔnsɔ́:vɔtizm] *n.* hoshushugi (*-ism*).

conservative [kɔnsɔ́:vɔtiv] *a.* hoshu no ; (*C-*) hoshutō no. *n.* hoshushugisha ; (*C-*) hoshutō-in.

conservatoire [kɔnsɔ́:vɔtwa:] *n.* (*Fr.*) ongaku gakkō.

conservatory [kɔnsɔ́:vɔtəri] *n.* onshitsu (*greenhouse*) ; ongaku gakkō.

conserve [kɔnsɔ́:v] *v.* hozon suru ; satōzuke ni suru. ⌊gakkō.

consider [kɔnsídə] *v.* jukkō suru ; omonzuru (*pay regard to*).

considerable [kɔnsídərəbl] *a.* jūyōna ; yohodo no ; mushi deki-nai. ~**bly** *ad.* yohodo ; sōtō ni.

considerate [kɔnsídərit] *a.* omoiyari aru ; shinchōna.

consideration [kɔnsidəréiʃən] *n.* jukuryo ; omoiyari ; sonkei.

considering [kɔnsídəriŋ] *prep.* ...o omoeba ; ...ni shite wa.

consign [kɔnsáin] *v.* watasu ; itaku suru (*entrust*). ~**ment** [-mənt] *n.* itaku. ⌈*of goods*).

consignee [kɔns(a)iní:] *n.* takusareta mono ; niukenin (*receiver*

consigner, ~**or** [kɔnsáinə] *n.* itakusha (*truster*) ; nizumi-nushi.

consist [kɔnsíst] *v.* naritatsu (*of*) ; ni aru (*in*) ; itchi suru (*with*). ~**ence,** ~**ency** *n.* kenjitsu (*firmness*). ~**ent** *a.* kenjitsuna. ~**ently** *ad.* kenjitsuni.

consolation [kɔnsəléiʃən] *n.* nagusame.

consolatory [kɔnsɔ́lətəri] *a.* nagusame no.

console [kɔnsóul] *v.* nagusameru ; itawaru. [kɔ́nsoul] *n.* (oru-gan, rajio, terebi, nodo no) dai ; sotobako ; irebako.

consolidate [kɔnsɔ́lideit] *v.* kyōkoni suru ; katamaru.

consolidation [kɔnsɔlidéiʃən] *n.* jigatame ; kyōka. ~ **funds** seiri kikin.

consols [kɔ́nsoul] *n.* (*pl.*) Eikoku seiri kōsai (*3 per cent bonds*).

consommé [kɔsɔ́mei] *n.* (*Fr.*) konsomé (sumashi sūpu).

consonance [kɔ́ns(ə)nəns], **consonancy** [kɔ́ns(ə)nənsi] *n.* (*mus.*) waon. chōwa (*harmony*). ⌈shiin (shion).

consonant [kɔ́ns(ə)nənt] *a.* itchi suru ; chōwa suru. *n.* (*phon.*)

consort [kɔ́nsɔ:t] *n.* haigūsha ; ryōkan (onaji kantai no). *v.* [kɔnsɔ́:t] tsuresou (-sowasu). *prince* ~, *queen* no haigūsha. *queen,* ~ kōgō ; ōhi.

conspicuous [kɔnspíkjuəs] *a.* medatsu ; chomeina. ~**ly** *ad.*

medatte. ~ness [-nis] chomei.

conspiracy [kənspírəsi] n. kyōbō ; imbō ; hangyaku.

conspirator [kənspírətə] n. kyōbōsha ; muhonnin.

conspire [kənspáiə] v. kyōbō suru ; muhon o okosu.

constable [kʌ́nstəbl] n. junsa. ⌈(tai).

constabulary [kənstǽbjuləri] a. keikan (junsa) no. n. keisatsu

constancy [kʌ́nstənsi] n. fuhen ; seijitsu.

constant [kʌ́nstənt] a. fuhenna ; taema nai. ~ly ad. fuhenni.

constellation [kɔ̀nstəléiʃən] n. (astr.) seiza ; meishi no shūgō.

consternation [kɔ̀nstə(:)néiʃən] n. odoroki ; urotae.

constipate [kʌ́nstipeit] v. bempi saseru. ~ation [kɔ̀nstipéiʃən] n. bempi.

constituency [kənstítjuənsi] n. senkyomin ; senkyoku.

constituent [kənstítjuənt] a. soshiki suru ; senkyoken no aru n. senkyonin ; yōso (element).

constitute [kʌ́nstitjuːt] v. kōsei suru ; seitei suru ; kimeru.

constitution [kɔ̀nstitjúːʃən] n. kempō ; soshiki ; taishitsu. ~al [əl] a. umaretsuki no ; kempōno : ~ government [-əl gʌ́vəːnmənt] n. rikken seitai. ~alism ['-əlizəm] n. rikken seiji. ~ally ad. umaretsuki ; kempō de.

constrain [kənstréin] v. shiiru ; sokubaku suru (compel). ~ed [-d] a. murina ; osaetsuketa. ~edly [-idli] ad. murini.

constraint [kənstréint] n. kyōsei ; kōsoku.

constrict [kənstríkt] v. asshiku suru.

constriction [kənstríkʃən] n. asshiku.

construct [kənstrʌ́kt] v. kumitateru ; tsukuritateru. ~ion [kənstrʌ́kʃən] n. kensetsu ; (gram.) bun no kumitate. ~ive [-iv] a. kensetsuteki no. ~ively [-ivli] ad. kensetsutekini.

construe [kʌ́nstruː] v. kaishaku suru ; ...to iu imi ni yomu.

consul [kʌ́ns(ə)l] n. (Anc. Rome) shiseikan ; ryōji (consul). ~general n. sō-ryōji. ~ship [-ʃip] n. ryōji no shoku.

consular [kʌ́nsjulə] a. ryōji no.

consulate [kʌ́nsjulit] n. ryōji-shoku ; ryōji-kan. ~general n sōryōji no shoku ; sōryōjikan.

consult [kənsʌ́lt] v. sōdan suru ; shiraberu ; ~ a dictionary, jisho o hiku. ~ a doctor, (isha ni) kakaru.

consultation [kənsəltéiʃən] n. sōdan.

consume [kənsjúːm] *v.* kui (nomi)tsukusu ; shidaini naku-naru. ~**dly** [-idli] *ad.* hijōni. ~**r** *n.* shōhisha.

consummate [kənsʌ́meit] *v.* kansei suru. [-mit] *a.* kanzenna. ~**ly** *ad.* kanzenni.

consummation [kənsʌméiʃən] *n.* kambi ; kansei.

consumption [kənsʌ́m(p)ʃən] *n.* shōhi ; shōmō (*waste*) ; hai-kekkaku.

consumptive [kənsʌ́m(p)tiv] *a.* shōhi no ; haibyō no.

contact [kóntækt] *n.* sesshoku. *v.* sesshoku suru (sareru). ~ **lens** *n.* hamekomi megane.

contagion [kəntéidʒən] *n.* densen ; densen-byō (*disease*).

contagious [kəntéidʒəs] *a.* densensei no.

contain [kəntéin] *v.* fukumu ; ireru ; yokusei suru (*sustain*). ~**er** [-ə] *n.* iremono.

contaminate [kəntǽmineit] *v.* yogosu (*defile*).

contamination [kəntæminéiʃən] *n.* kitanaku suru koto.

contemn [kəntém] *v.* anadoru ; iyashimu.

contemplate [kóntempleit] *v.* jukushi suru ; kangaeru ; moku-romu (*plan*).

contemplation [kóntempléiʃən] *n.* meisō ; jukkō (*consideration*) ; jukushi (*gazing at*).

contemplative [kóntempleitiv/-témplət-] *a.* chinshi suru.

contemporaneous [kəntèmpəréinjəs] *a.* dō-jidai no.

contemporary [kəntémp(ə)rəri] *a.* dō-jidai no. *n.* onaji-jidai.

contempt [kəntém(p)t] *n.* keibetsu. ~**ible** *a.* asamashii. ~**uous** [kəntém(p)tjuəs] *a.* keibetsu subeki. ~**ly** ['-tjuəsli] *ad.*

contend [kənténd] *v.* arasou ; ronsō suru (*argue*). Lōheini.

content [kəntént] *v.* manzoku saseru. *n.* manzoku. *a.* manzoku shita ; amanjite iru. ~**edly** [-idli] *ad.* manzoku shite ; aman-jite. ~ **edness**, ~**ment** *n.* manzoku.

content [kəntént] *n.* yōseki ; yōryō ; (*pl.*) [kóntents] naiyō ; mokuji (*table of contents*).

contention [kənténʃən] *n.* arasoi ; ronsō.

contentious [kənténʃəs] *a.* kenkazuki no ; gironzuki no.

conterminous [kəntə́ːminəs] *a.* rinsetsu suru ; onaji kyōkai no.

contest [kóntest] *n.* arasoi ; shōbu (*victory or defeat*) ; sōron (*debate*). *v.* [kəntést] arasou ; ronsō suru (*dispute*). ~**ant** [kəntéstənt] *n.* kyōsōsha.

context [kɔ́ntekst] *n.* (*gram.*) bummyaku ; ato saki no bun no

contiguity [kɔ̀ntigjúiti] *n.* sesshoku ; sekkin. ⌊tsunagari.

contiguous [kɔntígjuəs] *a.* sesshoku suru ; tsuzuku (*to*). ~**ly**
ad. sesshoku shite.

continence [kɔ́ntinəns] *n.* jisei (*self-restraint*).

continent [kɔ́ntinənt] *a.* jisei suru. *n.* tairiku ; (*the* C-) Oshū
Tairiku. ~**ly** *ad.* jisei shite.

continental [kɔntinént(ə)l] *a.* tairiku no. ⌈koto.

contingency [kɔntín(d)ʒənsi] *n.* gūzen no koto ; man'ichi no

contingent [kɔntíndʒənt] *a.* gūzen no ; man'ichi no (*emergent*).
n. warimae (*quota*) ; bunkentai (*quota of troops*).

continual [kɔntínjuəl] *a.* taenai ; himpanna. ~**ly** *ad.* himpan-
ni ; taezu.

continuance [kɔntínjuəns] *n.* nagaku tsuzuku koto.

continuation [kɔntinjuéiʃən] *n.* keizoku (ippen yamete mata
tsuzuku).

continue [kɔntínju:] *v.* tsuzuku ; todomaru (*remain*) ; tsuzukeru.

continued [kɔntínju:d] *a.* tsuzuite iru, tsuzuki no.

continuity [kɔntinjú(:)iti] *n.* renzoku ; (eiga, radio no) daihon.

continuous [kɔntínjuəs] *a.* renzoku shita ; togirenai. ~**ly** *ad.*
taezu tsuzuite.

contort [kɔntɔ́:t] *v.* nejiru ; mageru. ~**ed** [-id] *a.* nejireta.

contortion [kɔntɔ́:ʃən] *n.* nejiru koto ; nejire ; yugami. ~**ist**
n. te, ashi o jiyūni mageru koto. ⌈sen.

contour [kɔ́ntuə] *n.* gaikei ; rinkaku. ~ line, (chizujō no) tōkō

contraband [kɔ́ntrəbænd] *a.* kinshi no. *n.* yunyū-kinseihin. ~
of war, senji kinseihin.

contraception [kɔ̀ntrəsépʃən] *n.* hinin (*birth control*).

contract [kɔ́ntrækt] *n.* keiyaku ; keiyaku-sho ; ukeoi. *v.* [kɔntrǽkt] keiyaku suru. ~**ible** [-ibl] *a.* chijimaru. ~**ile** [-tail] *a.*
chijimaru seishitsu no. ~**ion** [kɔntrǽkʃən] *n.* shūshiku ; shō-
ryaku. ~**or** *n.* keiyakusha ; ukeoinin.

contradict [kɔntrədíkt] *v.* hantai suru ; mujun suru.

contradiction [kɔntrədíkʃ(ə)n] *n.* hampaku ; mujun.

contradictory [kɔntrədíktəri] *a.* hantai no ; mujun no (*inconsistent*). ~**ily** *ad.* mujun shite.

contradistinction [kòntrədistíŋkʃən] *n*. taishō-kubetsu.

contradistinguish [kòntrədistíŋgwiʃ] *v*. kurabete kubetsu suru.

contralto [kəntrá:ltou] *n*. (*mus*.) ichiban hikui josei on ; chū-on-bu.

contrariety [kòntrəráiəti] *n*. haichi (*disagreement*) ; mujun.

contrariwise [kɔ́ntrəriwaiz] *ad*. ni hanshite ; hantai ni.

contrary [kɔ́ntrəri] *a*. hantai no. *n*. hantai. on *the* ~, kore ni hanshite. ~ *to*..., ...ni hanshite. ~rily *ad*. ni hanshite. ~riness *n*. hantai.

contrast [kɔ́ntræst] *n*. taishō. [kəntrǽst] *v*. taihi suru ; kiwa-datte chigau.

contravene [kɔ̀ntrəví:n] *v*. somuku.   ⌊datte chigau.

contravention [kɔ̀ntrəvénʃən] *n*. ihai ; hantai.

contribute [kəntribjú(:)t] *v*. kifu suru ; kikō suru (*an articles to a magazine*). kōken suru.

contribution [kɔ̀ntribjú:ʃən] *n*. kōken ; kifu (*subscription*) ; kifu-kin (~ *money*).

contributive [kəntríbjutiv] *a*. kōken suru ; joryoku suru (*help*).

contributor [kəntríbjutə] *n*. kōkensha ; kizōsha ; kikōsha. ~y [kəntríbjutəri] *a*. kōken suru ; kifu no.

contrite [kɔ́ntrait] *a*. kaikon no ; kuiru ; kōkai shita (*sorrowful for sin*). ~ly *ad*. kōkai shite.

contrition [kəntríʃən] *n*. kaikon ; kaigo.

contrivance [kəntráivəns] *n*. kufū ; shikake (*device*) ; keikaku (*plan*).   ⌈suru.

contrive [kəntráiv] *v*. kufū shite tsukuru ; kōan suru ; kufū

contriver [kəntráivə] *n*. anshutsusha ; kōansha.

control [kəntróul] *n*. seigyo ; tōsei ; seigen ; sōjū (*airplane*) ; (*pl.*) sōjūsōchi. *v*. sōjū suru. ~lable [-ləbl] *a*. osaerareru. ~ler [-lə] *n*. torishimarinin ; kanrinin.

controversial [kɔ̀ntrəvə́:ʃ(ə)l] *a*. ronsō no ; giron no.

controversy [kɔ́ntrəvə(:)si] *n*. ronsō.

controvert [kɔ́ntrəv:t] *v*. rombaku suru ; hitei suru (*deny*).

contumacious [kɔ̀ntju(:)méiʃəs] *a*. wagamamana ; iu koto o kikanai.

contumacy [kɔ́ntjuməsi] *n*. wagamama ; katakuna.

contumely [kɔ́ntjumli] *n*. gōman burei (*insolent*).

contuse [kəntjú:z] *v*. dabokushō o owaseru.

contusion [kəntjúːʒən] *n.* dabokushō.

conundrum [kənándrəm] *n.* nazo ; nammondai (*difficult problem*).

convalesce [kònvəlés] *v.* kaihō ni mukau (*byōki ga*).

convalescence [kònvəlésəns] *n.* byōki no kaifukuki.

convalescent [kònvəlés(ə)nt] *a.* kaihō ni mukatte iru. *n.* kaifuku-ki no kanja (*patient*).

convene [kənvíːn] *v.* shōshū suru ; atsumaru.

convenience [kənvíːniəns] *n.* benri ; tsugō. *at one's early* ～, tsugō no tsuki shidai.

convenient [kənvíːniənt] *a.* benrina ; tsugō no yoi. ～**ly** *ad.* benrini ; tsugō yoku.

convent [kɔ́nvənt] *n.* amadera. ～**icle** [kənvɔ́ntikl] *n.* himitsu shūkaijo (*religious*).

convention [kənvénʃən] *n.* shūkai ; kaigi ; shikitari.

conventional [kənvénʃ(ə)nəl] *a.* kanrei no ; arikitari no. ～**ism** [-izm] *n.* inshū ; kanrei. ～**ly** *ad.* kanrei ni shitagai. ～**ity** [kənvénʃ(ə)nǽliti] *n.* kanrei ni yoru koto. ～**ize** [kənvénʃ(ə)nəlaiz] *v.* kanrei ni yoraseru.

converge [kənvɔ́ːdʒ] *v.* yori-atsumaru ; yose-atsumeru. ～**nce** [-əns] *n.* yori-atsumari. ～**nt** [-ənt] *a.* yori-atsumaru.

conversant [kɔ́nvəs(ə)nt/kənvɔ́ː-] *a.* yoku shitte iru ; kuwashii (*with*).

conversation [kɔ̀nvəséiʃən] *n.* kaiwa. ～**al** [-əl] *a.* kaiwa no.

converse [kənvɔ́ːs] *v.* danwa suru ; kaiwa suru (*with*) (*to*). *n.* [kɔ́nvəːs] kaiwa. *a.* gyaku no. ～**ly** *ad.* gyaku ni.

conversion [kənvɔ́ːʃən] *n.* kaishū (*shūshi o kaeru*).

convert [kənvɔ́ːt] *v.* kaeru (*kawaraseru*) ; kaishū suru (*saseru*). [kɔ́nvəːt] *n.* kaitōsha ; kaishūsha. ～**ed cruiser,** *n.* kasō jun'yōkan. ～**ible** [kənvɔ́ːtibl] *a.* kae uru ; kōkan dekiru.

convex [kɔ́nvéks] *a.* nakadaka no ; deppatte iru. ～**ity** [kənvéksiti] *n.* nakadaka.

convey [kənvéi] *v.* okuru ; tsutaeru ; hakobu. ～**able** *a.* umpan dekiru. ～**ance** [-əns] *n.* yusō ; umpan. ～**ancer** *n.* umpan-sha. ～**er,** ～**or** *n.* konveyā ; umpan suru sōchi (*shikumi*).

convict [kənvíkt] *v.* yūzai to kimeru. [kɔ́nvikt] *n.* (*prove guilty*) hanzainin ; shūjin. ～**ion** [kənvíkʃən] *n.* yūzai no hanketsu ; ugokanu shinnen (*belief*).

convince [kənvíns] *v.* nattoku saseru. ~**cible** [kənvínsibl] *a.* nattoku saseuru. ~**cing** [kənvínsiŋ] *a.* nattoku saseru yōna. ~**cingly** *ad.* nattoku suru yōni.

convivial [kənvívial] *a.* sakamori no ; yōkina (*jovial*). ~**ly** *ad.* yōkini ; tanoshiku (*merrily*). ~**ity** [kənvìviǽliti] *n.* tanoshimi.

convocation [kɔnvokéiʃən] *n.* shōshū ; shūkai (*assembly*) ; (*C-*) (*Church of England* no) bōsan no kaigi.

convoke [kənvóuk] *v.* shōshū suru (*Congress, Parliament* o).

convoy [kɔnvɔ́i] *v.* keigo (goei) suru (*escort*). [kɔ́nvɔi] *n.* keigosha ; gosōsen (~*ship*).

convulse [kənváls] *v.* shindō saseru ; keiren o okosaseru. ~**sion** [kənválʃən] *n.* shindō ; dōran ; (*med.*) keiren. ~**sive** [kənválsiv] *a.* keiren o okosu.

cony [kóuni] *n.* usagi ; usagi no kegawa (*rabbit fur*).

coo [ku:] *v.* koi (*love*) o sasayaku. *n.* hato (*dove*) no nakigoe.

cook [kuk] *v.* ryōri suru. *n.* ryōrinin. ~ *up*, netsuzō suru. ~**ery** [kúkəri] *n.* ryōrihō. ~**ing** *a.* ryōri no ; kappō no.

cool [ku:l] *a.* suzushii (~ *weather*) ; tsumetai (~ *water*) ; reitanna (*half-hearted*) ; zūzūshii (*impudent*). (*col.*) shōmi no. *v.* hiyasu ; shizumeru. ~ *million dollars*, shōmi 100-man doru. ~**er** *n.* reikyakuki. ~**headed** [⊥hédid] *a.* ochitsuita. ~**ly** *ad.* hiyayakani. ~**ness** *n.* reisei ; ochitsuki ; reitan.

coolie, cooly [kú:li] *n.* ninsoku ; kūrii.

coon [ku:n] *n.* (*zoo.*) araiguma ; (*Am.*) zurui yatsu ; kokujin

coop [ku:p] *n.* toya ; torikago. *v.* toya ni ireru.

cooper [kú:pə] *n.* oke-ya.

co-operate [ko(u)ɔ́pəreit] *v.* kyōryoku suru. ~**tion** *n.* kyōryoku. ~**tive** [ko(u)ɔ́pərətiv] *a* kyōryokutekina. ~**tor** [ko(u)-ɔ́pəreitə] *n.* kyōryokusha.

co-ordinate [ko(u)ɔ́:dineit] *v.* dōtō ni suru (naru). *a.* [ko(u)-ɔ́:dinit] dōtō no. *n.* dōtō no hito (mono). ~**tion** [ko(u)ɔ:di-néiʃən] *n.* dōtō ; onaji de aru koto.

coot [ku:t] *n.* (*bird*) ōban ; kurogamo ; (*col.*) baka (*fool*).

cop [kɔp] *n.* (*col.*) junsa. *v.* (*sl.*) nusumu.

copal [kóupəl] *n.* isshu no jushi (kiyani-*resin*) (wanisu ni tsukau ; kōparu.

copartner [koupá:tnə] *n.* kyōryokusha ; kumiai-in. ~**ship** *n.*

kyōryoku ; kumiai.

cope [kóup] *v.* arasou ; tachimukau : *to* ~ *with*, tatakau ; u-

copeck [kóupek] *n. Soviet* no kahei (*coin*). ⌊chikatsu.

coping [kóupiŋ] *n.* kasa ; hei (*wall*) no yane.

copious [kóupiəs] *a.* takusan no. ~**ly** *ad.* takusan ; hōfuni. ~**ness** *n.* hōfu.

copper [kópə] *n.* (*min.*) dō ; dōka (~*coin*) ; dōki (~*vessel*) ; *v.* dō de ōu (*cover with* ~). ~**head** [-hed] *n. N. Am.* no dokuhebi (*snake*). ~**plate** [-pleit] *n.* dō-ban ; dō-ban zuri (-*print*). ~**smith** [-smiθ] *n.* dōki seizōnin (-*maker*).

copperas [kópərəs] *n.* (*chem.*) ryokuban.

coppice [kópis], **copse** [kóps] *n.* zōkibayashi.

copra [kóprə] *n.* kopura ; hoshita yashi no tane(mi).

copula [kópjulə] *n.* (pl. -s ; -lae [-li:]) (*gram.*) keiji ; renji ; (futsū *be, link verb.*) ; *link-verb.*

copulate [kópjuleit] *v.* kōsetsu suru ; kōbi suru. ~**tion** *n. copulate* suru koto. ~**tive** *a.* tsunagu ; musubitsukeru.

copy [kópi] *n.* utsushi ; nisemono (*imitation*). ~**book** [-buk] *n.* shūji no hon. ~**ing ink** [-iŋ iŋk] *n.* fukusha-yō inki. ~**-ing paper** [-iŋ péipə] *n.* fukusha-shi. ~**-ing press** [-iŋ pres] *n.* tōshaki. ~**ist** *n.* shajisei. ~**right** [-rait] *n.* chosaku-ken. *v.* hanken o motsu.

coquet [kɔkét] *v.* betatsuku ; fuzakeru. ~**ry** [kóuketri] *n.* betatsuki, ichatsuki. ~**tish** [kɔkétiʃ] *a.* adappoi.

coquette [kɔkét] *n.* uwaki onna.

coral [kórəl] *n.* sango ; sango-shoku (-*color*) ; *a.* sango no. ~**line** [kóləlain] sango no (yōna).

cord [kɔ:d] *n.* tsuna ; nawa (*rope*) ; himo (*string*) ; ~**age** [-idʒ] *n.* tsunagu.

cordate [kɔ́:deit] *a.* (*bot.*) shinzō-gata no (*heart-shaped*).

cordial [kɔ́:diəl] *a.* kokoro kara no ; shinsetsuna. *n.* kōfunzai (*stimulant*) (-*liquor*). ~**ly** *ad.* kokoro kara. ~**ness** *n.* shinsetsu. ~**ity** *n.* seijitsu ; shinsetsu.

cordon [kɔ́:dən] *n.* hijō-sen (*of police*) ; jushō ; himo-kazari : *the Grand C*~ *of the Rising Sun,* Kyokujitsu Daijushō.

cordovan [kɔ́:dəvən] *n.* kōdobagawa (Cordova san no) kawa) (*leather.*)

corduroy [kɔ́:djurɔi] *n.* kōruten ; (*pl.*) kōruten no zubon (*trousers*). ～*road*, maruta no dōro (numachi nado no).

core [kɔ:/kɔə] *n.* shin ; shinzui (*gist*). *v.* shin o nuku.

corespondent [kɔ̀rispɔ́ndənt] *n.* (*leg.*) kyōdō hikoku (rikon so-shō no) (*divorce lawsuit*).

Corinthian [kərínθiən] *a.* Korinto (*Corinth*) no ; Korinto-shi-ki no. *n.* Korintojin.

cork [kɔ:k] *n.* korukugashi (-*oak*) no kawa ; sen (-*stopper*). *v.* koruku (-*stopper*) o sasu ; kanjō (*feeling*) o osaeru. ～**screw** [-skru:] *n.* koruku nuki. *v.* rasen-jō ni susumu. ～y[kɔ́:ki] *a.* koruku no yōna ; koruku kusai.

corm [kɔ:m] *n.* (*bot.*) kyūkei ; chikakei.

cormorant [kɔ́:mərənt] *n.* (*bird*) u ; don'yokuna hito (*greedy* 　　　　　　　　　　　　　　　　　　　　　　　　　　　　*person*).

corn [kɔ:n] *n.* (*Am.*) tōmorokoshi ; (*Brit.*) komugi ; tako. ～ **cockle** *n.* (*flower*) muginadeshiko. ～**bread** [-bred] *n.* tōmorokoshi-pan. ～**chandler** [-tʃɑ́:ndlə] *n.* kokumotsu-shōnin. ～**cob** *n.* tōmorokoshi no hojiku. ～**factor** [-fǽktə] *n.* kokumotsu ton'ya. ～**field** [-fi:ld] (*Brit.*) komugibatake, (*Am.*) tō-morokoshi-batake. ～**flower** [-flauə] *n.* (*flower*). yaguruma-giku. ～**meal** [-mi:l] *n.* kokufun ; (*Scotland*) ōtomiiru (*oatmeal*) ; (*Am.*) tōmorokoshi-ko (*powder*). ～**stalk** [-stɔ:k] *n.* tōmorokoshi no kuki. ～**starch** [-stɑ:tʃ] *n.* tōmorokoshi no nori ; tōmorokoshi ko (-*powder*).

cornea [kɔ́:niə] *n.* (*anat.*) kakumaku (*of eye*).

corner [kɔ́:nə] *n.* kado ; sumi (*nook*). *v.* yarikome : rukaishime. ～*in wheat*, mugi no kaishime. ～**stone** [-stoun] sumi-ishi. ～**wise** [-waiz] *ad.* naname ni.

cornet [kɔ́:nit] *n.* korunetto.

cornice [kɔ́:nis] *n.* jabara ; noki-jabara (*eaves*).

cornucopia [kɔːnjukóupjə] *n.* Zeus ga kodomo no toki chi-chi o nomashita yagi. (*Gk. myth.*) ; mono no hōfuna *symbol.*

corolla [kərɔ́lə] *n.* (*bot*) kakan.

corollary [kərɔ́ləri] *n.* kei. teiri (*theorem*) kara shizenni deru meidai (*proposition*).

corona [kəróunə] *n.* (*pl.* -**nae** [-ni:]) byakkō ; taiyō (*sun*) ya tsuki (*moon*) no shūi no wa.

coronach [kɔ́rənæk] *n.* (*Scotland* no) banka ; sōshiki no uta.

coronation [kɔrənéiʃən] *n.* taikan-shiki ; sokui-shiki.　　　ʃri).

coroner [kɔ́rənə] *n,* kenshi-kan (shigai no shinsa o suru kan-

coronet [kɔ́rənət] *n.* chiisai kammuri (kizoku nado no kaburu).

corporal [kɔ:p(ə)rəl] *n.* gochō. *a.* nikutai no : ～ *punishment*, tai-kei. ～**ly** *ad.* nikutaiteki ni.

corporality [kɔ̀:pərǽliti] **corporeality** [kɔ:pòuriǽliti]. *n.* kan-kaku (*senses*) de mitomerareru mono ; nikutai.　　　ʃjin.

corporate [kɔ́:pərit] *a.* danketsu no ; ～**body** *or* body～ *n.* hō-

corporation [kɔ̀:pəréiʃən] *n.* dantai ; hōjin ; kaisha (*company*).

corporeal [kɔ:pɔ́:riəl] *a.* yūkei no ; busshitsuteki no (*material*).

corps [kɔ:] *n.* (*pl.* [kɔ:z]) heidan ; dantai (*party*). army ～, gundan. ～ **diplomatique** *n* (*Fr.*) gaikōdan.

corpse [kɔ:ps] *n.* shitai.

corpulence [kɔ́:pjuləns] ～**cy** [-si] *n.* himan ; debu-butori.

corpulent [kɔ́:pjulənt] *a.* himan shite iru (*being fat*).

corpus [kɔ́:pəs] *n.* (*pl.* **corpora**) karada ; shintai ; shitai (*dead body*) ; ...shū (*whole collection of writings*). ～ **delicti** [-dilíktai] *n.* hanzai no shutai.

corpuscle [kɔ́:pʌskl], **corpuscule** [-pʌ́skju:l] *n.* kekkyū (～ *of the blood*) ; white ～, hakkekkyū. red ～, sekkekkyū.

corpuscular [kɔ:pʌ́skjulə] *a.* kekkyū no. (*of blood corpuscle*).

corral [kɔrǽl] *n.* kachiku o ireru kakoi ; (yaei no) kuruma okiba.

correct [kərékt] *v.* machigai o naosu. kyōsei suru, (*cure of fault*). *a.* seikakuna. ～**ly** *a.* seikakuni. ～**ness** seikakusa. ～**or** *n.* teiseisha ; kōseisha. ～**ive** [kəréktiv] *a.* kyōseitekina.

correction [kərékʃən] *n.* teisei ; kōsei ; kyōsei.

correlate [kɔ́rileit] *v.* kankei suru.

correlation [kɔriléiʃən] *n'* sōgo kankei ; kōgo sayō (*interaction*).

correlative [kɔrélətiv] *a.* sōkan no. *n.* sōkanshi : (*gram.*) " both ...and " ; " either...or " nado no yōni itsu mo isshoni tsuka-wareru mono. ～**ly** *ad.* sōkantekini.

correspond [kɔ̀rispɔ́nd] *v.* chōdo...ni ataru ; tagaini tegami no yaritori o suru (*with*) ; tagaini kimochi (*mood*) ga au. ～**ing** *a.* fugō suru ; tsūshin suru. ～**ence** [-əns] *n.* tsūshin ; itchi. ～**ent** [-ənt] *n.* tsūshin'in.

corridor [kɔ́ridɔ:l] *n.* rōka.

corrigible [kɔ́ridʒibl] *a.* aratamerareru ; kyōsei dekiru.

corroborate[kərɔ́bəreit] *v.* tashikameru ; kakushō suru (*confirm*).

corroboration [kərəkəréiʃən] *n.* tashikame ; kakushō.

corroborative [kərɔ́bərətiv] *a.* tashikameru ; kakushō suru.

corrode [kəróud] *v.* fushoku suru.   ⌈iku.

corrosion [kəróuʒən] *n.* fushoku ; shinshoku ; zutto kusatte

corrosive [kəróusiv] *a.* shinshokusei no. *n.* (*chem.*) fushokuzai.

corrugate [kɔ́rjugeit] *v.* shiwa o yoraseru. [kɔ́r(j)ugit] *a.* shiwa no aru (*wrinkled*) ; namigata no (*wavy*), ~d iron, namigata teppan.

corrupt [kərʌ́pt] *v.* fuhai saseru ; baishū suru (*buy off*). fuhai suru. *a.* fuhai shita (*depraved*) ; ~ible *a.* fuhai (daraku) shi yasui. ~ness *n.* fuhai.

corruption [kərʌ́pʃən] *n.* fuhai ; haitoku ; kotoba no namari.

corsage [kɔ́:sidʒ] *n.* (fujin-fuku no) dōgi ; mune no hanataba.

corsair [kɔ́:sɛə] *n.* kaizoku ; kaizokusen (-*ship*).

corse [kɔ:s] *n.* shitai (*arch.*) = **corpse**.

corselet [kɔ́:slit] *n.* dō dake no yoroi ; kyōkō.

corset [kɔːsit] *n.* fujin no dōgi ; koruset.

Corsican [kɔ́:sikən] *n.* Korushikajin.   ⌈tendants).

cortége [kɔːtéiʒ] *n.* (Fr.) gyōretsu ; robo ; gubuin (*train of at-*

cortex [kɔ́:teks] *n.* (*pl.* -**tices** [kɔ́:tisi:z]) gaihi ; hishitsu ; juhi ; ki no kawa (*bark*).

corundum [korʌ́ndən] *n.* kōgyoku ; kongōsha (-*sand*).

coruscate [kɔ́rəskeit] *v.* pikat-to hikaru ; hirameku.

coruscation [kɔrəskeiʃən] *n.* senkō : kirari-to hikaru hikari ; hirameki.

corvette [kəːvét] *n.* mukashi no kaibōkan (*coast defence ship*).

cosecant [kousí:kənt] *n.* (*math.*) yokatsu ; kosekant.

cosey [kóuzi] *a.* kojimmari shita ; igokochi no yoi.

cosignatory [kó(u)sígnətəri] *a.* rensho suru. *n.* renshosha.

cosily [kóuzili] *a.* kokoroyoku ; anrakuni.

cosine [kóusain] *n.* (*math.*) yogen ; kosain.

cosmetic [kəzmétik] *n.* keshōhin (bihatsuyō no).

cosmic(al) [kɔ́zmik(əl)] *a.* uchū no ; kōdai-muhenna.

cosmogony [kəzmɔ́gəni] *n.* uchū kaibyaku setsu (-*theory*) ; u-chū no sōzō

cosmopolitan [kòzmopólitən] *n.* sekai-jin. *a.* sekai o wagaya to suru.

cosmopolite [kòzmópəlait] *n.* sekai o wagaya to suru hito.

cosmorama [kòzmrorá:mə] *n.* sekai fūzoku (*manners and customs*) nozoki megane (*a peep-show*).

cosmos [kózmɔs] *n.* uchū (*universe*) ; me ni mi, mimi ni kiku subete no mono. (*flower*) kosumosu.

Cossack [kósæk] *n.* Kassakujin ; Kossakukihei (*-cavalrymen*).

cosset [kósit] *n.* tegai no kohitsuji (*pet lamb*). *v.* amayakasu.

cost [kɔ(:)st] *n.* nedan ; genka (dekiagari made no hiyō) (*prime ~ or ~ price*)*~s* ; *v.* kane rōryoku nado ga kakaru. *at all ~s or at any ~*, zehi tomo ; ikura kakatte mo. *at the ~ of*, o gisei to shite. **~free** [-frí:] *ad.* muryō de. **~ly** *a.* kōkana. **~liness** *n.* hiyō no kakaru koto.

costal [kóst(ə)l] *a.* rokkotsu no ; abarabone no. (*of ribs*).

coster(monger) [kóstə(mʌ̀ŋɡə)] *n.* (kudamono (*fruit*), gyorui (*fish*) nado o yobiuri suru) gyōshōnin.

costive [kóstiv] *a.* bempi no. **~ness** *n.* bempi. ⌈ru hito.

costume [kóstju:m] *n.* ifuku. **~r** [kóstjumə] *n.* ishō o tsuku-

cosy [kóuzi] *a.* kojimmari shita (*snug*) ; igokochi no yoi (*comfortable*). *see* : **cozy.**

cot [kɔt] *n.* koya ; akambō no nedoko (*swinging cot*).

cotangent [kóutǽndʒənt] *n.* (*math.*) yosetsu ; kotanjento.

cote [kout] *n.* (hitsuji, hato, nado no) koya.

coterie [kóutəri] *n.* nakama ; kumi ; ippa (*group*). ⌈ku.

cotillion [kótiljən] *n.* hachinin de suru butō ; *cotillion* no kyo-

cottage [kótidʒ] *n.* inaka-ya ; koya (*small hut*).

cotton [kótn] *n.* wata ; menshi (*-thread*). **~yarn** [-jɑ:n] *n.* menshi. *raw ~*, menka. **~gin** [-dʒin] *n.* watakuri kikai. **~mill** [-mil] *n.* bōseki kōjō. **~ plant** [plænt], wata no ki. **~tail** [-teil] *n.* (*Am.*) nousagi.

cotyledon [kòtəlí:dən] *n.* (*bot.*) shiyō (*seed lead*).

couch [kautʃ] *n.* shindai ; ne-isu (*lounge*). *v.* yokotaeru (yokotawaru) ; machibuse suru (*lie in wait for*). kagamu (*stoop*).

couchant [káutʃənt] *a.* atama (*head*) o motagete uzukumatta. (*lion*, neko no yōni) (*cf.* dormant). ⌈do.

cough [kɔ:f] *n.* seki. *v.* seki o suru. **~ up**, shiharau (kane na-

could [kud] *aux. v. see* : **can.**

couldn't [kudnt]=**could not.**   ⌈yō tan'-i.).

coulomb [ku:lɔ́m] *n.* (*elec.*) kūron (denryō (*quantity*) no jitsu-

council [káuns(i)l] *n.* kaigi : *city* (*or municipal*) ~, shisanjikai. ~ *of war*, gunji kaigi ; ~**chamber** [-tʃémbə] *n.* kaigishitsu. ~**man** [-mən] *n.* gi-in ; shikai gi-in.

council(1)or [káunsilə] *n.* giin ; kyōgiin ; komonkan.

counsel [kauns(ə)l] *n.* sōdan ; *v.* jogen (*advise*) suru ; susumeru (*recommend*).   ⌈(*lawyer*).

counsel(1)or [káunsələ] *n.* komon ; hōritsu komon ; bengoshi

count [kaunt] *v.* kazoeru ; jūyōna hito ni kazoeru. shinrai su-ru (*rely on, or upon*). *n.* keisan ; (C~) Hakushaku ~**less** *a.* ka-zoerarenai hodo musū no. ~**out** [-aut] (*boxing*) kesshō byō-sū (*seconds*) ; (10 *seconds* o kazoeru.

countenance [káuntinəns] *n.* yōbō ; kao-tsuki. *v.* shōrei suru.

counter [káuntə] *n.* keisansha ; keisanki. *v.* samatageru ; han-tai suru. *a.* hantai no. *ad.* hantai ni. ~**act** [kàuntərǽkt] *v.* sa-matageru. ~**attack** [-'ətæk] *v.* hangeki suru. ~**balance** [káun-təbæ̀ləns] *n.* tsuriai. ~**claim** *n.* hantai yōkyū. ~**clockwise** [-klɔ́kwaiz] *a.* tokei no hari to gyaku ni mawaru. ~**feit** [-fit] *a.* mozō no. ~**feiter** [káuntəfitə] *n.* gizōsha. ~**intelligence** [-intélidʒəns] *n.* shōgaikatsudō nado. ~**mand** [-máːnd] *n.* hantaimeirei. ~**march** [-mɑːtʃ] *n.*, *v.* kōtai (suru). ~**pane** *n.* kakebuton. ~**part** *n.* tsui no mono no kataippō ; sei-futsu 2-tsū. no uchi no 1-tsu. ~**plot** *n.* teki no ura o kaku keikaku. ~**revolution** *n.* hankakumei. ~**poise** *v.* ...to tsuriawaseru. ~**sign** [-sain] *n.* aikotoba. ~**offensive** [kauntərəfénsive] *n.*

countess [káuntis] *n.* hakushaku fujin.   ⌊gyakushū.

counting [káuntiŋ] *n.* keisan. ~**house** [-haus] *n.* chōba ; kai-kei shitsu. ~**machine** [-məʃíːn] *n.* keisanki.

countrify [kántrifai] *v.* inakafū ni suru.

country [kántri] *n.* inaka ; kuni ; *go to the* ~, sō-senkyo o su-ru. ~**dance** [-dɑːns] chihō odori. ~**house** [-haus] *n.* bessō. ~**man** [-mən] *n.* inaka mono ; dōkoku-jin (*compatriot*). ~**seat** [-síːt] *n.* bessō.

county [kaunti] *n.* (*Am.*) gun ; (*Brit.*) shū.

coup [kuː] *n.* (*Fr.*) " *blow* " no imi. ~**d'état** [kúːde(i)táː] " *blow* *of state* "; budan seiryaku ; hijōshudan.

coupé [kú:pei] *n.* futari-nori no yonrin-basha ; jidōsha.

couple [kápl] *n.* fūfu ; ittsui ; tsugai (*pair*). *v.* awaseru ; tsunagu. ~**r** *n.* renketsuki ; renketsushu.

couplet [káplit] *n.* (shi (*poem*) no) tsui-ku ; renku. ┌~).

coupling [kápliŋ] *n.* renketsu ; renketsu-ki ; nejitsugite (*screw* ~).

coupon [kú:pɔːŋ] *n.* ri-fuda ; kiritori-fuda, kūpon.

courage [kárɪdʒ] *n.* yūki : *take* (or *pluck up*) ~, genki o dasu. ~**ous** [kəréidʒəs] *a.* isamashii. ~**ously** *ad.* isamashiku. ~-**ousness**, yūki.

courier [kúriə] *n.* haya-bikyaku ; isogi no tsukai.

course [kə:s] *n.* hōkō (*direction*) ; katei shoku (*meal*) no hitoshina. *v.* hashiru (*run*). ~ *of things* = *of course*, mochiron.

court [kə:t] *n.* saibansho ; kyūtei ; teikyūjō (*tennis* ~) ~**dress** kyūchū fuku. *go to* ~, sandai suru. ...ni iiyoru (*woo*). ~**eous** [kɔ́:tiəs] *a.* reigi no aru ; teineina. ~**eously** *ad.* teineini. **house** [-haus] *n.* saibansho. ~**ly** *ad.* teineini (*polite*). ~**ship** *n.* kigen-tori ; kyū-ai ; kyū-kon (*woo*). ~**yard** [-jɑːd] *n.* na-

courtesan, courtezan [kɔ̀:tizǽn] *n.* baishō-fu. └ka-ni-wa.

courtesy [kɔ̀:tisi] *n.* teinei ; kō-i (*good will*).

courtier [kɔ́:tjə] *n.* chōtei no tsukaibito.

court-martial [kɔ́:tmáːʃəl] *n.* (*pl.* **courts-**) gumpō kaigi. *v.* gumpō kaigi ni kakeru.

cousin [kázn] *n.* itoko ; second ~, mata-itoko.

cove [kouv] *n.* chiisai irie (*inlet*).

covenant [kávinənt] *n.* keiyaku ; keiyakusho (*written* ~) ; seikyō keiyaku (*Orthodox*) ; sei-yaku. *v.* keiyaku suru. ~**er** *n.* keiyakusha.

cover [kávə] *v.* ue kara ōu ; yōgo suru ; tsugunau (jūbunni) (*the cost*). *n.* ōi ; fū (*seal*) ; futa (*lid*) ; (hon (*book*) no) hyōshi (*binding*). ~ *up*, kakusu.

coverlet [kávəlit] *n.* kake-buton.

covert [kávət] *a.* hisokana ; kakureta hogo sarete iru. *n.* kakureba (*shelter*). ~**ly** *ad.* sore towa nashi ni.

covet [kávət] *v.* hoshigaru ; musaboru (*be greedy*).

covetous [kávitəs] *a.* gōyokuna (*avaricious*). ~**ly** *ad.* yokubatte. ~**ness** *n.* yokubari.

covey [kʌ́vi] *n.* kotori no mure. (uzura (*quail*) shako, (*partridge*) nado no).

cow [kau] *n.* meushi (sai, zō, kujira nado no) mesu. *v.* odokasu. ～**boy** [-bɔi] *n.* ushi-kai; (*Am.*) kaubōi. ～**catcher** [-kætʃə] *n.* (*Am.*) (kikansha (*engine*) no) mae ni tsuita haishō-ki. ～**herd** [hə:d] *n.* ushi-kai. ～**hide** [-haik] *n.* gyūhi; muchi (gyūhi no *whip*). ～**slip** [-slip] *n.* (*flower*) kibana no kurin-sakurasō.

coward [káuəd] *a.* okubyōna. *n.* okubyōmono. okubyō. ～**ly** *a.* okubyōna. *ad.* hikyō nimo. ～**ice,** ～**liness** *n.* okubyō.

cower [káuə] *v.* chijikomaru.

cowl [kaul] *n.* sō (*priest*); sō no zukin (*hood*); zukin no tsuita sō no kimono. (*Am.*) jidōsha no shatai (*car-body*) no mae no bubun (*front part*).

co-worker [ko(u)wə:kə] *n.* kyōryokusha; dōryō (*comrade*).

cowrie, cowry [káuri] *n.* (*zoo.*) koyasugai; tairagai zoku (*genus*) no isshu.

coxcomb [kɔ́kskoum] *n.* sharemono; (*flower*) keitō.

coxswain [kɔ́kswein / kɔ́ksn] *n.* tantei-chō; *boat* no dashu (*helmsman*).

coy [kɔi] *a.* hanikamu; uchikina. ～**ly** *ad.* hanikanda. **coyness** *n.* hanikami.

coyote [kɔióuti] *n.* (*zoo.*) ōkami no isshu (Hokubei-san).

cozen [kʌ́zn] *v.* damasu; damashite toru

cozy [kóuzi] *a. see*: **cosy.** ～**ily** *ad.* kokoroyoku; anrakuni. ～**iness** *n.* igokochi no yosa; kiraku.

CPI shōhisha kakaku shisū (*Consumer's Price Index*).

crab [kræb] *n.* kani; kijūki (*winch*).

crabbed [kræbid] *a.* iji no warui; kimuzukashii; hinekureta shofū (*style of penmanship*) ～**ly** *ad.* iji waruku. ～**ness** *n.* kimuzukashisa.

crack [kræk] *v.* wareru; pachitto iwaseru; shaberu (*chat*). *n.* wareme; hibi (*chap*). seishinsakuran. *ad.* pachitto iu. ～**brained** [-breind] *a.* ki no kurutta. ～**ed** [-t] *a.* wareta; hibi no haitta. ～**er** *n.* bakuchiku; usu-bisuket.

crackle [krǽkl] *n.* hibi-yaki no tōki (*china*). *v.* pachi, pachi oto

crackling [krǽkliŋ] *n.* pachi, pachi to iu oto. ⌊o tateru.

cradle [kréidl] *n.* yurikago ; yōran ; hasseichi (*place of origin*)
v. yurikago ni irete, nemuraseru.

craft [krɑ:ft] *n.* jukuren (*skill*) ; shugei (*handicraft*). warudakumi. ~**sman** [krɑ́:ftsmən] *n.* shokkō ; gijutsusha.

crafty [krɑ́:fti] *a.* kōkatsuna. **craftily** [krɑ́:ftili] *ad.* jōzuni ; zuruku. ⌐tsu no.

crag [kræg] *n.* iwa. **craggy** [krǽgi] *a.* iwa darake no ; ganku-
cram [kræm] *v.* tsumekomu ; akiru hodo kuu ; (*slang*) itsuwaru ; uso o yū.

cramp [kræmp] *n.* kasugai ; (*med.*) keiren. *v.* kasugai de shimeru : *be* ~*ed in the calf*, ashi ga komuragaeri suru.

cranberry [krǽmbəri] *n.* (*bot.*) tsurukokemomo.

crane [krein] *n.* (*bird*) tsuru ; kijūki. *v.* kubi o nobasu.

cranial [kréiniəl] *a.* zugai no.

craniology [kreiniólədʒi] *n.* zugaikotsugaku ; zugai-gaku.

cranium [kréiniəm] *n.* (*pl.* **-nia**) (*anat.*) zugai.

crank [kræŋk] *n.* magari-e ; kuranku ; myōna iimawashi. kawarimono. *a.* (*naut.*) tempuku shisōna. *v.* magari-e de ugokasu. ~**shaft** [-ʃæft] *n.* magari-e jiku. ~**y** [krǽŋki] *a.* kimagurena ; tempuku (*capsize*) shi sōna ; yura yura suru (*swinging*).

cranny [krǽni] *n.* wareme ; hibi (*chinks*).

crape [kreip] *n.* chirimen ; moshō. ~**d** [-t]*a.* chijinda.

crash [kræʃ] *v.* gachari to kowasu (kudaku) ; kudakeru. gata-
gata to kuzureru. *n.* isshu no arai asanuno.

crass [kræs] *a.* soakuna ; atsui ; (*fig*) gudonna (*stupid*). ~**ly**
ad. nibuku. ⌐suru.

crate [kreit] *n.* eda de anda ōkina kago ; *pack in a* ~, de hōsō

crater [kréitə] *n.* funkakō ; kakō ; funsenkō.

cravat [krəvǽt] *n.* nekutai.

crave [kreiv] *v.* setsubō suru ; setsuni (*eagerly*) nozomu ; kongan suru. ⌐*ly*).

craven [kréivn] *n.* okubyōmono (*coward*). *a.* okubyōna (*coward-*
craving [kréiviŋ] *n.* kongan ; setsubō ; netsubō

craw [krɔ:] *n.* ebukuro (*crop*).

crawfish [krɔ́fiʃ], **crayfish** [kréifiʃ] *n.* zarigani.

crawl [klɔ:l] *n.* hofuku (hatte iku koto) ; soro soro aruki ; ku-
rōru (oyogi.) *v.* hau ; kossori susumu ; umaku toriiru. ~**y** *a.*

muzumuzu suru.
crayon [kréion] *n.* kureyon ; iroempitsu ; kureyon-ga.
craze [kreiz] *v.* hakkyō saseru (suru) ; hibiyaki ni suru. *n.* nekkyō ; dairyūkō.
crazy [kréizi] *a.* hakkyō shita ; ki ga kurutta. ~**ily** *ad.* hakkyō shite ; nekkyōtekini. ~**iness** *n.* hakkyō.
creak [kri:k] *n.* kiikii naru oto ; kishiri. *v.* kishiru. ~**ly** *a.* kii-
kii iu ; kishiru.
cream [kri:m] *n.* kuriimu ; ichiban ii bubun. *v. cream* o sukutte toru ; *cream* ni naru (suru). ~**ery** [-əri] *n. cream* nado no
seizōsho. ~**ly** *a.* kuriimu ni nita.
crease [kri:s] *n.*, *v.* hida (o tsukeru) ga tsuku ; shiwa ni naru.
create [kri(:)éit] *v.* hajimete tsukuru ; tsukuridasu.
creation [kri(:)éiʃən] *n.* sōzō (*act of creating*).   ⌈*creating*).
creative [kri(:)éitiv] *a.* sōzōryoku no aru (*having the powder of*
creator [ki(i)éitə] *n.* sōzōsha ; zōbutsushu (*creator*).
creature [krí:tʃə] *n.* sōzōbutsu ; ningen ; dōbutsu (*what is creat-
ed*). ~ **comforts**, i-shoku-jū (*clothing, food, house, etc.*).
crèche [kreiʃ] *n.* takujisho.
credence [krí:dəns] *n.* shin'yō ; shinnin ; *letter of* ~, shinnin-
credential [kridénʃəl] *n.* (*pl.*) shinninjō.   ⌊jō.
credibility [krèdibíliti] *n.* shin'yō suru ni taru koto.
credible [krédibl/-dəb-] *a.* shinzuru ni taru ; shinjirareru. ~
ly *ad.* tashikani.
credit *n.* shin'yō ; saiken (*bond*) ; shin'yō-gashi ; ~**bureau**
[-bjúərou] *n.* kōshinjo. *v.* shin'yō suru. ~**able** *a.* homete
yoi ; kanshinna. ~**ably** *ad.* kanshinni. ~**or** *n.* saikensha.
credulity [kridjú:liti/kred-] *n.* karugarushiku shinzuru koto ;
keishin.   ⌈ru.
credulous [krédjuləs] *a.* ukkari (ikinari) shinzuru ; keishin su-
creed [kri:d] *n.* shinkōkajō ; kōryō.
creek [kri:k] *n.* irie ; chiisai wan. (*Amer.*) ogawa (*rivulet*).
creel [kri:l] *n.* biku (*angler's basket*).
creep [kri:p] *v.* **crept ; creeping.** *v.* hau ; sorosoro ugoku. *n.*
hara(m)bai ; sorosoro aruki. (*pl.*) mushi no hau yōna kokochi.
~**er** *n.* tsurukusa. ~**hole** [-houl] *n.* haikomiana ; kakureru
ana. ~**ly** *a.* hau ; muzumuzu suru.

cremate [kriméit] v. kasō ni suru ; shitai o yaku. ～**tion** [kri-méiʃən] n. kasō.

crematory [krémətəri] n. kasōjo ; kasō suru basho.

Creole [krí:oul] (*Am.*) hakujin-kei no ainoko ; *Fr. Sp.* no ijū-sha.

creosote [krí:əsout] n. kureosōto. └sha.

crêpe [kreip] n. kureipu ; chirimen.

crepitate [krépiteit] v. pachi pachi iu.

crept [krept] *see* : **creep.**

crescendo [kriʃéndou] n. (*mus.*) shidaini tsuyoku naru oto. *a. ad.* shidaini tsuyoi (tsuyoku).

crescent [krésnt/-znt] n. mikazuki ; shingetsu ; Toruko (no ha-ta). *a.* mikazuki no katachi no.

cresol [krí:sol/-səl] n. kurezōru ; kureosōto.

cress [kres] n. (*bot.*) tagarashi ; koshōsō (*etc.*).

cresset [krésit] n. kagaribi ; taimatsu.

crest [krest] n. tosaka ; maetate ; yama no teppen. ～**fallen** [⊥fɔ́:ln] *a.* shombori, genki o ushinatta.

cretaceous [kritéiʃəs] *a.* hakua (*chalk*) -shitsu no.

cretonne [kretɔ́n/krétən] n. sarasa no isshu.

crevasse [kriváes] n. wareme ; sakeme.

crevice [krévis] n. wareme.

crew [kru:] n. norikumiin ; nakama.

crewel [krú(:)əl] n. futako-ito.

crib [krib] n. kaibaoke ; kodomo no shindai. (*Am.*) kokumo-tsu chozōshitsu. (*also v.*) toranomaki (o tsukau).

cribbage [kríbidʒ/-edʒ] n. isshu no torampu asobi.

crick [krik] n. kata ya kubi no kori ; isshu no *leumatis.*

cricket [kríkit] n. kōrogi ; kuriketto.

crier [kráiə] n. kōkokuya ; yobidashiyaku.

crime [kraim] n. tsumi ; (hōritsujō no) hanzai.

criminal [krímunal] *a.* tsumi o okashita ; yūzaino. n. hanzai-sha. ～**action** n. keijisoshō ; kokuso. ～**law** n. keihō. ～**ly** *ad.*

criminality [krìmináeliti] n. hanzai ; yūzai.

criminate [krímineit] v. tsumi o owaseru ; yūzai to suru.

crimination [krìminéijən] n. tsumi o owaseru koto ; kokuso ; yūzai to suru koto.

criminology [krìminɔ́lɔkʒi] n. hanzaigaku ; keijigaku.

crimp [krimp] *v.* chijiraseru ; damashite heishi ni suru. *n.* chijiregami ; yūkaisha.

crimple [krímpl] *n.* shiwa ; hida.

crimpy [krímpi] *a.* chijireta.

crimson [krímzn] *n.* makkana iro. *a.* shinku no ; makkana. *v.* makkani suru (naru).

cringe [krindʒ] *n.* hetsurai ; ishuku. *v.* hetsurau ; ishuku suru.

crinkle [kríŋkl] *n.* chijire ; shiwa. *v.* chijire saseru ; shiwa o yoraseru ; shiwa ga yoru.

crinkly [kríŋkli] *a.* chijireta ; shiwa no yotta.

crinoline [krínəlin] *n.* fujin no sukāto ni mochiiru katai kire (kōfu, katai nuno) ; kōfu-sei no sukāto.　〔suru.

cripple [krípl] *n.* fugusha ; izari ; bikko. *v.* bikko (fugu) ni

crisis [kraisis] (*pl.* -ses [-si:z]) *n.* daijina (*grave*) kikai (*chance*) (byōki, kiken, seiji nado no).

crisp [krisp] *a.* katakute moroi ; paripari suru ; hikishimaru ; ~ *air* mi no hikishimaru yōna kūki. *v.* chijirasu ; moroku suru.

crispy [kríspi] *a.* moroi ; chijirete iru ; maatarashii (shihei) moroi ; chijireru yōna.

crisscross [krískrəs/krɔ́:s] *n.* jūmonji. *a., ad.* jūmonji no (ni) ; kimuzukashii. *v.* kōsasuru.　　　　　　　　　　〔koro.

criterion [kraitíəriən] *n.* (*pl.* -ria or -s) hyōjun ; kijun ; yorido-

critic [krítik] *n.* hihyōka ; kokuhyōka. ~**al** *a.* hihyō no ; kantei no ; me no takai ; kiwadoi. kitoku no. ~**ally** *ad.*

criticism [krítisizm] *n.* hihyō ; hyōron ; hinan.

criticize [krítisaiz] *v.* hihyō suru ; hinan suru.

critique [kritík] *n.* hihyō.

croak [krouk] *v.* karasu ga naku (fukitsuna) *n.* sono nakigoe.

crochet [króuʃei/-ʃi] *n.* kagibari ami ; kuroshē amimono.

crock [krɔk] *n.* kame ; tsubo ; doki no hahen ; haijin ; haiba.

crockery [krɔ́keri] *n.* doki ; tōki.

crocodile [krɔ́kədail] *n.* wani. ~ **tears** *n.* (*pl.*) soranamida.

crocus [króukəs] *n.* safuran.

crone [kroun] *n.* shiwakucha babā.

crony [króuni] *n.* shin'yū. (*intimate friend*).

crook [kruk] *n.* e no magatta tsue ; wankyoku ; zurui takura-

mi; sagishi. *v.* mageru; magaru. ～**back** *n.* semushi. ～**ed**
[krúkid] *a.* magatta; nejiketa.

croon [kr:n] *v.* hikui koe de utau; kuchizusamu.

crop [krɔp] *n.* shūkaku; sakumotsu; muchi (*whip*) no e; tori
nado no ibukuro. *v.* karu; tsumitoru. ～**per** *n.* kosakunin.

croquet [króukei/-ki] *n.* isshu no kogai yūgi; kurokkē.

croquette [kroukét] *n.* korokke (*cuisine*).

crosier [króuʒə] *n.* jūjikei no shakujō.

cross [krɔs/krɔːs] *n.* jūjika (+); kunan (*tribulation*). *a.* naname no; gyaku no; okorippoi; ijiwaru no. *ad.* yokogitte; gyaku-
kuni. *v.* yokogiru; jama suru; jūji o kiru; kōsa suru. ～**bar**
[-bɑ:] *n.* kannuki. ～**bill** [-bil] (*bird*) *n.* isuka. ～**bow** [-bou]
n. ishiyumi. ～**breed** [-kri:d] *n.* zasshu. ～**country** [-kʌntri] *n.*
inaka o tōru. ～**cut** [-kʌt] *n.* ichiban chikai kyori ～**examin-**
ation [-igzæmínéiʃən] (*leg.*) *n.* (shōnin no) hantai jimmon. ～
eyed [-aid] *a.* yabunirami no. ～**fire** [-faiə] *n.* jūji-hōka. ～
grained [-greind] *a.* sakame no. ～**ing** *n.* fumikiri; kōsaten.
～**legged** [-legid] *a.* ashi o kunde. ～**ly,** *ad.* ～**ness,** *n.* ～
piece [-pi:s] *n.* yokogi. ～**purpose** [-pə:pəs] *n.* hantai no mokuteki. ～**question** *v.* hantai jimmon o suru. ～**road** [-roud]
n. yotsutsuji. ～**sea** [-si:] *n.* yokonami. ～**section** [-sekʃən] *n.*
ōdan-men. ～**stitch** [-stiʃ] *n.* chidorigake. ～**way** [-wei] *n.* =
cross road. ～**wind** [-wind] *n.* mukaikaze. ～**wise** [-waiz] *ad.*

crotch [krɔtʃ] *n.* (ki nado no) mata (*fork*).   butchigai ni.

crotchet [krɔ́tʃit] *n.* henna kangae; toppina omoitsuki; (*mus.*)
shibuompu. ～**y** [krɔ́tʃiti] *a.* monozukina.

crouch [kráutʃ] *v.* uzukumaru. *n.* uzukumari.   tōen.

croup(e) [kru:p] *n.* (tokuni uma no) dembu; kuruppu-sei kō-

crow [krow] *n.* karasu; keimei (*cock crow*); akambō no kansei
(yorokobi). *v.* toki o tsukuru. ～**bar** [-bɑ:] kanateko. ～**foot**
[-fut] (*bot.*) kimpōge. ～**'s-foot** [-sfut] *n.* mejiri no shiwa
(*wrinkles*). ～**'s-nest** hobashira no ue no miharibansho.

crowd [kraud] *n.* gunshū; zattō. *v.* gunshū saseru (suru).

crown [kraun] *n.* kammuri; kunshu. ～**prince** [-prins] *n.* ōji;
kōtaishi. ～ **princess,** kōtaishi-hi. **C**～ **Office** ～ɔ́fis] *n.* keijibu.

crozier, crosier [króuʒə] *n.* (sōjō no motsu) jūjikei no shakujō.

crucial [krú:ʃiəl/-ʃəl] *a*. kibishii ; jūjikeino.

crucible [krú:sibl] *n*. rutsubo.

crucifix [krú:sifiks] *n*. Kirisuto haritsuke no zō.

crucifixion [krù:sifikʃən] *n*. haritsuke ; (*the* ~) *Christ* no jūjika no ue de no shi.

cruciform [krú:sifɔ:m] *a*. jūjikei no.

crucify [krú:sifai] *v*. jūjika ni tsukeru ; haritsuke ni suru.

crude [kru:d] *a*. tennen no mama no ; mijukuna. ~**ly** *ad*. ~**ness** *n*. ~ **oil** (*or* **petroleum**) *n*. gen'yu.

crudity [krú:diti] *n*. nama ; katai koto ; mijuku.

cruel [krúəl/krúil] *a*. zankokuna. ~**ly** *ad*. mugoku. ~**ness,** ~**ty** *n*. zankoku ; zankokuna okonai. ⌈dai.

cruet [krúit] *n*. yakumi o ireru bin. ~ **stand,** yakumi-bin no

cruise [kru:z] *n*. junkō, *v*. junkō suru. ~**r** [kru:zə] *n*. jun'yōkan ; rajio o motta keisatsu-jidōsha.

crumb [krʌm] *n*. chiisana kire ; pankuzu ; goku wazuka. *v*. konagona ni suru.

crumble [krʌmbl] *v*. kudaku ; kudakeru ; kuzureru.

crumbly [krʌ́bmli] *a*. kudakeyasui ; boroboro suru.

crummy [krʌ́mi] *a*. (*Brit. col*) (onna ga) nikuzuki no yoi ; kanemochi no ; fukuyōkana. (*Am. col*) shirami darake no.

crumpet [krʌ́mpit] *n*. isshu no karuyaki-sembei ; (*sl*.) atama.

crumple [krʌ́mpl] *v*. shiwa(-kucha) ni suru (naru).

crunch [krʌntʃ] *v*. oto o tatete kamu ; zukazuka to aruku. *n*. kamikudaku koto.

cruor [krú:ɔ] *n*. chi no katamaru koto.

crupper [krʌ́pə] *n*. uma no shirigai ; shiri.

crusade [kru:séid] *n*. Jūjigun (ni kuwawaru). ~**er** [kruséidə] Jūjigun no heishi.

cruse [kru:z] *n*. kobin ; tsubo.

crush [krʌʃ] *v*. oshitsubusu ; funsai suru : *n*. funsai ; (*Am*.) zattō. (*Am*.) kubittake. ~**ed** *a*. kudakete iru. ~**ing** *a*. attōteki.

crust [krʌst] *n*. gaihi ; (pan nado no) katai kawa ; chikaku. *v*. kawa ni naru ; kawa de ōu. ~**ly** *ad*. kowabatte. ~**iness** *n*. katai koto. ~**ly** *a*. katai ; buaisōna. ⌈rui no.

Crustacea [krʌstéiʃiə] *n*. (*pl*.) kōkakurui. ~**n** [-n] *a*. kōkaku-

crutch [krʌtʃ] *n*. matsubazue ; kuratchi.

crux [krʌks] *n.* (*pl.* **-xes** [-kses/-ksis] ; **-ces** [kru:si:z]) nazo ; nammon ; nanji.

cry [krai] *v.* sakebu ; naku. *n.* sakebi ; nakigoe. ~**ing** *a.* sakebu ; naku. ~ *down*, kenasu. ~ *on*, kongan suru. ~ *up*, hometateru. *a far cry* enkyori. ┌tsu no.

crypt [kript] *n.* chikarō ; chikashitsu. ~**ic** *a.* kakureta ; himi-

cryptogam [kríptogæm] *n.* (*bot.*) inka shokubutsu.

cryptogram [kríptougræm] *n.* angō (*cipher*) ; aikotoba.

cryptograph [kríptougrɑːf/græf] *n.* angō (hō). ~**ic** [kripto-gréfik] *a.* angō no. ~**y** [kriptógrəfi] *n.* angōbun.

crystal [krístl] *n.* kesshōtai ; suishō. *a.* suishō no ; tōmeina. **rock**~ [rɔkkrístəl] *n.* suishō. (*col.*) uranai. ~**gazing** [-géiziŋ] *n.* suishō uranai.

crystalline [krístəlain./-lin] *a.* suishō no ; suishō no yōna ; tōmeina. ~ **lens** [-lenz] me no suishōtai.

crystallization [krístəlaizéiʃən] *n.* kesshō ; kessōtai.

crystallize [krístəlaiz] *v.* kesshō suru (saseru). ┌kesshō.

crystalloid [krístəlɔid] *a.* kesshō no yōna ; tōmeina. *n.* kari-ct. [cent(s)] sento (*cent*).

cub [kʌb] *n.* (kuma ; kitsune nado no) ko ; busahōna otoko no ko. ~ **reporter** [-ripɔːtə] *n.* shimmai no shimbun kisha. **unlicked** ~ [ənlíktkʌb] *n.* mukeikenna wakamono.

Cuban [kjúːbən] *a.* Kyūba no. *n.* Kyūbajin.

cube [kjúːb] *n.* rippōtai ; sanjō ; rippō. *v.* sanjō suru.

cubic [kjúːbik] *a.* rippōtai no ; sanjō no.

cubism [kjúːbizm] *n.* rittaiha. ~**ist** *n.* rittaiha-gaka.

cubit [kjúːbit] *n.* udeshaku (18~22 *inches*).

cuckoo [kúkuː] *n.* kakkōdori ; hototogisu. **little** ~ [litlkúkuː] *n.* hototogisu. ~ **clock** [-klɔk] *n.* kakko dokei.

cucumber [kjuːkəmbə] *n.* (*veg.*) kyūri.

cud [kʌd] *n.* tabemodoshi ; hansū.

cuddle [kʌdl] *v.* dakishimeru ; dakiau. *n.* dakishime.

cudgel [kʌdʒəl] *n.* kombō. *v.* kombō de utsu. ~ *one's brains*, nōmiso o shiboru. *take up the* ~*s for*, ...o bengo suru tame ni tatsu. ┌anji.

cue [kjuː] *n.* o ; bempatsu ; serifu no owari no go ; kikkake ;

cuff [kʌf] *v.* hirate de utsu. *n.* hirateuchi ; kafusu ;

cuirass [kwirǽs] *n.* (dō)yoroi ; dōmawari dake no yoroi.

cuirasier [kwirəsíə] *n.* (do)yoroi kihei.

cuisine [kwi:zí:n] *n.* ryōriba ; ryōri no shikata.

cul-de-sac [kúldəsǽk] *n.* (*Fr.*) fukuro-machi ; fukuro-ji.

culinary [kjú:linəri] *a.* daidokoro no ; ryōri no.

cull [kʌl] *v.* tsumu (hana nado o) ; yoridasu. *n.* yori noke

culm [kʌlm] *n.* kusa no kuki ; wara ; sekitan kuzu. ⌊mono.

culminate [kálmineit] *v.* zetchō ni tassuru (noboru).

culminating [kálmineitiŋ] *a.* kyokudo no ; zetchō no.

culmination [kàlminéiʃən] *n.* kyokuten ; massakari.

culottes [kju:lóts/lá-] *n.* (*pl.*) (*Am.*) zubon shiki sukāto.

culpability [kàlpəbíliti] *n.* togamu beki koto ; yūzai.

culpable [kálpəbl] *a.* semu beki ; futodoki no. **~bly** *ad.* futodoki nimo.

culprit [kálprit] *n.* hanzaisha ; hanzai kengisha.

cult [kʌlt] *n.* gishiki ; saishiki ; ...kyō, ...shū.

cultivate [káltiveit] *v.* tagayasu ; saibai suru ; kyōka suru.

cultivation [kàltivéiʃən] *n.* kōsaku ; baiyō ; kyōka ; shūren.

cultivator [káltiveitə] *n.* kōsakusha ; yōseisha.

culture [káltʃə] *n.* kōsaku ; saibai ; kyōyō ; kyōiku ; bunka.

culvert [kálvət] *n.* chika-suiro ; ankyo. ⌈*a.* urusai.

cumber [kámbə] *v.* jama suru ; komaraseru. **~-some** [sʌm]

cumbrous [kámbrəs] *a.* yakkaina ; jamana ; atsukainikui.

cumulate [kjú:mjuleit] *v.* tsumu ; tsumikasaneru.

cumulation [kjù:mjuléiʃən] *n.* tsumikasane ; chikuseki.

cumulative [kjú:mjulətiv] *a.* kuwawaru ; fueru (chikara nado ga tsuyoku naru).

cumulus [kjú:mjuləs] *n.* sekiun (*clouds*) ; taiseki.

cuneiform [kjú:niifɔ:m/kjuní:ɔfɔ:m] *n.* kikkeimoji (*Babylon Assyria* no moji. *a.* kusabi moji no.

cunning [kániŋ] *a.* kōkatsuna ; takumina ; (*Am.*) omoshiroi. *n.* zurui koto. **~ly** *ad.* zuruku.

cup [kʌp] *n.* koppu ; shōhai. **~ and ball**, kendama. **~board** [kábəd] *n.* todana. **~board love** [-lʌv] *n.* yokutokuzuku no ai. **~ful** *n.* koppu ippai.

Cupid [kjú:pid] *n.* ren'ai no kami.

cupidity [kju:píditi] *n.* don'yoku ; taiyoku.

cupola [kjú:pələ] *n.* (mune no ue ni deteiru) maru-yane ; yō-
cupping glass [kápiŋ glɑ:s] *n.* suifukube. ⌐tetsuro.
cupreous [kjú:priəs] *a.* dō (akagane) no ; dō no yōna.
cur [kə:] *n.* nora-inu ; gesu ; gerō.
curable [kjúərəbl] *a.* chiryō shi uru ; chiryō no kiku.
curaçao, curaçoa [kjùəsóu] *n.* kyurasō (Curaçao gensan no
   sake).
curacy [kjúərəsi] *n.* bokushiho no shoku ; chii.
curate [kjúərit] *n.* bokushiho. ⌐*n.* kusuri.
curative [kjúərətiv] *a.* chiryō no ; chiryō suru chikara no aru.
curator [kjuəréitə] *n.* kanrisha ; shuji ; daigaku hyōgiin.
curb [kə:b] *n.* tomezuna ; kōsoku. *v.* yokusei suru ; osaeru.
curbstone [kə́:bstoun] *n.* fuchiishi. ⌐tsubutsu.
curd [kəid] *n.* chichi no katamari ; gyōnyū ; ekitai no gyōke-
curdle [kə́:dl] *v.* gyōketsu saseru ; katamaraseru. *v.* katamaru.
cure [kjuə] *n.* chiryō ; zenkai. *v.* iyasu. kambutsu, shiomono,
   kunsei, nado ni suru. **cure-all** [kjúərɔ:l] *n.* bannōyaku.
curé [kjúərei] *n.* (*Fr.*) shunin shisai.
curfew [kə́:fju:] *n.* yūbe no (iriai no) kane.
curio [kjúəriou] chimpin ; kottōhin.
curiosity [kjùəriósiti] *n.* kōkishin ; chimpin (*rare or novel object*).
curious [kjúəriəs] *a.* shiritagaru ; sensakuzuki no ; mezurashii ; henna ; memmitsuna. ~ly *ad.* ~ness *n.*
curl [kə:l] *v.* chijirasu ; maku ; chijireru ; uzumaku. *n.* makige ; nejire ; uzumaki. ~ly *a.* chijireta ; makige no aru.
curlew [kə́:lu:] *n.* (*bird*) taishaku-shigi.
curling [kə́:liŋ] *n.* *Scotland* no suijō ishinage yūgi.
curmudgeon [kə:mádʒən] *n.* kechimbo ; shiwambo.
currant [kárənt] *n.* isshu no chiisai hoshibudō ; (*bot.*) suguri (aka, shiro, kuro nado iroiro no).
currency [kárənsi] *n.* tsūka ; jika. *fractional* ~, hojo-kahei.
current [kárənt] *a.* tsūyō suru ; ryūkō suru. *n.* nagare ; (denki, shio nado no) nagare. ~ly *ad.* ippanni ; tsuneni. ~ account [-əkaunt] *n.* tōzakanjō. ⌐(*L.*) rirekisho.
curriculum [kərikjurəm] *n.* katei (gakkō no). ~ vitae [váiti:]
currier [káriə] *n.* kawa shōnin (seizōnin).
curry [kári] *n.* karei (karē) ; karēko ; karē ryōri. ~ *favo(u)r with,*

...ni kobihetsurau. *v.* ~**comb** [kɔ́:rikoum] *n.* umagushi. *v.* chōsei suru (kawa o). ~**powder** [-páudə] *n.* kareiko. ~ *and rice=* ~*ied rice*, raisukarei.

curse [kə:s] *v.* **cursed** [kɔ́:sid] *or* **curst; cursing.** norou ; komaraseru. *n.* noroi ; nonoshiri ; tatari ; tembatsu. ~**d** [-id] *a.* norowareta ; noroubeki ; imaimashii.

cursive [kɔ́:siv] *a.* hashirigaki no. *n.* hashirigaki ; sōsho.

cursory [kɔ́:səri] *a.* soryakuna ; sozatsuna. ~**ily** *ad.* zatto ; zonzaini. ~**iness** *n.* soryaku ; sozatsu.

curst [kə:st] *see* : **curse.**

curt [kə:t] *a.* mijikai ; buaisōna. ~**ly** *ad.* mijikaku ; sokkena- ⌜ku. **curtail** [kə:téil] *v.* kiritsumeru. ~**ment** *n.* sakugen ; kiritsume.

curtain [kɔ́:tn/-tən/-tin] *n.* maku ; madokake. ~ **fire,** hō no dammaku. ~**lecture** [-lektʃə] *n* keichū no kogoto. ~**raiser** [-réizə] *v.* shuyōgeki no mae no mijikai geki.

curtsy [kɔ́:tsi] *n.* koshi o kagamete suru ojigi. *v.* ojigi o suru.

curvature [kɔ́:vətʃə] *n.* wankyoku ; magari. ⌜magaru.

curve [kə:v] *n.* magari ; sori ; kyokusen ; kābu. *v.* mageru ;

curvet [kə:vét / ké:vet] *vi.* chōyaku suru ; tobihaneru. *n.* tobihaneru koto.

curvilinear [kə:vílíniə] *a.* kyokusen no ; *curved line* no.

cushion [kúʃən] *n.* zabuton ; kusshon. *v.* zabuton ni nekaseru.

cusp [kʌsp] *n.* togatta saki ; togatta ten.

cuspid [kʌ́spid] *n.* inuba ; kenshi. ~**ate** [-eit] *a.* togatta.

cuspidor [kʌ́spidɔ:] *n.* tantsubo.

custard [kʌ́stəd] *n.* kasutādo. ~ **apple,** (*bot.*) banreishi no mi.

custodian [kʌstóudiən] *n.* kanshisha (-nin) ; kanrinin.

custody [kʌ́stədi] *n.* hogo ; hokan ; kōryū ; shūyō : *be in the* ~, no hokan (hogo) no moto ni aru. *in* ~, kōryū sarete. *take into* ~, kōin suru.

custom [kʌ́stəm] *n.* shūkan ; tokui. ~**er** *n.* otokui ; (*pl.*) kanzei. ~**house** [kʌ́stəmhaus] zeikan.

customarily [kʌ́stəmərili] *ad.* tsune ni ; tsūrei ni.

customary [kʌ́stəməri] *a.* tsūrei no ; zairai no ; itsumo no.

cut [kʌt] **cut, cuttng,** *v.* kiru ; karu : *I had my hair* ~, watashi wa kami o katte moratta. ~ *a road through a hill*, yama o hiraite michi o tsukeru. shiranai furi shite tōru : *he* ~ *me* *in the street*, kare wa machi de shiranu furi shite itta. *the cold wind* ~ *me to the bone*, kampū wa honemi ni kotaeta. ~*and run*, subayaku nigeru. ~ *a tooth*, ha ga haeru. ~ *both ways*, futamata kakeru. ~ *it fine*, girigiri ni kiritsumeru. ~ *out*, kiri nozoku ; kitte awaseru. (*Am. sl.*) aru koto o yameru. ~ *short*, totsuzen chūshi suru. ~ *under*, nebiki shite uru. ~ *up*, fuzakeru. **short** ~, chikamichi. ~ *off*, jidō kaiheiki. ~**purse** [kʌtpɔːs] *n.* suri. ~**throat** [kʌtθrout] *n.* hitogoroshi ; satsugaisha. ~**ting** [kʌtiŋ] *n.* shimbun nado no kirinuki. ~**ty** [kʌti] mijikai ; tankina. ~**water** [kʌtwɔːtə] *n.* senshu no namikiri. ~**worm** [kʌtwɔːm] *n.* nekirimushi.

cutaneous [kju(ː)téiniəs] *a.* hifu no.

cut back [kʌt bæk] *n.* karikomi (ki nado) ; keiyaku nado tochū de yameru koto.

cute [kjuːt] *a.* nukeme no nai ; rikōna. (*Am.*) kawairashii.

cuticle [kjúːtikl] *n.* hyōhi ; jōhi (*epidermis*).

cutlass [kʌ́tləs] *n.* isshu no tanken.

cutler [kʌ́tlə] *n.* hamono-shi ; hamono-ya (tsukutte uru). ~**y** *n.* hamono ; hamonoshō.

cutlet [kʌ́tlit] *n.* usui niku no kire ; katsuretsu.

cutter [kʌ́tə] *n.* ifuku o tatsu hito ; chiisana sori ; gunkan yō no chiisai *boat*.

cuttlebone [kʌ́ltboun] *n.* ika no kō.

cuttlefish [kʌ́tlfiʃ] *n.* ika.

C.W.O. genkin sakibarai no chūmon (*cash with order*).

cwt. hundredweight ; (*Brit.*) **avoiredupois** [æ̀vədəpɔ́iz] 112 pondo no ryaku ; (*Am.*) 100 pondo.

cyanide [sáiənaid] *n.* shian kagōbutsu.

cyanogen [saiǽnədʒin] *n.* shianojin ; seiso ; yūdoku gasu.

cyclamen [síkləmən] *n.* (*bot.*) shikuramen.

cycle [sáikl] *n.* junkan ; hitomeguri ; jitensha. *v.* junkan suru ; jitensha ni noru. ~**car** [kɑː] *n.* kei jidō jitensha ; ōto sanrinsha.

cyclical [síklic(əl), sáik-] *a.* rinten suru ; junkan suru.

cyclist [sáiklist] jitensha nori.

cyclometer [saiklómitə] *n.* kaiten kirokukei ; sōtei kyorikei.

cyclone [sáikloun] *n.* sempū ; tatsumaki ; taifū. ⌐no.

cyclonic [saiklónik] *a.* sempū no ; sempūteki ; sempū no shita

cyclop(a)edia [sàiklopí:diə] *n.* hyakka-jiten.

cyclop(a)edic [sàikropí:dik] *a.* hyakka-jiten no ; kōhanna.

Cyclops [sáiklɔps] *n.* (*sing. pl.*) hitotsu me no kyojin (*giant*).

cyclotron [sáiklotrən] *n.* saikurotoron.

cygnet [sígnit] *n.* hakuchō no hina.

cylinder [sílində] *n.* entō ; enchū.

cylindrical [silíndrikəl] *a.* entōjō no.

cymbals [símbɔlz] *n.* (*pl.*) shimbaru ; nyōhachi.

cyme [saim] *n.* (*bot.*) shūsanka.

cynic [sínik] *n.* reishō-ka ; (C-) kenjugakuha no hitobito. ~**al** *a.* hinikuna ; (C-) kenjugakuha no. ~**ally** *ad.* reishōtekini ; hinikuni.

cynicism [sínisizm] *n.* reishōheki ; hiniku ; (C-) kenju shugi.

Cynosure [sínəzjuə/sáinəzjuə/-sjuə] *n.* Kogumaza ; (c-) chūmoku no mato ; sambi no mato.

cypher [sáitə] *n. see* : **cipher.**

cypress [sáipris, -rəs] *n.* (*bot.*) itohiba ; sono eda.

cyst [sist] *n.* suibun o fukunda, hifu (*dermal*) no odeki.

Czar [zɑ:] *n.* moto Roshia kōtei no yobina ; (c-) kōtei ; sensei kunshu.

Czareivitch [zá:rivitʃ], **Czarewitch** [zá:riwitʃ] *n.* kyū Roshia no kōtaishi.

Czarevna [zɑ:révnə] *n.* kyū Rosia no yobina.

Czarina [zɑ:rí:nə] kyū Roshia kōgō.

Czech [tʃek] *n.* Chekkujin ; Chekkugo. ~**ic** = ~**ish** *a.* Chekkujin no ; Chekkugo no.

Czecho-Slovak [tʃékou-slóuvæk] *n.* chekkosurovakiajin (-go). *a.* Chekkosurovakia no.

D

D, d [di:] *n.* (*pl.* D's, Ds, [di:s], d's ds [di:z]). Eigo alphabet dai-4-bamme no moji.

d. *a.* [di:] *date ; degree ; denarius* (=*penny, pence*) Rōma sūji=500.

dab [dæb] *v.* karuku tataku. *n.* karui tataki. (*sl.*) tatsujin (*at*).

dabble [dǽbl] *v.* mizu o haneru ; shimesu ; chotto te o dasu.

dabchick [kǽbtʃik] *n.* kaitsuburi (*water fowl*).

dace [deis] *n.* (*fish*) hae.

dachshund [dǽkshund] *n.* ashi ga mijikaku karada no nagai inu ; dakusufundo.

dacoit [dəkɔ́it/dæk-] *n.* Indo matawa Biruma no hizoku.

dactyl [dǽktil] *n.* yō, yoku, yoku kaku. (—‿‿). "shi" no *foot*.

dad [dæd] *n.* **daddy** ; papa ; tōchan. ⌈gumo.

daddy [dǽdi] *u.* tōchan. ~ **longlegs** [-lɔ́ŋlegz] (*ins.*) mekura-

dado [déidou] *n.* (*archi.*) koshihame ; yuka kara 1 m. ijō no takasa ni hatta hameita ; enchū daiza no shikakuna tokoro.

daffodil [dǽfədil] *n.* (*bot.*) kizuisen ; kiiroi hana no suisen.

daft [da:ft] *a.* bakana ; kichigai no.

dagger [dǽgə] *n.* tanken ; † insatsu ni tsukau shirushi. *at* ~*s drawn*, tsuyoku tekii (*hostile feeling*) o idaite.

daguerreotype [dəgérətaip] *n.* gimban-shashin-hō ; gimban-shashin (*photograph of an old type*).

dahlia [déiljə] *n.* (*flower*) daria ; tenjikubotan.

Dail Eireann [dail/dɑ:l/dɔ:l/éərən] Airurand (*Ireland*) kain (*the House of Commons*).

daily [déili] *a., ad.* mainichi (no). *n.* nikkan shimbun (*newspaper*).

dainty [déinti] *a.* umai ; bimyōna ; chūmon no komakai (*fastidous*). *n.* umai mono (*nice thing to eat*). ~**tily** [déintili] *ad.* yūbini ; umasōni.

dairy [déəri] *n.* rakunō ; gyūnyūten (*milk-shop*). ~ **farm** [-fɑ:m] *n.* rakunōjō. ~ **maid** [-meid], *dairy* de hataraku onna. ~ **man** [-mən] *n* *dairy* de hataraku otoko.

dais [déiis] *n.* kamiza (ichidan takai tokoro no (*platform* no)

daisy [déizi] *n.* (*flower*) hinagiku.

dale [deil] *n.* tanima.

dalliance [dǽliəns] *n.* guzutsuki ; ichatsuki (*flirtation*).

dally [dǽli] *v.* guzutsuku ; ichatsuku (*with*).

Daltonism [dɔ́(:)ltənizm] *n.* (*med.*) shikimō (*colour blindness*).

dam [dæm] *n.* seki ; dam. *v.* sekitomeru.

damage [dǽmidʒ] *n.* songai. (*pl.*) (*leg.*) baishōkin (*-money*) ; (*sl.*) hiyō ; *What is the* ~? Hiyō ikura? ~**able** [dǽmidʒəbl] *a.* songai o ukeyasui. ~**bly** *ad.*

damascene [dǽməsí:n], **damaskeen** [-kí:n] *n.* kin-gin o zōgan (*inlay*) shita saiku.

Damascus [dəmǽskəs] (mukashi no) *Syria* no shuto. ~ **steel**, **Damask** ~, ken o tsukuru ni mochiita nie iri kōtetsu.

damask [dǽməsk] *n. a.* donsu (no) ; aya ori (no). sekichiku iro (no). = *Damascus steel*.

damaskeen [dǽməskí:n], **damascene** [dǽməsí:n] *v.* tetsu, hagane nado ni nie o ukasu. ~**ing** *n.* kinzoku zōgan.

dame [deim] *n.* kifujin ; fujin.

damn [dæm] *inter.* (noroi no go) chikushō jigoku ni ochiro ! ~**able** [-əbl] *a.* norou beki. ~**ably.** *ad.*

damnation [dæmnéiʃən] *n.* noroi ; tsuyoi hinan.

damnatory [dǽmnət(ə)ri] *a.* jigoku-yuki no.

damned [dæmd] *a.* norowareta ; nikukute tamaranai.

damnification [dæmnifikéiʃən] *n.* (*leg.*) songai ; shōgai (*injury*).

damnify [dǽmnifai] *v.* (*leg.*) songai o ataeru ; kizu tsukeru (*injure*).

damp [dæmp] *n.* shikke ; dokki (*poisonous air*). *v.* shike saseru. ~**ish** [dǽmpiʃ] *a.* shimerike no. ~**ly** [-li]. *ad.* ~**ness** *n.*

dampen [dǽmpən] *v.* shimeru (-rasu) ; kujiku (*discourage*).

damper [dǽmpə] *n.* ro (*furnace*) no kūki chōsetsu sōchi ; *piano, violin* no jakuon sōchi.

damsel [dǽmz(ə)l] *n.* (*lit.*) shōjo (otome).

damson [dǽmz(ə)n] *n.* (*fruit.*) sumomo.

dance [dɑ:ns] *n.* butō ; odori. *v.* odoru ; odoraseru. ~**r** [dɑ́nsə] *n.* odoriko ; dansā.

dancing [dɑ́:nsiŋ] *n.* butō. ~ **girl** odoriko. ~ **room,** butō ⌊shitsu.

dandelion [dǽndilaiən] *n.* (*flower*) tampopo.

dander [dǽndə] *n.* (*col.*) kanshaku.

dandle [dǽndl] v. (shōni (*baby*) o) ayasu ; kawaigaru.

dandruff [dǽndrəf] n. fuke (atama (*head*) no).

dandy [dǽndi] a. n. shareta (otoko) ; (*Am.*) sutekina (mono) ～**ism** [-ism] n. oshare ; oshare suru koto.

Dane [dein] n. Demmākujin.

danger [déindʒə] n. kiken : *be in* ～, abunai ; kikenna. *out of* ～, kiken o nogarete. ⌐**ness.** n.

dangerous [déin(d)ʒ(ə)rəs] a. kikenna ; kiken de. ～**ly** ad. ～

dangle [dǽŋgl] v. burasagaru (-sageru). ～ *about* (*or after*), onna (*woman*) ni tsuki matou.

Daniel [dǽnjəl] n. (Kyūyaku Seisho (*The Old Testament*) no) Danieru ; mei-hangan (*upright judge*). ⌐*cf.* Dane.

Danish [déiniʃ] a. Demmāku no. n. Demmākugo (*language*).

dank [dæŋk] a. jimetsuita ; shimeppoi.

daphne [dǽfni] n. (*bot.*) gekkeiju ; jinchōge.

dapper [dǽpə] a. kogireina ; ki no kiita.

dapple [dǽpl] v. buchi (madara) ni suru. ～**grey** [grei] n. kurige no uma.

darbies [dáːbiz] n. (*pl.*) (*Brit. sl.*) tejō. (*handcuffs*).

dare [dɛə] **dared** *or* **durst, dared ; daring** v. omoikitte suru. idomu (*challenge*) ; mushisuru (*ignore*) : *I* ～ *say*, tabun. *D*～ *he do it*? kare ni yaru yūki ga aru ka na? *He dares to insult me*, kare wa watashi ni bureina koto o suru no da. ～**devil** [déə-dèvl] n. mukōmizu.

daring [déəriŋ] adj. daitanna ; omoikitta. n. daitan ; kibatsu : *a* ～ *idea*, kibatsuna omoitsuki.

dark [daːk] a. kurai ; fukakaina (*mysterious*) ; mikai no (*savage*). n. ankoku ; yūgata (*nightfall*). ～**en** [dáːkn] v. kuraku naru (suru) ; gomakasu. ～**horse** [-hɔːs] n. jitsuryoku no wakaranu uma. ～**ling** [dáːkliŋ] a. bōtto shita. ～**ly** ad. ～**ness** [-nis] n. ～**some** [-sʌm] a. usugurai. ～**y** [dáːki] v. kokujin.

darling [dáːliŋ] a. kawaii. n. aijin ; itoshigo (*precious child*).

darn [daːn] n. (hokorobi (*rip*) o) kagatta basho. v. nui tsukurou ; kagaru.

dart [daːt] n. nageyari : tosshin (*going rapidly*). v. nage-yari (*spear*) o nageru ; tosshin suru.

dash [dæʃ] v. buttsukeru (tatakitsukeru) : *He dashed his enemy* *to the ground*, kare wa teki o jimen ni tatakitsuketa. mizu nado o bukkakeru. ikioi yoku buttsukaru. *n.* butsukari : *the ∼ of the rain against the window*, mado ni buttsukaru amé. chotto no mazari : *water with a dash of whisky*, chotto *w.* o watta mizu. ∼**ingly** isamashiku. (—) no kigō. tankyori kyōsō : *the 100-meter ∼*, 100-m. kyōsō. *cut a ∼*, mie o haru. *make a ∼ for*, ni mukatte buttsukaru. ∼**board** [-bɔ:d] sori, kuruma no mae no dorohane.

dashing [dǽʃiŋ] *a.* isamashii ; hadena (*gay*). ∼**ly** *ad.*

dastard [dǽstəd] *n.* okubyō mono. *a.* okubyōna. ∼**ly** *ad.*

data [déitə] *datum* no fukusū ; hakkiri wakatta jijitsu. ∼**book** sankō shiryō

date [deit] *n.* hizuke ; (*Am.*) au yakusoku. natsume-yashi (no mi *fruit*). *down* (*or up*) *to ∼*, konnichi made. *out of ∼*, jidai okure no. *v.* hizuke o kaku ; ji-ki o yakusoku suru. *∼ back to* …ni sakanoboru. ∼**less** [déitlés] *a.* hizuke no shitenai (furui). ∼**palm** [-pɑ:m] (*bot.*) natsume yashi.

dative [déitiv] *n. a.* (*gram.*) yokaku (no).

datum [déitəm] *n.* (*pl.* **-ta**) ronkyo ; shiryō ; jijitsu.

daub [dɔ:b] *n.* shikkui ; hetana e (*unskilful painting*). *v.* nuru (*cover*) ; heta ni kaku (*paint*).

daughter [dɔ́:tə] *n.* musume. ∼**-in-law** [dɔ́:təinlɔ:] *n.* yome. ∼**ly** [dɔ́:təli] *a.* musume-rasshi.

daunt [dɔ:nt] *v.* odosu ; (eiki (*energy*) o) kujiku. ∼**less** [-lis] *a.* osore o shiranai.

dauphin [dɔ́:fin] *n. France* kōtaishi. ∼**ess** [-is] (*Fr.*) kōtaishihi.

davenport [dǽvnpɔ:t] *n.* (*Brit.*) kazari (*decoration*) tsuki kozukue. (*Am.*) shindai (*sleeping berth*) ken'yō no nagaisu.

Davis cup [déividʒ cʌp] Dēbis kappu (*cup*). Teikyū no Sekai yūshō-sha no morau (*cup*).

davit [dǽvit] *n.* bōto o tsurushite oku ittsui no tetsu no hashira.

Davy Jones [déivi dʒɔ́unz] *n.* kaijin (umi no kami) ; kaima (*sea devil*) : *go to ∼ locker*, kaitei no mokuzu to naru.

Davy lamp [dévi læmp] Dēvii-tō. *Davy* no hatsumei shita tankōyō (*used for a coal-mine*) anzentō.

daw [dɔ:] *n.* (*bird*) kokumaru-garasu.

dawdle [dɔ́:dl] *v.* norakura sugosu. *∼ away*, jikan o kūhi suru. ~r [dɔ́:dlə] *n*. namakemono.

dawn [dɔ:n] *n*. yoake; shokō (*incipient gleam*). *v*. yo ga akeru.

day [dei] *n*. hiru; jidai (*period of time*). shōri (*victory*) : win (*lose*) *the* ~, shōri o uru (makeru). ~**break** yoake. ~**dream** [-dri:m] kūsō (*reverie*). ~**labo(u)ror** [-léibələ] *n*. hiyatoi rōdōsha. ~ **scholar** [-skɔlə] chūkan gakusei. ~**time** [taim] hiruma.

daylight [déilait] *n*. nikkō; hiruma (*daytime*); akegata (*dawn*). ~**saving time** (*Am*.) kaki jikan (*summer time*).

daze [deiz] *n*. genwaku; kirameki. *v*. mabushiku suru; bon-yari saseru (*stupefy*).

dazzle [dǽzl] *v*. mabushiku suru. *n*. genwaku. ~**ing** [dǽzliŋ] *a*. mabushii.

D.D., D/D. [dimá:nd drá:ft] ichiran-barai tegata (*demand draft*).
DDT *dichloro-diphenyl trichloro-ethane* [-éθein] (ni-enka-butsu).

deacon [dí:k(ə)n] *n*. (*rel*.) (kyōkai no) shitsuji.

dead [ded] *a*. shinda; sutareta : ~ *ball* (*baseball*), shikyū. ~**freight** kara-ni unchin. ~**heat** gokaku no kyōsō; mushōbu. ~ **language** mukashi no gengo. ~ **letter** haitatsu funō no tegami. ~**loan** [-loun] kashidaore. ~**man** (*soldier sl*.) kara no sakebin. ~**pan** [-pæn] muhyōjōna kao. ~**weight** fūtai. ~**beat** [-bi:t] tsukarekitta. ~**drunk** deisui shite. ~**line** shisen. ~**lock** ikizumari. ~**ly** *a*. inochi ni kakaru. ~**liness** *n*. chimeiteki.

deaden [dédn] *v*. nibuku suru; (yuka nado *floor*) oto no shinai yōni suru. hikaranu yōni suru (*make no brightness*).

deaf [def] *a*. mimi (*ear*) no tōi; kikiirenu (~ *to all appeals*). ~**en** [défn] *v*. tsumbo ni suru. ~**ening** [défniŋ] tsumbo ni naru hodo no. ~**mute** *n*. rōa.

deal [di:l] *v*. **dealt; dealing.** wakeru; dageki o kuwaeru (*deliver*); akinau (*in*); torihiki suru (*do business*). *n*. torihiki; (*Am*.) keizai seisaku; mitsu yaku (*secret job*). *a*. good (*great*) ~ *of*, takusan no. ~**er** *n*. shōnin. ~**ing** [-iŋ] *n*. toriatsukai; shō-bai.
dealt [delt] *see : deal.*

dean [di:n] *n*. (*rel*.) shisaichō; fukukantoku; (daigaku) gaku-chō (*president*); gakubuchō. ~**ery** [dí:nəri] *n*. shisai no chō no shoku.

dear [díə] *a*. (nedan ga) takai; itoshii (*darling*). *n*. aijin (*lover*);

kawaii mono (*lovely child*, ~ *thing*). ~ **me**, oya, oya! ~**ly** [díɔri] *ad.* kōka ni ; takai nedan de.

dearth [dɔ:θ] *n.* ketsubō ; shokumotsu no tarinai (*lack of food*) ; kikin (*famine*).

death [deθ] *n.* shi ; shikei (~ *penalty*). ~**bed** [-bed] rinjū. ~ **blow** [-blou] chimei no dageki. ~**less** [-les] *a.* shinanai. ~ **like** [-laik] *a.* shinda yōna. ~**ly** *a.* = ~**-like**. ~**mask** [-mɑ:sk] desu-masuku. ~**rate** [-reit] shibōritsu. ~**s head** [déθshed] *n.* zugaikotsu ; dokuro. ~**warrant** [-wɔrənt] shikei shikkōmeirei. ~**watch** [-wɔtʃ] *n.* rinjū no kango.   ⌜do no).

debacle [deibá:kl] *n.* (*Fr.*) sōkuzure (seifu, ichiba, guntai na-**debar** [dibá:] *v.* kobamu ; kinzuru (*from*). ~**ment** [-mənt] *n* kinshi ; soshi.

debarkation [di:bɑ:kéiʃən] *n.* jōriku ; rikuage (*landing*).

debase [dibéis] *v.* (hinsei, neuchi nado o) otosu ; (kahei (*coin*) o) henzō suru (*adulterate*). ~**ment** [-mənt] *n. debase* suru koto.

debate [dibéit] *n.* tōron. tōron suru (*discuss thoroughly*) ; jukkō suru (*consider*). ~**able** [dibéitəbl] *a.* ronsō no tane to naru.

debauch [dibɔ́:tʃ] *v.* daraku (*downfall*) saseru ; yūwaku (*temptation*) suru. *n.* hōtō. ~**ed** daraku shita. ~**ery** [dibáutʃəri] *n.* hōtō.

debauchee [dèbɔ:tʃí:] *n.* hōtōmono ; dōrakumono.   ⌜hōtō.

debenture [dibéntʃə] *n.* shasaiken ; saiken.

debilitate [dibíliteit] *v.* suijaku saseru ; yowaraseru (*weaken*).

debility [debíliti] *n.* byōjaku ; suijaku.

debit [débit] *n.* fusai ; harai ; karikata (boki). *v.* chōbo no karikata ni kinyū suru.

debonair(e) [débənnéə] *a.* kaikatsuna (*cheerful*) ; yūgana.

debouch [dibáutʃ/dibú:ʃ] *v.* semai, seigen sareta tokoro kara hiroi tokoro e dete kuru ; kawa nado ga hiroi tokoro e na-garekomu.

debris [débri:/dəbrí:] *n.* kuzu ; hahen (*scattered fragments*) ; kowaremono no kozumi.

debt [det] *n.* shakkin ; saimu. ~**or** *n.* saimusha ; karikata.

debunk [di:bʌ́ŋk] *v.* (*Am. sl.*) bakuro suru ; suppanuku.

debut [déibju] *n.* (*Fr.*) hatsubutai ; omemie. ~**ant** [débjutá:nt] *n.* hatsubutai no hito. ~**ante** *n.* hatsubutai no onna no hito.

decade [dékeid/-kəd] *n.* jū ; jūnenkan (*period fo ten years*).

decadence [dékədəns/dikéid-] *n.* taihai ; daraku (*deterioration*).

decadent [dikéidənt] *a.* taihaiteki ; bungei taihaiki no. *n.* (19 seikimatsu *France* no) dekadanha no geijutsuka.

decagon [dékəgən] *n.* (*math.*) jikkaku-kei ; jippenkei.

decagram(me) [dékəgræm] *n.* deka guramu (*10 grammes*).

decahedron [dèkəhí:drən] *a.* 10-mentai no. *n.* jūmentai.

decaliter, -tre [dékəli:tə] *n.* deka-rittoru (10 rittoru).

Decalogue [dékəloug] *n.* (*rel.*) jukkai (*Ten Commandments*).

decameter, -tre [dékəmi:tə] *n.* deka-mētoru (10 mētoru).

decamp [dikémp] *v.* jin'ei o hikiharau ; nigete shimau.

decant [diként] *v.* shizukani sosogu ; uwasumi o toru.

decanter [dikéntə] *n.* dekanta ; sen (*stopper*) no aru garasubin.

decapitate [diképiteit] *v.* kubi o kiru (*behead*).

decapitation [dikæpitéiʃən] *n.* kubikiri ; menshoku (*dismissal*).

decay [dikéi] *v.* otoroeru (-sasu) ; kusaru (-rasu). *n.* suibi (*loss of power*).

decease [disí:s] *n.* shi ; shibō (*death*). *v.* shibō suru. ⌈no X.

deceased [disí:st] *a.* naku natta ; naki (*late*) : the ~ X, moto

deceit [disí:t] *n.* azamuki ; sagi. ~**ful** *a.* sagi no ; peten no. ~ fully *ad.* sagiteki ni.

deceive [disí:v] *v.* azamuku ; damasu.

decelerate [di:séləreit] *v.* gensoku suru ; sokudo ga ochiru. *cf.* **accelerate.**

December [disémbə] *n.* Jūnigatsu.

decency [di:sənsi] *n.* reigi ; reigi-tadashisa ; jōhinsa ; taimen. *for* ~*cy's sake*, taimenjō. *the decency*, reigi-sahō.

decennial [disénial] *a.* jūnenkan no ; jūnen goto no.

decent [dí:sent] *a.* reigitadashii ; jōhinna ; yasashii (*kindly*).

decentraliztion [di:sèntrəlizéiʃən] *n.* chihō bunken seido.

deception [disépʃən] *n.* manchaku ; sagi ; giman.

deceptive [diséptiv] *a.* madowasu ; sagitekina ; ate ni naranai. ~**ly** *ad.* giman teki ni.

decide [disáid] *v.* kettei suru. ~**ed** [disáidid] *a.* meikakuna (*definite*) ; ketteiteki no. ~**edly** *ad.* meihakuni ; danko to shite.

deciduous [disídjuəs] *a.* (*bot. zool.*) datsurakusei no ; rakuyōsei no. ~ *teeth*, nyūshi. *cf.* **evergreen.**

decigram(me) [désigræm] *n.* deshi-guramu ; 0.1 *gramme*.

deciliter, -tre [désilitr] *n.* deshi rittoru ; 0.1 *litre.*

decimal [désiməl] *a.* jisshinhō no ; shōsū no. ~**fraction** [frǽkʃən] *n.* shōsū. *circulating (or recurring)* ~**s,** junkan shōsū. ~**ly** *ad.* jisshinhō de ; shōsūtekini. ~**ization** [dèsiməlizéiʃən] jisshinhō ni suru koto.

decimate [désimeit] *v.* jū kara ichi o erabu ; jūnin kara hitori o korosu ; ōku no hito o korosu.

decimation [desiméiʃən] *n.* jūnin ni hitori erande korosu koto ; ōku no hito o korosu koto.

decimeter, -tre [désimi:tə] *n.* deshi mētoru ; 0.1 mētre.

decipher [disáifə] *v.* (angō o) yomitoku ; handoku suru. ~ *the letter,* tegami no imi ga wakaru. ~**ment** *n.* imi no yomi-

decision [disíʒən] *n.* kettei ; hanketsu ; ketsudan. ⌐toki

decisive [disáisiv] *n.* ketteiteki no ; ketsuzen taru ; meikakuna (*definite*). ~**ly** *ad.* ketteitekini ; danko to shite.

deck [dek] *n.* kampan. *v.* kazaru (*adorn*), (*with*) kampan o haru. *clear the* ~ *for action,* sentōjumbi o suru.

declaim [dikléim] *v.* (kanjō o komete) benji tateru ; rōdoku suru (*recite*) ; hinan suru (~ *against*).

declamation [dèkləméiʃən] *n.* (tōtō taru) enzetsu ; netsuben ; rōdoku ; anshō. ⌐no.

declamatory [diklǽmətəri] *a.* enzetsu kuchō no ; rōdokufū

declaration [dèkləréiʃən] *n.* sengen ; fukoku ; senseisho. **the Declaration of Independence,** dokuritsu sengen.

declarative [diklǽrətiv] *a.* sengen suru ; chinjutsu no. ~ *sentence* (*gram.*) jojutsubun.

declare [diklɛ́ə] *v.* sengen (fukoku, shinkoku, dangen) suru (*assert*). ~ *oneself,* shoshin o noberu.

declension [diklénʃən] *n.* (*gram.*) gobi henka (meishi, daimeishi nado no). suibi (*declineing*).

declinable [dikláinəbl] *a.* gobi henka ga dekiru. ⌐kaku.

declination [dèklinéiʃən] *n.* katamuki (*slope*) ; keisha ; hōi-

decline [dikláin] *v.* kotowaru : *I am sorry I must* ~ *your invitation to dinner, dinner* e no goshōtai o zannen nagara gojitai (okotowari) mōshi masu. otoroeru : *His strength slowly* ~**ed,** kare no chikara wa shidaini otoroeta. (*gram.*) gobi o henka suru. *n.* katamuki ; suijaku (toshi no tame ni).

declining [dikláiniŋ] *a.* katamuku ; otoroeru.

declivity [diklíviti] *n.* keisha ; kudarizaka. *cf.* **acctivity.**

decoction [dikɔ́kʃən] *n.* senji-gusuri ; nidashi.

decode [dì:kóud] *v.* (angō o) hon'yaku suru.

décolleté [deikɔ́ltei] *a.* (*Fr.*) kata to kubi o arawashita. *robe* ~, (rōbu dekorute) (shikujo-yō no eri nashi reifuku).

decolo(u)r [di:kʌ́lə] *v.* iro o nuku ; hyōhaku suru (*bleach*).

decompose [dikɔ́mpouz] *v.* bunkai suru ; kusaru (-raseru) ; bunkai suru.

decomposition [dìkɔmpəzíʃən] *n.* bunkai ; fuhai.

decorate [dékəreit] *v.* kazaru ; kunshō o sazukeru.

decoration [dìkəréiʃən] *n.* sōshoku ; kunshō.

decorative [dikɔ́rətiv] *a.* sōshoku no.

decorous [dékələs] *a.* reigi tadashii ; jōhinna (*decent*). ⌐tadashiku. ~ly reigi

decorum [dikóurəm] *n.* reigi ; reisetsu (*etiquette*).

decoy [dikɔ́i] *n.* esa ; otori. *v.* obiki yoseru ; tsuri dasu.

decrease [dikrí:s] *n.* genshō (*diminution*). *v.* heru ; herasu.

decree [dikrí:] *n.* meirei ; hōrei ; kokuji ; hanketsu. **Imperial** ~, chokurei. *v.* hōrei de kimeru ; fukoku suru.

decrepit [dikrépit] *a.* rōsui shita ; rōkyū no.

decrepitude [dikrépitju:d] *n.* rōsui ; rōkyū.

decrial [dikráiəl] *n.* hinan ; batō.

decry [dikrái] *v.* kenasu (*censure*) ; hinan suru.

dedicate [dédikeit] *v.* kenjō suru ; sasageru (mi o). ~ *oneself to*, ni mi o sasageru.

dedication [dèdikéiʃən] *n.* kenjō ; kenshin ; tōtoi mokuteki ni mi o sasageru koto..

dedicatory [dédikətəri] *a.* kenshinteki no ; sasageru.

deduce [didjú:s] *v.* suiron suru (*infer*) ; en'eki suru (*from, out of*) ; suji o oshihakaru.

deduct [didʌ́kt] *v.* hiku ; nozoku ; waribiki suru ; kōjo suru.

deduction [didʌ́kʃən] *n.* waribiki ; sashihiki ; suitei ; (*log.*) en'-ekironri.

deductive [didʌ́ktiv] *a.* suitei no ; (*log.*) en'ekironri no.

deed [di:d] *n.* kōi ; jigyō ; kōseki ; jijitsu ; *in* (*very*) ~, jissai ni.

deem [di:m] *v.* minasu ; kangaeru (*consider*).

deep [di:p] *a* fukai ; fukasa…no ; shin'enna (*profound*) ; tsūsetsuna (*intense*) ; haraguroi (*sly*) ; (koe) futoi, hikui ; (iro) koi. *n.* umi no fukami ; umi ; mannaka. *ad.* fukaku. ~**ly** *ad.* fukaku. ~**ness** *n.* fukasa. ~**-laid** [leid] *a.* fukaku takuranda. ~**-rooted** [-rú:tid] *a.* nebukai. ~**sea** [-si:] *a.* fukai umi no. ~**-seated** [-si:tid] *a.* nebukai ; fuji no (byōki nado no).

deepen [dí:pn] *v.* fukaku suru ; (iro) koku suru ; (koe) futoku hikuku suru. fukaku (koku ; muzukashiku) naru (suru).

deer [diə] *n.* (*sing. pl.*) shika. ~**skin** [-skin] *n.* shikagawa.

deface [diféis] *v.* gaimen o kizutsukeru. ~**ment** *n.* kison ; surikeshi.

defalcate [di(:)fǽlkeit] *v.* itakukin o shōhi suru (tsukai komu).

defalcation [di:fælkéiʃən] *n.* itakukin shōhi (tsukaikomi).

defamation [dèfəméiʃən] *n.* meiyo kison ; chūshō ; warukuchi.

defamatory [difǽmətəri] *a.* meiyo kison no.

defame [diféim] *v.* meiyo o kison suru ; chūshō suru (*slander*) *cf.* **libel.**

default [difɔ́:lt] *n.* taiman ; saiban e no kesseki ; ketsubō : *in* ~ *of*, no nai tame ; no fusokuna toki wa. *judgment by* ~, kesseki saiban. *make* ~, saiban o kesseki suru. *v.* saimu o rikō shinai. ~**er** *n.* furikōsha ; itakukin shōshisha.

defeat [difí:t] *n.* haiboku ; zasetsu (*frustration*). *v.* uchiyaburu ; zasetsu saseru ; (jōken nado o) mukō ni suru (*annul*). ~**ism** [-izm] *n.* haibokushugi. ~**ist** [-ist] *n.* haiboku shugisha.

defect [difékt] *n.* ketten (*fault*) ; ketsubō, fusoku. *in* ~ *of*, ga nai baai niwa.

defection [difékʃən] *n.* hainin ; hensetsu (*apostasy*) ; dattō.

defective [diféktiv] *a.* ketten no aru ; fukanzenna (*imperfect*) ; (*gram.*) katsuyō kei o kaita. ~**ly** *ad.* fukanzenni.

defend [difénd] *v.* fusegu ; bengo suru (*vindicate*). ~**ant** *n.* bengosha ; hikoku. ~**er** *n.* yōgosha ; bengosha.

defence (*Brit.*), **defense** (*Am.*) [diféns] *n.* bōgyo ; bengo ; hikoku no tōben. *in* ~ *of*, o mamotte ; o bengo shite. ~**less** [-lis] *a.* bōbi no nai ; bōgyo no michi no nai.

defensible [difénsibl] *a.* bōgyo shi uru ; bengo shi uru.

defensive [difénsiv] *a.* bōgyoteki ; bengo no. *n.* shusei. ~**ly** *ad.* bōeitekini.

defer [difɔ́:] *v.* enki suru (*put off*) ; nobiru ; nagabiku (*delay*).

shitagau (*yield*) [*to*] : ∼*ed telegram*, kansō dempō. ∼**ment** *n.*
enki (*postponement*) ; yūyo.

deference [défərəns] *n.* fukujū ; sonkei. (*respect*).

deferential [dəfərénʃəl] *a.* kenjō no ; kensonna.

defiance [difáiəns] *n.* chōsen ; hankō teki taido.

defiant [defáiənt] *a.* bureina ; bōjakubujin no ; hankōteki. ∼
ly *ad.* chōsentekini.

deficience [difíʃəns], ∼**cy** [-si] *n.* ketsubō ; fusoku. ∼**disease**
[difíʃənsidizi:z] *n.* eiyōshitchō.

deficient [difíʃənt] *a.* fusoku no ; fukanzenna. ∼**ly** *ad.* fukan-
deficit [défisit] *n.* fusoku ; akaji. *cf.* **surplus.** ⌊zenni.

defier [difáiə] *n.* chōsensha ; hankōsha.

defile [difáil] *n.* semai michi (tanima nado no). *v.* ichiretsu ni
susumu (michi ga semai tame).

define [difáin] *v.* gentei suru ; teigi o kudasu.

definite [définit] *a.* kakuteitekina ; meikakuna. ∼**ly** *ad.* kaku-
teitekini ; meikakuni. ∼**ness** *n.* kakutei ; meikakusei.

definition [dəfiníʃən] *n.* teigi ; (rajio nado no) meiryōdo (*degree
of clearness*).

definitive [difínitiv] *a.* ketteitekina ; saigotekina (*final*). ∼**ly**
ad. ketteitekini. ∼**ness** *n.* saigoteki. ⌈ku o toru.

deflate [difléit] *v.* kūki o nuku ; shukushō suru ; *deflation* seisa-
deflation [difléiʃən] *n.* kūki o nuku koto ; tsūka shikushō.

deflect [deflékt] *v.* sorasu (-reru) ; yugameru (-mu).

deflection [difléksən] *n.* katayori ; sore.

deflower [difláwə] *v.* hana o tsumi toru ; bi o ubau ; kegasu
(*virginity* o ubau).

deform [difɔ:m] *v.* minikuku suru ; fugu ni suru.

deformation [difɔ:méiʃən] *n.* katachi o waruku suru koto. fugu ; henkei.

deformity [difɔ:miti] *n.* kikei ; fugu ; kekkan. ⌈(*cheat*).

defraud [difrɔ:d] *v.* azamuki toru ; sagi ni kakeru ; kataru

defray [difréi] *v.* shiharau (*pay*). ∼**ment** *n.* shiharai.

deft [deft] *a.* kiyōna ; jōzuna ; takumina (*dexterous*). ∼**ly** *ad.*
kiyōni.

defunct [difʌ́ŋkt] *a.* shinda : *the*∼ shisha ; kojin (*the deceased*).

defy [difái] *v.* idomu ; mushi suru ; kobamu (*resist*) ; zasetsu saseru.

degeneracy [digénərəsi] *n.* taiho; daraku.

degenerate [didʒénəreit] *v.* waruku naru; daraku suru; taiho suru. *a.* daraku (taiho) shita. *n.* daraku shita mono.

degeneration [didʒənəréiʃən] *n.* taiho; daraku; henshitsu.

deglutition [dì:glu:tíʃən] *n.* enka; mono o nomikudasu sayō.

degradation [dègrədéiʃən] *n.* teika; daraku; ganseki no hōkai (*weathering*). ⌈suru.

degrade [digréid] *v.* kurai o sageru; hin'i o otosu; kakusage

degrading [digréidiŋ] *a.* hin'i o sageru; geretsuna (*debasing*).

degree [digrí:] *n.* tōkyū; doai; (kandankei nado no) do; gakui; chii (*rank*); (*math.*) -ji; (*gram.*) kyū, *comparative, supertive* ~).

degression [digréjən] *n.* zengen; dandan ni sagaru (heru).

degressive [digrésiv] *a.* zengenteki; zengen suru.

deification [dì:ifikéiʃən] *n.* shinseina mono to suru koto; kami to agameru koto.

deify [dí:ifai] *v.* kami ni matsuru; kami to agameru.

deign [dein] *v.* (katajikenaku mo) ...shitamou; kudashi tamawaru : *The King deigned to accept the offer,* Ō wa sono kenjōhin o uke tamōta.

deism [dì:izm] *n.* shizenshinkyō; shizen o kami to suru oshie.

deist [dí:ist] *n.* shizen shinkyō shinja. ~**ic** *a.* shizenshinkyō ⌊no.

deity [dí:iti] *n.* kami (*god*).

deject [kidʒékt] *v.* shogesaseru; gakkari saseru (*dishearten*). ~**edly** [-idli] *ad.* sugosugo.

dejection [didʒékʃən] *n.* rakutan; gakkari. haisetsu. ⌈ment).

delay [diléi] *v.* nobasu; okuraseru. *n.* chitai; yūyo (*postpone-*

delectable [diléktəbl] *a.* ureshii; yukaina. ~**bly** *ad.* yukaini; tanoshiku; ureshiku.

delectation [dìlektéiʃən] *n.* yukai; kanraku.

delegate [déligeit] *v.* dairi to shite ikaseru (yaru); (kenri nado o) inin suru. *n.* iin (*commissioner*) daihyōsha; dairi (*deputy*).

delegation [déligéiʃən] *n.* dairi haken; iin haken; iin-dan; daihyō-dan; inin.

delete [dilí:t] *v.* sakujo suru; massatsu suru (*erase*).

deleterious [dèlitíəriəs] *a.* yūgaina (*harmful*). ~**ly** *ad.* yūgaide.

deliberate [dilíbəreit] *v.* jukkō suru; hyōgi suru. *a.* shiryo aru (*cautious*); koi no (*intentional*). ∼**ly** *ad.* shinchō ni; koini. ∼**ness** *n.*

deliberation [dilibəréiʃən] *n.* jukkō; hyōgi; shinchō. 「no.

deliberative [dilíbərətiv] *a.* jukkōshita; shingi (gōgi) no ue

delicacy [dilíkəsi] *n.* umami (*tastefulness*); fudezukai (*penman ship*) nado nimo iu). umasa; oishii teido; kayowasa (*weak liness*); yūga (*refinement*); binkan (*sensitiveness*); shinchōsa (*consideration*).

delicate [délikit] *a.* yūbina (*fine*); oishii; seikōna (*exquisite*), yowayowashii (*feeble*); binkanna (*sensitive*); saishin no chūi o yōsuru, bimyōna (*subtle*), toriatsukai no muzukashii. ∼**ly** *ad.*

delicious [dilíʃəs] *a.* oishii; tanoshii (*enjoyable*). ∼**ly** *ad.*

delight [diláit] *n.* yorokobi; tanoshimi. *v.* yorokobu; tanoshi mu. ∼**ed** [-id] *a.* yorokonde; tanoshinde.

delightful [deláitful] *a.* yorokobashii; yukaina. ∼**ly** *ad.* ure shiku; yukaini. ∼**ness** *n.* yukai.

delineate [dilí:nieit] *v.* byōsha suru; jojutsu suru.

delineation [dilinéiʃən] *n.* byōsha; jojutsu; ryakuzu (*sketch*).

delinquency [dilíŋkwənsi] *n.* taiman (*neglect*); kashitsu.

delinquent [dilíŋkwənt] *a.* gimu o okotaru; tsumi no aru (*guilty*); namakeru; ihan shita.

deliquesce [dèlikwés] *v.* yūkai suru; chōkai suru; tokeru.

deliquescence [dèlikwésens] *n.* yōkai; chōkai (sei).

deliquescent [dèlikwésənt] *a.* yōkai suru; chōkaisei no.

delirious [dilírios] *a.* muga muchū no; seishin sakuran no.

delirium [dilíriəm] *n.* seishin sakuran; muchū; nekkyō.

deliver [dilívə] *v.* sukuidasu (*save*). haitatsu suru: *postman* ∼**s** *letters*, yūbin'ya ga tegami o kubaru. naguru: ∼ *a blow*, naguru. kōen suru: ∼ *a lecture*, kōgi o suru.

deliverance [dilívərəns] *n.* kyūjo (*rescue*); shakuhō (*release*), chinjutsu (*formal expression of opinion*).

deliverer [dilívərə] *n.* kyūjosha; hikiwatashinin; haitatsusha.

delivery [dilívəri] *n.* hikiwatashi; haitatsu; bumben; tōkyū (*baseball*).

dell [del] *n.* kyōkoku (*small valley*); semai taniai.

delta [déltə] *n.* deruta (Girisha moji no 4 bamme *Δ δ*); san kakusu.

delude [diljú:d] *v.* azamuku; mayowaseru (*mislead*).
deluge [délju:dg] *n.* dai-kōzui : *the D ~*, Noa no Daikōzui.
v. afure saseru; sattō suru.
delusion [diljú:ʒən] *n.* damashi (*deception*); mōsō; omoi chigai.   ⌜nai.
delusive [diljú:siv] *a.* magirawashii; mayowasu; ate ni nara-
delve [delv] *v.* (*arch.*) (suki nado de) horu (*dig*).
Dem. Amerika minshutōin (no) (*Democrat(ic*)).   ⌜*tor*).
demagogue [déməgoug] *n.* sendōka (*mob orator ; political agita-*
demand [dimǽnd] *v.* yōkyū suru; jimmon suru. *n.* yōkyū;
seikyū; shitsumon (*inquiry*).
demarcation [dima:kéiʃən] *n.* genkai-kettei; kyōkai-kubun.
demean [dimí:n] *v.* iyashiku suru (*debase*); furumau (*behave*).
demeanor [dimí:nə] *n.* kyodō; taido (*one's bearing*), hinkō (*behavior*).
demented [diméntid] *a.* hakkyō shita; kichigai no (*insane*).
dementia [dimén ʃiə] *n.* seishin sakuran; hakkyō (*insanity*).
demerit [di:mérit] *n.* ketten (*defect*); gakkō no batten.
demesne [diméin/dimí:n] *n.* shoyū; shoyūchi; katsudō han'i.
demigod [démigəd] *n.* hambun kami de hambun ningen.
demijohn [démidʒən] *n.* hosokuchi no ōbin. (kago-zaiku de
tsutsunda mono).
demilitarize [di:mílitəraiz] *v.* hibusōka suru.
demimonde [démimɔ́nd/dəmimō:də] *n.* (*Fr.*) karyūkai.
demise [dimáiz] *v.* hōgyo (*death of emperor or empress*) (shukensha ga kawaru).
demobilization [dímòubil(a)izéiʃən] *n.* fukuin; (shōshū sareta hei ga kaeru koto).
demobilize [di:móubilaiz] *v.* fukuin sareru; heitai o kaesu.
democracy [dimɔ́krəsi] *n.* minshu seitai; minshushugi, (D-)
(*Am.*) Minshutō (no shugi, seisaku).
democrat [déməkræt] *n.* minshushugisha. *~ic* [dəməkrǽtik]
minshu seitai no; minshushugi no.
demolish [dimɔ́liʃ] *v.* hakai suru (*destroy*); kuitsukusu (*eat up*).
demolition [demolíʃən] *n.* hakai; (*pl.*) kōhai no ato.
demon [dí:mən] *n.* akuma (*devil*) *~iac* [di(:)móuniæk] *n.* akuma ni tsukareta hito; kichigai. *a.* akuma no yōna; kyōaku-

na. ∼**ology** [di:mənólədʒi] *n*. akuma kenkyū.

demonetize [di(:)mɔ́nitaiz / -mʌ́n-] *n*. tsūka no shikaku o u-shinawaseru.

demonstrable [démənstrəbl/dimɔ́n-] *a*. shōmei no dekiru. ∼**bly** *ad*. meiryōni.

demonstrate [démənstreit] *v*. shōmei suru (*prove*); (kanjō nado o) arawasu, (mokei nado de) setsumei suru. jiiundō suru.

demonstration [demənstréiʃən] *n*. shōmei; hyōji (*display*); ji-tsu butsu setsumei; jiiundō.

demonstrative [dimɔ́nstrətiv] *a*. shōmei no; shiji no. ∼ *pro-noun*, (*gram.*) shiji daimeishi. ∼**ly** *ad*. ronshōtekini; meihakuni.

demoralization [dimɔ̀rəlaizéiʃən] *n*. fūki binran; shiki sosō.

demoralize [dimɔ́rəlaiz] *v*. fūkiomidasu; shiki o kujiku.

demur [dimɔ́:] *v*. hantai (suru) (*object*); kōben suru (*contradict*).

demure [dimjúə] *a*. majimena (*sober*). ∼**ly** *ad*. majimeni; o-chitsuite; fushizenna majimesano.

demurrage [dimʌ́ridʒ] *n*. nissū chōka no warimashi kin; ka-sha ryūchiryō.

den [den] *n*. dōkutsu (*cavern*); shosai.   ⌜nau koto.

denationalization [di:næ̀ʃ(ə)nəl(à)izéiʃən] *n*. kokuseki o ushi-

denationalize [di:nǽʃ(ə)nəraiz] *v*. kokuseki o hagu; koku-min no kenri o ubau.   ⌜nozoku.

denaturalize [di:nǽtʃ(ə)ralaiz] *v*. honshō o kaeru; kokuseki o

denature [di:néitʃə] *v*. seishitsu o kae saseru.

denial [dináiəl] *n*. hinin (*disavowal*); hitei; kyozetsu (*refusal*).

denizen [dénizn] *n*. kōmin (*citizen*); shimin.

Denmark [dénmɑ:k] *n*. Demmāku.

denominate [dinɔ́mineit] *v*. na o tsukeru; meimei suru.

denomination [dinəminéiʃən] *n*. namae o tsukeru koto; dō-rui no mono ni na o tsukeru koto. shūkyō no ippa : *What re-ligious denomination does he belong to?* nan to iu shūha ni haitte iru no? namae (kane, omosa nado no tan'i no).

denominator [dinɔ́minèitə] *n*. na o tsukeru hito. (*math.*) bumbo : *common* ∼, kō bumbo.

denotation [di:noutéiʃən] *n*. shiji; meishō (*designation*); imi (*meaning*); monji no shimesu seikakuna imi : *The ∼ of ' home ' is " place where one lives ", " home "* towa hito ga sumu basho to iu koto da.

denote [dinóut] *v.* shimesu; imi suru (*mean*).

dénouement [déinu:ma:ŋ/denú:ma:ŋ] *n.* (*Fr.*) shōsetsu, gekinado no) daidan'en; rakuchaku; (*epilogue*).

denounce [dináuns] *v.* kōzen to hinan suru (*accuse*); tekihatsu suru; hantai no sengen o suru.

dense [dens] *a.* shigetta; missei shita; koi (*thick*): *a dense fog*, koi kiri. usunoro no (*stupid*). ~**ly** *ad.* mitsuni; koku. ~**ness** *n.* chimitsu; gudon.

density [déns(i)ti] *n.* chimitsu; kosa; nōdo; nibusa. *traffic* ~, kōtsūryō. ⌈*dent* = *tooth*.

dent [dent] *n.* kubomi; haguruma no ha. *v.* kubomasu (*Fr.*)

dental [dént(ə)l] *a.* ha no, *n.* (*phon.*) shiin, shiin (ha o tsukatte dasu on) no. =shion.

dentifrice [déntifris] *n.* hamigakiko; nerihamigaki; mizuha- ⌈migaki.

dentine [dénti:n] *n.* ha no zōgeshitsu. ⌊

dentist [déntist] *n.* haisha; shikai. ~**ry** *n.* shikaijutsu.

dentition [dentíʃən] *n.* ha no hassei; hanarabi; ha no katachi.

denudation [di:nju(:)déiʃən] *n.* hadaka ni suru koto; roshutsu.

denude [dinjú:d] *v.* hadaka ni suru; hakudatsu suru (*strip*).

denunciation [dinʌnsiéiʃən] *n.* kōzen to suru tsuyoi hinan; kokuhatsu (*charge*). ⌈suru.

deny [dinái] *v.* uchikesu; kobamu (*refuse*): ~ *oneself*, gaman suru.

deodorize [di:óudəraiz] *v.* nioi (kusami) o kesu; bōshū suru, ~**r** [diódəraizə] *n.* kusamidome; bōshūzai.

depart [dipá:t] *v.* shuppatsu suru; ko no yo o saru (*die*); (shūkan nado kara) hanareru. ~**ed** [-id] *a.* kako no; kono yo ni inai. ~**ment** *n.* bumon; shō; ken. ~**ment store** hyakkaten.

departure [dipá:tʃə] *n.* shuppatsu; seikyo (*death*): *new* ~, shin'an; shinhōshin.

depend [dipénd] *v.* burasageru; miketsu de aru (*be pending*). ~*on* (or *upon*) ni tayoru: *We* ~ *on Australia for wool*, warera wa yōmō o *Aust.* ni aogu (tayoru).

dependant [dipéndənt] *a.*, *n.* =**dependent**.

dependence [dipéndəns] *n.* irai; shinrai.

dependency [dipéndənsi] *n.* jūzoku butsu; zokkoku.

dependent [dipéndənt] *a.* tayoru; jūzoku no. *n.* jūsha; isōrō (*hanger on*); fuyō kazoku.

depict [dipíkt] *v.* byōsha suru (*describe*); jojutsu suru.

deplete [diplí:t] *v.* karappo ni suru (*empty*); tsukai tsukusu (*exhaust*).

depletion [diplí:ʃən] *n.* ketsubō; kokatsu (*exhaustion*).

deplorable [diplɔ́:rəbl] *n.* nagekawashii; awarena. ~**bly** *ad.* awareni; nagekawashiku.

deplore [diplɔ́:ə] *v.* kanashimu; nageku (*lament*).

deploy [diplɔ́i] *n.* [*mil.*] (tai no) tenkai. *v.* (tai o) tenkai suru.

deponent [dipóunənt] *a.* (*gram.*) judōkei de nōdō no imi no aru : ~*verb* konoyōna dōshi. *n.* (*leg.*) senseisha; shōnin; chikatta hito. ⌈yōni suru.

depopulate [di:pɔ́pjuleit] *v.* jūmin o tayasu (herasu); fuenai

depopulation [di:pɔpjuléiʃən/dí:-] *n.* jinkō genshō.

deport [dipɔ́:t] *v.* (kokugai ni) tsuihō suru (*banish*); furumau (*behave*).

deportation [dì:pɔːtéiʃən] *n.* tsuihō; yusō (*transportation*).

deportment [dipɔ́:tmənt] *n.* hinkō; furumai.

depose [dipóuz] *v.* taii saseru; menshoku suru (*dethrone*); shōgen suru (*testify*).

deposit [dipɔ́zit] *v.* azukeru (ginkō nado ni kane o). *n.* itakubutsu; tetsukekin; yokin : *current* ~, tōzayokin. *fixed* ~, teiki yokin. *petty current* ~, koguchi tōza yokin.

depositary [dipɔ́zit(ə)ri] *n.* azukarinin; chōzōjo.

deposition [depəzíʃən] *n.* menshoku; taii (*dethronement*); shōgen suru (*testify*). ⌈gen.

depositor [dipɔ́zitə] *n.* yokinsha; kyōtakusha.

depository [dipɔ́zit(ə)ri] *n.* okiba; chōzōjo (*storehouse*).

depot [dépou/dí:pou] *n.* sōko (*storehouse*); rentai hombu; teishajō (*railway station*).

deprave [dipréiv] *v.* daraku saseru; waruku suru. ~**ed** [-d] *a.* daraku shita; furyō no.

depravity [diprǽviti] *n.* daraku; fuhai; akufū.

deprecate [déprikeit] *v.* ...no nai yōni negau (tanomu; inoru) : ~ *his anger*, ikari o nadameru yōni negau. hinan suru; hantai suru : *such a trend of youngmen is much to be* ~*ed*, kono yōna wakōdo-tachi no keikō wa hanahada negawashiku nai.

deprecation [deprikéiʃən] *n.* hinan; hantai; nai yōni inoru koto.

deprecatory [déprikətəri] *a.* fusansei no; aigan teki no.

depreciate[diprí:ʃieit] *v.* kachi o sageru; kenasu; geraku suru. *cf.* **appriciate.**

depreciatingly [diprí:ʃieitiŋli] *ad.* hinan shite.   ⌈ru koto.

depreciation [diprí:ʃiéiʃən] *n.* neuchi no teiraku; karuku mi-

depreciative [diprí:ʃiətiv] *a.* kenasu; misageru.

depredate [déprideit] *v.* ryakudatsu suru (*plunder*); arasu.

depredation [dəpridéiʃən] *n.* ryakudatsu. (*pl.*) ryakudatsu-kōi.

depredator [déprideitə] *n.* ryakudatsusha.

depress [diprés] *v.* sageru; genki o naku saseru (*make dull*); geraku saseru. ∼**ed** [diprést] *a.* genki no nai. ∼**ing** [-iŋ] *a.* osaetsukeru; omokurushii.   ⌈teikiatsu.

depression [dipréʃən] *n.* oshisageru koto; kubomi; fukeiki;

deprivation [dèprivéiʃən] *n.* ryakudatsu; sōshitsu (*the deprived*);

deprive [dipráiv] *v.* ubau; shoku o ubau : ∼ *someone of something, s.o.* kara *s.th.* o ubau.

Dept. = **Department.**

depth [depθ] *n.* fukasa : *beyond one's* ∼, sei no tatanai fukasa. iro no kosa. fukai umi. mannaka : *in the* ∼ *of winter*, fuyu no mannaka; mafuyu.

depurge [dipə́:dʒ] *n. purge* o toku; tsuihō kaijo ni naru (suru).

deputation [dèpjutéiʃən] *n.* dairi; daihyōdan.

depute [dipjú:t] *v.* dairi o meizuru; itaku suru (*commit*).

deputize [dépjutaiz] *v.* dairi o suru (*for*); dairi o meizuru.

deputy [dépjuti] *n.* dairi; (Furansu nado de) daigishi.

derail [diréil] *v.* dassen saseru (suru). ∼**ment** *n.* dassen.

derange [diréindʒ] *v.* midasu; hakkyō saseru. ∼**ment** *n.* hak-kyō.

Derby [dá:bi] *n.* Eikoku no *Epson* de maitoshi okonau kei-ba; dai keiba; (d-) (*Am.*) yamataka-bōshi.

derelict [dérilikt] *a.* uchisuterareta. *n. derelict* sareta mono.

dereliction [dèrilíkʃən] *n.* taiman; utcharu koto; hōki.

deride [diráid] *v.* chōrō suru; azakeru. ∼**dingly** *ad.* chōrō-

derision [diríʒən] *n.* chōrō; chōrō no mato.   ⌊tekini.

derisive [diráisiv] *a.* chōrō suru; azakeru.

derivation [dèrivéiʃən] *n.* dedokoro; kigen; (*gram.*) (go no) hasei, bumpa.

derivative [dirívətiv] *a.* hasei shita. *n.* haseigo.

derive [diráiv] *v.* hiki dasu; yurai suru (*from*); kigen o tazuneru. **Decimal** *and* **December** *are derived from the Latin word* **decem,** *which means " ten ".* Decimal to December wa L. no 10 to iu imi no *decem* kara deta no desu.

dermatology [də:mətɔ́lədʒi] *n.* hifubyōgaku.

derogate [dérogeit] *v.* tori saru; neuch, hyōban nado ga sagaru; shitsu ga waruku naru.

derogation [dèrogéiʃən] *n.* kison; daraku.

derogatory [dirɔ́gətəri] *a.* kachi o genzuru; neuchi ga sagaru.

derrick [dérik] *n.* nagai ude no kijūki; derikku. (derekki)

derringer [dérindʒə] *n.* (*Am.*) mijikai pisutoru.

dervish [də̀:viʃ] *n.* takuhatsu-sō (*of the* [*Islam*]).

descant [diskǽnt] *v.* kuwashiku nobetateru; utau. ʃei.

descend [disénd] *v.* kudaru; tsutawaru. ~-ant *n.* shison, kō-

descent [disént] *n.* kudaru (oriru) koto; kudari zaka; ochibure; sujō; kōei.

describable [diskráibəbl] *a.* jojutsu (byōsha) shi uru.

describe [diskráib] *v.* byōsha suru; jojutsu suru.

description [diskrípʃən] *n.* kijutsu; byōsha; shurui; ninsō gaki; jojibun.

descriptive [diskríptiv] *a.* jojutsu shita; kiji no. ~ly *ad.* kijutsutekini.

descry [diskrái] *v.* mitsukeru; mieru.

desecrate [désikreit] *v.* kamisama no mono o zokuyō ni tsukau; shinsei o kegasu.

desecration [dèsikréiʃən] *n.* zokuyō (*the use for worldly life*); shinsei bōtoku (*violation of sanctity*).

desert [dézət] *n.* sabaku. *a.* sabaku no.

desert [dizé:t] *v.* misuteru; tachisaru. *n.* (*usu. pl.*) shinshō hitsubatsu (*deserving reward or punishment*). ~-er *n.* tōbōsha.

desertion [dizɔ́:ʃən] *n.* uchisuteru koto; arehateru koto.

deserve [dizɔ́:v] *v.* ni ataisuru. ~dly *ad.* [-idli] sōtō ni; tōzen.

deshabille [déizæbi:ei], **dishabille** [di-] *n.* (*Fr.*) fudangi.

desiccate [désikeit] *v.* himono ni suru; kawaku; kawakasu.

desiccator [désikeitə] *n.* kansōki; himono (*dried fish*) o tsukuru hito.

desideratum [dizìdəréitəm] *n.* (*pl.* **-ta**) tsuyoku hoshigaru mono.

design [dizáin] *v.* kuwadateru; sekkei suru; shitazu o kaku. *n.* sekkei; zuan. ∼**edly** [-idli] *ad.* wazato. ∼**er** *n.* sekkeisha. ∼**ing** *a.* takurami no aru.

designate [dézigneit] *v.* shimesu; nazasu (namae o iu).

designation [dèzignéiʃən] *n.* shitei; shimei; meishō.

desirable [dizáiərəbl] *a.* nozomashii. ∼**bly** *ad.* ∼**ness** *n.*

desire [dizáiə] *v.* negau; nozomu. *n.* shomō; yokubō; yōkyū.

desirous [dizáiərəs] *a.* hoshigaru.

desist [dizíst] *v.* yameru; omoi-todomaru.

desk [desk] *n.* tsukue; (*Am.*) sekkyōdan. ∼**telephone** [desk télifoun] *n.* takujō denwaki.

desolate [désoleit] *v.* kōhai saseru; arehate saseru.

desolate [désolit] *a.* arehateta; hito no ikanai; sabishii; kokorobosoi. ∼**ly** *ad.* ∼**ness** *n.*

desolation [dèsəléiʃən] *n.* kōhai; kōryō; arechi.

despair [dispéə] *n.* zetsubō (*utterly hopeless*). *v.* omoikiru; zetsubō suru. ∼**ing** *a.* jibōjiki no. ∼**ingly** *ad.*

despatch, dis- [dispǽtʃ] *n.* haken; hassō; tebayai shori. **happy** ∼ seppuku. *v.* haken (hassō) suru; tebayaku shori suru.

desperado [dèspərá:dou/-réid-] *n.* narazumono; bōkan. (*Am.*) inochi-shirazu.

desperate [déspərət] *a.* jibōjiki no; inochi shirazu no. ∼**ly** *ad.* inochigake de. ∼**ness** *n.* hisshi; inochigake.

desperation [dèspəréiʃən] *n.* hisshi; inochigake.

despicable [déspikəbl] *a.* iyashimu beki, hiretsuna. ∼**bly** *ad.*

despise [dispáiz] *v.* keibetsu suru; mikubiru.

despite [dispáit] *n.* urami; nikumi. *in* ∼ *of…*, ni mo kakawarazu. ∼**ful** *a.* nikunikushii.

despoil [dispóil] *v.* ryakudatsu suru (*rob*).

despond [dispónd] *v.* chikara o otosu; rakutan suru. ∼**ence**, ∼**ency** [-əns/-si] *n.* rakutan; iki shōchin. ∼**ent** *a.* gakkari shita. ∼**ently** *ad.* genki naku. ∼**ingly** *ad.* chikara o otoshite.

despot [déspət] *n.* sensei kunshu. ∼**ic** [despótik] *a.* sensei no;

bōgyakuna. **～ically** *ad.* **～ism** [déspətizm] *n.* sensei ; sensei seiji.

dessert [dizə́:t] *n.* dezāto ; shokugo no kashi, kudamono.

destination [dèstinéiʃən] *n.* yuku-saki ; todoke-saki ; mokute-kichi.

destine [déstin] *v.* sadameru ; yotei suru ; ummei o sadameru.

destiny [déstini] *n.* ummei.

destitute [déstitju:t] *a.* hidoku mazushii. **～of** …ga nai.

destitution [dèstitjú:ʃən] *n.* ketsubō ; gokuhin.

destroy [distrɔ́i] *v.* hakai suru ; horobosu ; tayasu. **～er** *n.* ha-kaisha ; kowashite.

destructible [distrʌ́ktibl] *a.* hakai shi uru ; kowaseru.

destruction [distrʌ́kʃən] *n.* hakai ; metsubō kujo.

destructive [distrʌ́ktiv] *a.* hakaiteki no ; yūgaina. **～ly** *ad.*

desuetude [disjú(:)itju:d/dí:swi-] *n.* haishi ; fuyō : *fall into* ～, sutareru. ┌na. **～ily** *ad.*

desultory [désɔltəri] *a.* renraku no nai (*unconnected*) ; samman-

detach [ditǽtʃ] *v.* hanasu ; haken suru ; **～ed palace** rikyū. **～able** *a.* torihazushi no dekiru ; bunri shi uru. **～ment** *n.* bunri ; koritsu : *cf.* **attach.**

detail [dí:teil/ditéil] *v.* kuwashiku noberu. *n.* kuwashii koto. (*pl.*) shōsai ; saimoku ; sembatsu-tai.

detain [ditéin] *v.* hiki tomeru ; kōryū suru.

detect [ditékt] *v.* mitsukeru ; minuku.

detection [ditékʃən] *n.* hakken ; minuku koto.

detective [ditéktiv] *a.* tansaku suru ; tantei no. **～story,** tantei shōsetsu. *n.* tantei. **private ～,** himitsu tantei.

detention [diténʃən] *n.* hikitome ; chien ; kōryū.

deter [ditə́:] *v.* samatageru, omoi todomaraseru (*from*).

detergent [ditə̀:dʒent] *a.* yokuarau. *n.* senjōzai.

deteriorate [ditíəriəreit] *v.* waruku suru (naru).

deterioration [ditìəriəréiʃən] *n.* akka ; teika ; daraku.

determinate [ditə́:minit/-et] *a.* ittei no ; ketteiteki no. **～ly** *ad.*

determination [ditə́:minéiʃən] *n.* kettei ; kakutei ; kesshin.

determine [ditə́:min] *v.* kessuru ; kesshin suru. **～d** [-d] *a.* ketsuzen tatsu ; kesshin shita. **～dly** *ad.* ┌mono.

deterrent [ditérənt] *a.* samatageru ; hikitomeru. *n.* hikitomeru

detest [ditést] *v.* kirau; ken'o suru; nikumu. **~able** *a.* ken'o su beki. **~ably** *ad.* nikunikushiku.

detestation [di:testéiʃən] *n.* ken'o; zōo; nikushimi.

dethrone [diθróun] *v.* taii suru (saseru). **~ment** *n.* (kokuō nado o) haisuru koto.

detonate [détouneit] *v.* (ōkina oto o tatete) bakuhatsu suru (saseru).

detonation [dètonéiʃən] *n.* bakuhatsu; bakuon.

détour [deitúə/déituə] *n.* (*Fr.*) mawari michi; ukai. *v.* mawari michi suru.

detract [ditrǽkt] *v.* herasu; genzuru; genshō saseru.

detraction [ditrǽkʃən] *n.* kizutsukeru koto; kison; warukuchi.

detriment [détrimənt] *n.* songai; gai. **~al** [détriməntl] *a.* gai ni naru. *n.* (*Brit. sl.*) konomashiku nai kyūkonsha.

detritus [ditráitəs] *n.* kudaketa ganseki; iwakuzu.

deuce [dju:s] *n.* niten; jūsu; akuma. *D. take it!* shimatta!

devaluate [di:vǽljueit] *v.* kachi o sageru; heika o kirisageru.

devaluation [di:vǽljuéiʃən] *n.* heika kirisage.

devastate [dévəsteit] *v.* arasu; kōhai saseru.

devastation [dèvəstéiʃən] *n.* jūrin; kōhai.

develop [divéləp] *v.* kaihatsu suru; hatten suru (saseru); hattatsu suru (saseru); genzō suru. **~er** *n.* kaihatsusha. (*photo*) genzō-eki. **~ment** *n.* hattatsu; hatten; genzō.

deviate [dí:vieit] *v.* hazureru; soreru; jadō ni hairu. **~tion** *n.* [dì:viéiʃən] dassen; hensa.

device [diváis] *n.* kufū; keikaku.

devil [dévl] *n.* akuma; gokuakunin. **~ish** [dévliʃ] *a.* akuma no yōna; gokuaku hidōna. **~ly** *ad.* **~ry** *n.* gokuaku hidō. **~-fish** *n.* itomakiei; ankō.

devious [dí:viəs] *a.* tadashii michi o hazureta. **~ly** *ad.*

devise [diváiz] *v.* kufū (keikaku) suru. yuigon shite yuzuru. *n.* yuigon (de yuzuru).

devisee [dəvizí:/diváizi:]*n.* izō o uketa hito.   ⌐hito).

devisor [dəvàizí:/diváizɔ:] *n.* (*leg.*) izōsha (yuigon de yuzuru

devitalize [di:váitəlaiz] *v.* katsuryoku o ubau.

devoid [divóid] *a.* (...no) nai, (...o) kaita (*of*).

devoir [dəvwá:/dévwɑ:] (*Fr.*) *n.* gimu; (*pl.*) keii; reigi.

devolve [divólv] *v.* watasu; yuzuru.

devote [divóut] *v.* sasageru; yudaneru; makaseru.

devoted [divóutid] *a.* nesshinna; chūjitsuna. ~**ly** *ad.* ~**ness** *n*

devotee [dèvoutí:] *n.* nesshinka; kiesha (*of.*)

devotion [divóuʃən] *n.* kenshin; nesshin; shinjin; (*pl.*) inori. ~**al** *a.* keikenna; kitō no.

devour [diváuə] *v.* musabori kuu; horobosu.

devout [diváut] *a.* keikenna; nessei no. ~**ly** *ad.* ~**ness** *n.* keiken; nessei.

dew [dju:] *n.* tsuyu; tsuyu o musubu; ~**claw** [-klɔ:] *n.* (inu no) uwa zume. ~**drop** [-drɔp] *n.* tsuyu no shizuku. ~**point** [-pɔint] roten.

dewlap [djú:læp] *n.* (ushi nado no) nodo no tareniku.

dewy [djú:i] *a.* tsuyu o obita; tsuyu no yōna; sawayakana.

dexter [dékstə] *a.* migite no. ~**ity** [dekstériti] *n.* kiyō; binshō; migikiki.

dexterous [dékstərəs] *a.* kiyōna; kōmyōna; binshōna. ~**ly**

dextrin [dékstrin] *n.* kosei (nori ni naru). ⌐*ad.* ~**ness** *n.*

dextrose [dékstrous] *n.* budōtō; *glucose.*

dextrous [dékstrəs] *a.* kiyōna; binshōna.

diabetes [dàiəbí:ti:z] *n.* (*med.*) tōnyōbyō.

diabolic(al) [dàiəbólik(l)] *a.* akuma no yōna; kiwamete warui. ~**ally** *ad.*

diabolism [daiǽbəlism] *n.* mahō; akuma sūhai.

diabolo [diá:bəlou/-ǽb-] *n.* diaboro; kūchū koma.

diacritical [dàiəkrítikl] *a.* kubun suru; kubetsu no. ~**marks** hatsuon fugō (kyūshiki).

diadem [dáiədem] *n.* ōkan; ō no kammuri; ōken.

diaeresis [daiíərəsis], **dieresis** *n* (*pl.* -ses [si:z]) bun'ompu(··).

diagnose [dáiəgnouz] *v.* shindan suru.

diagnosis [dàiagnóusis] *n.* (*pl.* -ses [si:z]) shindan.

diagnostic [dàiəgnóstik] *a.* shindan no; *n.* shindan; (yamai no) chōkō. (*pl.*) shindangaku.

diagonal [daiǽgənl] *a.* taikaku-sen no; hasu no. *n.* taikaku-sen; ayaori. ~**ly** *ad.* suji chigai; nanameni.

diagram [dáiəgræm] *n.* zuhyō; zushiki; sakuzu. *v.* zuhyō de shimesu. ~**atic** [dàiəgrəmǽtik] *a.* zuhyōno; zushiki no.

dial [dáiəl] *n.* hidokei; moji-ban; *v.* memori-ban de hakaru; jidōshiki denwa o kakeru.

dialect [dáiəlekt] *n.* hōgen. ～**al** *a.* hōgen no.

dialectic, ～**al** [dàiəléktikəl] *a.* benshōteki no. ＝*dialectic; dialectal.* ～**s** [dàiéktiks] benshōhō.

dialogue [dáiəlɔg] *n.* taiwa; taiwa geki.

diameter [daiémitə] *n.* chokkei.

diametrical [dàiəmétrikl] *a.* chokkei no; seihantai no. ～**ly** *ad.* seihantai ni.

diamond [dáiəmənd] *n.* daiyamondo; kongōseki. *a.* daiyamondo iri no; hishigata no.

Diana [daiénə] *n.* Daiana.

diapason [dàiəpéisn/-zn] *n.* on no kōtei no chōwa (*melody*).

diaper [dáiəpə] *n.* hishigata-moyō no asanuno; fukin; omu-ʃ tsu.

diaphanous [daiéfənəs] *a.* tōmeina; sukitōtta. ⌊tsu.

diaphragm [dáiəfræm] *n.* ōkakumaku.

diarist [dáiərist] *n.* nikki gakari.

diarrhea, **-rhoea** [dàiəríə] *n.* (*med.*) geri.

diary [dáiəri] *n.* nikki.

diastase [dáiəsteis] *n.* (*chem.*) jiasutāze; diostaze.

diatonic [dàiətónik] *a.* zen'onkai no. ～**scale** zenonkai.

diatribe [dáiətraib] *n.* hageshii giron; tsūba; hinan.

dibasic [daibéisik] *a.* (*chem.*) nienki no.

dibble [díbl] *v.* anahoridōgu de ana o horu. *n.* anahoridōgu.

dice [dais] *n.* (*pl.* of **die** [dai]) saikoro; tobaku. ～**box** [dais bɔx] *n.* sai zutsu. *v.* *dice away*, tobaku de shinsho o suru (*gamble away one's fortune.*)

dicker [díkə] *v.* butsu butsu kōkan suru; negiru. *n.* shō torihiki; butsu butsu, kōkan.

dickey, **dicky** [díki] *n.* Y-shatsu no mune ate; (Basha no) kō-bu gyosha seki. ⌈chikuonki.

Dictaphone [díktəfoun] *n.* chikuonki no *trade mark*; rōkan

dictate [diktéit] *v.* sashizu suru; kakitori o suru. *n.* meirei. ～**tion**, *n.* sashizu; kōjō; kakitori. ～**tor** *n.* meireisha, dokusai shiseisha. ～**orial** [diktətóuriəl] *a.* sendan no; ōheina.

diction [díkʃən] *n.* kotobazukai; iimawashi.

dictionary [díkʃənri/-ʃənəri] *n.* jisho; jibuki; jiten.

dictograph [kíktəgrɑ:f/-græf] *n.* himitsuchōshūki; himitsu o nusumigiki suru kikai.

dictum [díktəm] (*pl.* **-ta** [-tə], **-tums**) *n.* hanji (*judge*) no iken; kakugen.

did [did] *v. see* : **do**.

didactic [didǽktik] *a.* kyōkuntekina. ~**ally** *ad.* ~**s** *n.* kyōkunhō; kun'ikugaku.

die [dai] *v.* **died** ; **dying**. shinu; kareru; taeru. ~**away** (or **down**), kieru; shizumaru. ~**out** taeru; sutareru.

die [dai] *n.* (*pl.* **dice** [dais] *see* : **dice**) sai ; sai no hitofuri : *The die is cast*, koto sude ni kessu.

die [dai] *n.* (*pl.* **dies** [daiz]) gokuin ; igata ; neji gata.

die-hard [dai hɑ:d] *n.* saigo no shunkan made teikō suru (gambaru).

dieresis [daiíərisis] *n.* bun'ompu. *cf.* **diaeresis** (··).

diet [dáiət] *n.* tabemono ; gikai ; kokkai.

dietary [dáiətəri] *a.* (byōin, kōba nado no) shokuji ni kansuru. ~ **cure**, shokuji ryōhō.

dietetic [dàiitétik] *a.* shokuji no ; shokuji ryōhō no. **dietetics** [dàiətétiks] *n.* inshokuron ; shokuji ryōhō.

differ [dífə] *v.* chigau ; (iken nado) itchi shinai.

difference [dífrəns] *n.* chigai (futatsu no aida no). *v.* chigai o hakkiri suru. tsu ni.

different [dífrənt] *a.* chigau ; shuju no. ~**ly** *ad.* kotonatte ; be-

differential [difərénʃəl] *a.* sabetsu suru ; tokutei no. ~**calculus** bibun. ~**duties** tokutei kanzei. *n.* (*math.*) bibungaku.

differentiate[dìfərénʃieit] *v.* kubun (bibun) suru.

differentiation [difərenʃiéiʃən/-siéi-] *n.* kubetsu ; bibun.

dfficult [dífikəlt] *a.* muzukashii ; konnanna.

difficulty [dífikəlti] *n.* konnan ; sashisawari ; zaisei konnan.

diffidence [dífidəns] *n.* jibun de utagau koto ; uchiki ; enryo.

diffident [dífidənt] *a.* jishin no nai ; enryo-gachi no. ~**ly** *ad.*

diffraction [difrǽkʃən] *n.* (*phys.*) kussetsu ; hikari no kussetsu (bunsan).

diffuse [difjú:z] *v.* makichirasu ; hiromeru. *a.* chitta ; kudoi.

diffusion [difjú:ʒən] *n.* dempa ; man'en ; chirakari.

diffusive [difjú:siv] *a.* sampusei no ; yukiwataru.

dig [dig] *v.* dug *or* (*arch.*) ~**ged** ; ~**ging**. horu ; horisageru (hiyuteki nimo) tankyū suru. *n.* atɛkoṣuɛ̣i; mōbenkyō. sai-kutsu.

digest [didʒést/dai] *v.* (tabemono ga) shōka suru; shōkaryo-ku. *n.* [dáidʒest] yōryō o toridashita mono.

digestible [didʒéstibl] *a.* shōka suru; shōka no yoi. ⌈suru.

digestion [didʒéstʃən/dai-] *n.* shōka; shōka nōryoku; shōka

digestive [didʒéstiv/dai-] *a.* shōkaryoku no aru; shōka o tasukeru. *n.* shōka o tasukeru mono.

digger [dígə] *n.* horu hito; horu kikai; (D~) ki no ne o tabe-ru Hoku-Bei genchijin.

digit [dídʒit] *n.* te, ashi no yubi; sūji; yubi haba. ~**al** *a.* yubi no; yubi no yōna katachi no. ~**ate** [-eit(id)] *a.* yubijō no; tenohira no katachi no.

digitalis [dìdʒitéilis] *n.* (*flow.*) jigitarisu (-no kawakashita ha).

dignify [dígnifai] *v.* igen o tsukeru; mottai o tsukeru. ~**ied** *a.* igen no aru; kōki no (*of nobility*).

dignitary [dígnitəri] ~**ary** *n.* kōki no hito; kōsō (*prelate*).

dignity [dígniti] *n.* igen; kōi; (*high rank*) kōi, kōkan no hito (*nobility*).

digraph [dáigrɑ:f/-græf] *n.* niji de ichion ni natte iru tsuzu-riji (*ch, sh, ea* no yōni). ⌈(*from*).

digress [daigrés/di:-] *v.* mondai o hanareru; shiyō ni wataru

digression [daigréʃən] *n.* edaha ni wataru koto.

digressive [daigrésiv] shiyō no. ~**ly** shiyō ni watatte.

dike [daik] *n.* teibō; mizo; hori.

dilapidate [dilǽpideit] *v.* arasu; areru; kōhai suru.

dilapidation [dilæ̀pidéiʃən] *n.* kōhai.

dilatation [dàileitéiʃən], **dilation** [dailéiʃən] *n.* kakuchō; bō-chō; fuen.

dilate [dailéit/di-] *v.* bōchō saseru (-suru); kakuchō saseru (-suru); fuen suru.

dilatoriness [dílətə:rinis] *n.* chien; chitai; kamman.

dilatory [dílətəri] *a.* osoi; guzutsuku.

dilemma [dilémə/dai-] *n.* ryōtō rompō; itabasami.

dilettante [dìlitǽnti] (*pl.* -**ti** [-ti:]) *n.* shirōto geijiutsuka; shirōto gakusha; kōzuka. ⌈kajiri.

dilettantism [dìlitǽntizm] *n.* bijutsuzuki; bungeizuki; nama-

diligence [dílidʒəns] *n.* benkyō.

diligent [dílidʒənt] *n.* kimbenna. ~**ly** *ad.* seidashite; kushin shite.

dill [dil] *n.* (*bot.*) inondo. ~**pickle** *n.* inondozuke.

dillydally [dílidæli] *v.* guzutsuku; chūcho suru.

dilute [dailjú:t/dil-] *v.* mizu o waru; usuku suru (-naru). *a.* kihakuna (*thin*).

dilution [dailjú:ʃən/dil-] *n.* usumeru koto; usuku natta mono.

diluvial[dailjú:viəl/dil-], ~**vian** [-viən] *a.* daikōzui no; tokuni Noa no kōzui no.

dim [dim] *a.* usugurai; mōrōtaru; me ga kasunda. ~**ly** *ad* usuguraku; kasukani. ~**ness** *n.*

dime [daim] *n.* jissento ginka. ~ **novel,** sammon shōsetsu.

dimension [diménʃən/dai-] *n.* sumpō (nagasa, hirosa, atsusa no); yōseki; menseki.

diminish [dimíniʃ] *v.* genzuru; genshō saseru (-suru); chiisaku suru (-naru).

diminuendo [dìminjuéndou] *ad.* (*mus.*) shidai ni yowaku.

diminution [dìminjú:ʃən] *n.* genshō; sukunaku naru koto.

diminutive [dimínjutiv] *a.* chiisai, kogata no. *n.* aishō ni tsukau go.

dimity [dímiti] *n.* ukijima ori mempu.

dimple [dímpl] *n.* ekubo; kubomi. *v.* ekubo ga dekiru.

din [din] *v.* mimi o rōsuru; nari hibiku; urusaku iu. *n.* sawagi.

dine [dain] *v.* seisan (ōgochiso) o taberu; shokuji suru; seisan o kyōsuru.

diner [dáinə] *n.* shokuji suru hito; shokudōsha (kisha no) : ~ (*in train*).

ding [diŋ] *v.* narasu; hibikaseru; gangan naru.

dingdong [díŋdòŋ] *n.* kān kān; janjan (kane no oto).

dingey, dinghy [díŋgi] *n.* gunkan ni tsunda chiisai bōto; gorakuyō bōto.

dingle [díŋgl] *n.* ki nado no shigetta tanima (*wooded deep valley*).

ding wagon [díŋ wǽgən] *n.* kuruma tsuki no shokki dai. (*wheeled plate-rack*).

dingy [díndʒi] *a.* usuguroi; yogoreta.

dining [dáiniŋ] *a.* shokuji suru. ~ **car** [kɑ:] *n.* shokudōsha. ~**room** [-ru:m] *n.* shokudō. ~**table** [-teibl] *n.* shokutaku.

dinner [dínə] *n.* seisan. ~ **bell** [-bél] shokuji-doki ni narasu kane. ～ **hour** [dínə auə] shokuji-doki. ～ **party**, gosankai ; bansankai.

dinosaur [dáinəsɔ:] *n.* kyōryū (ōmukashi no hachūrui).

dint [dint] *n.* utta ato no hekomi : *by* ～ *of*, ...no chikara de ; ...ni yotte. *v.* utte ato o tsukeru (hekomaseru).

diocese [dáiəsi(:)s] *n.* kantoku (**bishop**). ～(**e**)**an** [daiɔ́sisən] *a.* kantoku (shikyō, shukyō) kanku no. *n.* kantoku ; shikyō ; shukyō.

diorama [dàiərá:mə] *n.* jiorama ; tōshiga.

dioxide [daiɔ́ksaid/dái-] *n.* (*chem.*) nisankabutsu.

dip [dip] *v.* hitasu ; shinrei o kureru ; shizumu. *n.* hitasu koto ; abiru koto.

diphtheria [difθíəriə] *n.* (*med.*) jifuteria. ┌boin no.

diphthong [dífθəŋ/díp-] *n.* nijū boin. ～**al** [difθɔ́ŋgəl] *a.* nijū

diploma [diplóumə] *n.* menkyojō ; sotsugyō shōsho ; kunki.

diplomacy [diplóuməsi] *n.* gaikō ; gaikō shuwan ; kakehiki.

diplomat [dípləmæt] *n.* gaikōka ; gaikōkan. ～**ic** [dìpləmǽ-tik] *a.* gaikō no ; gaikō shuwan no aru. ～**ically** *ad.* ～**ist** [diplóumətist] *n.* gaikōka ; gaikokan.

dipper [dípə] *n.* hishaku no rui ; (*bird*) kawa-garasu. (D-) Ho-kuto Shichisei. ┌sha.

dipsomania [dìpsouméiniə] *n.* inshukyō ; arukōru chūdoku-**dire** [daiə] *a.* osoroshii ; hisanna.

direct [dirékt/dai-] *a.* chokusetsu no ; massuguna ; ～**action** [d(a)irektǽkʃən] *n.* chokusetsu kōdō. ～ **current**, chokuryū. *v.* sashimukeru ; shidō suru. ～**ly** *ad.* ～**ness** *n.*

direction [dirékʃən/dai-] *n.* hōkō ; naate (tegami no).

director [díréktə/dai-] *n.* shidōsha ; torishimari yaku ; eiga kantoku. ～**ate** [diréktərit] *n.* shidōshoku ; rijiren ; torishi-mariyaku-tachi.

directory [diréktəri] *n.* jimmeiroku ; (D-) (*France* kakumei jidai no) 5 shissei-naikaku. **telephone** ～ denwa chō.

direful [dáiəful] *a.* osoroshii ; hisanna.

dirge [də:dʒ] *n.* banka ; sōsōka ; sōshiki no toki no uta.

dirigible [díridʒibl/dirí-] *a.* sōjūshiuru. ～**balloon** *n.* hikōsen no. *n.* hikōsen ; sōjū kikyū.

dirk [də:k] *n.* tanken ; mijikai ken.

dirt [dǝ:t] *n.* fuketsu-butsu ; kitanai mono : *eat* ~, kutsujoku o shinobu.

dirty [dǝ́:ti] *a.* fuketsuna ; inwaina ; are-moyō no (*weather*) ; geretsuna. *v.* yogosu ; kegasu. ~**ily** *ad.* fuketsuni ; birōni ; iyashiku. ~**ness** *n.* fuketsu.

disability [dìsǝbíliti] munō ; munōryoku.

disable [diséibl] *v.* yakuni tatanaku suru ; fugu ni suru. (*leg.*) munōryokuni suru ; mushikaku ni suru.

disabuse [dìsǝbjú:z] *v.* mayoi o toku.

disadvantage [dìsǝdvá:ntidʒ] *n.* furi ; furina kyōgū ; sonshitsu. ~**ous** [disædrǝ:ntéidʒǝs] *a.* furina. ~**ously** *ad.*

disaffected [dìsǝtéktid] *a.* fumanna ; fuheina.

disaffection [dìsǝtékʃǝn] *n.* fuman ; fuhei ; fufuku.

disagree [dìsǝgrí:] *v.* awanai ; arasou. ~**able** *a.* kini kuwanu. ~**ably** *ad.* fukaini ; omoshiromi naku. ~**ment** *n.* sōron ; fuchōwa.

disallow [dísǝláu] *v.* yurusanu ; kyakka suru ; kyoka shinai.

disappear [dìsǝpíǝ] *v*, mienaku naru ; shōshitsu suru. ~**ing** gun inken hō. ~**ance** [-rǝns] *n.* shōshitsu ; shissō.

disappoint [dìsǝpóint] *v* shitsubō saseru ; samatageru. ~**ing** *a.* shitsubō saseru. ~**ment** *n.* shitsubō.

disapprobation [dìsæprobéiʃǝn] *n.* fusansei ; funinka.

disapproval [dìsǝprú:vǝl] *n.* =**disapprobation.**

disapprove [dísǝprú:v] *v.* fukyoka ni suru.

disapproving [dísǝprú:viŋ] *ad.* fuka to shite ; fu sansei de.

disarm [dìsá:m] *v.* busō kaijo suru ; jōbi ni fukusareru ; shikushō suru. ~**ment** [disá:mǝment] *n.* busō kaijo ; gumbi shikushō.

disarrange [dísǝréindʒ] *v.* midasu ; konran saseru. ⌊kushō.

disarray [dísǝréi] *v.* midasu. *n.* ranzatsu ; konran.

disaster [dizá:stǝ] *n.* fukō ; sainan ; saigai. ~**trous** *a.* [-trǝs] fukōna ; sainan no. ~**rously** *ad.*

disavow [dísǝváu] *v.* hinin suru ; kyohi suru.

disband [dìsbǽnd] *v.* kaisan suru (tai, kaisha nado o). ~**ment** *n.* jotai ; kaisan.

disbar [disbá:] *v.* bengoshi no shikaku o ubau.

disbelief [dìsbilí:f] *n.* fushinjin (bushinjin) ; giwaku (*doubt*). *n.* shinjinai koto ; fushinkō.

disbelieve [dìsbilí:v] v. shinjinai ; utagau.

disburden [dìsbá:dn] v. omoni o orosu ; andosaseru. (*cf. burden*)

disburse [dìsbá:s] v. shiharau. ~**ment** n. shishutsu ; shiharai.

disc [disk] n. hirattai emban ; rekōdo (*disk*).

discard [diská:d] v. (muyō da to shite) suteru (*give up*).

discern [dizá:n] v. miwakeru. ~**ible** [-ibl] a. miwakerareru. ~**ing** [-iŋ] a. shikibetsuryoku no aru. ~**ment** n. shikibetsu.

discharge [distʃá:dʒ] v. temoto kara hanatsu ; kaijo suru ; shiharau. n. hassha ; kaijo.

disciple [disáipl] n. deshi ; montei.

disciplinarian [disiplinέəriən] a. kunren no ; kiritsu no. n. kiritsu tadashii hito.

disciplinary [dísiplinəri] a. kunren no ; chōkaitekina.

discipline [dísiplin] n., v. kunren, tanren, chōbatsu, chōkai (suru).

disclaim [diskléim] v. (kenri o) hōki suru ; hinin suru. ~**er** n. hinin, hōki suru hito.

disclose [disklóuz] v. (himitsu nado o) abaku.

disclosure [disklóuzə] n. bakuro ; morasareta mono.

discolo(u)r [dìskálə] henshoku (-suru) saseru.

discolo(u)ration [dìskʌləréiʃən] n. henshoku ; shimi (*stain*).

discomfit [diskámfit] v. rōbaisaseru (ura o kaite) ; bikkuri saseru.

discomfiture [diskámfitʃə] n. (zetsubōteki) haiboku.

discomfort [diskámfət] v. fukaini suru. n. fuan ; fuyukai ; kurushimi. 〔suru.

discommode [diskəmóud] v. komaraseru (*distrub*) ; fujiyūni

discompose [diskəmpóuz] v. kokoro o sawagasu. ~**dly** [diskəmpóuzdli] ad. ki o torimidashite.

discomposure [diskəmpóuʒə] n. fuan ; konwaku.

disconcert [dìskənsá:t] v. samatageru ; tōwaku saseru.

disconnect [dìskənékt] v. bunri suru ; renraku o kiru. ~**ed** [-id] a. renraku ga naku.

disconnection [dìskənékʃən] n. bunri ; tachikiru koto.

disconsolate [diskónsəlit] a. kibō (tanoshimi) no nai.

discontent [dìskəntént] n. fuman ; fuhei. v. manzoku shinai.

~**ed** [-id] *a.* fuman no.

discontinuance [dìskəntínjuəns] *n.* chūshi ; teishi (*cessation*).

discontinue [dískəntínju(:)] *v.* yameru ; chūshi suru.

discord [dískɔːd] *n.* fuitchi ; nakatagai ; chōshi hazure. ~**ance** [-əns] *n.* fuchōwa ; chōshihazure. ~**ant** [-ənt] *a.* chōwa shinai ; chōshihazure no. ~**antly** *ad.* chōshihazure ni.

discount [dískaunt] *n.* waribiki ; shinshaku. *v.* waribiki (shinshaku) suru. ⌐nai.

discountenance [diskáuntinəns] *v.* iikao o shinai ; sansei shi-

discourage [diskʌ́ridʒ] *v.* rakutan saseru ; omoi tomaraseru (*prevent*) ; jama suru. ~**ment** [-mənt] *n.* rakutan ; samatage.

discouraging [diskʌ́ridʒiŋ] *a.* rakutan saseru ; hariai no nai.

discourse [disɔ́ːs] *n.* danwa ; enzetsu ; rombun (*treatise*). *v.* enzetsu suru ; ronjutsu suru.

discourteous [diskɔ́ːtiəs/-ɔ́ː t-] *a.* shitsureina. ~**ly** *ad.*

discourtesy [dìskɔ́ːtisi/-ɔ́ːt-] *n.* shitsurei ; burei.

discover [diskʌ́və] *v.* hakken suru ; (kakushiteta mono o) abaku (*disclose*). ~**er** *n.* hakkensha.

discovery [diskəʌ́vəri] *n.* hakken ; bakuro ; hakkaku.

discredit [diskrédit] *n.* fushin'yō ; fumeiyo. *v.* shinjinai. ~**able** [-əbl] *a.* shin'yō o kizutsukete iru. ~**ably** *ad.*

discreet [diskríːt] *a.* shiryo aru ; shinchōna. ~**ly** *ad.*

discrepancy [diskrépənsi] *n.* sōi ; mujun (*contradiction*).

discrepant [diskrépənt] *a.* sōi shita ; mujun shita.

discrete [diskríːt] *v.* bunri shiteru ; bekko no. ⌐ryo.

discretion [diskréʃən] *n.* fumbetsu ; shiryo ; shinchō no hai-

discriminate [diskrímineit] *v.* shikibetsu suru ; kubetsu suru ; bembetsu suru (*distinguish*).

discriminating [diskrímineitiŋ] *a.* shikibetsuryoku no aru ; sabetsutekina.

discrimination [diskrìminéiʃən] *n.* kubetsu ; shikibetsuryoku : *racial* ~, jinshuteki sabetsu ⌐(*distinctive*).

discriminative [diskríminətiv] *a.* shikibetsu suru ; tokushu no

discrown [diskráun] *v.* ōkan o ubau ; taii saseru.

discursive [diskɔ́ːsiv] *a.* sammanna ; toritome no nai. ~**ly** *ad.* manzen to shite ; bosatto shite. ~**ness** *n.* manzen.

discus [dískəs] *n.* emban. ~ *throw*, emban-nage.

discuss v. [diskʌ́s] ronzuru; tōron suru. (col.) ajiwau (shokumotsu o). ⌈shimu koto.

discussion [diskʌ́ʃən] n. rongi; (col.) shōmi; yoi aji o tano-

disdain [disdéin] n., v. keibetsu (suru). ~ful a. mikudashite;
keibetsu suru (teki). ~fully ad. ōheini; keibetsu shite.

disease [dizí:z] n. yamai; byōki. ~ed [-d] a. byōki no.

disembark [dìsimbá:k] v. jōriku (suru) saseru (land).

disembarkation [dìsimba:kéiʃən] n. rikuage; jōriku.

disembarrass [dísimbǽrəs] v. (shimpai goto nado o) torisaru;
anshin saseru.

disembody [dìsimbódi] v. nikutai kara hanasu (tamashii o);
kaitai suru (disband).

disembowel [dìsimbáuəl] v. harawata o nuku. ⌈illusion).

disenchant [dísintʃá:nt] v. mahō o toku; mayoi o samasu (dis-

disencumber [dìsinkʌ́mbə/dis] v. yakkai barai o suru.

disengage [dísingéidʒ/dis-] v. hazusu; kaiyaku suru. ~ment
n. kaiyaku; kaihō.

disentangle [dísintǽŋgl] v. hodoku; kaiketsu suru.

disfavo(u)r [dísféivə] n. reigū; funinki. v. sansei shinai; kirau : be in ~ with him, kare ni ki ni irarete inai. fall into
~, ninki o otosu.

disfigure [disfígə] v. minikuku suru; katachi o kizutsukeru.

disfranchise [dísfrǽntʃaiz] v. senkyoken o ubau; kōminken
o ubau. ⌈into).

disgorge [disgó:dʒ] v. hakidasu; (kawa (river) ga) sosogu (flow

disgrace [disgréis] n. fumeiyo. v. hazukashimeru. ~ful a. fu-
memmokuna. ~fully ad.

disgruntled [disgrʌ́ntld] a. fukigen no.

disguise [disgáiz] n. hensō; kakotsuke. v. hensō suru.

disgust [disgʌ́st] v. hidoku iyaki ga suru. in ~, iya ni natte.
be ~ed iya ni naru. be ~ed at (or by or with), ga iya ni naru. n. zōo; fukai. ~ful a. unzari suru. ~ing a. kimochi no
waruku naru.

dish [diʃ] n. ōzara, domburi, kozara, nado tabemono o irete
taberu utsuwa; dish ni motta shokumotsu. v. dish ni irete taberu.

dishabille, deshabille [des-], [dìsæbí:l] n. fudangi (no fukusō). ～, kinagashi no mama de.

disharmony [dishá:məni] *a.* chōwa no umaku ikanai.

dishcloth [díʃklɔθ] *n. dish* o arau kire.

dishearten [dishá:tn] *v.* rakutan saseru; yūki o kujiku.

dishevel(l)ed [diʃév(ə)ld] *a.* shiwakucha ni natte; (kami o) midashite; minari no darashi no nai.

dishonest [disɔ́nist] *a.* fushōjikina; futeina. ～ly *ad.* ～ni.

dishonesty [disɔ́nisti] *n.* fushōjiki; fusei.

dishono(u)r [disɔ́nə] *n.* fumeiyo; (tegata nado no) fuwatari. *v.* hazukashimeru (*disgrace*); shiharai o kobamu. ～able hazubeki; fumeiyona. ～ed bill [disɔ́nədbil] fuwatari tegata.

disillusion [disil(j)ú:ʒən] *n.* kakusei; mayoi o samasu koto. *v.* mayoi o samasu. ⌜koto.

disinclination [dìsinklinéiʃən] *n.* kinori-usu; ki ga susumanu

disincline [dìsinkláin] *v.* iya ni naraseru; ki ga mukanaku suru. ⌜doku no. *n.* shōdokuzai.

disinfect [dìsinfékt] *v.* (sakkin) shōdoku suru. ～ant *a.* shō-

disinfection [dìsinfékʃən] *n.* shōdoku; sakkin.

disingenuous [dísindʒénjuəs] *a.* fushōjikina; seii no nai.

disinherit [dìsinhérit] *v.* haichaku suru; kandō suru. ～ance *u.* haichaku; kandō. ⌜(sareru).

disintegrate [disíntigreit] *v.* kuzusu; kuzureru; bunri suru

disintegration [dìsintigréiʃən] *n.* hōkai; bunri.

disinter [dísintɔ́:] *v.* horidasu; yo ni dasu.

disinterested [disíntristid] *a.* kōheina; mukanshinna; kyōmi no nai. ～edly [-idli]*ad.* ～ness *n.*

disjoin [disdʒɔ́in] *v.* hanasu; barabara ni suru. ⌜suru.

disjoint [disdʒɔ́int] *v.* kansetsu o hazusu; (kikai o) kaitai

disjunctive [disdʒʌ́ŋktiv] *a.* bunri suru. *n.* (*gram.*) risetsuteki : ～ *conjections*, risetsu (setsuzokushi [*but*, *yet*, *either*, *or* nado); (*log.*) sengen teki.

disk [disk] *n.* hei emban; emban; rekōdo. (*cf. disc.*)

dislike [disláik] *v.* kirau. *n.* kirai; dai-kirai. ⌜dasu.

dislocate [dísləkeit] *v.* ichi o utsusu; kansetsu o hazusu; mi-

dislocation [dísləkéiʃən] *n.* ichi no idō; dakkyū; konran.

dislodge [dislɔ́dʒ] *v.* aite no kakurega (*hiding*) kara oidasu. ～ment [-mənt] *n.* oitate.

disloyal [dislói(ə)l] *a.* fuchūna; fuchūjitsuna; fushinjitsuna. ～**ly** *ad.* fuchūjitsuni. ～**ty** *n.* fuchūjitsu.

dismal [dízm(ə)l] *a.* inkina; monosugoi. *n.* in'utsuna kibun. ～**ly** [dízməli] *ad.* in'utsuni; monosugoku.

dismantle [dismǽntl] *v.* sōbi o torinozoku; kimono o nugi-
dismast [dismá:st] *v.* hobashira o ubaitoru. ⌊suteru.

dismay [disméi] *n.* rōbai (*consternation*). *v.* rōbai saseru.

dismember [dismémbə] *v.* te-ashi o kirihanasu; (kuni nado o) bunkatsu suru; jomei suru. ～**ment** *n.* te-ashi setsudan (*amputation*).

dismiss [dismís] *v.* kaiko suru; kaisan suru; (kangae nado o) suteru. ～**al** *n.* menshoku. ～**ible** *a.* kaisan dekiru.

dismount [dismáunt] *v.* oriru (uma, kuruma o); gesha suru; waku kara hazusu; orosu. ⌈soku.

disobedience [dìsəbí:djəns] *n.* fujūjun; oya fukō; ihan; han-
disobedient [dìsobí:djənt] *a.* fujūjunna; meirei ihan no. ～**ly** *ad.* jūjun de naku; meirei ni somuite.

disobey [dísobei] *v.* iu koto o kikanai; ...ni ihan suru. ～**er** [-ə] *n.* meirei o mamoranai mono. ⌈rau.

disoblige [dísobláidʒ] *v.* fushinsetsuni suru; kimochi ni saka-
disobliging [disobláidʒiŋ] *a.* fushinsetsuna; bureina. ～**ly** *ad.* ～**ness** *n.* ⌈naru.

disorder [disó:də] *n.* ranzatsu; byōki. *v.* midasu; byōki ni
disorganization [disɔ̀:gən(a)izéiʃən] *n.* (soshiki no) gakai; konran.

disorganize [disó:gənaiz] *v.* gakai saseru; chitsujo o midasu.

disown [disóun] *v.* jibun no mono de nai to iu; hinin suru (*disclaim*).

disparage [dispǽridʒ] *v.* kachi o otosu; kenasu.

disparity [dispǽriti] *n.* fukinkō (*incongruity*); sōi.

dispassionate [dispǽʃənit] *a.* ochitsuita; kōheina (*impartial*).

dispatch [dispǽtʃ] *n.*, *v.* haken (suru) (*despatch*).

dispel [dispél] *v.* chirasu; oiharau (*disperse*).

dispensary [dispénsəri] *n.* yakkyoku; kusuri o ataeru tokoro.

dispensation [dispenséiʃən] *n.* bumpai; kusuri o wakete yaru koto (haizai).

dispense [dispéns] *v.* bumpai suru; kusuri o chōgo suru, chōzai suru; menjo suru (*exempt*) : ~ **with,** nashi de yatte iku.

disperse [dispə́:s] *v.* happō ni chirasu (chiru); bunsan suru.

dispersion [dispə́:ʃən] *n.* sanran; hikari no bunsan.

dispirit [dispírit] *v.* rakutan saseru; ki o kujiku (*discourage*).

displace [displéis] *v.* basho o kaeru; menshoku suru. irekawaru. ~**(e)able** [-əbl] okikaerareru. ~**ment** [-mənt] *n.*

display [displéi] *v.* miseru; misebirakasu; ōyorokobi de miseru. *v.* chinretsu; hyōji.　　　　　　　　　　　　　　　　┌(nau).

displease [displí:z] *v.* fukai ni suru; gokigen o sokoneru.

displeasing [displí:ziŋ] *a.* fuyukaina; haradatashii (*provoking*).

displeasure [displéʒə] *n.* fukai; rippuku.

disport [dispó:t] *v.* asobu; tanoshimaseru; nagusameru : ~ *oneself,* tanoshimu.

disposable [dispóuzəbl] *a.* shori shiuru; jiyūni naru.

disposal [dispóuz(ə)l] *n.* haichi; shori.

dispose [dispóuz] *v.* haichi suru; shori suru : ~ *of,* shobun suru. *feel* ~*d,* ki ga muku. ~**r** [dispóuzə] *n.* shori suru hito.

disposition [dispəzíʃən] *n.* haichi; shobun; seishitsu; keikō (*inclination*).

dispossess [dispəzés] *v.* (tochi ya, ie o) ōryō suru (*oust*).

dispossession [dìspəzéʃən] *n.* ōryō; oitate.

disproof [dísprú:f] *n.* hanshō (*refutation*); hantai.

disproportion [disprəpó:ʃən] *n.* fukinkō; futsuriai.　　┌sōōni.

disproportionate [dísprəpó:ʃ(ə)nit] *a.* futsuriaina. ~**ly** *ad.* fu-

disprove [dísprú:v] *v.* hanshō o ageru; rompa suru (*refute*).

disputable [díspjutəbl] *a.* giron no yochi aru.

disputant [díspju:tənt] *n.* ronsōsha. *a.* ronsō suru.

disputation [dispju(:)téiʃən] *n.* ronsō; tōron.

disputatious [dispju(:)téiʃəs], **disputative** [dispjú:tətiv] *a.* ronsōteki; sōron-zuki no.　　　　　　　　　　　　┌sō; kenka.

dispute [dispjú:t] *v.* ronsō suru; igi o tonaeru; kisou. *n.* ron-

disqualification [diskwɔ̀rifikéiʃən] *n.* shikaku o hakudatsu suru; fugōkaku.　　　　　　　　　　　　　　　　　┌suru.

disqualify [diskwɔ́lifai] *v.* shikkaku to suru; mushikaku ni

disquiet [diskwáiət] *v.* (kokoro nado o) midasu; fuan ni suru. *n.* fuan; shimpai. ~**ing** [-iŋ] *a.* fuanna.

disquietude [diskwáiitju:d] *n.* fuan; shimpai.

disquisition [dìskwizíʃən] *n.* tankyū (*investigation*); rombun.

disregard [dísrigá:d] *v.* mushi ṣuru (*ignore*). *n.* mushi; mutonjaku.

disreputable [disrépjutəbl] *a.* fuhyōban no; (gaibun) no warui. ～**ly** *ad.*

disrepute [dísripjú:t] *n.* fuhyōban; akuhyō; omei (*discredit*).

disrespect [dísrispékt] *n.* burei; shitsurei. ～**ful** [-ful] *a.* bureina. ～**fully** *ad.*

disrupt [disrápt] *v.* bunretsu saseru; (kokka o) gakai saseru

disruption [disrápʃən] *n.* bunretsu; gakai.

disruptive [disráptiv] *a.* bunretsu suru; bunretsusei no.

dissatisfaction [di(s)sætisfǽkʃən] *n.* fumanzoku; fuhei.

dissatisfactory [dìssætisfǽktəri] fumanzokuna (*unsatisfactory*).

dissatisfy [dìssǽtisfai] *v.* fumanzokukan o idakaseru : *a ～ed look*, fumanna kaotsuki.

dissect [disékt] *v.* kaibō suru; shōsai ni shiraberu.

dissection [disékʃən] *n.* kaibō; komakaku shiraberu koto.

dissemble [disémbl] *v.* kakusu (*conceal*); misekakeru; shira-bakureru.

disseminate [disémineit] *v.* (tane o) hiroku maku; hiromeru.

dissension [disénʃən] *n.* iken no sōi; funsō (*strife*).

dissent [disént] *v.* iken ga chigau. *n.* fudōi; Eikoku Kokkyō hantai. ～**er** *n.* Eikoku kokkyō hantaisha. ～**ient** [disénʃənt] *a.* hantaisha. ～**ience** [-ʃəns] *n.* hantai.

dissertation [disə(:)téiʃən] *n.* ronsetsu; rombun.

dissever [disévə] *v.* wakeru; bunkatsu suru (*sever*).

dissidence [dísidəns] *n.* fuitchi; fudōi (*disagreement*).

dissident [dísidənt] *a.* (iken, seishitsu nado o) koto ni suru. *n.* fudōi; hantai iken no hito.

dissimilar [dísímilə] *a.* kotonaru. ～**ly** *ad.* kotonatte.

dissimilarity [dìssimilǽriti] *n.* niteinai koto; sōiten.

dissimulate [dísímjuleit] *v.* sora-tobokeru (*dissemble*); furi o suru.   ⌈boke.

dissimulation [disimjuléiʃən] *n.* shira o kiru koto; sora-to-

dissipate [dísipeit] *v.* chirasu; rōhi suru; hōtō suru. ～**ed** *a.* hōtō shita.

dissipation [disipéiʃən] *n.* rōhi; hōtō; kibarashi.

dissociate [disóuʃieit] *v.* kankei o tatsu ; hanareru.

dissociation [disousiéiʃən] *n.* bunkai ; (*chem.*) kairi.

dissoluble [disóljubl] *a.* bunkai shi uru ; yōkai dekiru.

dissolute [dísɔlu:t] *a.* hōtō no. ~**ly** *ad.* mi o mochikuzushite. ~**ness** *n.* jidaraku ; hōtō. ⌜kaisan.

dissolution [disɔljú:ʃən] *n.* bunkai ; yōkai ; (gikai nado no)

dissolve [dizólv] *v.* bunkai suru ; tokasu (tokeru) ; kaisan suru ; (maryoku o) yaburu (*destroy*).

dissonance -cy [dísɔnəns] *n.* fuchōwa ; fukyōwaon.

dissonant [dísɔnɔnt] *n.* chōwashinai ; itchishinai ; fukyōwa no.

dissuade [diswéid] *v.* omoikiraseru ; omoitodomaraseru.

dissuasion [diswéiʒɔn] *n.* omoitodomaraseru ; chūkoku ; kandissuasive [diswéisiv] *a.* omoitodomaraseru ; seishi no. ⌊gen.

dissyllable [disíləbl] *n.* nionsetsugo.

distaff [dísta:f] *n.* itomakibō ; (*the* ~) onna no ryōbun.

distance [dístəns] *n.* kyori : *keep one at a* ~, tōzakeru. *keep one's* ~, narenare shiku shinai. *v.* empō ni oku ; kyōsō de ai-te ni katsu. ⌜nai.

distant [dístənt] *a.* tōi ; yosoyososhii ; tōen no ; hakkiri shi-

distaste [distéist] *n.* kirai ; iyaki (*for*). ~**ful** [-fʌl] *a.* (aji ga) mazui ; iyana (*disagreeable*). ~**fully** [-fʌli] *ad.* iya de.

distemper [distémpə] *n.* fukigen ; inu no byōki ; nikawa e-nogu.

distend [disténd] *v.* fukuramasu ; fukuramu.

distension, distention [dísténʃən] *n.* bōchō ; fukureagari.

distich [dístik] *n.* (*poet.*) tsuiku ; nigyō renku.

distil(l) [dístíl] *v.* jōryū suru ; shitatari ochiru : *distilled water*, jōryūsui.

distillation [distiléiʃən] *n.* jōryū ; jōryūhō ; sono eki (*liquid*).

distillery [dístíləri] *n.* jōryūsho. ⌜akirakani.

distinct [dístíŋkt] *a.* meiryōna ; kotonatta. ~**ness** *n.* ~**ly** *ad.*

distinction [dístíŋ(k)ʃən] *n.* sabetsu ; (yoi imi de) hoka to chi-gau koto : *people of* ~, chomeina hitobito. ⌜*istic*).

distinctive [dístíŋ(k)tiv] *a.* sabetsu aru ; tokushu no (*character-*

distinguish [distíŋgwiʃ] *v.* kubetsu suru ; miwakeru. ~ *oneself*, na (*name*) o ageru. ~**able** [-əbl] *a.* kubetsu dekiru. ~**bly** *ad.* ~**ed** [-t] *a.* hiideta ; nadakai. ~**ing** tokushuna.

distort [distó:t] *v.* yugameru ; yugande uketoru. ∼**ed** *a.* kojitsuketa. ∼**edly** *ad.* ∼**edness** *n.* kojitsuke. ∼**er** *n.* kojitsukeru hito. ⌈no.

distortion [distɔ:ʃən] *n.* yugami ; kojitsuke. ∼**al** *a.* kojitsuke

distract [distrǽkt] *v.* chūi o sorasu ; kangae o hikkakimidasu. ∼**ed** [-id] *a.* hakkyō shita. ∼**edly** *ad.* kokoro ga midarete. ∼**ing** [-iŋ] *a.* ki ga kurui sōna. ∼**ive** [-iv] *a.* madowasu.

distraction [distrǽkʃən] *n.* kibarashi ; konwaku ; kyōki.

distress [distrés] *n.* kurushimi. *v.* kurushimeru. ∼**ing** *a.* kuru-

distribute [distríbju(:)t] *v.* bumpai suru ; sampu suru. ⌊shii.

distribution [distribjú:ʃən] *n.* bumpai(butsu) ; haikyū hōhō.

distributive [distríbjutiv] *a.* bumpai suru ; (*gram.*) bumpaiteki no *collective* ni tairitsu suru ; koko no. ∼*adjectives* bumpai keiyōshi (*each, every, either, etc.*).

distributor [distríbjutə] *n.* bumpaisha ; haikyūsha.

district [distríkt] *n.* chihō (*region*) ; (*Am.*) senkyo-ku.

distrust [distrást] *n.* giwaku ; fushin'yō ; utagai. ∼**ful** *a.* utagaibukai. ∼**fully** *ad.*

disturb [distó:b] *v.* midasu ; fuanni suru. ∼**ance** [-əns] *n.* sōran ; jōran. ∼**er** *n.* hikkakimawasu hito.

disunion [dísjú:njən] *n.* bunretsu ; atsureki (*discord*).

disunite [disju(:)náit] *v.* bunretsu suru (saseru).

disuse [disjú:s] *v.* [disjú:z] *n.* fuyō : *fall into* ∼, sutareru.

ditch [ditʃ] *n.* mizo ; hori (*trench*).

ditto [dítou], **do.** *n.* dōjō ; ue ni onaji.

ditty [díti] *n.* kouta ; shōkyoku. ⌈nichi

diurnal [daió:n(ə)l] *a.* mainichi no. ∼**ly** [daió:nəli] *ad.* mai-

divan [divǽn/dáivən] *n.* nagaisu ; kaigishitsu.

dive [daiv] *n.* (suichū) moguri ; tobikomi ; (kūchū) kyūkōka. *v.* **dived**, (*Am. col.* Brit., *dial.* **dove**, o *past tense* ni dake tsukau.) ∼ *bomber*, kyūkōka bakugekiki. *a fancy* ∼ (*ing*), suiei no kyokutobi. *an oyster* ∼, (*Am.*) yasuryōriya. *an opium* ∼, ahenkutsu. ⌈suikan.

diver [dáivə] *n.* sensui-fu ; mizu ni moguru tori (*bird*) ; sen-

diverge [daivó:dʒ] *v.* wakarete deru ; hanareru.

divergence [daivó:dʒ(ə)ns] *n.* bumpa ; bunshutsu.

divergent [daivó:dʒ(ə)nt] *a.* wakarete deru ; chigatta....

divers [dáivə(:)z] *a.* shujuna ; iroirona.

diverse [d(a)ivə́:s] *a.* kotonatta ; shuju no (*various*).

diversify [d(a)ivə́:sifai] *v.* henka saseru. ⌐undō.

diversion [daivə́:ʃən] *n.* kibuntenkan ; kibarashi ; (*mil.*) kensei

diversity [daivə:s(i)ti] *n.* fudō ; zattana koto ; iroirosamazama.

divert [daivə́:t] *v.* ta ni tenzuru ; ki o harasu. ⁓**ing** *a.* kibara-

divest [daivést] *v.* ubau ; hagitoru (kimono nado). ⌐shi no.

divide [diváid] *v.* wakeru ; wakareru ; saiketsu suru. *n.* (*Am.*) bunsuikai (*watershed*).

dividend [dívidend] *n.* (*math.*) hijosū ; warareru sū ; haitōkin.

divider [diváidə] *n.* bunkatsusha ; (*pl.*) ryōkyaku-ki (*compasses*).

divination [divinéiʃən] *n.* uranai ; yogen (*prediction*).

divine [diváin] *v.* minuku ; yogen suru. *a.* kami no ; shinseina (*holy*). *n.* shingakusha. ⁓**r** [diváinə] *n.* ekisha ; uranai.

diving [dáiviŋ] *a.* sensuiyō no. *n.* tobikomi. ⁓**bell** [dáiviŋ-bel] *n.* tsurigane-gata sensuiki.

divinity [divíniti] *n.* kōgōshisa ; (*the* ⁓) kami (*God*) ; shingaku.

divisible [divízibl] *a.* wakerareru ; (*math.*) hakkiri warikireru.

division [divíʒən] *n.* kubun : ⁓ *of labour*, bungyō. ...-bu (*section*) ; (*math.*) warizan ; (*mil.*) shidan. ⁓**al** [divíʒənəl] *a.* bumpai no ; (*mil.*) shidan no.

divisor [diváizə] *n.* (*math.*) josū : *common* ⁓, kōyakusū.

divorce [divɔ́:s] *n.* rikon. *v.* rikon suru.

divulge [diváldʒ] *v.* himitsu (*secret*) o morasu.

dizzy [dízi] *a.* memai suru. ⁓**ly** *ad.* ⁓**nss** *n.* memai.

do [du:/də] *v.* did, done ; doing. (1) okonau ; suru : ⁓ *your work*, kimi no shigoto o nasai. ⁓*or die*, yare yo, de nakyā shine. (2) sumu : *That's done*, soitsā sunda. (3) tsukuru : *Walt Disney did a movie about seven dwarfs*, Walts Disney wa 7-nin no kobito no eiga o tsukutta. (4) gen'in o suru : *Your work does you credit*, anata no saku wa anata no shin'yō o takame masu. (5) furumau : ⁓ *wisely*, kashikoku furumau koto desu ne. (6) niau ; kakkō suru : *This hat will* ⁓, kono bōshi wa niai masu ne. (7) teshita ni naru : ⁓ *homage to*, ni teshita ni naru. (8) yarareru : *I'm afraid you've been done*, yararetan ja ari masen ka na? (9) tsuyomeru iikata : *I* ⁓ *want to go*, ore (nani ga nan demo) iki taitte iun da yo. (10) ippan dōshi no kawari ni : *My dog goes where I* ∼. (11) *negative adverb* no ato ni : *Rarely did she laugh*, mettani ano kata wa warawanakatta.

docile [dóusail] *a.* oshie yasui ; yoku oshie o mamoru.

docility [do(u)síliti] *n.* sunaosa ; yoi seishitsu (*gentle disposition*).

dock [dɔk] *n.* dokku ; (*Am.*) hatoba (*wharf*) ; hikokuseki.

docket [dɔ́kit] *n.* soshō jiken ichiranhyō ; naiyō tekiyō no fuda. *v.* *docket* ni kakitsukeru.

doctor [dɔ́ktə] *n.* isha ; hakase. *v.* isha (*chiryō*) o suru. ∼**ate** [dɔ́ktərit] *n.* hakase-gō.

doctrinal [dɔktráin(ə)l] *a.* kyōgi (=oshie) no ; kyōkun no.

doctrine [dɔ́ktrin] *n.* kyōri ; kyōgi (*-ism*) ; gakusetsu (*theory*).

document [dɔ́kjumənt] *n.* shōkodateru shorui : *human* ∼, ningen kiroku. ∼**al** [dɔkjuméntəl], ∼**ary** [-təri] *a.* bunsho no ; kiroku no.

dodge [dɔdʒ] *n.* gomakashi ; iinuke ; katasukashi. *v.* hirari to mi o kawasu ; gomakasu ; iinukeru ; katasukashi o kuwasu. ∼**r** [dɔ́dʒə] *n.* gomakasu hito.

doe [dou] *n.* mejika (*female deer*) ; me-usagi (*female rabbit*).

doer [dú(:)ə] *n.* jikkōsha ; jikkō suru hito.

does [dʌz] do no 3-ninshō, tansū, genzai no katachi.

doff [dɔf] *v.* bōshi (*hat*) o nugu =*do off*.

dog [dɔg] *n.* inu : *go to the* ∼, hametsu suru. *He hasn't a word to throw to a* ∼, kare wa hidoku mukuchina otoko da. *v.* ato o tsukeru. ∼**cart** [-kɑːt] nirimbasha. ∼**cheap** [-tʃíːp] muchani yasui. ∼ **days** natsu no doyō (*hottest season*). ∼**eared** [-iəd] kami no sumi ga oreta. ∼ **fancier** [-fӕnsiə] *n.* aikenka ; inu shōnin. ∼**fish** [-fiʃ] *n.* same. ∼**sleep** [-sliːp] *n.* mezatoi hito. ∼**tired** [-taiəd] *a.* tsukarekitta. ∼**tooth** [-tuːθ] *n.* inuba ; itokiriba. ∼**'s-eared**=**dog-eared**.

doge [doudʒ] *n.* kyōwasei sōtoku (*Anc. Venice* no).

dogfight [dɔ́gfait] *n.* (*col.*) (kogata sentōki no) kūchūsen.

dogged [dɔ́gid] *a.* gōjōna. ∼**ly** [-li] *ad.* gōjōni.

doggerel [dɔ́gərəl] *n.* hetana shi ; hebo-shi (*poet*). *a.* hetana.

doggie, doggy [dɔ́gi] *n.* koinu ; wanchan.

doggish [dɔ́giʃ] *a.* inu no yōna ; hiretsuna ; iji no warui (*cross, ill-natured*).

doghouse [dɔ́ghaus] *n.* inugoya. *in the* ∼, (*Am. col.*) ninki (*popularity*) no nai koto.

dogma [dɔ́gmə] *n.* kyōri; teiri; dokudansetsu.

dogmatic [dəgmǽtik] *a.* kyōri no; dokudantekina. ~**cally** [-kəli] *ad.* dokudantekini. ~**ics** [-iks] *n.* kyōriron.

dogmatism [dɔ́gmətizm] *n.* dokudan; dokudanron.

dogmatist [dɔ́gmətist] *n.* dokudanka; kyōgigakusha.

dogmatize [dɔ́gmətaiz] *v.* dokudan suru.

doily [dɔ́ili] *n.* shokutaku-yō no chiisai napkin.

doing [dú(:)iŋ] *n.* kōi, okonai (*pl.*); furumai (*behaviour*).

doldrum [dɔ́ldrəm] *n.* (*pl.*) (sekidō (*the Equator*) fukin no) mufūtai. iki shōchin (*depression of spirits*): *be in the* ~, fusagi konde iru.

dole [doul] *v.* sukoshi zutsu bumpai suru. *n.* shitsugyōsha ni ataeru bumpaikin. ~**ful** [dóulful] *a.* kanashii. ~**fully** kana-**doll** [dɔl], **dolly** [dɔ́li] *n.* ningyō.   [shiku.

dollar [dɔ́lə] *n.* doru (Beikoku no kahei tan'i): *almighty* ~, **dolo(u)r** [dɔ́lə] *n.* hiai (*poet.*).   [ōgon bannō.

dolorous [dɔ́lərəs] *a.* kanashii.

dolphin [dɔ́lfin] *n.* (*zoo.*) iruka.

dolt [doult] *n.* baka; orokamono.

domain [doméin] *n.* kuni no shihaiken no oyobu tochi.

dome [doum] *n.* maruiyane.

domestic [doméstik] *a.* katei no; kokunai no; kokusan no; hito ni nareta (*tame*). *n.* meshitsukai.   [*lize*).

domesticate[doméstikeit]*v.* kainarasu; tochi ni nareru (*natura-***domesticity** [dò(u)mestísiti] *n.* katei seikatsu; (*pl.*) kaji, *the domesticities*; kafū.

domicile [dɔ́misail] *n.* jūsho; honseki. *v.* jūsho o sadameru.

domiciliary [dòmisíljəri] *a.* idokoro no: ~ *visit*, kataku sōsaku.

dominant [dɔ́minənt] *a.* shihai suru; yūryokuna (*prevailing*).

dominate [dɔ́mineit] *v.* shihai suru; sobieru (*tower above*).

domination [dòminéiʃən] *n.* shihai; tōchi (*rule*); shuken (*sovereignty*).

domineer [dòminíə] *v.* senseiseiji o suru. ~**ing** *a.* kenryoku o furimawasu.   [no sō (*priest*).

Dominican[domínikən] *a.* Dominiko Kyōdan no. *n.* Dominican **dominie** [dɔ́mini] *n.* kyōshi (*Scotland* de); bokushi.

dominion [domíniən] *n.* shuken ; ryōdo (*territory*).

domino [dɔ́minou] *n.* zukin tsuki hōi ; (*pl.*) domino asobi.

don [dɔn] *n.* Spein no kizoku no keishō (*title*). *v.* kimono o

donate [dóuneit] *v.* ataeru ; kifu suru. ⌊kiru (*do on*).

donation [do(u)néiʃən] *n.* kifu ; okuri mono.

done [dʌn] *v. see :* **do**

donkey [dɔ́ŋki] *n.* roba ; baka (*a fool*). ⁓**-engine,** hojo kikan.

donor [dɔ́nə] *n.* kifu o kureta hito.

don't [dóunt] =**do not.**

doom [du:m] *n.* kanashii ummei (*fate*) ; hametsu ; shi. ⁓**sday** [-zdei] *n.* Saigo no hi ; Sabaki no Hi.

door [dɔ:] *n.* tobira ; ikken no ie ; ikko : *three* ⁓*s off,* sangen mukō. *live next* ⁓, tonari awase ni sumau. *in* ⁓**s,** ie no uchi ni. ⁓ **bell,** genkan no *bell.* ⁓**keeper** [-ki:pə] *n.* momban. ⁓**plate** [-pleit] *n.* hyōsatsu. ⁓**mat** [dɔ́ːmæt] kutsufuki. ⁓**way** toguchi. ⁓**knob** [-nɔb] *n. door* no nigiri. ⁓**man** *n.* hotel na-do de kyaku no jidōsha nado no okurimukae o suru mono. ⁓**money** [-mʌnə] kidosen. ⁓**nail** *n.* mukashi to ni utta kugi. *as dead as a doornail,* kanzenni shinde iru.

dormancy [dɔ́:mənsi] *n.* suimin ; tōmin (*hibernation*) ; sempuku (*hiding*). ⌈shain.

dormant [dɔ́:mənt] *a.* nemutte (iru) : ⁓ *partner,* tokumei

dormer [dɔ́:mə] *n.* (*archi.*) yane mado.

dormitory [dɔ́:mit(ə)ri] *n.* kishikusha ; ryō.

dormouse [dɔ́:maus] *n.* (*pl.* ⁓**mice** [-mais]) risu no yōna, tō-min suru nezumi.

dorsal [dɔ́:s(ə)l] *a.* senaka no. ⁓**fin** [-fin] uo no sebire.

dory [dɔ́:ri] *n.* (*Am.*) gyosen fuzoku no hirazoko-bune.

dose [dous] *n.* (*med.*) ippuku ; *v.* kusuri o moru.

dost [dʌst] *v.* (*arch., poet.*) 2 ninshō tansū ('*thou*') ni musubu **do** no genzai-kei..

dot [dɔt] *n.* ten (·). *v.* ten o utsu.

dotage [dóutidʒ] *n.* mōroku (*senility*).

dotard [dóutəd] *n.* mōroku shita hito.

dote [dóut] *v.* mōroku suru.

doth [dʌθ] (*arch., poet.*,) =**does.**

doting [dóutiŋ] *a.* ai ni oboreta.

double [dÁbl] *n. a.* nijū (no) ; nibai (no) ; futae (no) : ～ *play*, *baseball* no ippen ni *out* o 2-ri tsukuru koto. ～**barrel**(l)**ed** [-bærəld] *n.* ni-rempatsu no. ～**dealer** [-díːlə] *n.* futagokoro no aru hito. ～**edged** [-edʒd] *a.* moroba no. ～**quick** [-kwik] *n.* kakeashi. ～**tongued** [-tÁŋd] nimaijita no.

doublet [dÁblit] *n.* onaji gogen kara deta futatsu no tango. 16 seiki ni otoko no kita uwagi. futago no kataippō nado.

doubloon [dʌblúːn] *n.* Spein no furui kinka no namae.

doubly [dÁbli] *ad.* 2-bai ni ; futatsu-ori ni.

doubt [daut] *n.* utagai. *v.* utagau. ～**ful** [-ful] *a.* okashii ; utagawashii. ～**fully** [-fuli] *ad.* okashiku ; utagawashiku. ～**fulness** *n.* giwaku ; utagai. ～**less** *ad.* utagai naku. ～**lessly** [-li] *ad.* utagai mo naku.

dough [dou] *n.* neriko ; (*Am. sl.*) kinsen (*money*). ～**boy** [-bɔi] (*sl.*) hohei. ～**nut** [-nʌt] dōnats. (isshu no kashi)   ⌈shiku.

doughty [dÁuti] *a.* tsuyoi ; gōtanna (*bold*). ～**ily** *ad.* isama-

doughy [dóui] *a.* koneta mugiko no yōna ; nibui (*dull*).

douse [daus] *v.* mizu (*water*) ni tsukkomu ; mizu o abiseru.

dove [dʌv] *n.* hato. ～**cot** [-kɔ́t], ～**cote** [-kout] *n.* hatogoya.

dovetail [dÁvteil] *n.* arizashi ; (kenchiku de) tsugiawaseru to-koro. *v.* arizashi ni suru.

dowager [dáuədʒə] *n.* taikō ; zen-kokuō no mibōjin : *Empress* ～, kōtaikō.

dowdy [dáudi] *a.* darashinai fukusō (*dress*).   ⌈*perty*).

dower [dáuə] *n.* shinda (*diceased*) otto (*husband's*) no isan (*pro-

down [daun] *n.* tori no (*bird's*) watage ; sakyū (*sandhill*). box. daun. *a.* kudari no : ～ *train*, kudari ressha. *a* ～ *slope*, kuda-rizaka. *ad.* leave the blind ～, to o oroshite oku. *bring* ～ *the price*, nedan o sageru. *ups and* ～*s*, uki-shizumi. *go* ～ *the river*, kawa o kudaru. ～**cast** [-kɑːst] *a.* unadareta. ～**fall** [-fɔːl] *n.* tsuiraku. ～**hearted** [-háːtid] *ad.* gakkari shite. ～**hill** [-hil] *n.* kudarizaka. ～**pour** [-pɔː] *n.* doshaburi. ～**right** [-rait] *a.* akarasamano. ～**stairs** [-stɛəs] *a. ad. n.* kaika (no) ～**stream** [-striːm] *a.* kawashimo e. ～**town** [-taun] *a. ad.* shitamachi (no ; e). ～**trod**(**den**) [-trɔ̀d(n)] *a.* fuminijirareta. ～**ward**, ～**wards** [-wəd(z)] *ad., a.* shitamuki ni (no).   ⌈(*wideawake*).

downy [dauni] *a.* mukuge no ; yawarakai ; nukeme no nai

dowry [dáu(ə)ri]=**dot** [dɔt] *n.* kekkon jisankin; umaretsuki no chie (*natural gift*).

doxology [dɔksɔ́lədʒi] *n.* kami (*God*) o tataeru shi (*poem*).

doyen [dwáje:ŋ] *n.* (Fr.) kosansha; mae kara iru hito (*senior member*).

doze [douz] *v.* inemuri suru. *n.* inemuri.

dozen [dʌ́zn] *n.* ichi-dāsu (12).

dozy [dóuzi] *a.* nemui (*sleepy*); nemusōna (*looking sleepy*).

Dr. karikata (*debit*): saimusha (*debtor*). Hakase: *Dr. Smith*, Smith Hakase.

drab [dræb] *n.* darashi no nai onna (*slut*); kasshoku. *a.* kas-shoku.

drachm, dram [dræm] *n.* dorama (jūryō no na) (*weight*)=1.88 guramu; yakuryō (*medicine dose*) dewa 3.888 guramu.

Draconian [dreikóunjən] *a.* Draco no yōna; kibishii; kako-kuna; Draco (*Athens* no rippōsha).

draff [dræf] *n.* kasu; sakekasu (*lees*).

draft [drɑ:ft], *v.* **draught** [drɑ:ft] kisō suru (*prepare*); shita-e o kaku (*draw rough sketch*). *n.* sōkō (*rough copy*); (*mil.*) sembatsu sareta tai; (*Am.*) chōhei. kawase tegata (*bill of exchange*). ~**board** [-bɔ.d] *n.* seiyō goban. ~**sman** [-smən] *n.* kisōsha.

drag [dræg] *v.* hiku; saguru (*the bottom of water*); hikizuru. *n.* ken'in; maguwa (*harrow*); yontō basha (*carriage*). ~**net** [-net] *n.* hikiami.

draggle [drǽgl] *v.* hikizuru; hikizuri yogosu.

dragoman [drǽgəmən] *n.* tsūyaku annainin (*interpreter*).

dragon [drǽg(ə)n] *n.* ryū; genkakuna kanshinin (*severe watch-er*). *the Old* ~, ma-ō. ~**fly** [-flai] *n.* tombo. ⌈gai suru.

dragoon [drəgú:n] *n.* ryūki-hei. *v.* *dragoon* de nayamasu; haku-

drain [drein] *v.* haisui suru; zaigen (*funds*) o karasu (*exhaust*). *v.* shitatari deru. ~**age** [dréinidʒ] *n.* haisui. ~**ing** [-iŋ] *n. a.*

drake [dreik] *n.* (*bird.*) osu-gamo. ⌊haisui (suru).

drama [drɑ́:mə] *n.* gikyoku; gekishi.

dramatic [drəmǽtik], **dramatical** [drəmǽtikl] *a.* gikyoku no; gekiteki no.

dramatis personae [drǽmətis pəsóuni] (L.) tojō jimbutsu.

dramatist [drǽmətist] *n.* geki (gikyoku) sakka.

dramatize [drǽmətaiz] *v.* gikyoku ni tsukuru; kyaku shoku

drank [drǽŋk] *v. see*: **drink**. ⌊suru.

drape [dreip] *v.* nuno (*cloth*) de ōu; chōsei suru (*prepare*). *n.* kāten (*curtain*).

draper [dréipə] *n.* gofukushō. ⌈no (*hanging*).

drapery [dréipəri] *n.* tammono; gofuku (*trade*); kake nuno

drastic [drǽstik] *a.* shunretsuna (*violent*); omoikitta (*decisive*).

draught [drɑ:ft] = draft.

draughts [drɑ:fts] *n.* (*pl.*) (*Brit.*) seiyō shōgi (*Am. checkers*).

draw [drɔ:] *v.* **drew, drawn; drawing** hiku; hiki nuku (*pull out*); kumu (*-water*); (tegata (*bill*)) furidasu; egaku (*delineate*); (kawase (*money-order*) o) furidasu. ~ *back*, kaishū suru. shirizoku (*fall back*). ~ *down*. (maku (*curtain*) o) hiki orosu. ~ *in*, hiki ireru; (ichinichi ga) kureru. ~ *near*, chikazuku. ~ *on*, sasoi dasu. ~ *out*, seiretsu saseru; nobasu (*stretch*).

drawback [drɔ́:bæk] *n.* koshō; furieki (*disadvantage*); harai modoshi kin (*repayment money*).

drawbridge [drɔ́:bridʒ] *n.* hanebashi (*swing-bridge*).

draw-well [drɔ́:wel] *n.* tsurube (*well-bucket*) ido.

drawee [drɔ:í:] *n.* tegata shiharai nin. ⌈tsukue no).

drawer [drɔ́:(ə)] *n.* tegata haraidashinin; hikidashi (tansu ya

drawing [drɔ́:iŋ] *n.* e; zuga. ~**board**, seizu ban. ~**paper**, zugayōshi. ~**pen**, karasuguchi. ~**pin**, ga-byō. ~**room**, ōsetsu shitsu.

drawl [drɔ:l] *v.* noronoro hanasu. *n.* monougena hanashiburi.

drawn [drɔ:n] : *see* **draw**. ~ *sword*, nuita katana. ~ *face*, shikameta. ~ *game*, mushōbu.

dray [drei] *n.* nibasha. ⌈*shy of*).

dread [dred] *n.* kyōfu. *a.* osoroshii. *v.* osoreru; habakaru (*be*

Dreadnought [drédnɔ:t] *n.* dokyū senkan (*fear nothing*). ~**cruiser** dokyū jun'yōkan.

dream [dri:m] *n.* yume. *v.* yume o miru; ~ *away*, yume utsutsu ni sugosu. ~ *of*, no koto o yume ni miru. *I little ~ed of it*, sonna koto yume nimo omowanakatta.

dreamily [drí:mili] *ad.* yume no yōni.

dreamy [drí:mi] *a.* yume no yōna; kūsō ni fukeru (*fanciful*).

drear [driə]=**dreary** [dríəri] *a.* mono sabishii; taikutsuna; omoshiroku nai.

dredge [dredʒ] *n.*, *v.* shunsetsuki de sarau.

dredger [drédʒə] *n.* shunsetsuki ; shunsetsusen (~*ship*).

dregs [dregz] *n.* (*pl.*) ori ; chinden-butsu ; kasu.

drench [drentʃ] *v.* hitasu ; gyūba ni mizugusuri o nomaseru. *n.* sui-yaku no ikkaibun.

dress [dres] *v.* kiseru ; kikazaru ; hōtai suru (*bandage*) ; chōri suru (*cook*). ~**coat** [-kout] *n.* reifuku ; embifuku. **full** ~ [fúldres] reifuku ; seisō. ~ **circle** [sə:kl] jōtō sajiki.

dressing [drésiŋ] *n.* kimono ; sakana ya niku nado ni kakeru sōsu ; tori nado ni tsumeru pankuzu nado ; kusuri ya hōtai (kizu no teate no) ; hiryō ; koyashi (*to plants*). ~ **case** [-keis] *n.* keshō bako. ~ **gown** [-gaun] *n.* keshō-gi. ~ **room** [-ru:m] *n.* keshōbeya.

dressy [drési] *a.* ishō gonomi no ; ikina (*stylish*).

drew [dru:] *v. see* : **draw.**

dribble [dríbl] *v.* shitataru ; shitataraseru ; yodare o tarasu ; (*football*) doriburu suru. *n.* shitatari, shizuku, doriburu.

drib(b)let [dríblit] *n.* shōryō ; shōgaku ; sukoshi.

drier, dryer [dráiə] *n.* kawakasu hito ; kansōki ; kansōzai.

drift [drift] *n.* mizu, kūki nado no nagare ; nagare ga motte kita mono (gomi). *v.* hyōryū saseru ; fukiyoseru. ~**ice** [-ais] *n.* ryūhyō. ~**wood** [-wud] *n.* ryūboku.

drill [dril] *n.* kiri ; kunren ; tanemaki-ki ; isshu no mempu *v.* kiri de ana o akeru. kunren suru.

drily [dráili] *ad.* sugenaku ; mumikansō ni.

drink [driŋk] *v.* **drank, drunk** ; **drinking.** nomu ; sake o no-mu ; shikuhai o ageru. ~ sake ; hitonomi ; (*Am. sl.*) taiyō ; mizuumi ; kawa. ~ *money*, sakate. ~**able** [-əbl] *a.* nomeru. ~**able** *n.* (*pl.*) nomimono. ~**er** [-ə] *n.* nomu hito ; sakenomi.

drinking [dríŋkiŋ] *n.* mizu (sake nado) o nomu koto. ~**bout** [-baut] *n.* sakamori. ~**fountain** [~ fàuntin] (*n.* (kōen nado no) mizu nomi funsui. ~ *water* [~ wɔ́:tə] *n.* inryōsui.

drip [drip] *n.* shitatari ; shizuku. *v.* shitataru ; shizuku o tarasu (*with*). ~**ping** *n.* shitatari ; shizuku ; (*pl.*) yakiniku no tare-shiru.

drive [dráiv] *v.* karitateru ; muri ni…saseru ; (kugi nado o) utsu ; nerau (*at*) : *I can't make out what he is driving at. n.* kuru-ma o unten suru koto ; doraibu. (*Am.*) ~**in** *n.* noriireshiki no mise. ～**way** [⌐wei] *n.* doraibu dōro; jidōsha dōro.

drivel [drívl] *n. v.* yodare (o tarasu).

driven [drívn] *v. see :* **drive.**

driver [dráiuə] *n.* gyosha; untenshu.

drizzle [drízl] *v.* (ame ga) shitoshito furu. *n.* kirisame.

drizzly [drízli] *a.* shitoshito furu; kirisame no furu.

droll [droul] *a.* odoketa. ～**ery** [-əri] *n.* odoke; dōke.

dromedary [drʌ́məd(ə)ri/drɔ́m-] *n.* hitokobu rakuda. *cf.* **camel.**

drone [droun] *n.* (*insect*) osu no mitsubachi; namake mono; bunbun unaru oto. *v.* bunbun unaru; namakeru.

droop [dru:p] *v.* taresagaru; shioreru. *n.* unadareru koto; shioreru koto. ～**ing** *a.* unadareta; tareru.

drop [drɔp] *n.* shizuku; tsuiraku; doroppu (*baseball, soccer, cake etc.*). *v.* tarasu; otosu; (tegami nado o) kaki okuru; futo morasu; shitatariochiru : ～ *in,* tachiyoru. ～ **curtain** [-kə́:tin] *n.* donchō. ～**scene** [-si:n] *n.* tsurisage haikei; sage maku.

dropsical [drɔ́psik(ə)l] *a.* mizubukure no.

dropsy [drɔ́psi] *n.* mizubukure; suiki.

dros(h)ky [drɔ́ʃki] *n.* Soren no yonrin basha; Doitsu no tsuji basha

dross [drɔs] *n.* kanekuzu; tetsu o tokashite ue ni uku kuzu.

drought [draut], **drouth** [drauθ] *n.* kambatsu; hideri.

drove [drouv] *v. see :* **drive.**

drover [dróuvə] *n.* kachiku o ichiba ni otte iku hito; kachiku-shō.

drown [draun] *v.* oboresasu; hitasu. *be* ～*ed,* dekishi suru. ～ *oneself,* minage suru.

drowse [drauz] *n.* inemuri. *v.* inemuri o suru.

drowsy [dráuzi] *a.* nemui. ～**ily** [-ili] *ad.* nemuku; utouto to. ～**iness** [-nis] *n.* nemui koto; madoromi.

drub [drʌb] *v.* bō de utsu; makasu; renda suru (*beat*); ashibumisuru. *n.* ōda.

drudge [drʌdʒ] *v.* akuseku hataraku. *n.* akuseku hataraku hito.

drudgery [drʌ́dʒəri] *n.* honeori shigoto.

drug [drʌg] *n.* yakuhin; masuizai. *v.* masuiyaku o nomaseru. ～**gist** [-′ist] *n.* yakuzaishi; kusuriya. ～**store** [⌐stɔ:] *n.* (*Am.*) kusuriya (kissaten kengyō no).

Druid [drú(:)id] *n.* kodai Keruto-zoku no sōryo.

druidical [dru(:)ídik(ə)l] *a. Druid* no.

drum [drʌm] *n.* taiko; komaku (*of ear*); kodō. *v.* taiko de sō-suru (kyoku o); yakamashiku kurikaeshite iu. ~**mer** [-ə] *n.* koshu; taiko o utsu hito; (*Am.*) chūmontori.

drunk [drʌŋk] *v.* see : **drink**. *a.* yopparatte

drunkard [drʌ́ŋkəd] *n.* yopparai.

drunken [drʌ́ŋk(ə)n] *a.* yotte iru; nondakure no.

dry [drai] *v.* kawakasu; kawaku; hikarabiru : ~ *up*, hoshi-ageru; damaru. *a.* kawaita; kawaki no; (*Am.*) kinshusei o shiku; *n.* (*pl.*) kinshuhō sanseisha. ~ **battery** [bǽtəri] *n.* ~**cell** [-sél] *n.* kandenchi. ~**goods** [-gudz] *n.* gofukurui. **dry nurse** *n. Am.*; **dry-nurse** *n. Brita.*, *v. Am.*; *v. Brit.* ~**nurse** [-nəːs] *n.* jibun no chichi o yaranai uba. *v.* **dry-urse** to shite hataraku. ~**plate** [-pleit] *n.* kampan (shashin no). ~**-shod** [-ʃód] *a.* (kutsu) kutsu o nurasanai de (*shod* = *shoed*). ~**ing** *a.* kansō saseru. ~**ly** *ad.* reitanni. ~**ness** *n.* kansō.

dryard [dráiəd] *n.* shinrin no megami; ki no sei (Girisha Shin-wa no)

dual [djú(ː)əl] *a.* futatsu no; nijū no; nigen no. ~**personality** nijūjinkaku. ~**ism** [-izm] *n.* nigenron; nishinkyō. ~**ist** [-ist] *n.* nigenronsha.

duality [dju(ː)ǽliti] *n.* nijūsei; nigensei.

dub [dʌb] *v.* shakui o ataeru.

dubiety [djuːbáiəti] *n.* ginen; utagai. ⌐**ness** *n.*

dubious [djúːbiəs] *a.* utagawashii. ~**ly** *ad.* utagawashiku. ~

ducal [djúːk(ə)l] *a.* kōshaku no. ⌐**joō**).

duchess [dʌ́tʃis] *n.* kōshaku fujin; kōhi (kōkoku *dukedom*) no

duchy [dʌ́tʃi] *n.* kōshakuryō (*dukedom*).

duck [dʌk] *v.* mizu ni moguru; hyoi to atama o sageru. *n.* hyoi to atama o sageru koto; kamo (mesu) : *domestic* ~, ahiru. *make ducks and drakes*, kinsen o yumizu no yōni shōhi suru. *wild* ~, kamo. ~**bill** [-bil] *n.* kamo no hashi. ~**ling** [-liŋ] *n.* kogamo.
duct [dʌkt] *n.* kuda; dōkan. ⌐*n.* kogamo.

ductile [dʌ́ktil] *a.* hikinobashi yasui; shinayakana; sunaona.

ductility [dʌktíliti] *n.* shintensei; shinayakasa; jūjun.

dude [djuːd] *n.* (*Am.*) sharemono; mekashiya.

dudgeon [dʌ́dʒ(ə)n] *n.* rippuku : *in high* ~, ōini rippuku shite.

due [djuː] *a.* tōzen shiharau beki; suru koto ni natte iru : ~

date, (tegata nado no) kijitsu. *ad.* tadashiku; seitō ni. *n.* tōzen haraubeki mono; fusai; gimu.

duel [djú:il/djú(:)əl] *n.* kettō. *v.* kettō suru.

duenna [dju(:)énə] *n.* (Spein no katei de no) shōjo kantoku fujin; tsukisoi fujin.

duet [dju(:)ét], **duetto** [duétto] *n.* nibu gasshō (kyoku); nibu-gassō (kyoku).

dug [dʌg] *v. see* : **dig**.

dugout [dʌ́gaut] *n.* marukibune; hottate-goya; zangō.

duke [dju:k] *n.* kōshaku. ～**dom** [⌐dəm] *n.* kōkoku; kōshaku-ryōchi; kōshaku no kurai.

dulcet [dʌ́lsit] *n.* chōshi no yoi; onshoku no utsukushii.

dulcimer [dʌ́lsimə] *n.* kinzoku no gen o hatta gakki (*piano* no genkei).

dull [dʌl] *a.* nibui; noroi. ～**ish** [dʌ́liʃ] *a.* nibui; noroi, seishitsu no. ～**ard** [dʌ́ləd] *n.* nibui hito. ～**ness** [-nis] *n.* rodon. ～**brained** [-breined] atama no unten no nibui. ～**sighted** [-saitid] *a.* shiryoku no nibui.

dully [dʌ́li] *ad.* nibuku; noroku; fukappatsuni.

duly [djú:li] *ad.* masashiku; tōzen(ni); tashikani.

Duma [dú:mə] *n.* (kakumei mae no) Roshia gikai. (1906 n. ni hajimari 1917 n. ni haishi sareta).

dumb [dʌm] *a.* oshi no; kuchi no kikenai. ～**show** dammari geki. ～**bell** [-'bel] *n.* arei. ～**found** [-'faund] *v.* bikkuri saseru; akire saseru. ～**founded** [-'fáundid] *a.* bōzen taru; akire saserareta; dogimo o nukareta. ～**ly** [⌐li] *ad* mokumoku to shite. ～**ness** [⌐nis] *n.* oshi; mugon.

dumdum [dʌ́mdʌm] *n.* damdandan. ┌*a.* nise no.

dummy [dʌ́mi] *n.* oshi; nisemono kazari ningyō; nisemono.

dump [dʌmp] *n.* gomi no yama; gomi-suteba; rinji no dan'yaku okiba; (*pl.*) yūutsu. *in the* ～*s*, fusaide; genki naku. *v.* (gomi nado o) nagesuteru; dampingu suru.

dumping [dʌ́mpiŋ] *n.* (gomi nado o) nagesuteru koto; nageuri; dampingu.

dumpy [dʌ́mpi] *a.* zunguri shita; futokute mijikai.

dun [dʌn] *n.* saisoku suru hito; shiharai tokusoku. *v.* yakamashiku saisoku suru. *a.* kogecha iro no.

dunce [dʌns] *n.* orokamono; baka.

dune [dju:n] *n.* sakyū (umibe no *sandhill*).

dung [dʌŋ] *n.* fun; tsumitate. **~hill** [-ʰhil] taihi.

dungeon [dʌ́ndʒ(ə)n] *n.* tsuchirō; chikarō.

dunk [dʌŋk] *v.* (*Am. col.*) hitasu (taberu toki pan nado o cha, kōfii nado ni).

duodecimo [dju(:)o(u)désimou] *n.* 12-mai ni otta hon.

duodenum [du(:)o(u)díːnəm] *n.* (*pl.* -na [-nə]) (*anat.*) jūni-shichō.　　　　　　　　　　　　　　　　　　　Ⅎmasu.

dupe [dju:p] *n.* damasareru hito; manuke. *v.* azamuku; da-

duplex [djúːpleks] *a.* nijū (futae) no; niren shiki no.

duplicate [djúːplikeit] *v.* nijū ni suru; fukusha suru; utsushi o toru. *a.* [djúːplikit] nijū no; fuku no. *n.* aitaisuru mono; tōhon. *duplicating paper*, fukushashi.

duplication [djuːplikéiʃən] *n.* bai; nijū; fukusha; fukusei.

duplicity [djuːplísiti] *n.* futagokoro; nimaijita; kagehinata; uraomote.

durability [djùərəbíliti] *n.* taikyūsei; taikyūryoku.

durable [djúərəbl] *a.* mochi no yoi; kenrōna. **~bly** [djúərə-bli] *ad.* eizokutekini.

duralumin [dju(ə)rǽljumin] *n.* jurarumin.

duration [dju(ə)réiʃən] *n.* taikyū; keizoku.

durbar [dɔ́ːbɑ] *n.* (Indo shokō no) ekken; inken shitsu.

duress [dju(ə)rés/djúːres] *n.* kyōhaku; kankin.

durian [djúəriən/dúríːən] *n.* dorian no mi; so no ki.

during [djúəriŋ] *prep.* ...no aida jū; no aida ni.

durst [dɔːst] *v. see* : **dare**.

dusk [dʌsk] *n.* usugurai; tasogare : *at* **~**, higure ni. **~ily** [dʌ́skili] *ad.* usuguraku. **~iness** [dʌ́skinis] *n.* usuguraiyami;

dusky [dʌ́ski] *a.* usugurai.　　　　　　　　　　　　　Ⅎusugurasa.

dust [dʌst] *n.* chiri; hokori; kona; shitai : *bite the* **~**, taoreru; korosareru. *v.* chiri o harau; kona o furikakeru. **~brand** [-ʰbrænd] kurobobyō. **~er** [-ə] *n.* chiritori. **~ coat** [kout] *n.* chiriyoke gaitō. **~bin** [-bin] *n.* (*Brit.*) gomiire. **~hole** [-houl] *n.* chiridame. **~ing** [-iŋ] chirihirai. **~man** [-mæn] *n.* chiritori nimpu.

dusty [dʌ́sti] *a.* hokorippoi; gomidarake no.

Dutch [dʌtʃ] *n.* Orandajin (-go). *a.* Orandajin (go) no.
Dutchman [dʌtʃmən] *n.* Orandajin (hitori no).
duteous [djú:tjəs] *a.* kōkōna ; teisetsuna.
dutiable [djú:tiəbl] *a.* kanzei o haraubeki ; yūzei no.
dutiful [djú:tiful] *a.* chūjunna ; teisetsuna. ～**ly** [-li] *ad.* chū-
junni ; uyauyashiku. ～**ness** *n.* uyauyashisa.
duty [djú:ti] *n.* hombun ; nimmu ; kanzei. ～**-free** [-fri:] *a.*
menzei no. ～**-paid** [-péid] *a.* nōzei-zumi no.
dwarf [dwɔ:f] *n.* issumbōshi ; chiisana dōbutsu ; shokubutsu.
v. seichō o samatageru. ～**ish** [-iʃ] *a.* kobito no yōna.
dwell [dwel] *v.* sumu : ～ **on**, aru mondai ni itsu made mo
torikumu. ～**er** [-ə] *n.* kyojūsha.
dwelling [dwéliŋ] *n.* kyojū ; sumika. ～ **house** [-haus] jūtaku. ～ **place** [-pleis] *n.* jūsho.
dwindle [dwíndl] *v.* dandan heru ; dandan yaseru (otoroeru).
dye [dai] *v.* **dyed ; dyeing.** someru (maru). *n.* senryō. **dyeing**
[dáiiŋ] *n.* somekata ; somemonogyō. ～**r** [daiə] *n.* somemo-
noshi. ～ **stuff,** *n.* senryō. ～ **works** [-wɔ:ks] *n.* (*s.* & *pl.*)
somemono kōjō.
dying [dáiiŋ] *n.* rinjū ; shinikakatte iru : *his* ～ *wish,* kare no
rinjū no negai. (*col.*) hidoku sō shitagatte iru.
dynamic [dainǽmik] *a.* rikigaku no ; chikarazuyoi.
dynamics [dainǽmiks] *n.* (*sci.*) rikigaku (*kinetics*←→*statics*).
dynamite [dáinəmait] *n.* dainamaito.
dynamo [dáinəmou] *n.* chokuryū hatsudenki ; dainamo.
dynastic [dinǽstik] *a.* ōchō no ; ōke no.
dynasty [dínəsti] *n.* rekidai no ōchō.
dysentery [dísəntri] *n.* (*med.*) sekiri.
dyspepsia [dispépsiə], **dyspepsy** [dispépsi] *n.* shōka furyō
(*indigestion*).
dyspeptic [dispéptik] *n.* i no yowai hito. *a.* shōka furyō no.

E

E [i:] *n.* (*pl.* E's, Es [i:z], *E's*, e's, es [iiz]). Eigo *alphabet* no dai-5-bamme no moji.

each [i:tʃ] *a.* meimei no. *pron.* onoono : ～ *has his merits*, hito niwa sorezore chōsho (torie) ga aru. ～ **other** otagaini.

eager [í:gə] *a.* nesshinna; netsubō suru. ～**ly** *ad.* nesshinni. ～**ness** [-nis] *n.* nesshin; setsubō.

eagle [í:gl] *n.* (*bird.*) washi. (*Am.*) 10-doru kinka. **double** ～, *n.* 20-doru kahei. ～**eyed** [-aid] *a.* me no surudoi.

eaglet [í:glit] *n.* washi no ko.

ear [iə] *n.* mimi; (mizusashi nado no) torite (=totte); (mugi nado no) ho. *over head and* ～*s* (*or*) *up to the* ～*s*, muchū ni natte; kubi no mawaranu hodo (shakkin nado de). *prick up one's* ～*s*, kikimimi o tateru; mimi o sobadateru. ～**ache** [-eik] *n.* mimi no itai koto. ～**drop** [⌐drɔp] *n.* mimikazari. ～**drum** [-drʌm] *n.* (*anat.*)chūji; komaku. ～**lobe** [⌐loub] *n.* mimitabu. ～**mark** [⌐mɑːk] *n.* mimijirushi (hitsuji no mimi ni tsuketa shirushi, (torinokete oku mono). ～**phone** [⌐foun] *n.* hochōki. ～**ring** [⌐riŋ] *n.* mimiwa. ～**shot** [⌐ʃɔt] koe no kikoeru kyori (*distance*). ～**trumpet** [⌐trʌ́mpet] *n.* hochōki.

earl [ə:l] *n.* (*Brit.*) Hakushaku no kurai (ryōchi).

early [ə́:li] *a.* hayai; hajimegoro. ～**bird** (*or* **riser**) *n.* hayao ki no hito. *keep* ～ *hours*, hayane hayaoki suru. *ad.* hayaku.

earn [ə:n] *v.* kasegu; hataraite eru.

earnest [ə́:nist] *a.* nesshinna; majimena. *n.* nesshin. *in* ～, honki de. **ly** [-li] *ad.* honki de. ～**money** [-mʌ́ni] *n.* tetsukekin; shōkokin. ～**ness** *n.* honki; nesshin.

earnings [ə́:niŋz] *n.* (*pl.*) shūnyū; kasegi.

earth [ə:θ] *n.* chikyū; konoyo; tsuchi. *v.* tsuchi o kabuseru. ～**born** [⌐bɔːn] *a.* chi kara umareta; ukiyo no. ～**en** [ə́:θ(ə)n] *a.* tsuchi de dekita; tōki no. ～**enware** [á:θ(ə)nwɛə] *n.* doki; tōki. ～**iness** [ə́:θinis] *n.* doshitsu; zokuakusa (*vulgarity*). ～**liness** [ə́:θlinis] *n.* genseteki de aru koto. ～**ly** [ə́:θli] *a.* chikyū no; kono yo no. ～**nut** [ə́:θnʌt] *n.* rakkasei. ～**quake**

[ɔ́:θkweik] *n.* jishin; dai hendō. ~**ward**(s) [ɔ́:θwəd(z)] *ad.* daichi ni mukatte. ~**work** [ɔ́:θwə:k] *n.* do-rui; daiba. ~ ~**worm** [ɔ́:θwə:m] *n.* mimizu. ~**y** [ɔ́:θi] *a.* tsuchi no; yahina; tsuchikusai.

ease [i:z] *n.* anraku; kurō ya kutsū no nai koto. *v.* rakuni suru; yurumeru. *at (one's)* ~, kiraku ni. *to be ill at* ~, ochitsuki ga nai. *with* ~ rakuni; yōini.

easel [í:zl] *n.* gaka.

east [í:st] *n.* higashi. *a.* higashi no. *ad.* higashi ni. *the E*~, Tōyō. *the Far E*~, Kyokutō. *the Near* ~, Kintō.

Easter [í:stə] *n.* Fukkatsusai. ~**egg** [-eg] (Fukkatsusai no) iro o nutta tamago. ~**ly** [-li] *a., ad.* tōhō (ni); higashi kara (no). ~**tide** [í:stətaid] *n.* fukkatsusai jibun.

eastern [í:stən] *a.* higashi no; Tōyō no.

eastward [í:stwəd] *a.* tōhō e (no); higashi no. ~**s** [-z] *ad.* higashi ni (e).

easy [í:zi] *a.* rakuna; yuttari shita; surasura shita (buntai na-do ga). ~ **chair** *n.* anrakuisu. ~**going** [-góuiŋ] *a.* kirakuna; nonkina. ~**iness** [-nis] *n.* yasashisa; kigarusa. ~**ily** [í:zili] *ad.* yōini. ~**money** (*Am.*) *n.* rakuna mōke shigoto.

eat [í:t] *v.* ate [et/eit], **eaten**; **eating**. taberu; shokuji suru; kuikomu (*into*); kusaru. ~ *one's words*, zengen o torikesu. ~ **able** [-əbl] *a.* taberareru. ~**ables** *n.* taberareru mono.

eaten [í:tn] *see :* **eat.**

eating [í:tiŋ] *see :* **eat.** *n.* taberu koto; shokumotsu. ~**house** [haus] *n.* inshokuten; ryōriten. ~ **room** [ru(:)m] *n.* shokudō.

eaves [i:vz] *n.* (*pl.*) nokiba. ~**drop** [-drɔp] *v.* nokishita ni hisomu; tachigiki suru. ~**dropper** [-drɔpə] *n.* tachigiki suru hito. ~**dropping** [-drɔpiŋ] *n.* tachigiki; nusumi-giki.

ebb [eb] *n.* hikishio; otoroe (*declining*). *v.* (shio ga) hiku; otoroeru (*decline*). ~**tide** [-taid] *n.* hikishio; kanchō (*reflux of tide*).

E-boat [í:bout] *n.* =**enemy's boat** kōsoku-gyoraitei (*high speed mortor torpedo boat*).

ebon [ébən] *a.* kokutan no; makkuro no.

ebonite [ébənait] *n.* kōka gomu; ebonaito.

ebonize [ébənaiz] *v.* kokutan'iro ni suru.

ebony [ébəni] *n.* kokutan. *a.* makkurona.
ebullience [ibÁliəns], **-ency** [-ənsi] *n.* futtō (*boiling*) ; nekkyō.
ebullient [ibÁljənt] *a.* netsuretsuna ; futtō suru (*boiling*).
ebullition [ebəlíʃən] *n.* futtō (*boiling*) ; gekihatsu (*of passion*, kanjō no) ; boppatsu (*outburst of passion*).
Ecce Homo [éksi hóumou] *n.* ibara no kammuri o kabutta Kirisuto no zō. (*L.=Behold the Man!*) kono hito o miyo.
eccentric [ikséntrik/ek-] *a.* chūshin o hazureta ; namihazure no. *n.* henjin ; kijin. ∼ *person*, henjin ; kijin. ∼**ally** [-əli] *ad.* chūshin o hazurete ; fūgawari ni.
eccentricity [èksentrísiti] *n.* fūgawari ; hijōshiki (*lack of common sense*).
ecclesiastic [ikli:ziǽstik] *n.,* *a.* seishoku (no) ; bokushi (no).
ecclesiastical [ikli:ziǽstik(ə)l] *a.* kyōkai no ; ∼**ly** [-li] *ad.* kyōkai no kenchi kara.
echelon [éʃələn/-lə] *n.* teikei.
echo [ékou] *n.,* *v.* kodama (suru) ; hankyō (suru) ; mane (ru).
eclat [éiklɑ:/éklɑ] *n.* hanabanashii ; seikō ; dai kassai.
eclectic [ekléktik] *a.* setchū no ; *n.* setchūgakuha no hito.
eclipse [iklíps] *n.* (nisshoku nado no) shoku. *solar* (*lunar*) ∼, nis(ges)shoku. *v.* eclipse ga aru. (hito no me nado o) ōu ; hikari o ubau. ⌐kei aru.
ecliptic [iklíptik] (*astr.*) *n.* kōdō. *a.* kōdō no ; shoku ni kan-
eclogue [éklɔg] *n.* bokka ; den'enshi (*idyll ; pastoral poem*).
economic [i:kənɔmik/ek-] *a.* keizaigaku no ; keizaijō no. ∼**al** [-əl] *a.* keizaitekina ; keizaijō no. ∼**ally** [-əli] *ad.* keizaiteki ni ; ken'yaku shite. ∼**s** [-s] *n.* keizaigaku. ⌐su hito.
economist [i(:)kɔnəmist] *n.* keizaigakusha ; ken'yakuni kura-
economize [i(:)hɔnəmaiz] *v.* setsuyaku suru ; yūekini tsukau.
economy [i(:)kɔnəmi] *n.* ken'yaku ; keizai. **domestic** ∼ [dəméstik i(:)kɔnəmi] *n.* kasei. **political** ∼ *n.* keizaigaku.
ecstasy [ékstəsi] *n.* tōsui ; kōkotsu ; uttori ; mugamuchū.
ecstatic [ikstǽtik/ek-] *a.* kōkotsu taru ; mugamuchū no.
ecumenical [i:kju(:)ménik(ə)l] *a.* zempantekina ; zen Kiristo-
eczema [éksimə/égzi-] *n.* (*anat.*) shisshin. ⌐kyōsha no.
eddy [édi] *n.* tsumuji kaze ; (chiisai) uzumaki. *v.* uzumaku.
Eden [í:dn] *n.* Eden no Rakuen ; gokuraku.

edge [edʒ] *n.* ha; fuchi; heri. *v.* ha (*edge*) o tsukeru; sorosoro susumu. ~**ways** [-weiz], ~**wise** [-waiz] *ad.* ha to ha o mukai awaseru.

edging [édʒiŋ] *n.* fuchi o tsukeru koto; fuchikazari.

edible [édibl] *a.* taberareru; shokuyō no.

edict [í:dikt] *n.* chokurei; fukoku; chokugo (*imperial edict*).

edification [edifikéiʃən] *n.* kyōkun; keihatsu; kuntō.

edifice [édifis] *n.* ōkina kenchikubutsu.

edify [édifai] *v.* toku (*virtue*) ni michibiku; kuntō suru.

edit [édit] *v.* henshū suru.

edition [idíʃən] *n.* kankō-bon; hakkōbusū; han (*prints*). ~**de luxe** [edisjónd(ə) ləks] *n.* (*Fr.*) gōkaban; zeitakubon.

editor [édita] *n.* henshūsha; henshūchō. **chief** ~, *n.* shuhitsu. ~**ship** *n.* henshūsha no chii; shuhitsu no shoku.

editorial [editó:riəl] *a.* henshūsha no; henshū no. *n.* shasetsu; ronsetsu.

educate [édju(:)keit] *v.* kyōiku suru; oshiekomu.

education [edju(:)kéiʃən] *n.* kyōiku. ~**al** [-əl] *a.* kyōikujō no.

educative [édjukeitiv/-kətiv] *a.* kyōikuteki.

educator [édju(:)keitə] *n.* kyōikusha.

educe [i(:)djú:s] *v.* hikidasu (kakurete iru sainō nado o).

eel [i:l] *n.* unagi; su ni waku senchū.

e'en [i:n] *n. ad.* =**even.**

e'er [ɛə] *ad.* =**ever.**

eerie, eery [íəri] *a.* okubyōna; sugoi; kimi no warui.

efface [iféis] *v.* kesu. ~**able** [-əbl] *a.* keseru. ~**ment** *n.* massatsu; sakujo.

effect [ifékt] *n.* kekka; kōka; inshō. (*pl.*) dōsan. *v.* kekka o motarasu. *for* ~, kōka o neratte. *in* ~, jissai niwa. *come* (*or go*) *into* ~, jisshi sareru.

effective [iféktiv] *a.* yūryokuna; yūkōna. ~**ly** *ad.* yūkō ni; jissaijō. ~**ness** *n.* yūkō; yūryoku.

effectual [iféktjuəl] *a.* yūkōna; kōka no aru. ~**ly** *ad.* yūkōni; jissai ni.

effectuate [iféktjueit] *v.* yūkōni suru; shitogeru.

effeminacy [iféminəsi] *n.* memeshisa; nyūjaku.

effeminate [iféminit] *a.* memeshii; nyūjakuna·

efferent [éfərənt] *a.* enshinsei no : ～ *nerve, n.* enshinsei shinkei.

effervesce [èfəvés] *v.* awadatsu(-dateru) ; kōfun suru.

effervescence [èfəvésns] *n.* awadachi ; futtō ; kōfun.

effervescent [èfəvésnt] *a.* awadatsu ; futtō suru.

effete [efí:t] *a.* seiryoku tsukita ; tsukarehateta ; munōryoku no.   ⌈[-nis] *n.* yūkō.

efficacious [efikéiʃəs] *a.* yūkōna. ～**ly** *ad.* yūkōni. ～**ness**

efficacy [éfikəsi] *n.* kikime ; kōryoku.

efficiency [ifʃíənsi] *n.* nōritsu.

efficient [ifíʃənt] *a.* kōryoku aru ; jitsuryoku aru. ～ **ly** [-li] *ad.* yūkōni ; yūryokuni.

effigy [éfidʒi] *n.* shōzō ; hito no nigao (*image*).

effloresce [èflɔrés] *v.* hana ga hiraku ; fūka suru.

efflorescence [èflɔrésəns] *n.* kaika ; fūka.

effluence [éfluəns] *n.* nagare deru koto ; nagashi dasu koto.

effluent [éfluənt] *a.* nagarederu. *n.* nagarederu mono (mizu).

effluvium [eflú:viəm] *n.* (*pl.* -**via**) akushū ; iyana nioi.

efflux [éflʌks] *n.* ryūshutsu ; ryūshutsu-butsu.

effort [éfət] *n.* doryoku ; rikisaku ; rippana seiseki.

effrontery [efrʌ́nt(ə)ri] *n.* tetsumempi.

effulge [efʌ́ldʒ], **effulgence** [efʌ́ldʒəns] *n.* hikari ; kagayaki.

effulgent [efʌ́ldʒənt] *a.* hikaru ; kagayaku. ～**ly** *ad.* hikari kagayaite.

effuse [ifjú:z] *v.* nagare deru ; hotobashiri deru. **effusion** [efjú:ʒən] *n.* hotobashiri deru koto.

effusive [ifjú:siv/ef-] *a.* netsujōtekini happyō suru. ～**ly** *ad.* netsujōtekini. ～**ness** *n.* happyō.

eft [eft] *n.* (*insect*) imori ; chiisai tokage.   ⌈*ample*)

e.g. [i:dʒi] [fɚ̀rigzǽ:mpl] (L.＜*exempli gratia*) tatoeba. (*for ex-*

egg [eg] *n.* tamago ; tōkabakudan. *bad* ～, yakuza mono ; damena keikaku. *v.* hagemasu ; sendō suru (*on, to do*). ～**plant** [-plɑːnt] *n.* nasu. ～**shell** [-ʃel] *n.* tamago no kara.

eglantine [égləntain] *n.* isshu no nobara.

ego [égou/í:gou] *n.* jiga. ～**ism** [égouizm/í:go(u)-] rikoshugi ; jibunkatte. ～**ist** [-ist] *n.* rikoshugisha ; jibunkattena hito.

egoistic [ego(u)ístik] *a.* rikotekina ; jibunkattena.

egotistic [ego(u)tístik] *a.* rikotekina ; unubore tsuyoi.

egregious [igrí:dʒiəs] *a.* hōgaina; bakagekitta. ~**ly** *ad.* jitsuni hidoku.

egress [í:gres] *n.* dete iku koto; deguchi; gaishutsu.

egret [í:gret] *n.* (*bird*) shirasagi; *egret* no hanege (umō).

Egyptian [idʒípʃən] *a.* Ejiputo no. *n.* Ejiputojin; Ejiputogo.

eh [ei] *in.* e? nan datte? dō?

eider [áidə] *n.* (*bird*) kewatagamo. ~**down** [-daun] *n.* kamo no kewata. ~ **duck** [-dʌk] *n.* kewatagamo.

eight [eit] *a.* yattsu no. *n.* yattsu; hachi. ~**fold** [-fould] *a. ad.* hachibai.

eighteen [éití:n] *n. a.* jūhachi (no). ~**th** [-θ] *a.* dai jūhachi bamme no; jūhachibun no ichi no. *n.* dai jūhachi; jūhachi nichi; jūhachi bun no ichi.

eighth [eitθ] *a.* hachibamme no. *n.* daihachi; (tsuki no yōka.) ~**ly** [⊥li] *ad.* hachibamme ni.

eightieth [éitiiθ] *a.* daihachijū no; hachijūbamme no. *oneeightieth*, hachijūbun no ichi.

eighty [éiti] *a.* hachijū no. *n.* hachijū.

Einstein [ainstáin] *n.* Albert, (1879-1955) Doitsu-umare no Amerika no butsurigakusha. **E**~ **theory** Ainstain setsu, sōtaisei riron (*theory of relativity*).

either [áiðə/í:ðə] *a. pron.* (futatsu no uchi no) dochira ka? dochira mo; onoono no. *conj.* ~ ...*or*, dochira ka; dochira mo. *If you do not go, I shall not go* ~, kimi ga ikanai nara watashi mo ikanai.

ejaculate [idʒǽkjuleit] *v.* sakebidasu; ekitai ga fukidasu (karada kara). ⌐tobideru koto.

ejaculation [idʒækjuléiʃən] *n.* zekkyū; ekitai no shashutsu.

ejaculator [idʒǽkjuleitə] *n.* (totsuzen) zekkyū suru hito.

ejaculatory [idʒǽkjuleitəri/-lət-] *a.* zekkyūteki no.

eject [i(:)dʒékt] *v.* oidasu; haishutsu suru. ~**ment** *n.* hōshutsu (*forcing out*); hōshutsubutsu.

ejection [idʒékʃən] *n.* haiseki; haisetsu butsu (*things ejected*).

ejective [idʒéktiv] *a.* haishutsu suru.

eke [i:k] *v.* oginau; karōjite seikei o tateru. ~ *out one's salary with odd job*, aimashigoto o shite kyūryō no tashi ni suru. ~ *out a scanty livelihood*, hosoboso to seikei o tateru.

elaborate [iléb(ə)reit] *v.* tansei shite tsukuru; rikisaku o suru. [ilǽbərit] *a.* nyūnen no; seikōna. ~**ly** *ad.* (kushin shite) seikōni. ~**ness** *n.* nyūnen; tansei. ⌐ku.

elaboration [ilæbəréiʃən] *n.* kushin no saku (doryoku); rōsa-**elaborative** [ilǽbəreitiv/-rət-] *a.* nyūnen no; tansei kometa.

eland [í:lənd] *n.* (*zoo.*) (Minami Afurika san no) ō-kamoshika.

elapse [ilǽps] *v.* (toki ga) sugiru; keika suru.

elastic [ilǽstik/-lá:s-] *a.* danryokusei no; keikaina. *n.* gomu ito (himo). ~**ally** [-əli] *ad.* shinshiku jizaini.

elasticity [èlæstísiti] *n.* danryoku; shinshuku ryoku.

elate [iléit] *a.* genki o tsukeru; gōzen to shite (*proud*). *v.* tokuigaraseru. ~**ed** [⸗id] *a.* tokui ni natte; sondaina. ~**ly** [-li] *ad.* sondaini kamaete.

elation [iléiʃən] *n.* ikiyōyō; kono ue nai tokui.

elbow [élbou] *n.* hiji. *at one's* ~, soba ni. *out at* ~*s*, misuborashiku. *v.* hiji de osu. ~ **grease** [gri:s] *n.* honeorishigoto. ~**room** [-rum] *n.* hiji ga jiyū ni tsukaeru yochi; yoyū.

elder [éldə], *a.* **older** toshiue no; kosan no. *n.* nenchō-sha; sempai. (*bot.*) niwatoko. ~**ly** [-li] *a.* sukoshi toshitotta. *cf.* **elder, eldest.** ⌐no.

eldest [éldist] *a. see;* **elder.** ichiban toshiue no : sainenchō

elect [ilékt] *v.* erabu; senkyo suru. *a.* erabareta. *the* ~, kami no semmin (Isuraerujin).

election [ilékʃən] *n.* senkyo; kami no sembatsu.

electioneer [ilèkʃ(e)níə] *v.* senkyo undō o suru hito.

elective [iléktiv] *a.* sentaku ni yoru; senkyo no. *n.* sentaku kamoku.

elector [iléktə] *n.* yūkensha. ~**al** [-rəl] *a.* senkyonin no; senkyo no. *electoral college* (*Am.*) Daitōryō senkyo botai. ~**ate** [ilékt(ə)rit] *n.* senkyomin; yūkensha. Senteikō no kurai (ryōdo).

electric [iléktrik] *a.* denki no. ~ **battery** [-bǽtəri] *n.* denchi. (*galvanic cell*). ~**bell** [-bel] *n.* denrei. ~**chair** *n.* (shikei yō no) denki isu. ~**car** [ka:] *n.* densha (*cf.* **tram**~; *street*~; *trolley*~). ~**fan** [-fæn] *n.* sempūki. ~**clock** [-clɔk] *n.* denkidokei. ~**current** [-kɔ:rənt] *n.* denryū. ~**eel** [-i:l] *n.* denki-unagi. ~**heater** [-hi:tə] *n.* dennetsuki. ~**potential** [pɔténʃəl] *n.*

den'i. ~jar [-dʒɑ:] *n.* chikudembin. ~ lamp, dentō. ~
light, dentō. ~ railway (*Am.*) ~ railroad. denkitetsudō
~shock [-ʃɔk] *n.* kanden. ~ spark [-spɑ:k] *n.* denki hibana.
~ wave [-weiv] *n.* dempa. ~wire [-waiə] *n.* densen.
electrical [iléktrik(ə)l] *a.* denki no. ~ly *ad.* denki de; denki-
gakujō.
electrician [ì(:)lektríʃən] *n.* denki-gakusha; denki-gishi.
electricity [i(:)lektrísiti] *n.* denki; denkigaku. frictional ~
[fríkʃənəl-] *n.* masatsu denki. galvanic ~ [gəlvǽnik-] *n.*
ryūdenki. negative ~ [négətiv-] *n.* indenki. positive ~
[pɔzitiv-] *n.* yōdenki.
electrification [ilèktrifikéiʃən] *n.* jūden; denka.
electrify [iléktrifai] *v.* denki o tsūjiru; denka suru; kandō
saseru.
electrize [iléktraiz] *v.* =electrify.   ʃni.
electro [iléktrou] *n.*, *v.* (*sl.*) electroplate, electrotype no imi
electrobath [iléktrobɑ:θ] *n.* denki mekki yōeki.
electrochemistry [iléktro(u)kémistri] *n.* denki kagaku.
electrocute [iléktrəkju:t] *v.* denki shikei ni suru.
electrocution [ilèktro(u)kjú:ʃən] *n.* kandenshi; denki shikei.
electrode [iléktroud] *n.* denkyoku.
electrodynamic [ilèktro(u)dainǽmik] *a.* denkirikigaku no. ~
s [-s] *n.* denkirikigaku.
electrokinetics [iléktro(u)kainétiks] *n.* dōdengaku.
electrolier [ilèkrolíə] *n.* hanadentō; shūgōdentō; shanderia.
electrolyse [iléktro(u)laiz] *v.* denki-bunkai suru.
electrolysis [ilektrólisis/elek-] *n.* denki-bunkai; denkai.
electrolyte [iléktro(u)lait] *n.* denkaishitsu; denkaieki.
electromagnet [iléktro(u)mǽgnit] *n.* denjishaku. ~ism *n.*
denjiki; denjikigaku.
electromotive [iléktro(u)móutiv] *a.* kiden no; dendō no.
electromotor [iléktro(u)móutə] *n.* dendōki; dengen.
electron [iléktrɔn] *n.* denshi; erekutoron.
electronics [ilektróniks] *n.* denshigaku.
electropathy [i(:)lèktrópəθi] *n.* denkiryōhō.
electroplate [iléktro(u)pleit / -pléit] *v.* denkimekki suru. *n.*
denkimekki shita mono.

electrotype [iléktrətaip] *n.* denkiban. *v.* denkiban (ni suru.)
eleemosynary [élii:mɔ́sinəri] *a.* gienkin no; kyūjutsu o uke-ru; kifu o ukeru.
elegance [éligəns] *n.* yūbi: kihin. ⌐bini.
elegant [éligənt] *a.* yūbina; kihin no takai. ∼ly [-li] *ad.* yū-
elegiac [èlidʒáiək] *a.* banka no; kanashii (*sad*); aitō no. ∼s *n.* (*pl.*) hika; banka; aitō no uta.
elegy [élidʒi] *n.* hito o ushinatta kanashimi no uta; banka.
element [élimənt] *n.* (uchū o tsukuru) genso (*earth, water, fire, wind*). (*pl.*) uchū (*universe*) no chikara. (*pl.*) genri (*fundamental principles*); Seisan (*the Sacrament*) no pan (*bread*) to budō-shu (*wine*).
elemental [elimént(ə)l] *a.* genso no; kihonteki no; shizen-ryoku no.
elementary [eliméntəri] *a.* shoho no; kihon (*basic*) no. ∼ school, *n.* shōgakkō. ⌐no
elephant [élifənt] *n.* (*zoo.*) zō : *white* ∼, shiroi zo. yakkai mo-
elephantine [elifǽntain] *a.* zō no yōni subarashiku okii.
elevate [éliveit] *v.* ageru; chii (*social position*) o ageru; kōshō-ni suru (*ennoble*); agaru. ∼d [éliveitid] *a.* takai; agerareta. ∼ railway [-réilwei] kōkatetsudō.
elevation [elivéiʃən] *n.* takasa (*height*); kōchi (*plateau*).
elevator [éliveitə] *n.* erebētā. (*Brit.* lift).
eleven [ilévn] *a.* jūichi no. (11)jūichi.
eleventh [ilévnθ] *a* dai jūichi no. *n.* jūichi-bamme.
elf [elf] (*pl.* elves [elvz]) *n.* chiisai sennyo-tachi; shōyōsei.
elfin [élfin] *a.* shōyōsei no. *n.* itazurakko (*mischievous child*).
elfish [élfiʃ] *a.* shōyōsei no yōna; waru-itazura no (*mischie-vous*). ⌐(*draw out*).
elicit [ilísit] *v.* shin'ri o hikidasu; henji (*answer*) o sasoi dasu
elide [iláid] *v.* boin (*vowel*) ya onsetsu o habuku.
eligibility [elidʒibíliti] *n.* senkyo sareru shikaku; tekininsha.
eligible [élidʒibl] *a.* hisenkyo shikaku no aru; tekitōna (*suit-able*).
eliminate [ilímineit] *v.* haijo suru (*exclude*); nakama ni irenai.
elimination [iliminéiʃən] *n.* haijo; nokeru koto.
eliminator [ilímineitə] *n.* denchi no iranai jushinki.

elision [ilíʒən] *n.* boin ya onsetsu no shōryaku.

elite [eilí:t] *n.* (*Fr.*) erinuki (*chosen*) no.

elixir [ilíksə] *n.* renkinyakueki (*alchemy*) ; furōfushi (*eternal youth*) no kusuri.

Elizabethan [ilizəbí:θən] *a.* Erizabesu no ; Erizabesu jidai no.

elk [élk] *n.* (*zoo.*) ōshika.

ell [el] *n.* mukashi no nagasa no tan'i ; erujaku (45 inchi gurai. ima wa fuyō).

ellipse [ilíps] *n.* daen ; daenkei (*shape*).

ellipsis [ilípsis] *n.* (*pl.* ～ses [ilípsi:z]) shōryakuhō.

elliptic(al) [ilíptik((ə)l)] *a.* shōryaku no ; daen (kei) no. ～ **ally** *ad.* shōryaku shite ; daenkei ni.

elm [elm] *n.* (*bot.*) nire ; nirezai.

elocution [eləkjú:ʃən] *n.* enzetsuhō ; hanashikata. ～**ary** [-əri] enzetsuhō no ; hanashikata no. ～**ist** [-ist] *n. elocution* no sensei.

elongate [í:lɔŋgeit] *v.* nobasu ; nagaku suru.

elongation [i:lɔŋgéiʃən] *n.* enchō (sen) ; nobashiuru doai.

elope [ilóup] *v.* kakeochi suru. ～**r** [-ə] *n.* kakeochimono. ～**ment** [-mənt] *n.* kakeochi.

eloquence [éləkwəns] *n.* yūben.

eloquent [éləkwənt] yūbenna. ～**ly** *ad.* yūbenni.

else [els] *a.* hoka no. *ad.* hoka ni. *conj.* de naito : *He finally decided that the book was somebody ～'s,* kare wa sono hon wa hoka no dare ka no mono da to dantei shita. ～**where** [-ːhwɛə] *ad.* doko ka hoka no tokoro ni.

elucidate [il(j)ú:sideit] *v.* akirakani suru ; setsumei suru.

elucidation [il(j)u:sidéiʃən] *n.* setsumei ; bemmei.

elude [il(j)ú:d] *v.* sakeru.

elusion [il(j)ú:ʒən] *n.* sakeru koto ; gomakashi ; iinuke.

elusive [il(j)ú:siv], **elusory** [il(j)ú:səri] *a.* tsukamae-dokoro no nai.

Elysian [ilíziən] *a.* (*Gk. myth*) gokuraku no.

Elysium [ilíziəm] (*Gk. myth*) gokuraku.

'em [əm] *pron.* =(*col.*) them.

emaciate [iméiʃieit] *v.* shōsui saseru ; yaseotoroe saseru. ～(**e**)**d** [id] *a.* shōsui shita ; yasekoketa.

emaciation [imeisiéiʃən] *n.* shōsui ; yase otoroeru koto.

emanate [éməneit] *v.* hassan suru (*from*).

emanation [emənéiʃən] *n.* hassan ; hassan suru busshitsu.
emancipate [imǽnsipeit] *v.* kaihō suru ; ridatsu saseru.
emancipation [imǽnsipéiʃən] *n.* kaihō ; jiyūni suru koto. ～
ist *n.* dorei kaihō ronsha.
emasculate [imǽskjuleit] *v.* kyosei suru ; ikujinashi ni suru.
a. [imǽskjulit] memeshii.
emasculation [imǽskjuléiʃən] *n.* nyūjaku.
embalm [imbáːm] *v.* kusuri de miira ni suru.
embank [imbǽŋk] *v.* dote o kizuku. ～**ment** [-mənt] *n.* dote ; ⌐teibō.
embargo [embáːgou] *v.* fune ga minato ni de-hairi suru no o kinzuru ; fune no tsumini o toriageru. *n.* fune no de-iri kinshi (*prohibition*).
embark [imbáːk] *v.* jōsen suru (*ship*) ; fune ni noseru.
embarkation [embaːkéiʃən] *n.* jōsen ; noseru koto.
embarrass [imbǽrəs] *v.* komarasu ; jama suru (*hinder*) ; zaisei konnan (*financial trouble*) ni ochiirasu. ～**ing** *a.* komaru. ～**ment** *n.* tōwaku ; zaisei konnan.
embassador＝ambassador
embassy [émbəsi] *n.* taishikan ; taishi no shoku ; taishikan no zen'in ⌐kabe o kizuita.
embattled [imbǽtld] *a.* (*mil.*) senjin o shiita ; jūgan-tsuki no
embed [imbéd] ＝**imbed** *v.* umeru.
embellish [imbéliʃ] *v.* kazaru. ～**ment** *n.* kazari.
ember [émbə] *n.* (*pl.*) moesashi. ～ **days,** (*Roman Catholic*) de danjiki shite kitō o suru hi.
embezzle [imbézl] *v.* tsukaikomu ; chakufuku suru. ～**ment** *n.* itakukin shōhi.
embitter [imbítə] *v.* tsuraku suru ; kurushii omoi o saseru.
emblazon [imbléiz(ə)n] *v.* monshō (*crest*) de kazaru ; hadeni kazaru. ～**ment** *n.* monshō no kazari. ～**ry** [-ri] *n.* utsukushii sōshoku.
emblem [émbləm] *n.* shōchō ; kishō (*badge*) ; monshō ; ～ **atise** [-ətaiz] *v.* hyōji suru ; gutaitekina katachi de shimesu.
emblematic(al) [emblimǽtik(ə)l] *a.* shōchō no ; kishō no ; monshō no ; hitome de wakaru.
embodiment [imbódimənt] *n.* katachi ni arawasu koto.
embody [imbódi] *v.* yūkei ni suru ; ganchiku suru (*implicate*).

embolden [imbóuldn] *v.* daitanni suru.

embosom [embúzm] *v.* mune ni idaku; kokoro ni tomeru.

emboss [imbɔ́s] *v.* uki-bori zaiku o suru.

embower [imbáuə] *v.* kokage (*shade*) ni kakusu.

embrace [imbréis] *v.* dakishimeru; dakiau. *n.* hōyō. dakiai. ∼ **cery** [-səri] *n.* (*leg.*) (baishinkan nado no) dakikomi; baishū.

embrasure [imbréiʒə] *n. fort.* hōgan; jūgan; hazama.

embrocate [émbrokeit] *v.* (*med.*) kusuri o nuritsukeru.

embrocation [embrokéiʃən] *n.* nuritsukeru koto; sono kusuri.

embroider [imbrɔ́idə] *v.* shishū suru.

embroidery [imbrɔ́idəri] *n.* shishū; nuihaku. ∼ **frame** shishū waku.

embroil [imbrɔ́il] *v.* funkyū saseru (*bring into confusiton*).

embryo [émbriou] *n.* hai; taiji; dō-shokubutsu no ichiban hajime no jō-tai (katachi); onaka no kodomo.

embryology [embriɔ́lədʒi] *n.* taiseigaku; hasseigaku ∼**gist** [-dʒist] *n.* hasseigakusha.

emend [i(:)ménd] *v.* suikō (tensaku) suru; ∼**able** [-əbl] *a.* tensaku subeki (-shiuru). ∼**ator** [i:məndéitə] *n.* tensakusha. ∼ **atory** [iméndətəri] *a.* tensaku (suikō) suru.

emendation [i:mendéiʃən] *n.* tensaku; suikō suru koto.

emerald [emər(ə)ld] *n.* emerarudo (ryokugyoku). ∼**Isle** Airurand no yobina (imyō).

emerge [imɔ́:dʒ] *v.* dete kuru; arawareru (mizu nado kara).

emergency [imɔ́:dʒ(ə)nsi] *n.* jihen (*event*); hijō no baai; fui no dekigoto (*sudden case*). ∼**fund** [-fʌnd] *n.* yobi-kin.

emeritus [i(:)méritəs] *a.* taishoku no. ∼ **professor** [-prɔ́fésə] *n.* meiyo kyōju.

emersion [i(:)mɔ́:ʃən] *n.* shutsugen (*appearance*); (*astr.*) saigen (*reappearance after eclipse*).

emery [éməri] *n.* kongōsha. ∼ **cloth** [klɔ́θ] yasurinuno. ∼ **paper** [péipə] yasurigami; kamiyasuri.

emetic [imétik] *a.* hakike ga deru. *n.* hakukusuri.

emigrant [émigrənt] *n.* ijūmin; imin. *a.* imin no.

emigrate [émigreit] *v.* ijū suru.

emigration [emigréiʃən] *n.* ijū; imin.

eminence [eminəns] *n.* takai tokoro; takai kurai. **E∼** =

Eminence, Kakka (*Cardinal* ni taisuru sonshō).

eminent [éminənt] *a.* sugureta; chomeina (*famous*). **~ly** *ad.* sugurete.

emir [emíə] *n.* shōgun (Arabia no) ōzoku no sonshō; ōzoku (*prince*); shūchō (*chieftain*).

emissary [émis(ə)ri] *n.* misshi; shisha; kanchō.

emission [imíʃən] *n.* hassha; tama o utsu koto.

emit [imít] *v.* hassha suru; hakkō suru. ⌈itamidome.

emollient [imɔ́liənt] *a.* yawarakani suru. *n.* (*med.*) chintsū-zai;

emolument [imɔ́ljumənt] *n.* kyūryō; teate.

emotion [emóuʃən] *n.* jōsho; kanjō.

emotional [imóuʃ(ə)n(ə)l] *a.* jōsho no; kandōtekina.

emperor [émpərə] *n.* kōtei.

emphasis [émfəsis] (*pl.* **-ses** [-si:z]) *n.* tsuyosa (*strength*). kyōsei; (tsuyoi) gosei (*stress*).

emphasize [émfəsaiz] *v.* chikara o irete iu; rikisetsu suru.

emphatic [imfǽtik] *a.* chikara o ireta iikata no. **~cally** [-kəli] *ad.* chikara o irete. **E~ Day** Victoria Joō no tanjōbi no shikujitsu.

empire [émpaiə] *n.* teikoku.

empiric [empírik] *n.* keiken shugisha. **~al** [-kəl] keiken shugi no. ⌈ni ijutsu).

empiricism [empírisizm] *n.* keiken-shugi; keikenron (omo

emplacement [impléismənt] *n.* taihō no daiza; suetsukeru basho. ⌈rete.

employ [implɔ́i] *v.* yatou. *n.* yatoiire : *in the* **~** *of*, ni yatowa-

employé [əmplɔ́iei], **employee** [àmplɔii:] *n.* yatoinin; yato-wareta hito ; jūgyōin.

employer [implɔ́iə] *n.* yatoi nushi; koyōsha.

employment [implɔ́imənt] *n.* koyō; shigoto (*work*). **~agency** shokugyō shōkaijo : *in the* **~** *of* ni yatowarete.

emporium [impɔ́:riəm] *n.* (*pl.* **~s** *or* **~ia**) shōgyō chūshin -chi; dai-shōten.

empower [impáuə] *v.* kenryoku (*power*) o ataeru.

empress [émpris] *n.* jo(nyo)-tei; kōgō.

emptiness [émptinis] *n.* karappo; nani mo nai koto; kūkyo.

empty [ém(p)ti] *a.* kūkyona; karappo no; *v.* kara ni suru

(naru). ～handed [-hǽndid] a. tebura de; karate de. ～head-
ed [-hedid] a. atama ga karappo no.
empyreal [èmpairí(:)əl] a. Tenjōkai (*uppermost sky*) no.
empyrean [empairí:ən] n. Tenjōkai. a. Tenjōkai no (*empyreal*).
emu [í:mju:] n. (*bird*) emyū (dachō no tsugi ni ōkii tori).
emulate [émjuleit] v. kyōsō suru; onaji yōni narō to hagemu.
～tive [imjú:lətiv] a. kachikina.
emulation [emjuléiʃən] n. kyōsō; hariai; hagemu koto.
emulator [émjuleitə] n. kyōsōsha.
emulous [émjuləs] a. kyōsōtekina; be ～ of, o nesshinni maneru; to kisou. ～ly ad. kisotte; isshōkemmeini. ～ness
[-nis] n.   [zaika-sayō.
emulsification [imʌlsìfikéiʃən] n. nyūzai ni suru koto; nyū-
emulsify [imʌlsifai] v. nyūzai ni suru.
emulsion [imʌlʃən] n. nyūzai; (tokeawanai kongōeki).
emulsive [imʌlsiv] a. nyūzai no; nyūzaishitsu no.
en- [en] *prefix*. …. " suru " to iu imi o tsukekuwaeru settōgo.
enable [inéibl] v. dekiru yōni suru.
enact [inǽkt] v. (*leg.*) gian o tōsu; hōritsu ni suru; no yaku
o enzuru. ～ment [-mənt] n.(hōrei no) seitei; rippō.
enamel [inǽm(ə)l] n. enameru; hōrō; hōrō-zaiku. v. enameru
o kakeru. ～(l)ed [-d] ironware, n. hōrōtekki. ～ware [-wɛə]
n. setohiki.
enamo(u)r [inǽmə] v. horekomaseru; miwaku suru : be ～ed
of…, …ni horekomu.
en bloc [ɑn blɔk] (*Fr.*) sōkatsu shite : resignation ～, sōjishoku.
encamp [imkǽmp] v. jindoru; yaei suru (saseru). ～ment
[-mənt] n. yaei.
encase [inkéis] v. yōki (utsuwa) ni ireru.
enchain [intʃéin] v. kusari (*chain*) de tsunagu.
enchant [intʃá:nt] v. mahō o kakeru; miwaku suru. ～er [in-
tʃá:ntə] n. mahōtsukai. tamashii o ubau mono. ～ing a.
uttorisaseru. ～ress [-ris] n. mahō tsukai no onna.
encircle [insə́:kl] v. tori-maku; mawaru.
enclose [inklóuz] v. kakomu; tsutsumu.
enclosure [inklóuʒə] n. fūnyū shita mono; kakoi.
encomiast [inkóumiəst] n. homeru hito; gokigentori.

encomium [enkóumiəm] *n.* sanji ; sambi no kotoba.

encompass [inkʌ́mpəs] *v.* torimaku. ～**ment** *n.* hōi ; torimaki.

encore [ɔŋkɔ́:] *n.* (*Fr.*) ankōru.

encounter [inkáuntə] *n.* deai ; sōgūsen. *v.* deau ; dekkuwasu ; shōtotsu suru.

encourage [inkʌ́ridʒ] *v.* shōrei (kobu) suru ; yūkizukeru. ～**ment** *n.* kobu ; shōrei. ～**ing** *a.* kobusuru. ～**ly** *ad.* hagema-shite.

encroach [inkróutʃ] *v.* shingai (sanshoku) suru (*on*). ～**ment** [-mənt] *n.* shingai ; sanshoku.

encrust [inkrʌ́st] *v.* katai kawa (*crust*) de ōu.

encumber [inkʌ́mbə] *v.* jama o suru.

encumbrance [inkʌ́mbrəns] *n.* jama mono ; isōrō ; (*leg.*) fudō-san-jō no futan. ～**r** [i-sə] *n.* hito no tochi ni teitōken o motsu hito.

encurtain [inkə̀:tin] *v.* maku (*curtain*) o harimegurasu.

～ency [-ensi] *suf.* seishitsu, arisama o shimesu setsubigo (*suffix*) rei : *dependency* (ison) ; *frequency* (himpan).

encyclical [ensáiklik(ə)l] *n.* (Rōma Hō-ō (*Pope*) no) kaijō. (mawashibumi). *a.* kairan no ; kaisō no. ⌈jiten.

encyclop(a)edia [ensàikləpí:diə] *n.* hyakkazensho ; hyakka-

encyclop(a)edic [insaikləpí:dik] *a.* hyakkazenshoteki ; chishi-ki no hiroi.

end [end] *n.* haji ; owari : *at one's wit's* ～, tohō ni kurete. *come to an* ～, shūryō suru (owaru). *in the* ～ kekkyoku. *put an* ～ *to*, o yameru ; ochitsuku ; korosu (*kill*). *v.* oeru (owaru).

endanger [indéindʒ] *v.* ayauku suru.

endear [indíə] *v.* natsukashiku omowaseru ; aijō o kanji sase-ru : ～ *oneself to*, ni aisareru ; ni shitawareru. ～**ing** *a.* aijō o arawasu ; shin'ai no. ～**ment** *n.* shin'ai ; aibu.

endeavo(u)r [indévə] *n.* doryoku. *v.* chikara o tsukusu.

endemic [endémik] *n.* fūdo-byō (*-illness*). *a.* fūdosei no ; fū-

endive [éndiv] *n.* (*bot.*) kikujisa. ⌊do-byō no.

endless [éndlis] *a.* eien no. ～**ly** *ad.* hateshi naku.

endorse [indɔ́:s] *v.* uragaki suru ; hoshō suru ; zenin suru. ～**ment** *n.* hoshō ; uragaki.

endow [indáu] *v.* kihonkin o kifu suru ; sazukeru : *He is* ～*ed* *with genius*, kare niwa tempu no sainō ga aru. ~**ment** *n*. kifukin; kihonzaisan. ~**ment insurance** *n*. yōrōhoken.

endue [indjú:] *v*. (kimono o) kiseru; sazukeru (*give*).

endurable [indjúərəbl] *a*. gaman dekiru.

endurance [indjúərəns] *n*. nintai; nintairyoku : *beyond* ~, gaman dekinai hodo.

endure [endjúə] *v*. taeru; shimbō suru.

enduring [indjúəriŋ] *a*. shimbō suru; eikyū no. ~**ly** *ad*. eikyūni.

endways [éndweiz], **endwise** [éndwaiz] *ad*. chokuritsu shite; haji to haji o kuttsukete.

enema [énimə] *n*. (*med*.) kanchō; kanchō-ki.

enemy [énimi] *n*. teki; tekihei.

energetic [enədʒétik] *a*. seiryoku no aru; kibikibi shita (*spirited*). ~**ally** [-əli] *ad*. konki yoku; seiryokutekini.

energize [énədʒaiz] *v*. ikioi o tsukeru.

energy [énədʒi] *n*. seiryoku; (*pl*.) katsudōryoku; nōryoku : *devote* (*apply*) *one's* ~*ies to*, ni seiryoku o katamukeru : *mental* ~, seishinryoku. *act* (*speak*) *with* ~, genki ni okonau (hanasu).

enervate [énə:veit] *v*. yowaraseru; otoroesaseru. *a*. [énə:vit/inó:-] chikara no nai.

enervation [enə:véiʃən] *n*. suijaku; mukiryoku.

enfeeble [infí:bl] *v*. yowaku suru; otoroe saseru.

enfilade [infiléid] *n*. jūsha. retsu o tate ni jūgeki suru.

enfold [infóuld] *v*. tsutsumu.

enforce [infó:s] *v*. jisshi (shikō) suru; kyōsei suru. ~**ment** *n*. jishi; shikō; kyōsei.

enfranchise [infrǽntʃaiz] *v*. kaihō suru; senkyoken o ataeru.

engage [ingéidʒ] *v*. yakusoku suru; kon'yaku suru. ~ *oneself to*, chikau; jūji suru. ~**ment** *n*. yakusoku.

engaging [ingéidʒiŋ] *a*. aikyō no aru (*charming*).

engender [indʒéndə] *v*. hassei saseru; hikiokosu (*arouse*).

engine [éndʒin] *n*. kikan; kikai (*machine*); kikansha. ~ **driver** [-dráivə] *n*. (*Brit*.) kikanshi, (*Am*. *locomotive engineer*). ~ **house,** *n*. kikanko.

engineer [endʒiníə] *n*. kōgakusha; gishi; kikanshi; kōhei (*a* *corps* [kɔ:] *of*~). **civil** ~. *n.* doboku-gishi. ~**ing**, *n.* kōgaku : civil ~. *n.* doboku kōgaku.

England [íŋgliʃ] *a. England* no; Eikoku no; Eigo no. *n.* Eigo; **the E**~, Eikokujin. ~ **woman** [wúmən] *n.* Eikoku fujin.

engrave [ingréiv] *v.* chōkoku suru. kokoro (*mind*) ni meiki ⌊suru.

engraver [ingréivə] *n.* chōkoku-shi.

engraving [ingréiviŋ] *n.* chōkoku-jutsu; mokuhan (*wood* ~), dōban (*copperplate*) nado.

engross [ingróus] *v.* ōmoji de kaku. muchūni naru. ~**ment** *n.* bottō; muchū; ōmojigaki.

engulf [ingʌ́lf] *v.* suikomu; nomikomu (*swallow*).

enhance [inhá:ns] *v.* masu; tsuyomeru; (nedan o) tsuriageru. ~**ment** *n.* zōshin; zōkyō; (nedan no) tōki.

enigma [iníɡmə] *n.* nazo.

enigmatic(al) [eniɡmǽtik(əl)] *a.* nazo no yōna; wakarinikui. ~**cally** [-kli] *ad.* nazo no yōni.

enjoin [indʒɔ́in] *v.* meizuru; kinshi suru (*prohibit*).

enjoy [indʒɔ́i] *v.* kyōraku suru; tanoshimu. ~**able** *a.* yukaina. ~**ment** *n.* tanoshimi; kyōraku.

enkindle [inkídl] *v.* hi (*fire*) o tsukeru; sendō suru.

enlarge [inlá:dʒ] *v.* ōkiku suru; shōjutsu suru (*on, upon*). ~**ment** *n.* kakudai. (*photo.*) hikinobashi.

enlighten [inláitn] *v.* keihatsu suru; hikari o ataeru. ~**ed** [-d] *a.* keihatsu sareta. ~**ment** *n.* keihatsu.

enlist [inlíst] *v.* hyō (*list*) ni noseru; heiseki ni hairu. ~**ment** [-mənt] *n.* narabete kaku koto; ōbo; chōhei tōroku.

enliven [inláivn] *v.* kakki o tsukeru; nigiyakani suru.

en masse [ɑ̃:(ŋ) más] *ad.* (*Fr.*) ikkatsu shite. **resignation** ~ *n.* ⌊sōjishoku.

enmity [énmiti] *n.* tekii; nikushimi.

ennoble [inóubl] *v.* takameru; kizoku ni ressuru.

ennui [ɑ̃:núi] *n.* (*Fr.*) taikutsu.

enormity [inɔ́:miti] *n.* kyodai; hōgai (*excessive*); gokuakuhidō.

enormous [inɔ́:məs] *a.* kyodaina; hōgaina. ~**ly** *ad.* hōgaini.

enough [inʌ́f] *a., n.* ...ni tariru; jūbun. *ad.* jūbunni.

enquire, in- [inkwáiə] *v.* tazuneru; shiraberu.

enrage [inréidʒ] *v.* okoraseru. ~**d** [-d] *a.* gekido shite.

enrapture [inrǽptʃə] *v.* kyōki saseru; kōkotsu to saseru.

enrich [inrítʃ] *v.* tomaseru; yutakani suru; eiyōka o takameru. ~**ment** *n.* hiyoku.

enrol, enroll [inróul] *v.* -**rolled**; -**rolling.** meibo ni kinyū (tōroku) suru. ~ ment [-mənt] *n.* meibo ni kinyū.

en route [ū: rú:t] (*Fr.*) *ad.* tochū (de).

ensconce [inskɔ́ns] *v.* anchi suru; kakusu. ~ *oneself in,* ni osamaru; ochitsuku.

ensemble [ū:nsā:(m)bl] *n.* (*Fr.*) zentai; (*mus.*) gasshō; gassō.

enshrine [inʃráin] *v.* anchi suru; hizō suru.

enshroud [inʃráud] *v.* kyōkatabira o kiseru; tsutsumu.

ensign [énsain/énsn] *n.* hata; (*Am.*) [énsn] kaigun shōi (*a navy second lieutenant*).

ensilage [énsilidʒ] *n.* nama no bokusō no. *silo* [sáilou], sono chozō shita bokusō. ⌐ru.

enslave [insléiv] *v.* dorei ni suru : *be* ~*d to,* ...no dorei ni naru.

ensnare [insnéə] *v.* wana ni kakeru; yūwaku suru. ⌐toshi.

ensue [insú:] *v.* tsuzuite okoru : *the* ~*ing year,* sono tsugi no

ensure [inʃúə] *v.* kakujitsu ni suru; hoshō suru. ⌐hō).

entablature [entǽblətʃə] *n.* nageshi; hashira no jōbu (ue no

entail [intéil] *n.* (*leg.*) gentei sōzoku (zaisan no). *v.* (*leg.*) gentei sōzoku o suru.

entangle [intǽŋgl] *v.* kongaragaru (-garaseru); komarasu. ~ **ment** *n.* konran. ⌐koku.

entente [ū:(n)tā:t] *n.* (*Fr.*) kyōshō; ~**cordiale** *n.* kyō-yaku

enter [éntə] *v.* hairu; kuwawaru; hajimeru : ~*into,* o hajimeru; chakushu suru. ~ *on* (*upon*), o hajimeru (*story*);

enteric [entérik] *a.* chō no : ~ **fever** [intɜ̀rik fí:və] *n.* (*med.*) ⌐chōchibusu.

enteritis [entəráitis] *n.* (*med.*) chōen.

enterprise [éntəpraiz] *n.* jigyō; kigyōshin. ~**ing** [-iŋ] *a.* kigyōshin no aru; shinshutekina.

entertain [entətéin] *v.* motenasu; tanoshimaseru; kokoro ni idaku (*cherish*). ~**ing** *a.* yorokobaseru; tanoshimaseru. ~**ment** *n.* gochisō; kantai; yokyō.

enthral(l) = **inthral(l)** [inθrɔ́:l] *v.* miwaku suru; dorei ni suru.

enthrone [inθróun] *v.* kurai ni tsukaseru.

enthusiasm [inθ(j)ú:ziæzm] *n.* nesshin; nekkyō.

enthusiast [inθ(j)ú:ziæst] *n.* nesshinka; nekkyōsha.

enthusiastic [inθ(j)ùːziǽstik] a. nesshinna ; nekkyōtekina. ~
ally ad. nesshinni.

entice [intáis] v. sasou ; yūwaku suru. ~ment n. yūwaku. ~
ing a. kokoro o mayowasu. ~ingly [-iŋli] ad. yūwakutekini.

entire [intáiə] a. kanzenna ; zentai no. n. (Brit.) kuro-biiru no
isshu. ~ly mattaku ; zembu.

entirety [intáiəti] n. kanzen ; sōgaku.

entitle, in- [intáitl] v. title o ataeru ; kenri o ataeru.

entity [éntiti] n. jittai ; hontai.

entomb [intúːm] v. haka (a grave) ni umeru ; ...no haka to na-

entomologist [èntəmɔ́lədʒist] n. konchūgakusha.   Lru.

entomology [èntəmɔ́lədʒi] n. konchūgaku.

entourage [ɔ̀nturáːʒ/ùturáːʒ] n. (Fr.) kankyō ; zuikōsha ; zui-

entrails [éntreilz] (pl.) n. naizō.   Lkōin.

entrance [éntrəns] n. hairu koto ; iriguchi.

entrance [intrάːns] v. uttori saseru ; uchōtenni suru.

entrap [intrǽp] v. wana ni kakeru ; otoshiireru.

entreat [intriːt] v. kongan (tangan) suru.

entreaty [intríːti] n. kongan ; tangan.

entrée [ɔ́(ː)ntrei] n. (Fr.) nyūjō kyoka ; nyūjōken ; (cooking)
fukushoku-hin.

entrench [intréntʃ] v. zangō de kakomu. ~ment n. zangō o
megurashita jinchi. (encampment).

entrust [intrΛ́st] v. yudaneru ; makaseru.

entry [éntri] n. hairu koto ; hairiguchi ; tōroku (registration).

entwine [intwáin] v. karamu ; karamaseru.

enumerate [injúːməreit] v. kazoeageru ; rekkyo suru.

enumeration [injːməréiʃən] n. keisan ; maikyo.

enunciate [inΛ́nsieit] v. sengen suru ; hatsuon suru (pronounce).

enunciation [inΛnsiéiʃən] n. hatsuon (no shikata).

enure [injúə], inure [injúə] v. narau (nareru) ; tanren suru.

envelop [invéləp] v. tsutsumu ; kakomu. ~ment n. hōi.

envelope [énvəloup] n. fūtō.

envenom [invénəm] v. doku (poison) o ireru ; zōo (nikushimi)
ni michiru (fill with hatred).   ⌈shiku.

enviable [énviəbl] a. urayamashii. ~bly [-bli] ad. urayama-

envious [énviəs] *a.* urayamashi garu; shitto-bukai.

environ [inváiərən] *v.* torimaku. ～**ment** [-mənt] *n.* kankyō; mawari no jijō. ～**s** [énvirənz] *n.* (*pl.*) ...no mawari; kingō; shūi.

envoy [énvəi] *n.* shisetsu; zenkenkōshi. ～ *extraordinary and minister plenipotentiary,* Tokumei Zenkenkōshi.

envy [énvi] *v.* netamu; urayamu. *n.* shitto.

enzyme [énzaim] *n.* (*chem.*) kōso.

Eos [i:əs] *n. Gk. myth* no megami, Rōma no *Aurora*: yoake ⌈no megami.

epaulet(te) [épo(u)let] *n.* kenshō. (gunjin no, *soldiers'*)

ephemeral [ifémərəl] *a.* ichinichi kagiri no; hakanai.

epic [épik] *n.* joji-shi. *a.* joji-shi no; yūsōna.

epicure [épikjuə] *n.* tsūjin; bishoku-ka (*man of dainty tooth*).

epicurean [epikju(ə)rí(:)ən] *a.* kairaku-shugi no. *n.* kairaku-shugisha. ～**ism** [epikjú(ə)riənizm] *n.* kairaku-shugi.

epidemic [epidémik] *n.* densembyō; ryūkō. *a.* densensei no.

epidermis [èpidə́:mis] *n.* hyōhi; uwakawa.

epiglottis [epiglɔ́tis] *n.* (*anat.*) ēnnankotsu.

epigram [épigræm] *n.* keiku; suntetsu-shi (*short pointed witty saying; short poem*).

epigrammatic [èpigrəmǽtik] *a.* suntetsu-shi no; kikei no.

epigraph [épigræf] *n.* hibun; (bohi (*tombstone*) nado no) daimei; daishi (*motto*).

epilepsy [épilepsi] *n.* (*med.*) tenkan.

epileptic [epiléptik] *a.* tenkan no. *n.* tenkan kanja.

epilogue [épiləg] *n.* ketsuron; engeki no owari no kōjō.

episcopacy [ipískəpəsi] *n.* kantoku seido; *bishop*-tachi no kantoku-dantai. ⌈no.

episcopal [ipískəpəl] *a.* kantoku no; (*E*～) kantokukyōkai-ha

Episcopalian [ipìskəpéiliən] *a.* kantokuha no. *n.* sono ha no hito.

episcopate [ipískəpit] *n.* kantoku shoku; sono ninki.

episode [épisoud] *n.* sōwa (chotto naka ni hasamu); sōwateki dekigoto.

episodic(al) [episɔ́dik(l)] *a.* sōwa no.

epistle [ipísl] *n.* shinsho (*letter*); (*E*～) Shitosho (*in the Bible*).

epistolary [ipístələri/ep-] *a.* tegami no; tegamibuntai no.

epitaph [épitɑːf] *n.* himei ; hakaishi ni kaita monji.

epithet [épiθet] *n.* keiyō no goku ; adana.

epitome [ipítəmi/ep-] *n.* kōgai ; arasuji ; shukuzu : *man, the world's* ~, sekai no shikuzu taru ningen. ~**mize** [ipítəmaiz] *v.* yōyaku suru (*summarize*).

epoch [íːpɔk/épɔk] *n.* shin-kigen ; jidai : ~**-making** [-méikiŋ] *a.* shin-kigen o hiraku.

equability [ə̀kwəbíliti/ìːk-] *n.* ichiyō ; dōyō.

equable [ékwəbl/íːk-] *a.* mura no nai ; heiseina. ~**bly** *ad.*

equal [íːkwəl] *a.* hitoshii ; byōdōna. *n.* dōhai ; onaji mono. *v.* hitteki suru. ~**ly** *ad.* hitoshiku.

equality [i(ː)kwóliti] *n.* dōtō ; byōdō ; kintō.

equalization [ìːkwəlaizéiʃən/liz-] *n.* hitoshiku suru koto.

equalize [íːkwəlaiz] *v.* hitoshiku suru ; dōten ni naru.

equanimity [ìːkwənímiti] *n.* kokoro no ochitsuki ; itsumo to kawaranu koto.

equate [ikwéit] *v.* byōdō ni suru ; heikin suru.

equation [ikwéiʃən] *n.* hitoshiku suru koto ; (*math.*) hōteishiki.

equator [ikwéitə] *n.* sekidō ; chūya-heibunsen.

equatorial [èkwətóːriəl/ìːk-] *n.* sekidō no.

equestrian [ikwéstriən/ek-] *n.* bajutsu no ; bajō no. *n.* bajutsuka.

equidistant [íːkwidístənt] *a.* dōkyori no ; kyori ga onaji.

equilateral [íːkwilǽtərəl] *a.* (*math.*) tōhen no ; hen no nagasa no hitoshii.

equilibrium [ìːkwilíbriəm] *n.* heikin ; tsuriai.

equine [íːkwain/ék-] *n.* uma no ; uma ni nita.

equinoctial [ìːkwinɔ́kʃəl/ə̀k] *n., a.* chūya heibun (no) ; higan (no). ~ **gales** [-geilz] *n.* higan arashi. ~ **line** [-lain] chūya heibun-sen ; sekidō.

equinox [íːkwinɔks/ék-] *n.* chūya heibunji. **autumnal** ~ *n.* Aki no Higan ; Shūbun. **vernal** ~ *n.* Haru no Higan ; Shumbun.

equip [ikwíp] *v.* shitaku suru ; gisō suru. ~**ment** *n.* jumbi.

equipage [ékwipidʒ/-edʒ] *n.* basha-uma ; tomo mawari yōgu isshiki.

equipoise [ékwipɔiz/íːk-] *n.* tsuriai ; heikin ; heikō.

equitable [ékwitəbl] *a.* kōheina ; seitōna. ～**bly** *ad.* ～**ness** *n.*

equity [ékwiti] *n.* kōhei ; seitō ; (*leg.*) kōheihō.

equivalence [ikwívələns] *n.* dōtō.

equivalent [ikwívələnt] *a.* dōtō no ; dōigi no. *n.* dōtō no mono ; dōgigo (*synonym*).

equivocal [ikwívəkəl] *a.* aimaina ; utagawashii. ～**ly** *ad.*

equivocate [ikwívəkeit] *v.* futatōri no imi ni toreru go o mochiiru ; kotoba o nigosu.

equivocation [ikwìvəkéiʃən] *n.* gomakashi.

era [íərə] *n.* kigen ; nendai ; jidai.

eradicate [irǽdikeit] *v.* konzetsu (bokumetsu) suru.

eradication [irædikéiʃən] *n.* konzetsu ; bokumetsu.

erase [iréiz] *v.* nuguikesu ; sakujo suru ; bōkyaku suru. ～**r** [-ə] *n.* keshigomu ; kokubanfuki.

ere [ɛə] *prep. conj.* maeni ; …suru izenni.

erect [irékt] *a.* massuguna. *v.* tateru ; kensetsu (konryū) suru ; setsuritsu suru. ～**er** [iréktə] *n.* kensetsu(konryū)sha ; setsuritsusha.

erection [irékʃən] *n.* chokuritsu ; kensetsu ; konryū ; bokki.

eremite [érimait] *n.* intonsha.

ergot [ɔ́ːgət/-gət] *n.* bakkaku ; bakkakubyō (*disease of ergot.*)

ermine [ɔ́ːmin] *n.* ten ; ten no kegawa (*fur*) ; hōkan no hōfuku (*robes of judges*) ; mata wa chii, mibun (*judicial office*).

erode [iróud/er-] *v.* shinshoku suru (*consume*) ; fushoku suru.

erosion [iróuʒən/er-] *n.* shinshoku ; fushoku (*corrosion*).

erosive [iróusiv/er-] *a.* shinshoku (fushoku) suru.

erotic [irɔ́tik/er-] *a.* ren'ai no ; shikijō no ; aiyoku no. ⌐ku.

ERP (＝*European Recovery Program*) Yōroppa Fukkō Keikaku.

err [ɔː] *v.* ayamaru ; machigai o suru (*make mistakes*) ; tsumi o okasu (*do wrong*).

errand [érənd] *n.* tsukai ; stukai no yōmuki ; shimei : *go on an* ～, tsukai ni iku. ～ **boy** [-bɔi] *n.* hashirizukai (no shōnen).

errant [érənt] *a.* henreki suru (*travelling about*) ; mayotta ; machigatta (*mistaken*). ⌐goto).

errantry [érəntri] *n.* musha-shugyō (musha-shugyōsha no shi-

errattic [irǽtik/er-] *a.* nami hazure no ; kikyōna ; utsurigi no (*not steady*). ～**ally** *ad.*

erratum [iréitəm,/irúː-] *n.* (*pl.* **-ta** [-te]) gobyū ; goji.

erroneous [iróunjəs/er-] *a.* ayamatta ; fuseina. ∼**ly** *ad.*

error [érə] *n.* ayamari ; kokoroe chigai ; kashitsu.

erudite [éru(ː)dait] *a.* hakugakuna. ∼**ly** *ad.*

erudition [əru(ː)díʃən] *n.* hakugaku (*acquired knowledge*).

erupt [irÁpt/er-] *v.* funka suru ; ha ga haeru (*a tooth breaks through the gum*).

eruption [irÁpʃən/er-] *n.* bakuhatsu ; funka ; funshutsubutsu (*things thrown up*) ; hasshin (*rash*).

eruptive [irÁptiv/er-] *a.* funshutsu suru ; hasshinsei no. ∼ **fever** *n.* hasshin chibusu (*eruptive typhus*).

erysipelas [ərisípiləs] *n.* (*med.*) tandoku.

ESB (= *Economic Stabilization Board*) Keizai Antei Hombu ; Keizai Antei Kyoku.

escadrille [əskədríl] *n.* shō-kantai ; hikōtai (*a small fleet of airplanes or warships*).   ⌈go [*ladder*].

escalade [əskəléid] *n.* untei ; (shiro no kabe o noboru) hashi-

escalator [éskəleitə] *n.* esukareitā ; jidō kaidan.

escapade [éskəpéid] *n.* dassen ; itazura ; rambō ; hompō (*breaking loose*) ; itazura (*prank*).

escape [iskéip] *v.* nigedasu. *n.* tōbō ; dasshutsu. ∼ **stair** *n.* hinan kaidan. **hairbreadth** (**narrow**) ∼, kyūshi ni isshō. ∼**ment** [-mənt] *n.* (tokei no haguruma no) nigashi dome.

escapee [èskəpíː] *n.* tōbōsha.

escapism [iskéipizm] *n.* tōbōshugisha.

eschew [istʃúː] *v.* sakeru ; tōzakeru.

escort [éskɔːt] *n.* goei(sha) ; goei(hei) ; goeikan. *v.* [iskɔ́ːt] go-ei suru ; gosō suru.

escritoire [əskri(ː)twáː] *n.* (hikidashi tsuki ∼*with drawers*) no shajidai (*kakimono-zukue*).

esculent [éskjulənt] *a.* shokuyō ni tekisuru (*edible*).

escutcheon [iskÁtʃən] *n.* monshō no tsuita tate (*a shield with a coat of arms*).

Eskimo, [éskimou] **Esquimau** (*pl. eskimo*(*s*), Esquimaux [-z]) *n.* Esukimōjin. ∼ **dog** *n.* Eskimōjin ga sori (*sledge*) o hikaseru tsuyoi inu.

esophagus [iːsɔ́fəgəs] *n.* (*anat.*) shokudō.

esoteric [èsoutérik] *a.* okugi no; himitsu no; hiden no (*understood only by the select few*).

especial [ispéʃəl/es-] *a.* tokubetsu no; kakubetsu no. ~**ly** *ad.* tokuni; koto ni.

Esperanto [èsporá:ntou/-ræn] *n.* Esuperantogo.

espial [ispáiəl/es-] *n.* tantei; tansaku (*act of watching*).

espionage [əspiəná:ʒ/éspiənidʒ/ispáiənidʒ] *n.* tantei; tansaku.

esplanade [ésplənéid/-ná:d] *n.* yūhochi; shōyōchi (*a roadway by river or sea*).

espousal [ispáuzəl/es-] *n.* kon'yaku.

espouse [ispáuz/es-] *v.* metoru; yome ni yaru; shiji suru; yōgo suru : ~ *a new religion*, shinkyō o shiji suru.

esprit [éspri:] *n.* seishin; kakki; saichi.

espy [ispái/es-] *v.* mitsukeru; miyaburu.

esquire, Esq. [iskwáiə/es-] *n.* (*honorific*—keishō) sama; dono.

essay [eséi/ései] *v.* kokoromiru; tamesu. *n.* [ései, -sei] rombun; kokoromi; kokoromi. ~**ist** *n.* zuihitsuka.

essence [ésns] *n.* honshitsu; shinzui; ekisu.

essential [isénʃəl/es-] *a.* honshitsutekina; komponteki; ekisu no : *be* ~ *to*, ni nakute wa naranu. *n.* honshitsu; yōten; yōken. ~**ly** *ad.* honshitsutekini.

establish [istǽbliʃ/es-] *v.* setsuritsu suru; kakuritsu suru; aratani mōkeru; mi o ochitsukaseru. ~**ed** [-t] *a.* kakuritsu shita; tashikana. **E**~**ed Church** *n.* Eikoku kokkyōkai. ~**ment** [-mənt] *n.* kakuritsu; kensetsu; kensetsubutsu : **peace** (**war**) ~**ment.** *n.* heiji (senji) hensei.

estate [istéit/es-] *n.* zaisan; shoyūchi; mibun. **fourth** ~ *n.* shimbun kisharen; shimbun. **personal** ~ *n.* dōsan. **real** ~ *n.* fudōsan. **the third** ~ *n.* heimin.

esteem [istí:m/es-] *n.* sonchō. *v.* sonchō suru; omou.

esthete [í:sθi:t] *n.* yuibishugisha; bigakusha; bijutsuka-buru.

estimable [éstiməbl] *a.* sonchō subeki. ⌊hito.

estimate [éstimeit] *v.* mitsumoru; hyōka suru. *n.* [-mit] mitsu mori; hyōka; yosan.

estimation [estiméiʃən] *n.* hyōka; handan; sonchō.

estrange [istréindʒ/es-] *v.* tōzakeru; rikan suru (*to make strange*).

estuary [éstjuəri/-tʃu-] *n.* kakō; kawaguchi (*river mouth*).

et cetera, etc. [itsétərə/et-] unɒun; nado-nado (*and so forth or on*).

etch [etʃ] *v. etching.* (kagakusayō de sen ya e nado o kinzoku, garasu nado ni dasu). **~ing** *n.*etchingu; shokuru-jutsu.

eternal [itə́:nəl] *a.* eien no; itsu made mo. **~ly** *ad.* eienni.

eternity [i(:)tə́:niti] *n.* eien; fushi; fumetsu.

ether [í:θə] *n.* ēteru; reiki.

ethereal [i(:)θíəriəl] *a.* ēteru no; karui; tenjō no; reitekina. **~ize** [-aiz] *v.* ēteru ni suru. **~zation** [ì:θəriəlaizéiʃən] *n.* ēteru no jōtai ni suru koto.

etherize [í:θəraiz] *v.* ēteru ni suru; ēteru de mahi saseru.

ethic(al) [éθik(əl)], *a.* rinri nɒ; rinrigaku no. **~ally** *ad.* rin-ethics [éθiks] *n.* rinri; rinrigaku. └ritekini; rinrigakujō.

ethnic [éθnik], **~al** [-əl] *a.* jinshu no; jinshuteki no.

ethnography [eθnɔ́grəfi] *n.* iroirona shurui no ningen no kagakuteki kijutsu to bunrui.

ethnologic(al) [èθnəlɔ́dʒik(əl)], *a.* jinshugakujō no.

ethnologist [eθnɔ́lədʒist] *n.* jinshugakusha.

ethnology [eθnɔ́lədʒi] *n.* jinshugaku.

etiquette [étikét] *n.* reigi; sahō; yononaka no kimari.

Eton [í:tn] *n.* Eikoku no toshi no na. └shinsha.

Etonian [i:tóunjən/-niən] *n.* Etonkō no seito; Etonkō shus-

étude [etjú:d] *n.* (*Fr.*) renshū; renshū kyoku.

etymological [ètiməlɔ́dʒikl] *a.* gogen no; hinshiron no.

etymologist [ètimɔ́lədʒist] *n.* gogen gakusha.

etymology [ètimɔ́lədʒi] *n.* gogen; gogengaku; gogenron.

eucalyptus [jù:kəlíptəs] *n.* (*pl.* **-es, -ti** [-tai]) (*bot.*) yūkari-ju.

Eucharist [jú:kərist] *n.* Seisan (*Lord's Supper*); Seisan no pan to budōshu (*bread & wine*).

euchre [jú:kə] *n.* isshu no torampu asobi.

eugenics [ju(:)dʒéniks] *n.* yūseigaku; jinshu-kairyōgaku.

eulogist [jú:lədʒist] *n.* hometataeru hito.

eulogistic [jù:lədʒístik] *a.* shōsan no; homeageru.

eulogize [jú:lədʒaiz] *v.* homeru; shōsan suru; sanji o tate-

eulogy [jú:lədʒi] *n.* sanji; shōsan no kotoba. └matsuru.

eunuch [jú:nək] *n.* kangan; kyosei sareta otoko (*castrated man* *in charge of harem*). ⌈kotoba.

euphemism [júːfəmizm] *n.* enkyokuna iikata; enkyokuna

euphemistic [jùːfimístik] *a.* enkyokuna. ⌈ad.

euphonic(al) [ju(ː)fɔ́nik(əl)/ju(ː)fóu-] *a.* onchō no yoi. ~**ally**

euphonious [juːfóuniəs] *a.* mimizawari no yoi. ~**ly.** *ad.*

euphonize [júːfənaiz] *v.* onchō o yoku suru.

euphony [júːfəni] *n.* yoi onchō; yoi gochō.

European [jùərəpíː(ː)ən/jɔ́ːr-] *a.* Yōroppa no. *n.* Yōroppajin.

evacuate [ivǽkjueit] *v.* akewatasu; iten suru; kara ni suru; haisetsu suru; tettai suru.

evacuation [ivæ̀kjuéiʃən] *n.* akewatashi; tettai; karappo.

evacuee [ivæ̀kjuiː] *n.* sokaisha. ⌈suru.

evade [ivéid] *v.* sakeru; iinukeru; kuguru. ~ *a tax,* datsuzei

evaluate [ivǽljueit] *v.* nebumi o suru; kachi o kimeru.

evanesce [ivænés] *v.* iro ga aseru; dandan ni kieru.

evanescence [iːvənésns/èv-] *n.* shōmetsu; shōsan; hakanasa.

evanescent [ìːvənésnt/èv-] *a.* shidai ni kieru; hakanai.

evangel [ivǽndʒəl] *n.* fukuin. ~**ism** *n.* fukuin no dendō. ~**ist** *n.* fukuin dendōsha.

evangelic(al) [ìːvændʒélik(-əl)/è-], *a.* fukuin no.

evaporate [ivǽpəreit] *v.* jōhatsu suru (saseru); suibun o nuku; chitte kieru.

evaporation [ivæ̀pəréiʃən] *n.* jōhatsu; dassui; kansō.

evaporator [ivǽpəreitə] *n.* jōhatsu-ki; jōhatsukansō-ki.

evasion [ivéiʒən] *n.* nigeru; iinuke; nigeguchi.

evasive [ivéisiv] *a.* kaihi suru; iinuke no. ~**ly** *ad.*

eve [iːv] *n.* saijitsu no mae no ban (zen'ya); yūbe; ban.

even [íivən] *a.* tairana; dekoboko no nai; ichiyōna. *v.* tairani suru. *ad.* demo; sae. ~ *if,* tatoe...to iedomo. ~**ly** *ad.* tairani; kōheini. ~**ness** *n.* heitan; kōhei.

even [íːvən] *n.* (*poet.*) yūbe; ban. ~**song** [íːvnsɔŋ] *n.* yūbe no inori. ~**tide** [-taid] *n.* (*poet.*) yūbe.

even-handed [íːvnhǽndid] *a.* kōheina.

evening [íːvniŋ] *n.* yūbe; ban. ~**dress** [-dres] *n.* yakaifuku. ~**paper** [-péipə] *n.* yūkan shimbun. ~**primrose** [-prímrouz] *n.* (*bot.*) tsukimisō. ~**star** [-staː] *n.* yoi no myōjō (*Venus*).

event [ivént] *n.* dekigoto; jiken; hito shōbu. *at all* ~*s,* dō shite mo. **~ful** *a.* tajina. *in any* ~, donna koto ga atte mo. *in either* ~, dochira ni shite mo. *in the* ~ *of*, no baai niwa. **double ~s**, isshoni okotta koto.

eventual [ivéntjuəl/-tʃu-] *a.* shūkyoku no; okoru kamo shirenai. **~ly** *ad.* kekkyoku.

eventuality [ivèntjuǽliti] *n.* omowanu jiken; gūhatsusei.

eventuate [ivéntjueit] *v.* kekka ni naru; ...to iu koto ga okoru.

ever [évə] *ad.* katsute; itsu ka; tsuneni; iyashiku mo. ~ *so*, taisō (*very*). ~ *since*, sono go zutto. *for* ~, eien ni. *hardly* ~, mettani...shinai. **~glade** [-gleid] *n.* numachi. **~green** [-gri:n] *a.* fuyugareshinai. *n.* tokiwagi. **~lasting** [-lá:stiŋ] *a.* eien ni tsuzuku. **~more** [-mɔ́:/-mɔ́ə] *ad.* tsuneni; eikyū ni.

every [évri] *a.* onoono no; subete no. **~body** [-bɔ́di] *n.* dare demo; minna. **~day** [-dei] *a.* mainichi no; fudan no. **~thing** [-θiŋ] *n.* nan demo; issai. **~where** [-hwɛə] *ad.* doko nimo.

evict [i(:)víkt] *v.* toriageru; oidasu (shakuyanin nado o).

eviction [i(:)víkʃən] *n.* toriageru koto; oidashi.

evidence [évidəns] *n.* shōko; keiseki. *v.* shōmei suru; wakaru yōni suru.

evident [évidənt] *a.* akirakana. **~ly** *ad.* akirakani.

evil [í:vl] *a.* warui; yūgaina; fukitsuna. *n.* gai; wazawai; jaaku; akuhei. *the social* ~, imbai. *ad.* waruku. **~disposed** [-dispóuzd] *a.* shō no warui. **~doer** [-dú:ə] *n.* akunin. **~eyed** [-áid] *a.* dokudokushii metsuki no. **~minded** [-máindid] *a.* haraguroi; jaaku no. **~ speaking** [-spi:kiŋ] *n.* warukuchi; akkō; zambō.

evince [ivíns] *v.* arawasu; shimesu (*show clearly*).

eviscerate [ivísəreit] *v.* chō (*intestine*) o nuku; (giron nado o) honenuki ni suru.

evocation [èvəkéiʃən] *n.* yobidashi.

evoke [ivóuk] *v.* yobidasu; hikiokosu; kanki suru; (*leg.*) jōkyū saibansho ni jiken o utsusu.

evolution [ì:vəljú:ʃən] *n.* hatten; tenkai. **~ism** *n.* shinkaron. **~ist** *n.* shinkaronja.

evolutional [ì:vəljú:ʃn(ə)l], **evolutionary** [ì:vəljú:ʃənəri/èv-] *a.* hatten no; shinka no.

evolve [ivólv] *v.* tenkai (shinka) suru (saseru).

ewe [ju:] *n.* (*zoo*) mehitsuji (*female sheep*).

ewer [jú(:)ə] *n.* mizusashi ; mizugame.

ex- [eks/egz] *prefix.* (*out of*) kara deta ; (*from*) kara.

exacerbate [eksǽsə(:)beit/egzǽs-] *v.* akka saseru ; iradataseru.

exact [igzǽkt/eg-] *a.* seikakuna ; gemmitsuna. *v.* (kimari o) kyōyō suru ; shiiru. ~**ing** *a.* kyōyōtekina ; hone no oreru. ~**ly** *ad.* seikakuni ; gemmitsuni ; kimaridōri ni. ~**ness** *n.*

exaction [igzǽkʃən/eg-] *n.* yusuri ; muridori.

exactitude [igzǽktitju:d/eg-] *n.* seikaku ; gemmitsu.

exaggerate [igzǽdʒəreit/eg-] *v.* ōgesani iu ; kochō suru.

exaggeration [igzǽdʒəréiʃən/eg-] *n.* kochō.   ⌐daina.

exaggerative [igzǽdʒərretiv/eg-/-rət-] *a.* ōgesana ; shinshōbō-

exalt [igzɔ́:lt/eg-] *v.* takameru ; homeru ; tokuini saseru ; kō-shōni suru. ~**ed** *a.* tōtoi mibun no ; kōshōna ; uchōten no.

exaltation [ègzɔ:ltéiʃən] *n.* takameru koto ; iki yōyō ; tokui.

exam [igzǽm/eg-] *n.* shiken. < **examination.**

examination [igzæminéiʃən/eg-] *n.* kensa ; chōsa ; shiken ; shimmon.

examine [igzǽmin/eg-] *v.* torishiraberu ; shiken suru ; shim-mon suru ; shinsatsu suru.

examinee [igzæminí:/eg-] *n.* jukensha ; shiken o ukeru mono.

examiner [igzǽminə/eg-] *n.* kensakan ; shinsakan ; shiken iin.

example [igzá:mpl/eg-] *n.* mihon ; tehon ; mohan ; zenrei ; reidai.

exasperate [igzá:spəreit/eg-/-zǽs-] *v.* akka saseru ; okoraseru.

exasperation [igzá:spəréiʃən/-zǽs] *n.* gekika ; akka ; gekikō.

excavate [ékskəveit] *v.* horidasu ; horu.

excavation [èkskəvéiʃən] *n.* hakkutsu ; horaana ; kiridōshi ; horu koto ; hotta ana.

exceed [iksí:d/ek-] *v.* masaru ; koeru ; do o kosu. ~**ing** *a.* hijōna. ~**ingly** *ad.* hanahada ; hijōni.

excel [iksél/ek-] *v.* sugureru ; takuetsu suru.

excellence [éksələns] *n.* takuetsu ; yūshū ; biten ; chōsho.

excellency [éksələnsi] *n.* takuetsu ; biten ; (*Brit.*) shōgō (kakka).

excellent [éksələnt] *a.* sugureta ; yūryōna. ~**ly** *ad.*

excelsior [eksélsiə:/ik-] *inter. a.* sarani takaku！ sarani kōjō！ *n.* (*Am.*) jōtōna kannakuzu (tsumemono ni mochiiru).

except [iksépt/ek-] *v.* nozoku; jogai suru; hantai suru. *prep.* o nozoite; no hoka. ~ing *prep.* ...o nozoite; no hoka.

exception [iksépʃən/ek-] *n.* reigai; jogairei. ~able *a.* hantai serareru. ~al *a.* reigai no; ijōna. ~ally *ad.* regaitekini.

excerpt [iksə́:pt] *v.* bassui suru; in'yō suru. *n.* [éksə:pt] bassui; basshō; batsuroku.

excess [iksés/ek-] *n.* chōka; kado; ōsugi; chōkaryō.

excessive [iksésiv/ek-] *a.* kado no. ~ly *ad.* kado ni.

exchange [ikstʃéindʒ/eks-] *v.* kōkan suru; ryōgae suru; tori-kawasu. *n.* kōkan; ryōgae; kawase torihikijo; denwa kōkan kyoku. ~able *a.* kōkan ga dekiru. ~rate [-reit] *n.* kawase sōba.

exchequer [ikstʃékə] *n.* Ōkurashō; kokko (*national treasury*); (*col.*) zaigen. *Chancellor of the E*~, Igiris no Okuradaijin. ~bill, Ōkurashō shōken. ~bond kokko saiken.

excise [eksáiz] *n.* naikoku shōhizei. *v.* zei o kakeru. kiri-toru (ki no eda nado o). ~man [-mən] *n.* shūzeiri.

excision [eksíʒən/ik-] *n.* (*med.*) setsudan; kiritoru koto (geka shujitsu de).

excitable [iksáitəbl/ek-] *a.* gekishi yasui; ki no hayai.

excitant [éksitənt/iksáitənt] *a.* shigeki suru. ~ *n.* shigeki butsu.

excitation [èksitéiʃən] *n.* shigeki; kōfun; gekirei.

excite [iksáit/ek-] *v.* sendō (shigeki) suru; hikiokosu (saseru); kōfun suru (saseru). ~ment [-mənt] *n.* kōfun.

excited [iksáitid/ek-] *a.* kōfun shita; gekikō shita. ~ly *ad.* kōfun shite. ⌈shiroi.

exciting [iksáitiŋ/ek-] *a.* kōfun saseru; shigeki suru; omo-

exclaim [ikskléim/eks-] *v.* sakebu; ōgoe de iu. ⌈tan fugō.

exclamation [èkskləméiʃən] *n.* sakebi; (*gram.*) kantanshi; kan-

exclamatory [ekskláemətəri] *a.* zekkyō no; kantan no.

exclude [iksklú:d/eks-] *v.* kobamu; kyozetsu suru; jogai suru; oidasu. ⌈chiku.

exclusion [iksklú:ʒən/eks-] *n.* kyozetsu; haijo; haiseki; hō-

exclusive [iksklú:siv/eks-] *a.* haitatekina; dokusen no; sen'-etsu no; takaku tomatta. ~ *of*, o nozoite. ~ly *ad.* moppara.

excommunicate [èkskəmjú:nikeit] *v.* Seisan (*Lord's Supper*) o teishi suru; hamon suru.

excommunication [èkskəmjùːnikéiʃən] *n.* Seisan teishi ; hamon ; jomei.

excoriate [ekskɔ́ːrieit/iks-/-kɔ́r-] *v.* kawa o hagu ; surimuku ; kokuhyō (*severe criticism*) o kudasu.

excoriation [ekskɔ(ː)riéiʃən] *n.* kawahagi ; surimuki.

excrement [ékskrimənt] *n.* (*pl.*) haisetsubutsu. ～**al** *a.* haisetsubutsu no.

excrescence [ikskrésəns/eks-] *n.* ibo ; kobu no yōna dekimono ; kobu ; yokeina mono.　　　　　　　　　　　⌈mudana.

excrescent[ikskrésənt/eks-] *a.* muyōni tobidashita ; muyō no ;

excrete [ekskríːt] *v.* haisetsu suru ; bumpi suru.

excretion[ekskríːʃən] *n.* haisetsu ; bumpi ; haisetsubutsu ; bumpi butsu.

excretive [ekskríːtiv] *a.* haisetsu suru ; bumpi suru.

excretory [ekskríːtəri/iks-] *a.* haisetsu no ; bumpi no.

excruciate [ikskrúːsieit/eks-] *v.* gōmon suru (*torture*) ; kurushimeru.

excruciation [ikskrùːʃiéiʃən/eks-/-siéi-] *n.* gōmon.

exculpate [ékskʌlpeit] *v.* muzai to naru ; muzai ni suru.

exculpation [èkskʌlpéiʃən] *n.* muzai no bemmei ; benkai.

exculpatory [ekskʌ́lpətəri/ékskʌlpeitəri] *a.* benkai suru ; benkai no tame no.

excursion [ikskɔ́ːʃən/eks-] *n.* ensoku ; yūran ; ensoku dantai.

excursive [ekskɔ́ːsiv/iks-] *a.* hondai o hanareta ; manzen taru.

excusable [ikskjúːzəbl/eks-] *a.* kamben dekiru ; mōshiwake no tatsu.

excuse [ikskjúːz/eks-] *v.* tsumi o yurusu ; benkai suru. *n.* kamben ; benkai ; wabi ; kōjitsu.

execrable [éksikrəbl] *a.* norou beki ; jitsu ni hidoi. ～**bly** *ad.*

execrate [éksikreit] *v.* norou ; imi kirau.

execration [èksikréiʃən] *n.* noroi ; zōo ; juso.

execute [éksikjuːt] *v.* jikkō suru ; kansei suru ; shikei o shikkō suru ; jōto suru.

execution [èksikjúːʃən] *n.* jōju ; shukkō ; shikei shukkō. ～**er** *n.* shikei shikkōnin.

executive [igzékjutiv/eg-] *a.* jikkō (shukkō) suru ; gyōseijō no. *n.* gyōseibu ; gyōseikan. **the E**～ *n.* (*Am.*) Daitōryō.

executor [igzékjutə/eg-] *n.* (*leg.*) shitei yuigon shukkōnin.
exegesis [èksidʒí:sis] *n.* (*pl.* **-ses** [-si:z]) chūshaku ; keiten no
exemplar [igzémplə] *n.* mohan ; tehon ; ruirei. ⌊chūkai.
exemplary [igzémpləri] *a.* mohan ni naru ; miseshime no.
exemplification [igzèmplifikéiʃən/eg-] *n.* reishō ; rei o agete
  shōmei suru koto.
exemplify [igzémplifai/eg-] *v.* reishō suru.
exempt [igzémpte/g-] *v.*, *a.* menjo suru (sareta). *n.* menjo
exemption [igzémpʃən/eg-] *n.* menjo. ⌊sareta mono.
exercise [éksəsaiz] *n.* jikkō ; renshū ; undō ; shiki. *v.* jikkō
  suru ; hatarakasu ; renshū (suru) saseru ; shimpai saseru. undō suru.
exert [igzə́:t] *v.* hatarakasu ; mochiiru : ∼ *oneself to the utmost*,
  zenryoku o tsukusu.
exertion [igzə́:ʃən] *n.* hataraki ; jinryoku.
exeunt [éksiənt] *v.* (*L.*) taijō suru (*stage direction to the actors*).
exhalation [èkshəléiʃən/ègzəl-] *n.* jōhatsu ; jōhatsuki (*vapour*).
exhale [ekshéil/egzéil] *v.* jōhatsu suru ; hassan suru ; haki
  dasu.
exhaust [igzə́:st] *v.* kara ni suru ; tsukai tsukusu ; shōmō suru ; hirō suru. *n.* (kikan kara) haishutsu ; haiki sōchi. ∼**ing** *a.*
  hone no oreru. ∼**ing pipe** [-paip] *n.* haiki-kan.
exhaustible [igzə́:stibl/eg-] *a.* tsukaitsukusu koto no dekiru.
exhaustion [igzə́:stʃən/eg-] *n.* shōmō ; hirō ; tsukarehateru
  koto.
exhaustive [igzə́:stiv/eg-] *a.* nokorinai ; tetteitekina.
exhibit [igzíbit/eg-] *v.* (soto ni dashite) miseru ; (shite) miseru ; chinretsu suru. *n.* tenji ; shuppimbutsu ; shōkobukken. ∼
  -ion [eksibíʃən] *n.* hirogete miseru koto ; hakurankai ; tenrankai. ∼**or** [igzíbitə/eg-] *n.* shuppin-nin.
exhilarate [igzíləreit/eg-] *v.* yōkini suru ; ki o hikitateru. ∼
  tion [igzìləréiʃən/eg-] *n.* genkizukeru koto ; yukai ; yōki.
exhort [igzə́:t, eg-] *v.* susumeru ; kunkai suru. ∼**ation** [ègzɔ:t-
  éiʃən/èks-] *n.* kankoku ; kunkai.
exhumation [èkshju:méiʃən] *n.* hakkutsu.
exhume [ekshjú:m/igzjú:m] *c.* hori dasu ; hakkutsu suru.
exigence [éksidʒəns/égz-] *n.* kikyū (*urgent need*) ; kinkyū.

exigent [éksidʒənt/égz-] *a.* kinkyū no; sashisematta.

exile [éksail/égz-] *n.* tsuihō (*being banished*); ruzainin, nagashimono, bōmeisha. *v.* tsuihō suru.

exist [igzíst/eg-] *v.* sonzai suru; seison suru. ~**ence** [igzístəns/eg-] *n.* sonzai; seison; seikatsu : *struggle of* ~, seison kyōsō. ~**ent** [igzístənt/eg-] *a.* sonzai suru; genson no. ~**entialism** [igzisténʃəlizm] *n.* jitsuzonshugi. ~**ing** *a.* sonzai suru; seison suru; genson no.

exit [éksit] *n.* deguchi; taikyo; shikyo; taijō.

exodus [éksədəs] *n.* kuni o deru koto; (E-) (*Brit.*) Isuraerujin no Ejiputo taikyo; Shutsu Ejiputoki.

exonerate [igzɔ́nəreit/eg-] *v.* omoni o torinozoite yaru; hinan kara kaihō suru; muzai ni naru.

exoneration [igzɔ̀nəréiʃən/eg-] *n.* muzai; menzai.

exorbitance [igzɔ́:bitəns/eg-] *n.* kado; do ga sugiru koto; ⌈muhō.

exorbitant [igzɔ́:bitənt/eg-] *a.* hōgaina. ~**ly** *ad.* hōgaini.

exorcise, ~**cize** [éksɔ:saiz/ekz-] *v.* mayoke o suru; harai kiyomeru.

exorcism [éksɔ:sizəm/ékz-] *n.* mayoke. ⌊meru.

exordium [eksɔ́:diəm/egz-] (*pl.* -**dia**, -**s**) *n.* shogen; bōtō.

exoteric [èksoutérik] *a.* soto no; kōkai no; tsūzokutekina.

exotic [egzɔ́tik/eks-] *a.* gairai no; gaikokusan no; ikokufū no. *n.* gairaibutsu; gairaigo.

expand [ikspǽnd/eks-] *v.* hirogeru (garu); kakuchō suru; fukuramu. ⌈koto.

expanse [ikspǽns/eks-] *n.* hirogari; bōchō; soto ni hirogaru

expansible [ikspǽnsibl/eks-] *a.* hirogari uru; bōchōsei no.

expansion [ikspǽnʃən/eks-] *n.* kakuchō; bōchō; hirogari.

expansionist [ikspǽnʃənist] *n.* bōchōronja; (*Am.*) ryōdo kakuchōronja.

expansive [ikspǽnsiv/eks-] *a.* bōchō suru; hiroi; kōdaina.

expatiate [ekspéiʃieit] *v.* fuen shite toku.

expatiation [ekspèiʃiéiʃən/iks-] *n.* fuen.

expatriate [ekspǽtrieit/-péit-] *v.* tsuihō suru. *n.* tsuihō sareta mono; bōmeisha.

expatriation [ekspǽtriéiʃən/-péit-] *n.* tsuihō; kokuseki ridatsu.

expect [ikspékt] *v.* kitai suru; omou; sōzō suru.

expectancy [ikspéktənsi] *n.* kitai.

expectant [ikspéktənt] *a.* kitai suru; suitei no.
expectation [èkspektéiʃən] *n.* kitai : ~ *of life,* heikin jumyō.
expectorate [ekspéktəreit/iks-] *v.* tsuba ya tan o haku.
expectoration [ekspèktəréiʃən/iks-] *n.* tsuba ya tan o haku koto; tsuba; tan.
expedience, -ency [ikspí:diəns, -ənsi] *n.* bengi; tokushitsu; tsugō; tokusaku; bengi shugi.
expedient [ikspí:diənt] *a.* bengi no; rinki no. *n.* shudan; hōben. ~ly *ad.* bengijō; hōbentekini.
expedite [ékspidait] *v.* saisoku suru; hakadorasu; hassō suru.
expedition [ekspidíʃən] *n.* ensei; tanken; tankentai. jinsoku ~ary [-əri] *a.* ensei no; tanken(tai) no.
expeditious [ekspidíʃəs] *a.* jinsokuna. ~ly *ad.* jinsokuni. ~ness *n.* jinsoku.
expel [ikspél/eks-] *v.* oidasu; hassha suru.
expend [ikspénd/eks-] *v.* tsuiyasu; shōhi suru (*on*).
expenditure [ikspénditʃə/eks-] *n.* shōhi; keihi; shishutsugaku.
expense [ikspéns/eks-] *n.* shōhi; shuppi; (*usu. pl.*) hiyō : *at the ~ of,* no kane de; ni meiwaku o kakete.
expensive [ikspénsiv/eks-] *a.* hiyō no kakaru; kōkana. ~ly *ad.* tagaku no hiyō o kakete. ~ness *n.* kane no kakaru koto; kōkani tsuku koto.
experience [ikspíəriəns/eks-] *n.* keiken. *v.* keiken suru.
experienced [ikspíəriənst/eks-] *a.* keiken no aru; rōrenna.
experiment [ikspérimənt/eks-] *n.* jikken kokoromi. *v.* jikken suru.
experimental [ikspèrimént(ə)l/eks-] *a.* jikken no. ~ly *ad.* jikkentekini; jikkenjō.
expert [ékspə:t] *n.* rōrenka; semmonka. ~ [ikspə́:t/eks-] *a.* rōrenna. ~ly [ikspə́:tli] *ad.* tegiwayoku; kōmyōni. ~ness [ikspə́:tnis] *n.* semmonka taru koto; jukuren.
expiate [ékspieit] *v.* tsumi o aganau; tsugunau. ~tion [ekspiéiʃən] *n.* hoshō; tsumihoroboshi. ~tory [ékspiətəri] *a.* aganai no; tsumihoroboshi no.
expiration [ekspəréiʃən] *n.* iki o hakidasu koto; kigen ga o-waru koto; manki; manryō. ⌈naru.
expire [ikspáiə/eks-] *v.* iki o haku; iki ga taeru; manki ni

explain [ikspléin/eks-] *v.* (riyū o) setsumei suru.
explanation [eksplənéiʃən] *n.* setsumei ; bemmei ; shakumei.
explanatory [iksplǽnətəri/eks-] *a.* setsumei no.
expletive [iksplí:tiv/eks-] *a.* tsuikateki no. *n.* muimina go.
explicable [éksplikəbl] *a.* setsumei dekiru.
explicit [iksplísit/eks-] *a.* meihakuna ; akarasama no. **~ly**
ad. meihakuni ; hanzen to. **~ness** *n.* meihaku ; akarasamana
koto.
explode [iksplóud/eks-] *v.* bakuhatsu saseru (suru).
exploit [iksplóit/eks-] *v.* (rikotekini) riyō suru. ~ [éksplɔit]
n. yūkanna okonai ; tegara ; kōseki. ⌈riyō.
exploitation [eksplɔitéiʃən] *n.* shigen no kaihatsu ; rikoteki no
exploration [eksplɔːréiʃən] *n.* tanken ; tōsa.
explore [iksplɔ́ː/eks-] *v.* tanken suru ; saguru ; tōsa suru. **~r**
[-rə] *n.* tankenka.
explosion [iksplóuʒən/eks-] *n.* bakuhatsu ; haretsu.
explosive [iksplóusiv/eks-] *a.* bakuhatsu no ; (*phon.*) haretsuon
no. *n.* bakuretsubutsu ; bakuyaku ; (*phon.*) haretsuon.
exponent [ekspóunənt] *n.* setsumeisha ; daihyōsha (tenkeiteki) ; (*math.*) shisū (*index*).
export [ékspɔːt] *n.* yushutsu ; yushutsuhin (*usu. pl.*). *v.* [eks-
pɔ́ːt] yushutsu suru. **~able** [-pɔ́ːtəbl] *a.* yushutsu muki no.
~er [ikspɔ́ːtə] *n.* yushutsusha. **~ation** [ekspɔːtéiʃən] *n.* yushutsu.
expose [ikspóuz/eks-] *v.* sarasu (*leave unprotected*) ; abaku chinretsu suru : ...*be* ~*d to ridicule*, waraimono ni naru. *have one's
secret* ~*d*, himitsu ga abakareru. ~ *something for sale*, aru
mono o uri ni dasu.
exposé [ekspóuzeì] *n.* (*Fr.*) jijitsu no mōshitate ; bakuro.
exposition [ekspozíʃən/-pɔz-] *n.* setsumei ; tenran ; hakurankai.
expositor [ikspózitə] *n.* setsumeisha ; kaisetsusha.
expository [ikspózitəri] *a.* kaishaku no ; setsumei no.
expostulate [ikspóstjuleit/eks-] *v.* isameru (*with*) : ~ *with someone about* (*on*) *something*, aru koto ni tsuite aru hito o isameru.
expostulation [ikspɔstjuléiʃən/eks-] *n.* isame ; kangen.
exposure [ikspóuʒə/eks-] *n.* sarasu (*expose*) koto ; bakuro ;
tekihatsu ; roshutsu.

expound [ekspáund/iks-] v. kaishaku suru; setsumei suru.

express [exprés/iks-] v. iiarawasu; shiboridasu; shikyūbin de okuru. a. meihakuna; tokushu no; kyūkō no: *an ~ company*, tsūungaisha. n. sokutatsu; (*Am.*) kyūkōressha (*~ train*); kyūshi. **~age** [-idʒ] n. (*Am.*) sokutatsu; sokutatsuryō. **~ly** ad. meihakuni; hakkiri to.

expression [ikspréʃən/eks-] n. hyōgen; hyōjō; iiarawashi (kata); jiku; goku.

expressive [iksprésiv/eks-] a. arawasu (*of*); hyōgenryoku ni tomu; imi shinchōna. **~ness** n. hyōgenryoku no yutakasa; imi shinchō.

expulsion [ikspʌ́lʃən/eks-] n. tsuihō; nakama kara nozoku koto; jomei; joseki.

expunge [ikspʌ́ndʒ/eks-] v. nuguikesu; massatsu suru.

expurgate [ékspə(:)geit] v. sakujo suru; (futekitōna kasho) o **expurgation** [ekspə(:)géiʃən] n. sakujo. ⌊kezuru.

exquisite [ékskwizit/ekskwízit] a. zetsumyōna; kotta; surudoi; subarashii. n. mekashiya; sharemono. **~ly** ad. subarashiku; konoue naku. **~ness** n. subarashisa; seikō; zetsumyō.

extant [ekstǽnt/ékstənt] a. genson no; genni nokotte iru. *cf.* extinct.

extemporaneous [ekstempəréinjəs] a. sokuseki no; sokkyō no (*extempore*).

extemporary [ikstémpərəri/eks-] a. sokuseki no; sonoba no.

extempore [ekstémpəri] a., ad. sokuseki no(ni); sokkyō no(ni); buttsuke homban.

extemporize [ekstémpəraiz] v. rinki ni suru; sokuseki ni tsukuru; sokuseki ni hanasu. ⌈su).

extend [iksténd/eks-] v. nobasu; hirogeru (garu); oyobu (bo-**extensible** [iksténsibl] a. hirogaru; nobiru.

extension [iksténʃən/eks-] n. kakuchō; enchō; hirogari; zōchiku. **~ladder,** n. kuridashi hashigo. **university ~,** n. daigaku kōkai kōza.

extensive [iksténsiv/eks-] a. hiroi; tebiroi; endaina. **~ly** [-li] ad. hiroku; daikiboni. **~ness** n. hirosa; daikibo; enchō.

extent [ikstént/eks-] n. hirosa; gendo; han'i. *to a certain ~,* ikubun ka; tashō. *to the* ～ *of*, ...made;...hodo.

extenuate [iksténjueit/eks-] *v. (take the circumstances into consideration)* jōjō o shakuryō suru; karuku shiyō to iiwake o suru.

extenuation [ikstenjuéiʃən/eks-] *n.* keigen; shakuryō.

exterior [ekstíəriə] *a.* soto no; hyōmen no. *n.* gaimen; gaikan.

exterminate [ekstə́:mineit] *v.* bokumetsu suru; konzetsu suru *(destroy completely).*

extermination [ekstə̀:minéiʃən] *n.* bokumetsu; konzetsu *(complete destruction).*

external [ekstə́:n(ə)l] *a.* gaibu no; gaikai no; hyōmen no; gaikoku no. *n. (pl.)* gaikan; gaikei. ～**ly** *ad.* gaimen ni; gaikenjō.

extinct [ikstíŋ(k)t/eks-] *a.* kieta; zetsumetsu shita. ⌈tsubō.

extinction [ikstíŋkʃən/eks-] *n.* shōmetsu; zetsumetsu; me-

extinguish [ikstíŋgwiʃ/eks-] *v.* kesu (hikari nado o); zetsumetsu suru; chimmoku saseru; (fusai o) haraimodosu. ～**able** [-əbl] *a.* kesu koto ga dekiru. ～**er** [-ə] *n.* shōkaki.

extirpate [ékstə:peit] *v.* bokumetsu suru; (akufū nado) o nedayashi ni suru.

extirpation [ekstə:péiʃən] *n.* konzetsu; bokumetsu.

extol(l) [ikstól/eks-/tóul] *v.* homeageru(-soyasu); gekishō suru *(praise highly).*

extort [ikstó:t/eks-] *v.* kyōyō suru; yusuritoru *(obtain by threats, etc.)*; kojitsukeru *(of sophistry).*

extortion [ikstó:ʃən/eks-] *n.* kyōyō; gōdatsu; sakushu *(extort de te ni ireru koto).*

extortionate [ikstó:ʃ(ə)nit/eks-] *a.* gōdatsuteki; hōgaina *(by way of something like extortion).*

extra [ékstrə] *a.* yobun no; rinji no; tokubetsuna. *n.* yobun no mono; warimashi-kin; gōgai; 〈shimbun ya (zashi nado no) tokubetsu-gō.

extract[ékstrækt] *n.* chūshutsu-butsu; ekisu; bassui. [ekstrǽkt] *v.* hikinuku; nukitoru; chūshutsu suru; bassui suru.

extraction [ikstrǽkʃən/eks-] *n.* nukitori; tekishutsu; bassui *(extracting)*; umare; sujō *(descent).*

extradite [ékstrədait] *v.* tōbōsha *(a fugitive)* o sono kuni no tōkyoku *(legal authority)* ni hikiwatasu *(deliver).*

extradition [ekstrədíʃən] *n.* tōbō hannin hikiwatashi (*surrender of fugitive to the legal authority*).

extraneous [ekstréinjəs] *a.* gaibu kara kita (*from outward*) ; mukankei no (*foreign*). ~**ly** *ad.* gaibutekini.

extraordinary [ekstrɔ́:dinəri/ikstrɔ́:dn(ə)ri] *a.* hijōna ; hōgaina ; tokubetsuna (*specially employed*). *n.* (*pl.*) tokubetsu-teate (*special allowance*). ~**rily** [ikstrɔ́:d(i)nərili/eks-] *ad.* hijōni (*most unusually*) ; odoroku bakari ni (*astonishingly*).

extraterritorial [ékstrətèritó:riəl/eks-] *a.* ryōdogai no (*beyond territorial limits*) ; chigaihōken no. ~**lity** [ékstrətèritɔ:riǽliti] *n.* chigaihōken.

extravagance [ikstrǽvəgəns/-si/eks-], ~**ancy** [-ənsi] *n.* shashi (*luxury*) ; rampi (*lavish spending*) ; musessei.

extravagant [ikstrǽvəgənt/eks-] *a.* kado no (*excessive*) ; hōgai no (*unreasonable*) ; zeitakuna (*luxurious*) ; rampi no (*lavishing*). ~**ly** *ad.* hōgai ni ; zeitaku ni ; rōhitekimi.

extravaganza [ekstrævəgǽnzə] *n.* kyōkijimita bungaku (*fantastic play*) ; kyōtai (*peculiar behavior*).

extreme [ikstrí:m/eks-] *a.* kyokutanna ; kagekina. *n.* kyokutan (*pl.* ryōkyokutan) : ~**s** *meet*, ryōkyokutan wa tsune ni itchi suru. *go to* ~**s** = *run to an* ~, kyokutan ni hashiru. *in the* ~, kyokutanni ; kiwamete. ~**ly** *ad.* kyokutanni ; hijōni.

extremist [ikstrí:mist] *n.* kagekironja ; kyokutanshugisha.

extremity [ikstrémiti/eks-] *n.* mattan ; hate ; kyokutan ; kyokudo ; kyūchi. (*pl.*) teashi. saigo no shudan : *at the* ~ *of*, no mattan ni. *proceed* (*go*) *to* ~**ies**, saigo no shudan o toru. *the* ~**ies**, shishi ; teashi. *to the last* ~, zettai zetsumei no tokoro made.

extricate [ékstrikeit] *v.* sukuidasu ; manukaresasu (*from*).

extrication [ekstrikéiʃən] *n.* sukuidashi ; kaihō ; dasshutsu.

extrinsic [ekstrínsik] *a.* gaibu no ; tsuketashi no ; koyū de nai. ~**ally** [-əli] *ad.* futaitekini ; gaibu kara.

extrude [ekstrú:d] *v.* oshidasu ; oidasu)

exuberance [igzjú:bərəns/eg-] *n.* hammo ; hōfu ; juntaku.

exuberant [igzjú:bərənt/eg-] *a.* hammoshita ; shigetta ; hanayakana. ~**ly** *ad.* oishigette ; hōfuni ; yutakani.

exudation [eksju(:)déiʃən] *n.* shimideru koto ; bumpibutsu.

exude [igzjú:d/eksjú:d] *v.* shimidasaseru; shimideru.

exult [igzʌ́lt/eg-] *v.* hijōni yorokobu; kachihokoru.

exultant [igzʌ́ltənt/eg-] *a.* ōyorokobi no; kachihokoru (*exult in one's victory*).

exultation [ègzʌltéiʃən/èksʌl-] *n.* ōyorokobi.

exultingly [igzʌ́ltiŋli] *ad.* ōyorokobi de; kyōki shite.

eye [ai] *n.* me. kansatsuryoku; shiryoku; me no katachi o shita mono, hari no medo. *be all eyes*, isshin ni chūi suru. *have an ~ to*, ni me o tsukeru (yashin o motsu); o nerau. *in one's ~s*. ...no miru tokoro dewa. ~**ball** [⌐bɔ:l] *n.* gankyū. ~**brow** [⌐brau] *n.* mayu; mayuge. ~**glasses** [⌐glɑ:siz] (*pl.*) *n.* gankyō; megane. ~**hole** [-houl] *n.* ganka; nozoki-ana. ~**lash** [⌐læʃ] *n.* matsuge. ~**let** [⌐lit] *n.* himotōshiana. ~**lid** [-lid] *n.* mabuta. ~**piece** [⌐pi:s] *n.* me ni kuttsuite iru megane. ~**shot** [⌐ʃɔt] *n.* shikai; me no todoku han'i. ~**sight** [⌐sait] *n.* shiryoku; shiya. ~**sore** [⌐sɔ:] *n.* mezawari. ~**tooth** [⌐tu:θ] kenshi; itokiriba. ~**water** [⌐wɔ:tə] *n.* megusuri; senganzai. ~**witness** [⌐witnis] *n.* mokugekisha.

eyre [ɛə] *n.* junkai; junkai saibansho.

eyrie, aerie [ɛ́əri/áiəri] *n.* mōkinrui no su; hina.

F

F, f [ef] *n.* (*pl.* **E's, fs** [efs]) Eigo *alphabet* no dai-6-bamme
no moji.

f., fr. [fræŋk] furan (*Fr.* no kahei).

Fabian [féibiən] *a.* (Rōma no) *Febius* shōgun no. *n.* Febian
Kyōkai-in : **~Society,** Febian Kyōkai (Igirisu no shakaishugisha no dantai).

fable [féibl] *n.* gūwa ; tsukuribanashi. *v.* tsukuribanashi o
suru. **~d** [feibld] *a.* monogatari de yūmeina ; densetsuteki.

fabric [fǽbrik] *n.* orimono ; kireji. kōzō. tatemono. **~ant**
[-ənt], **~ator** [-eitə] *n.* seizōsha ; kumitatenin. **~ate** [-eit] *v.*
tsukuritateru. **~ation** [-éiʃən] *n.* seisaku. gizō (*forgery*).

fabulist [fǽbjulist] *n.* gūwasakusha.

fabulize [fǽbjulaiz] *v.* gūwa o tsukuru.

fabulous [fǽbjuləs] *a.* densetsutekina. shinjirarenai ; hōgaina.
~ly *ad.* densetsutekini. uso no yōni. **~ness** *n.* densetsuteki
de aru koto.

facade [fəsáːd] *n.* shōmen (tatemono (*building*) no) ; shōmen kara mita tokoro.

face [feis] *n.* kao. memboku. mojiban (*of clock*). gakumen (*face-
value*) : *in* (*the*) **~** *of,* ni mo kakawarazu ; ni sakaratte. *make*
~s, ironna kao o suru. *pull* (*or make*) *a long* **~,** kanashisōna kao
o suru. *put a bold* **~** *on,* nani kuwanu kao o suru. *put a good*
~ *on,* umaku tori tsukurou ; gaman suru. *set one's* **~** *against,*
…ni hankō suru. *show one's* **~,** kao o dasu. **~** *down,* odoshitsukeru. **~** *it out,* daitanni oshitōsu. **~ache** [⌣eik] *n.* gammen shinkeitsū. **~** **guard,** *n.* kendō no men. **~** **powder,**
oshiroi.

facer [féisə] *n.* (*box.*) kao e no dageki. fui no nankan.

facet [fǽsit] *n.* hōseki nado no ōku no men ; kizami. **~ed**
[-id] *a.* ōku no men no (konchū no fukugan no yōni).

facetious [fəsíːʃəs] *n.* kokkeina ; odoketa. **~ly** *ad.* odokete. **~
ness** [-nis] *n.* odoketa koto.

facia [fǽʃiə] *n.* (*Brit.*) (tentō no) kamban.

facial [féiʃəl] *a.* kao no. *n.* (*Am. col.*) gammen.

facile [fǽsail/-sil] *a.* yasashii. binshōna ; jōzuna. kumishiyasui.

facilitate [fəsíliteit] *v.* yōini suru ; tsugō yoku suru.

facilitation [fəsìlitéiʃən] *n.* yōini suru koto ; benri.

facility [fəsíliti] *n.* yasashisa ; yōina koto : *with* ～, yōini ; sura-sura to.

facing [féisiŋ] *n.* hogo ya sōshoku no tame ni kabuseru mono ; keshō omote : *go through one's* ～*s*, ude o tamesareru ; kunren o ukeru. *put a person through his* (*her*) ～*s*, hito no giryō o tamesu ; shimpei o kunren suru.

facsimile [fæksímili] *n.* mosha ; fukusha ; ikiutsushi.

fact [fækt] *n.* jijitsu ; jissai. (*pl.*) ronkyo : *as a matter of* ～, jissai wa ; jitsu wa. *in* ～, jissai wa ; yōsuru ni. *in point of* ～, jijitsu-jō. *in the* ～, okonatte iru saichū ni. ⌐(teki) no.

faction [fǽkʃən] *n.* tōha ; totō ; tōhashin. ～al [-(ə)l] *a.* tōha

factious [fǽkʃəs] *a.* tōhateki ; hankōteki no. ～ly *ad.* tōha o kunde. ⌐de nai.

factitious [fæktíʃəs] *a.* jin'iteki no ; hito no tsukutta ; shizen

factitive [fǽktitiv] *a.* sakuiteki no ; (*gram.*) mokuteki hogo (*complement*) o hitsuyō to suru tadōshi (*factitive verb*), sakui-dōshi.

factor [fǽktə] *a.* dairishō ; ton'ya. (*math.*) inshi ; insū. anzen-ritsu. ～**ship** [-ʃip] *n.* ton'ya.

factory [fǽkt(ə)ri] *n.* kōjō. dairiten : **F～ Law** (*or* **Acts**), *n.* kō-jōhō. ～ **ship**, kōsakusen.

factual [fǽktjuəl] *a.* jijitsu no ; jissai no.

faculty [fǽk(ə)lti] *n.* nōryoku ; sainō ; karada no hataraki ; (daigaku no) gakubu ; kyōjudan ; shokuin ; tokken.

fad [fæd] *n.* monozuki ; ichiji no ryūkō ; dōraku.

fade [feid] *v.* iro aseru, asesaseru ; (hana ga) shibomu ; usuragu ; kieru. ～-**in** [-in] *n.* yōmei, gamen nado ga shidaini hakkiri naru (eiga). ～-**out** [-aut] *n.* yōan (shidai ni kuraku naru (eiga).

faecal [fí:kəl] *a*, **faeces** [fí:si:z] *n.* =**fecal, feces.**

fag [fæg] *v.* akuseku hataraku. tsukaresaseru. (kakyūsei o) kokitsukau. *n.* kurushii shigoto. hirō. jōkyūsei ni tsukawa-reru kakyūsei. (*sl.*) kamimaki-tabako. ～ **end**, (mono no) mattan ; nokorikuzu.

fag(g)ot [fǽgɔt] *n.* makitaba ; soda. *v.* tabaneru.

Fahrenheit [fúːrənhait] *n.*, *a.* Kashi kandankei (no).

fail [feil] *v.* fusoku suru. otoroeru. shisokonau (*in*). hasan suru.
n. shippai : *without* ~, kanarazu. ~**ing** *n.* ketten. shippai ;
hasan. *conj.* …no nai toki wa. ~**ure** [-jə] *n.* shippai. shippai-
sha. suijaku.

fain [fein] *a.* *ad.* yorokonde.

faint [feint] *a.* yowai. kasukana ; kizetsu suru (*away*). *n.* kizetsu.
~**ing** *n.* kizetsu. ~**ly** *ad.* kasukani. yowayowashiku. ~**-
ness** *n.* kasuka. suijaku. mukiryoku.

fair [feə] *n.* teiki-ichi. (*Am.*) hakurankai. *a.* kireina ; irojirona.
jōtenki no ; kōmeiseidaina ; kanari no : *ad.* teineini ; kōmei-
seidaini. ~ **copy** *n.* seisho. ~**play** *n.* kōmei seidaina yarikata. **the** ~ **sex** *n.* josei. ~**ly** *ad.* tadashiku ; sōtōni ; kireini
~**ness** [-nis] *n.* irojiro ; kōhei ; junchō. ~**-spoken** [-spóuk-
(ə)n] *a.* kuchisaki no umai ; jōhinna.

fairy [fέəri] *n.* shinsen ; yōsei. *a.* shinsen no. sōzōjō no. yūbina.
~**land** [-lænd] otogi no kuni ; senkyō. ~**tale** [-teil] *n.* otogi
banashi ; dōwa.

faith [feiθ] *n.* shinkō ; shinnen. **bad** ~ *n.* fujitsu ; haishin. ~
less [fέiθlis] *a.* shinnen no nai ; fu(chū)jitsuna ; giman no.

faithful [fέiθf(u)l] *a.* chūjitsuna. ~**ly** *ad.* chūjitsuni. ~**ness**
chūjitsu ; magokoro.

fake [feik] *n.* sagi ; gomakashi ; kyohō ; gomakashi-mono. *v.*
gomakasu ; umaku koshiraeageru. *a.* (*Am.*) inchiki no.

faker [fέikə] *n.* petenshi ; ikasamashi ; daidō shōnin.

fakir [fέikə/fəkíə] *n.* (Kaikyō no) takuhatsusō.

falchion [fɔ́ːl(t)ʃən] *n.* engetsu-tō ; seiryū-tō.

falcon [fɔ́ː(l)kən/fɔ́ːkn] *n.* (*bird*) taka ~**er** [-ə] *n.* takashō ; taka-
tsukai. ~**ry** [-ri] *n.* takatsukaijutsu. taka-gari.

fall [fɔːl] *v.* **fell, fallen; falling.** *v.* ochiru ; taoreru ; horobiru ;
(dekigoto ga) okoru ; daraku suru : ~ *away*, tōzakaru. ~
back, shirizoku. ~ *back on* (*upon*), ni tayoru. ~ *calm*, shizumaru. ~ *in*, ochikomu. ~ *in with*, futo deau. ~ *off*, ochiru ;
genjiru. ~ *on* (*or upon*), no mi ni furikakaru ; o kōgeki suru.
(aru hi ga) …ni ataru. ~ *out*, arasou ; okoru (*happen*) ; retsu

o hanareru. ～ *over*, taoreru. ～ *through*, shippai suru. ～ *to*,
kyūni hajimeru; o ukeru. *n.* rakka; geraku; daraku; shik-
kyaku; taki. (*Am.*) aki. fōru (*wrestling*) *a.* aki no.

fallacious [fəléiʃəs] *a.* fugōrina; itsuwari no. ～**ly** *ad.* giman-
fallacy [fǽləsi] *n.* ronrijō no ayamari; kyogi; ⌊tekini.

fallen [fɔ́:ln] *v. see* : **fall**. *a.* taoreta; daraku shita; shinda.

fallibility [fælibíliti] *n.* machigaiyasui koto.

fallible [fǽlibl] *a.* ayamariyasui; ate ni naranai.

falling [fɔ́:liŋ] *a.* rakka suru. *n.* rakka; daraku. ～ **star**, ryūsei.
～ **sickness** *n.* tenkan.

fallow [fǽlou] *a.* kōsaku o yasunde iru; kyūsaku shite iru
n. kyūkanchi. *v.* kyūkan suru; yasumete aru tochi.

false [fɔ:ls/fɔls] *a.* fushōjikina; itsuwari no; ayamatta; fuhōna; nise no. ～ **key**, *n.* aikagi. ～ **tooth**, *n.* gishi. ～**hearted**
[⸝hɑ́:tid] *a.* itsuwari no kokoro o idaite iru; nise no. ～
hood [⸝hud] *n.* itsuwari; uso. ～**ly** *ad.* itsuwatte. ～**ness** *n.*
giman; fujitsu.

falsetto [fɔ(:)lsétou] *n.* (*mus.*) uragoe.

falsification [fɔ(:)lsifikéiʃən] *n.* gizō; bunshogizō.

falsify [fɔ́:lsifai] *v.* gizō suru; itsuwaru; itsuwari de aru koto
o shōmei suru.

falsity [fɔ́:lsiti] *n.* kyogi; uso; itsuwari.

falter [fɔ́:ltə] *v.* yoromeku. domoru; kuchigomoru. ～**ing**
[-riŋ] *a.* yoromeku. kuchigomoru; domoru. ～**ingly** [-riŋli]
ad. yoromeki nagara; domori nagara. ⌈yūmeina.

fame [feim] *n.* meisei; hyōban. *v.* nadakaku suru. ～**d** [-d] *a.*

familiar [fəmíljə] *a.* shitashii. nichijō no. *n.* shin'yū. mahō
tsukai ni tsukawareru ma. ～**ly** *ad.* shitashiku.

familiarity [fəmiliǽriti] *n.* shimmitsu; kon'i.

familiarize [fəmíljəraiz] *v.* narasu; najimaseru.

family [fǽmili] *n.* kazoku. iegara. ichimon. (ryōshin o nozoite)
shijo. zoku; ka (seibutsu) : *in a* ～ *way*, uchitokete. *in the* ～
way, ninshin shite.

famine [fǽmin] *n.* kikin; ketsubō; ue; kiga.

famish [fǽmiʃ] *v.* ueru; uesaseru.

famous [féiməs] *a.* yūmeina. ～**ly** *ad.* yūmeini.

fan [fæn] *n.* sensu; sempūki; mi (*winnow*); (*col.*) (kyōgi, eiga

nado no) fan; nesshinna aikōka : *movie* ～, eigakyō. *v.* aogu;
sendō suru; mi de fukiwakeru.
fanatic [fənǽtik] *n.* kyōshinsha; nekkyōsha. *a.* kyōshinteki
(na). ～**al** [-(ə)l] *a.* nekkyōtekina. ～**ally** [-əli] *ad.* nekkyō
shite. ～**ism** [-sizm] *n.* nekkyō; kyōshin.
fancy [fǽnsi] *a.* ishō o korashita. kimagure no. *v.* sōzōsuru;
unuboreru; ...shitagaru. ～ **ball** [-bɔ:l] kasō butōkai. ～ **dress**
n. kasōfuku. ～**goods** *n.* komamono. *n.* sōzō; kūsō; kimagure; shikō; konomi; dōraku : *take a* ～ *to*, o suku; ni ho-
reru. the ～ *n.* kōzurenchū. ～**ied** [-d] *a.* kūsō no. ～**ier** [-ə]
n. kūsōka; kōzuka; (hana, tori, inu nado no) aikōsha. ～**ful**
[-f(u)l] *a.* kūsō ni fukerigachina; kūsōtekina; kakūna. ～
fully [-fəli] *ad.* kūsōtekini.
fane [fein] *n.* jiin; shinden.
fanfare [fǽnfeə] *n.* fanfāre; hanayakana rappa no suisō.
fang [fæŋ] *n.* (inu nado no) kiba; (hebi no) dokuga.
fantasia [fæntéiziə] *n.* (*mus.*) gensōgaku.
fantastic [fæntǽstik] *a.* kūsōtekina; toritome no nai. ～**ally**
[-əli] *ad.* iyōni; gensōtekini.
fantasy [fǽntəsi] *n.* kūsō; kimagurena kangae; gensōkyoku.
fantoccini [fɑ:ntotʃí:ni] *n.* (*pl*) ayatsuri ningyō.
FAO (*Food and Agricaltural Organization*) Kokuren Shokuryō
Nōgyō Kikō.
far [fɑ:] *a.* harukana; tōi : *ad.* harukani. *a* ～ *cry*, taihen empō.
as ～ *as*, dake; made. *by* ～, ōini. *so* ～, kore made wa. *so* ～
as, ...dake dewa; ...suru kagiri wa. ～**away** [-ʃrəwéi/-rəwei] *a.*
empō no. ～**famed** [fá:feimd] *a.* nadakai. ～**fetched** [-fétʃt]
a. kojitsuke no; fushizenna. ～**reaching** [fá:rí:tʃiŋ] *a.* tōku
e oyobosu; endaina. ～**seeing** [fá:sí:iŋ] *a.* senken no mei
ga aru. ～**sighted** [fá:sáitid] *a.* enshigan no; senken no mei
farce [fɑ:s] *n.* dōke shibai; kudaranu koto. ⌊aru.
farcical [fɑ:sik(ə)l] *a.* kokkeina. ～**ly** [-li] *ad.* kokkeini.
fare [feə] *n.* chingin; jōshachin. jōkyaku. inshoku butsu; ryōri.
v. kurasu. taberu. ryokō suru.
farewell [féəwél] *a.* sōbetsu no; kokubetsu no. *inter.* sayōnara.
n. kokubetsu; sōbetsu.
farina [fəráinə/fərí:nə] *n.* kona; kafun; dempun; fummatsu-

jō no mono.

farinaceous [færinéiʃəs] *a.* kokumotsu no kona no; dempun shitsu no; kona no yōna.

farm [fɑːm] *n.* nōjō; nōen. *v.* kōsaku(o) suru. **~er** [-ə] *n.* nōfu; sozei toritate ukeoinin. **~house** [-́háus] *n.* nōjō no kaoku; nōka. **~ing** [-iŋ] *n.* nōjō. **~yard** [-́jɑ́ːd] *n.* nōka no niwa.

faro [féərou] *n.* isshu no torampu asobi. ⌈tetsujo.

farrier [fǽriə] *n.* teitetsukō; jūi. **~y** [-ri] *n.* teitetsujutsu; teifarrow [fǽrou] *n.* (buta ga) ko o umu koto; (buta no) hitoharago. *v.* (buta ga) ko o umu.

fart [fɑːt] *n.* he; hōhi. *v.* hōhi suru.

farther [fɑːðə] *a.* motto tōi. sono ue no. *ad.* motto tōku. sono ue ni (*besides*): **~** *on,* motto saki ni (de); ato de. *No* **~***!* mō yoi! mō wakkata! **~most** [-moust] *a.* ichiban tōi.

farthest [fɑːðəst] *a.* mottomo tōi. *ad.* tōku.

farthing [fɑːðiŋ] *n.* (*Brit.*) dōka; 1/4 *penny.* goku wazuka.

fasces [fǽsiːz] *n.* kodai Rōma de mochiita kōkan no shirushi (tabaneta bō no naka ni ono no ha o nozokashita mono).

fascinate [fǽsineit] *v.* sukumaseru (*by terror*). *a snake* **~***s its prey,* hebi ga emono o sukumaseru. nōsatsu suru (*charm*). **~ting** [-tiŋ] *a.* miwakutekina; uttori saseru. **~tion** [fæsinéiʃən] *n.* miryoku; hito no kokoro o toraeru chikara.

fascine [fəsiːn] *n.* makitaba (zangō nado ni uzumeru).

Fascism [fǽsizm] *n.* Fasizumu (Mussorini no kokusui-shugi).

Fascist [fǽsist] *n.* Italia kokusuitō-in.

fashion [fǽʃən] *n.* fukusō (*dressing*); gyōgi-sahō (*manners*); ippan no hayari. *after (in) a* **~**, tonikaku mā. **~able** [-əbl] *a.* hayari no. **~ably** [-əbli] *ad.* hayari ni.

fast [fɑːst] *a.* hayai; (tokei ga) susunde iru. *adv.* hayaku; shikkari to. *n.* danjiki: **~ day** [-dei] danjikibi.

fasten [fɑːsn] *v.* shikkari shimeru; musubitsukeru. **~ing** [-iŋ] *a.* tomeru.

fastidious [fæstídiəs] *a.* kimuzukashii. **~ly** [-li] *ad.* kimuzukashiku. **~ness** kimuzukashisa.

fat [fæt] *a.* koeta; aburakkoi: **~** *job,* miiri no ii shigoto. *n.* shibō; abura. *v.* futoru; koeru.

fatal [féitl] *a.* inochi ni kakawaru; un no warui. **~ist** [-ist] *n.* ummeironja. ~**ly** *ad.* un waruku.

fatality [fətǽliti] *n.* shukumei (*destiny*).

fate [feit] *n.* mae kara kimatte iru ummei. ~**ful** [-ful] *a.* ummei o sadameru ; ketteitekina ; jūdaina.

father [fáːðə] *n.* chichi ; sosen : the ~ *n* kami (*God*) ; shimpu. *v.* chichioya to naru. ~**hood** [-hud] *n.* chichi taru koto. ~ **-in-law** [ɂinlɔ̀ː] *n.* giri no chichi ; yōfu. ~**land** [-lænd] *n.* sokoku. ~**less** [-lis] *n.* chichinashigo.

fathom [fǽðəm] *n.* hiro (*old popular measure, about 1.828 m.*). *v.* tsuna de fukasa (*depth*) o hakaru. ~**less** [-lis] *a.* soko no shirenai. ~**able** [-əbl] *a.* hakari uru.

fatigue [fətíːg] *n.* hirō. *v.* hirō saseru.

fatling [fǽtliŋ] *n.* (shokuyō ni futoraseta) koushi nado.

fatten [fǽtn] *v.* futorasu ; futoru.

fatty [fǽti] *a.* aburakkoi (*greasy*). *n.* debu ; futotcho.

fatuity [fətjú(ː)iti] *n.* baka ; bakageta koto.

fatuous [fǽtjuəs] *a.* bakana ; pokan to shita.

faucet [fɔːsit] *n.* taru no nomikuchi (*tap*).

fault [fɔːlt] *n.* ayamari. tsumi (*crime*). ara (*defect*). ~**finder** [ɂfàində] *n.* arasagashiya. ~**finding** [-fàindiŋ] *n.* arasagashi. ~**less** *a.* ketten no nai. ~**lessly** *ad.* mōshibun naku.

faulty [fɔ́ːlti] *a.* ketten darake no.

faun [fɔːn] *n.* makiba no kamisama.

fauna [fɔ́ːnə] *n.* (ichi chihō (*district*), ichi jidai (*age*) dake no) dōbutsu.

favo(u)r [féivə] *n.* chōai ; kōi (*good will*). *v.* favour o arawasu : by ~ of, ni takushite. in ~ of, ni sansei shite ; tame ni. ~**able** [féivərəbl] *a.* yūbōna ; tsugō no yoi. ~**bly** [-bli] *ad.* tsugō yoku ; kōi o motte. ~**ed** [-d] *a.* megumareta : *the most* ~*ed nation clause*, saikeikoku jōkan. ~**er** [féiv(ə)rə] *n.* kōi o yoseru hito. ~**ite** [féiv(ə)rit] *n.* okiniiri ; ninkimono. shikōbutsu. *a* kiniiri no. ~**itism** [féiv(ə)ritizm] *n.* ekohiiki ; jōjitsu.

fawn [fɔːn] *n.* kojika ; sono iro. *v.* ko o umu ; jaretsuku.

fealty [fíː(ə)lti] *n.* chūgi.

fear [fiə] *n.* kyōfu ; shimpai. *v.* osoreru ; kizukau. ~**ful** [fíəf(u)l] *a.* osoroshii. ~**less** osorenai. ~**lessly** *ad.* osorezuni. ~**some** [fíəsəm] *a.* osoroshii ; okubyōna (*cowardly*).

feasibility [fi:zibíliti] *n.* kanōsei ; jikkō dekiru (*practicable*)
feasible [fízibl] *a.* kanōna ; jikkō dekiru.   ⌊koto
feast [fì:st] *n., v.* omatsuri ; oiwai. (o suru).
feat [fi:t] *n.* shuren. kōseki (*exploit*).
feather [féðə] *n.* hane ; chōrui (*birds*). show the white ~, hiru-
    mu ; hane o tsukeru ; hane ga haeru. ~y [-ri] *a.* hane no ha-
    eta ; hane no yōna.
feature [fí:tʃə] *n.* tokushoku ; chisei (*geographical*) ; me, hana
    nado. (*pl.*) kao (*face*). *v.* tokushoku o motsu.
febrifuge [fébrifju:dʒ] *n.* (*med.*) genetsu-zai ; netsusamashi.
febrile [fí:brail] *a.* netsu no.
February [fébruəri] *n.* Nigatsu.
fecal [fí:kl] *a.* kasu no ; fun, nyō no.
feces [fí:si:z] (*pl.*) *n.* kasu. haisetsubutsu.
fecund [fékənd] *a.* takusan dekiru ; tochi no koeta (*fertile*).
fecundity [fi:kʌnditi] *n.* tasan ; umi fuyasu chikara (*produc-
fed [fəd] *v. see :* **feed**.   ⌊*tiveness*).
federal [féd(ə)rəl] *a.* rempō no. (*F*~) (*Am.*) hokubu rempō
    dōmei no. ~**ism** [-izm] rempō-shugi ; rempō seido.
federate [fédərit] *a.* dōmei no. *v.* [fédəreit] dōmei saseru.
federation [fedəréiʃən] *n.* dōmei ; rempō (seifu *government*).
fee [fi:] *n.* shareikin ; nyūkaikin (*entrance* ~) ; jugyōryō (*school*
    ~).
feeble [fí:bl] *a.* kayowai. ~**ness** *n.* yowayowashisa. ~**ly** *ad*
    yowaku.
feed [fí:d] *v.* yashinau ; kau (*keep*). *n.* shokuryō. ~**er** [-ə] *n.*
    kaite. ~**ing-bottle** [-iŋ bɔtl] *n.* honyūbin.
feel *v.* [fí:l] **felt ; feeling.** kanzuru ; sawaru ; kandō suru (*be
    moved*). *n.* kanji. ~**er** [fí:lə] *n.* anji ; shokkaku. ~**ing** [fí:l-
    iŋ] *n.* kankaku ; kanjō.
feet [fi:t] *n.* foot no fukusū.
feign [fein] *v.* ...no furi o suru : He ~ed himself mad, kare
    wa kichigai no furi o shita.
feint [feint] *n.* misekake. *v.* itsuwaru ; furi o suru.
fel(d)spar [fel(d)spɑ:] *n.* (*min.*) chōseki.
felicitate [filisiteit] *v.* iwau ; iwai o suru
felicitation [filisitéiʃən] *n.* shukuga ; (o)iwai.

felicitous [filísitəs] *a.* tekisetsuna; kōfukuna (*happy*).

felicity [filísiti] *n.* kōfuku; keiji (*happy event*); meimonku (*well chosen phrase*).

feline [fí:lain] *a.* neko no; neko no yōna (*like a cat*).

fell [fel] *see*; **fall.** *a.* zanninna. *n.* jūhi; kemono no kawa.

fell [fel] *v.* ki o kiritaosu (*cut down*).

fellow [félo(u)] *n.* nakama (*mate*), (Eikoku daigkaku no) tokubetsu kenkyūin; tokutai kōyū. *a.* nakama no. ~ **countryman** [-kántrimən] *n.* dōkokujin. ~ **creature** [-krí:tʃə] *n.* ningen dōshi. ~ **feeling** [-fí:linŋ] *n.* dōjō. ~**ship** [-ʃip] *n.* yūjō, (*Brit.*) *fellow* no chii (kenkyū-hi). shōgaku shikin.

felly [féli], **felloe** [félou] *n.* sharin (*wheel*) no wa-buchi.

felon [félən] *n.* jūzainin; akunin. (*med.*) hyōso (*whitlow*). *a* kyōakuna.

felonious [filóuniəs] *a.* kyōakuna. jūzai no. ~**ly** *ad.* kyōakuni.

felony [féləni] *n.* jūzai; omoi tsumi.

felt [feit] *v. see* : **feel.** *n.* feruto. ~**hat** [-⸍hæt] feruto no bōshi. ~**ing** *n.* feruto no tsukurikata; zairyō.

female [fí:meil] *n.* onna; mesu. *a.* onna (mesu) no.

feminine [féminin] *a.* josei (mesu) no. memeshii (*womanish*) nyūwana (*gentle*). ~ **gender** (*gram.*) *n.* josei.

femininity [femiṇíniti] *n.* onna taru koto; josei (*woman*); nyū-femoral [fémər(ə)l] *a.* momo no; daitaikotsu no. ⌊wa.

femur [fí:mə] *n.* (*anat.*) daitaikotsu.

fen [fen] *n.* numachi.

fence [fens] *n.* kakine; kobaisha (*a buyer of stolen goods*). *v.* kakine de kakomu; bōgyo (*protect*) suru; kenjutsu (*swordman-*
fencer [fénsə] *n.* kendōka. ⌊*ship*) o tsukau.

fencing [fénsiŋ] *n.* kenjutsu. heigakoi (*fence*).

fend [fend] *v.* (*arch.*) fusegu (*defend*); sakeru (*avoid*). ~ **for oneself**, jikatsu suru.

fender [féndə] *n.* sutōbu (*stove*) no hai (*ashes*) dome; doroyoke.

fennel [fen(ə)l] *n.* (*bot.*) uikyō (*used in medicine and cooking*).

fenny [féni] *a.* numa no; numa no ōi.

feoff [fef], **fief** [fi:f] *n.* ryōdo; ryōchi.

ferment [fə(:)mént] *v.* hakkō saseru (suru); sawagu (gaseru); dōran suru (*stir up*). [fá:ment] *n.* sawagi. kōbo; hakkō.

fermentation [fə:mentéiʃən] *n.* hakkō ; dōran ; gekkō.

fern [fə:n] *n.* (*bot.*) shida. ~**y** [fə́:ni] *a.* shida no shigetta.

ferocious [fəróuʃəs] *a.* dōmōna. zanninna (*cruel*). ~**ly** *ad.* dōmōni ; mugotarashiku.

ferocity [fərɔ́siti] *n.* dōmōsa ; zanninsei (*savagery.*)

ferret [férit] *n.* (*zoo.*) shiro-itachi. *v.* shiro-itachi o tsukatte kari o suru (*hunt with a* ~) ; usagi o karid su (*a* ~ *rabbits out*)

ferriage [fériidʒ] *n.* watashi. funa chin (*fare*).

ferrule [féru:l] *n.* kanawa. ishizuki (*of sticks or umbrellas*).

ferry [féri] *n.* watashiba. watashibune. *v.* fune de watasu (-ru). ~**boat** [-bout] *n.* watashibune. ~**man** [-mən] *n.* (watashiba no) watashimori.

fertile [fɔ́:tail] *a.* hiyokuna.

fertility [fə:tíliti] *n.* hiyoku ; hōfu (*richness*). ⌈sayō.

fertilization [fə:tilaizéiʃən] *n.* hiryō o yaru koto. jusei(-tai)

fertilize [fɔ́:tilaiz] *v.* hiyokuni suru ; jusei(tai) saseru. ~**r** [-ə] *n.* hiryō. jusei baikaibutsu.

ferule [féru:l] *n.* (kodomo o korashimeru) kibera ; muchi.

fervency [fɔ́:v(ə)nsi] *n.* netsujō.

fervent [fɔ́:v(ə)nt] *a.* netsujō o shimesu ; netsuretsuna.

fervid [fɔ́:vid] *a.* atsui ; nesshinna. ~**ly** *ad.* nesshinni.

fervo(u)r [fɔ́:və] *n.* netsuretsu. netsujō.

festal [fést(ə)l] *a.* matsuri no. tanoshii (*joyous*). yōkina (*gay*).

fester [féstə] *n.* kaiyō (*pus ga tamaru odeki*). *v.* umu ; umaseru.

festival [féstiv(ə)l] *a.*, *n. a.* (o)matsuri (no).

festive [féstiv] *a.* (o)iwai no.

festivity [festíviti] *n.* iwatte nomi, sawagu koto (*merriment*).

festoon [festú:n] *n.* hanazuna (hana to tsunaida kazari).

fetch [fetʃ] *v.* itte motte kuru (*things*) ; itte tsurete kuru (*person*) ; yoi ne ni naru : *These eggs will* ~ *a good price*, kono tamago wa ii kane ni naru. ~**ing** *a.* hikitsukeru : *she wore a* ~ *hat*, kanojo wa me ni tsuku bōshi o kabutte ita.

fête [feit] *n.* matsuri ; shikuen (*great entertainment*). *v.* kyōō suru ; motenasu.

fetid [fétid] *a.* kusai ; nioi no suru.

fetish [fí:tiʃ] *n.* monogami (yabanjin ga kami to agameru mono). meishin.

fetlock [fétlɔk] *n.* kezumege (uma no hizume (*hoof*) no ue ni haeru ke (*tufty hair*). kyūsetsu (kezumege no haeru basho).

fetter [fétə] *n.* ashikase. (*pl.*) shūjin. *v.* ashikase o kakeru.

fettle [fétl] *n.* guai ; jōtai : *The horse is in (good) fine* ~.) uma wa hijōni chōshi (genki) ga ii.

fetus, foetus [fí:təs] *n.* hai ; taiji (haha no onaka no ko).

feud [fju:d] *n.* ryōchi (*fief*) ; arasoi ; nakatagai : *at* ~ *with*, hammoku shite.

feudal [fjú:d(ə)l] *v.* ryōchi no. hōkenteki. ~**lord** [-lɔ:d] *n.* ryōshu. ~**system** *n.* hōken seido. ~**ism** [fjú:dəlizm] *n.* Hōkenseido. ~**ist** [-ist] *n.* hōkenronja.

feudatory [fjú:dət(ə)ri] *a.* hōken no ; kashin no (*of retainer*). *n.* kashin (*retainer*). han (*clan*).

fever [fí:və] *n.* netsu. netsubyō : *in a* ~, netsu ni ukasarete ; nekkyō shite. *v.* hatsunetsu suru. ~**ed** [fí:vəd] *a.* netsu no aru ; nekkyō shita. ~**ish** [fí:v(ə)riʃ] *a.* netsuppoi ; nekkyō shita.

feverfew [fí:vəfju:] *n.* (*bot.*) natsu-shiragiku.

few [fju:] *a.* sukunai ; ikura mo nai : *a* ~, shōsū no. ~**ness** shōsū.

fez [fez] *n.* Torukobō.

fiancé [fiã:(n)séi] *n.* (*Fr.*) kon'yaku shita otoko.

fiancée [fiã:(n)sei] *n.* (*Fr.*) kon'yaku shita onna.   ⌈shippai.

fiasco [fiǽskou] *n.* (sōgaku-ensō (*musical performance*) de) dai-

fiat [fáiæt] *n.* meirei ; ninka (*authorization*). ~ **money** [fáiət-máne] *n.* (*Am.*) fukanshihei (*paper money*).

fib [fib] *n.* tsumi no nai uso (*white lie*). *v.* fib o tsuku.

fiber, fibre [fáibə] *n.* sen'i. ~**board** [-bɔ:d] sen'i no ita ; fai-
fibrin [fáibrin] *n.* sen'i-so.   ⌊vā-ita.

fibrinous [fáibrinəs] *a.* sen'i soshitsu no ; sen'i-so kara naru.

fibroid [fáibrɔid] *a.* sen'i-sei no ; sen'ijō (-*state*) no.

fibrous [fáibrəs] *a.* sen'i no.

fibula [fíbjulə] (*pl.* **-lae** [-li:], **las**) *n.* hikotsu ; sune no hone.

fickle [fíkl] *a.* ki no kawari yasui. ~**ness** *n.* ~ ki no kawari yasui koto.

fictile [fíktail] *a.* nette tsukutta. tōdosei no.

fiction [fíkʃən] *n.* shōsetsu ; tsukuri-goto (*invention*). ~**al** [-əl] *a.* tsukurigoto no.

fictitious [fiktíʃəs] *a.* kari no (*assumed*); sōzō no (*imaginary*). ~ ly shōsetsutekini.

fiddle [fidl] *n.* = **violin**. *as fit as a* ~, genki de. *play first* ~. (*col.*) hito no ue ni tatsu. *play second* ~, (*col.*) shita-yaku ni naru. *v.* ~ o hiku. ~-**de-dee** [fídldidí:] *inter.* bakana !. ~**stick** [-stik] *n. violin* no yumi. tsumaranu koto.

fiddler [fídlə] *n. violin* ensōsha.

fidelity [faidéliti] *n.* chūjitsu; seikaku.

fidget [fídʒit] *v.* mojimoji suru; sekaseka suru (*be uneasy*).

fidgety [fídʒiti] *a.* sowasowa suru. kimuzukashii (*fastidious*).

fiduciary [fidjú:ʃəri] *a.* kakkotaru; shinnin sareta. ~**loan** [-loun] *n.* shintaku kashitsuke.

fie [fai] *inter.* keibetsu, daikirai o arawasu hatsuon.

fief [fi:f] *n.* ryōdo *cf.* **feud**.

field [fi:ld] *n.* nohara; hatake. senjō (*battle* ~); (*baseball*) gaiya (*outfield*). ~**allowance** [fíldə/áuəns] *n.* senjō teate. ~**glass** [-glas] *n.* sōgankyō. ~ -**gun** [-gʌn] *n.* yasenhō. ~ -**hospital** [hóspitəl] *n.* yasembyōin. ~**ing** [-iŋ] (*base.*) shubi. ~ **marshal** [-má:ʃəl] *n.* rikugun-gensui. ~ **officer** [-ɔ́fisə] *n.* rikugun-sa kan. ~**sport** [-spɔ:ts] *n.* yagaiundō. ~**work** [-wə:k] *n.* yagai-sagyō.

fiend [fi:nd] *n.* akuma (*satan*). (*Am. col.*) tandekisha (*a drug*-~).

fierce [fiəs] *a.* hageshii (*wild*); mōakuna (*ferocious*). ~**ly** [-li] *ad.* dōmōni; ken'akuni. ~**ness** *n.* dōmō; zannin; rambō.

fierily [fáiərili] *ad.* hi no yōni hageshiku.

fieriness [fáiərinis] *n.* mōretsu. tanki (*short temper*).

fiery [fáiəri] *a.* hi (*fire*) no yōna; hageshii. bakuhatsu shiyasui (*be easy to explode*).

fife [faif] *n.* yoko-bue. ~**er** [fáifə] *n.* yokobue-fuki.

fifteen [fífti:n] *n., a.* jūgo (15) (no).

fifteenth [fíftí:nθ] *a.* jūgobamme no. jūgobun no ichi ($\frac{1}{15}$) no. *n.* dai jūgo; jūgobun no ichi ($\frac{1}{15}$); jūgo-nichi (*fifteenth day of the month*).

fifth [fifθ] *a.* gobamme no; gobun no ichi no ($\frac{1}{5}$). *n.* dai go. gobun no ichi. itsuka (*the* ~ *day of the month; the* ~ *colmun*) dai go-retsu. ⌈gojū; gojūbun no ichi.

fiftieth [fíftiiθ] *a* gojūbamme no; gojūbun no ichi no. *n.* dai

fifty [fífti] *a.* gojū no. *n.* gojū(50). ~-**fifty** [-fífti] *a.* (tōbun) hanhan no. *ad.* hanhan ni.

fig [fig] *n.* ichijiku : *don't care a* ~, sukoshi mo kamawanai.

fight [fait] *v.* **fought; fighting.** tatakau; tatakawaseru (*make one fight*); shiki suru (*direct*); tatakau : ~ *it out*, shōbu no tsuku made tatakau. *n.* ikusa. kenka (*quarrel*). ~**er** [fáitə] *n.* senshi. sentōki (*airplane*). ~**ing** [fáitiŋ] *a.* tatakai no. *n.* sentō.

figment [fígmənt] *n.* koshiraegoto.

figurative [fígjurətiv] *a.* hiyu no. keiyō no ōi. hanayakana (~ *style*). tengi no (*metaphorical*). ~**ly** [-li] hanayakani.

figure [fígjə] *n.* sūji. katachi. moyō (*design*). hitokage : *a* ~ *emerged.* (*great* ~), daijimbutsu. ~**head** [-hed] *n.* senshu-kazari. myōmokujō no tōshu (*nominal chief*).

filament [fíləmənt] *n.* chiisai sen'i no ito. (denkyū no naka no) sen.

filbert [fílbə(:)t] *n.* (*bot.*) hashibami no mi.

filch [filtʃ] *v.* choromakasu; kapparau.

file[1] [fail] *n.* shorui sashi; tojikomi : ~ *of the Times*, Times no tsuzuri. *v.* seiri shite shimatte oku : *rank and* ~, zen kashikan to hei.

file[2] [fail] *n., v.* yasuri (o kakeru).

filial [fíljəl] *a.* kodomo no; kōkōna : (~ *piety*), kōkō.

filibuster [fílibʌstə] *n.* ryakudatsu-hei. (*Am.*) giji bōgai giin; giji bōgai. *v.* ryakudatsu suru. (*Am.*) giji shinkō o bōgai suru (*obstruct*).

filigree [fíligri:] *n.* kin, gin no sen de tsukutta saikumomo; kirei da ga yaku ni tatanai mono.

filing [fáiliŋ] *n.* yasuri kake; yasuri kuzu (*waste*). ~-**cabinet** [-kæbinit] *n.* bunsho-yōki.

Filipino [filipí:nou] *n.* Firippin-jin.

fill [fil] *v.* mitasu; ippai ni suru (-naru). ~**er** [fílə] *n.* tsumeru hito (mono).

fillet [fílit] *n.* himo; ribon (*ribbon*). hireniku (*tenderloin*).

fillip [fílip] *n.* tsumahajiki. shigeki (*stimulus*). *v.* yubi de hajiku. shigeki suru. (*tomboy*).

filly [fíli] *n.* mesu (*female*) no komma; (*col.*) otemba-musume.

film [film] *n.* usui kawa; firumu. eiga (*moving picture*). *v.* usukawa de ōu. ~**y** [fílmi] *a.* usukawa no; bon'yari shita.

filter [fíltə] *n.* rokaki; kosu kikai. *v.* roka suru; kosu.

filth [filθ] *n.* obutsu; aka (*dirt*). ~**y** [fílθi] *a.* fuketsuna. midarana (*improper*).

filtrate [fíltreit] *v.* kosu. *n.* roka-eki.

filtration [filtréiʃən] *n.* roka. shintō; shimitōru koto.

fin [fín] *n.* hire.

final [fáin(ə)l] *a.* saigo no. *n.* kesshō (*sport*). (*pl.*) shiai; (shiken nado no) saishū.

finale [finá:li] *n.* owari; (*mus.*) shūsetsu; shūkyoku; ōzume (geki de).

finality [fainǽliti] *n.* shūkyoku; saigo no kettei.

finance [finǽns/fái-] *n.* zaisei (gaku); (*pl.*) sainyū (*annual revenue*); shotoku (*income*): ~ **bill,** *n.* zaisei hōan. (*Am.*) kin'yūtegata. **Minister of F~.** Ōkura Daijin. *v.* shihon (*capital*) o dasu; kin'yu suru; yūshi suru.

financial [f(a)inǽnʃ(ə)l] *a.* zaisei no: ~ **year,** *n.* kaikei nendo. ~**ly** *ad.* zaiseijō ni.

finacier [finǽnsiə] *n.* zaimukan. shihonka (*capitalist*).

finch [fín(t)ʃ] *n.* (*bird*) uso.

find [faind] *v.* **found, finding.** miidasu; kizuku. *n.* hakken. horidashimono (*a good* ~). ~**ing** *n.* hakken.

finder [fáində] *n.* hakkensha. (*range* ~) (kansatsubutsu no ichi o misadameru) kyorisokuteiki.

fine [fain] *a.* rippana; komakai. *n.* bakkin. ~**snow,** *n.* komakai yuki. ~**ness** *n.* rippasa. jundo (kin, gin nado).

finery [fáinəri] *n.* kazari; bifuku.

finesse [finés] *n.* (*Fr.*) kōmyōna gijutsu; sakuryaku.

finger [fíŋgə] *n.* yubi. (tokei no) hari: *have at one's* ~*s ends,* jukuchi suru. *v.* ijiru; nusumu (*steal*). ~ **alphabet** [-ǽlfəbet] yubi-moji. ~**board** [bɔːd] *n.* violin nado no yubiita. ~**bowl** [-boul], ~**glass** [-glas] *n.* shokuji no ato de yubi o arau hachi. ~**ing** *n.* ijiru koto. ~**post** [-poust] *n.* yubi o kaite hōkō o shimeshita mono. ~**print** *n.* shimon.

finial [fíniəl] *n.* ie no mune ya tō nado no sumi ni tsuketa kazari.   ⌈*in details*).

finical [fínik(ə)l] *a.* muzukashii. nen'iri sugita (*too much finished*

finis [fáinis] *n.* shūketsu; oshimai.

finish [fíniʃ] *v.* oeru. shitogeru. *n.* shiage. ~**-line** [⌐ləin] *n.*

(*Am.*) kyōsō (*race*) no kesshō-sen (*finishing-line*). ～ **ed** [fíniʃt]
a. owatta ; sunda.

finite [fáinait] *a.* yūgen no ; genkai no aru.

Finn [fin] *n.* Finland-jin. ～**ic** [fínik] *n.* Fin rando no. ～**ish** *n.*
Finland-jin(go).

finny [fíni] *a.* hire (*fin*) no aru ; uo (*fish*) ga ōku sunde iru.

fiord, fjord [fjɔ:d] *n.* semai irie.

fir [fɔ:] *n.* (*bot.*) momi no ki.

fire [faiə] *n.* hi ; kaji ; happō. *v.* hi o tsukeru (*set on fire*) ; happō
suru. ～ **alarm** *n.* kasai-hōchiki. ～**arms** [fáiərɑːmz] *n.*
(*pl.*) (jū, hō, nado no) buki. ～ **bell** *n.* hanshō. ～**brand**
[◦brænd] *n.* moesashi ; taimatsu ; sendōsha. ～**brick** [◦brick
n. taika renga. ～**brigade** [◦brigèid] *n.* shōbōtai. ～**cracker**
[◦krǽkə] *n.* bakuchiku ; kanshakudama. ～**damp** [-dæmp] *n.*
bakuhatsu-gasu. ～**dog** [-dɔg] *n.* ro no mae no takigikake. ～
drill [-dril] *n.* shōbō enshū. ～**escape** [◦eskèip] *n.* kaji hinan-
bashigo. ～**extinguisher** [◦ikstìŋgwiʃə] *n.* shōkaki. ～**fly**
[-flai] *n.* hotaru. ～ **insurance** [◦inʃùərəns] *n.* kasai hoken. ～
man *n.* shōbōtaiin ; kafu. ～**place** [◦pleis] *n.* danro (*stove*).
～**plug** [◦plʌg] *n.* shōkasen. ～**policy** [◦pɔlisi] *n.* kasai hoken
shōsho. ～**proof** [◦pruːf] *n.* hi ni moe nikui mono. ～**side**
[◦said] *n.* rohen ; irori no hata. ～**wood** [◦wud] *n.* maki. ～
works *n.* (*pl.*) hanabi. ～**worship** [◦wɔːʃip] *n.* hi o kami to
agameru shūkyō ; haika(kyō).

firing-line [fáiəriŋ láin] *n.* kasen ; hō-retsu (*gun-line*.).

firkin [fɔ́:kin] *n.* ko-oke ; yōryō no tan'i (ichi bareru no 1/4).

firm [fɔ:m] *n.* shōkai. *a.* shikkari shita ; fuhen no. ～**ness** *n.*
kenjitsusa.

firmament [fɔ̀:məmənt] *n.* aozora ; ōzora.

firman [fɔ:mən] *n.* Toruko-ō (*Turkish King=the Sultan*) no
chokurei ; ryokō menjō (*passport*). menkyo (*licence*).

first [fɔ:st] *a.* saisho no ; dai-ichi no ; saijō no (*highest*) : at ～
hand, chokusetsu ni. at ～ *sight*, ikken shite. ～ *aid*, ōkyū
teate. *for the* ～ *time*, haijmete. *in the* ～ *place*, mazu dai-ichi
ni. *the* ～ *thing*, nani yori mo saki ni. *n.* dai-ichi ; tsuitachi
(*the* ～ *day of the month*). at (*the*) ～, saisho wa. *from the* ～, saisho kara. *ad.* daiichini. ～ *and last*, zutto hajime kara oshimai made. ～ *of all*, massaki ni, nani yori saki ni.

firth [fə:θ] *n.* umi ga semaku hairikonda tokoro; irie.

fiscal [físk(ə)l] *a.* kokko keizai no. ~ **stamp** shūnyū inshi. ~ **year**, kaikei nendo.

fish [fiʃ] *n.* (*pl.* **fish, -es** [-iz]*s*) uo; sakana; gyo-niku: *F*~ *is cheap*, sakana wa yasui. (*col.*) yatsu (*fellow*). *v.* sakana o toru; tsuru. sagashidasu (*search*): ~ *in troubled waters*, dosakusa magire ni umai koto o suru. ~**culture** [-kʌltʃə] *n.* yōgyo. ~ **hook** [-huk] *n.* tsuribari. ~**monger** [-mʌŋgə] *n.* sakanaya. ~ **pond** [-pɒnd] *n.* yōgyo ike. ~**wife** [-waif] *n.* uo-uri onna. ~**y** [fíʃi] *a.* (nioi ya aji ga) uo no yōna; (*col.*) utagawashii.

fisher [fíʃə] *n.* (*arch.*)=~**man** [-mən] *n.* ryōshi. ~**y** [-ri] *n.* gyogyō; gyojō (*fishing-ground*); (*leg.*) gyogyōken (-*right*); gyogyō-gaisha (*fishing establishment*)

fishing [fíʃiŋ] *n.* gyokaku; uotsuri. ~**boat** [-bout] *n.* tsuribune. ~**line** [lain] *n.* tsuriito. ~**rod** [-rɒd] *n.* tsurizao. ~ **tackle** tsuridōgu. ~ **village** gyoson.

fissure [fíʃə] *n.* wareme. *v.* waru; wareru.

fist [fist] *n.* genkotsu. ~**ic** [fístik] *a.* kentō no.

fisticuffs [fístikʌfs] (*pl.*) *n.* naguriai; rantō.

fit [fit] *v.* guai yoku au (awaseru); jumbi suru: *This school* ~*s students for college*, kono gakkō wa daigaku nyūgaku jumbi o suru. ~ *in*, hameru. ~ *out*, fune o gisō suru. *a.* tekitōna. *n.* hossa (*paroxysm*). ~**ful** [fítful] *a.* hossateki no. kanketsuteki no (*intermittent*); kimagure no (*capricious*). ~**ter** [fítə] *n.* kikai (*machine*) kumitate shokkō; toritsuke-nin. ~**ly** *ad.* tekitōni. ~**ness** *n.* tekitō.

fitting [fítiŋ] *a.* tekitōna. ~**s** [-z] *n.* (*pl.*) toritsuke-mono; fuzoku-hin. ~**ly** [-li] *ad.* tekitōni.

five [faiv] *a.* itsutsu (go) no. *n.* go(5). ~**fold** [fáivfould] *a.* gojū (gobai) no (=*five times*).

fix [fiks] *v.* suetsukeru; ugokanai yōni suru; kotei suru (~ *a loose plank*), yurunda ita o shikkari tomeru. ~**ed** [fíkst] *a.* kotei shita. **well-**~ [wélfíkst] *ad.* (*Am.*) (*be well off*) rakuni kurasu. ~**ture** [fíkstʃə] *n.* zōsaku (*a house to let with* ~), zōsakutsuki kashiya.

fizz [fíz] *n.* shūtto iu oto; shūtto oto o tateru nomimono. *v.* shūtto oto o tateru.

fizzle [fízl] *n.* shippai. *v.* shūtto iu ; *(col.)* shikujiru.

flabby [flǽbi] *a.* tarunda ; nanjakuna. ～**biness** *n.* nanjaku.

flaccid [flǽksid] *a.* tarunda (hifu, niku nado).

flaccidity [flæksíditi] *n.* nanjaku ; mukiryoku.

flag [flæg] *n.* hata : *black* ～, kaizokusen ; shikei shikkō no shirushi. *white* ～, hakki *(of truce)*. *v.* hata o tateru. ～**officer** *n.* kaigun shōkan. ～**ship** *n.* kikan. ～**staff** *n.* hatazao. ～ **stone** hirattai shikiishi.

flagellant [flǽdʒələnt] *n.* jibun de muchiutsu hito.

flagellate [flǽdʒileit] *v.* muchi *(whip)* de utsu.

flagellation [flædʒiléiʃən] *n.* muchiuchi.   ⌈fue.

flageolet [flǽdʒo(u)lét] *n.* fue ; ana ga 6 (muttsu) aru. chiisai

flagging [flǽgiŋ] *n.* shikiishi (hosō) o suru koto.   ⌈na.

flaggy [flǽgi] *a.* hata no yōna ; ita-ishi no yōna. shōbu no yō-

flagitious [flədʒíʃəs] *a.* gokuaku no ; hazu beki *(disgraceful)*. ～**ly** [-li] *ad.* hajishirazu ni. ～**ness** [-nis] *n.* hajishirazu ; go-

flagon [flǽgən] *n.* hosokuchi-bin.   ⌊kuaku budō.

flagrancy [fléigrənsi] *n.* gokuaku hidō.

flagrant [fléigrənt] *a.* kakurenaki. gokuaku no. ～**ly** [-li] *ad.* ～**ness** [-nis] *n.* gokuaku hidō *(itself)*.

flail [fleil] *n.* karazao. *(a farming tool, beating grains off)*. *v.* kara-zao de utsu.

flak [flæk] *n.* kōshahō no hōka *(antiaircraft gun's fire)*.

flake [fleik] *n.* hakuhen *(thin broad piece peeled off)*.

flaky [fléiki] *a.* hakuhen no.

flambeau [flǽmbou] *n.* *(pl.* **-s**, **-beaux** [-bouz]) taimatsu.

flamboyant [flæmbɔ́iənt] *a.* kareina ; honō no yōna *(like flame)*.

flame [fleim] *n.* honō. netsujō *(passion)* ; koi-bito *(sweetheart)*.

flamen [fléimen] *n.* *(pl.* **-mines** [flǽminiz]) *(anc. Rome)* kami o matsuru hito.

flaming [fléimiŋ] *a.* moeru yōna.

flamingo [fləmíŋgou] *n.* *(bird)* beni-zuru.

flange [flændʒ] *n.* tsuba ; fuchi ; marui fuchi.

flank [flæŋk] *n.* yokobara ; sokumen *(side)*. *v.* sokumen o …su-

flannel [flǽn(ə)l] *n.* furan-neru.   ⌊ru.

flap [flæp] *n.* hirahira suru mono *(flattering)*. *v.* hirahira ugoku.

flapper [flǽpə] *n.* hae-tataki. *(col.)* komusume *(little girl)*. *(slang)* otemba-musume (*tomboy*).

flare [flεə] *n.* yuragu hikari (*unsteady glaring light*). *v.* yuragu (~ *up*); moeagaru. ~**bomb** [-bɔm] *n.* shōmeidan.

flash [flæʃ] *n.* senkō; pikatto suru hikari (*a ~ lightning*); *v.* pikatto hikaru. ~**light** [-lait] *n.* pikatto suru tōdai (*lighthouse*) nado no hikari; kaichūdentō. ~ **point** [-pɔint] *n.* hi no tsuku ondo. ~**y** [flǽʃi] *a.* hirameku. kabina (*gaudy*).

flask [flɑ:sk] *n.* furasuko; suitō (*water-bottle*).

flat [flæt] *a.* tairakana : *fell* ~, bettari taoreta. ~ *against the wall*, kabe ni pittari kuttsuite; daku-on no (*a ~ consonant*). *ad.* murisoku de; tairani. *n.* heimen; hiratai bubun.

flatten [flǽtn] *v.* tairani suru; tanchōni suru (naru) (*make monotonous*).

flatter[flǽtə] *v.* kobi hetsurau; tokui garasu. ~**er**[-rə] *n.* obekka tsukai. ~**ing** [-iŋ] hetsurai o iu. ~**y** [-ri] *n.* hetsurai.

flatulence [flǽtʃuləns], **flatulency** [flǽtʃulənsi] *n.* gasu ga ichō no naka ni tamaru koto.

flatulent [flǽtʃulənt] *a.* kūki de okoru; kūkyona (*vapid*).

flaunt [flɔ:nt] *v.* misebirakasu.

flavo(u)r [fléivə] *n.* fūmi; omomuki (*savour*); yakumi (*spice*). *v.* fūmi o soeru.

flaw [flɔ:] *n.* hibi; ketten (*fault*); (*leg*) kekkan : ~ *in the indictment*, kiso tetsuzuki no fubi. *v.* hibi ga hairu; mukō ni suru. ~**less** [-lis] *a.* kizu no nai.

flax [flæks] *n.* ama; ama-nuno (*linen*). ~**en** [-n] *a.* ama no; awai kiiro no. ~ **seed** [-si:d] *n.* ama no tane.

flay [flei] *v.* kawa o hagu; kokuhyō suru (*criticize*).

flea [fli:] *n.* nomi; *a* ~ *in one's ear*, iyami. ~**bite** [⊥bait] *n.* nomi no kutta ato.

fleck [flek] *n.* hanten; oten (*stain*). *v.* madara ni suru.

fled [fled] *v. see* : **flee**.

fledge [fledʒ] *v.* hane ga haeru. ~**(e)ling** [flédʒliŋ] *n.* hane no haetate no hina.

flee [fli:] *v.* **fled**; **fleeing**. nigeru; sakeru (*avoid*).

fleece [fli:s] *n.* hitsuji no ke; yōmō. *v.* yōmō o karu; damashitoru (*swindle*).

fleecy [flí:si] *a.* yōmō no yōna; yōmō de ōwareta.

fleer [fliə] *v.* azakeri warau (*jeer*). *n.* gurō; azakeri.

fleet [fli:t] *v.* tobi saru; jinsokuni sugisaru. *a.* kaisoku no. *n.* (1) kantai. (2) sentai; irie; chiisai wan. ~ *in being.* genson kantai : ~ **paymaster** *n.* kaigun shukei chūsa. ~ **surgion** *n.* kaigun gun'i chūsa. ~**ing** *a.* shissō suru; sugisaru.

Flemish [flémiʃ] *a.* Furandoru no; Furandorujin no; Furandorugo no. *n.* Furandorujin; Furandorugo.

flesh [fleʃ] *n.* niku; nikutai; nikuryoku; jinrui; kudamono no niku : *gain (or put on)* ~, ...futoru. *in* ~, futotte; koete. ~**colo(u)r** [fléʃ-kálə] nikuiro. ~**iness** [fléʃinis] *n.* taniku; himan (*fat*). ~**ly** *a.* nikuyoku no; konoyo no. ~**y** [fléʃi] *a.* futotta; koeta; niku no yōna; tanikushitsu no.

fleur-de-lis [fləː-də-líː] *n.* (*bot.*) ichihatsu.

flew [flúː] *v. see* : **fly**.

flex [fleks] *v.* mageru (garu). *n.* mageyasui densen (*flexible wire*).

flexibility [fləksibíliti] *n.* jūnansei; yūzūsei; yoku magaru seishitsu.

flexible [fléksibl] *a.* mageyasui; jūnanna. ~**bly** *ad.*

flexion, flection [flékʃən] *n.* kukkyoku; kukkyokubu (*cf. inflexion*).

flexure [flékʃə] *n.* kukkyoku; kukkyokubu.

flick [flik] *n.* pachitto utsu koto; yubi de hajiku koto. *v.* pachitto utsu; yubi de hajiku.

flicker [flíkə] *n.* hikari no yuragu koto; (ki no ha nado no) soyogi. *v.* chiratsuku; yuragu; soyogu.

flier, flyer [fláiə] *n.* tobu mono; tōbōsha; hikōka.

flight [flait] *n.* hikō; tōsō; hikō shita kyori; agaridan; makete nigeru koto : *put to* ~, haisō saseru. *take (to)* ~, tōbō suru. ~**y** [fláiti] *a.* sowasowa shita; utsurigina; ki no kawariyasui. ⌈na.

flimsy [flímzi] *n.* shikiutsushigami. *a.* hakujakuna; usuppera-

flinch [flíntʃ] *v.* shirigomi suru; hekieki suru.

flinders [flíndəz] *n.* (*pl.*) hahen; saihen.

fling [fliŋ] *v.* **flung; flinging.** tosshin suru; nageru; nonoshiru; funzen to shite saru. *n.* nagenawa (ishi no); isshu no kappatsuna butō : *have a* ~ *at*, ...o kōgeki suru; ...o batō suru. *have one's* ~, shitai hōdai o suru.

flint [flint] *n.* hiuchiishi. ～ **glass** *n.* namari garasu. ～**lock** [⊥lɔk] *n.* hinawajū. ～**y** [flínti] *a.* hiuchiishi-shitsu no; gankona; reikokuna.

flip [flip] *n.* tsumahajiki; oyayubi to nakaiyubi de narasu oto; isshu no atsui nomimono. *v.* gui to hipparu; yubi de kahei o haneageru.

flippancy [flípənsi] *n.* keisotsu; taben; oshaberi.

flippant [flípənt] *a.* keisotsuna; tabenna. ～**ly** *ad.* keisotsuni.

flipper [flípə] *n.* azarashi nado nɔ hirejō no ashi; mizukaki.

flirt [fləːt] *v.* (hazumi o tsukete) hyoi to nageru; furiugokasu; ichatsuku; honrō suru. *n.* uwaki-onna. ～**ation** [fləːtéiʃən] *n.* jaratsuki; ichatsuki. [suru.

flit [flit] *v.* hirahira to tobu; tobimawaru; tobi sugiru; iten

flitch [flitʃ] *n.* buta no wakibara o shiozuke ni shita mono.

float [flout] *n.* fuwari to uite iru mono; ikada; uki (*on the fishing line*) (hikōtei no) ukibune (furōto). *v.* ukaberu (-bu). ～**er** *n.* nijū-tōhyōsha. ～**ation** [-éiʃən] *n.* ukabu koto. ～**ing** [flóutiŋ] *a.* ukande iru; ugoite iru : ～**ing capital,** *n.* ryūdō shihon. ～**ing bridge** *n.* ukihashi. ～**ing light** *n.* …tōdaisen.

flock [flɔk] *n.* (1) mure; Kirisuto kyōkai, (*sheep flock*); kaishū. (2) ke no fusa. *v.* muragaru.

floe [flou] *n.* ōkina uita hyōzan; *floe* no uitere umi; uita kōri no katamari. [to.

flog [flɔg] *v.* muchiutsu. ～**ging** [flɔ́giŋ] *n.* muchi de utsu ko-

flood [flʌd] *n.* ōmizu. ōmizu. the Flood Noa no Kōzui. *v.* hanran suru; kangai suru; sattō suru. ～**gate** [-geit] *n.* suimon.

floor [flɔː/flɔə] *n.* yuka; giinseki; hatsugenken; saitei kakaku. **first** ～ *n.* (*Brit.*) nikai; (*Am.*) ikkai; ～ **leader** (*Am.*) innai sōmu. **second** ～ *n.* (*Brit.*) sangai; (*Am.*) nikai. *v.* tokoita o haru. ～**ing** *n.* neda; tokobari. ～**walker** [⊥wɔ̀ːkə] *n.* ten-nai torishimarinin.

flop [flɔp] *v.* patari to oto o tateru (ochiru). *n.* taoreru oto; shippai. [dai no).

flora [flɔ́ːrə] *n.* shokubutsu (tokubetsu no basho mata wa ji-

floral [flɔ́ːrəl] *a.* hana no; hana no yōna; hana ni kansuru.

Florentine [flɔ́rəntain] *a.* *Florence* (Furorensu) no. *n.* Florence-

floriculture [flɔ́ːrikʌltʃə] *n.* hanasaibai; hanazukuri. [jin.

florid [flórid] *a.* akami no sashita; hanayakana; kesshoku no yoi. ~**ly** *ad.* hanayakani.

florin [flórin] *n.* mukashi no *Florence* no kinka; Eikoku no ginka (2s.); mukashi no Eikoku no kinka.

florist [flórist] *n.* kaki saibaisha, hanaya.

floss [flɔs] *n.* mawata; (tōmorokoshi nado no) hige: ~ *silk*, mawata. ~**y** [flɔ́si] *a.* mawata no yōna; fuwafuwa suru.

flotage [flóutidʒ] *n.* furyoku; fuyūbutsu.

flotation [floutéiʃən] *n.* (*Brit.*) ukabu koto; uru koto; uri ni dasu koto.

flotilla [floutíɾə] *n.* shōkantai; kobune no teitai.

flotsam [flɔ́tsəm] *n.* hyōryū shite iru fune no hahen; ukini.

flounce [flauns] *n.* susokazari; mimodae; *v.* mizu ni tobikomu. okotte pui to dete iku. hida kazari o tsukeru: *She* ~*d out of the room in a rage*, kanojo wa kankanni natte heya kara pui to dete itta.

flounder [fláundə] *v.* mogaku; agaku. *n.* mogaki; magotsuku koto; (*fish*) hirame no rui.

flour [flauə] *n.* kona; merikenko (o furikakeru): ~ **mill**, seifunjo; konaya.

flourish [flʌ́riʃ] *n.* (katana nado no) furimawashi; patto shita utsukushisa; shareta monji; (*mus.*) hanayakana bubun: *in full* ~, hanjō shite; genki ōsei de; misebirakashite. *v.* hanayakana monku o tsukau; hammo suru; hanjō suru.

floury [fláuəri] *a.* kona no; kona mamire no.

flout [flaut] *v.* chōrō suru. *n.* chōrō.

flow [flou] *v.* nagareru; ryūchōni deru; (shio ga) sasu: ~ *like water*, oshige mo naku sosogu. *n.* nagare; sashishio. ~**ing** [flóuiŋ] *a.* nagareru; ryūchōna: ~ *tide*, age shio.

flower [fláuə] *n.* hana; massakari. *v.* hana ga hiraku. hana (hana moyō) de kazaru. ~**bed**, *n.* kadan. ~**show** *n.* hana no himpyōkai. ~ **vase** *n.* kabin. ~**ing** *a.* hana no (saku) aru.

floweret [fláuərit] *n.* chiisai hana.

flowery [fláuəri] *a.* hana no ōi; hanayakana.

flown [floun] *v. see* **fly**.

flu [flu:] *n.* (*col.*) ryūkōsei-kambō (=*influenza*).

fluctuate [flʌ́ktjueit] *v.* dōyō suru; hendō suru.

fluctuation [flʌktjuéiʃən] *n.* dōyō (hendō) suru koto.

flue [flu:] *n.* kemuridashi no ana ; endō ; paipu. ryōshi-ami no

fluency [flú(:)ənsi] *n.* nōben ; ryūchō. ⌊isshu.

fluent [flú(:)ənt] *a.* nōbenna ; ryūchōna. ~**ly** *ad.* nōbenni.

fluff [flʌf] *n.* keba ; watage ; ubuge. ~**y** [flʌfi] *a.* keba no yō-na ; yawarakai ; watage no.

fluid [flú(:)id] *n.* ryūdōtai (ekitai, kitai). *a.* nagareru. ~**ify** [-ifai] *v.* ekitaika suru. ~ **dram** [dræm] *n.* 1/8 onsu. ~ **ounce** [-auns] ekitai masume no tan'i de, 1 *pound* no 1/16.

fluidity [flu(:)íditi], **fluidness** [flú:idnis] *n.* ryūdōsei ; ryūdō-shitsu.

fluke [flu:k] *n.* kōun. kachiku no kanzō jistoma. (*fish*) Hira-me no isshu. *win by a* ~, kōun de katsu.

flume [flu:m] *n.* keiryū ; yōsuiro ; tanigawa.

flummery [flʌ́məri] *n.* ōtomiiru-sei no jerii ; isshu no puddin-gu ; tawagoto.

flung [flʌŋ] *see :* **fling.**

flunk(e)y [flʌ́ŋki] *n.* shikise o kita jūboku ; obekkamono.

fluorescence [flù(:)ərésns] *n.* keikō ; keikōsei.

fluorescent [flù(:)ərésnt] *a.* keikōsei no. ~ **lamp** [-læmp] *n.* keikōtō. ~ **screen** [-skri:n] *n.* keikōban.

fluoridate [flú:ərideit] *v.* fusso o kuwaeru (mushiba yobō no

fluorine [flúəri:n/-rain] (*chem.*) *n.* fusso. ⌊tame ni).

fluorite [flúərait] *n.* keiseki.

flurry [flʌ́ri] *n.* rōbai ; ichijin no shippū : *in a* ~, awatete. *v.* rōbai saseru. ~**ied** *a.* awatete iru ; awatadashii.

flush [flʌ́ʃ] *v.* patto akarameru ; kōfun saseru ; mizu ga hoto-bashiru ; nagashite arau ; tobitatsu. *a.* takusan aru : *He is* ~ *with money,* kane o unto motte iru.

fluster [flʌ́stə] *n.* rōbai ; (shinkeishitsu no kōfun). *v.* kōfun suru ; rōbai suru (saseru).

flute [flu:t] *n.* fue. hashira no mizo. *v.* fue o fuku ; fue no chōshi de utau. mizo o tsukeru.

flutist [flú:tist] *n.* fuefuki.

flutter [flʌ́tə] *v.* habataki suru ; hirugaeru ; hirahira tobu ; sawagu ; magotsuku. myaku ga yowaku, fukisoku ni utsu : *her pulse* ~*ed,* kanojo no myaku wa fukisoku de yowakatta.

n. habataki ; hirameki ; magotsuki ; dōyō.

fluty [flú:ti] *a.* fue no oto no yōna sunda.

fluvial [flú:viəl] *a.* kawa no ; kawa ɲi shōzuru ; kawa ni sumu.

flux [flʌks] *n.* ryūshutsu ; ryūdō ; ageshio ; hendō ; (*med.*) geri ; ketsuben. *v.* tokasu ; nagarederu ; tokeru.

fly [flai] *v.* flew, flown; flying. tobu (tobaseru) ; nigeru ; hirugaeru ; ageru ; hanatsu. *n.* hae ; kabari ; (*pl.*) kei-basha ; hikō ; botan kakushi ; hikyū. ~**blow** [⌐blou] *n.* hae no tamago. ~**leaf** [⌐li:f] *n.* mikaeshi. ~**speck** [⌐spek] *n.* hae no fun no oten. ~**wheel** [⌐hwi:l] *n.* hazumiguruma.

flyer, flier [fláiə] *n.* tobu mono.

flying [fláiiŋ] *a.* tobu ; hikō suru ; hirugaeru ; awatadashii *a.* hikō. F~ **Dutchman** *n.* yūreisen. F~ **Fortress** *n.* sora no yōsai. *with* ~ *colors,* gaika o sōshite ; jōshubi ni. ~**fish** [⌐fiʃ] *n.* tobiuo. ~ **machine,** kōkūki.

foal [foul] *n.* (uma, roba nado no) ko.

foam [foum] *n.* awa ; abuku ; tama no ase. *v.* awadataseru ; awadatsu. ~**y** [fóumi] *a.* awadatta ; awa no yōna.

F.O.B., f.o.b. honsen watashi (*free on board*).

fob [fɔb] *n.* (zubon no) tokei-kakushi ; mijikai tokei-gusari. *v.* azamuku ; oshitsukeru.

focal [fóukəl] *a.* shōten (*focus*) no ; shōten ni aru. ~ *length* (*or distance*) shōten kyori. ~**ize** [-aiz] *v.* shōten ni atsumeru.

focus [fóukəs] (*pl.* **-ci** [-sai] ; **-es**) *n.* shōten ; chūshin. *v.* shōten o awaseru.

fodder [fɔ́də] *n.* magusa. *v.* magusa o ataeru.

foe [fou] *n.* kataki ; tekigun. ~**man** [-mən] *n.* tekihei.

foetus [fí:təs] *n.* =**fetus.**

fog [fɔg] *n.* kiri ; (*photo.*) kaburi. *v.* kiri de tsutsumu ; konwaku saseru (*purplex*) ; mōrō to naru. ~**horn** [⌐hɔ:n] *n.* nōmu keiteki (shingō). ~ **signal** [-sígnəl] nōmu shingō.

foggy [fɔ́gi] *a.* kiri no fukai ; nōmu no. ~**ily** *ad.* kiri fukaku ; mōrō to.

fogy, fogey [fóugi] *n.* kyūheina hito (=*old* ~) ; gankona hito.

foible [fɔ́ibl] *n.* jakuten ; katana no mae hambun.

foil [fɔil] *n.* (kin, gin no) haku ; *fencing*-yō no ken ; kemono no ashiato. *v.* haku o tsukeru; kemono ga nioi o keshite nigeru.

foist [fɔist] *v.* kossori hamekomu; gomakashite nisemono nado o yaru.

fold [fould] *n.* otta hida. hitsuji-goya; hitsuji no mure. *v.* orikasaneru; ude o kumu. koya ni ireru.

folder [fóuldə] *n.* kamibasami; oritatami-shiki no mono.

folding [fóuldiŋ] *a.* tatamu; oritatami no: ~*chair*, oridatami-isu. ~*doors*, kannombiraki no to; orido.

foliage [fóuliidʒ] *n.* ki no ha.

foliate [fóuliit] *a.* ha no ōi; haku ni nobeta.

foliation [fòuliéiʃən] *n.* ha o shōzuru koto; haku ni suru koto.

folio [fóuliou] *n.* zenshi futatsuori-ban no hon: *in* ~, *folio* ban de. *a.* futatsuori-ban no.

folk [fouk] *n.* hitobito. (*pl.*) kazoku; ichizoku. ~*lore* [-lɔ:/lɔə] *n.* densetsu; minzokugaku. ~**song** [-sɔŋ] *n.* min'yō. ~**tale**, ~**story** [stóuri] minkan densetsu; minwa.

follow [fólou] *v.* tsuite iku; tsuzuku; ato o ou; jūji suru; rikai suru: *as follows*, tsugi no gotoshi. *n.* tsuite iku koto.

follower [fólouə] *n.* jūsha; zuiin; shinja; monjin; gakuto; kōkeisha.

following [fólouiŋ] *n. follower*-tachi. *a.* tsuite iku.

folly [fóli] *n.* bakana okonai.

foment [foumént] *v.* musu; unagasu; chōhatsu suru (*instigate*).

fomentation [fòumentéiʃən] *n.* ampō; chōhatsu (*instigation*).

fond [fɔnd] *a.* baka ni kawaigaru, jō ni amai: *be* ~ *of*, o konomu; o suku. ~**ly** *ad.* ~**ness** *n.*

fondle [fóndl] *v.* kawaigaru; aibu suru.

font [fɔnt] *n.* senrei no mizu o ireru utsuwa; abura-tsubo.

food [fu:d] *n.* tabemono. ~**stuff** [-stʌf] *n.* shokuryō.

fool [fu:l] *n.* bakamono; dōkemono; honrō sareru hito. *v.* baka ni suru; bakana koto o suru: ~ *away*, rōhi suru; mudani tsukau. ~**ery** [-rəri] *n.* bakana okonai (*behavior*). ~**hardy** [-hà:di] *a.* mukōmizuna; muteppōna.

foolish [fú:liʃ] *a.* orokana; bakageta. ~**ly** *ad.* ~**ness** *n.*

foolscap [fú:lzkæp] *n.* dōke mono no bōshi; ōban no kami.

foot [fut] *n.* (*pl.* **feet** [fi:t]) ashi; (*mil.*) hohei; fumoto; ichi fūto; (*poet.*) tan'i to naru onsetsu. *v.* aruku; odoru; (*col.*) shiharau. ~**ball** [⌐bɔːl] *n.* shūkyū. ~**board** [⌐bɔːd] *n.* fumidai; fumiita. ~**fall** [⌐fɔːl] *n.* ashioto. ~**gear** [⌐giə] *n.* hakimono. ~**hill** [-hil] *n.* sanroku; sanroku no ko-oka. ~**hold** [⌐hould] *n.* ashiba; ashigakari. ~**lights** [⌐laits] *n.* (*pl.*) futtoraito; kyakkō. ~**man** [⌐mən] *n.* hohei; jūboku. ~**note** [⌐nout] *n.* kyakuchū. ~**pace** [⌐peis] *n.* namiashi. ~**pad** [⌐pæd] *n.* oihagi. ~**passenger** [-pǽsindʒə] *n.* tsūkōnin. ~**path** [⌐paθ] *n.* hodō. ~**pound** [⌐paund] *n.* fūto pondo. ~**print** [⌐print] *n.* sokuseki; ashiato. ~**race** [⌐reis] toho kyōsō. ~**sore** [⌐sɔə] *a.* ashi o itameta. ~**step** [⌐step] *n.* ayumi; ashioto; ashiato. ~**stool** [⌐stuːl] *n.* ashidai; fumidai.

footing [fútiŋ] *n.* ashiba; tachiba; ugokanai chii.

fop [fɔp] *n.* sharemono; niyaketa otoko. ~**pery** [fɔ́pəri] *n.* mekasu koto; oshare. ~**pish** [fɔ́piʃ] *a.* mekashita; niyaketa.

for [fɔː] boin no mae; [fə] yowai hatsuon. *prep. act* ~ *a person*, ni kawatte hataraku. *He was returned* ~ *Birmingham*, kare wa Bāmingamu *kara* daigishi ni erabareta. *I will give you a horse* ~ *your gun*, boku wa kimi no jū *no kawari ni* uma o ageyō. *to dance* ~ *joy*, ureshisa no *tame* odoru. ~ *want of*, no nai *tame*. *to send* ~ *a doctor*, isha o mukai ni yaru. *to go out* ~ *a walk*, sampo *ni* dekakeru. *This book is too difficult* ~ *me to read*, kono hon wa watashi *niwa* yomu no ni konnan da, (=muzukashikutte yomenai). *hunger* ~ *knowledge*, chishiki ni *taisuru* yokkū. *the train* ~ *London*, London *e no* (e iku) kisha. *word* ~ *word*, go ni *taishite* go o. *Shall I read the letter* ~ *you*, anata ni (*kawatte*) kono tegami o yomi mashō ka? *respect* ~ *his teacher*, sensei ni *taisuru* sonkei. *smoking is not good* ~ *your throat*, tabako wa anata no nodo *niwa* yoku nai. *They chose A* ~ *their leader*, karera wa A o shidōsha *to shite* (or *ni* eranda.

forage [fɔ́ridʒ/-edʒ] *n.* magusa; ryōmatsu no chōhatsu. *v.* ryōshoku o ubau; magusa o ataeru.

forasmuch as [fərɔzmátʃ əz] *conj.* .. de aru yue ni.

foray [fɔ́rei] *v.* shinryaku (jūrin) suru. *n.* shinryaku (*pillage*).

forbade [fɔbáid/-bǽd] *v. see* : **forbid**.

forbear, forebear [fɔːbέə] *v.* forbore, forborne ; forbearing taeru; gaman suru; hikaeru (*from*). ~**ance** [-rəns] *n.* nintai;

gaman. ～ing [-riŋ] a. gamanzuyoi.

forbid [fəbíd/fɔbíd] v. forbade [-bæd] or forbad; forbidden [-bidn] or forbad; forbidding. kinzuru; samatageru. *God (or Heaven)* ～! ...nakare kashi!

forbidden [fəbídn/fɔ:b-] v. *see*: forbid.

forbidding [fəbídiŋ/fɔ:b-] a. iyana; chikazuki gatai: *a forbidding coast*, chikazuki nikui kaigan.

forbore [fɔ:bɔ́:/-bɔ́ə] v. *see*: forbear.

forborne [fɔ:bɔ́:n] v. *see*: forbear.

force [fɔ:s] n. chikara; ikioi; bōryoku; heiryoku. (*pl.*) guntai: *by* ～, chikarazuku de. *in* ～, jisshichū; yūkō de. v. shiiru: ～ *one's way*, ni oshiiru. ～d [-t] a. kyōseiteki no; chikara o kometa; muri no: ～d labo(u)r n. kyōsei rōdō. ～d march n. kyōkōgun. ～d smile n. tsukuriwarai. ～ful [fɔ́:s-ful] a. chikarazuyoi. ～meat [fɔ́:smi:t] n. (tsumemono ni suru) hikiniku.

forceps [fɔ́:seps] n. pinsetto; kenuki; hanuki nado.

forcible [fɔ́:sibl] a. chikara no aru; murina. ～bly ad.

ford [fɔ:d] v. wataru; kachiwataru. n. asase.

fore [fɔ:/fɔə] a. mae no. n. zembu; mae no bubun. ad. mae ni. *inter. Fore!* sore ii kai! *prep.* no mae ni. **fore-and-aft** [fɔ́:rəndá:ft] a., ad. hesaki kara tomo made.

forearm [fɔ́:a:m] n. ni no ude. v. [fɔ:rá:m] busō suru; (arakajime) yōi suru: *To be forewarned is to be* ～*ed.* = *Forwarned is* ～*ed*, keikai wa sentōjumbi da.

forebear [fɔ́:bɛə] n. (1) (*usu. pl.*) sosen; senzo. (2) =**forbear.**

forebode [fɔ:bóud] v. zenchō to naru; yochi suru: *these black clouds* ～ *a storm*, kono kurokumo wa taifū no zenchō da.

foreboding [fɔ:bóudiŋ] n. zenchō; yokan.

forecast [fɔ́:kɑst] v. forecast or forecasted; forecasting. yosō suru; senken suru; yohō suru. [fɔ́:kɑst] n. yosō; yohō: **weather** ～ n. tenki yohō.

forecastle [fóuksl] n. zenkampan (gunkan no).

foreclose [fɔ:klóuz] v. jogai suru; shimedasu (*of*); teitōnagare ni suru.

foreclosure [fɔ:klóuʒə] n. (*leg.*) teitōbutsu torimodoshiken no heisa-tetsuzuki; teitō nagare.

forefather [fɔ́:fɑ́:ðə] *n.* (*pl.*) sosen; senzo. *cf. forebear.*

forefinger [fɔ́:fíŋgə] *n.* hitosashiyubi; shokushi.

forefoot [fɔ́:fut] *n.* mae ashi (kemono no, *beast*); fune no hesaki no namikiri.

forefront [fɔ́:frʌnt] *n.* saizembu; saizensen.

forego *v.* [fɔ:góu] **forewent, foregone; foregoing.** sakidatsu. ～**ing** *a.* jōki no; mae ni itta (nobeta).

foregone [fɔ:gɔ́n] *v. see :* **forego.** *a.* sudeni kimatta. ～ **conclusion.**, kitei no ketsuron hajime kara wakatte iru koto.

foreground [fɔ́:graund] *n.* zenkei; mottomo medatsu ichi.

forehead [fɔ́rid/-red] *n.* hitai.

foreign [fɔ́rin] *a.* gaikoku no; gairai no. ～**er** *n.* gaikokujin.

foreknew [fɔ:nju:] *v. see :* **foreknow**

foreknow [fɔ:nóu] *v.* **foreknew, foreknown; foreknowing.** maemotte shiru; yochi suru.

foreknowledge [fɔ́:nɔ́lidʒ] *n.* senken; yochi.

foreknown [fɔ:noun] *v. see :* **foreknow.**

foreland [fɔ́:lənd] *n.* misaki (*cape*).

forelock [fɔ́:lɔk] *n.* maegami. ⌐kōchō; kantoku.

foreman [fɔ́:mən] *n.* sekininsha; baishinchō (*of jury*); shok-

foremast [fé:mɑ:st] *n.* zenshō; (fune no) mae no hobashira.

foremost [fɔ́:moust] *a.* massaki no. *ad.* massaki ni.

forenoon [fɔ́:nu:n] *n.* gozen; hirumae.

forensic [fərénsik] *a.* hōtei ya kōkai-tōron ni yakudatsu.

foreordain [fɔ́:rɔ:déin] *v.* maemotte kimeru; yotei suru.

foreordination [fɔ́:rɔ:dinéiʃən] *n.* yotei; yotei no ummei.

forerun [fɔ:rʌ́n] *v.* **foreran, forerun; forerunning.** senku suru; yohō suru (*formerly informing*). ⌐(an omen).

forerunner [fɔ́:rʌ́nə] *n.* senku (*person that goes before*); zenchō

foresail [fɔ́:seil] *n.* (*schooner* de) mae no *mast* no daiichi no ho.

foresee [fɔ:sí:] *v.* **foresaw, foreseen; foreseeing.** senken suru; mitōsu; yochi suru. ⌐sage).

foreshadow [fɔ:ʃǽdou] *v.* no zenchō to naru; yochi suru (*pre-*

foreshorten [fɔ:ʃɔ́:tn] *v.* (*in painting*) enkin o tsukete e (*picture*) o kaku.

foreshow [fɔ:ʃóu] *v.* **foreshowed, foreshown; foreshowing.** maemotte shimesu (miseru).

foresight [fɔ́:sait] *n.* senken. yōjin; shōsei (jū no).

forest [fɔ́rist] *n.* shinrin; sanrin; mori; kariba.

forestall [fɔ:stɔ́:l] *v.* kisen o seisuru; dashinuku. kaishimeru (*take the initiative of*).

forester [fɔ́ristə] *n.* rimmukan; sanrin no jūnin.

foretaste [fɔ:téist] *v.* maemotte ajiwau (tamesu); yosō suru. *n.* [fɔ́:teist] saki dameshi; yosō.   ⌈suru.

foretell [fɔ:tél] *v.* **foretold; foretelling.** yogen suru; yochi

forethought [fɔ́:θɔ:t] *n.* shinryo; yōjin; mae motte iroiro no. koto o kangaeru koto.

foretoken [fɔ́:toukən] *n.* zenchō. *v.* [fɔ:tóukən] zenchō ga aru.

forever [fərévə] *ad.* eienni; tsuneni.

forewarn [fɔ:wɔ́:n] *v.* arakajime keikoku suru.

forewent [fɔ:went] *v. see* : **forego.**

foreword [fɔ́:wə:d] *n.* jobun; hashigaki.

forfeit [fɔ́:fit] *v.* namakete ushinau (chii, kenri nado o). *a.* ushinatta; bosshū sareta. *n.* bakkin.

forfeiture [fɔ́:fitʃə] *n.* (chii, kenri, rieki, meiyo nado) sōshitsu; bosshū; bakkin; bosshū butsu.

forgather [fɔ:gǽðə] *v.* atsumaru; majiwaru; shitashimu (*with*).

forgave [fəgéiv] *v. see* : **forgive.**

forge [fɔ:dʒ] *n.* kajikōba. *v.* kitaeru; gizō suru; jojoni susumu; kitaeru. ～**er** *n.* gizōsha. ～**ry** [fɔ́:dʒəri] *n.* gizō; bunsho-gizō.

forget [fəgét] *v.* **forgot, forgotten; forgetting.** wasureru. ～**ful** *a.* wasureppoi. ～**fully** *ad.* ～**fulness** *n.* kembōshō; fuchūi.

forget-me-not [fəgétminɔ̀t] *n.* (*flow.*) rurisō; wasurenagusa.

forgive [fəgív] *v.* **forgave, forgiven; forgiving.** yurusu. ～ **ness** *n.* yōsha; yurushi.

forgiven [fəgívn] *v. see* : **forgive.**   ⌈(*merciful*).

forgiving [fəgíviŋ] *v. see* : **forgive.** *a.* kandaina; nasakebukai

forgo [fɔ:góu] *v.* **forwent, forgone; forgoing.** nashi de sumasu; sashihikaeru.

fork [fɔ:k] *n.* niku sashi; fōku; futamata; bunkiten; onsa. *v.* mata ni wakareru. ～**ed** [-t] *a.* mata-jō no; futamata no.

forlorn [fəlɔ́:n] *a.* misuterareta : ～ **hope**, kesshitai.

form [fɔ:m] *n.* sugata; katachi; shoshiki; yōshi; keishiki; keitai; soshiki; shurui; reishiki; **telegraph** ～, *n.* raishinshi.

v. katachizukuru; hensei suru; soshiki suru; kangae dasu.
∼less [fɔ́:mles] *a.* katachi no nai.

formal [fɔ́:məl] *a.* seishiki no; kyorei ni kodawaru. **∼ism** [fɔ́:məlizm] *n.* kyorei; keishiki-ron. **∼ly** *ad.* seishiki ni; aratamatte; keishikitekini.

formaldehyde [fɔ:mǽldihaid] *n.* (*chem.*) gisan arudehiido.

formality [fɔ:mǽliti] *n.* gishiki baru koto; (*pl.*) tetsuzuki.

formation [fɔ:méiʃən] *n.* katachizukuru koto; katachizukura-reta soshiki.

formative [fɔ́:mətiv] *a.* keisei suru.

former [fɔ́:mə] *a.* izen no; mae no; zensha no. **∼ly** *ad.*

formidable [fɔ́:midəbl] *a.* osoroshii; anadori-gatai. **∼bly** *ad*

Formosa [fɔ:móusə] *n.* Taiwan.

Formosan [fɔ:móusən] *a.* Taiwan (jin) no. *n.* Taiwanjin.

formula [fɔ́:mjulə] *n.* (*pl.* **-s; -lae** [li:]) kōshiki; shiki; (*med.*) shohō. **∼ry** *n.* kōshikishū. *a.* kōshiki no.

formulate [fɔ́:mjuleit] *v.* shiki ni tsukuru; shiki de shimesu. **∼tion** [fɔ:mjuléiʃən] *n.* keishikika; kōshikika.

fornicate [fɔ́:nikeit] *v.* shitsū suru.

fornication [fɔ́:nikéiʃən] *n.* shitsū (*unmarried sexual relation*).

forsake [fəséik/fɔ:séik] *v.* **forsook; forsaken, forsaking.** suteru; misuteru; dannen suru.

forsooth [fəsú:θ/fɔ:s-] *ad.* tashikani (furui yōhō).

forswear [fɔ:swéə] *v.* **forswore; forsworn, forswearing.** chikai o tateru; chikatte yameru.

forswore [fɔ:sóə] *v. see* : **forswear.**

forsworn [fɔ:swɔ́:n] *v. see* : **forswear.**

fort [fɔ:t] *n.* yōsai; toride.

forte [fɔ:t] *n.* chōsho, tokui. *ad., a.* (*mus*) [fɔ́:ti] tsuyoku; tsuyoi.

forth [fɔ:θ] *ad.* mae e; zempō ni; saki ni; soto e; mieru tokoro ni. *and so* **∼**, unnun (*etc.*); nadonado; tō.

forthcoming [fɔ:θkʌ́min] *a.* kore kara no; kondo no; tejika ni : *She needed help but no one was* **∼**, kanojo wa tasuke ga hoshikatta ga, kite kureru mono ga dare mo nakatta.

forthwith [fɔ́:θwíθ/-wíð] *ad.* tachidokoro ni; tadachini.

fortieth [fɔ́:tiiθ] *a.* dai shijū (yonjū) (bamme) no. *n.* dai shijū (yonjū); yonjū (shijū)-bun no ichi (*one fortieth*).

fortification [fɔ:tifikéiʃən] *n.* chikujō; chikujōjutsu (gaku);

(pl.) hōrui ; yōsai.

fortify [fɔ́:tifai] *v.* yōsai o mōkeru ; kengo ni suru : ～**ied port,** *n.* gunkō. ～**ied zone** *n.* yōsaichitai.

fortissimo [fɔ:tísimou] *ad.* (*mus.*) mottomo tsuyoku.

fortitude [fɔ́:titju:d] *n.* kennin fubatsu ; fukutsu (*never yielding*).

fortnight [fɔ́:tnait] *n.* jūyokka ; nishūkan. ～**ly** *a.*, *ad.* nishūkan goto no (ni).

fortress [fɔ́:tris] *n.* yōsai.

fortuitous [fɔ:tjúitəs] *a.* gūzen no ; igai no. ～**ly** *ad.*

fortuity [fɔ:tjúiti] *n.* gūzen ; gūzen no dekigoto.

fortunate [fɔ́:tjunit/-et] *a.* shiawasena ; kōunna. ～**ly** *ad.* saiwaini.

fortune [fɔ́:tʃən/-tju:n] *n.* ummei ; kōun ; shiawase ; zaisan ; (*F.*) ummei no megami ; (*pl.*) eiko seisui : ～**hunter** [hʌ́ntə] zaisan meate ni tsuma o motomeru hito. ～**teller** [-tèlə] *n.* ekisha. ～**telling** [-tèliŋ] *n.* uranai.

forty [fɔ́:ti] *a.*, *n.* shijū yonjū (no). ～ **winks,** hirune. shokugo no

forum [fɔ́:rəm] *n.* (kōdai Rōma) no hiroba ; soko e atsumatte hanashiatta tokoro ; saibansho ; rondan (*the platform*).

forward [fɔ́:wəd] *v.* okuru ; tensō suru : *Please ～ my mail to my new address,* yūbimbutsu wa atarashii banchi e okutte kudasai. *a.* mae no ; susunda ; sōjuku no ; desugita. ～**ing business** *n.* unsōgyō. ～**ly** *ad.* mae ni ; sashidegamashiku. ～**ness** *n.* namaiki. ～(**s**) [-d(z)] *ad.* mae no hōni ; saki ni ; deshabatte.

forwent [fɔ:wént] *see* : **forgo.**

fosse, foss [fɔs] *n.* hori ; unga.

fossil [fɔ́sl/-sil] *n.* kaseki ; kyūheijin. *a.* kaseki no ; chimpuna.

fossilize [fɔ́silaiz] *v.* kaseki ni suru (naru) ; furukusaku suru (naru).

foster [fɔ́stə] *v.* yashinau ; sodateru : ～ **brother** *n.* chi(chi) kyōdai. ～**child** *n.* yashinaigo ; satogo. ～ **father** *n.* yōfu. ～ **mother,** *n.* yōbo.

fought [fɔ:t] *see* : **fight.**

foul [faul] *v.* yogosu ; shōtotsu suru. *a.* kitanai ; fuseina ; hiwai na ; minikui. ～ *play,* hansoku ; fusei kōi. *n.* shōtotsu ; hansoku. ～**ly** *ad.* ～**-mouthed** [-mauðd] *a.* kuchi-gitanai. ～**ness** *n.*

foulard [fú:lɑ:d] *n.* usui kinu ; reiyon ; momen nado no kire.

found [fáund] *see* : **find.**

found [fáund] *v.* kiso o oku; dodai o tsukuru; sōritsu suru; chūzō suru (*cast*).

foundation [faundéiʃən] *n.* dodai; kiso; kifukin; kifukin de dekita mono; zaidan. ⁓**stone** [-stoun] dodaiishi; kontei.

founder [fáundə] *n.* sōritsusha; chūzōsha. *v.* shinsui (chimbotsu) suru; chimba ni naru.

foundling [fáundliŋ] *n.* sutego.

foundry [fáundri] *n.* chūzō; chūzōjo.

fount [faunt] *n.* izumi; gensen; katsuji no hitosoroi (*a set*).

fountain [fáuntin] *n.* izumi; funsui; minamoto. ⁓**head** [-hed] *n.* suigen. ⁓**pen** [-pen] *n.* mannenhitsu.

four [fɔ:/fɔə] *a.* yottsu no; yonko no. *n.* shi (yottsu-yon, 4) : on *all* ⁓*s*, yotsumbai ni natte; hitoshiku. ⁓**fold** [⁻fould] *a.* yonjū no; yombai no; yotsuori no. ⁓**-in-hand** [-inhʌnd] *n.* yontōbasha. ⁓ **o'clock** [-əklɔk] *n.* (*bot.*) oshiroibana. ⁓**square** [-skwɛə] *a.* shikaku no; fudō no.

fourteen [fɔ́:tí:n] *a.* jūshi (jūyon) no. *n.* jūshi (jūyon, 14).

fourteenth [fɔ́:tí:nθ] *a.* dai jūshi (yon) no; (jūyon) bamme no; *n.* dai jūshi; jūyombun no ichi; jūyokka.

fourth [fɔ:θ] *a.*, *n.* yombamme (no). dai shi (no).

fowl [faul] *n.* niwatori; (*pl.*) kakin; tori.

fowling [fáuliŋ] *n.* toriuchi. ⁓ **net,** *n.* tori ami. ⁓ **piece**, tori o utsu jū.

fox [fɔks] *n.* (*zoo*) kitsune; kitsune no kegawa; kōkatsuna hito. ⁓**glove** [⁻glʌv] *n.* (*bot.*) jigitarisu. ⁓**hound** [⁻haund] *n.* ryōken no isshu. ⁓**sleep** [-sli:p] *n.* tanukineiri. ⁓**y** *a.* kitsune no yōna; kōkatsuna; kitsuneiro no.

foyer [fɔ́iə] *n.* kankyaku yūhojō; kyūkei shitsu.

fracas [frǽkɑ:/fréikəs] *n.* (*sing.*, & *pl.*) kenka; sōdō.

fraction [frǽkʃən] *n.* hahen; shōryō; (*math.*) bunsū.

fractional [frǽkʃənəl] *a.* hampana; wazukana; bunsū no.

fractious [frǽkʃəs] *a.* okorippoi; kimuzukashii.

fracture [frǽktʃə] *n.* hasai; zashō; kossetsu. *v.* kudaku; kudakeru; kujiku. ⌈liti] *n.* kyojaku; morosa

fragile [frǽdʒail] *a.* moroi; kyojakuna. ⁓**ly** *ad.* ⁓**ity** [fredʒí-

fragment [frǽgmənt] *n.* hahen; dampen. ⁓**ary** [frǽgméntəri] *a.* dampenteki; barabara no.

fragrance [fréigrəns] *n*. hōkō ; yoi nioi ; kaori ; kōki.

fragrant [fréigrənt] *a*. kambashii ; kaori no yoi. ~**ly** *ad*.

frail [freil] *a*. moroi ; kyojakuna ; teisō no yowai. ~**ty** [fréilti] *n*. zeijaku ; jakuten ; ishi hakujaku.

frame [freim] *n*. soshiki ; honegumi ; waku ; kibun. *v*. kumitateru ; waku o tsukeru. ~**work** [wə:k] *n*. honegumi ; soshiki

franc [fræŋk] *n*. furan (*France* no kahei).

franchise [frǽntʃaiz] *n*. tokkyo ; senkyoken ; sanseiken

frank [fræŋk] *a*. shōjikina. *n*. shōjiki ; muryō sōtatsu no yūbin. *v*. yūzei (*postage*) o menjo suru. *to be* ~ *with you*, uchi akete iu to. ~**ly** *ad*. shōjikini ; sotchokuni. ~**ness** *n*.

Frank [fræŋk] *n*. Seiyōjin (*European*). ~**ish** *a*. *Frank* zoku no ; Seiyōjin no.

frankfurter [frǽŋkfə:tə] *n*. sōsēji (*sausage*) no isshu.

frankincense [frǽŋkinsens] *n*. nyūkō (*milk* no kaori).

franklin [frǽŋklin] *n*. (*Brit*. chūsei no) gōshi ; chiisai jinushi.

frantic [frǽntik] *a*. kichigaijimita. ~**ally** [-kəli] *ad*. kichigaijimite.

fraternal [frətɔ́:nəl] *a*. kyōdai no.

fraternity [frətɔ́:niti] *n*. kyōdai no aijō (*amity*) ; daigakusei no *club* ; dantai ; kumiai ; nakama.

fraternize [frǽtənaiz] *v*. shitashiku majiwaru.

fraud [frɔ:d] *n*. sagi ; sagishi (*impostor*).

fraudulence [frɔ́:djuləns] *n*. sagi. ~**ent** *a*. sagi no. ~**ly** *ad*.

fraught [frɔ:t] *a*. ni o tsunde (iru) ; jūman shita (*with*).

fray [frei] *v*. kosuru ; hotsureru (*become loose*). hogusu. *n*. sōjō ; kenka (*fight*). *v*. sōdō (*commotion*).

freak [fri:k] *v*. madara ni suru. *n*. kimagure ; kikei : ~ *of nature*, kikei ; zōka no tawamure. ~**ish** [fri:kiʃ] *a*. kimagureno ; kimyōna (*odd*). ~**ly** [-li] *ad*. kimagure ni.

freckle [frékl] *n*. sobakasu. *v*. sobakasu ga dekiru.

free [fri:] *a*. jiyūna ; hima no (~ *time*) ; enryo no nai (*unreserved*) ; monooshimi senu (*generous*) ; muzei no (~ *tax*) ; muryō no (~ *ticket*). *v*. jiyū ni suru. *ad*. jiyū ni ; muryō de. ~**board** [fri:bɔ:d] *n*. (*marine*) kan-gen. (fune no mizu to kampan to no aida). ~**booter** [fri:bu:tə] *n*. kaizoku. ~**born** [fri:bɔ́:n] *a*. jiyū no mi ni umareta. ~ **fight** *n*. naguriai. ~**-hand** [fri:hǽnd] *a*., *u*. te de egaita (e—*picture*) ; jizai (no

(~ *drawing*). ~**hold** [fríːhould] *n.* (*leg.*) jiyūhoyū fudōsan.
~**holder** [fríːhóuldə] *n.* (jiyūhoyū fudōsan) shoyūsha. ~**ly**
[fríːli] *ad.* jiyūni. ~**man** [fríːmən] *n.* jiyūjin; kōminken o
motte iru hito. ~**stone** [⌐stoun] *n.* sekkaiseki (*lime-stone*). ~
thinker [⌐θiŋkə] *n.* jiyū shisōka.

freedom [fríːdəm] *n.* jibun no omou yōni dekiru koto; jiyū;
jishu; buenryo (enryo no nai koto); tokkyo; tokken.

Freemason [fríːmeisn] *n.* Furiimēson kyōsai kumiai-in. ~**ry**
[fríːmeisnri] *n.* Furiimēson kyōsai kumiai sei.

freeze [friːz] *v.* **froze, frozen; freezing.** kōraseru; kogoeru;
kogoesaseru; issai no ugoki o nakusuru (hiyuteki ni mo).

freezing [fríːziŋ] *a.* kōritsuku; reitanna. ~ **point** *n.* hyōten
(cf. *boiling point*).

freight [freit] *n.* un'yu; kamotsu (*goods*); unchin (*rates*). *v.* kamotsu o tsumu. ~**age** [fréitidʒ] *n.* kamotsu unsō; unchin.
~**car** [fréitkaː] *n.* (*Am.*) kasha.

French [frentʃ] *a.* Furansu no; Furansujin no. *take* ~ *leave*,
shujin ni aisatsu sezu ni kaeru koto. *n.* Furansugo: The ~,
n. France kokumin. ~**man** [⌐mən] *n.* Furansujin (hitori no).

frenzy [frénzi] *v.* hakkyō saseru. *n.* kyōki.

frequency [fríːkwənsi] *n.* hindosū (kurikaesu dosū; shūha-sū,
of electric wave).

frequent [fríːkwənt] *a.* tabitabi no. *v.* [frikwént] tabitabi iku.
~**ly** *ad.* tabitabi. ~**er** [frikwéntə] *n.* otokui.

fresco [fréskou] *n.* hekiga-hō (*way*); hekiga (*wall painting*).

fresh [freʃ] *a.* atarashii; keiken no nai; sōkaina (*invigorating*);
nama no: ~ **herring** *n.* nama nishin. (*Am. col.*) namaikina.
~**ly** [-li] *ad.* aratani. ~**man** [-ʃmən] *n.* shin'nyūsei. ~**ness**
n. atarashisa. ~ **water,** tansui.

freshen [fréʃn] *v.* atarashiku suru; genkizukeru (*encourage*);
shinsenni naru; ikioi o masu; (*wind*) tsuyoku naru; shioke
(*salt*) o ushinau.   「*melting snow*).

freshet [fréʃit] *n.* ōmizu; kōzui (*flood caused by heavy rain or*

fret [fret] *v.* kuyokuyo suru; nayamasu; nayamu; namidatasu
(*ruffle*); raimon (*design*) de kazaru. *n.* iradachi (*irritation*);
(*arch.*) raimon. ~**work** [⌐wəːk] *n.* raimon kazari; sukashi
zaiku.

fretful [frétf(u)l] *a.* iradatsu; kimuzukashii. ∼**ly** *ad.* iradatte. ∼**ness** [frétfulnis] *n.* iradachi.

friable [fráiəbl] *a.* moroi; kudakeyasui. ∼**ness, friability** [fraiəbíliti] *n.* morosa.

friar [fráiə] *n.* takuhatsu-sō; shūdōsō (*the Franciscan Order*).

friary [fráiəri] *n.* shūdō-in; sō-an.

fricative [fríkətiv] *a.* masatsu de shōzuru. *n.* masatsu-on (f, ∫, θ, ӡ nado no shiin (*consonant*)).

friction [fríkʃən] *n.* masatsu; fuwa; atsureki (*disagreement*).

Friday[fráidi] *n.* Kin'yōbi. **Good F.** Kirisuto junan no hi (*day*).

friend [frend] *n.* tomodachi; sanjosha (*patron*); (*rel.*) Quaker no kai-in (*Society of* F∼). ∼**less** [⌐is] *a.* tomodachi no nai. ∼**liness** [⌐linis] *n.* yūjō; shimmitsu (*intimacy*). ∼**ly** *a.* shinzen no; kōtsugōna (*propitious*). ∼**ship** [⌐ʃip] *n.* yūjō.

frieze [fri:z] *v.* kebadatasu; chijirasu (*curl*). *n.* (katamen ni keba (*nap*) no aru) rasha (*woollen cloth*); (*arch.*) e-moyō.

frigate [frígit] *n.* mukashi no sambon-bashira no gunkan; (*Brit.*) goeikan.

fright [frait] *n.* kyōfu; osoroshii mono; (*col.*) minikui mono. ∼**en** [fáitn] *v.* kyōfu saseru; odorokasu. ∼**ful** [fráitf(u)l] *a.* osoroshii; kikaina (*shockingly ugly*). ∼**fully** *ad.* [fráitf(u)li] osoroshiku.

frigid [frídӡid] *a.* samui; reitanna (*apathetic*). ∼**ity** [fridӡíditi] *n.* kanrei; reitan; teichō ∼**ly** *ad.* tsumetaku; reitanni. ∼ **zone** *n.* kantai.

frill [fril] *n.* kazari; (*Am.*) kyoshoku; (*col.*) kidori.

fringe [frindӡ] *n.* fusa; fuchikazari (*margin decoration*). *v.* fusa o tsukeru : *bushes* ∼*d the road*, michi o yabuga fuchidotte.

frippery [frípəri] *n.* yasupikamono.

frisk [frisk] *n.* hanemawari. *v.* hanemawaru; (*Am. sl.*) te de sawatte shojihin (*personal effects*) o shiraberu. ∼**y** [⌐i] *a.* hanemawaru.

frith [friθ]=**firth** [fə:θ] *n.* semai irie; kaimon (*estuary*).

fritter [frítə] *n.* karui agemono. komagire. *v.* komakani kiru; (jikan, kane nado) o mudazukai suru (*waste*).

frivolity [frivóliti] *n.* kudaranu okonai (kangae).

frivolous [frívələs] *a.* karugarushii, fuhakuna, kudaranai. ∼

ly *ad.* ⌈keba (*nap*) datasu.

friz(z) [friz] *n.* chijirege (*curl*); kebadatta kireji. *v.* chijirase

frizzle [frízl] *n.* chijirege. *v.* chijirasu; jūjū abura de ageru.

fro [frou] *ad.* achira e (*away*). *to and* ∾, atchi ittari kotchi kitari.

frock [frɔk] *n.* fujin, kodomo no fuku; sōryo no koromo. *v.* koromo o kiru. ∾ *coat*, tsūjō-reifuku.

frog [frɔg] *n.* kaeru; *France*jin (keibetsu shita iikata).

frolic [frɔ́lik] *a., v.* jareru; tawamureru; fuzakeru. *v.* tawamure, ∾*some* [⌐səm] *a.*

from [frɔm] *prep.* kara; ...no tame ni (*suffer* ∾). irai zutto; riyū de. *a train* ∾ *New York, N. Y.* kara no ressha. ∾ *that time forward*, sono toki konokata zutto. *act* ∾ *a sense of duty*, gimu no kannen kara okonau.

frond [frɔnd] *n.* (*bot.*) shida (*fern*). kaisō (*seaweeds*) nado no ha.

front [frʌnt] *n.* shōmen; jinchū; hitai (*forehead*). *a.* shōmen no. *v.* mukau; men suru. *have the* ∾, atsukamashiku mo... suru. *in* ∾ *of*, no shōmen ni. *show a bold* ∾, zūzū shiku kamaeru.

frontage [frʌ́ntidʒ] *n.* tatemono ya tochi no omote; tatemono to tōri ya kawa nado to no aida no jisho.

frontal [frʌ́nt(ɔ)l] *a.* mae no; hitai (*forehead*) no; shōmen no.

frontier [frʌ́ntiə] *n.* kokkyō. *a.* kokkyō no.

frontispiece [frʌ́ntispi:s] *n.* hon no tobira no e; kuchie.

frontlet [frʌ́ntlit] *n.* hitai kazari (*forehead* ni tsukeru mono); dōbutsu (*animal*) no hitai.

frost [frɔ́(:)st] *n.* shimo; samusa; (*col.*) shippai (*failure*). *v.* shimo de ōu; shimo no gai o ukeru. ∾*bite* [frɔ́(:)s(t)bait] *n.* shimoyake. ∾*bitten* [⌐bitn] *a.* shimoyake no. ∾*ed* [frɔ́(:)stid] *a.* satō(*sugar*)-kake no; shimo no gai o uketa; shimoyake ni kakatta; tsuya-keshi no (∾ *glass tumblers*). ∾*work* [-wə:k] *n.* shimo moyō no kazari. ∾*y* [frɔ́(:)sti] *a.* shimo no furi sōna; reitanna (*chilling nature*).

froth [frɔ́(:)θ] *n.* awa; kudaranai mono. *v.* awadataseru; awadatsu. ∾*y* [-i] *a.* awadatsu; kūkyona (*empty*).

froward [frɔ́(u)əd] *a.* gankona; wagamamana.

frown [fraun] *n., v.* mayu o hisomeru (koto).

frowzy [fráuzi] *a.* kitanai (*dirty*); kabikusai (*musty*).

froze [frouz] *see* : **freeze.**

fructify [fráktifai] *v.* mi o musubu (musubaseru).

frugal [frú:g(ǝ)l] *a.* ken'yaku suru ; shissona. *be* ~ *of,* o setsuyaku suru. ~**lity** [fru:gǽliti] *n.* kenyaku ; setsuyaku. ~**ly** [frú:gǝli] *ad.* setsuyaku shite ; tsumashiku. ~ **meal** *n.* shissona shokuji.

fruit [fru:t] *n.* kudamono (kajitsu) ; kekka (*result*). *v.* mi o musubu. ~ **sugar** [frú:t sjú:gǝ] *n.* katō. ~**age** [frú:tidʒ] *n.* kajitsu ; kekka (*result*). ~**erer** [-⌐ǝrǝ] *n.* kudamonoshō. ~**ful** [-f(u)l]*a.* ōku minoru ; kōka no ōi (*profitable*). ~**less** [-lis] *a.* minoranu ; muekina (*useless*). ~**lessly** [-lisli] *ad.* mi o musubanai de ; kōka naku(*vainly*). ~**y** [-i] *a.* kajitsu no yōna ; kajitsu no aji ga suru (*taste*).

fruition [fru:íʃǝn] *n.* ketsu-jitsu ; jitsugen (*realization*).

frustrate [frástreit] *v.* kujiku ; shikujiraseru ; mukō ni suru.

frustration [frʌtréiʃǝn] *n.* zasetsu ; shippai..

frustum [frástǝm] (*pl.* **-tums, -ta** [-tǝ]) *n.* ensuikei no jōbu o teihen ni heikōni kirisuteta mono.

fry [frai] *v.* abura (*oil*) de ageru. *n.* furai. waka-uo no mure (*shoal*) ; kodomo-tachi.

frying-pan [fráiiŋ pæn] *n.* furainabe (*pan*).

ft. = **feet, foot.**

fuchsia [fjú:ʃǝ] *n.* (*bot.*) fukushia ; tsuriuki-sō.

fuddle [fʌdl] *v.* meitei (saseru, suru). *n.* meitei.

fudge [fʌdʒ] *n.* tawagoto (*nonsense*) ; chokorēto (*chocolate*) iri kyandei (*candy*). *inter.* bakana ! (*bosh !*).

fuel [fjúil] *n.* nenryō.

fugitive [fjú:dʒitiv] *a.* tōbō suru ; sonoba kagiri no (*occasional*) ; hakanai (*fleeting*) ; *n.* tōbōsha ; bōmeisha.

fugue [fju:g] *n.* (*mus.*) tonsōkyoku.   ⌐shiten.

fulcrum [fʌlkrǝm] (*pl.* **-crums** ; **-cra** [-krǝ]) *n.* tekomakura.

fulfil(l) [fulfíl] *v.* hatasu ; jōju suru. ~**ment** *n.* rikō ; shūryō.

full [ful] *a.* ippai no ; kanzenna (*perfect*). *n.* jūbun. *ad.* jūbunni ~ *age,* seinen. ~ **dress,** *n.* reifuku. ~ **binding,** sōgawa seihon. ~**-blown** [fúlblóun] *a.* mankai no. ~**-grown** [-gróun] *a.* jūbunni seichō shita. ~**-hearted** [-há:tid] *a.* yūki ni michita. ~**stop,** *n.* shūshifu. ~**y** [fúli] *ad.* jūbunni.

fulminate [fʌlmineit] *v.* bakuhatsu saseru (suru) ; pikatto hikaru (*flash*) ; narihibiku. *n.* (*chem.*) raisan'en ; bakuyaku (*explosives*).

fulmination [fʌlmínéiʃən] *n.* raimei ; bakuhatsu ; okotte donaru (*angry roar*).

ful(l)ness [fúlnis] *n.* jūman ; ippai ; kanzen : *in the ～ of one's heart*, ureshisa no amari.

fulsome [fulsəm] *a.* shitsukkoi ; iyarashii. ～**ly** *ad.* shitsuk- ⌐koku.

fumble [fʌmbl] *v.* saguru ; hema o suru (*handle awkwardly*) ; tori sokonau (tama o).

fume [fju:m] *n.* nioi no aru kemuri (*smoke*) ; gekido (*rage*). *v.* kemuru ; jōhatsu suru. *be in a ～*, pumpun okoru ; ikimaku.

fumigate [fjú:migeit] *v.* ibusu ; kō o taku (*burn incense*).

fumigation [fju:migéiʃən] *n.* ibusu koto ; shōdoku (*disinfection*).

fun [fʌn] *n.* tawamure : *be good (or) great ～*, jitsu ni omoshiroi. *for (or in) ～*, jōdan ni. *half in ～*, omoshiro hambun ni. *make ～ of*, o karakau.

function [fʌ́nkʃən] *n.* hataraki ; kannō ; kinō (*faculty*) ; (*math.*) kansū. *v.* yakume o hatasu. ～**al** [-əl] *a.* kannō no ; shokumu no. ～**ary** [-əri] *n.* kanri ; shokuin.

fund [fʌnd] *n.* shikin ; (*pl.*) kōsai ; takuwae. *v.* shikin ni mukeru ; kōsai ni suru. ～**holder** [-hould́ə] *n.* (*Brit.*) kōsai shoyūsha.

fundamental [fʌndəmént(ə)l] *a.* kihontekina. *n.* genri. ～**ly** [fʌndəméntali] *ad.* kompontekini ; hataraki no.

funeral [fjú:n(ə)r(ə)l] *n.* sōshiki. *a.* sōshiki no.

funereal [fjuníəriəl] *a.* sōshiki ni fusawashii ; inkina (*gloomy*).

fungous [fʌ́ŋgəs] *a.* baikin no ; kin no yōna.

fungus [fʌ́ŋgəs] *n.* (*pl.* -**gi** [-dʒai]) ; -**guses** [-gəsiz] kin.

funk [fʌŋk] *n.* osore ; okubyōmono (*coward*). *v.* furueagarasu ; kowagaru (*be afraid of*).

funnel [fʌ́n(ə)l] *n.* jōgo ; fune no entotsu (*chimney*).

funnily [fʌ́nili] *ad.* okashiku ; (*popularity*) kimyōni.

funny [fʌ́ni] *a.* okashina ; kimyōna.

fur [fə:] *n.* ke ; kegawa ; shita (*tongue*) no koke. *v.* kegawa o tsukeru. ～ **coat** [-kóut] *n.* kegawa no gaitō.

furbelow [fə́:bilou] *n.* fujinfuku no susokazari ; (*pl.*) keba-

kebashii kazari.
furbish [fɔ́:biʃ] v. migaku; mata yaku ni tatsu yōni suru.
furious [fjúɔriəs] a. ikari kuruu; sōzōshii (*noisy*).
furl [fɔ:l] (ho (*sail*) nado o) tatamu (maku).
furlough [fɔ́:lou] n., v. kyūka (o ataeru).
furnace [fɔ́:nis] n. ro; kamado; yōtetsuro; shiren (*severe test*).
furnish [fɔ́:niʃ] v. kyōkyū suru; sonaetsukeru (*fit up*). ～ings
[-iŋz] n. (*pl.*) kagu; shitsunai no sonaetsuke.
furniture [fɔ́:nitʃə] n. kagu; shitsunai no dōgu; naiyō (*of*).
furor [fjúɔrɔ:] n. nekkyō; nekkyōtekina shōsan (*praise*).
furrier [fʌ́riə] n. kegawashō.
furrow [fʌ́rou] n. mizo; sukiato; shiwa (*deep wrinkle*).
furry [fɔ́:ri] a. kegawa de ōwareta; kegawa de tsukutta.
further [fɔ́:ðə] a. sono ue no. ad. sara ni. v. susumeru. ～ance
[fɔ́:ðərəns] n. zōshin; sokushin; hakadoraseru koto. ～more
[-mɔ̀ə] ad. sono ue ni. ～most a. mottomo tōi.
furthest [fɔ́:ðist] a. ichiban tōi. ad. mottomo tōku.
furtive [fɔ́:tiv] a. hisokana; naisho no. ～ly [-li] ad. sotto.
fury [fjúɔri] n. funnu; fungeki; kyōbō (*violence*); (F～, *usu.*
Furies fukushū no megami (*goddess of revenge*) : in a ～, fungeki
shite. *like* ～, hageshiku.
furze [fɔ:z] n. (*bot.*) harienishida.
furzy [fɔ́:zi] a. harienishida no shigetta.
fuse [fju:z] v. tokasu; tokeru. n. dōkasen; (*elec.*) fyūzu.
fusee [fju:zí:] n. taifu matchi (atama ga ōkikute kaze de kienai).
fuselage [fjú:zəlidʒ/-lɑ:dʒ] n. hikōki (*airplane*) no dōtai.
fusel oil [fjú:z(ə)l ɔil] (*chem.*) fūzeru-yu (*oil*).
fusibility [fjù:zəbíliti] n. tokeyasui teido; tokeyasui seishitsu.
fusible [fjú:zibl] a. yōkai suru; tokeru.
fusillade [fju:ziléid] n., v. issei shageki o suru.
fusion [fjú:ʒən] n. yōkai; yūgō; gappei.
fuss [fʌs] n. ōsawagi. v. sawagu; iraira saseru (*get nervous*). ～y
[fʌ́si] a. kimuzukashii; komakai; chūi no urusai.
fustian [fʌ́stʃən] n. momen ya asa no arai orimono; fasuchian'-
ori. a. fasuchian'ori no.
fusty [fʌ́sti] a. kabikusai (*musty*); furukusai. ～iness n. kabikusai koto.

futile [fju:tail] *n.* mudana ; patto shinai. ～**ity** [fju:tíliti] *n.* mu-eki ; muda.

future [fjú:tʃə] *n.* mirai ; shōrai ; (*pl.*) (*trade*) sakimono. *a* mi-rai no. ～**ism** [fjú:tʃərizm] *n.* (*art*) miraiha. ～**ist** [-ʃərist] *n.* miraiha no geijutsuka (*artist*). ～**ity** [fju:tjúəriti] *n.* mirai ;

fuze, fuse [fjú:z] *n.* fyūzu ; dōkakan.

fuzz [fʌz] *n.* keba ; mukuge (*fluff*). ～**y** [fʌzi] *a.* fuwafuwa shita. raise (*time to come*).

G

G, g [dʒi:] *n.* (*pl.* **G's, gs** [dzi:z]) Eigo *alphabet* no dai-7-bamme no moji.

g. guramu=**gram.**

G.A., g.a. kyōdō kaison (*general average*)

gab [gæb] *n.* muda-banashi; oshaberi.

gabardine [gæbədí:n] *n.* gyabajin; ke (*wool*) ya, men (*cotton*) no isshu no orimono; yuruyakana nagai uwagi (*Jews* no chūseiki no kimono).

gabble [gæbl] *n.* hayakuchi no oshaberi. *v.* pechakucha shaberu (*babble*).

gabion [géibiən] *n.* ishigamachi; jakago (ishi o tsumete teibō nado o kizuku toki tsukau) entōkei no kago.

gable [géibl] *n.* (*archi.*) kirizuma. ~ **board** [-bɔ:d] (*archi.*) hafū. ~ **roof,** kirizuma yane (*roof*). ~ **window** [-windou] hafū mado.

gad [gæd] *v.* buratsuku. ~**fly** [⸗flai] *n.* (*insect*) abu.

gadget [gǽdʒit] *n.* (*col.*) kufū; kōan.

Gaelic [géilik] *a.* Gēru-zoku (*the Gael tribe*) no. *n.* Gērugo.

Gaels [geilz] *n.* (*pl.*) Gēru-zoku (*Scotland* kōchi-chihō ni sumu minzoku).

gaff [gæf] *n.* uokagi (gyofu ga uo o hikiageru tame no saka kagi no aru tsuyoi kagi); isshu no hogeta.

gag [gæg] *n.* sarugutsuwa; (*Brit., sl.*) ba-atari no serifu (*speech*); (*sl.*) peten; itazura. *v.* sarugutsuwa o hameru; hakike o jitto gaman suru; genron o appaku suru.

gage [geidʒ] *n.* teitō butsu; jōgi (*measurement*). *v.* hakaru; hyōka suru (*value*); teitō ni ireru (*mortgage*).

gaiety [gé(i)əti]=**gayety** *n.* kaikatsusa; nigiyakana asobi.

gaily=**gayly** [géili] *ad.* kaikatsuni; nigiyakani.

gain [gein] *n.* rieki; shimpo. *v.* mōkeru; katsu ~**ed** katta. *My watch* ~*s five minutes a day,* watashi no tokei wa ichinichi ni 5 fun susumu. ~*on* (*upon*) chikayoru. ~*over,* tokitsukete mikata ni suru; tassuru. ~ *the summit,* yama no chōjō ni tassuru. ~**ful** [-f(u)l] *a.* rieki no aru.

gainsay [geinséi] *v.* hantai suru.

gait [geit] *n.* arukitsuki ; (*Am.*) hosoku (*pace*).

gaiter [géitə] *n.* gētoru ; kyahan.

gal(1) garon (**gallon, gallon**(s).

gala [géilə] *n.* omatsuri. *a.* omatsuri suru. ~**day**, saijitsu.

galantine [gǽlənti:n] *n.* garantiin (reiniku ryōri (*cold meat dish*) no isshu).

Galaxy [gǽləksi] *n.* (*astr.*) Ginga (*the Milky Way*) ; hanayakana hitobito no mure (*brilliant group*).

gale [geil] *n.* kyōfū. ōkaze.

galena [gəlí:nə] *n.* (*min.*) hōenkō (i(w)ō to namari o fukunda [kōseki].

gall [gɔ:l] *n.* tanjū ; urami (*rancour*) ; (*Am. col.*) tetsumempi (*impudence*). dip one's pen in ~, dokuhitsu o furuu. ~ *and worm-wood*, daikiraina mono. *v.* surimuku ; okoraseru (*make angry*). ~**stone** [gɔ́:lstoun] *n.* (*med.*) tanseki.

gallant [gǽlənt] *a.* yūkanna ; rippana ; fujin ni teineina. *n.* sharemono (*dandy*) ; [gəlǽnt] iro-otoko. ~**ly** *ad.* yūkanni ; fujin ni teineini.

gallantry [gǽləntri] *n.* yūki ; fujin (*ladies*) ni teineina koto.

galleon [gǽliən] *n.* mukashi no Spein no ōkina homaesen.

gallery [gǽləri] *n.* sajiki ; rōka (*croister*) ; bijutsuhin chinretsu-shitsu. [*ing type*).

galley [gǽli] *n.* garii-sen ; fune no ryōribeya ; gerazuri (*print-*

Gallic [gǽlik] *a.* Gōru no ; Gōrujin (*people*) no ; *France* no.

gallipot [gǽlipɔt] *n.* kusuri tsubo ; (*col.*) kusuriya.

gallivant [gǽlivænt] *v.* kairaku o tazunete mawaru ; ochitsu-kanai de aruki mawaru.

gall(**nut**) [gɔ́:lnʌt], **gall** [gɔ:l] *n.* mushi no tsukuru kobu ; mu-shikobu ; fushi.

gallon [gǽlən] *n.* garon (*English measure :* 4,545 *litre*).

galloon [gəlú:n] *n.* hosohimo ; kinsuji, ginsuji nado.

gallop [gǽləp] *n.* uma no kakeashi : *at a* ~, kake ashi de. *v.* (uma o) kakesaseru.

gallows [gǽlouz] *n.* (*pl*) kōshudai. ~ **bird** [-bə:d] *n.* (*col.*) kō-shukei ni narubeki yatsu.

gallstone [gɔ́:lstoun] *n.* tanseki ; tannō ni dekiru ishi.

galop [gǽləp] *n.* (*Fr.*) butō (*dance*) no namae.

galore [gəlɔ́:] *a.* (*pl.*) takusan no; hōfuna. *ad.* takusan ni.

galosh [gəlɔ́ʃ] *n.* (*usu.* **galoshes**) gomu (*gum*) sei no uwagutsu; ōba-shūzu.

galvanic [gælvǽnik] *a.* dōdenki no. **~ism** *n.* dōdenki.

galvanize [gǽlvənaiz] *v.* denki o kakeru; denki mekki suru.

galvanometer [gὰlvənómitə] *n.* denryūkei.

gamble [gǽmbl] *v.* kakegoto de nakusuru; kakegoto o suru. *n.* tobaku; bōken (*risk*). **~r** [-lə] *n.* tobakusha.

gamboge [gambú:ʒ] *n.* kiiroi ki no yani (ganryō) (-cosmetics).

gambol [gǽmb(ə)l] *n.* hane-mawari. *v.* hane-mawaru.

game [geim] *n.* kyōgi; yūgi; shōbu; emono (*in hunting*). (*pl.*) kyōgikai. **~of chance**, ichi-roku shōbu. *a.* yūkanna. *v.* shōbu-goto o suru. **~bag** [⊥bæg] *n.* emono-bukuro. **~bird** [⊥bə:d] *n.* ryōchō. **~cock** [⊥kɔk] *n.* keai-dori. **~keeper** [géimki:pə] *n.* ryōba no bannin. **~some** [⊥səm] *a.* asobi-zuki na.

gamester [géimstə] *n.* shōbu no aite; bakuchi-uchi.

gamin [gǽmin] *n.* (*Fr.*) furōji.

gammon [gǽmən] *n.* shio-buta no momoniku; kunsei-ham (*cured ham*); tawagoto (*nonsense*).

gamut [gǽmət] *n.* (*mus.*) zen'onkai; zenhan-i (*whole extent*).

gamy [géimi] *a.* ryō no emono ga ōi; tori kemono kusai; isa-mashii (*brave*).　　　　　　　　　　　　　　　⌐(*fool*).

gander [gǽndə] *n.* osu (*male*) no gachō; orokamono; manuke.

gang [gæŋ] *n.* hito kumi; ittai; tōrui. **~way**, *n.* (*marine*) gem-mon.

gangling [gǽŋgliŋ] *a.* bukakkōni sei ga takakute hosoi.

ganglion [gǽŋgliən] (*pl.* **-lia; -s**) *n.* shinkei-setsu.

gangplank [gǽŋplæŋk] *n.* fune ni noru tame ni tsukau, ugo-ku hashigo.

gangrene [gǽŋgri:n] *n.* (*med.*) karada no ichibu ga kusaru (*decay*) byōki; eso; dasso.

gangster [gǽŋstə] *n.* (*Am.*) akutō (*criminal gang*) no ichi-in (*member*).

gannet [gǽnit] *n.* (*bird*) katsuodori (*a large, fish eating bird*).

gantlet [gɔ́:ntlit/gǽn/gɑ:n-] *n.* kote; naga-tebukuro (*gloves*); muchi de utsu keibatsu. (ni-retsu ni naranda tokoro o ha-

shitte tōru toki muchi ya bō de utsu mukashi guntai de
okonawareta) (*cf.* **gauntlet**).

gantry [gǽntri] *n.* taru no dai ; kosen-kyō (*overbridge ; railway
signals*).

gaol [dʒeil] *n.* (*Brit.*) rōgoku. *v.* tōgoku suru.

gap [gæp] *n.* wareme ; sankyō (*deep ravine*) ; kankaku.

gape [geip] *n.* pokan to (*blankly*) kuchi (*mouth*) o hiraku koto ;
akubi (*yawn*). *v.* akubi o suru ; sakeru (*burst open*).

garage [gǽrɑːdʒ] *n.* (*Fr.*) jidōsha no shako ; kakunōko (*for
airplane*). ⌐jū.

Garand rifle [gǽrənd ráifl] *n.* America rikugun no han-jidō-

garb [gɑːb] *n.* fukusō. *v.* kimono o kiseru ; yosoou.

garbage [gáːbidʒ] *n.* kuzumono.

garble [gáːbl] *v.* eriwakeru ; shorui o kakikaeru (tsukuri-kae-
ru = *falsify*).

garden [gáːdn] *n.* niwa, sosai-en. (*vegetable* ~), kaju-en (*fruit*
~). *v.* niwa o tsukuru. ~ **city**, den'en toshi. ~ **party** *n.*
en'yūkai. ~**er** [-ə] *n.* uekiya. ~**ing** *n.* niwatsukuri ; engei.
~**stuff** [⌐stʌf] *n.* sosai.

gargle [gáːgl] *n.* ugai-gusuri. *v.* ugai o suru.

garish [gέəriʃ] *a.* giragira suru ; kebakebashii (*gaudy*).

garland [gáːlənd] *n.* hanawa ; keiku-shū (*anthology*).

garlic [gáːlik] *n.* (*veg.*) ninniku.

garment [gáːmənt] *n.* gaii ; ifuku.

garner [gáːnə] *n.* kokumotsu-gura. *v.* kokumotsu gura (*granary*)
ni osameru.

garnet [gáːnit] *n.* zakuro-ishi ; ankō-shoku (*dark red*).

garnish [gáːniʃ] *n.* sōshokuhin ; shokuhin no tsuma. *v.* sōshoku suru ; kazaru. ~**ment** [-mənt] *n.* sōshoku ; (*leg.*) sashiosae no shirase (*attachment*). ⌐nin.

garnishee [gàːniʃíː] *n.* (*leg.*) dai san saimu-sha ; zaisan jutaku-

garret [gǽrət] *n.* yaneurabeya (*attic*).

garrison [gǽris(ə)n] *n., v.* (*mil.*) shubitai (o oku).

garrotte [gərɔ́t], **garote** [gəróut/gərɔ́t] *n.* Spein no kōsatsu
kei ; *v.* kōsatsu suru ; nodo o shimete shoji-hin o ubau.

garrulity [gərúːliti] *n.* oshaberi ; taben.

garrulous [gǽruləs], *a.* oshaberi no. ~**ly** *ad.* taben ni ; oshaberi ni ; kudokudo to.

garter [gá:tə] *n.* kutsushita-dome. *the Order of the* ∼, Gātā kun'i ; G. kunshō (*decoration*).

gas [gæs] *n.* gasu ; kitai ; (*Am. col*) gasorin (*gasoline*). *v.* mudabanashi suru (*gossip*) ; gasu o kyōkyū suru ; chūdoku suru (*be poisoned*). ∼**station**, (*Am.*) gasorin-hambaijo ; gasorin-stando. ∼**burner** [gǽsbə:nə] gasutō-higuchi. ∼ **engine,** gasu-kikan. ∼**fitter** [gǽsfitə] *n.* gas shokkō. ∼**helmet** [gǽshèlmit], ∼ **mask** [∠mɑ:sk] *n.* bōdoku masuku. ∼**-light** [∠lait] *n.* gasutō. ∼**mantle** [mǽntl] *n.* gasutō no higuchi no ishiwata. ∼ **sed** [-t] **yarn,** gasu ito.

gasconade [gǽskənéid] *n., v.* jiman suru.

gaseous [gǽsiəs/géiz-] *n.* gasu (jō) no. ∼**ness** *n.*

gash [gæʃ] *n., v.* fukade (o owaseru).

gasify [gǽsifai] *v.* gasu ni suru.

gasket [gǽskit] *n.* gasuketto (kuda no tsugime o fusagu mono, gomu (*gum*) asa (*hemp*) nado o mochiiru).

gasolene, gasoline [gǽsoli:n] *n.* gasorin ; kihatsuyu.

gasometer [gæsɔ́mitə] *n.* gasu-tanku.

gasp [gɑ:sp] *n.* aegi. *v.* aegu ; aeginagara iu.

gassy [gǽsi] *a.* gasu no yōna ; gasu no michita (*full of gas*).

gastric [gǽstrik] *a.* i (*stomach*) no. ∼ **juice** [-dʒu:s] *n.* i-eki.

gastritis [gæstráitis] *n.* i-en.

gastronomy [gæstrɔ́nəmi] *n.* bishokuhō. ryōrihō.

gate [geit] *n.* mon ; kippu (*ticket*) no uriage daka. ∼**way** [-wei] mon, kado-guchi.

gather [gǽðə] *v.* atsumeru ; suisoku suru (*infer*) ; kanō suru umu. *n.* (*pl.*) hida. ∼ *sticks for a fire,* koeda o atsumete hi o taku. atsumaru : *tears* ∼*ed in her eyes,* me ni namida ga tamatta. ∼ *head,* kanō suru. ∼ *way,* sokuryoku o masu. ∼ **ing** *n.* shūkai ; haremono.

Gatling [gǽtling] *n. gatoring* kikanhō (*gun*).

gauche [gouʃ] *a.* (*Fr.*) hetana ; busahōna. 　　　　⌈hadena.

gaud [gɔ:d] *n.* yasupika mono. ∼**ily** [∠ili] *ad.* hadeni. ∼**y** *a.*

gauge [géidʒ] *n.* monosashi ; hakari ; (*railroad*)-*rail* no aida **broad** ∼, *n.* kōki. *take the* ∼ *of,* o mitsumoru. *v.* hakaru. ∼**r** [-ə] *n.* kenryō kan (do-ryō-kō no kikai o shiraberu hitō).

Gaul [gɔ:l] *n.* Gōrujin ; Furansujin.

gaunt [gɔ:nt] *a.* yasekoketa. ~**let** [gɔ́:ntlit] *n.* kote (*armoured glove*) : *fling* (or *throw*) *down the* ~., ikusa o idomu (shikakeru). *pick* (or *take*) *up the* ~, chōsen ni ōzuru. *run the* ~, chikei (muchi no kei) o ukeru. (*cf.* **gantlet.**)

gauze [gɔ:z] *n.* sha ; gāze (*bandage*). ~**zy** [gɔ́:zi] *a.* usui ; gāze.

gave [geiv] *v. see* : **give.**   [no yōna.

gavel [gǽvəl] *n.* (*Am.*) gichō no utsu tsuchi ; kyōbainin (*auctioneer*) no tsuchi.

gavotte [gəvɔ́t] *n.* isshu no butō.

gawk [gɔ:k] *n.* noroma. *v.* bakana mane o suru. ~**y** [gɔ́:ki] *a.* noroma(no) ; bukiyōna (*awkward*). *n.* noroma.

gay [gei] *a.* yōkina ; hadena. ~**ety** [géiəti] *n.* yukai ; tanoshimi. ~**ly** [géili] *ad.* yōkini.

gaze [geiz] *v.* gyōshi. *v.* mitsumeru.

gazelle [gəzél] *n.* (*zoo.*) kamoshika no isshu.

gazette[gəzét] *n.* shimbunshi ; kampō. (*official* ~). *v.* kampō ni noseru ; nimmei suru. ~**er** [gæzitíə] *n.* chimei jisho.

G.B. Eikoku (*Great Britain*).

gear [giə], *n.* (*machine*) sōchi ; haguruma (~ *wheel*). dōsan (*movables*). chōshi (*condition*). *v.* rendō saseru (suru) ; kamiawaseru. *throw out of* ~, konran saseru. ~**ing** [gíəriŋ] *n.* (*machine*) rendōki. ~**wheel** [˗hwi:l] *n.* haguruma.

gee [dʒi:] (gyosha yōgo (*driver's terms*). mae e ! migi (*right*) e muke ! achira(*there*) e ! *n.* (*col.*) uma (*horse*).

gelatin(e) [dʒelətí:n] *n.* jerachin ; nikawa.

geld [geld] *v.* kyosei suru. ~**ing** [géldiŋ] *n.* kyosei shita uma.

gem [dʒem] *n.* hōseki. *v.* hōseki de kazaru.

geminate [dʒémineit] *v.* nijū ni suru ; futatsu ni suru.

gemination [dʒèminéiʃən] *n.* nijū ni suru koto ; hampuku ; shiin (*consonant*) o kasaneru koto.

Gen. *n.* shōkan no shōgō.

gendarme [ˈʒɑ̄:(n)dɑ:m] *n.* (*Fr.*) kempei.

gender [dʒéndə] *n.* (*gram.*) sei (dansei, josei no)

genealogical [dʒi:niəlɔ́dʒikəl] *a.* keizu no. ~ **tree** *n.* keitō-zu.

genealogist [dʒì:niǽlədʒist] *n.* keizu-gakusha.

genealogy [dʒì:niǽlədʒi] *n.* keizu ; keizugaku.

genera [dʒénərə] *n. see* : **genus.**

general [dʒén(ə)rəl] *a.* ippan no ; futsū no. ~ **tariff,** kokutei zeiritsu. *in* ~, ippan ni. *(mil.)* n. rikugun taishō ; shōkan. gaishitei eba. **full** ~, rikugun taishō. ~**ly** *ad.* ~*ly speaking,* taigai ; ippan ni. ~ **ship** *n.* taishō no shoku ; taishō taru jimbutsu.

generalissimo [dʒenərəlísimou] *n.* daigensui.

generality [dʒènərǽliti] *n.* ippanteki de aru koto ; yōten o zembu atsumeta mono *(abstracted)* ; kōgai ; daibubun.

generalization [dʒènərəl(a)izéiʃən] *n.* ippanka ; gaikatsu (ka).

generalize [dʒénərəlaiz] *v.* ippantekini suru ; sōgō suru ; hiromeru *(popularize).*

generate [dʒénəreit] *v.* umu ; shōzuru ; okosu. ~**ting station** [-tiŋstéiʃən] *n.* hatsudensho.

generation [dʒénəréiʃən] *n.* sanshutsu ; hassei ; shison ; (yaku 30 nen) jidai ; dōjidai no hitobito. **rising** ~ *n.* seinen ; wakai hitobito.

generative [dʒénəreitiv/-rət-] *a.* seisan suru ; seishoku no.

generator [dʒénəreitə] *n,* seishokusha ; hasseiki. *(elect.)* hatsudenki.   ⌜shurui ni yotte.

generic [dʒinérik] *a.* zoku no ; ippan(teki) no. ~**ally** *ad.*

generosity [dʒènərɔ́siti] *n.* kandai ; kimae no yosa ; ōmaka.

generous [dʒénərəs] *a.* kandaina ; hōfuna. ~**ly** *ad.*

genesis [dʒénisis/-siz] *n.* hassei ; hajime (G-) *(Bible* no) Sōseiki.

genetic [dʒinétik] *a.* hasseiteki ; genshi no ; hasseigakuteki.

genial [dʒí:niəl/-njəl] *a.* nikoyakana ; onwana ; shinsetsuna. ~**ity** *n.* shinsetsu. ~**ly** *ad.* onwani ; shinsetsu ni.

genie [dʒí:ni] *n.* (*pl.* **genii** [dʒí:niai]) mashin *(demon)* ; reiki.

genital [dʒénitl] *a.* seishoku ni kansuru ; seishoku no.

genitive [dʒénitiv] *n., a. (gram.)* zokkaku (no).

genius[dʒí:njəs] *n.* (*pl.* ~**es**) tensai ; tempin ; tokuchō ; tokushitsu ; tokushu no nōryoku ; kojin ya minzoku no tokuchō. (*pl.* **genii** [dʒí:niai]) mamorigami ; rei (zendama, akudama nado no) tamashii.   ⌜jin.

Genoese [dʒèno(u)í:z] *a.* Itaria Jenoa no. *n. (sing. & pl.)* Jenoa

genre [ʒɑ̃:ŋr] *n.* (Fr.) shurui ; yōshiki *(daily life)* o kaita e. fūzoku e.

gens [dʒenz] *n.* (*pl.* **gentes** [dʒénti:z]) (kodai Rōma de) onaji sosen kara deta to iu kazoku-gun (*group of families*).

genteel [dʒentí:l] *a.* shitsuke no yoi ; jōhin-butta.

gentian [dʒénʃiən] *n.* (*bot.*) rindō.

gentile [dʒéntail] *n.* (Yudayajin igai no) ihōjin (*non-Jew*) *a.* ihōjin no ; ikyōto no.

gentility [dʒentíliti] kyōyō no aru ; jōryū no hito.

gentle [dʒéntl] *a.* iegara no yoi ; jōhinna ; odayakana. ∼**folk** [-fɔ:k] *n.* (*pl.*) mibun aru hitobito. ∼**man** [-mən] *n.* shinshi. ∼**manlike,** ∼**manly.** *a.* shinshi rashii ; reigitadashii. ∼**iness** *n.* shinsetsu ; jōhin ; odayakasa ; nyūwa. ∼**woman** [-wumən] *n.* kifujin. ∼**womanlike,** ∼**womanly** *a.* shitoyakana.

gentry [dʒéntri] *n.* shinshi shakai ; jōryū shakai ; hitobito ; renchū.

genuflect [dʒénjuflekt] *v.* hiza (*knee*) o mageru (raihai).

genuflexion [dʒènjuflékʃən], ∼**tion** *n.* hiza o mageru koto ; kihai (hiza o magete inoru koto).

genuine [dʒénjuin] *a.* junsui no ; hommono no. ∼**ly** *ad.* junsuini. ∼**ness** *n.* junsui de aru koto ; majime ; hommono de aru koto. ⌈zoku.

genus [dʒí:nəs/dʒén-] (*pl.* **genera** [dʒénərə]) *n.* shurui ; rui ;

geocentric [dʒìouséntrik] *a.* (*astr.*) chikyū chūshin de mita.

geodesy [dʒi(:)ódisi] *n.* sokuchigaku ; rikuchi sokuryō.

geographer [dʒiógrəfə] *n.* chirigakusha. ∼**phical** [dʒiəgréfikl] *a.* chirigaku no. ∼**phically** *ad.*

geography [dʒiógrəfi] *n.* chirigaku ; chisei..**physical** ∼ [fízikl-] *n.* shizen chirigaku ; **political** ∼ [pəlítikl] *n.* seijichirigaku ; jimmon chirigaku.

geological [dʒiəlódʒik(ə)l] *a.* chishitsugakujō no ; chishitsu no. ∼**ist** *n.* chishitsu-gakusha. ∼**ly** *ad.* chishitsugakutekini.

geology [dʒiólədʒi] *n.* chishitsugaku.

geometer [dʒiómitə] *n.* kikagakusha.

geometric(al) [dʒiəmétrik(əl)] *a.* (*math.*) kikagaku(teki)no. ∼ **progression** [-prəgréʃən] *n.* kikakyūsū. ∼ **proportion** [prəpó:ʃən] *n.* kika hirei. ∼**ally** *ad.* kikagakutekini.

geometrician [dʒìo(u)metríʃən] = **geometer**

geometry [dʒiómitri] *n.* kikagaku.

geophysics [dʒèəfíziks] *n.* chikyu-butsurigaku.
geopolitic(al) [dʒì:opolítik(l)] *a.* seijichiri no.
geopolitics [dʒì:opólitiks] *n.* chiseigaku; seijichirigaku.
georgic [dʒɔ́:dʒik] *a.* nōgyō ni kansuru. *n.* nōgyō ni kansuru shi (*poem*). ⎡aoi.
geranium [dʒiréinjəm] *n.* (*bot.*) zeranyūmu; seiyō aoi. tenjiku
gerfalcon [dʒɔ́:fɔ:(l)kən] *n.* (*bird*) isshu no ōhayabusa.
germ [dʒə:m] *n.* yōga; hai; saikin; byōkin; baikin.
German [dʒɔ́:mən] *a.* Doitsu no; Doitsijin no; Doitsugo no. *n.* Doitsujin; hakudō; Doitsugo. **G~ silver** *n.* yōgin.
german [dʒɔ́:mən] *a.* dō(so)fubo o motsu. **brothers ~**, (*sister ~*, *etc.*) (dōitsu no fubo kara deta) kyōdai (shimai). ⎡na.
germane [dʒə:méin] *a.* missetsuna kankei no aru; tekisetsu
Germanic [dʒə:mǽnik] *a.* Doitsujin no; Chūton-minzoku no. *German* zoku no.
germicide [dʒɔ́:misaid] *n.* sakkinzai; *a.* sakkinryoku no aru.
germinal [dʒɔ́:minəl] *a.* me (*germ.*) no; yōga no; kongen no.
germinate [dʒɔ́:mineit] *v.* hatsuga suru (saseru).
germination [dʒɔ̀:minéiʃən] *n.* hatsuga; mebae.
gerrymander [gérimændə/dʒé~] *v.* (senkyoku o) jibun no tō ni yūri ni aratameru; tsugō no yoi yōni (*convenienty*) tekagen suru. *n.* senkyoku fusei kaitei; tekagen.
gerund [dʒérənd] *n.* (*gram.*) gobi ga **ing** de owaru Eigo no dō meishi. **~ial** [dʒirʌ́ndiəl] *a.* dōmeishi no.
gesticulate [dʒestíkjuleit] *v.* temane de hanasu; miburi suru. **~ion** [dʒèstikjuléiʃən] *n.* miburi; temane. ⎡arawasu.
gesture [dʒéstʃə] *n.* miburi. *v.* temane de hanasu; miburi de
get [get] *v.* got, got *or* (*Am.*) gotten; getting. eru; uketoru; ...saseru; shitemorau; ankisuru; tassuru; tsuku. **~ at**, ni te ga todoku; o mitsukeru. **~away**, saru. **~ back**, torimodosu; kaeru. **~ behind**, (*Am.*) ushirodate (kōen) suru. **~ by**, (*Am. colloq.*) umaku nigeru. **~ down**, oriru. **~ in**, ni hairu; toriireru. **~ off**, nogareru. **~ on**, susumu; noru; seikōsuru. **~ out**, dasu; deru; suru. **~ to**, ni tsuku. **~ together**, atsumaru; atsumeru. **~ up**, okiru; noboru. **have got**=(*col.*) **have.** ⎣motsu.
getup [gétʌp] *n.* migoshirae; teisai.
gewgaw [gjú:gɔ:] *n.* yasupika mono; omocha (*toy*).

geyser [gáizɔ] *n.* kanketsu (on)sen; funsen.

ghastly [gá:stli] *a.* osoroshii; monosugoi; aozameta. *ad.* ao-zamete; monosugoku.

ghost [goust] *n.* yūrei; bōrei. ~**ly** *a.* yūrei no (yōna.)

ghoul [gu:l] *n.* haka o abaku hito; zanninna hito.

G.H.Q ; GHQ. Sōshireibu (*General Head Quarters*).

GI., GI *a.* (*Am.*) (*mil.*) kankyū no; gunki ni yoru; (*general issue* "ippan shikyū hin" mata wa *government issue* "kankyū hin" no ryaku). *n.* (*Am.*) kashikanhei; heisotsu. **GI haircut** *n.* heitaigari. **GI shoes** *n.* guntaigutsu.

giant [dʒáiənt] *n.* kyojin; kyodaina. *a.* kyodaina; idaina. ~**ess** *n.* onna no kyojin; ōonna.

gibber [dʒíbə] *v.* berabera wakaranai koto o iu. ~**ish** [dʒíbər-iʃ/dʒi-] *n.* tawagoto.

gibbet [dʒíbit] *n.* kōshudai. *v.* shimekorosu; hazukashimeru.

gibbon [gíbən] *n.* (*zoo.*) tenagazaru. (*a sort of monkeys*).

gibbous [gíbəs] *a.* totsumen no; semushi no. ~**moon** *n.* ⌐hangetsu.

gibe [dʒaib] *n.* chōrō (suru), azakeri. *v.* azakeru. ⌐hangetsu.

giblets [dʒíblits] *n.* (*pl.*) (*fowl*) kakin no zōmotsu (*entrails*).

giddy [gídi] *a.* memai ga suru; keisotsuna. ~**dily** *ad.* memai ga shite; keisotsuni. ~**diness** *n.* memai; keisotsu.

gift [gift] *n.* okurimono; tempu no sainō. ~**ed** [-tid] *a.* tempu no sainō aru.

gig [gig] *n.* ittō biki nirimbasha; keikaina bōto.

gigantic [dʒaigǽntik] *a.* kyodaina; subarashii; bōdaina.

giggle [gígl] *n.* kusukusu-warai. *v.* kusukusu warau.

gild [gild] *v.* gilt *or* gilded; gilding. kimmekki o suru; hika-raseru; funshoku suru. *n.* kumiai; girudo. **the Gilded Chamber,** Eikoku no jōin. ~**ing** *n.* mekki; kimpaku; kyo-shoku. ⌐no ami).

gill [gil] *n.* (*usu. pl.*) era (sakana no). ~**net** *n.* sashiami (isshu

gill [dʒil] *n.* jiru; ekiryō no tan'i (*unit*). shōjo; musume.

gillyflower [dʒíliflauə] *n.* (*bot.*) araseito.

gilt [gilt] *a.* mekki shita. *n.* mekki; uwabe dake no utsukushi-sa; ōgon; kane (=*money*). ~**-edged** [⌐edʒd] *a.* kimbuchi no; saijōtō no. ⌐sōchi.

gimbals [dʒímb(ə)lz] *n.* (rashimban nado) suihei o tamotsu

gimcrack [dʒímkræk] *a.* mikakedaoshi no. *n.* yasupika mono.

gimlet [gímlit] *n.* tegiri; nejirigiri.

gimp [gimp] *n.* sasaberi.

gin [dʒin] *n.* wata kuriki; kuiuchiki; sankyaku kijūki; wana; jin (sake). *v.* watakuriki de tane o toru; wana de toraeru.

ginger [dʒíndʒə] *n.* shōga; hajikami. **~bread** [-bred] *n.* shōga iri kashipan. **~ly** *ad.* yōjin shite; osoruosoru; kossori to.

gingham [gíŋəm] *n.* gingamu; shima-mempu.

ginseng [dʒínseŋ] *n.* (*bot.*) chōsen (*Corea*) ninjin.

gipsy [dʒípsi] *n.* jipushii (moto Indo kara deta hōrō no tami).

giraffe [dʒirá:f] *n.* (*zoo*) jirafu; kirin.

gird [gə:d] *v.* **girt; girding.** matou; maku; kakomu. **~one-self** obi o shimeru; kinchō suru. (*cf.* **girdle.**)

girder [gə́:də] *n.* keta; ōbari; ōtsubari (*main supporting beam*).

girdle [gə́:dl] *n.* obi. *v.* obi de maku; obi o shimeru.

girl [gə:l] *n.* shōjo; jochū; koibito. **~hood** [-hud] *n.* shōjo jidai. **~ish** [-iʃ] *a.* shōjo no; shōjo rashii.

girt [gə:t] *v. see* : **gird.**

girth [gə:θ] *n.* haraobi; ningen no dōmawari; shūi; *man of large* ~ dōmawari no ōkii otoko.

gist [dʒist] *n.* yōten; gammoku.

give [giv] *v.* **gave, given,** *v.* **giving.** (mono o hoka no mono ni) watasu; ataeru; yaru; yuzuru; hōki suru. ~ *back*, kaesu. ~ *forth*, ōyake ni suru. ~ *in*, shiraseru; kuppuku suru. **~oneself** *up*, kakugo suru; fukeru; bottō suru. ~ *out*, iifurasu; tsukareru; tsukiru. ~ *over*, hikiwatasu; yameru. ~ *up*, suteru; watasu; dannen suru. ~ *way*, kuzureru; oreru; (kabuken nado) ne ga sagaru; kowareru. **~r** *n.* ataeru hito.

giveaway [gívəwèi] *n.* (*Am. col.*) kuchi o suberasu koto; kataru ni ochiru koto.

given [gívn] *see* : **give.** *a.* ataerareta; kimatta dake no. *be* ~ *to*, ni fukette iru. ⌈shaku.

gizzard [gízəd] *n.* (*zoo.*) tori no sunabukuro (*stomach*); so-**glacé** [glǽsei] *a.* (*Fr.*) satō o mabushita (kudamono, kashi): tsuya no aru. *n.* kōtaku aru usui kinu no nuno.

glacial [gléisiəl/gléiʃ(i)əl] *a.* kōri no; hyōga no; reitanna.

glaciated [glsǽieitid] *a.* hyōga-sayō o uketa; kōri de ōwareta.

glacier [glǽsjə] *n.* hyōga.

glacis [glǽsis] *n.* nadarakana saka.

glad [glæd] *a.* ureshii. *be* ~, ureshii. ~**hand** *n.* (*Am. col.*) kangei no akushu no te. ~**hander** [glæ̀dhǽndə] (*Am. col.*) *n.* minna ni aisō yoku suru hito. ~**ly** *ad.* yorokonde. ~**ness** *n.* yorokobi. ~**some** *a.* yorokobashii.

gladden [glǽdn] *v.* yorokobu; yorokobaseru.

glade [gleid] *n.* hayashi no naka no akichi.

gladiator [glǽdieitə] *n.* (kodai Rōma no) kenshi, tōshi.

gladiolus [glæ̀dióuləs] *n.* (*pl.* **-es ; -i**) (*bot.*) guradiorasu.

glair [glɛə] *n.* (tamago no shiromi) (*albumen*).

glamo(u)r [glǽmə] *n.* fushigina miryoku. ~**ous** [-rəs] *a.* miwakutekina.

glance [glɑːns] *n.* chirari to hitome ; mekubase. *v.* hirameku ; chirari to miru.

gland [glænd] *n.* (*anat.*) sen (chi (*blood*) kara karada (*body*) ni daijina yōbun (*nutriment*) o wakeru yakume o suru kikan).

glanders [glǽndəz] *n.* (*vet.*) bisobyō (*a serious contagious disease of horses, mules, etc.*)

glandular [glǽndjulə], **glandulous** [glǽndjuləs] *a.* sen no (*of gland*) sen (*a gland*) no (yōna).

glare [glɛə] *n.* mabushii me no itai yōna tsuyoi) hikari ; niramitsukeru me. *v.* giragira hikaru ; niramitsukeru.

glaring [glɛ́əriŋ] *a.* mabayui ; niramitsukeru ; meihakuna. ~**ly** *ad.* giragira to ; medatte.

glass [glɑːs] *n.* garasu ; garasu de tsukutta kigu ; kagami (*mirror*) ; opera-gurasu ; sōgankyō. (*pl.*) megane. *v.* garasu o hameru. ~**blower** [-ˈblo(u)ə] *n.* garasukō. ~**cutter** [-ˈkʌtə] *n.* garasu kiri ; garasu kiri shokunin. ~**ful** *n.* koppu ippai. ~**ware** [-wɛə] *n.* garasu seihin. ~**y** [glɑ́ːsi] *a.* garasu no ; garasu-shitsu no ; kagami no yōni odayakana.

glaze [gleiz] *v.* garasu o hameru ; uwagusuri o kakeru ; garasu no yōni naru. *n.* uwagusuri.

glazier [glɛ́iziə] *n.* garasuya.

glazing [glɛ́iziŋ] *n.* garasu o hameru koto ; tōki ni uwagusuri o kakeru koto ; kōtaku-tsuke.

gleam [gliːm] *n.* hitosuji no hikari. *v.* pikari to suru.

glean [gli:n] *v.* ochibo o hirou; karinokori o atsumeru.

glebe [gli:b] *n.* kyōkai (otera) no ryōchi; (*poet.*) tochi; hatake.

glee [gli:] *n.* ōyorokobi. (*mus.*) gasshōkyoku.

glen [glen] *n.* kyōkoku (*narrow valley*).

glib [glib] *a.* yoku shaberu; ryūchōna. **~ly** *ad.* surasura to; yodomi naku.

glide [glaid] *n.* suberi; kūchū-kassō; suberidai (*phon.*) watari no on. *v.* sūtto ugoku; kūchū-kassō suru. **spiral ~** *n*, senkai kassō. **~-bomb** [⸗bɔm] *v.* (*Am.*) kyūkōka-bakugeki o kuwaeru. **~r** [-ə] *n.* suberu hito (mono); guraidā.

glimmer [glímə] *n.* yowai hikari; usuakari. *v.* bon'yari hikaru. ⌠miru.

glimpse [glim(p)s] *n.* bekken; chiratto miru koto. *v.* chiratto

glint [glint] *v.* pikatto hikaru; hansha suru. *n.* kirameki.

glisten [glísn] *v.* hikaru; hansha suru. *n.* kirameki; senkō.

glitter [glítə] *n.* kōki (hikari kagayaku koto); kaiten tōdai no hikari ga hansha suru yōna hikari. *v.* pikapika hikaru.

gloaming [glóumiŋ] *n.* (yūgata no) usuakari; tasogare.

gloat [glout] *v.* (manzoku sōni) nagameru; jitto miru.

globe [gloub] *n.* kyū; (*the ~*) chikyū; (rampu no marui) hoya. **celestial ~** *n.* tentaigi. **terrestrial ~** *n.* chikyūgi. **~fish** [⸗fiʃ] *n.* fugu. ⌠o obita.

globose [gloubóus], **globular** [glóbjulə] *a.* kyūjō no; marumi

globule [glóbju:l] *n.* chiisana tama; gan'yaku.

gloom [glu:m] *n.* usukuragari; in'utsu. *v.* kuraku suru (naru); inkini suru (naru). **~ily** *ad.* kuraku; inkini. **~iness** *n.* usukuragari; inki. **~y** [glú:mi] *a.* usugurai; inkina; fusaida.

glorification [glɔ̀:rifikéiʃən] *n.* sambi; eikō; eiyo.

glorify [glɔ́:rifai] *v.* sambi suru; eikō o tataeru; tegara (*merit*) o homeageru. ⌠ad. migotoni.

glorious [glɔ́:riəs] *a.* eikō aru; kagayakashii; sutekina. **~ly**

glory [glɔ́:ri] *n.* hikaru tegara; homare to meiyo; han'ei; gokō. *v.* hikaru; tokuini naru; hokoru. ⌠ku suru.

gloss [glɔs] *n.* kōtaku. chūshaku. *v.* tsuya o tsukeru. chūsha-

glossary [glɔ́səri] *n.* goi; chiisai tangoshū.

glossy [glɔ́si] *a.* nameraka de kōtaku no aru; mottomo rashii. **~sily** *ad.* tsuyatsuya shite; teisai yoku. **~siness** *n.* kōtaku (tsuya) no aru koto; mottomo rashisa.

glottal [glɔ́t(ə)l] *a.* (*anat.*) seimon no; nodo no; inkō no.

glottis [glɔ́tis] *n.* (*anat.*) kōtō; seimon.

glove [glʌv] *n.* tebukuro; *take up the* ~, chōsen (*challenge*) ni ōzuru. *throw down the* ~, chōsen suru.

glover [glʌ́və] *n.* tebukuro seizōnin; tebukuroshō (*merchant*).

glow [glou] *n.* hakunetsu; shakunetsu; manzokukan; netsuretsu; kagayaki. *v.* makkani naru. ~**ing** [glóuiŋ] *a.* shakunetsu shite iru; netsuretsuna; ikiikishita. ~**lamp** [-læmp] *n.* hakunetsutō. ~**watch** *n.* yakō tokei. ~**worm** [-wəːm] *n.* tsuchi hotaru; yami de hikaru mushi.

glower [gláuə] *v.* okotte niramu.

gloze [glouz] *v.* iitsukurou; mottomo rashii setsumei o suru.

glucose [glúːkous] *n.* budōtō.

glue [gluː] *n.* nikawa. *v.* nikawazuke ni suru. ~**y** *a.* nikawa o nutta; nikawashitsu no.

glum [glʌm] *a.* fusaide iru; kimuzukashii. ~**ly** *ad.* muttsuri shite; fukigen ni. ~**ness** *n.* muttsuri; fukigen.

glume [gluːm] *n.* (*bot.*) (momigara no yōna) kara.

glut [glʌt] *n.* jūbun ni aru koto; ari sugiru koto. *v.* michitaraseru; mampuku saseru. ~ *oneself with*, o hōbaru. ~ *the market*, ichiba ni mono o dabutsukaseru.

gluten [glúːtən] *n.* (*chem.*) guruten; fushitsu.

glutinosity [glùːtinɔ́siti] *n.* nenchaku-sei.

glutinous [glúːtinəs] *a.* nenchakusei no; nebaneba suru.

glutton [glʌ́tən] *n.* taishokukan; kentanka. ~**ous** *a.* taishoku suru; kuishimbō no. ~**y**, *n.* ōgui; kuishimbō.

glyceric [glisérik] *a.* guriserin no.

glycerin(e) [glísəriːn] *n.* guriserin.

G-man [dʒíːmæn] *n.* (*Am. sl.*) Rempō Kensatsukyoku no keiji, (*Government man* no ryaku). ⌈fushidarake no.

gnarl [naːl] *n.* fushi; kino kobu. ~**ed** [-d] *a.* fushi no aru;

gnash [næʃ] *v.* hagishiri suru; ha o kuishibaru.

gnat [næt] *n.* ka; buyo; (*Brit.*) ka (*mosquito*).

gnaw [nɔː] *v.* kajiru; fushoku suru; kurushimeru.

gneiss [(g)nais] *n.* (*min.*) hemmangan. ⌈(*spirit*).

gnome [noum] *n.* chijō no rei; issumbōshi; chi (*earth*) no sei.

gnomon [nóumɔn] *n.* (hidokei no) toki o sasu hari.
Gnosticism [nɔ́stisizm] *n.* Nosuchikku-kyō (shoki Kirisuto-kyōchū no isshu no shimpi tetsugaku).
gnu [nju:] *n.* (*zoo*) tsunouma.
go [gou] *v.* **went, gone; going.** iku; hoka no basho e utsuru. *n.* shinkō; genki; kokoromi. ~ **to school,** gakkō e iku; ~ *mad,* kichigai ni naru. *be* ~ *ing to,* ...suru tokoro da. ~ *about,* chakushu suru. ~ *around,* ugokimawaru. ~ *at,* kōgeki suru; (shigoto ni) torikakaru. ~ *back,* kaeru. ~ *back on,* (*Am. col.*) yakusoku o yaburu. ~ *behind,* jijitsu o kentō suru. ~ *by,* sugiru. ~ *down,* sagaru. ~ *for,* o yobi ni iku. ~ *in,* ni hairu. ~ *in for,* ni sansei suru; shiyō to suru. ~ *into,* nakama ni naru; kenkyū suru. ~ *off,* saru; otoroeru. ~ *on,* susumu; tsuzukeru. ~ *out,* soto e deru; kieru. ~ *over,* wataru; fukushū suru. ~ *round,*ikiwataru. ~ *through,* o tsūka suru; owari made taeru. *let* ~, hanasu. *all the* ~, daihyōban. *a pretty* ~, komatta koto. *no* ~, dame, shippai. ~**-ahead** [-'ɔhed] *a.* shinshuteki; katsudōteki. ~**between** [⌐bitwi:n] *n.* assensha; nakōdo. ~ **cart** [⌐kɑ:t] *n.* (kodomo no) tsukamari-kuruma.
goad [goud] *n,* (kachiku o ou tame no) tsukibō; shigekibutsu. *v.* tsukibō de tsuku; odateru.
goal [goul] *n.* kesshōten (sen, hyō); gōru; mokutekichi.
goat [gout] *n.* yagi. ~**ee** [-í:] *n.* yagihige; agohige. ~**herd** [⌐hɔːd] *n,* yagi kai. ~**ish** *a.* yagi no yōna; inranna.
gob [gɔb] *n.* (*Am. sl.*) suihei (*Jack*).
gobble [gɔ́bl] *n.* (shichimenchō no nakigoe) gorogoro. *v.* gorogoro iu; musaborikuu; unomi ni suru.
gobbler [gɔ́blə] *n.* shichimenchō no osu; ōgui suru hito.
goblet [gɔ́blit] *n.* dai-tsuki no sakazuki.
goblin [gɔ́blin] *n.* oni.
god [gɔd] *n.* kami. (*G*~) tentei. **God's acre,** hakaba. ~**child** [-tʃaild] *n.* (senrei no) natsuke kodomo. ~**dess** [⌐is] *n.* megami. ~**father** [⌐fɑ́:ðə] *n.* kyōfu (*godchild* ni taisuru shūkyōjō no otōsan). ~**head** [⌐hed] *n.* (*G*~) kami; kami no honshitsu. ~**hood** [hud] *n.* kamitaru shikaku. ~**less** *a.* fushinkōno. ~**like** [⌐laik] *a.* kami no yōna; kōgōshii. ~**liness** *n.* kami o uya mau koto; shinjin. ~**ly** *a.* kami o uyamau; ~**mother**

[‿mʌðə] *n.* kyōbo (*cf. godfather*). ~**parent** [pὲərənt] *n.* kyōfu, kyōbo; naoya. ~**send** [-send] *n.* ten no okurimono. ~**son** [-sʌn] *n.* otoko no *godchild.* ~**speed** [‿spìːd] *n.* dōchū heian no inori.

godown [góudaun] *n.* sōko (*warehouse*).

gof(f)er [góufə] *n.* hida; chijimi. *v.* hida o tsukeru; chijimeru.

goggle [gɔ́gl] *v.* medama o guruguru mawasu. ~**-eyed** [-aid] *a.* deme no; dongurime no. ~**s** *n.* (*pl.*) gomiyoke megane; iromegane.

goiter, ~**tre** [gɔ́itə] *n.* (*med.*) kōjōsen no hare.

gold [gould] *n.* kin; ōgon; kinka; tomi (*wealth*). *a.* kin no; kin'iro no. ~**beater** [‿bìːtə] *n.* kimpakushi. ~ **dust,** sakin; kimpun. ~**finch** [‿fintʃ] *n.* (*bird*) kawarahiwa. ~**fish** [-fiʃ] *n.* kingyo. ~ **lace** [‿leis] *n.* kimmōru. ~**smith** [‿smiθ] *n.* kinzaikunin.

golden [góuldən] *a.* kin no; koganeiro no; tōtoi. ~ **mean** chūyō. ~**rod** [‿rɔd] *n.* (*bot.*) aki no kirinsō; awatake-sō. ~ **rule** *n.* kingen; ōgonritsu.

golf [gɔlf] *n.* gorufu. ~ **club** gorufuyō no bō; gorufu kurabu. ~**links** *n.* gorufujō. ~**er** [gɔ́lfə] *n.* gorufu o suru hito.

Goliath [goláiəθ] *n. David* ni korosoreta *Philistine* no kyojin. (g~) kyojin. idōkijūki.

golliwog [gɔ́liwɔg] *n.* bukakkōna sugoi ningyō; sugoi kao no hito; bakemono.

gondola [gɔ́ndələ] *n.* gondora-bune (Venisu no hirabune). (*Am.*) mugaikasha; hirazokobune.

gondolier [gɔ̀ndəlíə] *n.* gondora no sendō.

gone [gɔn, gɔːn] *v. see*: **go.** *a.* ~ *case,* nozomi no nai jiken. misutemono; sutarimono.

gong [gɔŋ] *n.* dora.

good [gud] *a.* yoi; shinsetsuna; tanoshii; jōzuna. *n.* zen; rieki; kōfuku. (*pl.*) nimotsu; kamotsu; shōhin. ~**speed,** kōun; seikō. *do* ~, hito ni shinsetsu ni suru. *for* ~ (*and all*), eikyū-ni. ~**strain** (*Brit.*)kamotsu ressha. ~**-by(e)** [gú(d)bái/gu(d)-bái] *inter.* sayōnara. *n.* wakare. ~**-for-nothing** ‿[fənʌθiŋ] *a.* mueki no; yakuzana. *n.* rokudenashi. ~**humo(u)red** [‿hjuː-məd] *a.* kigen no yoi. ~**ly** *a.* utsukushii; shitsu no yoi :

a ∼*ly gift*, sōtōna gaku no : (*a* ∼*ly sum*). ∼**-natured** [⌐néitəd] *a*. hito no yoi ; onkōna. ∼**naturedly** *ad*. shinsetsuni ; otonashiku. ∼**ness** [-nis] *n*. zenryō ; shinsetsu. *for* ∼' *sake*, goshō da kara. ∼**-tempered** [⌐témpəd] *a*. yasashii ; otonashii. ∼**will** [-wil] *n*. kōi ; shinsetsu. ∼**y** [gúdi] *a*. shushōgena ; zenryōna. *n.* (*pl.*) kyandē. *inter.* subarashii !

goose *n*. [gu:s] (*pl.* **geese** [gi:s]) gachō. ∼**berry** [gúzbəri] *n*. suguri ; guzuberii. ∼**flesh** [-fleʃ] *n*. torihada. ∼**herd** [⌐hə:d] *n*. gachō no mure o sewa suru hito. ∼**neck** [⌐nek] *n*. ippan ni gachō no kubi ni nita mono.

G.O.P., GOP Amerika Kyōwa-tō no adana (*Grand Old Party*).

gopher [góufə] *n*. (*Am*.) isshu no jinezumi.

gore [gɔ:/gɔə] *v*. tsuno de tsuku (ushi nado ga) ; sankakukei ni kiru ; sasu ; tsuku. *n*. sankakukei no nunogire ; okumi ; machi ; sankakukei no jimen. chi (*blood*) no katamari.

gorge [gɔ:dʒ] *v*. musaborikuu. *n*. intō ; nodo ; yamaai ; nomikudashita mono.

gorgeous [gó:dʒəs] *a*. kabina. ∼**ly** *ad*. kabini ; utsukushiku. ∼**ness** *n*. kirabiyakana koto (*being showy in dressing.*)

Gorgon [gó:gən] *n*. tōhatsu ga hebi no majo (mita hito wa minna ishi ni naru to iu) ; minikui kao no onna.

gorilla [gərílə] *n*. gorira ; dai-shōjō.

gormandize [gó:məndaiz] *v*. gatsugatsu kuu.

gorse [gɔ:s] *n*. (*bot.*) harienishida.

gory [gó:ri] *a*. kizudarake no ; chidarake no.

goshawk [góshɔ:k] *n*. (*bird*) tsubasa no mijikai ōtaka.

gosling [gózliŋ] *n*. gachō no hina.

gospel [gósp(ə)l/-pel] *n*. fukuin ; (G∼) fukuinsho (*Bible*).

gosport [góspɔ:t] *n*. tsūwakan (hikōki nai no).

gossamer [gósəmə] *n*. chiisai kumo no su (yabu nado ni kaketa) ; fujin'yo bōsuifuku.

gossip [gósip] *n*. zatsudan ; goshippu ; oshaberi (ya). *v*. shaberu. ∼**ly** *a*. oshaberi no.

got [gɔt] *v*. *see* : **get** (*Am. gotten*).

Goth [gɔθ] *a*. Gōtojin ; yabanjin.

Gothic [góθik] *a*. Gōtojin no ; Gōtogo (*word*) no ; Goshikku shiki no. *n*. Gōtogo ; Goshikkushiki (*arch it* kenchiku yōshiki).

gouge [gaudʒ] *n.* marunomi (daiku no); petenshi; *v.* marunomi de horu; kane o makiageru.

gourd [guəd] *n.* hyōtan : **bottle** ~, *n.* hyōtan.

gourmand [gúəmənd] *n.* taishokuka; bishokuka.

gourmet [gúəmei] *n.* shokutsū; saketsū (*connoisseur*).

gout [gaut] (*med.*) *n.* tsūfū. ~**y** *a.* tsūfū ni kakatte iru.

govern [gávən] *v.* osameru; shihai suru; kanri suru. ~**ment**
n. seiji; shihai; seifu; naikaku. ~**mental** [gàvənmént(ə)l] *a.*

governess [gávənis] *n.* onna kyōshi; onna kateikyōshi.

governor [gávənə] *n.* tōchisha; sōsai; chiji; sōtoku; chōsei-
ki. ~ **general** [-dʒén(ə)rəl] *n.* sōtoku.

gown [gaun] *n.* nagaiuwagi; gaun; hōfuku; daigaku-fuku.
town and ~, shimin to daigaku no hitobito   ⌈*Pay-Oo*⌉

G.P.U. [géipéiú:] Soren no kyū Kokka Keijihoambu. (*Gay-*

grab [græb] *n.* kyū ni tsukamu koto. *v.* kyū ni tsukamu; hittakuru.

grace [greis] *n.* onchō; onten; jōhin de kedakai koto; shoku-
zen, shokugo no kansha no inori. (G~) kakka (keishō); shinsetsu; shiharai-yūyo. *v.* kazaru; agameru. **good** ~**s.** *n.* kōi.
with a bad ~, iyaiya. *with a good* ~ isagiyoku. ~**less** *a.* migurushii. ~**ful** [gréisf(u)l] *a.* yūbina. ~**fully** *ad.* yūbini;
jōhinni. ~**fulness** *n.* yūbi; jōhin.

gracious [gréiʃəs] *a.* jōhinna; jihibukai; shinsetsuna. ~**ly**
ad. yūgani; jōhinni. ~**ness** *n.* yūga; jōhin.

grackle [grækl] *n.* (*bird*) isshu no mukudori.

gradation [grədéiʃən] *n.* dankai no aru koto. (*gram.*) boin hensa. (*art*) bokashi.

grade [greid] *n.* tōkyū; gakunen; kurai; kōbai. *v.* tōkyū o
sadameru; narasu.

gradient [gréidiənt/-dʒənt] *n.* keisha (*slant*) no doai; kōbai;
henka (*change*) no doai.

gradual [grǽdju(ə)l/-dʒu(ə)l] *a.* dandan no : ~ *improvement in
health*, kenkō ga dandan kaifuku suru koto. ~**ly** *ad.* jojoni.

graduate [grǽdjueit/-dʒu-] *v.* memori suru; tōkyū o tateru;
sotsugyō suru. *n.* [grǽdjuit/-dʒu] *n.* sotsugyō-sei.

graduation [grædjuéiʃən-/dʒu-] *n.* memori; tōkyū-zuke; sotsugyō; gakui juyo (shiki).   ⌈*suru.*⌉

graft [graːft] *n.* tsugiki. (*Am.*) oshoku; shūwai. *v.* tsugiki

grail [greil] *n.* sakazuki ; ōzara. *Holy* ~, Seihai.

grain [grein] *n.* tsubu ; kokumotsu ; gurein (0.0648 gr.) shō-ryō ; mokume ; ishime : *against the* ~, iyaiya nagara ; i ni hanshite.

gram(me) [græm] *n.* guramu.

grammar [grǽmə] *n.* bumpō. ~**ian** [grəmɛ́əriən] *n.* bumpō-gakusha. ~**school** (*Brit.*) bumpō gakkō, kōritsu chūgakkō. (*Am.*) shotō chūgakkō. ~**tical** [grəmǽtik(ə)l] *a.* bumpō no ; bumpō ni atte iru. ~**tically** *ad.* bumpōjō ; bumpōtekini.

gramophone [grǽməfoun] *n.* chikuonki.

grampus [grǽmpəs] *n.* (*zoo.*) sakamata ; shachi.

granary [grǽnəri] *n.* kokumotsugura.

grand [grænd] *a.* sōdaina ; dōdōtaru ; kanroku no aru. ~**duke**, taikō. ~**child** [⊥tʃaild] *n.* mago. ~**daughter** [⊥dɔːtə] *n.* mago musume. ~**father** [-fáːðə] *n.* sofu. ~**ly** *ad.* sōdaini ; dōdō to. ~**mother** [-mʌ́ðə] *n.* sobo. ~**parent** [⊥pɛ́ərənt] *n.* sofu(-bo). ~**sire** [-saiə] *n.* (*arch.*) sofu ; sosen. ~**son** [⊥sʌn] *n.* mago musuko.

grandee [grændíː] *n.* taikō (Spein saikōi no kizoku).

grandeur [grǽndʒə/-djuə] *n.* sōdai ; sōgon.

grandiloquence [grændíləkwəns] *n.* ōgesani iu koto ; jiman.

grandiloquent [grændíləkwənt] *a.* kochō no ; taigen sōgo

grandiose [grǽndious/-djous] *n.* sōdaina ; kidotta. ⌊suru.

grange [greindʒ] *n.* nōjō ; gōnō no teitaku. (G~) (*Am.*) nō-min kyōsai kumiai.

granite [grǽnit] *n.* (*min.*) kakōgan ; mikageishi.

granivorous [grənívərəs] *a.* kokumotsu o taberu.

grant [graːnt] *n.* hojokin ; ninka ; shōdaku ; jōto shōmeisho. *v.* yurusu ; ataeru ; jōto suru. ~**ee** [-íː] *n.* yuzuri ukenin ; yu-rusareta hito. ~**tor** [-ɔː/gráːntə] *n.* yuzuri watashinin.

granular [grǽnjulə] *a.* kotsubu de dekite iru ; tsubujō no.

granulate [grǽnjuleit/-njəl-] *v.* tsubu ni suru (naru) ; hyōmen ga zaratsuku. ⌈suru koto.

granulation [grænjuléiʃən] *n.* tsubu ni naru koto ; tsubujō ni

granule [grǽnjuːl] *n.* kotsubu ; tsubujō.

grape [greip] *n.* budō. ~**shot** [⊥ʃɔt] *n.* budōdan. ~**stone** [⊥stoun] *n.* budō no tane. ~**sugar**, budōtō (*glucose*). ~**vine**

graph 315 **gravitation**

[⌐vain] *n.* budōzuru; budō no ki.

graph [græf/grɑːf] *n.* gurafu; zuhyō. ～**ic** *a.* zukai no; zu ni kaita; e (*picture*) o miru yōna.

graphite [grǽfait] *n.* (*min.*) sekiboku; kokuen,

grapnel [grǽpnəl] *n.* chiisai ikari (*anchor*); tetsukagi; tsukami-kikai. ⌐uchi; tsukamiai.

grapple [grǽpl] *v.* tsukamiau; kagi de hikkakeru. *n.* kumi-

grasp [grɑːsp] *v.* nigiru; etoku suru; imi o yoku tsukamu. *n.* tsukami; rikairyoku; haakuryoku. ～ *at*, tsukamō to do-ryoku suru; nesshin ni uketoru. ～**ing** *a.* yokufukai.

grass [grɑːs] *n.* kusa; bokusō; sōgen. ～**hopper** [⌐həpə] *n.* is-shu no batta; kirigirisu. ～**y** *a.* kusabukai; kusa no yōna.

grate [greit] *n.* irori no higōshi; tetsugōshi. *v.* suriawaseru; suri kudaku; kanjō o gaisuru. ～**r** [gréitə] *n.* oroshigane; orosu hito. ～**ting** [gréitiŋ] *n.* kōshi; madogōshi. *a.* kishi-ru; shinkei o shigeki suru.

grateful [gréitf(u)l] *a.* kansha suru; ureshii (*glad*); arigatai to omou. *be* ～ *for*, ni shai o arawasu. ～**ly** *ad.* kanshashite.

gratification [grætifikéiʃən] *n.* manzoku; yorokobi.

gratify [grǽtifai] *v.* manzoku saseru; yorokobasu. ～**ing** *a.* yorokobashii; manzokuna.

gratis [gréitis] *ad.* tada de (*free of charge*).

gratitude [grǽtitjuːd] *n.* kansha; arigatasa.

gratuitous [grətjúː(i)təs] *a.* muryō no; hitsuyō no nai; muhō-shū no; riyū no nai.

gratuity [grətjúː(ː)iti] *n.* hōbi; kokorozuke.

grave [greiv] *v.* **graved** *or* **graven**; **graving**. chōkoku suru; kokoro ni kizamu. *n.* haka. *a.* jūdaina; majimena. ～**clothes** [⌐klouðz] *n.* shinin (*dead body*) ga kite hōmurareru kimono. ～**digger** [-dìgə] *n.* haka hori (nin). ～**ly** *ad.* majimeni; ogo-sokani. ～**r** [gréivə] *n.* chōkokushi; chōkoku-tō (*knife*). ～**stone** [-stoun] *n.* hakaishi. ～**yard** [⌐jaːd] *n.* bochi; hakaba.

gravel [grǽv(ə)l] *n.* jari. *v.* jari o shiku. ～**ly** *a.* jari no ōi.

graven [gréivn] *v. see* : **grave**.

gravitate [gr(ə)ǽviteit] *v.* jūryoku ni hikareru; soko (*battom*) made hikareru; shizen ni hikitsukerareru. ⌐chikara).

gravitation [grævitéiʃən] *n.* inryoku; jūryoku (hikitsukeru

gravity [grǽviti] *n.* genshikusa ; jūryoku. *center of* ~, jūshin. *force of* ~, jūryoku. **specific** ~, *n.* hijū.

gravure [grɔvjúə/gréivjə] *n.* grabia-ban ;

gravy [gréivi] *n.* gureivii ; niku no shiru. ~**boat** [-bout] *n.* ~ ya *sauce* o ireru mono (fune no katachi o shita).

gray (*Am.*), **grey** [grei] *a.* haiiro no ; shiraga no. *n.* haiiro. ~ **beard** [-biəd] *n.* shiroku natta hige ; rōjin.

graze [greiz] *v.* kusa o kuwaseru ; hōboku suru ; surimuku ; kasuru. ⌈*the market*).

grazier [gréiziə] *n.* bokuchikugyōsha (*one who grazes cattle for*

grease [gri:s] *n.* shibō. *v.* [gri:z] abura o nuru ; zōwai suru. ~**r** [-ə] *n.* abura o sasu hito ; (*Am. sl.*) Mekishikojin mata wa Speinkei no Beijin.

greasy [grí:zi/grí:si] *a.* aburagitta ; aburajimita ; aburakkoi.

great [greit] *a.* ōkii ; idaina ; *G~ Bear*, (*astr.*) ōkuma-za (Hokutosei no betsumei). *G~ Britain*, Dai-Ei-Teikoku. ~**aunt** [-ɑ:nt] *n.* ōoba (sofubo no shimai). ~**coat** [-kóut] *n.* ōgaito. ~**hearted** [-há:tid] *a.* kokoro no ōkii ; genkina. ~**ly** *ad.* ōini ; kedakaku. ~**ness** *n.* idai ; takuetsu. ~**-uncle** [-ʌ́ŋkl] *n.* ōoji (sofubo no kyōdai).

greaves [gri:vz] (*pl.*) *n.* suneate.

Grecian [grí:ʃ(ə)n] *a.* Girisha no. *n.* Girishago gakusha.

greed [gri:d] *n.* don'yoku. ~**ily** *ad.* gatsugatsu to ; yokubatte. ~**iness** *n.* don'yoku. ~**y** *a.* kuishimbō no ; yoku no fukai ; setsubō suru.

Greek [gri:k] *a.* Girisha no ; *n.* Girishajin ; Girishago.

green [gri:n] *a.* midori iro no ; midori ni ōwareta ; genkina. *v.* midori iro ni suru (naru). *n.* midori ; kusachi ; (*pl.*) midori no ha, eda ; aomono. ~**back** [-bæk] *n.* (*Am.*) ura ga midori no shihei. ~**ery** *n.* (*collective*) aoba ; ryokuju. ~**hand** [-hænd] *n.* mijukumono. ~**-eyed** [-áid] *a.* shittobukai. ~**grocer** [-gròusə] *n.* aomonoshō ; yaoya. ~**horn** [-hɔ:n] *n.* manuke ; aonisai. ~**house** [-haus] *n.* onshitsu. ~**ing** *n.* midoriiro ringo. ~**ish** *a.* midorigakatta. ~**ly** *ad.* midoriiro ni. ~**ness** *n.* midoriiro ; shinsen ; mijuku. ~**room** [-ru:m] *n.* (gekijō no) gakuya. ~**sward** [-swɔ:d] *n.* shibafu. ~**wood** [-wud] *n.* midori no mori.

greet [gri:t] *v.* aisatsu ; keirei suru. ~**ing** *n.* aisatsu ; keirei.

gregarious [gregέəriəs] *a.* gunkyo suru ; shakōtekina. ~**ly** *ad.* shūdantekini.

grenade [grinéid] *n.* (*mil.*) shuryūdan.

grenadier [grènədíə] *n.* (*mil.*) tekidanhei (*grenade* o nageru hei).

grenadine [grénəd:in] *n.* isshu no usui sha.

grew [gru:] *v. see* : **grow**.

grey [grei] (*Brit.*) *n. a.* haiiro (no). ~**hound** [-haund] *n.* ryōken no isshu. (*cf.* **gray**.)

grid [grid] *n.* kōshi ; aburiko ; (shinkūkan no) guriddo.

griddle [grídl] *n.* (chokusetsu no hi de pan, kashi nado o yaku) isshu no furaipan.

gride [graid] *v.* suru ; kishiru.

gridiron [grídàiən] *n.* tekkyū ; aburiki ; (*Am.*) shūkyūjō.

grief [gri:f] *n.* kanashimi ; hitan. *come to* (*great*) ~, sainan ni au.

grievance [grí:v(ə)ns] *n.* kujō ; nangi : *a popular* ~, seken no hinan (kujō ; fuhei). *have a* ~ *against someone*, aru hito ni taishi fuhei o idaku.

grieve [gri:v] *v.* kanashimu (-maseru) ; nayamu (-masu).

grievous [grí:vəs] *a.* kanashii ; hitsūna : ~ *news*, kanashii shirase : *a* ~ *cry*, hitsūna nakigoe. ~**ly** *ad.* kanashiku.

griffin [grífin] *n.* (*Gk. myth.*) hanshin washi (*eagle*), hanshin raion (*lion*) no kaibutsu.

grill [gril] *n.* aburiko ; yakiniku (no) ryōri. *v.* aburu. ~**room** [-rum] *n.* guriru ; shokudō ; yakiniku shokudō.

grille [gril] *n.* kōshi ; tetsugōshi.

grim [grim] *a.* yōbō no kowai ; zanninna ; arai ; fukitsuna. ~**ly** *ad.* mugoku ; monosugoku.

grimace [griméis] *v.* kao o yugameru ; *n.* ikari ni yugameta kao.

grime [graim] *n.* (hifu (*skin*) ni) shimi konda yogore.

grimy [gráimi] *a.* yogoreta ; kitanai.

grin [grin] *v.* ha o dashite warau ; ha o mukidasu. *n.* ha o dashite suru azawarai.

grind [graind] *v.* **ground** ; **grinding**. *v.* suru ; togu ; (kona o) hiku. *n.* hiku koto ; togu koto. ~**er** *n.* hiku hito ; togu hito ; okuba. ~**stone** [-stoun] *n.* toishi.

grip [grip] *n.* nigiri ; tsukamu koto. (*Am.*) tesage kaban (= *gripsack*). *v.* nigiru ; tsukamu.

gripe [graip] *n.* shikkari nigirishimeru koto. *v.* kunō o ataeru ; kurushimeru.

grippe [grip] (*med.*) *n.* infuruenza ; ryūkōsei kambō.

grisly [grízli] *a.* miburui suru hodo osoroshii.

grist [grist] *n.* hiita kokumotsu ; seihen zairyō.

gristle [grísl] (*anat.*) *n.* nankotsu (*cartilage*).

grit [grit] *n.* suna ; komakai ishi (gohan ni haitta). *v.* kishiru (raseru). (*pl.*) hikiwari.

grizzled [grízld] *a.* haiiro no ; shiraga majiri no.

grizzly [grízli] *a.* haiiro no. *n.* (*zoo.*) haiiro no kuma.

groan [groun] *n.* umeki. *v.* unaru ; fusansei de tsubuyaku ; umeku.

groat [grout] *n.* mukashi no Eikoku-ginka (ima no 4 pensu ̄ni ataru) ; sukoshi.

groats [grouts] *n.* (*pl.*) hikiwarimugi nado no shokumotsu.

grocer [gróusə] *n.* kambutsuya ; shokuryōhinten. ～**y** [-ri] *n.* (*usu. pl.*) shokuryōzakkarui. (*Am.*) shokuryō zakkaten.

grog [grɔg] *n.* mizu o watta (*brandy*) tsuyoi sake. ～**gy** [-́gi] *a.* sake ni yotta ; chidoriashi no.

groin [grɔin] *n.* (*anat.*) momo no tsukene.

groom [gru(:)m] *n.* batei ; hanamuko. *v.* (uma nado no) teire o suru. ～**sman** [-zmən] *n.* hanamuko ; tsukisoinin.

groove [gru:v] *n.* (ki, kinzoku nado ni hotta) mizo. *v.* mizo o horu.

grope [group] *v.* tesaguri suru ; anchūmosaku suru.

gross [grous] *a.* arai ; somatsuna ; hidaina ; hanahadashii. *n.* (*sing. pl.*) gurosu (12×12, 12 dāsu) : *in the* ～, gaishite ; daitai ; sōtai ni(no) : ～ *profits*, sōtai no rieki : ～ *injustice*, hanahadashii fusei. ～**ly** *ad.* hidoku. ～**ness** *n.* sozatsu ; futorisugi.

grotto [grɔ́tou] *n.* gankutsu ; dōkutsu.

ground [graund] *n.* tsuchi ; jimen. *v.* kiso o oku ; zashō suru. **baseball** ～, yakyūjō. *grounds for a statement,* shuchō no ronkyo. *coffee* ～*s*, kōhii no dashigara.. *give* ～, jōho suru. *go to the* ～, shippai suru. ～**crew** (*Am.*) chijō seibiin. ～**loop,** (*Am.*) hikōki no kyūtenkai. ～ **hog** [hɔg] *n.* yamanezumi. ～**less** *a.* konkyo no nai. ～**ling** [-liŋ] *n.* suitei ni sumu sakana ; teikyū-na kankyaku. ～**work** [-́wə:k] *n.* kiso ; kontei.

ground [graund] *v. see* : **grind**.

grounder [gráundə] *n. (baseball)* goro .

group [gru:p] *n.* mure ; shūdan ; nakama. *v.* atsumaru (-meru) ; bunrui suru.

grouse [graus] *n. (bird)* raicho no rui.

grout [graut] *n.* shikkui ; usui ekijō no shikkui.

grove [grouv] *n.* chiisana mori ; kodachi ; chiisai.

grovel [grÁvl/grÓvl] *v.* harabau ; heifuku suru. ⌢(l)er *n.* hiretsuna hito.

grow [grou] *v.* **grew, grown; growing.** seichō suru ; naru ; sodatsu ; haeru ; tsukuru.

growl [graul] *n.* unari. *v.* unaru. ⌐jin ; otona.

grown [groun] *v. see* : **grow.** ⌢up [⌐Áp] *a.* seichōshita. *n.* seichōshita hito.

growth [grouθ] *n.* seichō ; hattatsu ; hare mono. *(tumor)* a ⌢ *of weeds,* zassō no seichō.

grub [grÁb] *v.* horu ; sesseto hataraku ; jimichini benkyō suru. *n.* jimushi ; *(worm) (pl.) (sl.)* shokumotsu.

grudge [grÁdʒ] *n.* akui ; ikon. *v.* iyagaru ; oshimu.

grudgingly [grÁdʒinli] *ad.* iyaiya nagara ; shibushibu.

gruel [grúəl] *n.* (o)kayu.

gruesome [grú:səm] *a.* miburui suru hodo kimi no warui ; zotto suru yōna.

gruff [grÁf] *a.* arai ; bukkirabōna : ⌢ *voice,* arai koe. ⌢ *manner* sobona taido. ⌢ly *ad.* araarashiku ; bukkirabōni.

grumble [grÁmbl] *n.* fuhei. (tōi kaminari no) gorogoro. *v.* fuhei o narasu. (enrai nado ga) gorogoro naru.

grumpy [grÁmpi] *a.* ijiwarui ; kimuzukashii.

grunt [grÁnt] *n.* (buta, nado no) būbū iu koe ; *v.* bukigen ni butsubutsu iu ; būbū iu. ⌢er [grÁntə] *n.* buta ; buta no yōna koe o dasu (fuhei o iu) hito.

guano [gwá:nou/gju(:)á:nou] *n.* kaichō no fun ; hiryō.

guarantee [gærəntí:] *n.* hoshō ; tampo ; hi-hoshōnin. *v.* ho-
guarantor [gærəntɔ:/gərǽntɔ:] *n.* hoshōnin. ⌊shō suru.

guaranty [gǽrənti] *n.* hoshō ; tampo. *v.* hoshō suru.

guard [ga:d] *n.* mihari ; bampei. *(pl.)* bōei ; konoetai ; bōgyobutsu. *v.* miharu ; bōeisuru ; yōjin suru. ⌢ *of hono(u)r,* gijōhei. [⌐id] ⌢ed *a.* yōjimbukai. ⌢house [-haus] *n.* eiheijo ;

ryūchijo. ～**room** [⌐rum] *n.* eiheijo; eiso ～**sman** [⌐zmən/ -mæn] *n.* konoe hei.

guardian [gá:diən] *n.* kōkennin; hogosha. ～ **angel** *n.* shugo- shin. ～**ship** *n.* kōken; shugo.

guava [gwá:və] *n.* (*bot.*) banjirō (Amerika nettai chihō san).

gubernatorial [gju:bənətɔ́:riəl] *a.* chiji no; chihōchōkan no.

gudgeon [gʌ́dʒən] *n.* (*fish*) kawagisu; (kawagisu no yōni ra- kuni tsukamatte e ni sareru yōna) amai ningen; noroma; fune no kaji no ukegane; jikutō (*top*).

guerdon [gɔ́:dən] *n.* hōshū; hōbi. *v.* hōshū o ataeru.

Guernsey [gɔ́:nzi] *n.* keito de anda shatsu (*shirts*).

guerrilla [gərílə] *n.* gerirahei (butai); fuseikihei.

guess [ges] *n.* suisatsu. *v* suisoku suru; (*Am.*) omou. ～**work** [⌐wə:k] *n.* atezuiryō; atezuppō.

guest [gest] *n.* kyaku; shukuhakunin. *paying* ～, (*Brit.*) geshu- kunin.

guffaw [gʌfɔ́:] *n.* ōwarai; geragera-warai. *v.* geragera warau.

guidance [gáidəns] *n.* annai; shidō.

guide [gaid] *n.* annaisha; shidōsha. *v.* annai suru; shidō su- ru. ～**book** [-buk] *n.* ryokō-annai. ～**post** [⌐poust] *n.* michi- shirube. ～ **rope** [-roup] *n.* yūdōzuna.

guild [gild] *n.* (chūsei no) dōgyōkumiai; girudo. ～**hall** [⌐hɔ:l] *n.* dōgyō kumiai shūkaijo; shikai gijidō.

guilder [gíldə] *n.* Oranda no ginka.

guile [gail] *n.* kokkei; kōkatsu; warudakumi. ～**ful** *a.* kōka- tsuna. ～**less** *a.* mujakina.

guillotine [gìlətí:n/gílətì:n] *n.* girochin; kōshudai. *v.* girochin de kubi o kirareru. ～**cutter,** *n.* bōru (kami) dansaiki.

guilt [gilt] *n.* tsumi. ～**ily** [gíltili] *ad.* yūzai ni. ～**iness** *n.* yū- zai; zaiaku. ～**less** *a.* muzai no. *be* ～*less of,* o shiranai; no keiken ga nai; ga nai. ～**y** *a.* yūzai no.

guinea [gíni] *n.* mukashi (Igilisu) de tsukawareta kinka (gen- zai no 21 shiringu). ～**fowl** [⌐faul], ～ **hen** [-hen] *n.* (*bird*) ho- rohorochō. ～ **pig** [pig] *n.* tenjikunezumi. (*Am.*) jikkenshiryō.

guise [gaiz] *n.* (ippan ni) gaimenteki fukusō nado. gaikan; sugata. *in the* ～ *of,* ni misekakete.

guitar [gitá:] *n.* gita (gakki).

gulch [gʌltʃ/gʌlʃ] *n.* fukaku kiritatta semai tani.

gules [gju:lz] *n.* akage kegawa no erimaki; *a.* pink iro (no); aka iro (no).

gulf [gʌlf] *n.* wan; rikuchi ni irikonda umi. *a* ~ *between old friends,* kyūyū no aida no mizo.

gull [gʌl] *n.* (*bird*) kamome; damasareyasui hito. *v.* damasu.

gullet [gʌlit] *n.* (*anat.*) shokudō (*esophagus*).

gullibility [gʌlibíliti] *n.* damasare yasui koto.

gullible [gʌləbl] *a.* damasare yasui. ~**bly** [-li] *ad.* damasare yasuku. ⌈fukai tani.

gully [gʌli] *n.* kyōkoku; nagareru mizu ga tsukutta mizo;

gulp [gʌlp] *n.* guinomi. *v.* ōini aoru; gokuri to nomu.

gum [gʌm] *n.* gomu; gomu nori. (*pl.*) haguki. (*Am.*) chūingamu. ~**arabic** *n.* Arabiya gomu. *v.* gomu o nuru. ~ **tree** [-tri:] *n.* (*bot.*) yūkari.

gummy [gʌmi] *a.* gomu no yōna; fukureta; jushi no ōi.

gumption [gʌm(p)ʃən] *n.* jōshiki; shinshuteki kishō; chie.

gun [gʌn] *n.* jū; hō. *v.* (*Am.*) (*air.*) hatsudōki no shiboriben o hiraku. ~ **barrel** [-bærəl] *n.* hōshin; jūshin. ~**boat** [⌐bout] *n.* hōkan. ~ **carriage** [-kæridʒ] *n.* hōsha. ~**cotton** [⌐kɔtn] *n.* menkayaku. ~**fire** [-faiə] *n.* hōka; hōgeki. ~**man** [⌐mæn, -mən] *n.* (*Am.*) pisutoru shoji no akukan. ~ **metal** [-metl] *n.* seidō.; hōkin ~**powder** [⌐paudə] *n.* kayaku. ~ **room** [-ru:m] *n.* (gunkan no) shikanjishitsu. ~**shot** [⌐ʃɔt] *n.* hōgeki; chakudankyori. ~**smith** [-smiθ] *n.* teppōkaji. ~**stock** [⌐stɔk] *n.* jū- **gunner** [gʌnə] *n.* hōshu; chief ~, *n.* hōjutsuchō. ⌊shō.

gunnery [gʌnəri] *n.* hōjutsu; hōgehi. ~ **lieutenant,** *n.* hōjutsuchō. ~ **ship,** hōjutsu renshūkan.

gunny [gʌni] *n.* isshu no zukku; nankimbukuro; tsuyoi, arai nuno no fukuro.

gunwale=**gannel** [gʌnəl] *n.* funaberi.

gurgle [gə́:gl] *n.* gobogobo (*sound*). *v.* gobogobo iu.

gush [gʌʃ] *n.* funshutsu. *v.* wakideru. ~**er** *n.* fukidashi yuden; (*oil well*).

gusset [gʌsit] *n.* (kimono no) machi; okumi.

gust [gʌst] *n.* reppū; (kanjō no) gekihatsu (*fit*). ~**y** [gʌsti] *a.*

gustation [gʌstéiʃən] *n.* mikaku; ajiwai. ⌊reppū no.

gustatory [gʌ́stətəri] *a*. mikaku no. ~ **sensation**, mikaku.

gusto [gʌ́stou] *n*. shumi ; fūmi ; shikō.

gut [gʌt] *n*. harawata ; semai tsūro. (*sl.*) yūki. *v*. harawata o toridasu ; naibu o hakai suru. **blind** ~, (*anat.*) mōchō.

gutta-percha [gʌ́təpə́:tʃə] *n*. perucha-gomu ; guttapercha.

gutter [gʌ́tə] *n*. amadoi ; gesui ; oke. *v*. mizo o tsukeru ; rō (*wax*) ga tareru ; mizo ga dekiru.

guttural [gʌ́t(ə)rəl] *a*. nodo no. *n*. nodo kara deru (koe).

guy [gai] *n*. (aru mono ni shikkari tsuketa) nawa (*rope*) ya kusari (*chain*). (*Am.*) otoko ; yatsu.

guzzle [gʌ́zl] *v*. gabugabu nomu. ~**r** *n*. ōzakenomi.

gym [dʒim] *n*. (*sl.*) taiikukan ; taisō.

gymnasium [dʒimnéiziəm] (*pl*. **-sia** ; **-s**) *n*. taiikukan ; (Doitsu no) kōtō-gakko ; daigaku-yobikō.

gymnast [dʒímnæst] *n*. taisō kyōshi. ~**ic** [dʒimnǽstik] *a*. taisō no. ~**ics** (*sing. pl.*) taisō.

gypsum [dʒípsəm] (*min.*) *n*. sekkō.

gypsy, gipsy [dʒípsi] *n*. jipushii.

gyrate [dʒai(ə)réit] *v*. senkai suru ; mau (odoru).

gyration [dʒai(ə)réiʃ(ə)n] *n*. senkai ; kaiten ; gurugurumawari. ~**tory** [dʒáirətəri] *a*. senkai no.

gyropilot [dʒáiərəpailət] *n*. jidō sōjūki (*of aeroplane*).

gyroscope [dʒáiərɔskoup/gái-] *n*. kaitenki ; jairosukōpu.

gyve [dʒaiv] *n*. (*usu. pl.*) ashikase. *v*. ashikase o hameru.

H

H, h [eitʃ] *n.* (*pl.* **H's, Hs,** [éitʃiz]). Eigo *alphabet* no dai-8-bamme no moji.

ha [hɑ:] *inter.* hō! hō! (odoroki, yorokobi, tamerai nado o arawasu hassei).

habeas corpus [héibiæs kɔ́:pɔs] *n.* (*You may have the person*); aru hito ga hōritsujō kōkin sareru beki ka dō ka o kimeru tame ni hōtei (*court*) ni kuru yōni to iu reijō; migara teishutsu reijō.

haberdasher [hǽbədæʃə] *n.* komamonoya. (*Am.*) danshi sō-shingusho.

habiliment [həbílimənt] *n.* (*pl.*) fukusō; ifuku.

habit [hǽbit] *n.* shūkan; seishitsu; kuse; fujin jōba fuku. *v.* (kimono o) kiseru; sumawasu.

habitable [hǽbitəbl] *a.* sumu ni tekishita.

habitant [hǽbitənt] *n.* sunde iru hito. ka.

habitat [hǽbitæt] *n.* gensanchi; jūsho (*address*); homba; sumi-ka.

habitation [hæbitéiʃən] *n.* jūsho; sumai. ~ly *ad.*

habitual [həbítjuəl] *a.* itsumono; higoro no; shūkanjō no.

habituate [həbítjueit] *v.* narasu (naresaseru).

habitude [hǽbitju:d] *n.* karada ya kokoro no tokushuna (*characteristic*) jōtai; shūkan; seishitsu; taishitsu.

hack [hæk] *v.* tataki kiru; kirikizamu. shitabataraki suru. *n.* kirikizami. kashibasha.

hackle [hækl] *n.* asa-nado o suku kushi; tori no kubi no ho-sonagai hanege. *v.* asa nado o sukiwakeru; hiki saku.

hackney [hǽkni] *n.* kashi-uma; jōba. *v.* tsukai furusu. ~-coach [-koutʃ] *n.* kashi basha. ~ed [-d] *a.* arifureta; chimpuna.

had [hæd/həd] *v. see* : **have.**

haddock [hǽdək] *n.* (*fish*) tara no isshu.

Hades [héidi:z] *n.* (*Gk. myth.*) gekai; jigoku; meifu.

haft [hɑ:ft] *n.* e (*handle*; *hilt*). tsuka *v.* e (mata wa tsuka) o tsukeru.

hag [hæg] *n.* minikui (*ugly*) rōba (*old woman*); majo (*witch*). (*fish*) yatsume unagi no rui.

haggard [hǽgəd] *a.* yatsureta; yasekoketa.

haggle [hǽgl] *v.* negiru (shōhin no nedan o yasuku saseru; make sasu); ii arasou.

hail [heil] *n.* arare; hyō; kassai. (*inter.*) banzai! (*hurrah!*) *v.* arare ga furu. aisatsu suru. ～ *from,* kara kuru; no shusshin. ～**-fellow** [-félou] *a.* naka no yoi. *n.* shin'yū. ～**stone** [-stoun] *n.* hyō.

hair [hɛə] *n.* ke; tōhatsu. ～**breadth** [-bredθ], ～**sbreadth** [-zbredθ] *n.*, *a.* ke hodo no kyori; kanhatsu o ire nai. ～**do** [-du:] *n.* (*Am.*) kamiyui. ～**dresser** [-dresə] *n.* rihatsushi. ～ **pin** [-pin] atama ni sasu pin. ～**splitting** [-splitiŋ] *a.* sasaina koto ni kōdei suru. *n.* herikutsu; tsumaranu koto ni kōdei suru koto. ～**spring** [-spriŋ] *n.* (tokei no) hige zemmai.

hairy [hɛəri] *a.* kebukai; ke no yōna.

hake [heik] *n.* (*fish*) tara no isshu.

halation [həléijən] *n.* harēshon; (shashin no) boyake.

halberd [hǽlbəd] ～**bert** [-bət] *n.* hoko (ono to yari ni naru). ～**ier** [hǽlbədíə] *n.* kono buki o motta heitai.

halcyon [hǽlsiən] *a.* odayakana. *n.* (*bird*) kawasemi (ōnami o shizumeru to omowarete ita tori).

hale [heil] *a.* kenkōna; genkina.

half [ha:f] *n.* hambun. *a.* hambun no. *ad.* nakaba. ～**-and-**～ [⌐(ə)n(d)há:f] *a.* hampa no, hanhan no. ～**back** [-bǽk] *n. footb.* de hāfu bakku; chūei. ～**binding** [-baindiŋ] *n.* kado to se ga kawa no sōtei (no hon). ～**blood** [⌐blʌd] *n.* kataoya chigau kyōdai. ～**-bound** [-báund] *a.* hankawa sōtei no. ～**breed** [⌐bri:d] *n.* zasshu; konketsuji. ～**brother** [⌐brʌðə] *n.* ifubo kyōdai. ～**crown** [-kraun] *n.* (Eikoku no) han-kuraun ginka. ～**-hearted** [⌐há:tid] *n.* fu-nesshinna; reitanna. ～**holiday,** han-kyūji. ～**mast** [⌐má:st] *n.* hanki no ichi : *flag at* ～**mast,** hanki; chōki. ～**moon** [⌐mú:n] *n.* hangetsu. ～ **note** [-nout] *n.* nibu-ompu. ～ **pay** [-péi] *n.* hankyū. ～**penny** [héip(ə)ni] *n.* han-penni. ～**sister** [⌐sisteə] *n.* harachigai no ane, imōto. ～**track** [⌐trǽk] *n.* mugen kidō; (*Am.*) mugen kidō tsuki yusōyō jidōsha. ～**way** [-wéi] *ad.*, *a.* chūto de (no); hampani (na). ～**witted** [-wítid] *a.* manukena.

halibut [hǽlibət] (*fish*) *n.* hirame no rui.

halitosis [hælitóusis] *n.* aku(warui)-shū (nioi) no aru iki (*breath*).

hall [hɔ:l] *n.* kaikan; ōhiroma; genkan. (*Am.*) gakuin; (*British Univ.* no) shokudō; (*Brit.*) (jinushi no) teitaku.

halleluiah, hallelujah [hælilú:jə] *inter. & n.* harerūya (Kami o tataeru sakebi). ⌐kokuin.

hallmark [hó:lmá:k/hó:lmɑ:k] *n.* (kin, gin no) jundo shōmei

hallo(a) [həlóu, hǽlóu] *int.* moshi moshi! oi!

halloo [həlú:/hæl-] *int.* oi! moshi moshi! *v.* yobi kakeru; kowadaka ni yobu; yobikakeru. *n.* yobikake.

hallow [hǽlou] *v.* shinseini suru; sonkei suru.

hallucination [həlù:sinéiʃən/-lju:-] *n.* gensō; maboroshi; mō-
halo [héilou] *n.* (taiyō, tsuki no) kasa; gokō. ⌊sō.

halt [hɔ:lt/hɒlt] *n.* tachidomari; chūcho; teishi. *v.* tomaru (tomeru); chūsha suru.

halter [hó:tə/hóltə] *n.* tsuna (kemono ni tsukeru). *v.* tsuna o tsukeru; tsuna de shibaru.

halve [hɑ:v] *v.* nitōbun suru; seppan suru. ∼s *n.* '*half*' no fukusū (*pl.*). ⌐ge suru tsuna.

halyard [hǽljəd] *n.* hikizuna (hogeta; ho; hata nado o agesa-
ham [hæm] *n.* momo; shio buta niku; hamu.

hamlet [hǽmlit] *n.* chiisai mura; buraku; shōson (toku ni kyōkai no nai).

hammer [hǽmə] *n.* tsuchi. *v.* tsuchi (de tataku): ∼ *out*, tsuchi de utte katachi o tsukuru; (*fig.*) kangae dasu; sesseto hataraku (*at*).

hammock [hǽmək] *n.* tsuridoko; hammokku. ⌐ōkago.

hamper [hǽmpə] *v.* samatageru; jama suru. *n.* futa-tsuki no

hamstring [hǽmstriŋ] *n.* hiza (*knee*) no ushiro no suji (*tendon*). *v.* hamstring o kitte bikko (*cripple*) ni suru.

hand [hænd] *n.* te; kaita moji; tokei no hari; shiyōnin; hito-
de : *at first* ∼, chokusetsu ni. *at* ∼, tejika ni. *at second* ∼, hito no te o hete; ofuru. *change* ∼s, mochinushi ga kawaru. *clean* ∼, keppaku. *come to* ∼, uketoru; te ni ireru. *free* ∼, jiyū kōdō. *from* ∼ *to mouth*, sonohi-gurashi. ∼ *in* ∼, te o tsunaide. *Hands off!* te o fureru na! *have a* ∼ *in*, ni kankei suru. *in* ∼, torikakatte; jikkōchū de. *off one's* ∼, te o hanarete; sunde

on the other ～, ichi men niwa. *wash one's* ～ *of*, …kara te o hiku. *v.* te de tasukeru; te de watasu. ～ *down*, tsutaeru. ～ *on*, junguri ni mawasu. ～**bag** [bæg] *n.* tesage kaban. ～**bill** [￪bil] *n.* hiki fuda; bira. ～**book** [-buk] *n.* benran; annaisho. ～**cuffs** [-kəf] *n. (usu. pl.)* tejō; tejō o kakeru. ～**ful** [-ful] *n.* hito tsukami; shōsū. ～**loom** [￪lu:m] *n.* teori bata. ～**made** [￪meid] *a.* tesei no. ～**maid** [￪meid], **maiden** [-méidn] *n.* jochū. ～**-me-down** [￪midàun] *n.* dekiai no; yasumono no. *n.* dekiai fuku; furugi. ～**organ** [￪ó:gən] tefūkin. ～**out** [￪aut] *n.* toguchi de kojiki ni ataeru tabemono (kimono, etc.). ～**rail** [-reil] *n.* tesuri. ～**shake** [-ʃeik] *n.* akushu. ～**spike** [-spaik] *n.* teko. ～**-to-**～ [-təhænd] *a.* tsukami ai no (ikkiuchi). ～**work** [-wə:k] *n.* te zaiku. ～**writing** [-ràitiŋ] *n.* hisseki; shofū.

handicap [hǽndikæp] *n.* handikappu; furina jōken. *v. handicap* o tsukeru; furi no chii ni oku.

handicraft [hǽndikrɑ:ft] *n.* tezaiku; shukō; tesaki no jukuren. ～**sman** [hǽndikrɑ:ftsmən] *n.* tezaikunin; teshokunin.

handie-talkie [hǽnditò:ki] *n. (Am.)* keitaiyō kogata musen denwaki.

handiwork [hǽndiwə:k] *n.* shukō; tezaiku.

handkerchief [hǽŋkətʃif/-tʃii:] *n.* hankachi.

handle [hǽndl] *n.* e; totte; handoru; jōzu beki kikai *(chance)*; kōjitsu. *v.* ijiru; toriatsukau.

handsel [hǽnsəl], **hansel** [hǽnsəl] *n.* otoshidama; omemie no temiyage; iwaihin.

handsome [hǽnsəm] *a.* rippana; tanreina; sōtōna : *a* ～ *sum of money*, sōtōna gaku no kane *(money)*. ～**ly** *ad.* na.

handy [hǽndi] *a.* keibenna; chōhōna; benrina; jōzuna; kiyō-hang [hæŋ] *v.* **hung** *or* **hanged**; **hanging**. kakaru; kakeru; tsurusu; korosu; miketsu ni suru. ～ *about*, buratsuku. ～ *back*, guzuguzu suru. ～ *on (upon)*, …ni yorikakaru. ～ *together*, gōdō suru. ～ *up*, (juwaki o) kakeru. *n.* kakari guai; atsukai kata; kotsu. ～**dog** [￪dog] *n.* hiretsukan. *a.* gesu no. ～**man** [-mən] *n.* kōshukei shikkōnin. ～**nail** [-neil] *n.* sasakure.

hangar [hǽŋə] *n.* (hikōki no) kakunōko.

hanger [hǽŋə] *n.* kagi; kei shukkōnin *(hangman)*; koshigatana. ～**-on** [-ón] *n.* isōrō; yakkai mono.

hanging [hǽŋiŋ] *n*. ishi; kubikukuri; kōshukei. (*pl.*) kakenuno; kakemono. *a*. burasagatta; kōshukei ni sarerubeki. ～ **committee** (kaiga tenrankai nado no) shinsa in.

hank [hæŋk] *n*. hitotaba no ito; kaseito. ⌈**crave.**

hanker [hǽŋkə] *v*. setsubō suru (*wish*); akogareru (*after*). = **hansel** [hǽnsel] *n*.= **handsel** otoshidama; iwaihin.

hansom [hǽnsəm] *n*. isshu no nirin basha. ⌈**fuunna.**

hap [hæp] *n*. gūzen; kōun. *v*. fui ni okoru. ～**less** [⊥lis] *a*.

haphazard [hǽphæzəd] *n*., *ad*. gūzen (ni) : *at* ～, muyamini; ikiatari battari ni.

happen [hǽpən] *v*. okoru; shōzuru.

happily [hǽpili] *ad*. saiwaini; tanoshiku; tekisetsu; shiawase.

happy [hǽpi] *a*. kōfukuna; ureshii; tekisetsuna. ～**-go-lucky** [-gou-lʌ́ki] *a*. nonkina.

harangue [hərǽŋ] *n*. batō enzetsu. *v*. netsuben o furuu.

harass [hǽrəs] *v*. komaraseru; hampuku kōgeki suru.

harbinger [há:bindʒə] *n*. senkusha (*forerunner*).

harbo(u)r [há:bə] *n*. minato; hinanjo. *v*. kakumau; idaku (akui nado o). ～**age** [-ridʒ] *n*. teihakusho; minato. ～**master** *n*. kōmubuchō.

hard [ha:d] *a*. katai; shikkari shimatta : ～ *knot*, katai musubime. ～ *problem*, muzukashii mondai. *to be* ～ *on a person*, hito ni kibishiku ataru ～ *faced*, kibishii kao. *a* ～ *worker*, yoku hataraku hito. ～ *water*, sekken no tokenai. arukōru no do no tsuyoi : ～ *liquor*, do no tsuyoi sake. (*phon*.) haretsu on no *k. g., etc. ad*. kataku. *frozen* ～, kataku kōtte. *hold* ～, shikkari nigitta. konnanni : *breath* ～, kokyū konnan. omoku : *the taxes that bear* ～ *upon us*, warera ni omoku kakatte kuru zeikin. shikkari honeotte (*try* ～). chikaku ni : *the house stands* ～ *by the bridge*, ie wa (*house*) hashi no chikaku ni aru. ～ *and fast*, genjūna. *go* ～ *on*, tsuraku ataru. ～ *of hearing*, sukoshi mimi ga tōi. ～**ness** *n*. katasa; mujō; taegatai koto; muzukashisa. ～**ship** *n*. konku; shinku; shinsan. ～**tack** [-tæk] *n*. katapan. ～**ware** [-wɛə] *n*. kana mono. ～**wood** [-wud] *n*. katagi. ～*up*, (*col*.) hidoku seikatsu ni komatte iru. ～**bitten** [-bítn] *a*. gankona. ～**boiled** [-bɔild] *a*. nakiotoshi no kikanai. ～**headed**

[-hédid] *a*. kantanni wa ugokanai. ~**-hearted** [⌐ha:tid] *a*. rei-kokuna.

harden [há:dn] *v*. kataku suru (naru) ; mujōni suru.

hardy [há:di] *a*. yūkanna ; kantanni kusshinai. ~**dihood** *n*. ~**diness** *n*.

hare [hɛə] *n*. (*zoo.*) no-usagi : ~*and hounds*, kami maki kyōsō. ~**bell** [⌐bəl] *n*. (*bot.*) hotarubukuro. ~**brained** [breind] *a*. keisotsuna ; sokotsuna. ~**lip** [⌐lip] *n*. mitsukuchi.

harem [héərem] *n*. (Kaikyōkoku de) fujimbeya ; keibō ; sokoni sumu fujin-tachi.

hark [ha:k] *v*. kiku. *Hark!* okikinasai.

harlequin [há:likwin] *n*. (H-) (mugon-geki no) dōke yakusha ; dōke mono.

harlot [há:lət] *n*. shūgyōfu.

harm [ha:m] *n*. gai ; songai ; gaiaku. *v*. gai suru. ~**less** [⌐lis] *a*. mugai no ; akui no nai. ~**ly** *ad*.

haul [hɔ:l] *v*. hipparu. (fune ga) hōkō o kaeru ; kaze no muki ga kawaru.

harmonic [ha:mónik] *a*. chōwa shita. *n*. kaion ; (*pl.*) waseigaku ; k(w)aseigaku. ~**ally** *ad*. chōwa shite.

harmonica [ha:mónikə], ~**con** [-kən] *n*. hāmonika.

harmonious [ha:móuniəs] *a*. mutsumajii ; chōwa shita ; chōshi no yoi.

harmonize [há:mənaiz] *v*. chōwa saseru ; wagō saseru ; kaichō ni suru ; wagō suru (*with*) ; chōwa suru (*with*).

harmony [há:məni] *n*. chōwa ; wagō ; (*mus.*) wasei ; k(w)asei.

harness [há:nis] *n*., *v*. bagu (o tsukeru) : *in* ~, hataraite.

harp [ha:p] *n*. tategoto. *v*. ~ o hiku : ~ *on* (*upon*), kudoku iu.

harpoon [ha:pú:n] *n*. mori. (kujiratori nado ni tsukau).

harpsichord [há:psikɔ:d] *n*. piano no zenshin (*forerunner*).

Harpy [há:pi] *n*. (*Gk. myth.*) karada ga tori, kao ga hito no onna no katachi no kaibutsu (bakemono) ; (h-) gōyoku na hito.

harrier [hǽriə] *n*. usagi gariyō no ryōken no isshu.

harrow [hǽrou] *n*. maguwa : *under the* ~, nanjū shite. *v*. maguwa de narasu. ijiwaru o suru. ~**ing** *a*. hisanna. ⌐masu.

harry [hǽri] *v*. hito o osotte bōryoku de ubau ; arasu ; nayaharsh [ha:ʃ] *a*. araarashii (koe nado), mimizawarina hidoi shiuchi no. ~ly ad. ~ness n.

hart [hɑːt] n. osu (*male*) no akajika.

hartshorn [háːtʃhɔːn] n. shika no tsuno (izen wa ammonia o toru no ni tsukawareta); mizu ni toketa ammonia.

harum-scarum [héǝrǝm-skéǝrǝm] a. sosokkashii; muchana. ad. muchakuchani.

harvest [háːvist] n. shūkaku; toriire. ~ **home,** shūkakusai (matsuri): ~ **moon,** chūshū no mangetsu. ~er n. shūkaku sha; karitori-ki (*machine*).

has [hæz/hǝz/ǝz/z] v. **have** nɔ dai (3) sanninshō, tansu, genzai jojitsu-hō. no katachi.

hash [hæʃ] n. komagire niku-no gotamaze ryōri: *make* (*a*) ~ *of*, ...o gocha-gocha ni suru. v. komagire ni suru.

hasheesh, -ish [hǽʃiːʃ] n. hashiishi (Indo ōasa kara totta eki-su; saiminzai; nemuku naru (suru) ni kikime ga aru).

hasp [hɑːsp] n. kakegane. v. kakegane de shimeru.

hassock [hǽsǝk] n. daiza; hizabuton.

haste [heist] n. isogi; shikyū: *in* ~, isoide; awatete.

hasten [héisn] v. isogu (-gaseru); sekitateru.

hasty [héisti] a. kyū no; sekkachina; keisotsuna. ~tily ad. isoide. ~tiness n. ōisogi.

hat [hæt] n. bōshi. ~band [⸚bænd] n. bōshi no hachimaki.

hatch [hætʃ] v. tamago o kaesu; (*fig.*) hakaru; takuramu. n. hito hara no hina. (fune de kampan no) origuchi. ~way [⸚wei] n. sōkō.

hatchet [hǽtʃit] n. teono: *bury the* ~, waboku suru.

hate [heit] n. zōō, nikushimi. v. nikumu; kirau. ~ful [⸚f(u)l] a. nikui; nikumu beki. ~fully ad. nikuku.

hatred [héitrid] n. zōō; nikushimi.

hatter [hǽtǝ] n. bōshi seizōnin; bōshi-shōnin.

hauberk [hɔ́ːbǝːk] n. kusarikatabira.

haughty [hɔ́ːti] a. gōmanna; ōheina. ~tily ad. ~tiness n.

haul [hɔːl] v. hipparu: ~*logs to a mill with horses*, uma de ma-ruta o seizaisho made hiite iku. kazamuki ga kawaru (fune ga hōkō o kaeru). n. tsuyoku hiku koto; hito taguri; hito ami.

haunch [hɔːntʃ/hɑːntʃ] n. koshi no mawari; (dōbutsu dewa) ashi to koshi. (*archit.*) serigoshi.

haunt [hɔ:nt] *n.* yoku iku tokoro. *v.* yoku iku (aru basho ni) : ～*ed house*, bakemono yashiki.

hautboy [óuboi/hóu-] *n.* (*mus.*) ōboe (mokkan gakki).

hauteur [outóː] *n.* (*Fr.*) kōman.

have [hæv/hәv] *v.* **had ; having.** motsu ; motte iru ; tanoshi-mu ; umu ; taberu : ～ *on*, kite iru ; haite iru. ～ *to do*, seneba naranu. *aux. v.* (*have had*) = kanryōkei. (*cf.* **has.**)

haven [héivn] *n.* minato ; hinansho (hinanjo).

haversack [hǽvasæk] *n.* seoibukuro ; zatsunō.

havoc [hǽvәk] *n.* hakai ; kōhai : *make* (*play*) ～ *with*, o sanzan ni arasu.

haw [hɔ:] *n.* sanzashi no mi.

Hawaiian [hɑːwáiiәn] *a.* Hawai (jin) no. *n.* Hawaijin (go).

hawk [hɔ:k] *n.* (*bird*) taka. *v.* taka gari o suru. yobi uri suru. tan o haku. ～**er** *n.* taka tsukai. gyōshōnin.

hawse [hɔ:z] *n.* (*ship*) (ikari ana) no aru senshubu. ～**hole** [⌐houl] *n.* byōsakō. **hawser** [hɔ́ːzә] *n.* byōsakō ; ikari zuna.

hawthorn [hɔ́ːθәːn] *n.* (*bot.*) sanzashi no ki.

hay [hei] *n.* hoshi kusa. ～**cock** [⌐kәk] *n.* hoshi kusa no yama. ～**loft** [⌐lɔ(:)ft] *n.* hoshi kusa okiba. ～**stack** [⌐stæk] *n.* hoshi kusa-zumi.

hazard [hǽzәd] *n.* kiken ; ichiroku-shōbu ; gūzen no koto : *at all* ～, bannan o haishite. *at* ～, detarameni. *run the* ～, ichi ka bachi ka yatte miru ; ummei o kakeru. *v.* kake o suru. ～**ous** [-әs] *a.* bōkentekina. ～**ously** *ad.*

haze [heiz] *n.* moya ; bon'yari. *v.* bon'yari saseru ; shinnyūsei o kokitsukau (*to force freshman to do unnecessary or ridiculous tasks*) (*Am.*) ijimeru.

hazel [héizl] *n.* (*bot.*) hashibami. ～**nut** [-nut] *n.* hashibami no mi.

hazy [héizi] *a.* kasunda ; kiri no kakatta. ～**izness** *n.*

H-bomb [éitʃbɔm] *n.* suiso bakudan (*hydrogen bomb*).

he [hi:] *pron.* **he, his, him.** kare wa ; kare ga (*3rd pers. sing.*)

head [hed] *n.* atama (nan demo ichiban ue) (*the top part of every-thing*) ; ichiban ue no hito (*chief person*) : *The crowned* ～ *of En-gland*, Eikoku no ōkan o itadaita atama = *kings or queens. taller by a* ～, ...dake takai. *cannot make* ～ *or tail of*, no shōtai ga wakaranai. *a good* ～ *for business*, jigyō ni taisuru ii kangae (ude). *it cost him his* ～, sore wa kare no inochitori ni natta. *the* ～ *of the lake*, mizuumi no minakuchi (nagarekomu tokoro). *ten* ～s *of cattle*, ushi jittō. *to bring matters to a* ～, kotogara o ketsuron ni motte kuru. *go to one's* ～, atama ga konran suru; gomakasareru. *be out of one's* ～ (*or mind*), (*Am.*) atama ga baka ni naru. *lay* ～s *together*, atama o atsumete sōdan suru. *lose one's* ～, urotaete wakaranaku naru. *take into one's* ～, omoitatsu; omoitsuku. ～**band** [⌐bænd] *n.* hachimaki. ～**gear** *n.* uma no atama no, dōgu no zentai. ～**ing** *n.* hyōdai. ～**light** *n.* mae no *lamp.* ～**long** *ad.* muyamini. mukōmizu ni. massakasama ni. ～**master** [⌐máːstə] *n.* kōchō. ～ **most** [⌐moust] *n.* massaki no. ～**office** [-ɔ́fis] *n.* hombu. ～ **quarters** [⌐kwɔ́ːtəz] hombu; shireibu. ～**strong** *a.* [⌐strɔŋ] gōjōna. ～**water** *n.* suigen. ～**y** [hédi] *a.* (sugu you) mōretsuni tsuyoi (*sake*).

heal [hiːl] *v.* iyasu; wakai saseru; byōki ga ieru.
health [helθ] *n.* kenkō. ～**ful** *a.* kenzenna; kenkōna. ～**fully**
healthy [hélθi] *a.* kenkōna. ～**ily** *a.* -**iness** *n.* ⌐*ad.*
heap [hiːp] *n.* tsumikasane. *v.* tsumikasaneru.
hear [hiə] *v.* **heard; hearing.** kiku; kikoeru; *Hear! Hear!* kinchō! kinchō! *I hear*, da sō da; no …yoshi. ～**er** [híərə] *n.* kikite hito.
heard [həːd] *v.* see : **hear.**
hearing [híəriŋ] *n.* chōshū; shimmon; chōryoku. **public** ～ (*to*). kōchōkai.
hearken [háːk(ə)n] *v.* (*arch.*) keichō suru; mimi o katamukeru
hearsey [híəsei] *n.* fūbun; uwasa.
hearse [həːs] *n.* reikyūsha.
heart [haːt] *n.* shinzō; kokoro; aijō. **at** ～ soranjite. *have a* (*or the*) ～, dōjō suru; genki ga aru. *lose* ～, ki o otosu. ～**ache** [-eik] *n.* shintsū. ～**beat** [⌐biːt] *n.* dōki. ～**break** [⌐breik] *n.* hitan; danchō no omoi. ～**broken** [⌐bróuk(ə)n] *a.* hitan ni kureta. ～**burn** [-bəːn] *n.* munayake. ～**felt** [-felt] *a.* kokoro kara no. ～**less** [-lis] *a.* mujōna. ～**rending** [-réndiŋ] *a.* danchō no. ～**sick** [⌐sik] *a.* hitsūna; yarusenai. ～**sore** [⌐sɔː] *a.* mune no itamu. ～**stricken** [-strikn] *a.* kanashimi ni mune utareru. ～**strings** [⌐striŋz] *n.* fukai dōjō. ～**throb** [⌐θrɔb] *n.* ureshisa ni mune tokimekasu. ～ **to** ～ *a.* mune no uchi o hanashiatte iru. ～**wood** [-wud] *n.* mokuzai no shin (*center*).

hearten [háːtn] *v.* genkizuku (*up*); hagemasu.

hearth [haːθ] *n.* irori; katei. ~**stone** [-stoun] *n.* kamado o tsukuru ishi; katei; robata.

hearty [háːti] *a.* atatakai; shinjitsu no : *a* ~ *welcome*, kokoro kara no kangei. gatchiri tsuyoi. *the old man is still hale and* ~, rōjin wa madamada tassha de gatchiri shite iru; genki de harikitte iru. *a loud* ~ *laugh*, genkina, ōkina waraigoe. *a* ~ *meal*, tappuri aru shokuji; haraippai no shokuji. ~**tily** *ad.* kokoro nokori naku. ~**tiness** *n.*

heat [hiːt] *n.* netsu; atsui tenki : ~ *of day*, hi no sakari. *v.* nessuru; gekkō saseru; atsuku naru. ~**ed** [-id] *n.* hageshii. ~**er** *n.* dambō-sōchi (dennetsu ki; sutōbu nado).

heath [hiːθ] *n.* hiisu; hikui yabu no ippai aru arechi.

heathen [híːðən] *n.* ikyōjin; chigau shūkyō no shinja. **the** ~ ikyōto. *a.* ikyō no. ~**dom** [híːðn(ə)dəm] *n.* ikyōkoku; ikyōto. ~**ish** [híːðəniʃ] *a.* ikyō no. ~**ism** [híːðənizm] *n.* ikyō.

heather [héðə] ~**y** *a.* Scotland ya Kita Igilisu no *heath* ni aru yabu. *heather* (yabu) no.

heave [hiːv] *v.* ageru ; ~ *a heavy box into a wagon*, omoi hako o basha ni hikiageru. tameiki o tsuku (*sigh*). *n.* ageru koto ; (umi no) nami no uneri. ~**s** (*pl.*) uma no zensoku.

heaven [hévn] *n.* ten; tengoku. H~, Kami. ~**ly** *a.* ten no ; shinseina ;. ~ **body,** tentai.

heavily [hévili] *ad.* omoku; dokkari to.

heavy [hévi] *a.* omoi; ōkina; hageshii; omokurushii; omoomoshii; nibui; utsuutsu taru; arukinikui (dōro nado). ~ **artillery,** jūhō; jūhō-tai. ~**-armed** [⌐aːmd] *a.* jū-sōkō no. ~ **weight** [-weit] *n.* jū-taijū kentōka.   ⌐go (*Hebrew*) no.

Hebraic [hi(ː)bréiik/heb] *a.* Heburaijin (*Hebrew*) no ; Heburai-

hecatomb [hékətoum/-tuːm] *n.* ichido ni ushi 100-tō no sonaemono (ikenie) ; dai-gyakusatsu.

heckle [hékl] *v.* kitsumon suru.

hectare [héktaː] *n.* hekutā ; 10,000 heihō mētoru.

hectic [héktik] *a.* kao ga akaku natte ; netsuppoi.

hecto- [hektou] *prefix* (100-) no imi.

hectogram(me) [hékto(u)græm] *n.* hekutoguramu (100 *gram*).

hectograph [hékto(u)graːf] *n.* zerachin-ban ; konnyakuban.

hectoliter, -tre [héktolì:tə] *n.* hekutorittoru (100-*litre*).
hectometer, -tre [héktomì:tə] *n.* hekutométoru (100-*m*).
hector [héktə] *v.* odoshitsukeru; shikaritsukeru.
hedge [hedʒ] *n.* ikegaki; magaki. *v.* magaki de kakou; seki-nin o kaihi suru; nigeru. ∼**hog** [⌐həg] *n.* (*zoo.*) harinezumi. ∼**-hop** [⌐həp] *v.* taihen hikui hikō o suru. ∼**row** [⌐rou] *n.* ichi retsu no kamboku, ∼ **sparrow** [-spǽrou] *n.* magaki suzume.
hedonism [hí:dənizm] *n.* kairaku shijōshugi.
heed [hi:d] *n.* chūi; yōjin. *v.* ki o tsukeru. ∼**ful** *a.* chūi bukai. ∼**less** *a.* fuchūina; keisotsuna.
heel [hi:l] *n.* kakato : *Achilles'* ∼, yuiitsu no jakuten. *be at* (*or on*) *the* ∼*s of*, ...ni oisemaru. *down at* (*the*) ∼, darashinai su-gata de. *have the* ∼*s of*, ...o oikosu. *show a clean pair of* ∼*s*, nigeru.
heft [heft] *n.* (*col.*) mekata. *v.* mochiagete omosa o hakaru.
hegemony [hi(:)gémɔni/hédʒim-] *n.* shidōken; haken.
Hegira [hédʒirə/hədʒái-] *n.* Mahomet ga nigeta koto; tōsō L(*flight*).
heifer [héfə] *n.* mada ko o umanai wakai meushi.
heigh-ho [héi-hóu/hai-] *inter.* oya, oya ! yare, yare ! (odoroki, hitan, kōfun, hirō nado ni).
height [hait] *n.* takasa; takai koto. ∼**en** [háitn] *v.* takameru; masu; (kokoro o) kōshō ni suru.
heinous [héinəs] *a.* gokuaku no. ∼**ly** *ad.*
heir [ɛə] *n.* sōzokunin; atotsugi-shishi.
held [held] *v. see :* **hold.**
helicopter [hélikɔ̀ptə] *n.* herikoputā; suichoku jōshō no hikō- Γki.
heliograph [hí:lio(u)grà:f] *n.* kaiten shingōki.
heliotrope [hí:ljɔtroup] *n.* (*flow.*) kidachirurisō; usu murasaki iro. (*min.*) kesseki.
helium [hí:ljəm] *n.* heriumu.
hell [hel] *n.* jigoku; tobaku yado; makutsu (*brothel.*).
hell-cat [hélkæt] *n.* tsumaranai onna.
hellebore [hélibɔ:] *n.* (*flow.*) Xmas rōzu; baikeisō.
Hellene [héli:n] *n.* Girishajin ippan.
Hellenic [helí:nik] *a.* Girisha-(jin, go) no; Girisha bungei no (773-323 BC).
Hellenism [hélinizm] *n.* Girishafū; Girishagofū.

Hellenist [hélinist] *n.* Girishagakusha. ⌈to yobu (*call*).
hello [hélou/hálóu] *int.* moshi, moshi !, oya !, oi, oi ! *v. "hello"*
helm [helm] *n.* kaji. *v.* kaji o toru. ~**sman** [-zman] *n.* dashu ; kajitori. ⌈poreonbō.
helm [helm], **helmet** [hélmit] *n.* kabuto ; fuchi no semai na-
help [help] *v.* tasukeru ; tetsudau : *cannot* ~ *-ing*, ...sezaru o enai. ~ *on*, ...o hakadoraseru. ~ *oneself to*, ...o katte ni toru. *Please* ~ *yourself* (*to a candy*), *candy* o hitotsu ikaga. *n.* kyūjo ; joryoku ; tetsudai. *second* ~, okawari. *There is no* ~ *for it*, shikata ga nai. ~**ful** *a.* tasuke ni naru ; yaku ni tatsu. ~
less *a.* dō nimo naranai. ~**lessly** *ad.* ~**mate** [-meit], ~**meet** [-mi:t] *n.* kyōryokusha ; tsuma matawa otto.
helter-skelter [héltəskéltə] *ad.* awate futameite.
helve [helv] *n.* ono (*ax*) nado no e (*handle*).
hem [hem] *n.* fuchi ; hida ; heri. *v.* fuchi o toru ; torimaku. ~ *out*, shime dasu.
hemisphere [hémisfiə] *n.* chikyū no hambun ; hankyū. (katsudō no) han'i (*sphere*).
hemlock [hémlək] *n.* (*bot.*) doku ninjin ; hokubei-san tsuga.
hemoglobin [hì:mo(u)glóubin] *n.* kekkyū so ; hemogurobin.
hemorrhage [héməridʒ] *n.* shukketsu (hanaji nado no yōni).
hemorrhoids [hémərɔidz] *n.* (*pl.*) ji (=*piles*).
hemp [hemp] *n.* asa ; taima ; o. ⌈suru.
hemstitch [hémstitʃ] *n., v.* ito o nuite kagatta fuchi kazari (o
hen[hen] *n.* mendori. ~**coop**[-ku:p] *n.* toya. ~**pecked** [-ˊpèkt] *a.* kakā tenka no.
henbane [hénbein] *n.* (*bot.*) hiyosu (dokusō).
hence [hens] *ad.* kono yue ni ; kore kara. ~**forth** [-fɔ́:θ] *ad.* ~**forward** [-fɔ́:wəd] *ad.* igo.
henchman [héntʃmən] *n.* shimobe ; jūsha.
hepatic [hipǽtik/he-] *a.* (*med.*) kanzō (*liver*) no.
hepcat [hépkæt] *n.* suwingu (*jazz*) gakudan no gakushu.
heptagon [héptəgən] *n.* shichikakkei ; shichihenkei. ~**al** *a.* shichihen kei no.
her [həː] *pron.* kanojo no ; kanojo o (ni). ~**self** [-sélf] *pron.* kanojo jishin : *She* ~ *did it*, kanojo jibun ga shitan da.
herald [hérəld] *n.* denreikan ; senkusha. *v.* dentatsu suru ; sa-

kibure suru. ～**ry** *n.* monshōgaku.

herb [hə:b] *n.* kusa; yakusō. ～**al** *a.* kusa no.

herbaceous [hə:béiʃəs] *a.* kusa no; kusa no ha jō no.

herbage [hə́:bidʒ] *n.* kusa; bokusō.

herbarium [hə:bέəriəm] *n.* (*pl.* -**s**; -**ria**) shokubutsu hyōhon shū (-bako); hyōhonshitsu (kan).

herbivorous [hə:bívərəs] *a.* sōshoku no (=kusa o taberu).

Herculean [hə̀:kjulí:ən/hə:kjú:liən] *a.* Herukyūrēsu (*Hercules*) no yōna; chikara no aru; hijōni konnanna.

herd [hə:d] *n.* (ushi, hitsuji nado no) mure : *the* ～, gunshū. *v.* (ushi, hitsuji nado no) ban o suru. ～**sman** [-zmən] *n.* bokusha.

here [hiə] *ad.* koko ni; koko made; gense de. **Here !** hai (henji). ～**about** [-əbáut] *ad.* konohen ni.

hereditary [hiréditəri] *a.* seshū no; iden no.

heredity [hiréditi] *n.* iden.

heresy [hérəsi] *n.* chigau shūkyō.

heretic [hérətik] *n.* ikyōto. ～**al** [-əl] *a.* ikyō no.

heritable [héritəbl] *a.* daidai yuzurareta; sōzoku subeki.

heritage [héritidʒ] *n.* sōzoku zaisan.

hermaphrodite [hə:mǽfrədait] *n.* danjoryōsei o motte iru; (*bot.*) shiyū-ryōsei-ka.

hermetic [hə:métik] ～**al** [-əl] *a.* renkinjutsu no; mippū shita. ～**ally** *ad.* mippei shite; kūki no hairanu yōni.

hermit [hə́:mit] *n.* inja. ～**age** *n.* anshitsu. ～**crab** [kræb] *n.* yadokari.

hernia [hə́:njə] *n.* (*med.*) heruniya; datchō.

heroic [hiró(u)ik/hər-] *a.* sōretsuna; ooshii. ～**ally** *ad.*

heroine [héro(u)in] *n.* reppu; jojōfu; onna shujin kō (shōsetsu no). ⌈kaesu basho.

heron [hér(ə)n] *n.* aosagi. ～**ry** [hérənri] *n.* *heron* ga tamago o

herpetology [hə̀:pitólədʒi] *n.* hachūrui dake o atsukau *zoology*.

herring [hériŋ] *n.* nishin. ～**bone** [-boun] *a.* yahazugata no.

hers [hə:z] *pron.* kanojo no mono.

hesitancy [hézit(ə)nsi], **hesitance** [hézit(ə)ns] *n.* chūcho.

hesitant [hézit(ə)nt] *a.* chūcho shita; guzutsuita. ～**ly** *ad.*

hesitate [héziteit] *v.* chūcho suru; kuchi gomoru.

hesitation [hezitéiʃən] *n.* chūcho.

Hesperus [héspərəs] *n.* yoi no myōjō; Kinsei. (*cf. Venus.*)

Hessian [hésiən, -sjən] *a.* Doitsu Hesse no. *n.* Hessejin; Doitsujin yōhei. ┌*n.* itan; hi-seitō setsu.

heterodox [hét(ə)rədəks] *a.* itan no; seitōsetsu hitei no. ~y

heterogeneous [hétərodʒí:njəs] *a.* ishu no; shurui no chigau; chigatta rui no.

hew [hju:] *v.* **hewed, hewed** *or* **hewn; hewing.** (ono nado de) kiru; kiri taosu; kitte katachi o tsukuru: ~ *stone for building*, biruding no ishi o kiru.

hewn [hju:n] *v. see*: **hew.** ┌penkei no.

hexagon [héksəgən] *n.* rokkakkei; roppenkei. ~al *a.* rophexameter [heksǽmitə/-kzǽ-] *n.* roppokaku (no shi).

hey [hei] *inter.* hē ! yā ! sate ! (odoroki, chūi, yorokobi, gimon, nado no). ~day [-dei] *inter.* suteki! (yorokobi, odoroki no kansei). *n.* zenseiki: ~ *of youth*, wakazakari. *in the* ~ *of his power*, kensei ryūryū taru toki.

H. H. *His* (*Her*) *Highness*; *His Holiness.* Denka; Geika.

H H H H, 4H kurabu (*Head*, atama; *Heart*, kokoro; *Hand* te; *Health*, kenkō).

H. I. *Hawaiian Islands* (Hawai guntō).

hiatus [haiéitəs] *n.* (*pl.* -tus; -tues [-təsiz]) wareme; sakeme; datsu-bun; datsu-ji.

hibernal [haibə́:n(ə)l] *a.* fuyu no.

hibernate [háibə:neit] *v.* fuyu gomori suru; tōmin suru.

hibernation [haibə:néiʃ(ə)n] *n.* tōmin; fuyugomori.

hic-cough, hic-cup [híkʌp] *n.* shakkuri. *v.* shakkuri suru.

hickory [híkəri] *n.* (*bot.*) hikkori.

hid [hid] *v. see*: **hide.**

hidden [hídn] *v. see*: **hide.** *a.* kakureta; himitsu no.

hide [haid] *v.* **hid, hid** *or* **hidden; hiding.** kakusu (-reru); kakumau. *n.* jūhi; kegawa. ~-and-seek [-ʌnsí:k] *n.* kakurembō. ~bound [-́baund] *a.* katakunana; henkyō de genkakuna.

hideous [hídiəs/-djəs] *a.* osoroshii; zotto suru yōna. ~ly *ad.* ~ness *n.*

hiding [háidiŋ] *n.* intoku; kakusu koto; muchi-utsu koto.

hie [hai] *v.* isogu; isoide iku.

hierarchy [háiərɑ:ki] *n.* sōryo seiji; kyōshoku-ren; sōryo; sono taikei (soshiki, *system*).

hieroglyph [háiərəglif] *n.* e-monji. ～**ic** [hàiərəglífik] *a.* e-monji no. *n. (pl.)* e-monji.

higgle [hígl] *v.* negiru; kake-hiki suru.

higgledy-piggledy [hígldipígldi] *ad.* mecha-kuchani.

high [hai] *a.* takai; kōkina; kōshōna; hageshii. ～ **school**, chūgakkō; kōtōgakkō. ～ **seas**, taikai; kōkai. ～ **tea**, niku ryōri no deru gogo no tii. ～ **tide**, (or water) taka shio. ～**time**, chōdo yoi toki. *ad.* takaku; ōini. ～**-flown** [-floun] *a.* erabutta; kodaina. ～**-handed** [-hǽndid] *a.* kōatsutekina. ～**land** [-lənd] *n.* kōchi. ～**lander** [-ləndə] *n.* kōchijin. (H～) *Scotland* no kōchijin. ～**light** [-lait] *n.* mottomo akarui bubun (e=*picture*); ichiban kyōmi aru tokoro. ～**ly** *ad.* takaku; ōini. ～**minded** [-máinded] *a.* kedakai; kōshōna. ～**ness** *n.* takai koto; (H～) denka. ～**road** [-roud] *n.* daidō. ～**speed** [-spi:d] *a.* kōsokudo no. ～**-spirited** [-spíritid] *a.* yūkanna; genki no yoi. ～**strung** [-stráŋ] *a.* shinkei shitsuna; kōfun shita. ～**-toned** [-tóund] *a.* chōshi no takai kōketsuna (*noble*). (*Am.*) igen no

higher [háiə] *a.* motto takai. (*cf.* **high**.) ⌐aru.

highest [háiist] *a.* saikō no; ichiban takai. (*cf.* **high**.)

highway [háiwèi] *n.* daidō. ～**man** [-mæn] *n.* oihagi.

H. I. H. *His Imperial Highness.* Denka.

hike [haik] *v.* toho (=aruite) ryokō o suru. *n.* toho ryokō. ～*r n.* toho ryokōsha.

hilarious [hiléəriəs] *a.* yōkina; hashagitatta.

hilarity [hilǽriti] *n.* yōki; bakasawagi.

hill [hil] *n.* koyama; oka; tsuka. ～ **side** [-said] *n.* sampuku. ～**y** *a.* koyama no ōi.

hillock [hílək] *n.* chiisai oka; ko-oka.

hilt [hilt] *n.* tsuka; (*up*) *to the* ～, zembu; zentai.

him [him] *pron.* kare o; kare ni. ～**self** [-sélf] *pron.* kare jishin. *see :* **he.**

H. I. M. *His* (or *Her*) *Imperial Majesty.* Heika, keigo).

Himalayas [himəléiəz] *n. (pl.)* Himaraya Sammyaku.

hind [haind] *a.* ushiro no; ato no. *n.* (*zoo.*) akajika no mesu (tōnen ni(2)-san(3)-saigo). sakuotoko; nōfu. ～**most** [háind-

moust] *a.* ichiban ushiro no.
hinder [[háində] *a.* ato no; ushiro no.
hinder [híndə] *v.* samatageru; jama ni naru.
hindrance [híndr(ə)ns] *n.* bōgai; shōgai; jama mono (*to*).
Hindu; Hindoo [híndú:] Indo ni sumu Aryanjin; Indokyō no shinja.
hinge [hindʒ] *n.* chōtsugai. *v.* chōtsugai de ugoku.   ⌈(*at*).
hint [hint] *n.* anji; atekosuri: *take a* ∼, satoru. *v.* anji suru
hinterland [híntəlænd] *n.* okuchi; minato (*port*) de, kaigan (*coast*) de nai tokoro.
hip [hip] *n.* shiri. (*bot.*) nobara no mi. *inter.* "*hurrah*" no mae ni. "*hip, hip, hurah!*" to yobu sakebigoe.
hippo [hípou] *n.* kaba (*hippopotamus*).
hippodrome [hípədroum] *n.* (*Greek, Rome* no jidai no) keibajō; kyokubajō.
hippopotamus [hìpəpótəməs] (*pl.* -**mi** [-mai]) *n.* (*zoo.*) kaba.
hire [háiə] *n.* chin-gashi (gari); chin; kashiryō. *v.* chin-gari (gashi) suru; yatou. ∼**ling** *n.* yatowareta hito.
hirer [háiərə] *n.* chin-garinin; karite; yatoi nushi.
hirsute [hə́:sju:t] *a.* kebukai; nagai ke de ōte.
his [hiz] *pron.* kare no (mono). *cf.* **he.**
hiss [his] *inter.* sh...sh.... *v.* sh...sh...to iu. *n.* shū; shi.
hist [hist] *inter.* shii! shizuka ni.
historian [histɔ́riən] *n.* rekishika.
historic [histɔ́rik] *a.* rekishijō yūmeina; rekishiteki. ∼**al** *a.* rekishi no, rekishijō no. ∼**ally** *ad.*
history [híst(ə)ri] *n.* rekishi; shigaku.
histrionic [hìstriónik] *a.* haiyū no; engeki no.
hit [hit] *v.* **hit; hitting.** utsu; ataru : ∼ *off*, sokuza ni tsukuru ("e" ya "shi" nado o). ∼ *on* (*or upon*), ni omoiataru. ∼ *out*, genkotsu de utsu. *n.* meichū; seikō anda. *happy* ∼, tekihyō. ∼ *and run*, (*baseball*) hitto ando ran. (untenshu no hikinige) : ∼*-and-rnn driver*, hikinige untenshu.
hitch [hitʃ] *v.* gui to hipparu : ∼ *up*, hippari ageru. *to* ∼ *up one's trousers*, zubon o hippari ageru. *n.* gui to hipparu koto. hikiage; koshō.
hither [híðə] *ad.* kochira e. ∼ *and thither*, achikochi e. *a.* ko-

chira no. ～to [híðətú:/hið-] *ad.* ima made.

hive [haiv] *n.* mitsubachi no subako; mitsubachi no mure; hachi no su mitaina tokoro. *v.* subako ni ireru; su ni atsume-

hives [haivz] *n. pl.* (*med.*) hasshin; jimmashin. ⌊ru.

ho(a) [hou] *inter.* hou! (chūi o hiku tame no; yorokobi no; aruiwa reishō no koe).

hoar [hɔ:/hɔə] *a.* haiiro no; masshiro no (kamige). ～**frost** [-frɔ:st] *n.* shiroi shimo.

hoard [hɔ:d] *n.* takuwae; chikuseki; tameta zaisan. *v.* hataraite tameru; takuwaeru. ⌈**ness** *n.*

hoarse [hɔ:s] *a.* shiwagareta; shiwagaregoe no. ～**ly** *ad.* ～

hoary [hɔ́:ri] *a.* haiiroatama no; hakuhatsu no; furui.

hoax [houks] *v.* ippai kuwasu; *n.* katsugu koto.

hobble [hɔ́bl] *v.* bikko o hiite aruku; tobo, tobo aruku; ashi o issho ni shibaru (uma nado). *n.* uma no ashi kase.

hobbledehoy [hɔ́bldihɔ́i] *n.* (otona to shōnen no aida no) seinen; aonisai.

hobby [hɔ́bi] *n.* jūhachiban; ohako. ～**horse** [-hɔ:s] *n.* mokuba; batō no tsuita omocha no takeuma.

hobgoblin [hɔ́bgɔ̀blin/hɔbgóblin] *n.* yōkai; kooni.

hobnail[bɔ́bneil] *n.* byōkugi; kutsuzoko o hogo suru tame no atama no ōkii kugi.

hobnob [hɔ́bnɔb] *v.* uchitokete nomu; mutsumajiku suru.

hock [hɔk] *n.* kemono no ushiroashi. nibamme no kurubushi; kansetsu. shiro budōshu no isshu.

hockey [hɔ́ki] *n.* hokkei.

hocus-pocus [hóukəs-póukəs] *n.* tejina; tejinashi no kakegoe; gomakashi. ⌈sumi tori.

hod [hɔd] *n.* hoddo (renga, shikkui nado o hakobu utsuwa).

Hodge [hɔdʒ] *n.* Igirisu no daihyōteki sakuotoko; tagosaku.

hodgepodge [hɔ́dʒ-pɔdʒ] *n., a.* gochagocha; gotta kaeshita.

hoe [hou] *n.* kuwa. *v.* kuwa de suku.

hog [hɔg] *n.* buta. don'yokusha. funasoko sōji hōki.

hoggish [hɔ́giʃ] *a.* kitanai; rikoteki na; gatsu, gatsu kuu.

hogshead [hɔ́gzhed] *n.* hogguzuhed 52½ garon; ōtaru (*barrel*).

hoist [hɔist] *v.* ageru; hikiageru. *n.* hikiageru koto; shōkōki (*elevator*).

hoity-toity [hóiti tóiti] *inter.* odoroki to keibetsu-gimi no hyō-gen. *a.* keihakuna ; gōmanna.   『*icecream.*

hokeypokey [hóukipóuki] *n.* machi de utte iru yasumono no

hold [hould] *v.* **held ; holding.** sasae motte iru : ~ *a child,* ko-domo o jitto daite iru. ~ *the prisoner,* horyo o osaete oku. ~ *your head on one side,* atama o ippō ni katamukete i nasai. *This pillar* ~*s this platform,* kono hashira ga kono dan o sasaete iru no da. *The speaker held their attention,* benshi wa chōshū no chūi o (toraete, tsukande, nigitte) ita. ~ *him to his word,* kare o jibun no kotoba ni shibaritsukeru. *He* ~*s the office of mayor,* kare wa shichō no shoku ni tsuite iru. *We* ~ *a meeting this evening,* konseki kai o hiraki masu. *This bottle* ~*s a quart,* kono bin wa 1 q. hairi masu. *He* ~*s a belief,* kare wa hitotsu no shinnen o idaite iru. *I hold your statement to be untrue,* watashi wa kimi no sono hanashi wa hontō de nai to omotte iru. ~ *back,* tomeru. ~ *down,* osaeru. (*Am. sl.*) ~ *down a job,* zutto sono shigoto o yatte iru. ~ *forth,* senden suru. ~ *good,* yaku ni tatsu ; tekiyō saseru. ~ *in,* gaman suru. ~ *off,* tōzakeru. ~ *on,* tsuzukeru. ~ *one's own,* jōho shinai. ~ *out,* tsuzukeru ; kōsan shinai. ~ *over,* kōdō o enki suru. ~ *to,* o koshu suru. ~ *together,* issho ni suru. ~ *up,* ageru ; sasaeru. *catch* ~ *of,* o tsukamaeru. *lose one's* ~, tegakari o ushinau. ~**all** [-ɔːl] *n.* kimono ire ; gassaibukuro (ryokōyō). ~**er** *n.* shoyūsha. sasaeru jiku, dai, ~**ing** *n.* motte iru koto ; shoyū.

hole [houl] *n.* ana. *pick* ~*s in,* ara o sagasu. *v.* ana o akeru ; ana ni hairu. ~ *up,* fuyugomori suru.

holiday [hólidi] *n.* kyūjitsu ; (*pl.*) kyūka (*vacation*).

holiness [hóulinis] *n.* shinsei ; (H-) geika (*honorific to Pope*) (*His H* ~ *Pope Leo,* Hō-ō Reo Geika).

Holland [hólənd] *n.* Oranda. ~**er** [-ə] *n.* Orandajin.

hollo [hólou], **horoa** [hálou] *inter.* ōi !, ōi ! *v.* ōi to yobu.

hollow [hólou] *v.* utsuro ni suru. ~ *out,* kurinuku. *n.* ana ; kubomi ; kubochi. *a.* utsurona ; kubonda (*concave*). *ad. to beat someone all* ~, aru hito o sanzanni uchinomesu.

holly [hóli] *n.* (*bot.*) seiyō hiiragi. ~**hock** [-hɔk] *n.* tachiaoi.

holocaust [hóləkɔːst] *n.* hansai (maruyakimatsuri) no kumo-tsu ; daigyakusatsu (*great slaughter*).

holster [hóulstə] *n.* kenjū-(*pistol*)-yō kawabukuro.
holy [hóuli] *a.* shinseina. *H~ Ghost*, seirei.
homage [hɔ́midʒ] *n.* fukujū; sonkei (*reverence*) : *pay ~ to a great leader*, idaina kunshu ni fukujū o hyōmei suru.
home [houm] *n.* katei; kokyō; homba (*habitat*). *at ~*, uchi ni iru. *bring ~*, akirakani suru. *bring oneself ~*, jibun no mono o torimodosu. *come ~*, kaeru. *~keeping* [-kí:piŋ] *a.* uchi ni bakari iru. *~less* [-lis] *a.* yadonashi. *~like a.* wagaya no yōna. *~bred n.* hongoku sodachi no. *~brew a.* jika jōzō no. *~ economics* [-ikənɔ́miks] *a.* katei keizai. *~land* [-lænd] *a.* hongoku. *~ly a.* katei no; shissona; kazari no nai. *~made* [-méid] *a.* uchi de tsukutta. *~opathy* [hòumiɔ́pəθi] = **homoeopathy** *n.* (*med.*) kateiyōjō; teyōjō. *~plate* [-pleit] *home base. ~r* [houmə] *a home run. ~ rule* ['-ru:l] chihō jichi. *~spun* [hóumspʌn] jikasei no. *~stead* [hóumsted] *a.* jisakunōka. *~stretch* [-stretʃ] *n.* kyōsō no saigo no kōsu (*course*). *~work* [houmwə:k] *n.* shukudai.
homesick [hóumsik] *a.* kaikyō-byō no. *~ness* [hóumsiknis] *n.* kaikyō-byō; kyōshū (*nostalgia*).
homicidal [hòmisáid(ə)l] *a.* satsujin no.
homicide [hɔ́misaid] *n.* satsujin (sha); hitogoroshi.
homiletics [hɔmilétiks] *n.* sekkyō jutsu.
homily [hɔ́mili] *n.* sekkyō.
homing [hóumiŋ] *a.* ie ni kaeru. *n.* ie ni kaeru koto. *~ pigeon* [-pidʒən] *n.* denshobato.
hominy [hɔ́mini] *n.* (*Am.*) hikiwari tōmorokoshi.
homo [hóumo(u)] *n.* (*L.*) ningen; hito (*man.*)
homogeneity [hòmo(u)dʒení:əti] *n.* dōshu (taru koto).
homogeneous [hòmdʒí:njəs] *a.* dōshu no; onaji seibun de dekita. *~ness n.*
homologous [hɔmɔ́ləgəs] *a.* sō-ō suru (basho to neuchi ga); uma no maeashi to, tori no tsubasa to wa *homologous* de aru.
homonym [hɔ́mənim] *n.* dō-on igigo (*meet, meat*).
homophone [hɔ́məfoun] *n.* "c" to "k" no yōni ji wa betsu demo on ga onaji mono.
hone [houn] *n.* toishi. *v.* toishi de togu.
honest [ɔ́nist] *a.* shōjikina; tadashii (*just*). *~ly ad.* shōjikini.

honesty [ɔ́nisti] *n.* shōjiki.

honey [hʌ́ni] *n.* hachimitsu ; (*Am.*) aijin (*darling*). ⁓**bee** [hʌ́ni-bi:] *n.* mitsubachi. ⁓**comb** [hʌ́nikoum] *n.* mitsubachi no su. ⁓**moon** [hʌ́nimu:n] *n.* kekkon go (*after marriage*) no ikka-getsu (shinkon ryokōjū). ⁓**suckle** [hʌ́nisʌkl] *n.* (*bot.*) suika-zura.

honeyed [hʌ́nid] *a.* (hachi-)mitsu no ōi ; amattarui (*sweet*).

hong [hɔŋ] *n.* Chūgoku no shōkwan.

honk [hɔŋk] *n.* gan (*wild goose*) no nakigoe (*cry*) ; onaji yōna oto : ⁓ *of a taxi*, takusi no keiteki.

hono(u)r [ɔ́nə] *n.* meiyo ; sonkei (*respect*) ; (H-) Kakka ; tei-setsu (*chastity*) : ⁓*s of war*, tōkōhei ni ataeta tokuten. *in* ⁓ *of*, no kinen ni ; ni keii o hyōshite (*respect*). *point of* ⁓, taimen ni kansuru koto. *v.* sonkei suru ; (kawase tegata (*draft*) nado o) shiharau. ⁓**able** [⌐rəbl] *a.* sonkei subeki ; keigo ni (*as the honorific*). *the Honorable Robert M. La Follette.*

honorarium [ɔnərɛ́əriəm] (*pl.* **-s ; -ria**) *n.* hōshūkin (gaku no kettei shite nai shareikin).

honorary [ɔ́nərəri] *a.* meiyo no ; meiyo shoku no (*titulary*).

honorific [ɔnərífik] *a.* keishō no *n.* keigo.

hood [hud] *n.* zukin ; horo (*car*).

hoodlum [hú:dləm] *n.* (*Am. col.*) machi no gurentai. ⁓**ism** [hu:dlʌmizm] *n.*

hoodoo [hú:du:] *n.* bimbōgami.

hoodwink [húdwiŋk] *v.* mekakushi o suru ; damasu.

hoof [hu:f] (*pl.* **-s** [hu:fs] ; *rarely* ⁓**oves** [hu:vz]) hizume (uma, ushi, hitsuji nado no).

hook [huk] *n.* kagi ; kagi-bari (*fish-*⁓). *v.* kagi de hikkakeru ; tsuno (*horn*) de tsuku ; kagi no yōni magaru (*bend*). ⁓**worm** [-wə:m] *n.* jūnishichōchū.

hookah [húkə] *n.* mizu-giseru.

hookup [húkʌp] *n.* (muden (*wireless*)) kumitate haisen ; (*Am.*) teikei (*co-operative*) : *a* ⁓ *between nations*, kokka-kan no teikei

hooligan [hú:ligən] *n.* buraikan ; furyōshōnen. ⌐shinwa

hoop [hu:p] *n.* taga ; wa (*of barrel*) ; kujira no hone ya hagane no wa (*for skirt of ladies dress*). ⁓**ing cough** [hú:piŋ kɔ(:)f] hyakunichi-zeki.

hoot [hu:t] *v.* sakebi azakeru. *n.* hōhō to naku (*owl*); fukuro (*owl*) no nakigoe; hito no kotoba o mushi shite ageru azakeri no koe (*shout in contempt*).

hop [hɔp] *v.* tobu (kataashi de); ryōashi soroete: *many birds* ∼, ōku no tori wa *hop* o suru. ∼, *step and jump*, Olympic no sandantobi. ∼s [hɔps] *n.* biiru ni aji o tsukeru *hops*.

hope [houp] *n.* kibō; kibō o kakerareru hito (*person*), mono (*thing*): *past* ∼, zetsubōteki de. *v.* kibō suru. *I* ∼ *not*, dewa nakarō to omou. ∼**ful** [hóupf(u)l] *a.* yūbōna. ∼**less** [⸲lis] *a.* mikomi no nai.   「nado no).

hopper [hɔ́pə] *n.* tobu hito; tobu mushi (*insect*); jōgo (seifunki

hopple [hɔ́pl] *n.* (ushi, uma nado no) ashikase; ushi, uma nado no ashi o shibaru; ashikase suru. (*cf.* **bobble**.)

horde [hɔ:d] *n.* yūbokumin no mure; gunshū (*crowd of nomad*).

horizon [horáiz(ə)n] *n.* chiheisen; genkai (*limits*). ∼**tal** [hɔrizónt(ə)l] *a.* chiheisen no; yoko no: *a* ∼ *union* (= *a craft union*), shokugyōbetsu kumiai. ∼**ly** *ad.* suiheini.

horn [hɔ:n] *n.* tsuno; horun (*musical instrument*): *drinking* ∼, tsunosei no sakazuki. ∼ *of plenty*, hōjō no tsuno (*cf.* **cornucopia**). *v.* tsuno de tsuku. ∼**ed** [hɔ:nd] *a.* tsuno no aru. ∼**et** [hɔ́:nit] *n.* ōkumabachi. ∼**less** [hɔ́:nlis] *a.* tsuno no nai. ∼**pipe** [hɔ:npaip] *n.* mukashi *Wales* de mochiita ki no fue; isshu no odori.

horny [hɔ́:ni] *a.* kaku-(tsuno)-shitsu no; tsuno sei no.

horologe [hɔ́rələdʒ] *n.* tokei (ironna shurui no).

horologer [hɔrɔ́lədʒə] *n.* hoshiuranai semmonka.

horology [hɔrɔ́lədʒi] *n.* hoshiuranai no jutsu.

horoscope [hɔ́rəskoup] *n.* hoshiuranai.

horrendous [hɔréndəs] *a.* osoroshii; kowai.

horrible [hɔ́rəbl] *a.* osoroshii; (*col.*) hidoi; iyana. ∼**bly** [hɔ́ribli] *ad.* monosugoku; furueru yōni osoroshii.

horrid [hɔ́rid] *a.* osoroshii; (*col.*) iyana. ∼**ly** [hɔ́ridli] *ad.* oso-

horrific [hɔrifík] *a.* mi no ke mo yodatsu.   「roshiku.

horrify [hɔ́rifai] *v.* kowagaraseru; zotto saseru.

horror [hɔ́rə] *n.* kyōfu; (*col.*) daikirai. ∼**-stricken** [hɔ́rə-stríkn] *a.* kyōfu ni osowareta.

hors d'oeuvre [ɔ:də̀:vr] (*F.*) zensai.

horse [hɔ:s] *n.* uma; ashi no aru monokake. kihei. *v.* uma ni noru; uma de iku. ~**back** [hɔ́:sbæk] uma no senaka; uma ni notte. ~**breaker** [hɔ́:sbrèikə] n. chōbashi. ~**car** [hɔ́:skɑ:] n. basha. ~ **coper** [hɔ́:skoupə] n. bakurō. ~ **dealer**, uma no urikainin; bakurō. ~**fly** [hɔ́:sflai] n. umabai; abu. ~**hair** [hɔ́:shɛ́ə] n. uma no ke. ~**laugh** [hɔ́:slɑ:f] n. bakawarai. ~ **latitudes** [-lǽtitjudz] n. chikyūjō 2 no basho. koko dewa hijōni tenki ga yoi. Minami to Kita no ido 30do no tokoro. ~**leech** [hɔ́:sli:tʃ] umabiru; don'yokuna hito. ~**man** u. uma ni noru hito. ~**manship** [hɔ́:smænʃip] bajutsu. ~**pistol**, kihei no *pistol*. ~**play** [hɔ́:splèi] n. rambōna, sōzōshii yūgi. ~**power** [hɔ́:spáuə] n. enjin no chikara no tan'i. ~**radish** [hɔ́srǽdiʃ] n. wasabi.

horticultural [hɔ:tikʌ́ltʃ(ə)rəl] a. engei-jutsu no. ⌐gei-ka.
horticulture [hɔ́:tikʌltʃə] n. engei-jutsu. ~(**e)ist** [-ist] n. en-
hosanna [houzǽnə] inter. n. hozana!; kami (*god*) o home tatae-ru kotoba (*praising term*).

hose [houz] n. (*pl.* **hose** [houz] (*formerly*) **hosen** [hóuzn]) n. na-gakutsushita n. (*pl.* ~**s** [houziz]); hōsu (*Indianrubber*, hōsu). no baai. *pl.* ni mochiiru. v. hōsu de mizu (*water*) o kakeru.

hosier [hóuʒə] n. kutsushitaya; meriyasuya. ~**y** [hóuʒəri] n. kutsushita-rui; meriyasu rui (*knitted goods*).

hospitable [hɔ́spitəbl] a. motenashi no yoi. ~**bly** [hɔ́spitəbli] ad. taigū yoku.

hospital [hɔ́spit(ə)l] n. byōin; dōbutsu (*animal*) byōin.

hospitality [hɔ̀spitǽliti] n. teineina taigū.

host [houst] n. shujin; gunzei (*army*); (H-) Misa (Seisan) no
hostage [hɔ́stidʒ] n. hitojichi; teitō. ⌐pan.

host(e)l [hɔ́stəl] n. (*Am.*) gasshuku-jo; shukusha (*hotel*).

hostelry [hɔ́st(ə)lri] n. yadoya; ryokan.

hostess [hóustis] n. onna aruji; okami (*female host*).

hostile [hɔ́stail] a. tekii no aru. ⌐(*warfare*)
hostility [hɔstíliti] n. teki-i; tekigaishin (*enmity*); (*pl.*) sensō
hostler [ɔ́slə] n. (ryokan (*inn*) no) batei.

hot [hɔt] a. atsui; karai (*pepper, etc.*); tankina (*short-tempered*); netsuretsuna : ~ *spring*, onsen. ~**bed** [⊥bed] n. onshō : ~ of *criminal*, zaiaku no onshō. ~**blooded** [⊥blʌ́did] a. tankina. ~**foot** [⊥fut] ad. (*col.*) ōisogi de. ~**headed** [hɔ́thédid] a. gekishi yasui. ～**house** [⌣haus] *n.* onshitsu.

hotchpot [hɔ́tʃpɔt], **hotchpotch** [hɔ́tʃpɔtʃ] *n.* gottani ; kongō

hotel [houtél] *n.* ryokan ; hoteru.   ⌊(*mixture*).

hough, hock. [hɔk] *n.* **hock** *n.*

hound [haund] *n.* ryōken. *v.* ryōken de karu (*hunt*) ; keshika-keru (*set a dog at quarry*).

hour [áuə] *n.* ichijikan ; toki. ～**glass** [áuəglɑːs] *n.* suna-dokei. ～**hand** [áuəhænd] *n.* tanshin. ～**ly** [áuəli] *a.* maiji no. *ad.* ichijikan goto ni.

house [haus] *n.* ie (*building*) ; katei. ～ *of worship*, raihaijo. ge-kijō. -ke (*lineage*). shōkan. *a large* (*or full*) ～, ō-iri no. *bring down the* ～, manjō no kassai o hakusuru. *keep the* ～, ie ni iru. *the House of Commons*, Eikoku no Kain. *the House of Lords*, Jō-in (Eikoku no). *the House of Representatives*, Ka-in (Amerika no). *v.* [hauz] ie ni ireru ; shūyō suru (*accommodate*) ; mamoru (*protect*). ～**breaker** [háusbreikə] *n.* kataku-shinnyūsha ; gōtō (*robber*). ～**hold** [háus(h)ould] *n.* kazoku. *a.* kazoku no. ～**holder** [háus(h)ouldə] *n.* koshu. ～**keeper** [⌣kiːpə] *n.* shufu ; kaseifu. ～**keeping** [⌣kiːpiŋ] *n.* kasei. ～**maid** [⌣meid] *n.* jo-chū. ～**rent** [háusrent] *n.* yachin. ～**work** [⌣wəːk] *v.* kaji (sōji (*cleaning*), ryōri (*cooking*)) suru.

housewife [háuswaif] *n.* shufu. [házif] haribako. ～**ly** [háus-waifli] *a.* shufu rashii ; ken'yaku suru (*economical*). ～**ry** [háus-waifəri] *n.* kasei.

housing [háuziŋ] *n.* ie o teikyō suru koto ; ie : ～ *problem*, jūtaku mondai. uma no kazari.

hove [houv] *v. see :* **heave.**

hovel [hʌ́v(ə)l] *n.* koya ; monooki (*shed*).

hover [hʌ́və] *v.* sora ni mau (*bird*) ; urotsuku (*loiter*) ; chūcho suru (*hesitate*).

how [hau] *ad.* dōshite ; dorehodo ; mā ! ～ *many?* ikutsu?

howbeit [háubíːt] *conj.* towa ie ; ...nimo kakawarazu.

howdah [háudə] *n.* zō (*elephant*) no senaka ni noru hito no su-waru basho (*seat*).   ⌈domo.

however [hauévə] *ad.* ...da to itte mo ; ikani...demo. *conj.* kere-

howitzer [háuitsə] *n.* (*mil.*) kyokushahō.

howk [hauk] *v.* ana o horu.

howl [haul] v. hoeru (inu (*dog*), ōkami (*wolf*)); dogō suru; nakiwameku (*yell*)!

howsoever [hauso(u)évə] ad. ikani...demo; =**however.**

hoy [hɔi] inter. ōi! (buta nado o ou toki ni).

hoyden [hɔ́idn], **hoiden** a. sōzōshii. n. otemba musume.

HQ., H.Q., h.q. shireibu (*headquarters*).

hub [hʌb] n. sharin no koshiki (*center*.); chūshin.

hubba-hubba [hʌ́bʌ-hʌ́bʌ] inter. (*Am. sl.*) hayaku hayaku! suteki da (*fine! wonderful!*).

hubbub [hʌ́bʌb] n. gaya gaya; sōdō.

huckle [hʌ́kl] n. daitaibu. ~**bone** [hʌ́klboun] n. zakotsu.

huckster [hʌ́kstə] n. gyōshō; shōnin (yasai, kudamono nado no).

huddle [hʌ́dl] v. (~ *together*) gotagota kaki atsumeru; (~ *up*) isoide yaru He ~d himself up close to the stove, stove no soba de chijikomatta. n. gochagocha; komiai; ranzatsu (*disorder*).

hue [hju:] n. iroai; sakebi-goe (*cry*) : ~ *and cry*, zainin (*criminal*) tsuiseki no sawagi no koe.

huff [hʌf] n. rippuku; ikari : *take* ~, rippuku suru. ~**y** [hʌ́fi] a. okorippoi; fukigenna.

hug [hʌg] v. dakishimeru; koshitsu suru (*cherish*).

huge [hju:dʒ] a. kyodaina; hijōna. ~ *difference*, ōkina sōi. ~**ly** [hjú:dʒli] ad. hijōni. ~**ness** n. kyodai; bakudai.

Huguenot [hjú:gənɔt] n. Yūgunō (*Protestants in the 16, 17th century in France*).

hula [hú:lə] n. Hawai no fura dansu (*Hawaiian dance*).

hulk [hʌlk] n. furuku natta fune. ~**ing** [⌐iŋ] a. kasabaru; bukakkōna (*ungainly*).

hull [hʌl] n. kawa; kara; ōi (*cover*); hikōsen no dōtai. v. kawa

hullabaloo [hʌ̀ləbəlú:] n. ōsawagi.　　　　　　　　Lo muku.

hullo [hʌ́lóu], **hello** [helóu] inter. moshi, moshi!

hum [hʌm] v. bun-bun (*sound*) iu; kakki ga aru; (*be all astir*) (~ *a tune*) hanauta o utau. n. bunbun iu oto.

human [hjú:mən] a. hito no; ningentekina. ~**ism** [hjú:mənizm] n. jindōshugi; jimbungaku (*literary culture*). ~**ist** n. jindōshugisha; jimbun gakusha (*scholar*). ~**kind** [⌐káind] n.

ningen. ~**ly** [hjú:mənli] *ad.* ningen rashiku (...to shite).

humane [hju(:)méin] *a.* ninjō no aru. ~**ly** [hju(:)méinli] *ad.* shinsetsuni. ~**ness** [hju(:)méinnis] *n.* shinsetsu.

humanistic [hjù:mənístik] *a.* ninjō no ; jindōteki ; jimbun-gaku no.

humanitarian [hju(:)mӕnitéəriən] *n.* jindō-shugisha. *a.* jindō-tekina ; hakuai no. ~**ism** [hju(:)mӕnitéəriənizm] *n.* jindō-shugi ; hakuaishugi (*philanthropy*).

humanity [hju(:)mӕniti] *n.* jinsei (*human nature*), life ; ninjō (*feeling*) ; jinrui ; (*pl.*) koten bungaku.

humanize [hjú:mənaiz] *v.* ningen rashiku suru ; kyōka suru (*educate to be kind and merciful*).

humble [hámbl] *a.* hikui ; kensonna (*modest*). *v.* iyashimeru (*abase*) ; humble ni suru (*humiliate*). ~**bly** [hámbli] *ad.* kenson shite.   ⌈*v.* damasu.

humbug [hámbʌg] *n.* peten ; gomakashi ; sagishi (*impostor*).

humdrum [hámdrʌm] *a.* kyōmi no nai ; heibonna ; taikutsu suru.   ⌈(*forearm*).

humerus [hjú:mərəs] *n.* (*anat.*) jōhakkotsu (~*bone*) ; jōhaku

humid [hjú:mid] *a.* shikke no aru (*moist*).

humidity [hju(:)míditi] *n.* shikke.

humiliate [hju(:)mílieit] *v.* hazukashimeru ; hokori (*pride*) ya igen (*dignity*) o sageru (*to lower*).

humiliating [hju(:)mílieitiŋ] *a.* humiliate suru yōna.   ⌈koto.

humiliation [hju(:)mìliéiʃən] *n.* fumemmoku ; humiliate suru

humility [hju(:)míliti] *n.* kenson ; (*pl.*) kensonna kōi (*acts*).

hummingbird [hámiŋbə:d] *n.* (*bird*) hachi-suzume.

hummock [hámək] *n.* marui oka ; chiisai oka.

humo(u)r [hjú:mə] *n.* kigen ; omoshiromi ; okashimi (*comic*) : be out of ~, kigen ga warui. *v.* kigen o toru. *a sick person has to be ~ed,* byōnin wa kigen o totte yaraneba naranai. geigō suru (*indulge*). ~**ist** [hjú:mərist] *n.* kokkeika. ~**ous** [hjú:-mərəs] *a.* kokkeina. ~**ously** [hjú:mərəsli] *ad.* omoshiroku.

hump [hʌmp] *n.* (senaka (*back*) no) kobu. ~**back** [hámpbӕk] *n.* semushi (no hito).

humus [hjú:məs] *n.* (*L.*) fushokudo ; kusatta tsuchi (*fertilizer*).

Hun [hʌn] *n.* Kyōdojin ; (*col.*) Doitsu hei (*German soldiers*).

hunch [hʌntʃ] *n.* kobu (=*hump*); (*Am. col.*) yokan (*presentiment*). *v.* (senaka (*back*) o) mageru. ~**back** [hʌntʃbæk] *n.* semushi no hito.

hundred [hʌndrəd] *a.* hyaku no. *n.* hyaku. ~**th** [hʌndrədθ] *a.* hyaku-bamme no. *n.* dai-hyaku; hyaku-bun no ichi ($1/100$). ~**weight** [hʌndrədweit] *n.* omosa no tan'i.

hung [hʌŋ] *v. see :* **hang.**

Hungarian [hʌŋgéəriən] *a.* Hangariyajin (go) no. *n.* Hanga-[riyajin (go).

hunger [hʌŋgə] *n.* kūfuku; katsubō (*strong desire*). *v.* kūfuku ni naru; katsubō suru (*for, after*).

hungry [hʌŋgri] *a.* ueta; katsubō suru; fumō no (*barren*). ~**rily** [hʌŋgrili] *ad.* kūfuku ni; gatsugatsu to.

hunk [hʌŋk] *n.* (*col.*) ōkina kire (*piece*).

hunt [hʌnt] *v.* karu; okkakeru, ou (~ *a thief*). sagasu (*scour*); kari o suru : ~ **down**, oitsumeru. ~ **out**, sagashi dasu. *n.* kari (shuryō); sōsaku. ~**sman** [hʌntsmən] *n.* karyūdo.

hunter [hʌntə] *n.* ryōshi; karyūdo; ryōken (-*dog*); ryōba (-*horse*); tsuikyūsha (~ *after glory*).

hunting [hʌntiŋ] *n.* kari; shuryō; tankyū (*search*). ~ **cap** [hʌntiŋkæp] toriuchi-bō.

huntress [hʌntris] *n.* onna-ryōshi.

hurdle [hə́:dl] *n.* sunoko; shōgai butsu; (*pl.*) shōgaibutsu kyōsō. *v.* mabarana kakine (*fence*) o suru. ~ **race** [hə́:dlreis] *n.* shōgaibutsu kyōsō.

hurl [hə:l] *n.* nagetsukeru koto. *v.* nageru; (akkō (*abuse*) o) haku; (*baseball*) tōkyū suru.

hurly-burly [hə́:li bə̀:li] *n.* sawagi; gotagota.

hurrah [hurá:] *inter.* banzai! furē! *n.* kanko. *v.* banzai o sa-[kebu.

hurricane [hʌrikən] *n.* bōfū; ōkaze.

hurriedly [hʌridli] *ad.* isoide.   [*ad.* awatete.

hurry [hʌri] *v.* isogaseru; isogu. *n.* isogi. ~-**scurry** [hʌriskʌ́ri]

hurt [hə:t] *n.* kizu; itami; songai. *v.* kizu tsukeru; kanjō (*feeling*) o kizutsukeru. ~**ful** [hə́:tf(u)l] *a.* gai ni naru. ~**fully** [hə́:tfuli] *ad.* yūgaini; songai o ataete. ~**less** [hə́:tlis] *a.* gai ni naranu.

hurtle [hə́:tl] *v.* tsuki ataru; tosshin suru (*rush*): *the spears* ~*d against shields,* yari ga tate ni gachiri to tsukiatatta.

husband [házbənd] *n.* otto. *v.* setsuyaku suru. ~**man** [házbən(d)mən] *n.* nōfu. ~**ry** [házbəndri] *n.* nōgyō ; setsuyaku.

hush [hʌʃ] *n.* seishuku. *v.* shizumeru ; shizukani ! ~ *up*, momikesu. ~ **money** [háʃmʌni] *n.* kuchidomeryō.

husk [hʌsk] *n.* kawa ; (*Am.*) tōmorokoshi no kawa (*of corn*). *v.* kawa o muku. ~**y** [háski] *a.* kawa no (*yōna*) ; shiwagaregoe no (*hoarse*) ; (*Am. col.*) ganjōna.

hussar [huzáː] *n.* keikihei.

hussy [házi] *n.* otemba musume ; abazure onna (*a minx*).

hustings [hástiŋz] *n.* (*pl.*) senkyo enzetsu no endan.

hustle [hásl] *v.* oshihiraite tōru (*jostle rudely*) ; isogu (*hurry*). *n.* [hʌt] *n.* koya ; kari-hei.⌐oshiai.

hutch [hʌtʃ] *n.* usagi (*rabbit*) no ori ; hako (*box*). *v.* hutch ni ireru. ⌐mukaeru.

huzza [huzáː] *inter.* banzai ! *n.* banzai. *v.* banzai o sakende

hyacinth [háiəsinθ] *n.* (*bot.*) hiyashinsu.

Hyades [háiədiːz] *n.* (*pl.*) (*astr.*) Hiyadesu (Oushi-za no hoshi no gun (*stars*). ⌐(*word*).

hybrid [háibrid] *n.* zasshu ; ainoko (*crossbred child*) ; konsei-go

hydra [háidrə] *n.* (H-) (*Gk myth.*) 9 no atama o motta hebi ; konzetsu shigatai wazawai (*disaster*) ; (*zoo.*) hidora ; mizu-hebi.

hydrangea [haidréindʒiə] *n.* (*flow.*) murasaki ajisai.

hydrant [háidr(ə)nt] *n.* suidōsen ; shōkasen (*fire* ~).

hydraulic [haidrɔ́ːrik] *a.* suiryoku no ; sui-atsu no (*pressure*) : ~ *press*, suiatsuki. ~**s** [haidrɔ́ːliks] *n.* suiryokugaku.

hydride [háidraid] *n.* (*chem.*) suiso kagōbutsu.

hydroairplane [háidrouɛ́əplein] *n.* suijō-hikōki.

hydrocarbon [háidro(u)káːbən] *n.* tankasuiso.

hydroelectric [háidruiléktrik] *a.* suiryoku denki no.

hydroelectricity [háidrəilektrísiti] *n.* suiryoku denki.

hydrogen [háidrədʒən] *n.* (*chem.*) suiso.

hydrography [haidrɔ́grəfi] *n.* suirogaku ; suiro sokuryōjutsu.

hydrometer [haidrɔ́mitə] *n.* ekitai hijūkei ; ekitai ukibakari.

hydropathic [hàidropǽθik] *a.* suichiryōhō no (*a water-cure*).

hydrophobia [háidrəfóubiə] *n.* (*med.*) kyōsui-byō ; kyōken-byō.

hydroplane [háidroplein] *n.* suijō-kassōtei.

hydroponics [hàidrəpóniks] *n.* (*Am.*) (*agric.*) suichū yōshoku.

hydrostat [háidrostæt] *n.* kikan-bakuretsu-bōshiki.
hydrostatics [hàidrostǽtiks] *n.* ryūtai-seirikigaku.   ⌈hito.
hyena = **hyaena** [ha(i)í:nə] *n.* (*zoo.*) haiina; ryōku; zanninna
Hygeian [haidʒí:ən] *a.* kenkō (*health*) no megami (*goddess*);
　Haijin no; (h-) hoken no; eisei no.
hygiene [háidʒi:n] *n.* eisei-gaku.
hygienic [haidʒí:nik] *a.* eiseigaku no; eiseijō no. **~s** [hai-
　dʒí:niks] *n.* eiseigaku.
hygrometer [haigrómitə] *n.* shitsudo-kei.
Hymen [háimen] (*Gk. myth.*) kon'in no kami. "*hymen*" wa
　shojomaku no imi.
hymeneal [hàiminí(:)əl] *a.* kekkon no.   ⌈bika-shū.
hymn [him] *n.* sambika. *v.* sambi suru. **~al** [hímnəl] *n.* sam-
hymnology [himnólədʒi] *n.* sambika-gaku.
hyperbola [haipó:bələ] *n.* (*math.*) sōkyokusen.
hyperbole [haipó:bəli] *n.* (*rhet.*) kochōhō; e.g. (*Waves mountain
　high broke over the reef*, yama no yōna ōnami ga anshō no ue
　ni kudaketa).   ⌈no; ōgesana.
hyperbolical [hàipə(:)bólikəl] *a.* sōkyokusen no; kochōhō
hypercritical [háipə(:)krítik(ə)l] *a.* kokuhyō suru.
hypercriticism [háipə(:)krítisizm] *n.* kokuhyō.
hyphen [háif(ə)n] *n.* haifun; tsunagi (-).
hyphenate [háifəneit] *v.* haifun (*hyphen*) de tsunagu. **~d**
　Americans, gaikoku-kei Beijin.
hypnosis [hipnóusis] *n.* saimin (-jōtai).
hypnotic [hipnótik] *a.* saiminjutsu no.
hypnotism [hípnətizm] *n.* saiminjutsu.
hypnotize [hípnətaiz] *v.* saiminjutsu o kakeru.
hypochondria [hàipokóndriə] *n.* (*med.*) yūutsushō.
hypochondriac [hàipokóndriæk] *a.* yūutsushō no. *n.* yūutsu-
hypocrisy [hipókrəsi] *n.* gizen.   ⌊shō no kanja.
hypocrite [hípəkrit] *n.* gizensha.
hypocritical [hìpəkrítikəl] *a.* gizen no.
hypodermic [hàipədó:mik] *n.* hika no. **~ injection** [-indʒék-
　ʃən] hikachūsha.
hypotenuse [haipótinju:z] *n.* (*math.*) gen; shahen.
hypothec [haipóθek] *n.* teitōken : **~ bank**, kangyō ginkō.

hypothecate [haipɔ́θikeit] *v.* teitō ni ireru.
hypothesis [haipɔ́θisis] *n.* (*pl.* ∼ses [-si:z]) kasetsu.
hypothetic(al) [hàipoθétik(ə)l] *a.* kasetsu no. ∼**ally** [haipǝ-θétikǝli] *ad.* kari ni.
hyssop [hísǝp] *n.* (*bot.*) hisoppu.
hysteria [histíǝriǝ], **hysterics** [histériks] *n.* (*med.*) hisuterii.
hysteric(al) [histérik(ǝ)l] *a.* histerii no.

I

I, i [ai] *n.* (*pl.* I's, Is, [aiz]) Eigo *alphabet* no dai-9-bamme no moji.

I [ai] *pron.* wata(ku)shiwa; wata(ku)shi ga.

iambic [aiǽmbik] *n.* (*poet.*) jaku-kyō-kaku (× ⌣) no shi (*poem*). *a.* tanchō kaku no.

iambus [aiǽmbəs] *n.* (*pl.* **-bi -bai** [bai]; or ~**ses** [aiǽmbəsiz]) *n.* (*poet.*) tan-chō-kaku; jaku-kyō-kaku (× ⌣).

ibex [áibeks] *n.* (*zoo.*) *Alps* no yasei yagi.

ibis [áibis] *n.* (*bird*) toki.

ice [ais] *n.* kōri. *v.* kōrasu; kōri de oū (*over*); satō-goromo (*sugar*) o kakeru. ~**berg** [áisbə:g] *n.* hyōzan. ~**boat** [áisbout] *n.* saihyō-sen. ~**bound** [áisbaund] *a.* kōri ni kakomareta. ~**box** [áisbɔks] *n.* (*Am.*) reizōko. ~**breaker** [áisbreikə] *n.* saihyōsen. ~**cream** [áiskrí:m] *n.* aisu-kuriimu. ~**house** [áishaus] *n.* hyōshitsu.　　　　　　　　⌈chi (*bee*).

ichneumon [iknjú:mən] *n.* (*zoo.*) neko-itachi; (*insect*) himeba-

ichthyology [ikθiɔ́lədʒi] *n.* gyoruigaku.

icicle [áisikl] *n.* tsurara.

icily [áisili] *ad.* kōri no yōni; tsumetaku (*coldly*).

icing [áisiŋ] *n.* (kashi no) satōgoromo.

ICJ Kokusai Shihō Saibansho (*International Court of Justice*).

icon [áikɔn] *n.* Kiristo-kyō seijin-tachi no gazō.

iconoclasm [aikɔ́noklæzm] *n.* gūzō-hakai no seishin to kōi.

iconoclast [aikɔ́noklæst] *n.* gūzō-hakaisha.

iconoscope [aikɔ́nəskoup] *n.* (terevijon no) okuri shinkūkan.

icy [áisi] *a.* kōri no; tsumetai (*cold*); reitanna.

idea [aidíə] *n.* kannen; gainen; kangae.

ideal [aidíəl] *a.* risō no; kannentekina. *n.* risō. ~**ism** [aidí(:)əl izm] *n.* risōshugi; yuishinron. ~**ist** [aidíəlist] *n.* risōshugi-sha; yuishinronja.

idealistic [aidìəlístik] *a.* risōshugi no; yuishinron no; kan-nenron no.

ideality [àidiǽliti] *n.* kannenjō ni sonzai suru jōtai.

idealize [aidíəlaiz] *v.* risōka suru.

identical [aidéntik(ə)l] *a.* dōitsu no; dōyōna. ~**ly** [aidénti-kəli] *ad.* dōitsuni.

identification [aidèntifikéiʃən] *n.* dōitsu da to suru koto; aru mono o dōitsu to mitomeru koto.

identify [aidéntifai] *v.* onaji mono (dōitsu) to suru, mitomeru.

identity [aidéntiti] *n.* dōitsusei; itchi (*agreement*).

ideogram [ídiougræm], **ideograph** [ídiougræf] *n.* hyōi(shō-kei)moji.

ideology [àidiólədʒi] *n.* kannen keitai; ikkan shita seishin.

ides[aidz] (*pl.*) *n.* (Ko-Rōma no koyomi de) 3, 5, 7, 10 no tsuki no 15ch. to sono ta no tsuki no 13ch. (*the 15th of March, May, July and October, and the 13th of the other months*).

idiocy [ídiəsi] *n.* hakuchi.

idiom [ídiəm] *n.* kan'yōgo; jukugo dokutoku no iikata.

idiomatic [ìdiomǽtik] *a.* kan'yōgo no; tokushu no.

idiosyncrasy [idiosínkrəsi] *n.* aru hito (mono) no tokushitsu.

idiot [ídiət] *n.* hakuchi; baka.　　　　　　　　　　　⌈no yōni

idiotic [idiótik] *a.* hakuchi no. ~**ally** [idiótikəli] *ad.* hakuchi

idle [áidl] *a.* namaketa. *v.* namakeru. ~ *away*, muda ni suru. karamawari suru. ~**ness** [áidlnis] *n.* taida. ~**r** [áidlə] *n.* namakemono.

idly [áidli] *ad.* namakete; munashiku (*in vain*).

idol [áidl] *n.* gūzō.

idolater [aidólətə] *n.* gūzō sūhaisha; sūhaisha (*adorer*).

idolatress [aidólətris] *n.* gūzō sūhai suru onna.

idolatrous [aidólətrəs] *a.* gūzō sūhai o suru.

idolatry [aidólətri] *n.* gūzō sūhai; sūhai (*admiration*); shinsui.

idolize [áidolaiz] *v.* aite o kamisama no yōni shinjikiru koto.

idyl(l) [áidil] *n.* den'en-shi; bokkateki jōkei (*scene*).

idyllic [aidílik] *a.* den'en-shi no.

i. e. [ai i:] *i. e.* (L. *id est*) [ðǽt iz] sunawachi.

if [if] *conj.* moshi...naraba. ...*wonder*...*if*, ...darō ka shiran.

igloo, iglu [íglu:] *n.* Esukimō (*Eskimo*) jin no ie.

igneous [ígniəs] *a.* hi (*fire*) no; hi no yōna (*like*); kasei no; hi (*fire*) de dekita (*produced by fire*).

ignis fatuus [ígnis fǽtjuəs] *n.* (*pl.* (L.) **ignes fatui** [ignes fatūi])

yamiyo nado ni chirachira to mieru hi.
ignite [ignáit] *v.* hi o tsukeru; makkani nessuru.
ignition [igníʃ(ə)n] *n.* shakunetsu (*white heat*).
ignoble [ignóubl] *a.* iyashii; teikyūna (*mean*). ∼**bly** [ignóubli]
    ad. iyashiku. ∼**ness** [ignóublnis] *n.*
ignominious [ignəmíniəs] *a.* fumembokuna; geretsuna (*vul-
    gar*). ∼**ly** [ignəmíniəsli] *ad.* geretsuni.
ignominy [ignəmini] *n.* fumemboku; hazubeki kōi (okonai).
ignoramus [ìgnəréiməs] *n.* muchina hito; shittakaburi o suru
    hito (*pretentious*).
ignorance [ígn(ə)r(ə)ns] *n.* muchi; mugaku; shiranai koto.
ignorant [ígn(ə)r(ə)nt] *a.* muchina; mugaku no; shiranai.
    ∼**ly** [ígnərəntli] *ad.* mugaku de.
ignore [ignɔ́:] *v.* mushi suru; (*leg.*) kyakka suru (*throw out*).
iguana [ìgwá:nə] *n.* (*zoo.*) nettai Amerika no ōtokage.
iliac [íliæk] *a.* (*anat.*) koshibone no hiroi bubun.
Iliad [íliəd] *n. Homerus* no "*Troy* Seibatsu Monogatari".
ilium [íliəm] *n.* (*anat.*) chōkotsu (koshi no hone, hiroi tokoro).
ill [il] *a.* byōki; yokunai; warui. *an* ∼ *deed*, warui okonai. ∼ *at
    ease*, ochitsukanai; igokochi no warui. ∼**-advised** [-ədváizd]
    a. orokana. ∼**-bred** [-bréd] *a.* sodachi no warui. ∼**breeding**
    [-bri:diŋ] *a.* gyōgi no warui. ∼**-fated** [-féitid] *a.* un (*fate*) no
    warui. ∼**-favored** [-féivəd] bukiryōna. ∼**gotten** [-gɔ́tn] *a.*
    fusei de eta. ∼**-humored** [-hjú:məd] *a.* kigen no warui;
    fuyukaina. ∼**-mannered** [-mǽnəd] *a.* busahōna. ∼**-natured**
    [-neitʃ-əd] *a.* seishitsu no warui. ∼**ness** *n.* byōki. ∼**temper-
    ed** [-témpəd] *a.* kimuzukashii. ∼**-treat** [-trí:t] *v.* warui toria-
    tsukai (gyakutai) suru. ∼**use** [-júz] *v.* warui atsukai o suru.
I'll=**I will, I shall.** no shōryaku (*abbreviated form*).
illegal [ilí:g(ə)l] *a.* fuhōna. ∼**ly** [ilí:gəli] *ad.* fuhōni.
illegality [ili(:)gǽliti] *n.* hōritsu mushi.
illegibility [ilidʒibíliti] *n.* yominikui koto.
illegible [ilédʒəbl] *a.* yomenai; yominikui. ∼**bly** [ilédʒəbli]
    ad. yominikuku. ∼**ness** *n.* awanai.
illegitimacy [ìlidʒítiməsi] *n.* rikutsu ni awanai; hōritsu ni
illegitimate [ilidʒítimit] *a.* shiseiji no.
illiberal [ilíb(ə)r(ə)l] *a.* kechina; kokoro no semai; gehinna

(base). ∾ly *ad.* kitanaku. ∾ness [ilíberəlnis] *n.* kechi; rinshoku.

illiberality [ilibərǽliti] *n.* rinshoku; kechimbō; kyōryō.

illicit [ilísit] *a.* hō de yurusarenai *(legally prohibited).* ∾ly [ilísitli] *ad.* hōritsu de tomerarete. ∾ness [ilísitnis] *n.* hōritsuno kinshi. ⌈kagiri naku.

illimitable [ilímitəbl] *a.* kagiri no nai. ∾bly [ilímitəbli] *ad.*

illiteracy [ilít(ə)rəsi] *n.* mugaku; yomi-kaki no dekinai koto.

illiterate [ilít(ə)rit] *a.* yondari, kaitari no dekinai; gehinna *(base).* ⌈ni.

illogical [ilódʒik(ə)l] *a.* fugōrina. ∾ly [ilódʒikəli] *ad.* fugōri

illuminant [il(j)ú:minənt] *n.* hakkōtai; hikari o dasu mono. *a.* hikaru.

illuminate [il(j)ú:míneit] *v.* hikaraseru; irumineishon o tsukeru; setsumei suru *(explain)*; kazaru *(decorate).*

illumination [il(j)ù:mínéiʃən] *n.* shōmei; irumineishon; kei-

illumine [il(j)ú:min] *v.* terasu; hikaru. ⌊hatsu.

illusion [il(j)ú:ʒən] *n.* gen'ei; sakkaku; machigatte miru koto.

illusive [il(j)ú:siv], **illusory** [il(j)ú:səri] *a.* machigatte miru; ayamatta.

illustrate [íləstreit] *v.* setsumei suru; sashie o ireru. ∾d [íləstreitid] *a.* e-iri de setsumei suru.

illustration [iləstréiʃən] *a.* setsumei; sashie.

illustrative [íləstreitiv] *a.* setsumei suru; setsumei o tasukeru. ∾ly [íləstreitivli] *ad.* akirakani.

illustrious [ilʌ́striəs] *a.* hiideta; yūmeina. ∾ly [ilʌ́striəsli] *ad.* yūmeini. ∾ness [ilʌ́striəsnis] *n.* yūmei.

I.L.O. Kokusai Rōdō Kikō *(International Labor Organization).*

I'm [áim]=**I am.**

image [ímidʒ] *n.* shōzō. *v.* zō o tsukuru; utsusu *(mirror).*

imagery [ímidʒ(ə)ri] *n.* shinshō (kokoro ni egaku sugata).

imaginable [imǽdʒ(i)nəbl] *v.* kokoro no uchi ni egaku koto no dekiru *(be able to imagine).*

imaginary [imǽdʒin(ə)ri] *a.* sōzōjō no.

imagination [imǽdʒinéiʃən] *n.* sōzō (ryoku).

imaginative [imǽdʒ(i)nətiv] *a.* sōzō ryoku ni tomu.

imagine [imǽdʒin] *v.* sōzō suru; omou.

imago [iméigou] *u (inst.)* seichū. ⌈mono.

imbecile [ímbisail] *a.* nyūjakuna; teinō no *(foolish)*. *n.* baka

imbecility [ìmbisíliti] *n.* teinō; nyūjaku *(weekness)*.

imbed, embed [imbéd] *v.* shikkari hamekomu (shikkui, tsuchi nado ni).

imbibe [imbáib] *v.* nomu; kyūshū suru *(drink in)*; kokoro ni ⌈kakitomeru.

imbricate *a.* [ímbrikit] orikasanatte iru. *v.* [ímbrikeit] kawara no yōni kasanaru.

imbrication [imbrikéiʃən] *n.* kawara *(tile)* no yōni kasanaru koto; uroko gata *(scale-shaped)*.

imbroglio [imbróuliou] *n.* funkyū; kongaragari.

imbue [imbjú:] *v.* someru; shimikomaseru *(inspire)*; fukikomu: *He ～d his son's mind with his ambition to succeed*, kare wa musuko ni jibun no kōjōshin o fukikonde ato o tsugashi-

imitable [ímitəbl] *n.* mane ga dekiru. └ta.

imitate [ímiteit] *v.* maneru; gizō suru *(counterfeit)*. ～**d** [-id] *a.* mozō no.

imitation [imitéiʃ(ə)n] *n.* mane; mozōhin; nisemono. ～**al** [imitéiʃən(ə)l] *a.* nise no; mozōhin no.

imitative [ímitətiv] *a.* mane no. ～**ly** [ímitətivli] *ad.* manete.

imitator [ímiteitə] *n.* mohōsha.

immaculate [imǽkjulit] *a.* muku no; shōjōna; ketten no nai *(faultless)*. ～ *Conception*, Seibo Mariya no jutai.

immanence [ímənəns] *n.* kokoro no uchi ni tamotte iru koto.

immanent [ímənənt] *a.* naizai suru. ～**ly** *ad.* naizai shite.

immaterial [imətíəriəl] *a.* mukei no; jisshitsuteki de nai.

immature [ìmətjúə] *a.* mijukuna. ～**ly** [ìmətjúəli] *ad.* mikan-

immaturity [imətjúəriti] *n.* mijuku. └seini (de).

immeasurable [iméʒ(ə)rəbl] *a.* hakarenai. ～**bly** [iméʒərəbli] *ad.* hakarenai hodo ni.

immediate [imí:djət] *a.* chokusetsu no; shikyū no. ～**ly** [imí:djətli] *ad.* chokusetsuni; suguni. ～**ness** [imí:djətnis] *n.* chokusetsu. ⌈inai.

immemorial [ìmimó:riəl] *a.* taiko (furui mukashi) no; oboete

immense [iméns] *a.* bakudaina. ～**ly** [iménsli] *ad.* bakudaini.

immensity [iménsiti] *n.* tohō mo naku ōkii koto.

immerse [imɔ́:s] *v.* hitasu; ni fukeru: *be ～d in*, ni hamari konde iru. ～ *oneself*, fukeru.

immersion [imə́ːʃ(ə)n] *n.* shinnyū ; netchū.

immigrant [ímigr(ə)nt] *n.* ijūsha ; imin.

immigrate [ímigreit] *v.* ijū suru ; aru kuni (chihō) kara ijū shite kuru. ⌜1918 nen no imindan.

immigration [imigréiʃ(ə)n] *n.* ijū ; imindan ; *the* ～ *of 1918,*

imminence [íminəns] *n.* sashisemaru koto ; shōbi no kyū.

imminent [íminənt] *a.* seppaku shita ; sashisematta.

immobile [imóubail] *a.* ugokashi nikui ; *mobile* shigatai.

immobility [imoubíliti] *n.* fudō (-sei) ; ugokanai koto. ⌜gaini.

immoderate [imɔ́d(ə)rit] *a.* hōgaina. ～**ly** [imɔ́dəritli] *ad.* hō-

immodest [imɔ́dist] *a.* daitan de bureina. ～**ly** [imɔ́distli] *ad.* buenryō de. ～**y** [imɔ́disti] *n.* wagamama ; buenryo.

immolate [ímoleit] *v.* ikenie (*sacrificial*) to shite korosu.

immolation [imoléiʃ(ə)n] *n.* kami ni ikenie to shite korosu (korosareru) koto. ⌜*ad.* fuhinkō de.

immoral [imɔ́rəl] *a.* futokugi no ; fuhinkōna. ～**ly** [imɔ́rəli]

immorality [imɔrǽliti] *n.* fudōtoku ; fuhinkō (*misconduct*) ; wai-setsu (*lewdness*). ⌜fumetsuni.

immortal [imɔ́ːt(e)l] *a.* fukyū no ; fushi no. ～**ly** [-təli] *ad.*

immortality [imɔːtǽliti] *n.* fushi ; fumetsu.

immortalize [imɔ́ːtəlaiz] *v.* fukyū ni suru ; fushi ni suru.

immovable [imúːvəbl] *a.* ugokashi nikui ; shikkari shita. *n.* (*pl.*) (*leg.*) fudōsan.

immune [imjúːn] *a.* men'eki no ; sozei menjo no.

immunity [imjúːniti] *n.* sozei menjo ; men'eki (*epidemic*).

immure [imjúə] *v.* tojikomeru ; yūhei suru.

immutability [imjuːtəbíliti] *n.* fuhensei ; fudō.

immutable [imjúːtəbl] *a.* kawaranai ; ugokanai.

imp [imp] *n.* oni no kodomo ; wampaku kozō.

impact [ímpækt] *n.* shōgeki (*striking*) ; shōtotsu (*collision*) : *the* ～ *of the two swords broke both of them,* futatsu no ken no uchi-ai de ken wa tomoni oreta.

impair [impéə] *v.* gaisuru (*harm*) ; genzuru (*take off*).

impale [impéil]*v.* tsukisashite korosu. ～**ment** [impéilmənt] *n.* sashi tsuranuku koto.

impalpable [impǽlpəbl] *a.* shokkaku ni kanjinai ; komakai

(-*powder*); ryōkai shinikui : *sunbeams are* ~, taiyō no hikari wa te ni torenai. ~**bly** [impǽlpəbli] *ad.* shokkaku ni kanjinai yōni ; komakaku.   ⌈mae (*name*) o kinyū suru.

impanel [impǽn(ə)l] *v.* baishin'in (*jury*) meibo (*list*) ni na-

impart [impá:t] *v.* ataeru ; tsutaeru ; *rich furnishing that* ~ *elegance to a room*, heya ni gachi o soeru rippana chōdo. shiraseru : ~ *a secret*, himitsu o shiraseru.

impartial [impá:ʃ(ə)l] *a.* kōheina. ~**ly** [impá:ʃəli] *ad.* kōhei ni.

impartiality [ímpa:ʃiǽliti] *n.* kōhei.

impassable [impá:səbl] *a.* tōrenai.

impasse [æmpá:s] *n.* (*Fr.*) nukerarenai ; fukurokōji ; nankyoku.

impassible [impǽsibl] *a.* mukankakuna ; kanjō no nai.

impassioned [impǽʃ(ə)nd] *a.* kangeki shita ; netsuretsuna.

impassive [impǽsiv] *a.* kutsū o kanjinai ; heiseina (*calm*).

impatience [impéiʃ(ə)ns] *n.* tanki.

impatient [impéiʃ(ə)nt] *a.* shimbō dekinai ; tankina (*short tempered*). ~**ly** *ad.* kimijikani.

impeach [impí:tʃ] *v.* kokuso suru ; kōgi suru (*protest*). ~**ment** *n.* dangai ; kokuso ; kōgi.

impeccable [impékəbl] *a.* ketten no nai.

impecuniosity [ímpikju:niósiti] *n.* bimbō ; mu-ichimon.

impecunious [ímpikju:niəs] *a.* bimbōna ; mu-ichimon no.

impede [impí:d] *v.* fusegu ; jama o suru.

impediment [impédimənt] *n.* bōgai ; geng(y)o-shōgai.

impel [impél] *v.* oshisusumeru ; hagemasu (*drive forward*) ; shiite ...saseru.

impend [impénd] *v.* sashisemaru (*approach*). ~**ing** [impéndiŋ] *a.* tarekakatta (*hanging over*) ; sashisematta (*pressing*).

impenetrability [impènitrəbíliti] *n.* (*phys.*) fukanyūsei.

impenetrable [impénitrəbl] *a.* tsukitōsenai ; fukanyū-seino aru ; oku no shirenai (-*forests*). ~**ness** [impénətrəblnis], **impenetrability** [ìmpenitrəbíliti] *n.* ~**bly** [impénətrəbli] *ad.* hakarishirenaiyōni.

impenitent [impénit(ə)nt] *n.* kuiaratameru kokoro no nai ; gōjōna. **impenitence**, ~**cy**, ~**ness** *n. kuiaratame* no kokoro no nai koto. ~**ly** *ad.* kuiaratamenai de.

imperative [impérətiv] *a.* meireitekina ; (*gram.*) meirei-hō

no. *n. (gram.)* meirei-hō. ∼**ly** [impérətivli] *ad.* meireitekini.
imperceptible [ìmpəsépt(ə)bl] *a.* **mitomerukoto** no dekinai.
∼**bly** [ìmpəséptibli] *ad.* jojoni ; me ni tsukanai hodo ni.
imperfect [impə́:fikt] *a.* fukanzenna. ∼**ly** [impə́:fiktli] *ad.* fu-
imperfection [ìmpəfékʃ(ə)n] *n.* fukanzen. ⌊kanzenni.
imperial [impíəriəl] *a.* teikoku no ; kōshitsu no. ∼ *salute*, kō-
reihō *(gun). n.* kōtei hige. ∼**ism** [impíəriəlizm] *n.* teisei
(rule) ; teikoku shugi *(ism).* ∼**ist** [impíəriəlist] *n.* teikoku
imperialistic [impìəriəlístik] *a.* teikoku shugi no. ⌊shugisha.
imperil [impéril] *v.* ayauku suru ; kikenni sarasu. ⌈*(urgent).*
imperious [impíəriəs] *a.* ōheina ; meireitekina ; kinkyū no
imperishable [impériʃəbl] *a.* eikyūteki no. ∼**bly** [impériʃə-
bli] *ad.* eikyūtekini.
impermanent [impə́:mənənt] *a.* ichijiteki no.
impermanence, -cy [impə:mənəns(i)] *n.* ichijisei ; hi-eikyūsei.
impermeable [impə́:miəbl] *a.* fushintō no ; tōtte ikenai ; naka ni tsukiiru koto no dekinai.
impersonal [impə́:s(ə)n(ə)l] *a.* hijinkakuteki no ; hakkiri shita
ninshō no nai baai : " *first come, first served* " *is an* ∼ *remark,*
" *first…served* " wa hininshōteki iikata da. *Electricity is an* ∼
power, denki wa hijinkakuteki chikarada. ∼**ity** [impè:sənǽl-
iti] *n.* hijinkakusei. ∼**ly** *ad.*
impersonate [impə́:səneit] *v.* koe nado o maneru : ∼ *the well-
known news commentator,* shirewatatte iru *news* kaisetsusha o
maneru. ∼ *Hamlet on the stage,* butai de (on) *Hamlet* no
' yaku o suru ' *(impersonate).*
impersonation [impè:sənéiʃ(ə)n] *n.* jinkaku o ataeru koto ; funsō *(impersonate)* suru koto.
impertinence -cy [impə́:tinəns(i)] *n.* futekitō ; busahō *(bad
manner) ;* namaiki ; zūzūshisa ; atsukamashisa.
impertinent [impə́:tinənt] *a.* zūzūshii ; shitsureina. ∼**ly** [im-
pə́:tinəntli] *ad.* busahōnimo.
imperturbability [ímpə(:)tə̀:bəbíliti] *n.* ochitsuki ; heisei ;
muyamini agaranai. ⌈∼**bly** *ad.*
imperturbable [impə(:)tə́:bəbl] *a.* ochitsuita ; reiseina *(calm).*
impervious [impə́:vjəs] *a.* (mizu nado no tōranai ; giron nado
ni shinai *(not open to argument).*

impetuosity [impètjuósiti] *n.* sekkachi de hageshii seishitsu.

impetuous [impétjuəs] *a.* sekkachi de hageshii. ~**ly** *ad.*

impetus [ímpitəs] *n.* gendōryoku; shigeki (*stimulation*).

impiety [impáiəti] *n.* fushinjin; oyafukō (*lack of filial piety*).

impinge [impíndʒ] *v.* tsuki ataru; utsu : *rays of light* ~ *on the eye*, kōsen ga me o tsuku (shigeki suru).

impious [ímpiəs] *a.* fushinjinna; ja-aku no (*wicked*); oya fukōna (*lack of filial piety*).

impish [impiʃ] *a.* ko-oni no yōna; waru-itazura o suru.

implacable [implǽkəbl] *a.* wakai dekinai; shūnen-bukai (*grudge*).

implant [implá:nt] *v.* uetsukeru; oshiekomu (*inculcate*).

implement [ímplimənt] *n.* dōgu.

implicate [ímplikeit] *v.* kankei suru (saseru); makikomu; fukumu : *be* ~*d in*, ni renza suru.

implication [ìmplikéiʃən] *n.* kankei suru koto. igi; ganchiku; kakariai.

implicit [implísit] *a.* ganchiku suru; zettai no (*complete*). ~**ly** [implísitli] *ad.* ammoku no uchi ni.

implied [impláid] *a.* imi o fukunde iru : *her* ~ *smile that she had forgiven us*, wareware o yurushite kurete iru to iu imi no kanojo no hohoemi. ~**ly** [impláidli] *ad.* ammoku no uchi ni.

implore [implɔ́:] *v.* kongan suru.

imply [implái] *v.* imi o fukunde iru; imi suru (*mean*).

impolite [impəláit] *a.* shitsureina. ~**ly** [impəláitli] *ad.* busahōni. ~**ness** [impəláitnis] *n.* busahō.

impolitic [impɔ́litik] *a.* futokusakuna; hemana.

imponderable [impɔ́nd(ə)rəbl] *a.* omosa o hakaru koto no dekinai (amari karui node).

import [ímpɔ:t] *n.* yunyūhin (tsūjō fukusū); imi (*meaning*); jūyōsei (*importance*). *v.* [impɔ́:t] yunyū suru; imi suru (*mean*); jūyō de aru. ~**able** [-əbl] *a.* yunyū no dekiru. ~**er** *n.* [ə] yunyūshō.

importance [impɔ́:t(ə)ns] *n.* jūyō. *man of* ~, seiryoku no aru hito. *relative* ~, hikakutekina jūyōsei. *with an air of* ~, mottaibutte.

important [impɔ́:t(ə)nt] *a.* jūyōna; mottai buru (*pompous*). ~**ly**

[impɔ́:təntli] *ad.* jūyōni; mottai butte.

importation [impɔ:téiʃən] *r.* yunyū; yunyūhin (*-goods*).

importunate [impɔ́:tjunit] *a.* shitsukkoi; urusai. ∼ly *ad.* shitsukkoku; urusaku.

importune [impɔ:tjú:n] *v.* shitsukoku (*persistently*) nedaru; sebiru. ⌈shitsuyō.

importunity [ìmpɔ:tjú:niti] *n.* shitsukkoi (*obstinate*) yōkyū;

impose [impóuz] *v.* oku; zei (*tax*) o kasuru; shiiru (*upon, on*); azamuku (*deceive*).

imposing [impóuziŋ] *a.* dōdō taru. ∼ly [li] *ad.* dō- dō to shite.

imposition [impəzíʃ(ə)n] *n.* wariate (*levy*); sagi (*swindle*); omoni (*burden*).

impossibility [impɔ̀səbíliti] *n.* fukanō; fukanō de aru koto.

impossible [impɔ́səbl] *a.* fukanōna; deki uru koto de nai.

impost [ímpoust] *n.* zei (*tax*); yunyūzei (*an import duty*).

impostor [impɔ́stə] *n.* sagi-shi.

imposture [impɔ́stjuə] *n.* sagi. ⌈(*med.*) in'i.

impotence [ímpətəns] *n.* mukiryoku; kyojaku (*weakness*);

impotent [ímpət(ə)nt] *a.* mukiryokuna; (*med.*) in'i no.

impound [impáund] *v.* ori (*cage*) ni ireru; yūhei suru (*shut up*); ōshū suru (*confiscate*).

impoverish [impóv(ə)riʃ] *v.* bimbō ni suru; hihei saseru. ∼ment [impóv(ə)riʃmənt] *n.* hihei.

impracticable [impræktikəbl] *a.* jikkō fukanō no.

imprecate [ímprikeit] *v.* norou (*call down evil upon others*).

imprecation [imprikéiʃ(ə)n] *n.* noroi.

impregnability [impregnəbíliti] *n.* chikarazuku dewa katenai koto; kengo.

impregnable [imprégnəbl] *a.* chikarazuku dewa katenai. seme yoserarenai (*fortress*); an ∼ fortress; an ∼ argument, yaburenai giron.

impregnate [imprégneit] *v.* jutai saseru; shimikomasu (*imbue*); inshōzukeru (*with*).

impresario [ìmprezá:riou] *n.* kageki kōgyōshu (*opera manager*).

impress [imprés] *v.* inshō zukeru; kammei saseru (*move deeply*). *n.* [ímpres] natsu-in; inshō (*impression*).

impressible [imprésibl] *a.* kanji yasui.

impression [impréʃən] *n.* natsu-in; inshō : *the first ~s of Japan,* Nippon no daiichi inshō. insatsu (*printing*). **~able** [impréʃ-(ə)nəbl] *a.* kanji yasui. **~ism** [impréʃ(ə)nizm] *n.* inshōha. **~ist** [impréʃ(ə)nist] *n.* inshōha no gaka (*painter*), chōkokuka (*sculptor*), sakka (*writer*), *etc.*

impressive [imprésiv] *a.* kammeitekina. **~ly** [imprésivli] *ad.* inshōtekini.

imprint [ímprint] *n.* oshita atokata; shuppansha no namae. *v.* [imprínt] insatsu suru.

imprison [imprízn] *v.* tōgoku suru; kankin suru (*shut up*). **~ment** [impríznmənt] *n.* tōgoku; kankin.

improbability [imprɔ̀bəbíliti] *n.* arisō mo nai koto.

improbable [imprɔ́bəbl] *a.* arisō mo nai. **~bly** [imprɔ́bəbli] *ad.* arisō mo naku.

impromptu [imprɔ́m(p)tjuː] *a.* sokuseki no. *n.* sokuseki no enzetsu (*speech*), ensō (*musical performance*), sokkyō shi (*poem*); sokkyō kyoku (*melody*). *ad.* sokuza ni. (*in readiness.*).

improper [imprɔ́pə] *a.* futekitōna; midarana (*immoral*). **~ly** [imprɔ́pəli] *ad.* futekitōni.

impropriety [imprɔpráiəti] *n.* fuontō; busahō (*rudeness*).

improvable [imprúːvəbl] *a.* kairyō-dekiru.

improve [imprúːv] *v.* kairyō suru; riyō suru (*make use of*). **~ment** [imprúːvmənt] *n.* kairyō; shimpo (*progress*).

improvidence [imprɔ́vid(ə)ns] *n.* senken no mei no nai koto; rōhi (*waste*).

improvident [imprɔ́vid(ə)nt] *a.* ukatsuna; rōhi no. **~ly** [imprɔ́vidəntli] *ad.* ukatsuni.

improvisation [ìmprəvaizéiʃ(ə)n] *n.* sokkyōshi (*-poem*); sokkyō ensō; sokkyō-kyoku. [*ptu*).

improvise [ímprəvaiz] *v.* sokuseki ni tsukuru; utau (*improm-*

imprudence [imprúːd(ə)ns] *n.* ukatsu; fukinshin.

imprudent [imprúːd(ə)nt] *a.* ukatsuna; fukinshinna. **~ly** [imprúːdəntli] *ad.* ukatsuni; fukinshinni.

impudence [ímpjud(ə)ns] *n.* tetsumempi; namaiki; zūzūshi-[*sa.*

impudent [ímpjud(ə)nt] *a.* atsukamashii. **~ly** [ímpjud(ə)ntli] *ad.* atsukamashiku; zūzūshiku.

impugn [impjúːn] *v.* hinan suru.

impulse [ímpʌls] *n.* shigeki ; shōdō (*shock*).

impulsion [impʌlʃ(ə)n] *n.* shigeki ; shōdō ; ikioi (*impetus*).

impulsive [impʌlsiv] *a.* shōdōtekina. ~ly [impʌlsivli] *ad.* shōdōtekini.

impunity [impjú:niti] *n.* batsu (*punishment*) o manukareru koto ; buji. *with* ~, batsu o ukezu ni ; buji ni.

impure [impjúə] *a.* fuketsuna ; midarana (*obscene*). ~ly [impjúəli] *ad.* fuketsuni. ~ness [impjúənis] *n.* fuketsu.

impurity [impjúəriti] *n.* fuketsu ; fujun ; inwai (*obscenity*).

imputable [impjú:təbl] *a.* tenka shi uru (*to*) ; (tsumi nado o) nasuritsukeru koto ga dekiru. ⌈(*ascription*).

imputation [impju(:)téiʃ(ə)n] *n.* (tsumi o) owaseru koto ; tenka

imputative [impjú:tətiv] *a.* (tsumi o) kiserareta ; owasareta (*imputed*). ⌈ireru.

impute [impjú:t] *v.* kisuru ; owaseru (tsumi nado o) ; kazu ni

in [in] *prep.* ~ *the box*, hako ni. *go* ~ *the house*, ie ni hairu. *a dress* ~ *silk*, kinu no (de dekita) kimono. *act* ~ *self-defense*, jiko bōei no tame ni suru. *a book* ~ *American history* A. rekishi ni kansuru hon. ~ *the present time*, gendai ni oite wa. ~ *crossing street*, tōri o yokogiru toki. ~ *that*. sore de ; dakara. *n.* ~*s and outs*, yotō to yatō. ichibushijū.

in-¹ [in] *prefix.* de nai (*not*) ; ga nai no imi. *in-, un-* wa uchikeshi (*negative*) no imi ni yoku tsukau ; *incapable*, dekinai ; *inactive, active* de nai ; *inanimate*, kakki ga nai, *etc.*

in-² [in] *prefix.* naka ni ; *into* ; nado no imi : *indoor* ; *inland, etc.*

inability [ìnəbíliti] *n.* munō. ⌈(*accessible*).

inaccessibility [ínæksèsibíliti] *n.* chikazuki nikui koto. (*cf.*

inaccessible [ínəksésəbl] *a.* chikazuki nikui ; egatai.

inaccuracy [inækjúrəsi] *n.* fuseikaku ; zuzan (*cf. accuracy*).

inaccurate [inækjurit] *a.* fuseikakuna, zuzanna (*not accurate*). ~ly *ad.*

inaction [inækʃən] *n.* fukatsudō ; taida (*cf. action*).

inactive [inæktiv] *a.* katsudō shinai (*not active*) ; isogashiku nai. **ly** *ad.*

inactivity [ìnæktíviti] *n.* fukatsudō ; daki ; taida.

inadequacy [inædikwəsi] *n.* futekitō ; fujūbun (*cf. adequacy*).

inadequate [inædikwit] *a.* futekitōna ; fujūbunna. ~ly *ad.*

inadmissible [ìnədmísəbl] *a.* yurusarenu (*not admisible*).

inadvertence [ìnədvə́:t(ə)ns] *n.* fuchūi ; taida ; sosō ; teochi (*cf. advertence*). ⌜ly *ad.*

inadvertent [ìnədvə́:t(ə)nt] *a.* fuchūina ; taidana ; gūzen no. ~

inalienable [inéiljənəbl] *a.* yuzurenu (*not alienable*).

inane [inéin] *a.* mi no nai ; munashii ; orokana.

inanimate [inǽnimit] *a.* musei no ; kakki no nai (*cf. animate*).

inanition [ìnəníʃ(ə)n] *n.* genki no nai jōtai ; eiyō furyō.

inanity [ìnǽniti] *n.* kūkyo ; atama no warui koto ; bakageta mono.

inappeasable [ìnəpí:zəbl] *a.* nadame gatai ; yawaragerarenai (*cf. appeasable*). ⌜applicable).

inapplicable [inǽplikəbl] *a.* tekiyō dekinai ; ōyō shigatai (*cf.*

inappreciable [ìnəprí:ʃiəbl] *a.* hyōka shigatai (*not appreciable*) ; toru ni taranu.

inappropriate [ìnəpróupriit] *a.* futekitōna (*not appropriate*). ~ ly *ad.* ~ness *n.*

inapt [inǽpt] *a.* futekitōna (*not apt*) ; hetana. ~ly *ad.*

inaptitude [imǽptitju:d] *n.* futekitō ; futekinin.

inarticulate [ìnɑːtíkjulit] *a.* hatsuon fumeiryō no ; kuchi no kikenai. ~ly *ad.* ~ness *n.* hatsuon fumeiryō (*not articulate*).

inartistic [ìnɑːtístik] *a.* bijutsuteki de nai (*not artistic*).

inasmuch (as) [inəzmǽtʃ əz] ...de aru kara ; ...no yue ni.

inattention [ìnəténʃ(ə)n] *n.* fuchūi ; buaisō (*cf. attention*).

inattentive [ìnəténtiv] *a.* fuchūina ; buaisōna. ~ly *ad.*

inaudible [inɔ́:dəbl] *a.* kikitorenai. ~bly *ad.* kiki torenai yōni (*cf. audible*).

inaugural [inɔ́:gjur(ə)l] *a.* shūnin no ; kaishi no. ~ **address** shūnin aisatsu. ⌜o suru.

inaugurate [inɔ́:gjureit] *v.* shūnin-shiki o suru ; kaigyō-shiki

inauguration [inɔ̀:gjuréiʃ(ə)n] *n.* shūnin (kaigyō) shiki ; (shūnin, kaigyō, hirō, rakusei nado hajimeru toki no) shiki

inauguratory [inɔ́:gjureitəri] *a. inauguration* no. ⌜(ceremony).

inauspicious [ìnɔːspíʃəs] *a.* fukitsuna, warui koto no maebure no (*not auspicious*). ~ly *ad.*

inborn [ínbɔ́:n] *a.* tempu no ; umaretsuki no.

inbred [ímbréd] *a.* seirai no ; umaretsuki no.

inc. *inclusive ; inclosure ; incorporated ; increase,* nado no ryaku.

Inca [íŋkə] *u.* Inkajin (Perū no genjūmin) ; Inkazoku no ō.

incalculable [inkǽlkjuəbl] *a.* musū (no *not calculable*) ; ate ni naranai. ∼**bly** *ad.* kazoe kirenai hodo ōku.

incandescence [ìnkændésns] *n.* hakunetsu ; shakunetsu.

incandescent [ìnkændésnt] *a.* hakunetsu no ; makkani yake- [ta.

incantation [ìnkæntéiʃ(ə)n] *n.* majinai ; jumon.

incapability [inkèipəbíliti] *n.* dekinai koto (*cf. capability*).

incapable [inkéipəbl] *a.* dekinai. chikara ga nai : *He is* ∼ *of work in this factory,* kare wa kono kōba dewa yaku ni tatanai. shikaku ga nai : *A foreigner is* ∼ *of becoming president of the United States,* gaikokujin wa U.S. no daitōryō niwa narenai.

incapacitate [ìnkəpǽsiteit] *v.* shikaku, nōryoku o ubau (*disable*), dekinai yōni suru (*cf. capacitate*).

incapacity [ìnkəpǽsiti] *n.* nōryoku no nai, shikaku ga nai.

incarcerate [inkάːsəreit] *v.* rō ni ireru ; kankin suru.

incarceration [inkὰːsəréiʃ(ə)n] *n.* tōgoku ; kankin.

incarnate [inkάːneit] *v.* gutaika suru ; nikutai o ataeru. *a.* [inkάːnit] gonge no ; keshin no.

incarnation [ìnkɑːnéiʃ(ə)n] *n.* gonge ; gugentai.

incase [inkéis] *v.* hako ni ireru ; zembu tsutsumu. [∼**ly** *ad.*

incautious [inkɔ́ːʃəs] *a.* karuhazumina ; fuchūina (*not cautious*).

incendiarism [inséndjərizm] *n.* hōka ; sendō (*to incite*).

incendiary [inséndjəri] *a.* hōka no ; sendōtekina. ∼ *shell,* shōidan. *n.* hōka-hannin ; sendōsha.

incense [ínsens] *n.* kō ; kaori ; kōki. *v.* kō o taku (*burn incense*).

incense [inséns] *v.* gekkō saseru ; okoraseru.

incentive [inséntiv] *a.* shigeki suru ; yūhatsu suru. *n.* shigeki ;

inception [insépʃ(ə)n] *n.* hajime ; hottan ; hajimari. [yūin.

incertitude [insə́ːtitjuːd] *n.* fukakujitsu (*cf. certitude*).

incessant [insésnt] *a.* taema no nai (*cessation*). ∼**ly** *ad.* taezu.

incest [ínsest] *n.* kinshin sōkan.

inch [intʃ] *n.* inchi ; $\frac{1}{12}$ foot. =2.54 senchi mētoru) ; shōryō ; sukoshi ; ∼**worm** [-wəːm] *n.* shakutorimushi.

inchoate [inkóu)it] *a.* hajimatta bakari no (*not yet disciplined.*)

incidence [ínsid(ə)ns] *n.* dekigoto (tochū tsuketashi no) ; sashi-komi (hikari nado no).

incident [ínsid(ə)nt] *a.* okori yasui : *hardship* ～ *to the life of an explorer,* tankensha no seikatsu ni okoriyasui konnan. tōsha no ; nyūsha no. *n.* dekigoto ; jiken ; futai jiken.

incidental [ìnsidéntl] *a.* gūhatsu no ; futai no. ～**ly** *ad.* gūzen ni ; futaitekini.

incinerate [insínəreit] *v.* yaite hai ni suru.

incineration [insìnəréiʃ(ə)n] *n.* yaite hai ni suru koto.

incipience [insípiəns], ～**cy** [insípiənsi] *n.* hajimeru tokoro ;

incipient [insípiənt] *a.* hajime no ; shoki no.   ⌊hajimari.

incise [insáiz] *v.* kirikomu ; horikomu ; kizamu.

incision [insíʒ(ə)n] *n.* horikomi ; kirikuchi ; sekkai.

incisive [insáisiv] *a.* surudoi ; shinratsuna : ～ *criticism,* surudoi hihyō. ～**ly** *ad.* surudoku.

incisor [insáizə] *n.* (*teeth*) monshi ; maeba.

incitation [ìnsaitéiʃ(ə)n] *n.* gekirei ; shōrei.

incite [insáit] *v.* hagemasu ; gekirei suru. ～**ment** *n.* gekirei.

incivility [ìnsivíliti] *n.* busahō (*cf.* civility).

inclemency [inklémənsi] *n.* mujihi ; (tenki, kikō nado no) ge-kiretsu : *The* ～ *of weather kept us at home,* hidoi tenkō na no-de uchi ni ita (*cf.* clemency).   ⌈ciless)

inclement [inklémənt] *a.* mujihina ; kibishii ; ken'akuna. (*mer-*

inclinable [inkláinəbl] *a.* katamuki yasui ; keikō aru.

inclination [ìnklinéiʃ(ə)n] *n.* keikō ; seiheki ; shikō ; katamuki.

incline [inkláin] *v.* katamuku (-keru) ; keikō ga aru ; kono-mu. *n.* shamen ; kōbai ; saka.   ⌈*v.,* *n.* kakoi o suru (koto).

inclose, enclose [inklóuz] ; **inclosure, enclosure** [inklóuʒə].

include [inklú:d] *v.* fukumu ; hōgan suru.

inclusion [inklú:ʒən] *n.* naka ni fukumu koto ; naka ni fuku-mu mono ; hōgan ; gan'yū ; gan'yū-butsu.

inclusive [inklú:siv] *a.* fukumete ; sore mo irete (*of*). ～**ly** *ad.* minna issho ni komete.

incognito [inkógnitou] *ad.* dare tomo shirenai yōni shite ; oshinobi de ; tokumei de. *a.* bikō no ; tokumei no. *n.* (*pl.* **-ti** [-ti:]) bikō suru hito ; tokumei no hito.

incoherence [ìnko(u)híər(ə)ns] *n.* renraku no nai koto (*cf.* coherence).   ⌈～**ly** *ad.*

incoherent [ìnko(u)híər(ə)nt] *a.* renraku no nai ; mujun shita.

incombustibility [ìnkəmbʌ̀stəbíliti] *n.* funensei ; moenai seishitsu (*cf. combustibility*).

incombustible [ìnkəmbʌ́stəbl] *a.* moenai ; funensei no.

income [ínkəm] *n.* (kimatte hairu) shūnyū ; shotoku (*cf. in-²*).

incomer [ínkʌ̀mə] *n.* atarashiku kita hito ; shinnyūsha ; shimmai.

incommensurable [ìnkəménʃ(ə)rəbl] *a.* kurabe hakarenu ; hikaku dekinai ; fugôrina (*cf. commensurable*).

incommensurate, -able [ìnkəménʃurit] *a.* tsuriawanai. (*cf.
commensurable*).

incommode [ìnkəmóud] *v.* meiwaku o kakeru ; komaraseru
(*cf. commode*).

incommodious [ìnkəmóudiəs] *a.* fubenna (*not commodious*).

incommunicable [ìnkəmjú:nikəbl] *a.* tsutaerarenai (*cf. com-
municablity*).

incomparable [inkɔ́mp(ə)rəbl] *a.* kuraberarenai ; hikaku dekinai ; muhi no (*not comparable*). ～**bly** *ad.*.

incompatibility [ínkəmpæ̀təbíliti] *n.* ai-irenai koto ; mujun
(*compatible*).

incompatible [ìnkəmpǽtəbl] *a.* ai-irenai ; ryōritsu shi gatai ;
issho ni shigoto ga dekinai.

incompetence, -cy [inkɔ́mpit(ə)ns/si] *n.* futekitō ; mushikaku ;
munôryoku (*cf. competence*).   ⌜**ly** *ad.*

incompetent [inkɔ́mpit(ə)nt] *a.* futekitōna ; mushikaku no. ～

incomplete [ìnkəmplí:t] *a.* fukanzenna. ～**ly** *ad.* (*cf. complete*).

incompletion [ìnkəmplí:ʃən] *n.* fukanzen ; mikansei.

incomprehensible [ìnkɔ̀mprihéns(ə)bl] *a.* wakari nikui. ～**bly**
ad. wakari kanete.

inconceivable [ìnkənsí:vəbl] *a.* sōzō no dekinai (*not conceivable*) ; omoi mo yoranai. ～**bly** *ad.* sōzō dekinai hodo ni

inconclusive [ìnkənklú:siv] *a.* mikettei no ; kettei dekinai. ～
ly *ad.*

incongruity [inkɔŋgrú:iti] *n.* fuchōwa ; futsuriai (*cf. congruity*).

incongruous [inkɔ́ŋgruəs] *a.* chōwa shinai. ～**ly** *ad.*

inconsequence [inkɔ́nsikwəns] *n.* renraku no nai koto ; mujun
(*cf. consequence*).

inconsequent [inkɔ́nsikwənt], ～**ial** [inkɔ́nsikwénʃ(ə)l] *a.* tsujitsuma no awanai.

inconsiderable [ìnkənsídərəbl] *a.* toru ni tarinai. ～**bly** *ad.* (*cf. considerable*). ⌈*considerate*).

inconsiderate [ìnkənsídərit] *a.* omoiyari no nai. ～**ly** *ad.* (*cf.*

inconsistency [ìnkənsístənsi] *n.* mujun (*cf. consistency*).

inconsistent [ìnkənsístənt] *a.* itchi shinai ; mujun shita (*not consistent*).. ～**ly** *ad.*

inconsolable [ìnkənsóuləbl] *a.* nagusame enai ; akiramerare-nai (*cf. consolable*). ⌈～**ly** *ad.*

inconspicuous [ìnkənspíkjuəs] *a.* medatanai (*not conspicuous*).

inconstancy [ìnkɔ́nst(ə)nsi] *n.* kawari yasui koto ; uwaki ; gu-ratsuki (*cf. constancy*). ⌈～**ly** *ad.*

inconstant [ìnkɔ́nst(ə)nt] *a.* kawari yasui ; futeina (*not constant*)

incontestable [ìnkəntéstəbl] *a.* arasowarenai ; kakujitsuna ; (*not contestable*).

incontinence [ìnkɔ́ntinəns] *n.* fusessei ; inran ; (*cf. continence*).

incontinent [ìnkɔ́ntinənt] *a.* fusessei no ; inran no.

incontrovertible [ìnkɔntrəvə́ːtəbl] *a.* ronsō no yochi no nai ; meikakuna (*not controvertible*).

inconvenience [ìnkənvíːnjəns, -si], *n.*, *v.* fuben (ni suru) ; men-dō (ni suru) ; komaraseru ; (*not convenience.*) -**cy** [-si] *n.*

inconvenient [ìnkənvíːnjənt] *a.* fubenna ; tsugō no warui (*not convenient*). ～**ly** *ad.*

inconvertible [ìnkənvə́ːtibl] *a.* torikae no dekinai. *paper curency* fukan shihei (*cf. convertible*).

incorporate [inkɔ́ːp(ə)rit] *a.* hōjin-soshiki no. *v.* [inkɔ́ːpəreit] hōjinsoshiki ni (gattai) suru ; danketsu suru ; gōdō suru.

incorporation [inkɔ̀ːpəréiʃ(ə)n] *n.* gappei ; hōjin (soshiki) kai-sha. ⌈*real*).

incorporeal [ìnkɔːpóːriəl] *a.* jittai no nai ; mukei no (*not corpo-*

incorrect [ìnkərékt] *a.* tadashiku nai ; machigatta. ～**ly** *ad.* ～**ness** *n.* (*cf. correct*). ⌈*corrigible*).

incorrigible [inkɔ́ridʒəbl] *a.*, *n.* kyōsei shi gatai (hito) (*not*

incorruptibility [ínkərʌ̀ptibíliti] *n.* kusaranu koto ; seiren ; baishū dekinai hito (*cf. corruptiblty*). ⌈*dekinai*).

incorruptible [ìnkərʌ́ptəbl] *a.* fuhai shinai ; seirenna ; baishū

increase [ínkriːs] *n.* zōka ; zōshin. *v.* [inkríːs] zōka suru ; masu.

~ingly [inkrí:siŋli] ad. (cf. decrease).

incredible [inkrédəbl] a. shinjirarenai (not credible). ~bly ad.

incredulity [inkridjú:liti] n. yōi ni shinjinai koto (cf. credulity).

incredulous [inkrédjuləs] a. yōini shinjinai; utagai bukai; (not credulous).

increment [ínkrimənt] n. zōdai; zōka; fueru koto.

incriminate [inkrímineit] v. tsumi o kiseru; tsumi ni otoshi ireru. (cf. criminate).　　　　　　　　　　　　　　┌meru.

incrust [inkrΛst] v. kara ni hairu; zōgan o hodokosu; chiriba-
incrustation [ìnkrΛstéiʃən] n. kawa de ōu koto; hikaku; ke-shō-bari (as marble coating).

incubate [ínkjubeit] v. (tori ga) su ni tsuku (sit on eggs).

incubation [ìnkjubéiʃən] n. su ni tsuku koto.

incubator [ínkjubeitə] n. furanki.

incubus n. [íŋkjubəs] (pl. -es [-siz], -bi [b-ai]). yume (dream) ni haitte (coming) kuru akuma (evil spirit).

inculcate [ínkΛlkeit] v. oshie-komu (implant).　　┌repetition).

inculcation [inkΛlkéiʃ(ə)n] n. oshie-komu koto (impressing by
inculpate [ínkΛlpeit] v. hinan suru; tsumi ga aru to suru.

incumbency [inkΛmbənsi] n. zaishoku; zaishoku no kikan.

incumbent [inkΛmbənt] n. bokushi; jūshoku. a. gimu de(aru) (on, upon); gimu to shite kakaru (on, upon); It is ~ on a judge to be just, tadashiku aru to iu koto wa saibankan no gimu de aru.

incur [inkɔ́:] v. kōmuru; ukeru; maneku; the hunter ~red a great danger in killing a tigar, karyūdo wa sono tora o korosu no ni hijōna kiken ni atta.

incurable [inkjúərəbl] a. naosu koto no dekinai; naoranai.

incursion [inkɔ́:ʃ(ə)n] n. shinnyū; oshiiri; fuji no shūgeki (sudden attack).

indebted [indétid] a. shakkin ga aru; ongi ga aru (ongi no debt); on o ukete iru.

indecency [indí:snsi] n. busahō; waisetsu (lack of decency).

indecent [indí:sənt] a. mittomo nai; hiwaina. ~ly ad.

indecision [ìndisíȝ(ə)n] n. fu-ketsudan; shunjun; ketsudan no nai koto; (lack of decision) yūjūfudan.

indecisive [ìndisáisiv] a. kettei shinai; yūjūfudan no (waving).

~ly *ad.* ⌐*able*).

indeclinable [ìndikláinəbl] *a.* gobi katsuyō no nai; (*not declin-*

indecorous [indékərəs/indikɔ́:rəs] *a.* busahōna (*not decorous*).

indecorum [indikɔ́:rəm] *n.* busahō (*lack of decorum*).

indeed [indí:d] *ad.* jitsu ni. *inter.* hontō ni! sō kai? masaka!

indefatigability [ìndifætigəbíliti] *n.* futō-fukutsu.

indefatigable [indifǽtigəbl] *a.* futō no; fukutsu no.

indefeasible [indifí:zəbl] *a.* haki dekinai; mukō ni shi (*annul*) gatai (*difficult to*). ⌐*sible*).

indefensible [indifénsəbl] *a.* bōgyo (bengo) dekinai. (*cf. defen-*

indefinable [indifáinəbl] *a.* sadamerarenu; teigi dekinai (*not to be defined*).

indefinite [indéfinit] *a.* futei no; hakkiri shinai. ~ly *ad.*

indelible [indélibl] *a.* kesarenai; nuguigatai. ⌐*licacy*).

indelicacy [indélikəsi] *n.* gehin; waisetsu; busahō (*lack of de-*

indelicate [indélikit] *a.* gehinna; midarana. ~ly *ad.*

indemnification [indèmnifikéiʃən] *n.* baishō (*compensation*).

indemnify [indémnifai] *v.* tsugunau; baishō suru.

indemnity [indémniti] *n.* baishō; songai baishō; baishōkin.

indent [indént] *v.* gizagiza o tsukeru; keiyakusho o irete hōkō saseru. *paragraph* no hajime o chotto hikkomeru. ~**ed** [-id] *a.* gizagiza no aru; dekoboko no aru.

indentation [ìndentéiʃ(ə)n] *n.* kizamime; gizagiza; hekomi.

indenture [indéntʃə] *n.* keiyakusho o ireta neṇikibōkō. *v.* keiyakusho o irete hōkō saseru.

independence [ìndipéndəns] *n.* dokuritsu. **I.Day** (*Am.*) Dokuritsu Kinembi (7 gatsu 4 ka). ⌐*shite.*

independent [ìndipéndənt] *a.* dokuritsu no. ~ly *ad.* dokuritsu

indescribable [ìndiskráibəbl] *a.* meijō dekinai; fude (*pen*) ya kotoba dewa arawasenai. ~**bly** *ad.* iu ni iwarenu hodo ni.

indestructible [ìndistrʌ́kt(ə)bl] *a.* kowasarenai; fumetsu no.

indeterminable [inditɔ́:minəbl] *a.* kettei (kakutei) dekinai; kimerarenai.

indeterminate [ìnditɔ́:minit] *a.* futashikana. ~ly *ad.*

indetermination [ìnditɔ̀:minéiʃ ơn] *n.* fuketsudan; yūjū-fudan.

index [índeks] *n.* (*pl.* -xes [-ksi:z], -ces [-i:si:z]) sakuin; hitosashi-yubi; shisū; shishin; shihyō. *v.* sakuin o tsukeru. ~

finger [-fiŋgə] *n.* hitosashi-yubi.

Indian [índjən/-diən] *a.* Indo no ; Higashi Indo no ; Amerika dojin no. ~ *corn*, tōmorokoshi. ~ *summer*, (hokubei no) ban-shū no jikō ; koharu. *n.* Indojin ; higashi-Indojin ; Amerika dojin.

India-rubber [índjərʌ́bə] *n.* dansei gomu.

indicate [índikeit] *v.* sashi shimesu ; kantanni noberu.

indication [ìndikéiʃən] *n.* shiji ; chōkō ; kizashi ; yōsu.

indicative [indíkətiv] *a.* shiji suru ; (*gram.*) jojutsuhō no.

indicator [índikeitə] *n.* sashishimesu hito (mono).

indict [indáit] *v.* (*leg.*) kiso suru ; kokuhatsu suru. ~**ment** *n.* kiso ; kisojō.

indifference [indífərəns] *n.* mukankei ; mutonjaku ; reitan.

indifferent [indífərənt] *a.* dō demo yoi ; kanshin o motanai ; katayoranai ; mutonjakuna ; yosoyososhii. ~**ly** *ad.*

indigence [índidʒəns] *n.* bimbō ; kyūbō.

indigenous [indídʒinəs] *a.* (sono tochi) koyū no ; shizen no.

indigent [índidʒənt] *a.* mazushii ; bimbōna.

indigestible [ìndidʒést(ə)bl] *a.* fushōka no ; shōka shi nikui.

indigestion [ìndidʒéstʃən] *n.* fushōka ; shōka furyō (*cf. diges-*

indignant [indígnənt] *a.* fungai shiteiru. ~**ly** *ad.*   [*tion.*

indignation [ìndignéiʃən] *n.* fungai ; seigi no ikidōri.

indignity [indígniti] *n.* bujoku ; ken' i o kizutsukeru koto.

indigo [índigou] *n.* ai ; aiiro.

indirect [ìndirékt/-dai-] *a.* massugu de nai ; kansetsu no, tō-mawashi no. (*gram.*) ~ *object* (*dative case*) ; "ni-" kaku no mokutekigo. ~**ly** *ad.*

indirection [ìndirékʃən] *n.* kansetsuteki shudan ; fusei shu-

indiscernible [ìndisə́:nibl] *a.* hakkiri miwake nikui.   [dan.

indiscreet [ìndiskrí:t] *a.* fumbetsu no nai ; fukinshinna (*not discreet*). ~**ly** *ad.*

indiscretion [ìndiskréʃən] *n.* mufumbetsu ; fukinshin ; chūi no tarinai koto (himitsu nado o sugu hakken sareru).

indiscriminate [ìndiskríminit] *a.* sabetsu no nai : ~ *in one's friendships*, kōsai ga musabetsuna ; yatarana ; ~ *slaughter*, mechakuchana gyakusatsu. ~**ly** *ad.*

indiscrimination [índiskriminéiʃən] *n.* musabetsu ; nani mo ka mo gochagocha.

indispensable [ìndispénsəbl] *a.* hitsuyōna; nakutewa naranai; *air is ~ to life*, kūki wa seikatsu ni nakute wa naranai. ~**bly** *ad.* kanarazu; zehitomo.

indispose [ìndispóuz] *v.* futekitōni suru; suru ki o nakusaseru. ~**d** *a.* kagen ga warui; guai ga warui.

indisposition [ìndispəzíʃ(ə)n] *n.* fukai; chotto shita fukagen; iyake; ken'o.

indisputable [ìndispjú:təbl] *a.* giron no yochi ga nai; meihakuna. ~**bly** *ad.* meimei hakuhaku ni.

indissoluble [ìndisóljubl] *a.* yōkai shi gatai; nagatsuzuki suru.

indistinct [ìndistíŋkt] *a.* hakkiri shinai. ~**ly** *ad.* bon'yari to.

indistinguishable [ìndistíŋgwiʃəbl] *a.* kubetsu no tsukanai.

indite [indáit] *v.* tsukuru; kaku. ~**ment** *n.* sakubun; chosaku.

individual [ìndivídjuəl] *a.* koko no; dokuji no. *n.* kojin; kotai. ~**ism** *n.* kojinshugi. ~**ly** *ad.* koko ni; sorezore; bekko ni.

individuality [ìndivìdjuǽliti] *n.* kosei; meimei no mochimae.

individualize [ìndivídjuəlaiz] *v.* kosei o ataeru; koko ni kubetsu suru.

indivisible [ìndivízəbl] *a.* wari kirenai (*not divisible*).

Indo-China [índoutʃáinə] *n.* Indo-Shina.

indoctrinate [indóktrineit] *v.* oshiekomu; oshieru.

Indo-European [índoujùərəpí(:)ən] *a.* Indo-Yōroppa gozoku

indolence [índələns] *n.* taida; namake. ⌊no.

indolent [índələnt] *a.* taidana; namaketa. ~**ly** *ad.*

indomitable [indómitəbl] *a.* fukutsuna; kachiki no tsuyoi. ~ *spirit*, makeji-damashiino. ⌈ajin.

Indonesian [indouni:ʃən/-ʒən] *a.* Indoneshia no. *n.* Indoneshi-

indoor [índɔ:] *a.* shitsunai no; okunai no. ~**s** [índɔ́:z/-dɔ́:z] *ad.* okunai ni; *keep indoors*, gaishutsu shinai.

indorse [indɔ́:s] *v.* =**endorse**. ~**ment** *n.* =**endorsement**.

indorsee [indɔ:síː] *n.* hi-uragakinin; uragaki shōsho o yuzuri-uketa hito.

indubitable [indjú:bitəbl] *a.* utagai nai; akirakana. ~**bly** *ad.*

induce [indjú:s] *v.* sasou; yūdō suru. ~**d current** *n.* yūdō denryū. ~**ment** *n.* yūdō; kan'yū; yūin; dōki.

induct [indʌ́kt] *v.* hikiireru; michibiku; shūshoku saseru.

induction [indʌkʃ(ə)n] *n.* yūdō; (*elec.*) kannō; (*log.*) kinōhō. ~ **coil** [-kɔil] *n.* yūdōsen no wa; kannō koiru.

inductive [indʌktiv] *a.* yūdō-suru; yūdōsei no; kinōteki no.

indue [indjú:], **endue** *v.* chikara, sainō nado ga ataerareru.

indulge [indʌldʒ] *v.* kimamani saseru; *to* ~ *a sick person*, byōnin o kimama ni saseru. fukeru (*in*). *to* ~ *in tobacco*, tabako ni me ga nai. *He* ~*d our desire*, kare wa wareware no netsubō o kiite kureta. ⌐zai.

indulgence [indʌldʒ(ə)ns] *n.* kimama; tandeki; onkei; men-

indulgent [indʌldʒ(ə)nt] *a.* amayakasu; kandaina. *The* ~ *mother brought her boy everything he wanted*, amai okāsan wa kodomo ni hoshii mono wa nan demo ataeta. ~**ly** *ad.*

indurate [indjuəreit] *v.* gōjōni suru (naru)

industrial [indʌstriəl] *a.* kōgyō no; sangyō no; jitsugyō no. ~**ism** *n.* kōgyōshugi; kōgyō netsu. ~**ist** *n.* jitsugyōka. ~**ization** [indʌstriəlizéiʃ(ə)n] *n.* kōgyōka seisaku. ~**ize** [indʌstriəlaiz] *v.* kōgyōka suru.

industrious [indʌstriəs] *a.* kimbenna. ~**ly** *ad.*

industry [índəstri] *n.* kimben; kōgyō; sangyō.

indwell [índwél] *v.* uchi ni sumu; yadoru; uchi ni komoru.

inebriate [iní:brieit] *v.* yowaseru. [iní:briit] *a.* yotta. *n.* nondakure; seishinteki tōsui.

inebriety [ini(:)bráiəti], **inebriation** [inì:briéiʃən] *n.* meitei.

ineffable [inéfəbl] *a.* iiarawashi enai; iu ni iwarenu. ~**bly** *ad.*

ineffaceable [ìniféisəbl] *a.* keshi nikui.

ineffective [ìniféktiv] *a.* kitai shita kōka no nai; muryokuna (*not effective*). ~**ly** *ad.*

ineffectual [ìniféktjuəl] *a.* muekina; kōka no nai (*cf. effectual*).

inefficacious [inefikéiʃəs] *a.* kitai shita kōryoku no nai; kikime no nai. (*cf. efficacious*). ⌐ficient). ~**ly** *ad.*

inefficient [ìnifíʃ(ə)nt] *a.* kōryoku no nai; munōna. (*not efficient*).

inelastic [ìniléstik/-lá:s-] *a.* danryoku no nai (*not elastic*).

inelegant [inéligənt] *a.* yūbi de nai; bufūryūna. (*not elegant*).

ineligibility [ìnèlidʒəbíliti] *n.* mushikaku (*cf. eligibility*).

ineligible [inélidʒ(ə)bl] *a.* shikaku no nai.

ineloquent [inéləkwənt] *a.* totsubenna (*not eloquent*).

ineluctable [ìnilʌktəbl] *a.* nigerarenai. ~**bly** *ad.* ~**bility** [inilàktəbíliti] *n.* nigeru koto fukanō.

inept [inépt] *a.* futekitōna ; orokana. ～**ly** *ad.*

ineptitude [inéptitju:d] *n.* futekitō ; gudon (futekitōna koto).

inequality [ìni(:)kwóliti] *n.* fubyōdō ; fuheikin ; dekoboko.

inequitable [inékwitəbl] *a.* fukōheina ; fukōsei no (*cf. equita-*

inequity [inékwiti] *n.* fukōsei ; fukōhei (*cf. equity*). ⌊*ble*).

ineradicable [ìnirǽdikəbl] *a.* konzetsu shinikui (*cf. eradicable*).

inert [inə́:t] *a.* jidōryoku no nai ; katsudōryoku no nai ; nibui ; bushōna. ～**ly** *ad.*

inertia [inə́:ʃjə] *n.* (*phys.*) dasei.

inestimable [inéstiməbl] *a.* hyōka dekinai ; konoue mo naku tōtoi. ～**bly** *ad.* (*cf. estimable ; priceless*). ⌈ranu. ～**bly** *ad.*

inevitable [inévitəbl] *a.* sakerarenai (*not eviaded*) ; noppikina-

inexact [ìnigzǽkt] *a.* fuseikakuna (*not exact*). ～**ly** *ad.* ～**ness** *n.*.

inexcusable [ìnikskjú:zəbl] *a.* iiwake no tatanai ; kannin naranu (*cf. excusable*).

inexhaustible [inigzɔ́:stəbl] *a.* tsukiru koto no nai ; (*not exhaustible*). mujinzō no.

inexorable [inéks(ə)rəbl] *a.* gan to shite ugokanai ; mujōna.

inexpedient [ìnikspí:djənt] *a.* fubenna ; futokusaku no (*not expedient*).

inexpensive [ìnikspénsiv] *a.* hiyō no kakaranai (*cf. expensive*).

inexperience [ìnikspíəriəns] *n.* mukeiken ; mijuku. ～**d** [-t] *a.* mijukuna.

inexpert [ìnekspə́:t] *a.* mijukuna ; hetana (*cf. expert*).

inexpiable [inékspiəbl] *a.* tsugunawarenai. *murder is an ～ crime*, satsujin wa tsugunae nai hanzai da (*not expiable*).

inexplicable [inéksplikəbl] *a.* setsumei dekinai (*cf. explicable*).

inexpressible [ìniksprésəbl] *a.* iiarawasenai (*cf. expressible*).

inextinguishable [ìnikstíŋgwiʃəbl] *a.* kesu koto no dekinai (*cf. extinguishable*).

inextricable [inékstrikəbl] *a.* tokenai ; hodokenai ; kaiketsu dekinai (*cf. extricable*).

infallibility [infæ̀ləbíliti] *n.* gobyū zetsumu ; machigai ga hitotsu mo nai koto.

infallible [infǽləbl] *a.* machigai ga nai (*not fallible*). ～**bly** *ad.*

infamous [ínfəməs] *a.* akumei no takai ; gokuaku no.

infamy [ínfəmi] *n.* omei ; shūbun ; akumei.

infancy [ínfənsi] *n.* akambojidai ; kodomojidai ; miseinen.

infant [ínfənt] *n.* yōji ; miseinensha. *a.* yōji no.

infanticide [infǽntisaid] *n.* akambogoroshi.

infantile [ínfəntail], **infantine** [ínfəntain] *a.* yōchina.

infantry [ínf(ə)ntri] *n.* hohei ; hoheitai.

infatuate [infǽtjueit] *v.* mayowasu ; netchū saseru.

infatuation [infæ̀tjuéiʃən] *n.* uchōten ; wakudeki ; tandeki.

infect [infékt] *v.* kansen saseru (suru).

infection [infékʃ(ə)n] *n.* densen ; densembyō ; aku-eikyō.

infectious [infékʃəs], **infective** [inféktiv] *a.* densensei no ; utsuri yasui.

infelicitous [ìnfilísitəs] *a.* futekitōna ; shiawase de nai.

infelicity [ìnfilísiti] *n.* fukō ; futekitō ; futekitōna mono.

infer [infə́ː] *v.* suiron suru. ∼**able** *a.* suiron dekiru (*from*).

inference [ínf(ə)r(ə)ns] *n.* suiron ; ketsuron.

inferential [ìnfərénʃ(ə)l] *a.* suiron no ; suiri no. ∼**ly** *ad.*

inferior [infíəriə] *a.* katō no ; warui hō no ; otoru. *n.* meshita no mono.   ⌈ka.

inferiority [infìərióriti] *n.* shitsu no ototte iru koto ; toshiwa-

infernal [infə́ːn(ə)l] *a.* jigoku no ; gokuaku hidō no.

inferno [infə́ːnou] *n.* jigoku ; jigoku no yōna basho. ⌈meru.

infest [infést] *v.* (warui mono ga) habikoru ; arasu ; kurushi-

infidel [ínfid(ə)l] *a.* mushinkō no ; ikyōto no. *n.* shinkō no nai hito ; ikyōto.

infidelity [ìnfidéliti/-fai-] *n.* fushinjin ; chūjitsu de nai ; chigau shinkō no mono.

infield [ínfiːld] *n.* (*base*) naiya. ∼**er** *n.* naiyashu.

infiltrate [ínfiltreit] *v.* shimikomu (-maseru) ; mogurikomu.

infinite [ínfinit] *a.* mugen no ; musū no ; hijōna. *n.* mugen ; (*math.*) mugendai. ∼**ly** *ad.* mugenni ; ōini.

infinitesimal [ìnfinitésim(ə)l] *a.* mugen ni chiisai ; kyokushō (mugen-shō).

infinitive [infínitiv] *a.*, *n.* (*gram.*) futeishi (no). *n.* (*gram.*) futeihō. *split* ∼ (*gram.*) bunri futeishi.   ⌈mugendai.

infinitude [infínitjuːd], **infinity** [infíniti] *n.* mugen ; (*math.*)

infirm [infə́ːm] *a.* yowai ; yūjūfudan no (*irresolute*). ∼**ly** *ad.*

yowayowashiku.

infirmary [infɔ́:məri] *n.* byōin; fuzoku byōin.

infirmity [infɔ́:miti] *n.* byōjaku; dōtokuteki fukenzen.

infix [infíks] *v.* naka ni sashikomu. *n.* ichigo (*one word*) no nakani ireru " on " ya " onsetsu."

inflame [infléim] *v.* moeru; moyasu; moetataseru.

inflammable [inflǽməbl] *a.* moeyasui; kōfunshiyasui.

inflammation [ìnfləméiʃ(ə)n] *n.* nenshō; (*med.*) enshō.

inflammatory [inflǽmət(ə)ri] *a.* enshōsei no; sendōteki no.

inflate [infléit] *v.* bōchō saseru; tokui garaseru.

inflation [infléiʃ(ə)n] *n.* bōchō; tokui; tsūka bōchō.

inflect [inflékt] *v.* mageru; (*gram.*) (gokei o) henkasasaseru, henka suru; katsuyō suru. (*cf. conjugation*).

inflection [inflékʃ(ə)n] *n.* kukkyoku; yokuyō; (*gram.*) gobi henka. ∼**al** *a.* kukkyoku no; (*gram.*) gobihenka no.

inflective [infléktiv] *a.* (*gram.*) gobihenka no aru.

inflexibility [infleks(ə)bìliti] *n.* magerarenai koto; hirumanai koto (*cf. flexiblity*). ⌈renai.

inflexible [infléksəbl/-sib-] *ad.* gankona; fukutsu no; magera-

inflexibly [infléks(ə)bli] *a.* magerarenai yōni; hirumanai de.

inflexion [inflékʃ(ə)n] *n.* =**inflection**.

inflict [inflíkt] *v.* (dageki, batsu nado o) ataeru; kasuru (batsu nado o).

infliction [inflíkʃ(ə)n] *n.* (batsu nado o) ataeru koto; shobatsu.

inflorescence [ìnflɔ:résns] *n.* kaika; hana no kajo; hana.

influence [ínfluəns] *n.* eikyō; eikyō o oyobosu hito (mono). *v.* eikyō o oyobosu.

influential [ìnfluénʃ(ə)l] *a.* eikyō o oyobosu; yūryokuna.

influenza [ìnfluénzə] *n.* (*med.*) ryūkōsei kambō.

influx [ínflʌks] *n.* nagarekomi (mizu nado).

infold [infóuld] *v.* tsutsumu; tsutsumikomu; idaku.

inform [infɔ́:m] *v.* shiraseru; kakkizukeru; kokuhatsu suru. ∼**ant** *n.* hōkokusha. ∼**er** *n.* kokuhatsusha.

informal [infɔ́:m(ə)l] *a.* seishiki de nai; uchiwa no.

informality [ìnfɔ:mǽliti] *n.* ryakushiki.

information [ìnfəméiʃən] *n.* tsūchi; kokuhatsu; jōhō.

infraction [infrǽkʃ(ə)n] *n.* hansoku; hōritsu ihan.

infrared [ínfrəréd] *a.* (*phys.*) sekigaisen no. ～**ray** *n.* sekigaisen.

infrequent [infrí:kwənt] *a.* marena ; tama no (*not frequent*). ～**ly** *ad.* mareni.

infringe [infríndʒ] *v.* yaburu ; shingai suru (chosakuken nado o). ～**ment** *n.* ihan ; shingai.

infuriate [infjúərieit] *v.* gekido saseru ; kankanni okoraseru.

infuse [infjú:z] *v.* sosogu ; furidasu ; fukikomu : *The captain ～d his own courage into his soldiers*, taii wa jibun no yūki o sono hei tachi ni tsugikonda.

infusible [infjú:zəbl] *a.* sosogiuru ; yōkaishinai.

infusion [infjú:ʒ(ə)n] *n.* chūnyū ; senjishiru.

ingenious [indʒí:njəs] *a.* dokusōtekina ; jōzuna ; hatsumei no

ingenue [ǽnʒenjú:] *n.* (*Fr.*) mujakina shōjo. ⌊sai aru.

ingenuity [indʒinjú(:)iti] *n.* hatsumei no sai ; kiyō ; kōmyō.

ingenuous [indʒénjuəs] *a.* sotchokuna ; mujakina ; kazarikke no nai. ～**ly** *ad.* sotchokuni.

inglorious [ingló:riəs] *a.* fumeiyona ; yo ni kikoenai.

ingot [íŋgət] *n.* katamari (kin ; -gin ; nado no). *gold* ～, kinkai.

ingraft [ingrá:ft] *v.* tsugiho suru.

ingrain [ingréin] *v.* someru ; *a.* [íngrein] kizome no ; fukaku-shimikonda. ～**ed** [-d] *a.* nebukai ; umaretsuita.

ingrate [ingréit] *n.* on o shiranai hito. *a.* on o shiranai.

ingratiate [ingréiʃieit] *v.* ki ni iru yōni suru ; no kōi o eru : ～ *oneself with*, ni toriiru.

ingratitude [ingrǽtitju:di] *n.* on o shiranai koto ; bōon.

ingredient [ingrí:djənt] *n.* seibun ; yōso.

ingress [íngres] *n.* shinnyū ; irikuchi ; nyūjō no kenri.

ingulf [ingʌ́lf] *v.* =**engulf.**

inhabit [inhǽbit] *v.* sumu ; sonzai suru. ～**able** *a.* sumai ni te-kisuru. ～**ant** *n.* jūnin ; jūmin.

inhabitation [inhæbitéiʃ(ə)n] *n.* kyojū ; jūkyo ; jūsho.

inhalation [in(h)əléiʃ(ə)n] *n.* kyūnyū ; kyūnyūbutsu.

inhale [inhéil] *v.* kyūnyū suru. ～**r** *n.* kyūnyūsha ; kyūnyūki.

inharmonious [ìnhɑːmóunjəs/-niəs] *a.* fuchōwana ; fuwa no (*not harmonious*).

inhere [inhíə] *v.* umaretsuki motte iru. ⌈iru kosei).

inherence [inhíər(ə)ns] *n.* koyū ; tempu (umaretsuki motte

inherent [inhíər(ə)nt] *a.* koyū no; umaretsuki no.

inherit [inhérit] *v.* sōzoku suru; iden suru. ~**able** *a.* sōzoku dekiru; iden suru. ~**ance** [-əns] *n.* sōzoku; sōzokuzaisan; iden. ~ **or** *n.* sōzokunin.

inhibit [inhíbit] *v.* kinshi suru; osaeru : *the soldier's sense of duty ~ed his impulse to run away*, sono heishi no gimukan ga ni-gedashitai shōdō o osaeta. ⌈buaisōni.

inhospitable [inhóspitəbl] *a.* buaisōna; arehateta; ~**bly** *ad.*

inhospitality [inhòspitǽliti] *n.* buaisō; reigū.

inhuman [inhjú:mən] *a.* funinjōna; zanninna.

inhumanity [ìnhju(:)mǽniti] *n.* funinjō; zannin.

inimical [inímik(ə)l] *a.* tekii no aru; gaii no aru.

inimitable [inímitəbl] *a.* mane no dekinai (*not imitable*); murui ⌊no

iniquitous [iníkwitəs] *a.* fuseina; jaakuna.

iniquity [iníkwiti] *n.* fusei; jaaku.

initial [iníʃ(ə)l] *a.* hajime no. *n.* kashiramoji. ~**ly** *ad.* hajimeni.

initiate [iníʃieit] *v.* hajimeru; kanyū saseru; tehodoki suru.

initiation [iníʃiéiʃ(ə)n] *n.* kaishi; nyūkai; nyūkai(nyūsha)-shiki.

initiative [iníʃiətiv/-ʃjə-] *a.* hajime no. *n.* dai ippo; chakushu; hatsugiken : *on one's own* ~, jihatsutekini. *on the* ~ *of*, no ha-tsui de. *take the* ~, sossen suru.

initiatory [iníʃiət(ə)ri/-ʃjə-] *a.* hajime no.

inject [indʒékt] *v.* chūsha suru. ~**or** *n.* chūshaki.

injection [indʒékʃ(ə)n] *n.* chūsha; chūshaeki.

injudicious [indʒu(:)díʃəs] *a.* kemmei de nai; shiryo no nai.

injunction [indʒʌ́n(k)ʃ(ə)n] *n.* meirei; kinshimeirei (hōritsute-kini ataerareta).

injure [índʒə] *v.* gaisuru; kison suru. ⌈ni; fui ni.

injurious [indʒúəriəs] *a.* gai ni naru; yūgaina. ~**ly** *ad.* fuho

injury [índʒ(ə)ri] *n.* songai; shōgai; bujoku; kenri shingai.

injustice [indʒʌ́stis] *n.* fusei; tadashiku nai koto (okonai).

ink [iŋk] *n.* inki. *v.* inki de kaku; yogosu. ~**stand** [-stænd] *n.* inki tsubo. ~**y** *a.* inki no; makkurona.

inkling [íŋkliŋ] *n.* anji; usuusu shitteiru koto (*vague notion*).

inlaid [ínléid] *a.* zōgan no; chiribameta.

inland [ínlənd/ínlænd] *n.* naichi; okuchi. *a.* naichi no; kokunai no. ～ *sea*, naikai. *ad.* naichi (okuchi) ni.

inlay [ínléi] *v.* chiribameru; hamekomu. *n.* zōgan. ～**ing** *n.* zōgan; jūten.

inlet [ínlet] *n.* irie; iriguchi; zōganbutsu.

inmate [ínmeit] *n.* dōkyonin; (rōya, byōin, yōikuin nado ni) shūyō sareta hito. 　　　　　　　　　　⌈no negai.

inmost [ínmoust] *a.* ichiban oku no : ～ *desire*, kokoro no oku

inn [in] *n.* yadoya. ～**keeper** *n.* yadoya no shujin.

innate [ínéit] *a.* umaretsuki no; koyū no. ～**ly** *ad.* umaretsuki.
　～ *talent for drawing*, e no sainō.

inner [ínə] *a.* naibu no; naishin no : *a person's* ～ *life*, hito no naibu seikatsu. ～**most** [-moust] *a.* ichiban oku no.

inning [íniŋ] *n.* (*baseball*) dagekiban, inningu; kai ; (*Brit. pl.*) zaishoku-kikan.

innocence [ínəs(ə)ns] *n.* mujaki ; tsumi ya aku o shiranai koto.

innocent [ínəs(ə)nt] *a.* mujakina ; keppakuna. *n.* mujakina koto ; ohitoyoshi. ～**ly** *ad.* tsumi naku.

innocuous [inókjuəs] *a.* mugai no. ～**ly** *ad.* mugai ni.

innovate [ínouveit] *v.* isshin suru; kaikaku suru.

innovation [inovéiʃən] *n.* kakushin; kaishin; shinkufū.

innovator [ínouveitə] *n.* kakushinsha.

innoxious [inókʃəs] *a.* gai no nai.

innuendo [inju(:)éndou] *n.* fūshi, atekosuri : *scandal by* ～ *against someone*, aru hito no akuhyō o fūshitekini tateru.

innumerable [injú:m(ə)rəbl] *a.* musū no; kanjō ni naranu hodo ōku no.

inoculate [inókjuleit] *v.* tsugiki suru; (shisō nado o) uetsukeru; yobōchūsha o suru.

inoculation [inɔkjuléiʃən] *n.* shutō; tsugiki.

inodorous [inóudərəs] *a.* sukoshi mo kusaku nai.

inoffensive [inəfénsiv] *a.* gai ni naranai; waruge no nai.

inoperative [inópərətiv] *a.* yaku ni tatanai. 　　　　　⌈ashiku.

inopportune [inɔpətjú:n/inópətju:n] *a.* ainiku no. ～**ly** *ad.* ori-

inordinate [inó:dinit] *a.* futsū de nai; kado no; hōgaina. ～**ly** *ad.* tohō mo naku. 　　　　　　　　　　⌈muki kagaku.

inorganic [ìnɔ:gǽnik] *a.* muki no. ～ *chemistry* [kémistri]

inpatient [ínpeiʃənt] *n.* nyūin kanja (opp. *outpatient*.

inquest [ínkwest] *n.* jimmon; shinri.

inquietude [inkwáiətju:d] *n.* fuan; jitto shite irarenai (*restlessness*).

inquire, en- [inkwáiə] *v.* tazuneru; chōsa suru. ~ *after*, ampi o tou. ~ *for*, menkai o motomeru.

inquiring [inkwáiəriŋ] *a.* sensakuzukina; tazuneru; kegen sōna. ~**ly** *ad.* fushin sōni.

inquiry [inkwáiəri] *n.* shitsumon; shōkai; chōsa. *court of* ~, samon kaigi. ~ *agency*, kōshinjo. ~ *office*, uketsuke.

inquisition [inkwizíʃən] *n.* chōsa; jimmon; (*the I-*) shūkyō saibansho.

inquisitive [inkwízitiv] *a.* kikitagaru; shiritagaru. ~**ly** *ad.* (nehori hahori) kiki tagaru.

inquisitor [inkwízitə] *n.* jimmonsha; (*I-*) shūkyō saibankan.

inquisitorial [inkwizitó:riəl] *a.* (*Roman Catholic Church* no) shūkyō saibankan no yōna; urusaku kiku.

inroad [ínroud] *n.* shinnyū. shingai : *expenses* ~ *upon savings*, shishutsu ga chokin ni kuikomu.

inrush [ínrʌʃ] *n.* totsunyū. rannyū.

insane [inséin] *a.* hakkyō shita; hijōshikina. ~**ly** *ad.* kyōki no yōni. 〔*sanitary*〕.

insanitary [insǽnitəri] *a.* kenkō ni yoku nai; hieiseiteki (*not*

insanity [insǽniti] *n.* hakkyō.

insatiable [inséiʃəbl] *a.* manzoku shinai; don'yokuna. ~**bly** *ad.* akukoto naku; yokufukaku; don'yokuni.

insatiate [inséiʃiit] *a.* manzoku o shiranai; don'yokuna.

inscribe [inskráib] *v.* kizamu; kaku; tōroku suru; (*math.*) nai-

inscription [inskrípʃən] *n.* mei; hibun. Lsetsu saseru.

inscrutable [inskrú:təbl] *a.* hakarishirenai; fushigina; etai tsumaranu yatsu. Lno shirenai.

insect [ínsekt] *n.* konchū; tsumaranu yatsu. Lno shirenai.

insecticide [inséktisaid] *n.* satchūzai.

insectivorous [insektívərəs] *a.* mushirui o taberu.

insecure [insikjúə] *a.* fuanteina; anzen de nai (*not secure*). ~**ly** *ad.* fuanzenni.

insecurity [insikjúəriti] *n.* fuantei.

inseminate [insémineit] *v.* tane o maku; nae o ueru.

insensate [insénseit/-sit] *a.* chikaku no nai; kanjō o motanai;

zanninna.

insensibility [insènsibíliti] *n.* mukankaku; muishiki; donkan.

insensible [insénsibl] *a.* reitanna; mukankaku no; me ni mienai hodo no : *the room grew cold by ~ degrees*, heya wa kanjirarenai teido de samuku natte itta.

inseparable [insép(ə)rəbl] *a.* hanasarenai.

insert [insə́:t] *v.* sashikomu. *n.* [ínsə:t] sashikomi.

insertion [insə́:ʃən] *n.* sōnyū; sashikomi-bira.   ⌈shikomu.

inset [ínset] *n.* sashikonda mono; sashikomi-pēji. *v.* [insét] sa-

inshore [ínʃɔ́:] *a.* kaigan ni chikai : *~ fishing*, kinkai gyogyō.

inside [ínsáid] *a.* naibu no. *ad.* naibu ni. *prep.* [ínsáid] no naibu ni. *n.* naibu; rimen.

insidious [insídiəs/-djəs] *a.* inkenna; zurui; hisokani susumu. *~ly ad.* suki o neratte.

insight [ínsait] *n.* dōsatsuryoku; ganshiki; meisatsu.

insignia [insígniə] *n. pl.* erishō; shirushi; kunshō.

insignificance [insignífikəns] *n.* muimi; toru ni taranu koto.

insignificant [insignífikənt] *a.* muimina; jūyō de nai. *~ly ad.* muimini.

insincere [insinsíə] *a.* seii no nai; gizenteki. *~ly ad.* seiinaku.

insincerity [ìnsinsériti] *n.* fuseijitsu; gizen.

insinuate [insínjueit] *v.* itsu to naku hairikomu; umaku toriiru; honomekasu. *~ing* [insínjueitiŋ] *a.* umaku toriiru. *~ voice*, neko-nade-goe de. *~ly ad.* kobiru yōni.

insinuation [insinjuéiʃən] *n.* umaku toriiru koto; atekosuri.

insipid [insípid] *a.* aji no nai; kyōmi no nai.

insipidity [insipíditi] *n.* aji no nai koto; kakki no nai koto.

insist [insíst] *v.* shuchō suru; iiharu. *~ence n.* kataki shuchō. *~ent a.* iiharu; medatsu.

insnare, en- [insnéə] *v.* wana ni kakeru.

insole [ínsoul] *n.* kutsu no nakazoko.

insolence [ínsələns] *n.* ōhei; gōman.

insolent [ínsələnt] *a.* ōheina; gōmanna; zūzūshii. *~ly ad.* ōheini; bureini.   ⌈koto.

insolubility [insòljubíliti] *n.* tokenai seishitsu; wakaranai

insoluble [insóljubl] *a.* tokenai; kaiketsu dekinai.

insolvency [insólv(ə)nsi] *n.* shiharai funō; hasan.

insolvent [insólvənt] *a.* shiharai funō ; hasan shita. *n.* shiharai funōsha ; hasansha.

insomnia [insómniə] *n.* fumin (shō).

insomuch [inso(u)mátʃ] *ad.* sonna teido made ; sore hodo ni.

inspect [inspékt] *v.* kensa suru no ; shisatsu suru. ~or *n.* shisatsusha ; kantokusha : *school* ~, shigaku.

inspection [inspékʃən] *n.* shisatsu ; kensa ; sankan.

inspiration [inspiréiʃən] *n.* iki o suikomu koto. reikan ; kobu gekirei suru chikara.

inspire [inspáiə] *v.* iki o suikomu ; kobusuru ; reikan o ataeru.

inspiring [inspáiəriŋ] *a.* kobu suru ; isamashii.

inspirit [inspírit] *v.* kobu suru ; genki o tsukeru.

inspissate [inspíseit/ínspi-] *v.* koku suru ; nōkōni suru.

instability [instəbíliti] *n.* fuantei ; utsurigi (*cf. stability*).

install [instɔ́:l] *v.* nimmei suru ; suwaraseru ; setsubi suru.

installation [instɔ:léiʃən] *n.* nimmei ; shūnin ; setsubi.

instal(l)ment [instɔ́:lmənt] *n.* bunkatsu-barai, (bunsatsu shuppan nado no) ikkai bun.

instance [ínstəns] *n.* zenrei : *at the* ~ *of*, no susume (irai) de. *court of first* ~, daiisshin saibansho. *for* ~, tatoeba. *v.* rei ni hiku.

instant [ínstənt] *n.* sokuji ; tadaima. *a.* sokuji no : *an* ~ *need of action*, sokkoku kōdō (*action*) no hitsuyō. ~ly *ad.* tadachini.

instantaneous [instəntéinjəs] *a.* sokuji no.

instanter [instǽntə] *ad.* tadachini (*joc.*).

instead [instéd] *ad.* kawari ni ; ...shinai de. *let him go* ~, kawari ni kare o oyari yo. ~ *of studying, she read a book*, kenkyū o shinai de hon o yonde ita.

instep [ínstep] *n.* ashi no kō ; kutsu, kutsushita nado no kō.

instigate [ínstigeit] *v.* sosonokasu ; sendō suru : *foreign agents* ~*ed a rebellion*, kaigai kara no tesaki ga nairan o sosotta.

instigation [instigéiʃən] *n.* kyōsa ; sendō.

instigator [ínstigeitə] *n.* sendōsha ; chōhonnin.

instil(l) [instíl] *v.* sukoshizutsu tarasu ; (kanjō nado o) fukikomu : *reading a good book* ~*s a love of literature*, yoi hon o yomu koto wa bungaku-ai o sodateru. ⌐koto.

instillation [instiléiʃ(ə)n] *n.* shitataraseru koto ; oshiekomu

instinct [ínstiŋ(k)t] *n.* honnō; shōdō. *a.* [instíŋ(k)t] hatsuratsu taru; moetatsu.

instinctive [instíŋ(k)tiv] *a.* honnōteki no. ~**ly** *ad.* honnōteki-ni.

institute [ínstitju:t] *n.* gakkai; kaikan; kenkyūjo. *v.* hajimeru; tateru.

institution [ìnstitjú:ʃ(ə)n] *n.* setsuritsu; bunkasetsubi; kōkyō dantai (kyōkai, gakkō, byōin no yōna); kanrei; kitei; hōritsu; shūkan (*custom*) nado. ~**al** [-n(ə)l] *a.* seido no; kōkyō-dantai no.

instruct [instrʌ́kt] *v.* oshieru; sashizu suru.

instruction [instrʌ́kʃ(ə)n] *n.* kyōju; (*pl.*) kunrei; sashizu.

instructive [instrʌ́ktiv] *a.* kyōkunteki; kyōikujō yūekina.

instructor [instrʌ́ktə] *n.* kyōshi; kyōjusha.

instrument [ínstrumənt] *n.* shudan; dōgu; gakki.

instrumental [ìnstruméntl/-trəm-] *a.* yaku ni tatsu; gakki no. ~**ist** *n.* gakki o hiku hito.

instrumentality [ìnstrumentǽliti] *n.* tasuke; shudan; dōgu; yakuni tatsu koto.

insubordinate [ìnsəbɔ́:dinit] *a.* jūjun de nai; hankōteki.

insubordination [ìnsəbɔ:dinéiʃ(ə)n] *n.* fukujū shinai koto.

insufferable [insʌ́f(ə)rəbl] *a.* gaman dekinai; nikurashii (*cf. sufferable*).

insufficiency [ìnsəfíʃi(ə)nsi] *n.* fujūbun; fusoku. ⌐jūbunni.

insufficient [ìnsəfíʃ(ə)nt] *a.* fusokuna; fujūbunna. ~**ly** *ad.* fu-

insular [ínsjulə] *a.* shima no; shimaguni konjō no; henkyō-na; kyōryōna.

insularity [ìnsjulǽriti] *a.* shimaguni de aru koto; shimaguni konjō; henkyō. ⌐suru (*electricity*).

insulate [ínsjuleit] *v.* shima ni suru; kakuri suru; zetsuen

insulation [ìnsjuléiʃ(ə)n] *n.* kakuri; zetsuen.

insulator [ínsjuleitə], *n.* kakuri suru hito (mono); zetsuentai.

insult [ínsʌlt] *n.* bujoku; burei. *v.* [insʌ́lt] bujoku suru. ~**ing** *a.* bureina.

insuperable [insjú:p(ə)rəbl] *a.* uchikatenai; kokufuku dekinai (*not superable*).

insupportable [ìnsəpɔ́:təbl] *a.* taerarenai (*unbearable*).

insurance [inʃúər(ə)ns] *n.* hoken; hokenryō; hokenshōken.

fire ~, kasai hoken. *life* ~, seimei hoken.

insure [inʃúə] *v.* ukeau; hoshō suru; hoken o tsukeru. *the* ~*d*, hihokensha. ~*r* n. hokengyōsha.

insurgency [insɔ́:dʒ(ə)nsi] *n.* muhon; hanran.

insurgent [insɔ́:dʒ(ə)nt] *a.* muhon suru; bōdō no. *n.* muhon-nin; bōto. ⌐*able*).

insurmountable [ìnsə(:)máuntəbl] *a.* uchikatenai (*cf.* surmount-

insurrection [ìnsərékʃ(ə)n] *n.* hanran; bōdō. ~*ary* *a.* muhon no; bōdō no.

insusceptible [insəséptəbl] *a.* ...o yurusanai; ...o kanjinai (*not*

intact [intǽkt] *a.* higai no nai; kanzenna. ⌐*susceptible*).

intaglio [intǽljou / -tá:liou] *n.* horikomi hōseki; horikomi moyō. (*cf. cameo*) ⌐ryō.

intake [ínteik] *n.* (mizu, kūkinado no) toriireguchi; toriire

intangible [intǽndʒəbl] *a.* sawaru koto no dekinai; kokoro de yōini tsukamenai.

intangibility [intæ̀ndʒəbíliti] *n.* tsukamenai koto.

integer [íntidʒə] *n.* kanzenna mono. (*math.*) seisū.

integral [íntigr(ə)l] *a.* hitsuyōna; kanzenna; (*math.*) seisū no *n.* kanzen seisū. ⌐kibun suru.

integrate [íntigreit] *v.* kanzenni suru; tōgō suru; (*math.*) se-

integration [ìntigréiʃ(ə)n] *n.* kansei; ketsugō; sekibun.

integrity [intégriti] *n.* kanzen; shōjiki.

integument [intégjumənt] *a.* gaihi, hifu; kaigara no yōna gaibu no ōi.

intellect [íntilekt] *n.* chiryoku (*power of knowing*).

intellectual [ìntiléktjuəl] *a.* chitekina; sōmeina. *n.* chishikijin. ~*ly* *ad.* chitekini.

intelligence [intélidʒ(ə)ns] *n.* rikairyoku; takai chiryoku; chishiki (*high mental ability*). ~ *bureau*, jōhōkyoku. ~ *office* shokugyō shōkaijo. ~ *quotient*, chinō shisū. ⌐ni.

intelligent [intélidʒ(ə)nt] *a.* sōmeina; rikōna. ~*ly* *ad.* sōmei

intelligentsia [intèlidʒéntsiə, -gén-] *n.* chishiki kaikyū.

intelligible [intélidʒəbl] *a.* wakariyasui; meiryōna. ~*bly* *ad.* wakariyasui; meiryōni.

intemperance [intémp(ə)r(ə)ns] *n.* fusessei; bōin; ōzake.

intemperate [intémp(ə)rit] *a.* fusessei no; ōzake o nomu.

intend [inténd] *v.* ...suru tsumori de aru; kuwadateru; imisuru.

intendency [inténdənsi] *n.* kantoku no shoku (shigoto).

intendant [inténdənt] *n.* kantokusha; kanrisha.

intense [inténs] *a.* hageshii; netsuretsuna. ～ly *ad.* hageshiku.

intensify [inténsifai] *v.* hageshiku suru; zōdai suru.

intension [inténʃ(ə)n] *n.* (kokoro no) kinchō; doryoku; tsuyosa.

intensity [inténs(i)ti] *n.* gekiretsu; kyōdo; tsuyosa.

intensive [inténsiv] *a.* tsuyoi; tetteitekina; kyōretsuna. *n.* kyōdo (*emphatic*).

intent [intént] *n.* ishi; shui : *to all intents and purposes,* hotondo arayuru hōhō de. *a.* kokoro o kometa; nesshinna. ～ly *ad.* nesshinni.

intention [inténʃ(ə)n] *n.* ikō; kangae; kokoro no tsumori; mokuteki; imi. (*pl.*) shitagokoro.

intentional [inténʃən(ə)l] *a.* koi no. ～ly *ad.* wazato.

inter [intə:] *v.* maisō suru. ～ment *n.* maisō.

inter- [intə] *pref.* tagaini...shiau; issho ni.

interact [intərǽkt] *v.* tagai ni sayō suru; tagai ni eikyō suru.

interaction [intərǽkʃ(ə)n] *n.* sōgosayō.

intercalary [intə́:kələri/intəkǽləri] *a.* urū no; aida ni ireta : *February 29 is an* ～ *day,* 2 (ni) gatsu 29 nichi wa urū no hi da.

intercalate [intə́:kəleit] *v.* aida ni ireru.

intercede [intə(:)sí:d] *v.* chūsai suru; torinasu.

intercept [intə(:)sépt] *v.* saegiru; yokodori suru; toki o osaeru. ～ive *a.* tochū de yokodori suru; bōgai no.

interception [ìntəsépʃ(ə)n] *n.* tochū de yokodori suru koto; bōgai.

intercession [ìntəséʃ(ə)n] *n.* chūsai; torinashi.

intercessor [intəsésə, íntəsəsə] *n.* chūsaisha; torinashi o suru hito. ～y chūsai no.

interchange [intə(:)tʃéindʒ] *v.* tagaini kōkan suru; kōtai suru. *n.* [íntə(:)tʃeindʒ] kōkan; kōtai. ～able [i-əbl] *a.* taikō no. kōkan dekiru; kōtai dekiru. ⌈taikō no.

intercollegiate [intə(:)kəlí:giit] *a.* daigakukan no; daigaku no.

intercolonial [intə(:)kəlóuniəl] *a.* shokuminchi kan no.

intercom [intəkɔ́m] *n.* (*sl.*) kōkūki, fune nado de tagaini hanaseru denwaki.

intercommunication [íntə(:)kəmjù:nikéifən,] *n.* sōgo no kōtsū; kōsai.

intercostal [ìntə(:)kɔ́st(ə)l] *a.* (*anat.*) rokkotsu no aida no.

intercourse [íntəkɔ:s/-kɔɔs-] *n.* kōtsū; kōsai; tsūshō; jōkō.

interdependence [ìntə(:)dipéndəns] *n.* sōgo izon (tagaini tasukeau koto).

interdependent [ìntə(:)dipéndənt] *a.* tagai ni irai suru.

interdict [ìntə(:)díkt] *v.* kinzuru; hamon suru; samatageru. *n.* [íntə(:)dikt] kinshi; hamon.

interdiction [ìntə(:)díkʃən] *n.* kinshi; teishi.

interest [íntrist/íntərest] *n.* kyōmi; kanshin; rigai; rishi. *v* kyōmi o okosaseru; kankei saseru: *be ~ed in*, ni kyōmi o motte iru; ni kankei shiteiru. **~ing** *a.* kyōmi aru; omoshiroi.

interfere [ìntəfíə] *v.* kanshō suru; samatageru; shōtotsu suru. *~ with*, jama o suru.

interference [ìntəfíər(ə)ns] *n.* shōtotsu; kanshō; bōgai.

interfering [ìntəfíəriŋ] *a.* kanshō suru; jama ni naru.

interim [íntərim] *n.* aima; sono aida. *a.* kari no; ichiji no: *in the ~*, sono aida ni.

interior [intíəriə] *a.* naibu no; naichi no. *n.* naibu; naichi; naishin (*at heart*).

interject [ìntə(:)dʒékt] *v.* aida ni ireru; fui ni saegiru; sashihasamu (kotoba nado o).

interjection [ìntə(:)dʒékʃ(ə)n] *n.* (*gram.*) kantōshi; kantanshi.

interlace [ìntə(:)léis] *v.* kumiawaseru; orimazeru; mazaru.

interlard [ìntə(:)lá:d] *v.* mazaru (*mix*): *~ his speech with English*, hanashi ni Eigo o mazeru.

interlay [ìntə(:)léi] *v.* aida ni ireru.

interleave [ìntə(:)lí:v] *v.* aida ni kami o hasamu.

interline [ìntə(:)láin] *v.* gyō no aida ni (*between lines*) kaku.

interlinear [ìntə(:)líniə] *a.* gyōkan ni kaita.

interlock [ìntə(:)lɔ́k] *v.* dakiau; ketsugō suru; renketsu suru.

interlocutor [intəlɔ́kjutə] *n.* taiwasha; taidansha.

interlocutory [ìntə(:)lɔ́kjut(ə)ri] *a.* taiwa no; chūkan no. *~ judgment*, chūkan hanketsu.

interlude [íntə(:)lu:d/-lju:d] *n.* makuai (no kyōgen); kansōkyoku. ⌈kekkon.

intermarriage [ìntə(:)mǽridʒ] *n.* ketsuzoku-kekkon; kinshin-

intermarry [ìntə(:)mǽri] *v.* ketsuzoku-kekkon o suru.

intermeddle [ìntə(:)médl] *v.* kanshō suru; deshabaru.

intermediary [ìntə(:)míːdjəri] *a.* chūkan no; baikai no. *n.* bai-

kaisha; nakōdo.

intermediate [ìntə(:)míːdjət] *a.* chūkan no. *n.* chōteisha. ～ly

ad. chūkan ni.

intermediation [ìntə(:)mìːdiéiʃ(ə)n] *n.* chūkai; chōtei.

interminable [intə́ːminəbl] *a.* hateshi no nai (*not terminable*).

intermingle [ìntə(:)míŋgl] *v.* mazeru; mazaru.

intermission [ìntə(:)míʃ(ə)n] *n.* chūshi; chuzetsu.

intermit [ìntə(:)mít] *v.* ichiji tomaru; chūshi suru.

intermittent [ìntə(:)mít(ə)nt] *a.* danzoku suru. ～ly *ad.* danzo-

kutekini; ma o oite.

intermix [ìntə(:)míks] *v.* mazeru; mazeawaseru (*with*). ～ture

n. kongō; kongōbutsu.

intern, interne [intə́ːn], *v.* byōin no kenkyūsei o tsutomeru;

yokuryū suru. *n.* (*Am.*) byōin no kenkyūsei; yokuryūsha.

～ment *n.* yokuryū.

internal [intə́ːn(ə)l] *a.* naibu no; seishinteki; kokunai no. ～

combustion *a.* nainen no. ～-**combustion engine** *n.* nainen

kikan. ～ly *ad.* naibu ni; kokunai de.

international [ìntə(:)nǽʃ(ə)n(ə)l] *a.* kokusai no; bankoku no.

～*law*, kokusaihō. *n. International Labour Organization.* Kokusai

Rōdōsha Kikō (*cf.*) I.L.O..

internecine [ìntə(:)níːsain, -sin] *a.* satsujinteki; tagai ni ko-

roshiau; hakai.

interphone [ìntə(:)fóun] *n.* shanai (*or* kannai) denwa.

interpolate [intə́ːpo(u)leit] *v.* kinyū suru; kakiire o shite (*text*);

hombun nado o kaeru.

interpolation [intə̀ːpo(u)léiʃ(ə)n] *n.* kakiire; sōnyū; kakiire

shite hombun ga kawaru koto.

interpose [ìntə(:)póuz] *v.* sōnyū suru. igi o sashihasamu. chū-

sai ni hairu. ⌈sai.

interposition [intə̀ːpəzíʃ(ə)n] *n.* sōnyū; kanshō (*intefere*); chū-

interpret [intə́ːprit] *v.* kaishaku (tsūyaku) suru.; enshutsu suru. ~er *n.* tsūyaku; setsumeisha. ⌜k⸳ı.

interpretation [intɔ:pritéiʃ(ɔ)n] *n.* kaishaku; setsumei; tsūya-

interregnum [intɔrégnɔm] *n.* (*pl.* -s; -na) kūi-kikan (kokuō nado ga hōgyo mata wa taii shite, mada kōkeisha no kimaranai kikan); nagayasumi no kikan.

interrogate [intérɔgeit] *v.* shitsumon (jimmon) suru.

interrogation [intèrɔgéiʃ(ɔ)n] *n.* shitsumon; gimon : ~ *mark* (*or point*) gimon-fu (?).

interrogative [intɔrógɔtiv] *a.* gimon no. *n.* (*gram.*) gimon-shi. ~ly *ad.* fushinsōni.

interrogatory [intɔrógɔt(ɔ)ri] *a.* shitsumon no. *n.* shitsumon; jimmon. ⌜togireta.

interrupt [intɔrʌ́pt] *v.* samatageru; sashideguchi suru. ~ed *a.*

interruption [intɔrʌ́pʃ(ɔ)n] *n.* chūshi; tochū de yameru koto; bōgai; shadan suru mono.

intersect [intɔ(:)sékt] *v.* yokogiru; aimajiwaru.

intersection [intɔ(:)sékɔn] *n.* kōsa; ōdan; kōten.

intersperse [intɔ(:)spɔ́:s] *v.* makichirasu : *bushes were ~ed here and there among trees,* kigi no aida ni yabu ga choichoi atta.

interspersion [intɔ(:)spɔ́:ʃ(ɔ)n] *n.* makichirasu koto; sampu.

interstate [intɔ(:)stéit] *a.* (*Am.*) kakushū no aida no : ~ *commerce,* shū to shū no aida no shōtorihiki.

interstice [intɔ́:stis] *n.* sukima; wareme; sakeme.

intertwine [intɔ(:)twáin] *v.* karamiau (awaseru). ~ment *n.* karamiai. ⌜doki.

interval [íntɔv(ɔ)l] *n.* aima; hedatari, yasumijikan. *at* ~s, toki-

intervene [intɔ(:)ví:n] *v.* aida ni hairu; chōtei suru; kanshō suru (*interfere*). ⌜kanshō.

intervention [intɔ(:)vénʃɔn] *n.* aida ni hairu koto; chōtei;

interview [íntɔ(:)vju:] *n.* kaiken; kaikendan. *v.* kaiken (kaidan) suru.

interweave [ìntɔ(:)wí:v] *v.* -wove, -woven; -weaving. orimazeru; kongō suru.

interwove [intɔ(:)wóuv] *v. see* : **interweave.**

interwoven [intɔ(:)wóuvn] *v. see* : **interweave.** ⌜no shinin.

intestate [intéstit/-teit] *a.* yuigonjō no nai. *n.* yuigonjō nashi-

intestinal [intéstin(ɔ)l] *a.* chō no; harawata no.

intestine [intéstin] *a.* naibu no; kokunai no. *n.* (*anat.*) chō; harawata.

inthrall, enthrall [inθró:l] *v.* seifuku suru; miwaku suru.

inthrone, enthrone [inθróun] *n.* ōza ni tsuku (*sit on the throne*).

intimacy [íntiməsi] *n.* shimmitsu; kon'i; fukai majiwari.

intimate [íntimit] *a.* shitashii. *n.* shin'yū. *v.* [íntimeit] honomekasu; kōhyō suru.

intimation [intiméiʃən] *n.* tsūchi; anji.

intimidate [intímideit] *v.* odosu; kyōhaku suru.

intimidation [intìmidéiʃən] *n.* kyōhaku.

into [íntu(:)] *prep.* no uchi ni; ni; ...no naka ni.

intolerable [intól(ə)rəbl] *a.* taerarenai. ~**bly** *ad.* gaman dekinai hodo ni.

intolerance [intólər(ə)ns] *n.* gaman dekinai koto; chigau kangae o irenai koto; kyōryō.

intolerant [intólərənt] *a.* taerarenai; isetsu o irenai; kyōryōna.

intomb, entomb [intú:m] *v.* maisō suru. [no yokuyō.

intonation [ìnto(u)néiʃən] *n.* hanashi no chōshi; ginshō; oto

intone [intóun] *v.* ginshō suru; yokuyō o tsukeru.

intoxicant [intóksikənt] *n.* nonde you mono; sakerui.

intoxicate [intóksikeit] *v.* yowaseru; muchū ni naraseru.

intoxication [intòksikéiʃ(ə)n] *n.* meitei; muchū.

intractable [intræktəbl] *a.* toriatsukai nikui; gōjōna.

intransitive [intrá:ns(i)tiv/-træn-] *a.* (*gram.*) jidō no. ~ *verb*, jidōshi. ~**ly** *ad.* jidōshitekini (*opp. transitive*).

intrench, entrench [intréntʃ] *v.* zangō de kakomu; kengoni mi o mamoru. ~**ment** *n.*

intrepid [intrépid] *a.* osore o shiranai; daitanna. ~**ly** *ad.*

intrepidity [ìntrepíditi] *n.* gōki; daitan. [daitanni.

intricacy [íntrikəsi] *n.* fukuzatsu; komiitta mono.

intricate [íntrikit] *a.* komiitta; fukuzatsuna. ~**ly** *ad.* komiitte. [fugi o suru.

intrigue [intrí:g] *n.* imbō; mitsugi. *v.* imbō o kuwadateru;

intrinsic [intrínsik] *a.* honrai no. ~**ally** *ad.* honrai.

introduce [ìntrədjú:s] *v.* shōkai suru; toriireru; denrai suru. ~**r** *n.* shōkaisha. ~ *a story into the conversation*, kaiwa no naka ni monogatari o toriireru.

introduction [intrədák∫(ə)n] *n.* shogen. *n.* shōkai ; yunyū. toriire : *the* ~ *of steel made tall buildings easy to build,* kōtetsu o toriireta koto wa takai tatemono o tateru koto o yōini shita.

introductory [ìntrədáktəri] *a.* shōkai no ; maeoki no. ~ *remarks,* hashigaki ; maeoki.

introspect [ìntro(u)spékt] *v.* naisei suru ; jiko-kansatsu suru.

introspection [ìntro(u)spék∫(ə)n] *n.* naimen-kansatsu ; naisei.

introspective [íntro(u)spéktiv] *a.* naisei no ; jiko kansatsu no.

introspectory [ìntrəspéktəri] *a.* jiko naisei suru.

introversion [ìntrəvə́:∫(ə)n] *n.* gaikai yori no jiko kansatsu ; naisei ni kyōmi o motsu keikō.

introvert [íntrd(u)və:t] *n.* naiseitekina hito.

intrude [intrú:d] *v.* oshiiru ; jamasuru ; deshabaru. ~**r** *n.* shinnyūsha ; chinnyūsha.

intrusion [intrú:ʒ(ə)n] *n.* chinnyū ; deshabari ; jama.

intrusive [intrú:siv] *a.* deshabaru ; jama suru.

intrust, entrust [intrást] *v.* shinjite makaseru.

intuition [intjú(:)i∫(ə)n] *n.* chokkaku ; chokkan. ~**al** *a.* chokkaku no ; chokkan no.

intuitive [intjú(:)itiv] *a.* chokkantekina. ~**ly** *ad.* chokkanteki

intwine, entwine [intwáin] *v.* karamiau. ⌊ni.

inundate [ínʌndeit] *v.* afureru ; hanran suru.

inundation [inʌndéi∫(ə)n] *n.* kōzui ; hanran.

inure [injúə] *v.* narasu ; kitaeru ; yakudatsu.

invade [invéid] *v.* shinnyū suru. ~**r** *n.* shinnyūsha.

invalid [ínvəli:d] *n.* byōnin. *a.* byōjakuna. [ìnvǽlid] *a.* chikara no nai ; shigoto no dekinai. *v.* [ìnvǽli:d/ìnvǽli:d] byōjaku ni suru ; heieki o menjo suru. ~**ate** [invǽljdeit]. *v.* mukō ni suru. ~**ity** [ìnvəlíditi] *n.* mukō ; muryoku.

invaluable [invǽlju(ə)bl] *a.* hyōka dekinai ; hyōka dekinai hodo kichōna.

invariable [invéəriəbl] *a.* fuhen no ; ittei no. ~**bly** *ad.* kisokutekini ; itsumo kawaranaide.

invasion [invéiʒ(ə)n] *n.* shinryaku ; shingai ; osoikakaru koto.

invective [invéktiv] *n.* akkō ; dokuzetsu.

inveigh [invéi] *v.* warukuchi o iu ; nonoshiru. ~ *against democracy, democracy* o mechakucha ni kokiorosu.

inveigle [invéigl/-ví:-] *v.* obikikomu; yūwaku suru; damasu.

invent [invént] *v.* hatsumei suru. ∼**or** *n.* hatsumeisha.

invention [invénʃ(ə)n] *n.* hatsumei (hin); netsuzō; tsukuri-ba-

inventive [invéntiv] *a.* hatsumei no sai aru; kiyōna. ⌊nashi.

inventory [ínvəntri] *n.* shōhin mokuroku; zaikohin. *v.* mokuroku o tsukuru; zaiko shirabe o suru.

Inverness [ìnvənés] *n.* imbanesu; nijūmawashi.

inverse [ínvə́:s] *a.* hantai no; gyaku no. ∼**ly** *ad.* gyakuni;
abekobeni.

inversion [invə́:ʃ(ə)n] *n.* gyaku; uragaeshi; (*gram.*) tōchihō.

invert [invə́:t] *v.* gyaku ni suru; uragaesu. ∼**ed commas**, in'yōfu. (' ' *or* " ").

invertebrate [invə́:tibrit] *a.* sekitsui no nai; memeshii. *n.* mu-
sekitsuidōbutsu.

invest [invést] *v.* kiseru; kakomu: *Darkness* ∼*s the earth at
night*, yami ga yoru ni chikyū o tsutsumu. tōshi suru: *people
∼ their money in stocks*, hitotachi wa sono kane o kabu ni tōshi suru. ∼**ment** *n.* tōshi; hōi; kakomi; ifuku. ∼**or** *n.* tōshi-
sha, hōisha.

investigate [invéstigeit] *v.* kenkyū suru; chōsa suru.

investigation [invèstigéiʃ(ə)n] *n.* chōsa; kenkyū.

investigator [invéstigeitə] *n.* kenkyūsha; chōsasha.

investiture [invéstitʃə] *n.* nimmeishiki; sazukeru koto.

inveteracy [invét(ə)rəsi] *n.* nebukai koto; mansei; nagai urami.

inveterate [invét(ə)rit] *a.* nebukai; mansei no; urami no aru.
∼**ly** *ad.* nebukaku.

invidious [invídiəs] *a.* iyana; fukaina; shaku ni sawaru.

invigorate [invígəreit] *v.* genki o tsukeru; kobu suru.

invigoration [invìgəréiʃ(ə)n] *n.* gekirei; genki o tsukeru koto.

invincible [invínsəbl] *a.* uchikachi gatai; mutekina. ∼**bly** *ad.*
uchikachi gataku.

inviolable [inváiələbl] *a.* okasu koto no dekinai; shinseina.
∼**bly** *ad.* okasu bekarazaru.

inviolate [inváiəlit] *a.* kegare no nai; shinseina; okashigatai.

invisibility [invìzəbíliti] *n.* me ni mienai koto.

invisible [invízəbl] *a.* me ni mienai. ∼**bly** *ad.* me ni mienai

invitation [invitéiʃ(ə)n] *n.* shōtai(jō).   ⌊yōni.

invite [inváit] *v.* shōtai suru; yūwaku suru; (iken nado o) motomeru : *He* ~*d our opinion of his work,* kare wa kare no shigoto ni tsuite wareware no iken o motometa.

inviting [inváitiŋ] *a.* kokoro o sosoru; tobitsukitai yōna.

invocation [invo(u)kéiʃən] *n.* kigan; kitō; inori.

invoice [ínvɔis] *n.* okurijō; shikirijō. *v.* okurijō o tsukuru, ⌐shikiru.

invoke [invóuk] *v.* inoru; ...ni uttaeru. └shikiru.

involucre [ínvəlu:kə] *n.* (*anat.*) himaku. (*bot.*) hana (*flower*) no chiisai kawa; sōhō.

involuntary [invɔ́ləntri] *a.* muishiki no; kokoro-narazu no. ~ *manslaughter,* kashitsu satsujinzai. ~ *muscle* (*anat.*) fuzuiikin. ~**rily** *ad.* muishikitekini; fuhon'i nagara.

involute [ínvəl(j)u:t] *a.* komiitta; uchimaki no.

involution [ìnvəl(j)ú:ʃ(ə)n] *n.* makikomu koto; uchimaki; sakusō; (*math.*) jijōhō.

involve [invɔ́lv] *v.* makikomu; fukumu; imi suru. *be* ~*d in,* ni renza suru; kankei suru.

invulnerable [inváln(ə)rəbl] *a.* fujimi no; kizutsukerarenai.

inward [ínwəd] *a.* uchigawa e no; kokoro no uchi e no. *ad.* uchi e n. (*pl.*) (*anat.*) chō; naizō. ~**ly** *ad.* uchi ni; kokoro no uchi de.

inwards [ínwədz] *ad.* =**inward.**

inwrought [ínrɔ́:t] *a.* orikonda; shishū shita; yoku mazatta.

iodide [áiədaid] *n.* (*chem.*) yōkabutsu.

iodine [àiədi:n] *n.* (*chem.*) yōso; yōdo.

iodoform [aiɔ́dəfɔ:m] *n.* yōdohorumu.

ion [áiən] *n.* ion. ⌐jin.

Ionian [aióunjən] *a.* Ioniya no; Ioniyajin (shiki) no. *n.* Ioniyaiota

iota [aióutə] *n.* Girisha-moji no 9 (kyū)bamme (*I*); sukoshi; └wazuka.

IOU., I.O.U. shakuyō shōsho (*I owe you*).

I. Q. chinō keisū (*intelligence quotient*).

ir-=in-, *pref.* not no imi.

irascibility [iræ̀sibíliti/ai(ə)r-] *n.* kanshaku; tanki.

irascible [irǽsibl/ai(ə)r-] *a.* okorippoi; tankina.

irate [ai(ə)réit] *a.* okotta; rippuku shita.

ire [áiə] *n.* ikari. ~**ful** *a.* okotta; funzen to shita.

iridescence [ìridés(ə)ns] *n.* niji-iro; shinju no kōtaku.

iridescent [ìridés(ə)nt] *a.* niji-iro no.

iridium [àirídiəm] *n.* (*chem.*) irijium (genso) (*chemical element*).

iris [áiəris] *n.* (*anat.*) gankyū no kōsai ; niji. (*flow.*) ichihatsu no hana ; (*Gk. myth.*) niji no megami.

Irish [áiəriʃ] *a.* Airurando no. *n.* Airurandojin ; Airurandogo. ~**ism** *n.* Airurandofū. ~**man** *n.* Airurandojin. ⌈mendōna.

irk [ə:k] *v.* taikutsu saseru ; nayamasu. ~**some** *a.* unzari suru ;

iron [áiən] *n.* tetsu ; airon. (*pl.*) ashikase. *a.* tetsu no ; katai. *v.* airon o kakeru ; ashikase (mata wa tekase) o kakeru ; tetsu de ōu. ~**bound** [⸕báund] *a.* tetsu de maita ; kengona. ~**clad** *a.* sōkō saseru. ~**foundry** *n.* seitetsujo. ~ **lung** *n.* tetsu no hai. ~**monger** [⸕máŋgə] *n.* kanamonoya. ~**mongery** [⸕máŋgəri] *n.* tekkirui ; kanamono. ~**sides** [⸕said] *n.* gōkina hito. ~**stone** [⸕stoun] *n.* tekkō. ~**ware** [⸕wɛə] *n.* tekki ; kanamono. ~**wood** *n.* kōshitsu zai (sono jumoku). ~**work** [⸕wə:k] *n.* tetsu-kanamono. ~**works** [⸕wə:ks] *n.* tekkōjō ; seitetsujo.

ironical [ai(ə)rɔ́nik(ə)l] *a.* hango no ; hinikuna. ~**ly** *ad.* hangotekini ; hinikuni.

irony [áiərəni] *n.* hango ; hiniku. ⌈kagayaku.

irradiate [iréidieit] *v.* terasu ; keihatsu suru ; hikari o hassuru ;
irradiation [ireidiéiʃ(ə)n] *n.* hikari kagayaku koto.

irrational [iræʃ(ə)n(ə)l] *a.* risei no nai ; fugōrina. *n.* (*math.*) murisū. ~**ly** *ad.* risei naku ; fugōrini.

irrationality [iræʃənǽliti] *n.* risei ketsubō ; fugōri. ⌈dekinai.

irreclaimable [ìrikléiməbl] *a.* torikaeshi no dekinai ; kyōka

irreconcilable [irékənsailəbl] *a.* wakai dekinai ; mujun suru.

irrecoverable [irikáv(ə)rəbl] *a.* torikaeshi no tsukanai (*cf. recoverable*).

irredeemable [ìridí:məbl] *a.* shōkan dekinai ; saiken nado ga shōkan sarenai ; shihei nado ga genkin ni kaerarenai.

irredentism [ìridéntizm] *n.* Itariya-Minzoku Tōgōshugi. ~**tist** *n.* Itariya-Minzoku-Tōitsutōin. ⌈kusarenai (*cf. reducible*).

irreducible [iridjú:səbl] *a.* herasu koto no dekinai ; (*math.*) ya-
irrefragable [iréfrəgəbl] *a.* arasoenai ; tashikana ; rompa deki-nai. ⌈nai.

irrefutable [iréfjutəbl/irifjú:təbl] *a.* iiyaburenai ; rompa deki-

irregular [irégjulə] *a.* fukisokuna ; fuhōna ; ranzatsuna. *n.* fuseiki-hei ; (*pl.*) sono guntai. ~**ly** *ad.* fukisokuni ; fuhōni.

irregularity [irègjulǽriti] *n.* fukisoku; fuhō.

irrelevancy [irélivənsi] *n.* futekisetsu; kentōchigai; mukankei.

irrelevant [irélivənt] *a.* futekisetsuna; kentōchigai no; suji-chigai no.

irreligious [ìrilídʒəs] *a.* mushūkyō no; fushinjinna.

irremediable [ìrimí:diəbl] *a.* chiryō dekinai; kyōsei dekinai.

irreparable [irép(ə)rəbl] *a.* kaifuku dekinai; torikaeshi no tsu-

irrepressible [ìriprésəbl] *a.* osaekirenai; te ni oenai. ⌊kanai.

irreproachable [ìripróutʃəbl] *a.* hinan no yochi no nai; mō-shibun no nai. ⌈nai.

irresistible [ìrizístəbl] *a.* teikō dekinai; osaeru koto no deki-

irresolute [irézəlju:t/-lu:t] *a.* ketsudan no nai; guzuguzu shi-ta. ∼ly *ad.* guzuguzu shite.

irresolution [irèzəljú:ʃ(ə)n, -lú:] *n.* yūjūfudan; guzu.

irrespective [ìrispéktiv] *a.* ni kankei naki; o kaeriminai. ∼ly *ad.* ni kakawarazu; to kankei naku.

irresponsibility [írispɔ̀nsibíliti] *n.* musekinin.

irresponsible [ìrispɔ́nsibl] *a.* sekinin no nai; iikagenna.

irretrievable [ìritrí:vəbl] *a.* kaifuku no muzukashii; tsugunai

irreverence [irév(ə)r(ə)ns] *n.* fukei; burei. ⌊gatai.

irreverent [irév(ə)r(ə)nt] *a.* fukeina; bureina.

irreversible [ìrivé:s(ə)bl] *a.* gyakumodori dekinai; haishi deki-nai; henkō dekinai.

irrevocable [irévəkəbl] *a.* torikesenai; henkō dekinai.

irrigate [írigeit] *v.* mizu o hiku; kangai suru.

irrigation [irigéiʃ(ə)n] *n.* kangai.

irritability [iritəbíliti] *n.* tanki; shigeki e no kanjusei; sugu okoru koto.

irritable [íritəbl] *a.* okorippoi; shigeki ni kanji yasui.

irritant [írit(ə)nt] *a.* shigeki suru. *n.* shigeki butsu.

irritate [íriteit] *v.* okorasu; iraira saseru; shigeki suru. *His foolish questions* ∼*d me*, kare no tsumaranu shitsumon ga bo-ku o okorashita.

irritating [íriteitiŋ] *a.* shaku ni sawaru; shigeki suru.

irritation [irìtéiʃ(ə)n] *n.* ikari; iradachi; shigeki. ⌈*in*).

irruption [irʌ́pʃ(ə)n] *n.* totsunyū; shinnyū; rannyū (*bursting*

is [iz] *v.* ' be ' no dai sanninshō tansū genzai.

isinglass [áiziŋglà:s] *n.* nibe; ummo.
Islam [íslэm/ízlɑ:m] *n.* Isuramukyō; Kaikyōto; Kaikyōkoku.
～**ism** *n.* Kaikyō no kyōgi.
island [áilэnd] *n.* shima. ～**er** *n.* shimabito.
isle [ail] *n.* shima; kojima.
isobar [áiso(u)bɑ:] *n.* (tenkizu no) tōatsusen.
isolate [áisэleit] *v.* kakuri suru; koritsu saseru. ～**d** [-id] *a.*
hanarete iru; koritsu no.
isolation [àisэléiʃ(э)n] *n.* kakuri; kōtsū shadan. ～ **hospital**
hibyōin. ～**ist** *n.* koritsu-shugisha.
isolator [áisэléitэ] *n.* zetsuentai.
isosceles [aisɔ́sэli:z] *a.* nitōhen no. ～ **triangle** [tráiэŋgl] *n.*
(*math.*) nitōhen sankakukei.
isotherm [áiso(u)θэ:m] *n.* tōonsen.
isothermal [àiso(u)θэ́:m(э)l] *a.* tōonsen no. ┌Yudayajin.
Israel [ízreiэl] *n.* Isuraeru; Yudaya. ～**ite** [-ait] *n.* Isuraerujin.
issuance [íʃju(:)эns] *n.* hasshutsu; hakkō.
issue [íʃju:/íʃu:] *n.* hakkō; hakkōdaka. shison; deguchi; kekka; keisō mondai : *at* ～, ronsō ni kakaru; mondai taru : *join*
～ *with*, to iken o tatakawaseru. *v.* hassuru; deru. *smoke issues*
from the chimney, kemuri ga entotsu kara deru. shōzuru; kekka...to naru; happyō suru. hakkō suru : *the government* ～*s*
stamps, seifu wa kitte o hakkō suru.
isthmus [ísmэs, ísθm-] *n.* chikyō.
it [it] *pron.* sore wa; sore ga; sore ni; sore o.
Italian [itǽljэn] *a.* Itaria no. *n.* Itariajin; Itariago. ┌katsuji.
italic [itǽlik] *a.* itarikkutai katsuji no. ～**s** *n.* (*pl.*) itarikkutai
italicize [itǽlisaiz] *v.* itarikkutai katsuji de insatsu suru.
itch [itʃ] *n.* kayui koto; hizen; katsubō. *v.* netsubō suru.
itchy [ítʃi] *a.* kayui; katsubō suru.
item [áitem] *n.* kajō; kōmoku : ～ *of business*, eigyō kamoku.
itemize [áitэmaiz] *v.* kajō gaki ni suru; kōmoku ni wakeru.
iterate [ítэreit] *v.* kurikaesu.
iteration [itэréiʃ(э)n] *n.* kurikaeshi.
iterative [ítэrэtiv/-reit-] *a.* kurikaeshi no.
itinera(n)cy [itín(э)rэ(n)si/ai-] *n.* junkai.
itinerant [itín(э)r(э)nt/ai-] *a.* junkai suru. *n.* junkaisha.

itinerary [aitín(ə)rəri] *n.* ryokō-annai ; rotei. *a.* junkai suru ;
itinerate [itínəreit/ai–] *v.* junkai suru. ⌊dōchū no.
its [its] *pron.* (**it** no shoyū kaku) sore no ; are no.
it's [its] =**it is.**
itself [itsélf] *pron.* sore jishin : *by* ～, sore dake de ; jibun de.
in ～, honshitsutekini ; honrai. *of* ～, shizen ni ; hitoride ni.
I've [aiv] =**I have.**
ivied [áivid] *a.* kizuta de ōwareta.
ivory [áivəri] *n.* zōge ; zōge-iro ; (*pl.*) zōge-zaiku no mono ; ha.
～ **nut**, zōge-shuro no mi. ～ **palm**, zōge-shuro.
ivy [áivi] *n.* kizuta.
izzard [ízəd] *n.* z-ji no furui namae (yobikata).

J

J, j [dʒei] *n.* (*pl.* J's, Js, [dʒeiz]) Eiji *alphabet* no dai-10-bamme no monji.

J. j. *joule* nado no ryakuji.

jab [dʒæb] *v.* tsuku ; sasu. *n.* tsuki.

jabber [dʒǽbə] *v.* hayakuchi ni hanasu ; shaberu.

jack [dʒæk] *n.* *John* no zokushō ; suifu ; suihei ; kijūki ; mizu-sashi. ～ *in office*, nariagari yakunin. ～ *of all trades*, yorozuya. ～**ass** [-æs/-ɑːs] *n.* osu no roba ; bakamono. ～**boot** [-buːt] *n.* ō-nagagutsu. ～**daw** [-dɔː] *n.* (*bird.*) kogarasu. ～**-in-the-box** [⌐in-ðə-bóks] *n.* bikkuri-bako. ～**knife** [⌐naif] *n.* kaigun-naifu. ～**-o'-lantern** [-əlǽntən] *n.* onibi. (*Am.*) kabocha-jōchin.

jackal [dʒǽkɔːl] *n.* (*zoo.*) yamainu no rui.

jackanapes [dʒǽkəneips] *n.* namaiki-mono.

jacket [dʒǽkit] *n.* jaketsu ; mijikai uwagi.

Jacobite [dʒǽkəbait] *n.* (*Brit. hist.*) *James II* (gawa) no tōin.

jade [dʒeid] *n.* (*min.*) kōgyoku ; yakuza uma ; abazure-onna. *v.* hidoku tsukaresaseru ; oitsukau.

jag [dʒæg] *n.* gizagiaz. *v.* gizagiza o tsukeru.

jagged [dʒǽgid], **jaggy** [dʒǽgi] *a.* gizagiza no aru.

jaguar [dʒǽgwə] *n.* (*zoo.*) Amerika-hyō.

jail [dʒeil] *n.* kangoku. *v.* tōgoku suru (*put in* ～). ～**bird** [⌐bəːd] *n.* shūjin. ～**er** *n.* gokuri. ～**break** [-breik] (*col.*) rōyaburi.

jalopy [dʒəlópi] *n.* (*Am. sl.*) boro-jidōsha ; boro-hikōki.

jam [dʒæm] *v.* oshitsukeru ; hasamu ; ugokanaku suru ; tsume-komu. *n.* jamu ; zattō.

jamb, jambe [dʒæm] *n.* wakibashira (doa no waki nado no).

jamboree [dʒæmbəríː] *n.* (*Am. sl.*) *Boy Scout* no taikai. (*Am. sl.*) ōsawagi no enkai.

jangle [dʒǽŋgl] *n.* bakasawagi ; kenka. *v.* sawagu ; kōron suru.

janitor [dʒǽnitə] *n.* momban ; (*Am.*) kanrinin.

January [dʒǽnju(ə)ri] *n.* Ichigatsu.

Jap [dʒæp] *n.* Nippon-jin (*Japanese* no ryakuji).

japan [dʒəpǽn] *n.* urushi; shikki. *v.* urushi o nuru. (**Japan**, **Nippon**).

Japanese [dʒæpəní:z] *a.* Nippon no. *n.* Nipponjin; Nippon-go. ⌐chika.

Japanophile [dʒəpǽnəfail] *n.* Nippon biiki no hito; shinni-jape [dʒeip] *v.* jōdan o iu; hiyakasu. *n.* jōdan; karakai.

japonica [dʒəpónikə] *n.* (*bot.*) tsubaki.

jar [dʒɑː] *n.* kame; tsubo; mimizawarina, kasakasa shita oto; *v.* gishigishi oto o tateru; kosuru.

jardinière [ʒàːdinjéə] *n.* (*Fr.*) bonsai-dana; kabin; uekibachi.

jargon [dʒáːgən] *n.* tawagoto; (tōzoku nakama nado no) ingo; mazekoze kotoba. ⌐kei.

jasmin(e), jessamine [dʒǽsmin/dʒǽz-] *n.* (*bot.*) jasumin; so-jasper [dʒǽspə] *n.* (*min.*) hekigyoku (*green quartz*).

jaundice [dʒɔ́:ndis/dʒáːndis] *n.* (*med.*) ōdan. **~d** *a.* ōdan ni kakatta; higanda (*prejudiced*).

jaunt [dʒɔːnt] *n.* ensoku. *v.* ensoku suru.

jaunty [dʒɔ́:nti] *a.* kaikatsuna (*carefree*). **~ily** *ad.* kaikatsuni; kidotte (*stylish*).

javelin [dʒǽvlin] *n.* nageyari.

jaw [dʒɔː] *n.* ago. (*pl.*) kuchi. **~bone** [⏄boun] *n.* (*anat.*) ago-bone; gakkotsu.

jay [dʒei] *n.* (*bird*) kakesu; oshaberi (-na hito); baka.

jazz [dʒæz] *n.* jazu.

jealous [dʒéləs] *a.* shitto-bukai; sonemu: *be ~ of*, ni yaki-mochi o yaku; o sonemu; o netamu. **~ly** *ad.* **~y** *n.* shitto; yakimochi.

jean [dʒiːn] *n.* ayaori-mempu. (*pl.*) (*Am.*) zubon; sagyō fuku.

jeep [dʒiːp] *n.* (*Am.*) gun'yō kogata jidōsha; jiipu. *v.* (*Am.*) jiipu o hashirasu.

jeer [dʒiə] *n.* azawarai. *v.* azawarau (*at*).

Jehovah [dʒihóuvə] *n.* Ehoba; Tentei.

jejune [dʒidʒú:n] *a.* hinjakuna; fumō no; mumi kansōna.

jell [dʒel] (*Am. sl.*) *v.* jerii ni naru. *n.* jerii.

jelly [dʒéli] *n.* jerii (nikawa-shitsu no mono). *v.* katamaru; jerii ni naru. **~fish** [-fiʃ] *n.* kurage.

jennet, gennet [dʒénit] *n.* Spein san no kouma.

jenny [dʒéni] *n.* bōsekiki (=*spinning jenny*); idō kijūki. (*zoo.*) roba nado no mesu.

jeopardize [dʒépədaiz] *v.* ayauku suru : *soldiers ～ their lives in war*, gunjin-tachi wa sensō ni seimei no kiken o okasu.

jeopardy [dʒépədi] *n.* kiken.

jerk [dʒɔ:k] *v.* gui to hiku. *n.* gui to hiku koto.

jerkin [dʒé:kin] *n.* mijikai uwagi ; chokki (sode no aru mono ; nai mono).

jerky [dʒɔ́:ki] *a.* kimagurena ; kyūni ugoku.

jerry-building [dʒéri-bildiŋ] *n.* yasu-bushin.

Jersey [dʒé:zi] *a. Jersey*-tō (shima) no. *n.* Jāzishu no ushi ; fujin'yō jaketsu.

jess [dʒes] *n.* taka (*hawk*) no ashi ni tsuketa (*fastened*) himo

jessamin(e) [dʒésəmin] *n.* =**jasmine**. ⌊(*string*).-

jest [dʒest] *n.* jōdan. *v.* jōdan o iu ; chakasu. ～**er** *n.* dōkemo no ; ozamochi (*hōkan*).

Jesu [dʒí:zju:] *n. Jesus* no shitekina namae.

Jesuit [dʒézjuit] *n.* Jesuitto-Kaiin (*Roman Catholic*) ; imbōka. ～**ical** *a.* Jesuitto-Kai no ; inkenna ; kōkatsuna. ～**ism** *n.* Jesuitto no kyōgi ; inken ; kōkatsu.

Jesus [dʒí:zəs] *n.* **Jesus**.

jet [dʒet] *n.* (*min.*) kokugyoku ; kurodama. jōki nado ga ikkini ikioi yoku fukidasu koto. *a.* kurodama (sei) no. *v.* hotobashiri deru. ～**-airplane** (*or* **-plane**) jettoki. ～**-black** [⸺blæk] *a.* makkurona. ～**-propelled** [⸺prəpéld] *a.* funsha-suishinshiki no. ～**ty** [dʒéti] *n.* haridashi ; hatoba ; tottei. *a.* kokugyoku no ; kurodama sei no ; makkurona (*see* : **jet**).

jetsam [dʒétsəm/-sæm] *n.* (nansen no toki (*when shipwrecked*) fune o karuku (*to lighten*) suru tame nageta) kamotsu (*cargo*).

Jew [dʒu:] *n.* Yudayajin. ～**ish** *a.* Yudayajin no ; Yudayajinfū no. ～**'s-harp** [dʒú:z-hɑ:p] *n.* kōkin ; kuchi ni kuwaete yubi de kanaderu *Jew* no gakki.

jewel [dʒú(:)əl] *n.* (*min.*) hōseki ; kikinzoku (*precious metals*). daijina hito (mata wa mono) ; tokei no ishi. *v.* hōseki de kazaru (*put on*). ～**(l)er** [dʒú:ələ] *n.* hōseki-kō ; hōsekishō. ～**ry,** ～**lery** [dʒú(:)əlri, dʒú(:)ilri] *n.* hōgyoku zaiku ; hōseki rui.

jib [dʒib] *n.* (kijūki no) ude. *(naut.)* senshu no sankaku-ho. *v.* (uma ga) saki e susumanu.

jibe [dʒaib], **gibe** *n.* chōrō; azakeri. *v.* fune no ho no muki o kaeru. chōshi o awaseru.

jiffy [dʒifi] *n.* shunkan; chotto no ma.

jig [dʒig] *n.* jiggu (chōshi no hayai isshu no) dansu; isshu no tsuribari. *v.* jiggu o odoru furui ni kakeru.

jigger [dʒigə] *n.* fune de tsukau tsuna to kassha; tamatsukibō no dai; chiisai garasu no koppu; *(zoo.)* sunanomi.

jiggle [dʒigl] *v.* ugoitari, hippattari, jitto shite irarenai.

jigsaw [dʒigsɔ:] *n.* magatte hiku nokogiri.

jilt [dʒilt] *n.* otoko-tarashi. *v.* otoko o furu *(give the mitten)*.

jingle [dʒingl] *v.* (suzu nado ga) rinrin naru (narasu); chinchin naru (narasu). *n.* rinrin; chinchin (oto); kotoba no dōonhampuku.

jingo [dʒingou] *n.* shinryakuteki gaikō ronja (sha); shusenronsha. **~ism** *n.* shinryakuteki gaikōron; shusenron.

jinks [dʒinks] *n.* (*pl.*) sawagi. **high ~,** *n.* donchan sawagi.

jinx [dʒinks] *n.* (*Am. sl.*) engi no warui mono (mata wa hito).

jitney [dʒitni] *n.* (5 *c.*) no hakudōka; 5 *c.* noriai jidōsha.

jitterbug [dʒitəbʌg] *n.* (*Am. sl.*) *swing*-ongaku kichigai *v.* (*Am. sl.*) hageshii miburi de odoru.

jitters [dʒitəz] *n.* (*pl.*) (*Am. sl.*) shinkei-kabin-shō.

jittery [dʒitəri] *a.* (*Am. sl.*) shinkei-kabin no.

jive [dʒaiv] *n.* (*Am. sl.*) *swing*-ongaku semmon go. *v.* (*Am.*) *swing*-ongaku no ensō suru.

job [dʒɔb] *n.* shigoto; chin'uke-shigoto. *v.* chin-shigoto o suru; chingari suru. **~ber** [dʒɔbə] *n.* temachin shigoto o suru hito. **~bery** [dʒɔbəri] *n.* kōeki *(official)* no na no moto ni shiri o itonamu *(graft)* koto. **~master** [-mɑːstə] *n.* kashi bashaya.

jockey [dʒɔki] *n.* (keiba ni deru) kishu; bakurō. *v.* azamuku.

jocose [dʒɔkóus/dʒou-] *a.* gokigen no; kokkeina. **~ly** *ad.*

jocosity [dʒo(u)kɔsiti/dʒə-] *n.* kokkei; gokigen no jōtai.

jocular [dʒɔkjulə] *a.* kokkeina; jōdan o iu; odoketa. **~ity** [dʒɔkjulǽriti] *n.* kokkei; jōdan.

joccund [dʒɔkənd/dʒóuk-] *a.* kaikatsuna; yōkina. **~ly** *ad.*

jog [dʒɔg] *v.* sotto chūi suru : *give one's memory a* ～ = ～ *the memory*, omoidasaseru. ～**gle** *n.* karui yure ; sotto tsutsuku koto. *v.* yusuburu ; kosokoso aruku.

John Bull [dʒɔn bul] *n.* Eikokujin no adana.

Johnny [dʒɔ́ni] *n. John* no zokushō ; yatsu ; oshare otoko.

johnnycake [dʒɔ́nikèik] *n.* (*Am.*) tōmorokoshi no kona (*flour*) no pan.

join [dʒɔin] *v.* issho ni naru ; gappei suru ; tsunagu. ～**er** [dʒɔ́inə] *n.* sashimonoshi. *club* ya kai (*society*) nado o tsukuru hito. ～**ery** [dʒɔ́inəri] *n.* sashimonogyō ; mokkō-shoku ; sono shigoto (*work*).

joint [dʒɔint] *n.* tsugime ; kansetsu. *a.* rengō (byōdō) no. *v.* tsugu ; kansetsu kara kiru. ～ *comittee*, Ryōin Iinkai. ～**ed** [-id] *a.* tsugime no aru. ～**ly** *ad.* rengō shite. ～**stock** [-stɔk] *a.* gōshi (*jointstock company*) kabushiki kaisha.

joist [dʒɔist] *n.* keta ; neda ; utsubari.

joke [dʒouk] *n.* jōdan ; share. *v.* karakau ; jōdan o iu. ～**r** [dʒóukə] *n.* kokkeika.

jokingly [dʒóukiŋli] *ad.* jōdan ni.

jollification [dʒɔ̀lifikéiʃ(ə)n] *n.* yukai ; yūkyō.

jollity [dʒɔ́liti] *n.* yōki ; shuen ; sakamori.

jolly [dʒɔ́li] *a.* yukaina ; yōkina ; (*Brit. col.*) sutekina. *v.* karakau ; (*Am.*) odateru.

jolt [dʒoult] *v.* gatagata yureru. *n.* dōyō ; gatatsuki.

jonquil [dʒɔ́ŋkwil] *n.* (*flow.*) ki-zuisen ; usugiiro.

joss [dʒɔs] *n.* Chūgokujin no *god* no gūzō. ～**stick** [-stík] senkō.

jostle [dʒɔ́sl] *n.* oshiai. *v.* (hiji nado de) osu ; oshiau (*against*).

jot [dʒɔt] *n.* wazuka ; sukoshi. *v.* zatto kakitomeru (*note*).

joule [dʒu:l/dʒaul] *n.* denki enerugii no tan'i (*unit*).

jounce [dʒauns] *v. n.* gatagata suru (koto).

journal [dʒə́:n(ə)l] *n.* shimbun ; zasshi. ～**ism** [-izəm] *n.* shimbun (zasshi) gyō (*publication in all*). ～**ist** [-ist] *n.* shimbun (zasshi) kisha. ～**istic** [-ístik] *a.* shimbun (zasshi) kisha no.

journey [dʒə́:ni] *n.* ryokō ; ryotei. *v.* ryokō suru. ～**man** [-mən] hiyatoi shokkō ; ichinimmae no shokunin.

joust [dʒaust/dʒu:st] *n.* bajō shiai. *v.* bajō shiai o suru.

Jove [dʒouv] *n. Jupiter* no betsu no na : *by* ～, chikatte.

jovial [dʒóuvjəl] *a.* kaikatsuna; yōkina; yukaina. ~ly *ad.*

jowl [dʒaul] *n.* hō; ago.

joy [dʒɔi] *n.* yorokobi. *v.* yorokobu. ~ful *a.* ureshii; tanoshigena. ~fully *ad.* ~fulness *n.* ~ous *a.* yorokobashii; ureshisōna. ~ously *ad.* ~ousness *n.*

J.T.B. Nihon Kōtsū Kōsha (*Japan Travel Bureau*).

jubilant [dʒú:bilənt] *a.* gaika o sōsuru; kanko suru; yorokobi no koe o ageru.

jubilation [dʒù:biléiʃ(ə)n] *n.* gaika; kanko.

jubilee [dʒú:bili:] *n.* gojūnensai; shukuten (iwai).

judaism [djú:deiizm] *n.* Yudayakyō. ⌠dan suru.

judge [dʒʌdʒ] *n.* saibankan; shimpankan. *v.* saiban suru; hanjudg(e)ment [dʒʌ́dʒmənt] *n.* hanketsu; handan.

judicature [dʒú:dikətʃə/dʒudík-] *n.* shihō; saibansho.

judicial [dʒu(:)díʃ(ə)l] *a.* saibansho no; shihō no; kōheina : ~police, *n.* shihō keisatsu. ~ly *ad.*

judiciary [dʒu(:)díʃiəri] *a.* saibansho no; saibankan no. *n.* shihōken; shihōkan.

judicious [dʒu(:)díʃəs] *a.* shiryo no aru; rikutsu no tadashii. ~ly *ad.* ~ness *n.*

judo [dʒú:dòu] *n.* jūdō. (*cf.* **jūjutsu**).

jug [dʒʌg] *n.* mizusashi; saketsugi; kame.

Juggernaut [dʒʌ́gənɔ:t] *n.* Indo Kurishuna-Shin no gūzō; hito o gisei (metsubō) ni michibiku shūkan; sono seido nado.

juggle [dʒʌ́gl] *n.* kijutsu; tejina; manchaku. *v.* tejina o tsukau; manchaku suru. ~r *n.* kijutsushi; sagishi. ~ry *n.* kijutsu; tejina; sagi.

jugular [dʒʌ́gjulə] *a.* kubi no atari no. ~ vein (*anat.*) keijōjuice [dʒu:s] *n.* shiru; eki; jūsu. ⌊myaku.

juicy [dʒú:si] *a.* shiruke no ōi.

jujube [dʒú:dʒu(:)b] *n.* (*bot.*) natsume (no mi); natsume jerii.

jūjutsu [dʒu:dʒtsu] *n.* Nippon no (mukashi no) jūdō.

julep [dʒú:lep] *n.* (*Am.*) isshu no seiryō inryō (*sugar*+*crushed*July [dʒu(:)lái] *n.* Shichigatsu. ⌊*ice*).

jumble [dʒʌ́mbl] *n.* kongō; ranzatsu. *v.* gotamazeni suru (naru) : *things strangely ~d together*, mono ga omoshiroku isshoni mazekoze ni natte.

jump [dʒʌmp] v. tobiagaru; bōtō suru; tobikosu; tobaseru. n. tobu koto; bōtō. *prices* ~*ed*, bukka ga bōtō shita. ~ *a claim*, tanin no kenri o yokodori suru. ~ *at*, tobitsuku (yorokonde). ~*off*, tettai suru. ~ *on*, hidoku hinan suru. ~**er** [dʒʌmpə] n. tobu hito (mushi); jampā; (fujin'yō no) yurui *blouse*.

junction [dʒʌ́ŋ(k)ʃ(ə)n] n. rengō-ten; kōsaten; (kawa no) gōryūten : ~ **station**, n. norikae-eki; renraku eki.

juncture [dʒʌ́ŋ(k)tʃə] n. setsugōten; toki; baai; kyūba.

June [dʒuːn] n. Rokugatsu.

jungle [dʒʌ́ŋgl] n. yabuchi; janguru.

junior [dʒúːnjə] a. toshishita no; kōshin no. n. kakyūsha; (Amerika no yonen-sei daigaku no) sannensei; chichi to dōmei no musuko. ~ **high school**, n. (Am.) kakyū chūgakkō. ~**college**, n. tanki daigaku.

juniper [dʒúː(ː)nipə] n. (bot.) nezu; muro no rui.

junk [dʒʌŋk] n. furui kanamono, boro; (Am. sl.) garakuta; jankubune (sen).

junket [dʒʌ́ŋkit] n. isshu no gyūnyūsei no kashi; ō-gochisō no enkai. (Am.) kampi-ryokō.

Juno [dʒúːnou] n. (Rom. myth.) Jūnō (Jupiter no tsuma).

junta [dʒʌ́ntə] n. (Spein nado no) gikai. = Junto.

junto [dʒʌ́ntou] n. totō; imbōdan.

Jupiter [dʒúːpitə] n. kodai Rōma no kami-gami no Kami; (astr.) Mokusei; Girisha no Zeus.

juridical [dʒ(u)(ə)rídik(ə)l] a. saibanjō no; hōritsujō no (juristic) : ~ **person**, n. hōjin.

jurisdiction [dʒùərisdíkʃ(ə)n] n. saibanken; kankatsu kuiki (extent of authority).

jurisprudence [dʒùərisprúːd(e)ns] n. hōritsugaku.

jurist [dʒúerist] n. hōgakusha.

juror [dʒúərə] n. baishin'in.

jury [dʒúəri] n. baishin (in). ~**man** n. baishin'in no hitori.

just [dʒʌst] a. tadashii; tekitōna. ad. chōdo; imashigata (~ now); honno (only). ~**ly** [ɪtli] ad. tadashiku. ~**ness** n. tadashisa.

justice [dʒʌ́stis] n. seigi; saibankan : shihōkan. **court of** ~, n.

saibansho. *do* ～ *to*, ni kōheina handan o kudasu.

justiciary [dʒʌstíʃiəri] *n.* saibankan.

justifiable [dʒʌstifaiəbl] *a.* mottomona ; seitōna. ～**bly** *ad.*

justification [dʒʌstifikéiʃən] *n.* seitōka suru (sareru) koto ; bemmei ; bengo (*advocacy*).

justificatory [dʒʌstifikeitəri] *a.* bemmei no.

justify [dʒʌstifai] *v.* tadashii to suru : bemmei suru. *The fine quality of the cloth* ～*es the high price*, kiji no yūshūna koto ga sono takane o seitōka suru ; kiji ga sutekini iin da kara, ne no takai no mo tōzen da. *be* ～*ed*, sashitsukae nai. ～ *oneself*, iihiraki o suru.

jut [dʒʌt] *n.* tosshutsu. *v.* tosshutsu suru.

jute [dʒuːt] *n.* (*bot.*) tsunaso ; Indo-asa.

Jute [dʒuːt] *n.* Jūtojin.

juvenescence [dʒùːvinésns] *n.* wakagaeri ; wakasa (*youth*).

juvenescent [dʒùːvinésnt] *a.* wakagaeru.

juvenile [dʒúːvinail] *a.* shōnen no. *n.* shōnen ; koyaku ; shōnen muki no shomotsu. ～**ly** shōnen muki ni. ～ **court,** shōnen shimpansho.

juxtapose [dʒʌkstəpouz] *v.* narabete oku.

juxtaposition [dʒʌkstəpəzíʃ(ə)n] *n.* heichi ; narabete oku koto.

K

K, k [kei] *n* (*pl.* K's, Ks, [keiz]) Eigo *alphaqet* no dai-11-bamme no monji.

k *kalium*, *kilo* nodo no ryakuji.

kadi, cadi [káːdi/kéidi] *n.* Toruko (*Turkey*) no saibankan (*judge*).

Kaf(f)ir [kǽfə] *n.* Kafirujin (*Negro in South Africa*); Kafirisu-tanjin (*in Asia*).

Kaiser [káizə] *n.* kōtei; (K-) kyū Doitsu no kōtei no shōgō (*title*).

kale [keil] *n.* (*bot.*) habotan no isshu.

kaleidoscope [kəláidəskoup] *n.* mangekyō.

kaleidoscopic [kəlàidəskópik] *a.* iroiro chigatta.

kangaroo [kæŋgərúː] *n.* (*zoo.*) kangarū.

Kantian [kǽntiən] *a. Immanuel Kant* no; Kanto-tetsugaku (*philosophy*) no. *n. Kant* gaku-ha no hito.

kaolin [kéiəlin] *n.* tōki, jiki o tsukuru genryō.

kapok [kéipɔk] *n.* kinu mitaina sen'i; pan'ya (*nettaichihō no ki no mi o ou mono.

kappa [kǽpə] *n.* Girisha moji (K, κ).

karma [káːmə] *n.* (*Skt.*) inga-ōhō.

katydid [kéitidid] *n.* (*insect*) kutsuwamushi.

kauri [káuri] *n.* (*bot.*) kauri-matsu.

kayak [káiæk] *n.* Esukimōjin no mochiiru gyosen (*fishing-boat*).

Kc., kc, kirosaikuru (*kilocycle(s)*).

kedge [kedʒ] *n.* (*naut.*) chiisai ikari (*small*). *v.* ikari no tsuna o tagutte fune o susumeru.

keel [kiːl] *n.* ryūkotsu. *v.* ryūkotsu o tsukeru. ～ *over*, fune ga hikkurikaeru; sottō suru (*swoon*). ～**son** [kélsn] *n.* (*ship*) nai-ryūkotsu.

keen [kiːn] *a.* nesshinna; eibinna. ～**ly** [-li] *ad.* nesshinni; surudoku. ～**ness** [-nis] *n.* surudosa.

keep [kiːp] *v.* **kept**; **keeping.** (kisoku, yakusoku nado o) ma-moru; iwau (*celebrate*); tsuzukeru. *n.* hozon; ryōshoku. tenshukaku. ～ *standing*, tachi tsuzukeru. ～ *servants*, yatoinin o tsukau ; yatou. ~ *back*, hikaeru. ~ *down*, shizumeru ; suetsukeru (setsubi). ~ *off*, yobōsuru. ~ *on*, tsuzukeru. ~ *to*, o koshu suru. ~ *up*, tsuzukeru. ~ *up with*, to hitteki suru. *to work for my* ~, shokuhi ni hataraku. ~**er** [kíːpə] *n.* kanshu ; bannin ; kainushi : ~ *of the Great Seal* (*Brit.*) Kokuji Shōsho. ~ *of the Privy Seal* (*Brit.*) Gyoji Shōsho. ~**ing** *n.* hokan. ~**sake** [⌐seik] *n.* katami (*memento*) ; kinen-hin.

keg [keg] *n.* chiisai taru.

kelp [kelp] *n.* kaisō ; kaisō o yaita hai.

Kelt, Celt [kelt] *n.* Kerutojin. ~**ic** [kéltik] *a.* Kerutojin no. *n.* Kerutogo (*language*).

ken [ken] *n.* gankai ; chishiki no han'i. *v.* (*arch.*) miru.

kennel [kénl] *n.* inugoya.

kerchief [kəːtʃif] *n.* fujin no zukin ; kubimaki (*muffler*). (*poet.*) hankechi. 　　　　　　　　　　　　　　　　　⌐sence].

kernel [kəːn(ə)l] *n.* kaku ; kokuryū (naka no tane) ; shinzui (*essence*).

kerosene [kérəsiːn] *n.* tomoshibi no abura ; tōyu ; sekiyu.

kersey [kəːzi] *n.* isshu no rasha (*a sort of woolen cloth*).

kestrel [késtrəl] *n.* (*bird*) magusodaka (chiisai yōroppa no taka).

ketch [ketʃ] *n.* nihon-masuto no homaesen. 　　　⌐ka).

ketchup [kétʃəp] *n.* kechappu.

kettle [kétl] *n.* yuwakashi : *a pretty* (*nice, fine*) ~ *of fish*, komatta koto. ~**drum** [kétldrʌm] *n.* kama-gata no ōdaiko.

key [kiː] *n.* kagi ; tebiki (*manual*) ; piano nado no ken. *v.* (gakki no) chōshi o awaseru. ~ *industry*, jūyō sangyō. ~**board** [⌐bɔːd] *n.* kemban. ~**hole** [⌐houl] *n.* kagi-ana. ~**less** [⌐lis] *a.* kagi no nai ; ryūzumaki no tokei (*watch*). ~**note** [⌐nout] *n.* shuon ; shugan (*chief aim*). ~**stone** [⌐stoun] *n.* kusabi-ishi.

Kg., kg. kiroguramu (1000 g.). kodaru (*kegs*).

khaki [káːki] *n.* kākii-iro no fuku ; fuku-ji (*cloth*).

Khan [kɑːn] *n.* Chūō Ajia (*Central Asia*) no tōchisha no shōgō (*ruler's title*). 　　　　　　　　　　　　　　　　⌐general].

khedive [kədíːv] *n.* Torukojin no Ejiputo-sōtoku (*governor-*

kibe [kaib] *n.* (*med.*) kagato no akagire (*chaps*).

kibitz [kíbits] *v.* (*Am. col.*) iranu sewa o yaku ; shōbugoto ni kuchi o dasu.

kick [kik] *v.* keru; hantai suru (*be opposed to*). *n.* keru koto; teikō (*opposition*). ∼**off** [kíkɔ́(:)f] *n.* (shūkyū (*football*) no) shiai kaishi.　　　　　　　　　　　　　⌈(*fancy dish*).

kickshaw [kíkʃɔ:] *n.* chiisai tsumaranai mono; kotta ryōri

kid [kid] *n.* (*zoo.*) koyagi; koyagi no kawa; kodomo (*child*). *v.* karakau; fuzakeru. ∼**nap** [⸴næp] *v.* yūkai suru. ∼**nap(p)er** [⸴næpə] *n.* yūkaisha.

kidney [kídni] *n.* (*anat.*) jinzō; seishitsu (*nature*); shurui.

kill [kil] *v.* korosu : ∼ *time*, taikutsu o shinogu. ∼**ing** [kíliŋ] *a.* nōsatsu suru : *a* ∼ *glance*.

kilogram(me) [kíl(ə)græm] *n.* kiroguramu; 1.000 gr. yaku 266.6 momme.

kilogrammeter, ∼**tre** [kílográmì:tə] *n.* kiroguramu mētoru.

kiloliter, ∼**tre** [kílolì:tə] *n.* kirorittoru; 1000 *liters* (-*tre*); yaku 5.5425 koku.

kilometer, ∼**tre** [kílomì:tə] *n.* kiromētoru; 1000 *meters*; yaku 9 chō 10 ken.

kilostere [kíləstiə] *n.* kirosutēru mētoru; 1000 rippō mētoru.

kilowatt [kíləwət] *n.* (*elec.*) kirowatto.

kilt [kilt] *n. Scotland*-jin no kiru mijikai sukāto.

kin [kin] *n.* shinzoku; dōzoku. *a.* shinzoku no; dōzoku no. ∼**sfolk** [kínzfouk] *n.* (*pl.*) shinrui. ∼**ship** [kínʃip] *n.* dōzoku de aru koto. ∼**sman** *n.* shinseki.

kind [kaind] *a.* shinsetsuna. *n.* shurui (*sort*); zokusuru seishitsu (*nature*). ∼**-hearted** [káindhá:tid] *a.* shinsetsuna. ∼**ly** [káindli] *a.* shinsetsuna. *ad.* shinsetsuni; dōzo (*please*). ∼**ness** [káindnis] *n.* shinsetsu.　　　　　　　　　　⌈hobo.

kindergarten [kíndəgà:tn] *n.* yōchien. ∼**er** [kíndəga:tnə] *n.*

kindle [kíndl] *n.* hi (*fire*) o tomosu; (jō (*passion*) o) ugokasu

kindling [kíndliŋ] *n.* takitsuke.　　　　　　　　⌊(*inflame*).

kindred [kíndrid] *n.* shinzoku. *a.* shinseki no; ruiji no : *We are studying about dew, frost, and* ∼ *facts of nature*, wareware wa tsuyu, shimo, nado onaji shurui no shizen genshō (jijitsu) ni tsuite kenkyū shite iru.

kine [kain] *n.* (*pl.*) meushi.

kinematics [k(à)inimátik] *n.* (*phys.*) undō-gaku (dō-gaku).

kinematograph [k(à)inimátəgra:f] *n.* eiga; (*Am.*) eiga-satsueiki; (*Brit.*) eishaki (*cinematograph*). 「*film.*

kinescope [káiniskoup] *n.* (terevijon (*television*) no) eizō no

kinetic [k(à)inétik] *a.* undō o okosu. ~**s** *n.* (*phys.*) dōrikigaku.

king [kiŋ] *n.* ō; ōdatemono : ~ *of the country-side*, chihō no ōdatemono; ō-shō (*of chess*). *K*~'*s Bench* (*Brit.*) Kōtō-Hōin, saibansho. *K*~'*s English*, Hyōjun Eigo. ~**-craft** [⌐krɑːft] *n.* ōsei; ōdō. ~**dom** [⌐dəm] *n.* ōkoku; -kai (*animal* ~), dōbutsukai. ~**fish** [⌐fiʃ] *n.* (*Am. col.*) ryōshū (seikai, *political world*); oyakata; Taiheiyō, Taiseiyō de toreru aru shu no ōkina sakana. ~**fisher** [⌐fiʃə] *n.* (*bird*) kawasemi. ~**ly** [⌐li] *a.* ō no; ō rashii (*kinglike*). ~**ship** [⌐ʃip] *n.* ō-i, ō-ken (*sovereign power*).

kink [kiŋk] *n.* motsure; kimagure (*whim*). *v.* motsureru.

kiosk [kiɔ́sk] *n.* (*Toruko* no) azumaya; azumaya-fū no shimbun-uriba (*newspaper shop*); ongaku-dō (*band-stand*).

kip [kip] *n.* wakai kemono no kawa.

kipper [kípə] *n.* kunsei shita sake, nishin. *v.* himono ni suru; kunsei ni suru.

kirk [kəːk] *n.* (*Scot.*) kyōkai.

kismet [kízmet] *n.* ummei; temmei (*fate*).

kiss [kis] *v.* seppun suru; sesshoku suru. *n.* seppun; sesshoku.

kit [kit] *n.* teoke (*small pail*); biku (*fish basket*); dōgubako (*a tool-chest*).

kitchen [kítʃin] *n.* daidokoro. ~**garden** [⌐gáːdn] *n.* saien. ~**maid** [-meid] *n.* gejo.

kite [kait] *n.* (*bird*) tobi; tako : *fly a* ~, tako o ageru. ~ **balloon** [bəlúːn] *n.* kikyū-dako.

kith [kiθ] *n.* shirai. ~ *and kin*, shinseki hōyū.

kitten [kítn] *n.* koneko. ~**ish** [kítniʃ] *a.* koneko no yōna; jaretagaru (*playful*).

kittiwake [kítiweik] *n.* (*bird*) mitsu-yubi kamome.

kitty [kíti] *n.* koneko (aishō, *pet name*).

kl. *see* : **kiloliter**

kleptomania [klèpto(u)méinjə] *n.* (*med.*) settōkyō; tōheki.

kleptomaniac [klèpto(u)méiniæk] *n.* settōkyōsha.

knack [næk] *n.* kokyū; kotsu (*art ingenuous*).

knag [næg] *n.* (ki no) fushi (*knot in wood*).

knapsack [nǽpsæk] *n.* hainō.

knapweed [nǽpwiːd] *n.* (*flow.*) yagurumagiku. ⌜akuji.

knave [néiv] *n.* warumono; akkan. ∼**ry** [néivəri] *n.* fusei;

knavish [néiviʃ] *a.* akkan (warumono) no yōna; fuseina.

knead [niːd] *v.* koneru (kashi nado yaku mae, mugiko o).

knee [niː] *n.* (*anat.*) hiza : *bring to one's* ∼, kuppuku saseru. *fall on one's* ∼*s*, hizamazuku. ∼**breeches** [níːbritʃiz] (*pl.*) han-zubon. ∼**cap** [níːkæp], ∼**pan** [níːpæn] *n.* (*anat.*) shitsugai-kotsu.

kneel [niːl] *v.* **knelt, kneeling ;** hizamazuku. ⌞kotsu

knell [nel] *n.* kane (*bell*) no oto; kyōchō (*evil omen*).

knelt [nelt] *v. see :* **kneel.**

knew [njuː] *v. see :* **know.**

knickerbockers [níkəbɔkəz], **knickers** [níkəz] *n.* (*pl.*) yurui (*loose*) han-zubon. ⌜mono (*trifle*).

knick-knack, nick-nock [níknæk] *n.* omocha; tsumaranai

knife [naif] *n.* (*pl.* **-ves** [naivz]) kogatana; naifu; hōchō (*kitchen* ∼).

knight [nait] *n.* mukashi no kishi; "*Sir*" no shōgō (*title*) o yurusareta kizoku. -shōgi (*chess*) no keima. *v.* kishi no sha-kui o sazukeru. ∼**errant** [náitərənt] yūreki-kishi. ∼**er-rantry** [náitér(ə)ntri] *n.* musha-shugyō. ∼**hood** [-hud] *n.* kishidō; kishi no shakui. ∼**ly** *a.* kishi no; kishi rashii.

knit [nit] *v.* amu; musubitsukeru (*unite*); ∼ *one's brows*, mayu o hisomeru. ∼**ted** [nítid] *a.* meriyasu no; ∼ **goods,** meri-yasu rui. ∼**ting** [nítiŋ] *n.* amimono; meriyasu. ∼**ting-ne-edle** [nítiŋniːdl] *n.* ami-bari.

knob [nɔb] *n.* fushi; doa no torite.

knock [nɔk] *v.* utsu. *n.* utsu koto; to o tataku (koto) : *He* ∼*ed him on the head*, kare wa are no atama o nagutta. ∼ *about*, uchi tsuzukeru; kozuki mawasu. ∼ *down*, rakusatsu suru. ∼ *off*, yameru. ∼*out*, tataki nomesu ; (*cigarette-end* o) haizara ni oto-su; nokku-auto ni suru. ∼ *up*, tataki okosu; tsukaraseru (*make one tired*). ∼**down** [nɔ́kdaun] *v.* tataki taosu. ∼**er** [nɔ́kə] *n.* toguchi no nokka (tataki-gane). ∼ **kneed** [-niː(d)] *a.* uchiwani-ashi no. ∼**out** [nɔ́kaut] *v.* (*boxing*) nokku-auto suru; kyōbai de otosu.

knoll [noul] *n.* marui (*round*) koyama.

knop [nɔp] *n.* marui (*round*) totte ; tsubomi.

knot [nɔt] *n.* musubi-me ; shūdan. fushi (*board* ~) ; ichikairi ; (*nautical mile*, yaku 1853 mētoru (*meters*)). *v.* musubu : *cut the Gordian* ~, ittō-ryōdan no shochi o suru. *a* ~ *of people*, ichigun no hitotachi. ~**ted** [nɔ́tid] *a.* fushi no aru. ~**ty** [nɔ́ti] *a.* fushi no ōi ; konnanna.

knout [naut] *n.* muchi (Kodai Roshia no keibatsu no).

know [nou] *v.* knew, known ; knowing. shiru ; shitte iru. ~**all** [nóuɔːl] *n.* monoshiri-gao no hito. ~**-how** [nóuhau] *n.* (*Am. col.*) semmon no chishiki (*knowledge*) to gijutsu (*skill*). ~**ing** [nó(u)iŋ] *a.* yoku shitte iru (*well informed*) ; kosui (*cunning*). ~**ingly** [nó(u)iŋli] *ad.* waza to ; josai naku. ~**-nothing** [nóunʌθiŋ] *n.* muchi no hito.

knowledge [nɔ́lidʒ] *n.* chishiki ; gakumon (*learning*) : *come to a person's* ~, hito ni shireru. *have no* ~ *of*, o sukoshi mo shiranai. *to my* ~, watakushi no shiru kagiri dewa. *without the* ~ *of*, (hito) ni shirasezu ni. ~**able** [nɔ́lidʒəbl] *a.* (*Am. col*) chishiki no aru.

known [noun] *v. see* : **know**.

knuckle [nʌ́kl] *n.* yubi kansetsu ; hiza kansetsu : ~ *down* (*or under*) kōsan suru. ~**bone** [-boun] *n.* yubi kansetsu no hone.

knurl [nəːl] *n.* fushi ; kobu (*knot*). ~**y** [nɔ́ːli] *a.* fushi no ōi.

kodak [kóudǽk] *n.* kogata shashinki. *v. kodak* de utsusu.

Kohinoor [kó(u)inuə] *n.* Eikoku Koushitsu no *diamond*.

kola, cola [kóulə] *n.* (*bot.*) kora (*cola*) no ki. ~**nut** [-nʌt] *n.* kora no ki no mi.

kolkhoz [kɔlkɔ́(ː)z] *n.* koruhōzu ; Soren (*the Soviet Union*) no shūdan-nōjō (*farm*).

konzern [kontsérn] *n.* (*Ger.*) kontserun ; kigyō no tōitsu soshiki.

kope(c)k [kóupek] *n.* Soren (*the Soviet Union*) no kahei (*money*)

Koran [kɔ́(ː)rɑːn] *n.* Kōran ; Kaikyō no *Bible*. no na.

Koranic [kɔrǽnik] *o.* Kōran no.

Korea [kɔríə] *n.* Chōsen ; Kankoku.

kosher [kóuʃə] *a.* kiyorakana (Yudayakyō de).

kotow [kóutáu/kautáu], **kowtow** [kóutáu] *n.* kōtō no rei. (*in China*). *v.* kōtō suru ; obekka o suru.

kraal [krɑːl] *n.* Minami Afurika no dojin no mura ; kachikugoya (*pen*).

Kremlin [krémlin] Roshia no toride (*fortress*); Kremlin no kyūden (*palace*).

kreutzer [krɔ́itsə] *n.* mukashi Minami Doitsu ni okonawareta chiisai dōka (*copper coin*).   [*ver coins*].

krone [króunə] *n.* Demmāku, Nōruwē, Swēden no ginka (*silku-klux-klan* [kjú:klʌ́ksklǽn] *u.* K.K.K. himitsu kessha.

kumiss [kú:mis] *n.* Ajia no yūbokumin (*nomads*) ga nomu, milk o hakkō (*ferment*) sashita sake.

L

L, l [el] *n.* (*pl.* L's, Ls, [elz]) Eigo *alphabet* no dai-12-bamme no moji.
L, l [el] *Latin*, *lady*, *lake*, *law*, *liter* (rittoru) nado ni tsukawareru kashira-moji.
label [léib(ə)l] *n.* harigami ; harifuda ; retteru. *v.* haru.
labial [léibiəl] *a.* kuchibiru no. *n.* shin'on ([p], [b] nado.)
labo(u)r [léibə] *n.* rōdō ; shigoto. *v.* rōdō suru ; hataraku ; kushin suru ; osan de kurushimu (*travail*) ; tateyoko ni yureru (*ship*). ⁓**er** [léibərə] rōdōsha. ⁓**ing** [léibəriŋ] *a.* rōdō suru ; osan de kurushimu ; hidoku yureru (*ship*) : *the* ⁓ *classes*, rōdō kaikyū. ⁓**ly** [léibəriŋli] *ad.* ⁓**-saving** [⸺sèiviŋ] *a.* rōdō o herasu.
laboratory [ləbɔ́rət(ə)ri] *n.* jikkenshitsu ; kenkyūjo ; seiyakulaborious [ləbɔ́:riəs] *a.* hone no oreru ; benkyō suru. ⁓**ly** *ad.* hone otte. ⌐jo.
labyrinth [lǽbərinθ] *n.* meizu ; meiro (*maze*). ⁓**ine** [læbərínθain] *a.* irikunda (*mazy*).
lac [lǽk] *n.* rakku ; rakku o nutta kigu (*utensil*).
lace [leis] *n.* uchihimo ; reisu. *v.* himo de shimeru ; reisu de kazaru ; (*col.*) muchi (*whip*) de utsu. ⁓**d boots** amiagegutsu.
lacerate [lǽsəreit] *v.* hikisaku (*tear*) ; kizutsukeru (*wound*) ; kurushimeru (*distress*).
laceration [lǽsəréij(ə)n] *n.* hikisaki ; kunō (*suffering*).
lachrymal [lǽkriməl] *a.* namida no. ⁓ **gland,** (*anat.*) ruisen.
lachrymatory [lǽkrimət(ə)ri] *a.* sairui no. ⁓ **bomb** *n.* sairui dan. ⌐su.
lachrymose [lǽkrimous] *a.* namidagunda ; namida o moyō
lacing [léisiŋ] *n.* himo ; reisu.
lack [lǽk] *v.* tarinai ; kakeru (*be short of*). *n.* ketsubō.
lackadaisical [læ̀kədéizik(ə)l] *a.* mono omowashigena ; kanashigena ; bon'yari shita.
lackey, lacquey [lǽki] *n.* genan ; jūsha (*servant*).
laconic [ləkɔ́nik] *a.* kanketsuna (kotoba ya goku no.)

lacquer [lǽkə] *n.* urushi; rakkā; shikki (∼*ware*).

lacrosse [ləkrɔ́s/lɑ:] *n.* tama-asobi (*game*).

lactation [lǽktéiʃən] *n.* junyū; chichi o nomaseru. junyūki.

lacteal [lǽktiəl] *a.* nyūjō no (∼ *fluid*). *n.* (*anat.*) nyūbikan.

lactic [lǽktik] *a.* chichi no; ∼ *acid*, nyūsan.

lactose [lǽktous] *n.* nyūtō.

lacuna [lɔkjú:nə] *n.* sukima; datsubun (*missing part in a book or sentence*).

lad [læd] *n.* wakamono; shōnen (*youth*).

ladder [lǽdə] *n.* hashigo; shusse (*rising in the world*) no tezuru.

lade *v.* [leid] **laded, laden** *or* **laded; lading.** tsumu; kumikomu (*dip into*); kumidasu (*dip out*).

lading [léidiŋ] *n.* funa-zumi (*loading*); tsumini (*freight*).

ladle [léidl] *n.* hishaku. *v.* hishaku de kumidasu.

lady [léidi] *n.* fujin; shikujo. ∼**bird** [léidibə:d], ∼**bug** [léidibʌg] *n.* (*insect*) tentomushi. ∼**killer** [léidikilə] *n. sl.* onnagoroshi; irootoko (*handsome man*). ∼**like** [léidilaik] *a.* teishukuna. ∼**ship** [léidiʃip] *n.* fujin no sonshō (*title of honour*); chii ya kaikyū. *Ladyship* to keishō nimo tsukau.

lag [læg] *n.* okureru koto. *v.* noronoro (*slowly*) aruku; guzuguzu suru (*go slowly*).

lager [lá:gə] *n.* yowai (*weak*) biiru (*beer*).

laggard [lǽgəd] *a.* guzuguzu suru. *n.* noroma; guzuguzu shite rakugo suru mono.

lagoon [ləgú:n] *n.* gata; numa (*swamp*); sangoshō no naka no mizuumi (*lake in coralisland*).

laic(al) [léiikəl] *a.* zokujin no (sōryo to kubetsu suru tame ⌊ni).

laid [léid] *v. see* : **lay.**

lain [lein] *v. see* : **lie.**

lair [leə] *n.* kedamono (*beast*) no sōkutsu (nedoko) (*living place*).

laird [leəd] *n.* (*Scot.*) jinushi (*land-owner*).

laissez-faire [léiseifeə] *n.* (*Fr.*) mu-kanshō shugi; hōnin shugi.

laity [léiiti] *n.* zokujin; mongaikan (*unprofessional people*).

lake [leik] *n.* (1) mizuumi; kōen nado no ike. (2) shinkōshoku : (iro). ∼ *District, England* hokubu (*northern part*) no kosuichihō.

lam [læm] *n.* (*Am. col.*) tōbō : *on the* ～, nigete ; kakurete. *v.* (*Am. col.*) tōbō suru ; (tsue (*stick*) de) utsu.

lama [láːmə] *n.* Tibet ya Mōko no Rama-kyō no sō : *Grand* ～, Darai Rama. ～**ism** [láːmaizm] *n.* Rama-kyō.

lamb [læm] *n.* ko-hitsuji ; *The Lamb, Christ.* ko hitsuji no niku (*meat*). *v.* ko-hitsuji o umu. ～**kin** *n.* ko-hitsuji.

lambaste [ləmbéist] *v.* (*sl.*) tataki nomesu ; hidoku shikaru.

lambent [lǽmbənt] *a.* hi no hikari ga yuragu ; hikaru : kei-myōna. *moonlight is* ～, tsuki no hikari ga yawarakani terasu.

lame [leim] *a.* bikko no ; chōshi no awanai : *go* ～, bikko o hiku. *v.* bikko ni suru (naru).

lament [ləmént] *n.* hitan. *v.* kanashimu : *we* ～*ed his absence*, kare no rusu o kuyanda. ～**able** [lǽməntəbl] *a.* kanashii ; nagekawashii : ～ *able accident*, nagekawashii dekigoto.

lamentation [læməntéiʃ(ə)n] *n.* hitan ; koe o tatete naku koto ; nageki ; (*pl.*) (*L*～) Eremiya Aika (Kyūyaku Seisho).

lamina [lǽminə] *n.* (*pl.* **-nae** [-niː]) (kinzoku nado no) ita. (*bot.*) ha no usui hiratai tokoro.

laminate [lǽmineit] *v.* usuita ni suru (naru) ; haku ni suru (naru). *a.* usuita no.

lamp [læmp] *n.* rampu ; akari : *smell of the* ～, kushin no ato ga mieru. *hand* (*pass*) *on the* ～, bunka no shimpo ni tsukusu. ～**black** [◦blǽk] *n.* yuen. ～**lighter** [◦laitə] *n.* tentō-fu.

lampoon [læmpúːn] *n.* hiniku ; fūshibun ; rakushu. *v.* fūshi ⌐suru.

lamprey [lǽmpri] *n.* (*fish*) yatsumeunagi.

lance [lɑːns] *n.* yari. *v.* yari de tsuku ; ransetto de sasu. ～**-corporal** [lɑːnskɔ́ːpərəl] *n.* gochō kimmu jōtōhei.

lancer [láːnsə] *n.* sō (yari) kihei. (*pl.*) isshu no butō.

lancet [láːnsit] *n.* (*med.*) ransetto.

land [lænd] *n.* riku ; jimen ; kuni ; jisho. *v.* jōriku suru (saseru) ; chakuriku suru (saseru) ; oriru (orosu) (norimono kara). tsukamaeru ; tōchaku suru. ～ **breeze** rikunampū (riku kara umi e fuku soyo-kaze). ～**ed** [◦id] *a.* tochi o motte iru ; jisho no : *landed proprietor*, jinushi. ～**-holder** [◦houldə] *n.* jinushi ; shakuchinin. ～**ing** *n.* jōriku ; chakuriku ; hatoba ; kaidan no odoriba. ～**ing field** (*or* **ground**), chakurikujō. ～**ing party** *n.* rikusentai. ～**lady** [◦leidi] *n.* yadoya no onna shujin. ∼**locked** [⌐ˈlɔkt] *a.* riku ni kakomareta. ∼**lord** [⌐ˈlɔːd] *n.* ryokan no shujin ; jinushi. ∼**mark** [⌐ˈmɑːk] *n.* kyōkaihyō. ∼**slide** [⌐ˈslaid], ∼**slip** [⌐ˈslip] *n.* jisuberi ; riku no hō e. ∼**sman** [⌐ˈzmən] *n.* rikujō-seikatsusha ; fune ni narenai hito. ∼ **tax,** chiso. ∼**ward** [-wəd] *ad.* riku no hō e. *a.* rikuchi no hō e.

landau [lǽndɔː] *n.* randō basha (isshu no yon (4)-rimbasha).
landaulet [lǽndɔːlét] *n.* kogata randō basha ; randō gata jidōsha.
landscape [lǽn(d)ske(i)p] *n.* fūkeiga ; keshiki.
lane [lein] *n.* komichi ; semai michi ; *red* ∼, (*sl.*) nodokubi. *the* ∼, London no "*Drury* [drúəri] *Lane*" gekijō. ⌐kashi.
langsyne [lǽŋsáin] *ad.* (*Scot.*) hisashii mae ni (*long since*). *n.* mu-**language** [lǽŋgwidʒ] *n.* gengo ; kotoba. ⌐naku.
languid [lǽŋgwid] *a.* daraketa ; kakki no nai. ∼**ly** *ad.* genki **languish** [lǽŋgwiʃ] *v.* otoroeru ; shibomu ; omoi nayamu ; kogareru. ∼**ing** *a.* shidai ni otoroeru ; omoi nayamu.
languor [lǽŋgə] *n.* darui koto ; hirō ; kentai : *long illness causes* ∼, nagai byōki wa akiaki suru. ∼**ous** *a.* darui ; taikutsuna.
lank [læŋk] *a.* yaseta ; hossori shita ; massuguna. ∼**y** [⌐i] *a.* hyoronagai.
lantern [lǽntən] *n.* chōchin ; tōrō. ∼ **jaws,** yasehosotta ago (kao). **magic** ∼ *n.* gentō. ⌐nawa.
lanyard [lǽnjəd] *n.* (*Am.*) hikinawa (taihō hassha no) ; shime-**lap** [lǽp] *n.* hiza ; maekake ; ito no hitomaki ; keibajō no hitomawari. *v.* orikasanaru ; (nami ga) kishi o arau. orekasanaru. **lap-dog** [lǽpdɔg], chin ; daki-inu.
lapel [ləpél/lǽp(e)l] *n.* uwagi no eri no orikaeshi.
lapidary [lǽpidəri] *n.* hōseki shokunin.
lapis lazuli [lǽpis lǽzjulai] *n.* (*miner.*) ruri.
lappet [lǽpit] *n.* tare ; hida (kimono ; mimitabo nado).
lapse [læps] *n.* keika ; kashitsu ; (*leg.*) (kenri nado no) sōshitsu. *v.* toki ga tatsu ; daraku suru. (*leg.*) hitode ni wataru ; mukō ni naru.
lapwing [lǽpwiŋ] *n.* (*bird*) nabegeri. ⌐Asia).
LALA kōnin Ajia kyūsai kikan (*Licensed Agency for Relief of*
larboard [lúːbɔːd/-bəd] *n.* (*naut.*) sagen. (*cf. starboard*).
larch [lɑːtʃ] *n.* karamatsu.
lard [lɑːd] *n.* rādo ; buta no abura. *v.* butaniku o naka ni

tsumeru; kazaru.

larder [láːdə] *n.* shokuryō shitsu; nikuire todana.

large [lɑːdʒ] *a.* ōkii; hiroi; tasū no : *at* ∼, torawarenai; ippan-ni. ∼**-hearted** [⌐háːtid] *a.* kokoro no ōkii. ∼**ly** *ad.* ōini. ∼**ness** *n.* ōkisa.

largess [láːdʒes] *n.* okurimono (kimae no yoi).

largo [láːgou] *ad.* (*mus.*) kiwamete yukkuri. *n.* rarugō. *a.* yuk-kuri shita utsukushii.

lark [lɑːk] *n.* (*bird*) hibari : *rise with the* ∼, hayaoki suru. ∼**spur** [⌐spəː] *n.* (*flow.*) hiensō.

larva [láːvə] *n.* (*pl.* -vae [-viː]) yōchū (otamajakushi no yōna). *a.* yōchū no.

laryngeal [ləríndʒiəl] *a.* (*anat.*) kōtō no; nodo no.

laryngitis [lèrindʒáitis] *n.* kōtōen (*disease*).

laryngoscope [ləríŋɡəskoup/lær-] *n.* kōtōkyō (kōtō o miru kagami).

larynx [lǽriŋks] *n.* (*anat.*) kōtō.

lascivious [ləsíviəs] *a.* midarana. ∼**ly** *ad.* waisetsuni. ∼**ness** *n.* kōshoku; nikuyoku.

lash [lǽʃ] *n.* (muchi (*whip*) no) himo; muchiuchi; matsuge; tsūretsuna hinan. *v.* muchiutsu; nonoshiru; hageshiku utsu; tosshin suru. ∼**ing** *n.* muchiuchi; shibaru koto.

lass [lǽs] *n.* wakai musume; koibito.

lassitude [lǽsitjuːd] *n.* tsukare; ki no susumanai koto.

lasso [lǽsou] *n.* (*pl.* -s) wanawa; nagenawa.

last [lɑːst] *a.* saigo no; kono mae no; saigo no. *ad.* saigo ni; kono mae. *n.* saigo. kutsuya no ashigata. *v.* tsuzuku; mochi ga yoi. ∼ *day of*, no saigo no hi. *at* ∼, tsui ni. *breathe one's* ∼, iki o hikitoru. *to the* ∼, saigo made. ∼**ing** *a.* eikyū no; mochi no yoi. ∼**ly** *ad.* saigo ni.

latch [lǽtʃ] *n.* sashijō. *v.* kakegane o orosu.

latchet [lǽtʃit] *n.* kutsu no kawa himo.

late [leit] *a.* osoi. mae no; shinda; chikagoro no; yoru osoi. *ad.* osoku. *keep* ∼ *hours*, yofukashi suru. *of* ∼, chikagoro. ∼**spring** *n.* banshun. ∼ **riser** asanebō. ∼**ly** *ad.* chikagoro. ∼**ness** *n.* osoi koto.

latency [léit(ə)nsi] *n.* sempuku shita jōtai (jōken) aruiwa sei-shitsu.

latent [léit(ə)nt] *a.* kakurete iru ; sempuku shite iru. ~ **heat,** sennetsu.

later [léitə] *ad.* ato de : ~ *on,* ato de. *a.* motto osoi.

lateral [lǽtər(ə)l] *a.* yoko no ; sokumen no. ~ **attack** *n.* sokumen kōgeki.

latest [léitist] *a.* saikin no ; ichiban osoi : *at the* ~, osoku tomo. ⌈no mono).

lath [lɑːθ] *n.* kizuri ; komai (tenjō (*ceiling*) o motaseru tame

lathe [leið] *n.* darai-ban ; semban : *turning* ~, semban.

lather [lǽðə/láːðə] *n.* sekken no awa ; ase no awa. *v.* awadatsu (-dateru) ; ase o kaku.

Latin [lǽtin] *n.* Latenjin no ; kodai Rōmajin no : ~ *Church,* Rōma-kyō ; Tenshukyō. *n.* kodai Rōmajin ; Latengo. ~**ism** *n.* Latengofū. ~**ist** *n.* Latengo gakusha. ~**ize** *v.* Latengo no yōni suru. ~ **Quarter** bunshi ya bijutsuka no ōzei atsumatte iru machi. (*Quartier Latin*).

latitude [lǽtitjuːd] *n.* ido ; jiyū ; han'i : *you are allowed much* ~, (*fig.*) kimi wa hiroi han'i no jiyū ga ataerarete iru.

latitudinal [lætitjúːdin(ə)l] *a.* ido no.

latitudinarian [lætitjùːdinéəriən] *a.* jiyūshugi no ; kyōgi nado ni torawarenai. *n.* jiyūshugisha.

latter [lǽtə] *a.* ato no ; kōsha no ; kōhan no : *the* ~, kōsha. (*cf. former.*) ~**ly** *ad.* kono goro ; bannen ni.

lattice [lǽtis] *n.* kōshi ; kōshimado. *v.* kōshi o tsukeru. ~**d** *a.* kōshi tsukuri no. ~**work** [-wəːk] *n.* kōshizaiku, kōshi moyō.

laud [lɔːd] *v.* homeru. *n.* sambi ; sambi no uta. ~**able** *a.* kanshinna. ~**ably** *ad.* rippani.

laudanum [lɔ́d(ə)nəm] *n.* ahenchinki ; ahenzai (itami o yawarageru (*lessen*) kusuri).

laudation [lɔːdéiʃ(ə)n] *n.* sambi ; shōsan ; hometatae.

laudatory [lɔ́ːdət(ə)ri] *a.* sambi no.

laugh [lɑːf] *n.* warai. *v.* warau : ~ *at,* warau. ~**able** *a.* okashina. ~**ably** *ad.* omoshiroku. ~**ing stock,** waraigusa.

laughter [lɑ́ːftə] *n.* warai ; waraigoe.

launch [lɔːntʃ/lɑːntʃ] *v.* shinsui suru ; chakushu suru ; hassha suru ; noridasu. *n.* shinsui ; ranchi ; chiisai jōkisen.

launder [lɔ́ːnd(ə)] *v.* sentaku suru (*clothes*).

laundress [lɔ́:ndris/lɑ́:n-] *n.* sentaku onna.

laundry [lɔ́:ndri/lɑ́:n-] *n.* sentakuya ; sentaku-mono.

laureate [lɔ́:riit/lɔ́r-] *a.* gekkeikan o itadaita : *poet* ~, keikan-shijin.

laurel [lɔ́r(ə)l] *n.* gekkeiju ; gekkeikan ; eiyo.

lava [lɑ́:və] *n.* yōgan (kazan kara fukidashita).

lavatory [lǽvət(ə)ri] *n.* semmenjo.

lave [leiv] *v.* arau.

lavender [lǽvində] *n.* (*flow.*) rabendā ; usumurasaki iro.

lavish [lǽviʃ] *a.* kimae no yoi (*liberal*) ; rōhi suru. *v.* rōhi suru ; kimae yoku ataeru. ~**ly** *ad.* oshigenaku ; midarini. ~**ness** *n.* ōmakasa ; rōhisei.

law [lɔ:] *n.* hōritsu ; hōgaku : *go to* ~, kokuso suru. *have (or take) the* ~ *of*, kiso suru. ~**ful** *a.* gōhō no ; hōritsujō no. ~**giver** [⸜givə] *n.* rippōsha. ~**less** *a.* hōritsu no nai ; fuhōna. ~**suit** [⸜sju:t/⸜su:t] *n.* soshō.

lawn [lɔ:n] *n.* shibafu. kanreisha no rui. ~**-tennis** teikyū.

lawyer [lɔ́:jə] *n.* hōritsuka ; bengoshi.

lax [læks] *a.* yurui ; tenurui ; aimaina.

laxative [lǽksətiv] *a.* tsūji o tsukeru. *n.* bentsū no kusuri.

laxity [lǽksiti] *n.* yurui koto ; darashi no nai koto ; aimaisa.

lay [lei] *v.* **laid** ; **laying.** oku, yokotaeru ; (sekinin nado o) owaseru ; kasuru (*charge*) ; (tamago o) umu ; yokotaeru. shizumaru. *n.* ichi (*situation*) ; uta. *a.* zokujin no. *your effort* ~ *the ghost*, kimi no doryoku de shizumatta ; ~ *about (one)*, mōretsuni dageki o kuwaeru. ~ *aside*, katazukeru ; yameru. ~ *by*, takuwaeru ; yameru. ~ *down*, fusetsu suru ; yameru ; takuwaeru ; keikaku o tateru. ~ *out*, naraberu ; sekkei suru. tsuiyasu ; nōkan no yōisuru ; ~ *up*, takuwaeru. ~ **figure,** jintai mokei ; deku no bō ; kairai. ~**man** [⸜mən] *n.* zokujin ; shirōto.

lay [lei] *v. see* : **lie.**

layer [lé(i)ə] *n.* tsumu hito ; tamago o umu niwatori : *a bad* ~, tamago o umanai niwatori.

layer [léə] *n.* (*stratum*) sō ; kasane ; nuri ; toriki (engei no).

layoff [léiɔ(:)f] *n.* (*Am.*) ichijiteki kaiko (*temporary dismiss*).

layout [léi-aut] *n.* sekkei. (*Am.*) tori hirogerareta mono : *the* ~ *of the house,* ie no sekkei.

lazar [lǽzə] *n.* raibyō no kojiki.

lazaret(to) [læzərétou] *n.* densembyōin ; raibyōin.

lazy [léizi] *a.* namakeru ; mo**n**ougena. ∼**bones** [-′bounz] *n.* (*col.*) namakemono. ∼**ily** *ad.* namakete ; bushōni. ∼**iness** *n.* taida. ∼ **tongs** [′-tɔŋz] *n.* bushō-basami.

lb. pondo (*pound, apothecaries' weight*).

L/C. l/c. (*com.*) shin'yōjō (*Letter of Credit*).

lea [li:] *n.* (*poet*) kusachi ; bokusōchi.

leach [li:tʃ] *v.* kosu (*filter*) ; mizu de sarasu. *n.* kosu koto ; mizu-koshioke.

lead [led] *n.* namari ; empitsu no shin. *v.* namari o kabuseru ; namari o tsumeru. ∼ **line,** (mizu no fukasa o hakaru) soku-ensen. ∼ **pencil** *n.* empitsu.

lead [li:d] *v.* michibiku ; annai suru ; hikiiru ; sasou. *v.* sendō suru. *n.* sendō ; kachikoshi. ∼ **to,** dōro ga…ni itaru ; o shō-zuru. ∼**ing** *a.* sendō suru ; dai ichii no ; omona. ⌐nai.

leaden [lédn] *a.* namari no ; omokurushii ; darui ; kakki no

leader [lí:də] *n.* sendōsha ; shikisha ; shimbun no shasetsu ; suidō tekkan ; sentō no uma.

leaf [li:f] *n.* (*pl.* **leaves** [li:vz]) ha ; (shomotsu no) ichimai ; (kin, gin nado no) haku. ∼**age** [lí:fidʒ] *n.* konoha. ∼**let** [′-lit] *n.* chiisana ha ; orikomi insatsubutsu ; shōsasshi. ∼**stalk** [′-stɔ:k] *n.* yōhei. ∼**y** *a.* ha no ōi ; shigette iru.

league [li:g] *n.* dōmei ; remmei ; riigu (yaku 4.83 kiro mētoru). *v.* dōmei suru. *the L*∼ *of Nations,* Kokusai Remmei.

leak [li:k] *n.* moriguchi ; morimizu. *v.* moru : ∼ **out,** moreru. ∼**age** [′-idʒ] *n.* mori ; moridaka ; (himitsu nado no) rōei.

leaky [lí:ki] *a.* more yasui ; himitsu no mamorenai ; oshaberina.

lean [lí:n] *a.* yaseta ; shūkaku no sukunai ; wari ni awanai. *v.* **leaned** *or* **leant, leaning,** katamuku ; yorikakaru ; tayoru ; tatekakeru. ∼**-to** [′-tú:] *n.* sashikake-goya ; geya.

leant [lent] *v. see :* **lean.**

leap [li:p] *v.* tobu ; tobikoeru ; tobaseru. *n.* chōyaku ; chōyaku no takasa ; habatobi. ∼ **year,** uruu-doshi. ∼**frog** [′-frɔg] *n.* kaerutobi ; umatobi.

learn [lə:n] *v.* **learned** *or* **learnt** [lə:nt] ; **learning.** manabu ; shiru ; kiku ; …ni naru ; oboeru. ∼**ed** [′-id] *a.* gakumon no aru. ∼**ing** *n.* gakumon ; gakushiki.

learnt [lə:nt] *v. see* : **learn.**

lease [li:s] *n.* shakuchi keiyaku ; shakuchiken ; shakuyō kikan. *v.* kasu ; kariru. ∼**hold** ['-(h)ould] *n.* shakuchi ; shakuchiken. ∼**holder** [-'(h)ouldə] *n.* shakuchinin ; chinshakunin.

leash [li:ʃ] *n.* kawahimo. *v.* kawahimo de tsunagu.   ⌐naku.

least [li:st] *a.* saishō no. *n.* saishō ; saishōryō. *ad.* ichiban suku-

leather [léðə] *n.* kawa ; kawa seihin. *a.* **kawa** no ; kawa no yō-na. ∼**ette** [lèðərét] *n.* mozō no kawa. ∼**y** *a.* kawa no yōna.

leave [li:v] *v.* **left ; leaving.** nokosu ; oite iku ; saru ; makaseru. *n.* kyoka ; kyūka ; itomagoi. ∼ *off,* yameru. ∼ *out,* habuku ; mushi suru. *take* ∼, itomagoi suru.   ⌐oyobosu.

leaven [lévn] *n.* kōbo ; pan-dane. *v.* hakkō saseru ; eikyō o

leavings [lí:viŋz] *n.* (*pl.*) nokorimono ; nuka ; kuzu.

lecher [létʃə] *n.* hōtōmono. ∼**ous** [-rəs] *a.* kōshoku no.

lecture [léktʃə] *n.* kōgi ; kōen ; (*fig.*) kogoto. *v.* kōgi (kōen) suru ; *read a* ∼, kunkai suru. ∼**r** [-rə] *n.* kōensha ; kunkaisha.

led [led] *v. see* : **lead.**

ledge [ledʒ] *n.* tana. anshō (*ridge of rock*) ; kōmyaku (*lode*). *window* ∼, mado no deppari.

ledger [lédʒə] *n.* motochō ; gembo.

lee [li:] *n.* kazashimo ; kazakage.

leech [li:tʃ] *n.* hiru ; kyūketsuki ; kōrikashi.

leek [li:k] *n.* nira : *eat the* ∼, (*fig.*) kutsujoku o shinobu.

leer [liə] *n.* yokome ; irome. *v.* irome o tsukau.

lees [li:z] *n.* (*pl.*) ori (*dregs*) ; kuzu ; haibutsu.   ⌐*ward.*)

leeward [lí:wəd] *a.* kazashimo no. *ad.* kazashimo e. (*cf. wind-*

leeway [lí:wei] *n.* fūatsu-sa (*side movement of a ship*) ; kaze de fune ga ukeru eikyō ; jikan no sonshitsu ; okure ; (*col.*) yoyū ; yochi.

left [left] *v. see* : **leave.** *a.* hidari no ; ∼ *bank,* (karyū ni mu-katte) hidarigishi. *n.* hidari ; zaiyatō (*non-government*) ; (*baseball*) sayoku (shu). ∼**-handed** ['-hǽndid] *a.* hidari-giki no.

leftist [léftist] *n.* sayokuha ; kyūshintōin.

leg [leg] *n.* ashi ; sune. *v.* (*col.*) aruku ; hashiru.

legacy [légəsi] *n.* isan (daidai no) ; katami.

legal [lí:g(ə)l] *a.* hōritsujō no ; ∼ *tender,* hōtei kahei.

legality [li(:)gǽliti] *n.* tekihō ; seitōna koto ; gōhō.

legalize [líːgəlaiz] *v.* kōnin suru; hōritsuka suru.
legate [légit] *n.* tai (kō) shi; kokushi; Rōma Hōō no shisetsu.
legatee [lègətíː] *n.* isan uketorinin. ⌊(tsukai).
legation [ligéiʃən] *n.* kōshikan; kōshikan zen'in.
legato [legáːtou] *ad.* (*mus.*) namerakani; enkatsuni.
legend [lédʒ(ə)nd/-dʒind] *n.* densetsu. ~**ary** *a.* densetsu no; kōtō-mukei no.
legerdemain [lédʒədəméin] *n.* tejina; gomakashi; manchaku.
leggings [léginz] (*pl.*) *n.* kyahan; suneate.
legibility [lédʒibíliti] *n.* yomiyasui koto; meiryōna koto.
legible [lédʒəbl] *a.* yomiyasui; meiryōna. ~**bly** *ad.* meiryōni.
legion [líːdʒən] *n.* guntai; kodai Rōma no gundan; ōzei. ~**ary** *a.* gundan no. *n.* kodai Rōma no gundan hei.
legislate [lédʒisleit] *v.* hōritsu o seitei suru. ⌈tsu.
legislation [lèdʒisléiʃən] *n.* hōritsu seitei; seitei sareta hōri-
legislative [lédʒisleitiv] *a.* rippōken no aru; rippō no.
legislator [lédʒisleitə] *n.* rippōsha; rippōin-giin.
legislature [lédʒisleitʃə] *n.* rippōbu; gikai.
legitimacy [lidʒítiməsi] *n.* gōhō; seitō; chakushutsu.
legitimate [lidʒítimit] *a.* gōhō no; chakushutsu no.
legume [légjuːm/legjúːm] *n.* saya; sayamame; (*pl.*) yasai.
leguminous [ligjúminəs/le-] *a.* saya no; mameka no.
lei [léi] (*pl.* ~**is**) *n.* rei (Hawai no hanawa).
leisure [léʒə/líː-] *n.* hima; tsugō no yoi toki. *a.* himana. ~**d** *a.* hima no aru. ~**ly** *ad.* yūzen to.
lemon [lémən] *n.* remon. *a.* remon-iri no; remon iro no.
lemonade [lemənéid/léməneid] *n.* remonsui; remonēdo; ramune.
lend [lend] *v.* **lent; lending.** kasu; ataeru. *banks* ~ *money and charge interest,* ginkō wa kane o kashite risoku o toru. ~**er** *n.* kashite. *a becoming dress* ~*s charm to a girl,* yoku niau kimono wa shōjo ni miryoku o ataeru.
Lend-Lease Act [léndlíːs ækt] (*Am.*) gunjuhin taiyohō.
length [leŋθ/leŋkθ] *n.* nagasa: *at* ~, tsui ni. ~**en** *v.* nagaku-suru; nagaku naru. ~**wise** ['-waiz] *ad.* tate ni. ~**y** *a.* nagatarashii; kudokudoshii.
leniency [líːnjənsi/-njənsi] *n.* kandai; onwa.

lenient [líːniənt/-njənt] *a.* kandaina ; onwana.

lens [lenz] *n.* renzu ; suishōtai ; megane.

lent [lent] *v. see* : **lend.**

Lent [lent] *n.* Shijun sai (Fukkatsusai mae 40 (shijū)nichi kan). ～**en** [-(ə)n] *a.* Shijunsai no.

lentil [léntil] *n.* (*veg.*) renzu mame.

leopard [lépəd] *n.* (*zoo*) hyō.

leper [lépə] *n.* raibyō kanja. ～ **house** ['-haus] *n.* raibyōin.

leprosy [léprəsi] *n.* (*med.*) raibyō ; fuhai ; daraku.

leprous [léprəs] *a.* raibyō ni kakatta ; minikui ; fuketsuna.

lese-majesty [líːzmǽdʒisti] *n.* fukeizai ; daigyakuzai.

lesion [líːʒ(ə)n] *n.* songai ; sonshō ; shōgai ; byōgai.

less [les] *a.* issō chiisai ; issō sukunai ; ototte iru. *ad.* yori sukunaku. ～**en** *v.* chiisaku suru ; herasu ; chiisaku naru ; heru.

lessee [lesíː] *n.* chingarinin ; shakuchinin ; shakuyanin.

lesson [lésn] *n.* nichinichi no gakka ; kyōkun ; (*pl.*) jugyō.

lessor [lésɔː/lésɔ́ː] *n.* kashinushi ; kashi-jinushi ; kashi-yanushi.

lest [lest] *conj.* (～...*should*) ...shinai yō ni ; suru to ikenai kara.

let [let] *v.* **let ; letting.** ...saseru ; kasu : ～ **down,** sageru. ～ **in,** ireru. ～ **into** =～ **in,** ireru ; tōsu. ～ **me see,** hatena ; chotto matte. ～ **off,** hanatsu ; yurusu. ～ **out,** dasu ; orosu (kimono no age).

letdown [létdaun] *n.* (*Am.*) yurumi ; tarumi ; rakutan.

lethal [líːθəl] *a.* chimeitekina : ～ *weapon,* kyōki.

lethargic [leθáːdʒik] *a.* konsuijōtai no ; nemutai ; bon'yari shita ; donkanna.

lethargy [léθədʒi] *n.* (fushizenna) konsui(byō) ; mukiryoku.

Lethe [líːθi(ː)] *n.* (*Gk. Myth.*) Wasuregawa ; monowasure ; bōkyaku.

letter [létə] *n.* moji ; tegami ; (*pl.*) gakumon ; bungaku ; moji-dōri no imi : *man of* ～*s,* bungakusha. ～ **book,** tegami hika-echō. ～ **box,** yūbimbako. ～ **card,** *n.* fūkan-hagaki. ～**ed** *a.* gakumon no aru. ～**head** ['-hed] *n.* binsen no jōbu no insatsu monku.

lettuce [létis] *n.* chisa ; retasu.

letup [létʌp] *n.* (*Am. col.*) teishi ; tomari.

Levant [livǽnt] *n.* tōhōshokoku (*Italy* yori higashi no chichūkai no kuni).

Levantine [lévəntain] *n.* tōhōshokoku no. *n.* tōhōkokujin.

levee [lévi] *n.* (kokuō, daitōryō nado no) sekken no shiki; shōtaikai.

level [lévəl] *n.* suiheimen; onaji takasa o motte iru koto; suijunki. *a.* tairana; suiheina. *v.* suiheini suru; byōdōni suru.

lever [lí:və] *n.* teko. *v.* teko de ugokasu; kojiakeru. ~**age** [‿ridʒ] *n.* teko no sayō; teko sōchi.

leviable [léviəbl] *a.* zei o kakeru.

leviathan [liváiəθ(ə)n] *n.* (*Old Test.*) ōkina umi no dōbutsu; kyodaina mono.

levitate [léviteit] *v.* kūchū ni ukabiagaru.

levity [léviti] *n.* keisotsu; fuhaku. ⌐kazei suru.

levy [lévi] *v.* toritateru; shōshū suru : *n.* kazei. ~ *taxes on,*

lewd [lu:d] *a.* midarana; geretsuna. ~**ly** *ad.* midarani. ~**ness** *n.* irogonomi.

lexicography [lèksikógrəfi] *n.* jisho hensan. ~**pher** [lèksikógrəfə] *n.* jisho hensansha.

lexicon [léksikən] *n.* jisho (Girisha, Raten, Heburai-go no).

liability [làiəbíliti] *n.* sekinin ; (*pl.*) fusai : *limited* ~, yūgen sekinin. *unlimited* ~, mugen sekinin.

liable [láiəbl] *a.* sekinin ga aru; ukeru beki; shigachina.

liaison [li(:)éizɔ:ŋ] *n.* nareai; renraku; (*gram.*) mae to ato no go no hatsuon ga tsunagaru koto.

liar [láiə] *n.* usotsuki.

libation [laibéiʃ(ə)n] *n.* omiki ya mizu o chijō ni sosogu koto (kami o matsuru tame ni); kono sake ya mizu.

libel [láib(ə)l] *n.* soshiru koto. *v.* hibōsuru. ~**ous** [láibələs] *a.* hibō suru; chūshōteki.

liberal [líbərəl] *a.* kimae no yoi; kandaina. *n.* jiyūshugisha; (*L-*) Jiyūtō(in). ~**ism** *n.* jiyūshugi. ~**ly** *ad.* jiyūni.

liberality [lìbəræliti] *n.* kandai (kimae no yoi koto).

liberate [líbəreit] *v.* jiyū ni suru; hanashite yaru.

libertine [líbə(:)tain/-tin] *n.* hōtōmono; dōrakumono.

liberty [líbəti] *n.* jiyū : *take the* ~ *of,* shitsurei nagara...suru. *land of* ~, jiyū no kuni.

librarian [laibréəriən] *n.* toshokan'in; shisho.

library [láibrəri] *n.* toshokan; shosai; zōsho; bunko.

libretto [librétou] *n.* kageki (*opera*) no kashi; kageki kyakuhon.

license, licence [láis(ə)ns] *n.* kyoka; menjō; menkyojō; hōjū; kimama. *v.* menkyo suru. *to drive a car*, unten menkyo. **~d house**, kyoka o motte iru ie; joroya. **~e** [lais(ə)nsí] *n.* menkyo sareta hito; sakerui hambai menkyonin.

licentiate [laisénʃiit/-ʃjət] *n.* menkyojō shoyūsha; gakushi.

licentious [laisénʃəs] *a.* kimamana; hōtō no.

lichen [láiken/-kin/lítʃin] *n.* koke; taisen.

lick [lik] *n.* nameru koto. *v.* nameru. (*col.*) naguru; uchikatsu.

licorice [líkəris] *n.* (*bot.*) kanzō.

lid [lid] *n.* futa; mabuta (*eye-lid*).

lie [lai] *v.* **lay, lain ; lying.** yokotawaru; neru; ...ni aru; **~** *at the heart*, ki ni kakaru. *n.* ichi (*position*); hōkō (*direction*).

lie [lai] *n.,* *v.* **lied ; lying.** uso o tsuku.

lief [li:f] *ad.* yorokonde. *had* (*or would*) *as* **~** *go there as anywhere else*, doko e iku yori soko e iku hō ga mashida.

liege [li:dʒ] *n.* tonosama. *my* **~** *!* waga kimi! *a.* kunshu taru;

lien [lí(:)ən/li:n] *n.* ryūchiken; shichiken. ⌐chūjitsuna.

lieu [lju:/lu:] *n.* basho. *in* **~** *of*, no kawari ni. ⌐chii).

lieutenancy [lefténənsi/lif-] *n.* *lieutenant* no shoku (shigoto).

lieutenant [lefténənt/ljú(:)t-] *n.* jōkandairi; rikugun chūi; (*Am*). kaigun taii; (*Brit*). kaigun shōsa. **~** *colonel*, rikugun chūsa. **~** *commander*, kaigun shōsa. **~** *general*, rikugun chūjō.

life [laif] *n.* inochi; shōgai; isshō; kurashi : *to the* **~**, shin ni sematte. **~ belt** ['-belt] *n.* kyūmeitai. **~boat** ['-bout] *n.* kyūmeitei. **~ buoy** ['-bɔi] *n.* kyūmei ukibukuro. **~guard** ['-gɑːd] *n.* (*Brit*.) konoe hei; (*Am*.) suinan kyūjoin. **~like** ['-laik] *a.* shin ni semaru; ikiutsushi no. **~ line** ['-lain] *n.* seimei sen. **~long** ['-lɔŋ] *a.* isshō no. **~ preserver** ['-prizə:bə] *n.* kyūmeigu. **~saving** ['-seiviŋ] *a.* kyūmei no; (*Am*.) suinan kyūjo no. **~-size** ['-sáiz] *a.* jitsubutsudai no. **~time** ['-taim] *n.* shōgai; zommeichū.

lift [lift] *v.* ageru; takameru; **agaru.** (kiri nado ga) hareru. *n.* mochiageru koto; risshin shusse. (*Brit*.) =*elevator*; kijūki. *this window does not* **~**, kono mado wa agaranai. *give a person a* **~**, te o kasu; (kuruma ni) binjō saseru.

ligament [lígəment] *n.* himo ; jintai.
ligature [lígətʃuə/-tʃə/-tjuə] *n.* himo ; (*surg.*) nuiawase-ito ; (*print*) renji (æ, fi), *etc.*
light [lait] **lighted** *or* **lit, lighting,** *v.* akari o tsukeru ; akaruku naru. *n.* hikari ; akarusa ; nikkō ; akari. *a.* akarui ; karui ; tegaruna ; assari shita ; binshōna ; tegiwa no yoi ; keisotsuna ; uwaki no ; sasaina. *ancient* ~*s*, (*leg.*) akari o toru kenri ; saikō-ken. *between the* ~*s*, tasogare ni. *between two* ~*s*, yakan ni. *bring to* ~, ōyake ni suru. *come to* ~, akiraka ni naru. *see the* ~, yo ni deru. *make* ~ *of*, o karonzuru. ~ *up*, (hi) akari o tsukeru ; tabako ni hi o tsukeru. ~ **headed** [⸝-hédid] *a.* atama no henna. ~ **hearted** [⸝-há:tid] *a.* kaikatsuna. ~ **horseman** [⸝-hó:smən] *n.* keikihei. ~**house** [⸝-haus] *n.* tōdai. ~ **minded** [⸝-máindid] *a.* keisotsuna ; utsurigina. ~**ship** [⸝-ʃip] *n.* tōdai sen. ~**some** *a.* kaikatsuna ; jōhinna. ~**ly** *ad.* karuku ; sotto ; subashikoku.
lighten [láitn] *v.* hikaru ; akaruku naru (suru) ; karuku naru (suru) ; genkizukeru.
lighter [láitə] *n.* hashike ; hi o tsukeru hito ; raitā.
lightning [láitniŋ] *n.* denkō ; inazuma : ~ *rod*, (*Am.*) hiraishin.
lignite [lígnait] *n.* kattan ; atan (isshu no sekitan (*coal*)).
like [laik] *a.* dōyōna. *prep.* ...to dōyō ni ; ...no yōni. *conj.* (*col.*) to dōyōni. *n.* dōyōna hito mata wa mono. (*pl.*) konomi. *v.* konomu ; ki ni iru. ~**ly** *ad.* arisōna ; ...no mikomi no aru ; tekitōna. *ad.* tabun. *feel* ~*ing*, shitai ki ga suru. ~**ness** *n.* ruiji ; shōzō ; nigao. ~**wise** [⸝-waiz] *ad.* dōyōni ; mata.
likelihood [láiklihud] *n.* arisōna koto ; mikomi : *in all* ~, tabun ; jitchū hakku.
liken [láikən] *v.* tatoeru ; nisaseru.
liking [láikiŋ] *n.* shumi ; konomi (*for, to*) ; yōsu.
lilac [láilək] *n.* (*bot.*) murasaki hashidoi ; usumurasaki iro.
Lilliputian [lìlipjúʃjən] *a.* shōjinkoku no ; hijōni chiisai. *n.* kobito ; issumboshi.
lilt [lilt] *v.* kaikatsuni utau. *n.* keikaina uta.
lily [líli] *n.* yuri. ~ *of the valley*, suzuran.
limb [lim] *n.* teashi ; tsubasa ; ōeda.   ⌈guruma.
limber [límbə] *a.* shinayakana. *n.* (hōsha, *gun-carriage* no) mae-

limbo [límbou] *n.* jigoku (*Hades*) no inaka (senrei o ukenai kodomo nado ga shigo iku tokoro).

lime [laim] *n.* (*min.*) sekkai. torimochi. (*bot.*) bodaiju ; (remon ni nita) kajitsu.

limit [límit] *n.* gendo ; han'i. *v.* kagiru ; seigen suru.

limitation [lìmitéiʃ(ə)n] *n.* seigen ; gendo ; kigen.

limn [lim] *v.* egaku ; kotoba de egaku.

limousine [límu(:)ziːn] *n.* (*Fr.*) yūgai (ōi no aru) jidōsha.

limp [limp] *a.* jūnanna ; gunya-gunya no ; yowai. *n. v.* bikko (o hiku).

limpet [límpit] *n.* isshu no kai (*shell*) ; suzumegai.

limpid [límpid] *a.* kiyoi ; sunda.

linden [líndən] *n.* shina no ki ; bodaiju.

line [lain] *n.* ito ; tsuna ; sen ; gyō ; ippitsu ; mijikai tegami ; shi no ichigyō ; ku ; kyōkai ; (kisha, basu nado no) -sen ; michisuji ; kettō ; keiretsu ; shōbai. *v.* sen o hiku ; ichiretsu ni naraberu ; ura o tsukeru ; tsumekomu.

lineage [líniidʒ] *n.* kettō ; keitō ; chisuji.

lineal [líniəl] *a.* chokkei no ; senzo kara no ; sen no.

lineament [líniəmənt] *n.* (*usu. pl.*) mehanadachi ; gaikei ; rinkaku.

linear [líniə] *a.* sen no ; senjō no. ⌊kaku.

linen [línin] *n.* rinneru (seihin) ; shatsurui. ~ **draper** [-dreipə] *n.* rinnerushō ; shatsurui shōnin.

liner [láinə] *n.* teikisen ; teikihikōki ; (*base.*) rainā.

linger [língə] *v.* guzuguzu suru ; nagabiku.

lingo [língou] *n.* kiite mo wake no wakaranai kotoba (gaiko-kugo nado no yōni). ⌈n, l, r).

lingual [língwəl] *a.* shita no. *n.* (*phon.*) zetsuon(ji) (t, d, th, s,

linguist [língwist] *n.* gengo gakusha.

linguistic [lingwístik] *a.* gengo no ; gogaku no. ~**s** *n.* gengo-

liniment [línimənt] *n.* nuri-gusuri. ⌊gaku.

lining [láiniŋ] *n.* (ifuku no) ura ; uraji ; (saifu nado no) naka-mi. ⌈nagu-(garu).

link [liŋk] *n.* (kusari no) wa ; renketsu ; kafusu-botan. *v.* tsu-

links [liŋks] *n.* (*pl.*) gorufujō ; sukētojō.

linnet [línit] *n.* beni-suzume. ⌈mono).

linoleum [línóuljəm/lain-] *n.* rinoryūmu (yuka no shiki-

linotype [láinotaip] *n.* rainotaipu.

linseed [línsi:d] *n.* amani. ~ **oil**, amaniyu.

lint [lint] *n.* rinto (gekayō hōtai); kuzuito.

lintel [líntl] *n.* hisashi (mado, irikuchi nado no ue no yokogi).

lion [láiən] *n.* shishi. ninkimono; meisho; meibutsu: ~'s *share*, rikutsu ni awanai wakemae. ~**ess** *n.* mesu no shishi. ~**ize** *v.* motehayasu; meisho o miru.

lip [lip] *n.* kuchibiru; (*pl.*) kuchi; heri. ~**stick** [lípstik] *n.* bō-kuchibeni.

liquefaction [likwifǽkʃən] *n.*, *v.* ekitai (ni suru):

liquefy [líkwifai] *v.* tokasu. tokeru. ekika saseru.

liqueur [likjúə] *n.* rikyūrushu.

liquid [líkwid] *a.* ekitai no; ryūchōna. (*phon.*) ryūon no: ~ *fire*, moeru (ekijō no) kaen. *n.* ekitai; nagareru honoo.

liquidate [líkwideit] *v.* shiharau. seisan suru; issō suru.

liquidation [likwidéiʃən] *n.* seisan; shiharai; seiri.

liquor [líkə] *n.* ekitai; sake (nomimono).

lira [líərə] *n.* (*pl.* **lire** [líəri]; **-ras** [-rəz]) rira (Itaria no kahei).

lisle [láil] *n.* katayori no momen'ito: ~ *thread*, rairu-ito.

lisp [lisp] *n.* shita-tarazu; katakoto. *v.* fukanzenni hatsuon suru; shita-motsure de hanasu.

list [list] *n.* mokuroku; meibo; shiaijō (shiai no basho); (nuno no) mimi. *v.* mokuroku no naka ni ireru; heri o tsukeru; (*poet.*) mimi o katamukeru; kiku. ~**less** [lístlis] *a.* ki no nai; taigisōna.

listen [lísn] *v.* chūi shite kiku: ~ *in*, hito ga denwa de hanasu no o kiku; tōchō suru; rajio o chōju suru.

lit [lit] *v. see* : **light**.

lit. *liter, literal, literary.*

litany [lítəni] *n.* (*rel.*) kaishū ga onaji yōni inoru inori.

liter, litre [li:tə] *n.* rittoru (yaku 5 gō 5 seki). ⌈koto.

literacy [lítərəsi] *n.* yomi kaki no nōryoku; gakumon no aru-

literal [lít(ə)rəl] *a.* moji no; mojidōri no; seikakuna.

literary [lít(ə)rəri] *a.* bungaku no; bungaku ni tsūjita.

literate [lítərit] *a.* yomi-kaki no dekiru; kyōiku no aru.

literatim [litəréitim] (*L.*) *ad.* ichiji, ichiji, mojidōri ni.

literature [lít(ə)rətʃə] *n.* bungaku; bunken.

lithe [laið] *a.* shinayakana ; gunyagunya no. ～some [láizsəm] *a.* shinayakana ; binshōna. 　　　　　　　　　　　⌐tsu).

lithium [líθiəm] *n.* (*chem.*) richūmu (kinzoku-genso no hito-

lithograph [líθəgra:f] *v.* sekiban. ～er [liθógrəfə] *n.* sekibangi-shi. ～ic [liθográfik] *a.* sekibanzuri no. ～y [liθógrəfi] *n.* se-

litigant [lítigənt] *a.* (*leg.*) soshō no; soshōsha. ⌐kiban-jutsu.

litigation [litigéiʃən] *n.* (*leg.*) soshō.

litigious [litídʒəs] *a.* soshōzukina ; ronsōzukina ; soshō no.

litmus [lítməs] *n.* ritomasu (senryō) : ～ *paper*, ritomasu shi-kenshi.

litter [lítə] *n.* tanka ; kago ; newara ; (buta nado no) hitohara no ko; konran. *v.* newara o shiku ; chirakasu ; ko o umu.

little [lítl] *a.* (**less** *or* **lesser** (*attr. only*), **least**) chiisai ; tsuma-ranai ; sukoshi no. *ad.* sukoshiku ; hotondo...nai. *n.* sukoshi. *a* ～, sukoshi wa aru.

littoral [lítərəl] *a.* kaigan no. *n.* enkaichi no.

liturgical [litó:dʒik(ə)l] *a.* reihaishiki (rai-) no.

liturgy [lítə(:)dʒi] *n.* reihai (rai-) no keishiki.

live [liv] *v.* sumu ; ikite iru ; o jōshoku to suru (*on*) ; de seikei o tateru (*on*) ; sugosu. [laiv] *a.* ikite iru ; kakki no aru ; (sumi-bi nado no) okotte iru. ～ *stock*, kachiku. ～long, [lívlɔŋ], (*poet.*) *a.* hisashii. ～ly [láivli] *a.* kappatsuna ; nigiyakana. *ad.* kap-

livelihood [láivlihud] *n.* kurashi ; seikei. ⌐patsuni.

liveliness [láivlinis] *n.* genki no yoi koto ; kaikatsu ; azaya-

liver [lívə] *n.* seikatsusha ; kyojūsha. (*anat.*) kanzō. ⌐kasa.

livery [lívəri] *n.* soroi no fuku. kashi-uma-gyō.

livid [lívid] *a.* namari-iro no ; aoguroi.

living [lívíŋ] *a.* ikite iru ; gendai no ; tannen no ; kakki no aru. *n.* seikatsu ; bokushi no teate. ～room [⌐rum] *n.* (*Am.*)

lizard [lízəd] *n.* tokage : *house* ～, yamori. ⌐ima

llama, lama [lá:mə] *n.* (*zoo.*) rama.

llano [lá:nou/lja:-] *n.* Nam-Bei no dai-sōgen (kusahara).

load [loud] *n.* nimotsu ; sekisairyō ; jū ni kometa tama ; (*pl.*) takusan. *v.* ni o tsumu ; (dan'yaku nado o) komeru. ～ing [lóudiŋ] *n.* tsumikomi ; nimotsu ; sōten.

loadstar [lóudsta:] *n.* hokkyokusei ; shidō genri.

loadstone, lodestone [lóudstoun], *n.* tennen jishaku.

loaf [louf] *n.* (*pl.* **loaves** [louvz]) *n.* (pan nado no) hito kata-mari. *v.* norakura kurasu. **~er** [lóufə] *n.* norakuramono; furōnin.

loam [loum] *n.* suna to nendo no ii dojō. *v.* *loam*-do de mitasu.

loan [loun] *n.* kashitsuke; kōsai. *v.* kasu. **~ syndicate** [-síndi-kit] *n.* kashitsuke zaidan.

loath [louθ] *a.* iyana. **~e** [louð] *v.* kirau; nikumu. **~ing** [lóuðiŋ] *n.* daikirai. **~some** [lóuðsəm] *a.* mune no waruku naru; imawashii.

lobby [lóbi] *n.* (*arch.*) genkan; hikaeshitsu; rōka; (*Am.*) in-gaidan. *v.* hikaeshitsu de giin ni undō suru. **~ist** *n.* gian tsūka undōsha; ingai undōin.

lobe [loub] *n.* mimitabu; marui deppari.

lobster [lóbstə] *n.* iseebi.

local [lóuk(ə)l] *a.* chihō no; kyokubu no. **~ize** [lóukəlaiz] *v.* kyokubu ni todomeru; basho o kimeru; chūi o shūchū suru.

locality [lo(u)kǽliti] *n.* shozaichi; basho.

locate [lo(u)kéit] *v.* oku; basho o tsukitomeru. (*Am.*) teijū suru. *he* ~*d his new store on main street*, kare wa atarashii mise o ōdōri ni oita.

location [lo(u)kéiʃən] *n.* oku koto; basho; yagai satsuei.

lock [lɔk] (1) *n.* kami no fusa; makige. (2) *n.*, *v.* fune ga sui-mon (o tōru); (3) jō (o orosu); tojikomeru. **~jaw** [lókdʒɔ:] *n.* soshakukin no keiren; hashōfū. **~ out** [lókáut] *n.* kōjō heisa. **~smith** [-smiθ] *n.* jōmaeya. **~up** [-ʌp] *n.* mongen; ryūchijō.

locker [lókə] *n.* jō o orosu hito; (jōmae-tsuki no) todana.

locket [lókit] *n.* roketto; kazarikobako.

locomotion [loukəmóuʃən] *n.* undō; unten.

locomotive [lóukəmoutiv] *a.* undō suru; unten no. *n.* kikan-sha.

locust [lóukəst] *n.* (*ins.*) inago; (*Am.*) semi (*bot.*) harienjyu (na-lo).

locution [lokjú:ʃən] *n.* hanashikata; kan'yō gohō.

lode [loud] *n.* kōmyaku; suiro.

lodestar [lóudstɑ:] *n.* hokkyokusei; shidō genri. (*cf. loadstar*).

lodge [lɔdʒ] *n.* koya; shūkaijo (himitsu-kessha nado no). *v.* geshiku suru; (dangan nado ga) karada ni tomaru. *n.* shikuhaku-nin; dōkyo-nin. **~house** [-haus] *n.* geshikuya.

lodging [lódʒiŋ] *n.* geshiku; shikuhaku; (*pl.*) kashima. **~**

lodg(e)ment [lɔ́dʒmənt] *n.* shikusho; (tampo -*security*) (nado) azukeru koto; chokin; taiseki (butsu). (*mil.*). senryō; shita kyoten.

loft [lɔ(:)ft] *n.* yaneurabeya; yanebeya. ～**ily** [lɔ́:ftili] *ad.* takaku; kōshōni; kōmanni. ～**iness** [lɔ́(:)ftinis] *n.* takai koto; kōshō; kōman. ～**y** [lɔ́(:)fti] *a.* sobietatsu; kōshōna; kōmanna.

log [lɔg] *n.* maruta; noroma. (*naut.*) sokuteigi; kōkainisshi. *v.* kitte maruta ni suru; kōkai nisshi ni kinyū suru. ～**book** [lɔ́gbuk] *n.* kōkai nisshi. ～**wood** [˗wud] *n.* hematokishinboku (senryōzai).

logarithm [lɔ́gəriðm] *n.* (*math.*) taisū : *table of* ～*s*, taisūhyō.

loggerhead [lɔ́gəhed] *n.* bakamono.

logging [lɔ́giŋ] *n.* (*Am.*) maruta kiridashi; bassairyō.

logic [lɔ́dʒik] *n.* ronrigaku; ronri. ～**al** *a.* ronrijō no; ronritekina. ～**ally** *ad.* ronri ni kanatte; dōdō to.

logician [lo(u)dʒíʃən] *n.* ronrigakusha.

loin [lɔin] *n.* (*pl.*) koshi; (ushi nado no) koshi-niku. ～**cloth** [lɔ́inklɔ(:)θ] *n.* fundoshi; shitaobi.

loiter [lɔ́itə] *v.* burabura aruku; burabura kurasu.

loll [lɔl] *v.* darari to tareru : ～ *on sofa,* darari to *sofa* ni yorikakaru. *a dog's tongue* ～*s out in hot weather,* inu no shita ga atsui toki wa darari to sagaru.

Londoner [lʌ́ndənə] *n.* London-shinin; London-jin.

lone [loun] *a.* sabishii; hito no sumanai. ～**ly** *a.* kodoku no; sabishii. -**liness** *n.* sabishisa; kodoku. ～**some** *a.* sabishii; hitozato hanareta.

long [lɔŋ] *a.*, *da.* nagai; tōku ni todoku : ～ *dozen,* 13 ko. *ad.* nagaku. ～**-lived** [lɔ́ŋl(ə)ivd] *a.* chōmei no; eizoku suru. ～**-sighted** [˗sáitid] *a.* senken no mei aru. ～**-standing** [˗stǽndiŋ] *a.* naganen no. ～**-suffering** [˗sʌ́fəriŋ] *a.* shimbōzuyoi. ～ **winded** [˗wíndid] *a.* nagatarashii; iki no nagai.

long [lɔŋ] *v.* setsubō suru; o shitau (*for, after*). ～**ing** *n.* setsubō; akogare. *a.* natsukashi.

long-distance [lɔ́ŋdístəns] *a.* chōkyori no : ～ *cruise,* en'yō kōkai.

longevity [lɔndʒéviti] *n.* chōmei; jumyō.

longhand [lɔ́ŋhænd] *n.* futsū no kakikata (*cf. shorthand*).

longitude [lɔ́ndʒtju:] *n.* keido; keisen.

longitudinal [lɔndʒitjúːdin(ə)l] *a.* keido (keisen) no; tate no.

longshoreman [lɔ́ŋʃɔːmən] *n.* (*Am.*) okinakashi; hatoba ninsoku.

look [luk] *v.* miru; kao o suru. *n.* kaoiro; yōsu; ikken. ～ *after*, sewa o suru; kitaisuru. ～ *into*, shiraberu. ～ *out*, soto o miru; chūi suru. ～ *over*, zatto me o tōsu; ōme ni miru. ～ *sharp*, kiotsukeru; isogu. ～ *through*, me o tōsu; minuku; misukasu. ～ *up*, sagasu; hōmon suru. ～ *up to*, miageru; uyamau. ～**er-on** [lúkərɔ́n] *n.* bōkansha; kembutsunin. ～**ing glass**, kagami. ～**out** [-áut/ˊaut] *n.* mihari; miharijo; miharinin.

loom [luːm] *n.* hata; hataorikikai. *v.* bōtto mieru; kimiwaruku semaru.

loon [luːn] *n.* namakemono; neuchi no nai hito. (*bird*) kaitsuburi (kaitsumuri).

loony [lúːni] *a.*, *n.* kichigaijimita (hito).

loop [luːp] *n.* (himo nado no) wa; wankyoku; (*airpl.*) chūgaerihikō. *v.* wa ni suru. ～ *the* ～, jitensha de kyokunori o suru; (*airpl.*) chūgaeri suru. ～**hole** [ˊ-houl] *n.* jūgan; hazama.

loose [luːs] *a.* jiyūna; yurui. *v.* hodoku; hanasu; yurusu. ～ *leaf* rūzuriifu. ～**ly** *ad.* yuruku; darashinaku.

loosen [lúːsn] *v.* yurumeru; kandai ni suru.

loot [luːt] *n.* senrihin; fuseiritoku. *v.* ryakudatsu suru.

lop [lɔp] *v.* eda o kiru: eda o tareru. ～**-sided** [ˊ-sáidid] *a.* kinkō no torete inai.

lope [loup] *n.*, *v.* ōmata-kakeashi (de hashiru).

loquacious [loukwéiʃəs] *a.* tabenna. ～**ly** *ad.* berabera to shaberu. ～**ness** *n.* taben.

loquacity [lókwǽsiti] *n.* taben; oshaberi.

lord [lɔːd] *n.* kunshu; ryōshu; Kirisuto; shujin; (*L-*) Kyō (keishō). *v.* ibarichirasu. ～**s** *spiritual*, (*Brit.*) seishoku; jōin giin. ～**s** *temporal*, (*Brit.*) jōin ni seki o motsu kizoku. **my lord** [milɔ́ːd/milʌ́d] Kakka (kizoku, kantoku, *London* Shichō, saibankan nado ni). ～ *it over*, haba o kikasu. ～**ly** *a.* sondaina. ～**liness** *n.* tonosama rashisa. ～**ship** *n.* tonosama rashisa. *his* (*or your*) ～**ship**, kakka (taiwa no toki).

lore [lɔː/lɔə] *n.* furui densetsu nado ni tsuite no gakumon.

lorgnette [lɔ́:njét] *n.* (*Fr.*) e (*handle*) no tsuita megane; opera-
lorn [lɔ:n], =**forlorn** *a.* suterareta; kodoku no. ⌊gurasu.
lorry [lɔ́:ri] *n.* kōzan no torokko: 4 (yon)-rinsha; jidōsha; to-
Los Angeles [lɔ(:)s ǽŋgələs] *n.* Losanzerusu. ⌊rakku.
lose [lú:z] *v.* **lost; losing.** ushinau; (tokei ga) okureru; makeru; michi ni mayou.
loss [lɔ(:)s] *n.* sonshitsu: *at a* ~, tōwaku shite; son shite. ~
leader [-li:də] *n.* kakuyasuhin; otori shōhin.
lost [lɔ(:)st] *v. see* : **lose.** *a.* ushinatta; maketa; michi ni mayotta; muchū ni natta. ⌈suru. *draw* ~*s*, kuji o hiku.
lot [lɔt] *n.* kuji; ummei; hito-yama. *v.* kubun suru; bumpai
loth, loath [louθ] *a.* iyagaru; iyaiya no (*unwilling; reluctant*).
lotion [lóuʃən] *n.* araigusuri; keshōsui.
lottery [lɔ́təri] *n.* tomikuji; un.
lotus [lóutəs] *n.* hasu (*flow*.). ⌈kakuseiki.
loud [laud] *a.* koedakai; hadena. ~-**speaker** [-spí:kə] *n.*
lounge [laundʒ] *n.* sampo; yūhojō; kyūkeishitsu; neisu;
nagaisu. *v.* burabura aruku; norakura kurasu.
lour, lower [láuə] *v.* kao o shikameru; ken'akuni naru.
louse [laus] *n.* (*pl.* **lice** [lais]) shirami. ~**y** *a.* shirami no ōi.
lout [laut] *n.* bukotsumono; inakamono. ~**ish** *a.* bukotsuna.
lovable [lʌ́vəbl] *a.* airashii.
love [lʌv] *n.* ai; koi; aijin. (teikyū nado de) mutoku ten. *v.*
aisuru, koisuru; konomu. ~**child** [-tʃaild] *n.* shiseiji. ~**lock**
[-lɔk] *n.* aikyō-kamige. ~**ly** *a.* airashii; rippana. ~**r** [lʌ́və] *n.*
koisuruotoko; aikōsha. koibito-doshi. ~**ing** [lʌ́viŋ] *a.* aisuru. ~**ly** *ad.* aishite : shinsetsuni.
low [lou] *a.*, *ad.* hikui (-ku); iyashii (-ku); yasui (-ku); genki
no nai. *n.* ushi nado no nakigoe. *v.* (ushi nado ga) naku. ~
bred [-bred] *a.* sodachi no warui; shitsuke no warui. ~**land**
[-lənd] *n. a.* teichi (no). ~**ly** *a.* kensonna. *ad.* kenson shite.
~-**spirited** [-spírited] *a.* genki no nai.
lower [ló(u)ə] *a.* (1) shita no; rettōna: *L*~ *House*, Kain. *v.* sageru; kujiku; iyashiku suru. (2) [lauə] kao o shikameru.
ken'aku ni naru.
lowering [láuəriŋ] *a.* aremoyō no; fukigenna.
loyal [lɔ́i(ə)l] *a.* chūgina; chūjitsuna. ~**ist** *n.* chūshin. ~**ly** *ad.*

chūjitsuni. ～**ty** [lɔ́jəlti] *n.* chūgi ; chūjitsu. ⸢suri).

lozenge [lɔ́zindʒ] *n.* hishigata ; hishigata no kashi ; jōzai (ku-
Ltd., ltd. [limitid] yūgen kaisha (*limited*).

lubber [lʌ́bə] *n.* bukotsumono. ～**ly** *a., ad.* bukakōna (-ni).

lubricant [lúbrikənt/ljú:-] *n.* namerakani surumono ; junkatsu-
yu. ⸢o yaru.

lubricate [lúbrikeit/ljú:-] *v.* nameraka ni suru ; kokoro zuke

lubrication [lu:brikéiʃ(ə)n/lju:-] *n.* namerakani suru koto ; chū-
yu (abura o sasu).

lubricator [lú:brikeitə/lju:-] *n.* aburasashi.

lucerne [lu:sɔ́:n] *n.* (*flower*) murasaki umagoyashi.

lucid [lú:sid/ljú:-] *a.* kagayaku ; sunda ; shōki no.

lucidity [lu:síditi/lju:-] *n.* tōmei ; hikari kagayaku koto.

Lucifer [lú:sifə] *n.* (*astr.*) Ake no Myōjō ; akuma ; (l-) ōrin
matchi.

luck [lʌk] *n.* un ; kōun. ～**ily** *ad.* shiawase nimo. ～**less** *a.* fuunna. ～**y** *a.* un no yoi ; engi no yoi.

lucrative [lú:krʌtiv/ljú:-] *a.* rieki no aru. ～**ly** *ad.* yūri no ;

lucre [lú:kə/ljú:-] *n.* rieki ; don'yoku. ⸤mōkatte.

lucubration [lùkju(:)bréiʃən/lju:-] *n.* yofukete no benkyō. (*usu.
pl.*) kushin no mieru sakuhin.

ludicrous [lú:dikrəs/ljú:-] *a.* kokkeina ; bakabakashii.

luff [lʌf] *v.* senshu o kazakami ni mukeru.

lug [lʌg] *v.* chikara-makase ni (*forcibly*) hiku ; hikizuru (*drag*).
n. mimi (tabu) ; tosshutsubu. chikarazuyoku hiku koto. (*pl.*)
(*Am. col.*) mottaiburu koto.

luggage [lʌ́gidʒ] *n.* (*Brit.*) nimotsu ; tenimotsu.

lugubrious [lu:gjú:briəs] *a.* awarena ; inkina (*mournful*).

lukewarm [lú:kwɔ:m/ljú:k-] *a.* namanurui ; funesshinna.

lull [lʌl] *n.* koyami ; nagi. *v.* nadameru ; shizumeru.

lullaby [lʌ́ləbai] *n.* komoriuta.

lumbago [lʌmbéigou] *n.* senki ; yōbu shinkeitsū.

lumbar [lʌ́mbə] *a.* koshi no. ～ *vertebra.* yōtsui.

lumber [lʌ́mbə] *n.* zaimoku ; garakuta. *v.* garakuta o tsumekomu ; jama suru ; ki o kiridasu. doshindoshin to aruku.
～**ing** *v.* mechakucha ni tsumu. ～**man** *n.* zaimokushō.

luminary [lú:minəri/ljú:-] *n.* hakkōtai (tokuni taiyō, tsuki).

luminous [lú:minəs/ljú:-] *a.* hikaru ; akarui.

lump [lʌmp] *n.* katamari ; kobu ; fushi : *in the* ～, hikkurumete ; komi de. *v.* sōkatsu suru ; komi de kau. ～**ish** *a.* motatsuita. ～**y** *a.* katamari no ōi ; bon'yari shite iru ; bukotsuna.

lunacy [lú:nəsi] *n.* fūten ; seishin sakuran ; kichigai.

lunar [lú:nə/ljú:-] a. tsuki no ; hangetsu no.

lunate [lú:nit/ljú:-] *a.* shingetsujō no ; hangetsujō no.

lunatic [lú:nətik] *a.* kichigai no. *n.* kyōjin ; kichigai.

lunch [lʌnt∫] *n.* chūshoku ; keishoku. *v.* ranchi (*lunch*) o taberu.

luncheon [lʌ́n(t)∫ən] *n.* ohiru ; bentō.

lung [lʌŋ] *n.* (*anat.*) haizō ; hai.   ⌜suru.

lunge [lʌndʒ] *n.* tsuki (*fencing*). *v.* ken nado de tsuku ; tosshin

lurch [lə:t∫] *n.* keisha ; yoromeki. *v.* katamuku : *leave in the* ～, konnanna jōtai ni hōtte oku.

lure [ljuə/luə] *n.* yūwaku ; esa. *v.* obikiyoseru ; yūwaku suru.

lurid [ljúərid/lúər-] *a.* makkani yaketa. monosugoi ; susamajii : ～ *crime*, osoroshii hanzai.

lurk [lə:k] *v.* kakureru ; hisomu (*about, in, under*).

luscious [lʌ́∫əs] *a.* umai ; amasugiru ; shitsukkoi.

lush [lʌ∫] *a.* mizumizushii ; aokusa no ōi.   ⌜no.

lust [lʌst] *n.* yoku ; shikijō. *v.* katsubō suru. ～**ful** *a.* kōshoku

luster, lustre [lʌ́stə] *n.* kōtaku ; kōtaku aru orimono. shande-

lustrous [lʌ́strəs] *a.* kōtaku no aru ; kagayaku.   ⌊ria.

lusty [lʌ́sti] *a.* jōbuna ; kappatsuna.   ⌜to.

lute [lju:t/lu:t] *n.* ryūto (gitājō no gengakki). isshu no semen-

Luxemburg [lʌ́ksəmbə:g] *n.* Doitsu, Furansu, Belugii no ai-da no kuni.

luxuriance, -cy [lʌgzjúəriəns/lʌksjú-, -si], *n.* hammo ; hōfu.

luxuriant [lʌgzjúəriənt/lʌksj] *a.* shigetta ; hōfuna ; kenrantaru.

luxuriate [lʌgzjúərieit/lʌksj-] *v.* oishigeru ; zeitaku o suru ; (…ni) fukeru (*in*).

luxurious [lʌgzjúəriəs/lʌksj-] *a.* zeitakuna.

luxury [lʌ́k∫uri/-k∫(ə)r-] *n.* zeitaku ; manzoku.

lyceum [laisi(:)əm] *n.* kōdō (*auditorium*) ; gakkai (*society of the specialists*) ; bunka dantai ; (*L-*), *Aristotle* no gakuen.

lye [lai] *n.* aku ; sentaku-yō arukari-eki.

lying [láiiŋ] *v. see* : **lie.** *a.* uso o tsuku ; uso no.

lying-in [láiiŋin] *n.* osan no toko ni tsuku koto. ～ **hospital,** sankabyōin.

lymph [limf] *n.* (*anat.*) rimpa (eki).

lymphatic [limfǽtik] *a.* rimpa no ; fukappatsuna. *n.* rimpasen.

lynch [lin(t)ʃf] *v.* rinchi o kuwaeru. *n.* shikei ; rinchi.

lynx [liŋks] *n.* (*zoo.*) yamaneko. (*animal*)

lyre [láiə] *n.* shichigenkin ; (*the* ～) jojōshi.

lyric [lírik] *a.* jojōteki ; jojōshi chō no. *n.* jojōshi ; uta. ～**al** *a.* =**lyric.** ～**ly** *ad.* jojōtekini. ～**ism** [lírisizm] *n.* jojōshi-chō.

lysol [láisəl] *n.* rizōru-eki.

M

M, m [em] *n.* (*pl.* M's, Ms, [emz]) Eigo *alphabet* no dai-13-bamme no moji.

ma [mɑ:] *n.* (*col.*) okāsan; kāchan.

ma'am [mæm/mɑ:m] *a.* madam no yaku.

macadam [məkǽdəm] *n.* kudaita ishi; shikiishi no dōro. ~**ize** *v.* koishi o shiku.

macaroni [mækəróuni] *n.* makaroni; Itariya udon.

macaroon [mækərú:n] *n.* makaroi (bisukettofū no kashi, hatankyō, rampaku, satō nado de tsukuru).

macaw [məkɔ́:] *n.* (*bird*) kongō inko.

mace [meis] *n.* tsuchiboko; shokken o arawasu tsue; isshu no tamatsukibō. kawakashita *nutmeg* no kawa (kōryō ni mochiiru).

Macedonian [mæsidóuniən] *a.* Makedonia no. *n.* Makedoniajin.

macerate [mǽsəreit] *v.* hitashite yawarakani suru; yaseotoroe saseru.

Machiavellian [mæ̀kiəvéliən] *a.* *Machiavelli* no (kembō jussaku no). ~**lism** [-lizm] *n.* *Machiavelli*-shugi.

machination [mæ̀kinéiʃən] *n.* imbō; warudakumi.

machine [məʃí:n] *n.* kikai; (kikai ippan). ~**gun** [-́gʌn] *n.* kikanjū. ~**ry** [məʃí:nəri] *n.* kikai (shūgōteki kikō).

machinist [məʃí:nist] *n.* kikaishi; kikaikō.

mackerel [mǽkrəl] *n.* (*fish*) saba.

mackintosh [mǽkintɔ́ʃ] *n.* (zukin tsuki) gomubiki amagaitō.

mad [mæ(:)d] *a.* ki no kurutta; kichigai no; nekkyō shita. ~**cap** [mǽdkæp] *n.* abaremono. ~**den** [mǽdn] *v.* hakkyō saseru (suru); okoru (raseru). ~**house** [-́haus] *n.* seishimbyōin. ~**ly** *ad.* kichigaijimite. ~**man** [-́mən] *n.* kyōjin. ~**ness** *n.* kyōki.

madam, madame [mǽdəm] *n.* fujin; okusama.

madame [mǽdəm/mədá:m] *n.* (*Fr.*) (*pl.* **mesdames** [medá:m/ méidæm]) okusamagata (yobikake); …okusama.

madder [mǽdə] *n.* (*bot.*) akane.

made [meid] *v. see* : **make**. *a.* tsukurareta; de dekita. ～-**up** [-ʌp] *a.* tsukutta; koshiraeta.

mademoiselle [mæ̀dməzél/mədmwəzél] *n.* (*Fr.*) ojōsan.

Madonna [mədónə] *n.* Seibo Maria (no zō).

madrigal [mǽdrigəl] *n.* mijikai shi; koiuta.

maelstrom [méilstroum] *n.* ōuzumaki; kore ni nita shinkyō (*mental state*); *Norway* no nishikita kinkai no uzumaki.

maestro [mɑ:éstrou] *n.* (*It.*) dai-ongakka; dai-sakkyokka; daishikisha; kyōshi.

magazine [mæ̀gəzí:n] *n.* sōko; dan'yakko; zasshi.

magenta [mədʒéntə] *n.* anirin-aka (murasakippoi aka. *purplish red*).

maggot [mǽgət] *n.* uji; kūsō. ～**y** *a.* uji darake no.

magic [mǽdʒik] *n.* mahō; kijutsu. *a.* ～**al** mahō no. **a** ～ **lantern**, gentō.

magician [mədʒíʃən] *n.* mahōtsukai.

magisterial [mæ̀dʒistíəriəl] *a.* chōkan no; ifū no aru; genzen taru; ōheina.

magistracy [mǽdʒistrəsi] *n.* chōkan no shoku.

magistrate [mǽdʒistrit/-reit] *n.* chōkan; chian-hanji.

Magna C(h)arta [mǽgnə kú:tə] (*Brit. hist.*) Dai Kenshō.

magnanimity [mæ̀gnənímiti] *n.* kannin taido; kōketsu.

magnanimous [mægnǽniməs/məg-] *a.* kandaina; kōketsuna.

magnate [mǽgneit] *n.* kijin; tōtoi katagata; gōshō.

magnesia [mægní:ʃjə] *n.* (*chem.*) sanka-maguneshūmu.

magnesium [mægní:ziəm/ʃiəm] *n.* (*chem.*) maguneshūmu.

magnet [mǽgnit] *n.* jishaku; jitetsu. ～**ic** *n.* [mæ̀gnétik/məg-] *a.* jishaku no; miryoku aru. ～**ics** jikigaku. ～**ism** [mǽgnítizm] *n.* jiki; miroyku. ～**ize** [mǽgnitaiz] *v.* jiryoku o tsukeru; (*fig.*) saiminjutsu o kakeru; jiki o ukeru. ～**o** [mægní:tou] *n.* chiisai hatsudenki.

magnificence [mægnífisns] *n.* sōrei; utsukushiku sakan.

magnificent [mægnífisnt] *a.* sōreina; subarashii. ～**ly** *ad.*

magnifier [mǽgnifaiə] *n.* kakudaikyō.

magnify [mǽgnifai] *v.* kakudai suru; ōgesani hanasu. ～**ing glass** [mǽgnifaiiŋglɑ:s] *n.* kakudaikyō.

magniloquent [mægnílokwənt] *a.* ōgesana; kodaina.

magnitude [mǽgnitju:d] *n.* futosa; (hoshi no hikari no) tō-kyū.

magnolia [mægnóuljə] *n.* (*bot.*) mokuren no isshu.

magpie [mǽgpai] *n.* kasasagi (*hardwood*).

mahogany [məhógəni] *n.* (*bot.*) mahogani.

maid [meid] *n.* jochū; *old* ~ ...rōjo.

maiden [méidn] *a.* shojo no; muku no. ~**hair** [-həə] *n.* isshu no shida. ~**hood** [-hud] *n.* shojo-sei. ~**ly** *a.* shojo rashii; uchikina. ~ **voyage,** shojo-kōkai.

mail [meil] *n.* kusari-katabira; yoroi; yūbin. *v.* yūsō suru. yoroi o kiseru. ~ **cart,** yūbin-basha. ~**chute** [-ʃu:t] *n.* yūbin otoshi; mērushūto. ~**coach** [-koutʃ] *n.* yūbin basha.

maim [meim] *v.* fugu (katawa) ni suru. ~**ed** *a.* fugu no.

main [mein] *n.* ōkuda; honkan. *a.* omona; daiichi no. *in the* ~ ..., taigai. *with might and* ~... zenryoku o tsukushite. ~**land** [-lænd] *n.* tairiku; hondo. ~**ly** *ad.* omoni; moppara. ~**mast** [-mæst] *n.* ōhobashira. ~**sail** [-seil] *n.* shuhan; daiichi ni ōkii ho. ~**spring** [-spriŋ] *n.* ōzemmai. ~**stay** [-stei] *n.* ōhobashira no sasaezuna.

maintain [mentéin/mein-] *v.* sasaeru; iji suru; shuchō suru.

maintenance [méintinəns] *n.* iji; fuyō; shuchō.

maize [meiz] *n.* tōmorokoshi.

majestic [mədʒéstik] *a.* sōgonna; dōdō taru. ~**ally** *ad.*.

majesty [mǽdʒisti/-dʒəs-] *n.* ifū; sōgon. *His (Her) M*~ *the Emperor (Empress),* Tennō (Kōgō) Heika.

majolica [mədʒólikə] *n.* majorika yaki (no tōki).

major [méidʒə] *a.* ōkii hō no; jūyōna; nenchō no. *n.* rikugun shōsa. *v.* (*Am,*) senkō suru (*in*). ~**domo** [-doumou] *n.* karō; karei. ~**general,** rikugun shōshō.

majority [mədʒóriti] *n.* tasū; kahansū; rikugun shōsa no kurai; otona ni naru toshi.

make [meik] *v.* **made; making.** tsukuru; ...saseru; ...ni naru; suru; susumu. *n.* koshirae; kakkō; deki. ~ *away with,* ...o nusumu; o korosu. ~ *light of,* ...o karonzuru. ~ *much of,* ... o omonzuru. ~ *one's way* ...susumu. ~ *out,* ...rikai suru; kaku; seikō suru; (*Am. sl.*) dō nika kurasu. ~ *over,* ...

yuzuri watasu. ～ *up*, ...oginau ; okeshō suru. ～ *up one's mind*, kesshin suru. ～ *up to*, ...ni chikazuku. ～**-believe** [⌐bili:v] *n.* kakotsuke ; kōjitsu. *a.* itsuwari no. ～**r** [méikə] *n.* seisakunin ; furidashi-nin ; (M～) zōbutsusha. ～**shift** [⌐ʃift] *n.* ichiji no maniawase. ～**-up** [⌐ʌp] *n.* (haiyū no) tsukuri.

making [méikiŋ] *n.* seikō no gen'in ; seisaku ; sono zairyō ; *in the* ～, sono tochū ni.

maladministration [mælədminìstréiʃ(ə)n] *n.* shissei ; akusei.

maladroit [mælədróit] *a.* hetana ; bukiyōna.

malady [mælədi] *n.* yamai ; byōki.

malapropos [mæləprəpóu] *a.* ori no warui. *ad.* ori ashiku.

malaria [məléəriə] *n.* (*med.*) marariya netsu.

malcontent [mælkəntènt] *n.* fuheika. *a.* fumanzokuna.

male [meil] *a.* otoko no ; osu no. *n.* otoko ; osu.

malediction [mælidíkʃən] *n.* juso ; noroi ; akkō.

malefactor [mǽlifæktə] *n.* zainin ; hannin ; akunin.

malevolence [məlévələns] *n.* akui ; akushin.

malevolent [məlévələnt] *a.* akui no. ～**ly** *ad.*

malfeasance [mælfí:zəns] *n.* (tokuni kōmuin no) fuseikōi.

malice [mǽlis] *n.* akui ; tekii. *of* ～ *prepense (aforethought)*, (*leg.*) arakajime kagai suru i o motte.

malicious [məlíʃəs] *a.* akui no aru ; akui no.

malign [məláin] *v.* soshiru. *a.* akui no aru.

malignancy [məlígnənsi], **malignity** [məlígniti] *n.* akui ; akusei.

malignant [məlígnənt] *a.* akui no aru ; akusei no.

malinger [məlíŋgə] *v.* kebyō o tsukau.

mall [mɔ:l/mæl] *n.* kokage no sampomichi.

mallard [mæləd] *n.* (*bird*) magamo.

malleable [mæliəbl] *a.* kitae uru ; uchinobashi uru ; jūjunna.

mallet [mǽlit] *n.* kizuchi.

mallow [mǽlou] *n.* zeniaoi (*flower*).

malnutrition [mælnju(:)tríʃən] *n.* eiyō fusoku ; eiyō furyō.

malt [mɔ(:)lt] *n.* bakuga ; moyashi ; kōji. ～ **liquor,** bakuga shu : biiru.

Malthusian [mælθjú:ziən/-zjən] *a.* Marusasu (*Malthus*) (Igirisu no keizai gakusha) no. *n.* Marusasushugisha. ～**ism** *n.*

Marusasushugi ; Marusasu jinkōron.

maltreat [mæltríːt] *v.* gyakutai suru. ~**ment** *n.* gyakutai.

malversation [mælvəːséiʃən] *n.* tokushoku ; kōkin-shōhi.

mamma [məmáː] *n.* okāchan ; kāchan.

mammal [mǽməl] *n.* honyū-dōbutsu.

mammalian [mæméiljən] *a.* honyū-dōbutsu no.   ⌈mi.

mammon [mǽmən] (yokoshimana kokoro no) Fuku no Ka-

mammoth [mǽməθ] *n.* mammosu (taiko no kyozō). *a.* kyodai-

mammy [mǽmi] *n.* (*Am.*) kokujin no uba ; kāchan.   ⌊na.

man [mæn] *n.* (*pl.* **men** [men]) ningen ; otoko ; (otoko no) otona : (*pl.*) buka ; kimi (yobikake). *v.* hito o wariateru ; fune ni hito o norikomaseru. ~ *the side* (*or yards*), tōgenreishiki o okonau. ~**at-arms** [mæn-ət-áːmz] *n.* heishi ; jūkihei. ~**ful** *a.* otokorashii. ~**hood** [-hud] *n.* jinkaku ; seijin ; gōyū. ~ *suffrage*, seinen danshi senkyoken. ~**kind** [mænkáind] *n.* jinrui no sōshō ni *man* o tsukau. ~**liness** [mǽnlinis] *n.* otokorashisa. ~**ly** *a.* yūkanna ; otokorashii. ~**nish** *a.* otoko no yōna. ~**of-war** [-əv-wɔ́ː] *n.* gunkan.

manacle(s) [mǽnəkl] *n.* (*pl.*) tejō. *v.* tekase (tejō) o hameru ; sokubaku suru.

manage [mǽnidʒ] *v.* shori suru ; kanri suru ; yatte iku. **managing director,** semmu torishimariyaku. ~**able** *a.* atsukai yasui. ~**ment** *n.* toriatsukai ; (*the m-*) keieisha. ~**r** [-dʒə] *n.* shihainin ; riji ; kantoku. ~**rial** [mænəgzíəriəl] *a.* toriatsukai no ; kanri no.

mandarin [mǽndərin] *n.* (chūgoku no) mukashi no kōkan ; (*M*~) (chūgoku no) kanwa. mikan. ~ **duck,** (*bird*) oshi-

mandate [mǽndeit/-dit] *n.* meirei ; inin.   ⌊dori.

mandatory [mǽndətəri] *a.* meirei no ; inin no. ~ **administration,** inin tōchi.

mandible [mǽndibl] *n.* shitaago ; ue mata wa shita no kuchi-

mandolin [mǽndəlin] *n.* mandorin.   ⌊bashi.

mandrake [mǽndreik] *n.* (*flower*) mandarage.

mandrel [mǽndril] *n.* (semban no) shinjiku ; shimbō.

mane [mein] *n.* tategami. ~**d** *a.* tategami no aru.

manes [méiniːz] *n.* (*pl.*) (kodai Rōma) kami ni sareta shisha no reikon.

maneuver [mənúːvə] *n.* sakusen-kōdō (guntai, kantai no) ; (*pl.*) kidō-enshū. *v.* enshū suru ; kōdō saseru (guntai, kantai o).

manganese [mǽŋgəniːs] *n.* (*min.*) mangan.

mange [méindʒ] *n.* (kachiku no) kaisen.

manger [méindʒə] *n.* umabune ; magusaoke.

mangle [mǽŋgl] *v.* zutazutani kiru ; mechakuchani suru. [mǽŋgl] *v.* kikai de tsuya o tsukeru. *n.* tsuyadashi kikai.

mango [mǽŋgou] *n.* mangō (*fruit*). ⌐no ki).

mangrove [mǽŋgrouv] *n.* (*bot.*) mangurōbu (nettaichihōsan

mangy [méindʒi] *a.* kaisen ni kakatta ; musakurushii.

mania [méiniə] *n.* kyōki ; netchū ; ...netsu ; ...heki. ∼**c** [méiniæk] *a.* kyōki no. *n.* kyōjin. ∼**cal** [mənáiəkl] *a.*

manicure [mǽnikjuə] *n., v.* tsumemigaki (o hodokosu).

manifest [mǽnifest] *a.* meihakuna. *v.* shimesu ; hyōji suru. *n.* tsumini ; mokuroku.

manifestation [mæ̀nifestéiʃ(ə)n] *n.* hyōmei ; hyōmei no gutairei : *Diving in to rescue the child was a* ∼ *of courage*, kodomo o tasukeru tame ni mizu ni tobikomu no wa yūki no aru shō-

manifesto [mæ̀niféstou] *n.* sengen ; kōji. ⌐ko da.

manifold [mǽnifould] *a., n., v.* iku tōrimo (tsukuru) ; fukusha (suru).

man(n)ikin [mǽnəkin] *n.* kobito ; issumbōshi ; =**mannequin**.

manipulate [mənípjuleit] *v.* te de atsukau ; gomakasu.

manipulation [mənìpjuléiʃ(ə)n] *n.* sōsa ; sōjū ; gomakashi.

manna [mǽnə] *n.* mana (Isuraerujin ga kōya o ryokōchū ni kami kara megumareta shokumotsu).

mannequin [mǽnəkin] *n.* manekin ; moderu-ningyō.

manner [mǽnə] *n.* hōhō. (*pl.*) gyōgi ; sahō ; fūshū : *in a* ∼, ikubun ka (furui) : *in a* ∼ *of speaking,* =*so to speak*, iwaba. ∼**ism** *n.* furui shikitari ; mannerizumu. ∼**ly** *a.* gyōgi no yoi.

manoeuvre [mənúːvə] *n., v.* =**maneuver**.

manor [mǽnə] *n.* sōen ; kizoku no ryōchi. ∼ **house,** ryōshu no yashiki. ∼**ial** [mənɔ́riəl] *a.* kizoku no ; ryōchi no ; sōen no.

mansard [mǽnsɑːd] *n.* nidan kōbai no yane ; sono yaneura

manse [mæns] *n.* bokushikan. ⌐no heya.

mansion [mǽnʃən] *n.* yakata ; yashiki ; (*pl.*) sō.

manslaughter [ménslɔ̀ːtə] *n.* hitogoroshi ; kosatsu.

mantel [méntl] **-piece** [-piːs] *n.* danro no maekazari.

mantilla [mæntílə] *n.* fujin no kami-ōi ; (*cape*).

mantle [méntl] *n.* gaitō ; manto ; (gasutō no) mantoru. *v.* ōu.

manual [ménjuəl] *a.* te de suru. *n.* tebiki ; benran ; (buki no) atsukaikata. ∼**ly** *ad.* te de.

manufactory [mæ̀njufǽktəri] *n.* seisakujō.

manufacture [mæ̀njufǽkt∫ə] *v.* seizō suru. *n.* seizō ; seihin. ∼**r** *n.* seizōsha.

manumit [mæ̀njumít] *v.* (dorei o) kaihō suru.

manure [mənjúə] *n.* hiryō. *v.* hiryō o hodokosu.

manuscript [ménjuskript] *a.* te de kaita. *n.* shahon ; genkō. MS., Ms., (*pl.*) MSS, Mss. to ryakusu.

many [méni], *a., n.* **more ; most.** tasū(no), takusan(no).

map [mæp] *n., v.* chizu (de arawasu). ∼ *out,* meiki suru.

maple [méipl] *n.* kaede. ∼ **sugar,** kaedetō.

mar [mɑː] *v.* dainashi ni suru. *n.* kison ; koshō.

marathon [mǽrəθən] *n.* chōkyori kyōsō (*Marathon*).

maraud [mɔːrɔ́ːd] *v.* ryakudatsu suru. ∼**er** *n.* ryakudatsusha.

marble [mɑ́ːbl] *n.* dairiseki ; (*pl.*) dairiseki chōkokubutsu ; hajikiishi. *a.* dairiseki no ; (*fig.*) dōjō no nai. *v.* dairiseki moyō o tsukeru.

march *n.* kōshin ; kōshinkyoku ; kokkyō no semai tochi. *v.* kōshin suru. ∼ *past,* bunretsu shiki.

March [mɑːt∫] *n.* Sangatsu.

marchioness [mɑ́ː∫ənis] *n.* kōshaku fujin.

marconi [mɑːkóuni] *n.* marukoni-shiki musendenshin. ∼**gram** [-grǽm] *n.* musendenshin. ∼**nism** *n.* marukoni-shiki musendenshinhō.

mare [mɛə] *n.* meuma (mesu uma).

margarine [mɑ̀ːdʒəríːn/mɑ́ːdʒərin] *n.* jinzō-batā ; māgarin.

margin [mɑ́ːdʒin] *n.* fuchi ; rangai ; rizaya. ∼**al** *a.* fuchi no ; rangai no. ∼**al notes,** rangaichū, bōchū. (**foot note**)

marguerite [mɑ̀ːgəríːt] *n.* (*flow.*) māgaretto (*daisy* no isshu).

marigold [mǽrigould] *n.* (*flow.*) kinsenka.

marine [məríːn] *a.* umi no ; kaijō no. *n.* kaihei ; kaiji ; kaigun ; sempaku. ∼**r** [mǽrinə] *n.* suifu ; sen'in.

marionette [mæriənét] *n.* ayatsuri-ningyō.

marital [məráitl/mǽritl] *a.* otto no; kekkon no.

maritime [mǽritaim] *a.* kaijō no; kaiun no. ～ **insurance**, kaijō hoken. ～ **law**, kaijōhō.

mark [ma:k] *n.* shirushi; kigō; hyōteki; tensū; (Doitsu) maruku kahei. *v.* shirushi o tsukeru; tensū o tsukeru; chūi suru. ～**out**, shiji suru. ～**ed** [-t] *a.* medatta. ～**edly** [-idli] *ad.* medatte. ～**ing** *n.* moyō; hanten. ～**sman** [-smən] *n.* shashu; shateki no meishu.

market [má·kit] *n.* ichiba; hanro; sōba. *v.* baibai suru; ichiba (shijō) ni dasu. ～ **place**, ichiba. ～ **price** sōba. **public** ～, kōsetsui chiba.

marl [ma:l] *n.* deikaido (semento, hiryō nado no).

marline [má:lin] *n.* hosoi tsuna. ～**-spike** [-spaik] *n.* tsunatōshi-yō no tetsubō.

marmalade [má:məleid] *n.* māmareido (orenji, remon no jamu).

marmot [má:mət] *n.* morumotto no isshu.

maroon [mərú:n] *n.* nigeta kokujin. *v.* mujintō ni suteru; *a.* kuriiro no; ebichairo no.

marplot [má:plɔt] *n.* (tanin no jama ni naru) osekkaiya.

marquee [ma:kí:] *n.* dai-temmaku; (*Am.*) (iriguchi no) ōhisashi.

marquetry [má:kitri] *n.* hamegi-zaiku.

marquis [má:kwis] *n. see* : **Duke.** kōshaku (*Duke*, no tsugi no).

marriage [mǽridʒ] *n.* kekkon. ～**able** *a.* toshigoro no; kekkon dekiru. ～**d** [-d] *a.* kekkon shite iru (otoko, onna).

marrow [mǽrow] *n.* (*anat.*) zui; kotsuzui; (hone no ana ni tsumatte iru).

marry [mǽri] *v.* kekkon suru (saseru). *inter.* mā! jitsu ni! (odoroki mata wa dantei ni iu).

Mars [ma:z] *n.* (*Rom. myth.*) gunshin; (*astr.*) Kasei.

Marseilles [ma:séilz] *n.* Maruseiyu (*France* no minato).

marsh [ma:ʃ] *n.* numa; shitchi. ～**y** *a.* numa no ōi. ～ **mallow** [mǽlou] *n.* mashimaro (kashi).

marshal [má:ʃəl] *n.* shikibukan; rikugun gensui; (*Am.*) Rempō Saibansho shikkōkan. *v.* seiretsu saseru.

marsupial [ma:sú:piəl] *n.* (*zoo.*) (*kangaroo* no yōna) yūtaijū.

mart [ma:t] *n.* ichiba; shōbai no chūshinchi.

marten [mάːtin] *n.* (*zoo.*) ten; ten no kawa.

martial [mάːʃəl] *a.* gunji no; gunshin no; (*astr.*) Kaʊei no. ∼ **law** *n.* kaigen-rei. ∼**ly** [-ʃəli] *ad.* isamashiku.

martin [mάːtin] *n.* (*bird*) tsubame no rui.

martinet [màːtinét] *n.* kiritsu tadashii hito; genkakuna hito.

martingale [mάːtiŋgeil] *n.* (uma no) munagai.

martyr [mάːtə] *n.* junkyōsha. *v.* (shinkō no tame ni) shokei suru; hakugai suru. ∼**dom** [-dəm] *n.* junkyō.

marvel [mάːvəl] *n.* fushigi. *v.* fushigini omou. ∼(l)**ous** [mάː-viləs] *a.* fushigina; subarashii.

mascara [mæskǽrə] *n.* matsuge-zome(-zai). ⎡(hito).

mascot [mǽskət] *n.* masukotto; mamori; engi no yoi mono

masculine [mάːskjulin/mǽs-] *a.* dansei no; osu no.

mash [mæʃ] *n.* moyashi-jiru; biiru no genryō; kachikushiryō. *v.* tsukimazeru.

mask, masque [mɑːsk] *n.* men; kamen; kamen-geki.

mason [méisn] *n.* ishiya; sekkō; rengakō. *Free M*∼, himitsu kessha. ∼**ry** *n.* sekkō-jutsu; ishi-zaiku.

masquerade [mæskəréid] *n.* kamen butōkai. *v.* kore ni haitte odoru; itsuwaru (*as*); kasō suru (ni=*as*).

mass [mæs] *n.* katamari; tairyō; shūdan; the ∼**es** taishū. (*cathol.*) misa. *v.* atsumeru (-maru); katamari ni naru (suru).

massacre [mǽsəkə] *n.* gyakusatsu. *v.* gyakusatsu suru.

massage [mǽsɑːʒ/mæsάːʒ] *n.*, *v.* massāji (o suru).

massive [mǽsiv] *a.* ōkina katamari no; dosshiri shita; chikarazuyoi.

mast [mɑːst] *n.* hobashira; donguri; kuri nado buta no esa. *before the* ∼, futsū no funanori to shite. ∼**head** [‑hed] *n.* shōtō; shōtō miharinin.

master [mάːstə] *n.* shujin; kashira; kōchō; kyōshi; senchō; meijin; taika. *v.* katsu; osaeru; yoku shitte iru. *a.* shu to shite. **the** ∼, Kirisuto. *be* ∼ *of oneself*, jisei suru. ∼**ful** *a.* eraburi tai. ∼**fully**, *ad.* eraburi taku. ∼**key** [-kiː] *n.* oyakagi. ∼**piece** [-piːs] *n.* kessaku. ∼**y** [-ri] *n.* shihai; rentatsu.

mastic [mǽstik] *n.* nyūkō; isshu no shikkui.

masticate [mǽstikeit] *v.* soshaku suru.

mastication [mὰstikéiʃən] *n.* soshaku.

mastiff [máːstif/mǽs-] *n.* isshu no mōken (*fierce dog*).
mastodon [mǽstədɔn] *n.* ōmukashi no ōkina zō; masutodon.
mat [mæt] *n.* matto; mushiro; shikimono. *v.* mushiro o shiku; kumiawasu. *a.* nibui; kōtaku no nai.
matador(e) [mǽtədɔː] *n.* tōgyūshi.
match [mætʃ] *n.* matchi; nakama; kyōgi. *v.* tsuresowaseru; ataraseru; tsuriau; tsuresou. ~**less** *a.* muni no. ~**lock** [⌐lɔk] *n.* hinawajū. ~**maker** [⌐meikə] *n.* baishakunin. ~**making** [⌐meikiŋ] *n.* baishaku.
mate [meit] *n.* nakama; ittsui no katappō; untenshi. *v.* nakama ni suru (naru).
material [mətíəriəl] *a.* jisshitsu no; busshitsu no. *n.* zairyō; shiryō. ~**ism** *n.* yuibutsuron; jitsuri-shugi. ~**ist** *n.* yuibutsuronsha. ~**istic** [mətìəriəlístik] *a.* yuibutsuron no. ~**ize** *v.* yūkeini suru (naru). ~**ly** *ad.* jisshitsutekini.
maternal [mətэ́ːnəl] *a.* haha no; bosei no. ~ **love,** *n.* boseiai.
maternity [mətэ́ːniti] *n.* haha taru koto; bosei.
mathematical [mæ̀θəmǽtikl] *a.* sūgaku(jō) no. ~**ly** *ad.* sūgaku- Ⱡkujō.
mathematician [mæ̀θəmətíʃən] *n.* sūgakusha.
mathematics [mæ̀θəmǽtiks] *n.* sūgaku.
matin [mǽtin] *n.*, *a.* asa no inori (no).
matinée [mæ̀tinéi] *n.* hiru-kōgyō; machinē.
matricide [méitrisaid] *n.* hahaoya-goroshi.
matriculate [mətríkjuleit] *v.* nyūgaku o yurusu.
matriculation [mətrikjuléiʃən] *n.* nyūgaku kyoka.
matrimonial [mæ̀trimóuniəl] *a.* kekkon no.
matrimony [mǽtrimouni] *n.* kekkon.
matrix [méitriks] *n.* (*pl.* -ces [-siːz]), igata; jibo.
matron [méitrən] *n.* obasan; toji; kangofu-chō. ~**ly** *a.* toji rashii; genshukuna; ochitsuita.
matter [mǽtə] *n.* kotogara; jiken; busshitsu; jūyō. *v.* jūyō de aru; kankei suru. ~**of-course** [-əvkóus] *a.* muron no koto. ~**of-fact** [-əvfǽkt] *a.* jijitsu no; jissai no.
matting [mǽtiŋ] *n.* mushiro; tatami; korera no zairyō.
mattock [mǽtək] *n.* ryōtō-guwa.
mattress [mǽtris] *n.* futon; shitone.
maturate [mǽtʃureit] *v.* (*med.*) kanō suru (saseru).

mature [mətjúə] *a.* enjuku shita. *v.* jukusaseru; (tegata nado) manki ni naru. ～**ly** *ad.* seijuku shite; jukuryo shite.

maturity [mətʃúriti] *n.* seijuku; kansei; manki.

maudlin [mɔ́:dlin] *a.* namidamoroi. *n.* namida-morosa

maul [mɔ:l] *n.* ō-zuchi. *v.* kokuhyō suru.

maunder [mɔ́:ndə] *v.* urotsukimawaru; butsubutsu iu.

mausoleum [mɔ̀:səlí:əm] *n.* (*pl.* -s; -lea [li:ə]) reibyō; mita-maya. ⌈saki.

mauve [mouv] *n.* akamurasaki no anirin-senryō; akamura-

maw [mɔ:] *n.* i; (tori no) sonō (sunabukuro).

mawkish [mɔ́:kiʃ] *a.* iyana; hakike o moyōsu.

maxim [mǽksim] *n.* kakugen; kotowaza.

maximum [mǽksiməm/-kzi-] (*pl.* -s; -ma) *n.*, *a.* saidaigen

May [mei] *n.* Gogatsu. ～**day** [-dei] gosaku-setsu: rōdō-sai. ～**flower** [-flauə] *n.* gogatsu no hana. (*Brit.*) sanzashi. (*Am.*) iwanashi. ～**pole** [-poul] *n.* meipōlu (hana mata wa himo de kazatta hashira) (sono mawari o odoru). ～ **queen**, goga-tsuhime.

may [mei] *aux. v.* **might**. ...shitemo yoi; ...ka mo shirenu; ...suru koto mo dekiyō. (*it*) ～ *be*, tabun.

maybe [méibi:] *a.* tabun; osoraku.

mayonnaise [mèiənéiz] *n.* mayonēzu (sōsu no isshu).

mayor [meə] *n.* shichō. ～**alty** [méərəlti] *n.* shichō no shoku; ninki. ～**ess** [méəris] *n.* shichō fujin.

maze [meiz] *n.* meiro; konwaku; funkyū.

mazy [méizi] *a.* meiro no yōna; mayoiyasui.

M/D., m/d. tsuki-okure (*months' date*). tsuki okure no onaji hi.

M-day [émdèi] *n.* (*Am.*) dōimbi; sensō kaishi no hi.

me [mii] *n.* (*I* no mokutekikaku) watashi ni, watashi o.

mead [mi:d] *n.* mitsubachi-zake. (*poet.*) =**meadow.**

meadow [médou] *n.* kusachi; bokusōchi. ～**ly** *a.* kusachi no.

meager, -gre [mí:gə] *a.* yaseta; toboshii; hinjakuna.

meal [mi:l] *n.* isshoku; shokuji; shokuji-doki; hikiwari.

mealy [mí:li] *a.* hikiwari no yōna; konajō no. ～**-mouthed** [-mauðd] *a.* akarasamani iwanu; kuchisaki no umai.

mean [mi:n] *a.* chūkurai no; heikin no; jūdai de nai. *n.* chū-yō; chūkurai. (*pl.*) zaisan. *v.* to omou; tsumori de aru. *by all*

~s, zehi tomo. *by any* ~s, dō demo shite. *by no* ~s, kesshite
...shinai. *by* ~s *of*, ni yori; de. ~**ly** *ad.* herikudatte.. ~**ness**
n. teikyū; hikui teido. ~**time** [-taim], ~**while** [-hwail] *ad.*
sono ma ni; tokaku suru uchi (aida) ni.

meander [miǽndə] *v.* magarikunette nagareru; sozoro-aruki
suru; *n.* magari-kuneri.

meaning [mí:niŋ] *n.* imi; kangae. *a.* imiarigena. ~**less** *a.* i-
mi no nai. ~**ly** *ad.* imi arigeni.

measles [mí:zlz] *n.* (*med.*) hashika; mashin.

measurable [méʒərəbl] *a.* sokuryō dekiru; tekido no.

measure [méʒə] *n.* monosashi; shakudo; masu; doryō; hodo; masume; sokutei; keiryō; yakusū. (*poet.*) inritsu; hyōshi. (*pl.*) hōhō; shochi. *v.* hakaru; sokuryō suru; sumpō o
toru. *beyond* ~, hijō ni. *half* ~s, bihōsaku. *in a great* ~, yohodo. *in a* ~, tashō. ~**less** *a.* muryō no. ~**ment** *n.* sokuryō;
sokutei hō; ryō; sumpō; futosa.

measuring-worm [méʒəriŋwə:m] *n.* (*insect*) shakutorimushi.

meat [mi:t] *n.* (shokuyō no) niku; tabemono.

mechanic [mikǽnik] *n.* kikaikō; gishi. ~**al** *a.* kikai no. ~
ally *ad.* ~**ian** [məkəníʃən] *n.* kikaikō; gishi. ~**s** *n.* kikai-
gaku; rikigaku.

mechanism [mékənizəm] *n.* kikai sōchi; kikō.

mechanize [mékənaiz] *v.* kikaika suru.

medal [médl] *n.* kishō; medaru. ~**lion** [midǽljən/med-] *n.*
dai shōhai; enkei sōshoku.

meddle [médl] *v.* kanshō suru; ijiru. ~**some** [-səm] *a.* kan-
shōzuki no; osekkai no.

mediaeval, medieval. [mèdií:vəl/mì:d-] *a.* chūsei no.

medial [mí:diəl], **median** [mí:diən] *a.* chūō no; chūkan no.

mediate [mí:di:t/-et] *v.* chūsai suru; chōtei suru.

mediation [mì:diéiʃən] *n.* chūsai; chōtei.

mediator [mí:dieitə] *n.* chūsainin.

medical [médikəl] *a.* igaku no; iyaku no. ~**ly** *ad.*

medicament [medíkəmənt/médik-] *n.* iyaku.

medicate [médikeit] *v.* kusuri de chiryō suru; kusuri o ireru.

medicinal [medísinəl] *a.* yakuyō no; kusuri ga kiku.

medicine [médsin/médisin] *n.* igaku; ijutsu; yakuzai.

medieval [mèdiíːvəl/mìːd] *a.* chūsei no.
mediocre [míːdioukə/mìːdióukə] *a.* tsūjō no ; heibonna.
mediocrity [mìːdiókriti/mèd-] *n.* heibon ; bonjin.
meditate [méditeit] *v.* jitto kangaeru ; kuwadateru.
meditation [mèditéiʃən] *n.* meisō ; kōsatsu ; (*pl.*) meisōroku.
meditative [méditeitiv] *a.* mokusō no ; tanoshimu.
Mediterranean [mèditəréinjən/-niən] *a.* Chichūkai no.
medium [míːdiəm] *n.* baikaibutsu ; baitai ; hōhō ; shudan. *a.* chūkan no.
medley [médli] *n.* kongō ; konsei kyoku ; konsei ka. ∼ **race**, kongō kyōsō (-ei).
medulla [medʌlə/mi-] *n.* (*pl.* **-lae** [-li]) (*anat.*) kotsuzui ; mokuzui. ⌈shū.
meed [miːd] *n.* (*poet.*) sōtō suru mukui (*what one deserves*) ; hō-
meek [miːk] *a.* nyūwana ; otonashii.
meerschaum [míəʃəm] *n.* (mizu ni uku) kaihō-seki (no paipu).
meet [miːt] *v.* **met ; meeting.** au ; demukae ni yuku. ∼ *with*, pattari deau. ∼ *together*, yoriatsumaru. *the plan* ∼*s with approval*, keikaku wa kangei sareta.
megalomania [megəlo(u)méiniə] *n.* (*med.*) kodaimōsōkyō.
megalosaurus [mégəlousóːrəs] *n.* (*zoo.*) kodai no kyōryū.
megaphone [mégəfoun] *n.* megahon.
megaton [mégətən] *n.* 1,000,000 ton no bakuhatsuryoku ; gen-shi heiki no bakuhatsuryoku tan'i (*unit*).
melancholia [melənkóuliə] *n.* (*med.*) yūutsushō.
melancholy [mélənkəli] *n.* yūutsu. *a.* yūutsuna ; inkina (*gloomy*).
mêleé [mélei] *n.* (*Fr.*) rantō ; hageshii ronsen. ⌊my.
mellifluous [melífluəs] *a.* ryūchōna ; mitsu no yōna chōshi no.
mellow [mélou] *a.* jukushita ; yawarakana ; hōjunna. *v.* juku suru.
melodious [milóudiəs] *a.* chōshi no ii ; ongakutekina (*musical*).
melodrama [meloudráːmə] *n.* amai tsūzokugeki ; merodora-
melody [mélədi] *n.* (*mus.*) senritsu ; kyoku (*tune*). ⌊ma.
melon [mélən] *n.* (*veg.*) makuwauri ; meron.
melt [melt] *v.* tokasu ; tokeru.
member [mémbə] *n.* shitai (te, ashi nado). kaiin ; nakama. ∼-**ship** [-ʃip] *n.* kaiin taru koto.

membrane [mémbrein] *n.* (*anat.*) usui maku.
membraneous [membréiniəs] *a.* maku no.
memento [miméntou] *n.* kinembutsu; katami (*keepsake*).
memoir [mémwɑ] *n.* denki. *pl.* jijoden.
memorable [mémərəbl] *a.* kioku subeki. ~**bly** [mémərəbli] *ad.* nadakaku.
memorandum [memərǽndəm] *n.* bibōroku; oboegaki (*note*).
memorial [mimɔ́:riəl] *a.* kinen no. *n.* kinembutsu. *pl.* bibō-roku. ~**ize** [mimɔ́:riəlaiz] *v.* o kinen suru; kengi (seigan) suru.   ⌈*by heart*).
memorize [méməraiz] *v.* kiroku suru; (*Am.*) anki suru (*learn*
memory [méməri] *n.* kiokuryoku.
menace [ménəs] *v.* odosu. *n.* ikaku; kyōhaku.
menagerie [minǽdʒəri] (*Fr.*) *n.* yajū dōbutsuen; dōbutsu no misemono.
mend [mend] *v.* naosu; shūzen suru. *n.* shūzen.
mendacious [mendéiʃəs] *a.* uso no.
mendacity [mendǽsiti] *n.* uso; usotsuki.
mendicancy [méndikənsi] *n.* kojiki; kojiki seikatsu.
mendicant [méndikənt] *a.* kojiki no. *n.* kojiki. ~**friar,** taku-hatsusō.
menial [mí:niəl] *n.,* *a.* meshitsukai (no).
menses [ménsi:z] *n.* (*pl.*) gekkei.
menstrual [ménstruəl] *a.* gekkei no; tsuki-zuki no (*monthly*).
mensuration [mensju(ə)réiʃən] *n.* sokuryō; (*math.*) kyūsekihō.
mental [méntl] *a.* seishin no. ~ **arithmetic,** anzan. ~**ity** [mentǽliti] *n.* chiryoku. ~**ly** [méntəli] *ad.* kokoro de. ~ **test,** chinō kensa.
menthol [ménθəl] *n.* hakkanō; mentōru.
mention [ménʃən] *n.* happyō. *v.* noberu; shirusu (*write down*). *Don't* ~ *it,* dō itashi mashite.
mentor [méntɔ:] *n.* komon; sōdan'yaku.
menu [mén(j)u:] *n.* kondate; kondate-hyō (*bill of fare*).
mephitic [mifítik] *a.* akushū no aru.
mercantile [mɔ́:k(ə)ntail] *a.* shōnin no; shōbai no (*commercial*). ~ **agency,** kōshinjo.
mercantilism [mɔ́:kəntailizm] *n.* jūshōshugi.

mercenary [mə́:sinəri] *a.* kane no tame ni hataraku. *n.* yōhei.

mercer [mə́:sə] *n.* (*Brit.*) gofukushō.

merchandise [mə́:tʃəndaiz] *n.* shōhin.

merchant [mə́:tʃənt] *n.* shōnin. ∼**man** [-mən] *n.* shōsen. ∼ **ship** [ʃip] *n.* shōsen ; bōekisen.

merciful [mə́:siful] *a.* jihibukai. ∼**ly** *ad.* jihibukaku.

merciless [mə́:silis] *a.* mujihina. ∼**ly** *ad.* mujihini.

mercurial [mə:kjúəriəl] *a.* (*M*∼) Mākyuri (*Mercury*) shin no ; (*M*∼) (*astro.*) Suisei no ; suigin no.

mercury [mə́:kjuri] *n.* suigin ; (*M*∼) (*astr.*) Suisei ; Mākyurii (*Rom. myth*) shōbai no kami.

mercy [mə́:si] *n.* jihi. *be at the* ∼ *of*, ni sayū saseru ; no suru mama ni naru.

mere [miə] *a.* hon no (sukoshi) ; tanni (...ni suginai). ∼**ly** [míəli] *ad.* tada ; tanni.

meretricious [mèritríʃəs] *a.* zokuakuna.

merge [mə:dʒ] *v.* nomikomu. ni natte shimau. *twilight* ∼*s into darkness*, yūgure ga yami ni tokekomu.

meridian [merídiən] *n.* shigosen ; zetchō (*top*).

merino [mərí:nou] *n.* (*zoo.*) merinohitsuji ; sono keorimono.

merit [mérit] *n.* neuchi ; yosa. *v.* ni ataisuru.

meritorious [meritɔ́:riəs] *a.* kōseki no aru ; kanshinna.

mermaid [mə́:meid] *n.* ningyo (onna).

merman [mə́:mæn] *n.* ningyo (otoko).

merrily [mérili] *ad.* tanoshigeni.

merriment [mérimənt] *n.* yukai ; ōwarai ; tanoshimi.

merry [méri] *a.* yōkina ; *make* ∼, gochisō o tabete yukai o tsukusu. *make* ∼ *over*, o karakau. ∼**-andrew** [-ǽndru:] *n.* dōkemono. ∼**go-round** [-gouráund] *n.* kaiten mokuba. ∼ **making** [-méikiŋ] *n.* omatsuri sawagi. *a.* yukaina.

mesh [meʃ] *n.* (ami no) me ; (*pl.*) ami. *v.* ami de toraseru.

mesmeric [mezmérik] *a.* saiminjutsu no.

mesmerism [mézmərizm] *n.* saiminjutsu.

mesmerize [mézməraiz] *v.* saiminjutsu o kakeru.

meson [mésɔn], **mesotron** [mésɔtrɔn] *n.* meson ; chūkanshi.

mess [mes] *n.* isshoku-bun ; kaishokusha. *v.* kaishoku suru ; yaru. yogosu (*spoil*). *make a* ∼ *of it*, hema o yaru ∼**mate**

[mésmeit] *n.* kaishokusha.
message [mésidʒ] *n.* dengon; tsūshin (*news*); kyōsho.
messenger [mésindʒə] *n.* tsukai.
Messiah [misáiə] *n.* kyūseishu; Kirisuto (*Christ*).
messieurs [mesəz] *n.* **monsieur** no fukusū.
Messrs. [mésəz] **messieurs** no ryaku.
mestizo [mestí:zou] Speinjin to *Am. Indian* no konketsuji.
met [met] *v. see* : **meet**.
metabolism [mitǽbəlizm] *n.* (*physiol.*) shinchintaisha; dōkasa- ⌜yō.
metal [métl] *n.* kinzoku; sozai. ∼**lic** [mitǽlik] *a.* kinzoku no.
metalliferous [metəlífərəs] *a.* kinzoku o fukunda, sansuru.
metallurgic [metəlǝ́:dʒik] *a.* yakin-gaku (jutsu) no.
metallurgy [metǽlədʒi] *n.* yakin-gaku (-jutsu).
metamorphic [metəmɔ́:fik] *a.* henka no; hentai no.
metamorphose [metəmɔ́:fouz] *v.* henkei suru; *The witch* ∼*ed people into animals*, majo ga hitobito o kemono ni kaeta.
metamorphosis [metəmɔ́:fəsis] *n.* henkei.
metaphor [métəfə] *n.* (*rhet.*) hiyuhō (mono ni tatoeta iikata). ∼**ical** [metəfɔ́rik(ə)l] *a.* anni tatoeta iikata no.
metaphysical [metəfízikəl] *a.* keijijōgaku no; junsei-tetsuga- ku no. ⌜gakusha.
metaphysician [mètəfizíʃən] *a.* keijijōgakusha; junsei-tetsu-
metaphysics [metəfíziks] *n.* keijijōgaku; junsei-tetsugaku.
mete [mi:t] *v.* sokutei suru (*measure*); wariateru. *n.* kyōkai.
meteor [mí:tiə] *n.* ryūsei; nagare-boshi. ∼**ic** [mì:tiórik] *a.* ryū- sei no; ichiji hanabanashii (∼ *life*). ∼**ite** [mí:tjərait] *n.* inseki.
meteorological [mì:tiərəlɔ́dʒikəl] *a.* kishōgaku no.
meteorology [mì:tiərɔ́lədʒi] *n.* kishōgaku.
meter [mí:tə] *n.* keiryōki; mētoru; (*poet.*) inritsu.
methinks [miθíŋks] *v.* **methought** (*p.*) (*archa.*) watakushi wa omou. (=*it seems to me*).
method [méθəd] *n.* hōhō; junjo (*order*).
methodical [miθɔ́dikəl] *a.* kiritsu tadashii. ∼**ly** [-li] *ad.* kiri- tsu tadashiku.
Methodism [méθədizm] *n.* Mesojisutoha.
Methodist [méθədist] *n.* Mesojisuto kyōto; (m-) kisoku o ma- moru hito.

methought [miθɔ́:t] *see* : **methinks.** sono kako.

methyl [méθil] *n.* (*chem.*) mechiru; mokusei (*wood-alcohol*). ～ alcohol, *n.* mechiru arukōru.

meticulous [mitíkjuləs] *a.* nen o iresugiru.

metre, meter [mí:tə] *n.* mētoru.

metrical [métrik(əl)] *a.* mētoru (*metre*) no. inritsu no.

metronome [métrənoum] *n.* (*mus.*) metoronōmu.

metropolis [mitrópəlis] *n.* shufu; shuto (*capital*).

metropolitan [mètrəpólitən] *a.* shufu (shuto) no.

mettle [métl] *n.* yūki. ～some [-səm] *a.* kekki ni hayaru.

mew [mju:] *n.* taka-kago (*hawk cage*); (*bird*) kamome; neko (*cat*) no nakigoe.⌐jin.

Mexican [méksikən] *a.* Mekishiko (*Mexico*) no. *n.* Mekishiko-

miasma [maiǽzmə] *n.* (*pl.* -s; -ta). yūkibutsu no fuhai kara

mica [máikə] *n.* (*min.*) ummo.⌐deru gas.

Michaelmas [míklməs] *n.* Mikaeru-sai (*Sept. 29,*).

microbe [máikroub] *n.* biseibutsu.

microcopy [máikrəkòpi] *n.* (*Am.*) kogata shashin no fukusha.

microcosm [máikro(u)kɔzm] *n.* shō-uchū; ningen shakai.

microcosmic [maikrokɔ́zmik] *a.* shō-uchū no.

micrometer [maikrómitə] *n.* sokubi-kei; maikurōmētā.

microphon [máikrəfoun] *n.* maikurofōn.

microscope [máikrəskoup] *n.* kembikyō.

microscopic [maikrəskɔ́pik] *a.* kembikyō no.

mid [mid] *a.* mannaka no. ～day [⌐dei] *n.* shōgo. ～land [⌐lənd] *n.,a.* naichi (no). ～night [⌐nait] *n.,a.* mayonaka (no). ～summer [⌐sʌmə] *n.* geshi. ～way [⌐wei] *a.* chūto no. *ad.* chūto ni. ～winter [⌐wintə] *n.* tōji; mafuyu.

middle [mídl] *a.* mannaka no. *n.* mannaka.

middling [mídliŋ] *a.* chūto no; chūgurai no.

midge [midʒ] *n.* (*insect*) ka; buyo (*gnat*); chiisai hito (*man*).

midget [mídʒit] *n.* issumbōshi; kogata no mono.

midriff [mídrif] *n.* (*anat.*) ōkakumaku.

midshipman [mídʃipmən] *n.* (*Brit.*) kaigun-shōi kōhosei (*naval cadet*); (*Am.*) kaigun heigakkō seito.

midst [midst] *n.* mannaka; massaichū.⌐tsu.

midwife [mídwaif] *n.* samba. ～ry [mídwaif(ə)ri] *n.* sambaju-

mien [mi:n] *n.* fūsai ; yōsu.

might [mait] *aux. v. see :* **may.** kamo shirenu ; …shite mo yoi. *n.* chikara ; iryoku. ～**y** [máiti] *a.* yūryokuna ; kyōdaina. *ad.* ōini.

migrant [máigrənt] *a.* ijū suru. *n.* ijūsei no tori ya kedamono.

migrate [maigréit] *v.* ijū suru.

migration [maigréiʃən] *n.* ijū.

migratory [máigrətəri] *a.* ijū suru ; ～ **bird,** watari-dori.

milch [miltʃ] *a.* chichi (*milk*) no deru. ～ **cow,** nyūgyū.

mild [maild] *a.* onwana ; odayakana.

mildew [míldju:] *n.* kabi.

mile [mail] *n.* mairu. ～**age** [máilidʒ] *n.* mairusū ; mairu keisan (*calculating*) no unchin (*carriage charges*). ～**stone** [⊥stoun] *n.* ［mairuhyō.

militant [mílitənt] *a.* tatakau.

military [mílitəri] *a.* ikusa no ; gun no ; gunji no ; tatakai no ; gunjin no. *n.* heitai ; guntai. ～**riism** *n.* gunkokushugi.

militate [míliteit] *v.* hataraku ; (tasukete *or* jama shite) hataraku.

militia [milíʃə] *n.* giyū-gun. ～**man** [-mən] *n.* kokuminhei.

milk [milk] *n.* chichi ; nyūzai *v.* chichi o sū ; chichi o shiboru. ～**maid** [⊥meid] *n.* chichishibori no onna. ～**man** [⊥mən] *n.* gyūnyū-haitatsunin. ～**sop** [⊥sɔp] *n.* ikuji-nashi. ～**tooth** [⊥tu:θ] *n.* nyūshi.

milky [mílki] *a.* chichi no ; nyūhaku no. ～ **Way,** *n.* (*astr.*) Amanokawa ; ginga.

mill [mil] *n.* hiki usu (*hand-*～) ; suisha goya (*water-*～) ; (*Am.*) ($1/10$ *cent*). *v.* kona o hiku. ～**er** [mílə] *n.* konaya. ～**stone** [-stoun] *n.* usuishi.

millennium [miléniəm] *n.* issennen ; shifuku issen nen (*the highest good, a second coming of Christ*).

millet [mílit] *n.* (*bot.*) kibi ; awa ; tōmorokoshi.

milligram(me) [mílɡræm] *n.* miriguramu ($1/1000$ *gram*).

milliliter, ～**-tre** [mílili:tə] *n.* miririttoru ($1/1000$ *liter*).

millimeter, ～**-tre** [mílimi:tə] *n.* mirimētoru ($1/1000$ *meter*).

milliner [mílinə] *n.* fujin-bōshiten ; fujin-sōshingushō. ～**y** [-ri] *n.* fujin-bōshi-rui.

million [míljən] *n.* hyakuman ; musū (*countless*). ～**aire** [miljənéɔ] *n.* hyakuman chōja ; fugō.

milt [milt] *n.* (*anat.*) hizō (*spleen*) ; shirako (*roe*).

mime [maim] *n.* miburi-kyōgen ; dōkemono (*mimic*).

mimeograph [mímiogræf] *n.* tōshaban. *v.* tōshaban de suru.

mimic [mímik] *a.* mane tagaru. *n.* hitomane o suru hito ; dō-kemono (*mime*). *v.* mane suru. ~**ry** [-ri] *n.* mane.

minaret [mínəret] *n.* (Kaikyō-jiin no) sentō.

mince [mins] *v.* komakani kiru ; hikaemeni iu. ~**meat** [⸗miːt] *n.* minsu niku. (hikiniku, ringo, shibō, kōryō o mazeta mono).

mind [maind] *n.* kokoro. *v.* ki o tsukeru (*take care of*). *give one's* ~ *to,* ni kokoro o komeru. *Never* ~ ! daijōbu. ~**ful** [⸗f(u)l] *a.* chūibukai. ~**less** [⸗lis] *a.* mushiryona. ~**lessness** fuchūi-na koto.

mine [main] *pron.* **I** no shoyū daimeishi. *n.* kōzan (*mine*) ; (*mil.*) jirai. *v.* kōseki o horu ; jirai o shiku. ~**layer** [máinleiə] *n.* suirai fusetsu-kan. ~**r** [máinə] *n.* kōfu ; jirai o shiku kōhei ; suirai (*torpedo*) fusetsusen (*ship*). ~**ral** [mínərəl] *n.* kōbutsu. *a.* kōbutsu no. ~**ral water,** *n.* tansansui. ~**ralogy** [minərælədʒi] *n.* kōbutsugaku. ~ **sweeping** [máinswiːpiŋ] *n.* sōkai.

mingle [míŋgl] *v.* mazeru ; mazaru (*mix*).

miniature [míni(ə)tʃə] *n.* shikuzu. *a.* kogata no.

minim [mínim] *n.* yakuekiryō no tan'i (¹/₁₆ *dram*) ; biryō.

minimize [mínimaiz] *v.* kyokushō ni suru (*understate*) ; keishi suru. ⌐gendo.

minimum [míniməm] *n.* (*pl.* -ma [mínimə]) saishōryō ; saitei

mining [máiniŋ] *n.* saikō ; kōgyō ; ~ **company,** *n.* kōgyō-ka-⌐isha.

minion [mínjən] *n.* okiniiri ; tesaki (*tool*) ; chōji.

minister [mínistə] *n.* daijin (*cabinet* ~) ; kōshi ; (*relig.*) bokushi (*priest*). *v.* yakudatsu ; hōshi suru. ~**ial** [ministíəriəl] *a.* daijin no ; naikaku no. ~ **resident,** benri kōshi.

ministration [ministréiʃən] *n.* hōshi ; shokumu.

ministry [mínistri] *n. minister* no shoku ; seifu ; naikaku.

minnow [mínou] *n.* (*fish*) togeuo.

minor [máinə] *a.* chiisai ; toshishita no ; jūyō de nai. *n.* misei-nensha ; (*mus.*) tanchō. ~**ity** [mainóriti] *n.* miseinen ; shōsū (*small number*).

minster [mínstə] *n.* dai-garan; sōin no kaidō.

minstrel [mínstrəl] (chūsei no) gin'yū shijin (*musician*). ～sy [-si] *n.* koto o hiite utau koto; sono uta.

mint [mint] *n.* zōheikyoku. *v.* kahei o tsukuridasu. ～age [-idʒ] *n.* kahei o tsukeru ryōkin.

minuet [minjuét] *n.* yuruyakana buyō; sono kyoku.

minus [máinəs] *a.* (*math.*) gen no; fu no. *prep.* o hiite; nashi de.

minute [mainjú:t] *a.* komakai; shōsaina. ～ly *ad.* komakani.

minute [mínit] *n.* fun (jikan, kakudo no tan'i); oboegaki (*memorandum*). ～book [-buk] *n.* gijiroku. ～hand [-hænd] *n.* (tokei no) funshin.

minutia [mainjú:ʃiə] *n.* (*pl.* ～tiae [-ʃii:]) (*pl.*) saimoku; shōsai (*details*).

minx [miŋks] *n.* otemba-musume; uwaki-musume.

miracle [mírəkl] *n.* kiseki; odoroku beki mono mata wa hito; kiseki geki (*drama*).

miraculous [mirékjuləs] *a.* kisekiteki no; odoroku beki.

mirage [mirá:dʒ] *n.* (*astr.*) shinkirō.

mire [máiə] *n.* doro. *v.* doro ni hamaru; tōwaku saseru.

mirror [mírə] *n.* kagami; (*fig.*) mohan. *v.* hansha suru; kagami ni utsusu. ～writing, *n.* sakasa-gaki.

mirth [mə:θ] *n.* tanoshimi; yukai. ～ful [-f(u)l] *a.* yukaina. ～fully [-(fu)li] *ad.* yukaini.

miry [máiəri] *a.* doromamire no; fuketsuna (*dirty*).

misadventure [mísədvéntʃə] *n.* fukō; fukōna dekigoto.

misadvise [mísədváiz] *v.* machigatta chūkoku o suru.

misalliance [mísəláiəns] *n.* mibunchigai no (tokuni) kekkon (*marriage*).

misanthrope [mízənθroup] *n.* ningengirai. ～pic *a.* ningen-girai no. ～py [mizénθropi] *n.* ningengirai; ensei.

misapply [mísəplái] *v.* mochiikata o ayamaru (*misuse*).

misapprehend [mísæprihénd] *v.* gokai suru; omoichigaeru.

misappropriate [mísəpróuprieit] *v.* ran'yō suru; jibun no mono no yōni tsukau.

misbehave [mísbihéiv] *v.* busahōni furumau (*behave badly*).

misbelief [mísbili:f] *n.* machigatta shinkō (*wrong belief*); jakyō.

misbeliever [mísbilí:və] *n.* ikyōto; shinjinai.

miscarriage [miskǽridʒ] *n.* shippai (*failure*); ryūzan (*abortion*); haitatsu chigai : ~*of goods, letters.*

miscarry [miskǽri] *v.* shippai (ryūzan) suru; todokanai.

miscellaneous [misiléiniəs] *a.* shuju no; iroiro no.

miscellany [mísiləni] *n.* zatta no·(*mixed*) mono no atsumari (*collection-in one book*).

mischance [mistʃá:ns] *n.* fukō : *by* ~, fukō nimo.

mischief [místʃif] *n.* itazura; meiwaku, yakkai.

mischievous [místʃivəs] *a.* yūgaina; itazurana.

miscible [mísəbl] *a.* gochagochani nari yasui.   ⌈ru.

misconceive [miskənsí:v] *v.* gokai suru; kangaechigai o su-
misconduct [miskóndʌkt] *n.* fugyōseki. [mìskəndʌ́kt] *v.* fugyōseki o suru.

misconstrue [miskónstru:/-strú:] *v.* imi o torichigaeru; gokai
miscreant [miskriənt] *n.* akkan; warumono.   ⌊suru.

misdeed [misdí:d] *n.* warui okonai; hanzai (*crime*).

misdemeanou(u)r [mìsdimí:nə] *n.* karui hanzai; hikō.

misdirect [mìsdirékt] *v.* ayamatta sashizu o suru.

miser [máizə] *n.* kechina hito; monooshimi suru hito. ~ly
a. rinshokuna.

miserable [mízərəbl] *a.* awarena; mijimena. ~ly *ad.* awareni; mijimeni.

misery [mízəri] *n.* fukō; konkyū (*poverty*).

misfeasance [misfí:zəns] *n.* (*leg.*) fuhōkōi; hōritsu no akuyō.

misfortune [misfɔ́:tʃ(ə)n] *n.* fuun.

misgiving [misgíviŋ] *n.* shimpai : *have* ~ *about their safety,*
ampi ga shimpai de aru.

mishap [míshæp] *n.* fukō. *without* ~, buji ni.

misjudge [misdʒʌ́dʒ] *v.* handan o ayamaru.

mislay [misléi] *v.* oita basho o wasureru : ~ *a sweater,* suetā
o oita basho o wasureru.

mislead [mislí:d] *v.* madowasu; chigatta michi e tsurete iku.

mismanage [mìsmǽnidʒ] *v.* kanri o ayamaru. ~ment [mis-
mǽnidʒmənt] *n.* kanri no futegiwa.

misogamy [misógəmi] *n.* kekkongirai.

misogyny [misódʒəni] *n.* onnagirai.

misprint [misprínt] *n.* goshoku. *v.* goshoku o suru.

misprision [misprízən] *n.* fuhōkōi; kanri *(officials)* no taiman *(neglect)*.

misrule [mísrú:l] *n.* ayamatta seiji. *v.* ayamatta seiji o suru.

miss [mis] *n.* shippai; yarisokonai. *A ~ is as good as a mile*, chotto no machigai ichi mairu. *v.* yarisokonau.

miss [mis] *n.* kekkon shinai onna. *Miss Tsuji*, *(pl.) the Misses Tsuji*, *=the Miss Tsujis*, Tsujis san no ojōsan-tachi.

missal [mís(ə)l] *n. (Roman Catholic)* ichinenjū no Mass (misa) no koto o kaita hon.

missile [mísail] *n.* misairu; yūdōdan.

mission [mísən] *n.* shimei; shisetsu ikkō. **~ary** [mísənəri] *a.* dendō no. *n.* senkyōshi.

missis [mísis], **missus** [mísiz] *n. (col. dial.)* okusan.

missive [mísiv] *n.* shojō; kōbunsho *(official letter)*; shinsho.

mist [mist] *n.* kiri; me no kasumi. *v.* kiri ga oriru. **~y** [místi] *a.* kiri no kakatta.

mistake [misteik] *v.* **mistook, mistaken; mistaking.** machigaeru. *n.* machigai.

mistaken [mistéik(ə)n] *v. see*: **mistake.** *a.* ayamatta: *a ~ idea.*

Mister [místə] *n.* Dono; San; *Mr. X*, X San.

mistletoe [mízltou/-sl-] *n.* yadorigi *(plant)*.

mistress [místris] *n.* shufu; (M~) fujin (" Mrs." to kaku); jōfu *(sweetheart)*; jokyōshi. *M~ of Robe*, kyūchū nandogakari no jokan. ⌠bukai.

mistrust [místrʌst] *n.* fushin. *v.* utagau. **~ful** [-ful] *a.* utagai-

misunderstand [mísʌndəstǽnd] *v.* gokai suru. **~ing** *n.* gokai.

misuse [misjú:z] *v.* ran'yō suru; gyakutai suru. [misjú:s] *n.* ran'yō; gyakutai.

mite [mait] *n.* dani; uji; kozeni. *not a ~*, sukoshi mo...nai; dani.

miter, -tre [máitə] *n.* shikyō no kammuri (dai sōjō nado no). *v.* shikyō kammuri de kazaru.

mitigate [mítigeit] *v.* yawarageru; genzuru; karuku suru.

mitigation [mitigéiʃən] *n.* kanwa; chinsei; keibetsu.

mitt [mit], **mitten** [mitn] *n.* yubi-nashi-tebukuro; mitto.

mix [miks] *v.* mazeru; mazaru.

mixed [mikst] *a. (pp. of* **mix)** ironna mono no mazatta. **~**

bathing, kon'yoku. ~ **school,** danjo kyōgaku.

mixture [míkstʃə] *n.* kongō; kongōbutsu (*thing*).

miz(z)en [mízn] *a.* sembi no. ~**mast** [-mɑ:st] *n.* sembi hobashira. *n.* (*naut.*) ichiban hikui ho; sambon-masuto no ichiban ushiro no mono.

Mlle., mlle. [mædməzél] (*Fr.*) *mademoiselle*=*Miss.* ojōsan.

Mme. [mædɑm] =**madame** fujin (=*Mrs.*). okusan.

Mmes. [me:dáːm] *n.* (*pl.*) =**mesdames. madame** no fukusū.

mnemonic [ni(:)mónik], *a.* kioku (jutsu) no. ~**s** [ni(:)móniks] *n.* kiokujutsu.

moan [moun] *v.* umeku. *n.* umeki.

moat [mout] *n.* hori. *v.* hori de kakomu.

mob [mɔb] *n.* bōmin; bōto. *v.* mure o nashite osou.

mobile [móubail] *a.* ugoki (kawari) yasui. ~ *mind adapts itself quickly,* ugokiyasui kokoro wa sugu sono ki ni naru. ~**ity** [məbíliti] *n.* dōyōsei. ~ *and nobility,* minshū to kizoku.

mobilization [moubilaizéiʃən] *n.* dōin. ~**orders,** *n.* dōinrei.

mobilize [móubilaiz] *v.* dōin suru.

mock [mɔk] *v.* chōrō suru; maneru. *n.* chōrō; chōrō no mato, (*laughing stock*). *a.* nise no. ~**ery** [⁻əri] *n.* chōrō; manete azakeru shigusa. ~**ingbird**[⁻iŋbəːd] *n.* monomanedori. ~**ingup** [⁻iŋʌp] *n.* (*Am.*) jitsubutsu-dai no mokei.

mode [moud] *n.* hōhō; ryūgi (*a style*); ryūkō (*fashion*).

model [mɔ́dl] *n.* mokei; mohan (*example*). *v.* moderu ni suru.

moderate [mɔ́dəreit] *v.* kagen suru; chōsetsu suru. *a.* [mɔ́d(ə)rit] tekido no; onwana.

moderation [mɔdəréiʃən] *n.* onwa; sessei (*temperance*); tekido (*suitableness*).

moderator [mɔ́dəreitə] *n.* chūsaisha (*mediator*); kaichō (*chairman*); chōsetsuki; ~ **lamp,** *n.* sekiyu chōsetsu rampu.

modern [mɔ́dən] *a.* kinsei no; gendai no. *n.* gendaijin. (~ *people.*) ~**ism** [-izm]. *n.* gendaishugi. ~**ize** [-aiz] *v.* gendaifūni suru.

modest [mɔ́dist] *a.* tsutsushimibukai; nedan ga takaku nai; shissona; jimina; enryogachina; uchikina.

modesty [mɔ́disti] *n.* kenson. *a.* deshabaranai (*not forward*).

modicum [mɔ́dikəm] *n.* kinshō; shōryō.

modification [mədifikéiʃən] *n.* henkō; seigen (*limit*); (*gram.*) shūshoku. ⌐*adv.* nado).

modifier [módifaiə] *n.* shūseisha; (*gram.*) shūshokugo (*adj. or*

modify [módifai] *n.* shūsei suru (*alter*); shūshoku suru; ka-

modish [móudiʃ] *a.* ryūkō no; tōseifu no. ⌐gen suru.

modulate [módjuleit] *v.* chōsetsu suru. (*mus.*) chōshi o kaeru.

modulation [módjuléiʃən] *n.* chōsetsu; chōon. (*mus.*) tenchō.

Mogul [mo(u)gál/móugəl] *n.* Mōkojin; (*Am.*) jūyō-jimbutsu (*an important person*).

Mohammedan [mo(u)hǽmidən] *a.* Kaikyō no. *n.* Kaikyōto. ～**ism** *n.* Kaikyō.

moiety [móiəti] *n.* hambun; ichibubun (*a part*).

moil [moil] *v.* honeoru; akuseku hataraku. *toil and* ～, sesse-to hataraku.

moist [moist] *a.* nureta. ～**en** [móisn] *v.* nureru, nurasu. ～**ure** [móistʃə] *n.* shimeri; namida (*tears*).

molar [móulə] *v.*, *a.* kudaki tsubusu. *n.* okuba (～*teeth*).

molasses [mələ́siz] *n.* tōmitsu; sharibetsu.

mold, mould [mould] *n.* hiyokuna tochi; kabi; igata. *v.* ka-bi ga haeru; kata o tsukuru. ～**er** [móuldə] *v.* kusatte kuzu-reru. ～**ing** [móuldiŋ] *n.* igata. ～**y** *a.* kabita.

mole [moul] *n.* hokuro; aza; mogura; bōhatei (*breakwater*). ～**hill** [-hil] *n.* mogura-zuka.

molecule [móulikju:l] *n.* bunshi; biryō.

molest [mələ́st] *v.* kurushimeru; jama suru (*disturb*); kanshō

molestation [moulestéiʃən] *n.* jama; bōgai. ⌐suru.

mollification [molifikéiʃən] *n.* kanwa; keigen.

mollify [mólifai] *v.* yawarageru. ～ *his wrath*, kare no ikari o yawarageru.

mollusc, mollusk [móləsk] *n.* (*zoo.*) nantai-dōbutsu.

mollycoddle [mólikɔdl] *n.* ikujinashi; nyūjakuna mono (ko-domo).

molt, moult [moult], *v.* nukekawaru (hane ya kawa ga); *n.* nukekawari.

moment [móumənt] *n.* shunkan; nōritsu (*efficiency*); jūyōsei (*importance*). ～**arily** [-ərili] *ad.* chotto no aida; jiji kokukoku ni (*every moment*). ～**ary** [-(ə)ri] *a.* shunkan no. ～**ous** [mo(u) méntəs] *a.* jūdaina. ~**ously** *ad.* jūdaini. ~**ousness** *n.* jūdai ; jūyō.

momentum [mo(u)méntəm] *n.* (*pl.* ~**s** ; **-ta**) (*mach.*) undōryō.

Mon. = **Monsignor** [mɔŋsiɲɔːr(e)] Hōō-Chō (*the Vatican*), kōkan (*high official*) no keishō (*honorific*).

monad [mónəd] *n.* monado ; ikka genso ; tansaibō seibutsu.

monarch [mónək] *n.* kunshu. ~**al** [mɔnáːk(ə)l] *a.* kunshu no. ~**ism** [-izm] *n.* kunshu-shugi. ~**ical** [mɔnáːkikəl] *a.* kunshu seiji no. ~**y** *n.* kunshu seitai. *an absolute* ~, sensei seiji. *a constitutional* ~, rikken seiji.

monastery [mónəstri] *n.* shūdōin.

monastic [mɔnǽstik] *a.* shūdōin no ; sōryo no (*of priest*). ~**ism** [mɔnǽstisizəm] *n.* sōinseido ; sōinseikatsu.

Monday [mándi]. *n.* Getsuyōbi. [*cial*).

monetary [mánit(ə)ri] *a.* kahei no (*of money*) ; kin'yū no (*finan-*

monetize [mánitaiz] *v.* kahei to sadameru.

money [máni] *n.* kahei ; kane ; ~ **market,** kin'yū shijō. ~ **changer** [-tʃéindʒə] *n.* ryōgaeya. ~**ed** [-d] *a.* kanemochi no. ~**-making** [-meikiŋ] *n.* kanemōke. ~**order** [-ɔ́ːdə] *n.* yūbin kawase.

monger [máŋgə] *n.* ...shōnin. "**-monger**" to shite yoku tsukau ; *fish*~ ; *iron*~, *etc.*

Mongol [móŋgɔl], **Mongolian** [mɔŋgóuliən] *a.* Mōko no. *n.* Mōkojin. ~**ia** [mɔŋgóuliə] *n.* Mōko.

mongrel [máŋgrəl] *n.* zasshu. *a.* zasshu no (*anim. & plant.* dōshoku-butsu).

monism [mónizm] *n.* (*phylos.*) ichigenron.

monition [mo(u)níʃən] *n.* kunkai ; keikoku.

monitor [mónitə] *n.* kankokusha ; kyūchō (*chief of the class*) ; rajio no kanshi. *v.* kanshi sōchi de kanshi suru. ~**man**[-mən] *n.* tōkii satsueijō no onkyōgishi.

monk [mʌŋk] *n.* shūdōshi.

monkey [máŋki] *n.* saru ; itazurakko (*imp*). *v.* itazura suru.

monochrome [mónəkroum] *n.* tansaiga ; hitoiro no ga (e).

monocle [mónəkl] *n.* katamegane.

monody [mónədi] *n.* banka ; shisha (dead) o kanashimu uta.

monogamous [mɔnógəməs] *a.* ippu-ippu no (hitori no otto to hitori no tsuma no).

monogamy [mɔnɔ́gɔmi] *n.* ippu ippu seido.

monogram [mɔ́nɔgræm] *n.* kumiawase moji.

monograph [mɔ́nɔgræf] *n.* senkō-rombun; (aru mondai (*subject*) ni tsuite no rombun).

monologue [mɔ́nɔlɔg] *n.* (*aside*) hitori de iu serifu (*play for a single actor*).

monomania [mɔ́no(u)méiniɔ] *n.* henshitsukyō. ～**c** *n.* sono kanja (*patient*).

monoplane [mɔ́nɔplein] *n.* tan'yō hikōki.

monopolist [mɔnɔ́pɔlist] *n.* dokusensha; sembaisha.

monopolize [mɔnɔ́pɔlaiz] *v.* dokusen suru; sembai suru.

monopoly [mɔnɔ́pɔli] *n.* dokusen; sembaiken (～ *right*).

monosyllabic [mɔ́nɔsilǽbik] *a.* (*phon.*) tan'onsetsu no.

monosyllable [mɔ́nɔsìlɔbl] *n.* (*phon.*) tan'onsetsu.

monotheism [mɔ́nɔθi:izm] *n.* isshinkyō. ～**ist** [mɔ́nɔθi:ist] *n.* isshinronja.

monotone [mɔ́nɔtoun] *n.* tanchō; henka no nai chōshi.

monotonous [mɔnɔ́t(ɔ)nɔs] *a.* tanchōna; henka no nai.

monotony [mɔnɔ́t(ɔ)ni] *n.* tanchō.

monotype [mɔ́nɔtaip] *n.* katsuji (*type*) o jidōtekini chūzō suru

monsieur [mɔsjɔ́] *n.* (*Fr.*) ...Kun; ...Sama (=*Mr.*). ⌊kikai.

monsoon [mɔnsú:n] *n.* kisetsufū; Indo no uki (*rainy season*).

monster [mɔ́nstɔ] *n.* kaibutsu; (*fig.*) zanninna hito (*cruel person*).

monstrosity [mɔnstrɔ́siti] *n.* kimyōna katachi; ayashii mono.

monstrous [mɔ́nstrɔs] *a.* kikei no (*deformed*); kyodaina (*huge*); bakemono no yōna. ～**ly** *ad.* ～**ness** *n.*

montage [mɔ(:)ntɑ:ʒ] *n.* montāju; (tokuchō o atsumete) tsukutta shashin.

month [mʌnθ] *n.* tsuki: *two months* [-θs], nikagetsu (futatsuki).

monthly [mʌ́nθli] *a. ad.* maitsuki no (*once a month*) *n.* gekkan zasshi (*monthly magazine*).

monument [mɔ́njumɔnt] *n.* kinenhi; kinen-butsu. ～**al** [mɔnjuméntɔl] *a.* kinenhi no. ～**ally** *ad.* kinen ni.

mood [mu:d] *n.* yōshiki; (*gram.*) hō; iikata kibun (*temper*). **subjunctive** ～, (*gram.*) setsuzokuhō; kateihō. *in the* ～ *for,* suru ki ni natte. ～y [mú:di] a. fukigen no. ～iness [mú:d-inis] n. fukigen.

moon [mu:n] n. tsuki. ～**light** [⌐lait] n. gekkō. ～**lit** [⌐lit] a. tsuki ni terasareta. **-shiner** [⌐ʃainə] n. (Am. col.) sakerui mitsuzō sha. ～**struck** [mú:nstrʌk] a. hakkyō shita.

Moor [muə] n. Mūajin.

moor [muə] n. arenohara. v. fune o tsunagu. ～**age** [⌐ridʒ] n. teihakujo. ～**cock** [⌐kək] n. (bird) aka-raichō no osu. ～**hen** [⌐hen] sono mesu. ～**ings** [⌐riŋz] n. (pl.) teihakujo. ～**land** [⌐lænd] n. numachi ; arenohara.

moose [mú:s] n. ōjika.

moot [mu:t] v. tōron suru (renshū no tame). n. gakusei tōronkai. ～ **point**, ronten.

mop [məp] n. e (handle) no tsuita zōkin (house-cloth). shikamezura. v. moppu de sōji suru (clean). kao o shikameru. ～ ana mow, kao o shikameru.

mope [moup] v. fusagikomu. n. shombori shite iru hito ; fusagikonde iru hito.

moraine [moréin] n. hyōga de dekita taiseki.

moral [mɔ́r(ə)l] a. dōtokujō no. n. kyōkun ; shūshin (～s). ～ certainty, tashikani machigai no nai koto. ～**ist** [mɔ́rəlist] n. dōtokuka. ～**ize** [mɔ́rəlaiz] v. dōtoku kyōka suru (～ the heathen). ～**ly** [mɔ́rəli] ad. dōtokujō. ～**ity** [mərǽliti] n. tokkō ; dōtoku. ～ **science** [-sáiəns] n. rinri.

morale [mɔ́ra:l] n. fūki.

morass [mərǽs] n. numachi. ┌enki (rei).

moratorium [mɔrətɔ́:riəm] n. (pl. **-ria** [-riə] ; **-s** [-s]) shiharai

morbid [mɔ́:bid] a. byōki no. ～**ity** [mɔ:bíditi] n. byōki de aru koto ; aru chihō no byōnin no percentage.

mordant [mɔ́:dənt] a. shinratsuna (hiniku) ; iro o (asenai yōni) tomeru. n. hiniku ; irodome.

more [mɔ:] a., ad., a. see : **many** and **much**. a. motto ōi. ad. motto ōku. ～ and ～, masumasu. ～ or less, tashō.

moreover [mɔ:róuvə] ad. sono ue.

morganatic [mɔ:gənǽtik] a. mibun-chigai no kekkon o suru ; ～ **marriage**, kodomo ni sōzokuken no nai kekkon.

morgue [mɔ:g] n. (Fr.) shitai (dead body) kōji (hito ni miseru) basho; (*Am.*) (shimbunsha no) chōsabu.

moribund [mɔ́ribʌnd] *a.* shinikakatta. ⌐shū.

Mormon [mɔ́:mən] *a.* Morumonkyō no. ~ism *n.* Morumon-

morn [mɔ:n], (*poet.*) **morning** [mɔ́:niŋ] *n.* asa. ~ing glory,

(*flow.*) asagao. ~ing star, *n.* ake no myōjō.

Morocco [mərɔ́kou] *n.* Morokko. (Morokko-yagi no kawa).

morose [məróus] *a.* ki-muzukashii.

morphia [mɔ́:fiə], **morphine** [mɔ́:fin] *n.* (*chem.*) moruhine.

morphology [mɔːfɔ́lədʒi] *n.* (*biol.*) keitaigaku; (*gram.*) keitai-ron (*accidence*).

morrow [mɔ́rou] *n.* (*poet.*) yokujitsu.

morsel [mɔ́:s(ə)l] *n.* hitokuchi; hitokire (*fragment*).

mortal [mɔ́:təl] *a.* shinubeki; inochi no yaritori o suru; ino-chi ni kakawaru (~ *wound*). *n.* ningen. ~ly [-li] *ad.* ~ity [mɔ:tǽliti] *n.* shinubeki koto; shibōritsu (*death-rate*).

mortar [mɔ́:tə] *n.* shikkui; morutaru; usu (*hand-mill*). *v.* mo-rutaru de katameru.

mortgage [mɔ́:gidʒ] *n.* teitō; teitōken. *v.* shichi ni ireru. ~r, ~or [mɔ:gədʒɔ́:] *n.* teitō (shichi) ken setteisha.

mortician [mɔ:tíʃən] *n.* (*Am.*) sōgiya.

mortification [mɔ̀:tifikéiʃən] *n.* (*med.*) eso; dasso. nangyō ku-gyō. **mortify** [mɔ́:tifai] *v.* kurushii koto ni taeru. ⌐gyō.

mortise [mɔ́:tis] *n.* (*archi.*) hozoana. *v.* hozo o akeru.

mortuary [mɔ́:tuəri] *n.* shitai kari-okiba. *a.* shitaimaisō no.

mosaic [məzéiik/mouz-] *n.* yosegi zaiku; mozaiku.

Moslem [mɔ́zlem] *n.*, *a.* Kaikyōto (no).

mosque [mɔsk] *n.* Kaikyō jiin.

mosquito [məskí:tou] *n.* (*insect*) ka. ~net, kaya.

moss [mɔs] *n.* koke. ~y *a.* koke no haeta.

most [moust] *a.* see : **many** *and* **much.** mottomo ōi; taitei no. *ad.* ichiban. *n.* ichiban takusan. at (*the*) ~, ōkute; takadaka. ~ly *ad.* taigai.

mot [mou] *n.* (*Fr.*) kichi (*wit*) ni tonda iikata. ⌐gomi.

mote [mout] *n.* chiisai ten (toku ni chiri no); goku chiisai

motel [moutél] *n.* (*Am.*) motor car goto tomaru *hotel.* ⌐*no ball.*

moth [mɔ(:)θ] *n.* (*insect*) ga; shimi. ~ball [-bɔ:l] *n.* nafutalin

mother [mʌ́ðə] haha. ~ country, *n.* bokoku. ~ tongue, bokokugo. ～**hood** [-hud] *n.* bosei. ～**in-law** [-in-lɔ́:] *n.* shūtome; gibo. ～**land** [-lænd] *n.* bokoku. ～**ly** *a.* haha no; jiai no. ～**-of-pearl** [-ǝv-pé:l] *n.* shinjugai no uchigawa no sō.

motion [móuʃǝn] *n.* undō; katsudō; dōgi. *v.* miburi de shimesu. ～**less** *a.* ugokanai. ～**picture** [-píktʃǝ] *n.* eiga.

motive [móutiv] *a.* ugokasu; undō no. *n.* shushi; dōki. ～ power, gendōryoku.

motley [mɔ́tli] *a.* madara no. *n.* madarana (ironna iro no) kimono.

motor [móutǝ] *n.* gendōryoku; hatsudōki; jidōsha. *v.* jidōsha de iku. ～ *coach*, (*Am.*) noriai jidōsha. ～**bicycle** [-bǽisikl]= *motorcycle*. ～**boat** [-bout] *n.* hatsudōkisen. ～**bus** [-bǝs] *n.* noriai jidōsha. ～**cab** [-kæb] *n.* tsujimachi jidōsha. ～**cade** [-keid] *n.* (*Am.*) jidōsha no gyōretsu. ～**car** [-kɑ:] *n.* jidōsha. ～**cycle** [-saikl] *n.* jidō jitensha. ～**ist** *n.* jidōsha sōjūsha. ～ man [-mǝn] *n.* (densha nado no) untenshu.

mottle [mɔ́tl] *v.* madara ni suru; zasshoku ni suru.

motto [mɔ́tou] *n.* kakugen; hyōgo; mottō.

mould, [mould] *v. see* : **mold**.

moult [moult] *v., n. see* : **molt**.

mound [maund] *n.* tsutsumi; dote; ko-oka; tōshuban (*baseball* no).

mount [maunt] *n.* yama; (shashin no) daishi. *v.* noboru, (uma ni) noseru; urauchi suru.

mountain [máuntin] *n.* yama; (*pl.*) sammyaku. ～**eer** [-íǝ] *n.* yamaguni no hito. tozanka. *v.* tozan suru. ～**ous** [-ǝs] *a.* yama no ōi; yama no yōna.

mountebank [máuntibæŋk] *n.* yamashi; horafuki.

mourn [mɔ:n/mɔǝn] *v.* kanashimu; tomurau. ～**er** *n.* aitōsha. ～**ful** *a.* kanashii. ～**fully** *ad.* ～**ing** *n.* kanashimi; mo.

mouse [maus] *n.* (*pl.* **mice** [mais]) hatsukanezumi; okubyōmono.

mouser [máuzǝ] *n.* nezumi o toru neko mata wa fukurō.

moustache [mǝstá:ʃ/mus-] *n. see* : **mustache**.

mouth [mauθ] *n.* kuchi; iriguchi. ～**ful** *n.* hitokuchi. ～**piece** [-pi:s] *n.* suikuchi; sōwaguchi.

movable [mú:vǝbl] *a.* ugokashiuru. ～ **property**, ～**s,** dōsan.

move [mu:v] *v.* ugoku; ugokasu; kandō saseru; dōgi o dasu;

tenkyo suru. ～r *n*. hatsugisha. ～ing picture, eiga. ～ment *n*. undō.

movie [mú:vi] *n*. (*Am. col.*) eiga (tsūjō *pl.*).

mow [mou] *n*. kusazumi. *v*. mowed, mown; mowing. kusa o karu. ～ing machine, kusakariki. ～er *n*. kusakariki (nin).

mown [moun] *v. see* : mow.

moxa [móksə] *n*. mogusa.

MP., m.p. *n*. kempei (*Military Police*).

M.P. *n*. kokkai giin (Igirisu no) (*Member of Parliament*).

mph., m.p.h. *n*. jisoku mairu (*miles per hour*).

Mr. [místə] =Mister, Mrs. [mísiz, mísis] =Mistress.

MRA. dōtoku saibusō (*Moral Re-Armament*).

M/S., m.s. =ichiran go tsuki barai (*months after sight*).

Msgr. =Monsignor.

Mt., mt. =Mount; mountain.

much [mʌtʃ] *a*. more, most. takusan no; taisōna. *n*. takusan. *ad*. taihen.

mucilage[mjú:silidʒ] *n*.(shokubutsu kara toru) nen'eki ; (*Am.*) ⌊gomunori.

muck [mʌk] *n*. taihi; taifun. *v*. yogosu.

mucous [mjú:kəs] *a*. nen'eki (*mucus*) o dasu.

mucus [mjú:kəs] *n*. nen'eki ; nebakkoi eki.

mud [mʌd] *n*. doro ; nukarumi. ～dy *a*. doro-darake no.

muddle [mʌdl] *v*. konran saseru ; mechamechani suru. *n*. konran.

muff [mʌf] *n*. mafu (ryōte o irete atatameru) ; tama no ukesokonai. *v*. tama o ukesokonau.

muffin [mʌfin] *n*. karuyaki pan ; maffin. ⌈mafurā.

muffle [mʌfl] *v*. tsutsumu ; me ya mimi o ōu. ～r *n*. erimaki ;

mug [mʌg] *n*. mimitsuki no sakazuki ; *mug* de nomu seiryō-

muggy [mʌgi] *a*. mushiatsui ; atsukurushii. ⌊inryō.

mulatto [mju(:)lætou] *n*. shirokuro no konketsuji.

mulberry [mʌlbəri] *n*. (*bot.*) kuwa ; kuwa no mi.

mulch [mʌltʃ] *n*. shikiwara (shokubutsu hogo no). *v*. shikiwara o shiku.

mulct [mʌlkt] *v*. bakkin o kasuru. *n*. bakkin. ⌈nai.

mule [mju:l] *n*. raba (*male* to *mare* no zasshu) ; kakato ōi no *slipper* ; (*col.*) gōjōna hito. ～teer [mjù:litíə] *n*. robaoi (bito).

mull [mʌl] *v.* ajitsukeshite atatameru (biiru nado o). *v.* (*Am. col.*) kuyokuyo suru (*over*).

mullet [mʌ́lit] *n.* (*fish*) bora.

multi- [mʌ́lti] ōku no; takusan no to iu imi no settōgo. ~**farious** [-féəriəs] *a.* iroiro no; zattana. ~**form** [-fɔːm] *a.* tayō no; ōku no; chigatta katachi no. ~**ple** [-pl] *a.* tasū no. ~**ple telegrams**, dōbun dempō. *n.* baisū. **common** ~, kōbaisū. **least common** ~, saishō kōbaisū (*L. C. M.*). ~**plex** [-pleks] *a.* tayō no; ikue mo no. ~**plicand** [-plikǽnd] *n.* hijōsū; 9×5 no baai no 9. ~**plication** [-plikéiʃən] *n.* kakezan; jōhō. ~**table**, kakezan kuku. ~**plicity** [mʌltiplísiti] *n.* tasū; ~**plier** [-plaiə] *n.* jōsū; hō (9×5 no baai, 5). ~**ply** [-plai] *v.* masu; hanshoku saseru (suru); jōzuru. ~**tude** [-tjuːd] *n.* tasū; taninzū; gunshū. ~**tudinous** [-tjúːdinəs] *a.* tasū no; samazama no.

mum [mʌm] *a.* mugon no; chimmoku no. *inter.* damare!

mumble [mʌ́mbl] *n.* tsubuyaki, *v.* mogumogu iu; mogumogu kamu.

mummy [mʌ́mi] *n.* miira. *beat to a* ~, uchinomesu.

mumps [mʌmps] *n.* (*pl.*) (*med.*) jikasen-en; otafukukaze.

munch [mʌntʃ] *v.* shikkari kamu; kuchakucha kamu.

mundane [mʌ́ndein] *a.* konoyo no; gense no.

municipal [mju(:)nísipəl] *a.* shisei no. ~**ity** [mju(:)nisipǽliti] *n.* shikai; shisei. 〔(*generosity*).

munificence [mju(:)nífisəns] *n.* kyokudo no (*extreme*) kandaisa.

munificent [mju(:)nífisənt] *a.* kyokudo ni ōyōna. 〔nado).

munitions [mju(:)níʃəns] *n.* (*pl.*) gunjuhin (jū, hō, dan'yaku...

mural [mjúərəl] *n.*, *a.* hekijō (no); kabe no ue (no); hekiga.

murder [mə́ːdə] *n.* satsujin; bōsatsu. *v.* korosu. ~**er** *n.* [-rə] satsugaisha. ~**ess** *n.* onna no satsujinhan. ~**ous** *a.* satsujin no.

murk [məːk] *a.* kurasa; inki. ~**y** [mə́ːki] *a.* inkina; kurai.

murmur [mə́ːmə] *n.*, *v.* sasayaki-ku); butsubutsu(iu).

murrain [mʌ́rin] *n.* gyūeki (ushi no densembyō).

muscle [mʌ́sl] *n.* (*anat.*) suji; kinniku.

Muscovite [mʌ́skəvait] *n.*, *a.* Roshiajin (no).

muscular [mʌ́skjulə] *a.* suji no; kinniku no. 〔shisai.

Muse [mjuːz] *n.* (*Gk. myth.*) Myūzu no Kami; (*M*~) shisō;

muse [mju:z] *v.* chinshi suru; mokusō suru (*on, upon*).

museum [mju(:)zíəm] *n.* hakubutsukan.

mushroom [mʌ́ʃrum] *n.* kinoko; kin; narikin. *v.* (*Am.*) kyūni sodatsu (*into*).

music [mjú:zik] *n.* ongaku; gakufu. **～al** *a.* ongaku no; ongakuzuki no. **～ hall,** ongakudō; engeikan. **～ian** [mju(:)zíʃ(ə)n] *n.* ongakuka; gakujin.

musk [mʌsk] *n.* jakō. **～deer** [-diə] *n.* jakō-jika. **～ melon** [-melən] *n.* (*veg.*) masukumeron.

musket [mʌ́skit] *n.* jū (kyūshiki no). **～ry** *n.* shageki(jutsu). **～eer** [mʌ́skətíːə] *n.* jū de busōshita heitai.

muslin [mʌ́zlin] *n.* men-merinsu; shin-mosu.

muss [mʌs] *n., v.* (*Am. col.*) gotagota (saseru).

mussel [mʌ́sl] *n.* (*zoo.*) igai. (sono kaigara kara botan ga deMussulman** [mʌ́slmən] *n.* Kaikyōto. ⌐kiru).

Mussulman [mʌ́slmən] *n.* Kaikyōto.

must [mʌst, məst] *aux. v.* seneba naranu; *n.* (*Am.*) hitsuyō jikō; gimu. *a.* (*Am.*) hitsuyōna. *man* **～** *eat to live,* hito wa ikiru tame ni tabeneba naranu. *He must have that book* kare wa sono hon o motte iru ni chigai nai. **～ book,** hitsudoku-sho.

mustache [məstáːʃ] *n.* hana no shita no hige.

mustard [mʌ́stəd] *n.* karashi.

muster [mʌ́stə] *n.* eppei; jin'intenko. *v.* atsumeru.

musty [mʌ́sti] *a.* kabita; kabikusai; furukusai.

mutability [mjù:təbíliti] *n.* kawariyasui koto; futei.

mutable [mjú:təbl] *a.* kawariyasui.

mutation [mju:téiʃən] *n.* henka; henten.

mute [mju:t] *a.* oshi no; on o dasanai. *n.* oshi no hito; mugon.

mutilate [mjú:tileit] *v.* (teashi nado o) setsudan suru.

mutilation [mjù:tiléiʃən] *n.* setsudan.

mutineer [mjù:tiníə] *n.* bōdōsha; jōkan-teikōsha.

mutinous [mjú:tinəs] *a.* bōdō no; jōkan-teikō no.

mutiny [mjú:tini] *n.* bōdō; jōkan-teikō. *v.* bōdō o okosu.

mutter [mʌ́tə] *n.* tsubuyaki; uramigoto. *v.* butsubutsu iu.

mutton [mʌ́tn] *n.* hitsujiniku; hitsuji.

mutual [mju:tjuəl] *a.* sōgo no; kyōtsū no. **～ly** *ad.* tagai ni.

muzzle [mʌ́zl] *n.* (kemono no) hanazura; kuchi-ami. *v.* kankōgu o kakeru. **～loader** [-loudə] *n.* jūkō kara tama o komeru jū (hō) ; uragome.

MVD. Sobietto Dōmei Naimushō (*Ministerstvo Vnutrennikh Del = the Ministry of Internal Affairs*).

my [mai] *pron.* (**I** no shoyūkaku) watashi no ; O ～! mā !, o-ya !, ara ! ～**self** [-sélf] *pron.* watashi jishin.

myopia [maióupiə] **myopy** [máiəpi] *n.* kinshigan.

myriad [míriəd] *n.* ichiman ; musū. *a.* musū no.

myrrh [məː] *n.* nettai ni sansuru kiyani ; nioi ga yoi (*mirra*).

myrtle [mə́ːtl] *n.* (*flow.*) tenninka.

mysterious [mistíəriəs] *a.* shimpi no ; fukashigina.

mystery [místəri] *n.* shimpi ; fukashigi ; (*pl.*) shūkyōgeki.

mystic [místik], *n.* shimpishugisha. *a.* = ～**al** shimpi no ; shimpisetsu no ; reikan no. ～**ism** *n.* shimpishugi ; shimpikyō.

mystify [místifai] *v.* shimpi ni suru ; mayowasu ; kemu ni maku.

myth [miθ] *n.* shinwa. **mythic**(**cal**) [míθik(əl)] *a.* shinwa no. **mythological** *a.* = **mythical**.

mythological [miθəlódʒikəl] *a.* shinwa no.

mythology [miθólədʒi] *n.* shinwagaku ; shinwashū ; shinwa.

N

N, n [en] *n.* (*pl.* N's, Ns, [enz]) Eigo *alphabet* no dai-14-bamme no moji.

nab [næb] *v.* (*sl.*) hobaku suru; hittsukamu.

nabob [néibɔb] *n.* hijōna kimmanka. (Indo no ichibu no chihō no ōsama).

nadir [néidiə/-də] *n.* (*rel.*) tenchō (*zenith*) no hantai ten; taishoten; donzoko.   ⌈ru.

nag [næg] *n.* uma; kouma (*pony*). *v.* kogoto bakari itte ijime-

naiad [náiæd] *n.* ((*Gk. & Rom. myth.*) mizu no sei (*nymph*).

nail [neil] *n.* tsume; kugi. *v.* kugi o utsu; (*col.*) toraeru.

naive [naíː v/naːíː v] *a.* adokenai; mujakina.   ⌈mujaki.

naiveté [naíː vtei/naːíː -], **~ty** [néivti] *n.* (*Fr.*) tenshin ramman;

naked [néikid] *a.* hadaka no; mukidashi no. ~ *eyes*, nikugan. ~ *sword*, hakujin; nukimi.

name [neim] *n.* na; namae; (*pl.*) akkō. *v.* meimei suru; shimei suru. *to call person* ~*s*, akkō suru. ~**less** *a.* na no (mo) nai; meijō shigatai. ~**ly** *ad.* sunawachi. ~**sake** [-seik] *n.* dōmei no hito.

nankeen [næŋkíː n] **-kin** [-kín] *n.* nankin momen.

nap [næp] *n.* utatane; keba (orimono nado no). *v.* madoromu.

nape [neip] *n.* unaji; bonnokubo.

naphtha [næfθə/næp-] *n.* nafusayu (kihatsu-yu).

naphthaline [næfθəlin] *n.* nafutarin.

napkin [næpkin] *n.* napukin.

Naples [néiplz] *n.* Napori (Itariya nambu no minato).

narcissus [naːsísəs] *n.* (*flow.*) suisen.

narcotic [naːkɔ́tik] *a.* masuisei no. *n.* masuizai.

narrate [næréit] *v.* hanasu; kataru; noberu.

narration [næréiʃən] *n.* hanashi; monogatari; (*gram.*) wahō.

narrative [nærətiv] *a.* monogatari no. *n.* hanashi; monogatari.

narrow [nǽrou] *a.* semai; henkyōna; gemmitsuna. *n.* seto; semai tokoro. *v.* semaku suru (naru). ~**gauge** [-géidʒ] *a.*

(railway) kyōki no. ～**ly** *ad.* karōjite; yatto. ～**minded** [-máindid] *a.* kokoro no semai.

nasal [néizəl] *a.* hana no. *(phon.)* bion no. *n.* bion.

nascent [nǽsnt] *a.* kore kara umareru; shoki no.

nasturtium [nəstə́:ʃəm] *n. (flow.)* inugarashi; kinrenka.

nasty [ná:sti] *a.* kitanai; midarana; iyana.

natal [néitl] *a.* shussei no; umareizuru.

natatorium [nèitətɔ́:riəm] *n. (pl.* **-s; -ria)** *(Am.)* okunai suiei-nation [néiʃən] *n.* kokumin; kuni; kokka. ⌐pūru.

national [nǽʃənəl] *a.* kokka no; kokumin no; kokuritsu no. ～**ism** *n.* kokkashugi. ～**ist** *n.* kokkashugisha. ～**ly** *ad.* kyo-koku itchi shite.

nationality [nὲʃənǽliti] *n.* kokuminsei; kokuseki. ⌐yū.

nationalization [nὲʃənəlizéiʃən]*n.* kokuminka; kokuei; koku-

nationalize [nǽʃənəlaiz] *v.* kokuminka suru; kika (saseru) su-ru; kokuyū ni suru.

native [néitiv] *a.* seirai no; sono kuni no; shizen no; tennen no. *n.* genchijin; genchi no (dō-shokubutsu).

nativity [nətíviti] *n.* shussei; tanjō; (N-) Kirisuto no tanjō.

NATO [nétou] Kita Taiseiyō Jōyaku Kikō. *(North Atlantic*

natty [nǽti] *a.* kogireina; seisona. ⌐*Treaty Organization).*

natural [nǽtʃurəl-tʃər-] *a.* shizen no; seirai no. *n.* seirai no hakuchi; *(mus.)* hon'i kigō. ～ **child,** shiseiji. ～ **history,** hakubutsugaku. ～**ism** *n.* shizen shugi. ～**ist** *n.* hakubutsu gakusha; shizenshugisha. ～**ly** *ad.* shizen ni; tōzen.

naturalization [nὲtʃurəlaizéiʃən] *n.* kika; nareru koto.

naturalize [nǽtʃurəlaiz] *v.* shizen ni suru; narasu.

nature [néitʃə] *n.* tensei; seishitsu; tennen; shizen.

naught [nɔ:t] *n.* mu; zero. **set at** ～, keibetsu suru.

naughty [nɔ́:ti] *a.* wampakuna; itazurana. ～**ily** *ad.* ～**iness** *n.*

nausea [nɔ́:siə-ʃiə] *n.* funayoi; hakike; mukatsuki.

nauseate [nɔ́:sieit-ʃieit] *v.* hakike o moyōsu.

nauseous [nɔ́:siəs-ʃiəs] *a.* hakike no aru; iyana.

nautical [nɔ́:tikəl] *a.* kōkai no; umi no ue no; sempaku no.

nautilus [nɔ́:tiləs] *(pl.* **-li** [lai]; **-es)** *n. (zoo.)* takobune.

naval [néivəl] *a.* kaigun no; fune no. ～ **architecture** *n.* zō-sengaku. ～ **brigate,** kaigun rikusentai. ～ **station,** chinjufu.

nave [neiv] *n.* (kuruma no) koshiki ; (*church* no) naijin.

navel [néiv(ə)l] *n.* heso ; chūshin. ~ *orange*, nēburu orenji.

navigable [nǽvigəbl] *a.* kōkai (kōkū) ni tekisuru.

navigate [nǽvigeit] *v.* kōkai (kōkū) suru. sōjū suru (fune ; hikōki o).

navigation [nævigéiʃ(ə)n] *n.* kōkū ; kōkai ; kōkai-jutsu.

navigator [nǽvigeitə] *n.* kōkaisha ; kōkaichō ; kōkaigakusha.

navvy [nǽvi] *n.* dokata ; nimpu.

navy [néivi] *n.* kaigun. ~yard [-jɑːd] *n.* kaigun zōsenjo.

nay [nei] *ad.* iya ; katsu mata ; mushiro ; nomi narazu nao. *n.* kyohi ; (hantai tōhyōsha). *we are willing* ~ *eager to go*, bokutachi sansei na dokoro ka ikitasa de ippai nan da.

Nazi [nɑ́ːtsi(i)] *n.* (*Ger.*) Doitsu Kokka Shakaitō ; sono tōin ; (ta no kuni no) Natsisu tōin.

neap [niːp] *a.* koshio no ; saitei no. *n.* koshio ; saitei no koshio.

near [niə] *a.* chikai. *ad.* chikaku ; sekkin shite. *prep.* chikaku. *v.* chikazuku. ~ly *ad.* hotondo ; yatto. ~ness *n.* ~-sighted [-saitid] *a.* kingan no ; kinshi no.

neat [niːt] *a.* seiketsuna ; kichin to shita ; jōhinna. ~ly *ad.*

nebula [nébjulə] *n.* (*pl.* -lae [-liː]) (*astr.*) seiun. ~r [-lə] *a.* seiun.

nebulous [nébjuləs] *a.* (*astr.*) seiun no yōna ; kasunda. ⌊no.

necessarily [nésisərili] *ad.* hitsuzentekini. *not* ~, kanarazu shimo … de nai.

necessary [nésisəri] *a.* hitsuyōna. *n.* hitsuyō-hin.

necessitate [nisésiteit] *v.* hitsuyō to suru.

necessitous [nisésitəs] *a.* bimbōna ; hinkyūna.

necessity [nisésiti] *n.* hitsuyō ; hitsuzen.

neck [nek] *n.* kubi ; chikyō. ~ *and* ~, ai narande. ~ *or nothing*, hisshini. ~band [-bænd] *n.* (shatsu nado no) eri. ~cloth [-klɔ(ː)θ] *n.* kubimaki ; erikazari. ~lace [-lis] *n.* kubikazari. ~tie [-tai] *n.* nekutai.

neckerchief [nékətʃif] *n.* nekkachiifu.

neckware [nékwɛə] *n.* *neck* ni tsukeru mono zembu.

necromancer [nékrəmænsə] *n.* yōjutsusha ; shinda hito to kōtsū shite yogen suru hito.

necromancy [nékrəmænsi] *n.* kōshinjutsu ; yōjutsu.

necrosis [nekróusis] *n.* (*med.*) eso ; dasso.

nectar [néktə] *n.* kami ga nomu osake ; amai osake.

need [ni:d] *n.* nyūyō ; hitsuyō. *v.* iru ; yōsuru. ~ *not*, ...suru ni oyobnai. ~**ful** *a.* hitsuyōna. ~**less** *a.* fuhitsuyōna. ~**ly** *a.* kinkyūna. ~**s** *ad.* kanarazu ; zehi.

needle [ní:dl] *n.* nuibari. *v.* hari de nuu ; tsukitōsu ; (*Am.*) nayamasu. ~**woman** [-wùmən] *n.* saihōfu ; oharionna. ~ **work** [-wə:k] *n.* harishigoto.

ne'er [nɛə] *ad.* = *never* .

nefarious [niféəriəs/ne-] *a.* kyōakuna ; gokuaku hidōna.

negation [nigéiʃən/ne-] *n.* hitei ; kyozetsu ; hantai.

negative [négətiv] *a.* hitei no ; shōkyoku no ; insei no ; (*math.*) fu no. *n.* kyozetsu. indenki ; inkyokuban ; inga. *v.* kyohi suru.

neglect [niglékt] *v.* okotaru ; keishi suru. *n.* taiman ; mushi. ~**ful** *a.* taimanna. ~**fully** *ad.*

négligé [négli(:)ʒei] *n.* (*Fr.*) fudangi ; heyagi. negurije.

negligence [néglidʒəns] *n.* taiman ; fuchūi ; nageyari.

negligent [néglidʒent] *a.* taimanna ; fuchūina ; nageyarina.

negligible [néglidʒibl] *a.* mushi shi uru ; tsumaranai.

negotiable [nigóuʃiəbl] *a.* jōto dekiru ; ryūtsū suru. ~ **bill**, ryūtsū tegata. ~ **instrument**, ryūtsū shōken.

negotiate [nigóuʃieit] *v.* sōdan suru ; kōshō suru ; dampan suru. *v.* kyōtei suru ; uru ; ryūtsū suru.

negotiation [nigòuʃiéiʃən] *n.* dampan ; jōto ; torihiki.

negotiator [nigóuʃieitə] *n.* shōgisha ; torihikinin.

negress [ní:gris] *n.* kokujin onna.

negro [ní:grou] *n.* kokujin ; niguro.

neigh [nei] *n.* uma no inanaki. *v.* inanaku.

neighbo(u)r [néibə] *n.* rinjin ; kinjo no hito. ~**hood** [-hud] *n.* kinjo. ~**ing** [-riŋ] *a.* tonari no ; kinjo no. ~**ly** *a.* rinjin no ; shinsetsuna. ~**liness** *n.* shinsetsu.

neither [naiðə/ní:ðə] *a.* (*neither...nor*) ...demo naku ... demo nai ; ...mo sezu ... mo shinai. ~ *statement is true*, dotchi no iibun mo hontō dewa nai. *conj.* ~ *you nor I will go*, kimi mo boku mo ikanai. *pron.* dochira mo ... de nai.

Nemesis [némisis] *n.* (*Gk. myth.*) fukushū no megami ; (*n~*) tembatsu ; ōhō. ⌐setsu.

neologism [ni(:)ɔ́lədʒizm] *n.* shingo o tsukau koto ; atarashii

neology [ni(:)ólədʒi] *n.* =**neologism**

neon [ní:ɔn/níən] *n.* neon.

neophyte [ní(:)oufait] *n.* shinkyōto; shoshinsha.

nephew [névju(:)/-fju(:)] *n.* oi.

nepotism [népɔtizm/nép-] *n.* enja-biiki; dōzoku tōyō.

Neptune [néptju:n/-tʃu:n] *n.* kaijin; (*astr.*) Kaiōsei.

Nereid [níɔriid] *n.* (*Gk. myth.*) umi no sei; umi no megami.

nerve [nɔ:v] *n.* (*anat.*) shinkei; seishinryoku; yūki; seiryoku; (*pl.*) shinkeikabin. *v.* chikara (yūki) o tsukeru. ~**center** [-séntɔ] shinkei chūsū. ~**less** *a.* kiryoku no nai; yūki no nai. *get on one's* ~, urusagaraseru; iradataseru.

nervous [nɔ́:vɔs] *a.* shinkei no; yūki no aru; shinkeishitsu no.

nescience [nésiɔns/nésjɔns] *n.* mugaku; muchi. (*phylos.*) fukanest [nest] *n.* su; sōkutsu; kumijū. *v.* su o tsukuru. ⌊chiron.

nestle [nésl] *v.* guai yoku osameru; kao nado o kosuritsukeru : ~ *up to one's mother*, okāsan ni amaeru.

nestling [néslin] *n.* kaeritate no hina; subina.

net [net] *n.* ami; amijō no mono; wana. jun'eki. *a.* shōmi no. *v.* ami de toraeru; wana ni kakeru; jun'eki o uru.

nether [néðɔ] *a.* anoyo no; meifu (yomiji) no.

Netherlands [néðɔlɔndz] *n.* Nēderurando (Oranda, Berugii)

netting [nétin] *n.* ami; ami-suki; ami-uchi. ⌊chihō.

nettle [nétl] *n.* iragusa (*hert.*) *v.* jiraseru; iraira saseru. ~**rash** [-ræʃ] *n.* (*med.*) jimmashin.

network [nétwɔ:k] *n.* ami zaiku; ami no me; (*Am.*) rajio hōsōmō. ~ *of railways*, tetsudō-mō.

neural [njúɔrɔl] *a.* (*anat.*) shinkei no; shinkei-kei no.

neuralgia [njuɔrǽldʒɔ] *n.* (*med.*) shinkeitsū.

neurasthenia [njùɔrɔsθí:niɔ] *n.* (*med.*) shinkei suijaku.

neuritis [njuɔráitis] *n.* (*med.*) shinkeien.

neurology [njuɔrólɔdʒi] *n.* shinkeigaku.

neuron [njúɔrɔn] *n.* shinkei-saibō.

neurosis [njuɔróusis] *n.* shinkeibyō.

neurotic [njuɔrótik] *a.* shinkei no; shinkeibyō no.

neuter [njú:tɔ] *a.* chūsei no. *n.* (*gram.*) chūsei meishi. (*zoo.*) chūsei dōbutsu.

neutral [njú:trɔl] *a.* (kyokugai) chūritsu no; kōheina. *n.* kyokugai chūritsusha; chūritsukoku (jin).

neutrality [njùːtrǽliti] *n.* (kyokugai) chūritsu.

neutralization [njùːtrəlaizéi∫ən]/-liz-] *n.* chūritsu no jōtai.

neutralize [njúːtrəlaiz] *v.* chūritsu saseru.

never [névə] *ad.* kesshite…nai. ~ **more** [-mɔ́ː/-mɔ́ə] *ad.* nido to …shinai. ~**theless** [-ðəlés] *conj.* sore nimo kakawarazu.

new [njuː] *a.* atarashii; aratana; chikagoro no. *ad.* aratani. ~ **comer**, shinzanmono. ~**ly** *ad.* aratani; chikagoro.

newel [njúːəl] *n.* (rasen kaidan no) oyabashira.

newfangled [njúːfæŋgld] *a.* shinki no; shin-ryūkō no.

news [njuːz] *n.* atarashii dekigoto; hōdō; nyūsu. ~ **agency**, tsūshin-sha. ~ **agent**, shimbun toritsuginin (ten). ~**boy** [-bɔi] *n.* shimbun uriko (haitatsunin) ~**cast** [-kɑːst] *n.* (*Am.*) nyūsu hōsō. ~**monger** [-màŋgə] *n.* kanabōhiki. ~**paper** [njúːspèipə] shimbunshi. ~**reel** [riːl] *n.* nyūsu eiga. ~**stand** [-stænd] *n.* (eki nado no) shimbun baiten. ~**y** [njúːzi] *a.* (*col.*) nyūsu no ōi.

newt [njuːt] *n.* imori.

New Year [njúːjiə] *n.* Shinnen; Ganjitsu. *New Year's Day*, New York [njúː jɔ́ːk] Nyūyōku. ⌊Gantan.

next [nekst] *a.* tsugi no. *ad.* tsugi ni.

N. G., n. g. dame (=*no good*).

nib [nib] *n.* pensaki; tori no kuchibashi. *v.* togarasu.

nibble [níbl] *n.* kajiru koto. *v.* sukoshi zutsu kamu.

nice [nais] *a.* kekkōna; seikōna. *a. a* ~ *distinction*, goku bisaina kubetsu. ~**ly** *ad.*

nicety [naisti] *n.* seimitsu; seikaku; umami. (*pl.*) shōsai. *to a* ~, seikakuni; chōdo yoku.

niche [nit∫/niːʃ] *n.* kabe no kubonda tokoro; tekitōna basho.

nick [nik] *n.* kirime; hekomi. *in the* ~ *of time*, chōdo yoi toki ni. *v.* kizamime o tsukeru; kangaemono o ateru.

nickel [níkl] *n.* nikkeru; hakudōka.

nickelodeon [nìkəlóudiən] *n.* (*Am.*) (5 *c.*) gosento gekijō; go sento jidō chikuonki.

nickname [níkneim] *n.*, *v.* adana (o tsukeru).

nicotine [níkəti:n/níkəti:n] *n.* nikochin.

nicotinism [níkəti:nizm] *n.* nikochin chūdoku.

niece [ni:s] *n.* mei.

niggard [nígəd] *n.*, *a.* kechi (na). ～**ly** *a.* kechina. *ad.* kechi-

nigger [nígə] *n.* (*col.*) kokujin; niguro.⠀⠀⠀⠀⠀⠀⠀⠀[kechi shite.

nigh [nai] *a.* chikai. *ad.* chikaku; hotondo.

night [nait] *n.* yoru; ankoku. ～ **blindness,** yamō; torime. ～ **cap** [⸝kæp] *n.* shinshitsu bōshi; nezake. ～**dress** [⸝dres]＝ ～**gown** [⸝gaun] *n.* (fujin, kodomo no) nemaki. ～**fall** [⸝fɔ:l] *n.* higure. ～**hawk** [⸝hɔ:k] *n.* yotaka; yofukashi suru hito. ～**ly** *a.* maiban no. *ad.* yogoto ni. ～**mare** [⸝mɛə] *n.* akumu. unasareru koto. ～**piece** [⸝pi:s] *n.* yoru no keshiki no ga(e). ～**shade** [⸝ʃeid] *n.* inuhōzuki. ～**soil** [⸝soil] shimogoe. ～**stool** [⸝stu:l] *n.* shinshitsu benki. ～**watch** [-wɔtʃ] yoban; shiku-choku. ～**work** [-wə:k] *n.* yagyō.

nightingale [náitiŋgeil] *n.* naichingēru (yoru-uguisu).

nihilism [náihilizm/náiəl-] *n.* kyomuron; kyomushugi. ～**ist** *n.* kyomuronsha; museifushugisha.

nil [nil] *n.* mu; kaimu; zero.

Nile [nail] *n.* Nairu gawa.

nimble [nímbl] *a.* subashikkoi; binshōna. ～**bly** *ad.*

nimbus [nímbəs] *n.* (*pl.* **-bi** [-bai]) amagumo; ran'un; gokō.

nincompoop [nínkəmpu:p] *n.* manuke; tomma.

nine [nain] *n.*, *a.* 9 (ku＝kyū) (no).

ninefold [náinfould] *a.* kyūbai no.

ninepins [náinpinz] *n. pl.* kyūchūgi (9-hon no hashira o tama de taosu yūgi); naimpin.

nineteen [naintí:n] *n.*, *a.* 19 (jūkyū, jūku) (no.)

nineteenth [naintí:nθ] *n.*, *a.* dai jūku (no); jūkyūbamme (no); jūkyūbun no ichi (no).

ninetieth [náintiiθ] *n.*, *a.* dai (90) kyūjū (no); (90) kyūjūbamme (no); kyūjūbun no ichi (no).

ninety [náinti] *n.*, *a.* (90) kyūjū＝kuju (no).

ninny [nini] *n.* baka; manuke.

ninth [nainθ] *n.*, *a.* dai (9) ku (no); kubamme (no); kyūbun no ichi (no).

nip [nip] *v.* tsumamu; kamu; itameru. *n.* tsumami; hasami; shimo no gai. (*frost damage*)

nippers [nípəz] *n.* (*pl.*) yattoko; kenuki; kuginuki.

nipple [nípl] *n.* chikubi (no yōna tokki).　　　　　　⌐ponjin.
Nipponese [nìpəníːz] *a.* (*Am.*) Nippon no. *n.* (*sing. & pl.*) Nip-
N. I. R. A. Sangyō Fukkōhō (*National Industrial Recovery Act*).
Nissen hut [nísən hát] kamaboko-heisha.
nit [nit] *n.* shirami (*lice*) nado chiisai mushi no tamago.
niter, nitre [náitə] *n.* (*min.*) shōseki.
nitrate [náitreit/-trit] *n.* shōsan'en. ⌐ *of silver,* shōsan-gin.
nitric [náitrik] *a.* shōseki no. ⌐ *acid,* shōsan.
nitrogen [náitridʒən] *n.* (*chem.*) chisso.
nitrogenous [naitrɔ́dʒinəs] *a.* chisso no; chisso o fukumu.
nitroglycerin(e) [náitrəglísərín/-glìsərín] *n.* nitoroguriserin.
nitrous [náitrəs] *a.* chisso no; chisso o fukumu; shōseki no;
　shōseki o fukumu. ⌐ *acid,* ashōsan. ⌐ *oxide,* issanka chisso.
nix [niks] *n.* mizu no sei; suima. *inter.* kitazo !
no [nou] *a.* sukoshi mo…de nai. *ad.* iie. *n.* kyozetsu; hantai.
NO., no. [námbə] (*pl.* **NOS., nos.** [námbəz]) numero (*num-
　ber*) no ryaku; **number.**
no-account [nouəkáunt] *a., n.* (*Am. dial.*) munōna (hito); nō-
nob [nɔb] *n.* (*sl.*) atama.　　　　　　　　　　⌐nashi (-bito).
nobility [noubíliti] *n.* kizoku-tachi.
noble [nóubl] *a.* kōshōna; tōtoi; rippana; kizoku no. *n.* ki-
　zoku. ⌐**man** [-mən] *n.* kizoku. ⌐**minded** [-máindid] *a.*
　kedakai kokoro no. ⌐**ness** *n.* kōshō; kōketsu.
nobly [nóubli] *ad.* kedakaku; rippani.　　　　　　⌐nai.
nobody [nóubədi/-bɔdi] *n.* namonai hito. *pron.* dare mo…de
nocturnal [nɔktə́:nəl] *a.* yoru no; yoru deru.　　　　⌐no e.
nocturne [nɔ́ktə:n] *n.* yumemiru yōna yoru no kyoku; yakei
nod [nɔd] *n.* unazuki; inemuri. *v.* unazuku; eshaku suru;
noddy [nɔ́di] *n.* baka; tomma.　　　　　　　⌐inemuri suru.
node [noud] *n.* fushi; kobu.
nodule [nɔ́dju:l] *n.* chiisai fushi; (katamari; kobu).
noggin [nɔ́gin] *n.* mokuhai; ippai no inryō; $^1/_4$ painto.
noise [nɔiz] *n.* sawagashii oto; sawagi; hyōban. *v.* furechirasu;
　iifurasu. ⌐**less** *a.* oto no nai; shizukana.
noisome [nɔ́isəm] *a.* yūgaina; kusai; iyana.
noisy [nɔ́izi] *a.* sōzōshii; sawagashii. ⌐**sily** *ad.* ⌐**siness** *n.*
nom [nɔ:m] *n.* (*Fr.*) namae. ⌐ *de guerre,* kamei; geimei. ⌐ *de*

plume, gō ; gagō (*pen name*).

nomad [nómæd/nóumæd] *n.* yūboku no tami. *a.* yūboku no ;

nomadic [noumǽdik] *a.* yūboku no. ⌊hōrō suru.

nomenclature [nóumenklèitʃə] *n.* kagakutekini meimei o suru hō. ⌈jō.

nominal [nóminəl] *a.* namae no ; meigi-jō no. ∼**ly** *ad.* meigi-

nominate [nómineit] *v.* shimei (nimmei) suru ; suisen suru.

nomination [nòminéiʃən] *n.* shimei ; nimmei ; suisen.

nominative [nóminətiv] *a.* shukaku no ; shimei sareta. *n.* shukaku ; shugo. ∼ *case*, shukaku.

nominator [nómineitə] *n.* shimeisha ; joninsha ; suisensha.

nominee [nòminí:] *n.* shimei sareta mono ; juninsha.

non- *pref.* mu-, fu-, hi- ; *negative* (hitei no) *prefix*.

nonage [nóunidʒ/nón-] *n.* miseinen. ⌈no hito.

nonagenarian [nòunədʒinéəriən] *a.* kyūjū-dai no. *n.* kyūjū-dai

nonce [nɔns] *n.* tōbun. *for the* ∼, sashiatari ; tōbun.

nonchalance [nónʃələns] *n.* mutonjaku ; reisei ; heiki.

nonchalant [nónʃələnt] *a.* reiseina ; heikina.

noncombatant [nɔnkɔ́mbətənt] *n.* hi-sentōin ; gunzoku.

noncommissioned [nɔnkəmíʃənd] *a.* ininjō no nai ; nimmei sarenai. ∼ *officer*, kashikan. ⌈kazu no.

noncommittal [nònkəmítl] *a.* genshitsu o ataenai ; dotchitsu-

nonconductor [nònkəndʌ́ktə] *n.* fudōtai ; netsu ya denki o dendō shinai mono.

nonconformist [nònkənfɔ́:mist] *n.* hi-kokkyō-to ; dokuritsu kyōha no hito.

nonconformity [nònkənfɔ́:miti] *n.* fuitchi ; kokkyō ni shitagawanai koto.

nondescript [nóndiskript] *a.* nan no tokushoku mo nai ; bakuzen to shita. *n.* tokushoku no nai koto.

none [nʌn] *ad., pron.* hitotsu mo nai ; chitto mo...shinai ; dare mo...shinai.

nonentity [nɔnéntiti] *n.* jitsuzai shinai mono ; toru ni taranu hito (mono).

nonfeasance [nɔnfí:zəns] *n.* gimu no furikō.

nonmetal [nónmetl] *n.* hikinzoku.

nonpareil [nónpərel] *a.* kuraberu mono ga nai hito (mono) ;

roku pointo katsuji.

nonplus [nónplʌ́s] *a.* nan tomo dekinai. *v.* komarikiru. *n.* tōwaku. *He was completely* ～*ed,* kare wa mattaku komarikitta.

nonsense [nónsəns] *n.* muimi ; tawagoto.

nonsensical [nɔnsénsikəl] *a.* bakageta ; tohō mo nai.

nonstop [nónstóp] *a.* tochū de tomaranai ; muchakuriku no. ～ *flight,* muchakuriku hikō.

nonsuit [nónsjú:t] *n.* kyakka ; soshō tekkai.

nonunion [nɔnjú:njən] *a.* rōdō kumiai ni kanyū shinai.

noodle [nú:dl] *n.* baka ; ahō. (*pl.*) hoshi-udon no rui.

nook [nuk] *n.* sumi ; kado ; kakureta tokoro ; hikkonda tokoro.

noon [nu:n] *n.* shōgo ; mahiru. ～**day** [‐dei] *a.* shōgo no. *n.* shōgo ; mahiru. ～**tide** [‐taid] *n.* shōgo ; nitchū.

noose [nu:s/nu:z] *n.* wanawa ; wana. *v.* wana de toraeru.

nor [nɔ:/nɔə] *conj.* mata...demo nai ; mata...mo shinai. *I have neither time* ～ *money,* watashi wa jikan mo kane mo nai.

norm [nɔ:m] *n.* kihan ; mohan ; hyōjun. *fulfil the* ～, hyōjun dake o suru.

normal [nɔ́:məl] *a.* kitei no ; hyōjun no. ～ *school,* shihan gakkō. ～**ly** *ad.* juntōni ; kisoku dōrini.

Norman [nɔ́:mən] *a. Normandy* no ; Noruman minzoku no. *n. Normandy*jin ; Norumanjin.

Norse [nɔ:s] *a.* Hokuō no. *n.* Hokuōgo. ～**man** [‐mən] *n.* Hokuōjin.

north [nɔ:θ] *n., a.* kita (no). ～ *light,* hokkyokkō. ～ *Star,* Hokkyokusei.

northeast [nɔ́:θí:st] *n.* tōhoku. *a.* tōhoku no. ～**er** *n.* tōhoku no bōfū. ～**ern** *a.* tōhoku no ; tōhoku kara. ～**ward** *ad.* tōhoku e. *a.* tōhoku e no. *n.* tōhoku.

northerly [nɔ́:ðəli] *a.* kita no ; kita e (kara) no ; *ad.* kita e.

northern [nɔ́:ðə(:)n] *a.* hoppō e no. ～ *light,* hokkyokukō. ～**er** *n.* hokkokujin ; (N-) (*Am.*) Gasshūkoku hokubu no hito. ～**most** *a.* saihoku no.

Northman [nɔ́:θmən] *n.* Hokuōjin.

northward [nɔ́:θwəd] *a.* kita (e) no. *ad.* hoppō e.

northwest [nɔ́:θwést] *n., a.* seihoku (no) ; seihoku kara no. ～**er** *n.* seihoku no kyōfū. ～**ern** *a.* seihoku no ; seihoku kara no.

Norwegian [nɔ:wí:dʒən] *a.* Noruwē no. *n.* Noruwējin (go).

nose [nouz] *n.* hana ; saki ; deppatta tokoro. *v.* kagu ; susumu. ∼**-dive** [-daiv] *n., a.* kyūkōka (no) ; (kakaku no) bōraku (no). ∼ **ring** [nóuzriŋ] hana kazari ; (ushi nado no) hana no wa.

nostalgia [nɔstǽldʒiə] *n.* kaikyōbyō (*homesickness*).

nostril [nɔ́stril] *n.* hana no ana.

nostrum [nɔ́strəm] *n.* baiyaku ; (gimanteki) seisaku.

nosy [nóuzi] *a.* (*col.*) sensakuzuki no.

not [nɔt,] *ad.* de nai ; shinai. ∼ *at all,* sukoshi mo ... nai ; dō itashi mashite. (*Am.*) *you are welcome.* ("*Thank you*" no henji).

notable [nóutəbl] *a.* nadakai. *n.* chomeina hito ; meishi. ∼**bly** *ad.* ichijirushiku.

notary [nóutəri] *n.* kōshōnin. ∼ *public*, kōshōnin.

notation [no(u)téiʃən] *n.* kigōhō ; gakufu ; kigō de kaku koto.

notch [nɔtʃ] *n.* kizamime ; yama no hazama. *v.* kizamime o tsukuru.

note [nout] *n.* chūi ; oboegaki ; shihei (*paper money*). *v.* chūisuru ; kakitomeru. *of* ∼, kenchona. ∼**book** [⊥buk] *n.* hikkichō. ∼**d** [-id] *a.* yūmeina. ∼**worthy** [⊥wə:θi] *a.* chūmoku subeki.

nothing [nʌ́θiŋ] *n.* nanimono mo nai ; mu ; zero ; tsumaranu mono mata wa hito. *ad.* sukoshi mo...de nai. *make* ∼ *of*, mono to mo shinai ; mondai ni shinai. ∼*but=only* tada...dake. ∼*else but* (*or than*) ni hokanaranai. ∼*to* kurabemono ni naranai. ∼**ness** *n.* mu ; mukachi ; jinji fusei.

notice [nóutis] *n.* chūmoku ; tsūchi ; keiji ; shōkai ; hihyō. *v.* mitomeru ; chūi suru ; shōkai suru ; hihyō suru ; tsūchi suru. ∼**able** *a.* hitome o hiku. ∼**ably** *ad.* ichijirushiku.

notification [noutifikéiʃən] *n.* tsūchi ; tsūchisho ; todoke.

notify [nóutifai] *v.* tsūchi suru ; todokeru.

notion [nóuʃən] *n.* kangae ; gainen. (*Am.*) ∼**s** *n.* komamono hin. ∼**al** *a.* kannen no.

notoriety [noutəráiəti] *n.* (warui imi de) yūmeina koto ; yūmeina hito.

notorious [no(u)tɔ́:riəs] *a.* (warui imi de) yūmeina ; naute no.

notwithstanding [nɔ́twiðstǽndiŋ] *conj., prep., ad.* nimo kakawarazu ; da ga. *he bought it* ∼ *its high price,* takane nimo kamawazu sore o katta.

nought, naught [nɔ:t] *n.* (*arch.*) mu ; zero.

noun [naun] *n.* (*gram.*) meishi.

nourish [nʌriʃ] *v.* yashinau ; jiyō o ataeru ; sodateru ; o motte iru. **~ing** *a.* jiyō ni naru. **~ment** *n.* jiyōbutsu.

novel [nɔ́v(ə)l] *a.* atarashii ; mezurashii. *n.* shōsetsu. **~ette** [nəvəlét/-vilét] *n.* tampen-shōsetsu. **~ist** [nɔ́vəlist] *n.* shōsetsuka. **~ty** *n.* meatarashisa. (mono).

November [no(u)vémbə] *n.* 11 (jūichi) gatsu.

novice [nɔ́vis] *n.* shoshinsha ; shimmai ; minarai.

novitiate [no(u)víʃi(e)t/nəv-] *n.* shinzan ; minarai-sō (ama) ; shūren kikan.

now [nau] *ad.* ima ; sate ; dore. *conj.* de aru kara. *n.* ima. **~ and then**, tokidoki. **~adays** [⌐ədeiz] *ad.* genzai dewa ; ima dewa.

nowhere [nóu(h)wɛə] *ad.* doko nimo…nai,

noxious [nɔ́kʃəs] *a.* yūgaina ; fukenzenna.

nozzle [nɔ́zl] *n.* hana ; kuchi ; tsutsusaki.

nuance [nju:ɑns] *n.* iroai ; bimyōna chigai.

nucleus [njú:kliəs] *n.* kaku (*core*) ; chūshin.

nude [nju:d] *a.* hadaka no ; ari no mama no. *n.* rataiga (zō).

nudge [nʌdʒ] *v., n.* hiji de karuku tsuku (koto).

nudity [njú:dity] *n.* ratai ; rataizō ; sekirara.

nugatory [njú:gət(ə)ri] *a.* tsumaranai ; taishite kachi no nai.

nugget [nʌ́git] *n.* (tennen no) kinkai ; nan demo kachi no aru mono. **~ of wisdom**, chie no katamari.   ⌐mono.

nuisance [njú:s(ə)ns] *n.* yakkaimono ; urusai mono ; komari.

null [nʌl] *a.* kachi no nai ; tokuchō no nai. **~ification** [-ifikéiʃən] *n.* mukōni suru koto ; torikeshi. **~ify** [nʌ́lifai] *v.* mukōni suru ; torikesu. **~ity** [nʌ́liti] *n.* mukō ; kachi no nai hito

numb [nʌm] *a.* shibireta. *v.* shibire saseru.   ⌐(mono).

number [nʌ́mbə] *n.* kazu ; sūji. (*pl.*) shi no ku (*verse*). *v.* kazoeru ; bangō o tsukeru. **~less** *a.* musū no.

numeral [njú:mərəl] *a.* kazu no. *n.* sūji. (*gram.*) sūshi.

numeration [nju:məréiʃən] *n.* keisan ; sū no yobikata.

numerator [njú:məreitə] *n.* keisansha ; (*math.*) bunshi.

numerical [nju:(:)mérik(ə)l] *a.* kazu no ; kazu de arawashita.

numerous [njú:mərəs] *a.* tasū no. **~ly** *ad.* kazu ōku.

numismatics [njù:mizmǽtiks] *n.* kosengaku (furui *coin* no kenkyū).

numismatist [nju(:)mízmətist] *n.* kosengakusha.

numskull [námskʌl] *n.* bakamono.

nun [nʌn] *n.* ama.

nuncio [nánʃiou] *n.* Rōma Hōō no shisetsu (*ambassador*).

nunnery [nánəri] *n.* amadera ; shūdōin.

nuptial [nápʃ(ə)l] *a.* konrei no. ~**s** *n.* (*pl.*) kekkonshiki.

nurse [nə:s] *n.* uba ; kangofu. *v.* chichi o nomaseru ; kango suru ; (kibō o) idaku. ~**(e)ling** [nɔ́:sliŋ] *n.* akambō. ~**ry** *n.* ikujishitsu ; naedoko ; yōgyojō ; yōseijo. ~**rytale** [nɔ́:səriteil] *n.* otogibanashi ; dōwa.   〔iku) suru.

nurture [nɔ́:tʃə] *n.* yōiku ; kyōiku ; eiyōbutsu. *v.* yōiku (kyō-**nut** [nʌt] *n.* kurumi, kuri nado, katai kawa no kudamono. tomeneji (natto). *a.* hard ~ to crack, nandai. ~**meg** [⊥meg] *n.* (*bot.*) nikuzuku.

nutriment [njú.trimənt] *a.* jiyō ni naru. *n.* jiyōbutsu.

nutrition [nju(:)tríʃən] *n.* eiyō ; jiyōbutsu. ~**al** *a.* jiyō no.

nutritious [nju(:)tríʃəs] *a.* eiyō ni tomu.

nutritive [njú:tritiv] *a.* eiyō no. *n.* eiyōbutsu.   〔tsu ni.

nutshell [nát-ʃel] *n.* katai ki no mi no kara. in a ~, kanke-

nuzzle [názl] *v.* hana de horu ; hana o suritsukeru.

nylon [náilən] *n.* nairon.

nymph [nimf] *n.* ninfu ; mori (izumi) no sei ; utsukushii shōjo ; sanagi. (yōchū ni tsukau koto mo aru).

O

O, o [ou] *n.* (*pl.* **O's, Os** [ouz]) Eigo *alphabet* no dai-15-bamme no moji.

oaf [ouf] *n.* hakuchi ; kikeiji. ～**ish** *a.* bakana.

oak [ouk] *n.* (*bot.*) kashiwa ; kashi. ～**en** [-(ə)n] *a.* kashisei no.

oakum [óuk(ə)m] *n.* maihada (fune no itanoma no tsumeniono).

oar [ɔː / ɔə] *n.* kai ; ōru ; kogite. *v.* kogu ; kai o tsukau. ～**sman** [-zmən] *n.* kogite.

oasis [o(u)éisis] *n.* (*pl.* **oases** [o(u)éisi:z]) oashisu (sabaku no naka no ryokuchi).

oat [out] *n.* (*usu. pl.*) embaku ; karasumugi. ～**en** [-n] *a.* embaku no. ～**meal** [-mi:l] *n.* ōtomiiru ; hikiwari karasumugi ; ōtomiiru no kayu.

oath [ouθ], (*pl.* **oaths** [ouðz]) *n.* seiyaku ; chikai ; noroi.

obduracy [ɔ́bdjurəsi] *n.* ganko ; reikoku.

obdurate [ɔ́bdjurit / əbdjúərit] *a.* gankona ; reikoku-mujōna. ～**ly** *ad.* gankoni ; reikokuni.

obedience [əbí:djəns] *n.* fukujū ; jūjun.

obedient [əbí:djənt] *a.* jūjunna ; sunaona. ～**ly** *ad.* sunaoni.

obeisance [obéis(ə)ns] *n.* ojigi ; sonkei ; fukujū.

obelisk [ɔ́bilisk] *n.* oberisuku ; hōsentō ; (*print.*) daggā (†).

obese [o(u)bí:s] *a.* debudebu shita.

obesity [o(u)bí:siti] *n.* himan ; debu.

obey [obéi] *v.* shitagau ; fukusuru.

obfuscate [ɔ́bfʌskeit] *v.* kuraku suru ; tōwaku saseru.

obituary [əbítjuəri] *a.* shibō no ; shinda hito no. *n.* shibōsha hōkoku ; shisha ryakuden.

object [əbdʒékt] *v.* hantai suru ; fufuku de aru.

object [ɔ́bdʒikt] *n.* jibutsu ; mokutekibutsu ; mokuteki ; kyakkan no taishō ; (*gram.*) mokutekigo. ～ **lesson,** chokkan kyōju ; jitsubutsu kyōiku. ～ **glass,** taibutsu renzu.

objection [əbdʒék∫(ə)n,] *n.* fufuku ; igi. ～**able** *a.* igi no aru ; futsugōna ; ki ni kuwanai.

objective [əbdʒéktiv / ob-] *a.* kyakkanteki ; buttai no ; *(gram.)* *n.*, *a.* mokutekikaku (no).

objurgate [ɔ́bdʒɔːgeit] *v.* shikaru ; hantai no hinan o suru.

objurgation [ɔbdʒɔːgéiʃ(ə)n] *n.* shisseki ; shikaru koto.

oblate [ɔ́bleit] *a.* *(math.)* hen'en no.

oblation [obléiʃ(ə)n] *n.* hōnō ; kumotsu ; sasagemono.

obligation [ɔbligéiʃ(ə)n] *n.* gimu ; saiken ; saimu ; ongi.

obligatory [ɔbligət(ə)ri] *a.* gimuteki ; hitsuyōna.

oblige [əbláidʒ] *v.* yoginaku saseru ; onkei o hodokosu ; man-zoku saseru. *I'm much* ~*d (to you)*, dōmo arigatō.

obliging [əbláidʒiŋ] *a.* shinsetsuna ; teichōna. ~**ly** *ad.* shin-setsuni ; teichōni.

oblique [əblíːk] *a.* naname no.

obliquity [əblíkwiti] *n.* keisha ; yugami ; fusei.

obliterate [əblítəreit] *v.* kesu ; atokata o nakusu.

obliteration [əblitəréiʃən] *n.* massatsu ; atokata o nakusu koto ; immetsu.

oblivion [əblíviən] *n.* bōkyaku ; wasuresaru koto ; immetsu.

oblivious [əblíviəs] *a.* wasureppoi ; bon'yari shita.

oblong [ɔ́bləŋ] *a.* chōhōkei no ; chōdaenkei no. *n.* chōhōkei.

obloquy [ɔ́bləkwi] *n.* warukuchi ; omei.

obnoxious [əbnɔ́kʃəs] *a.* iyana ; ki ni sawaru.

oboe [óubɔi / óubou] *n.* *(mus.)* ōboe.

obscene [əbsíːn] *a.* waisetsuna ; fuketsuna. 「kōi.

obscenity [əbsíːniti / -sén-] *n.* waisetsu ; *(pl.)* waidan ; waisetsu-

obscure [əbskjúə] *a.* hakkiri shinai ; kurai ; yo ni shirareani. *v.* kuraku suru ; ōu ; aimaini suru. ~**ly** *ad.* kuraku.

obscurity [əbskjúəriti / ob-] *n.* hakkiri shinai koto. ~ *passage*, hakkiri shinai tokoro.

obsequies [ɔ́bsikwiz] *n.* *(pl.)* sōshiki.

obsequious [əbsíːkwiəs] *a.* kobihetsurau ; kerai no yōna.

observance [əbzɔ́ːv(ə)ns / ob-] *n.* junshu ; gishiki ; shūkan. ~ *of the Sabbath*, Ansokunichi genshu.

observant [əbzɔ́ːv(ə)nt] *a.* chūibukai ; yoku mamoru.

observation [ɔbzə(ː)véiʃ(ə)n] *n.* kansatsu ; kansoku. ~ *car*, ten-bōsha.

observatory [əvzɔ́ːvət(ə)ri] *n.* kansokujo ; sokkōjo ; tenbōdai.

astronomical~, temmondai.

observe [əbzɔ́:v] *v.* (gishiki nado o) okonau ; kansatsu suru ; ki ga tsuku ; genshu suru.

obsess [əbsés] *v.* aru koto o shijū kangaete iru : be ~ed by,... aru koto ni toritsukarete iru.

obsession [əbséʃ(ə)n] *n.* toritsuku koto ; kyōhaku kannen.

obsolescent [ɔ̀bsəlés(ə)nt] *a.* sutare kakatta ; tsukawarenaku natta.

obsolete [ɔ́bsəli : t] *a.* sutareta ; tsukawarenai ; kyūshiki no.

obstacle [ɔ́bstəkl] *n.* shōgaibutsu ; koshō ; jamamono.

obstetric [əbstétrik] *a.* sanka no ; samba no ; ~s *n.* sankagaku ; sambajutsu.

obstinacy [ɔ́bstinəsi] *n.* ganko ; gankosa.

obstinate [ɔ́bstinit] *a.* gankona ; gōjōna.

obstreperous [əbstrép(ə)rəs] *a.* yakamashii ; sōzōshii ; abarete shimatsu no warui. an ~ mob, shimatsu ni oenu bōto.

obstruct [əbstrʌ́kt] *v.* saegiru ; bōgai suru. ~ive *a.* bōgai suru.

obstruction [əbstrʌ́kʃ(ə)n] *n.* bōgai ; shadambutsu.

obtain [əbtéin] *v.* te ni ireru ; tassei suru. ~able *a.* erareru ; tasseishiuru.

obtrude [əbtrú:d] *v.* oshitsukeru ; deshabaru.

obtrusion [əbtrú:ʒ(ə)n] *n.* oshitsuke ; deshabari.

obtrusive [əbtrú:siv] *a.* oshitsukegamashii ; deshabari no.

obtuse [əbtjú:s] *a.* donkaku no ; nibui ; gudonna. ~ly *ad.* nibuku.

obverse [ɔ́bvə:s] *n.* (kahei nado no) hyōmen. *a.* uragaeshi no ; (medaru nado no) hyōmen no.

obviate [ɔ́bvieit] *v.* jokyo suru ; torinozoku.

obvious [ɔ́bviəs] *a.* meihakuna ; ichijirushii.

occasion [əkéiʒən] *n.* baai ; kōki ; riyū. *v.* hikiokosu. the ~ of the quarrel, kenka no riyū wa.... ~al *a.* tokidoki no ; rinjino.

occident [ɔ́ksidənt] *n.* seihō ; (the O-) Seiyō.

occidental [ɔ̀ksidént(ə)l] *a.* (O-) Seiyō no ; seihō no.

occiput [ɔ́ksipʌt] *n.* (anat.) atama no ushiro no bubun.

occlude [əklú:d] *v.* fusagu ; kyūshū suru (absorb).

occult [əkʌ́lt] *a.* shimpitekina ; ōikakusareta. astrology and al-

chemy are ~ *sciences*, hoshiuranai ya renkinjitsu wa shimpi kagaku da.

occupancy [ókjupənsi] *n.* sen'yū ; senryō ; shoyū

occupant [ókjupənt] *n.* sen'yūsha ; kyojūsha.

occupation [ɔkjupéiʃ(ə)n] *n.* senryō ; ~ *of the town by the enemy*, teki ni yoru kono machi no senryō. shigoto ; shokugyō.

occupy [ókjupai] *v.* senryō suru ; kyojū suru ; (jikan, kūkan nado o) shimeru.

occur [əkə́:] *v.* okoru, shōzuru ; (kokoro nado ni) ukabu.

occurrence [əkə́r(ə)ns] *n.* (jiken ga) okoru koto ; dekigoto.

ocean [óuʃ(ə)n] *n.* taiyo ; ōkina umi ; hateshinai hirogari. ~**ic** [òuʃiǽnik] *a.* taiyō no.

ocher, -re [óukə] *n.* usui kiiro kei no shikiso to shite tsukawareru dosha.

o'clock [əklók] ...ji. 7 ~, 7 (shichi)ji.

octagon [óktəgən] *n., a.* hachihenkei(no) ; hakkakukei(no).

octahedron [ɔ̀ktəhí:dr(ə)n] *n.* (*math.*) 8 (hachi) mentai.

octane [óktein] *n.* (*chem.*) okutan.

octave [ókteiv] *n.* (*mus.*) okutābu ; 8 (hachi) do ontei.

octavo [əktéivou] *n.* okutaboban ; 8 (yatsu) oriban : okutabo ban no shomotsu.

October [ɔktóubə] *n.* Jūgatsu.

octogenarian [ɔ̀kto(u)dʒinéəriən] *a., n.* 80 (hachijū) dai no (hito).

octopus [óktəpəs / əktóupəs] *n.* tako ; yatsuashi.

octuple [óktju(:)pl] *a.* yae no ; 8 (hachi) bai no. *n.* 8 (hachi) bai ; yae.

ocular [ókjulə] *a.* me no ; shikakujō no.

oculist [ókjulist] *n.* ganka-i ; me no isha.

odd [ɔd] *a.* kisū no ; hampana. ~**ity** [óditi] *n.* fūgawari ; henjin. ~**s** *n.* (*sing. & pl.*) fubyōdō ; saikoro ; kachime : *be at* ~ *with*, to arasotte iru. ~**s and ends,** nokori ; garakuta.

ode [oud] *n.* jojōshi no isshu.

Odin [óudin] *n.* (Hoku-Ō shinwa no) shushin.

odious [óudjəs] *a.* nikurashii ; shūakuna.

odium [óudjəm] *n.* fuhyōban ; hankan ; nikumaremono.

odo(u)r [óudə] *n.* nioi ; hyōban ; kimi (*suspicion*).

odoriferous [òudərifərəs] *a*. kambashii. **~ly** *ad*. kambashiku.

odorous [óudərəs] *a*. (omoni, *poet*) kambashii.

oecumenical [ì:kju(:)ménik(ə)l] *a*. zempanteki ; fuhentekina (*ecumenical*).

oesophagus [i:sɔ́fəgəs] *n*. (*anat*.) shokudō (*esophagus*).

of [əv / əv] *prep*. ... no ; ... ni tsuite ; ... kara naru ; ... no uchi no.

off [ɔ:f / əf] *a*. hanareta ; yasumi no ; tōi hō no. *ad*. *prep*. hanarete ; achira ni ; ... no oki de. *be well* (*badly*) ~, kurashimuki ga yoi (warui). ~ *and on*, danzoku teki ni ; tokidoki. *inter*. atchi ike ! ike !

offal [ɔ́f(ə)l] *n*. zōmotsu ; kuzu ; kuzuniku ; katōna kozakana.

offence, offense [əféns] *n*. tsumi ; hansoku ; burei.

offend [əfénd] *v*. no ki o waruku suru ; sokonau ; tsumi o oka-
offense, [əféns] *n*.=see : **offence.** ⌊su.

offensive [əfénsiv] *a*. ki ni sawaru ; bureina. *n*. kōsei (*aggres-sion*). **~ly** *ad*. kizani ; kōgekitekini.

offer [ɔ́fə / ɔ́:fə] *v*. mōshideru ; kokoromiru. *n*. mōshide ; tsu-kene ; kokoromi.

offhand [ɔ́(:)fhǽnd] *a*. sokuseki no ; muzōsa no. *ad*. [ɔ́fhænd] sokuseki ni ; muzōsani.

office [ɔ́(:)fis] *n*. shokumu ; yakusho ; jimusho. (*pl*.) daidokoro. *good* ~*s*, sewa ; assen.

officer [ɔ́(:)fisə] *n*. kankōri ; yakunin ; shōkō ; kōkyū sen'in.

official [əfíʃ(ə)l] *a*. shokumujō no. ~ *gazette*, kampō. *n*. kan-ri ; yakuin.

officiate [əfíʃieit] *v*. shiki o okonau ; tsutomeru.

officious [əfíʃəs] *a*. osekkai no ; hikōshiki no ; kōiteki.

offing [ɔ́(:)fiŋ] *n*. oki ; okiai : *in the* ~, oki ni ; okiai ni.

off limits [əflimits] (*Am*.) tachiiri kinshi (chiiki).

offset [ɔ́(:)fset] *n*. umeawase ; daishōbutsu. ofusetto insatsu. *v*. sashihiki kanjō suru ; oginau ; ofusettoban ni suru.

offshoot [ɔ́(:)fʃu:t] *n*. wakaredeta eda ; bumpa ; haseibutsu.

offspring [ɔ́(:)fspriŋ] *n*. shison ; kekka.

oft [ɔ:ft], **often** [ɔ́(:)fn] *ad*. shibashiba ; tabitabi.

ogle [óugl] *n*. irome ; shūha. *v*. irome o tsukau.

ogre [óugə] *n*. hitokui-oni ; oni no yōna hito.

ogress [óugris] *n.* ogre no josei meishi.

oh [ou] *inter.* ō !, ū !, oi ! nado no kantanshi.

ohm [oum] *n.* ōmu (denki teikō no tan'i).

oil [ɔil] *n.* abura ; (*pl.*) abura-enogu ; aburae. *v.* abura o nuru ; namerakani suru. ～ **cake** [-keik] *n.* aburakasu. ～**cloth** [-klɔ(:)θ] *n.* tōyu-nuno. ～ **colo(u)r** [-kʌlə] *n*, abura-enogu ; aburae. ～ **painting** [-péintiŋ] *n.* aburae. ～**skin** [-skin] *n.* yufu ; kappa. ～**y** *a.* abura no.

ointment [ɔ́intmənt] *n.* nankō ; kōyaku.

O.K., OK [óukéi] *a.*, *ad.* (*Am. col.*) yoroshii ; kekkō (*all correct*). *v.* shōnin suru. *n.* shōnin.

old [ould] *a.* (～**er**, ～**est; elder, eldest**) toshi totta ; ... sai no ; rōrenna. ～**-fashioned** [óuldfǽʃənd] *a.* kyūshiki no.

oleaginous [òuliǽdʒinəs] *a.* aburashitsu no ; kuchisaki no umai.

oleander [òuliǽndə] *n.* (*bot.*) kyōchikutō.

olfactory [əlfǽktəri] *a.* kyūkaku no.

oligarch [ɔ́ligɑːk] *n.* katōseiji no shisseisha. ～**ic(al)** [ɔligɑ́:kik-(əl)] *a.* shōsū dokusaiseiji no. ～**y** *n.* shōsūdokusai-seiji.

olive [ɔ́liv] *n.* oriibu ; oriibu no iro ; botan ; kazaridome.

olympiad [oulímpiæd / -pjæd] *n.* Orimpia taikai ; 2(ni)-do no taikai no aida no 4(yo) nen kan.

Olympian [o(u)límpiən] *a.* *Olympia* yama no ; *Olympia* no. *n.* *Olympus* no kami.

Olympic [o(u)límpik] *a.* *Olympia* no ; *Olympic* kyōgi no. ～ **games**＝*Olympics*.

omega [óumigə / -mé-] *n.* omega (Girisha *alphabet* no saigo no Ω ω) ; owari ; saigo.

omelet(te) [ɔ́mlit] *n.* omuretsu (Seiyō ryōri no).

omen [óumen] *n.* zenchō. *v.* zenchō to naru ; yochi suru.

ominous [ɔ́minəs] *a.* fukitsuna ; yochi suru. ～**ly** *ad.*

omission [o(u)míʃ(ə)n] *n.* shōryaku ; shōryaku sareta mono.

omit [o(u)mít] *v.* shōryaku suru ; (ii)morasu ; (kaki) otosu.

omnibus [ɔ́mnibəs] *n.* noriaijidōsha. *a.* gochagocha ni morikonda.

omnipotence [ɔmnípət(ə)ns] *n.* zennō ; zennō no kami (*omnis* ＝*all*＋*potens*＝*be able*).

omnipotent [omnípət(ə)nt] *a.* zennō no ; zetsudai no chikara o motsu. *the O ~*, Kami.

omnipresence [ɔ̀mniprézəns] *n.* doko ni demo aru ; nai tokoro wa nai ; henzai.

omnipresent [ɔ̀mnipréz(ə)nt] *a.* doko ni demo iru (aru).

omniscience [ɔmnísi(ə)ns] *n.* zenchi ; hakushiki ; nan demo shitteru.

omniscient [ɔmnísiənt] *a.* zenchi no ; hakushiki no.

omnivorous [ɔmnív(ə)rəs] *a.* nan demo taberu ; nan demo gozare no : *an ~ reader*, nan demo yomu (randoku suru).

on [ɔn / ɒn] *prep.* no ue ni. *~ the desk, desk* no ue ni. *put the ring ~ her finger*, yubiwa o yubi ni hameru. ni sotte. *a house ~ the street*, tōri ni sotta ie. no hōkō e. *they marched ~ the capitol*, minna gijidō no hō e itta. no ue no. *the picture ~ the wall*, kabe no ue no e. no te kara, *This news is ~ good authority*, kono nyūsu wa shikkari shita tokoro kara no de desu. ni kansuru. *a book on animals*, dōbutsu ni kansuru hon. no mokuteki de. *He went ~ an errand*, kare wa otsukai de itta no da. no ue mata. *defeat ~ defeat*, haiboku no ue mata haiboku. no uchi ni. *Who is ~ the committee?*, iinkai no uchi ni dare ga iru? *~ Sunday*, Nichiyō ni. *~ our arrival*, watashi-tachi ga tōchaku suru to. *ad.* *hold ~ or you may fall*, tsukamatte oide, de naito okkochiru kamo shirenai zo. *march ~*, dondon ike. *turn the gas ~*, gas o tsukero. *from that day ~*, sono hi kara zutto. *and so ~*, nado nado.

once [wʌns] *ad.* katsute ; ichido. *at ~*, tadachi ni ; issho (dōji) ni. *~ and again*, ikudo mo kurikaeshite. *~ for all*, oshimaini ; mō ippen dake. *~ in a while*, tokiori.

one [wʌn] *n., a.* hitotsu (no) ; aru. *pron.* aru hito ; aru mono. *pron.* mono ; no. *~ and all*, minna. *~ by ~*, hitotsu zutsu. *all ~*, minna onaji.

onerous [ɔ́nərəs] *a.* yakkaina ; futan tsuki no.

oneself [wʌnsélf] *pron.* mizukara ; honnin jishin.

one-way [wʌ́nwéi] *a.* ippō kōtsū no.

onion [ʌ́njən] *n.* (*veg.*) tamanegi.

onlooker [ɔ́nlùkə] *n.* kembutsu-nin ; bōkansha.

only [óunli] *a.* yuiitsu no ; kiwamete sugureta. *ad.* tada tanni ; tsui ... ; chotto. *not* ～ ... *but (also)* ... nomi narazu (mata). *conj.* ... to iu koto sae nakereba. *if* ～, ... sae areba ii no da ga. ～ *too*＝*very. shi was* ～ *too glad to help us*, kanojo wa warera no enjo o suru koto o taihen yorokonde iru.

onomatopoeia [ɔ̀no(u)mætopí(:)ə] *n.* gion ; giseigo.

onset [ɔ́nset] *n.* totsugeki ; chakushu ; tehajime.

onslaught [ɔ́nslɔːt] *n.* kōgeki ; mōshū.

onus [óunəs] *n.* omoni ; futan ; sekinin.

onward [ɔ́nwəd] *a.* zenshin suru. *ad.* zempō e ; susunde.

onyx [ɔ́niks] *n. (min.)* shimamenō.

oolong [úːlɔŋ] *n.* ūron-cha.

ooze [uːz] *v.* daradara nagareru ; (kitai, ekitai ga) moreru ; shimidasu. *n.* bumpi (butsu) ; yawarakai doro.

oozy [úːzi] *a.* yawarakai doro no ; shimideru.

opacity [o(u)pǽsiti] *n.* futōmei ; gudon ; aimai.

opal [óup(ə)l] *n. (min.)* opāru ; nyūshoku (*milky white*) garasu.

opalescence [òupəlésns] *n.* nyūhakukō ; opāruiro no hikari.

opalescent [òupəlésnt] *a.* nyūhakushoku no.

opaque [o(u)péik] *a.* futōmeina ; gudonna.

ope [oup] *v. (poet)* open.

open [óup(ə)n] *a.* hiraita ; akeppanashi no ; mubōbi no. ～ *city*, mubōbi toshi. *v.* hiraku ; kōkai suru ; hajimeru ; kaitaku suru. *n.* hirobiro to shita basho ; akichi. ～**-air** [-ɛ́ə] *a.* kōgai no. ～**-armed** [-áːmd] *a.* magokoro kara no. ～**-door** [-dɔː] *a.* monko kaihō no. ～**-handed** [-hǽndid] *a.* kimae no yoi. ～**-hearted** [-háːtid] *a.* sotchokuna. ～**ing** *n.* hiraku koto ; hajimari ; akichi. ～**ly** *ad.* sotchokuni ; kōzen to.

opera [ɔ́pərə] *n.* kageki. ～ *glass* [-qláːs] *n.* sōgankyō. ～**hat** [-hæt] *n.* opera-bō. ～**house** [-háus] *n.* kagekijō.

operate [ɔ́pəreit] *v.* hataraku ; sayō suru ; kikime o arawasu ; shujutsu o suru.

operatic [ɔ̀pərǽtik] *a.* opera no ; kageki no.

operation [ɔ̀pəréiʃən] *n.* hataraki ; jisshi ; shujutsu.

operative [ɔ́p(ə)rətiv / -rèitiv] *a.* hataraku ; shujutsu no. *n.* hatarakite ; tantei.

operator [ɔ́pəreitə] *n.* gishi ; keieisha ; shujutsusha. *telephone*

~, denwa kōkanshu.

operetta [ɔ̀pərétə] *n.* kei kageki ; operetta.

ophthalmia [ɔfθǽlmiə / ɔpθ-] *n.* (*med.*) gan'en ; fūgan ; me no enshō.

ophthalmic [ɔfθǽlmik / ɔpθ-] *a.* gan'en no ; me no. *n.* megusuri.

opiate [óupiit / -pieit] *n.* megusuri. *a.* ahen no ; kutsū o shizumeru.

opine [o(u)páin] *v.* kangaeru ; handan suru.

opinion [əpínjən] *n.* iken ; kangae. *public* ~, yoron. **~ated** [əpínjəneitid] *a.* gankona ; kataijina (*opinionative*).

opium [óupjəm] *n.* ahen. ~ *den*, ahenkutsu. ~ *eater*, ahen jōyōsha.

opossum [əpɔ́səm] *n.* fukuro nezumi.

opponent [əpóunənt] *a.* tekitai suru. *n.* hantaisha.

opportune [ɔ̀pətjúːn / ɔ́pətjuːn] *a.* jiki o eta ; chōdo yoi. **~ly** *ad.* ori yoku.

opportunism [ɔ̀pətjuːnizm / ɔ́pətjuːn-] *n.* hiyorimi-shugi. **~ist** [ɔ̀pətjúːnist / ɔ́pətjun-] *n.* gotsugō-shugisha.

opportunity [ɔ̀pətjúːniti] *n.* kikai.

oppose [əpóuz] *v.* hantai suru.

opposite [ɔ́pəzit] *a.* mukōgawa no ; hantai no. *n.* hantaisha.

opposition [ɔ̀pəzíʃ(ə)n] *n.* hantai ; tairitsu ; hantaitō.

oppress [əprés] *v.* appaku suru ; shiitageru. **~ive** *a.* appaku suru. **~or** *n.* asseisha ; gyakutaisha.

oppression [əpréʃ(ə)n] *n.* assei ; appaku.

opprobrious [əpróubriəs] *a.* bureina ; kuchigitanai.

opprobrium [əpróubriəm / -əp-] *n.* omei ; akkō.

optative [ɔ́ptətiv] *a.* gambō o arawasu.

optic [ɔ́ptik] *a.* me no. *n.* me (*eye*). **~al** *a.* me no ; kōgakujō no. **~s** *n.* kōgaku.

optician [ɔptíʃ(ə)n] *n.* gankyōshō (megane shōnin).

optimism [ɔ́ptimizm] *n.* rakkanshugi.

optimist [ɔ́ptimist] *n.* rakkanshugisha ; nonkimono.

optimistic [ɔ̀ptimístik] *a.* rakkanshugi no.

option [ɔ́pʃ(ə)n] *n.* sentakuken ; nin'i. **~al** *a.* zuii no ; nin'i no.

opulence [ɔ́pjuləns] *n.* fuyū ; kanemochi.

opulent [ɔ́pjulənt] *a.* yūfukuna ; kanemochi no.

opus [óupəs] *n.* (*pl.* **opera** [ɔ́p(ə)rə]) sakuhin. *the violinist played his own* ~, *violinist* wa jibun no sakuhin o ensō shita.

or [ɔ: / ə] *conj.* arui wa ; mata wa ; sunawachi ; ... ka aruiwa. ~ *else*, samo nakereba.

oracle [ɔ́rəkl] *n.* kami no otsuge ; shintaku.

oracular [ərǽkjulə] *a.* shintaku no yōna.

oral [ɔ́:r(ə)l] *a.* kuchi no ; kōjutsu no. ~**ly** *ad.* kōtō de.

orange [ɔ́rindʒ] *n.* orenji (*fruit*) ; orenji-iro. *mandarin* ~, mikan. ~**ry** *n.* orenji saibaien.

orang-outang [ɔ́:rəŋu:tǽŋ] *n.* (*zoo.*) shōjō ; ruijin'en.

orate [ɔréit] *v.* (*col.*) enzetsu o suru ; erasōni hanasu.

oration [ɔ:réiʃ(ə)n] *n.* enzetsu ; kitō.

orator [ɔ́rətə] *n.* yūbensha ; enzetsusha. ~**ical** [ɔ̀rətórik(ə)l] *a.* enzetsu no ; shūjiteki. ~**y** [ɔ́rət(ə)ri] *n.* yūben (jutsu).

oratorio [ɔ̀rətɔ́:riou] *n.* (*pl.* ~**s**) oratorio (*solo, chorus, orchestra*).

orb [ɔ:b] *n.* kyū ; tentai.

orbit [ɔ́:bit] *n.* kidō ; ganka (*eyesocket*).

orchard [ɔ́:tʃəd] *n.* kajuen.

orchestra [ɔ́:kistrə] *n.* ōkesutora ; kangengaku (dan).

orchestral [ɔ:késtrəl] *a.* ōkesutora no.

orchid [ɔ́:kid], **orchis** [ɔ́:kis] *n.* (*flow.*) ran.

ordain [ɔ:déin] *v.* sadameru ; nimmei suru.

ordeal [ɔ:dí(:)əl] *n.* mukashi no saibanhō ; shiren.

order [ɔ́:də] *n.* meirei ; junjo ; seido ; kunshō ; chūmon ; kawase ; shūkyō dan. ~ *of the day*, giji nittei. *take the* ~*s*, sōryo ni naru. *v.* seiton suru ; meirei suru ; chūmon suru. ~ *from*, ... e chūmon suru. ~ *form*, chūmon yōshi.

orderly [ɔ́:dəli] *a.* junjo tadashii ; meirei no. *n.* denreikashi ; kangonin.

ordinal [ɔ́:dinl] *a.* junjo no (cf. *cardinal*). *n.* junjosū (~*number*) (cf. *cardinal*).

ordinance [ɔ́:dinəns] *n.* hōrei ; fukoku.

ordinarily [ɔ́:dinərili] *ad.* taitei ; tsūjō.

ordinary [ɔ́:dinəri] *a.* tsūjō no ; heibonna.

ordination [ɔ̀:dinéiʃən] *n.* nimmei ; bunrui. ⌈hin.

ordnance [ɔ́:dnəns] *n.* taihō ; buki (arayuru shurui no) ; gunju-

ordure [ɔ́:djuə] *n.* fun ; kitanai mono.
ore [ɔ: / ɔə] *n.* kōseki ; (*poet.*) kinzoku (ōgon).
organ [ɔ́:gən] *n.* kikan ; orugan ; kikanshi. ~**ism** *n.* yūkitai. ~**ist** [ɔ́:gənist] *n.* orugan ensōsha.
organdy, -die [ɔ́:gəndi] *n.* usude mosurin no isshu.
organic [ɔ:gǽnik] *a.* shintai no kikan no ; yūkitai no. ~**ally** [ɔ:gǽnikəli] *ad.* yūkitekini.
organization [ɔ̀:gənaizéiʃ(ə)n] *n.* soshiki ; kikō.
organize [ɔ́:gənaiz] *v.* kumitateru ; soshiki suru.
oriel [ɔ́:riəl] *n.* haridashi-mado.
orient [ɔ́:riənt] *a.* higashi no ; (*O-*) Tōyō no. *n.* higashi ; (*the O-*) Tōyō.
oriental [ɔ̀(:)riéntl] *a.* higashi no ; (*O-*) Tōyō no. *n.* (*O-*) Tōyō jin ; Ajiajin.
orientate [ɔ́:rienteit] *v.* higashi ni mukeru ; tadashii hōkō ni oku.
orientation [ɔ̀(:)rientéiʃ(ə)n] *n.* higashi ni mukeru koto ; monogoto o yoku tadashiku mukeru koto.
orifice [ɔ́rifis] *n.* (dōkutsu nado no) ana ; kuchi.
origin [ɔ́ridʒin] *n.* okori ; kigen ; kongen.
original [ərídʒən(ə)l] *a.* moto no ; jibun no omoitsuki no ; dokusōteki no ; ichiban saki ni suru. *n.* saisho no mono. ~**ity** [ərìdʒinǽliti] *n.* dokusōryoku, ~**ly** *ad.* moto wa ; honrai.
originate [ərídʒineit] *v.* hajimete okosu (tsukuru).
origination [ərìdʒinéiʃ(ə)n] *n.* hajimeru koto (hito no mada shinakatta koto o).
originator [ərídʒineitə] *n.* sōshisha ; hokkinin.
oriole [ɔ́:rioul] *n.* (*bird*) kōrai-uguisu.
Orion [oráiən] *n.* Orion (nampō no seiza).
ornament [ɔ́:nəmənt] *n.* sōshoku. *v.* [-ment] sōshoku suru. ~**al** [ɔ̀:nəméntl] *a.* sōshoku no. ~**ation** [ɔ̀:nəmentéiʃ(ə)n] *n.* sōshoku.
ornate [ɔ:néit / ɔ́:neit] *a.* kazari no ōi ; kabina.
ornithology [ɔ̀:niθɔ́lədʒi / -naiθ-] *n.* chōruigaku. ~**ist** [ɔ̀:niθ-ɔ́lədʒist] *n.* chōrui gakusha.
orphan [ɔ́:f(ə)n] *n.* koji. ~**age** [ɔ́:fənidʒ] *n.* kojiin.
orthodox [ɔ́:θədəks] *a.* seitō no ; (*O-*) Girisha Kyōkai no

Orthodox Church [ɔ́:θədəkstʃə:tʃ] *n. Pope* o shimpu to mito-menai *Greek Catholic* no shinja-tachi ; seikyōkai.

orthodoxy [ɔ́:θədəksi] *n.* seitōha (*Orthodox Church*) no hito-ta-chi.

orthoepy [ɔ́:θouepi / ɔ:θóuipi] *n.* seiongaku (ima no *phonetics or phonology*).

orthographer [ɔ:θógrəfə] *n.* seijihō-gakusha.

orthographical [ɔ̀:θográfikəl] *a.* seijihō no ; tetsujihō no.

orthography [ɔ:θógrəfi] *n.* seijihō ; mojiron.

oscillate [ɔ́sileit] *v.* shindō suru (saseru) ; dōyō suru (saseru).

oscillation [ɔ̀siléiʃ(ə)n] *n.* shindō ; dōyō.

oscillatory [ɔ́sileitəri / -lət(ə)ri] *a.* shindō suru.

oscillograph [əsíləgrɑ:f] *n.* onseikirokuki ; oshirogurafu.

osculate [ɔ́skjuleit] *v.* seppun suru ; sesshoku suru.

osier [óuziə] *n.* (*bot.*) kinuyanagi (no eda) ; (*Am.*) yamabōshi no rui.

osprey [ɔ́spri] *n.* (*bird*) misago.

osseous [ɔ́siəs] *a.* hone no ; hone no aru ; hone ni nita.

ossification [ɔ̀sifikéiʃ(ə)n] *n.* seikotsu ; hone ni naru koto.

ossify [ɔ́sifai] *v.* hone ni naru.

ostensible [əsténs(ə)bl] *a.* omotemuki no ; hyōmenteki no. ∼bly *ad.*

ostentation [ɔ̀stentéiʃ(ə)n] *n.* mie ; mikake ; kyoshoku.

ostentatious [ɔ̀stentéiʃəs] *a.* mie o haru ; kyoshoku no ; hade-na.

osteology [ɔ̀stiólədʒi] *n.* kotsugaku.

ostler [ɔ́slə] *n.* (ryokan no) batei (*hostler*).

ostracism [ɔ́strəsizm] *n.* tsuihō ; hōchiku. (*Athene* de mukashi yatta kaigara tōhyō.)

ostracize [ɔ́strəsaiz] *v.* tsuihō suru ; ... to zekkō suru.

ostrich [ɔ́stritʃ / -idʒ] *n.* dachō.

other [ʌ́ðə] *a., pron.* ta no (hito ; mono) ; (*the o-*) kataippō no. *every ∼ day* ... kakujitsu ni. *the ∼ day* ... senjitsu. *the ∼ way* ... abekobe ni. ∼**wise** [ʌ́ðəwaiz] *ad.* betsuni ; ta no hōhō de. *conj.* samo nai to.

otter [ɔ́tə] *n.* kawauso. *sea ∼* ... rakko.

ought [ɔ:t] *aux. v.* ... subeki de aru ; ... suru no ga tōzen da.

ounce [auns] *n.* onsu (28.35gr. arui wa 31.104gr.) ; shōryō.

our [áuə] *pron.* ('**we**' no shoyū-kakau) warera no. ∼**s** *pron.* warera no mono. ∼**selves** [-sélvz] *pron.* Chin mizukara. ∼**selves** [-selvz] *pron.* ; (*pl.*) warera jishin.

oust [aust] *v.* oidasu ; ubaitoru.

out [aut] *ad.* soto ni(e). *rush* ∼, tobidasu. naka ni nai : ∼ *of fashion*, ryūkō okure ; yabottai. *a young girl who came* ∼ *last season*, mae no *season* ni dete kita wakai musume. *fight it* ∼, tokoton saigo made tatakainuku. nan demo (a) soto ni ; (b) kotogara kara nukederu yōni " deru" to iu imi. ∼ *and away*, tōku e itteru. *at outs=on the outs*, nakatagai shite iru.

out-and-out [áutənáut] *a.* mattaku no. *ad.* zenzen.

outboard [áutbə:d] *a., ad.* sengai no (e) ; fune no soto (e).

outbreak [áutbreik] *n.* (sōdō no) bakuhatsu.

outburst [áutbə:st] *n.* haretsu ; boppatsu.

outcast [áutkɑ:st] *a.* oidasareta ; yadonashi no. *n.* tsuihōnin ; yadonashi.

outclass [áutklɑ́:s] *v.* harukani masaru.

outcome [áutkʌm] *n.* kekka ; seika.

outcrop [áutkrəp] *n.* rotō. *the* ∼ *of a vein of coal*, sekitan kōmyaku no rotō.

outcry [áutkrai] *n.* sakebi ; kyōbai ; sawagi.

outdate [autdéit] *v.* jidai okure ni naru.

outdistance [autdístəns] *v.* zutto oinuku.

outdo [autdú:] *v.* makasu ; katsu.

outdoor [áutdə: / -dəə] *a.* kogai no. ∼**s** *ad.* kogai de. *n.* kogai.

outer [áutə] *a.* soto no ; gaibu no. *the* ∼ *man*, fūsai. ∼**most** [-moust] *a.* ichiban soto no.

outfield [áutfi:ld] *n.* (*base.*) gaiya. ∼**er** *n.* gaiyashu.

outfit [áutfit] *n.* shitaku ; (nan demo) hitsuyōna dōgu. *v.* jumbi suru. ∼**ting** [-fitiŋ] *n.* shitaku ; jumbi.

outflank [autflǽŋk] *v.* sokumen o ukai (hōi) suru.

outgo [autgóu] *v.* tsuiyasu. [áutgou] *n.* shuppi.

outgoing [áutgòuiŋ] *n.* shuppatsu ; shuppi ; (*pl.*) dete iku tokoro. *a.* shuppatsu suru.

outgrow [autgróu] *v.* ... yori mo motto seichō suru ; nukeru (kuse kara). ∼**th** [áutgrouθ] *n.* hikobae.

outing [áutiŋ] *n.* gaishutsu ; ensoku.

outlandish [autlǽndiʃ] *a.* kawatta ; myōna ; gaikokufūna.

outlast [autlɑ́:st] *v.* ... yori mo nagamochi suru.

outlaw [áutlɔ:] *n.* muhōmono ; narazumono. *v.* ... kara hōritsu no hogo o ubau. **~ry** [áutlɔ̀:ri] *n.* taikyo meirei ; tsuihō.

outlay [áutlei] *n.* hiyō ; keihi ; shishutsu.

outlet [áutlet] *n.* deguchi ; hakeguchi.

outline [áutlain] *n.* gaikei ; rinkaku ; (*pl.*) kōgai ; aramashi. *v.* aramashi o kaku.

outlive [autlív] *v.* ... yori ikinobiru (nagaku ikiru).

outlook [áutluk] *n.* mihari ; miharisho ; miharashi ; zento no mikomi.

outlying [áutlàiiŋ] *a.* soto ni aru ; hanarete iru ; tōi tokoro no.

outnumber [autnʌ́mbə] *v.* kazu de katsu ; kazu ni oite masaru.

out-of-date [áut-əv-deit] *a.* kyūshikina.

out-of-door [áut-əv-dɔ́: / -dɔɔ] *a.* kogai no.

out-of-the-way [áut-əv-ðə-wéi] *a.* hempina ; katainaka no.

outpost [áutpoust] *n.* zenshō ; zenshinkichi.

outpour [áutpə: / -pɔɔ] *n.* ryūshitsu ; nagarederu koto.

output [áutput] *n.* seisandaka ; haisetsubutsu.

outrage [áutreidʒ / -ridʒ] *n.* rambō ; tegome. *v.* rambō suru. **~ous** [autréidʒəs] *a.* rambōna ; muhōna.

outrigger [áutrigə] *n.* (kanū) haridashi ukizai ; kaiuke.

outright [áutráit] *a.* an ~ *loss*, tetteitekina sonshutsu. sotchoku-na. *an ~ refusal*, nibe mo nai kyozetsu. *ad.* [autráit] tantekini.

outset [áutset] *n.* hajime.

outside [áutsáid] *n.* sotogawa ; gaikei ; kyokugen. *at the* ~, sei-izei. *a.* gaibu no. *ad.* soto ni. (*Am.*) o nozoite.

outsider [áutsáidə] *n.* kyokugaisha ; mongaikan ; shirōto.

outskirt [áutskə:t] *n.* basue ; kōgai (*usu. pl.*).

outspoken [autspóukn] *a.* fukuzōnaku hanasu ; sotchokuna.

outstanding [autstǽndiŋ] *a.* debatte iru ; medatsu ; kenchona ; miketchaku no.

outstrip [autstríp] *v.* oikosu ; ryōga suru.

outward [áutwəd] *a.* gaibu no ; gaimen no ; hisō no.

outward(s) [áutwəd(z)] *ad.* soto ni ; kokugai ni. ~ *bound* ... gaikoku yuki no ; gaikō no.

outwit [autwít] v. kisen o seisuru.

outwork [áutwə:k] n. gaihō ; gairui (*fortification* oshiro no).

outworn [áutwə:n] a. surikireta ; tsukai furushi no.

ouzel [ú:zl] n. (*bird*) tsugumi no rui.

oval [óuv(ə)l] a. tamagogata no ; daen no. n. daenkei.

ovary [óuvəri] n. shibō ; ransō.

ovate [óuveit] a. tamagogata no ; rankei no.

ovation [o(u)véiʃ(ə)n] n. dai kangei ; dai kassai.

oven [ʌ́vn] n. kama ; ro.

over [óuvə] *pref.* ue no mono ga shita no mono (*object of the preposition*) yori, ōkii, hiroi, nagai, (*surpass*) koto o arawasu. *the roof* ~ *one's head*, atama no ue no yane. *We have a captain* ~ *us*, warera no ue (*over*) ni *captain* ga iru. *A blush came* ~ *her face*, kao ga patto akaku natta. *leap* ~ *a wall*, kabe o tobikosu. *lands* ~ *the sea*, umi no mukō no kuni. *he fell* ~ *the edge of the cliff*, zeppeki no haji kara okkotta. *It costs* ~ *ten dollars*, 10(ju) doru ijō suru.

over- [óuvə] *pref.* " *too* " no imi.

overact [óuvərǽkt] v. yarisugiru ; kochōshite enzuru.

overage [óuvəre:dʒ] a. toshitori sugita. n. (*Am.*) kajō shōhin.

overall [óuvərɔ:l] a. zentai ni wataru. n. gaitō ; (*pl.*) sagyō zubon. ad. [òuvərɔ́:l] zentai de.

overawe [òuvərɔ́:] v. odoshitsukeru ; ikaku suru.

overbear [òuvəbéə] v. attō suru ; oshitsubusu. ~**ing** a. attō-tekina ; ōheina.

overboard [óuvəbə:d / òuvəbɔ́:d] ad. sengai ni ; suichū ni.

overcast [óuvəka:st] v. kumoraseru (kumoru) ; kuraku suru (naru) ; kukeru, nuiawaseru. a. kumotta ; kurai.

overcharge [óuvətʃáːdʒ] n. tsumini chōka. v. tsumi sugiru ; sōyaku jūten ga ōsugiru ; kakene o suru.

overcoat [óuvəkout] n. gaito.

overcome [òuvəkʌ́m] v. uchikatsu ; makasu.

overdo [òuvədú:] v. kochō suru ; yaki sugiru ; nisugiru ; yarisugiru.

overdose [óuvədous] n. karyō (kusuri no ōsugi).

overdraft [óuvədra:ft] n. tōza kashikoshi.

overdraw [óuvədrɔ́:] v. ōgesa ni iu ; furidashi sugiru (tegata o).

overdue [óuvədjú:] *a.* kigen o sugita ; enchaku shita. *the train is overdue*, ressha wa okurete iru.

overflow [òuvəflóu] *v.* afureru ; minagiru. *n.* [óuvəflou] kōzui, hanran.

overhang [óuvəhǽŋ] *v.* ue ni tsukideru ; odokasu. *n.* [óuvəhǽŋ] haridashi.

overhaul [ouvəhɔ́:l] *v.* kensa suru ; oitsuku. *n.* [óuvəhɔ:l] kensa.

overhead [óuvəhed] *ad.* ue ni takaku ; zujō ni.

overhear [òuvəhíə] *v.* morekiku ; tachigiki suru.

overland [óuvəlænd] *a.*, *ad.* rikujō no (o) ; rikuro no (o).

overlap [òuvəlǽp] *v.* kasanaru (-neru) ; chōfuku suru.

overlay [óuvəlei] *v.* shiku ; kabuseru ; mekki suru.

overload [óuvəloud] *v.* ni o tsumi sugiru.

overlook [òuvəlúk] *v.* miorosu ; kantoku suru ; ōme ni miru ; miotosu.

overnice [óuvənáis] *a.* kimuzukashii ; keppeki sugiru.

overnight [óuvənáit] *ad.* sakuban ; yodōshi. *a.* zen'ya no ; yoigoshi no.

overpower [òuvəpáuə] *v.* attō suru ; katsu.

overreach [òuvəríːtʃ] *v.* koeru ; ikisugiru ; damasu.

override [òuvəráid] *v.* noritsubusu ; mukō ni saseru. *a new rule* ~*ing all previous ones*, subete no jūzen no kisoku o mukō ni suru atarashii kisoku.

overrule [òuvərúːl] *v.* attō suru ; haki suru ; kyakka suru.

overrun [òuvərán] *v.* arasu ; ikisugiru ; afureru. *the speaker* ~ *the time set for him*, benshi wa kare ni atete atta jikan o chōka shita.

overseas [óuvəsíːz] *a.*, *ad.* kaigai no (ni) ; gaikoku no (ni).

oversee [óuvəsíː] *v.* kantoku suru ; kanri suru.

overseer [óuvəsi(:)ə] *n.* kantoku ; kanrisha ; torishimarinin.

overshadow [òuvəʃǽdou] *v.* kuraku suru ; ōu.

oversight [óuvəsait] *n.* kantoku ; miotoshi, tenukari.

overt [óuvəːt / ouvɔ́:t] *a.* mɛihakuna ; rekizen taru ; kōzen no.

overtake [òuvətéik] *v.* oitsuku ; totsuzen ni osou. *The storm* ~ *the children*, arashi ga totsuzen kodomo-tachi o osotta.

overtask [óuvətáːsk] *v.* murina shigoto o saseru.

overthrow [òuvəθróu] *v.* taosu ; horobosu. *n.* [óuvəθrou] tentō ; metsubō.

overtime [óuvətaim] *n.* teijigai no rōdōjikan ; chōka kimmu.

overture [óuvətjuə] *n.* mōshiide ; teian. *The enemy is making ~ for peace,* teki wa heiwa e no mōshiide o shite iru tokoro da. ⌐robosu.

overturn [óuvətə:n] *n.* tempuku ; kaimetsu. *v.* kutsugaesu ; ho-

overweening [òuvəwí:niŋ] *a.* unuboreta ; manshin shita.

overwhelm [òuvəhwélm] *v.* attō suru ; kujiku.

overwork [óuvəwə́:k] *v.* -worked *or* -wrought; -working. *~ oneself,* hataraki sugiru. *n.* karō ; hatarakisugi.

overwrought [óuvərɔ́:t] *a.* ~ nerves, tsukai sugita shinkei. *see :* overwork.

oviduct [óuvidʌkt] *n.* yurankan.

oviform [óuvifɔ:m] *a.* tamagogata no.

oviparous [o(u)vípərəs] *a.* ransei no.

ovoid [óuvɔid] *a.* rankei no ; tamagogata no.

ovule [óuvju:l] *n.* haishu ; chiisai tamago.

ovum [óuvəm] *n.* (*pl.* ova [óuvə]) ran ; ransaibō ; tamago.

owe [ou] *v.* fusai ga aru ; on ga aru.

owing [óuiŋ] *a.* kari ga aru ; ~ to...no tame ni.

owl [aul] *n.* (*bird.*) fukurō. ~et *n.* fukurō no ko. ~ish *a.* fukurō no yōna.

own [oun] *a.* jibun no. shoyū suru ; mitomeru. ~ up... sukkari hakujō suru.

owner [óunə] *n.* shoyūsha. ~ship *n.* shoyūken.

ox [ɔks] *n.* (*pl.* oxen [ɔ́ksən]) *n.* (*zoo.*) oushi ; kyosei oushi.

oxeye [ɔ́ksai] *n.* ōkina me ; (*flower*) furansugiku.

Oxford [ɔ́ksfəd] *n.* tangutsu no isshu (*Oxford shoe,* tomo iu).

oxidation [ɔ̀ksidéiʃən] *n.* sanka (sabi ; kinzoku no).

oxide [ɔ́ksaid] *n.* sankabutsu.

oxidize [ɔ́ksidaiz] *v.* sanka suru.

oxygen [ɔ́ksidʒən] *n.* sanso. ~ate *v.* sanka suru.

oyes, oyez [oujés / oujéz] *inter.* kike !, kinchō seyo !, shizukani !

oyster [ɔ́istə] *n.* kaki. ~ bed, kaki yōshokujō. ~ farm, kaki yōshokujō. ~ catcher, (*bird*) miyakodori. ⌐so.

ozone [óuzoun / ouzóun] *n.* ozon ; (*col.*) shinsenna kūki ; san-

P

P, p [pi:] *n.* (*pl.* P's, Ps [pi:z]) Eigo *alphabet* no dai-16-bamme no moji.

pabulum [pǽbjuləm] *n.* shokumotsu; jiyōbutsu; kokoro no kate.

pace [peis] *n.* hitoashi; hochō; (*about* 2$^1/_2$ *feet*). keep ~ *with*, ... to hochō o awaseru. *v.* hochō tadashiku aruku; hosoku suru.

pachyderm [pǽkidə:m] *n.* kawa no atsui (*thick skinned*) dōbutsu; donkanna hito.

pacific [pəsífik] *a.* heiwana; (P-) Taiheiyō no. *the* P ~ (*Ocean*), Taiheiyō. ~**ation** [pæsifikéiʃən] *n.* kōwa (-jōyaku); heitei.

pacifist [pǽsifist] *n.* heiwashugisha.

pacify [pǽsifai] *v.* heiwa ni suru.

pack [pæk] *n.* tsutsumi; nimotsu. *v.* tsutsumu; tsumekomu; shippu suru. ~**age** [⊥idʒ] *n.* komozutsumi; nimotsu. ~ **er** *n.* nizukurinin. ~**horse** [-hɔ:s] *n.* daba; niuma. ~**saddle** [⊥sædl] *n.* nigura. ~**ing** [pǽkiŋ] *n.* nizukuri; sono zairyō. ~ *house*... (*Am.*) kanzume kōjō; nizukurigyō.

packet [pǽkit] *n.* kozutsumi. ~**boat** [-bout] *n.* yūbinsen.

pact [pækt] *n.* keiyaku; jōyaku.

pad [pæd] *n.* ateru mono; (yawarakana mono no) taba; inu nado no ashiura; nikushi; sutampudai. *v.* tsumemono ni suru. ~ **ding** [pǽdiŋ] *n.* tsumemono o suru koto; tsumemono; umegusa. ~ **dock** [pǽdək] *n.* (chōbayō no) baba (*riding ground*). ~**lock** [pǽdlək] *n.*, *v.* ebijō, nankinjō (o kakeru).

paddle [pǽdl] *n.* kai. *v.* kai de kogu. ~**boat** [-bout] *n.* gairinsen. ~**wheel** [-hwi:l] *n.* kisen no gairin-sha.

padre [pá:dri] *n.* shimpu; bokushi.

paean [pí:ən] *n.* yorokobi no uta; tatae no uta.

pagan [péigən] *n.* ikyōto. *a.* ikyō (to) no. ~**ism** *n.* ikyō.

page [peidʒ] *n.* kyūji; pēji; kiroku. *v.* (*Am.*) na o yonde sagasu; pēji zuke o suru.

pageant [pǽdʒənt] *n.* pējento; yagai geki. ~**ry** misemono; omatsuri sawagi.

pagoda [pɔgóudə] *n.* tō ; pagoda.
paid [peid] *v. see* : **pay.** *a.* shiharaizumi no ; kyūryō o morau. **〜-up** [ʌ́p] *a.* haraikomizumi no.
pail [peil] *n.* oke, teoke. **〜ful** [-ful] *n.* oke ippai.
pain [pein] *n.* itami ; (*pl.*) jintsū ; honeori. *v.* kurushimeru. **〜ful** *a.* itai ; kurushii. **〜less** *a.* itami no nai. **〜staking** [-zteikiŋ] *a.* hone no oreru ; kushin no.
paint [peint] *n.* enogu ; penki. *v.* penki o nuru ; e o kaku. **〜er** *n.* gakya ; penkiya. **〜ing** *n.* kaiga.
pair [pɛə] *n.* ittsui ; futatsu de hitokumi ni naru mono. *v.* ittsui ni suru (naru).
pajamas [pɔjúːməz] *n.* (*pl.*) pajama ; (nemaki).
Pakistan [pǽkistæn] *n.* Pakisutan.
pal [pæl] *n.* (*sl.*) nakayoshi ; tomodachi. **pen 〜,** buntsū no to-modachi.
palace [pǽlis / -ləs] *n.* kyūden ; goten.
Paladin [pǽlədin] *n. Charlemagne* Taitei no 12 (jūni) nin no yūshi no hitori ; bukyōsha.
palankeen, palanquin [pæləŋkíːn] *n.* kago ; norimono.
palatable [pǽlətəbl] *a.* umai ; oishii ; ki ni itta.
palatal [pǽlətəl] (*phon.*) *a.* kōgai no. *n.* kōgai-no ([j] [ʃ] nado no yōna on).
palatalize [pǽlətəlaiz] *v.* kōgaika suru. **〜ation** kōgaika.
palate [pǽlit / -lət] *n.* kōgai.
palatial [pɔléiʃəl / -ʃiəl] *a.* kyūden no (yōna) ; kōdaina.
palaver [pɔlúːvə] *n., v.* dampan (o suru) (*Africa* nado de ryo-kōsha to genchijin to no shōbaijō nado no) ; mudana osha-beri (o suru).
pale [peil] *a.* aojiroi (kaoiro nado). *v.* aozameru. kaki nado o mōkeru. *n.* bōgui (saku nado ni suru). **〜 face,** hakujin. **〜ly** *ad.* **〜ness** *n.*
paleography [pæliógrəfi / pei-] *n.* komonjo-gaku (*study or an-cient writing*).
paleolithic [pæliɔlíθik / pei-] *a.* sekki-jidai no.
paleontology [pæliɔntɔ́lədʒi] *n.* koseibutsu-gaku ; kasekigaku.
palette [pǽlit -let] *n.* paretto ; (chōshoku-ban) hitokumi no enogu. **〜 knife,** parettonaifu, enogu chōshokuyō no naifa.

palfrey [pɔ́:lfri / pɔ́l-] *n.* fujin-nori no komma.
Pali [pá:li] *n.* Pāriigo (bongo no zokugo).
paling [péiliŋ] *n.* kuiuchi ; kui ; saku. *see :* **pale.**
palisade [pæliséid] *n.* kui ; yarai. *v.* saku o yū. ∼s [pǽliseidz]
(gake, kawappuchi nado no) saku.
pall [pɔ:l] *n.* (kan, oke ya haka nado ni kakeru) kire. *v.* ōu.
pall [pɔ:l] *v.* aji ga nakunaru ; mazuku naru ; akiru ; akisaseru.
pallet [pǽlit] *n.* warabuton. (tōkishi (*potter*) no) kote.
palliate [pǽlieit] *v.* yawarageru ; benkai suru.
palliation [pæliéiʃən] *n.* kanwa ; iiwake.
palliative [pǽljətiv] *a.* kanwa suru ; yawarageru.
pallid [pǽlid] *a.* aozameta. ∼ *complexion*, aoi kao (iro).
pallor [pǽlə] *n.* sōhakuni natta kaoiro.
palm [pɑ:m] *n.* tenohira ; shuro. *v.* tenohira ni kakusu ; naisho
ni uketoru. ∼ **Sanday,** Fukkatsusai mae no Nichiyōbi. ∼**er**
n. Palestina no seichi ; junreisha. ∼ **etto** [pælmétou] *n.* isshu
no shuro (Kita-Amerika nambu no san). ∼ **ist** [pɑ:mist] *n.*
tesōmi. ∼ **istry** [pá:mistri] *n.* tesōjutsu (*palm* no suji de
uranau). ∼ **oil,** shuro abura ; wairo. ∼**y** *a.* shuro no ōi ;
sakanna.
palpable [pǽlpəbl] *a.* te de sawatte wakaru ; sugu wakaru.
palpitate [pǽlpiteit] *v.* dōki ga suru ; mune ga dokidoki suru.
palpitation [pælpitéiʃən] *n.* dōki.
palsy [pɔ́:lzi / pɔ́l-] *n.* mahi ; chūki. *v.* mahi saseru.
palter [pɔ́:ltə / pɔ́l-] *v.* gomakashi o iu ; gomakasu ; negiru.
paltry [pɔ́:ltri / pɔ́l-] *a.* tsumaranai ; kachi no nai.
pampas [pǽmpəz] *n.* (*pl.*) pampasu (Minami Amerika no daisōgen).
pamper [pǽmpə] *v.* hara ippai gochisō o tabesaseru.
pamphlet [pǽmflit] *n.* panfuretto ; shō-sasshi ∼ **eer** [-íə] *n.*
panfuretto no sakusha.
pan [pæn] *n.* nabe ; hiranabe. (*P-*) (*Gk. myth.*) bokuyō no kami. *v.* nabe de ryōri suru ; kane o dasu. ∼ *out well*, umaku
iku.
panacea [pænəsí(:)ə] *n.* bannō-yaku.
panama [pænəmá: / pǽnəma:] *n.* panamabō ; (*P-*) Panamako-
ku. *the* ∼ *Canal*, Panama Unga.

Pan-American [pǽn-əmérikən] *a.* zembei no. **~ism** *n.* Hambeishugi.

pancake [pǽnkeik] *n.* pankēki (age sembei).

pancreas [pǽŋkriəs / -iæs] *n.* (*Anat.*) suizō.

pandemonium [pæ̀ndimóunjəm / -niəm] *n.* fukumaden; shurajō.

pander [pǽndə] *v.* baishun o torimotsu; akuji o tetsudau.

pane [pein] *n.* madogarasu.

panegyric [pæ̀nidʒírik] *n.* homekotoba. **~al** [-əl] *a.* homekotoba no.

panel [pǽnəl] *n.* hameita; itae; baishin'in meibo. **~(l)ing** *n.* hameita.

pang [pæŋ] *n.* kutsū; shintsū; kumon.

panic [pǽnik] *n.* kyōkō; rōbai; panikku. *a.* dai kyōkō no. **~stricken** [-strikən] *a.* kyōkō o kitashita.

pannier [pǽniə / -njə] *n.* (uma nado no) nikago.

panoply [pǽnəpli] *n.* katchū; yoroi kabuto; gusoku.

panorama [pæ̀nərá:mə] *n.* panorama; zenkei.

panoramic [pæ̀nərǽmik] *a.* panorama (shiki) no.

pansy [pǽnzi] *n.* (*flower*) sanshikisumire.

pant [pænt] *v.* aegu; dōki ga suru; akogareru; aegi aegi iu. *n.* aegi; ikigire.

pantaloons [pæ̀ntəlú:nz] *n.,* (*pl.*) (*Am.*) zubon.

pantheism [pǽnθi(:)izəm] *n.* hanshinron.

pantheist [pǽnθiist] *n.* hanshinronsha. **pantheic(al)** [pæ̀nθiik(əl)] *a.* hanshinron no.

Pantheon [pǽnθi(:)ən / pǽnθiən] *n.* Rōma no *Panteon* no dendō.

panther [pǽnθə] *n.* hyō; Amerika hyō.

pantomime [pǽntəmaim] *n.* mugon-geki; (miburi dake no geki).

pantry [pǽntri] *n.* shokki-shitsu; shokuryō-shitsu.

pants [pænts] *n.,* (*pl.*) (*Am. col.*) zubon; zubonshita; pantsu.

pap [pæp] *n.* chikubi; akambō no yawarakai shokumotsu.

papa [pəpá:] *n.* otōsan (kodomo no kotoba).

papacy [péipəsi] *n.* Rōma Hōō no shoku mata wa kurai; Hōōseiji.

papal [péipəl] *a*. Rōma Hōō no.

paper [péipə] *n*. kami; shimbun; sono hoka kami ni kaita (insatsu) shita mono. *v*. kami de haru; kami de tsutsumu. ~ *money*, *n*. shihei. ~**-hanger** [-hæŋə] kyōjiya.

papier-mache [pæpjei-máːʃei / -mæʃei] *n*. (*Fr*.) hariko; ikkambari. ~ *mould* [pæpjei-maːʃei mould], *n*. shikei. (*printing*).

papist [péipist] *n*. Kasorikku shinja (hantaisha no imi de)

papyrus [pəpáiərəs] *n*. (*pl.* **-ri**[-ai]) kamigusa. *Egypt* de mukashi kami o tsukutta zairyō.

par [paː] *n*. byōdō.

parable [pǽrəbl] *n*. tatoebanashi; gūwa. *Jesus taught in* ~.

parabola [pərǽbələ] *n*. hōbutsusen.

parabolic [pærəbɔ́lik] *a*. hōbutsusen no.

parachute [pǽrəʃuːt / pǽrəʃúːt] *n*. rakkasan. *v*. rakkasan de kōka suru (oriru).

parade [pəréid] *n*. misebirakashi; kampeishiki. *v*. koshi suru. *make a* ~ *of*, o misebirakasu.

paradigm [pǽrədaim] *n*. mohan; katsuyō-hyō.

paradise [pǽrədais] *n*. rakuen; (*P*-) Eden no Rakuen.

paradox [pǽrədɔks] *n*. gyakusetsu. ~**ical** [pærədɔ́ksikəl] *a*. gyakusetsu no.

paraffin [pǽrəfin, / fiin] *n*. parafin; parafin'yu (abura).

paragon [pǽrəgɔn] *n*. (kanseihin no) mohan; kikan; tehon.

paragraph [pǽrəgraːf] *n*. paragurafu; paragurafu kigō (¶).

parallel [pǽrəlel] *a*. heikō no. *n*. heikōsen; heikōfugō (∥). *v*. heikō suru. ~**ism** *n*. heikō; ruiji; heikōron. ~**ogram** [pèrəlélogræm] *n*. heikōshihenkei.

paralysis [pərǽlisis / -ləs-] *n*. (*med*.) mahi; chūbū.

paralytic [pærəlítik] *a*. mahi shita; chūbūyami no. *n*. chūbū kanja.

paralyze, paralyse [pǽrəlaiz] *v*. mahi saseru.

paramount [pǽrəmaunt] *a*. saikō no; shijō no; shuyōna.

paramour [pǽrəmuə] *a*. jōfu (*female or male*).

parapet [pǽrəpit] *n*. rankan; tesuri.

paraphernalia [pèrəfənéiliə] *n*. (*pl.*) fuzokubutsu; shodōgu; tsuma no dōgu (kimono nado.)

paraphrase [pǽrəfrəiz] *n*. parafureizu. *v*. iikaeru.

parasite [pǽrəsait] *n.* isōrō (shokkyaku) ; yadokari ; kiseichū.
parasitic(al) [pὲrəsítik(l)] *a.* isōrō no ; kisei suru.
parasol [pǽrəso(:)l] *n.* (fujin'yō no) higasa.
paratroop [pǽrətru:p] *n.* (*Am.*) rakkasan-butai.
par avion [pɑ:r ɑ(:)vjo(:)n] (*Fr.*) *ad.* kōkū-bin de (*by air-mail*).
parboil [pá:bɔil] *v.* hanjuku ni suru ; udarisugiru.
parcel [pá:sl] *n.* kozutsumi ; ichi-kukaku. *v.* bumpai suru (*out*).
~ **post** [pá:slpóust] *n.* kozutsumi-yūbin.
parch [pɑ:tʃ] *v.* aburu ; kogeru (*scorch*). ~**ment** [-mənt] *n.* hitsuji no kawa no kami ; sore ni kaita monjo (shorui).
pardon [pá:dn] *n.* yurushi ; shamen ; (*leg.*) taisha ; (*rel.*) menzai *v.* yurusu. ~**able** [-əbl] *a.* yōsha dekiru ; muri mo nai. ~**ably** [-əbli] *ad.* yurusu beki.
pare [pɛə] *v.* muku. ~ *an apple*, ringo no kawa o muku ; kiritsumeru. ~ *down expenses*, hiyō o sukoshi zutsu kiritsumeru.
paregoric [pærəgɔ́rik] *a.* itamidome no. *n.* (*med.*) chintsū-zai (itamidome no kusuri).
parent [pɛ́ərənt] *n.* oya. ~**age** [-idʒ] *n.* keizu ; chisuji. ~**al** [pərɛ́ntl] *a.* oya no. ~**ally** [pərɛ́ntəli] *ad.* oyarashiku.
parenthesis [pərɛ́nθisis] *n.* (*pl.* -ses [-si:z]) sōnyūku ; maru kakko ( ).
parenthetic(al) [pærənθétik(əl)] *a.* sōnyūku no.
paresis [pǽrisis] *n.* (*med.*) kyokubu-mahi.
pariah [pǽəriə / pəráiə] *n.* Indo no saikakyū no jimmin.
Paris [pǽris] *n.* Pari (*France* no shufu).
parish [pǽriʃ] *n.*, *a.* kyōku (no.) ~**ioner** [pərʃ́(ə)nə] *n.* kyōku-min.
parity [pǽriti] *n.* dōtō. *stand at* ~, dōtō de aru.
park [pɑ:k] *n.* kōen. *v.* ennai ni ireru ; jidōsha o chūsha suru. ~**ing lot**, chūshajō.
parlance [pá:ləns] *n.* hanashiburi ; kotoba.
parley [pá:li] *n.* sōdan (shōgi) ; dampan. *v.* shōgi suru ; dampan suru.
parliament [pá:ləmənt] *n.* gikai ; (P~) Eikoku Gikai. ~**ary** [pà:ləméntəri] *a.* gikai no ; giinhō ni yoru.
parlo(u)r [pá:lə] *n.* (*Am.*) kyakuma.
parochial [pəróukiəl] *a.* kyōku no. ~ *school*, kyōku no gakkō.
parody [pǽrədi] *n.* mojiri-uta ; kaeuta. *v.* mojiru.

parole [pəróul] *n.* sensei ; kaihō sensei ; karishutsugoku-kyoka. *v.* sensei (*oath*) sasete kaihō suru (*set free*).

paroxysm [pǽrəksizm] *n.* (*med.*) hossa ; gekihatsu. ~ *of laughter*, hossatekina warai.

parquet [pá:ki] *n.* hiradoma (*the pit*) ; yosegi-zaiku.

parricide [pǽrisaid] *n.* oya-goroshi (*parent-killer*).

parrot [pǽrət] *n.* (*bird*) ōmu.

parry [pǽri] *v.*, *n.* ukenagasu (koto) ; iinukeru (koto).

parse [pɑ:z] *v.* (*gram.*) bunkai suru (*analyse*).

parsimonious [pɑ:simóuniəs] *a.* kechina.

parsimony [pá:siməni] *n.* rinshoku ; kechimbō

parsley [pá:sli] *n.* (*veg.*) paseri.

parsnip [pá:snip] *n.* (*veg.*) Oranda bōfū. ⌐bokushi-kan.

parson [pá:sn] *n.* kyōku no bokushi (*rector*). ~**age** [-idʒ] *n.*

part [pɑ:t] *n.* bubun ; yakuwari (*role*). *v.* wakeru ; wakareru. *for my* ~, jibun wa. *for the most* ~, taigai. *in good* ~, zen'i ni. ~ *and parcel*, gammoku. ~ *of speech*, (*gram.*) hinshi. *take* ~ *with*, ni mikata suru. ~**ial** [pá:ʃ(ə)l] *a.* ichibubun no ; ekohiiki no. ~**iality** [pɑ:ʃiǽliti] *n.* ekohiiki. ~**ing** [-iŋ] *a.* wakare no. *n.* wakare ; wakare michi. ~**ly** [pá:tli] *ad.* ichibubun.

partake [pa:téik] *v.* shōban suru ; ... no kibun ga aru. ~**r** [-ə] *n.* aite o suru hito ; kankeisha.

parterre [pa:téə] *n.* (*Fr.*) kadan (*flower-beds*) ; sajiki (*pit*).

participant [pa:tísipənt] *a.* kankei suru. *n.* nakama.

participate [pa:tísipeit] *v.* nakama ni naru ; kankei suru (*in*).

participation [pa:tisipéiʃən] *n.* kankei ; nakamairi.

participator [pa:tísipeitə] *n.* kankeisha ; nakama.

participial [pà:tisípiəl] *a.* (*gram.*) bunshi no.

participle [pá:t(i)sipl] *n.* (*gram.*) bunshi. ⌐inter., etc.⌐.

particle [pá:tikl] *n.* bubunshi ; (*gram.*) fuhenkashi (*prep., conj.*).

parti-colo(u)red [pá:tikʌləd] *a.* somewake no (*variagated*).

particular [pətíkjulə] *a.* tokubetsu no ; kimuzukashii. *n.* komakai koto. ~**ize** [-raiz] *v.* shōsaini noberu.

partisan (**-zan**) [pa:tizǽn] *n.* tō-in ; ichimi no hito ; yūgekihei (*guerilla soldier*). ~**ship** [pa:tizǽnʃip] *n.* tōha-shin.

partition [pa:tíʃən] *n.* kubun ; shikiri. *v.* shikiru. ~ *wall*, majikiri no kabe.

partitive [pá:titiv] *a.* kubun suru ; (*gram.*) bubunteki no.

partner [pá:tnə] *n.* nakama ; haigūsha. ~**ship** *n.* kyōryoku.

partridge [pá:tridʒ] *n.* (*bird*) shako ; raichō.

parturient [pɑ:tjúriənt] *a.* shussan no.

parturition [pà:tju(ə)ríʃən] *n.* shussan. ⌈no kabe.

party [pá:ti] *n.* tōha ; nakama ; kai (*meeting*). ~**y wall**, kyōyū

parvenu [pá:vənju:] *n.* narikin. ⌈*ster Day*)no.

paschal [pá:sk(ə)l] *a.* Sugikoshi no iwai no ; Fukkatsusai (*Ea-*

pasha [pá:ʃə] *n.* (*Turk, Egypt* no) sōtoku.

pass [pɑ:s] *v.* toki ga tatsu ; tōtte iku ; sugite iku. *n.* nyūgaku ; tsūkōken ; ryokōmenjō ; pasu ; tōge. ~ *into*, dandan ... to naru. ~ *off*, keika suru. ~ *on*, susumu ; tsugi e watasu. ~**able** [-əbl] *a.* tsūka dekiru. ~**ably** *ad.* tsūka dekiru hodo ni. ~**book** [-buk] *n.* ginkōtsūchō. ~**port** [⊥pɔ:t] *n.* ryokōmenjō. ~**word** [⊥wɔ:d] *n.* aikotoba.

passage [pǽsidʒ] *n.* tsūkō ; tsūro ; (bun no) issetsu. ~**way** [-wei] *n.* tsūro ; (*Am.*) rōka.

passenger [pǽs(i)ndʒə] *n.* ryokaku ; tsūkōnin.

passer-by [pá:səbái] *n.* tsūkōnin.

passion [pǽʃən] *n.* jōnetsu ; jōyoku ; kanshaku. *have a ~ for*, o konomu. P~ *Sunday*, Shijunsetsu (*Lent*)-chū no dai-5(go) Nichiyōbi. P~ *Week*, Shijunsetsu-chū no dai-5(go) shūkan. ~**ate** [-it] *a.* tankina ; netsuretsuna. ~**ately** [-itli] *ad.* tankini ; kanjōtekini ; nesshinni. ⌈kutekini.

passive [pǽsiv] *a.* ukemi no ; (*gram.*) judōtai. ~**ly** *ad.* shōkyo-

Passover [pá:souvə] *n.* Sugikoshi no iwai. ⌈o sugite.

past [pɑ:st] *a.* kako no. *n.* kako no keireki (*career*). *prep. ad.*

paste [peist] *n.* nori ; mozō-hōseki. *v.* nori de haru. ~**board** [⊥bɔ:d] *n.* daishi ; itagami.

pastel [pǽstel] *n.* pasuteru.

pastern [pǽstə:n] *n.* uma (*horse*) no kurubushi no hone.

pasteurization [pæ̀stəraizéiʃən] *n.* teionsakkin.

pasteurize [pǽstəraiz] *v.* teion sakkin suru.

pastime [pá:staim] *n.* nagusami ; yūgi.

pastor [pá:stə] *n.* bokushi. ~**al** [-rəl] *a.* inaka no ; bokushi no. *n.* den'enshi. ~**ate** [-rit] *n.* bokushi no shoku.

pastry [péistri] *n.* neriko-gashi.

pasturage [pá:stʃuridʒ] *n.* bokujō (kusaki no shigette iru).

pasture [pá:stʃə] *n.* bokusō no aru bokujō. *v.* hōboku suru (*graze*).

pat [pæt] *a.* tekisetsuna. *a* ~*reply*, tekitōna henji ; (*Am.*) kotei shita (*fixed*). *n.* karuku tataku koto ; naderu koto *v.* aibu suru ; naderu.

patch [pætʃ] *n.* tsugihagi ; chiisai tochi ; kao no kizu ni tsuketa chiisai kire ; hatake (*farm*). *v.* tsugi o ateru. ~**work** [-wə:k] *n.* tsugihagi (zaiku.)

pate [peit] *n.* atama ; nōten (*head*).

patent [peit(ə)nt] *a.* sembaitokkyo no. *n.* sembaitokkyo. *v.* sembaitokkyo o ukeru. P~ *Office*, Tokkyokyoku.

patentee [peit(ə)ntí:] *n.* sembaitokkyo-ken shoyūsha.

paternal [pətə́:nl] *a.* chichioya (*father*) no. ⌈gen (*origin*).

paternity [pətə́:niti] *n.* chichioya (*father*) to naru koto ; kon-

paternoster [pǽtənə́stə] *n.* shu no inori. ⌈life).

path [pɑ:θ] (*pl.* -s [pɑ:ðz]) *n.* komichi ; jinsei-kōro (*course of*

pathetic [pəθétik] *a.* awarena. ~**ally** [-əli] *ad.* awareni.

pathology [pəθɔ́lədʒi] *n.* byōrigaku. ~**gical** [pæ̀θəlɔ́dʒik(ə)l] byōrigaku no.

pathos [péiθəs] *n.* aware o moyōsu chikara.

patience [péiʃ(ə)ns] *n.* nintai.

patient [péiʃ(ə)nt] *a.* shimbō-zuyoi. *n.* byōnin ; kanja.

patio [pá:tjou] *n.* (*Sp.*) uchi-niwa.

patois [pǽtwa:] *n.* (*Fr.*) hōgen.

patriarch [péitriɑ:k] *n.* kachō ; zokuchō (*head of clan*). ~**al** [peitriá:k(ə)l] *a.* kachō no.

patrician [pətríʃən] *n.* kodai Rōma no kizoku. *a.* kizoku no.

pathway [pá:θwei] *n.* ko-michi (*path*).

patricide [pǽtrisaid] *n.* chichi-goroshi. ⌈no ; seshū no.

patrimonial [pætrimóunjəl] *a.* senzo denrai no ; seshū zaisan

patrimony [pǽtriməni] *n.* seshū zaisan ; katoku ; kyōkai zaisan.

patriot [péitriət / pǽt-] *n.* aikokusha. ~**ic** [pæ̀triɔ́tik] *a.* aikoku no. ~**ism** [pǽtriətizm] *n.* aikokushin.

patrol [pətróul] *n.* junkai ; patorōru. *v.* junkai suru. ~**man** [-mən] *n.* junkai junsa (*policeman*).

patron [péitr(ə)n] *n.* patoron ; kōensha. *a.* kōen suru. : *a* ~*of* *the arts*, geijutsu kōensha; hiiki-kyaku. ～**age** [pǽtrənidʒ] *n.* kōen. ～**ize** [pǽtrənaiz] *v.* kōen suru.

patronymic [pæ̀trənímik] *a.* sosen (*ancestors*) no na (*name*) kara deta. *n.* myōji (*surname*).

patten [pǽtn] *n.* (nukarumi de kutsu no ue ni haku) kigutsu.

patter [pǽtə] *n.* patapata to iu oto; hayakuchi. *v.* patapata iu; hayakuchi ni shaberu.

pattern [pǽtən] *n.* mokei; mihon (*sample*). *v.* maneru (*imitate*);

paucity [pɔ́:siti] *n.* shōsū; shōryō; futtei (*scarcity*).

paunch [pɔ:ntʃ] *n.* hara; hoteibara.

pauper [pɔ́:pə] *n.* himmin. ～**ism** [-rizm] *n.* bimbō. ～**ize** [-raiz] *v.* bimbō ni saseru.

pause [pɔ:z] *n.* chūshi; kugiri (*punctuation*). *v.* kugiru.

pave [peiv] *v.* dōro o hosō suru. ～**ment** [⸍mənt] *n.* hosōdōro.

pavilion [pəvíljən] *n.* dai-temmaku. *bathing* ～, suieijō no dai-temmaku; yagai kyūgojo. ⌐moyō (*figure*) o tsukeru. ⌐de hikkaku.

paw [pɔ:] *n.* (kemono no) ashi; hito no te (*hand*). *v.* maeashi

pawl [pɔ:l] *n.* (gyakumodori senu yōni suru) ha-dome.

pawn [pɔ:n] *n.* teitōbutsu; fu (shōgi no.) ～**broker** [⸍broukə] *n.* shichi-ya. ～**shop** [⸍ʃɔp] *n.* shichi-mise.

pay [pei] *n.* shiharai. *v.* harau. **paid; paying.** harau. ～ *down*, sokkin de harau. ～ *off*, (*debt*), zembu o shiharau; fukushū suru. ～ *one's way*, shakkin sezu ni yatte iku. ～ *out*, shiharau. ～**able** [péiəbl] *a.* shiharai dekiru. ～**day** [⸍dei] *n.* shiharaibi; kyūryōbi. ～**ee** [-í:] *n.* tegata no uketorinin. ～**master** *n.* kaikeigakari. ～**ment** [-mənt] *n.* shiharai. ～**roll** [péiroul] *n.* kyūryōshiharaibo.

pea [pi:] *n.* (*pl.* -s *or* **pease** [pi:z]) endō-mame. ⌐haraibo.

peace [pi:s] *n.* heiwa. ～**able** [pí:səbl] *a.* heiwa o konomu. ～**ful** [pi:sf(u)l] *a.* heiwana.

peach [pi:tʃ] *n.* momo (*fruit*). *v.* (*col.*) tsugeguchi suru.

peacock [pí:kɔk] *n.* kuʃaku (osu).

peafowl [pí:faul] *n.* kujaku (*peacock or peahen*).

peahen [pí:hen] *n.* mesu (*female*) kujaku.

peak [pi:k] *n.* chōjō. ～**ed** [-t] *a.* togatta; *peak* no aru.

peal [pí:l] *n.* dodōn to iu hibiki. *v.* todoroku.

peanut [pí:nʌt] *n.* rakkasei; piinatsu.

pear [pɛə] *n.* (*bot.*) nashi.

pearl [pə:l] *n.* shinju; shinju-iro. ∼ **oyster** shinjugai.

peasant [péz(ə)nt] *n.* nōfu. ∼**ry** [-ri] *n.* nōmin (zentai to shite).

peat [pi:t] *n.* deitan (isshu no sekitan).

pebble [pébl] *n.* koishi. ∼**bly** [-i] *a.* koishi no ōi.

peccadillo [pèkədílou] *n.* bizai.

peck [pek] *n.* pekku (Igirisu no masume; 9.092 *litres*); tsuibami (*bird*). *v.* tsuttsuku. **wood-pecker** [wúdpèkə] *n.* kitsutsuki.

pectoral [péktərəl] *a.* mune no (∼ *muscles*). *n.* munakazari.

peculate [pékjuleit] *v.* itakukin o shōhi suru; kōkin o shōhi suru (*embezzle*). ∼**tion** [pekjuléiʃ(ə)n] *n.* kōkin shōhi.

peculiar [pikjú:ljə] *a.* dokutoku no. ∼**ly** *ad.* tokuni. ∼**ity** [pikjù:liǽriti] *n.* tokushoku (*speciality*); kuse.

pecuniary [pikjú:niəri] *a.* kinsenjō no.

pedagog(ue) [pédəgəg] *n.* sensei; kyōshi; gakushaburu hito (*pedantic person*).

pedagogy [pédəgəgi] *n.* kyōiku no riron to jissai.

pedal [pédl] *a.* pedaru no; ashi (*foot*) no. *n.* pedaru (piano, jitensha nado no.).

pedant [péd(ə)nt] *n.* esegakusha. ∼**ic** [pidǽntik] *a.* gakushaburu. ∼**ry** [-ri] *n.* gakushaburu koto.

peddle [pédl] *v.* gyōshō suru. ∼**r** [-ə] *n.* gyōshōnin.

pedestal [pédist(ə)l] *n.* dai (*stand*); kontei (*foundation*).

pedestrian [pidéstriən] *a.* toho no. *n.* tohozuki; hokōsha

pedigree [pédigri:] *n.* keizu; kigen (*derivation*);okori.

pedlar, peddler [pédlə] *n.* gyōshōnin.

peek [pi:k] *v.* sotto nozoku. *n.* sotto nozoku koto.

peel [pi:l] *n.* kawa. *v.* kawa o muku.

peep [pi:p] *n.* hiyoko no nakigoe; nozokimi. *v.* piyopiyo naku. nozoku. ∼ **show**, nozoki-karakuri.

peer [piə] *v.* jitto (*intently*) miru; mie hajimeru. *n.* dōhai (*one's equal*); kizoku (*nobleman*). *without a* ∼, murui no. ∼**age** [píəridʒ] *n.* kizoku kaikyū. ∼**ess** [píəris] *n.* kizoku fujin. ∼**less** [píəlis] *a.* murui no.

peevish [pí:viʃ] *a.* okorippoi. ［hataraku (*work hard*).

peg [peg] *n.* ki-kugi; kugi; kui (*tent* ∼). *v.* kugi o utsu; sesseto

pelagic [piládʒik] *a.* ōunabara no; tōi kaijō no.

pelf [pelf] *n.* fuseina zaisan (*ill-gotten wealth*).

pelican [pélikən] *n.* (*bird*) perikan. ⌐(*pill*).
pellet [pélit] *n.* chiisai tama; shō-dangan; chiisai gan'yaku
pell-mell [pélmél] *ad.* muyami ni; ōsawagi shite.
pellucid [peljú:sid] *a.* tōmeina; meiryōna (*clear*).
pelt [pelt] *n.* nama-gawa; kegawa. *v.* ame (*rain*) ga tsuyoku
(*heavily*) furu.
pelvis [pélvis] *n.* (*anat.*) kotsuban. ⌐(*food*).
pemmican [pémikən] *n.* (*Am.*) hoshita niku no keitai-kōryō.
pen [pen] *n.* pen; buntai. ori (*fold*). *v.* penned *or* pent; pen-
ning. kaku (*write*). tojikomeru ∼-name [‐neim] *n.* gagō.
P.E.N. Kokusai Pen Kurabu. (*International Association of Poets,
Playwriter, Editors, Essayists and Novelists.*)
penal [pí:nl] *a.* keibatsu no; keijijō no (*criminal*).
penalty [pénəlti] *n.* keibatsu; bakkin (*fine*).
penance [pénəns] *n.* kuiaratame (*repentance*); kugyō.
pence [pens] *n. see :* penny (péni)
penchant [pā:nʃā:ŋ] *n.* (*Fr.*) keikō; shumi (*taste*).
pencil [péns(i)l] *n.* empitsu.
pendant, pendent [péndənt] *n.* burasagaru mono; mimiwa.
a. tareta; mitei no. ⌐... no aida.
pending [péndiŋ] *a.* chūburarin no; mikettei no. *prep.* ...jū,
pendulous [péndjuləs] *a.* burasagatte iru; yureru.
pendulum [péndjuləm] *n.* (*clock* no) furiko.
penetrable [pénitrəbl] *a.* hairikomareru.
penetrate [pénitreit] *v.* hairikomu; shimikomu; minuku.
penetration [penitréiʃən] *n.* naka ni hairikomu koto. kampa.
penguin [péŋgwin] *n.* (*bird*) penginchō.
penicillin [pènisílin] *n.* (*med.*) penishirin. ⌐∼r *a.* hantō no.
peninsula [pinínsjulə] *n.* hantō (*P∼.* = *the Iberian Peninsula*)
penitence [pénit(ə)ns] *n.* kōkai (no nen).
penitent [pénit(ə)nt] *a.* kuiaratameta. ∼ial [peniténʃ(ə)l] *a.*
kōkai no. ∼iary [peniténʃ(ə)ri] *a.* kaigo no; (*Am.*) keimusho
(*prison*) iri no *n.* keimusho.
penknife [pénnaif] *n.* kaichū-naifu. ⌐*n.* shūji; hisseki.
penman [pénmən] *n.* shoka; chosakusha (*writer*). ∼ship
pennant [pénənt] *n.* saki no hosoi nagai hata; sankakuki.
pennon [pénən] *n.* hosonagai (*narrow*) sankakuki.

penny [péni] *n.* (*pl.* **pennies** [péniz] maisū ; **pence** [pens] kanedaka) (*Am.*) sent (*cent*). **～less** [-lis] *a.* mon-nashi no. **～wise** [wáiz] *a.* ichi-mon oshimi no (**～-and pound-foolish**).

penology [pi:nɔ́lədʒi] *n.* keibatsu-gaku.

pension [pénʃən] *n.* nenkin (*annuity*) ; onkyū ; onkyūkyoku (*The Bureau of P～s*). *v.* onkyū o ataeru. **～er** [-ə] *n.* onkyū juryōsha (*receiver*).

pensive [pénsiv] *a.* kangaekonde iru.

pent [pent] *v. see*: **pen**, tojikomeru. *a.* tojikomerareta. **～-up** [péntʌp] *a.* kitchiri shimatta.

pentagon [péntəgən] *n.* 5(go) kakukei ; 5(go) henkei.

Pentateuch [péntətju:k] *n.* Mōze (*Moses* [móuziz] *in the Bible* no 5)(go) sho ; Kyūyaku Seisho no saisho no 5kan.

Pentecost [péntikə(:)st] *n.* gojunsetsu (Yudayajin no matsuri) ; seirei kōrinsetsu.

penthouse [pénthaus] *n.* sashikake-yane (*roof*) ; (*Am.*) okujō-jūtaku.

penult [penʌlt / pí:nəlt] *n.* gobi kara 2-(ni)bamme no onsetsu (*syllable*).

penumbra [pinʌ́mbrə] *n.* (*pl.* **-brae** [-bri:] ; **-s**) taiyō ya tsuki no kage no mawari no han'in'ei.

penurious [pinjúəriəs] *a.* kechina (*stingy*).

penury [pénjuri] *n.* bimbō.

penwiper [pénwaipə] *n.* penfuki.

peon [pí:ən] *n.* shakkin (*debt*) no kata ni hataraku rōdōsha.

peony [píəni] *n.* (*bot.*) shakuyaku. **tree～** *n.* botan.

people [pí:pl] *n.* kokumin (*nation*). *v.* ...ni shokumin suru.

pep [pep] *v.* (*Am. col.*) genki-zukeru. *n.* genki.

pepper [pépə] *n.* koshō. *v.* koshō o furikakeru. **～mint** [-mint] *n.* hakka(-yu). **～y** [-ri] *a.* koshō no yōna ; karai (*pungent*).

peppy [pépi] *a.* genkiippai no.

pepsin [pépsin] *n.* pepushin ; i-eki-so.

peptic [péptik] *a.* shōka o yoku suru.

per [pə:] *prep.* ...ni tsuki.

peradventure [pərədvéntʃə] *ad.* osoraku. *n.* utagai ; gūzen.

perambulate [pərǽmbjuleit] *v.* arukimawaru.

perambulation [pərǽmbjuléiʃən] *n.* haikai ; junkai (*trip*).

perambulator [pərǽmbjuleitə] *n.* ubaguruma.

perceive [pə(:)síːv] v. chikaku suru ; wakaru ; satoru.

per cent [pə(:)sént] n. hyakubunritsu. *Only small ~ of the class was (or were) present,* kurasu no goku shōsū ga shusseki shi mashita. **percentage** [pə(:)séntidʒ] n. hyaku-bun ritsu.

per centum [pə séntəm] (*L.*) =**per cent.** (*La*). hyaku (*one hundred*) ni tsuki.

percept [pə́ːsept] n. chikaku no taishō. **~ible** [pə(:)séptəbl] a. ki ga tsuku hodo no. **~bly** [pə:séptəbli] ad. medatsu hodo. **~ion** [pə(:)sépʃən] n. ninshiki. **~ive** [pə(:)séptiv] a. chikaku suru ; satori no hayai.

perch [pəːtʃ] n. suzuki (*fish*) ; (*for bird*) tomarigi ; shakudo no tan'i (*5.03 meters*). v. tomaru.

perchance [pə(:)tʃáːns] ad. tabun (*maybe*).

percipience [pəːsípiəns] n. ninchi ; chikaku.

percipient [pə(:)sípiənt] a. ninchi suru ; chikaku suru.

percolate [pə́ːkəleit] v. kosu (*filter*) ; shimitōru.

percussion [pə(:)kʌ́ʃən] n. shōtotsu ; (taiko nado) utsu koto.

perdition [pəːdíʃən] n. hametsu (tamashii no) ; jigoku (*hell*).

peregrination [pèrigrinéiʃən] n. rurō (*wandering*) ; ryokō (*traveling*).

peremptory [pərém(p)t(ə)ri] a. danko to shita ; ketteitekina.

perennial [pəréniəl] a. eikyū no ; tanensei no.

perfect [pə́ːfikt] a. kanzenna. n. (*gram.*) kanryō jisei (*~ tense*). **~ible** [pə(:)féktibl] a. kansei dekiru. **~ly** [pə́ːfik(t)li] ad. zenzen ; sukkari. **~ion** [pə(:)fékʃ(ə)n] n. kanzen ; emman (*harmony*).

perfidious [pə(:)fídiəs] a. fujitsuna ; uragiru.

perfidy [pə́ːfidi] n. fujitsu ; uragiri (*treachery*).

perforate [pə́ːfəreit] n. ana o akeru ; tsuranuku.

perforation [pə̀ːfəréiʃən] n. ana o akeru koto ; tsukinukeru koto.

perforce [pə(:)fɔ́ːs] ad. chikara-zuku de ; zehi tomo (*by all means*).

perform [pəfɔ́ːm] v. okonau ; enzuru (geki o) ; sōsuru (*music*). **~ance** [-əns] n. jikkō ; ensō ; kōgyō. **~er** [-ə] n. jikkōsha ; yakusha.

perfume [pəfjúːm] v. nioi o tsukeru. n. [pə́ːfjuːm] kōryō ; kōsui. **~ry** [pəfjúːməri] n. kōsui. (seizōsho, hambaiten).

perhaps [pəhǽps] ad. tabun, osoraku.

perigee [péridʒi:] *n.* (*astr.*) kinchiten (tsuki no (*orbit*) unkō de ichiban chikyū ni chikai tokoro.)

perihelion [perihí:liən] *n.* (*astr.*) kinjitsuten. (*planet* no unkō de ichiban taiyō ni chikai ten.)

peril [péril] *n.* kiken. ⁓**ous** [-əs] *a.* kikenna.

perimeter [pərímitə] *n.* shūi ; shiya o hakaru kikai.

period [píəriəd] *n.* jidai ; kikan ; shūketsu ; shūshifu (*full stop*). ⁓**ic** [piəríɔdik] *a.* toki no (*cyclical*). ⁓**ical** [-(ə)l] *a.* teiki-kankōbutsu no. *n.* teiki-kankōbutsu. ⁓**ically** [-əlí] *ad.* teikini.

peripatetic [peripətétik] *a.* arukimawaru.

periphery [pərífəri] *n.* shūi ; gaimen. *The* ⁓ *of a circle is called circumference*, en no shūi wa enshū to ii masu.

periscope [périskoup] *n.* perisukōpu ; sembōkyō (sensuikan no nozoki-megane).

perish [périʃ] *v.* shinu (*die*) ; kusaru. ⁓**able** [-əbl] *a.* shinubeki (*mortal*) ; kusariyasui. ⁓**s** *n.* kusariyasui mono.

peritonitis [pèritənáitis] *n.* (*med.*) fukumaku-en.

perjure [pə́:dʒə] *v.* gishō suru (*oneself*). ⁓**r** [-rə] *n.* gishōsha.

perjury [pə́:dʒ(ə)ri] *n.* gishō ; gishōzai (*crime by* ⁓).

perk [pə:k] *v.* migirei ni suru ; kidoru (*smarten*).

permanence [pə́:mənəns] *n.* eikyū ; fuhen.

permanent [pə́:mənənt] *a.* eizoku suru ; fuhen no.

permeable [pə́:miəbl] *a.* shimitōru. ⁓**bly** [-bli] *ad.*

permeate [pə́:mieit] *v.* shimikomu ; fukyū suru (*spread*).

permeation [pə:miéiʃən] *n.* shintō (shimitōru).

permissible [pəmísibl] *a.* yurusu beki. ⁓**bly** [-bli] *ad.* yuru-
permission [pə(:)míʃən] *n.* kyoka. ⌊sarete.

permissive [pə(:)mísiv] *a.* kyoka suru ; kyoka sareta.

permit [pə:mít] *v.* kyoka suru. [pə́:mit] *n.* kyoka ; menkyojō (*licence*).

permutation [pə:mju:téiʃən] *n.* kōkan ; (*math.*) junretsu.

pernicious [pə:níʃəs] *a.* gaidoku no ; chimeiteki no (*fatal*).

peroration [pèrəréiʃən] *n.* (enzetsu ya tōron no) owari no bubun.

perpendicular [pə̀:p(ə)ndíkjulə] *a.* suichoku no. *n.* (*math.*) sui

perpetrate [pə́:pitreit] *v.* (tsumi o) okasu. ⌊sen ; suichoku.

perpetration [pə̀:pitréiʃən] *n.* hanzai.

perpetrator [pə́:pitreitə] *n.* hanzaisha.

perpetual [pəpétju(ə)l] *a.* eikyū no ; taezaru.

perpetuate [pə(:)pétjueit] *v.* eizoku saseru ; eikyūni nokosu.

perpetuation [pə(:)pètjuéiʃən] *n.* eizoku.

perpetuity [pə̀:pitjú(:)iti] *n.* eikyū ; eizoku ; shūshin nenkin.

perplex [pəpléks] *v.* komaraseru.

perplexity [pəpléksiti] *n.* tōwaku ; konran (*confusion*).

perquisite [pə́:kwizit] *n.* yakutoku ; teate (*allowance*) ; kokoro-zuke (*tip*).

persecute [pə́:sikju:t] *v.* kurushimeru ; hakugai suru.

persecution [pə̀:sikjú:ʃən] *n.* hakugai.

persecutor [pə́:sikju:tə] *n.* hakugaisha.

perseverance [pə̀:sivíərəns] *n.* kennin fubatsu ; nintai.

persevere [pə:sivíə] *v.* gaman suru ; shimbō suru (*endure*).

persiflage [pèəsiflá:ʒ] *n.* (*Fr.*) hiyakashi ; karui jōdan.

persimmon [pə:símən] *n.* (*fruit*) kaki.

persist [pə(:)síst] *v.* gambaru. ∼ence [-(ə)ns], ∼ency [-(ə)nsi] *n.* shitsukkoi koto ; taikyūsei. ∼ent [-(ə)nt] *a.* koshitsu suru ; eizokusei no (*ever lasting*).

person [pə́:sn] *n.* hito ; yōshi (*external appearance*) ; (*gram.*) ninshō. ∼able [-əbl] *a.* fūsai no yoi. ∼age [-idʒ] *n.* kōki no (*of high rank*) hito ; (geki no) jimbutsu. ∼al [-(ə)l] *a.* kojin no ; honnin no. ∼ality [pə̀:s(ə)næliti] *n.* jinkaku (*character*) ; kosei. ∼alty [-(ə)lti] *n.* (*leg.*) kojin no shoyūchi (*personal estate*). ∼ate [pə̀:səneit] *v.* yaku o tsutomeru. ∼ification [pə:sònifikéiʃən] *n.* gijin ; keshin ; jinkaku o ataeru. ∼ify [pə:sónifai] *v.* gijin suru (ningen toshite atsukau). ∼nel [pə̀:sənél] *n.* sono naka no hito-tachi o issho ni shite mita mono ; shokuin ; jin'

perspective [pə(:)spéktiv] *a.* enkinhō no. *n.* enkingahō. [in.

perspicacious [pə̀:spikéiʃəs] *a.* wakari no hayai ; sōmeina.

perspicacity [pə̀:spikǽsti] *n.* sōmei ; eibin.

perspicuity [pə̀:spikjú:iti] *n.* meiryō.

perspicuous [pə(:)spíkjuəs] *a.* meihakuna ; sugu wakaru.

perspiration [pə̀:spəréiʃən] *n.* ase (*sweat*) ; hakkan.

perspire [pəspáiə] *v.* ase ga deru ; hakkan suru.

persuade [pə(:)swéid] *v.* tokifuseru ; nattoku saseru.

persuasion [pə(:)swéiʒən] *n.* settoku ; kan'yū.

persuasive [pəswéisiv] *a.* kuchi no umai.

pert [pə:t] *a.* atsukamashii ; buenryona.

pertain [pə:téin] *v.* zoku suru ; kan suru.

pertinacious [pə:tinéiʃəs] *a.* gankona.

pertinacity [pə:tinǽsiti] *n.* ganko ; gōjō (*persistency*).

pertinence [pɔ́:tinɔns] *n.* tekisetsu ; tekitō.

pertinent [pɔ́:tinənt] *a.* tekisetsuna.

perturb [pə(:)tɔ́:b] *v.* konran saseru. *Mother was much ~ed by my illness,* haha wa watashi no byōki de hidoku urotaete i mashi-ta. **~ation** [pɔ̀:təbéiʃən] *n.* dōyō ; rōbai.

perusal [pərú:z(ə)l] *n.* jukudoku (*careful reading*).

peruse [pərú:z] *v.* jukudoku suru.

pervade [pə:véid] *v.* shintō suru ; hiroku fukyū suru (*spread*).

pervasion [pə(:)véiʒən] *n.* shintō (*permeating*) ; fukyū.

pervasive [pə(:)véisiv] *a.* yukiwataru (*spreading*).

perverse [pəvɔ́:s] *a.* konjō (*nature*) no magatta (*crooked*) ; iji-waru no (*cross*). ⌈born).

perversion [pə(:)vɔ́:ʃən] *n.* akka (*becoming worse*) ; kataiji (*stub-*

perversity [pə(:)vɔ́:siti] *n.* gōjō. ⌈raku ; akuyō.

pervert [pə(:)vɔ́:t] *v.* daraku suru (*degenerate*). *n.* [pɔ́:vɔ:t] da-

pervious [pɔ́:viəs] *a.* shimikomu (*permeable*). kanzuru. *Sand is easily ~ to water,* suna wa mizu o yōini shimikomaseru

peso [péisou] *n.* peso (Supein no kahei (*coin*)).

pessimism [pésimizm] *n.* enseishugi ; hikanshugi.

pessimist [pésimist] *n.* hikanshugisha. **~ic** [pèsimístik] *a. a.* enseiteki.

pest [pest] *n.* kokushibyō ; pesuto ; yakkaina hito (koto). **~house** [pésthaus] *n.* hibyōin.

pester [péstə] *v.* nayamasu ; komarasu.

pestiferous [pəstífərəs] *a.* densen suru ; yūdokuna (*noxious*).

pestilence [péstiləns] *n.* (pesuto, kōnetsubyō, tennentō nado no) densembyō. ⌈ful).

pestilent [péstilənt] *a.* chimeitekina (*deadly*) ; yūgaina (*harm-*

pestilential [pestilénʃəl] *a.* densembyō no (*epidemic*) ; yūgaina (*harmful*). ⌈(*pound*).

pestle [pes(t)l] *n.* kine ; nyūbō. *v.* kine (*pestle*) de tsuku

pet [pet] *n.* aigan dōbutsu ; fukigen (*ill humour*). *a.* kiniiri no.

v. chōai suru ; kawaigaru.

petal [pétl] *n.* (*bot.*) kaben, hanabira. ⌐ita).

petard [petá:d] *n.* bakuha sōchi (mukashi wa sensō ni mochi-

petition [pitíʃən] *n.* seigan. *v.* seigan suru.

petrel [pétrəl] *n.* (*bird*) umi-tsubame.

petrifaction [petrifǽkʃən] *n.* sekka (*petrifying*) ; kaseki (*fossil*).

petrify [pétrifai] *v.* kaseki suru ; ugokenaku naru (*fig*).

petrol [pétrəl] *n.* gasorin (*gasolene*).

petroleum [pitróuliəm] *n.* sekiyu.

petticoat [pétikout] *n.* (fujin no) shitagi.

pettifogger [pétifɔgə] *n.* sambyaku daigen.

pettish [pétiʃ] *a.* okorippoi ; ijiwaruna.

petty [péti] *a.* sukoshi no ; tsumaranai (*trifling*). ⌐*temper*).

petulance [pétjuləns], ∼**cy** [-si] *n.* suneru koto ; tanki (*quick-*

petulant [pétjulənt] *a.* okorippoi (*touchy*) ; tankina.

petunia [pitjú:njə] *n.* tsukubane asagao (*flow.*) ; kurai murasa-

pew [pju:] *n.* kyōkai (*church*) no zaseki (*seat*). ⌐ki-iro.

pewit [pí:wit] *n.* (*bird*) tageri ; isshu no kamome.

pewter [pjú:tə] *n.* hakurō (*alloy of tin and lead*).

phaeton [fé(i)tn] *n.* (isshu no) yonrin-basha ; jidōsha (*car*).

phalanx [fǽlæŋks] *n.* (*pl.* ∼**es** [-iz] ; ∼**langes** [-lændʒi:z]) (*Am.*) *Greek* no hōjin (*square formation*) ; misshūgun.

phantasm [fǽntæzm] *n.* maboroshi ; kūsō (*fancy*). ∼**al** [fæn-tǽzməl] *a.* maboroshi no ; kūsōteki.

phantasy [fǽntəsi] *n.* kūsō ; kimyōna (*strange*) ishō (*design*).

phantom [fǽntəm] *n.* yūrei ; sakkaku (*illusion*).

pharisaic(al) [færiséiik(əl)] *a.* Parisai (*Pharisee*)-ha no ; gizen no (*hypocritical*). ⌐sha (*hypocrite*).

Pharisee [fǽrisi:] *n.* Parisai-ha no hito-tachi (*fellow*) ; gizen

pharmaceutic [fɑ:məsjú:tik] *a.* chōzaihō no ; seiyaku no. ∼**s** *n.* chōzaigaku. ∼**al** [-əl] *a.* chōzaihō no.

pharmacopoeia [fɑ:məkəpí:ə] *n.* kusuri no shiyōhō o kaita

pharmacy [fá:məsi] *n.* yakugaku ; yakkyoku. ⌐hon.

pharynx [fǽriŋks] *n.* (*anat.*) intō ; nodo no jōbu.

phase [feiz] *n.* jōtai ; keisei. (mondai nado no) men.

pheasant [féznt] *n.* (*bird*) kiji.

phenacetin(e) [fináesətin] *n.* fenasetin ; genetsuzai.

phenix, phoenix [fí:niks] *n.* eikyūni shinanai tori.
phenomenal [finɔ́minəl] *a.* genshō no ; marena ; subarashii.
phenomenon [finɔ́minən] *n.* (*pl.* **-na**) genshō.
phial [fáiəl] *n.* garasubin (kogata no).
philanthropic [fìlənθrɔ́pik / -θrə-] *a.* hakuai no.
philanthropy [filǽnθrəpi] *n.* hakuai ; jinruiai. ∼**ist** *n.* jizenka.
philatelist [filǽtəlist] *n.* kitte nado atsumeru hito.
philharmonic [fìlhɑːmɔ́nik] *a.* ongakuzukina.
Philippine [fílipi:n] *a.* Firippin no. **the ∼ Islands.** Firippin Guntō.
philology [filɔ́lədʒi] *n.* bunkengaku. ∼**ical** *a.* ∼ no. ∼**ist** *n.*
philosopher [filɔ́səfə] *n.* tetsugakusha. ⌊∼ gakusha.
philosophic(al) [fìləsɔ́fik(əl)] *a.* tetsugaku no. ∼**ally** *ad.*
philosophize [filɔ́səfaiz] *v.* rikutsu o kiwameru.
philosophy [filɔ́səfi] *n.* tetsugaku.
philter, -tre [fíltə] *n.* horegusuri.
phlegm [flem] *n.* (kuchi kara deru) tan.
phlegmatic [flegmǽtik] *a.* tammochi no ; reiseina. ∼ **temperament,** nen'ekishitsu.
phoenix [fí:niks] *n. see* : **phenix.**
phone [foun] *n.* denwa. gengoon ; *v.* denwa o kakeru.
phonetic [founétik] *a.* onsei no. ∼ **alphabet,** hatsuon fugō. ∼**ally** *ad.* hatsuon dōrini ∼**s** *n.* onseigaku.
phonic [fóunik] *a.* onsei no.
phonograph [fóunəgrɑːf] *n.* chikuonki. ∼**ic** [fòunəgrǽfik] *a.* hyōon no ; chikuonki no. ∼**y** [founɔ́grəfi] *n.* sokkihō.
phosphate [fɔ́sfeit] *n.* (*chem.*) rinsan'en.
phosphorescence [fɔ̀sfərésns] *n.* (*min.*) rinkō ; keikō.
phosphorescent [fɔ̀sfərésnt] *a.* rinkō o hassuru.
phosphoric [fɔ̀sfɔ́(:)rik] *a.* rin no fukumu.
phosphorus [fɔ́sfərəs] *n.* (*pl.* **-ri** [rai]) (*chem.*) rin.
photo [fóutou] *n.* shashin. ∼**finish,** *n.* shashin ni yoru shōbu no hantei. ∼ **engraving** [-ingréiviŋ] *n.* shashin toppan jutsu. ∼**genic** [-dʒénik] *a.* shashin ni yoku utsuru. ∼ **montage** [-montá:ʒ] *n.* gōseishashin. ∼**graph** [fóutəgrǽf] *n.* shashin. *v.* satsuei suru ; shashin ni utsuru. ∼**graphy** *n.* shashinjutsu. ∼**telegraph** [-téləgræf] *n.* densō-shashin. ∼**telegraphy** *n*

densō-shashinjutsu.

phrase [freiz] *n.* ku ; jukugo. *v.* kotoba de noberu. ~**ology** [-ólədʒi] *n.* kotobazukai. ⌐kossōgakusha.

phrenology [frinólədʒi / fre-] *n.* kossōgaku. ~**ical** *a.* ~**ist** *n.*

physic [fízik] *n.* igaku. *v.* gezai o kakeru. ~**al** *a.* butsurigaku no ; nikutaiteki no. ~**s** *n.* butsurigaku. ~**ian** [fizíʃən] *n.* isha. ~**ist** [fízisist] *n.* butsurigakusha.

physiognomy [fìziógnəmi] *n.* ninsōgaku. ⌐chiri gakusha.

physiography [fìziógrəfi] *n.* shizenchirigaku. ~**er** *n.* shizen-

physiology [fìziólədʒi] *n.* seirigaku. ~**ical** *a.* ~**ist** *n.* seiri-

physique [fizíːk] *n.* taikaku. ⌊gakusha.

P.I. = Philippine Islands.

pianist [piǽnist] *n.* pianisuto.

piano [piǽnou], ~**forte** [piǽnoufɔ́:ti] *n.* piano.

piazza [piǽzə] *n.* (*It.*) hiroba ; ichiba.

picaresque [pikərésk] *a.* akkan o daizai ni shita.

piccolo [píkəlou] *n.* (*mus.*) pikkoro (kōon no fue).

pick [pik] *v.* tsutsuku ; hojiru. *n.* hojiru mono ; koyōji. ~**ax(e)** [⌐æks] *n.* tsuruhashi. ~**ing** *n.* saishū. ~**pocket** [⌐pɔkit] *n.* suri. ~**up** [píkʌp] *a.* (*Am.*) yoseatsume no. *n.* (*Am. col.*) horidashi-mono.

picket [píkit] *n.* kui ; pike. *v.* (uma nado o) kui ni tsunagu.

pickle [píkl] *n.* tsukeshiru ; (*pl.*) tsukemono. *v.* tsukeru. *in a*

picnic [píknik] *n.* pikunikku. ⌊*bad* ~, komatte.

picot [píːkou] *n.* pikotto (rēsu nado no fuchikazari).

pictograph [píktəgræf / -grɑːf] *n.* kaigamoji.

pictorial [piktɔ́:riəl] *a.* e no ; e no yōna. *n.* gahō ; eiri shimbun.

picture [píktʃə] *n.* e. *v.* e o kaku. ~**-card** [⌐káːd] torampu no

picturesque [piktʃərésk] *a.* e no yōna. ⌊efuda.

pidgin English [pídʒin íngliʃ] *n.* Chūgoku shōnin no katakoto Eigo.

pie [pai] *n.* pai (niku, kudamono nado o koneko ni tsutsunde yaita mono) ; (*bird*) kasasagi.

piebald [páibɔːld] *a.* shiro-kuro no ; buchi no.

piece [piːs] *n.* hito-kire. *v.* tsugu. ~**meal** [⌐miːl] *a.* sukoshi zutsu no ; kire-gire no. ~**work** [⌐wəːk] *n.* chin'uke shigoto.

pied [paid] *a.* madara no.

pier [piə] *n.* hatoba.

pierce [piəs] *v.* sasu ; tsukitōsu.

pierrot [pí(:)ərou] *n.* (*Fr.*) piero (dōke yakusha).

piety [páiəti] *n.* shinjingokoro.

pig [pig] *n.* buta. ~**gish** [pigiʃ] *a.* buta no yōna. ~**headed** [⊥hédid] *a.* baka-gōjōna. ~**iron** [-aiən] *n.* sentetsu ; yōkōro kara dete kita nama no sentetsu. ~**sty** [⊥stai] *n.* butagoya. ~**tail** [⊥tèil] *n.* neji tabako.

pigeon [pídʒin] *n.* hato. ~ **English = pidgin English.** ~**hearted** [-hɑ:tid] *a.* okubyōna. ~**hole** [-houl] *n.* (tana nado ⌊no) ichi-kukaku.

pigment [pígmənt] *n.* enogu.

pigmy [pígmi] *n.* kobito.

pike [paik] *n.* mijikai yari ; (*fish*) kamasu (atama no togatta uo). ~**staff** [⊥stæf / -stɑ:f] *n.* yari no e. *as plain as a* ~, kiwamete akirakana.

pilaster [piləéstə] *n.* kabebashira (kabe no ichibu de, kabe kara soto ni dete iru kakubashira).

pile [pail] *n.* tsumikasane. *v.* tsumikasaneru.

piles [pailz] *n.* (*pl.*) (*med.*) ji (byōki).

pilfer [pílfə] *v.* kusuneru (kosodoro).

pilgrim [pílgrim] *n.* junreisha. ~**age** [-idʒ] *n.* junrei no tabi.

pill [píl] *n.* gan'yaku ; (*pl.*) (*col.*) tamatsuki. ~**box** [⊥bɔks] *n.* ⌊gan'yaku-ire.

pillage [pílidʒ] *n.* ryakudatsu. *v.* ubaitoru.

pillar [pílə] *n.* hashira.

pillion [píljən] *n.* (ōtobai no ushiro no) kura-futon.

pillory [píləri] *n.* (zainin no) sarashidai. *v.* sarashimono ni

pillow [pílou] *n.* makura. *v.* makura o saseru. ⌊suru.

pilot [pailət] *n.* mizusakiannainin ; sōjūshi. *v.* annai suru.

pimp [pimp] *n.* baishun chūkaisha.

pimple [pímpl] *n.* nikibi ; fukidemono.

pin [pin] *n.* tomebari. *v.* (hari nado de) tomeru. ~**ball** [⊥bɔ:l] *n.* pachinko. ~**cushion** [⊥kuʃn] *n.* harisashi. ~**point** [⊥pəint] *n.* pin no saki ; goku chiisai mono. *a.* chiisai mokuhyō ni shōjun o awaseru. ~**up** [pínʌp] *a.* (e nado o) pin de tomete kabe o kazaru. *n.* sono e ya shashin nado (zokugo).

pinafore [pínəfɔ:] *n.* maekake (kodomo no).

pincers [pínsəz] *n.* (*pl.*) kuginuki.

pinch [pintʃ] *v.* tsuneru; kurushimeru; itamu. *n.* tsuneri. ～**beck** [⌐bek] *n.* (*metal.*) dō to aen no gōkin. ～**hitter** [⌐hitə] *n.* kawari no battā (*base*).

pine [pain] *n.* (*bot.*) matsu. *v.* akogareru. ～**apple** [-æpl] *n. painappuru.*

ping-pong [píŋpóŋ] *n.* pimpon.

pinion [pínjən] *n.* hane; tsubasa. *v.* tsubasa o shibaru.

pink [piŋk] *n.* (*flow.*) nadeshiko (no hana). usubeniiro; momoiro. *a.* usu beniiro no. *v.* koana o akeru.

pinnace [pínis] *n.* (2 hon *mast* no) shō-hansen.

pinnacle [pínəkl] *n.* (*arch.*) chōjō; shōsentō.

pint [paint] *n.* painto (ekiryō no tan'i).

pinwheel [pínhwi:l] *n.* (omocha no) kazaguruma.

pioneer [pàiəníə] *n.* kaitakusha.

pious [páiəs] *a.* shinjimbukai.

pipe [paip] *n.* fue; kuda. *v.* fue o fuku. ～**r** [-ə] *n.* fue-fuki.

pipkin [pípkin] *n.* chiisana dobin.

pippin [pípin] *n.* isshu no ringo.

piquant [pí:kənt] *a.* piri-piri suru.

pique [pi:k] *n.* rippuku. *v.* rippuku saseru.

piracy [páiərəsi] *n.* kaizoku-kōi.

pirate [páiərit] *n.* kaizoku. *v.* kaizoku o suru.

pirouette [pirwét] *n., v.* (*Fr.*) (butō de) tsumasaki senkai (de mawaru).

piscatorial [pìskətɔ́:riəl], **piscatory** [pískətɔ:ri] *a.* gyogyō kankei no.

pistil [pístil] *n.* (*flow.*) meshibe no chūshin no zui.

pistol [pístl] *n.* pisutoru. *v.* pisutoru de utsu.

piston [pístən] *n.* (kikai no) pisuton.

pit [pit] *n.* ana. *v.* ana ni ireru. ～**fall** [⌐fɔ:l] *n.* otoshiana.

pitch [pitʃ] *n.* kōrutā; ittei no doai; fune no tateyure nado. ～**er** *n.* tōshu (*base*). ～**fork** [⌐fɔ:k] *n.* e no nagai ōkumade.

piteous [pítiəs] *a.* awarena. ～**y** *a.* makkurona.

pith [piθ] *n.* (kusa-ki ya, dōbutsu no hone no naka no) zui. ～**y** *a.* zui no aru.

pitiable [pítiəbl] *a.* awarena.

pitiful [pítiful] *a.* nasakebukai.

pitiless [pítilis] *a.* nasake-gokoro no nai. ～**ly** *ad.*

pity [píti] *n.* awaremi. *v.* awaremu.

pivot [pívət] *n.* (kikai no) senkaijiku (sūjiku). *v.* mannaka no jiku o sonaeru; jiku de mawaru.

pix [piks] *n.* (*pl.*) shashin no yōgo ; *picture* no imi.

placable [pléikəbl] *a.* nadameyasui ; odayakana.

placard [plǽkkəd] *n.* harifuda. *v.* keiji suru.

placate [pléikeit] *v.* nadameru.

place [pleis] *n.* tokoro ; basho ; ichi. *v.* oku.

placer [plǽsə] *n.* chūseki-kōshō.

placid [plǽsid] *a.* odayakana.

placket [plǽkit] *n.* (sukāto nado no) wakiaki.

plagiarism [pléidʒiərizm] *n.* hyōsetsu. ~**ist** *n.* hyōsetsusha.

plagiarize [pléidʒiəriaz] *v.* (tanin no bunshō ya setsu o) nusumu ; hyōsetsu suru.

plague [pleig] *n.* ekibyō. *v.* kurushimeru (*afflict*).

plaid [plæd] *n.* kōshijima no rasha.

plain[plein] *n.* heichi ; heigen. *a.* tairana ; yasashii. *to be ~ with you*, enryo naku ieba. ~**ly** *ad.*

plaint [pleint] *n.* nageki ; kanashimi. ~**iff** [-if] *n.* (soshōjō no) genkoku. ~**ive** [pléintiv] *a.* kanashii.

plait [pleit] *n.* hida ; shiwa. *v.* hida o toru.

plan [plæn] *n.* keikaku. *v.* keikaku suru.

plane [plein] *a.* tairana. *n.* heimen ; hikōki. *v.* kanna o kakeru.

planet [plǽnit] *n.* (*astr.*) yūsei. ~**ary** [-əri] *a.* yūsei no.

plank [plæŋk] *n.* atsui ita. *v.* itabari ni suru.

plant [plænt] *n.* shokubutsu. setsubi ; kōjō. *v.* tane o maku.

plantain [plǽntin] *n.* (*herb.*) ōbako ; banana no isshu.

plantation [plæntéiʃən] *n.* ueru koto ; shokuminchi.

plaque [plɑːk] *n.* gaku (kabe nado ni kakeru).

plash [plæʃ] *n.* hane (mizu ya nado). *v.* haneru.

plasma [plǽzmə] *n.* (ketsueki no) kesshō.

plaster [plǽstə] *n.* kōyaku. *v.* kōyaku o haru.

plastic [plǽstik] *a.* yawarakai (seikeisareru). *n.* purasutikku. ~**ity**[plæstísiti] *n.* jūnansei.

plat [plæt] *n.* chiisana jimen.

plate [pleit] *n.* itagane. sara. *v.* kimbari (kabuse) ni suru.

plateau [plǽtóu] (*pl.* **-s ; -x** [-z]) *n.* kōgen.

platen [plǽtn] *n.* (insatsuki no) ōban taipuraitā no rūra.

platform [plǽtfə:m] *n.* dai ; purattofōmu (teishajō no).

platinum [plǽtinəm] *n.* (*met.*) hakkin.

platitude [plǽtitju:d] *n.* heibon ; sukoshi mo shimmi no nai.

Platonic [plətɔ́nik] *a.* Puraton no. ~**ism** *n.* Puraton tetsugaku.

platoon [plətú:n] *n.* hohei-shōtai.

platter [plǽtə] *n.* hiratai ōzara.

plaudit [plɔ́:dit] *n.* hakushu kassai.

plausible [plɔ́:zəbl] *a.* mottomo rashii. ~**bly** *ad.*

play [pléi] *n.* asobi ; engeki. *v.* asobu ; suru (undō ya yūgi nado) (shibai, engeki de … no yaku o) ; hiku *piano, violin* nado o). *double* ~, heisatsu (*base*). ~**er** *n.* ensōsha ; kyōgisha. ~**fellow** [⌐fèlou] *n.* asobi-tomodachi. ~**ful** *a.* fuzake-tagaru. ~**ground** [⌐graund] *n.* undōjō. ~**wright** [⌐rait]-*n.* gikyoku-sakka.

plaza [plɑ́:zə] *n.* (*Sp.*) hiroba.

plea [pli:] *n.* tangan ; (hōritsu (*law*) ni yoru) kōben.

plead [plí:d] *v.* shuchō suru ; tangan suru.

pleasant [pléznt] *a.* yukaina. ~**ry** *n.* kaikatsu ; jōdan.

please [plí:z] *v.* yorokobaseru ; yorokobu. dōzo.

pleasing [plí:ziŋ] *a.* tanoshii.

pleasure [pléʒə] *n.* tanoshimi ; goraku.

pleat [plí:t] *n.* hida. *v.* hida o tsukeru.

plebe [pli:b] *n.* (*Am.*) shikangakkō (heigakkō) no saikakyūsei.

plebeian [plibí:ən] *a.* heimin no. *n.* (Kodai Rōma no) heimin.

plectrum [pléktrəm] *n.* (*pl.* **-tra**) (gengakuki no) bachi.

pledge [plédʒ] *n.* shichigusa. *v.* shichi ni ireru.

Pleiades [plí:ədi:z] *n.* (*pl.*) (*astr.*) Subaru Seiza.

plenary [plí:nəri] *a.* kanzenna.

plenipotentiary [plènipəténʃəri] *n.* zenkentaishi. *a.* zenken o motsu.

plenitude [plénitju:d] *n.* jūbun ; kanzen.

plenteous [pléntiəs] *a.* takusan no.

plentiful [pléntiful] *a.* takusan no. ~**ly** *ad.*

plenty [plénti] *n.* takusan ; jūbun.

pleonasm [plí:ənæzm] *n.* yokeina koto.

plethora [pléθərə] *n.* kajō ; kata ; (*med.*) ketsueki-kajō.

pleurisy [plúrəsi] *n.* (*med.*) rokumakuen.

pliable [pláiəbl] *a.* shinayakana.

pliancy [pláiənsi] *n.* shinayakasa.

pliant [pláiənt] *a.* shinayakana.

pliers [pláiəz] *n.* (*pl.*) yattoko.

plight [plait] *n.* mijimena sugata. *v.* yakusoku suru.

plod [plɔd] *v.* tobotobo aruku.

plosive [plóusiv] *n.* (*phon.*) haretsuon.

plot [plɔt] *n.* jisho (*a piece of ground*). keikaku (*plan*). *v.* keikaku suru. ～**ter** [plɔ́tə] *n.* imbōsha (*evil*).

plough, plow [plau] *n.* suki. *v.* suku. ～ *through*, honeotte susumu. ～ *a lonely furrow*, kodokuna seikatsu o okuru. ～ *the sands*, mudabone o oru.

plover [plʌ́və] *n.* (*bird*) chidori no isshu.

plow [plau] *n.*, *v. see* : **plough**

pluck [plʌk] *n.* tsuyoi hippari. *v.* ke (*hair*) o nuku. ～ *up*, nekogi ni suru. ～**y** *a.* yūki no aru. ～**ily** *ad.* isamashiku.

plug [plʌg] *n.* sen (*of bottles*). *v.* sen o suru (*put in*).

plum [plʌm] *n.* (*fruit*) sumomo.

plumage [plú:midʒ] *n.* hanege (tori no).

plumb [plʌm] *n.* omori. *a.* suichoku no. *ad.* suichoku ni. *v.* suichoku ni suru. ～**er** *n.* enkan-shokkō ; haikankō.

plumbago [pləmbéigou] *n.* (*metal*) sekiboku.

plume [plu:m] *n.* hanege. *v.* jiman suru.

plummet [plʌ́mit] *n.* omori ; sageru namari. 「doshin to.

plump [plʌmp] *a.* marubotcha no. *v.* futoru ; futoraseru. *ad.*

plunder [plʌ́ndə] *n.* ryakudatsu. *v.* ryakudatsu suru.

plunge [plʌndʒ] *v.* otoshiireru ; tobikomu. *n.* tsukkomi.

plural [plúrəl] *n.* (*gram.*) fukusū. *a.* fukusū no.

plurality [plurǽliti] *n.* fukusū de aru koto (*being pl.*).

plus [plʌs] *prep.* ... o kuwaete. *a.* sei no ; purasu no. ～ *sign*,

plush [plʌʃ] *n.* kinuwata ; birōdo. 「sei no kigō (+).

plutarchy [plúta:ki] =**plutocracy**

plutocracy [plu:tɔ́krəsi] *n.* kinken-seiji ; kanemochi no seiji. **plutocratic** [plù:təkrǽtik] *a.* kinken seiji no.

plutonium [plu:tóuniəm] *n.* (*chem.*) purutoniumu.

ply [plai] *v.* sei o dasu ; ōfuku suru. *n.* hida (*pleat*).

P.M., p.m. gogo (*post meridiem*).

p.n., P/N, yakusoku tegata (*promissory note*).

pneumatic [nju(:)mǽtik] *a.* kūki no. ～ *tire*, (kūkiiri)-taiya.

pneumonia [nju(:)móunjə] *n.* (*med.*) haien.

P.O. Post Office, Yūbinkyoku.

poach [poutʃ] *v.* nettō de yuderu (tamago o). mitsuryō o suru. ~**er** *n.*mitsuryōsha.

pock [pɔk] *n.* (*med.*) hōsō (byōki). ~**mark** [⸗mɑːk] *n.* abata.

pocket [pókit] *n.* poketto. *v.* poketto ni ireru. **air** ~ *n.* ea-poket-
to. ~**book** [⸗buk] *n.* saifu. ~**money** [⸗mʌni] *n.* kozukaisen.

pod [pɔd] *v.* (*bot.*) saya ni naru.

poem [póuim] *n.* shi ; uta.

poesy [póuizi] *n.* shi no tsukurikata ; shi.

poet [póuit] *n.* shijin. ~**aster** [-æ̀stə] *n.* hebo-shijin. ~**ic(al)**
[pouétik(l)] *a.* shi no. ~**ics** [pouétiks] *n.* shihō ; shiron. ~**ry**
[póuitri] *n.* shiika. ⎵ *n.* shigaku.

poignancy [póinjənsi / -ig-] *n.* shinratsusa.

poignant [póinjənt / póignən-] *a.* surudoi ; shinratsuna.

point [pɔint] *n.* ten ; yōten. *v.* mukeru ; shiji suru. ~ *of view*,
kenkai. *to the* ~, yōryō ni pittari suru. ~**blank** [⸗blǽŋk] *a.*
matomoni. ~**constable,** kōtsūjunsa. ~**duty,** kōtsūseiri kimmu. ~**ed** *a.* togatta. ~**er** *n.* hōkō o shimesu hari ; (*zoo.*) ryōken (*hound*) no isshu. ~**less** *a.* nibui.

poise [pɔiz] *n.* tsuriai. *v.* tsuriai o toru. tsuriai ga toreru.

poison [póizn] *n.* doku. *v.* doku o ireru. ~**ing** *n.* dokusatsu.
~**ous** *a.* yūdoku no. ⎵(torampu) pōkā.

poke [pouk] *n.* tsuki. *v.* tsuku. ~**r** [-ə] *n.* hi o tsutsuku bō ;
pok(e)y [póuki] *a.* semakurushii.

polar [póulə] *a.* kyoku no. ~ **bear,** *n.* shirokuma. ~**ity** [po(u)-
lǽriti] *n.* kyokusei (jishaku no). ~**ization** [pòulərizéiʃən] *n.*
henkyoku ; katayori. ~**ize** [póuləraiz]*v.* hikari o katayoraseru.

pole [poul] *n.* kyokuchi. bō de sasaeru koto. sao-bashira.
North (**South**) ~ = Hok-(Nan) kyoku. ~-**jump** [⸗dʒʌmp],
~-**vault** [⸗vɔːlt] *n.* bōtakatobi. ~**star** [⸗stɑː] *n.* (*astr.*) Hokkyo-
polecat [póulkæt] *n.* (*Am.*) sukanku. ⎵kusei.

polemic [poulémik] *n.* ronsen. ~**al** *a.* ronsō no.

police [pəlíːs] *n.* keisatsu. ~**man** [-mən] *n.* keikan ; junsa. ~
policy [pólisi] *n.* seisaku. ⎵**station,** keisatsusho.

Polish [póuliʃ] *n.* Pōlando no. *n.* Pōlando-go (jin).

polish [póliʃ] *v.* migaku. *n.* tsuyadashi.

polite [pəláit] *a.* reigi tadashii ; teineina.

politic [pólitik] *a.* seijijō no. ~**al** [pəlítikəl] *a.* seijijo no. ~**s** *n.*

politician [pòlitíʃən] *n.* seijika. ⎵seiji.

polity [póliti] *n.* kokutai ; seitai.

polka [pólkə] *n.* poruka (butō no isshu).

poll [poul] *n.* atama. *v.* tōhyō suru. ~ **tax,** jintōzei.

pollen [pólən] *n.* (*bot.*) (hana no) kafun.

pollination [pòlinéiʃən] *n.* kafun o ataeru koto.

pollute [pəlú:t] *v.* kegasu ; yogosu.

polo [póulou] *n.* poro (bajō de okonau kyōgi).

poltroon [pɔltrú:n] *n.* okubyōmono. ~**ery** *n.* okubyō.

polyclinic [pòliklínik] *n.* sōgōbyōin.

polygamy [pəlígəmi] *n.* ipputasai.

polyglot [póliglɔt] *a.* sūkakokugo de kaita. *n.* sono hon.

polygon [póligən] *n.* tahenkei. ⌈taonsetsu no.

polysyllable [pólisiləbl] *n.* taonsetsugo. ~**bic** [pòlisilǽbik] *a.*

polytechnic [pòlitéknik] *a.* kōgei no. *n.* kōgei gakkō.

polytheism [póliθiizm] *n.* tashinkyō.

polytheist [póliθi:st] *n.* tashinronja.

pomade [pəmá:d / -meid], **pomatum** [pəméitəm] *n.* pomādo.

pomegranate [pómgrænit / pám-] *n.* (*bot.*) zakuro.

pommel, pummel [páml] *n.* tsukasaki (*end of the handle of a sword*). *v.* uchinomesu (*beat with such*).

pomp [pɔmp] *n.* hade. ~**osity** [pəmpósiti] *n.* gōsha. ~**ous** *a.* hadena ; gōshana. ōgesana ; mottaiburu (*put on airs*).

pom-pom [pómpóm] *n.* taikū sokushahō.

pond [pɔnd] *n.* ike.

ponder [póndə] *v.* jukkō suru.

ponderous [póndərəs] *a.* omoi ; omoomoshii.

poniard [pónjəd] *n.* tanken ; mijikai katana.

pontiff [póntif] *n.* shikyō ; kōsō. ⌈shikisho (*office book*).

pontifical [pɔntífikl] *a.* shikyō no. *n.* (*pl.*) ...no fuku ; ...no

pontoon [pɔntú:n] *n.* funabashi-yō no fune.

pony [póuni] *n.* komma.

poodle [pú:dl] *n.* (*zoo.*) isshu no mukuinu (*dog*).

pool [pu:l] *n.* mizutamari ; pūru. *v.* kyōdō-shusshi suru.

poop [pu:p] *n.* sembi no kampan (pūpu dekki) ; fune no tomo. *v.* (nami o) sembi ni ukeru.

poor [puə] *a.* mazushii ; hetana. ~-**box** [⌐bɔks] *n.* jizembako. ~-**house** *n.* yōikuin. ~**ly** *a.* mazushii *ad.* mazushiku. ~**ness**

n. ketsubō. **~-spirited** [⊥spíritid] *a.* okubyōna.

pop [pɔp] *v.* pon to naru ; pachin (pon-pon) to narasu. *ad.* pon to. **~corn** [⊥kɔːn] *n.* hajike tōmorokoshi. **~gun** *n.* kūkijū.

Pope [poup] *n.* Rōma Hōō.

popinjay [pɔ́pindʒei] *n.* oshaberina kidoriya.

popish [póupiʃ] *a. Pope* no.

poplar [pɔ́plə / pɑ-] *n.* (*bot.*) hakoyanagi (popura).

poplin [pɔ́plin] *n.* popurin.

poppy [pɔ́pi] *n.* (*flow.*) keshi. **~cock** [pɔ́pikɔk] (*Am. col.*) *n.* ┌mudabanashi.

populace [pɔ́pjuləs] *n.* minshū ; bōmin.

popular [pɔ́pjulə] *a.* ippan no ; ryūkō no ; hyōban no yoi. **~ity** [pɔpjulǽriti] *n.* ninki ; hayari. **~ize** [raiz] *v.* ryūkō saseru.

populate [pɔ́pjuleit] *v.* hito o sumawaseru.

population [pɔpjuléiʃən] *n.* jinkō.

populous [pɔ́pjuləs] *a.* jinkō no ōi ; nigiyakana.

porcelain [pɔ́:slin] *n.* jiki.

porch [pɔ:tʃ] *n.* genkan ; iriguchi.

porcupine [pɔ́:kjupain] *n.* (*zoo.*) yamaarashi.

pore [pɔ:] *v.* mitsumeru ; jukudoku suru. *n.* chiisai ana ; keana.

pork [pɔ:k] *n.* butaniku. **~er** [pɔ́:kə] *n.* (*zoo.*) shokuyō-buta.

porous [pɔ́:rəs] *a.* ana no ōi ; kikō no aru.

porphyry [pɔ́:firi] *n.* hangan (shiroi suishō o fukunda, aka ya, murasaki gakatta katai iwa).

porpoise [pɔ́:pəs] *n.* (*zoo.*) iruka (*a whale*).

porridge [pɔ́ridʒ] *n.* kayu (ōtomiiru nado de tsukutta). *keep one's breath to cool one's ~*, yokeina kuchidashi o shinai.

porringer [pɔ́rindʒə] *n.* kayu o ireru sara.

port [pɔ:t] *n.* poruto budōshu ; minato ; (gunkan taihō no) hōmon ; (shōsen no) nitsumiguchi ; sagen. *v.* sagen ni mukeru. *make a ~*, nyūkō suru. **~ admiral,** Chinjufu Shireichōkan. **~age** [pɔ́:tidʒ] *n.* umpan ; unchin ; umpambutsu. **~hole** *n.* hōmon ; tsuminiguchi.

portable [pɔ́:təbl] *a.* mochihakobi dekiru.

portal [pɔ́:təl] *n.* mon ; iriguchi.

portcullis [pə:tkʌ́lis] *n.* tsurimon.

portend [pɔ:ténd] *v.* zenchō to naru ; kizashi o miseru.

portent [pɔ́:tent] *n.* zenchō (kyōji no). **~ous** *a.* fukitsuna.

porter [pɔ́:tə] *n.* momban ; akabō. ～**age** [-idʒ] *n.* umpan ; un-
portfolio [pɔ:tfóuljou] *n.* kamibasami ; daijin no shoku. ⌊chin.
portico [pɔ́:tikou] *a.* genkan.
portiere [pɔ:tiéə] *n.* (*Fr.*) tobari ; donchō.
portion [pɔ́:ʃən] ichibubun ; *n.* wakemae ; ummei ; bumpai zaisan ; jisankin. *v.* bumpai suru.
portly [pɔ́:tli] *a.* himanshita ; dōdō taru. ～**liness** *n.* himan ; ifū.
portmanteau [pɔ:tmǽntou] *n.* (*pl.* **-s** ; **-x**) ryokō kaban.
portrait [pɔ́:trit] *n.* shōzō ; shōzōga. ～**ure** [-ʃə] *n.* shōzōga ;
shōzōgahō.
portray [pɔ:tréi] *v.* egaku. ～**al** *n.* byōsha ; shasei.
Portuguese [pɔ́:tʃugi:z] *a.* Porutogaru no ; Porutogarugo no.
n. Porutogarujin ; Porutogarugo.
pose [pouz] *n.* shisei. *v.* aru shisei o toraseru ; (toi o) hassuru ;
(giron o) shikakeru ; aru shisei o toru ; kidoru. ～**r** [-ə] *n.*
kidoriya ; nammon.
position [pəzíʃən] *n.* basho ; taido ; chii.
positive [pɔ́zitiv] *a.* danko taru ; sekkyokutekina ; ～ **pole**,
yōkyoku(+)(denki no).
possess [pəzés] *v.* shoyū suru ; sen'yū suru ; jitto koraeru. ～
oneself, jisei suru. ～**ion** [-ʃən] *n.* sho'yū ; senyū ; jisei ; (*pl.*)
zaisan. *take* ～ *of*, o senryō suru. ～ *is nine points of the law*,
sen'yū wa kubu no kachime. ～**ive** *a.* shoyū no. ～**ivecase**,
(*gram.*) shoyūkaku. ～**or** [-ə] *n.* mochinushi.
possibility [pɔsibíliti] *n.* kanōsei.
possible [pɔ́sibl] *a.* ariuru ; kanō no. ～**bly** *ad.* nantoka shite ;
dekiru dake. tabun ; arui wa.   ⌈kebyō o tsukau.
possum [pɔ́səm] *n.* kuronezumi. *play* ～, shinda furi o suru ;
post [poust] *n.* hashira ; ichi ; shokuba ; yūbin ; yūbimbako ;
tachiban no heitai. *v.* (hashira nado ni) haru ; keiji suru ; yusō
suru ; tōkan suru ; haichi suru ; ōisogi de tabi o suru ; isogu.
ad. ushiro ni. *be* ～*ed up in*, ni tsūjite iru. ～**card** *n.* yūbin-ha-
gaki. ～**age** [⌐idʒ] *n.* yūzei. ～**-chaise** [⌐ʃeiz] *n.* ekiden-basha.
～**er** *n.* kōkoku. ～**-free** [⌐frí:] *a.* yūzei menjo no. ～**haste**
[⌐héist] *ad.* ōisogi de. ～**man** *n.* yūbin shūhainin. ～**mark** *n.*
yūbin keshiin. ～**master** *n.* yūbinkyokuchō. ～**-office**, yūbinkyoku. ～**-bellum** [⌐belʌm] *a.* ikusa no ato ; sengo no. ～-

graduate[⌐grǽdjuit]*a.* daigaku sotsugyōgo no ; kenkyūka no. *n.* kenkyūsei ; daigakusei. ~-**mortem** [⌐mɔ́:tem] *a.* shigo no. ~-**war** [⌐wɔ: / ⌐wɔ́:] *a.* sengono. ~ **meridiem** [meridiem] *n.* gogo (*see* : **P.M., p.m.**).

posterior [pɔstíriə] *a.* ato no. *n.* kōbu ; (*pl.*) dembu.

posterity [pɔstériti] *n.* shison ; kōkei.

postern [póustə:n] *n.* uramon.

posthumous [pósthjùməs] *a.* chichi no shigo ni umareta ; shin-   ⌐da ato no (de).

postil(l)ion [pəstílən] *n.* hidari uma no gyosha.

postpone [póustpoun] *v.* enki suru ; atomawashi ni suru. ~-**ment** *n.* enki.

postscript [póustskript] *n.* tsuishin (tegami no).

postulate [póstjuleit] *v.* yōkyū suru ; katei suru. *n.* katei ; hitsuyō jōken ; (*math.*) kōri.   ⌐maeru.

posture [póstjuə] *n.* shisei ; taido. *v.* shisei o toraseru ; miga-

posy [póuzi] *n.* hana ; hanataba.

pot [pɔt] *n.* tsubo ; (fukai) hachi ; (fukai) nabe. *v.* tsubo ni ireru ; hachi-ue ni suru. iru ; utsu. ~-**herb** [⌐hə:b] *n.* yasai ni naru na (*greens*). *watched* ~ *never boils*, matteru nabe wa nakanaka nienai.

potash [pótæʃ] *n.* akujiru. **caustic** ~, (*chem.*) kasei kari. ~-**water**, (*chem.*) tansan-kari.

potassium [pətǽsiəm] *n.* (*chem.*) karushūmu ; pottashūmu.

potation [poutéiʃən] *n.* (sake o) nomu koto.

potato [pətéitou] *n.* jagaimo ; bareisho.

potency [póutənsi] *n.* chikara ; nōryoku ; kensei.

potent [póutnt] *a.* chikara no aru ; kensei no aru ; kōnō no aru. ~**ate** [póutənteit] *n.* shukensha ; kunshu.

potential [pəténʃ(ə)l] *a.* ikioi no aru ; ari uru ; kanō no. ~ **energy**, senseiryoku. ~**ity** [pətenʃéliti] *n.* nōryoku ; kanōsei.

pother [pɔ́ðə] *n.* sawagi ; sōdō.

potion [póuʃən] *n.* ippuku (kusuri no).

potsherd [póthə:d] *n.* tōki no kakera.

pottage [pótidʒ] *n.* yasaiiri no shichū (*stew*).

potter [pótə] *n.* tōki tsukuri. *v.* guzuguzu hataraku ; buratsuku.

pottery [pótəri] *n.* tōki (seizōjo).

pouch [pautʃ] *n.* tabakoire ; kaneire ; yūbin-bukuro ; hara-

bukuro (kangarū nado no); rōjin no me no shita no tarumi.
poultice [póultis] *n.* pappuzai; ampō; nurigusuri.
poultry [póultri] *n.* kakin (niwatori nado). ⌜tsukamikakaru.
pounce [pauns] *n.* nijimidome no kona; mōjū no tsume. *v.*
pound [paund] *n.* pondo (Eikoku no jūryōtan'i, 453.6 guramu); pondo (Eikoku no kahei tan'i, 20 shiringu); kemono
no ori; kōchisho. *v.* tsuku (kome nado o); dotari dotari aruku. ∼**er** [⊥ə] *n.* usu. ∼**-foolish** [⊥fú:liʃ] *a.* ichimon oshimi
no hyaku shirazu (*penny wise and* ∼ *foolish*).
pour [pɔə] *v.* tsugu (cha nado o); nagareru; doshaburi ni furu. *It never rains but it* ∼*s.*, fureba kanarazu doshaburi da;
sainan wa tsuzuite kuru mono da.
pout [paut] *n.* kuchi o togaraseru koto. *v.* kuchi o togaraseru.
poverty [póvəti] *n.* bimbō; hinkon.
powder [páudə] *n.* kona; kayaku; oshiroi. *v.* kona ni suru;
kona o hiku; oshiroi o tsukeru. ∼**y** [-ri] *a.* kona no; kona-
darake no.
power [páuə] *n.* chikara; kenryoku; kyōkoku; ininjō; dōryoku. (*math.*) beki. ∼**ful** *a.* tsuyoi; seiryoku no aru; yūryokuna.
powwow [páuwáu] *n.* (*N-Am.*) (dojin no aida de) majinaishi;
isha; sōryo; (byōki, senshō no) kiganshiki.
pox [pɔks] *n.* baidoku.
P.P. *per pro* (=*by proxy*) dainin shomei.
practicability [præktikəbíliti] *n.* jikkō kanō; jitsuyōsei.
practicable [præktikəbl] *a.* jikkō dekiru; jitsuyō ni naru.
practical [præktikl] *a.* jitsuyōmuki no. ∼ *joke*, itazura; warufuzake. ⌜*v.* (*Am.*).
practice, practise [præktis] *n.* jitsuyō; jikkō; renshū; shūkan.
practise [præktis] *v.* tsuneni okonau; jikkō suru; kaigyō suru (isha nado); narau. ∼**d** [-t] *a.* jukutatsu shita.
practitioner [præktíʃənə] *n.* kaigyōsha. (isha, bengoshi nado).
pragmatic(al) [prægmætik(əl)] *a.* jitsuyōteki no; osekkai no;
dokudanteki no. ∼**sanction,** *n.* kokuji; shōchoku.
pragmatism [prægmətizm] *n.* jitsuyōshugi.
prairie [préəri/-préri] *n.* daisōgen. ⌜mubeki; kanshinna.
praise [preiz] *n.* shōsan. *v.* homeru. ∼**worthy** [⊥wò:ði] *a.* ho-
pram [præm] *n.* ubaguruma (*perambulator*).

prance [præns] *v.* (uma o) odoraseru ; iki yōyō to kappō suru.

prank [præŋk] *v.* hadeni kazaru ; seisō suru. *n.* warufuzake.

prate [preit] *v.* becha-kucha shaberu. *n.* mudaguchi.

prattle [prǽtl] *n.* katakoto ; mudaguchi. *v.* katakoto o iu.

pray [prei] *v.* negau ; kigan suru. **～er** *n.* [prɛə] kitō (bun) ; oinori no kotoba. [pré(i)ə] inoru hito.

preach [pri:tʃ] *v.* sekkyō suru ; noberu. **～er** *n.* sekkyōsha.

preamble [pri:ǽmbl] *n.* jobun ; maeoki.　　　　　　⌐suru.

prearrange [pri:əréindʒ] *v.* arakajime tehazu o kimeru ; yotei

precarious [prikɛ́əriəs] *a.* futashikana ; fuanteina.

precaution [prikɔ́:ʃən] *n.* yōjin ; yobōsaku. **～ary** [-əri] *a.* yobō no ; keikai suru.

precede [pri(:)sí:d] *v.* saki ni yuku (tatsu). yūsen suru. **～ence** [prisí:dəns] *n.* zenrei ; jōseki ; yūsen (ken). **～ent** [prisí:dənt] *a.* mae no ; saki no. *n.* senrei. **～ing** [-iŋ] *a.* mae ni deta (itta).

precept [prí:sept] *n.* kyōkun ; kakugen. **～or** [priséptə] *n.* kyōkunsha ; kyōshi.　　　　　　　　　　　　　　　　　⌐fukin.

precinct [prí:sŋkt] *n.* keidai ; (*Am.*) kuiki (senkyo no) ; (*pl.*)

precious [préʃəs] *a.* kōkana ; kichōna ; daijina. *ad.* (*col.*) hidoku.

precipice [présipis] *n.* gake ; zeppeki.　　　　　⌐sama no.

precipitant [prisípitənt] *a.* ōisogi no ; keisotsuna ; massaka-

precipitate [prisípiteit] *v.* massakasama ni otosu ; shizumeru (shizumu) ; muyamini isogaseru. *a.* masshigura no ; keisotsuna. *n.* chindembutsu.

precipitation [prisìpitéiʃən] *n.* tsuiraku ; chinden (butsu) ; kōu (ryō) (ame ya yuki no furu ryō).

precipitous [prisípitəs] *a.* kewashii ; kakyū no ; ōisogi no.

precis [préisi:] *n.* (*Fr.*) tai-i ; gairyaku.

precise [prisáis] *a.* seikakuna ; kichōmenna.

precision [prisíʒən] *n.* seikaku ; kichōmen. **～ bombing,** (*Am.*) seishōjun bakugeki.

preclude [priklú:d] *v.* saegiru ; samatageru.

precocious [prikóuʃəs] *a.* sōjuku no ; maseta.

precocity [prikɔ́siti] *n.* sōjuku ; hayazaki.

preconceive [prì:kənsí:v] *v.* yosō suru ; mae motte kangaeru.

precursor [prikɔ́:sə] *n.* zenchō. **～y** [-ri] *a.* zenchō no. ⌐animals).

predatory [prédətəri] *a.* ryakudatsu suru (*preying upon their*

predecessor [predisésə] *n.* sempai ; senjin ; mae no hito.

predestinate [pri(:)déstineit] *v.* mae motte sadameru ; yotei

predestination [pri(:)destinéiʃən] *n.* shukumei. ⌊suru.

predestine [pri(:)déstin] *v.* yotei suru ; ummei o sadameru.

predicament [pridíkəment] *n.* kukyō ; konnanna, (kikenna) chii. ⌈(*gram.*) jutsugo.

predicate [prédikeit] *v.* dantei suru ; jojutsu suru. *n.* [prédikit]

predict [pridíkt] *v.* yogen suru ; yohō suru. ⌊n. [pridíkʃən]

predilection [pri:dilékʃən] *n.* hen'ai ; hiiki. ⌊n. yogen ; yohō.

predominance [pridóminəns] *n.* takuetsu ; yūsei.

predominant [pridóminənt] *a.* yūryokuna ; omona.

predominate [pridómineit] *v.* yūsei de aru ; takuetsu suru.

pre-eminence [pri(:)éminəns] *n.* kesshutsu ; takuzetsu.

pre-eminent [pri(:)éminənt] *a.* sugureta ; subarashii.

pre-emption [pri(:)émpʃən] *n.* sembai (sakini kau koto) ; sembai-ken.

preen [prí:n] *n.* (hane o) kuchibashi de totonoeru koto.

prefabricate [pri:fǽbrikeit] *v.* (*Am.*) kumitate-buhin o seizō suru. ～**d house,** *n.* kan'i kumitate jūtaku.

preface [préfis] *n.* jobun. *v.* maeoki suru.

prefatory [préfətəri] *a.* maeoki no ; jobun no.

prefect [prí:fekt] *n.* chōkan. ～**ure** [-tʃə] *n.* fu ; ken.

prefer [prifɔ́:] *v.* mushiro … o toru ; mushiro … no hō ga yoi. ～**able** [préfərəbl] *a.* mushiro toru beki ; madashimo yoi. ～**ably** *ad.* kononde ; mushiro. ～**ence** [préfərəns] *n.* erigonomi ; sentaku. ～**ment** *n.* shōshin ; agaru koto.

prefigure [pri:fígjə] *v.* yosō suru.

prefix [prí:fiks] *v.* mae ni tsukeru. *n.* [prí:fiks] (*gram.*) settōgo.

pregnancy [prégnənsi] *n.* ninshin ; hōfu ; ganchiku aru koto.

pregnant [prégnənt] *a.* ninshin shite iru ; kufū ni tonda.

prehensile [prihénsil / -sail] *a.* tsukamu ni tekishita ; haakuryoku aru.

prehistoric [prì:histórik] *a.* yūshiizen no (rekishi no nakatta).

prejudice [prédʒudis] *n.* henken ; sennyūkan. *v.* henken o idakaseru. ～**ial** [prèdʒudísiəl] *a.* gai ni naru ; furi no.

prelate [prélit] *n.* kōsō ; toku no takai bōsan. ⌈yobi-shiken.

preliminary [prilímineri] *a.* yobi no. *n.* (*pl.*) shitagoshirae ;

prelude [prélju:d] *n.* (*mus.*) jokyoku ; jomaku.

premature [prì:mətjúə] *a.* hayasugiru ; sōjikuna.

premeditate [pri(:)méditeit] *v.* mae motte jukkō suru.

premeditation [pri:meditéiʃən] *n.* arakajime kangaeru koto.

premier [prí:mjə] *a.* daiichi no ; ichiban ue no. *n.* Sōri-Daijin.

premiere [prəmiér] *n.* (*Fr.*) shibai no shonichi ; hanagata joyū.

premise [prémis] *n.* maeoki ; zentei ; (*pl.*) keidai ; kōnai. *v.* [primáiz] maeoki to suru ; zentei to suru.

premium [prí:mjəm] *n.* shōkin ; warimashikin. *at a* ～, gakumen ijō de ; puremiamu-tsuki de.

premonition [priməníʃən] *n.* yokoku.

premonitory [primónitəri] *a.* yokoku no ; zenchō no.

preoccupy [pri:ókjupai] *v.* senshu suru.

preparation [prèpəréiʃən] *n.* jumbi ; yōi.

preparatory [pripǽrətəri] *a.* jumbi no. yobi no.

prepare [pripéə] *v.* shitaku suru ; jumbi saseru ; jumbi suru.

prepense [pripéns] *a.* keikakuteki no ; koi no.

preponderance [pripóndərəns] *n.* issō omoi koto ; yūsei.

preponderant [pripóndərənt] *a.* issō omoi ; yūsei no.

preponderate [pripóndəreit] *v.* omosa (sūryō, rikiryō nado ni oite) masaru ; ippō ni katamuku.

preposition [prèpəzíʃən] *n.* (*gram.*) zenchishi.

prepossess [pri:pəzés] *v.* yoi inshō o ataeru ; (aru kangae ga) sennyūshu to naru. ～**ing** *a.* aikyō no aru.

preposterous [pripóstərəs] *a.* zengo tentō no ; fugōrina.

prerequisite [pri:rékwizit] *a.* arakajime shitsuyōna ; *n.* shitsuyōjōken.

prerogative [prirógətiv] *n.* tokken ; taiken (tōjisha no).

presage [présidʒ] *n.* yokan ; zenchō. *v.* yochi suru.

presbyter [prézbitə] *n.* (*rel.*) chōrō ; shisai (kyōkai no).

presbyterian [prèzbitíəriən] *a.* chōrōkyōkai no ; chōrōha no shinto.

presbytery [prézbiteri] *n.* (*rel.*) chōrōkai ; chōrōkanku.

prescience [préʃiəns] *n.* yochi ; senken.

prescient [préʃiənt] *a.* yochi suru ; senken no.

prescribe [priskráib] *v.* sashizu suru ; kitei suru ; shohōsen o ⌐kaku.

prescription [priskrípʃən] *n.* (*med.*) shohō. (*leg.*) jikō.

prescriptive [priskríptiv] *ad.* jikō ni yotte eta; kanrei no.

presence [prézns] *n.* sonzai; shusseki; tachiai; taido. ~ *of mind*, ochitsuki. *your* ~ *is requested*, goshusseki o negai masu.

present [prizént] *v.* sashidasu; okuru; zōtei suru; mukeru (jū nado o). *a.* [préznt] shusseki shite iru; genzai no. *n.* [préznt] genzai; okurimono. *at* ~, genzai. *for the* ~, tōbun. ~**able** *a.* teisai no yoi. ~**ation** [prèzəntéiʃən] *n.* zōtei; shintei; kannen; teiki; teishutsu; shōkai; (tegata no) teiji; enshutsu (geki no); jōen. ~**ly** *ad.* yagate. ~**ment** *n.* chinjutsu; jōen.

presentiment [prizéntimənt] *n.* yokan (nan to naku).

preservation [prèzəvéiʃən] *n.* hozon; takuwae; hokan.

preservative [prizə́:vətiv] *a.* hozon suru. *n.* yobōhō.

preserve [prizə́:v] *n.* satōzuke; uo no kinryōchi; ikesu. *v.* hozon suru; shio nado ni tsukeru.

preside [prizáid] *v.* shikai suru; shihai suru.

presidency [prézidensi] *n.* *President* no shoku (ninki).

president [prézidənt] *n.* daitōryō; kaichō, sōchō, shachō.

press [pres] *v.* oshitsukeru; shimetsukeru; oshisusumeru. *be* ~*ed for fund*, shikin ni kyūsuru. *n.* insatsuki; shuppan; appaku; zattō; shimbunshi. ~**ing** *a.* kinkyū no. ~**ure** [préʃə] *n.* atsuryoku; kyōsei; seppaku. ~**ure group**, (*Am.*) atsuryoku dantai. ~**urize** [préʃəraiz] *v.* hikōki nai no kiatsu o heijō ni tamotsu.

prestige [prestí:ʒ] *n.* ishin. *loss of* ~, ishin no shittsui (nakunaru).⌐⌐⌐⌐⌐⌐⌐⌐⌐⌐⌐⌐⌐⌐⌐⌐⌐⌐⌐⌐⌐ *ad.* tabun.

presumable [prizjú:məbl] *a.* suisoku sareru; arisōna. ~**bly**

presume [prizjú:m] *v.* minasu; aete...suru; deshabaru.

presumption [prizʌ́mpʃən] *n.* suitei; buenryo; sen'etsu.

presumptive [prizʌ́mptiv] *a.* suitei no; katei no.

presumptuous [prizʌ́mptʃuəs] *a.* unuboreta; atsukamashii.

presuppose [pri:səpóuz] *v.* katei suru; yosō suru.

presupposition [prì:səpəzíʃən] *n.* yosō; katei.

pretend [priténd] *v.* kōjitsu to suru; furi o suru; itsuwaru; yōsu o suru; uso o iu.

pretense, pretence [priténs] *n.* kōjitsu; sekentei.

pretension [priténʃən] *n.* misekake; kōjitsu.

pretentious [priténʃəs] *a.* unuboreta; mie o haru.

preterit(e) [prétərit] *n., a.* (*gram.*) kako. (no). (*past*). ⌐nai.

preternatural [prì:tənǽtʃərəl] *a.* kikei no ; fushigina ; futsū de

pretext [prí:tekst] *n.* kōjitsu ; kakotsuke.

prettiness [prítinis] *n.* kireisa ; kawairashisa.

pretty [príti] *a.* kireina ; kawairashii. *ad.* (*col.*) kanarini.

prevail [privéil] *v.* katsu ; kō o sōsuru ; ryūkō suru ; tokifuseru
  ~**ing** *a.* ippan no ; ryūko no ; yūseina.

prevalence [prévələns] *n.* yūsei ; ryūkō. ⌐no.

prevalent [prévələnt] *a.* yūseina ; ryūkō shite iru ; ippanteki

prevaricate [privǽrikeit] *v.* iimagirasu ; gomakasu.

prevarication [privæˌrikéiʃən] *n.* iinuke ; gomakashi.

prevent [privént] *v.* samatageru ; yobō suru.

prevention [privénʃən] *n.* samatage ; fusegitome ; yobōhō.

preventive [privéntiv] *a.* yobō no. *n.* yobōhō. *a* ~ *medicine,*

preview [prí:vju:] *n.* (*Am.*) eiga no shisha. ⌐yobōyaku.

previous [prí:vjəs] *a.* mae no ; izen no. *on the* ~ *night,* mae
no ban ni. ~**ly** *ad.* ; arakajime.

prevision [pri(:)víȝən] *n.* senken ; yochi.

prey [prei] *n.* ejiki ; senrihin. *v.* ejiki ni suru ; kurushimeru.

price [prais] *n.* bukka ; hōshū. *v.* ne o tsukeru. ~**less** [lis] *a.*
kiwamete kichōna ; hyōka dekinai. (*col.*) totemo omoshiroi.

prick [prik] *v.* sasu ; ana o akeru ; uma ni hakusha o kakeru ;
kokoro o itameru ; ki o momaseru ; sobadateru ; sasareru ;
chikuchiku itamu ; uma o katte susumu. *n.* sasu mono ; hari ; kiri ; toge.

prickle [prikl] *n.* toge ; hari. *v.* hirihiri itamu.

prickly [príkli] *a.* hari, toge (*thorn*) no ōi (*thorny*) ; hari-dara-
ke no (*full of prickles*). ~ **heat,** *n.* asemo. ~ **pear,** saboten
(*cactus*) no isshu. ⌐~, machigatta jisonshin.

pride [praid] *n.* jisonshin. *v.* hokoru ; jiman suru (*boast*). **false**

priest [pri:st] *n.* sōryo (*buddhist*) ; bokushi (*of Christianity*). ~
ess *n.* nisō ; ama. ~**hood** *n.* sōshoku. ~**ly** *a.* sōryo rashii.

prig [prig] *n.* kidoriya ; urusagata (*being too particular*).

prim [prim] *a.* katakurushii ; torisumashita (*stand aloof from*).

primacy [práiməsi] *n.* daiichii (*being first*) ; shui (*top*).

primadonna [prì:mədónə] *n.* kageki (*opera*) no hanagata kashu
(*star singer*).

primal [práiməl] *a.* saisho no (*first*); genshi no (*original*).
primary [práiməri] *a.* daiichi no (*first*); honrai no (*original*).
the original meaning of the word is..., kono go no honrai no imi
wa...de aru. ⌐rily *ad.* ⌐reichōrui no dōbutsu.
primate [práimit] *n.* (*rel.*) daishukyō (*archbishop*); daisōjō.
prime [praim] *a.* saisho no; saikō no; massakari. *n.* hajime;
(*math.*) sosū. *1, 3 and 5 are* ⌐*numbers.,* 1, 3, 5 nado wa sosū
desu. *in the* ⌐ *of life,* jinsei no massakari ni. ⌐ **cost** *n.* shiire
nedan. ⌐ **minister,** sōridaijin. ⌐cap.⌐
primer [prímə] *n.* tebiki (*introductory book*); raikan (*percussion-*
primeval [praimí:vl] *a.* genshi-jidai no (*of primitive age*).
primitive [prímitiv] *a.* genshi no; jōko (*ancient*) no; sobokuna
primordial [praimɔ́:diəl] *a.* genshi no; saisho no. ⌐ (*naive*).
primp [primp] *v.* mekasu; kikazaru (*dress up*).
primrose [prímrouz] *n.* (*flow.*) sakurasō.
prince [prins] *n.* ōji; shinnō; kōshaku (*duke*). **great** ⌐, taikō.
⌐**imperial,** kōtaishin. **merchant** ⌐, gōshō. ⌐ **royal,** daiichi-
ōji. ⌐**ss** [prinsés] *n.* kōjo; naishinnō; ōhi; kōshaku fujin.
principal [prínsəpəl] *a.* jūyōna. *n.* chō; kōchō (*schoolmaster*);
shubōsha (*ringleader*). **the** ⌐ **sum,** gankin. ⌐ity [prinsipǽliti]
n. kōkoku; *prince* no kuni. ⌐no aru.⌐
principle [prínsəpl] *n.* hongen; genri; shugi. ⌐d *a.* ...shugi
print [print] *v.* insatsu suru; shuppan suru; in o osu. *n.* in no
ato; insatsu; insatsubutsu; hanga; ezōshi. *in* ⌐, insatsu ni
natte. *out of* ⌐, zeppan ni natte. ⌐**er** *n.* insatsusha. ⌐**ing** *n.*
insatsu; insatsujutsu.
prior [praiə] *a.* saki no; mae no (*before in time*). *n.* shūdōin no
jichō. ⌐ity [praiɔ́riti] *n.* mae; jōi; yūsen. ⌐y [práiəri] *n.*
shūdōin.
prism [príz(ə)m] *n.* sankaku no garasu no hashira; purizumu;
bunkō-garasu (*divide into seven colors*); nanairo; (*kesshō*) hashira. ⌐**atic** [prizmǽtik] *a.* kakuchū no; purizumu de bunkai
shita.
prison [prízn] *n.* keimusho. ⌐**er** *n.* shūjin; horyo (*war captive*).
pristine [pristi(:)n] *a.* motono (*original*); genshiteki (*primitive*).
privacy [práivəsi] *n.* intai; intaijo; himitsu. *He told me his rea-
sons in strict* ⌐, kare wa sono riyū o gempi (*in strict* ⌐) to

shite watashi ni hanashita.

private [práivit] *a.* naisho no ; himitsu no ; shiritsu no ; kojin no heisotsu ; kojin. *in* ～, kossori ; nainai ni.   「kumiin.

privateer [pràivətíə] *n.* teki no fune o ubau fune ; sono nori-

privation [praivéiʃən] *n.* ketsubō ; fujiyū (*inconvenience*).

privet [prívit] *n.* (*bot.*) ibota.

privilege [prívilidʒ] *n.* tokken ; tokuten. *v.* tokken o ataeru ; menjo suru. ～ **classes,** tokken kaikyū.

privy [prívi] *a.* ichi kojin no. *n.* benjo. ～**council,** Sūmitsuin. ～**ily** *ad.* anni ; himitsuni. ～ **purse,** otemotokin.

prize [praiz] *n.* senrihin ; shōhin. *v.* hokaku suru ; homeru. ～ **essay,** kenshō rombun. *This is his most ～d possession.,* kore wa kare gojiman no mono desu.

pro [prou] *n.* sanseiron ; sanseisha. shokugyō senshu. (*professional*). ～ *and con. con* (*contre*), =sampi ryōron.

probability [prɔ̀bəbíliti] *n.* jijitsu rashisa ; mikomi ; kakuritsu.

probable [prɔ́bəbl] *a.* arisōna ; tashika rashii. ～**bly** *ad.* tabun ;

probate [próubeit] *n.* yuigon ninshō-kan.   「ōkata.

probation [proubéiʃən] *n.* minarai (kikan) ; shikkō yūyo ; hogo kansatsu. ～**ary** *a.* kokoromi no. ～**er** *n.* minarai (chū no hito).

probe [proub] *n.*, *v.* saguribari (de saguru.)

probity [próubiti] *n.* seijitsu.

problem [prɔ́bləm] *n.* mondai ; nammon (*hard quest*) ; sakuzudai. ～**atical** [-ǽtikl] *a.* mondai no ; utagawashii (*suspicious*).

proboscis [proubɔ́sis] *n.* (zō nado no) hana.

procedure [prəsí:dʒə] *n.* hōhō ; shochi ; shobun ; tetsuzuki.

proceed [prəsí:d] *v.* susumu ; hōhō o toru ; torikakaru. ～**ing** *n.* hōhō ; shochi ; (*pl.*) soshō tetsuzuki ; giji ; gijiroku. ～**s** [próusi:dz] *n.* (*pl.*) uriagekin.

process [próses] *n.* shinkō ; keika ; tetsuzuki ; hōhō ; seihō ; sayō ; (*anat.*). tokki ; ryūki *v.* shori suru.

procession [prəséʃən] *n.* gyōretsu. *in* ～, gyōretsu o tsukutte.

proclaim [proukléim] *v.* fukoku suru.

proclamation [prɔ̀kləméiʃən] *n.* sengen ; fukoku.

proclivity [prouklíviti] *n.* keisha ; seiheki.

procrastinate [proukrǽstineit] *v.* chien suru ; guzuguzu suru.

procrastination [proukræstinéiʃən] *n.* chien ; shunjun.

procreate [próukri(:)eit] *v.* shison o tsukuru ; ko o umu.

proctor [próktə] *n.* daisonin ; daigaku gakuseikan.

procurable [prəkjúərəbl] *a.* erareru ; chōtatsu dekiru.

procure[proukjúə] *v.* eru ; motomeru ; shūsen suru.

prod [prəd] *n.* sashibari ; kiri ; sasu koto. *v.* sasu ; tsuku.

prodigal [pródigəl] *a.* rōhi suru ; zeitakuna. *n.* dōrakumono. ～**ity** [prɔ̀digǽriti] *n.* mudazukai ; hōtō. [*mous*).

prodigious [prədídʒəs] *a.* tohōmonaku ōkii, tohōmonai (*enor*-
prodigy [pródidʒi] *n.* hibonna hito ; tensai ; shindō.

produce [prədjú:s] *v.* seisan suru ; (mi ga) naru. *n.* [pródju:s] sambutsu. ～**r** *n.* enshutsusha.

product [pródəkt] *n.* seihin ; kekka.

production [prədókʃən] *n.* seisan ; seisaku (*producing*).

productive [prədóktiv] *a.* ōku tsukuru ; seisantekina.

proem [próuem] *n.* shogen ; jobun.

Prof., prof. kyōju. (*professor*) [*fane holy things*).

profanation [prɔ̀fənéiʃən/prɔfənéiʃən,] *n.* shinsei-bōtoku (*pro*-
profane [prəféin] *a.* kegareta. *v.* kegasu.

profanity [prəfǽniti] *n.* bōtoku no kotoba ya okonai.

profess [prəfés] *v.* hakkiri iikiru. ～**ed** [-t] *a.* iikitta. ～**edly** [-idli] *ad.* kōzen to. ～**ion** [prəféʃən] *n.* shokugyō. ～**ional** *a.* semmon no. *n.* kurōto ; semmonka. ～**or** [-ə] *n.* kyōju. ～**orship** *n.* kyōju no shoku.

proffer [prófə] *v.* teikyō suru. *n.* teikyō.

proficiency [prəfíʃənsi] *n.* jōtatsu.

proficient [prəfíʃənt] *a.* jōtatsu shita. *n.* meijin.

profile [próufail] *n.* yokogao. *v.* yokogao o egaku.

profit [prófit] *n.* mōke ; rieki. *v.* rieki ni naru ; rieki o eru. ～**able** *a.* yūekina. ～**eer** [-i:ə] *n.* futōritokusha. *v.* kōri o musa-boru (*make inordinate profits*).

profligacy [prófligəsi] *n.* fumimochi.

profligate [prófligit] *a.* hōtō suru. *n.* hōtōmono.

profound [prəfáund] *a.* fukai (gakumon nado no).

profundity [prəfónditi] *n.* fukasa.

profuse [prəfjú:s] *a.* ōmakana.

profusion [prəfjú:ʒən] *n.* takusan.

progenitor [pro(u)dʒénitə] *n.* senzo (*ancestor*).

progeny [pródʒəni] *n.* shison ; kekka.

prognosis [prəgnóusis] *n.* yochi (yosoku) suru koto.

prognostic [prəgnóstik] *a.* maebure no ; zenchō no.

prognosticate [prəgnóstikeit] *v.* yogen suru.

prognostication [prəgnòstikéiʃən] *n.* yogen ; maebure.

program(me) [próugræm] *n.* bangumi ; puroguramu.

progress [próugris] *n.* shimpo ; shinkō. *v.* [prəgrés] susumu. ~ion [prəgréʃən] *n.* zenshin. ~ive [prəgrésiv] *a.* shimpo suru. *n.* shimpotekina hito.

prohibit [pro(u)híbit] *v.* kinshi suru. ~ion [pròuhibíʃən] *n.* kinshi. ~ionist *n.* kinshi-ronsha. ~tive [pro(u)híbitiv] *a.* kinshi no.

project [prədʒékt] *v.* uchidasu ; tsukideru. *n.* [pródʒekt] keikaku. ~ile [pródʒektail] *n.* dangan ; tama. *a.* hassha suru. ~ion [prədʒékʃ(ə)n] *n.* tōsha ; sekkei (*planning*). ~or [prədʒéktə] *n.* keikakusha.

proletarian [pròuletéəriən] *n.* puroretariya ; musansha.

proletariat(e) [pròuletéəriət] *n.* rōdōkaikyū.

prolific [prəlífik] *a.* kodomo o ōku umu.

prolix [próliks / proulíks] *a.* kudoi. ~ity [-líksiti] *n.* jōman.

prolog(ue) [próuləg] *n.* maeoki. ⌈enchō ; enki.

prolong [prəlóŋ] *v.* hikinobasu. ~ation [pròuləŋgéiʃən] *n.*

promenade [prɔminá:d] *n.* asobiaruki ; yūhojō.

prominence [próminəns] *n.* tokki ; takuetsu.

prominent [próminənt] *a.* ichijirushii.

promiscuous [prəmískjuəs] *a.* ranzatsuna ; sabetsu no nai.

promise [prómis] *n.* yakusoku. *v.* yakusoku suru ; *the crops ~ well.*, hōsaku rashii. ⌈tegata.

promissory [prómisəri] *a.* yakusoku no. ~ note, yakusoku

promontory [prómontəri] *n.* misaki.

promote [prəmóut] *v.* zenshin (shōshin) suru ; nobiru. ~r [-ə] *n.* shōreisha ; hokkinin.

promotion [prəmóuʃ(ə)n] *n.* shōrei ; hokki.

prompt [prɔmpt] *a.* jinsokuna. *v.* shigeki suru ; unagasu. ~itude [prómptitju:d] *n.* jinsoku. ~ly *ad.* jinsokuni.

promulgate [prómʌlgeit] *v.* happu suru.

promulgation [pròmʌlgéiʃ(ə)n] *n.* happu.

prone [proun] *a.* utsumuita ; ... shiyasui.
prong [prɔŋ] *n.* (fōku nado no) saki.
pronominal [prənɔ́minəl] *a.* (*gram.*) daimeishi no.
pronoun [próunaun] *n.* (*gram.*) daimeishi.
pronounce [prənáuns] *v.* hatsuon suru ; noberu. **～d** [-t] *a.* hakkiri shita. **～ment** *n.* senkoku.
pronunciation [prənʌnsiéiʃ(ə)n] *n.* hatsuon.   [*n.* kōseiyomi.
proof [pru:f] *n.* shōko ; kōsei. *a.* hoshōtsuki no. **～-reader** [-ⸯri:də]
prop [prɔp] *n.* sasae ; tsukkaibō ; shijisha. *v.* sasaeru.
propaganda [prɔ̀pəgǽndə] *n.* senden.
propagate [prɔ́pəgeit] *v.* dempan suru ; fueru.
propagation [prɔ̀pəgéiʃ(ə)n] *n.* dempan ; hirogari.
propel [prəpél] *v.* suishin suru. **～ler** *n.* suishinki ; puropera.
propensity [prəpénsiti] *n.* keikō ; katamuki ; kuse.
proper [prɔ́pə] *a.* tekitōna. **～ly** *ad.* tekitōni. **～ speaking,** hontō
property [prɔ́pəti] *n.* shoyūbutsu ; zaisan.   [o ieba.
prophecy [prɔ́fisi] *n.* yogen.
prophesy [prɔ́fəsai] *v.* yogen suru.   [*a.* yogensha no.
prophet [prɔ́fit] *n.* yogensha. **～ic** [prəfétik] **～** no. **～ical** [-ikl]
propinquity [prəpíŋkwiti] *n.* chikasa (*of time, distance*).
propitiate [prəpíʃieit] *v.* nadameru ; nagusameru.
propitiation [prəpiʃiéiʃən] *n.* wakai ; tokeai.
propitiatory [prəpíʃiətəri] *a.* nadameru.
propitious [prəpíʃəs] *a.* tsugō no yoi.
proponent [prəpóunent] *n.* teiansha.
proportion [prəpóːʃən] *n.* wariai ; hirei. *v.* hirei saseru. **～al** [-əl] *a.* tsuriatta. **～ate** [-it] *a.* tsuriatta. *v.* tsuriawaseru ; hirei saseru.
proposal [prəpóuzl] *n.* mōshikomi ; teian.
propose [prəpóuz] *v.* mōshikomu ; teian suru.
proposition [prɔ̀pəzíʃ(ə)n/prò-] *n.* teian ; keikaku ; meidai.
propound [prəpáund] *v.* teigi suru.
proprietary [prəpráiətəri] *a.* shoyūnushi no.
proprietor [prəpráiətə] *n.* shoyūsha. **～ship** *n.* shoyūken.
propriety [prəpráiəti] *n.* tekitōsei.
propulsion [prəpʌ́lʃ(ə)n] *n.* suishin suru koto (chikara.)
prorogue [prouróug] *v.* teikai suru (gikai o).
prosaic [prouzéiik] *a.* sambuntekina ; heibonna.

proscrible [prəskráib] *v.* hōritsu de hogo o shinai.

proscription [pro(u)skrípʃən] *n.* jinken (*personal rights*) no hakudatsu (*deprive*).

prose [prouz] *n.* sambun. *a.* sambun no. *v.* sambun de kaku.

prosecute [prɔ́sikju:t] *v.* yaritogeru.

prosecution [prɔ̀sikjú:(ə)n] *n.* jikkō.

prosecutor [prɔ́sikju:tə] *n.* jikkōsha ; kokusonin ; kenji.

proselyte [prɔ́silait] *n.* tenkōsha. *v.* kaishū saseru.

prosody [prɔ́sədi] *n.* sakushihō.

prospect [prɔ́spekt] *n.* mikomi ; miharashi. *v.* tōsa suru (*survey*). ～**ive** *a.* mikomi no aru.

prospectus [prəspéktəs] *n.* shuisho.

prosper [prɔ́spə] *v.* han'ei saseru (suru).

prosperity [prɔspériti] *n.* han'ei ; hanjō.

prosperous [prɔ́sperəs] *a.* hanjō suru.

prostitute [prɔ́stitju:t] *n.* baishunfu. *v.* baishun saseru (suru).

prostitution [prɔ̀stitjú:ʃən] *n.* baishun.

prostrate [prɔ́streit] *a.* taoreta ; hetabatta. *v.* (chijō ni) tata-

prostration [prɔstréiʃən] *n.* heifuku ; hetabari.   ⌊kinomesu.

prosy [próuzi] *a.* sambun no ; heibonna.

protagonist [proutǽgənist] *n.* shuyaku (geki nado no).

protean [prouti:ən] *a.* iroiro no katachi o suru.

protect [prətékt] *v.* hogo suru ; fusegu. ～**ion** [prətékʃən] *n.* hogo. ～**ive** *a.* hogo no (suru). ～**or** [-ə] *n.* hogosha ; hogo suru mono. ～**orate** [-ərit] *n.* hogoryō ; hogokoku.

protégé [próuteʒei] *n.* (*Fr.*) hi-hogosha.

protein [próuti(:)in] *n.* tampakushitsu.

protest [prətést] *v.* kōgi suru ; jisetsu o tsuyoku shuchō suru. ～**ation** [prɔ̀testéiʃ(ə)n] *n.* kōgi ; hantai no shuchō.

Protestant [prɔ́titstənt] *a.* shinkyō (Kirisutokyō no). *n.* shin-kyōto. ～**ism** *n.* shinkyō.

protoplasm [próutəplæzm] *n.* genkeishitsu (seibutsu no).

prototype [próutətaip] *n.* tehon.

protract [prətrǽkt] *v.* nagabikaseru.

protrude [prətrú:d] *v.* tsukideru ; dasu.

protrusion [prətrú:ʒən] *n.* tsukidashi ; tobidashi.

protuberance [prətjú:bərəns] *n.* tokki ; kobu.

protuberant [prɔtjúːbərənt] *a.* tsukideta. ⌐ad. tokuini natte.

proud [praud] *a.* tokui de. *be* ~ *of,* ... o tokui to suru. ~ly

prove [prúːv] *v.* shōmei suru.

provender [prɔ́vəndə] *n.* magusa ; kaiba. ⌐no.

proverb [prɔ́vəːb] *n.* kotowaza. ~**ial** [prɔvə́ːbjəl] *a.* kotowaza

provide [prɔváid] *v.* yōi suru ; kyōkyū suru. ~**d** [-id] *conj.*
moshi ... naraba (*that*).

providence [prɔ́vidəns] *n.* kami no kokoro.

provident [prɔ́vidənt] *a.* yōjin-bukai. ~**ial** [prɔ̀vidénʃ(ə)l] *a.*
kami no kangae no.

province [prɔ́vins] *n.* shū ; shō ; ken. (*pl.*) inaka ; chihō.

provincial [prɔvínʃəl] *a.* chihō no. *n.* inakamono. ~**ism** *n.*
okuninamari.

provision [prɔvíʒən] *n.* jumbi ; yōi ; (*pl.*) tabemono. *v.* tabemono o yōi suru. ~**al** *a.* kari no ; shibaraku no.

proviso [prɔváizo] *n.* tadashigaki.

provisory [prɔváizəri] *a.* jōkentsuki no.

provocation [prɔ̀vəkéiʃən] *n.* okoraseru koto. ; chōhatsu.

provocative [prɔvɔ́kətiv] *a.* okoraseru ; shigeki suru. *n.* shi-

provoke [prɔvóuk] *v.* okoraseru. ⌐gekibutsu.

provost [prɔ́vɔst] *n.* (daigaku no) gakuchō. [prɔvóu] (*mil.*)
kempei shōkō.

prow [prau] *n.* hesaki. *a.* isamashii. ~**ess** [⌐is] *n.* yūkan ; buyū.

prowl [praul] *v.* asari aruku.

prox. *see* : proximo.

proximate [prɔ́ksimit] *a.* mottomo chikai.

proximity [prɔksímiti] *n.* sekkin.

proximo [prɔ́ksimou] *ad.* raigetsu (*prox.*).

proxy [prɔ́ksi] *n.* kawari no hito.

prude [pruːd] *n.* tsutsushimibukai furi o suru onna.

prudence [prúːdəns] *n.* yōjin ; shinchō.

prudent [prúːdənt] *a.* yoku ki o kubaru. ~**ial** [pru:dénʃ(ə)l] *a.*

prudish [prúːdiʃ] *a.* enryo sugiru. ⌐chūibukai ; saishin no.

prune [pruːn] *v.* kireini karu (ki no eda nado o).

prurient [prúriənt] *a.* kōshoku no.

pry [prai] *n.* teko. *v.* kojiageru ; jiro-jiro miru.

P.S., p.s. ottegaki (tegami no).

psalm [sɑ:m] *n.* sambika. ~**ist** *n.* sambika sakusha. ~**ody** [sǽlmədi] *n.* sambika utai ; sambika no hon.

pseudonym [sjú:dənim] *n.* tokumei.

psyche [sáiki] *n.* reikon ; seishin. ⌈ku.

psychiatry [saikáiətri] *n.* seishimbyō chiryōhō ; seishimbyōga-**psychic(al)** [sáikik(əl)] *a.* reikon no.

psychoanalysis [sàikouənǽləsis] *n.* seishin bunseki (gaku).

psychology [saikɔ́lədʒi] *n.* shinrigaku. ~**ical** *a.* shinrigaku no. ~**ist** *n.* shinrigakusha.

P.T.A., PTA pii-tii-ei (*Parent-Teacher Association.*)

PT boat [pí:ti: bóut] *n.* (*Am.*) kōsoku suiraitei.

P.T.O., p.t.o. *please turn over.* ura o miyo.

ptomain(e) [tóumein] *n.* putomain (dokuso).

puberty [pjú:bəti] *n.* shishunki.

public [pʌ́blik] *a.* kōshū no. *n.* kōshū. ~**house**, izakaya. ~ **opinion**, *n.* yoron. ~ **school**, (*Am.*) kōritsu gakkō. *in* ~, kō-zen to. ~**an** [-ən] *n.* izakaya no shujin. ~**ation** [pʌ̀blikéiʃən] *n.* happyō ; hakkō. ~**ity** [pʌblísiti] *n.* kōhyō. ~**ize** [pʌ́blisaiz] *v.* kōhyō suru.

publish [pʌ́bliʃ] *v.* happyō suru. ~**er** *n.* shuppangyōsha ; shup-**Puck** [pʌk] *n.* pakku (itazurabōzu). ⌊pansha.

pucker [pʌ́kə] *v.* hida o toru ; subomaru. *n.* shiwa.

pudding [púdiŋ] *n.* puddingu (isshu no kashi).

puddle [pʌ́dl] *n.* mizutamari. *v.* doro o koneru.

puddling [pʌ́dliŋ] *n.* (kinzoku o) seiren suru koto.

pudgy [pódʒi/pʌ́dgi] *a.* zunguri shita.

puerile [pjúərail] *a.* kodomoppoi ; tawai mo nai.

puerility [pjùəríliti] *n.* yōchi ; kodomopposa.

puff [pʌf] *n.* hitoyaki fuki ; putto fukureru koto ; pafu (oshiroi no hake) ; karuyaki-manjū. *v.* putto fuku ; aegu ; fukiharau ; yatarani homeru. ~**y** [pʌ́fi] *a.* putto fuku ; kōdaina.

pug [pʌg] *n.* chin (inu no isshu) ; shishippana (*turned up nose*).

pugilism [pjú:dʒilizm] *n.* kentō ; bokushingu (*boxing*).

pugilist [pjú:dʒilist] *n.* kentōka. ~**ic** [pjù:dʒilístik] *a.* bokusā no. ~**ically** [pjù:dʒilístik(ə)li] *ad.* kentō de.

pugnacious [pəgnéiʃəs] *a.* kenkazukina.

puissance [pjú:isəns] *n.* chikara ; seiryoku ; kenryoku.

puissant [pjú:isənt] *a*. chikarazuyoi ; kyōryokuna.   ⌈tateru.
pule [pju:l] *v*. (byōki no kodomo no yōni) yowai nakigoe o
pull [pul] *v*. hiku ; hipparu ; saguru ; kogu. *n*. hiki ; hippari ;
    ōru no hitokogi. ~ *down*, hippari orosu ; kowasu. ~ *oneself*
    together, genki o kaifuku suru.~*together*, kyōryoku shite yaru.
pullet [púlit] *n*. wakai mendori.   ⌊~ *up*, tazuna o hiku.
pulley [púli] *n*. kassha.
pulmonary [pálmənəri] *a*. hai no ; haizō o motteru.
pulp [pʌlp] *n*. parupu ; (kudamono no) kaniku ; shizui (*inner-*
    part of a tooth). ~y [pálpi] *a*. kaniku no ; dorodoro shita.
pulpit [púlpit] *n*. sekkyōdan ; (*the p*~, sōryo) (*sermons*).
pulsate [palséit] *v*. (myakuhaku ga) utsu ; dōki suru.
pulsation [pəlséiʃən] *n*. myakuhaku ; dōki ; myakudō ; shindō.
pulse [pʌls] *n*. (*anat*.) myakuhaku ; (myaku no yōni) kisoku-
    tekina (*regularly*) ugoki. *v*. myaku utsu ; kodō suru.
pulverize [pálvəraiz] *v*. kona ni suru (naru) ; funsai suru.
puma [pjú:mə] *n*. (*zoo*.) Amerika-hyō (*beast*).
pumice [pámis] *n*. karuishi ; ukiishi.
pump [pʌmp] *n*. pompu ; butōgutsu. *v*. pompu de kumidasu ;
    (taiya nado ni) kūki o ireru.
pumpkin [pámpkin] *n*. (*vegetable*) kabocha.
pun [pʌn] *n*. share. *v*. share o iu.
punch [pʌntʃ] *n*. ponsu (iroiro mazeta nomimono) ; assakuki ;
    kippubasami ; ningyōgeki *Punch and Judy* no shujin kō ; man-
    ga zasshi. *v*. ana o akeru.
puncheon [pántʃən] *n*. ōoke (72—120 garon iri).
punctilious [pʌnktíliəs] *a*. kichitto shita.
punctual [páŋktʃəl] *a*. jikan o mamoru ; nichigen o chigaenai.
    ~ity [pàŋktʃuǽliti] *n*. jikan genshu ; kichōmen.
punctuate [páŋktʃueit] *v*. kutōten o tsukeru.   ⌈kutōhō.
punctuation [pàŋktʃuéiʃən] *n*. kutōten ; kutōten no tsukekata ;
puncture [páŋktʃuə] *n*. hari nado de sashita ana. *v*. hari nado
de sasu.   ⌈sa.
pungency [pándʒənsi] *n*. tsurasa ; shinratsu ; karasa ; hageshi-
pungent [pándʒənt] *a*. karai ; shigekisei no ; shinratsuna.
punish [pániʃ] *v*. bassuru ; korasu. ~ment *n*. chōba-tsu ;
    korashime.

punitive [pjú:nətiv], **punitory** [pjú:nitəri] *a.* keibatsu o kuwaeru; chōbatsu suru.

punt [pʌnt] *n.* isshu no hirasokobune. *v.* hirasokobune o sao de kogu; (*football*) kerikata no isshu.

puny [pjú:ni] *a.* chiisakute yowai; tsumaranai.

pup [pʌp] *n.* (zoo.) koinu (*young dog*); (azarashi nado no) ko.

pupa [pjú:pə] *n.* (*pl.* **-pae**) sanagi.

pupil [pjú:pl] *n.* seito; deshi. hitomi (*of eye*); dōkō.

puppet [pʌ́pit] *n.* ayatsuri-ningyō; tesaki ni tsukawareru hito.

puppy [pʌ́pi] *n.* inu no ko; namaikina kozō.

purblind [pə́:blàind] *a.* yoku me no mienai; hammekura no.

purchase [pə́:tʃeis] *v.* kau; doryoku shite toru. *n.* kaiire; kaimono. ～**r** [-ə] *n.* kaite; kainushi.

pure [pjuə] *a.* junsuina; seirenna; keppakuna; mattaku no. ～**ly** [⊥li] *ad.* junsuini; mattaku. ～**ness** *n.*

purgation [pə:géiʃən] *n.* kiyome; geri; kireini suru koto.

purgative [pə́:gətiv] *a.* kiyomeru; gezai no. *n.* gezai.

purgatory [pə́:gətəri] *n.* rengoku.

purge [pə:dʒ] *n.* kiyome; kudashi; gezai; shukusei; tsuihō. *v.* kiyomeru; shukusei suru; (furyō-bunshi o) tsuihō suru.

purification [pjùrifikéiʃən] *n.* kiyome; kiyome no shiki; seiren; jōka.

purify [pjú:rifai] *v.* kiyomeru; jōka suru; seisei suru.

puritan [pjú:ritən] *n.* Seikyōto; (*P*～) *Puritan* no nakama.

puritanical [pjùritǽnikl] *a.* seikyōto no; genkakuna.

purity [pjúəriti] *n.* muku; keppaku; junsei.

purl [pə:l] *n.* uzu; sarasara (nagareru oto). nuitori-beri; ura-ami. *v.* uzumaite nagareru : ura-ami suru.

purlieu [pə́:lju:] *n.* shinrin no shūhen; (*pl.*) machi-hazure; kōgai; himminkutsu.

purloin [pə:lɔ́in] *v.* nusumu; kusuneru.　　　　⌈takai kurai.

purple [pə́:pl] *a.* murasakiiro no; teiō no. *n.* murasakiiro.

purport [pə́:pə:t] *n.* shui; imi. *v.* [pə:pɔ́:t] imi suru.　⌈to suru.

purpose [pə́:pəs] *n.* mokuteki; shui. *v.* kokorozasu; … shiyō

purr [pə:] *v.* (neko nado) gorogoro iu. *n.* goro-goro.

purse [pə:s] *n.* saifu; gamaguchi. *v.* saifu ni ireru; shiwa ga yoru. ～**r** [pə́:sə] *n.* kaikei o atsukau hito.; (fune no) jimuchō.

pursuance [pə:sjúːəns] *n*. tsuiseki; zokkō; suikō. *in* ～ *of*, …
o suikō shite.

pursuant [pə:sjúːənt] *a*., *ad*. yotte; shitagatte; junjite (*to*).

pursue [pɔ́:sju:] *v*. tsuiseki suru; tsuikyū suru; motomeru;
suikō suru; jūji suru. ～**r** *n*. tsuiseki (tsuikyū) suru hito.

pursuit [pə:sjúːt] *n*. tsuiseki; zokkō; itonami; shigoto; kenkyū. *in* ～ *of*, motomete; tsuikyū shite.

pursy [pɔ́:si] *a*. ikigire suru; futotta.

purulent [pjúərələnt] *a*. (*med.*) kanō shita; nō ga deru.

purvey [pə:véi] *v*. chōtatsu (kyōkyū) suru; makanau. ～**ance**
[-əns] *n*. chōtatsu; ryōshoku; kyōkyū. ～**or** [-ə] *n*. goyō-
shōnin; goyōtatsu; shokumotsu chōtatsusha. *P*～ *to the Royal
Household*, Ōshitsu goyōtashi.

purview [pɔ́:vju:] *n*. kengen; han'i; shikai : yōkō.

pus [pʌs] *n*. (*med.*) nō; nōjū; umi.

push [puʃ] *v*. osu; tsuku; oshisusumeru; semaru. *n*. oshi;
tosshin; fumpatsu; kiryoku. ～**-button** [⸏bʌtn] *n*. (beru nado
no) oshi-botan. ～**-cart** [⸏kɑ:t] *n*. teoshiguruma. ～**ing** *a*.
osu; shinshuteki; kappatsuna. ～**-over** [⸏ouvə] *n*. (*Am. sl.*)
yariyasui koto; rakuni kateru aite.

pusillanimity [pjù:silənímiti] *n*. okubyō; hinsei rettō.

pusillanimous [pju:silǽniməs] *a*. hikyōna; okubyōna; hinsei-
puss [pus] *n*. neko; usagi; shōjō; komusume. ⎿rettōna.

pussy [púsi] *n*. neko. ～**willow**, nekoyanagi. ～**-foot** [-fut] *n*.
(*pl*. **-foots**) (*Am. sl.*) neko no yōni sottō chūi shite aruku
koto.

pustule [pústʃu:l / pʌ́-] *n*. kanō suru chiisai odeki; nōhō.

put [put] *v*. oku. ～ *about*, komaraseru. kōro o tenzuru; ～*ac-
cross*, umaku yaritōsu. ～ *down*, orosu; shizumeru; osaeru;
kakitomeru. ～ *in mind*, omoidasaseru. ～ *off*, nugu; nobasu;
enki suru; umaku hazusu. ～ *on* (*or upon*), kiru; kaburu; mi
ni tsukeru; obiru ～ *out*, dasu; oidasu; kesu; ōyake ni suru;
hakkō suru. ～ *through*, yaritōsu. ～ *to it*, shiite yaraseru; kyōsei suru. ～ *to rights*, naosu. ～ *up*, kakageru; shimau; haru
(temmaku o); tateru (ie o); shimeru (to o); yadoru. ～ *up
to*, o sendō suru. ～ *up with*, o gaman suru.

putrefaction [pjù:trəfǽkʃən] *n*. fuhai; fuhaibutsu.

putrefy [pjúːtrifai] *v.* kanō suru (saseru) ; kusaru ; kusaraseru.

putrid [pjúːtrid] *a.* fuhai shita. ~ity [pjuːtríditi] *n.* fuhai.

putt, put [pʌt] *v.* (*golf.*) ana ni hairu yō ni karuku utsu. *n.* kei-puttee, [pʌti] *n.* maki-geitoru.   └da.

putty [pʌti] *n.* pate ; tsugiawase-gusuri. *v.* pate de tsugi awa-seru.

puzzle [pʌzl] *v.* tōwaku saseru. *n.* nandai ; tōwaku ; nazo.

PX [píːéks] *n.* shuho (*Post Exchange*).   ┌kobito.

pygmy [pígmi] *n.* kobito ; issumbōshi ; (*P*~) Chūō Afurika no

pyjamas [pədʒúːməz] *n.* *see* : **pajamas.**

pylon [páilən] *n.* tōmon (Ejiputo kenchiku no) ; (kōatsusen yō) tettō ; (kūki yō) mokuhyō-tō ; mokuhyō-chū

pyramid [pírəmid] *n.* piramiddo ; kinjitō. *v.* piramiddo no ka-tachi ni tsumu. ~al [pirǽmidəl] *a.* piramiddo-kei no ; kakusui-kei no.

pyre [páiə] *n.* (shikabane o yaku tame no) maki no yama.

pyrites [pairáitiːz] *n.* (*min.*) ōdōkō (ōdō no kōzan).

pyrotechnic [pàiroutéknik] *a.* hanabi no ; hanabi seizō no ; hanabanashii. ~s *n.* hanabi seizōjutsu.

python [páiθən] *n.* nishikihebi.

Q

Q, q [kjuː]. *n.* (*pl.* Q's, Qs, [kjuːz]) Eigo *alphabet* no dai-17-bamme no moji.

quack [kwæk] *n.* gā gā (ahiru) no nakigoe; yabuisha; yamashi; horafuki. *v.* gāgā naku. ～**ery** [kwǽkəri] *n.* yabuisharyū no chiryō; ōbora; yamashiteki okonai (kōi). ～ **salver** [kwǽksælvə] *n.* horafuki; yabuisha.

quadrangle [kwɔ́dræŋgl] *n.* shikakkei; shihenkei; naka-niwa

quadrangular [kwɔ́dræ̀ŋgjulə] *a.* shikaku no.

quadrant [kwɔ́drənt] *n.* shibun'en; shibungi; zōgenki.

quadrat [kwɔ́dræt] *n.* komemono (insatsu ni tsukau).

quadrate [kwɔ́dreit] *a.* seihōkei no. ～ seihōkei. ⌈hōteishiki.

quadratic [kwɔdrǽtik] *a.* (*math.*) niji no. ～ **equation** *n.* niji-

quadrennial [kwɔdréniəl] *a.* 4 (yo) nen no; yonen goto no; yonen ikkai no (*every four years*).

quadrilateral [kwɔ̀drilǽtərəl] *n.*, *a.* shihenkei (no).

quadrille [kwɔdríl] *n.* kādoriru-butō; butō-kyoku.

quadroon [kwɔdrúːn] *n.* hakujin ³/₄ kokujin ¹/₄ no konketsu ji (ainoko).

quadrumanous [kwɔdrúːmənəs] *a.* yotsude no aru.

quadruped [kwɔ́drəped] *a.* yotsuashi no aru. *n.* yotsuashijū. ～**al** [kwɔdrúːpidl] *a.* yotsuashi no aru; yotsuashijū no.

quadruple [kwɔ́drupl] *a.* yombai no. *v.* yombai ni suru; 4 (yon) o jōzuru; yombai ni naru.

quaff [kwɔf] *v.* gabugabu nomu. *n.* gabu-nomi.

quagmire [kwǽgmaiə] *n.* numachi; doronuma. ⌈sareru.

quail [kweil] (*bird*) *n.* uzura. *v.* ki o otosu; hirumu; appuku

quaint [kweint] *a.* mukashifū no; kimyōna; okashii. ⌈suru.

quake [kwéik] *n.* senritsu; shindō. *v.* senritsu suru; shindō

Quaker [kwéikə] *n.* kweikākyōto; pūkaiha (*Friend*-ha) no to.

qualification [kwɔ̀lifikéiʃən] *n.* shikaku; jōken; seigen. ⌈no.

qualified [kwɔ́lifaid] *a.* shikaku aru; seigen aru; jōkentsuki

qualify [kwɔ́lifai] *v.* shikaku (kengen) o ataeru; gōkaku saseru; (suru) seigen suru. *v.* gōkaku shikaku o eru.

qualitative [kwɔ́liteitiv / -tə-] *a.* seishitsujō no; shitsutekina.

quality [kwɔ́liti] *n.* shitsu; hinshitsu; shikaku; chōsho.

qualm [kwɔːm] *n.* hakike; memai; kashaku.

quandary [kwɔ́ndəri] *n.* tōwaku (*dilemma* de komatta yōna).

quantitative [kwɔ́ntitətiv / -tei-] *a.* bunryōjō no; ryōtekina.

quantity [kwɔ́ntiti] *n.* ryō; bunryō; sūryō.

quantum [kwɔ́ntəm] *n.* teiryō; teigaku (dokuritsu ni sonzai shiuru enerugii no saiteiryō).

quarantine [kwɔ́rənti:n] *n.* ken'eki kikan; ken'ekijo; kōtsū-shadan. *v.* kakuri suru.

quarrel [kwɔ́rəl] *n.* kenka; kōron. *v.* kenka suru. **~some** [-sʌm] *a.* kenkazukina.

quarry [kwɔ́ri] *n.* ishikiriba. *v.* kiridasu.

quart [kwɔːt] *n.* kwōto (masume, yaku 1.14 rittoru).

quater [kwɔ́:tə] *n.* ¹/₄ (shibun no ichi); (*pl.*) jin'ei; (*pl.*) sentō busho; hōgaku; basho; jihi. *v.* yontōbun suru; yadoraseru; shukuei suru; yadoru. **~deck** [-dek] *n.* kōkampan. **~ly** *v.* nen yonkai no; maiki no. *n.* nen yonkai no kankōbutsu. *ad.* nen yonkai. **~master** [-mɑ:stə] *n.* kajitori; hokyūgakari.

quartet, quartette [kwɔ-tét] *n.* (*music*) shibu-gassō kyoku.

quarto [kwɔ́:tou] *n.* yotsuoriban no hon.

quartz [kwɔːts] *n.* sekiei.

quash [kwɔʃ] *v.* torikesu; mukō ni suru.

quasi [kwéisai] *conj. iwaba. a.* mikake no.

quasi- [kweisai] *pref.* jun-; **~-official,** jun-kanri. **~-humo(u)r,** namanie no share.

quaver [kwéivə] *v.* furueru; furuegoe o dasu; furuegoe de u-tau. *n.* furue; furuegoe.

quay [ki:] *n.* hatoba; futō; gampeki.

queen [kwi:n] *n.* kōgō; joō; joōbachi. **~ mother,** kōtaigō. **~ly** *a.* joō rashii; igen no aru.

queer [kwíə] *a.* henna; okashii; myōna.

quell [kwel] *v.* shizumeru; chintei suru.

quench [kwéntʃ] *v.* kesu; osaeru; shizumeru. **~** *thirst,* kawaki o tomeru. *Water will* **~** *a fire,* mizu ga kaji o kesu.

querist [kwíərist] *n.* jimmonsha; shitsumonsha.

querulous [kwéruləs] *a.* fuhei fuman no.

query [kwíəri] *n.* shitsumon; utagai. *v.* gimon o motsu.

quest [kwest] *n.* tansaku. *v.* tazunemawaru.

question [kwéstʃən] *n.* gimon; mondai. *in* ~, mondai no. *out of* ~, mochiron. ~**able** [-əbl] *a.* utagawashii; ayashii.

queue [kju:] *n.* osage; jumban o matsu gyōretsu.

quibble [kwíbl] *n.* herikutsu; share.

quick [kwik] *a.* hayai. *ad.* hayaku; jinsokuni. ~**en** [-ⁿn] *v.* hayameru; genkizukeru. ~**ening** [-ⁿniŋ] *n.* saisho no taidō (taiji no). ~**-eyed** [-ⁿaid] *a.* me no hayai. ~**-fire** [-ⁿfaiə] *n.* sokusha no. ~**-lime** [-ⁿlaim] *n.* seisekkai. ~**ly** *ad.* subayaku. ~**ness** *n.* jinsoku; binshō; tanki. ~**sand** [-ⁿsænd] *n.* yawarakai zuruzuru hairikomu suna. ~**silver** [-ⁿsilvə] *n.* suigin. ~**-tempered** [-ⁿtémpəd] *a.* tankina; sugu kātto naru. ~**-witted** [-ⁿwítid] *a.* atama no surudoi.

quid [kwid] *n.* (*Brit. sl.*) pondo kinka.

quiddity [kwíditi] *n.* honshitsu; herikutsu.

quidnunc [kwídnʌŋk] *n.* kikitagariya (hito); kanabō hiki.

quiescence [kwaiésəns] *n.* seijaku; fudō; mui.

quiescent [kwaiésənt] *a.* shizukana; ugokanai.

quiet [kwáiət] *a.* shizukana; ugokanai. *n.* shizukesa; seijaku (*stillness*) ochitsuki. *v.* shizumeru; yasunzuru. ~**ude** [-ju:d] *n.* seion; heian; chinchaku. ~**us** [kwaií:təs] *n.* shi; saigo no shūshifu. *The arrival of the militia gave the riot its* ~, mimpei no tōchaku de bōdō ga shizumatta.

quill [kwil] *n.* tori no hane (mukashi wa pen ni shita).

quilt [kwilt] *n.* futon.

quince [kwins] *n.* (*bot.*) marumero; sono mi.

quinine [kwáinain / kwiní:n] *n.* kiniine; kinaen.

quinquennial [kwiŋkwéniəl] *a.* 5 (go) nen goto no; gonenkan tsuzuku.

quinsy [kwínzi] *n.* (*med.*) hentōsen'en.

quintessence [kwintésəns] *n.* shinzui; okugi.

quintet, quintette [kwintét] *n.* gobu-gasshōkyoku.

quintuple [kwintʃúpl / kwíntjupl] *a.* 5 (go) bai no; gojū no.

quip [kwip] *n.* chōrō; hiniku; iinuke.

quire [kwáiə] *n.* (kami) ichijō.

quirk [kwəːk] *n.* kimagure; gomakashi; iinuke.

quisling [kwízliŋ] *n.* hangyakusha (kōi); uragirimono (kōi).

quit [kwit] *v.* **quit** *or* **quitted; quitting.** yameru ; suteru ; jinin suru. *a.* manukareta ; jiyūna ; gimu o hatashita.

quite [kwait] *ad.* mattaku ; marude ; hijōni.

quittance [kwítəns] *n.* menjo ; kaijo ; tsugunai. 「wananaku.

quiver [kwívə] *n.* yazutsu ; ebira ; furue ; wananaki. *v.* furueru ;

quixotic [kwiksɔ́tik] *a.* Donkihōte (*Don Quixote*) shiki no ; kūsōtekina.

quiz [kwiz] *n.* kangaemono ; hiyakashi ; (kyōshi no) shimon. *v.* karakau ; shimon suru.

quizzical [kwízikəl] *a.* chōshōteki no ; hentekona ; okashina.

quoin [kwɔin] *n.* sumiishi ; kusabi.

quoit [kwɔit] *n.* kanawa ; (*pl.*) kanawa nage.

quondam [kwɔ́ndəm] *a.* mae no ; izen no.

Quonset hut [kwɔ́nsit hʌt] *n.* kamaboko gata kumitate jūtaku.

quorum [kwɔ́ːrəm] *n.* teisū ; teiin.

quota [kwóutə] *n.* bubun ; wakemae ; wariateryō.

quotable [kwóutəbl] *a.* in'yō shiuru.

quotation [kwoutéiʃən] *n.* in'yō (bun, ku) ; *quotation* ni dekiru. ∼**marks** [-mɑːks] in'yōfu (" ") mata wa (' ').

quote [kwóut] *v.* (ta no goku o) in'yo suru.

quoth [kwóuθ] *v.* (*arch.*) 3 ninshō no **said.**

quotidian [kwoutídiən] *a.* mainichi no ; heibonna. ∼ **ague,** nippatsu netsu. 「∼**, chinō shisū.**

quotient [kwóuʃənt] *n.* shō ; warizan no kotae. **intelligence**

R

R, r [ɑː] *n.* (*pl.* R's, Rs [ɑːz]) Eigo *alphabet* dai-18-bamme no moji.

R.A. (*Royal Academy*) Eikoku Ōshitsu Gakushi-in.

rabbet [rǽbit] *n.* sanehagi (ita no tsugikata no isshu).

rabbi [rǽbai], **rabbin** [rǽbin] *n.* sensei (Yudaya rippō hakase).

rabbit [rǽbit] *n.* usagi ; kai usagi.

rabble [rǽbl] *n.* waiwairen ; yajimma ; katō shakai.

rabid [rǽbid] *a.* kyōbōna ; kyōsuibyō ni kakatta.

rabies [réibiːz] *n.* (*med.*) kyōsuibyō.

raccoon [rækúːn] *n.* (*zoo*) araiguma.

race [reis] *n.* minzoku ; kyōsō ; kōtei. *v.* kyōsō suru ; kyōsō saseru. **~-course** [-kɔːs] *n.* keibajō ; kyōsōro. **~-meeting** *n.*

racial [réiʃəl] *a.* shuzoku no ; jinshu no. ⌊keibakai

racily [réisili] *ad.* fūmi yoku ; piriri to. (*cf.* **racy**).

raciness [réisinis] *n.* fūmi no yoi koto (*being racy*) ; kyōmi ;

racism [réisizm] *n.* minzokuteki yūetsukan. ⌊kiryoku.

rack [ræk] *n.* gōmondai ; kutsū ; kōshi-dana ; (katana-, fude-) kake ; (uma no) karugake. *v.* (uma ga) karugake suru ; kurushimeru ; teashi o hippatte gōmon suru. **~ railway** [-réilwei] *n.* Abutoshiki tetsudō. **~-rent** [-rent] *n.* hōgai ni takai jidai.

racket [rǽkit] *n.* (teikyū no) raketto ; (*pl.*) isshu no dakyūgi ; raketto-gata yukigutsu. sawagi ; kinsen no yusuri ; fusei shudan. **~eer** [rækitíə] *n.* kyōkatsusha ; yusuri.

racy [réisi] *a.* fūmi no aru. *see :* **racily, raciness**.

radar [réidə] *n.* dempatanchiki

radial [réidiəl] *a.* kōsen no ; hōshanō ; hankei (*radius*) no ; (*anat.*) tōkotsu no. *n.* hōshabu (*radiating part*).

radiance, ~cy [réidiəns, -si] *n.* hakkō ; hikari ; kagayaki.

radiant [réidiənt] *a.* hikari kagayaku ; nikoniko suru ; hareyakana.

radiate [réidieit] *v.* hanatsu (hikari, netsu nado o) ; hōsha suru. *a.* hōsha suru ; fukushajō no.

radiation [reidiéiʃən] *n.* hakkō ; netsuhōsha ; fukusha.

radiator [réidieitə] *n.* hakkōtai ; hōshabutsu ; hōnetsuki ; jidōsha no hōnetsu-sōchi.

radical [rǽdikl] *a.* kompontekina ; kyūgekina ; ne kara haeru. (*ling.*) gokon no. *n.* kyūshintōin ; kyūshinronja. ～**ism** *n.* kagekiron ; kyūshin-shugi.

radio [réidiou] *n.* (musen) denshin, denwa ; rajio. *v.* muden o utsu ; musen-hōsō suru ; X-sen de satsuei suru ; radiumu de chiryō suru. *a.* musen no. ～**active** [réidio(u)ǽktiv] *a.* hōshanō no aru. ～**activity** [-æktíviti] *n.* hōshanō. ～ **beacon,** musen kōro hyōshiki. ～**broadcast** [-brɔːdkæst] *v.* hōsō suru. ～ **broadcaster** *n.* musen hōsōsha ; musen hōsō sōchi. ～**broadcasting** *n.* musen hōsō. ～ **compass,** musen rashimban. ～ **detector** [-ditéktə] *n.* kempaki. ～ **frequency,** musen shūhasū. ～**gram** [-græm] *n.* musen dempō. ～**graph** [-grǽf] *n.* hōshasen shashin ; X-sen shashin. *v.* X-sen shashin ni toru. ～**locator** [-loukéitə] *n.* dempatanchiki. ～**message** [-mésidʒ] *n.* musen denshin (denwa). ～ **operator,** musen denshin gishi. ～**phone** [-foun] *n.* musen denwa ; musen denwaki. ～ **photography** [-fətɔ́grəfi] *n.* shashin denso. ～**press** [-prés] *n.* rajio hōdō. ～ **receiver,** musen jushinki. ～**sonde** [-sɔnd] *n.* rajio zonde. ～**station,** musen denshin (hōsō) kyoku ; hōsōkyoku. ～**telegram** [-téləgræm] *n.* musen dempō. ～**telegraph** [-télə græf] *n.* musen denshin (-ki). *v.* musen denshin o utsu. ～**telegraphy** *n.* musen denshinjutsu. ～**telephone** [-téləfoun] *n.* musen denwa (-ki). ～**telephony** [-tələfəni] *n.* musen denwajutsu. ～**therapy** [-θérəpi] *n.* hōshasen ryōhō.

radish [rǽdiʃ] *n.* daikon (*vegetable*).

radium [réidiəm] *n.* rajūmu.

radius [réidiəs] *n.* (*pl.* **-dii** [-diai]) hōshasen ; (*anat.*) dōkotsu. (*bot.*) shashutsuka. (*math.*) hankei.

R.A.F., RAF *n.* Eikoku kūgun (*Royal Air Force*).

raffle [rǽfl] *n.* chūsen hambai. *v.* kujibiki de uru.

raft [rɑːft] *n.* ikada. *v.* ikada ni tsukuru ; ikada de unsō suru.

rafter [rɑːftə] *n.* taruki.

rag [ræg] *n.* boro ; borokire ; (*pl.*) borokimono ; warusawagi (*rumpus*). *v.* ijimeru (*tease*) ; shikaru (*scold*). ～**ged** [rǽgid] *a.*

yabureta; borogire (*rags*) o kita (*wore*). ⁓**weed** [rǽgwi:d] *n.* (*herb*) butakusa no rui.

ragamuffin [rǽgəməfin] *n.* boro kimono no hito; narazu mono (*disreputable fellow*).

rage [reidჳ] *n.* ikari; gekido (*violent anger*). ryūkōbutsu (*the fashion*). *v.* okoru; donaru.

raglan [rǽglən] *n.* ragurangata gaitō.

ragout [rægú:] *n.* isshu no shichū ryōri. **ragtime** [rǽgtaim] *n.* jazu ongaku.

raid [reid] *n.* shinnyū (*invasion*); shūgeki; (keikan no) teire. *v.* shigeki suru; teire suru : *air* ⁓, *n.* kūshū. *make a* ⁓ *upon*, ... o osou.

rail [reil] *n.* tesuri; rankan. tetsudō. *v.* tesuri o tsukeru. kidō o tsukeru; kisha de ryokō suru. nonoshiru; azakeru. ⁓**ing** *n.* tesuri; rankan; kaki; saku. ⁓**road** [⌐roud] (*Am.*), ⁓**way** [⌐wei] (*Brit.*) *n.*, *v.* tetsudō (de yusō suru).

raillery [réiləri] *n.* jōdan; karakai.

raiment [réimənt] *n.* ifuku; fukusō (furui; gishikibatta).

rain [rein] *n.* ame. *v.* ame ga furu; ame no yōni abiseru. ⁓**bow** *n.* niji. ⁓**coat** [⌐kout] *n.* amagaitō. ⁓**drop** [⌐drɔp] *n.* ame no shizuku. ⁓**fall** [⌐fɔ:il] *n.* kōu; amefuri. ⁓**storm** [⌐stɔ:m] *n.* bōfūu. ⁓**y** *a.* amefuri no; amegachina.

raise [reiz] *v.* ageru; okosu; takameru; kizuku (ie, ishigaki nado o); atsumeru; toru (zei o); sodateru. *n.* zōka; shōkyū.

raisin [réizn] *n.* hoshi-budō.

raison d'etre [reizon déitrə] (*Fr.*) sonzai no riyū.

raja, rajah [rá:dჳə] *n.* ō; kunshu.

rake [reik] *n.* kumade; maguwa; hōtōmono. *v.* keisha suru; kumade de kaku; kakiatsumeru.

rakish [réikiʃ] *a.* keikaina (fune ni iu); haikarana; ikina.

ralli-car(t) [rǽlika:(t)] *n.* yoninnori kogata nirinbasha.

rally [rǽli] *v.* atsumeru (yabureta mikata o); atsumaru; morikaesu; hiyakasu; karakau. *n.* kiryoku; kaifuku; morikaeshi; karakai; hiyakashi.

ram [ræm] *n.* ohitsuji; (R⁓) (*astr.*) Ohitsujiza. teki no shiro o yaburu tame no tsuchi (*battering ram*); shōkaku (gunkan no). *v.* tsuki ataru.

ramble [rǽmbl] *n.* sampo; shōyō. *v.* burabura aruku; toritome mo naku kaku. ~ing [rǽmbliŋ] *a.* buratsuku ; sammanna.

ramekin, ramequin [rǽməkin] *n.* chiizu, pankuzu, tamago nado o maze yakigata de yaita mono.

ramification [ræ̀mifikéiʃən] *n.* eda ga deru koto ; bumpa.

ramify [rǽmifai] *v.* eda o dasu ; wakareru ; bumpa suru.

ramp [ræmp] *v.* haneagaru ; (*bot.*) haiagaru. *n.* keisha shita rōka ; keishamen. ~**age** [⌐idʒ] *n.* abaremawaru koto. ~**ant** [⌐ənt] *a.* jiyūhompōna ; bakko suru (*unrestrained*).

rampart [rǽmpət] *n., v.* ruiheki (o megurasu).

ramrod [rǽmrɔd] *n.* (jūshin sōji-yō no) sakujō.

ran [ræn] *v. see* : **run.**

ranch [ræntʃ] *n.* bokuchikunōjō ; dainōjō. ~**er** [rǽntʃə] *n.* bokujō keieisha (shoyūsha) ; bokujō rōdōsha.

rancid [rǽnsid] *a.* kusarikakatta nioi no suru.

ranco(u)r [rǽŋkə] *n.* enkon ; urami.

rancorous [rǽŋkərəs] *a.* fukai urami o motta. 「mini.

random [rǽndəm] *n.* mukeikaku. *at* ~, ikiatari battari ; muyarang [ræŋ] *v. see* : **ring.**

range [reindʒ] *v.* naraberu ; retsu ni ireru ; narabu ; kurai suru. *n.* retsu ; kuiki ; bumpu han'i ; chishiki han'i ; tama no todoku (chakudan) kyori. **gas** ~, ryōriyō kamado. *in* ~ *with*, to narande. ~ **finder**, kyori sokuteiki. ~**r** [réindʒə] *n.* aruki mawaru hito ; haikaisha ; (*pl.*) yūgekihei.

rank [ræŋk] *n.* retsu ; kaikyū ; kurai ; (*pl.*) taigo. *v.* naraberu ; bunrui suru ; ressuru. *break* ~, retsu o midasu. ~ *and fashion*, jōryū shakai. *a.* hiyoku ni sugiru ; shigeri sugita. *land too* ~ *to grow corn*, amari koete ite kokumotsu ga uerarenai tochi.

rankle [rǽŋkl] *v.* itsu made mo tsuzuite mune o itamaseru : *That insult* ~*d him through his life*, sono bujoku ga isshō kare no mune o saranakatta.

ransack [rǽnsæk] *v.* tetteitekini sagasu : ~*ed the desk for the lost letter*, sono nakunatta tegami o mitsukeyō to tetteiteki ni tsukue no naka o sagashita.

ransom [rǽnsəm] *n.* baishō ; minoshirokin. *v.* miuke suru.

rant [rænt] *n.* bōgen. *v.* bōgen o haku. ~**er** *n.* kuchiyakama-
rap [ræp] *v.* tataku. *n.* tataku koto. 「shiya.

rapacious [rəpéiʃəs] *a*. gōyokuna; gōdatsu suru (*plunder*); ni-
rapacity [rəpǽsiti] *n*. don'yoku.   ⌊kushoku no.

rape [reip] *n*. gōdatsu; gōkan. (*bot*.) aburana. *v*. gōkan suru.

rapid [rǽpid] *a*. hayai; jinsokuna. *n*. kyūryū. ~**ity** [rəpíditi]
n. jinsoku; hayasa; sokudo.

rapier [réipiə] *n*. (isshu no) hosonagai ken.

rapine [rǽpin] *n*. gōdatsu; ryakudatsu.

rapt [rǽpt] *a*. uchōten no; kōkotsu taru. ~**ure** [rǽptʃə] *n*.
uchōten; kyōki (ōyorokobi). ~**urous** [rǽptʃərəs] *a*. ōyorokobi no; uchōten no.

rare [rɛə] *a*. marena; mezurashii; mettani nai; namanie no.
~**faction** [rɛərifǽkʃən] *n*. kihaku (kūki nado) kihakuka. ~**fy**
[rɛərifai] *v*. kihaku ni suru.

rarity [rɛəriti] *n*. mezurashii mono. kihaku.

rascal [rá:skl] *n*. akkan; (hajishirazu no) akutō. ~**ity** [rɑ:skǽ-
liti] *n*. hidōna okonai.

rash [rǽʃ] *n*. (*med*.) hasshin. *a*. keisotsuna.

rasher [rǽʃə] *n*. shiobuta no usui kirimi.   ⌈seru; jirasu.

rasp [rǽsp] *n*. ōmeyasuri. *v*. araku suru; kishiraseru; iradata-
raspberry [rǽzberi] *n*. (*fruit*) kiichigo; kuroichigo.

rat [rǽt] *n*. (*zoo*) nezumi. teikyūna shin'yō no nai otoko. *v*. nezumi o toraeru; nakama o uragiru. *smell a* ~, uron kusaku
omou. ~**sbane** [rǽtbein] *n*. nezumitorizai.

ratchet [rǽtʃit] *n*. ratchetto; tsumeguruma sōchi.

rate [reit] *n*. wariai; wariai de kimeru koto; wariate-ritsu. *v*.
wariai o hakaru; hyōka suru; shikaru; nonoshiru; kurai suru. *at any* ~, tonikaku.

rather [rǽðə] *ad*. mushiro. *I would* ~ *go today*, watashi wa mushiro kyō iki tai. *This is* ~ *for father to decide than you*, kore
wa kimi yori mushiro otōsama ni kimete itadaku beki da.

rathskeller [rá:tskelə] *n*. (*G*.) chikashitsu biya-hōru.

ratification [rǽtifikéiʃən] *n*. hijun; shōnin.

ratifier [rǽtifaiə] *v*. hijunsha; zeninsha.

ratify [rǽtifai] *n*. hijun suru; zenin suru.

rating [reitiŋ] *n*. hyōka; tōkyū. wariate; mitsumori. *the* ~ *of
a seaman*, aru kaiin (funanori) no kaikyū. *give a sound* ~, shi-
ratio [réiʃiou] *n*. hi; hiritsu; wariai.   ⌊karitobasu.

ratiocinate [ræ̀ʃiɔ́sineit] *v.* ronritekini suiri suru.
ratiocination [ræ̀ʃiɔsinéiʃən / -tiɔs-] *n.* ronriteki suiron.
ration [rǽʃən / rei-] *n.* ryōshoku no haikyū; teigaku; teiryō. *v.* wariateru.
rational [rǽʃənəl] *a.* risei no aru; gōritekina. ～**ism** *n.* gōrisetsu; junriron. ～**ist** *n.* junrironsha. ～**ity** [ræ̀ʃ(ə)nǽliti] *n.* gōrisei; junrisei. ～**ization** [ræ̀ʃ(ə)nəlaizéiʃ(ə)n / -li-] *n.* gōrika; ～ *of industry*, sangyō gōrika. ～**ize** *v.* gōrika suru; rirontekini kangaeru; junritekini setsumei suru; gōrika o okonau. ～**ly** *ad.* gōritekini.
ratline [rǽtlin], **ratling** [rǽtliŋ] *n.* (fune nado no) nawabashigo.
rattan [rætǽn] *n., a.* (*bot.*) tō; tōsei no.
rat-tat [rǽttǽt] *n.* ton-ton (tobira o tataku oto nado).
ratten [rǽtn] *v.* koso-koso itazura shite kurushimeru.
rattle [rǽtl] *v.* gara-gara naru (kuruma no oto nado); gata-gata iwaseru; hayaguchi ni shaberu; komaraseru. *n.* gara-gara; becha-kucha; shinigiwa no nodogoe. ～**r** *n.* gara-gara iu mono; dabenka; doshaburi. ～**snake** [-sneik] *n.* gara-garahebi.
rattling [rǽtliŋ] *a.* gara-gara iu; kappatsuna; genki no yoi; subarashii.
raucous [rɔ́:kəs] *a.* shagaregoe no.
ravage [rǽvidʒ] *n.* arasareta ato; mugotarashisa. *v.* arasu.
rave [reiv] *v.* tawagoto o iu; muchūni natte tokitateru.
ravel [rǽvl] *v.* toku; hogusu; tokeru; hogureru.
raven [réivn] *n.* (*bird*) watari garasu. [rǽvən] *v.* gōdatsu suru; gatsu-gatsu kuu. ～**ing** *a.* gatsu-gatsu kuu; gōyokuna. ～**ous** [rǽvinəs] *a.* gatsu-gatsu kuu; gōyokuna. ～**ously** *ad.* uekitte; hijōni.
ravine [rəví:n] *n.* kyōkoku; yamaai.
raving [réiviŋ] *a.* arekurū; kyōran no.
ravish [rǽviʃ] *v.* muchūni suru; uttori saseru; gōkan suru. ～**ing** *a.* kōkotsu (uttori) to saseru. ～**ment** *n.* kōkotsu; gōkan; ryakudatsu.
raw [rɔ:] *a.* nama no; genryō no mama no; mijukuna; kawa no muketa. ～**silk** *n.* kiito. *n.* kawa no suri muketa tokoro; itai tokoro. ～**boned** [-bóund] *a.* yasekoketa.
ray [rei] *n.* kōsen; netsusen. (*fish*) ei. *v.* shashitsu suru (kōsen nado o); kōsen o hōsha suru.
rayon [réiən] *n.* jinzō kenshi; reiyon.

raze [reiz] *v.* torisaru; hakai suru; (ke o) soru.
razor [réizə] *n.* kamisori. ∼**back** [-bæk] *n.* iwashikujira. han'-
yasei no buta (*pig*). ∼**edge** [réizərédʒ] *n.* kamisori no ha;
yama no se; bunsuirei. ∼**-strop** [-stróp] *n.* kamisori no
razz [ræz] *v.* hinan (warukuchi) suru; ijimeru.   ⌐kawado.
re [rei] *n.* (*mus*) chōonkai no daini (2) no on.
reach [ri:tʃ] *v.* nobasu (te, ashi o); watasu; tōchaku suru; todoku; itaru. *n.* todoku tokoro; kuiki : ∼ *after* (*or at*), ni tasshi
yō to tsutomeru.
react [ri(:)ækt] *v.* handō suru; hannō suru. ∼**ion** [-ǽkʃ(ə)n]
n. handō; hannō. ∼**ionary** [-ʃ(ə)nəri] *a.* handō no; gyakumodori no; hoshutekina.
read [ri:d] *v.* **read** [red]; **reading.** yomu; tokusho (do-)
suru. ∼**able** *a.* omoshiroku kaite aru. ∼**er** *n.* dokusha; do-
kushoka (t-). tokuhon. ∼**ing** *n.* dokusho (toku-); rōdoku;
kōdoku; yomimono; yomikata; kaishaku.
read [red] *v. see* : **read**.
readily [rédili] *a.* suguni; yōi ga dekite.
ready [rédi] *a.* yōi shite; jumbi shite. ∼**-made** [-méid] *a.*
dekiai no (sugu ni mani au). ∼**money** *n.* genkin.
reagent [ri(:)éidʒənt] *n.* shiyaku; aru mono no ari, nashi o tashikameru kusuri.
real [rí:əl] *a.* jissai no; hontō no; jitsuzai no. ∼ **estate,** fudōsan. ∼**ism** *n.* jitsuzairon; genjitsu shugi. ∼**ist** *n.* shajitsuha
no hito. ∼**istic** [ri(:)əlístik] *a.* jitsuzairon no; jissha no. ∼
ity [ri(:)ǽliti] *n.* shinjitsu; genjitsu; jittai; jijitsu. *in* ∼, shinni.
∼**ize** [rí(:)əlaiz] *v.* jitsugen suru; shōkin ni kaeru. ∼**ly** *ad.*
hontō ni. ∼**ty** [ríəlti] *n.* fudōsan.
realm [relm] *n.* kokudo; ryōdo.   ⌐(*kl.* ren).
ream [ri:m] *n.* ren (kami 480 *or* 500 mai). ima wa 1000 mai
reanimate [ri:ǽnimeit] *v.* sosei saseru; genki o torimodasu.
reap [ri:p] *v.* karitoru; shūtoku suru.
rear [riə] *n.* ushiro; kōjin. *v.* ageru; sodateru; (uma ga) ushiro
ashi de tatsu. ∼ **admiral,** *n.* kaigun shōshō. ∼ **guard**
[-gá:d] kōei. ∼**ward** [-wɔ:d] *a., ad., n.* ato no hō(no, ni); kōbu
ni (no, e). ∼**wards** *ad.* =∼*ward.*
reason [rí:zn] *n.* riyū; dōri. (*pl.*) jijō. *v.* ronzuru; wake o itte
kikaseru; ronkyū suru; suiri suru : *I have my* ∼*s to do this*,

kore o suru niwa wake (jijō) ga aru. ～**able** *a*. wake no wakaru ; dōri ni atta. ～**ing** *n*. suiron ; riron ; ronshō.

reassure [ri:əʃúə] *v*. sai-hoshō suru ; anshin saseru.

rebate [rí:bəit / ribéit] *n*. warimodoshi. *v*. waribiku.

rebel [rébl] *n*. hangyakunin. *a*. hangyaku no. *v*. [ribél] somuku. ～**lion** [ribéljən] *n*. muhon ; hanran. ～**lious** [ribéljəs] *a*. muhon shita ; hangyaku no.

rebirth [ri:bə́:θ] *n*. saisei ; fukkatsu. ⌈ta. *n*. hanekaeri ; handō.

rebound [rí(:)báund] *v*. hanekaeru ; hazumu. seihon shinaoshi-

rebroadcast [ri:brɔ́:dkæst] *v*. chūkei hōsō-suru ; chūkei suru.

rebuff [ribʌ́f] *n*. kyozetsu ; zasetsu. *v*. kyozetsu suru ; zasetsu

rebuke [ribjú:k] *v*. shikaru ; kenseki suru. *n*. kenseki. ⌊saseru.

rebus [rí:bəs] *n*. hanjie (*cat* + *log* no futatsu de '*catalog*' to yomu yōna).

rebut [ribʌ́t] *v*. hambaku suru. ～**tal** [-əl] *n*. genkoku (*plaintiff*) no rombaku (*refutation*) ; hambaku.

recalcitrant [rikǽlsitrənt] *a*. gōjōna ; hankō suru.

recall [rikɔ́:l] *n*. yobimodoshi ; rikōru. *v*. shōkan suru ; rikōru o suru ; torimodosu ; omoidasu. *ambassador was* ～*ed*, taishi wa (torikeshi) yobimodosareta.

recant [rikǽnt] *v*. torikesu ; tekkai suru : *After careful study the scholar* ～*ed his first opinion*, jikkuri kenkyū shite kara sono gakusha wa hajime no iken o kaeta. ～**ation** [ri:kæntéiʃən] *n*. iinaoshi ; torikeshi ; hensetsu.

recapitulate [rì:kəpítʃuleit] *v*., yōten (o tsukamu). ⌈to).

recapitulation [rí:kəpìtʃulé:ʃən] *n*. tekiyō (*recapitulate* suru ko-

recast [rí:káːst] *v*. inaosu ; *cast* (kata ni irete iru) shinaosu.

recede [risí:d] *v*. shirizoku ; te o hiku ; hikkomu.

receipt [risí:t] *n*., *v*. uketorisho (o watasu).

receivable [risí:vəbl] *a*. uketori uru ; shiharawareru.

receive [risí:v] *v*. uketoru ; mukaeru ; motenasu. ～**r** *n*. uketorinin ; settaisha ; iremono ; jushinki.

recent [rí:snt] *a*. atarashii ; chikagoro no. ～**ly** *ad*. chikagoro.

receptacle [riséptəkl] *n*. iremono ; (*bot*.) kataku (*calyx*).

reception [risépʃən] *n*. ukeire ; ōsetsu ; kangeikai.

receptive [riséptiv] *a*. ukeire-nōryoku no aru ; etoku no hayai.

receptivity [riseptíviti] *n*. kanjusei.

recess [risés] *n.* kyūkei; hikkonda tokoro; oku; toko-no-ma.
v. kubomi o tsukuru; kyūkei suru. ⁓**ion** [riséʃən] *n.* taikyo;
recipe [résipi] *n.* shohō; seihō; hiketsu.   ⌊kubomi.
recipient [risípiənt] *a.* ukeru; ukeireru. *n.* juryōsha.
reciprocal [risíprəkl] *a.* otagaini (tasukeau nado); henrei no.
⁓ **treaty** *n.* gokei-jōyaku.
reciprocate [risíprəkeit] *v.* tagaini torikawasu; mukuiru.
reciprocation [risìprəkéiʃən] *n.* kōgo sayō; kōkan.
reciprocity [resìprósiti] *n.* sōgo sayō; gokei shugi; rieki no
recital [risáitl] *n.* (anshō, ongaku nado) dokuenkai. ⌊kōkan.
recitation [rèsitéiʃən] *n.* anshō; ginshō.   ⌈shō-chō no.
recitative [rèsitəti:v] *n.* ginshō suru kotoba. *a.* [résiteitiv] gin-
recite [risáit] *v.* ginshō suru; hanasu; noberu.
reck [rek] *v.* chūi suru. ⁓**less** [⁻lis] *a.* fuchūina; mukōmizuna.
reckon [rékən] *v.* kazoeru; hyōka suru; minasu. ⁓ **on** (*or upon*), o ate ni suru. ⁓**ing** *n.* keisan.
reclaim [rikléim] *v.* yoi jōken ni kaesu; kaitaku suru; ume-
tateru. *n.* kyōsei; kaishin : *be past* ⁓, kaishun no mikomi no
nai.   ⌈fukki.
reclamation [rèkləméiʃən] *n.* kaifuku; kaishin; yoi jōtai e no
recline [rikláin] *v.* yorikakaru; yokotaeru; motareru.
recluse [riklú:s] *a.* ukiyo o suteta. *n.* yosutebito.
recognition [rəkəgníʃən] *n.* ninshiki; shōnin : *in* ⁓ *of*, ...no
shō to shite.
recognizance [rikógnizəns] *n.* shōnin (sho); hoshōkin.
recognize [rékəgnaiz] *v.* shōnin suru; mishiru; omoi dasu.
recoil [rikóil] *n.* (jū no) handō; atozusari. *v.* handō suru; ato-
shizari suru : *The gun* ⁓*ed, when I fired,* watashi ga happō shitara, jū ga handō shita. *He* ⁓*ed at seeing a snake,* kare wa hebi
o mite atozusari shita.
recollect [rèkəlékt] *v.* omoi dasu; kaisō suru. ⁓**ion** [-rèkə-
lékʃ(ə)n] *n.* tsuisō; kioku; omoide.
re-collect [rí:kəlékt] *v.* futatabi atsumeru; ochitsukaseru.
recommend [rèkəménd] *v.* suisen suru; susumeru. ⁓**ation**
[rèkəmendéiʃ(ə)n] *n.* suisen (jō).   ⌈nau.
recompense [rékəmpens] *n.* hōshū; baishō. *v.* mukuiru; aga-
reconcile [rékənsail] *v.* nakanaori saseru (suru); akirame saseru.

reconciliation [rèkənsiliéiʃən] *n.* chōtei; waboku; chōwa.

recondite [rékəndait] *a.* shinanna; wakarinikui.

recondition [ri:kəndíʃən] *v.* shūri suru.

reconnaissance [rəkónesəns] *n.* teisatsu (tai). **air ~,** kūchū teisatsu; kūchū sōsa. **~ machine,** teisatsu (hikō) ki.

reconnoiter, -tre [rékənəitə] *v.* teisatsu suru.

record [rékəd] *n.*, *v.* kiroku; (ōyake no) kiroku; chikuonki no rekōdo; (ningen ya dōbutsu sonota no shita jijitsu no) kiroku. *beat (or break) the* **~,** rekōdo o yaburu. *v.* [rikó:d] kiroku suru : *We* **~** *history in books,* warera wa rekishi o shomotsu ni kiroku suru. **~er** [rikó:də] *n.* kiroku gakari; kiroku sōchi. **~ bolder** *n.* saikō kiroku hojisha.

recount [rikáunt] *v.* kuwashiku (*minutely*) hanasu.

re-count [rí:káunt] *v.* kazoe naosu; mō ippen kazoeru (*count*).

recoup [rikú:p] *v.* sashihiku; aganau; benshō suru (*make up for*). 「**~ to,** ... ni tayoru.

recourse [rikó:s] *n.* irai; irai sareta hito mata wa mono : *have*

recover [rikávə] *v.* kaifuku suru; sosei saseru; honshin ni kaeru. **~y** [-ri] *n.* kaifuku; fukkatsu.

re-cover [rí:kávə] *v.* ōinaosu; hyōshi o tsukekaeru.

recreant [rékriənt] *a.* hikyōna; fujitsuna. *n.* hikyōmono; uragirimono. 「tanoshimu.

recreate [rékrieit] *v.* genki o tsukeru; kyūyō saseru (suru);

re-create [rí:kriéit] *v.* kaizō suru; tsukurinaosu.

recreation [rèkriéiʃən] *n.* kyūyō; hoyō; kibarashi; rekuriēshon.

recriminate [rikrímineit] *v.* tagaini tsumi o nasuriau.

recrimination [rikriminéiʃ(ə)n] *n.* tsumi no nasuriai.

recruit [rikrú:t] *v.* aratani hojū suru; kaiin o boshū suru. *n.* hojūhei; shinzan-mono.

rectal [réktəl] *a.* (*anat.*) chokuchō no.

rectangle [réklæŋgl] *n.* (*math.*) kukei; chōhōkei.

rectangular [rəktǽŋgjulə] *a.* (*math.*) kukei no; chōhōkei no.

rectification [rèktifikéiʃ(ə)n] *n.* kaisei; tadashiku (*right*) suru

rectify [réktifai] *v.* kyōsei suru; kaitei suru. 「koto (*to make*).

rectilinear [rèktilínia] *a.* chokusen no; chokusen de dekita.

rectitude [réktitju:d] *n.* jitchoku; seiren; seikaku.

rector [réktə] *n.* kyōkuchō; kōchō; daigaku sōchō. **~y** [-ri] *n.* kyōkuchō no jūtaku (shokubun).　⌈*intestines*).

rectum [réktəm] *n.* (*anat.*) chokuchō (*the lowest part of the large*

recumbent [rikámbənt] *a.* yoko ni natta (neta).　⌈hirō).

recuperate [rikjú:pəreit] *v.* kaifuku suru (byōki, kyokudo no

recuperation [rikjù:pəréiʃən] *n.* kaifuku.

recur [riká:] *v.* tokidoki okoru. ~**rence** [-rens] *n.* saihatsu;
tokidoki okoru koto.

red [red] *a.* akai; (R~) Sovietto Roshia no. *n.* akairo; aka-
enogu. ~**cap** [⊥kæp] *n.* (eki no) akabō. **Red Cross,** Seki-
jūji(sha). ~**den** *v.* akaku suru; akaku naru. ~**dish** [⊥iʃ] *a.*
akami o obita.

redeem [ridí:m] *v.* aganau; kaimodosu. ~**er** [-ə] *n.* aganai-
nushi; kaimodoshinin; (R-) kyūseishu.

redemption [ridémpʃən] *n.* kaimodoshi; miuke; shōkan; (tsumi no) aganai; sukui.　⌈shi yukashisa.

redolence, -cy [rédələns, -si] *n.* hōkō; kōbashii nioi; muka-

redolent [rédələnt] *a.* kambashii; mukashi yukashii. "*Ivanhoe*"
is a name ~ *of romance,* "Aivanhō" to ieba romantikkuna na-

redouble [ri(:)dʌ́bl] *v.* baimashi ni suru (naru).　⌊mae da.

redoubtable [ridáutəbl] *a.* osoroshii.

redound [ridáund] *v.* ... ni naru : shimai ni ... to naru.

redress [ridrés] *n.* kyōsei; kyūsai. *v.* tadasu; sukū.

reduce [ridjú:s] *v.* sageru (*bring down*); herasu (*make less*).

reducible [ridjú:səbl] *a.* genjirareru; chijimerareru; *reduce* de-

reduction [ridʌ́kʃən] *n.* genshō; waribiki.　⌊kiru.

redundancy [ridʌ́ndənsi] *n.* yobun; chōfuku.

redundant [ridʌ́ndənt] *a.* yobunna; yokeina; chōfuku shita.

reduplicate [ridjú:plikeit] *v.* nijūni suru; kurikaesu.

reed [ri:d] *n.* yoshi; ashi; ashi-bue.

reef [ri:f] *n.* anshō. *v.* shukuhan suru (ho o tatamu); mijikaku
suru. ~**er** *n.* shukuhan-sha; (*Am. sl.*) makitabako no isshu.
v. mijikaku susu; (*naut.*) ho o maku hito. isshu no mijikai
gaitō.　⌈yoi aku shū o hanatsu.

reek [ri:k] *n.* tsuyoi (*strong*) akushū (*unpleasant odo(u)r*). *v.* tsu-

reel [ri:l] *n.* itoguruma; itomaki. *v.* yoromeku; memai ga
suru; ito guruma ni maku; ayatsuru.

reenforce, reinforce [ri:nfɔ́:s] *v.*

reeve [ri:v] *v.* wa nado ni nawa o tōsu.

refection [rifékʃən] *n.* karui shokuji; chauke.

refectory [riféktəri] *n.* shokudō (sōin (*monastery*) nado no).

refer [rifə́:] *v.* toiawaseru; mukeru: makaseru: *Let's* ~ *the dispute to the umpire,* kono ronsō wa shimpan ni makaseyō. ~ *to your dictionary,* jisho (ni sōdan shi) o hiki nasai. ~**able** [réf(ə)rəbl / rəfə́:rəbl] *a.* kisuru; tayorareru; ni yudanerareru. ~**ence** [réfərəns] *n.* futaku; itaku; ronkyū; sankō; toiawase; sankōsho. ~**endum** [refəréndəm] *n.* kokumin ketsugiken; kokumin tōhyō.

referee [refərí:] *n.* shimpankan (shūkyū nado no).

refine [rifáin] *v.* yoku suru (naru); jōhinni naru (suru). ~**d** [-d] *a.* seiketsu de; seisei shita. ~**d sugar,** seisei shita satō. ~**ment** [-mənt] *n.* junsei; yūga; jōhin. ~**ry** [-əri] *n.* seirenjo; seiseijo (*refine suru basho*).

refit [rí:fít] *n.* shūri. *v.* shūri suru.

reflect [riflékt] *v.* hansha suru; utsusu (-ru); hansei suru. ~**ion, reflexion** [riflékʃ(ə)n] *n.* hansha; hansei; kangaete miru. ~**ive** [-iv] *a.* hanshateki; jukkō suru. ~**or** [-ə] *n.* hanshaki; hanshakyō.

reflex [rí:fleks] *a.* hannō; hansha suru. *n.* eizō (*image reflected*). ~**ive** [rifléksiv] *a.* hansha no; hanshateki; (*gram.*) saiki no: ~ **pronoun,** saiki daimeishi.

refluent [réfluənt] *a.* gyakuryū suru; shirizoku.

reflux [rí:flʌks] *n.* gyakuryū; hikishio.

reforest [ri:fɔ́rist] *v.* shokurin suru; ki o uetsukeru.

reform [rifɔ́:m] *v.* tsukurinaosu; naoru; kaishin suru. *n.* kaikaku; sasshin (tsukurinaoshi). ~**ation** [refəméiʃ(ə)n] *n.* kaikaku; tsukurikae; (*the R-*) Shūkyō Kaikaku. ~**ative** [rifɔ́:mətiv] *a.* kaikaku no; kanka no. ~**atory** [rifɔ́:mətəri] *n.* kankain. *a., n.* =**reformative.** ~**er** *n.* kaikakusha; (*R*~) Shūkyō Kaikakusha.

refract [rifrǽkt] *v.* kussetsu suru. ~**or** [-ə] *n.* kussetsu bōenkyō (kōsen ga). ~**ion** [rifrǽkʃ(ə)n] *n.* kussetsu; (hikari no) kussetsu. ~**ive** [-iv] *a.* kussetsu suru. ~**ory** [rifrǽktəri] *a.* iu koto o kikanai; gōjōna; tokenikui (*hard to melt*). 「orikaeshi ku.

refrain [rifréin] *v.* shinobu; tsutsushimu. *n.* uta no owari no

refresh [rifréʃ] *v.* aratani suru; taberu. ~**er** [-ə] *n.* kibun o sawayakani suru hito mata wa mono. ~**ment** *n.* genki kaifuku ; inshokubutsu ; saka (cha to kashi).

refrigerate [rifrídʒəreit] v. seiryō ni suru ; reizōko ni ireru ; kōru ; hiyasu ; hieru.

refrigeration [rifrìdʒəréiʃ(ə)n] n. seiryō ; reizō ; reitō.

refrigerator [rifrídʒəreitə] n. reikyakuki ; reizōko ; seihyōki.

refuge [réfju:dʒ] n. hogo ; kakurega ; hinanjo. ～e [rèfjudʒí:] n. hinansha ; bōmeisha.

refulgence [rifΛldʒəns] n. hikari ; kenran.

refulgent [rifΛldʒənt] a. kagayaku ; kenran taru.

refund [rí:fənd] n. haraimodoshi ; shōkan. v. [rifΛnd] shōkan suru ; haraimodosu.

refusal [rifjú:zəl] n. kyozetsu. ⌊suru ; haraimodosu.

refuse [rifjú:z] v. kyozetsu suru ; kotowaru. n. [réfju:s] zambu-

refutation [refjutéiʃən] n. hambaku ; rompa. ⌊tsu.

refute [rifjú:t] v. hambaku suru ; rompa suru. ⌈ru.

regain [ri(:)géin] v. torimodosu ; kaifuku suru ; futatabi tassu-

regal [rí:gəl] a. ō no ; ō no yōna ; dōdō taru ; rippana. ～ly ad.

regale [rigéil] v. tanoshiku motenasu ; gochisō o suru.

regalia [rigéiliə] n. (pl.) ō (king) de aru shirushi.

regard [rigá:d] n. me o yaru koto ; jitto miru koto ; chūshi ; sonkei. v. chūshi suru. ～ful [-ful] a. chūibukai. ～ing [-iŋ] prep. ... ni kanshite. ～less [-lis] a. fuchūina.

regatta [rigætə] n. (bōto mata wa yotto no) kyōsō (race).

regenerate [ridʒénəreit] v. saisei saseru (suru). a. [ridʒénərit]

regeneration [ridʒènəréiʃ(ə)n] n. saisei ; kaishin. ⌊saisei shita.

regent [rí:dʒənt] a. sesshō no. n. sesshō(sha).

regicide [rédʒisaid] n. shiigyaku(sha) ; taigyaku(sha).

regime [reʒí:m] n. seido ; seitai ; seifu no soshiki.

regimen [rédʒimən] n. sessei ; kenkō no tame no seikatsu.

regiment [rédʒimənt] n. (mil.) rentai. v. hensei suru. ～al [rèdʒiméntl] a. rentai no.

region [rí:dʒən] n. chihō ; chiiki (area) ; han'i (sphere).

register [rédʒistə] n. tōki ; tōroku ; tōroku kikai (kinsen nado) yōgu. v. tōki (tōroku) suru.

registrar [rédʒistra:] n. kirokusha ; tōkikanri.

registration [rèdʒistré:ʃən] n. tōki ; tōrokushasū.

registry [rédʒistri] n. kinyū ; tōroku.

regress n. [rí:gres] v. [rigrés] fukki ; atogaeri (suru).

regret [rigrét] *n*. kōkai; ikan. *v*. oshimu; kōkai suru. ～**ful** [-fəl] *a*. oshimu; zannen ni omou. ～**table** [-əbl] *a*. zannenna.

regular [régjulə] *a*. tadashii; kimarikitta; teiki no. *n*. seikihei. ～**ity** [règjulǽriti] *n*. kisoku tadashii koto.

regulate [régjuleit] *v*. chōsetsu suru; torishimaru.

regulation [règjuléiʃən] *n*. chōsetsu; seiri; jōrei.

regulator [régjuleitə] *n*. chōsetsuki; torishimaru hito.

rehabilitate [rèhəbíliteit] *v*. fukken saseru; fukushoku saseru.

rehearsal [rihə́:sl] *n*. fukushō; shitageiko; rihāzal.

rehearse [rihə́:s] *v*. fukushū suru; shitageiko suru.

Reichstag [ráiçsta:x] *n*. kyū-Doitsu no gikai.

reign [rein] *n*. shuken; kenryoku. *v*. shihai suru.

reimburse [rì:imbə́:s] *v*. benshō suru. ～**ment** [-mənt] *n*. haraimodoshi. ⌜kina yōni saseru.

rein [rein] *n*. (*pl*.) tazuna. *v*. iu koto o kikaseru. *give* ～ *to*, su-
reindeer [réindiə] *n*. (*zoo*.) tonakai.

reinforce [rì:infɔ́:s] *v*. engun o okuru. ～**ed concrete**, tekkin konkuriito. ～**ment** [-mənt] *n*. enjo; hokyō.

reinstate [rì:instéit] *v*. motodōrini suru.

reiterate [ri:ítəreit] *v*. kurikaeshite suru.

reiteration [rì:itəréiʃən] *n*. kurikaeshi. ⌜haiki; kyozetsu.

reject [ridʒékt] *v*. suteru; kyozetsu suru. ～**ion** [ridʒékʃ(ə)n] *n*.

rejoice [ridʒɔ́is] *v*. yorokobu; yorokobaseru (*make glad*).

rejoin [rí:dʒɔ́in] *v*. mata issho ni naru. [ridʒɔ́in] kotaeru; ōtō suru. ～**der** [-də] *n*. hentō.

rejuvenate [ridʒú:vəneit] *v*. wakagaeru (raseru).

rejuvenation [ridʒù:vənéiʃən] *n*. wakagaeri; genki kaifuku.

relapse [rilǽps] *n*. atomodori; daraku. *v*. daraku suru.

relate [riléit] *v*. hanasu (*tell*). kankei suru (saseru).

relation [riléiʃən] *n*. (*gram*.) kankei; setsuwa. (*pl*.) shinrui. ～**ship** [-ʃip] *n*. shinzoku kankei. ⌜kankeishi.

relative [rélətiv] *a*. kankei suru. *n*. shinrui; shinzoku. (*gram*.)

relativity [relətíviti] *n*. kankei aru koto. *the principle of* ～, sō-taiseigenri. ⌜rumi; kutsurogi.

relax [rilǽks] *v*. yurumu (meru). ～**ation** [rì:lækséiʃən] *n*. yu-
relay [ri:léi] *n*. rirei; tsugiuma. *v*. [riléi] tsugiuma suru. ～ **broadcast** [brɔ́:dkɑ:st], chūkeihōsō. ～ **race**, keisō. ～**ing**

station, (*radio*) chūkeikyoku. ⌜*tion*⌝; fūgiri.
release [rilí:s] *v.* kaihō suru; hanashite yaru. *n.* kaihō (*libera-*
relegate [réligeit] *v.* tsuihō suru (*banish*).
relent [rilént] *v.* yawaragu. ∼less [-lis] *a.* zankokuna; yurumi nai. ∼lessly [-lisli] *ad.* zankokuni; yurumi naku.
relevance, -cy [rélivəns, -si], *n.* tekisetsu (mondai ni taishite).
relevant [rélivənt] *a.* kanren suru; tekisetsuna.
reliable [riláiəbl] *a.* shinrai dekiru.
reliance [riláiəns] *n.* tanomi; tanomi to suru hito (mono).
relic [rélik] *n.* ibutsu; kinembutsu; katami.
relict [rélikt] *n.* mibōjin.
relief [rilí:f] *n.* kyūjo; anshin; ukibori; dekoboko. *The medicine
will give you* ∼, kono kusuri o nomeba rakuni nari masu.
bring out the facts in ∼, kotogara o ari no mama ni suru.
relieve [rilí:v] *v.* kyūjo suru; anshin saseru; kōtai suru; uki-
religion [rilídʒən] *n.* shūkyō; shinkō. ⌞agaraseru.
religious [rilídʒəs] *a.* shinjimbukai. *n.* sōryo; ama.
relinquish [rilíŋkwiʃ] *v.* yameru; suteru. ∼ment *n.* hōki.
relish [réliʃ] *v.* ajiwau; tanoshimu; aji ga aru. *n.* aji; shumi.
reluctance, -cy [riláktəns], *n.* kirai; teikō.
reluctant [riláktənt] *a.* kirau. ∼ly *ad.* iyaiya de.
rely [riláí] *v.* tanomi ni suru; shinrai suru (*on, upon*).
remain [riméin] *v.* nokoru; ... no mama de iru. *n.* (*pl.*) zam-
butsu. ∼der [-də] *n.* zan'yo; nokori. ⌜ru.
remand [rimá:nd] *v.* okuri kaesu; futatabi kōkin (ryūchi) su-
remark [rimá:k] *n.* chūi; kansatsu; hihyō. *v.* ki ga tsuku; chūmoku suru; noberu. ∼able [-əbl] *a.* chūi subeki; ichijirushii.
remediable [rimí:diəbl] *a.* chiryō no dekiru.
remedial [rimí:diəl] *a.* naosu; chiryō suru.
remedy [rémidi] *n.* kusuri; zengosaku. *v.* chiryō suru; tadasu.
remember [rimémbə] *v.* omoi dasu; kioku suru; dengon susuru.
remembrance [rimembrəns] *n.* mioboe, kioku; kinen; (*pl.*)
remilitarize [ri:mílitəraiz] *v.* saigumbi suru. ⌞dengon.
remind [rimáind] *v.* omoi dasaseru; nen o osu.
reminiscence [rèminísəns] *n.* tsuioku; kaisō; omoide.
reminiscent [rèminísənt] *a.* tsuioku no; kaikyū no.

remiss [rimís] *a.* taimanna. *v.* toku ; yurumeru. ~**ion** [rimíʃ(ə)n] *n.* menjo.

remit [rimít] *v.* sōkin suru ; yurusu. ~**tance** *n.* sōkin.

remnant [rémnənt] *n.* nokori.

remonstrance [rimɔ́nstrəns] *n.* kōgi ; chūkoku ; isame.

remonstrate [rimɔ́nstreit] *v.* kōgi suru ; chūkoku suru.

remorse [rimɔ́:s] *n.* kōkai. ~**ful** [-ful] *a.* kōkai shita. ~**less** [-lis] *a.* nanno hansei mo nai ; reikokuna.

remote [rimóut] *a.* tōi ; hanareta ; empō no.

removal [rimú:vəl] *n.* iten ; tettai ; menshoku.

remove [rimú:v] *v.* utsusu ; nozoku ; iten suru. *n.* iten.

remunerate [rimjú:nəreit] *v.* hōshū o ataeru ; tsugunai o suru.

remuneration [rimjù:nəréiʃən] *n.* hōshū ; baishō (tsugunai).

remunerative [rimjú:nərətiv] *a.* yūrina ; wari no yoi.

renaissance [rənéisəns] *n.* fukkō ; (R-) Bungeifukkō. *a.* (R-) Bungeifukkōjidai no.

renascence [rinǽsəns] *n.* kōsei ; (R-). =**Renaissance**.

rend [rend] *v.* **rent ; rending.** saku. (ki no kawa o) hagu ; sakeru.

render [réndə] *v.* kaesu ; watasu ; ataeru. teishutsu suru ; hon'yaku suru ; enshutsu suru.

rendezvous [rá:ndivú:] *n.* (*Fr.*) kaigōsho. *v.* kaigō suru ; deau.

renegade [rénigeid] *n.* haikyōsha ; dattōsha.

renew [rinjú:] *v.* aratani suru (naru). ~**al** *n.* kōshin ; shinaoshi.

renounce [rináuns] *v.* hōki suru ; uchisuteru.

renovate [rénouveit] *v.* atarashiku suru ; shinaosu.

renovation [rinouvéiʃən] *n.* kakushin ; sasshin.

renown [rináun] *n.* meisei ; yūmei. ~**ed** [-d] *a.* nadakai.

rent [rent] *n.* yachin ; shiyōryō. sakeme. *v.* kasu ; kariru.

rent *v., see* ; **rend.**

renunciation [rinʌnsiéiʃən] *n.* haiki ; kyozetsu ; dannen.

Rep., Repub. Amerika Kyōwatō in (no) (*Republic, Republican*).

repair [ripέə] *n.* shūzen. *v.* tsukurou. iku.

reparation [rəpəréiʃən] *n.* baishō.

repartee [repa:tí:] *n.* tōisokumyō no kotae.

repast [ripá:st] *n.* shokuji ; gochisō.

repatriate [ripǽtrieit] *v.* hongoku e sōkan suru.

repatriation [rìpǽtriéiʃən] *n.* hongokusōkan ; kikoku.

repay [ripéi] *v.* harai-modosu ; ongaeshi suru. ~**ment** *n.* ben-
repeal [ripí:l] *n.* haishi. *v.* haishi suru. ⌊sai ; hempō.
repeat [ripí:t] *n.* kurikaeshi. *v.* kurikaesu ; kasanete iu. ~**edly**
[-idli] *ad.* kurikaeshi. ~**er** *n.* rempatsujū ; junkanshōsū.
repel [ripél] *v.* oikaesu ; iyagaraseru. ~**lent** *a.* hanetsukeru ;
mizu o hajiku. ⌈kōkai shite iru.
repent [ripént] *v.* kōkai suru. ~**ance** [-əns] *n.* kōkai. ~**ant** *a.*
repertoire [répətwa:] *n.* engei mokuroku.
repertory [répətəri], **repertoire** [répətwa:] *n.* sōko ; takuwae.
repetition [repitíʃən] *n.* kurikaeshi.
repine [ripáin] *v.* guchi o iu (*at, against*).
replace [ripléis] *v.* moto no tokoro ni oku. ~**ment** *n.* okikae.
replenish [ripléniʃ] *v.* futatabi mitasu ; mata ippai ni suru.
replete [ripí:t] *a.* ippai tameta ; jūman shita.
repletion [riplí:ʃən] *n.* jūman.
replica [réplikə] *n.* (kaiga nado no) utsushi ; hikae.
reply [riplái] *n.* henji. *v.* kotaeru ; henjisuru.
report [ripó:t] *v.* shiraseru ; fukumei suru. *n.* hōkoku ; hyōban.
~ *oneself*, shuttō suru. ~**er** *n.* tsūshinnin.
repose [ripóuz] *v.* yasumaseru ; yasumu. *n.* kyūsoku.
repository [ripózitəri] *n.* chozōsho ; takuwaeru basho.
reprehend [riprihénd] *v.* shikaru ; hinan suru.
reprehensible [rèprihénsibl] *a.* hinan subeki.
reprehension [reprihén(ʃ)ən] *n.* shisseki ; hinan.
represent [rèprizént] *v.* daihyō suru ; byōsha suru. ~**ation**
[rèprizentéiʃən] *n.* hyōgen ; daihyō. ~**ative** [-ətiv] *a.* daihyō
suru. *n.* daihyōsha ; daigishi.
repress [riprés] *v.* chin'atsu suru ; osaete yamesasu. ~**ion**
[ripréʃən] *n.* chin'atsu ; yokusei. ~**ive** [-iv] *a.* chin'atsu suru ;
seishi suru.
reprieve [riprí:v] *n.* shikkō yūyo. *v.* shokei o nobasu.
reprimand [réprima:nd] *n.* kenseki. *v.* semeru ; shikaru.
reprint [ri:prínt] *n.* saihan ; nido no insatsu. *v.* han o kasaneru.
reprisal [ripráizəl] *n.* shikaeshi ; fukushū.
reproach [ripróutʃ] *n.* hinan. *v.* hinan suru ; semeru. ~**ful** *a.*
semeru. ⌈suru ; hinan suru
reprobate [réprəbeit] *a.* daraku shita. *n.* darakusha. *v.* kyozetsu

reprobation [reprəbéiʃ(ə)n] *n.* kyozetsu ; hinan.
reproduce [rìːprədjúːs] *v.* mata (*again*) tsukuru ; fukusei suru ; kodomo o fuyasu.
reproduction [rìːprədʌkʃ(ə)n] *u.* saisei ; fukusei ; seishoku.
reproductive [rìːprədʌktiv] *a.* saisei no ; fukusei no ; seisho-
reproof [riprúːf] *n.* kogoto ; hinan.   ⌊ku no.
reprove [riprúːv] *v.* shikaru ; satosu.   ⌈rui. hikyōmono.
reptile [réptil / -tail] *a.* haimawaru ; hiretsuna. *n.* (*zoo.*) hachū-
republic [ripʌ́blik] *n.* kyōwakoku. ∼**an** [-ən] *a.* kyōwakoku
no. *n.* kyōwasei-ronja ; R∼ *n.* (Amerika no) Kyowatōin.
repudiate [ripjúːdieit] *v.* suteru ; rien suru ; mitomenai.
repudiation [ripjùːdiéiʃ(ə)n] *n.* hōki ; rien ; hinin.
repugnance [ripʌ́gnəns] *n.* mujun ; ken'o (iyagari).
repugnant [ripʌ́gnənt] *a.* hantai no ; mujun suru ; iyana.
repulse [ripʌ́ls] *n.* gekitai suru ; kyozetsu suru.
repulsion [ripʌ́lʃən] *v.* gekitai ; hampatsu ; ken'o.
repulsive [ripʌ́lsiv] *a.* hanetsukeru ; iyana.
reputable [répjutəbl] *a.* hyōban no yoi ; rippana.
reputation [rèpjutéiʃən] *n.* yoi hyōban ; meisei.   ⌈sareru.
repute [ripjúːt] *n.* hyōban. *v.* (*be*∼*ed*) kangaerareru ; hyōban
request [rikwést] *n.* tanomi. *v.* motomeru ; yōkyū suru.
requiem [rékwiəm] *n.* chinkonsai ; tamashii no shizume.
require [rikwáiə] *v.* hitsuyō to suru ; yōkyū suru. ∼**ment** *n.*
yōkyū ; hitsuyōhin.
requisite [rékwizit] *a.* hitsuyō no. *n.* hitsuyōbutsu.
requisition [rèkwizíʃən] *n.* yōkyū. *v.* chōhatsu suru.
requital [rikwáitl] *n.* (*good*) hōshū ; (*bad*) fukushū.
requite [rikwáit] *v.* mukuiru ; fukushū suru.
rescind [risínd] *v.* haishi suru ; kaijo suru.
rescript [ríːskript] *n.* shōchoku (teiō no kotoba).
rescue [réskjuː] *n.* kyūjo ; sukui. *v.* sukū ; ubaikaesu.
research [risə́ːtʃ] *n.* kenkyū ; chōsa. *v.* kenkyū suru.
resemblance [rizémbləns] *n.* ruiji ; niyori.
resemble [rizémbl] *v.* niru ; ruiji suru.   ⌈urami.
resent [rizént] *v.* uramu. ∼**ful** *a.* urami o fukumu. ∼**ment** *n.*
reservation [rèzəvéiʃən] *n.* horyū ; mikettei. tadashigaki.
reserve [rizə́ːv] *v.* horyū suru. *n.* horyū ; hozon. ∼**d** [-d] *a.*

horyū shita ; uchikina.
reservist [rizə́:vist] *n.* yobihei.
reservoir [rézəvwɑ:] *n.* chosuichi ; suisō.
reside [rizáid] *v.* ni sumu. ⁓**nce** [rézidəns] *n.* kyojū ; jūtaku ; sumai. ⁓**nt** [rézidənt] *a.* kyojū suru. *n.* kyojūsha.
residual [rizídjuəl] *a.* nokori no.
residuary [rizídjuəri] *a.* amari no.
residue [rézidju:] *n.* nokori ; kasu ; zan'yo ; zankin.
residuum [rizídjuəm] *n.* zan'yo ; zanshi (kasu).
resign [rizáin] *v.* yameru ; jishoku suru. ⁓**ed** [-d] *a.* yameta.
resignation [rèzignéiʃən] *n.* jishoku ; dannen.
resilience [rizíliəns] *n.* hanekaeri ; hampatsuryoku.
resilient [rizíliənt] *a.* hanekaeru ; kaikatsuna.
resin [rézin] *n.* jushi (ki no yani). ⁓**ous** [-əs] *a.* jushishitsu no.
resist [rizíst] *v.* teikō suru ; taeru ; osaeru. ⁓**ance** [-əns] *n.* teikō. ⁓**less** [-lis] *a.* teikō (hankō) dekinai.
resolute [rézəljut] *a.* ketsudan no aru ; danko to shite.
resolution [rezəljú:ʃən] *n.* kesshin ; kaiketsu ; bunkai.
resolve [rizɔ́lv] *v.* kesshin suru ; bunkai suru. *n.* kesshin.
resonance [rézənəns] *n.* hankyō.
resonant [rézənənt] *a.* kyōmei suru.
resonator [rézəneitə] *n.* kyōmeitai ; kyōmei suru mono.
resort [rizɔ́:t] *n.* atsumaru basho ; tanomi : *the last*⁓, saigo no shudan. *summer (winter)* ⁓, hisho(hikan)-chi. *v.* iku ; tayoru.
resound [rizáund] *v.* hankyō suru. *n.* hankyō.
resource [risɔ́:s] *n.* hōhō ; shudan. (*pl.*) shisan ; shigen.
respect [rispékt] *n.* sonkei ; (*pl.*) sonkei no hyōjō (*show esteem*). *v.* uyamau. ⁓**able** [-əbl] *a.* rippana ; kanari no. ⁓**ful** [-fəl] *a.* reigi tadashii. ⁓**ing** [-iŋ] *prep.* ni kanshite. ⁓**tive** [-tiv] *a.* sorezore no.
respiration [rèspəréi(ʃə)n] *n.* kokyū ; iki o suru koto.
respiratory [réspirət(ə)ri / rispaiə-] *a.* kokyū no.
respire [rispáiə] *v.* kokyū suru ; kyūsoku suru.
respite [réspait] *n.* enki ; yūyo. *v.* kei no shikkō o enki suru.
resplendence [rispléndəns] *n.* kagayaki.
resplendent [rispléndənt] *a.* kagayaku.
respond [rispɔ́nd] *v.* kotaeru. *n.* taiō. ⁓**ent** [-ənt] *n.* kotaeru

hito ; (*leg.*) hikoku (*defendant*).
response [rispóns] *n.* hentō ; ōtō ; hannō.
responsibility [rispónsibíliti] *n.* sekinin ; futan.
responsible [rispónsibl] *a.* sekinin no aru ; sekinin no omoi.
responsive [rispónsiv] *a.* kotaeru ; ōjiru.
rest [rest] *n.* kyūsoku ; shukuhakujo ; amari ; nokori. *v.* yasumu ; shinrai suru ; yasumaseru. *among the* ~, nakanzuku. *the* ~, sonota no mono. ~**ful** [⌐fl] *a.* shizukana. ~**less** [-lis] *a.* ochitsukanu ; nemurenai.
restaurant [réstərənt] *n.* (*Fr.*) ryōriten ; shokudō.
restitution [rèstitjú:ʃən] *n.* baishō ; henkan ; kaifuku.
restive [réstiv] *a.* gōjōna ; iu koto o kikanai.
restoration [rèstəréiʃən] *n.* kaifuku ; fukkō ; (*the* R-) (*Englana* no) Ōseifukko.
restorative [ristó:rətiv] *a.* genki o tori modosu. *n.* kitsuke gu-
restore [ristó:] *v.* kaifuku suru ; tsugunau. ⌐[suri.
restrain [ristréin] *v.* yokusei suru ; kinzuru. ~ *oneself*, jisei suru. ~**t** [-t] *n.* yokusei ; gaman.
restrict [ristríkt] *v.* kagiru ; seishi suru. ~**ion** [-ʃ(ə)n] *n.* seigen ; sokubaku. ~**ive** [-iv] *a.* seigen suru.
result [risΛlt] *n.* kekka ; ketsugi. *v.* ... to iu kekka ni naru : *Eating too much often* ~*s in sickness*, kuisugi wa ōō byōki to iu kekka ni naru. *Sickness often* ~*s from eating too much*, byōki wa ōō kuisugi no kekka da. ~**ant** [-ənt] *n.* kekka ; (*phys.*) gō-
resume [rizjú:m] *v.* torikaesu ; futatabi hajimeru. ⌐[ryoku.
resume [rèzju:méi] *n.* (*Fr.*) yōryō ; kōgai.
resumption [rizΛmpʃən] *n.* torikaeshi ; kaishū.
resurrect [rèzərékt] *v.* sosei saseru (suru). ~**ion** [rèzərékʃ(ə)n] *n.* sosei ; kaifuku ; ikikaeri ; fukkatsu.
resuscitate [risΛsiteit] *v.* sosei suru (saseru).
resuscitation [risΛstéiʃ(ə)n] *n.* sosei ; kaifuku ; ikikaeri.
retail [rí:teil] *n.* kouri. *v.* [-⌐] kouri suru. ~**er** [-ə] *n.* kourishō.
retain [ritéin] *v.* mochitsuzukeru ; kioku suru. ~**er** [-ə] *n.* koshō ; jūsha bengoshi irairyō.
retaliate [ritǽlieit] *v.* shikaesu ; fukushū suru.
retaliation [ritǽliéiʃ(ə)n] *n.* hempō ; fukushū.
retard [ritá:d] *n.* chien. *v.* osoku suru ; okureru (raseru). ~**ation**

[ri:tɑːdéiʃən] *n.* chien.

retch [ri:tʃ] *v.* hakike o moyōsu ; hakidasu.

retention [riténʃən] *n.* hoyū ; hojiryoku ; kiokuryoku.

retentive [riténtiv] *a.* yoku tamotsu ; kiokuryoku no tsuyoi.

reticent [rétisənt] *a.* mukuchi no ; chimmoku no.

retina [rétinə] *n.* (*anat.*) (me no) mōmaku.

retinue [rétinju:] *n.* zuikōsha.

retire [ritáiə] *v.* shirizoku ; toko ni tsuku ; taishoku suru ; shirizokeru ; intai saseru. **～d** [-d] *a.* intai shita. **～ment** [-mənt] *n.* intai ; taishoku ; kaishū.

retiring [ritáiəriŋ] *a.* intai suru ; taishoku no ; enryobukai.

retort [ritɔ́:t] *v.* shikaeshi o suru ; iikaesu. *n.* kuchigotae ; hentō. (kagakuyō no) jōryūki ; retoruto.

retouch [ri:tʌ́tʃ] *v.* (shashin o) shūsei suru.

retract [ritrǽkt] *v.* hikkomaseru ; torikesu. **～ion** [-ʃ(ə)n] *n.* hikkomasu koto ; torikeshi.

retread [ri:tréd] *v.* (*Am.*) gomutaiya no wazoko o kaeru. *n.* [ríːtred] (*Am.*) wazoko o kaeta taiya.

retreat [ritrí:t] *n.* taikyaku ; intaibasho. *v.* shirizoku.

retrench [ritréntʃ] *v.* kiritsumeru ; sakujo suru.

retribution [rètribjúʃən] *n.* batsu ; ōhō (*just return for what one has done*). [no ; ōhō no.

retributive [ritríbju:tiv], **retributory** [ritríbju:təri] *a.* mukui ; kaisō.

retrievable [ritríːvəbl] *a.* kaifuku dekiru ; bankai dekiru.

retrieval [ritríːvəl] *n.* torikaeshi ; bankai ; tsugunai.

retrieve [ritríːv] *v.* kaifuku suru ; bankai suru ; tsugunau.

retroact [rìètrouǽkt] *v.* handō suru ; gyaku ni hataraku. **～ive** [-iv] *a.* mukashi ni sakanobotte kōryoku o motsu.

retrocede [rétrousiːd] *v.* (ryōdo o) kampu suru ; shirizoku.

retrograde [rétrougreid] *a.* kōtai suru. *v.* atomodori suru ; taiho suru.

retrogression [rètrougréʃən] *n.* kōtai ; gyakkō ; taiho.

retrospect [rétro(u)spekt] *v.* kaiko suru. *n.* kaiko. **～ion** [-ʃən] *n.* kaiko ; kaisō. **～ive** [-iv] *a.* kaikoteki no.

return [ritɔ́:n] *v.* kaeru ; modoru ; kotaeru ; kaesu. *n.* kaeri ; henkyaku ; hōshū. *by* **～** (*of post*), orikaeshi. **～ ticket** *n.* ōfu- [kukippu.

reunion [ri:júːniən] *n.* saikai ; konshinkai.

rev [rev] (*Am. col.*) *v.* enjin ya mōtā no kaiten. *v.* kaitensū o ┌masu (*up*), genzuru (*down*).
Rev. *see* : **Reverend**

revamp [rí:vǽmp] *v.* tsukurou ; (*Am. col.*) geki o kaisaku suru.

reveal [riví:l] *v.* arawasu ; morasu ; kami (*God*) ga kami no kotoba de shiraseru ; keiji suru.

reveille [rivǽli] *n.* kishō rappa.

revel [révəl] *n.* sakamori ; sokonuke-sawagi. *v.* sakamori suru ; sawagu ; ōini tanoshimu. ～ry [-ri] *n.* nomisugi.

revelation [rèviléiʃən] *n.* bakuro ; tekihatsu ; hakkaku ; mo-
revenge [rivéndʒ] *n.* fukushū. *v.* fukushū suru. ┌kushi.

revenue [révənju:] *n.* sainyū ; shūnyū ; nenshū.

reverberate [rivə́:bəreit] *v.* hankyō (hansha) suru ; kussetsu saseru (suru).

reverberation [rivə̀:bəréiʃən] *n.* hankyō ; yoin ; hansha.

revere [rivíə] *v.* sonkei suru ; agameru. ～nce [révərəns] *n.* sonkei ; keii ; itoku. *v.* sonkei suru. ～nd [révərənd] **Rev.** *a.* ...Shi no (sōryo ni taisuru sonshō). ～nt [revərənt], ～ntial [revərénʃəl] *a.* keiken no ; uyauyashii.

reverie [révəri] *n.* kūsō ; (ongaku no) gensōkyoku.

revers [rivíə] *n.* (*Fr.*) (*sing. pl.*) orikaeshi (yōfuku no).

reversal [rivə́:səl] *n.* gyakuten ; (hōritsu de) torikeshi.

reverse [rivə́:s] *v.* abekobe ni suru ; torikesu. *a.* gyaku no ; ura no. *n.* gyaku. ～ly *ad.*

reversion [rivə́:ʃən] *n.* fukki ; senzogaeri.

revert [rivə́:t] *v.* tachimodoru ; fukki suru.

revery [révəri] *n.* ＝**reverie**.

review [rivju:] *v.* ken'etsu suru. *n.* ken'etsu ; hyōron ; hyōron-
revile [riváil] *v.* nonoshiru. ┌ka. ～er [-ə] *n.* hyōronka.

revise [riváiz] *v.* kaitei (kaisei) suru ; kaeru. *n.* kaisei ; kaitei.

revision [riváiʒən] *n.* kaitei ; kaisei ; shūsei.

revival [riváivəl] *n.* fukkatsu ; fukkō ; (*R*～) Bungei-fukkō.

revive [riváiv] *v.* ikikaeru ; fukkō suru ; genki zukeru.

revocable [révəkəbl] *a.* haishi sareru ; torikesareru.

revocation [revoukéiʃən] *n.* haishi ; torikeshi.

revoke [rivóuk] *v.* haishi suru ; torikesu.

revolt [rivóult] *n.* hanran ; hankō. *v.* somuku ; mutto saseru.

revolution [revəljú:ʃən] *n.* kakumei. ～ary [-əri] *a.* kakumei no.

~**ist** [ist] *n*. kakumeitōin. ~**ize** [-aiz] *v*. kakumei o okosu.

revolve [rivɔ́lv] *v*. kaiten suru (saseru); junkan suru; shian suru. ~**r** [-ə] *n*. rempatsu-kenjū (pisutoru).

revue [rivjúː] (*Fr.*) revyū (ongaku-iri no karui kigeki).

revulsion [rivʌ́lʃən] *n*. gekihen; kyūhen.

reward [riwɔ́ːd] *n*. hōshū; mukui. *v*. sharei suru; bassuru.

rhapsody [rǽpsədi] *n*. kyōshi; (*mus.*) kyōsōkyoku; rapusodii.

rheostat [ríːəstæt] *n*. (*electr.*) denryū-chōsetsuki; reosutatto.

rhetoric [rétərik] *n*. shūjigaku; retorik(ku). ~**al** [ritórikəl] *a*. shūjigaku no. ~**ian** [rètəríʃən] *n*. shūjigakusha.

rheumatic [ruːmɔ́tik] *a*. (*med.*) ryūmachi no.

rheumatism [rúːmætizm] *n*. (*med.*) ryūmachisu.

Rhine [rain] *n*. (Doitsu no) Rain-gawa.

rhino [rainou], **rhinoceros** [rainɔ́sərəs] *n*. (*zoo*) sai.

rhododendron [ròudədéndrən] *n*. (*bot.*) shakunage.

rhomb [rɔmb, rəm], **rhombus** [rɔ́mbəs] *n*. (*math.*) hishigata; shahōkei.

rhubarb [rúːbɑːb] *n*. (*bot.*) daiō (ne ga gezai to naru).

rhyme, rime [raim] *n*. (shi (*poem*) de iu) in. *v*. shi o tsukuru; in ga au.; in o fumu.

rhythm [ríðəm] *n*. rizumu; (shi (*poem*) no inritsu; hyōshi; kuchō. ~**ical** [ríðmikəl] *a*. *rhythm* no aru; chōshi no yoi.

rib [ríb] *n*. (*anat.*) rokkotsu; (kasa no) hone. *v*. rokkotsu o tsukeru.

ribald [ríbəld] *a*. gebita. ~**ry** [-ri] *n*. gebita hanashi.

rib(b)and [ríbənd] *n*. =**ribbon**.

ribbon [ríbən] *n*. himo; ribon; obi. *v*. himo (*ribbon*) o tsukeru.

rice [rais] *n*. ine; kome. ~ **paper,** waragami; tōshi.

rich [ritʃ] *a*. tonda; kanemochi no; koiiro no; eiyō ni tomu. ~**es** [iz] *n*. (*pl.*) tomi; zaihō.

rick [rik] *n*. taiseki; inamura.

rickets [ríkits] *n*. (*med.*) kurubyō. ⌈suru.

rickety [ríkiti] *a*. kurubyō ni kakatta; semushi no; gura-gura

ricochet [rìkəʃéi] *n*. (*Fr.*) hanetobi. *v*. hanetobu.

rid [rid] *v*. rid *or* **ridded**; **ridding**. nozoku; kujo suru. *get* ~ *of*, o nozoku. *to be* ~ *of*, kara nogareru. ~**dance** [-ʒəns] *n*. jokyo. *good* ~, yakkai-barai.

riddle [rídl] *n.*, *v.* nazo o toku; nazo o kakeru. me no arai furui de furu.

ride [raid] *v.* **rode, ridden** *or arch.* **rid; riding.** (uma, kuruma, jitensha nado ni) noru. teihaku suru. *n.* noru koto. ~ *a hobby*, ohako o dasu. ~ *down*, nori tsubusu. ~**r** [ráidə] *n.* norite; kishu; ottegaki ⌈nagi.

ridge [ridʒ] *n.* yama no se; sammyaku. ~**pole** [⌐poul] *n.* muridicule [rídikjul] *n.* chōshō; azakeri (*mockery*). *v.* azakeru;

ridiculous [ridíkjuləs] *a.* okashii; bakageta; ⌊bakani suru.

riding [ráidiŋ] *n.* jōba. *a.* jōyō no. ~ **habit,** *n.* fujin'yōjōba-
rife [raif] *a.* ryūkō no; sakanna. ⌊fuku.

riffraff [rífræf] *n.* kuzu; iyashii hitobito.

rifle [ráifl] *n.* raifurujū; (*pl.*) jū-tai. *v.* shōjū de utsu; nusumu. ~**man** [-mən] *n.* shashu. ~ **range,** *n.* shatekijō. ~ **shot** [-ʃət] *n.* shōjūdan; (jōzuna) shashu.

rift [rift] *n.* sakeme; wareme. *v.* sakeru; saku.

rig [rig] *n.* gisō (fune nado o); fukusō. *v.* gisō suru; ifuku o kiru. ~ *the market*, sōba o kuruwaseru. ~**ging** *n.* sōbi; seibi.

right [rait] *a.* tadashii; massuguna. *ad.* chōdo. *n.* dōri; seigi; kenri. *v.* naosu; akashi o tateru; massuguni naru. ~ *over the head*, atama no ma ue. ~ *off*, tadachini. *by* ~, *by* ~s, tōzen. *set to* ~*s*, seiri suru; naosu. ~**about** [⌐əbaut] *n.* hantai no hōgaku. *send to the* ~, hanetsukeru. ~**angled** [⌐ǽŋgld] *a.* chokkaku no. ~**eous** [-tʃəs] *a.* tadashii; shōjikina. ~**eously** *ad.* tadashiku; massuguni. ~**eousness** *n.* seigi; renchoku. ~**ful** [-ful] *a.* seitōna. ~**fully** [-fuli] *ad.* seitōni. ~**hand** [⌐hænd] *n.*, *a.* migite (no). ~**handed** [⌐hǽndid] *a.* migikiki no. ~**ist** [ráitist] *n.* uyokuha no hito. ~**ly** *ad.* tadashiku. ~**minded** [⌐máindid] *a.* kokoro no tadashii; shōjikina. ~**ness** [ráitnis] *n.* renchoku; kōsei. ~**o,** ~ **oh** [ráitou] *inter.* (*Brit. col.*) =**all right.** ~**ward(s)** [⌐wəd(z)] *ad.* migigawa e.

rigid [rídʒid] *a.* katai; genkakuna. ~**ity** [ridʒíditi] *n.* katai koto; genkaku.

rigmarole [rígməroul] *n.* kudaranai (*worthless*) nagabanashi.

rigor [ráigə:] *n.* genkaku; kibishisa. ~**ous** [rígərəs] *a.* kibi-
rill [ril] *n.* ogawa (*rivulet*). ⌊shii; genkakuna.

rim [rim] *n.* heri; fuchi. *v.* fuchi o tsukeru.

rime [raim] *n.* shimo. *v.* shimo o musubu. (*cf.* **rhyme**.).
rind [ráind] *n.* kawa ; kara.

ring [riŋ] *n.* wa ; yubiwa ; kane no wa. (*bot.*) ki no nenrin. *v.*
rang, rung; ringing. torimaku ; narasu (beru o) ; hibiku. ∼
off, kiru (denwa nado). ∼ *up,* (denwa de) yobidasu. ∼**dove**
[⌐dəv] *n.* (*bird*) juzukakebato. ∼**ed** [-d] *a.* wa no aru. ∼ **finger,**
kusuriyubi. ∼**leader** [⌐li:də] *n.* chōhonnin. ∼**let** [⌐lit] *n.*
chiisai makige. ∼**worm** [-wə:m] *n.* (*med.*) tamushi (hifubyō).
rink [riŋk] *n.* kassōjō. *v.* (*rink* de) suberu.
rinse [ríns] *v.* susugu.

riot [ráiət] *n.* rambō ; bōdō. *v.* rambō suru. *run* ∼, abareru. ∼-
er [-ə] *n.* bōkōsha ; bōto. ∼**ous** [-təs] *a.* rambōna ; bōdō no.
rip [rip] *v.* saku ; sakeru ; yaburu ; yabureru. *n.* hokorobi ; sakeme. ⌐jukusaseru.
ripe [raip] *a.* jukushita ; jukutatsushita. ∼**n** [⌐n] *v.* juku suru ;
ripple [rípl] *n.* sazanami. *v.* sazanami o okosu ; sazanami ga
ripsaw [rípsɔ:] *n.* tatehiki nokogiri. ⌐tatsu.
rise [ráíz] *v.* rose,r isen ; **rising.** agaru ; takaku naru ; shusse
suru. *n.* takaku agaru koto. *give* ∼ *to,* ... o shōzuru. ∼**r** [-ə]
risen [rízn] *v. see* : **rise.** ⌐*n.* okiru hito (nedoko kara).
risibility [rizibíliti] *n.* warai-guse.
risible [rízibl] *a.* warai tagaru ; okashii.
rising [ráiziŋ] *a.* agaru ; shōshin suru. *n.* jōshō ; shutsugen.
risk [risk] *n.* kiken ; bōken. *v.* bōken suru. *at the* ∼ *of,* ... o toshite. ∼**y** [ríski] *a.* kikenna ; bōken suru.
rite [rait] *n.* gishiki. ⌐kishugi.
ritual [rítjuəl] *a.* gishiki no. *n.* gishiki. ∼**ism** [-izm] *n.* gishi-
rival [ráivəl] *n.* kyōsōsha. *a., v.* kyōsō suru. ∼**ry** [-ri] *n.* kyōsō.
rive [raiv] *v.* saku ; waru ; sakeru ; wareru.
river [rívə] *n.* kawa. ∼**bed** [-bed] *n.* kawadoko. ∼**side** [-said]
n. kahan ; kawagishi. ∼**wall** [-wɔ:l] *n.* teibō ; kawa no tsu-
rivet [rívit] *n.* byō. *v.* byō de tomeru. ⌐tsumi.
rivulet [rívjulit] *n.* ogawa.
roach [rout∫] *n.* (*pl.* **-es**) (*fish*) akahara.
road [roud] *n.* michi. ∼**bed** [⌐bed] *n.* (*Am.*) dōro ya senro
nado no jiban (*foundation*). ∼**show** [⌐∫ou] *n.* (*cinema* no) rōdo-
shō ; junkaikōgyō. ∼**stead** [⌐sted] *n.* (*naut.*) oki no teihakuchi.

～ster [⌐stə] *n.* zaseki hitotsu no mugai jidōsha. ～way [⌐wei]
roam [roum] *v.* bura-bura aruku.   ⌐*n.* dōro.
roan [roun] *a., n.* ashige no. (koma, *horse*).
roar [rɔ:] *v.* unaru ; hoeru ; sakebu. *n.* unarigoe.
roast [roust] *v.* yaku ; aburu. *a.* abutta. *n.* yakiniku.
rob[rɔb] *v.* nusumu ; gōtō suru. ～ber [rɔ́bə] *n.* tōzoku. ～bery
robe [roub] *n.* gaitō ; reifuku.   ⌐[rɔ́bəri] *n.* gōdatsu.
robin [rɔ́bin] *n.* (*bird*) komadori.
robomb [róubʌm] *n. see* : robot bomb.
robot [róubɔt] *n.* jinzō-ningen. ～bomb [-bʌm] *n.* mujin hikōki de hakobu bakudan.
robust [roubʌ́st] *a.* ganjōna ; kappatsuna.
rock [rɔk] *n.* iwa ; anshō. *v.* yusureru. *on the* ～*s*, kane ni komatte. ～ing chair, yuriisu. ～er [rɔ́kə] *n.* yusuru hito ; (*Am.*)
yuri-mokuba. ～y [rɔ́ki] *a.* iwa no ōi. the Rockies *n.* Rok-
rocket [rɔ́kit] *n.* noroshi ; rokketto.   ⌐kii Sammyaku.
rod [rɔd] *n.* sao ; muchi ; chōbatsu.
rode [róud] *v. see* : ride.
rodent [róudənt] *n.* (*zoo.*) kesshi-dōbutsu (nezumi, usagi nado
no yōna, ha no nobiru dōbutsu).   ⌐kyōgikai.
rodeo [roudéiou] *n.* (*Am.*) kachiku no kariatsume ; *cowboy* no
roe [rou] *n.* (*fish*) hararago (sakana no) ; (*zoo*) kojika.
Roentgen rays [rentgən réiz/-dʒen-] *n.* Rentogen-sen ; X-sen.
rogue [roug] *n.* akkan ; itazurakko.
rogury [róugəri] *n.* akuji ; warusa ; itazura.
roguish [róugiʃ] *a.* burai no ; fushōjikina.
roil [rɔil] *v.* kakimawasu ; funkyū saseru.
roister [rɔ́istə] *v.* ibarichirasu ; nomisawagu.
ROK Dai-Kamminkoku (*Republic of Korea*).
role [roul] *n.* (*Fr.*) (haiyū no) yakuwari ; nimmu.
roll [roul] *v.* korogasu ; korogaru ; maku ; (nami nado ga) u-
neru ; todoroku. *n.* kaiten ; makimono ; kiroku ; rōru. ～call
[⌐kɔ:l] *n.* tenko. ～er [róulə] *n.* rōrā ; makijiku ; ōkina nami
no uneri. ～ skate rōrā-suketo.
rollick [rɔ́lik] *v.* fuzakemawaru ; hashagu.
Roman [róumən] *n., a.* Rōma (no) ; Rōmajin (no).
romance [romǽns] *n.* denkishōsetsu ; jōwa ; rōmansu.

romantic [romǽntik] *a.* kūsōtekina ; denkishōsetsutekina ; jōji ni kansuru. **~ism** [romǽntisizm] *n.* kūsōtekina koto ; rōman-shugi.

Rome [roum] *n.* Rōma (Itaria no shufu).

romp [rɔmp] *v., n.* tobihaneru (koto) ; sawagu (koto).

rood [ru:d] *n.* jūjika (furui gokei). (menseki tan'i) ēkā no 1/4.

roof [ru:f] *n.* yane. *v.* yane o tsukeru.

rook [ruk] *n.* (*bird*) miyamagarasu. *v.* gomakasu.

rookery [rúkəri] *n.* miyamagarasu no su ; himminkutsu.

room [ru:m] *n.* heya ; basho ; yochi. (*pl.*) geshuku. *v.* (*Am.*) make ~ *for*, seki o yuzuru ; no yochi o tsukuru. **~y** [rú:mi] *a.* hirobiro to shita.

roost [ru:st] *n.* tomarigi. *v.* tomaru ; nemuru. *at* ~, negura ni tsuite. **~er** [rú:stə] *n.* (*Am.*) ondori. ~ *up*, nekogi ni suru.

root [ru:t] *n.* ne ; kiso. *v.* ne ga tsuku. *strike* ~, ne ga tsuku. ~

rope [roup] *n.* nawa : tsuna. *v.* rōpu de shibaru. **~-dancer** [⸍dɑ́:nsə] *n.* tsunawatarishi.

rosary [róuzəri] *n.* baraen. *Catholic* no juzu.

rose [rouz] *n.* bara ; barairo. **~ate** [róuziit] *a.* barairo no ; kō-fukuna. **~bud** [⸍bʌd] *n.* bara no tsubomi. **~tte** [rouzét] *n.* baramusubi ; marui hanakazari ; bara no yōni tsukutta kazari (shibashiba ribon de tsukuru). **~wood** [⸍wud] *n.* shitan. *v.*

rosin [rózin] *n.* kiyani ; jushi ; matsuyani. [*see* : **rise**.

roster [róstə] *n.* kimmusha-meibo.

rostrum [róstrəm] (*pl.* **-tra; -s**) *n.* kuchibashi ; hana. endan.

rosy [róuzi] *a.* barairo no ; yūbōna.

rot [rɔt] *v.* kusaru ; kusaraseru ; daraku suru. *n.* fuhai. **~ten** [rótn] *a.* kusatta ; kareta ; kusai.

rotary [róutəri] *a.* kaiten suru.

rotate [routéit] *v.* kaiten suru ; kōtai suru.

rotation [routéiʃən] *n.* (chikyū no) jiten ; junkan. *in* ~, jum-ban ni.

rote [rout] *n.* shigoto o kikaitekini suru koto (yoku oboete ite) ; anshō. *by* ~, anki shite ite.

rotund [routʌ́nd] *a.* maru-maru to shita. **~a** [-ə] *n.* maruyane no tatemono. **~ity** [ro(u)tʌ́nditi] *n.* maruyane ; kyūjō (tamajō no).

rouble [ru:bl] *n.* rūburu (Soren no kahei) =**ruble**.

rouge [ru:ʒ] *n.* beni ; benigara. *v.* beni o nuru (sasu).

rough [rʌf] *a.* arai ; zaratsuku ; sobōna. *n.* arai mono ; abare-

mono. **~-and-ready** [⌐ənrédi] *a.* maniawase no. **~en** *v.* araku suru (naru). **~hew** [⌐hju:] *v.* arakezuri suru. **~rider**
roulette [ru:lét] *n.* (*Fr.*) tamakorogashi. ⌐[⌐raidə] *n.* chōbashi.

round [raund] *a.* marui. *n.* marui mono; hitomawari; ippatsu. *ad.*, *prep.* mawatte. *v.* maruku naru; furimuku. *make one's* **~s**, junkai suru. **~about** [⌐əbaut] *a.* tōmawashi no. *n.* kaitenmokuba. **~house** *n.* enkei no ie. **~ robin**, enkei ni shomei shita tangansho. **~-table conferences**, entakukaigi. **~-trip** *n.*, *a.* kaiyū (no). **~up** [⌐əp] *n.* (*Am.*) kachiku no kariatsume.

rouse [rauz] *v.* me o samasaseru; okosu; me o samasu; okiru; furuitatsu.

roustabout [ráustəbaut] *n.* (*Am.*) hatoba-ninsoku; nakashi.

rout [raut] *n.* gunshū; ikusa ni makete nigeru guntai. *v.* uchi-
route [ru:t] *n.* michi; michisuji. ⌐yaburu.

routine [ru:tíːn] *n.* tetsuzuki; okimari; kanrei. *a.* nichijō no; okimari no.

rove [rouv] *v.* urotsuku. **~r** *n.* haikaisha; kaizoku.

row [rou] *n.* retsu; funaasobi. *v.* kai de kogu. **~boat** [⌐bout] *n.* kyōtei. **~lock** [rólək / rÁ-] *n.* kaiuke.

row rau] *n.* sawagi; sōdō. *v.* sawagu.

rowdy [ráudi] *n.* rambōmono. *a.* rambōna. **~dyish** *a.* rambōna. **~dyism** [róudiism] *n.* rambō.

rowel [ráuəl] *n.* (hakusha no) haguruma.

royal [rɔ́iəl] *a.* ō no; ōkoku no. **~ism** *n.* sonnōshugi. **~ist** *n.* kinnōka. **~ty** *n.* ōken; ōdō; shiyōryō; inzei.

rub [rʌb] *v.* kosuru; naderu; sureru; sawaru. *n.* masatsu; koshō. **~** *the wrong way*, okoraseru.

rubber [rÁbə] *n.* keshigomu; kokubanfuki.

rubbish [rÁbiʃ] *n.* kuzu; garakuta.

rubble [rÁbl] *n.* ishikuzu; sakanshigoto no kuzu.

ruble, rouble, rub [rúːbl] *n.* rūburu (*Soviet* no tsūka).

rubric [rúːbrik] *n.* hon no *chapter* (shō) nado ga akaku insatsu, matawa kaite aru mono; akazuri.

ruby [rúːbi] *n.* (*min.*) kōgyoku; rubii. ⌐kaji.

rudder [rÁdə] *n.* (fune no) kaji; hōkōda, (*direction*) o kimeru

ruddy [rÁdi] *a.* akai; akaranda.

rude [ru:d] *a.* somatsuna; shizen no mama no (*crude*); busahōna. ～ly *ad.* ～ness *n.*

rudiment [rú:dimənt] *n.* (*pl.*) kihon; shoho. ～ary [rù:di-mént(ə)ri] *a.* kihon (shoho) no.

rue [ru:] *n.* kanashimi; kui. *v.* kanashimu; nageku. ～ful *a.* kanashii; kanashisōna.

ruff [rʌf] *n.* hidaeri (kimono no); kubi no ke (tori nado no).

ruffian [rʌfiən] *n.* akkan. ～ism *n.* zanninsei. ～ly *a.*

ruffle [rʌfl] *v.* hida o toru; shiwakuchani suru (naru); rippu-ku saseru (suru). *n.* hidaeri.

rug [rʌg] *n.* (atsui rasha) jūtan.

Rugby [rʌgbi], **Rugger** [rʌgə] *n.* ragubii; ra-shiki shūkyū.

rugged [rʌgid] *a.* dekoboko no; rambōna. ～ly *ad.* ～ness *n.*

ruin [rú:in] *n.* hametsu; botsuraku; (*pl.*) haikyo. *v.* yaburu; arasu. ～ed *a.* kōhai shita; hasan shita. ～ation [ru:inéiʃ(ə)n] *n.* hametsu; reiraku. ～ous [-əs] *a.* kaimetsu shita; kōhai shita.

rule [ru:l] *n.* kisoku; shihai. *v.* shihai suru; sen o hiku. ～r [-ə] *n.* shihaisha; tōchisha; jōgi.

rum [rʌm] *n.* ramshu.

rumba, rhumba [rʌmbə] *n.* rumba (butō no isshu).

rumble [rʌmbl] *n.* goro-goro (oto); kōbuhojoseki (jitensha nado no). *v.* goro-goro to naru; todoroku.

ruminant [rú:minənt] *a., n.* (*zoo.*) hansū-dōbutsu (no); meisō suru (*meditate*).

ruminate [rú:mineit] *v.* hansū suru; omoi megurasu.

rumination [ru:minéiʃ(ə)n] *n.* meisō; hansū.

rummage [rʌmidʒ] *n.* garakuta; sōsaku. *v.* sagashinuku; kensa suru. ～ sale *n.* mikiriuri. ⌈tateru.

rumo(u)r [rú:mə] *n.* uwasa; hyōban. *v.* uwasa suru; hyōban o

rump [rʌmp] *n.* shiri; o (*tail*) no tsukene (tori ya kemono no).

rumple [rʌmpl] *n.* shiwa; hida. *v.* shiwa ni suru.

rumpus [rʌmpəs] *n.* bōdō; kōron (*noisy uproar*).

run [rʌn] *v.* **ran, run; running.** hashiru; nigeru; nagareru; unten suru; hashiraseru; keiei suru. *n.* hashiri; ryokō; unten; shinkō; ryūkō; hōkō. (jikan, okonai, seisan (*production*) no) tsuzuki. ～ down, kakeoriru; unten ga tomaru; otoroeru; attō suru. ～ over, afureru; shiku. ～ up, masu; kyūzō suru. *by the* ～, niwaka ni. *in the long* ～, kekkyoku; subete; ～ *for your* *life*, inochigake de nigeru. ∼ *a horse*, uma o hashiraseru. *Prices of hat* ∼ *as high as* $ 50, bōshi no nedan ga 50 (gojū) doru made agaru. *Vines* ∼ *along the sides of the road*, tsuru wa michibata ni sotte hatte iku. *time* ∼ *son*, toki wa sugiyuku. *my nose* ∼*s*, hanamizu ga tareru. ∼ *that report back to its source*, sono uwasa no dedokoro o tazuneru. *the well* ∼ *dry*, ido no mizu ga kareru. *shelves* ∼ *along the walls*, tana ga kabe no mawari ni zutto tsuite iru. *He* ∼*s a knife into his friend*, kare wa *knife* o tomodachi ni tsukitateru. *the streets* ∼ *blood*, tōri ni chi ga nagarete iru. *the color ran when the dress was washed*, kimono o arattara iro ga nijinda. *a lease to* ∼ *two years*, 2 (ni)-nenkan tsuzuku keiyaku. ∼ *a risk*, bōken suru. *How does the first verse* ∼*?* shi no daiichigyō wa nan to iu? *Enemy ships tried to* ∼ *the blockage*, teki no kantai wa fūsa o tsukiyaburō to shita. ∼ *rum*, ramushu no mitsuyu o suru. *he ran an ad in the evening paper*, kare wa yūkan ni chotto kōkoku o dashita. *a rope* ∼*s in a pulley*, nawa wa kassha o suru-suru tōru.

runaway [ránəwei] *n.* tōbōsha. *a.* tōbō shita. ∼ **knock,** to no tatakinige (itazura). ∼ **marriage,** kakeochi kekkon.

run-down [rándaun] *a.* tsukarehateta ; tomatta.

rune [ruːn] *n.* Hokuō no furui moji ; (*pl.*) Rūn-moji no shi.

rung [rʌŋ] *v. see :* **ring.** *n.* marui yokogi ; hashigo no yokogi.

runic [rúːnik] *a.* Rūn-moji no. *n.* Rūn-moji no mei (*inscription*).

runlet [ránlit], **runnel** [ránl] *n.* ogawa.

runner [ránə] *n.* (ichigo nado no) tsuru ; sōsha ; hashiri tsukai ; chūmontori. ∼-**up** [-ʌp] *n.* (kyōgi no) dainichaku.

running [rániŋ] *a.* hashiru ; keizoku suru. *n.* hashiru koto ; (*baseball*) tōrui ; sōrui.

runt [rʌnt] *n.* furui meushi.

runway [ránwei] *n.* sōro ; kassōro.

rupee [ruːpíː] *n.* rūpii (Indo no kahei).

rupture [ráptʃə] *n.* nakatagai ; haretsu. *v.* yaburu ; kankei o ta-tsu ; danzetsu suru.

rural [rúərəl] *a.* inaka no ; den'en no.

ruse [ruːz] *n.* (*Fr.*) sakuryaku.

rush [rʌʃ] *n., v.* tosshin (suru). sattō (suru). (*bot.*) tōshinsō. ∼-**light** [-lait] *n.* tōshinsō-rōsoku ; hizara no tōshin.

rusk [rʌsk] *n.* rasuku ; karui pan.

russet [rásit] *n., a.* kareha-iro (no).

Russian [rʌ́ʃ(ə)n] *n.*, *a.* Roshia (no); Roshiajin (no); Roshiago (no).

rust [rʌst] *n.* sabi ; sabiiro. *v.* sabiru (-saseru) ; niburu (-aseru). **～y** [rʌ́sti] *a.* sabita ; iro no sameta.

rustic [rʌ́stik] *n.*, *a.* inaka (no) ; inakafū (no). **～ate** [-eit] *v.* inaka ni iku ; inakazumai suru. **～ity** [rostísiti] *n.* inakafū ; bukotsu.

rustle [rʌ́sl] *a.*, *v.* sara-sara (to naru) ; gasa-gasa (iu).

rut [rʌt] *n.* wadachi (*track*). sakari (dōbutsu no).

ruth [ru:θ] *n.* (*arch.*) dōjō ; rembin. **～less** *a.* mujōna ; zanninna. **～ry** (*suffix*) shigoto, shokugyō, dōsa, seishitsu, jōken, gunshū, nado o arawasu. (*dentistry*, shika ijutsu. *chemistry*, kagaku. *mimicry*, monomane. *rivalry*, kyōsō. *jewelry*, hōsekirui. *peasantry*, nōmin-sōshō.

rye [rai] *n.* raimugi.

S

S, s [es] *n.* (*pl.* S's, Ss [esəz]). Eigo *alphabet* no dai-19-bamme no moji.

S.A. *Salvation Army; South Africa; South America.*

Sabbatarian [sæbətέəriən] *n., a.* ansokubi genshusha (no).

Sabbath [sǽbəθ] *n.* ansokubi (-jitsu).

saber, sabre [séibə] *n.* guntō; sāberu.

sable [séibl] *n.* (*zoo*) kuroten. kuroi kimono; mofuku.

sabotage [sǽbotɑːʒ] *n.* (*Fr.*) taigyō; shokuba ni ite namakeru koto; hakai kōsaku.

saboteur [sæbotə́ːr] *n.* (*Fr.*) taigyōsha; *sabotage* o suru mono.

sac [sæk] *n.* fukuro no yōna bubun.

saccharin(e) [sǽkərin] *n.* sakkarin (satō no daiyōhin).

sacerdotal [sæ̀səðdóutəl] *a.* sōryo (bōsan) no; sōken-sonchō no.

sachem [séitʃəm] *n.* (*America-Indian* no) shūchō.

sachet [sǽʃei / saʃέ] *n.* nioibukuro.

sack [sæk] *n.* nō; fukuro; tsutsumi; isshu no uwagi. *v.* ryakudatsu suru. ～**cloth** [˗klɔ:θ] *n.* arai asanuno. ～**ing** *n.* arai asanuno; zukku.

sacrament [sǽkrəmənt] *n.* genshikuna Kirisutokyōkai no shiki; (senrei, Seisanshiki nado) ～**al** [sæ̀krəméntl] *a.* shinseina; **sacred** [séikrid] *a.* shinseina. ⌊chikai no.

sacrifice [sǽkrifais] *n.* gisei; mikiriuri. *v.* kami ni sonaeru; sasageru. ～**hit**, (*baseball*) gisei-da. ～**cial** [sæ̀krifíʃ(ə)l]*a.* gisei

sacrilege [sæ̀krirídʒ] *n.* kami no bōtoku. ⌊no.

sacrilegious [sæ̀kilídʒəs] *a.* kami o okasu; fushinjin no.

sacristan [sǽkristən] *n.* seiki (*sacred vessels*) no bannin. (*in charge of*)

sad [sæd] *a.* kanashii; inkina (*gloomy*). ～**den** [sǽdn] *v.* kanashimu (-aseru); kanashiku naru.

saddle [sǽdl] *n.* kura. *v.* kura o tsukeru; omoni o owaseru. ～**r** [˗ə] *n.* bagushi (uma no kura nado o tsukuru hito). ～**ry** *n.* bagu (-shō).

sadiron [sǽdaiən] *n.* hinoshi; kote.

sadism [sǽdizm] *n.* gyakutai inranshō; sadizumu.

safe [seif] *a.* anzenna. *n.* kinko. ～ **hit,** (*baseball*) anda. ～**conduct** [￪kóndʌkt] *n.* (senji no) ryoken. ～**guard** *n.* hogo; yobō. *v.* hogo suru; goei suru. ～**ty** [￪ti] *n.* anzen; buji. ～**ty-valve,** anzemben. ～**ty zone,** anzenchitai.

saffron [sǽfrən] *n.*, *a.* safuran (no); ukon'iro (no); safuran'iro (no).

sag [sæg] *v.* tarumu; yurumu; *n.* yurumi; tarumi.

saga [sáːgə] *n.* (Kita Yōroppa) eiyūmonogatari.

sagacious [səgéiʃəs] *a.* sōmeina. ～**ly** *ad.* rikōni.

sagacity [səgǽsiti] *n.* sōmei; reiri.

sage [seidʒ] *a.* kashikoi (*clever*); kemmeina (*wise*). *n.* kenjin (*wiseman*).

sago [séigou] *n.* (*bot.*) sago-yashi (yashi no isshu).

sahib [sɑːib] *n.* danna (Indo de).

said [sed] *v. see :* **say.**

sail [seil] *n.* ho; fune; kōkai. *v.* kōkai suru; sōjū suru. *under* ～, kōkaichū. ～**ing** [séiliŋ] *n.* kōkai (ho de hashiru koto). ～**or** [séilə] *n.* suifu; kaiin.

saint [seint] *n.* seija; seito. ～**ly** [￪li] *a.* seito no yōna.

sake [seik] *n.* tame; riyū. *for the mercy's* ～, goshō da kara. *for the* ～ *of* …, no tame ni.

salaam [səlɑ́ːm] *n.* (hitai ni te o ateru) rei; aisatsu. *v. salaam* suru; rei o suru.

salable [séiləbl] *a.* uresōna; yoku ureru.

salad [sǽləd] *n.* namayasai no ryōri. ～**-days** [-deiz] *n.* wakai, mukeiken jidai.

salamander [sǽləməndə] *n.* hihebi (hi no naka ni sunde ita to iu hebi). sanshōuo, imori, nado.

salaried [sǽlərid] *a.* gekkyū-tori no. ～ **man,** hōkyū-seikatsu-sha.

salary [sǽləri] *n.* hōkyū; kyūryō.

sale [seil] *n.* hambai; ureyuki. ～**sman** [￪zmən] *n.* mise no uriko. ～**s-woman** [￪zwumən] *n.* fujin-hambaigakari.

salient [séiljənt] *a.* me ni tsuku. *n.* tobidashite iru tokoro : ～ *points in the speech,* hanashi no uchi no daijina ten.

saline [séilain] *a.* shio (*salt*) no; embun no.

saliva [səláivə] *n.* daeki; tsubaki.

sallow [sǽlou] *n.* nekoyanagi. *a.* kesshoku no warui.

sally [sǽli] *n.* totsugeki; ryokō; tawamure. *v.* totsugeki suru.

salmon [sǽmən] *n.* (*fish*) sake, shake; sakeiro.

salon [sǽlɔ̄ŋ] *n.* (*Fr.*) kyakuma. meishi no atsumari. *Paris Bi-jutsu Tenrankai*.

saloon [səlúːn] *n.* ōhiroma ; (kisha no) tembōsha ; chinretsujō.

salt [sɔːlt] *n.* shio ; tonchi. *v.* shio-kagen suru. *eat a person's* ∼, no kyaku to naru. *old* ∼, rōrenna suihei. *with a grain of* ∼, waribiki shite. ∼**cellar** [⌐selə] *n.* shioire. ∼**petre**, ∼**peter** [⌐piːtə] *n.* (*min.*) shōseki. ∼**y** [⌐ti] *a.* shioke no aru ; kichi no aru ; tonchi no ii.

salubrious [səljúːbriəs] *a.* kenkō ni yoi ; sawayakana.

salubrity [səljúːbriti] *n.* kenkō ni yoi koto.

salutary [sǽljutəri] *a.* kenkō ni yoi ; tame ni naru.

salutation [sæljutéiʃən] *n.* aisatsu ; keirei.

salute [səljúːt] *n.*, *v.* aisatsu (suru) ; keirei (suru).

salvage [sǽlvidʒ] *n.*, *v.* sempaku kyūjo (suru) ; sarubeiji (suru).

salvation [sælvéiʃən] *n.* kyūsai. *S*∼ *Army*, Kyūseigun.

salve [sɑːv] *n.* yawarakai kōyaku. *v.* yawarageru ; nagusameru.

salver [sǽlvə] *n.* (kinzokusei no) bon (*tray*).

salvia [sǽlviə] *n.* (*flower*) sarubia.

salvo [sǽlbou] *n.* jōken ; kōjitsu. isseishageki ; hakushu (*clap-ping hands*).

same [seim] *n.*, *a.* dōitsu (no) ; onaji (no).

sample [sæmpl] *n.* mihon. *up to* ∼, mihon dōri de.

sanative [sǽnətiv], **sanatory** [sǽnətəri] *a.* kaifuku suru ; naoru (*recover*) chikara no aru.

sanatorium [sænətɔ́ːriəm] *n.* ryōyōsho ; hoyōchi.

sanctification [sæŋktifikéiʃən] *n.* shinseika (*sanctifying*) ; reika (*spiritualizing*).

sanctify [sǽŋktifai] *v.* shinsei ni suru ; kiyomeru.

sanctimonious [sæŋktimóuniəs] *a.* shinseiburu ; shinjimburu.

sanctimony [sǽŋktiməni] *n.* seija kidori ; shinjimburu koto.

sanction [sǽŋkʃən] *n.* yurushi ; ninka. *v.* yurusu ; ninka suru.

sanctity [sǽŋktiti] *n.* shinsei (*sacredness*) ; kōketsu ; kedakasa (*nobleness*).

sanctuary [sǽŋktʃuəri] *n.* shinseina basho (*sacred place*).

sanctum [sǽŋktəm] *n.* shinseina basho ; jibun no heya.

sand [sænd] *n.* suna ; (*pl.*) sunawara. *v.* suna o maku. ∼**glass** [⌐glɑːs / glæs] *n.* suna-dokei. ∼**paper** [sǽn(d)peipə] *n.* kami-yasuri. ∼**y** *a.* suna no.

sandal [sǽndl] *n.* sandaru.
sandwich [sǽndwitʃ] *n.* sandoitchi. *v.* sandoitchi ni suru. ～ man, sandoitchiman.
sane [séin] *a.* kokoro no tashikana ; shōki no.
San Francisco [sǽn frənsískou] San Furanshisuko.
sang [sæŋ] *v. see :* sing.
sang-froid [sɑ̃frwɑ] *n.* (*Fr.*) heiki ; reisei.
sanguinary [sǽŋgwinəri] *a.* chinamagusai ; zankokuna.
sanguine [sǽŋgwin] *a.* kaikatsuna ; rakutentekina ; kesshoku no ii. ～ nature, rakutenka.
sanitarium [sænitéəriəm] *n.* sanatorium.
sanitary [sǽnitəri] *a.* eiseijō no ; hoken no.
sanitation [sænitéiʃən] *n.* kōshūeisei ; eiseisetsubi.
sanity [sǽniti] *n.* ki no tashikana koto.
sank [sæŋk] *v. see :* sink.
Sanskrit, Sanscrit [sǽnskrit] *n.* Bongo, Sanskuritgo.
sap [sæp] *n.* ki no yōeki ; seimei o ataeru yōeki. *v.* yowaraseru. *extreme heat sapped our strength*, hageshii atsusa ga tairyoku o shōmō saseru.
sapient [séipiənt] *a.* monoshirigao no ; kemmeina.
sapling [sǽpliŋ] *n.* wakagi ; wakamono.
saponify [səpɔ́nifai] *v.* sekkenka suru.
sapphire [sǽfaiə] *n.* (*min.*) seigyoku ; safaiya.
sappy [sǽpi] *a.* shiru no ōi ; bakana.
sapsucker [sǽpsʌkə] *n.* (*Am.*) *America* no chiisai kitsutsuki.
sarcasm [sɑ́:kæzm] *n.* atekosuri ; hiniku.
sarcastic [sɑ:kǽstik] *a.* fūshi no ; hiniku no.
sarcophagus [sɑ:kɔ́fəgəs] *n.* (*pl.* -gi [ʒdai]) kodai Girisha no ishi no kan.
sardine [sɑ:díːn] *n.* (*fish*) iwashi.
sardonic [sɑ:dɔ́nik] *a.* reishōtekina ; hinikuna.
sarsaparilla [sɑ:səpəríələ] *n.* (*bot.*) sarusa (nettaisan no yakusō).
sash [sæʃ] *n.* kazarimado ; mado no waku.
sassafras [sǽsəfræs] *n.* sasafurasu ; kusunoki.
sat [sæt] *v. see :* sit.
Satan [séitən] *n.* maō ; jamaika. ～ic [seitǽnik] *a.* Satan no.
satchel [sǽtʃəl] *n.* chiisana kaban ; tesagebukuro.
sate [seit] *v.* manzoku saseru ; tannō saseru. *be ～d with*, aki-a-

ki suru.
sateen [sæti:n] *n.* menjusu ; kejusu.
satellite [sǽtilait] *n.* jūsha ; eisei. ～ **country,** eiseikoku.
satiate [séiʃieit] *v.* akisaseru. *a.* [séiʃiit] (*poet*) akita.
satiety [sətáiəti] *n.* mampuku ; tannō.
satin [sǽtn] *n.*, *a.* shusu (no yōna).
satire [sǽtaiə] *n.* fūshishi ; fūshi.
satiric(al) [sətírik] *a.* fūshi no ; hinikuna.
satirist [sǽtərist] *n.* fūshi(shi) sakusha ; hinikuya.
satirize [sǽtəraiz] *v.* fūshi suru.   ⌈(*mental state*).
satisfaction [sætisfǽkʃən] *n.* manzoku ; michitarita shinkyō
satisfactory [sætisfǽktəri] *a.* manzokuna ; omou tōri no.
satisfy [sǽtisfai] *v.* manzoku saseru ; tokushin saseru.
satrap [séitræp] *n.* taishu ; chiji ; shū no *ruler*.
saturate [sǽtʃəreit] *v.* shimi saseru ; hōwa saseru.
Saturday [sǽtədi] *n.* Doyōbi.
saturnine [sǽtənain] *a.* inkina ; muttsuri shita ; namari no.
satyr [sǽtə] *n.* hanjin hanjū no mori no kami.
sauce [sɔːs] *n.* sōsu. *v.* aji o tsukeru. ～**pan** [⌐pæn] *n.* nagaetsuki no ryōrinabe ; furaipan. *What's* ～ *for the goose is* ～ *for the gander,* kotchi ni hontō nara sotchi nimo hontō. *Hunger is the best* ～, sukihara ni mazui mono nashi.
saucer [sɔ́ːsə] *n.* kōhiijawan nado no ukezara. *cup-and-*～.
saucy [sɔ́ːsi] *a.* namaikina ; desugita. ～**ciness** *n.* namaiki.
saunter [sɔ́ːntə] *n.* bura-bura aruki. *v.* bura-bura aruku.
saurian [sɔ́ːriən] *a.* (*zoo.*) tokagerui no. *n.* tokage ; ko no rui
sausage [sɔ́sidʒ] *n.* chōzume ; sōseiji.   ⌊no dōbutsu.
saute [sóutei] *a.* (*Fr.*) (ryōri de) karaage shita.
savage [sǽvidʒ] *a.* mikai no ; yabanna. *n.* yabanjin. *v.* mōgeki suru ; kamitsuku. ～**ly** *ad.* yaban ni. ～**ness** *n.* ～**ry** [-(e)ri] *n.* yaban ; mikai no jōtai ; *they live in* ～, karera wa mikai no jōtai de seikatsu shite iru.
savanna [səvǽnə] *n.* (Amerika nambu) daisōgen ; ki no nai
savant [sǽvənt] *n.* (*Fr.*) gakusha ; taika.   ⌊kusawara.
save [seiv] *v.* sukuu ; setsuyaku suru. *prep.*, *conj.* (*arch.*) …no hoka, …o nozoite.
saving [séiviŋ] *a.* chochiku suru. *prep.*, *conj.* …no hoka ; …o

nozoite. *n.* kyūjo; setsuyaku; (*pl.*) chokin. ~ **clause,** horyū-
Savio(u)r [séivjə] *n.* (*the* ~) sukuinushi; Kiristo. ⌊jōkō.

savo(u)r [séivə] *n.* aji; kaori. *a.*, *v.* aji (nioi) ga aru. ~**ry** [-ri]
a. fūmi no yoi. *n.* shiso-rui no shokubutsu (ryōri ni tsukau).

savoy [səvɔ́i] *n.* (*vegetable*) chirimen-jisha. ⌊~**ily** *ad.* ~**iness** *n.*

saw [sɔ:] *v.*[1] *see :* see. *v.*[2] **sawed, sawn; sawing.** nokogiri de
kiru. *n.* nokogiri; kakugen. ~**mill** [-mil] *n.* seizaisho. ~**dust**
[-dʌst] *n.* nokokuzu; ogakuzu. ~**yer** [-jə] *n.* kobiki.

saxifrage [sǽksifridʒ] *n.* (*bot.*) yukinoshita no isshu (*an alpine
Saxon [sǽksn] *n.*, *a.* Sakuson-jin (no). ⌊*plant*).

saxophone [sǽksfoun] *n.* sakisafōn.

say [sei] *v.* **said; saying.** iu; hanasu. ii tai koto; iibun. *I* ~,
kimi, kimi. *so to* ~, iwaba. *that is to* ~, sunawachi. *to* ~ *nothing of,* ...ni tsuite wa iwanu to shite. *n.* **the** ~, (*Am.*) ket-
teiken. ~**ing** [-iŋ] *n.* gen; setsu; kotowaza : *as the* ~ *is,* kotowaza no tōri. ~**ing and doing,** genkō.

SC. Anzen Hoshō Rijikai (*Security Council of United Nations*).

scab [skæb] *n.* kasabuta; hizen; sutoraiki fusanka shokkō.

scabbard [skǽbəd] *n.* (tōken no) saya. *v.* saya ni osameru.

scaffold [skǽfold] *n.* ashiba; sajiki. *v.* ashiba o kakeru; shikei
[skɔ:ld] *n.*, *v.* yakedo (suru); yuderu. ⌊ni suru.

scald

scale [skeil] *n.* uroko. memori. wariai. hashigo. (*pl.*) hakari.
v. uroko o otosu. hashigo de noboru. tembin de hakaru.
hagete ochiru (*off, away*). *turn the* ~, keisei ga kawaru.

scallop [skɔ́ləp] *n.* hotategai. *v.* scallop de ryōri suru.

scalp [skælp] *v.* atama no teppen (*top*) no kawa ya ke o hagu.
(*Am.*) rizaya o totte uru.

scalpel [skǽlpəl] *n.* gekayō no kogatana.

scaly [skéili] *a.* uroko no aru; urokogata no.

scamp [skæmp] *n.* yakuza; akkan. *v.* zonzaini suru.

scamper [skǽmpə] *n.* shissō; isogitabi; *v.* bata-bata hashiru.

scan [skæn] *v.* komakani shiraberu; jukushi suru.

scandal [skǽndl] *v.* shūbun; hinan. ~**ize** [-aiz] *v.* kanjō o sokonau. ~**ous** [-əs] *a.* hazubeki; kegarawashii.

scant [skænt] *v.* kagiru; kiritsumeru. *a.* toboshii; wazuka no.
~**ling** [-liŋ] *n.* kowari (koguchi sumpō no zaimoku); wazuka (*of*). ~**y** [-i] *a.* toboshii.

scapegoat [skéipgout] *n.* migawari.

scapegrace [skéipgreis] *n.* yakuza; rokudenashi.

scar [skɑ:] *n.* kizuato. *v.* kizuato ga nokoru.

scarce [skɛəs] *a.* toboshii; marena. **~ly** *ad.* karōjite; hotondo
…nai. *scarcely…before* (*when*), …suru ka shinai uchi ni.

scarcity [skéəsiti] *n.* fusoku; ketsubō; kikin.

scare [skɛə] *n.* odoshi. *v.* odokasu. **~crow** [⊥krou] *n.* kakashi.
~monger [⊥mʌŋgə] *n.* ryūgen (uwasa) o hanatsu hito.

scarf [skɑ:f] *n.* erimaki; katakake. *v.* setsugō suru (mokuzai nado). **~pin** [⊥pin] *n.* nekutai-pin. **~skin** [⊥skin] *n.* hyōhi.

scarlatina [skɑ:lətí:nə] *n.* (*med.*) shōkōnetsu.

scarlet [skɑ́:lit] *n.* shinku; hi-iro. *a.* shinku no. **~ fever,** (*med.*)
shōkōnetsu.

scarp [skɑ:p] *n.* kyūnakeisha *v.* kyūnakeisha o tsukeru.

scathe [skeið] (*arch.*) *n.* kizu. *v.* kizutsukeru. *without* **~,** buji ni.

scatter [skǽtə] *v.* chirasu; maku; risan suru.

scavenger [skǽvindʒə] *n.* gairosōjifu. *v.* (machi o) sōji suru.

scenario [sinɑ́:riou] *n.* (geki no) sujigaki; shinario; (eiga no)
kyakuhon.

scene [si:n] *n.* shiin; butaimen; bamen. *make a* **~,** katsugeki
o enzuru. **~ry** [⊥ri] *n.* keishiki; butaimen; haikei.

scenic [sí:nin] *a.* butai no; gekitekina fūkei no.

scent [sent] *n.* kaori; nioi. *v.* kagiwakeru; miyaburu.

scepter, ~tre [séptə] *n.* tsue; ōken. *v.* ō no tsue o sazukeru;
ōken o ataeru.   ⌈Am.⌉

sceptic, skeptic [sképtik] **a** utagai no (*the former Brit., the latter*

schedule [skédju:l] *n.* mokuroku; ichiranhyō; jikanwari. *v.*
mokuroku o tsukuru.

scheme [ski:m] *n.* keikaku; takurami; zukai. *v.* keikaku suru.

schism [sízm] *n.* bunri; (kyōkai no) bumpa. **~atic** [sizmǽtik]
n. shūha bunritsuronja. **~atical** *a.* bunri no; bumpa no.

schist [ʃist] *n.* (*geol.*) hengan (*easily splitted into layers*).

scholar [skɔ́lə] *n.* gakusei; gakusha. **~ly** *a.* gakushafū no. **~
ship** [⊥ʃip] *n.* gakuryoku; gakushiki.   ⌈tetsugakusha.

scholastic [skɔlǽstik] *a.* gakkō no. gakushabutta. *n.* Sukora-

school [sku:l] *n.* gakkō. **~ day** [skú:ldèi] *n.* gakusei jidai.
~fellow [skú:lfelou], **~mate** [skú:lmeit] *n.* gakkō nakama;

dōsōsei. ∼house [⌐haus] *n.* kōsha; kōchō no jūtaku. ∼ing kyōju; kyōiku; jugyōryō. ∼master (*m.*) [skú:lmà:stə], ∼mistress [skú:lmistris] *n.* sensei; kōchō. ∼room [⌐ru(:)m] *n.* kyōshitsu. ∼time [⌐taim] *n.* jugyōjikan.

schooner [skú:nə] *n.* sukūnā; 2(ni)-hon mata wa 3(sam)-bon *mast* no hansen.

sciatic [saiǽtik] *a.* (*med.*) zakotsu no; zakotsu-shinkeitsū no.

sciatica [saiǽtikə] *n.* (*med.*) zakotsu-shinkeitsū.

science [saiəns] *n.* kagaku; gakumon; shizenkagaku.

scientific [saiəntífik] *a.* kagaku no; kagakuteki no.

scientist [saíəntist] *n.* kagakusha.

scimitar [símitə] *n.* (Arabia no) mikazukigata no katana.

scintilla [sintílə] *n.* hibana; kirameki; wazukana konseki.

scintillate [síntileit] *v.* hibana o dasu; hirameku.

scintillation [sintiléiʃən] *n.* senkō; hibana.

scion [sáiən] *n.* wakaeda; yotsugi; shison.

scissor [sízə] *v.* hasami de kiru. ∼s [sízəz] *n.* (*pl.*) hasami.

scoff [skɔf] *n.*, *v.* chōshō (suru).

scold [skould] *n.* kuchigitanaku shikaru hito (tokuni onna). *v.* shikaru; gami-gami iu.

scollop [skɔ́ləp] *n.* hotategai.

sconce [skɔns] *n.* rōsokudai (kabe ni tsukideta).

scoop [sku:p] *n.* chiisana shaberu. tokudane; ōmōke. *v.* ku-scoot [sku:t] *v.* nigesaru. ∼er *n.* kogata-ōtobai. ⌊mu; sukū.

scope [skoup] *n.* han'i (chishiki, nōryoku no).

scorch [skɔ:tʃ] *v.* kogasu (-geru); karasu (-reru). ∼ed earth, shōdo-senjutsu.

score [skɔə] *n.* sukoā, kizamime; keisan. *v.* kizamime o tsukeru; tokuten suru; *on the* ∼ *of,* ... no wake de. ∼book [⌐buk]

scorn [skɔ:n] *n.*, *v.* keibetsu (suru). ⌊tokuten hyō.

scorpion [skɔ́:piən] *n.* sasori; (S-) (*astr.*) Sasoriza.

Scotch [skɔtʃ] *a.* *Scotland* no. *n.* *Scotland*-jin (-go). *v.* kasurikizu o owaseru. ∼man [-mən] *n.* *Scotland*-jin.

scot-free [skɔ́tfri:] *a.* batsu (gai) o ukenai. *go* ∼, batsu o ma-**Scots** [skɔts] *a.* *Scotland* no. *n.* *Scotland* go. ⌊nukareru.

scoundrel [skáudrəl] *n.* akutō; buraikan.

scour [skauə] *v.* kemma suru; togu. *n.* senjō; gezai.

scourge [skɔːdʒ] *n.* muchi ; tembatsu. *v.* muchiutsu ; bassuru. *the* ~ *of Heaven,* tembatsu.

scout [skaut] *n.* sekkō ; teisatsu. *v.* teisatsu (sekkō) suru. **Boy Scouts,** shōnen dan. **Girl Scouts,** joshi shōnen dan. ~**master** [⸋mæ̀stə] *n.* sekkōchō. ~**er** [skáutə] *n.* teisatsusha.

scow [skau] *n.* ōgata hirasokobune ; hakobune.

scowl [skaul] *n.* fukyōgao. *v.* nigai kao o suru.

scrabble [skrǽbl] *v.* kosuru ; kaku ; yojinoboru.

scramble [skrǽmbl] *v.* haiagaru. kakimazeru ; *n.* ubaiai (*for*).

scrap [skræp] *n.* kirikuzu. kirinuki. kenka. *a.* chiisai kirikuzu no. *v.* kenka suru. ~**iron** [⸋aiən] *n.* kuzutetsu ~**book** [⸋buk] *n.* kirinukichō. ⌜zuru koto.

scrape [skreip] *v.* kezuru ; kakiatsumeru ; ken'yaku suru. *n.* ke-

scratch [skrætʃ] *v.* hikkaku ; nagurigaki suru. *n.* hikkaita ato. *a.* niwaka-jitate no ; kyū-jitate no.

scrawl [skrɔːl] *n.* nagurigaki. *v.* hetani kaku.

scream [skriːm] *n.* sakebi ; kanakirigoe. *v.* sakebu ; kii-kii iu.

screech [skriːtʃ] *n.* kanakirigoe. *v.* sakebu.

screen [skriːn] *n.* sudare ; eishamaku. *v.* eisha suru.

screw [skruː] *n.* neji ; kechimbō. *v.* neji de shimeru ; mi o ne-jiru. ~ *propeller,* rasen (puropela) suishinki. ~**driver** [⸋drai-və] *n.* nejimawashi.

scribble [skríbl] *n.,* *v.* nagurigaki (suru) ; rakugaki (suru).

scribe [skraib] *n.* shoki ; daishonin.

scrimmage [skrímidʒ] *n.,* *v.* naguriai, kozeriai (suru).

scrimp [skrimp] *v.* kechikechi suru ; kiritsumeru. ~**y** [-i] *a.* ⌊kiritsumeta.

scrip [skrip] *n.* kamigire ; kari no shōken.

script [skript] *n.* sōshotai ; (*radio* hōsō nado no) daihon. ~**writer** [⸋raitə] *n.* hōsōgenkō-kisha.

Scriptual [skríptʃ(ə)rəl] *a.* Seisho (*Bible*) no.

Scripture [skríptʃə] *n.* seiten ; Bible.

scrivener [skrívnə] *n.* daisho ; kōshōnin ; kanekashi.

scrofula [skrɔ́fjulə] *n.* (*med.*) ruireki ; sembyō.

scrofulous [skrɔ́fjuləs] *a.* ruireki no ; sembyōshitsu no.

scroll [skroul] *n.* makimono ; makijiku ; uzumaki.

scrub [skrʌb] *n.* yabu ; akuseku to hataraku hito. *a.* katōna ; chiisai. *v.* migaku.

scrum [skrʌm], (*Brit.*) **scrummage** [⸌idʒ] *n.*, *v.* rambōna kenka ; rantō. ⎡ryo (suru).

scruple [skrú:pl] *n.*, *v.* chūcho (suru) ; tamerai (tamerau) ; en-

scrupulous [skrú:pjuləs] *a.* enryobukai ; tsutsushimibukai. ~

scrutinize [skrú:tinaiz] *v.* shiraberu ; kensa suru. ⎣**ly** *ad.*

scrutiny [skrú:tini] *n.* sensaku ; kensa.

scud [skʌd] *n.*, *v.* shissō (suru).

scuff [skʌf] *v.* ashi o agezuni aruku. ~**ing** [⸌iŋ] *n. scuff* suru ko-

scuffle [skʌfl] *n.*, *v.* kumiuchi (suru) ; rantō (suru). ⎣to.

scull [skʌl] *n.* (katate de motte kogu) kai ; *scull* de kogu kobune. *v. scull* de kogu.

scullery [skʌləri] *n.* shokki araiba ; nagashi (*sink*).

sculptor [skʌlptə] *n.* chōkokushi.

sculpture [skʌlptʃə] *n.* chōkoku (jutsu); horimono. *v.* chōko-

scum [skʌm] *n.* awa ; ukikasu ; kasu. ⎣ku suru.

scupper [skʌpə] *n.* (fune no dekki no) haisuikō.

scurf [skə:f] *n.* fuke ; aka. ~**y** [skə:fi] *a.* fukedarake no.

scurrilous [skə:riləs] *a.* kuchigitanai ; geretsuna. ~**ly** *ad.*

scurry [skə:ri] *v.* hashiru ; hashiraseru.

scurvy [skə:vi] *a.* geretsuna ; bureina. *n.* (*med.*) kaiketsubyō.

scutcheon [skʌtʃən], **escutcheon** [es-]*n.* monshō no tsuita tate.

scuttle [skʌtl] *n.* sekitan'ire ; funazoko no ana. *v.* awatete nigeru ; ana o akeru (fune no shizumeru tame nado).

scuttlebutt [skʌtlbət] *n.* (*sl.*) uwasa ; zatsudan.

scythe [saið] *n.* ōgama ; ōkina kama. *v.* ōgama de karu.

sea [si:] *n.* umi. *at* ~, kōkaichū. *by* ~, kairo de. ~ **anemone** [-ənémoni]*n.* isoginchaku. ~**board** [⸌bɔ:d] *n.* kaigan. ~ **breeze** [-ri:z] *n.* kainampū. ~**calf** [-ka:f] *n.* azarashi. ~**coast** [⸌koust] *n.* kaigan. ~**cow** [-kau] *n.* seiuchi. ~ **elephant** [⸌élifənt] *n.* kaizō. ~**farer** [⸌fèərə] *n.* funanori. ~**faring** [⸌fèəriŋ] *a.* funanori o shoku to suru ; kōkai no. ~ **fight** *n.* kaisen. ~**going** [-gouiŋ] *n.* kōkai ni jūji suru. ~**gull** [-gəl] *n.* kamome. ~**horse** [⸌hə:s] *n.* tatsunootoshigo. ~ **king** [-kiŋ] *n.* kaizokuō. ~ **level** [-levl] *n.* kaimen. ~ **lion** [⸌làiən] *n.* ashika. ~**man** [⸌mən] *n.* suihei. ~**manship** [⸌mənʃip] *n.* sempaku-un'yōjutsu. ~ **mew** [-mju:] *n.* kamome. ~ **mile** [mail] *n.* kairi. ~**piece** [-pi:s] *n.* umi no keshiki no e. ~**plane** [⸌plein] *n.*

suijō-hikōki. ～**-power** [⌐pauə] *n.* kaigunryoku. ～**room,** ka-ijō katsudō no yochi. ～**shore** [si:ʃɔ́: / -ʃɔ́:] *n.* kaigan. ～**sick** [⌐sik]*a.* funayoi suru. ～**sickness** [⌐siknis] *n.* funayoi. ～**side** [-said, ⌐sáid] *n.* umibe. ～**urchin** [ɔ́:tʃin] uni. ～**ward(s)** [⌐wə:d(z)]*ad.* umi no hō e. ～**weed**[-wi:d]*n.* kaisō. ～**worthy** [-wə:ði] *a.* kōkai ni tekisuru.

seal [si:l] *n.* azarashi. *n., v.* natsuin (suru); fūin (suru); kakushō (suru). ～**ling wax,** fūrō.

seam [si:m] *n.* nuime; shiwa. *v.* nuiawaseru. ～**stress** [⌐stris / sém-] *n.* saihōfu (onna). ～**y** *a.* nuime no aru. *the* ～*y side,* ura; ankokumen.

sear [siə] *a.* hikarabita. *v.* hikarabiru (-saseru); kogasu (-geru).

search [sɔ:tʃ] *n.* sōsaku; kensa. *v.* sagasu; sōsaku suru. ～**light** [⌐lait] *n.* tanshōtō. ～**-warrant** [⌐wɔ̀rənt] *n.* (kataku) sōsaku reijō.

season [si:zn] *n.* kisetsu; yoi ori. *v.* aji o tsukeru; yakudatsu yōni naru. *in* ～, dezakari de. ～**able** [si:znəbl] *a.* tekisetsuna. ～**ing** [si:zniŋ] *n.* chōmi (ryō).

seat [si:t] *n.* seki; isu; basho. *v.* chakuseki saseru.

sebaceous [sibéiʃəs] *a.* shibō (abura, *lard*) no.

secede [sisí:d] *v.* dattai suru; bunri suru (*from*).

secession [siséʃən] *n.* dattai; bunri. ～**ism** *n.* bunriron.

seclude [siklú:d] *v.* hikkomeru; intai saseru. ～**d** [-id] *a.* hito-**seclusion** [siklú:ʒən] *n.* kakuri; intai. [zato hanareta.

second [sék(ə)nd] *a.* dai-ni(2) no *ad., v.* hosa suru; kōen suru. *n.* dai-ni(2) no mono; (*pl.*) nikyūhin. byō. ～ *sight,* senken no mei. *in a* ～, tachimachi. ～**ary** [-(ə)ri] *a.* dai-ni no. *n.* hojosha. ～**hand** [-hǽnd] *a.* furute no. *n.* furumono; (tokei no) byōshin. ～**ly** *ad.* dai-ni ni. ～**rate** *a.* nitō no. *n.* niryūhin.

secrecy [sí:krəsi] *n.* himitsu; himitsushugi.

secret [sí:krit] *a.* himitsu no; kakureta. *n.* himitsu; hiketsu. ～**ariat** [-əriət] *n.* hishoka; kambō. ～**ary** [sékritəri] *n.* shoki; hisho; kanji; shokikan; dajiin; *S* ～ *of State,* (*Am.*) Kokumu Chōkan. ～**aryship** *n.* shokikanshoku. ～**ly** *ad.* himitsu ni; [naisho ni.

secrete [sikrí:t] *v.* hisuru; kakusu. [naisho ni.

secretion [sikrí:ʃən] *n.* intoku; impei; bumpi (tsu).

secretive [sikrí:tiv] *a.* kakushidate suru; bumpi o unagasu.

secretory [sikrí:təri] *a.* bumpi(tsu) suru ; bumpi(tsu) no.

sect [sekt] *n.* shūha ; gakuha. ⌈tsuyoi hito.

sectarian [sektéəriən] *a.* shūha (gakuha) no. *n.* shūhashin ⌐no

section [sékʃ(ə)n] *n.* setsudan ; bubun. **~al** *a.* bubun no. **~al-ism** *n.* bumpashugi ; habatsushugi.

secular [sékjulə] *a.* konoyo no ; sezoku no ; isseiki ichido no. **~** *affairs*, zokuji. **~ize** [-raiz] *v.* genzoku saseru. **~** *the school*, gakkō o shūkyō kara hanasu. ⌈suru.

secure [sikjúə] *a.* shimpai no nai. *v.* anzenni suru ; kakutoku

security [sikjúəriti] *n.* anzen ; hoshō ; teitōbutsu. (*pl.*) shōken.

sedan [sidǽn] *n.* kago. (*Am.*) sedan-gata jidōsha.

sedate [sidéit] *a.* shizukana ; ochitsuita.

sedative [sédətiv] *a.* shizukani osamaru. *n.* (*med.*) chinseiyaku.

sedentary [sédəntəri] *a.* suwarikiri no ; teijū suru. **~rily** *ad.*

sedge [sedʒ] *n.* (*bot.*) suge. ⌊**~riness** *n.*

sediment [sédimənt] *n.* ori ; chindembutsu.

sedition [sidíʃən] *n.* chiambōgai ; dōran no sendō.

seduce [sidjú:s] *v.* sosonokasu ; yūwaku suru.

seduction [sidʌkʃ(ə)n] *n.* (*pl.*) yūwaku(butsu) ; kudokiotoshi.

seductive [sidʌktiv] *a.* yūwaku suru. **~ly** *ad.* yūwakutekini. **~ness** *n.* yūwaku. ⌈kimben.

sedulous [sédʒuləs] *a.* kimbenna. **~ly** *ad.* umazuni. **~ness** *n.*

see [si:] *v.* **saw, seen ; seeing.** miru (me de) ; wakaru (kokoro de). **~** *that black cloud*, ano kurokumo o goran. *I* **~** *what you mean*, anata no kangae ga (wa) wakari masu. **~** *the girl home*, sono musume o uchi made miokuru. *Will you* **~** *him at his home?* ano hito no uchi de atte kudasai masu ka? **~** *through*, hontō no koto ga wakaru. *I* **~**, wakatta. *You* **~**, ne! wakattarō?

seed [si:d] *n.* tane ; tamago ; shison. *v.* tane o maku. **~ling** [-liŋ] *n.* mishō. **~y** *a.* tane no ōi.

seek [si:k] *v.* **sought ; seeking.** sagasu ; motomeru.

seem [si:m] *v.* mieru ; ...rashii. **~ing** [-iŋ] *a.* uwabe no. **~ing-ly** *ad.* uwabe wa. **~ly** *a.* niatta ; kakkō no. *ad.* fusawashiku.

seen [si:n] *v. see :* **see.**

seer [siə] *n.* yogensha.

seesaw [sí:sɔ] *n.* shiisō ; gikkon-battan. *v.* jōge ni ugoku.

seethe [si:ð] *v.* **seethed** *or* **sod, seethed** *or* (*arch.*) **sodden** ;

seething. futtō suru ; awadatsu. ⌈chokusen de kitta mono.
segment [ségmənt] *n.* dampen. (*math.*) kyūkei ; en no ichibu o
segregate [ségrigeit] *v.* bunri suru ; kakuri suru.
seignior [si:njər], **seigneur** [séinjə:] *n.* shukun ; ryōshu.
seine [sein] *n. v.* ōami (de uo o toru).
seismic [sáizmik] *a.* jishin no.
seismo- [sáizmə-] *prefix.* jishin no. **~gram** [-grəm] *n.* jishinkei no kiroku. **~graph** *n.* jishinkei. **~grapher** [saizmógrəfə]
  n. jishingakusha. **~graphical** [sàizmɔgræfikl] *a.* jishingaku
  no. **~graphy** *n.* jishingaku; jishinron, **~logy** [-ləgi] *n.* jishingaku. **~logical(ly)** [sàizmǝlódʒikl(i)] *a., ad.* jishingaku no (ni).
  ~gist [saizmólədʒist] *n.* jishingakusha. **~meter** [-mitə] *n.*
  jishinkei. **~metric(al)** [sáizmǝmétrik(l)] *a.* jishinkei no. **~**
  metry [saizmómǝtri] *n.* jishinkei. **~scope** [-skoup] *n.* jishinkei. **~scopic** [sáizmǝskópik] *a.* jishinkei no.
seize [si:z] *v.* toraeru.
seizure [sí:ʒǝ] *n.* hokaku ; sashiosae.
seldom [séldǝm] *ad.* mare ni ; metta ni...shinai.
select [silékt] *v.* erabu. *a.* sembatsu shita. **~tion** [-ʃ(ǝ)n] *n.* sentaku ; erinuki (*picked up*). **~ society,** jōryū shakai.
self [self] *n.* (*pl.* **selves** [-vz]) jibun jishin. *a.* onaji. **~con-**
  ceit [⸺kǝnsí:t] *n.* unubore. **~conscious** [-kónʃǝs] *a.* jikaku
  shite iru. **~contradictory** [⸺kɔntrǝdíktǝri] *a.* mujun no. **~**
  control [⸺kǝntróul] *n.* kokki. **~denial** [⸺dináiǝl] *n.* jisei. **~**
  ~educated [⸺édʒukeitid] *a.* dokugaku no. **~evident** [⸺évi-
  dǝnt] *a.* wakarikitta. **~explaining** [⸺ikspléiniŋ] *a.* wakarikitta. **~governing** [-gávǝniŋ] *a.* jichi no. **~help** [⸺hélp] *n.* jijo.
  ~interest [⸺íntǝrist] *n.* jibun no rieki. **~made** [⸺méid] *a.*
  jisaku no. **~possessed** [⸺pǝzést] *a.* reiseina. **~possession**
  [⸺pǝzéʃǝn] *n.* ochitsuki. **~taught** [⸺tɔ́:t] *a.* dokugaku no. **~**
  will [⸺wíl] *n.* wagamama. **~willed** [⸺wíld] *a.* wagamamana.
  ~winding [⸺wáindiŋ] *a.* jidōmaki no.
selfish [sélfiʃ] *a.* wagamamana.
selfsame [sélfseim] *a.* mattaku onaji no. ⌈baki.
sell [sel] *v.* **sold ; selling.** uru ; ureru. **~ing** *n.* hambai ; urisa-
selvage, selvedge [sélvidʒ] *n.* orihashi ; mimi (orimono no).
semaphore [sémǝfɔə] *n.* ūdegi no shingōki. *v.* shingō suru.

semblance [sémbləns] *n.* gaikan ; misekake.
semen [sí:mən] *n.* (*bot.*) tane ; (*physiol.*) seieki.
semester [siméstə] *n.* hannen gakki (niki seido).
semiannual [sémiænjuəl] *a.* hannen no ; hannengoto no.
semibreve [sémibri:v] *n.* (ongaku de) zen'ompu.
semicircle [sémisə̀:kl] *n.* han'en.
semicircular [sémisə̀:kjulə] *a.* han'en no.
semicolon [sémikóulən] *n.* semikoron (;).
semimonthly [sémimánθli] *a.* hantsuki ni ichido zutsu. *n.* hantsuki ikkai no shuppambutsu.
seminal [séminəl] *a.* tane no ; seieki no.
seminar [séminɑ:] *n.* zemināru ; kenkyūshitsu. ～y [ri] *n.* gakkō ; (toku ni) shingakkō.
semiofficial [semiəfíʃəl] *a.* hankantekina. ～ly *ad.*
semitone [sémitoun] *n.* (*mus.*) han'on no.
semiweekly [semiwí:kli] *a.* hanshūgoto no.
sempstress [sém(p)stris] *n.* saihō suru fujin (onna). *see :* seamstress [sémstris]
senate [sénit] *n.* genrōin ; jōin.
senator [sénətə] *n.* genrōin-giin. jōin-giin. ～ial [senətɔ́:riəl] *a.* genrōin(giin) no ; jōin(giin) no.
send [send] *v.* sent ; sending. okuru ; dasu. ～ for, yobi ni yaru. ～off [-ɔ:f] *n.* miokuri. ～off party sōbetsukai.
seneschal [sénəʃəl] *n.* karō ; shitsuji. (Yōroppa chūsei no).
senile [sí:nail] *a.* kōrei no ; rōsui no.
senility [siníliti] *n.* kōrei ; rōsui.
senior [sí:njə] *a.* nenchō no ; jōkyū no. *n.* nenchōsha ; sempai. ～ statesman, genrō. ～ity [sì:nióriti] *n.* nenchō ; jōkan.
senna [sénə] *v.* senna (*dried leaves, used as laxative*).
señor [senjɔ́:] *n.* (*Sp.*) Kun ; Sama.
señora [senjɔ́:rə] *n.* (*Sp.*) Fujin ; Okusama.
señorita [sènjɔ:rí:tə] *n.* (*Sp.*) jō ; Ojōsama.
sensation [senséiʃ(ə)n] *n.* kanji ; kankaku ; ninki ; hyōban. ～al [-əl] *a.* kankaku no ; kandō suru. hijōshikina.
sense [sens] *n.* kannō ; chikaku. *v.* kanjiru. ～less *a.* orokana ;
sensibility [sensəbíliti] *n.* kansei ; kanjusei ; kanzuru chikara.
sensible [sénsəbl] *a.* kanjiyasui ; wake no wakatta ; fumbetsu aru. nemurigusa.
sensitive [sénsitiv] *a.* kanjiyasui ; binkanna. ～ plant *n.* (*plant*)

sensitize [sénsitaiz] *v. sensitive* ni suru.

sensual [sénʃuəl] *a.* nikkan no ; seiyoku no.

sensuality [senʃuǽliti] *n.* kōshoku ; seiyoku ni fukeru koto.

sensuous [sénʃuəs] *a.* kankakutekina ; binkanna.

sent [sent] *v. see : send.* ⌈suru ; hanketsu suru.

sentence [séntəns] *n.* (*leg.*) senkoku. (*gram.*) bun. *v.* senkoku

sententious [senténʃəs] *a.* kanketsuna ; kingen no yōna.

sentient [sénʃənt] *a.* chikaku (kanjō) no aru.

sentiment [séntimənt] *n.* jōsō ; senren sareta kanjō. *man of* ∼,
  kanjōka. ∼**al** [sèntimént(ə)] *a.* jō ni moroi ; takanna. ∼**alism**

sentinel [séntinəl] *n.* bampei ; shōhei. ⌊*n.* kanjōshugi.

sentry [séntri] *n.* hoshō ; bampei.

Seoul [soul] *n.* Sōl (Keijō).

separable [sép(ə)rəbl] *a.* bunri shiuru. ∼**bly** *ad.* bunri shite.

separate [sépəreit] *v.* bunri suru ; wakareru. *a.* [sépərit] wakareta. ∼**tion** [sèpəréiʃ(ə)n] *n.* bunri ; bunrui. ∼**tist** [-ist] *n.* bun-
  rishugisha. ∼**tor** *n.* bunriki.

September [septémbə] *n.* Kugatsu.

septennial [septéniəl] *a.* shichinenkan no.

septic [séptik] *a.* fuhaisei no ; fuhai saseru.

septicemia [septisí:miə] *n.* (*med.*) haiketsushō.

septuagenarian [séptʃuədʒənéəriən], **septuagenary** [sèptʃuə-
  dʒí:nəri] *a.* nanajissai no. *n.* nanajissai no hito.

Septuagint [séptʃuədʒint] *n.* Girisha no kyūyakuseisho.

septum [séptəm] *n.* (*pl.* **-ta**) kakuheki ; kakumaku.

septuple [séptjupl] *a.* nanabai no. *n.* nanabai. *v.* nanabai ni su-

sepulcher, sepulchre [sépəlkə] *n.* haka. *v.* maisō suru. ⌊ru.

sepulchral [səpʌ́lkrəl] *a.* haka no ; maisō no.

sepulture [sépəltʃə] *n.* maisō ; haka.

sequel [sí:kwəl] *n.* tsuzuki ; nariyuki : *in the* ∼, kekkyoku.

sequence [sí:kwəns] *n.* keizoku ; renzoku ; kanren.

sequester [sikwéstə] *v.* sashiosaeru ; tonsei saseru.

sequestrate [sikwéstrəit] *v.* sashiosaeru ; bosshū suru.

sequestration [sì:kwestréiʃən / sè-] *n.* sashiosae ; bosshū.

sequin [sí:kwin] *n.* Ïtaria no mukashi no kinka ; kazari no
  kimmedaru. ⌈no heya. *cf.* **harem.**

seraglio [sirǽliou] *n.* (*pl.* **-s** ; **-li**) (Toruko no) kōkyū ; saishō

seraph [sérəf] *n.* (*pl.* **-s**; **-im**) saikōi no tenshi (*angel*). ~**ic**
sere [siə] *a.* hikarabita. └[seráefik] *a.* tenshifū no.
serenade [sèrənéid] *n.* (*music*) sayokyoku.
serene [səríːn] *a.* seirōna; seionna; yoku hareta.
serenity [səréniti] *n.* seirō; chinchaku.
serf [sɔːf] *n.* nōdo(*slave*). ~**dom** [⌐dəm] *n.* nōdo no mibun
serge [sɔːdʒ] *n.* ayaori no rasha; sāji.
sergeant [sáːdʒənt] *n.* gunsō; keibu. ┌shuppambutsu.
serial [síəriəl] *a.* tsuzuki (mono) no. *n.* tsuzukimono; teiki
series [síəriːz] *n.* (*sing.* & *pl.*) tsuzuki; kumi; rensa.
serious [síəriəs] *a.* genshukuna; majimena; jūdaina.
sermon [sɔ́ːmən] *n.* sekkyō; kunkai.
serous [síərəs] *a.* chishio no; mizu no yōna. ┌rikunetta.
serpent [sɔ́ːpənt] *n.* hebi. ~**ine** [-ain] *a.* hebi no yōna; maga-
serrate [séreit], **serrated** [séreitid] *a.* nokogiri no ha no yōna.
serried [sérid] *a.* misshū shita.
serum [síərəm] *n.* (*physiol.*) shōeki; (*med.*) kessei.
servant [sɔ́ːvənt] *n.* meshitsukai; yatoinin.
serve [sɔːv] *v.* tsukaeru; hōshi suru; yaku ni tatsu.
service [sɔ́ːvis] *n.* hōshi; kimmu. *at your* ~, go-jiyū ni. *take*
~, hōkō suru. ~**able** [-əbl] *a.* yaku ni tatsu.
servile [sɔ́ːvil] *a.* shimobe no; hikutsuna.
servility [sɔːvíliti] *n.* doreikonjō.
servitor [sɔ́ːvitə] *n.* boku; jūsha.
servitude [sɔ́ːvitjuːd] *n.* fukueki; chōeki.
sesame [sésəmi] *n.* goma.
session [séʃən] *n.* kaikai; kaitei. *congress is now in* ~, kokkai
wa ima kaikaichū da. ┌no 6-gyō.
sestet [sestét] *n.* (ongaku de) rokujūsō (shō); *sonnet* no saigo
set [set] *v.* **set**; **setting**. oku; sueru. *a.* kotei shita. *n.* kumi;
soroi; nakama. ~ *about*, torikakaru. ~ *against*, kuraberu. ~
aside, waki ni oku. ~ *by*, torinokete oku. ~ *down*, orosu; ka-
kiorosu. ~ *forth*, shimesu. ~*in*, hajimaru. ~ *off*, shuppatsu
suru. ~ *on*, sendō suru. ~ *one's teeth*, ha o kuishibaru. ~ *out*,
shuppatsu suru. ~ *to*, ni torikakaru. ~ *up*, tateru. ~ *up for*,
...to jishō suru. ~**back** [⌐bæk] *n.* zasetsu; taiho. ~**tee** [-tíː] *n.*
nagaisu (*sofa*). ~**ter** [⌐tə] *n. set* suru hito; sakkyokusha; sho-

kujikō. **～ting** [-ɪŋ] *n.* anchi ; suetsuke ; hamekomi. **～up** [-ʌp] *n.* kumitate ; soshiki.

settle [sétl] *v.* kata o tsukeru ; shokumin suru ; sadamaru (-eru) ; matomaru (-eru) ; kettei suru. *n.* senaka no takai isu. **～ing day** [-ɪŋ dei] seisambi ; kessambi. **～ment** *n.* kaiketsu ; shokuminchi. **～r** [-ə] *n.* kyojūsha.

seven [sévn] *n., a.* nanatsu(7) (no). **～fold** [-fould] *a.* nanabai no.

seventeen [sévntí:n] *n., a.* jūshichi(17) (no).

seventeenth [sévntí:nθ] *a.* dai-jūshichi(17) no. *n.* dai-jūshichi.

seventh [sévnθ] *a.* dai-shichi(7) no ; shichiban no. *n.* dai-shichi.

seventieth [sévntiiθ] *a.* dai-shichijū no ; shichijūban no. *n.* dai-shichijū.

seventy [sévnti] *a.* shichijū (70) no. *n.* shichijū.

sever [sévə] *v.* hanasu (-reru) ; kireru.

several [sévərəl] *a.* sūko no ; iroiro no.

severance [sévərəns] *n.* bunri ; setsudan.

severe [siviə] *a.* genjūna ; hageshii. **～ly** *ad.* kibishiku.

severity [səvériti] *n.* genjū ; kibishisa.

Sevres [séivrə] *a.* (*Fr.*) Sēburu-yaki no tōki.

sew [sou] *v.* **sewed, sewed** *or* **sewn** ; **sewing.** nuu ; tojiru. **～ing** *n.* saihō. **～ing machine,** mishin.

sewage [sjú:idʒ / sú:-] *n.* gesui de hakobareru obutsu.

sewer [sóuə] *n.* nuu hito. [sjú:ə] gesui. **～age** [sjúəridʒ] *n.* obutsu ga shori sareru koto.

sewn [soun] *v. see :* **sew.** ⌐no (aru) ; *sex* o motta.

sex [seks] *n.* sei. *the* **～** (shūgōtekini) josei. **～ual** [-ʃuəl] *a.* sei

sexagenary [sèksədʒénəri] *n.* rokujū(dai) no hito.

sexagesimal [sèksədʒésiməl] *a.* rokujū (60) no. rokujisshinhō no. *n.* rokujū-bunsū ; (*math.*) rokujū tan'i.

sexcentenary [sekssénténəri] *a.* roppyaku (600) nen no. *n.* roppyaku-nensai.

sexennial [seksénial] *a.* roku (6) nen tsuzuku.

sexfoil [séksfɔil] *n.* rokuyō shokubutsu (*six-leafed*).

sexillion [seksíljən], **sextillion** [sekstíljən] *n., a.* (*Fr., Am.*) 1 ni 0 no 21 tsuite iru kazu (no) ; (*Brit.*) 1 ni 0 no 36 tsuite iru [kazu (no). kazu (no).

sextant [sékstənt] *n.* en no rokubun no ichi. ⌐kazu (no).

sextet, sextette [sekstét] *n.* (*mus.*) rokujūsō (shō). *cf.* sō (*play with instruments*) ; shō (*sing each one's own part*).

sextillion [sekstíljən] *n.*, *a. see* : **sexillion.**
sexton [sékstən] *n.* teraotoko.
sextuple [sékstju:pl] *a.* roku (6) bai no.
shabby [ʃǽbi] *a.* misuborashii ; geretsuna. ~-**genteel** [-dʒentí:l] *a.* ochiburenagara mo teisai o kazaru.
shack [ʃæk] *n.* (*Am.*) marutagoya.
shackle [ʃǽkl] *n.* kase ; (*pl.*) tekase ; ashikase. *v.* kase o hameru.
shad [ʃæd] *n.* (*sing. & pl.*) nishin no rui no sakana.
shaddock [ʃǽdək] *n.* (*bot.*) zabon.
shade [ʃeid] *n.* kage ; hiyoke. *v.* kakusu. *the ~s of night were falling fast*, yoru no kage hayaku mo ochite kita. ~**less** [-lis] *a.* kage no nai. ~**y** [ʃéidi] *a.* kage no aru ; yami no. *on the ~ side of (forty)*, (40) no saka o koshite. ~ *character*, ikagawashii jimbutsu. ~**iness** [ʃéidines] *a.* kage no aru ; ushirogurai.
shadow [ʃǽdou] *n.* kage ; oboroge ; zenchō. *v.* kakusu ; bikō suru. ~ *of clouds*, kumo no kage (chijō ni ochita). *the ~s*, yūyami. ~**y** *a.* kage no aru ; kurai ; utagawashii.
shaft [ʃæft] *n.* yagara ; entotsu (hosonagai). jiku ; shimbō.
shag [ʃæg] *n.* arage ; mukuge. ~**gy** [ʃǽgi] *a.* kebukai ; arai ke no. ~**giness** *n.* kemukujara.
shagreen [ʃəgrí:n] *n.* samegawa (*shark skin.*).
shah [ʃɑ:] *n.* Perusha Ō no sonshō (*honorific*).
shake [ʃeik] *v.* furu ; yusuburu. *n.* furue ; yure. ~ *hands*, akushu suru. ~**down** [-daun] *n.* ma ni awase. ~**r** *n.* furu hito ; furueru
Shakespearian [ʃəikspíəriən] *a.* Shēkuspia (jidai, fū) no. ⌞hito.
shaky [ʃéiki] *a.* furueru ; guratsuku ; ate ni naranu.
shale [ʃeil] *n.* (*geol.*) ketsugan ; deibangan.
shall [ʃæl] **should** [ʃúd] *aux. v.* ... mashō ; ... subeki desu ; ... sase masu. (kuwashii koto wa furoku *Appendix* o goran kuda-
shallow [ʃǽlou] *a.* asai ; asahakana. *n.* asase. ⌞sai).
shalt [ʃælt] *anx. v.* **shall** no 2 nininshō tansū *thou shalt* to iu, *arch.* no katachi. ⌜mogisen ; enshū.
sham [ʃæm] *n.* misemono. *a.* itsuwari no. *v.* furi o suru. ~ **fight,**
shamble [ʃǽmbl] *v.* yorokete aruku. *n.* yoromeki. ~**s** [-z] *n.* (*often in sing.*) tosatsujō ; shurajō.
shame [ʃeim] *n.* haji ; chijoku. *v.* hazukashimeru ; bujoku suru. ~**faced** *a.* hazukashigaru. ~**ful** *a.* fumemboku no. ~**less**

a. haji-shirazu no ; harenchi no.

shampoo [ʃæmpú:] *n.* kamiarai ; kamiaraiko. *v.* kami o arau.

shamrock [ʃǽmsɑk] *n.* (*flower*) shirotsumegusa (*Ireland* no kokka).

Shangri-La [ʃǽŋgrilá:] *n.* kakū no risōkyō ; bakugeki-kichi.

shank [ʃæŋk] *n.* sune ; jiku (kagi, ikari nado no). ~'*s mare.* jibun no ashi ; hizakurige.

shanty [ʃǽnti] *n.* karigoya ; hottategoya.

shape [ʃeip] *n.* katachi ; gaikei. *v.* katachi o tsukuru ; kufū suru ; awaseru ; katachi o nasu. ~**less** *a.* katachi no nai ; bukakkōna. ~**ly** [ʃéipli]*a.* katachi no yoi. ~**liness** *n.* katachi no yoi koto.

shard [ʃɑ:d] *n.* (setomono no) kakera ; hahen.   ⌊yoi koto.

share [ʃɛə] *n.* bubun ; haitō ; kabushiki. *v.* bumpai suru ; azukaru. *go* ~ *s,* yamawake suru. ~**cropper** [⌐krɔpə] *n.* kosakunin. ~**holder** [⌐houldə] *n.* kabunushi.

shark [ʃɑ:k] *n.* same ; fuka. sagishi. *v.* sagi o hataraku.

sharp [ʃɑ:p] *a.* surudoi. ~**en** [ʃɑ́:pn] *v.* surudoku suru. ~**ness** [-nis] *n.* surudosa.

shatter [ʃǽtə] *v.* uchikudaku.

shave [ʃeiv] *v.* **shaved, shaved** *or* **shaven ; shaving.** hige o soru. *close* ~, abunai tokoro. ~**ing** [ʃéiviŋ] *n.* (*pl.*) higesori ;   ⌊kannakuzu.

shaven [ʃéivn] *v. see :* **shave.**

Shavian [ʃéiviən] *a. Bernard Shaw* (ryū) no.

shawl [ʃoul] *n.* katakake ; shōru.

she [ʃi:] *pron.* kanojo wa (ga) ; onna ; mesu (ippan ni).   ⌈neru.

sheaf [ʃi:f] *n.* (*pl.*) **sheaves** [ʃi:vz] *n.* (ine nado no) taba. *v.* taba-

shear [ʃiə] *n.* ōbasami. *v.* **sheared** *or arch.* **shore, shorn ; shearing.** hasami kiru.

sheath [ʃi:θ] *n.* saya ; hakama.   ⌊ing. hasami kiru.

sheathe [ʃi:ð] *v.* saya ni ireru.

sheave [ʃi:v] *n.* mizo no aru kassha no kuruma.

shed [ʃed] *v.* **shed ; shedding.** nagasu ; dasu. *n.* koya ; monooki. *the girl* ~ *tears,* shōjo wa namida o dashita. *that snake has just* ~, ano hebi wa ima kawa o nuida tokoro da.

sheen [ʃi:n] *n.* kagayaki ; kōtaku. ~**y** *a.* hikaru.

sheep [ʃi:p] *n.* (*pl.* onaji) men'yō ; hitsuji. ~**fold** *n.* hitsujigoya. ~**ish** *a.* hazukashigaru. ~**skin** *n.* hitsuji no kawa ; sotsugyō shōsho.   ⌈choku ni. ~. waki ni soreru.

sheer [ʃiə] *a.* sukitōru ; hontō no ; kiritatta. *ad.* mattaku ; sui-

sheet [ʃí:t] *n.* shikifu ; (kami) ichimai. *v.* shikifu o shiku. ~-

lightning *n.* inabikari. ～**ing** [ʃíːtiŋ] *n.* shikifu.

sheik, sheikh [ʃiːk] *n.* (Arabia) kachō, zokuchō.

shekel [ʃə́kl] *n.* kodai Hebrai no ginka.

sheldrake [ʃéldrəik] *n.* (*bird*) tsukushi-gamo no osu.

shelf [ʃelf] *n.* (*pl.* **-ves** [-vz]) *n.* tana ; su. *on the* ～, tana ni age-ru ; shimatte oku (*put aside*).

shell [ʃel] *n.* kaigara ; haretsudan. *v.* kara o muku. ～**back** *n.* rōsuifu. ～**-jacket**, rikugun shikan no tsūjōfuku. ～**-shock** [⌐ʃək] sensō chihōshō. ～**fish** [⌐fiʃ] *n.* kai ; kōkaku-rui (ebi,

shellac [ʃəlǽk] *n.*, *v.* sherakku (o nuru). ⌊kani, nado).

shelter [ʃéltə] *n.* kakureba. *v.* kabau ; (mi o) yoseru.

shelve [ʃelv] *v.* tana (*shelf*) ni noseru. (gian nado o) dasa nai ; shidaini katamuku.

Sheol [ʃíːoul] *n.* (Heburaijin no) meido (ano yo) ; haka.

shepherd [ʃépəd] *n.* hitsujikai ; bokushi. ～**ess** *n.* onna no hi-tsujikai.

sherbet [ʃə́ːbit] *n.* (kajū iri no) seiryō inryō ; sono aisukuriimu.

sheriff [ʃérif] *n.* Shū-chōkan ; keisatsu shochō.

sherry [ʃéri] *n.* sherii-shu ; shiro-budōshu.

shew, show [ʃou] *v.*, *n.* (*arch.*) *see : show*.

shibboleth [ʃíbəleθ] *n.* tokuchō ; aikotoba.

shield [ʃiːld] *n.* tate. *v.* tate de fusegu.

shift [ʃift] *v.* utsusu ; kaeru ; kawaru ; gomakasu. *n.* henkō. fu-jin no hadagi. kōtai-nakama. ～ *off*, hikinobasu. ～**ing** *a.* ka-wariyasui. ～**less** *a.* munō no ; ikuji nai. ～**ly** *a.* kawariyasui.

shilling [ʃíliŋ] *n.* shilingu (Igilisu no ginka).

shilly-shally [ʃíliʃæli] *n.* chūcho ; shunjun. *v.* guzutsuku. *ad.* guzutsuite.

shimmer [ʃímə] *n.* awai hikari. *v.* kasukani hikaru.

shin [ʃin] *n.* mukōzune ; sune. *v.* yojinoboru.

shine [ʃain] *v.* **shone** ; **shining**. hikaru ; kagayaku. *n.* hikari.

shingle [ʃíŋgl] *n.*, *v.* yane no kokeraita. *v.* ～ de fuku.

shiny [ʃáini] *a.* hikaru ; kagayaku.

-ship [ʃip] *suffix.* jōtai, mibun, kankei, shoku nado o arawasu.
governorship, (shoku) *kinship*, (jōtai, jōken). *horsemanship*. (juku-ren, nōryoku.) *cousinship*, (kankei) itokodōshi.

ship [ʃip] *n.*, *v.* fune ni noru (noseru). ～**building** *n.* zōsen.

~ment *n.* funazumi. ~wreck [⌐rek] *n.* nansen. ~wright [⌐rait] *n.* funa-daiku. ~yard [∫ípɑːd] *n.* zōsenjo.

shire [∫áiə] *n.* shū; Nippon no " gun " no yōna mono.

shirk [∫əːk] *v.* okotaru. *n.* namakemono.

shirt [∫əːt] *n.* shatsu. ~**ing** [∫ɔ́ːtiŋ] *n.* shatsuji.

shiver [∫ívə] *n.* kakera; miburui. *v.* kudakeru; furueru. ~**y** [-ri] *a.* furueru, samuke ga suru. ⌐tagui.

shoal [∫oul] *n.* taigun; asase. *v.* asase ni naru. *a* ~ *of fish*, uo no

shock [∫ɔk] *n.* shōtotsu; shōgeki. *v.* gyotto saseru. ~**ing** *a.*

shod [∫ɔd] *v. see :* **shoe.** ⌐gyotto suru.

shoddy [∫ɔ́di] *n., a.* saiseihin (no); mikakedaoshi (no).

shoe [∫uː] *n.* kutsu; uma no kutsu; jidōsha (no) taiya. *v.* **shod shod** *or* **shodden; shoeing.** kutsu o hakaseru; teitetsu o utsu. ~**black** *n.* kutsu migaki (nin). ~**blacking** *n.* kutsuzumi. ~**horn** [⌐hɔːn] *n.* kutsubera. ~**maker** *n.* kutsuya.

shone [∫ɔn / ∫oun] *v. see :* **shine.**

shook [∫uk] *v. see :* **shake.**

shoot [∫uːt] *v.* **shot; shooting.** ya o iru; teppō o utsu; iru yōni tobu; (kusaki no) me ga deru. *n.* hassha; shatekikai; mebae. ~**ing** *n.* hassha. ~**ing star** *n.* nagare-boshi.

shop [∫ɔp] *n.* mise; kōjō. *v. shop* e iku. ~**keeper** *n.* kouriten-shu. ~**lifter** [⌐liftə] *n.* mambiki (nin). ~**ping** [∫ɔ́piŋ] *n.* kaimono : *do one's* ~, kaimono o suru. *go* ~, kaimono ni iku. ~**worn** [⌐wɔːn] *a.* tanazarashi no. ~**py** [∫ɔ́pi] *a.* shōbai kusai (kotoba nado).

shore [∫ɔɔ] *n.* hamabe; nagisa; kaigan; tsukkaibō. *v.* tsukkaibō ⌐de sasaeru. *see :* **shear.**

shorn [∫ɔːn] *v. see :* **shear.**

short [∫ɔːt] *a.* mijikai; toboshii; fusokuna. *ad.* mijikaku; to-boshiku. *n.* gairyaku. (*pl.*) hanzubon; (*baseball*) yūgekishu. ~**age** [⌐idʒ] *n.* fusoku (daka); ketten. ~**cake** *n.* shōto keiki. ~**coming** [⌐kʌmiŋ] *n.* fusaku; fuyukitodoki. ~**en** [∫ɔ́ːtn] *v.* mijikaku suru; chijimeru. ~**hand** *n.* sokkihō. ~**lived** [⌐lívd] *a.* tammei no. ~**ly** *ad.* chikai uchi ni. buaisōni. ~**ness** *n.* kan-tan. ~**-sighted** [⌐sáitid] *a.* kingan no. ⌐sandanjū.

shot [∫ɔt] *v. see :* **shoot.** *n.* shageki; dangan. ~**gun** [⌐gʌn] *n.*

should [∫ud] *auxil. v. see :* **shall.** ...shita deshō; ...ta deshō ga; ...subekida.

shoulder [ʃóːldə] *n.* kata. *v.* katsugu ; sekinin o toru. **∼-blade,**
shout [ʃaut] *n.* sakebi. *v.* sakebu ; yobu.   ⌞ kenkōkotsu.
shove [ʃʌv] *v.* osu ; hageshiku osu. *n.* oshi.
shovel [ʃʌvl] *n.* shaberu ; jūnō. *v.* shaberu de sukū ; horu.
  ∼ful *n.* shaberu ippai. **∼er** *n.* shaberu de sukū hito.
show [ʃou] *v.* **showed** *or* (*arch.*) **shewed, shown** *or* (*arch.*)
  shewn ; showing. miseru ; annai saseru (suru). **∼** *in,* annai
  suru. **∼** *off,* misebirakasu. *n.* minna ni miseru koto ; misemono. **∼case** [∠keis] *n.* chinretsu-bako. **∼room** [∠ru(ː)m] *n.*
  chinretsu shitsu. **∼window** *n.* chinretsu mado.
shower [ʃáwə] *n.* niwaka-ame ; yūdachi ; sātto furu koto (mono). *v.* *shower* ga furu ; *shower* no yōni futte kuru.
shown [ʃóun] *v. see :* show.
showy [ʃóui] *a.* hadena ; medatsu ; miba no yoi.
shrank [ʃrǽŋk] *v. see :* shrink.
shrapnel [ʃrǽpnəl] *n.* ryūsandan.
shred [ʃred] *n.* kireppashi ; wazuka. *v.* hosoku kiru.
shrew [ʃruː] *n.* kuchi-yakamashii onna. jinezumi.
shrewd [ʃruːd] *a.* kibinna ; nukeme no nai ; surudoi.
shriek [ʃriːk] *n.* himei ; sakebi. *v.* sakebu ; himei o ageru.
shrift [ʃrift] *n.* (*arch.*) zange ; rinjū zange.
shrike [ʃraik] *n.* (*bird*) mozu.
shrill [ʃril] *a.* kanakirigoe no ; kandakai. *v.* kanakirigoe o dasu. **∼y** *ad.* kandakaku ; kanakirigoe de.
shrimp [ʃrimp] *n.* koebi.
shrine [ʃrain] *n.* zushi ; yashiro. *v.* anchi suru ; hōan suru.
shrink [ʃriŋk] *v.* **shrank, shrunk ; shrinking.** shiwa ga yoru ;
  shirigomi suru. *n.* shūshiku. **∼age** [∠idʒ] *n.* shūshiku ; teiraku.
shrivel [ʃrívl] *v.* shiwa ga yoru ; chijimu ; shinabiru.
shroud [ʃraud] *n., a.* kyō-katabira (de ōu).
shrub [ʃrʌb] *n.* kamboku ; kajū (*fruit juice*) ni ramushu nado o
  mazeta nomimono.
shrug [ʃrʌg] *v., n.* kata o sukumeru (shigusa).
shrunk [ʃrʌŋk] *v. see :* shrink.
shudder [ʃʌdə] *n., v.* miburui ; (suru) senritsu (suru).
shuffle [ʃʌfl] *v.* karuta o kiru ; noronoro aruku. *the old man* **∼***s*
  feebly along, ano rōjin wa ashi o yowayowashiku hikizutte a-

ruku. ~**board** [-bɔːd] *n.* fune no kampan de suru yūgi.

shun [ʃʌn] *v.* sakeru; imu. ⌐tsudō no).

shunt [ʃʌnt] *v.* michi o yokete tōsu; sorasu. *n.* tentetsuki (te-

shut [ʃʌt] *v.* **shut; shutting.** tojiru; shimeru (hon, mado, to nado) aite iru mono o). ~**down** [⌐daun] *n.* kyūgyō; heiten. ~**out** [⌐aut] *n.* shimedashi. ~**ter** [ʃʌtə] *n.* futa; tobira; shattā.

shuttle [ʃʌtl] *n.* hi (hataori no). ~**cock** *n.*, *v.* oibane (o suru); oibane (o uchiau.)

shy [ʃai] *a.* okubyōna; uchikina. *v.*, *n.* fuini michi o sakeru (koto). ~**ly** *ad.* okushite; u chikini.

Shylock [ʃáilɔk] *n.* gōyoku, mujihina kōrigashi.

shyster [ʃáistə] *n.* aku-bengoshi; sambyakudaigen. ⌐su).

sibilant [síbilənt] *n.*, *a.* ha no masatsuon (s, z, ʃ, ʒ nado) (o da-

sibyl [síbil] *n.* miko; onna yogensha. ~**line** [-liːn] *a.* miko no; yogentekina.

sick [sik] *a.* byōki no; mukatsuku. *v.* byōki ni naru; mukatsu-ku; akiru. ~**en** [síkn] *v.* byōki ni suru; aki saseru. ~**ish** *a.* byōki-gimi no. ~**ly** *a.* byōshinna. ~**ness** *n.* byōki; muka-

sickle [síkl] *n.* kama. ⌐tsuki.

side [said] *n.* waki; sokumen; katawara. *a.* soba no. *v.* mikata suru. ~**arms**, keitai buki. ~**board** [⌐bɔːd] *n.* shokki-dana; wakidana. ~**car** [⌐kɑː] *n.* (ōtobai no) saidokā. ~**long** [⌐lɔŋ] *ad.*, *a.* yoko ni (no); naname ni (no). ~**track** [⌐træk] *n.*, *v.* taihisen (ni ireru). ~**walk** [⌐wɔːk] *n.* (*Am.*) hodō; jindō. ~**ways**, ~**wise** *ad.*, *a.* yoko ni (no); naname ni (no).

sidereal [saidíəriəl] *a.* hoshi (*stars*) no; kōsei (*fixed star*) no; seiza (*constellation*) no. ~**day** *n.* kōsei-jitsu (23 *h.* 56 *m.* 4.09 *s.*).

sidle [sáidl] *v.* naname ni aruku. ~ *up to* …ni nijiriyoru.

siege [siːdʒ] *n.* shirozeme; rōjō. ~ *gun*, kōjō-hō.

sierra [siérə] *n.* nokogiri no ha no yōna sammyaku.

siesta [siéstə] *n.* hirune (atsui chihō no).

sieve [siv] *n.* furui; oshaberina hito. *v.* furū; kosu.

sift [sift] *v.* furui ni kakeru; shusha suru (*select*).

sigh [sai] *n.*, *v.* tameiki (o tsuku).

sight [sait] *n.* shiryoku; gankai; meisho; shōshaku. *v.* miru; shōjun suru; *payable at* ~, ichiran-barai. **second** ~, senri-gan. ~**less** *a.* me no mienai. ~**ly** *a.* kireina. ~**seeing** *n.*

kembutsu; kankō. ~seer *n.* kankōkyaku.

sign [sain] *n.* kigō; angō; temane; hata; kishō. ~board [⌐bc:d] *n.* kamban. ~away, shōsho ni shomei shite yuzuriwatasu.

signal [sígnəl] *n., a.* aizu (no); shingō (no); shingōki. (no). *v.* shingō (aizu) suru. ~-box, shingōshitsu. ~ fire, noroshi. ~ gun gōhō. ~ize *v.* medataseru. ~ly *ad.* ichijirushiku.

signatory [sígnətəri] *a.* shomei (chōin) shita. *n.* shomeinin.

signature [sígnətʃə] *n.* chōin; shomei.

signet [sígnit] *n.* in; chiisai han. *the order was sealed with the king's ~,* kono meirei niwa kokuō no in ga oshite atta.

significance [signífikəns] *n.* imi; yūigi; jūyō; jūdai.

significant [signífikənt] *a.* yūigina; jūyōna; jūdaina.

signification [sìgnifikiéʃ(ə)n] *n.* imi; igi.

significative [sígnífikətiv] *a.* igiaru; ishihyōji suru.

signify [sígnifai] *v.* arawasu; shimesu.

signor [sí:njɔ:] *n.* (*It.*) Kakka, Sama, Dono no keigo (*honorific*).

signora [si:njó:rə] *n.* (*It.*) Fujin; Okusama (*honorific*).

signore [si:njó:rei] *n.* (*It.*) kizoku; shinshi no yobikake.

signorina [si:njərí:nə] *n.* Ojōsama; Reijō no keigo (*honorific*).

Sikh [si:k] *n.* Shiiku kyōto (kita Indo no yūmeina shūha).

silage [sáilidʒ] *n.* hozon sareta aokusa no kaiba.

silence [sáiləns] *n., v.* chimmoku (saseru); seishiku (ni saseru). ~r [-ə] *n.* damaraseru hito; shōon-sōchi; shōon-ki.

silent [sáilənt] *a.* shizukana; mugon no; damatte iru.

silhouette [silu(:)ét] *n., v.* kage-e (de miseru.)

silica [sílikə] *n.* (*met.*) keisan; keido.

siliceous [silíʃəs] *a.* (*met.*) keisan no.

silicic [silísik] *a.* (*met.*) musui keisan no.

silicon [sílikən] *n.* (*met.*) keiso.

silk [silk] *n.* kiito; kinuito; kempu; kinumono. ~en [-ən] *a.* kinusei no. ~ hat, shiruku hatto. ~worm [⌐wə:m] *n.* kaiko. ~y [sílki] *a.* kinu no; kinu no yōna.

sill [sil] *n.* dodai; shikii; mado no shitawaku. window ~, madowaku.

silliness [sílinis] *n.* gudon; bakarashisa.

silly [síli] *n., a.* baka (na); orokamono (no).

silo [sáilou] *n.* (magusa) aokusa chozōko.

silt [silt] *n.* (mizu ga hakobu) komakai doro. *v. silt* de fusagu.

silva [sílvə] *n.* (*pl.*) jumoku (aru basho zentai).

silvan, sylvan [sílvən] *a.* mori no.

silver [sílvə] *n., a.* gin (no); ginka (no); gin'iro (no); ginsei (no). ~**smith** [-smiθ] *n.* (*Brit.*) ginzaikushi. ~**ware** *n.* ginseihin. ~**y** *a.* gin no yōna; gin'iro no; gin no suzu no yōna.

simian [símiən] *a.* saru no; saru no yōna. *n.* saru.

similar [símilə] *a.* dōyōna; nita. ~**ity** [sìmilǽriti] *n.* dōyō; ruiji. (*pl.*) ruijibutsu.

simile [símili] *n.* hiyu. "like" "as" no go de shimesareru tatoe (hiyu); *as cool as cucumber*, kyūri no yōni reiseini. *as poor as a church mouse*, kyōkai no nezumi no yōni bimbō de, nado koteishita mono ga takusan aru.

similitude [simílitju:d] *n.* dōyō; ruiji; hiyu.

simitar [símitə] *n.* wangetsutō; engetsutō (Arabiajin no katana).

simmer [símə] *v.* butsu-butsu to nie dasu; shizukani wakidasu; torobi de niru; butsu-butsu shizukana oto o tatete nieru. ~**ing anger**, shizukana ikari. ~**ing rebellion**, bakuhatsu mae no bōdō.

simoniac [simóuniæk] *n.* sōshoku o baibai shita mono (*one guilty of simony*). ~**al** [sàimənáiəkl] *a.* sōshoku baibai (urikai) no.

simonpure [sáimənpjúə] *a.* hommono no; ken'i aru.

simony [sáiməni] *n.* sōshoku (seishoku) baibai-zai (*offense*).

simoon [simú:n] *n.* Arabia chihō ni fuku neppū.

simper [símpə] *n., v.* tsukuri-warai (o suru).

simple [símpl] *a.* tanjunna; kantanna. ~**ness** *n.* tanjun; muchi. ~**ton** [símpltən] *n.* baka; tanjunna ningen.

simplicity [simplísiti] *n.* tanjun; kantan.

simplification [sìmplifikéiʃən] *n.* tanjunka (kantanka) suru koto.

simplify [símplifai] *v.* tanjunni (kantanni) suru koto.

simply [símpli] *ad.* tanjunni; tanni; tada assari to.

simulate [símjuleit] *v.* furi o suru. *a.* misekake no.

simulation [simjuléiʃ(ə)n] *n.* misekake; furi.

simultaneity [sàiməltəní:əti] *n.* dōji (-sei); dōji ni okuru koto.

simultaneous [sàiməltéinjəs] *a.* dōjini okoru; dōjisei no.

sin [sin] *n., v.* tsumi (*religious*, o okasu). ~**ful** *a.* tsumi no fukai. ~**less** *a.* tsumi no nai; keppakuna. ~**ner** [sínə] *n.* tsumibito (shūkyōjō no).

since [sins] *ad.* izen. *I heard that old joke long* ~, watashi wa a-no share wa zutto mukashi kiita. *prep.* irai. *package has been ready* ~ *noon*, tsutsumi wa ohiru kara dekite iru. *conj.* irai; igo. *he has not written* ~ *he left us*, kare wa wareware to wa-karete irai tegami o yokosanai.

sincere [sinsí:ə] *a.* shinjitsuna; seijitsuna.

sincerity [sinsériti] *n.* seijitsu; seii.

sine [sain] *n.* (*math.*) seigen; sain. ⌐no bokushishoku.

sinecure [sáinikjuə] *n.* himana chii (shigoto); meimoku dake

sine die [sáini:dáii:] *n.* (*L.*) shōrai no kōdō ni taishite hi o kimete nai. *the committee adjourned* ~, iinkai wa mukigenni enki sareta. ⌐tial).

sine quanon [sáini:kweinɔ́n] (*L.*) hissū jōken (*something essen-*

sinew [sínju:] *n.* (*anat.*) ken; kinniku; tairyoku. (*pl.*) kinniku; (*fig.*) tanomi no tsuna. ~y [-i] *a.* ken no; kinkotsu takuma-shii (*muscular*).

sing [siŋ] *v.* **sang (sung), sung; singing.** utau; saezuru. ~er *n.* kashu; shijin. ~**song** [´sͻ(:)ŋ] *n.* heboshi. *a.* tanchōna.

singe [sindʒ] *v.* kogasu. ~ *one's wings,* ...no meiyo o kizutsu-keru.

single [síŋgl] *n.,a.* hitotsu (no); tandoku (no). *ad.* tandoku de. ~-**handed** [´-hǽndid] *a.* katate no. ~**stick** *n.* bō, shiai; kenju-

singlet [síŋglit] *n.* hadagi; ura nashi chokki. ⌐tsu.

singly [síŋgli] *ad.* meimeini; tandokuni.

singular [síŋgjulə] *a.* tan'itsu no; hibon no. *n.* (*gram.*) tansū.

singularity [siŋgjulǽriti] *a.* tan'itsu; fūgawari; hibon; toku-

sinister [sínistə] *a.* hidari no; akui aru; fukitsuna. ⌐shu.

sink [siŋk] *v.* **sank** *or* **sunk, sunk** *or* **sunken; sinking.** shizu-mu; (kaze ga) nagu; unadareru; bossuru; (me, hoho nado ga) hekomu. *n.* gesui no mizo; (daidokoro no) nagashi. ~er *n.* omori (tsuriito no). ~**ing fund,** gensaikikin (shakkin o harau jumbi no kane). ⌐Chūgoku to no.

Sino-Japanese [sáinoudʒǽpəni:s] *a.* Nik-Ka no; Nippon to

sinuous [sínjuəs] *a.* magarikuneru; hajō no.

sip [sip] *n.* chibi-chibi nomi; hito-susuri. *v.* chibi-chibi nomu.

siphon [sáif(ə)n] *n.* saifon; saifon bin. ⌐susuru.

sir [sə:] *n.* anata; sensei; danna; *knight* ya *baronet* no keishō.

sire [saiə] *n.* heika ; chichi ; tane-uma. *v.* umaseru (*stallion*).

siren [sáiərən] *n.* Girisha Shinwa no megami ; sairen.

sirloin [sɔ́:lɔin] *n.* ushi no koshi (*loin*) no niku.

sirocco [sirókou] *n.* Shirokko (Afurika sabaku no) kaze.

sirup, syrup [sírəp] *n.* shiroppu ; tōmitsu.

sis [sis] *n.* (*Am. col*) ojōsan.

sister [sístə] *n.* shimai (onna kyōdai). **~hood** *n.* shimai taru koto ; fujin-kai. **~ly** *a.* shimai no yōna.

sit [sit] *v.* **sat ; sitting.** chakuseki suru ; suwaru ; isu ni tsuku. **~** *down,* chakuseki suru. **~down** [⏦daun] *n.* suwari-komi. **~ter** [sítə] *n.* chakusekisha. **~ting** *n.* kaikai ; kaitei ; tamago o daku koto. **~ting room,** ima.

site [sait] *n.* ichi ; shikichi ; shozaichi.

situated [sítjueitid] *a.* kurai suru ; okareta.

situation [situéiʃ(ə)n] *n.* ichi ; basho ; tachiba ; shokuba.

six [siks] *n., a.* roku (6) (no) ; muttsu (no).

sixteen [síkstí:n] *n., a.* jūroku (16) (no).

sixteenth [síkstí:nθ] *n., a.* dai jūroku (16) (no) ; jūroku bamme (no) ; jūroku bun no ichi (no) ; (tsuki no) jūroku nichi.

sixth [siksθ] *n., a.* dai roku (6) (no) ; rokubun no ichi (no) ; (tsuki no) muika.

sixtieth [síkstiiθ] *n., a.* dai rokujū (60) (no) ; rokujūbun no [ichi (no).

sixty [síksti] *n., a.* rokujū (60) (no).

size [saiz] *n.* ōkisa ; sumpō ; kata. *v.* norizuke suru.

sizzle [sízl] *n.* (*fry* no abura ga tateru) shūshū iu oto. *v.* shūshū oto o tateru.

skate [skeit] *n.* sukeito ; sukeitoyō no kutsu ; ei no isshu no uo. **~r** *n.* sukeito o suru hito. **~ rink,** sukeitojō.

skating [skéitiŋ] *n.* kōrisuberi ; sukeito.

skee, ski [ski: / ʃi:] *n., v. see* : **ski**

skein [skein] *n.* kase (ito) ; motsure (*tangle*).

skeleton [skélitən] *n.* kokkaku ; gaikotsu ; honegumi ; yasekoketa mono ; gairyaku. *a.* gaikotsu no ; yasekoketa ; yōryō no.

skeptic [sképtik] (*Am.*) *n.* kaigi-ronsha. **~al**[-l] *a.* kaigitekina. **~ism** [sképtisizm] *n.* kaigi(ron).

sketch [sketʃ] *n.* ryakuzu ; shaseizu ; genkō ; tampen. *v.* mitorizu o kaku ; shasei suru. **~book** *n.* shaseichō.

skew [skju:] *a.* naname no ; yuganda. ~**er** [skjú:ə] *n.*, *v.* yaki-gushi (ni suru).

ski [ski: / ʃi:] *n.*, *v.* sukii (de suberu). ~**er** [skíiə / ʃí:ə] *n.* sukiiyā.

skid [skid] *n.* hadome ; suberizai ; yokosuberi ; sori.

skiff [skif] *n.* kobune.   ⌈kuren shita.

skill [skil] *n.* myōgi ; jukuren ; tegiwa. **skilful** *a.* takumina ; ju-

skim [skim] *v.* uwakawa o sukuitoru ; zatsuni yomu ; kasuru. ~**mer** [skímə] *n.* ami shamoji ; sukui shamoji.   ⌈china.

skin [skin] *n.* kawa ; hifu. ~**ny** [-i] *a.* kawa no ; yaseta ; ke-

skip [skip] *v.* tobimawaru ; haneru ; tobu ; tobaseru. ~**per** [skípə] *n.* (kobune no) senchō.   ⌈~**er** *n.* sekkōhei.

skirmish [skə́:miʃ] *n.*, *v.* kozeriai ; chiisai shōtotsu (o suru).

skirt [skə:t] *n.* suso ; sukāto. *v.* sukāto o tsukeru ; fuchi ni aru.

skittish [skítiʃ] *a.* ki no yowai ; shinkeishitsu no ; utsurigi no.

skulk [skʌlk] *v.* kossori kakureru ; shinobu ; hisomu.

skull [skʌl] *n.* zugaikotsu (*bone*).

skunk [skʌŋk] *n.* sukanku. hiretsukan.

sky [skai] *n.* sora. ~**lark** [-lɑ:k] *n.* (*bird*) hibari. *v.* bakasawagi suru. ~**light** [-lait] *n.* akaritori. ~**rocket** *n.* uchiagehanabi. ~**scraper** [-skreipə] *n.* matenrō. ~**wards** [-wɔ:dz] *ad.* sora ni mukatte.

slab [slæb] *n.* sekiban ; itaishi.

slack [slæk] *a.* fuchūina ; taimanna ; **tarunda.** *n.* tarumi ; (*pl.*) dabudabu no zubon. *v.* ~**en**=*slack*, yurumu (-meru) ; osoku naru (suru). ~**weather,** hakkiri shinai tenkō. ~**er** [slǽkə] *n.* namakemono.

slag [slæg] *n.* kana-kuso.

slain [slein] *v. see :* **slay.**   ⌈~**d lime,** shōsekkai.

slake [sleik] *n.* kesu ; yawarageru ; (seisekkai o) shōwa suru.

slam [slæm] *v.* batan to shimeru (shimaru) ; batan to oku. *n.* batan to iu oto ; hageshii hihyō (*harsh criticism*).

slander [slǽndə] *n.*, *v.* warukuchi (o iu) ; hibō (suru).

slang [slæŋ] *n.* zokugo.

slant [slænt] *a.* katamuita ; naname no. *v.* katamuku (-keru) ; naname ni naru (suru). *n.* keisha ; keikō.

slap [slæp] *n.*, *v.* hirateuchi (o suru) ; pishari (to utsu). *ad.* pi-shari to ; dashinuke ni.

slash [slæʃ] *v.* fukaku kiru ; kirisaku. *n.*, *v.* mettagiri (mettauchi) (suru). ～ing *a.* mōretsuna ; shinratsuna.

slat [slæt] *n.* hosonagai usuita ; shikoroita ; kowariita.

slate [sleit] *n.* sekiban ; itaishi ; surēto ; kōhosha-meibo. *v.* surēto de yane o fuku.   ⌊darashinaku.

slattern [slǽtə(:)n] *n.* jidaraku-onna. ～ly *a.* darashinai. *ad.*

slaughter [slɔ́ːtə] *n., v.* zansatsu (suru) ; tosatsu (suru) ; boku-
satsu (suru). ～**house** *n.* tosatsujō.

Slav [slæv] *n.* Surabujin.

slave [sleiv] *n.* dorei. *v.* dorei no yōni hataraku. ～r [sléivə]
dorei bōekisen ; dorei baibaisha. ～ry [⌊ori] dorei no mibun ;
dorei seido. *be a ～ to*, no tame ni kurō o suru.

slavish [sléiviʃ] *a.* dorei no ; dorei no yōna ; iyashii.

slaw [slɔ:] *n.* kyabetsu no sarada.

slay [slei] *v.* **slew, slain ; slaying.** kirikorosu. ～er *n.* satsu-
sled [sled], **sledge** [sledʒ] *n.* sori.   ⌊gaisha ; geshunin.

sledge [sledʒ] *n.* ōzuchi, gennō ; =**sleigh.** ～ **hammer** [hǽmə],
n. gennō ; ōkikute chikarazuyoi mono.

sleek [sliːk] *a.* namerakana ; kōtaku no aru ; kuchisaki no umai.
v. namerakani suru ; kōtaku o dasu.

sleep [sliːp] *n.* nemuri. *v.* **slept ; sleeping.** nemuru ; nemuraseru. ～er *n.* nebō. shindai-sha. makuragi (tetsudō no).
～ing *n.* suimin. ～less *a.* nemuranai. ～y *a.* nemui. ～iness
n. nemui koto.

sleet [sliːt] *n., v.* mizore (ga furu). ～y [slíːti] *a.* mizore no furu.

sleeve [sliːv] *n.* sode (kimono no). *laugh in one's ～,* kage de
warau.   ⌊warau.

sleigh [slei] *n., v.* sori (de iku).

sleight [slait] *n.* shuren ; jukuren ; hayawaza. ～ *of hand,* tejina.

slender [sléndə] *a.* hosoi ; kayowai ; kyashana.

slept [slept] *r. see* : **sleep.**

slew [slu:] *r. see* : **slay.**

slice [slais] *n.* usui kire ; hōchō. *v.* usuku kiru.

slick [slik] *a.* namerakana ; kashikoi. *n.* katsumen (nameraka
na men). *v.* namerakani suru. ～er *n.* amagaitō ; petenshi.

slide [slaid] *v.* **slid, slidden ; sliding.** suberu ; suberaseru. *n.*
suberi ; jisuberi ; suberidai ; (gentōyō) suraido.

slight [slait] *a.* wazuka no ; sukoshi no. *n., v.* keibetsu (suru).

slim [slim] *a.* surari to shita ; hinjakuna.
slime [slaim] *n.* nendo. *v.* doro o nuru.
slimy [sláimi] *a.* nendo no yōna ; neba-neba suru ; **iyarashii.**
sling [sliŋ] *n.* furinage. *v.* **slung,** *or* (*arch.*) **slang, slung ;
slinging.** *sling* de nageru ; tsurusu ; tsuriageru.
slink [sliŋk] *v.* **slunk** *or* **slank, slunk ; slinking.** kossori nigeru.
slip [slip] *v.* suberu ; fumihazusu ; kossori nigeru. *n.* suberi ;
fumihazushi. fujin yō shitagi. sashiki. ~**shod** [⌐ʃɔd] *a.* darashi
no nai. ~**per** [slípə] *n.* uwagutsu ; surippa. ~**pery** [slípəri]
a. suberu ; toraedokoro no nai.
slit [slit] *n.* nagai kirikuchi ; sakeme. *v.* **slit ; slitting.** tate ni
sliver [slívə] *n.* hosonagai mokuhen. ⌐ kiru.
slobber [slɔ́bə] *n.,* *v.* yodare (o tarasu) ; guchi (o kobosu).
sloe [slou] *n.* (*bot.*) sumomo no rui ; sono mi.
slog [slɔg] *v.* tsuyoku utsu ; mettauchi suru. *n.* kyōda.
slogan [slóugən] *n.* senden-monku ; shugi ; shuchō ; tokinokoe.
sloop [slu:p] *n.* ippon-masuto no hansen.
slop [slɔp] *v.* kobosu (-reru). ~ **over,** nesshin sugiru. *n.* koboremizu ; (*pl.*) osui. ryūdōshoku. ~**py** [slɔ́pi] *a.* koboremizu
de nureta ; nukaru ; darashi no nai.
slope [sloup] *n.* keisha ; saka. *v.* keisha suru ; saka ni naru.
slosh [slɔʃ] =**slush.** *see* : **slush** [slʌʃ] *n.,* *v.* ⌐ guchi.
slot [slɔt] *n.* chiisai ana. ashiato ; (jidō-hambaiki no) kaneire-
sloth [slouθ] *n.* bushō. (*zoo.*) namakemono. ~**ful** *a.* bushōna.
slouch [slautʃ] *n.* (tattari, suwattari, aruitari no dōsa no) darashi
nai sugata. *v.* darashinai furumai o suru.
slough [slau] *n.* dobumichi ; nukarumi. shitsubō. ~ [slʌf] *n.*
(hebi nado no) nukegara ; dappi ; kusatta niku ; kasabuta. *v.*
dappi suru.
sloven [slʌ́vn] *n.* darashi no nai hito ; bushōmono. ~**ly** *a.*
darashi no nai ; bushōna.
slow [slow] *a.* osoi ; okureta. *v.* osoku naru. ~**ness** *n.* kamman.
sludge [slʌdʒ] *n.* doro ; dobudoro ; chiisai fuhyō. (kōri).
slug [slʌg] *n.* namekuji. ōda. *v.* naguru. ~**gard** [⌐əd] *n.* namakemono. ~**gish** [⌐iʃ] *a.* bushōna ; nibui.
sluice [slu:s] *n.* suimon. *v* suimon o hiraku.
slum [slʌm] *n.* uramachi ; himminkutsu.

slumber [slʌ́mbə] *n.* suimin. *v.* nemuru. ~**ous** [-rəs] *a.* nemui ; shizukana.

slump [slʌmp] *v.* dotto ochiru ; bōraku suru. *n.* bōraku.

slung [slʌŋ] *r. see* : **sling.**

slunk [slʌŋk] *r. see* : **slink.**

slur [slə:] *v.* zatto me o tōsu ; soshiru ; fumeiryōni tsuzukete mono o iu : *most persons* ~, " *How do you do?* " taitei no hito wa " *How···do?* " o *slur* ni iu. *n.* soshiri ; (*music*) surā ; renketsu-kigō (⌢).

slush [slʌʃ] *n.* nukarumi ; yukidokemichi. *v.* doro o haneru.

slut [slʌt] *n.* darashinai onna ; mesu-inu.

sly [slai] *a.* zurui ; ōchakuna. *on the* ~, kossori. ⌐tauchi suru.

smack [smæk] *n.* fūmi ; aji. isshu no gyosen. shitauchi. *v.* shismall [smɔ:l] *a.* chiisai ; bibitaru. ~ *talk*, seken-banashi. *feel* ~, katami no semai omoi o suru. ~**pox** [-pɔks] *n.* tennentō.

smart [smɑ:t] *a.* zuki-zuki itamu ; rikōna ; tsūkaina ; ikina. *v.* zuki-zuki itamu.

smash [smæʃ] *v.* kudaku ; butsukeru ; hasan suru. *n.* funsai ; hasan ; dai-shōtotsu ; (*blandy* to kōri to satō) no inryō.

smatter [smǽtə] *n.* shittakaburi. ~**er** [-rə] *n.* shittakaburi-ya. ~**ing** *n.* namakajiri.

smear [smiə] *n.* oten ; shimi. *v.* nuru ; yogosu.

smell [smel] *v.* **smelt** *or* **smelled; smelling.** kagu ; kagidasu ; saguridasu ; niou ; kaoru. *n.* kyūkaku.

smelt [smelt] *v. see* : **smell. smelt** [smelt] *v.* yōkai suru (tokeru) ; seiren suru. *n.* Sake no rui no chiisai umai sakana.

smile [smail] *v.* bishō suru ; reishō suru. *n.* bishō ; egao ; reishō.

smirch [smə:tʃ] *v.* yogosu. *n.* kegare ; yogore. ⌐shō.

smirk [smə:k] *n.*, *v.* tsukuriwarai (suru).

smite [smait] *v.* **smote** *or arch.* **smit, smitten** *or* **smite; smiting.** utsu ; hidoku utsu ; miserareru ; kyūni itasa o kanjiru.

smith [smíθ] *n.* kaji ; kajiya. ~**y** *n.* kajiba. ⌐mijin.

smithereens [smìðərí:nz] (*pl.*) *n.* kakera ; chiisai hahen ; koppa

smitten [smítn] *see* : **smite.** *a.* totsuzen tsuyoku ugogasareta.

smock [smɔk] *n.* fujinshatsu ; uwappari (kodomo no). ~**frock** *n.* noragi.

smoke [smouk] *n.* kemuri ; tabako. *v.* kemuru ; tabako o sū ; ibusu ; kunsei ni suru. ~**r** [smóukə] *n.* kunseisha ; kitsuensha.

~**less** *a.* muen no. ~ **screen**, emmaku.

smoky [smóuki] *a.* kemuru ; iburu ; kemui.

smolder [smóuldə] (*Am.*) *v.* iburu ; kusuburu. *n.* kemuri ; kusuburi.

smooth [smú:ð] *a.* namerakana ; yasashii. *v.* namerakani suru

smote [smout] *r. see* : **smite.** ⌊(naru).

smother [smʌ́ðə] *v.* chissoku saseru ; osaeru ; momikesu.

smoulder [smóuldə] *v., n.* (*Brit.*) =**smolder.**

smudge [smʌdʒ] *n.* ka-ibushi. oten. *v.* shimi o tsukeru ; yogo-

smug [smʌg] *a.* hitoriyogari no ; kogireina. ⌊su.

smuggle [smʌ́gl] *n., v.* mitsubōeki (suru) ; mikkō (suru). ~**r** *n.* mitsubōekisha ; mikkōsha.

smut [smʌt] *n.* obutsu. gebita hanashi. (*bot.*) kurohobyō. *v.* yo-gosu. ~**ty** [smʌ́ti] *a.* susu de yogoreta.

snaffle [snǽfl] *n.* kogata kutsuwa. ⌈tsukideta mono.

snag [snæg] *u.* suichū ni aru ki no eda nado ; surudoi, arai

snail [sneil] *n.* katatsumuri ; noroma. ⌈yōna.

snake [sneik] *n.* hebi ; inkenna hito. *v.* hebi no yōni une-une

snaky [snéiki] *a.* hebi no (yōna) ; magarikunetta ; inkenna.

snap [snæp] *v.* pokitto oru. *n.* pokitto (putsutto) oto o tateru koto. ~**shot** *n.* sokusha. hayatori-shashin.

snare [snɛə] *n., v.* wana (o kakeru) ; yūwaku (suru).

snarl [snɑ:l] *n.* unari ; igami. *v.* unaru ; bōgen suru. ⌈ru.

snatch [snætʃ] *v.* hittakuru ; hittsukamu. ~ **at**, tsukamō to su-

sneak [sni:k] *n.* hiretsuna yatsu ; koso-doro. *v.* kossori kuru ; nigeru ; nusumu.

sneer [sniə] *n., v.* chōshō (suru) ; batō (suru) ; azawarau.

sneeze [sni:z] *n., v.* kushami (suru).

snicker [sníkə], **snigger** [snígə] *n.* kusukusu-warai. *v.* kusu-

sniff [snif] *v.* nioi o kagu ; hana de ashirau. ⌊kusu warau.

snip [snip] *n.* kireppashi (*pieces*) ; (*Brit.*) shitateya ; (*Am.*) toru ni taranu hito. *v.* hasamikiru.

snipe [snaip] *n.* (*bird*) shigi.

snivel [snívl] *n., a.* hanamizu (o susuru) ; susurinaki (suru) ; hanagoe (o dasu). ~**er** [-ə] *n.* nakimushi.

snob [snɔb] *n.* shinshi-kidori no hito ; zokubutsu ; *strike* no fusankasha (shokkō). ~**bish** [-iʃ] *a.* ue ni hetsurai, shita ni ibaru ; shinshi-kidori no.

snoop [snu:p] *a.*, *v.* kossori (mimawasu).

snooze [snu:z] *n.*, *v.* inemuri (suru).

snore [snɔ:] *n.*, *v.* ibiki (o kaku).

snorkel [snɔ́:kl] *n.* sunōkeru (sensuikan no kūki toriire-sōchi).

snort [snɔ:t] *n.*, *v.* hana-arashi (o fuku) (uma nado ga) ; gera-

snot [snɔt] *n.* hanashiru ; yarō ; gesu.   ⌊gera (warau).

snout [snaut] *n.* (buta nado no) hana.

snow [snou] *n.* yuki ; yukifuri ; kōsetsu ; (*pl.*) sekisetsu. *v.* yuki ga furu. ~**bank** [⌐bæŋk] *n.* fuki-damari. ~**bound** [⌐baund] *a.* yuki ni tojikomerarete. ~**capped** [⌐kæpt] *a.* (teppen ni) yuki o itadaita. ~**drift** [⌐drift] *n.* fubuki. ~**drop** [-drɔp] *n.* (*bot.*) matsuyukisō. ~**flake** [⌐fleik] *n.* furu hane no yōna yuki. ~**plow** [-plau] *n.* yukikaki. ~**shoe** [-ʃú:] *n.* yuki-gutsu ; kanjiki. ~**storm** [⌐stɔ:m] *n.* ōfubuki. ~**y** [-i] *a.* yuki no yōna (ōi) ; kiyorakana.

snub [snʌb] *n.*, *v.* hiji-deppō (o kuwaseru) ; kentsuku (o ku-waseru) ; tsumetaku ashirau. *a.* shishippana no.

snuff [snʌf] *n.* rōsoku no koge-shin ; kagi-tabako. *v.* shin o kiru. kagi-tabako o sū (kagu) ; fufun to hana de ashirau.

snuffle [snʌfl] *n.*, *v.* hanagoe (de iu) ; hanazumari-goe (o dasu)

snug [snʌg] *a.* igokochi no yoi ; pittari shita.

snuggle [snʌ́gl] *v.* suri-yoru ; kosuri-tsuku.

so [sou] *ad.* sayōni ; sonnani ; sorehodo ; hanahada ; yohodo ; sōka ; soko o ; sono kurai. *conj.* soko de ; sono tame. ~ *ana* ~, soresore ; korekore. *Mr.* ~ *and* ~, *says that* ~ *and* ~ *is a cure of the cancer*, aru otoko ga korekore wa gan no isshu no chiryōhō da to iu. ~**called** [⌐kɔ̀:ld] *a.* iwayuru.

soak [souk] *v.*, *n.* hitasu (koto) ; shimaseru (koto) ; ōzake o nomu ; shintō suru.

soap [soup] *n.* sekken.   ⌊nomu ; shintō suru.

soar [sɔ:] *v.*, *n.* maiagaru (koto) ; takaku tobu (koto).

sob [sɔb] *n.*, *v.* susurinaki (o suru) ; beso (o kaku).

sober [sóubə] *a.* shirafu no ; kingenna ; jimina.

sobriety [səbráiəti] *n.* sesshu ; shirafu ; majime.

sobriquet [sóubrikei] *n.* (*Fr.*) adana.

soccer [sɔ́kə] *n.* sakkā ; assoshieishon-shiki no shūkyū (*foot-*
sociability [souʃəbíliti] *n.* kōsaizuki ; shakōsei.   ⌊*ball*).

sociable [sóuʃəbl] *a.* kōsaijōzuna ; shakōteki no.

social [sóuʃ(ə)l] *a.* shakai no. *n.* konshinkai. ~**ism** *n.* shakai-shugi. ~**ist** *n.* shakaishugisha. ~**istic** [sòusiəlístik] *a.* shakai-shugi(sha)teki. ~**ize** *v.* shakaiteki ni suru.

society [səsáiəti] *n.* shakai ; shakōkai.

sociology [sousiólədʒi] *n.* shakaigaku. ~**ical** [sòusjəlódʒikl] *a.* shakaigaku no.

sock [sɔk] *n.* mijikai kutsushita.

socket [sɔ́kit] *n.* ana ; ukeguchi ; soketto ; denkyūuke.

sod [sɔd] *n.* shiba ; shibafu. *v.* shibatsuchi de ōu.

soda [sóudə] *n.* (*chem.*) sōda ; tansansōda. ʃno.

sodden [sɔ́dn] *a.* mizu no shimita ; bon'yari shita ; manukegao

sodium [sóudiəm] *n.* (*chem.*)=**natrium** (kinzoku genso no hitotsu ; (shio, sōda wa kore o fukumu).

sofa [sóufə] *n.* nagaisu ; neisu ; sofâ.

soft [sɔft] *a.* yawarakana. *ad.* yawarakani. ~**pillow** *n.* yawa-rakana makura. ~ **hat** (*Am.*) nakaorebōshi. ~ **coal**, yūentan. ~**ly** *ad.* yawarakani. ~**ness** *n.* [sɔ́fn] *v.* yawarakani suru ; keigen su-

soggy [sɔ́gi] *a.* shimeta ; nureta. ʃru ; odayakani naru.

soil [sɔil] *n.* tsuchi ; doro. *v.* yogosu ; kitanaku suru.

soiree [swaré] *n.* (*Fr.*) yakai.

sojourn [sɔ́dʒəːn / sóudʒən] *n.* taizai. *v.* taizai suru.

sol [sɔl] *n.* (*mus.*) chōonkai no dai-5 (go) no on.

solace [sɔ́lis] *n.* isha ; nagusame. *v.* nagusameru.

solar [sóulə] *a.* taiyō no. ~ **system**, taiyōkei.

sold [sould] *v.* see : sell.

solder [sɔ́l(d)ə] *n.* handa. *v.* handa-zuke suru.

soldier [sóuldʒə] *n.* gunjin ; heishi. *v.* gunjin ni naru. ~**ly** *a.* gunjin rashii. ~**y** [-r] *n.* gunzei ; gunji kyōren.

sole [soul] *n.* ashi no ura ; kutsu no soko. *a.* tada hitotsu no. ~**ly** [sóuli] *ad.* tandokuni.

solecism [sɔ́lisizm] *n.* bumpō-ihan ; busahō.

solemn [sɔ́ləm] *a.* ogosokana ; jūdaina. ~**ity** [sɔlémniti] *n.* sōgon ; genshuku. ~**ize** [-naiz] *v.* sōgonni suru ; shiki o ageru.

solicit [sɔlísit] *v.* urusaku motomeru ; kongan suru. ~**ation** [səlìsitéiʃ(ə)n] *n.* konsei ; kongan. ~**or** [-ə] *n.* kan'yūsha ; ben-gosha ; soshō jumbisha. ~**ous** [-əs] *a.* isshōkemmei tanomu, negau ; shimpai suru. ~**ude** [-juːd] *n.* shimpai ; kenen.

solid [sɔ́lid] *a.* kotai no ; jūjitsu shita. *n.* kotai. ~ **foot,** ichi rippō futto. ~**arity** [səlidǽriti] *n*. rentai-sekinin. ~**ify** [sə-lídifai] *v*. kataku suru. ~**ity** [səlíditi] *n*. ganjōna koto.

soliloquize [səlíləkwaiz] *v*. hitorigoto o iu.

soliloquy [səlíləkwi] *n*. hitorigoto. ~**ist** *n*. hitorigoto o iu hito ; shibai nado de dokuhaku (hitori-zerifu) o suru hito.

solitary [sólitəri] *a*. hitori no ; sabishii. *n*. hitoribotchi (no). ~**ily** *ad*. hitori de.

solitude [sólitju:d] *n*. kodoku ; sabishisa.   [*voice*).

solo [sóulou] *n*. dokusō (*for one instrument*) ; dokushō (*for one*

solstice [sólstis] *n*. taiyō no (futatsu no) enjitsuten no hito-tsu. **summer** ~, geshi. **winter** ~, tōji.

solstitial [sɔlstíʃəl] *a*. geshi no ; tōji no.

solubility [sɔljubíliti] *n*. yōkaido ; yōkaisei.

soluble [sóljubl] *a*. tokeyasui ; tokeru.

solution [səlú:ʃən] *n*. yōkai ; kaiketsu ; (mondai) o toku koto.

solve [sɔlv] *v*. toku ; yōkai suru ; setsumei suru. ~**ncy** [sól-v(ə)nsi] *n*. yōkairyoku ; bensai nōryoku. ~**nt** [sólvənt] *n*. yōkairyoku ; kaiketsuryoku. *a*. *solvent* no aru.

somatic [soumǽtik] *a*. karada ni kansuru.

somber, ~**bre** [sómbə] *a*. usugurai ; inkina. ~**ness** *n*. usu-gurasa ; in'utsu.

some [sʌm] *a*., *pron*., *ad*. aru mono ; ikura ka ; karekore. ~**body** [⸗bɔdi, ⸗bɔdi] *pron*. aru hito ; dare ka. *n*. jūyōna hito. ~**how** *ad*. dō ni ka ; nan to naku. ~ *or other*, dō ni ka kō ni ka. ~**one** *pron*. aru hito ; dare ka. ~**thing** *n*. nani ka ; ikubun. ~**time** *ad*. itsuka. ~**times** *ad*. toki ni.... ~**what** *ad*. ikubun. ~**where** *ad*. dokoka de.

somersault [sʌ́məsoult] *n*., *v*. tombogaeri (suru).

Somerset [sʌ́məset] (*England*) Igirisu (*England*) minaminishi ni aru shū.

somnambulate [sɔmnǽmbjuleit] *v*. nemurinagara aruku. ~**bulism** *n*. muyūbyō. ~**bulist** *n*. muyūbyōsha.

somniferous [sɔmnífərəs] *a*. nemuri o moyōsu ; nemui. ~

somnolence [sómnələns] *n*. nemuke.   [**drug,** saiminzai.

somnolent [sómnələnt] *a*. nemui ; saimin no.   [yōshi.

son [sʌn] *n*. musuko ; shison. ~**-in-law** [sʌ́inlɔ:] *n*. muko ;

sonant [sóunənt] *a*. yūsei no ; dakuon no. *n*. yūseion ; dakuon.

sonata [sənɑ́:tə] *n*. (*mus*.) sōmeikyoku ; sonata.

song [sɔŋ] *n.* uta ; kakyoku. **~bird** [⌐bəid] *n.* meikin. **~ster** *n.* [sɔ́ŋstə] kashu ; shijin. **~stress** *n.* (onna no) kashu.

sonnet [sɔ́nit] *n.* sonetto ; 14 (jūshi)-gyō no shi.

sonorous [sənɔ́:rəs] *a.* (koe nado ga) rō-rō taru ; hibikiwataru.

soon [su:n] *ad.* sugu ; ma mo naku ; hodo naku. *as ~as*, ...suru to sugu. ...*no ~er...than...*, ...suru ya ina ya. *~er or later*, oso-soot [sut] *n.* susu ; baien. **~y** *a.* susuketa. ⌐kare hayakare.

sooth [su:θ] *n.* (*arch.*) shinjitsu. **~sayer** *n.* yogensha.

soothe [su:ð] *v.* nagusameru ; yawarageru.

sop [sɔp] *n.* mizu ; gyūnyū nado ni hitashita pan ; nagusame. *v.* hitasu ; zubunureni naru. **~py** [sɔ́pi] *a.* jikkuri nureta ; zu-sophism [sɔ́fizm] *n.* kiben. ⌐bunure no.

sophist [sɔ́fist] *n.* kiben gakusha (kodai Girisha no). **~ic** [səfístik] *a.* kiben no ; kiben o tsukau. **~icate** [səfístikeit] *v.* kiben de azamuku ; kiben o tsukau ; mazemono o suru. **~ication** [səfistikéiʃ(ə)n] *n.* kiben ; fujunni suru koto ; maze-mono ; nisemono. **~ry** [sɔ́fistri] *n.* kiben ; kibenjutsu.

sophomore [sɔ́feməɔ] *n.* daigaku no 2 (ni)-nensei. ⌐zai.

soporific [sóupərífik] *a.* nemuku suru ; saimin no. *n.* saimin-soprano [səprá:nou] *n.* sopurano kashu ; (*mus.*) josei saikōon ; **sorcerer** [sɔ́:sərə] *n.* mahōtsukai. ⌐sopurano.

sorceress [sɔ́:sres] *n.* (onna) mahōtsukai.

sorcery [sɔ́:səri] *n.* mahō ; majutsu.

sordid [sɔ́:did] *a.* kokoro no kitanai ; don'yokuna.

sore [sɔə] *a.* itai ; kanashii ; tsurai. *n.* haremono ; tsurai koto.

sorghum [sɔ́:gəm] *n.* (*bot.*) satōkibi-zoku no isshu.

sorority [sərɔ́riti] *n.* fujinkai (daigaku nado no).

sorrel [sɔ́rəl] *n.,* *a.* kuriiro (no) ; kurige (no).

sorrow [sɔ́rou] *n.* kanashimi ; kōkai ; nageki. *v.* kanashimu. **~ful** [-ful] *a.* kanashii ; awarena.

sorry [sɔ́ri] *a.* kawaisōni omotte ; kōkaishite ; dōjō shite.

sort [sɔ:t] *n.* shurui. *of ~s*, zasshu no. *out of ~*, (*col.*) kibun ga warui. *v.* bunrui suru ; chōwa suru.

sortie [sɔ́:ti] *n.* shutsugeki ; totsugeki (bōgyogun kara).

so-so [sóusou] *a.* iikagenna. *ad.* mā dōyara.

sot [sɔt] *n.,* *v.* nondakure(ru).

sough [sau] *n.* hyū-hyū (kaze no oto).

sought [sout] *v. see* : seek.

soul [soul] *n.* seishin; reikon; hito. ~**ful** *a.* seishin no ko-motta. ~**less** *a.* tamashii no nai.

sound [saund] *a.* kenzenna; seikakuna; jūbunna. ~ *sleep*, ju-kusui. *ad.* jūbunni. *n.* oto; onsei. *v.* hibiku; naru; narasu.

soup [su:p] *n.* nikujiru; suimono; sūpu.

sour [sauə] *a.* suppai; iyana. *v.* suppaku suru.

source [sɔ:s] *n.* minamoto; shussho.

souse [saus] *n.* shiomizu; mizubitashi. *v.* shiozuke ni suru.

south [sauθ] *n., a.* minami (no); nangoku (no). *ad.* minami e. ~**east** [˗í:st] *n.* tōnan. *a., ad.* tōnan no (e). ~**easter** *a.* tōnan kara no. ~**eastern** [-í:stən] *a.* tōnan no. ~**erly** [sʌðəli] *a.* minami e no. ~**ern** [sʌðən] *a.* minami no (ni). ~**erner** *n.* nangokujin. ~**ing** [sauðiŋ] *n.* minamimuki. ~**ward**, ~**wards** *ad.* minami e. ~**west** [˗wést] *n.* nansei. ~**western** [wéstən] *n.* seinampū. ~**westerly** *a.* seinan e no. ~**western** *a.* seinan no.

souvenir [sú:vəniə] *n.* (*Fr.*) kinenhin; miyage.   ⌈kaburn).

souwester [sauéstə] *n.* tsubabiro no bōsuibō (tokuni kaiin ga

sovereign [sóvrin] *n., a.* kokka no shihaisha (no); shukensha (no). ~**ty** [-ti] *n.* shuken; tōchiken.

Soviet [sóuviet] *n.* (*Russia*) hyōgikai. *the Union of* ~ *Socialist Republics*, Sobieto Shakaishugi Kyōwakoku Rempō (*USSR*).

sow [sou] *v.* sowed, sown; sowing. maku; tane o maku. ~**er** *n.* tane o maku hito; tanemaki-kikai. [sau] *n.* (*zoo.*) mesubuta.

soy [sɔi], **soya** [sɔ́iə] *n.* shōyu; daizu.

spa [spa:] *n.* kōsen; onsemba.

space [speis] *n.* jikan; kūkan; akibasho : *the earth moves through* ~, chikyū wa kūkan o tōtte unkō suru.

spacious [spéiʃəs] *a.* basho no ōi; hiroi; ōkina.

spade [speid] *n.* suki; (karuta no) supēdo.

spaghetti [spəgéti] *n.* (*It.*) supagetti; Itaria udon.

span [spæn] *n.* supan; oyayubi to koyubi no saki no nagasa; futatsu no mono no aida no kyori : *the arch has fifty-feet* ~, āchi wa ryōkyaku kan 50 (gojū) fiito aru.

spangle [spǽŋgl] *n.* kazari ni tsukeru kinzoku; nan demo hi-karu chiisai kireppashi : *this rock shows* ~*s of gold*, kono iwa

Spaniard [spǽnjəd] *n.* Spein-jin. ⌊niwa kin ga tsuite iru.
spaniel [spǽnjəl] *n.* inu no isshu; obekkamono.
Spanish [spǽniʃ] *a.* Supeinjin (-go) no. *n.* Supeinjin (-go).
spank [spæŋk] *v., n.* pishari to utsu (koto). ～**ing** *a.* shissō suru.
spar [spɑ:] *n.* usuku hageru ishi no sōshō. naguriai. fune no ho nado ni tsukau maruzai. *v.* (fune ni) maruzai o toritsukeru (*fix*). naguriai o suru.
spare [spɛə] *v.* ken'yaku suru; sukutte yaru. *a.* toboshii; teusuna; ken'yaku no. *n.* amari; yobihin.
spark [spɑ:k] *n.* hibana; hon no sukoshi. *a* ～ *from his match caused this fire,* kare no matchi no hi ga kono kaji o okoshita.
sparrow [spǽrou] *n.* (*bird*) suzume. ⌊*v.* hibana ga deru.
sparse [spɑ:s] *a.* mabarana. ～ *population,* mabarana jinkō.
Spartan [spɑ́:tən] *n.* Suparuta-jin. *a.* Suparuta no; shitsujitsu-gōkenna. ⌈no; hossateki.
spasm [spæzm] *n.* keiren; hossa. ～**odic(al)** [-ɔ́dik(əl)] *a.* keiren
spat [spæt] *n.* kaki no tamago; kozeriai; kuchigenka. *v. see :*
spate [speit] *n.* kōzui; doshaburi. ⌊**spit.**
spatial [spéiʃəl] *a.* kūkan no. ～**ly** *ad.* kūkantekini.
spatter [spǽtə] *v.* hanekasu. *n.* hane.
spatula [spǽtʃulə] *n.* kusuri o mazeru usui hera.
spavin [spǽvin] *n.* (uma no) nikushu.
spawn [spɔ:n] *n.* (uo no) tamago. *v.* (tamago o) umu.
speak [spi:k] *v.* **spoke, spoken; speaking.** iu; hanasu. ～**er** [spí:kə] hatsugensha; gichō. ～**ing** *a.* mono o iu. *n.* danwa.
spear [spiə] *n.* yari; yasu. *v.* yari de tsuku; hatsuga suru. ～**mint** [-mint] (*herb*) Oranda-hakka.
spec. [spek] =**speculation** *n.* (*Brit.*) tōki; omowaku.
special [spéʃ(ə)l] *a.* tokubetsuna; semmon no. *n.* tokuhain; to-kushi. ～**ist** *n.* semmonka. ～**ity** [spèʃiǽriti] *n.* tokuchō; toku-shuna ten. *make a* ～ *of,* o semmon ni suru. ～**ize** *v.* semmon-ni suru. ～**ty** *n.* tokushitsu; semmon.
specie [spi:ʃi] (*sing., pl.*) *n.* shōkin; kōka. *in* ～, seika de.
species [spi:ʃiz] (*sing., pl.*) *n.* shurui (*genus* no shita no bunrui).
specific [spisífik] *a.* tokushu no; shu no. *n.* tokukōyaku. ～**ally** *ad.* shu ni ōjite; tokubetsuni. ～**ation** [spèsifikéiʃ(ə)n] *n.* meisaisho (semmonteki no).

specify [spésifai] *v.* meiki suru ; kuwashiku shirusu.

specimen [spésimən] *n.* mihon (*example*).

specious [spí:ʃəs] *a.* shinjitsu rashii ; mottomo rashii.

speck [spek] *n., v.* hanten (o tsukeru) ; kizu (o tsukeru). ~le [spékl] *n., v.* (chiisana) hanten (o tsukeru). ⌐[-z] *n.* megane.

spectacle [spéktəkl] *n.* mimono ; misemono ; arisama. ~s

spectacular [spæktǽkjulə] *a.* mezamashii ; hanabanashii.

spectator [spektéitə] *n.* kembutsunin.

specter, -tre [spéktə] *n.* yūrei ; yōkai.

spectral [spéktrəl] *a.* yūrei no yōna ; *ad.* yūrei no yōni.

spectroscope [spéktrəskoup] *n.* bunkōki (*instrument for obtaining the spectrum*).

spectrum [spéktrəm] (*pl.* -tra ; -s) *n.* supekutoru ; kōsen (*beam*) o bunkai shita (*broken up*) obi (*band*).

speculate [spékjuleit] *v.* shisaku suru ; jukkō suru ; tōki o su-
speculation [spèkjuléiʃ(ə)n] *n.* shisaku ; tōki. ⌐ru.

speculative [spékjulətiv] *a.* shisaku no ; suiri no ; kūron no ; tōki no.

speculator [spékjuleitə] *n.* shisaku suru hito ; sōbashi.

speculum [spékjuləm] *n.* (*pl.* -la ; -s) hanshakyō ; kinzoku no kagami (*mirror of polished metal*).

sped [sped] *v. see* : **speed.** ⌐kuchi no kikenai.

speech [spi:tʃ] *n.* hatsugen ; gengo ; kōen ; enzetsu. ~less *a.*

speed [spi:d] *n.* sokudo ; hayasa. *at full* ~, zensokuryoku de. *v. sped* or **speeded** ; **speeding.** isogu, hayameru. ~ometer [-ómitə] *n.* sokudokei. ~way [-wei] *n.* kōsokudōro. ~y *a.* hayai.

spell [spel] *v.* **spelled** or **spelt** ; **spelling.** ji o tsuzuru (kaku). imi o motsu. ~ *the word*, sono go no tsuzuri o itte goran. *delay* ~s *danger*, nagabiku koto wa kiken o imi suru. ~ing bee [-iŋbi:] *n.* (*Am.*) spelling kyōsō.

spell [spel] *n.* mahō no kotoba. *cast a* ~ *on*, mahō no kotoba o iu. *under a* ~, sukkari mahō ni kakatte.

spell [spel] *n.* kimmujikan (*hour on duty*) ; (*col.*) nan demo kimatta jikan ; byōki nado ni natte ita jikan ; hoka no hito ga kawatta node yasunde iru jikan ; kyūkei jikan. *v.* hito ni kawatte hataraku. yasumijikan o ataeru.

spend [spend] *v.* **spent; spending.** kane o tsukau; rōhi suru. *earn before you* ~, tsukau mae ni mazu hatarake. ~**thrift** [-θrift] *n.* hōtōmono.

spent [spent] *v. see :* **spend.** *a.* tsukarekitta. *a* ~ *swimmer*, tsukare kitta oyogite (chikara o tsukai hatashita).

sperm [spɔ:m] *n.* seieki.

spermaceti [spɔ:məséti] *n.* kujira no nō (*brains of whale*) kara

spew [spju:] *v.* haku; oidasu; nageru. ⌊totta rō (*wax*).

sphagnum [sfǽgnəm] *n.* (*bot.*) mizugoke.

sphere [sfiə] *n.* kyū (tama); tentai; han'i.

spherical [sférikəl] *a.* kyūkei (tama no katachi) no; tentai no; tama ni kansuru (*pertaining to*).

sphericity [sfirísiti] *n.* kyūjō; tama no katachi.

spheroid [sfíərɔid] *n.* kaiten daentai.

sphincter [sfíŋktə] *n.* (*anat.*) katsuyakukin.

sphinx [sfíŋks] *n.* (*the S-*) Sufinkusu.

spice [spais] *n., v.* kōryō (o kuwaeru); yakumi (o ireru).

spicy [spáisi] *a.* kōryō o kuwaeta; kaori no aru.

spider [spáidə] *n.* kumo.

spigot [spígət] *n.* taru (*cask*) nado no sen; sashiguchi.

spike [spaik] *n., v.* ōkugi (o uchitsukeru); supaiku (o tsukeru).

spill [spil] *v.* **spilled** *or* **spilt; spilling.** kobosu; (chi o) nagasu. *n.* korogeochiru koto. ~**way** [-wei] *n.* hōsuiro.

spilt [spilt] *v. see :* **spill.**

spin [spin] *v.* **spun** *or* (*arch.*) **span, spun; spinning.** tsumugu; mawasu (koma nado o); (koma nado ga) mawaru.

spinach, spinage [spindʒ] *n.* hōrensō (*vegetable*).

spinal [spáinəl] *a.* sebone no. ~**column,** sebone.

spindle [spíndl] *n.* tsumu; supindoru; shimbō. ~**dling** *a.* hyoronagai. ~**legs** =~**shanks** [-ʃæŋks] *n.* sune ga hosokute

spine [spain] *n.* toge; sebone; se (hon no). ⌊nagai otoko.

spinster [spínstə] *n.* mikonfujin.

spiny [spáini] *a.* muzukashii; mendōna; sebone no aru.

spiral [spáirəl] *a.* rasenkei no; rasen.

spire [spaiə] *n.* sentō; hosoi saki no togatta tō (*pagoda*).

spirit [spírit] *n.* seishin; genki; kigen. *v.* hagemasu; yūkai suru. *Holy* ~, *the* ~, Seirei. *in high* ~*s*, genki yoku. ~**ed** *a.* [-id]

genkina. ~less *a*. kakki no nai. ~uous [spíritʃuəs] *a*. arukōru o fukunda.

spiritual [spíritjuəl] *a*. seishin no; kokoro no. ~ism *n*. yuishinron. ~ist [spiritjuǽliti] *n*. yuishinronja. ~ity *n*. reisei. ~ize *v*. seishintekini suru; kokoro o kiyoku suru.

spit [spit] *n*., *v*. yakigushi (ni sasu).

spit [spit] *v*. **spat; spitting.** tsuba (o haku). ~ on (*or* upon), o keibetsu suru. *a cat* ~*s when angry*, neko wa okoru to tsuba o tobasu.

spite [spait] *n*. akui. *v*. ijiwaru o suru. *in* ~ *of*, …nimo kakawarazu. ~ful [˗ful] *a*. akui no aru.

spittle [spítl] *n*. tsuba (ningen no).

spittoon [spitúːn] *n*. tantsubo.

splash [splæʃ] *v*. hanekakeru; bachan to tobu. *n*. hane.

splay [splei] *v*. naname ni suru; kirihiraku. *a*. bukakkōna. *n*. shamen. ~footed [˗fútid] *a*. hempeisoku no.

spleen [spliːn] *n*. hizō; fukigen; ijiwaru.

splendid [spléndid] *a*. subarashii; rippana : ~ *sight*, sōkan.

splendo(u)r [spléndə] *n*. migoto; hikari kagayaki.

splenetic [splinétik] *a*. hizō no; okorippoi. *n*. kimuzukashii hito.

splice [splais] *v*. tsugiawaseru. *n*. tsugiawase; setchaku.

splint [splint] *n*. soegi; ategi. *v*. soegi o suru.

split [split] *v*. tate ni waru; wareru. ~infinitive (*gram*.) " *to* " to " *v*." no aida ni " *adv*." ga haitta futeishi (tatoeba : *I want you to* clearly *understand that*…).

splutter [splʌ́tə], **sputter** [spʌ́tə] *see* : **sputter.**

spoil [spɔil] *v*. **spoiled** *or* **spoilt; spoiling.** ryakudatsu suru (kodomo nado amayakashite) dainashi ni suru. ~ed (*or* ~t) **child**, dadakko. ~sman [˗zmən] *n*. riken'ya.

spoilt [spɔilt] *v*. *see* : **spoil.**

spoke [spouk] *v*. *see* : **speak.**

spoken [spóukən] *v*. *see* : **speak.** *a*. kuchi de itta; kōgo no. ~spokesman [spóuksmən] *n*. daibensha.   [language, kōgo.

sponge [spʌndʒ] *n*. kaimen. *v*. kaimen de fuku; sū. ~ **cake**, kasuteira. ~y [spʌ́ndʒi] *a*. kaimenjō no.

sponsor [spónsə] *n*. hoshō suru hito; kōensha. *v*. *sponsor* to naru. ~**ial** [spɔnsɔ́:riəl] *a.* hoshōnin ; nazuke-oya.

spontaneity [spəntəní:ti] *n.* shizen no jijitsu (*fact*) ; jōtai (*state*) ; furumai (*action*).

spontaneous [spɔntéinjəs] *a.* shizen no ; tennen ni okoru. ~**ly** *ad.* shizenni. ~**ness** *n.*

spoof [spu:f] *v.* ippai kuwasu (itazurani).

spool [spu:l] *n., v.* itomaki (ni maku).

spoon [spu:n] *n.* saji. *v.* saji de sukuu. ~**ful** *n.* hitosaji.

sporadic(al) [spərǽdik(l)] *a.* sanzaisei no ; tokuhatsu no. tokidoki okoru. ~**outbreaks,** sampatsuteki no bōdō (sōdō).

spore [spɔə] *n.* hōshi ; shushi ; moto.   ⌐no aru).

sporran [spɔ́:rən] *n.* Kōchi *Scotland* no fukusō (mae ni fukuro

sport [spɔːt] *n.* yūgi ; kyōgi ; asobi. *v.* tanoshimu. ~**y** *a.* kyō-

sportive [spɔ́:tiv] *a.* fuzaketa ; karakau.   ⌊gitekina.

sportsman [spɔ́:tsmən] *n.* undōka. ~**like** [-laik] *a.* undōka rashii. ~**ship** *n.* undōka-seishin.

spot [spɔt] *n.* ten ; shimi. *v.* madarani suru (naru) ; shimi ga tsuku (o tsukeru). *a* ~ *of ink*, inku no shimi. *on the* ~, sono ba de. ~**less** [-lis] *a.* ketten no nai. ~**light** [-lait] *n.* supottoraito. ~**ter** *n.* (*Am.*) keiji (*detective*).

spouse [spauz] *n.* haigūsha (*husband or wife*).

spout [spaut] *n.* (kyūsu no) kuchi ; funsui. *v.* fukidasu.

sprain [sprein] *n* kujiki. *v.* kujiku ; nenza suru. ~ **fracture,** (*med.*) nenza ; kossetsu.

sprang [sprǽŋ] *v. see* : **spring.**

sprat [sprǽt] *n.* (*fish*) koiwashi (Taiseiyō-gan ni ōi sakana).

sprawl [sprɔ:l] *v.* funzorikaeru ; buzamani nesoberu.

spray [sprei] *n.* mizukemuri ; shibuki. *v.* mizukemuri o tataseru ; kiri o fuku.

spread [spred] *n. v.* **spread ; spreading.** hirogeru(-aru) ; hiraku ; tsutawaru. *n.* hirosa ; kakuchō ; man'en. ~ *oneself*, ii inshō o ataeru yōni honeoru ; jiman suru.

spree [spri:] *n.* sakamori. *on a* ~, ukarete.

sprig [sprig] *n.* koeda ; hikobae.

sprightly [spráitli] *a.* kaikatsuna. ~**liness** *n.*

spring [spriŋ] *v.* **sprang** *or* **sprung, sprung ; springing.** tobidasu ; haneagaru ; …kara deru. *n.* haru ; izumi ; bane ; supuringu. *a.* haru no; harumuki no. **~board** [⌐bɔːd] *n.* chōya-kuban. **~tide** [⌐taid], **~time** [⌐taim] *n.* shunki; haru. **~y** [spríŋi] *a.* danryoku no aru; wakasa ni michita; keikaina.

sprinkle [spríŋkl] *v.* (mizu o) makichirasu. *n.* kosame.

sprinkling [spríŋkliŋ] *n.* sampu; chirahora; parapara.

sprint [sprint] *v.* shissō suru. *n.* tankyori-kyōsō. **~er** *n.* tankyo-

sprite [sprait] *n.* kobito no yōsei; akki; yōsei. ⌊ri-sōsha.

sprocket [sprɔ́kit] *n.* kusariwa (yuki no hi nado no sharin no

sprout [spraut] *n.*, *v.* me (o dasu). ⌊suberi dome).

spruce [spruːs] *a.* kogireina. *v.* mekashitateru. *n.* momi-no-ki.

sprung [sprʌŋ] *v. see*: **spring.**

spry [sprai] *a.* subashikkoi. *a mouse is a* **~animal**, hatsukane-zumi wa subashikkoi dōbutsu da.

spume [spjuːm] *n.*, *v.* awa (-dateru).

spun [spʌn] *v. see*: **spin.** *a.* tsumuida. **~ glass,** garasu no ito. **~ rayon,** reiyon no ito. **~ silk,** kinu no tsumugiito. **~**

spunk [spʌŋk] *n.* yūki; hokuchi (*tinder*). ⌊**yarn** *n.* yoriito.

spur [spɔː] *n.* hakusha; kezume. *v.* hakusha o ireru (kakeru); uma o isogaseru. *on the* **~** *of the moment*, toki no hazumi de.

spurious [spjúəriəs] *a.* nise no; gizō no. *a* **~** *document*, gizō-bunsho (monjo).

spurn [spɔːn] *v.* ketobasu; hanetsukeru. *the judge* **~ed** *the bribe*, hanji wa wairo o hanetsuketa.

spurt [spɔːt] *v.* hotobashiru. *n.* fumpatsu. *the runners* **~ed** *near the end of the race*, senshu-tachi wa rasuto supāto o dashita.

sputnik [spútnik] 1957 *n.* 10 gt. 4 k no jinkō eisei no na.

sputter [spʌ́tə] *v.* pata-pata oto o tateru; tsuba o tobasu. *n.* ha-yakuchi.

sputum [spjúːtəm] *n.* (*pl.* -ta) kuchi kara tobasu tsubaki.

spy [spai] *n.* kanchō; supai. *v.* tantei suru. **~glass** [⌐glaːs], *n.* chiisai bōenkyō. **~master** [⌐maːstə] *n.* tanteichō.

squab [skwɔb] *a.* zunguri shita. *n.* hinadori (tokuni hato); zunguri shita hito.

squabble [skwɔ́bl] *n.*, *v.* kōron (suru), iiarasoi.

squad [skwɔd] *n.* han (*smallest group of soldiers*); buntai. **~ car,** patorōru-kā.

squadron [skwɔ́drən] *n.* kihei-chūtai; hikō-chūtai; kantai.

squalid [skwɔ́lid] *a.* kitanai.

squall [skwɔːl] *n.* hayate; sukōru. *v.* sukōru ga kuru. ōgoe de naku.

squalor [skwɔ́lə] *n.* mijime; musakurushisa.

squander [skwɔ́ndə] *v.* rōhi suru.

square [skwɛə] *n.*, *a.* seihōkei (no); hiroba (no). *v.* hōkei ni suru; tadasu. *ad.* shikaku ni. ～ **bracket,** kaku-gakko: [ ]. ～ **dance** *n.* sukweya-dansu: "*Virginia reel*" no yōna dansu. ～ **deal,** *n.* kōhei de tadashii toriatsukai. ～ **knot,** komamusubi. ～ **ed ring** *n.* (*col.*) kentōjō. ～ **meal,** jisshitsu no aru shokuji. ～ **ly** *ad.* kōmeiseidaini. ～ **measure,** (*math.*) heihōseki. ～ **ness** *n.* kōmeiseidai. ～ **shooter,** (*col.*) kōmeiseidaina hito.

squash [skwɔʃ] *v.* oshitsubusu. *n.* oshitsubusareta mono.

squat [skwɔt] *v.* shagamu; uzukumaru; ashi o mae ni kumu. *n.* uzukumari; agura. ～**ter** [skwɔ́tə] *n.* kenri ga nakute sumu hito. ～**ty** [skwɔ́ti] *a.* mijikaku atsui; hikukute hiroi.

squaw [skwɔː] *n.* (Hokubei genchijin no) onna; tsuma.

squawk [skwɔːk] *n.* niwatori ya ahiru no nakigoe (o suru).

squeak [skwiːk] *n.*, *v.* chū-chū, kii-kii (naku). *a mouse* ～*s.*

squeal [skwiːl] *n.*, *v.* kii-kii (naku). *a pig* ～*s.*

squeamish [skwíːmiʃ] *a.* mukatsuki yasui; kimuzukashii.

squeeze [skwiːz] *n.*, *v.* shimetsuke(ru); assaku (suru).

squelch [skweltʃ] *v.* magotsukaseru; chimmoku saseru. *she* ～*ed him with a look of contempt,* kanojo ga keibetsu no manazashi o okutta node kare wa damatte shimatta.

squib [skwib] *v.* kyo o tsuku; *n.* hiniku; fūshi (*sharp sarcasm*).

squid [skwid] *n.* yariika.

squint [skwint] *v.* me o hosomete miru. ～ *in the sun,* (mabushii node) hosome de miru. *n.* shashi.

squire [skwaiə] *n.* gōshi; ōjinushi.

squirm [skwəːm] *v.* notautsu; mogaku; karada o nejiru.

squirrel [skwírəl] *n.* risu.

squirt [skwəːt] *v.* mizu o kuda kara jā to dasu. *n.* mizudeppō; ss., s.s., s/s =*steamship.* funshutsu.

St. [seint] =*saint, street* no ryaku.

stab [stæb] *n.* sasu (tantō nado de) koto. *v.* sasu; gai suru; (*fig.*) hiyuteki ni mo mochiiru. ～ *in the back,* senaka o sasu; kageguchi o itte kizutsukeru.

stability [stəbíliti] *n.* kengo ; antei. ⌈saseru hito.

stabilize [stéibilaiz] *v.* antei saseru. ~**r** [-ə] *n.* anteisōchi ; antei-

stable [stéibl] *a.* kengona ; kotei shite iru. *n.* umaya. *v.* umaya ni ireru. ⌈tekini (na).

staccato [stəkɑ́:tou] *ad., a.* (*music*) sutakkato de (no) ; dan'on-

stack [stæk] *n.* inamura ; hondana. *a* ~ *of rifles,* sajū.

stadium [stéidiəm] *n.* (*pl.* **-dia** [-diə]) kyōsōjō ; kyōgijō.

staff [stɑ:f] *n.* (*pl.* **-s ; staves** [steivz]) buki ; tozan no tsue ; shikibō ; sambō ; bakuryō ; (shūgōteki ni) shokuin. ongaku

stag [stæg] *n.* o-jika. ⌊no fuhyō (*staves*).

stage [steidʒ] *n.* dai ; butai (engei no) ; eki ; jiken no atta ba-sho. *v.* jōen suru. ~**direction** *n.* butai-shiki. ~ **manager,** butai kantoku. ~**coach** [⊥koutʃ] *n.* ekibasha. ~**craft** [⊥krɑ:ft] *n.* gekisaku no sainō. ~**hand** [⊥hænd] *n.* gekijō dōgugata. ~ **whisper,** dokuhaku (kangae o kankaku ni wakaraseru tame no hitorigoto).

stagger [stǽgə] *v.* yorokeru ; tajirogu. *n.* yoromeki ; (*pl.*) me-

stagnant [stǽgnənt] *a.* yodonde iru ; fukeikina. ⌊mai.

stagnate [stǽgneit] *v.* yodomu ; fukeiki ni naru.

stagnation [stægnéiʃ(ə)n] *n.* yodomi ; fukeiki ; fushin.

staid [steid] *v. see* : **stay.** *a.* kokoro no shikkari shita ; ochitsu-ita. ~**ness** *n.* majime ; ochitsuki.

stain [stein] *v.* someru (somu) ; yogoreru (yogosu). *n.* yogore ; shimi. ~**less** *a.* yogore no nai ; mukizu no ; sabinai. ~**less steel** sabinai kōtetsu, stenres. ⌈*n.* kaidan.

stair [stɛə] *n.* hashigodan ; kaidan. ~**case** [⊥keis], ~**way** [⊥wei]

stake [steik] *n.* kui. hiaburi no kei no hashira. (*pl.*) kenshōkin. *v.* kui de shikiru. kakeru. *the* ~, hiaburi no kei. *pull up* ~*s,* jūsho o kaeru. *at* ~, kakerarete ; ayauku natte.

stalactite [stəlǽktait] *n.* (*min.*) shōnyūseki.

stalagmite [stəlǽgmait] *n.* (*min.*) sekijun.

stale [steil] *a.* ki no nuketa ; chimpuna. ⌈ibatte aruku.

stalk [stɔ:k] *n.* kuki ; jiku. shinobiyori. *v.* kossori to aruku.

stall [stɔ:l] *n.* umaya no hito-shikiri. roten. *v.* umaya ni ireru ; ugokanaku naru (hatsudōki nado ga).

stallion [stǽljən] *n.* taneuma.

stalwart [stó:lwət] *a.* jōbuna ; ganjōna.

stamen [stéimən] *n.* hana no oshibe.

stamina [stǽminə] *n.* kiryoku; konki; nagatsuzuki.
stammer [stǽmə] *n.*, *v.* domori (nagara iu).
stamp [stæmp] *n.*, *v.* ashibumi (suru); han (o osu); inshi (o haru).
stampede [stæmpí:d] *n.* (kachiku nado ga) odoroite nigedasu koto; dotto oshiyoseru koto.
stance [stæns] *n.* ashi no kamaekata (yakyū, gorufu nado de).
stanch [stɑ:ntʃ] *v.* (shukketsu o) tomeru. *a.* mizu o tōsanai. shikkari shita.
stanchion [stǽnʃən] *n.* tate no sasabashira. *v.* shichū de sasaeru.
stand [stænd] *v.* **stood; standing.** tatsu. gaman suru. shitagau. *n.* shuchō. tachiba. baiten. **~-by** [-bai] *n.* tanomi ni naru hito. **~ing** [stǽndiŋ] *a.* tatte iru; sadamatta. *n.* tachiba; chii. **~ing army** *n.* jōbigun. **~-point** [-pɔint] *n.* tachiba; kenchi. **~still** [-stil] *n.* tachidomari; teishi. **~up** [-ʌp] *a.* tatte iru; tachiagare!
standard [stǽndəd] *n.* hata. hyōjun. *a.* hyōjun no; mohan no. **~ coin,** hon'i kahei. **~ time,** hyōjunji. **~ization** [stændədaizéiʃ(ə)n] *n.* hyōjunka; kikaku tōitsu. **~ize** *v.* hyōjun ni awaseru.
stanza [stǽnzə] *n.* (shi no) issetsu.
staple [stéipl] *n.* shuyōsambutsu; genryō; sen'i; tomegane; kasugai. *a.* shuyō no. **~fiber** *n.* sufu; *fiber,* jinzōsen'i.
star [stɑ:] *n.* hoshi. ninkimono. hoshi-jirushi. *v.* hoshi de kazaru; hoshi no yōni kagayaku. *Stars and Stripes,* Seijōki. **~fish** [-fiʃ] *n.* hitode. **~ry** [-ri] *a.* hoshi no. **~-spangled** [-spæŋgld] *a.* hoshi de chiribameta.
starboard [stɑ:bə:d] *n.*, *a.* (fune no) ugen (no).
starch [stɑ:tʃ] *n.* dempun. nori. katakurushisa. *v.* nori o tsukeru. **~y** [-i] *a.* dempun-jō no; nori no yōna; katakurushii.
stare [stɛə] *n.* gyōshi (suru). *v.* jitto miru; mitsumeru.
stark [stɑ:k] *a.* kataku natta; mattaku no. *ad.* zenzen; sukkari.
start [stɑ:t] *v.* bikkuri suru; shuppatsu suru. **~er** *n.* shuppatsu-gakari.
startle [stɑ́:tl] *v.* bikkuri suru (saseru).
starvation [stɑ:véiʃ(ə)n] *n.* kiga; uejini; gashi.
starve [stɑ:v] *v.* gashi suru (saseru); uesaseru. **~ling** [stɑ́:vliŋ] *n.* ueta hito. *a.* ueta; yasekoketa.
state [steit] *n.* jōtai; kokka. *a.* kokka no; gishikiyō no. *v.* hanasu; noberu. **~ carriage,** gishikiyō basha. **~ criminal,**

kokujihan. ∼ly *a.* igen aru. ∼ment *n.* chinjutsu. ∼ room, ōhiroma. ∼sman [stéitsmən] *n.* daiseijika. S∼ house *n.* (*Am.*) shūgijidō. ⌈gaku.

static(al) [stǽtik(l)] *a.* seiteki no; seishi no. ∼s [-s] *n.* seiriki-station [stéiʃən] *n.* teishajō; keisatsusho; ichi. *v.* oku; haichi suru. ∼ary [-əri] *a.* ugokanai; isuwari no. ∼master ekichō.

stationer [stéiʃənə] *n.* bumbōgushō. ∼y [-ri] *n.* bumbōgu.

statistic(al) [stətístik(l)] *a.* tōkei no. ∼ian [stǽtistíʃən] *n.* tōkei-ka; tōkeigakusha. ∼s *n.* tōkei (-gaku).

statuary [stǽtʃuəri] *n.*, *a.* chōkoku (no).

statue [stǽtju:] *n.* zō; chōzō. ∼sque [stǽtjuésk] *a.* chōzō no yōna. ∼tte [stǽtjuét] *n.* chiisana chōzō.

stature [stǽtʃə] *n.* shinchō; minotake.

status [stéitəs] *n.* jōtai; mibun. ∼ quo [kwúo] (*L.*) genjō.

statute [stǽtju:t] *n.* hōrei. ∼ law *n.* seibunritsu (kaita hōbun).

statutory [stǽtjutəri] *a.* hōtei no; seiteihō no.

staunch [stɔ:ntʃ] *v.*, *a.* =stanch.

stave [steiv] *n.* oke (*barrel*) no ita. bō. (ongaku no) fuhyō. *v.* staved *or* stove; staving. oke o kowasu; ana o akeru.

stay [stei] *n.* taizai. sasae (bashira). ōkina tsuna. *v.* stayed *or* staid; staying. onaji jōtai de tomatte iru; taizai suru. sasaeru. ∼-at-home [-ət(h)oum] *a.*, *n.* gaishitsugirai. ∼sail [⌐sl] *n.* shisakuho; sankakkei no sasaezuna ni tsuita ho.

stead [sted] *n.* kawari. *in a person's* ∼, kawari ni. *stand a person in good* ∼, yaku ni tatsu. *in* ∼ *of*=instead of, kawari ni. ∼fast [⌐fəst] *a.* kakko taru; fubatsu no. ∼y [stédi] *a.* ugokanai; itsu mo kawaranai. *v.* shikkari ugokanu yōni suru.

steak [steik] *n.* yakiniku.

steal [sti:l] *v.* stole, stolen; stealing. nusumu. *n.* nusumi.

stealth [stelθ] *n.* himitsu. *by* ∼, hisoka ni. ∼y *a.* hisokana.

steam [sti:] *n.* jōki. *v.* musu; fukasu; jōhatsu suru. ∼boat *n.* kisen. ∼ engine, jōkikikan. ∼er *n.* kisen; kikan. ∼ship *n.* kisen.

steed [sti:d] *n.* uma (*horse for riding*); (*arch*) gumba.

steel [sti:l] *n.* hagane; kōtetsu. *v.* kataku suru. ∼y *a.* kōtetsu no. ∼yard *n.* saobakari.

steep [sti:p] *a.* kewashii. *n.* zeppeki. *v.* hitasu; tsukeru.

steeple [sti:pl] *n.* (kyōkai nado no) sentō. ～**chase** [‐ʧeis] *n.* yagai (shōgaibutsu) keiba.

steer [stiə] *n.* (osu no) koushi. *v.* kaji o toru ; fune o mukeru. ～ *clear of,* kirinukeru. ～**age** [‐ridʒ] *n.* santōsenshitsu ; fune ⌊no kajitori.

stellar [stélə] *a.* hoshi no ; hanagata no.

stem [stem] *n.* kuki. bunke. senshu. *v.* sekitomeru.

stench [stenʧ] *n.* akushū.

stencil [sténsil] *n.* tōshaban no genshi. *v.* tōsha suru.

stenograph [sténəgrɑ:f] *n.* sokkimoji. ～**er** *n.* sokki(ki)sha. ～**y** ⌊*n.* sokki-jutsu.

stentorian [stentɔ́:riən] *a.* ōgoe no.

step [step] *v.* aruku ; iku ; fumu ; odoru. *n.* ayumi ; kaidan. ～ *into a person's shoes,* atogama ni suwaru.

step- [step] *pref.* giri no. ～**brother** [‐brʌðə] *n.* gikyōdai. ～**child** *n.* mamako. ～**daughter** *n.* mamako (onna). ～**father** *n.* gifu. ～**mother** *n.* mamahaha. ～**sister** *n.* gishimai. ～**son** *n.* mamako (otoko).

steppe [step] *n.* areno ; (jumoku no nai) daisōgen.

stereopticon [stiəriɔ́ptikən] *n.* jittaigentōki.

stereoscope [stéəriəskoup] *n.* jittaikyō.

stereotype [stìəriɔ́taip] *n.* (*print*) suteroban ; emban. ～**d** [‐t] *a.* suteroban no ; kimarikitta.

sterile [stérail] *a.* fumō no ; ko no dekinai ; shōdoku shita.

sterility [steríliti] *n.* fumō ; shōdoku.

sterilize [stérilaiz] *v.* fumō ni suru ; sakkin suru.

sterling [stɔ́:liŋ] *n.* Igirisu no (jungin) kahei. ～ **silver,** jungin (gin no gan'yūryō, 92.5%).

stern [stə:n] *a.* kibishii. *n.* sembi ; fune (*ship*) no kōbu.

stethoscope [stéθəskoup] *n.* chōshinki.

stevedore [stí:vidɔ:] *n.* niagenimpu ; okinakashi.

stew [stju:] *v.* torobi de niru ; toro-toro nieru. *n.* shichūryōri.

steward [stjúəd] *n.* karei ; kyūji. ～**ess** *n.* kyūji (kisha, kisen, hikōki nado de onna no).

stick [stik] *n.* bō ; tsue ni naru ki no eda. *v.* **stuck; sticking.** sasu ; tsukisasu ; kuttsuku ; shūchaku suru ; kodawaru. *he* ～*s a flower in his button hole,* kare wa botan'ana ni hana o sashita.

stiff [stif] *a.* katai ; kowabatta ; gankona.～**en** [stífn] *v.* tsuyoku suru ; kowabaru ; gōjōni naru.

stifle [stáifl] *v.* iki o tomeru ; osaeru ; chissoku suru (saseru).
stigma [stígmə] *n.* rakuin. ~**tize** *v.* rakuin o osu ; omei o ki-
stile [stail] *n.* dan-dan ; fumidan. ⌊seru.
stiletto [stilétou] *n.* tanken (ha no semai). *v. stiletto* de sashi
korosu.
still [stil] *a.* ugokanai. *n.* shizukesa. *v.* damaraseru. *ad.* mada ;
yappari (yahari). ~ *waters run deep*, shizukana nagare wa soko
ga fukai. ~ *a crying child*, naku ko o damaraseru. ~**born**
[⌐bɔːn] *a.* shinde umareta ; shizan no. ~**y** *a.* [⌐li] shizukana.
ad. [⌐li] shizukani. ⌈ōgesana ; erasōna.
stilt [stilt] *n.* takeuma ; sagiashi. ~**ed** [⌐id] *a.* mottaibutta ;
stimulant [stímjulənt] *a.* shigeki suru. *n.* shigeki ; kōfunzai.
stimulate [stímjuleit] *v.* hagemasu ; shigeki suru.
stimulation [stìmjuléiʃən] *n.* gekirei ; shigeki.
stimulative [stímjulətiv] *a.* shigeki suru. *n.* shigekibutsu.
stimulus [stímjuləs] *n.* shigekibutsu ; shigeki.
sting [stiŋ] *v.* **stung**, **stinging**. sasu. *n.* toge ; kizu ; sasu koto.
stingy [stíndʒi] *a.* kechina ; toboshii. ⌈hassuru. *n.* akushū.
stink [stiŋk] *v.* **stunk** *or* **stank**, **stunk** ; **stinking**. akushū o
stint [stint] *v.* setsuyaku suru. *n.* kiritsume ; seigen.
stipend [stáipənd] *n.* hōkyū (bokushi nado no). ~**iary** [stai-
péndʒəri] *a., n.* hōkyū o ukeru (hito).
stipulate [stípjuleit] *v.* yōkyū suru ; yakujō suru ; jōken o mō-
stipulation [stìpjuléiʃ(ə)n] *n.* yakusoku ; kitei. ⌊keru.
stir [stəː] *v.* ugokasu ; sendō suru. *n.* sawagi. ~ *up*, shōrei
stirrup [stírəp] *n.* abumi. ⌊suru ; sendō suru.
stitch [stitʃ] *n., v.* kyūna itami (o kanjiru) ; hitohari (nū).
stock [stɔk] *n.* miki *(of tree)* ; takuwae *(for use, for sale)* ; kabushiki ; kachiku. *in* ~, zaiko. *out of* ~, shinagire. ~**holder**
[⌐houldə] *n.* kabunushi. ~**broker** [⌐broukə] *n.* kabushiki
nakagainin. ~**yard** [⌐jɑːd] *n.* kachiku okiba. ~**car** [⌐kɑː] *n.*
(Am.) kachiku o hakobu tetsudō no kasha. ~**man** [-mən]
n. kachiku o sodateru hito.
stockade [stɔkéid] *n.* saku ; yarai. *v.* saku de kakou.
stockinet [stɔkinét] *n.* meriyasu.
stocking [stɔkiŋ] *n.* nagakutsushita.
stocky [stɔki] *a.* zunguri shita. ⌈omoshiroku nai hon.
stodgy [stɔdʒi] *a.* omoshiroku nai ; gota-gota shita. *a* ~ *book*,

Stoic [stóuik] *n.*, *a.* Sutoa-gakuha no gakusha; kin'yoku shugisha. ~**al** [-l] *a.* Sutoa-gakuhafū no; kokkishugi no. ~**ism** [stóuisizm] *n.* Sutoa-tetsugaku; kokkishugi.

stoke [stouk] *v.* hi o taku; hi o kakitateru. ~**hole** [-houl], ~**hold** [-hould] *n.* kikan (kafu) shitsu. ~**r** *n.* kafu.

stole [stóul] *v.* see: **steal.** *n.* fujin no nagagaitō.

stolen [stóuln] *v.* see: **steal.**

stolid [stólid] *a.* donkanna. ~**ity** [stəlíditi] *n.* donkan; mushinkei.

stomach [stʌ́mək] *n.* i (no fu); konomi. *v.* shinobu. *I have no ~ for that kind of writing,* sono shu no saku niwa konomi wa nai. *he could'nt ~ such insults,* sonna bujoku wa gaman deki nakatta. ~**er** *n.* (fujin'yō) muneate.

stone [stoun] *n.* ishi; kinenhi. *v.* ishi de utsu. ~ **Age,** Sekki Jidai. ~**ware** [-wɛə] *n.* soakuna jiki. ~**henge** [-hendʒ, -éndʒ] *n.* Igirisu no rekishi izen no iseki. ~**work** *n.* sekizōkaoku; ishizaiku.

stony [stóuni] *a.* ishi no; ishi no ōi; mujōna.

stood [stud] *v.* see: **stand.**

stooge [stúːdʒ] *n.* (dōkeyaku no) hojoyaku.

stool [stuːl] *n.* shōgi; koshikake.

stoop [stuːp] *v.* kagamu; mageru; magaru. *n.* nekoze.

stop [stɔp] *v.* fusagu; tomeru (-aru). *n.* fusagu koto; owari. ~ *over,* tochūgesha suru. ~**cock** [-kɔk] *n.* jaguchi. (*faucet*) ~**page** [stópidʒ] *n.* tomari. ~**per** [stópə] *n.* sen. ~ **watch,** byōdokei; sutoppu wotchi.

storage [stó:ridʒ] *n.* chozō suru koto. **cold ~** reizōko (*refrigerator*). ~ **battery** *n.* chikudenchi.

store [stɔə] *n.* chozō; sō; mise. *v.* chozō suru. ~**house** [-haus] *n.* sōko. ~**room** *n.* chozōshitsu.

storey, story [stɔ:ri] *n.* kai; sō. **first ~,** (*Brit.*) nikai; (*Am.*) ikkai. (*Brit.*) ground floor=(*Am.*) 1st storey; (*Brit.*) 1st floor =(*Am.*) 2nd storey.

storied [stó:rid] *a.* monogatari (rekishi) ni nadakai. koto.

stork [stɔ:k] *n.* (*bird*) kōnotori. *visit from the ~,* shussan suru

storm [stɔ:m] *n.* arashi. *v.* aremawaru. ~ **boat** kōgekiyō shūtei. ~**y** *a.* arashi no yōna.

story [stɔ́:ri] *n.* hanashi.

stout [staut] *a.* futotte ōkii; jōbuna; ganjōna. *n.* kurobiiru; futotta hito.

stove [stouv] *v.* see: **stave.** *n.* stōbu; danro.

stow [stou] *v.* tsumikomu. ~**age** [-idʒ] *n.* tsumikomi. ~**away**

[⌐ɔwei] n. mikkōsha.   [ˈbismɔl] yabunirami no.

strabismus [strəbízməs] n. yabunirami. ∼**mal,** ∼**mic** a. [strə-

straddle [strǽdl] v. matagaru. n. matagari.

straggle [strǽgl] v. tsure ni hagureru ; mabara ni aru (ie na-do). samayoi aruku. ∼**r** n. furōsha ; rakugosha.

straight [streit] a. massuguna ; tadashii. ad. massuguni ; tada-chini. n. itchokusen. ∼**en** v. massuguni suru. ∼**forward** a. shōjikina. ∼**way** [⌐wei] ad. tadachini.

strain [strein] v. pin to hipparu ; tsukai sugiru ; tsutomeru. n. kinchō ; muri. ∼**ed** a. harikitta.

strait [streit] a. semai. n. kaikyō. ∼**en** v. semaku suru. ∼**jacket** [-dʒækit] n. pittari mi ni tsuita hogoyō no jaketsu.

strand [strænd] n. hama ; kishi. v. kishi ni noriageru ; zashō suru.

strange [streindʒ] a. yoso no ; mezurashii ; takoku no. ∼**r** n. mishiranu hito ; gaikokujin.

strangle [strǽŋgl] v. kubi o shimeru ; iki o tomeru.

strangulate [strǽŋgjuleit] v. shimekorosu.

strangulation [strǽŋgjuléiʃ(ə)n] n. kōsatsu.

strap [stræp] n. himo ; obi. v. kawahimo de shibaru.

strapping [strǽpiŋ] a. sei ga takaku, tsuyoku takumashii.

stratagem [strǽtədʒim] n. senryaku ; keiryaku.

strategic(al) [strətédʒik(əl)] a. senryakujō no.

strategist [strǽtidʒist] n. senryakuka.

strategy [strǽtidʒi] n. senryaku. ∼**unit** n. senryaku tan'i.

stratification [strætifikéiʃən] n. sō ga dekiru koto.

stratify [strǽtifai] v. sō o tsukuru.

stratosphere [strǽtəsfiə] n. (astr.) seisōken.

stratum [stréitəm] (pl. **-ta**) n. chisō.

stratus [stréitəs] n. sōun (sō (strata) o nashite iru kumo).

straw [strɔː] n. wara. not care a ∼, sukoshi mo kamawanai. ∼**berry** [⌐beri] n. Oranda-ichigo.

stray [strei] v. michi ni mayou. a. michi ni mayotta. n. hagu-reta kachiku. ∼ **bullets,** nagaredama.

streak [striːk] n. suji ; sō (layer). v. suji o tsukeru. like a ∼, (col.) zensokuryoku de (at full speed).

stream [striːm] n. nagare ; ogawa. v. nagareru ; nagasu. ∼**er** n.

nagai semai mono. ∼**let** [⌐lit] *n.* ogawa. ∼**line** [⌐lain] *v.*, *a.*
ryūsenkei (no). *v.* ryūsenkei ni suru.
street [striːt] *n.* machi ; gairo ; tōri. ∼ **Arab,** yadonashigo.
∼**car** [⌐kɑː] *n.* shigaidensha. ∼**walker** [⌐wɔːkɔ] *n.* baishunfu.
strength [streŋθ] *n.* chikara ; tsuyosa. *on* (or *upon*) *the* ∼ *of,* …
o tanomi to shite. ∼**en** *v.* tsuyoku suru ; tsuyoku naru.
strenuous [stréːnjuəs] *a.* chikara no kagiri no ; hone no oreru.
streptomycin [strèptəmáisin] *n.* sutoreputomaishin.
stress [stres] *n.* atsuryoku ; akusento ; kinchō. *v.* assuru.
stretch [stretʃ] *v.* nobasu ; nobiru ; haru ; hirogaru (-eru). *n.* kinchō. *at a* ∼, hitoikini. ∼**er** *n.* nobasu hito ; tanka.
strew [struː] *v.* **strewed, strewed** *or* **strewn; strewing.** furi-
maku ; makichirasu.   ⌐aru.
striate [stráieit] *v.* suji o tsukeru. ∼**d** [-id] *a.* (*streaked*) suji no
stricken [stríkn] *v. see* : **strike.**   ⌐gemmitsu ni ieba.
strict [strikt] *a.* genjūna. ∼**ly** *ad.* gemmitsu ni. ∼ *speaking,*
stricture [stríktʃɔ] *n.* (*med.*) kyōsaku. kokuhyō (*unfavorable*
strid [strid], ∼**den** [stridn] *see* : **stride.**   ⌐*criticism*).
stride [straid] *v.* **strode, strid** *or* **stridden; striding.** ōmata ni
aruku ; mataide kosu. *n.* ōmata ; hitomatagi.
strident [stráidnt] *a.* kii-kii iu.
strife [straif] *n.* kyōsō ; funtō.
strike [straik] *v.* **struck, struck** *or* **stricken; striking.** utsu ;
osou ; narasu ; shōtotsu suru. *n.* sutoraiki. ∼ *home,* kyūsho o
tsuku. *go on* ∼, dōmeihigyō (sutoraiki) suru. ∼**r** *n.* dōmeihi-
gyōsha. ∼**ing** *a.* ichijirushii.
string [striŋ] *v.* **strung, stringing** himo nado de shibaru. *n.*
ito ; himo. ∼**y** *a.* ito no ; himo no.
stringency [stríndʒ(ə)nsi] *n.* seppaku ; genkaku.
stringent [stríndʒənt] *a.* genjūna ; yakamashii.
strip [strip] *v.* hagu ; muku ; hadaka ni suru ; kimono o nugu.
n. (ribon no yōni) hosonagai kire.
stripe [straip] *n.* shima ; suji. *v.* suji o tsukeru.   ⌐koro).
stripling [strípliŋ] *n.* wakamono (shōnen kara otona ni naru
strive [straiv] *v.* **strove, striven; striving.** hagemu ; kisou.
striven [strivn] *v. see* : **strive.**
strode [stroud] *v. see* : **stride.**

stroke [strouk] *n.* hitouchi; hitotsuki; hitokogi. *v.* naderu; hida o nobasu. ⌐*take a* ∼, sampo suru.

stroll [stroul] *n.* bura-bura aruki; sampo. *v.* bura-bura aruku.

strong [strɔŋ] *a.* tsuyoi; jōbuna. ∼ **room,** (*Brit.*) kichōhin-shitsu. ∼**hold** [⊥hould] *n.* yōsai. ∼**ly** *ad.* kyōretsuni; tsuyoku.

strop [strɔp] *n.* kawato (*strap*). *v.* kawato de togu.

strove *v.* [strouv] *see* : **strive.**

struck [strʌk] *v. see* : **strike.**

structural [strʌ́ktʃərəl] *a.* kōzō no; soshikijō no.

structure [strʌ́ktʃə] *n.* kōzō; tsukurikata; soshiki.

struggle [strʌ́gl] *n.* mogaki; doryoku; tōsō. *v.* mogaku; fun-tō suru; kutō suru. ∼ *for existence,* seis(z)on kyōsō.

strung [strʌŋ] *v. see* : **string.**

strut [strʌt] *n.* kidoriaruki. (*archi.*) shichū. *v.* kidotte aruku.

strychnine [striknin] *n.* (*chem.*) sutorikiniine.

stub [stʌb] *n.* kirikabu; kabu. *v.* kabu o horinuku; nekogi ni suru. ∼**ly** *a.* zunguri shita.

stubble [stʌ́bl] *n.* karikabu; mijikaku kitta kami.

stubborn [stʌ́bən] *a.* gankona; gōjōna.

stucco [stʌ́kou] *n.* shikkui. *v.* shikkui o nuru.

stuck [stʌk] *v. see* : **stick.** ∼-**up** [⊥ʌp] *a.* tsun to shita.

stud [stʌd] *n.* taneuma; byō. *v.* kazarikugi o utsu. ∼**horse** [-hɔ:s] *n.* taneuma.

student [stjú:dənt] *n.* gakusei.

studied [stʌ́did] *a.* (**study** no *pp.*) koi no; takuranda.

studio [stjú:diou] *n.* shigotoba; shashinkan; sutajio.

studious [stjú:djəs] *a.* gakumonzukina; benkyō suru.

study [stʌ́di] *n.* benkyō; gakumon. shosai. *v.* manabu; kenkyū suru; chōsa suru.

stuff [stʌf] *n.* zairyō; buppin. *v.* tsumeru; fusagu.

stuffy [stʌ́fi] *a.* kazatōshi no warui. (*Am.*) fukuretsura shita.

stultify [stʌ́ltifai] *v.* bakarashiku miseru; muimi ni suru.

stumble [stʌ́mbl] *v.* tsumazuku (-aseru); futo dekuwasu. *n.* tsumazuki; kashitsu. ∼**bling block** [stʌ́mbliŋ blɔk] jama-mono; shōgai(-butsu).

stump [stʌmp] *n.* kirikabu; tsukaifurushi. *v.* kirikabu o shi-matsu suru. ∼**orator** (*Am.*) senkyo enzetsusha.

stun [stʌn] *v.* kizetsu saseru; tsumbo ni suru. ∼**ner** [stʌ́nə] *n.*

sutekina mono; sutekina bijin. ~ning [stániŋ] a. kizetsu sa-
stung [stʌŋ] v. *see*: **sting**. ⌊seru; subarashii.
stunk [stʌŋk] v. *see*: **stink**.
stunt [stʌnt] v. ijikesaseru; soshi suru; hanarewaza o suru. n.
stupefaction [stju:pifǽk∫(ə)n] n. mahi; konsui. ⌊myōgi.
stupefy [stjú:pifai] v. mahi saseru; chikaku o ushinawaseru.
stupendous [stju(:)péndəs] a. tohō mo nai; kyodaina.
stupid [stjú:pid] a. bakana; tsumaranu. ~ity [stju(:)píditi] n.
stupor [stjú:pə] n. jinjifusei; mahi; konsui. ⌊gudon; manuke.
sturdy [stə́:di] a. tsuyoi; ganjōna.
stutter [stʌ́tə] v. domoru. n. domori.
sty [stai] n. butagoya; (*med.*) monomorai.
style [stail] n. fū; yōshiki; sutairu. v. shōsuru; nazukeru. ~
book [⌐buk] n. sutairu bukku. ~ish [⌐i∫] a. ikina. ~ist n.
buntaika. ~ize [⌐aiz] v. *style* ni dōchō suru.
stylus [stáiləs] n. (chikuonki-yō no) hari.
styptic [stíptik] a. shukketsu o tomeru. n. chidomegusuri.
suasion [swéiʒən] n. settoku; kankoku.
suave [sweiv] a. nyūwana; onwana.
suavity [swéiviti] n. nyūwa; teinei.
sub [sʌb] n. hojūin. sensuikan.
sub- [sʌb], *prefix*. shita no; hojo no. ("*c, f, g, p, r*" no mae
dewa, "*suc, suf, sup, sur*" to nari; "*m*" no mae dewa, "*sum,
sub*"; "*s*" no mae dewa, "*sus, sub*" no dochira ka nimo
naru: *submarine*). ⌊kuryō.
subaltern [sʌ́bəltən] a. kakyū no; buka no. n. shitayaku; zo-
subconscious [sʌbkón∫əs] n., a. senzaiishiki (no).
subdivide [sʌ́bdiváid] v. kowake suru; saibun suru.
subdivision [sʌ́bdivíʒən] n. kowake; saibunrui.
subdue [səbdjú:] v. seifuku suru; yawarageru.
subject [səbdʒékt] v. shitagawaseru; ukeru. a. [sʌ́bdʒikt] zoku suru. n. shimmin; daimoku. ~ion [sʌbdʒék∫ən] n. seifuku; fukujū. ~ive [sʌbdʒéktiv] a. shukantekina; (*gram.*)
subjoin [sʌbdʒóin] v. soeru; tsuika suru. ⌊shukaku no.
subjugate [sʌ́bdʒugeit] v. seifuku suru; shizumeru.
subjugation [sʌ̀bdʒugéi∫ən] n. seifuku; chin'atsu.
subjunctive [səbdʒʌ́ŋktiv] n., a. (*gram.*) kateihō (no).

sublimate [sʌ́blimeit] v. junka suru. a. [-mit] junka shita. n. junka (butsu).

sublimation [sʌ̀bliméiʃən] n. (chem.) junka; shōka.

sublime [səbláim] a. sūkōna; yūdaina.

sublimity [səblímiti] n. sūkō; yūdai.

sublunary [sebljú:nəri] a. gekka no; kono yo no.

submarine [sʌ́bməri:n] a. kaichū no. n. sensuikan. ～ **cable,** kaiteidensen. ～ **mine,** fusetsusuirai.

submerge [səbmə́:dʒ] v. sensui suru; shizumu.

submergence [səbmə́:dʒəns] n. chimbotsu.

submerse [səbmə́:s] v. sensui suru (submerge).

submersion [səbmə́:ʃən] n. chimbotsu; shinsui.

submission [səbmíʃ(ə)n] n. kōfuku; fukujū; teishutsu.

submissive [səbmísiv] a. jūjunna; kuppuku suru [suru.

submit [səbmít] v. fukujū saseru (suru); makaseru; teishutsu

suborder [sʌ́bɔ:də] n. (biol.) amoku (class o waketa mono).

subordinate [səbɔ́:dinit] a. shita no; jūzoku suru. n. kakyū no hito. v. [səbɔ́:dineit] shita ni oku.

subordination [səbɔ̀:dinéiʃən] n. shita ni aru koto; jūzoku.

suborn [səbɔ́:n] v. gishō saseru; kyōsa suru; itsuwari no shō-mei o saseru. [suru.

subpoena [səbpí:nə] n. (leg.) shōkanjō; yobidashijō. v. shōkan

subscribe [sʌbskráib] v. shomei (kimei) suru; yoyaku suru; ōbo suru. ～r [-ə] n. kimeisha; kifusha; ōbosha.

subscription [səbskrípʃən] n. kimei; mōshikomi; yoyaku; ki-

subsequence [sʌ́bsikwəns] n. tsugi ni okoru koto. [fukin.

subsequent [sʌ́bsikwənt] a. tsugi no; sono ato no.

subserve [səbsə́:v] v. no yaku ni tatsu.

subservience [səbsə́:viəns] n. jūjun; zettai fukujū.

subservient [səbsə́:vjənt] a. jūjunna; zettai jūjun no.

subside [səbsáid] v. shizumu; ochikomu. ～**nce** [sʌbsídəns] n. chinka; kambotsu.

subsidiary [səbsídiəri] n., a. joshu (no); hojo (no).

subsidize [sʌ́bsidaiz] v. hojokin o kafu suru.

subsidy [sʌ́bsidi] n. hojokin.

subsist [səbsíst] v. sonzoku suru.

subsistence [səbsístəns] n. sonzoku; seikatsu; kurashi.

subsoil [sʌ́bsɔil] *n.* kasōdo ; sokotsuchi.

substance [sʌ́bstəns] *n.* hontai ; busshitsu ; honshitsu ; zaisan. *man of* ～, shisanka. ⌈ryō.

substantial [səbstǽnʃəl] *a.* jōbuna ; jisshitsutekina. *n.* (*pl.*) yō-
substantiate [səbstǽnʃieit] *v.* shōkodateru.

substantive [sʌ́bstəntiv] *a.* jitsuzai no. *n.* (*gram.*) jitsumeishi.

substitute [sʌ́bstitjuːt] *n.* dairisha ; daiyōbutsu. *v.* kaeru ; ka-
substitution [sʌ̀bstitjúːʃ(ə)n] *n.* daiyō ; kōkan. ⌊waru.

subterfuge [sʌ́btəfjuːdʒ] *n.* iinuke ; nigekōjō.

subterranean [sʌ̀btəréinjən] *a.* chika no.

subtitle [sʌ́btaitl] *a.* fukudai ; (eiga) (setsumei yō no) jimaku.

subtle [sʌ́tl] *a.* binkanna ; bimyōna ; kasukana. *a* ～ *odo*(*u*)*r of perfume,* kasukani niou ii kaori. ～**ly** *ad.* ～**ty** *n.* eibin ; bimyō.

subtract [səbtrǽkt] *v.* hiku ; genzuru. *10 subtracted 5 is 5.* 10 — 5＝5 (jū(10) hiku go(5) wa go(5)).

subtraction [səbtrǽkʃ(ə)n] *n.* kōjo ; hikizan ; gempō.

subtropical [sʌ́btrɔ́pikəl] *a.* a-nettai no ; nettai no tsugi no.

suburb [sʌ́bəːb] *n.* kōgai ; shigai. *in the* ～*s,* kōgai ni.

suburban [səbə́ːbən] *a.* kōgai no ; shigai no.

subvention [səbvénʃ(ə)n] *n.* (seifu no) hojokin.

subversion [səbvə́ːʃ(ə)n] *n.* tempuku ; hakai.

subversive [səbvə́ːsiv] *a.* tempuku suru ; hakaitekina.

subvert [səbvə́ːt] *v.* horobosu ; tempuku suru ; hakai suru.

subway [sʌ́bwei] *n.* chikadō ; (*Am.*) chikatetsudō (*underground railway*).

succeed [səksíːd] *v.* sōzoku suru ; seikō suru.

success [səksés] *n.* seikō ; seikōsha. ～**ful** *a.* seikō shita. ～**ion** [səkséʃ(ə)n] *n.* sōzoku ; keishō. ～**ive** [-iv] *a.* tsuzuku. ～**ively** *ad.* tsuzuite. ～**or** [-ə] *n.* sōzokusha ; atotsugi.

succinct [səksíŋkt] *a.* kanketsuna.

succo(u)r [sʌ́kə] *n.* kyūjo ; enjo. *v.* kyūen suru.

succulence [sʌ́kjuləns] *n.* takusan no shiru (eki).

succulent [sʌ́kjulənt] *a.* shiru (eki) no ōi (*juicy*) ; kyōmi no ōi.

succumb [səkʌ́m] *v.* makeru. *he* ～*ed to temptation,* kare wa yū-waku ni maketa.

such [sʌtʃ] *a.* kayōna ; sonna. *n.* kayōna hito. ～ *and* ～, kore kore no. ～ *as...,* no yōna. *and* ～, nado.

suck [sʌk] *v.* suu; shaburu. *n.* suu koto. **～er** *n.* suu hito; suite. **～le** [sʌkl] *v.* chichi o nomaseru; sodateru. **～ling** [sʌklij] *n.* chinomigo; aonisai.

sucrose [sjú:krous] *n.* kibisatō *(cane sugar)*.

suction [sʌ́kʃən] *n.* suikomi. **～ pump,** suiage pompu.

sudden [sʌ́dn] *a.* totsuzen no. *all of a* **～,** *on a (or the)* **～,** totsuzen. **～ly** *ad.* totsuzen.

suds [sʌdz] *(pl.) n.* (awadatta) sekkensui.

sue [su:] *v.* uttaeru; negau; kyūkon suru.

suede [sweid] *n.* suēdo-gawa (yagi no kawa).

suet [sú:it] *n.* ushi ya hitsuji no shibō (abura).

Suez Canal [su:éz kənǽl] *n.* Suezu Unga.

suffer [sʌ́fə] *v.* (gai o) ukeru; kōmuru; taeru; kurushimu. **～ from,** ...ni kakatte iru. **～able** [sʌ́f(ə)rəbl] *a.* taerareru. **～ance** [sʌ́f(ə)rəns] *n.* mokunin; nin'yō; kutsujū. **～er** *n.* risaisha; higaisha. **～ing** [-riŋ] *n.* kutsū; saigai.

suffice [səfáis] *v.* tariru; manzoku sareru.

sufficiency [səfíʃ(ə)nsi] *n.* jūbun; manzoku.

sufficient [səfíʃ(ə)nt] *a.* jūbunna; omou tōri no. **～ly** *ad.* jūbunni.

suffix [sʌ́fiks] *n.* setsubigo (*-able, -ment* nado no yōna).

suffocate [sʌ́fəkeit] *v.* chissoku saseru (suru).

suffocation [sʌfəkéiʃən] *n.* chissoku.

suffrage [sʌ́fridʒ] *n.* tōhyō; senkyoken. **woman ～,** fujinsan-seiken. **～tte** [sʌ̀frədʒét] *n.* (fujin) sanseikenronsha (ja).

suffragist [sʌ́frədʒist] *n.* (fujin) sanseiken kakuchōronsha (ja).

suffuse [səfjú:z] *v.* mitasu; afureru.

suffusion [səfjú:ʒ(ə)n] *n.* jūjitsu; biman; afureru koto.

sugar [ʃúgə] *n.* satō. *v.* satō o ireru. **～ cane,** satōkibi. **～-loaf** [-louf] *n.* bōsatō. **maple ～,** kaedesatō. **～-plum** *n.* bon-bon. **～ tongs,** kakuzatō-hasami. **～y** [-ri] *a.* satō no yōna; amai.

suggest [sədʒést] *v.* anji suru; teigi suru. **～ion** [-ʃ(ə)n] *n.* anji; teigen. **～ive** [-stiv] *a.* anji suru.

suicidal [sùisáidəl] *a.* jisatsu no. **～ policy,** jimetsuteki seisaku.

suicide [súisaid] *n.* jisatsu (-sha). *commit ～,* jisatsu suru.

suit [su:t] *n.* soshō; kyūkon. *v.* tekigō saseru. *...ni tekisuru.* **～able** *a.* tekitōna; sōtōna. **～ability** [-əbíliti] *n.* tekitō; tekihi. **～or** [sjú:tə] *n.* kisosha; kongansha; kyūkonsha.

suite [swi:t] *n.* hitokumi ; hitosoroi ; zui(kō)in.
sulfanilamide, sulpha- [sʌlfəníləmaid] *n.* (*chem.*) zurufon'a-sulfate [sʌlfit] *n.* (*chem.*) ryūsan'en. ⌊midozai.
sulfide [sʌlfaid] *n.* (*chem.*) ryūkabutsu.
sulfite [sʌlfait] *n.* (*chem.*) aryūsan'en.
sulfur, sulphur [sʌlfə] *n.* (*chem.*) iō.
sulfuret [sʌlfjuret] *n.* (*chem.*) ryūkabutsu. ⌈san.
sulfuric [səlfjúrik] *a.* (*chem.*) iō no ; iō o fukumu. ~ *acid*, ryū
sulfurous [sʌlfərəs] *a.* (*chem.*) iō o fukumu ; gekiretsuna.
sulk [sʌlk] *n.* (*pl.*) fukurettsura. *v.* suneru. ~**y** *a.* suneta.
sullen [sʌlən] *a.* buaisōna ; inkina.
sully [sʌli] *v.* yogosu ; kegasu (meiyo, hinsei nado o). ⌈ma.
sultan [sʌltən] *n.* Kaikyō no kunshu. *the S*~, Toruko no ōsa-
sultana [səltú:nə] *n.* Toruko no okisaki ; Kaikyō kunshu no
sultry [sʌltri] *a.* mushiatsui ; atsukurushii. ⌊haha.
sum [sʌm] *n.* sōkei ; kingaku. *v.* gōkei suru. *a large* (*small*) ~ *of*, ta (shō)gaku no. *in* ~, yōyaku sureba.
sumac(h) [ʃú:mæk] *n.* (*bot.*) urushi, haze no rui.
summarily [sʌmərili] *ad.* yōten wa ; tsuzumete ieba.
summarize [sʌməraiz] *v.* tekiyō suru ; yōyaku suru.
summary [sʌməri] *a.* yōten o ageru ; ryakushiki no. *n.* tekiyō.
summer [sʌmə] *n.* natsu. *v.* natsu o sugosu. ~ **time,** (*Brit.*) natsujikan. ~**house** [-haus] *n.* azumaya.
summit [sʌmit] *n.* chōjō ; kyokuten.
summon [sʌmən] *v.* shōkan suru. ~ *up*, furui okosu. *n.* (*pt.* **-s ; -ses**) shōkan(jō) ;yobidashi.
sumpter [sʌmptə] *n.* niuma ; ni o hakobu uma.
sumptuary [sʌmptʃuəri] *a.* hiyō setsugen no.
sumptuous [sʌmptʃuəs] *a.* zeitakuna ; hadena.
sun [sʌn] *n.* taiyō. *v.* hi ni sarasu. ~**beam** [-bi:m] *n.* nikkō. ~**burn** [-bə:n] *n.* hiyake. ~**burnt** [-bə:nt] *a.* hi ni yaketa. ~**down** [-daun] *n.* nichibotsu. ~**flower** [-flauə] *n.* himawari. ~**light** [-lait] *n.* nikkō. ~**lit** [-lit] *a.* hi ni terasareta. ~**rise** [-raiz] *n.* hinode. ~**set** [-set] *n.* nichibotsu. ~**shade** [-ʃeid] *n.* hiyoke. ~**shine** [-ʃain] *n.* nikkō. ~**spot** [-spɔt] *n.* taiyō no kokuten. ~**stroke** [-strouk] *n* .nisshabyō. ~**up** [-ʌp] *n.* hi-node.

sundae [sʌ́ndi / -dei] *n.* (*Am.*) sandē (aisukuriimu ni tsubu-shita kajitsu, satō nado o kaketa mono).

Sunday [sʌ́ndi] *n.* Nichiyōbi. ～ *best* (*or clothes*), haregi.

sundries [sʌ́ndriz] *n.* (*pl.*) zakka.

sundry [sʌ́ndri] *a.* iroiro no ; zattana. *all and* ～, kakujin mina.

sung [sʌŋ] *v. see* : **sing**.

sunk [sʌŋk] *v. see* : **sink**.

sunken [sʌ́ŋkn] *v. see* : *sink. a.* shizunda : *a* ～ *ship*, shizunda fune.

sunny [sʌ́ni] *a.* hiatari no yoi ; kaikatsuna.

sup [sʌp] *v.* suu ; yūshoku o kuu. *n.* hitosui ; hitosusuri. ～ *out*, soto de yūshoku o taberu.

superannuate [sjupərǽnjueit] *v.* rōkyūsha to shite taishoku saseru.

superb [sju:pə́:b] *a.* rippana ; migotona.

supercharge [sjú:pətʃɑ:dʒ] *v.* assakukūki o okuru.

supercilious [sjù:pəsíljəs] *a.* ōheina ; gōmanna. ～ly *ad.* ōhei-ni. ～**ness** *n.* gōman.

superdreadnought [sjù:pədrédnə:t] *n.* (*navy*) chō-dokyūkan.

superficial [sjù:pəfíʃ(ə)l] *a.* hyōmen no ; hisō no. ～ly *ad.* hyō-mentekini.

superfluity [sjù:(:)pəflú:iti] *n.* yobun ; muda no aru koto.

superfluous [sju(:)pə́:fluəs] *a.* yokeina ; mudana.

superhuman [sjù:pəhjú:m(ə)n] *a.* ningen ijō no ; chōjinteki no.

superimpose [sjú:pərimpóuz] *v.* ue ni noseru ; kuwaeru.

superintend [sjù:pəinténd] *v.* kanri suru ; kantoku suru.

superintendence [sjù:pərinténd(ə)ns] *n.* kantoku.

superintendent [sjù:pərinténd(ə)nt] *n.* kantokusha. ⌐pai.

superior [sju:píəriə] *a.* sugureta ; ue no chii no. *n.* jōkan ; sem-

superiority [sju(:)pìəriɔ́riti] *n.* yūetsu ; yūshū. ⌐jōkyū.

superlative [sju:pə́:lətiv] *a.* saijō no ; saikō no. *n.* (*gram.*) sai-

supernal [sju:pə́:n(ə)l] *a.* ue ni aru ; kami no kuni no.

supernatural [sju:pənǽtʃərəl] *a.* chō-shizen no.

supernumerary [sjù:pənjú:m(ə)rəri] *a.* teiingai no ; yokeina. *n.* teiingai no hito ; rinjiyatoi. ⌐kaku.

superscribe [sjú:pəskráib] *v.* uwagaki, atena, hyōdai nado o

superscription [sjù:pəskríp∫(ə)n] *n.* uwagaki ; hyōdai.

supersede [sju:pəsí:d] *v.* (totte) kawaru ; kōtetsu suru.

supersensitive [sjù:pəsénsitiv] *a.* byōtekini binkanna.

supersonic [sjú:pəsóunik] *a*. chō-onsoku (ningen no mimi de kikiuru ijō no ompa) no.

superstition [sjù:pəstíʃ(ə)n] *n*. meishin.

superstitious [sjù:pəstíʃəs] *a*. meishin no.

superstructure [sjú:pəstrʌktʃə] *n*. jōbu-kōzō.

supervene [sjù:pəví:n] *v*. fuzui shite okoru.

supervise [sjú:pəvaiz] *v*. kanri suru ; kantoku suru.

supervision [sju:pəvíʒ(ə)n] *n*. kantoku ; kanri.

supine [sju:páin] *a*. aomuke ni neta ; taidana.

supper [sʌ́pə] *n*. yūshoku. **Lord's ∼**, Shu no Bansan. **the Last ∼**, Saigo no Bansan.

supplant [səplǽnt] *v*. totte kawaru ; (chii nado o) ubaitoru.

supple [sʌ́pl] *a*. shinayakana ; jūjunna. *v*. otonashiku naru (suru).

supplement [sʌ́pləmənt] *n*. tsuika ; hosoku. *v*. [-ment] oginau. **∼al**, **∼ary** *a*. tsuika no ; hosoku no.

suppliant [sʌ́pliənt] *a*. tangan suru. *n*. tangansha.

supplicate [sʌ́plikeit] *v*. tangan suru ; (kami ni) inoru.

supplication [sʌ̀plikéiʃ(ə)n] *n*. tangan ; kigan.

supply [səplái] *n*., *v*. kyōkyū (suru) ; (*pl*.) ryōshoku ; kuni no hiyō. **∼ and demand**, kyōkyū to juyō.

support [səpɔ́:t] *n*. shiji ; enjo. *v*. sasaeru. **∼able** *a*. sasaerareru.

suppose [səpóuz] *v*. sōzō suru ; suisoku suru.

supposition [sʌ̀pəzíʃən] *n*. suisoku ; katei.

suppress [səprés] *v*. shizumeru ; kinshi suru. **∼ible** *a*. yoku-atsu dekiru. **∼ion** [səpréʃən] *n*. chintei ; yokusei.

suppurate [sʌ́pjureit] *v*. kanō suru ; nō ga tamaru.

suppuration [sʌ̀pjuréiʃ(ə)n] *n*. kanō.

supremacy [sjupréməsi] *n*. saijōi ; shuken (*ruling power*).

supreme [sju:prí:m] *a*. saijōi no. **∼ Court** *n*. Saikō Saibansho. *the ∼ Being n*. kami.

surcharge [sə́:tʃɑ:dʒ] *n*. tsumisugi. *v*. [sə:tʃɑ́:dʒ] nimotsu o ⌐tsumisugiru.

surcingle [sə́:siŋgl] *n*. (uma no) ueharaobi.

sure [ʃuə] *a*. tashikana. *be ∼ to*, kitto…suru. **∼ly** *ad*. tashikani. **∼ty** [ʃúəti] *n*. hoshōnin ; tampo. *of a ∼*, tashikani.

surf [sə:f] *n*. uchiyoseru nami ; isonami.

surface [sə́:ʃis] *n*. hyōmen ; uwabe. *a*. hyōmen no. *v*. hyōmen o tsukuru. ～ **tensin,** hyōmen chōryoku.

surfeit [sə́:fit] *n., v.* nomisugi(ru) ; tabesugi(ru).

surge [sə:dʒ] *n.* ōnami ; uneri. *v.* namiutsu ; oshiyoseru.

surgeon [sə́:dʒən] *n.* geka no isha ; gun'i.

surgery [sə́:dʒəri] *n.* geka ; shujutsu ; gekaiin.

surgical [sə́:dʒikəl] *a.* geka no.

surly [sə́:li] *a.* buaisōna ; kimuzukashii ; ōheina.

surmise [sə:máiz] *n.* suisoku. *v.* [sə:máiz] suisoku suru.

surmount [sə:máunt] *v.* uchikatsu. ～**able** *a.* uchikachiuru.

surname [sə́:neim] *n.* myōji ; sei.

surpass [sə(:)pá:s] *v.* sugureru. ～**ing** *a.* sugureta.

surplice [sə́:plis] *n.* (bōsan no) shiroi koromo (*gown*).

surplus [sə́:pləs] *n., a.* yobun (no) ; amari (no).

surprise [səpráiz] *n.* kishū ; odoroki. *v.* fuini osou ; odokasu. *be taken by* ～, fui o utareru.

surrender [səréndə] *v.* hikiwatasu ; kōsan suru. *n.* kōfuku.

surreptitious [sɔ́rəptíʃəs] *a.* ushirogurai. ～**ly** *ad.* nainaini.

surrogate [sə́:rəgit] *n.* dairinin.

surround [səráund] *v.* torikakomu. ～**ings** *n.* (*pl.*) kankyō.

surveillance [sə:véiləns] *n.* kanshi ; kantoku.

survey [sə́:vei] *n.* miwatashi ; kansatsu ; sokutei. *v.* [sə(:)véi] miwatasu ; kansatsu (sokuryō) suru.

survival [sə(:)váivəl] *n.* seis(z)on ; zanson ; nokotte iru koto.

survive [sə(:)váiv] *v.* ikinokoru ; ikinobiru.

survivor [sə:váivə] *n.* seis(z)onsha ; izoku.

susceptibility [səsèptəbíliti] *n.* binkan ; binkanshō.

susceptible [səséptibl] *a.* kanjiyasui ; …o ukeyasui.

suspect [səspékt] *v.* kanzuku ; utagau ; ayashimu. *n.* [sáspekt] yōgisha. *a.* utagawashii.

suspend [səspénd] *v.* chū ni burasagaru ; chūshi suru ; miawaseru. ～**ers** *n.* (*pl.*) zubontsuri.

suspense [səspéns] *n.* chūshi ; teishi ; ayafuya.

suspension [səspénʃ(ə)n] *n.* mitei ; chūshi ; teishi. ～**bridge** *n.* tsuribashi.

suspicion [səspíʃən] *n.* utagai ; kengi.

suspicious [səspíʃəs] *a.* ayashii ; utagawashii. ～**ly** *ad.*

sustain [səstéin] *v.* sasaeru ; fuyō suru ; ukeru. ～**ed efforts,** fudan no doryoku. ～**ing** *a.* nagaku motsu.

sustenance [sʌ́stinəns] *n.* shiji ; fuyō ; seikei.

sutler [sʌ́tlə] *n.* shuho no shōnin.

suture [sjúːtʃə] *n.* nuiawase ; awaseme. *v.* nuiawaseru.

suzerain [sjúːzərin] *n.* daimyō ; sono ryōchi. **∼ty** [sjùːzəríniti] *n.* daimyō no sōshuken.

swab [swəb] *n.* bōzōkin. *v.* sōji suru.　　　　　⌐maku.

swaddle [swɔ́dl] *v.* (akambō o nuno de) tsutsumu ; nuno de

swagger [swǽgə] *v.* ibatte aruku ; nosabaru.　　⌐wakamono.

swain [swein] *n.* (furui *or* shitekina iikata) koibito ; inaka no

swallow [swɔ́lou] *n.* (*bird*) tsubame ; hitonomi. *v.* nomikomu. **∼tailed** *a.* embijō no. **∼tailed coat,** embifuku.

swam [swæm] *v.* see : **swim.**

swamp [swɔmp] *n.* numachi. *v.* mizubitashi ni suru. **∼y** *a.* numachi no.

swan [swɔn] *n.* hakuchō. **∼song,** hakuchō no uta ; saigo no sakuhin.

swap [swɔp] *n., v.* (*col.*) butsubutsu kōkan (o suru).

sward [swɔːd] *n.* shibafu.

sware [swɛə] *v.* see : **swear.** (*arch.*)　　　　　　⌐garu.

swarm [swɔːm] *n.* hachi no mure (bumpō suru *bees*). *v.* mura-

swarthy [swɔ́ːθi] *a.* kurozunda ; iro no kuroi.

swash [swɔʃ] *n.* basha-basha. *v.* mizu o haneru.

swastika [swɔ́stikə] *n.* manjidomoe ; kagijūji.

swat [swɔt] *v., n.* pishari to utsu (koto).

swath [swɔːθ] *n.* ichiretsu no karikusa ; sono haba.

swathe [sweiŏ] *v.* hōtai. *v.* shibaru ; maku.

sway [swei] *v.* yureru. *n.* dōyō ; eikyōryoku ; shihai. *the tree* ∼*s in the wind,* ano ki ga kaze ni yureru.

swear [swɛə] *v.* **swore** *or* (*arch.*) **sware, sworn; swearing.** chikau, nonoshiru. *n.* noroi ; akkō zōgon.

sweat [swet] *n.* ase. *v.* **sweated** *or* (*Am.*) **sweat; sweating.** ase ga deru ; ase o nagasu. **∼er** *n.* shokkō o kokitsukau hito ;

Swede [swiːd] *n.* Swēdenjin.　　　　　　⌐sētā. **∼y** *a.* asejimita.

Swedish [swíːdiʃ] *n., a.* Swēden (no) ; Swēdengo (no).

sweep [swiːp] *v.* **swept; sweeping.** hōki de haku ; kosutte tōru. *n.* sōji ; miwatashi ; han'i. *the* ∼ *of the wind,* tsuyoi kaze no nagare. *the mountain is beyond the* ∼ *of one's eye,* sono yama wa mitōshi ga kikanai tokoro da. ～ing *a.* attōtekina. ～stakes [⌐steiks] *n.* (*sing.* & *pl.*) kakekin; kakeru mono.

sweet [swiːt] *a.* amai; yasashii. *n.* amai mono; amai kashi. ～bread [⌐bred] *n.* (koushi, kohitsuji no) suizō. ～heart [⌐hɑːt] *n.* koibito. ～ish [⌐iʃ] *a.* yaya amai. ～meat [⌐miːt] *n.* (*pl.*) amagashi. ～en [swíːtn] *v.* amaku suru (naru); kambashiku suru (naru); yasashiku suru. ～ pea, suwiitopii. ～ potato, satsumaimo.

swell [swel] *v.* **swelled** *or* **swollen; swelling.** fukureru; kasa ga masu. *n.* zōdai; tsuyomari. *a.* ichiryū no. ～dom [-dəm] *n.* ryūkōshakai. ～ing *n.* bōchō; haremono.

swelter [swéltə] *n.*, *v.* atsukurushisa (ni kurushimu).

swept [swept] *v. see*: **sweep.**

swerve [swəːv] *v.* soreru; soresaseru; yugamu. *n.* yugami; hizumi.

swift [swift] *a.* hayai. *n.* (*bird*) amatsubame no tagui.

swill [swil] *v.* arainagasu; gabu-gabu nomu. *n.* gabunomi; daidokoro no nokorimono.

swim [swim] *v.* **swam** *or* **swum; swimming.** oyogu. *n.* oyogi. ～mer *n.* oyogu hito. ～ming *n.* suiei. ～mingly *ad.* sura-sura to. ～raku.

swindle [swíndl] *n.* sagi; sagishi. *v.* kataritoru; sagi o hata

swine [swain] *n.* (*sing., pl.*) buta. ～herd [⌐həːd] *n.* butakai.

swing [swiŋ] *v.* **swung** *or* (*rare*) **swang, swung; swinging.** (furiko ga) furu; (doa no *hinge* ga) yawarakani ugoku. *n.* buranko. ～ *the bat,* batto o furu. *in full* ～, omou yōni furumau; massaichū de.

swinish [swáiniʃ] *a.* buta no yōna. ～ly *ad.* buta no yōni.

swirl [swəːl] *n.*, *v.* uzu (maku).

swish [swiʃ] *n.* (muchi nado no oto) hyup-hyup.

Swiss [swis] *a.* Suwisu no. *n.* Suwisujin (*Switzerland*).

switch [switʃ] *n.* shinayakana muchi; (*railway*) tentetsuki. (*electr.*) suwitchi. *v.* muchi utsu; furu. ～ *off,* kesu (dentō nado o). ～back [⌐bæk] *n.* (tetsudō no) tenkōsen. ～board [⌐bɔːd] *n.* (denshin, denwa no) kōkanki; haidemban. ～man [⌐mən] *n.* tentetsushu.

swivel [swívl] *n.* jizaijikuuke. ～ **chair,** kaiten'isu.

swollen [swóulən] *v. see*: **swell.** *a.* hareta; fukureta.

swoon [swu:n] *n.*, *v.* kizetsu (suru) ; sottō (suru).

swoop [swu:p] *v.* (tori ga emono o megakete) osoikakaru. *n.* shūgeki.

sword [sɔ:d] *n.* ken. ~**fish** [⌐fiʃ] *n.* (*fish*) mekajiki. ~**play** [⌐plei] *n.* kenjutsu. ~**sman** [⌐zmən] *n.* kenjutsu-tsukai ; ken-
swore [swɔ:] *v. see* : **swear.** ⌊kyaku.

sworn [swɔ:n] *v. see* : **swear.** *a.* chikatta.

swum [swʌm] *v. see* : **swim.**

swung [swʌŋ] *v. see* : **swing.**

sybarite [síbərait] *n.* zeitaku o konomu hito.

sycamore [síkəmɔ:] *n.* (*bot.*) kaede (*maple*) no isshu.

sycophancy [síkəfənsi] *n.* hetsurai ; obekka ; gokigentori.

sycophant [síkəfənt] *n.* obekkamono.

syllabary [síləberi] *n.* onsetsujihyō.

syllabic [siláebik] *a.* onsetsu no. ~**ation** [silàebikéiʃ(ə)n], **syl-labification** [silàebifikéiʃ(ə)n] *n.* onsetsu kubunhō.

syllabify [siláebifai] *v.* onsetsu ni wakeru.

syllable [síləbl] *n.* onsetsu.

syllabus [síləbəs] *n.* (*pl.* **-es ; -bi** [bai]) tekiyō ; jikanhyo.

syllogism [sílədʒizəm] *n.* (*log.*) sandanrompō.

sylph [silf] *n.* kūki no sei ; utsukushii fujin.

sylvan [sílvən] *a.* mori no. *n.* mori no sei.

symbol [símbəl] *n.* shirushi ; shōchō. ~**ical** [simbólik(ə)l] *a.* kigō no ; shōchō no. ~**ism** [-izəm] *n.* shōchōshugi. ~**ize** [-aiz] *v.* shōchō suru.

symmetrical [simétrikəl] *a.* kinsei no toreta ; taishō no.

symmetry [símitri] *n.* tsuriai ; kinsei.

sympathetic [sìmpəθétik] *a.* dōjō no aru ; kyōmei suru.

sympathize [símpəθaiz] *v.* dōjō suru ; omoiyaru.

sympathy [símpəθi] *n.* dōjō ; kyōmei ; dōkan.

symphony [símfəni] *n.* (*mus.*) waon ; kōkyōgaku.

symposium [simpóuziəm] *n.* (*pl.* **-sia**) tōronkai.

symptom [símptəm] *n.* chōkō ; kizashi. ~**atic** [sìmptəmáetik] *a.* chōkō no ; kizashi no.

synagogue [sínəgəg] *n.* Yudayajin no atsumari ; kaidō.

synchronism [síŋkrənizm] *n.* dōjihassei ; nempyō ; (*elect.*) dōki.

synchronize [síŋkrənaiz] *v.* dōji ni okoru ; (tokei o) awaseru.

syncopation [siŋkəpéiʃən] *n.* (*mus.*) shinkopeishon; setsubun-hō; (*philol.*) go no chūkan no monji (on) no shōryaku.

syncope [síŋkəpi] *n.* (*med.*) kashi; (*gram.*) go-tanshiku.

syndicalism [síndikəlizm] *n.* kakumeiteki rōdōkumiaishugi; sandikarizumu. ⌐shū hikiuke dantai.

syndicate [síndikit] *n.* kigyō-rengō; shinjikeito; kōshasai bo-

synod [sínəd] *n.* (*rel.*) shūkyōkaigi.

synonym [sínənim] *n.* dōgigo. ～ous [-əs] *a.* dōgi no.

synopsis [sinópsis] *n.* (*pl.* -ses [-siz]) gaiyō; tekiyō.

synoptic(al) [sinóptik(l)] *a.* tekiyō no; taii no.

syntactic(al) [sintǽktik(l)] *a.* (*gram.*) bunshōron no; bunshō

syntax [síntæks] *n.* (*gram.*) bunshō kōseihō. ⌐kōseihō no.

synthesis [sínθisis] *n.* (*pl.* -ses [si:z]) sōgō; kumiawase; (*chem.*)

synthetic(al) [sinθétik(l)] *a.* sōgōteki no; gōsei no. ⌐gōsei.

syphilis [sífəlis] *n.* (*med.*) baidoku.

Syrian [síriən] *a.* kodai (gendai) Shiria no. *n.* Shiriajin.

syringe [sírindʒ] *n.* (*med.*) chūshaki. *v.* chūsha suru; senjō suru.

syrup [sírəp] *n.* shirop; tōmitsu.

system [sístem] *n.* kumitate; soshiki; keitō; seido. ～atic [sìstəmǽtik] *a.* soshikiteki no; keitōteki no. ～actically *ad.* soshikitekini. ～atise, ～atize [sístəmətaiz] *v.* soshiki o tateru; keitōtekini suru. ～atic [sìstəmǽtik] *a.* keitō no; soshiki no; karada no.

T

T, t [ti:] *n.* (*pl.* T's, Ts [ti:z]) Eigo *alphabet* no dai-20-bamme
t. [ti:] *to a* T, seikakuni ; pittari to.   ⌊no moji.
tab [tæb] *n.* (bōshi no) mimi ōi ; tare. (*col.*) kanjō : *keep* ~*s on*,
    ...no kanjō o suru.
tabby [tǽbi] *n.* tabii-ori (*a kind of weave*). (mesu) neko.
tabernacle [tǽb(ə)nəkl] *n.* kariya ; temmaku ; reihaidō.
table [téibl] *n.* teiburu ; shokutaku. *turn the* ~*s*, keisei o ippen
    suru. *v.* takujō ni oku. ~**cloth** [˗klə:θ] *n.* teiburukake. ~**land**
    [˗lænd] *n.* kōgen. ~**spoon** [˗spu:n] *n.* shokutakuyō ōsaji.
tableau [tǽblou] *n.* (*pl.* -leaux, -s) katsujinga.
table d'hote [tá(:)bl dóut] *n.* (*Fr.*) teishoku.
tablet [tǽblit] *n.* genkōyōshi no issatsu : gaku : chiisai fuda ;
    hyōsatsu ; gan'yaku.
tabloid [tǽbləid] *n.* jōzai ; taburoido-ban insatsu.
taboo [təbú:] *n.* itte wa (shite wa) naranu kotoba (koto). *v.* kin-
    sei suru. *a.* kinsei no.
tabular [tǽbjulə] *a.* heiban no ; hiratai.
tabulate [tǽbjuleit] *v.* tairani suru.
tacit [tǽsit] *a.* mugon no. ~**ly** *ad.* ammoku ni.
taciturn [tǽsitə:n] *a.* mukuchi no. ~**ity** [tæsitə́:niti] *n.* mukuchi.
tack [tæk] *n.* hirabyō. (fune no) shinro. seisaku. *v.* byō de to-
    meru ; tsuketasu : *He* ~*ed a postcript to the end of his letter*, kare
    wa tegami no oshimai ni *P.S.* o tsuketashita.
tackle [tǽkl] *n.* dōgu ; kassha ; (*football*) takkuru. *v.* torikumu ;
    sesseto hajimeru.
tacky [tǽki] *a.* neba-neba suru. (*Am.*) misuborashii.
tact [tækt] *n.* kiten ; kotsu ; (*music*) hyōshi. ~**ful** *a.* kiten no
    kiku ; shuwan no aru.
tactical [tǽktikəl] *a.* senjutsu no ; kakehiki no umai.
tactician [tæktíʃən] *n.* senjutsuka ; sakushi.
tactics [tǽktiks] *n.* senjutsu ; kakehiki.
tactile [tǽktail] a. shokkaku no : (furete) kanjirareru.
tadpole [tǽdpoul] *n.* (*zoo.*) otamajakushi.

tael [téil] *n.* ryō (Chūgoku no kahei no tan'i).

taffeta [tǽfitə] *n.* kohakuori.

taffy [tǽfi] *n.* (*Am.*) satō to batā de tsukutta isshu no kashi (*toffee*). otsuishō (*flattery*). [⌐ɔ] *n.* onigokko no oni.

tag [tæg] *n.* tareta fuda; nifuda. onigokko. *v.* tsukeru. ~**ger**

tail [teil] *n.* shippo; hashi. *v.* shippo o tsukeru; tsuite iku. ~**light** [⌐lait] *n.* (densha; jidōsha no) bitō.

tailor [téilə] *n.* shitateya. *v.* shitateru. ~**bird** [⌐bɔːd] *n.* (*bird*) hanuidori. ~**made** [⌐méid] *a.* shitateyasei no.

taint [teint] *v.* yogosu; kegareru. *n.* yogore; daraku; byōdoku.

take [teik] *v.* **took, taken; taking.** toru; tsurete iku. ~ *after*, niru. ~ *for*, to omou; to machigaeru. ~ *in*, toriireru; damasu. ~ *off*, torisaru; ririku suru (hikōki). ~ *on*, hikiukeru; futi o suru. ~ *to*, ni iku; ni natsuku. ~ *up*, toriageru. ~**off** [⌐ɔf] *n.* mane; ririku chiten. ~**up** [⌐ʌp] *n.* itoshimedōgu.

taken [téikn] *v. see:* **take.**

talc [tælk] *n.* (*min.*) ummo (*mica*); kasseki.

tale [teil] *n.* hanashi; monogatari; uso: *tell* ~*s*, tsugeguch.suru. ~**bearer** [-béərə] *n.* tsugeguchiya.

talent [tǽlənt] *n.* sainō; giryō. ~**ed** [-id] *a.* sainō aru.

talisman [tǽlismən] *n.* omamori.

talk [tɔːk] *v.* kataru; hanasu. *n.* hanashi; uwasa. ~**ative** [⌐ətiv] *a.* hanashizukina; oshaberi no.

talkie [tɔ́ːki] *n.* hassei eiga; tōkii.

tall [tɔːl] *a.* sei no takai.

tallow [tǽlou] *n.* kemono no shibō (abura).

tally [tǽli] *n.* (moji no nai tokoro de oboe no tame ni kirikata o tsuketa) ki no bō; warifu. kanjō (*account*). *v.* kirikata o tsukeru.

talon [tǽlən] *n.* (mōkin no) tsume.

tamarack [tǽməræk] *n.* (*Am.*) (*bot.*) karamatsu.

tamarind [tǽmərind] *n.* (*bot.*) tamarindo.

tambour [tǽmbuə] *n.* taiko; shishū no waku.

tambourine [tæ̀mbərí:n] *n.* te-daiko; tambūrin.

tame [teim] *a.* nareta; otonashii. *v.* narasu.

tamp [tæmp] *v.* (nendo nado de) fusagu.

tamper [tǽmpə] *v.* iranu tedashi o suru. ~ *with*, baishū suru.

tan [tæn] *v.* (kawa o) namesu; hiyake saseru. *n.* hiyake shita iro.

tanager [tǽnədʒə] *n.* (*bird*) fūkinchō (America san no kotori)

tandem [tǽndəm] *n.* (uma nitō ga tate ni narande hiku) basha

tang [tæŋ] *n.* sasu yōna aji (nioi).

tangent [tǽndʒənt] *n.* (*math.*) sessen ; seisetsu ; tanjento.

tangential [tændʒénʃəl] *a.* seisetsu no. ～**ly** *ad.* sessen ni natte.

tangible [tǽndʒibl] *a.* furete wakaru ; fureuru. ～**bly** *ad.* akirakani. ⌈ta ; karanda.

tangle [tǽŋgl] *v.* motsuresasu. *n.* gotagota ～**gly** *a.* motsure-

tango [tǽŋgou] *n.* tango (*dance*).

tank [tæŋk] *n.* chosuichi ; mizutame ; sensha.

tankard [tǽŋkəd] *n.* (ōkii) koppu.

tanner [tǽnə] *n.* kawanameshinin. ～**y** *n.* nameshigawakōjō.

tannic [tǽnik] *a.* tannin no. ～ **acid** [-ǽsid] *n.* tanninsan.

tannin [tǽnin] *n.* tanninsan ; kawashibu.

tantalize [tǽntəlaiz] *v.* jirashite kurushimeru ; misebirakasu.

tantalum [tǽntələm] *n.* tantaru (haiiro no kinzokugenso).

tantamount [tǽntəmaunt] *a.* dōtō no.

tantrum [tǽntrəm] *n.* kanshaku : *go into one's*～, mutto suru.

tap [tæp] *n.* nomikuchi ; sen. *v.* nomikuchi o akeru.

tape [teip] *n.* tēpu ; himo. ～ **measure**, makijaku. ～**worm** [-wə:m] *n.* sanadamushi. ⌈hosoku suru (naru).

taper [téipə] *n.* chiisana rōsoku. *a.* saki no hosoi. *v.* dan-dan ni

tapestry [tǽpistri] *n.* tsuzureori ; tobari.

tapir [téipə] *n.* (*zoo.*) baku.

tapster [tǽpstə] *n.* sakaba no kyūjinin.

tar [ta:] *n.*, *v.* tāru (o nuru).

tarantula [tərǽntʃulə] *n.* fukurogumo (kumo no isshu).

tardy [tá:di] *a.* okureru ; noroi. ～**dily** *ad.* noro-noro to. ～**diness** *n.* kamman.

tare [tɛə] *n.* (*bot.*) yahazuendō. fūtai (nimotsu no).

target [tá:git] *n.* mato ; hyōteki.

tariff [tǽrif] *n.* kanzei ; kanzeihyō.

tarn [ta:n] *n.* yamanaka no chiisana mizuumi.

tarnal [tá:nəl], **tarnation** [tə:néiʃən] *a.*, *ad.* (*Am.*) (*sl.*) imaimashii ; berabōna (ni). *You tarnal thief!* imaimashii dorobō me! *Why are you in such a tarnation hurry?* nan datte kimi sō berabō-ni isogun dai?

tarnish [táːniʃ] *v.* kumoru (-aseru) ; sabiru (-raseru).
tarpaulin [taːpóːlin] *n.* bōsuifu ; bōsuibō.
tarpon [táːpɔn] *n.* (*fish*) nishin no isshu.
tarry [tǽri] *v.* taizai (nagai) suru.
tarry [taːri] *a.* tāru no ; tāru o nutta.
tarsus [táːsəs] *n.* (*pl.* **-si** [-sai]) fukotsu (kurubushi no hone).
tart [taːt] *a.* suppai. *n.* kudamonoiri no pai.
tartan [táːtən] *n.* kōshijima no rasha.
Tartar [táːtə] *n.* Dattanjin ; te ni oenu rambōmono. *a.* Dattan no. **~ious** [taːtéəriəs] *a.* Dattanjin no.
tartaric [taːskǽrik] *a.* shuseki no. **~** *acid*, shusekisan.
task [taːsk/tǽsk] *n.* kagyō ; shigoto. *take* (*or call*) *to* **~**, shikaritsukeru. *v.* shigoto o saseru. **~master** [‑máːstə] *n.* oyakata. **~work** [‑wəːk] *n.* ukeoi shigoto.
Tass [tæs] *n.* Soren no kokuei dempō tsūshinsha.
tassel [tǽsl] *n.* fusa.
taste [teist] *v.* ajiwau ; aji o miru. *n.* aji ; shumi. **~ful** [‑fəl] *a.* shumi no fukai. **~less** *a.* aji no nai.
tasty [téisti] *a.* fūmi (shumi) no aru.
ta-ta [táːtáː] *inter.* aba yo !, haichai !
tatter [tǽtə] *n.* boro. **~ed** *a.* boroboro no.
tatterdemalion [tætədiméiljən] *n.* boro o kita yatsu.
tatting [tǽtiŋ] *n.* tatchingu (isshu no rēsu-ami).
tattle [tǽtl] *n.* mudaguchi. *v.* oshaberi o suru. **~r** *n.* mudaguchi o tataku hito.
tattoo [tætúː] *n.* horimono. *v.* irezumi o suru.
taught [tɔːt] *v.* *see* : **teach.**
taunt [tɔːnt] *n.* nonoshiri. *v.* nonoshiru.
taut [tɔːt] *a.* harikitta ; genkakuna.
tautology [tɔːtɔ́lədʒi] *n.* onaji koto o kurikaesu koto.
tavern [tǽvən] *n.* izakaya.
taw [tɔː] *n.* ohajiki.
tawdry [tɔ́ːdri] *a.* kebakebashii ; akudoi.
tawny [tɔ́ːni] *a.* ōkasshoku (kiiro to kasshoku) no.
tax [tæks] *n.* zei. *v.* kazei suru. **~able** [‑əbl] *a.* kazei dekiru. **~ation** [tækséij(ə)n] *v.* kazei. **~-free** [‑friː] *a.* menzei no. **~payer** [‑peiə] *n.* nōzeisha.

taxi [tǽksi] *n.* **taxicab** no ryaku; takushii. *v.* takushii de iku. ～**cab** [tǽksikæb] *n.* takushii. ～**man** *n.* takushii untenshu.

taxidermy [tǽksidəːmi] *n.* hakuseijutsu. ～**mal**, ～**mic** *a.* hakusei no. ～**mist** *n.* hakuseisha.

taximeter [tǽksimìːtə] *n.* takushii no ryōkin-mētā.

taxonomy [tæksɔ́nəmi] *n.* bunruigaku.

tea [tiː] *n.* cha. ～**caddy** [-kǽdi] *n.* chazutsu. ～**cup** [˘kʌp] *n.* chawan. ～**kettle** [-kétl] *n.* chagama. ～ **party**, ocha no kai. ～**pot** [˘pɔt] *n.* kyūsu. ～**spoon** [˘spuːn] *n.* chasaji. ～-**things** [-θiŋz] *n.* (*pl.*) chadōgu.

teach [tiːtʃ] *v.* **taught; teaching.** oshieru; shikomu. ～**er** *n.* kyōshi. ～**ing** *n.* kyōju. (*pl.*) kyōkun; oshie.

teak [tiːk] *n.* (*bot.*) chiiku; chiikuzai. ⌈*n.* kyōdōsagyō.

team [tiːm] *n.* kumi. *v.* chiimu (tiimu) ni naru. ～**work** [˘wəːk]

tear [tiə] *n.* namida. ～ **shell** *n.* sairuidan. ～**drop** [˘drɔp] *n.* namida no shizuku. ～**ful** *a.* namidagunda. ～**less** *a.* namida no nai.

tear [tɛə] *v.* **tore, torn; tearing.** saku; sakeru; yaburu. *n.* kagizaki. ～**ing** [-riŋ]*a.* kurushii. ⌈*n.* ijimeru koto (hito).

tease [tíːz] *v.* suku (yōmō, asa nado o); kushikezuru. ijimeru.

teasel, teazel [tíːzl] *n.* kebadate kikai.

teat [tiːt] *n.* chichikubi; chibusa.

technic, technique [téknik] *n.* (*pl.*) semmongo; gijutsu.

technical [téknikəl] *a.* kōgei no; semmon no. ～**ity** [tèknikǽliti] *n.* semmontekina koto.

technician [tekníʃən] *n.* semmonka; gijutsuka.

technique [tekníːk] *n.* gikō; gijutsu =**technics**.

technocracy [teknɔ́krəsi] *n.* gijutsu shugi.

technological [tèknəlɔ́dʒikəl] *a.* kōgei no.

technology [teknɔ́lədʒi] *n.* kōgeigaku. ～**ist** *n.* kōgeika.

tedious [tíːdiəs] *a.* taikutsuna.

tedium [tíːdiəm] *n.* taikutsu; kentai.

teem [tiːm] *v.* ko (*child*) o umu (*bear*); jūman suru (*to be full*).

teens [tiːnz] *n.* (*pl.*) jūdai; 13 (jūsan) sai kara 19 (jūkyū) sai made no hito.

teeter [tíːtə] *v.* (*Am.*) **seesaw** zengo ni ugoku.

teeth [tiːθ] *n.*, *pl. of* **tooth.**

teethe [tiːð] *v.* ha ga haeru (*come out*).

teetotal [tiːtóutəl] *a.* zettaikinshu no. ～**ism** *n.* zettaikinshu shugi. ～**ler** *n.* zettaikinshusha.

tegument [tégjumənt] *n.* kawa.

telecast [téləkɑːst / -æ-] *n.*, *v.* (*Am.*) terevijon-hōsō (o suru).

telegram [téləgrəm] *n.* denshin; dempō.

telegraph [téləgræf] *n.* denshinki. *v.* dempō o utsu. ～**er** *n.* denshingishi. ～**ic** [tèləgrǽfik] *a.* denshin no; dempō no. ～**ist** [təlégræfist] *n.* denshingishi. ～**y** [-lég-] *n.* denshin.

telemark [téləmɑːk] *n.* (sukii no) teremāku.

telepathy [təlépəθi] *n.* seishinkannō.

telephone [téləfoun] *n.* denwa. *v.* denwa o kakeru.

telephonic [tèləfɔ́nik] *a.* denwa no.

telephony [təléfəni] *n.* denwajutsu. ～**ist** *n.* denwagishu.

telephoto [tèləfóutə] *a.* densōshashin no. ⌐shashinjutsu.

telephotograph [tèləfóutəgræf] *n.* densōshashin. ～**y** *n.* bōen-

telescope [téləskoup] *n.* bōenkyō. *v.* hamarikomu; hamekomu.

telescopic [tèləskópik] *a.* bōenkyō no; tōku ga mieru.

teleview [téləvjuː] *v.* (*Am.*) terebijonhōsō o miru.

televise [téləvaiz] *v.* terebijon de okuru.

television [téləvíʒən] *n.* terebijon.

tell [tel] *v.* told; telling. hanasu; shiraseru; iu. ～**er** [télə] *n.* hanashite; kinsensuitōgakari. ～**ing** *a.* kikime no aru. ～**tales**

telpher [télfə] *n.* denkisakudōsha   └[-teil] *see* : **tale.**

temblor [temblɔ́ə] *n.* (*Am.*) jishin.

temerity [təmériti] *n.* muteppō.

temper [témpə] *v.* kitaeru; hodoyoku suru. *n.* kibun; fukigen : *In her* ～ *she brake her vase,* fukigen de kabin o kowashita. *keep one's* ～, kigen yoku shite iru. *lose one's* ～, hara o tateru.

tempera [témpərə] *n.* temperaga.

temperament [témp(ə)rəmənt] *n.* kishitsu; kishō.

temperance [témp(ə)rəns] *n.* sessei; kinshu.

temperate [témp(ə)rit] *a.* hikaeme no; sessei suru.

temperature [témp(ə)rətʃə] *n.* ondo; atatakasa; taion.

tempest [témpest] *n.* ōarashi; ōkaze.

tempestuous [tempéstʃuəs] *a.* bōfūu no.

temple [témpl] *n.* shinden; jiin; otera.

tempo [témpou] *n.* (*It.*) tempo (sokudo).

temporal [témpərəl] *a.* kono yo no ; ukiyo no.

temporary [témpərəri] *a.* ichijitekina ; kari no.

temporize [témpəraiz] *v.* umaku dakyō suru.

tempt [tempt] *v.* yūwaku suru ; kokoromiru. ~**er** *n.* yūwaku-sha. *the Tempter*, akuma.

temptation [temptéiʃən] *n.* yūwaku ; kokoromi.

ten [ten] *n., a.* jū (10) (no). ~ *to one*, jū chū hakku.

tenable [ténəbl] *a.* sasaeeru ; mamoriuru.

tenacious [tənéiʃəs] *a.* nebarizuyoi ; katai.

tenacity [tənǽsiti] *n.* nebari ; gankyō. ⌈koto.

tenancy [ténənsi] *n.* (tochi no) shoyū kikan ; shakuchinin taru

tenant [ténənt] *n.* chingarinin ; kosakunin. *v.* chingari suru. ~**farmer** *n.* kosakunin. ~**ry** *n.* shakuchinin.

tend [tend] *v.* sewa o suru : *He* ~*s shop for his father*, otōsan no kawari ni mise no sewa o suru. katamuku : ~ *to*, ...suru kei-kō ga aru ; ...no yaku ni tatsu. ~**ency** *n.* keikō.

tender [téndə] *n.* sewanin ; bannin. *v.* omotedatte dasu ; nyū-satsu suru. *a.* yasashii. ~**foot** *n.* shimmai. ~-**hearted** [-hɑ́:tid] *a.* kokoro no yasashii. ~**loin** [-lɔin] *n.* ushi ya buta no koshi no yawarakai niku. ~**ly** *ad.* yasashiku. ~**ness** *n.* jūnan ; ya-

tendon [téndən] *n.* ken (ashi no). ⌊sashisa.

tendril [téndril] *n.* (*bot.*) makihige ; tsuru. ⌈nagaya.

tenement [ténəmənt] *n.* shakuchi ; shakuya. ~ **house,** apāto ;

tenet [ténit / tí:nit] *n.* kyōgi ; shugi (*doctorine*).

tenfold [ténfould] *n., a., ad.* jūbai (no, ni).

tennis [ténis] *n.* teikyū ; tenisu. ~ **court,** tenisu kōto.

tenon [ténən] *n., v.* hozo (o tsukuru).

tenor [ténə] *n.* shui ; taii (*general meaning*) ; (*music*) tenōru (*alto*, *baritone* no aida no koe).

tenpins [ténpinz] *n.* (*pl.*) (*Am.*) jitchū (hashira 10 jippon) asobi.

tense [tens] *n.* toki ; (*gram.*) jisei. *a.* kinchō shita. ~**ly** *ad.*

tensile [ténsail] *a.* hippari uru gendo (*limit of tension*) no ; hip-pari uru : ~ *strength*, hipparu tsuyosa ; kōchōryoku. ~ *stress*,

tension [ténʃən] *n.* kinchō ; harikiri. ⌊kōchōryoku.

tent [tent] *n., v.* temmaku (de ōu) ; tento (o haru).

tentacle [téntəkl] *n.* shokkaku.

tentacular [tentǽkjulə] *a.* shokkaku (shokushu) no.

tentative [téntətiv] *a.* tameshi no; kari no. *n.* tameshi; shiken.

tenth [tenθ] *n.*, *a.* dai-jū (10) (no); jūbun no ichi (no).

tenuity [tenjú:iti] *n.* hosoi koto; usui koto.

tenuous [ténjuəs] *a.* hosoi; usui.

tenure [ténjuə] *n.* hoyū; shakuchi; kigen (*limit of time*).

tepefy [tépifai] *v.* namanuruku (*lukewarm*) suru.

tepid [tépid] *a.* namanurui.

tercentenary [tə:sǽntinəri / tə:səntí:] *a.* (300-nen) sambyakunen no. *n.* sambyakunen-sai.

tergiversation [tə:dʒivəséiʃən] *n.* gomakashi; hensetsu.

term [tə:m] *n.* genkai. gakki. jutsugo. (*pl.*) jōken; aidagara : *bring to* ∼, oriai ga tsuku. *make* ∼ *s*, dakyō suru. *on good* (*bad*) ∼*s*, naka ga ii (warui). *on no* ∼, kesshite. *v.* nazukeru.

termagant [tə́:məgənt] *n.* kuchiyakamashii onna.

terminal [tə́:minəl] *a.* hashi no; gakki no. ∼ *station*, shūchakueki. *n.* hashi; shūten; gakki shiken. ∼**ly** *ad.* sue ni; gakki

terminate [tə́:mineit] *v.* yameru; oeru; owaru. ⌊goto ni.

termination [tə̀:minéiʃən] *n.* mattan; shūketsu; shūten.

terminative [tə́:minətiv] *a.* shūmatsu no.

terminator [tə̀:minéitə] *n.* shūketsu (butsu).

terminology [tə̀:minɔ́lədʒi] *n.* yōgo; jutsugo.

terminus [tə́:minəs] *n.* genkai; shūten.

termite [tə́:mait] *n.* shiroari.

ternary [tə́:nəri] *a.* mittsu no; mikumi no.

terra [térə] *n.* (*L.*) tochi; chikyū. ∼ **cotta** [térəkɔ́tə], akatsuchi-yaki. ∼ **firma**, rikuchi.

terrace [térəs] *n.* daichi; dan; terasu. *v.* dan o kizuku.

terrain [teréin] *n.* chihō; chisei.

terrapin [térəpin] *n.* (*zoo.*) suppon no tagui.

terrene [terí:n] *a.* chikyū no; kono yo no; gense no.

terrestrial [təréstriəl] *a.* chikyū no; chijō no; chijō ni sumu.

terrible [térəbl] *a.* osoroshii; hidoi. ∼**bly** *ad.* osoroshiku; hi-

terrier [tériə] *n.* inu no isshu. ⌊doku.

terrific [tərífik] *a.* osoroshii; monosugoi.

terrify [térifai] *v.* kowagaraseru; odokasu.

territorial [tèritɔ́:riəl] *a.* tochi no; ryōdo no; chihō no.

territory [térit(ə)ri] *n.* tochi ; ryōdo.

terror [térə] *n.* kyōfu ; osoroshii hito. ∼**ism** [-rizəm] *n.* bōsei ; kyōhaku. ∼**ist** [-rist] *n.* kyōfuseiji-shugisha. ∼**ize** *v.* appaku suru. ∼**-stricken,** ∼**-struck** [-strik(ə)n, -strʌk] *a.* kyōfu ni osowareta.

terse [təːs] *a.* kanketsuna. mijikakute surudoi. ∼**ly** *ad.* ∼**ness** *n.*

tertian [táːʃən] *a.* ichinichi oki no. *n.* kakujitsu. ∼ **ague** [-eigju:] *n.* kakujitsu *malaria*.

tertiary [táːʃəri] *a.* dai-san no ; dai-sanki no.

tessellate [tésəleit] *v.* mozaikku ni suru.

test [test] *n.* tameshi ; shiken ; shōko. *v.* shiken suru. ∼ **flight,** *n.* shikenhikō. ∼ **tube,** shikenkan. ∼ **working,** shiunten.

testacean [testéiʃən] *n.* yūkakudōbutsu (kai no tagui).

testaceous [testéiʃəs] *a.* kaigara no.

testament [téstəmənt] *n.* yuigon ; (T∼) seisho. *the New* (*Old*) T∼, Shin-(Kyū-)yaku Seisho. ∼**ary** [tèstəméntəri] *a.* yuigon-testate [tésteit] *a.* yuigonjō o nokoshita.   ⌊sho no.

testator [testéitə] (*fem.* **-trix**) *n.* yuigonjō o kaku hito.

tester [téstə] *n.* shikenkan ; shikenki.

testicle [téstikl] *n.* kōgan.

testify [téstifai] *v.* shōmei suru.

testimonial [testimóuniəl] *n.* shōmeisho ; shōjō.

testimony [téstiməni] *n.* shōgen. (*pl.*) kami no oshie.

testy [tésti] *a.* tankina ; okori-yasui.

tetanus [tétənəs] *n.* (*med.*) hashōfū.

tete-a-tete [téitətéit] *n.* (*Fr.*) mitsudan. *ad.* sashimukai de.

tether [téðə] *n.* tsunagi nawa. *v.* tsunagu.   ⌈kukei.

tetragon [tétrəgɔn] *n.* (*math.*) shikakukei. *a regular* ∼, sei-shika-tetragonal** [tetrǽgənəl] *a.* shikakukei no.

tetrahedral [tètrəhíːdrəl] *a.* shimentai no.

tetrahedron [tètrəhíːdrən] *n.* (*pl.* **-s ; -dra**) shimentai.

tetralogy [tetrǽlədʒi] *n.* (kodai *Gk.* no) yombugeki.

tetrameter [tetrǽmitə] *n.* (*poet.*) shihokaku no shikyaku.

tetter [tétə] *n.* (*med.*) shisshin.   ⌈zoku no. *n.* Chūtongo.

Teuton [tjúːtən] *n.* Chūton-minzoku. ∼**ic** [-tónik] *a.* Chūton-text** [tekst] *n.* hombun ; daimoku. ∼**book** [téks(t)buk] *n.* kyō-textile** [tékstail] *a.* orimono no. ∼ **fabrics,** orimono. ⌊kasho.

textual [tékstʃuəl] *a.* hombun no ; gembun no.

texture [tékstʃə] *n.* orimono no jihada.

than [ðæn] *conj.* yori ; yori mo.

thank [θæŋk] *n.* kansha. *v.* kansha suru. **～ful** *a.* kansha no. **～less** *a.* on o shiranai. **～sgiving** *n.* kansha. *Thanksgiving Day,* Kanshasai. 「...to iu koto o ; o ; to ; hodo.

that *pron.*, *a.* [ðæt] sore ; are ; sono. **～** *is,* sunawachi. *conj.* [ðət]

thatch [θætʃ] *n.* fukikusa. *v.* (wara, kaya nado de) yane o fuku.

thaumaturgy [θɔ́ːmətəːdʒi] *n.* majutsu ; kijutsu. **～ic** [-tɔ́ː-] *a.*

thaw [θɔː] *v.* tokeru ; tokasu. *n.* yukidoke. 「kisekiteki.

the [ðíː, ði, ðə] 1. teikanshi " *the* " wa, iu hito, kiku hito sore to iwanakute mo " dore " o sashite iru ka ga wakaru meishi no mae ni tsukeru : (1) *Once there lived an old man with three goats.* (2) *The old man...* no yōni (2) no baai sugu sono *old man* wa, iu hito, kiku hito ni yoku wakaru. 2. koyūmeishi ga fukusū (*pl.*) no toki. *The Alps.* 3. kawa no namae no mae ni. *the Thames.* 4. taitoru no ichibubun to shite. *the Duke of Wellington.* 5. tansū de sono shuzoku zentai o arawasu toki. *the horse is a domestic animal.* 6. keiyōshi ga meishi no shigoto o suru toki sono mae ni : *visit the sick.* 7. koyūmeishi no mae ni keiyōshi ga tsuku toki wa sono mae ni. *the good Washington helped to make a grand country of freedom,* kono baai, *young, little, old* nado no yōna baai wa tsukenai no ga futsū de aru. 8. meishi o naraberu toki kore o tsuyoku hibikase tai toki. *the color, the fragrance, and the beautiful patterns of the flowers...* nado.

theater, **-tre** [θíːətə] *n.* gekijō ; gemba. **～goer** *n.* shibai no jōren. **～going** *n.* shibai kembutsu.

theatrical [θiǽtrikl] *a.* engeki no. **～s** [-z] *n.* (*pl.*) (tokuni) shirōto shibai ; shibai ni kansuru koto.

thee [ðíː] *pron.* **thou** no mokutekikaku.

theft [θeft] *n.* settō. 「ra no mono.

their [ðɛə] *pron.* (**they** no shoyūkaku) karera no. **～s** *pron.* kare-**theism** [θíːizm] *n.* yūshinron. 「no.

theist [θíːist] *n.* yūshinronsha. **～ic(al)** [θiːistik(l)] *a.* yūshinron

them [ðem] *pron.* karera o ; karera ni. **～selves** [-sélvz] *pron.*

theme [θiːm] *n.* daimoku ; wadai ; ronsetsu. 「karerajishin.

then [ðen] *ad.*, *conj.* sono toki ni ; soko de ; sore kara.

thence [ðens] *ad.* sore kara ; soko kara. **～forth** [-fɔːθ], **～for-**

ward(s) [-fɔ́:wəd(z)] *ad.* sono go. ⌐seiji).

theocracy [θiɔ́krəsi] *n.* kami no dairisha ga suru seiji (shinken

theocratic [θi:əkrǽtik] *a.* shinkenseiji no ; shinsei no.

theodolite [θiɔ́dəlait] *n.* keiigi ; suichoku to heimen to o sokuryō suru kikai.

theology [θi:ɔ́lədʒi] *n.* shingaku. ⁓**ian** *n.* shingakusha. ⁓**ical**

theorem [θíərəm] *n.* hō ; teiri. ⌊[θiəlɔ́dʒikl] *a.* shingaku no.

theoretic(al) [θiərétik(l)] *a.* riron no ; rironjō no.

theoretics [θiərétiks] *n.* riron.

theorist [θíərist] *n.* rironka.

theorize [θíəraiz] *v.* riron o tateru.

theory [θíəri] *n.* riron ; gakuri ; setsu.

theosophic(al) [θi:əsɔ́fik(l)] *a.* sesshin no ; kami ni sesshita.

theosophist [θiɔ́səfist] *n.* sesshingaku zeninsha.

theosophy [θiɔ́səfi] *n.* sesshingaku.

therapeutic [θérəpjú:tik] *a.* chiryō no. ⁓**s** *n.* chiryōhō.

therapy [θérəpi] *n.* chiryō.

there [ðɛə] *ad.* asoko ni ; sora ! are ! ⁓**about(s)** *ad.* sono hen ni. ⁓**after** *ad.* sono go. ⁓**at** *ad.* sore yue ni. ⁓**by** *ad.* sore ni yotte. ⁓**fore** *ad.* sore yue ni. ⁓**from** *ad.* sore kara. ⁓**on** *ad.* sono ue ni. ⁓**upon** *ad.* soko de. ⁓**with** *ad.* sore o motte. ⁓**withal** *ad.* soko de ; sono hokani. ⁓ *is* (*are*), aru, iru.

therm [θə:m] *n.* netsuryō no tan'i. ⁓**al** *a.* netsu no. ⁓**ic** *a.* netsu no. ⌐*n.* netsurikigaku.

thermodynamic [θɔ́:moudainǽmik] *a.* netsurikigaku no. ⁓**s**

thermoelectricity [θɔ̀:mouilektrísiti] *n.* netsudenki.

thermometer [θə:mɔ́mitə] *n.* kandankei ; ken'onki.

thermos [θɔ́:məs] *n.* mahōbin.

thermostat [θɔ́:məstæt] *n.* ondochōsetsuki. ⌐(*book*) ; hōten.

thesaurus [θisɔ́:rəs] *n.* (*pl.* **-ri** [-rai]) takara no kura ; jiten

these [ði:z] *a.*, *pron.* this no *pl.* ⁓ *days*, chikagoro.

thesis [θí:sis] *n.* (*pl.* **-ses** [-si:z]) daimoku ; kadai ; rombun.

thews [θju:z] *n.* (*pl.*) tairyoku ; kinniku no chikara.

they [ðei] *pron.* (**he, she, it** no *pl.*) karera ; sorera.

thick [θik] *a.* atsui ; shigetta. *n.* shigemi. *ad.* atsuku ; koku. ⁓ *and fast*, hageshiku. ⁓**ly** *ad.* ⁓**ness** *n.* atsusa. ⁓**set** *a.* shigetta. ⁓**-skinned** [-́skind] *a.* kawa no atsui. ⁓**-headed** [-́hédid] *a.* noroi. ∼-**witted** [-wítid] *a.* noroi *n.* orokamono.

thicken [θíkən] *v.* atsuku suru (naru); koku suru (naru); shi-
thicket [θíket] *n.* shigemi; kusamura.   ⌊geru (shigeraseru).
thief [θiːf] *n.* nusubito; dorobō.
thieve [θiːv] *v.* nusumu. ∼**ry** *n.* settō.
thievish [θíːviʃ] *a.* tekuse no warui.
thigh [θai] *n.* mata; momo. ∼**bone** *n.* daitai-kotsu.
thill [θil] *n.* kuruma no nagae.
thimble [θímbl] *n.* yubinuki; hamewa.
thin [θin] *a.* usui; hosoi; yaseta. *v.* usuku suru. (-naru) ∼**ly**
ad. ∼**ness** *n.* ∼-**skinned** *a.* kawa no usui.
thine [ðain] *pron.* nanji no mono. 2 (ni)-ninshō tansū, (furui
yōhō). (*cf.* **thou.**)
thing [θiŋ] *n.* mono; koto. (*pl.*) jibutsu; ifuku; dōgu.
think [θiŋk] *v.* thought; thinking. omou; shinzuru. ∼**er** *n.*
shisōka. ∼**ing** *n.* kangae; shisaku.
third [θəːd] *n., a.* daisan (no); sambun no ichi (no). (*Am. col.*)
∼ *degree,* gōmon. ∼ *party,* daisansha. ∼**ly** *ad.* daisan ni.
thirst [θəːst] *n.* kawaki. *v.* nodo ga kawaku. ∼**y** *a.* nodo no
kawaita. ∼**ily** *ad.* nodo ga kawaite.
thirteen [θəːtíːn] *n., a.* jūsan (13) (no).
thirteenth [θəːtíːnθ] *n., a.* dai jūsan (no); jūsambun no ichi (no).
thirtieth [θə́ːtiiθ] *n., a.* daisanjū (no); sanjūbun no ichi (no).
thirty [θə́ːti] *a., n.* sanjū (30) (no).
this [ðis] *pron., a.* kore; kono.
thistle [θisl] *n.* (*bot.*) azami.
thither [ðíðə] *ad.* asoko e; achira e. ∼**wards** [ðíðəwɔːdz] *ad.*
tho [ðou] *conj., ad.* =**though.**   ⌊achira e.
thong [θɔŋ] *n.* kawahimo.
thoracic [θɔːræsik] *a.* mune no; kyōbu no.
thorax [θɔ́ːræks] *n.* (*pl.* -es; -races) kyōkaku; mune.
thorn [θɔːn] *n.* toge; ibara. ∼**y** *a.* toge no aru; konnanna.
thorough [θʌ́rou / -ə] *a.* tetteitekina; jūbunna; mattaku no. ∼-
bred *a.* junsuishu no *n.* junsuishu (uma). ∼**fare** *n.* ōdōri; dōro. ∼**going** [θʌ́rəgòuiŋ] *a.* tettei shita.
those [ðouz] *pron.* that no *pl. a.* sorera (no).
thou [ðau] *pron.* thy, thee, thine nanji; 2 (ni)-ninshō tansū

ima wa *poem* (shi) inori no hoka wa amari mochii nai.

though [ðou] *conj., ad.* de aru keredomo ; ...da ga. *What* ～, ...tomo nanno sono.

thought [θɔ:t] *v. see :* think. *n.* kangae ; iken. ～ful *a.* kangae no fukai. ～less *a.* kangae no nai. ～ **reading** *n.* tokushinjutsu.

thousand [θáuzənd] *n., a.* sen (1000) (no) ; musū (no). ～fold *a.* sembai no. ～th *n., a.* daiissen (no) ; sembun no ichi (no).

thrall [θrɔ:l] *n.* dorei ; sokubaku sarete iru hito. ～dom *n.* dorei no mibun.

thrash [θræʃ] *v.* utsu ; kurikaeshi utsu ; kokumotsu o uchi otosu. ～ *out,* jūbun ronjite kimari o tsukeru. ～ *over,* tabitabi onaji koto o suru. ⌐kireta ; furui.

thread [θred] *n.* ito ; sen'i. *v.* ito o tōsu. ～bare *a.* ito no suri-**threat** [θret] *n.* odokashi ; kyōhaku. ⌐suru.

threaten [θrétn] *v.* odokasu ; kyōhaku suru. ～ing *a.* kyōhaku

three [θri:] *n., a.* san ; mittsu (3) (no). ～bagger *n.* sanruida. (*base.*, *3-base hit*). ～fold *n., a.* sambai (no). ～pence [θrépəns] *n.* san pensu ～penny [θrépəni] *a.* san pensu no. ～score [θri:-skɔ:] *n., a.* rokujū (no) (*three* (*3*) *scores*).

threnody [θrénədi] *n.* banka ; kanashimi no uta.

thresh [θreʃ] *v.* dakkoku suru.

threshold [θréʃould] *n.* shikii ; irikuchi.

threw [θru:] *v. see :* throw.

thrice [θrais] *ad.* (*arch.*) sando.

thrift [θrift] *n.* ken'yaku ; keizai. ～less *a.* ken'yaku shinai. ～y *a.* ken'yaku suru ; han'ei suru.

thrill [θril] *v.* furue saseru ; zotto saseru. *n.* senritsu. ～er *n.* zotto saseru hito (mono). ～ing *a.* zotto suru.

thrive [θraiv] *v.* **throve,** *or* **thrived, thriven** *or* **thrived ; thriv-thriven** [θrívn] *v. see :* thrive. ⌐hanjō suru ; shigeru.

throat [θrout] *n.* inkō ; nodokubi ; shokudō.

throb [θrɔb] *n.* dōki ; kodō. *v.* dōki ga suru.

throe [θrou] *n.* gekitsū ; jintsū. *v.* hidoku kurushimu.

throne [θroun] *n.* ōi (ō no kurai) ; teii (tei no kurai).

throng [θrɔŋ] *n.* gunshū. *v.* gunshū suru ; dōtto atsumaru.

throttle [θrɔ́tl] *n.* (*anat.*) kikan ; nodobue. *v.* kubi o shimeru.

through [θru:] *prep.* ....o tōshite ; hete. *ad.* tōshite ; de. ～ *and* ～, zenzen. *a.* tōshi no. ～**ticket** *n.* tōshikippu. ～**train** *n.* chok-kōressha. ～**out** *prep.* …jū. *ad.* itaru tokoro ni.

throve [θróuv] *v. see :* **thrive.**

throw [θrou] *v.* **threw, thrown; throwing.** nageru. *n.* nage.

thrown [θroun] *v. see :* **throw.** ～*silk,* yoriito ; tsumugiito.

thrum [θrʌm] *v.* tsumabiki suru.

thrush [θrʌʃ] *n.* (*bird*) tsugumi.   ⌐*n.* oshi ; tsuki.

thrust [θrʌst] *v.* **thrust; thrusting.** tsukkomu ; osu ; tsuku.

thud [θʌd] (*onomat.*). dotan ; dosat. *v.* dotan to oto o tateru.

thug [θʌg] *n.* sekkaku (shikaku) ; koroshiya.

thumb [θʌm] *n.* oyayubi. *v.* oyayubi de mekuru. ～*a ride,* aizu shite nosete morau.   ⌐suru.

thump [θʌmp] gotsun ; dosun. *v.* gotsun to utsu ; dōki ga

thunder [θʌ́ndə] *n.* kaminari. *v.* kaminari ga naru ; donaru. ～**bolt** *n.* raiden. ～**clap** *n.* raimei. ～**cloud** *n.* raiun. ～**head** *n.* (*Am.*) sekiun. ～**ing** *a.* raimei suru. ～**ous** *a.* kaminari no yōna. ～**storm** *n.* dairaiu. ～**struck** *v.* dotan to tsubushita.

Thursday [θə́ːzdei] *n.* Mokuyōbi. |～**stricken** *a.* odoroita.

thus [ðʌs] *ad.* kakute. ～*far,* koremade wa. ～*much,* koredake.

thwack [θwæk] *v., n.* (bō nado de) hageshiku utsu (koto).

thwart [θwɔːt] *v.* samatageru ; kujiku. *a.* yoko no. *ad.* yoko-gitte.

thy [ðai] *pron. see :* **thou. thou** no shoyūkaku. ～**self** *pron.* nan-

thyroid [θáirɔid] *n., a.* (*anat.*) kōjōsen (no). |jijishin.

tiara [tiάːrə] *n.* Rōma-Hōō no kammuri.

tick [tik] *n.* dani. *v.* (tokei ga) kachi-kachi iu ; ten o utsu.

ticker [tíkə] *n.* kabushiki sōba hyōjiki.

ticket [tíkit] *n.* kippu ; jōshaken.

tickle [tíkl] *v.* kusuguru ; muzumuzu suru.

ticklish [tíkliʃ] *a.* kusuguttagaru ; okorippoi.

tidal [taidl] *a.* shio no. ～**wave** *n.* tsunami.

tide [táid] *n.* shio ; keikō. *v.* shio ni noseru. ～*over,* shubi yoku kirinukeru. ～**water** *n.* shiomizu. ～**way** *n.* shioji.

tidings [táidiŋz] *n.* (*pl.*) hōkoku ; tayori.

tidy [táidi] *a.* kichin to kireina. *n.* isu no seōi. *v.* kichin to suru.

tie [tai] *n.* musubime. (*pl.*) kizuna ; nekutai. *v.* musubu ; kuku-

tier [tiə] *n.* retsu ; narabi. |ru.

tie-up [táiʌp] *n.* teikei. (*Am. col.*) shokuba hōki ; kōtsu tozetsu.

tiff [tif] *n.* chotto shita kenka ; fukigen. *v.* chotto shita iiai o suru ; fukigen ni naru.

tiffin [tífin] *n.* chūshoku ; bentō. (Indo dewa bentō.)

tiger [táigə] *n.* (*zoo.*) tora. ~**ish** *a.* tora no yōna. ~**lily** *n.* (*bot.*) oniyuri.

tight [tait] *a.* kichin to shita ; katai ; kitsui. *ad.* shikkari to. ~**en** *v.* shimeru ; kataku suru. ~**ly** *ad.* shikkari to.

tights [taits] *n.* (*pl.*) nikujuban (*dancer*, karuwazashi no kiru).

tigress [táigris] *n.* mesu no tora.

tile [tail] *n.* kawara. *v.* kawara de fuku.

till [til] *prep., conj.* made. *n.* ko-hikidashi. *v.* tagayasu. ~**age**, [tílidʒ] *n.* kōsaku. ~**er** *n.* kōsakusha.

tilt [tilt] *v.* yari de tsuku ; tsuku. *n.* tsuki ; keisha (*slant*).

tilth [tilθ] *n.* kōsaku ; tagayasu koto.

timbal [tímbəl] *n.* kamagata-daiko ; *kettledrum* no furui kata-
timber [tímbə] *n.* zaimoku. (*Am.*) mori. ⌊chi.

timbrel [tí:mbrəl] *n.* tedaiko.

time [taim] *n.* toki ; jidai ; gendai ; do ; bai. *at* ~s, tokidoki. *for the* ~ *being*, tōbun. *in no* ~, tadachini. *in* ~, chōdo yoi toki ni. *v.* chōdo ii jiki ni suru. ~**hono(u)red** [⸺ɔ̀nəd] *a.* mukashi kara no. ~**keeper** [⸺kì:pə] *n.* tokei. ~**ly** *a.* yoi ori no. ~**piece** [⸺pì:s] *n.* tokei. ~**r** *n.* jikankirokugakari. ~**server** *n.* hiyorimishugi. ~**serving** [⸺sɔ̀:və] *a.* hiyorimi no. *n.* ~**table** jikanhyō.

timid [tímid] *a.* okubyōna. ~**ity** [timíditi] *n.* okubyō.

timorous [tímərəs] *a.* okubyōna ; ozuozu suru.

timothy [tíməθi] *a.* (*bot.*) ōawagaeri. (*named after Timothy*).

tin [tin] *n.* suzu ; buriki. ~**can**, *n.* (*Am.*) kuchikutei. ~**foil** *n.* suzuhaku. *v.* suzu o kiseru. ~**plate** *n.* buriki. ~**smith** *n.* burikiya. ~**ware** [⸺wɛə] *n.* burikiseihin.

tincture [tíŋktʃə] *n.* iro ; iroai ; chinkizai. *v.* iro o tsukeru ; fū-
tinder [tíndə] *n.* hokuchi. ⌊mi o tsukeru.

tine [tain] *n.* (fōku nado no) togatta saki.

tinge [tindʒ] *n.* aomi, akami nado iroai. *v.* iro o tsukeru ; chotto iro o kami suru.

tingle [tíŋgl] *v.* hiri-hiri itamu ; uzuku ; miminari ga suru.

tinker [tíŋkə] *n.* ikakeya ; hetana shokunin. *v.* ikakeya o suru.

tinkle [tíŋkl] *n.* (*onomat.*) chirin-chirin. *v.* chirin-chirin to naru.
tinned [tind] *a.* suzu o kabuseta.
tinny [tíni] *a.* suzu no yōna.
tinsel [tínsl] *n.* haku. *a., v.* yasupika (no) ; yasupika (de kazaru).
tint [tint] *n.* iroai. **autumnal ～s**, aki no iro ; kōyō. *v.* iro o ⌐tsukeru.
tiny [táini] *a.* chiisai.
tip [tip] *n.* sakippo. *v.* saki o tsukeru ; kokorozuke o yaru. ～ *over*, hikkuri kaesu. ～**off** [típɔf] *n.* naisho no jōhō. *v.* sore o morasu ; keikoku suru (*warn*). ⌐bōsan ga kakeru.
tippet [típit] *n.* kubi kara kata ni kakeru nagai kuroi *scarf* de
tipple [típl] *v.* chibi-chibi nomu. *n.* sake no chibinomi.
tipsy [típsi] *a.* yotta ; chidoriashi no.
tiptoe [típtou] *n.* tsumasaki. *on* ～, tsumasaki de ; kossori (aru- **tiptop** [típtóp] *n.* zetchō. *a.* saijō no. ⌐ku) ; sotto (aruku).
tirade [tiréid] *n.* nagadangi ; nagai batō enzetsu.
tire [táiə] *n.* gomuwa ; taiya. *v.* tsukarasu ; akisaseru. ～**d** *a.* tsukareta ; akita. ～**less** *a.* akinai. ～**some** *a.* taikutsuna.
'tis [tiz] " *it is* " no ryaku.
tissue [tíʃju:] *n.* usuorimono ; soshiki. ～ *paper* usuyōshi.
tit [tit] *n.* karuku utsu koto. ～ *for tat*, urikotoba ni kaikotoba.
Titanic [taitǽnik] *a.* Taitan no yōna. kyodaina ; kyōryokuna.
titbit [títbit] *n.* umaimono.
tithe [taið] *n.* jūbun no ichi ; jūbun no ichi no zeikin. *v. tithe*
titillate [títileit] *v.* kusuguru. ⌐o toritateru.
titillation [titiléiʃən] *n.* kusuguri ; kokoroyoi shigeki.
title [táitl] *n.* hyōdai ; shōgō. *v.* nazukeru. ～**d** *a.* katagaki no aru. ～**deed** *n.* chiken-shōmeisho. ～**page** *n.* hyōdaishi ; to- bira. ～**role** *n.* (shibai no) shuyaku.
titter [títə] *n.* shinobiwarai. *v.* kusukusu warau.
tittle [títl] *n.* gokuwazuka. ～**tattle** [⌐tǽtl] *n.* mudabanashi.
titular [títʃulə] *a.* katagaki dake no.
to [tu:, tə] *prep.* ...e ; ...ni ; ...made. ～ *and back*, ōfuku de. *go* ～ *the right*, migi e iku. *faithful* ～ *the end*, oshimai *made* chūjitsuni. *he came* ～ *the rescue*, kare ga kyūjo *ni* kita. ～ *her horror, the bear approached*, kanojo ga furueagatta *koto ni* wa, sono kuma ga chikazuita. *she tore the letter* ～ *pieces*, kanojo wa sono tegami o zutazuta *ni* yabutta. *we danced* ～ *the music*,

wareware wa ongaku *ni awasete* odotta. *the score was 9 ~ 7,* tokuten wa 9 (kyū) *tai* 7 (shichi) datta. *it is not ~ my liking,* watashi no konomi *ni* ai masen. *the key ~ my room,* watashi no heya *no* (mono de aru) kagi. *drink ~ the king,* ōsama o *shukufuku shite* ippai. *fasten it ~ the wall,* kabe *ni* tsukeru. *What did he say ~ that?* sore *ni tsuite* kare nan to itta? *four apples ~ the pound,* pondo *ni* ringo yottsu. *give the book ~ me,* watashi *ni* sono hon o kudasai.

toad [toud] *n.* hikigaeru. **~eater** [-íːtə] *n.* obekka mono. **~stool** [-stuːl] *n.* kinoko. ⌈**~ish** *a.* obekka no.

toady [tóudi] *n.* obekkamono. *v.* hetsurau. **~ism** *n.* obekka.

toast [toust] *n.* yakipan ; kampai ; tōsuto. *v.* yaku ; kampai suru. **~er** *n.* tōsuta. **~master** [-mɑ̀ːstə] *n.* (enkai no) shikaisha.

tobacco [toubǽkou] *n.* tabako. **~nist** *n.* tabakoya.

toboggan [təbɔ́gən] *n.* isshu no sori (saka nado kudaru toki

tocsin [tɔ́ksin] *n.* keishō ; kiken o shiraseru kane. ⌊tsukau.)

today [tədéi] *n., ad.* konnichi ; gendai.

toddle [tɔ́dl] *n., v.* choko-choko aruku (akambo nado ga).

toddy [tɔ́di] *n.* yashi no shiru de tsukutta sake.

toe [tou] *n.* ashiyubi ; tsumasaki. *v.* ashi o fureru. *on one's ~s,* yōi ga dekite iru. ⌈tsukutta kashi.

toffee [tɔ́fi] **taffy** [tǽfi] *n.* isshu no kashi ; satō, batā nado de

toga [tóugə] *n.* kodai-Rōma no yurui gaitō.

together [təgéðə] *ad.* tomo ni ; awasete.

toil [tɔil] *n.* honeori. *v.* kurō suru. **~ful, ~some** *a.* tsurai.

toilet [tɔ́ilet] *n.* keshō ; benjo. **~ry** *n.* keshōhinrui. **~te,** [twɑ̀ːlét] *n.* (F) keshō.

token [tóukən] *n.* shirushi ; shōko : *as a ~ of,* no shirushi ni.

told [tould] *v. see :* tell. ⌈man no dekiru hodoni.

tolerable [tɔ́lərəbl] *a.* gaman no dekiru ; sōōna. **~bly** *ad.* ga-

tolerance [tɔ́lərəns] *n.* kannin ; kan'yō.

tolerant [tɔ́lərənt] *a.* kandaina.

tolerate [tɔ́ləreit] *v.* kannin suru ; nintai suru.

toleration [tɔ̀ləréiʃən] *n.* kan'yō ; kannin shite yaru koto

toll [toul] *n.* tsūkōzei. *v.* (kane o) narasu.

tom [təm] *n.* osuneko. **~cat** [tɔ́mkæt] *n.* neko no osu.

tomahawk [tɔ́məhɔːk] *n.* masakari. *v.* masakari de kiru (Hoku-

Bei *Indian* no buki).
tomato [təméitou / -máː-] *n.* tomato.
tomb [tuːm] *n.* haka. *v.* hōmuru. **~stone** *n.* bohyō.
tomboy [tómbəl] *n.* otembamusume.
tome [toum] *n.* satsu ; kan (shomotsu).
tommy [tómi] *n.* shokumotsu. *T~ Atkins*, Eikokuhei.
tomorrow [təmórou] *n., ad.* asu ; myōnichi.
ton [tʌn] *n.* ton (jūryō no tan'i).
tone [toun] *n.* chōshi ; onshoku ; kifū. *v.* chōshi o awaseru.
tongs [tɔŋz] *n. (pl.)* hibashi (U-ji o sakasa ni shitayōna katachi).
tongue [tʌŋ] *n.* shita ; kokugo. *hold one's ~*, damaru.
tonic [tónik] *a.* onchō no ; onsei no. *v.* kyōsō ni suru. *n.* shu-
tonight [tənáit] *n., ad.* kon'ya ; komban. [chōon ; kyōsōzai.
tonnage [tʌ́nidʒ] *n.* sekisairyō ; tonsū.
tonsil [tónsil] *n.* hentōsen. **~lectomy** [tɔnsiléktəmi] *n. (med.)* hentōsen jokyoshujutsu. **~litis** [tɔnsiláitis] *n. (med.)* hentō-
tonsorial [tɔnsɔ́ːriəl] *a.* rihatsushi no. [sen'en.
tonsure [tónʃə] *n.* teihatsu (atama no teppen o maruku sotta mono). *v.* atama o soru.
too [tuː] *ad.* amari...sugiru ; mo ; mata.
took [tuk] *see :* **take.**
tool [tuːl] *n.* dōgu ; kōgu. *v.* dōgu de saiku suru.
tooth [tuːθ] *n. (pl.* **teeth** [tiːθ]) ha. *in the ~ of*, nimo kakawa-razu. *~ and nail*, hisshi ni. **~ache** [◡eik] *n.* haitami. **~brush** [◡brʌ] *n.* haburashi. **~ paste** *n.* nerihamigaki. **~ pick** *n.* ko-yōji. **~ powder,** hamigakiko. **~some** [◡sʌm] *a.* umai.
top [tɔp] *n.* koma ; chōjō ; atama. *v.* kamuraseru ; chōjō ni tas-suru. *a.* saikō no. **~ boots** *n.* isshu no nagagutsu. **~coat** [◡kout] *n.* gaitō. **~hat** *n.* reibō. **~ heavy** [◡hévi] *a.* atama no omoi. **~knot** [◡nɔt] *n.* mage. **~mast** *n.* (fune uo) naka hoba-shira. **~most** *a.* saikō no. **~notch** [◡nɔtʃ] *a.* ichiryū no. **~ping** *a.* saikō no. **~sail** [◡seil] *n. top* masuto no ho.
topaz [tóupæz] *n. (min.)* ōgyoku.
toper [tóupə] *n.* nondakure (*drunkard*)
topic [tópik] *n.* wadai. **~al** *a.* wadai no.
topographer [toupógrəfə] *n.* chikeigakusha.
topographical [təpəgrǽfikəi] *a.* chikeigakujō no.

topography [toupógrəfi] *n.* chishi ; chikeigaku.

topple [tópl] *v.* yoromeki taoreru ; nagetaosu : *The wrestler* ～*a his opponent,* sumō ga aite o nagetaoshita. 「ni (na).

topsy-turvy [tópsitə:vi] *ad., a.* abekobe ni (na) ; mechakucha

torch [tɔ:tʃ] *n.* taimatsu. ～**light** taimatsu no akari.

tore [tɔ:] *v. see : tear.* 「ijimeru.

torment [tɔ́:ment] *n.* kutsū ; kashaku. [tə:mént] *v.* nayamasu ;

torn [tɔ:n] *v. see : tear.*

tornado [tɔ:néidou] *n.* hageshii (*violent*) hakairyoku (*destructive*) no aru sempū (*whirl wind*).

torpedo [tɔ:pí:dou] *n.* suirai. shibireei. ～**boat** *n.* suiraitei. ～**tube** *n.* gyoraihasshakan (*from which* ～ *is discharged*).

torpid [tɔ́:pid] *a.* mukankakuna ; nibui. ～**ity** [tɔ:píditi] *n.* nemuri (*dormant*) ; fukappatsu (*sluggish*) na jōtai (*state*).

torpor [tɔ́:pə] *n.* mahi (*benumbedness*) ; mukankaku (*senseless*).

torrent [tɔ́rənt] *n.* honryū. ～**ial** [tɔrénʃəl] *a.* honryū no yōna (*like*).

torrid [tɔ́rid] *a.* ennetsu no ; yaketa (*sunburnt*). ～ *zone,* nettai.

torsion [tɔ́:ʃən] *n.* nejire. ～**al** *a.* nejireta (*twisted*).

tort [tɔ:t] *n.* shihan (*civil wrong*) ; fuhōkōi (*unlawful act*).

tortoise [tɔ́:təs] *n.* (*zoo.*) kame. ～**shell** *n.* bekkō.

tortuous [tɔ́:tʃuəs] *a.* nejireta (*twisted*) ; magarikunetta (*full of twists and turns*).

torture [tɔ́:tʃə] *n.* gōmon ; kutsū. *v.* kurushimeru (*torment*) ; gōmon ni kakeru (*inflict* ～ *on someone*).

Tory [tɔ́:ri] *n.* Ōtōin ; hoshutōin.

toss [tɔ:s] *v.* karuku nageru ; (nami ga fune o) yuru (*pitch a boat*). ～ *off,* wake naku shite shimau. hitokuchi ni nomihosu. *n.* nageageru koto ; hōriageru koto.

toss-up [tɔ́sʌp] *n.* okane o nageagete kimeru.

tot [tɔt] *n.* chibikko ; chiisana sakazuki. gōkei (*total*).

total [tóutəl] *n., a.* subete (no). ～**war** *n.* sōryokusen. ～**ity** [to(u)tǽliti] *n.* zentai. ～**ly** *ad.* kotogotoku. 「taishugi.

totalitarian [toutæ̀litéəriən] *a.* zentaishugiteki. ～**ism** *n.* zen-

tote [tout] *v.* hakobu ; hiku. *n.* hipparu koto ; umpan.

totem [tóutəm] *n.* tōtemu. ～ **pole** *n.* (uchi no mae ni tateru)

totter [tɔ́tə] *v.* yoromeku.   *totem*-bashira.

touch [tʌtʃ] *v.* fureru ; sesshoku suru ; eikyō o motsu (*related* *to*). *n.* tezawari ; shokkaku. ~**ing** *a.* itamashii (*arousing tender feeling*). *prep.* kanshite. ~ **stone,** shikinseki. ~**y** *a.* okorippoi.

tough [tʌf] *a.* katai ; ganjōna. ~**ly** *ad.* ~**ness** *n.*

toughen [tʌfn] *v.* kataku suru.

tour [tuə] *n., v.* man'yū (suru) ; ryokō (suru).

tourist [túərist] *n.* man'yūsha ; kankōkyaku (*sight-seer*).

tournament [túənəmənt] *n.* shiai ; kyōgi (*contest*).

tourney [túəni] *n.* kachinukishiai. *v.* shiai suru.

tourniquet [túənikət] *n.* (*med.*) shiketsuki ; chi o tomeru kikai.

tousle [táuzl] *v.* midasu ; gujaguja ni suru. ~*ed hair*, kushaku-sha no kami.

tout [taut] *v.* hisokani saguru. *n.* kyakuhiki ; jōhōsaguri.

tow [tou] *n.* nawa (tsuna) de hiku koto. *v.* hiku. ~**age** [-idʒ] *n.* hikifuneryō. ~**boat** *n.* hikifune. ~**path** [-pɑθ] *n.* hikifune-michi.

toward(s) [tóuədz] *prep.* no hō e ; chikaku. *a.* chikazuku. ~**s** *prep.* =*towards* (tokuni Igirisu).

towel [táuəl] *n.* taoru. ~**(l)ing** *n.* taoru-ji.

tower [táuə] *n.* tō ; yagura. *v.* sobieru. ~**ing** *a.* takaku sobie-ru.

town [taun] *n.* tokai ; machi. ~ **talk,** machi no uwasa. ~**sfolk** [táunsfouk] *n.* (*pl.*) chōmin. ~**ship** *n.* gunku. (gun o waketa).

toxic [tóksik] *a.* yūdoku no.

toxicology [tòksikólədʒi] *n.* dokubutsugaku.

toxin [tóksin] *n.* dokuso.

toy [tɔi] *n.* omocha. *v.* moteasobu ; omocha ni suru.

trace [treis] *n.* atokata. kawahimo ; kanagusari, nado. *v.* utsu-su ; tadori tsuku. ~**able** *a.* utsusu koto no dekiru.

tracery [tréisəri] *n.* madokazari.

trachea [tréikiə] *n.* kikan (*wind pipe*).

trachoma [trəkóumə] *n.* torahōmu. [*no kami.*

tracing [tréisiŋ] *n.* tōsha ; tsuiseki. ~ *paper n.* tōshashi (tōsha

track [træk] *n.* ashiato ; kuruma no tōtta ato (*mark left by a wheel*). *v.* ato o tsukeru. ~**age** [-idʒ] *n.* rail o tsukau kenri.

tract [trækt] *n.* tochi ; chihō.

tractable [trǽktəbl] *a.* sunaona. ~**bly** *ad.* sunaoni.

tractate [trǽkteit] *n.* chiisai rombun. [(kinzoku ni iu).

tractile [trǽktil] *a.* nagaku nobasu koto no dekiru (seishitsu)

traction [trǽkʃən] *n.* hippari ; ken'in ; ken'insha ; ken'in (hiku) suru chikara.

tractor [trǽktə] *n*. ken'injidōsha ; torəkutā.

trade [treid] *n*. shōgyō; bōeki. ~ **name** *n*. shōhimmei. ~ **school** *n*. jitsugyōgakkō. *v*. shōbai suru; bōeki suru. ~**mark**, [⹂mɑ:k] shōhyō. ~**r** *n*. shōnin. ~**sman** [⹁zmən] *n*. (kouri) shōnin. ~ **union**, rōdōkumiai. ~**wind** *n*. bōekifū. ~**-in** [⹂in] (*Am*.) shiharai (*payment*) to shite yaru mata wa toru mono. ~**people** [-pi:pl] *n*. miseban no shōbainin. to sono kazoku.

trading [tréidiŋ] *a*. akinai suru ; bōeki suru. ~**bank** shōgyōginkō. ~**post** *n*. (mikaichi no) bōekiten. ⌐no.

tradition [trədíʃən] *n*. densetsu ; inshū. ~**al**, ~**ary** *a*. densetsu

traduce [trədjú:s] *v*. chūshō suru. ~**ment** *n*. chūshō.

traffic [trǽfik] *n*. torihiki ; kōtsū. *v*. shōbai (torihiki) suru.

tragedian [trədʒí:diən] *n*. higeki haiyū ; higeki sakka.

tragedienne [trədʒì:dién] *n*. (*Fr*.) higeki-joyū.

tragedy [trǽdʒidi] *n*. higeki ; sanji.

tragic(-al) [trǽdʒikl], *a*. higeki no.

tragicomedy [trǽdʒikómidi] *n*. hikigeki. *The Merchant of Venice is a* ~. M, of V. wa hikigeki da.

trail [treil] *v*. ato o ou ; hikizuru. *n*. ato ; ashiato

trailer [tréilə] *n*. hikizuru hito (mono) ; tsuisekisha (*that follows a trail*).

train [trein] *v*. kunren suru ; keiko suru. *n*. ressha ; gyōretsu. ~**bearer** *n*. susomochi. ~**ed** *a*. narashita. ~**er** *n*. kunrensha.

training [tréiniŋ] *n*. kunren ; shikomi. ~ **college**, shihangakkō. ~**ship** *n*. renshūsen.

trait [trei / treit] *n*. tokushoku.

traitor [tréitə] *n*. hangyakusha. ~**ous** [-rəs] *a*. hangyakuteki.

trajectory [trədʒéktəri] *n*. suisei (*comet*), yūsei (*planet*) nado no kidō.

tram [trǽm] *n*. kidō; senro; tankōnai no 4 (yon)rinsha. *by* ~, densha de. ~**car** *n*. shigaidensha. ~**car stop**, densha teiryūjo. ⌐*v*. sokubaku suru.

trammel [trǽməl] *n*. hokakumō ; (*pl*.) sokubaku ; reigi (jama).

tramp [trǽmp] *v*. ashioto o tatete aruku. *n*. toho-ryokōsha.

trample [trǽmpl] *v*. fumitsukeru. ⌐jōtai.

trance [trǽns] *n*. kōkotsu (*dreamy, hipnostic condition*); konsui-

tranquil [trǽŋkwil] *a.* shizukana. ∼**ly** *ad.*

tranquil(l)ity [trænkwíliti] *n.* shizukesa (*stillness*); ochitsuki (*peacefulness*).

tranquil(l)ize [trǽŋkwilaiz] *v.* shizukani ochitsukaseru. ∼**ation** [trǽŋkwilizéiʃən] *n.* chinsei; shizukani ochitsuite iru koto.

transact [trænsǽkt] *v.* toriatsukau; shori suru. ∼**or** *n.* shorinin. ⌈no) kaihō (*transactions*).

transaction [trænsǽkʃən] *n.* shori; torihiki. (*pl.*) (gakkai nado

transalpine [trænzǽlpain] *a.* Alps o koeta mukō no.

transatlantic [trænzətlǽntik] *a.* Taiseiyō o koeta mukō no.

transcend [trænsénd] *v.* masaru. ∼**ence**, ∼**ency** *n.* yūetsu. ∼**ent** *a.* yūetsu shita. ∼**ental** [trænsendéntəl] *a.* chōetsu shita. ∼**entalism** [-éntəlizəm] *n.* senkenron. ⌈no mukō no.

transcontinental [trænzkəntinéntəl] *a.* tairikuōdan no; tairiku

transcribe [trænskráib] *v.* kakiutsusu; rokuon suru.

transcript [trǽnskript] *n.* utsushi.

transcription [trænskrípʃən] *n.* kakiutsushi; tōsha.

transept [trǽnsept] *n.* kyōkaidō no gaijin; soderō.

transfer [trænsfə́:] *n.* unsō; kakikae. ∼**ink** *n.* tenshayō-inku. **-paper** *n.* tenshashi. ∼**ticket** *n.* norikaekippu. ∼**slip** *n.* furikaedempyō. *v.* utsusu.

transferable [trænsfə́:rəbl] *a.* utsushi uru; jōto shi uru.

transferee [trænsfərí:] *n.* kaitorinin.

transference [trænsfə́rəns] *n.* idō; tensō; jōto.

transferrer [trænsfə́:rə] *n.* hikiwatashinin; jōtonin.

transfiguration [trænsfigjuréiʃən] *n.* henkei; yōsu o kaeru.

transfigure [trænsfí:gə] *v.* katachi o kaeru.

transfix [trænsfíks] *v.* tsukitōsu. ⌈saseru hito.

transform [trænsfɔ́:m] *v.* henkei (henka) saseru. ∼**er** *n.* henka

transformation [trænsfəméiʃən] *n.* henkei; henka. (*elect.*) hen'atsu.

transfuse [trænsfjú:z] *v.* tsugiutsusu (tsugikaeru); yuketsu suru. (*transfuse one's blood into another*).

transfusion [trænsfjú:dʒən] *n.* yuketsu.

transgress [trænsgrés] *v.* somuku; koeru; okasu. ∼**or** *n.* ihan-

transgression [trænsgréʃən] *n.* ihan; hanzai. ⌊sha.

transient [trǽnʒənt / -s-] *a.* ichiji no; hakanai.

transit [trǽnsit] *n.* tsūka ; unsō.

transition [trænzíʃən] *n.* utsurikawari. **~al** [əl] *a.*

transitive [trǽnsitiv] *a.* tadō no. **~** *verb*, (*gram.*) tadōshi.

transitory [trǽnzitə:ri] *a.* shibaraku no ; ichiji tekino.

translate [trænsléit] *v.* hon'yaku suru ; utsusu.

translation [trænsléiʃən] *n.* hon'yaku.

translator [trænsléitə] *n.* hon'yakusha. ⌈su).

translucent [trænslú:snt] *a.* hantōmei no (nakaba hikari o tō-

transmigration [trænsmaigréiʃən] *n.* ijū ; rinne.

transmissible [trænsmísəbl] *a.* okurareru ; tsutaerareru.

transmission [trænsmíʃən] *n.* kaisō ; dentatsu.

transmit [trænsmít] *v.* okuru ; dentatsu suru ; toritsugu. **~ter** *n.* okutte yaru hito.

transmutation [trænsmju:téiʃən] *n.* henkei ; henshitsu.

transmute [trænsmjú:t] *v.* henkei (henshitsu) suru.

transoceanic [trǽnzòuʃiǽnik] *a.* taiyō o koeta mukō no.

transom [trǽnsəm] *n.* (*Am.*) rammamado.

transpacific [trænspəsífik] *a.* Taiheiyō-ōdan no.

transparency [trænspɛ́ərənsi] *n.* tōmei ; sukashie.

transparent [trænspɛ́ərənt] *a.* tōmei no.

transpire [trænspáiə] *v.* jōhatsu suru ; haishutsu suru.

transplant [trænsplǽnt] *v.* uekaeru ; utsusu.

transport [trænspɔ́:t] *v.* yusō suru. [trǽnspə:t] *n.* yusō ; un'yu. **~er** *n.* unsōsha.

transportation [trænspə:téiʃən] *n.* yusō ; un'yu.

transpose [trænspóuz] *v.* okikaeru ; tentō suru.

transposition [trænspəzíʃən] *n.* okikae. (*math.*) ikō.

transship [trænsʃíp] *v.* hoka no fune ni utsuru. **~ment** *n.* tsumikae.

transsonic [trænsónik] *a.* ompa no sokudo ni chikai.

transubstantiate [trænsəbstǽnʃieit] *v.* henshitsu saseru.

transubstantiation [trænsəbstǽnʃiéiʃən] *n.* henshitsu.

transversal [trǽnsvə:sl] *a.* ōdan no. **~** ōdansen.

transverse [trǽnsvə:s] *a.* yoko no. **~ly** *ad.*

trap [træp] *n.* wana ; otoshiana. *v.* wana ni kakeru. **~ door**, ⌊otoshi-do.

trapeze [trəpí:z] *n.* isshu no buranko.

trapezium [trəpí:ziəm] *n.* futōhen-shihenkei.

trapezoid [trǽpizɔid] *n.* teikei ; futōhen-shihenkei.

trappings [trǽpiŋz] *n.* (*pl.*) kazari ; reifuku. ～s *of a king and his court*, kyūtei no hitotachi no seisō.

Trappist [trǽpist] *n.* Torapisuto-kai. *Trappist* no shūdōsha.

trash [trǽʃ] *n.* kuzu ; haibutsu ; mudabanashi. ～y *a.*

trauma [trɔ́:mə] *n.* (*pl.* -s ; -ta [-tə]) gaishō ; sotogawa ; no kizu. ～tic [trɔ:mǽtik] *a.* gaishō no. *n.* gaishō no kusuri.

travail [trǽveil] *n.* honeori. *v.* honeoru.

travel [trǽvl] *v.* ryokō suru. *n.* ryokō. ～(l)er *n.* ryokaku. ～(l)ing *n.* ryokō.

travelog(ue) [trǽvələ:g] *n.* ryokōdan ; kōen ; ryokō eiga.

traverse [trǽvə:s] *v.* yokogiru ; wataru. *n.* ōdan ; jamamono.

travesty [trǽvisti] *n.*, *v.* kokkeika suru.

trawl [trɔ:l] *n.* sokobikiami. *v.* torōruami o hiku. ～er *n.* torōrusen. ～ing *n.* torōru-gyogyō.

tray [trei] *n.* bon. ～ful *n.* bon ippai.

treacherous [trétʃərəs] *a.* hangyaku suru ; uragiru.

treachery [trétʃəri] *n.* hangyaku ; uragiri.

treacle [trí:kl] *n.* tōmitsu.

tread [tred] *v.* fumu ; ayumu ; odoru. *n.* fumiaruki.

treadle [trédl] *n.* fumigi. *v.* funde dōryoku o tsukuru.

treason [trí:zn] *n.* hangyaku.

treasure [tréʒə] *n.* zaihō. *v.* hizō suru. ～trove *n.* mochinushi-fumei no hakkutsu-zaihō.

treasurer [tréʒərə] *n.* kaikeigakari.

treasury [tréʒəri] *n.* hōko ; kinko ; sōko ; zaisei sekininsha (*one who is in charge of money*)

treat [tri:t] *v.* toriatsukau ; taigū suru. *n.* motenashi. **stand** ～ *v.* ogoru. ～ment *n.* toriatsukai ; shochi.

treatise [trí:tis] *n.* rombun ; riron.

treaty [trí:ti] *n.* jōyaku. ～power(s) *n.* teimeikoku ; jōyakkoku.

treble [trébl] *a.* sambai no. *n.* (ongaku de) saikōombu. *v.* sambai ni suru.

tree [tri:] *n.* ki. *up a* ～, shintai kiwamatte.

trefoil [trí:fɔil] *n.* (*bot.*) oranda-genge ; kometsubu umagoyashi.

trellis [trélis] *n.* yotsumegaki ; tana (*grape* nado no).

tremble [trémbl] *n.* furue. *v.* furueru.

tremendous [triméndəs] *a.* osoroshii ; subarashii. ～ly *ad.*

tremor [trémə] *n.* miburui.

tremulous [trémjuləs] *a.* furueru ; osore wananaku.

trench [trentʃ] *v.* mizo o (zangō o) horu. *n.* hori ; mizo.

trenchant [tréntʃənt] *a.* surudoi ; yoku kireru. ~ *wit*, zubari to

trend [trend] *n.* keikō. *v.* katamuku.   ⌊kireru surudoi chie.

trepidation [trepidéiʃən] *n.* furue ; kyōfu ; shinkeishitsu no kyōfu ; osore.

trespass [tréspəs] *n.* shinnyū ; oshiiri. *v.* shinnyū suru ; oshiiru.

tress [tres] *n.* kamige no hitofusa ; makige.

trestle [trésl] *n.* nosedai ; umagata no dai.

tri- [tri-] 3 (mittsu=san) no imi no settōgo.

triad [tráiæd] *n.* mikumi ; (*mus.*) san-waon (do, mi, so ; re, fa, la nado no yōna).

trial [tráiəl] *n.* kokoromi ; shiunten. **public** ~ *n.* kōhan. ~ **run** *n.* (*or trip*) shiunten. ~ **jury** *n.* baishin'in.

triangle [tráiæŋgl] *n.* sankakkei.

triangular [traiǽŋgjulə] *a.* sankakkei no.

tribal [tráibl] *a.* shuzoku no ; buzoku no.

tribe [traib] *n.* shuzoku ; buzoku ; minzoku.

tribulation [tribjuléiʃən] *n.* jūdaina kunan ; hijōna konku.

tribunal [traibjú:nəl] *n.* hōkanseki ; saibansho.

tribune [tríbju:n] *n.* (kodai Rōma no) gominkan ; endan.

tributary [tríbjuteri] *a.* mitsugi o osameru ; jūzoku suru. *n.* mitsugi suru kuni ; zokkoku. (*stream*) shiryū.

tribute [tríbju:t] *n.* mitsugi ; zei.

trice [trais] *v.* tsuriageru. *n.* shunkan. *in a* ~, tachimachi.

triceps [tráiseps] *n.* (*anat.*) santōkin.

trick [trik] *n.* warudakumi ; itazura ; kuse. *v.* azamuku ; meka-su. ~**ery** *n.* gomakashi. ~**y** *a.* zurui. ~**ster** *n.* sagishi ; akutō.

trickle [tríkl] *v.* shitataru (mizu nado ga). *n.* shitatari.

tricolo(u)r [tráikʌlə] *a.* sanshoku no. *n.* sanshokki

tricot [trí(:)kou] *n.* nikujuban ; isshu no uneori no juban.

tricycle [tráisikl] *n.* sanrinjitensha. *see* : **tri-**.

trident [tráidnt] *n.* mitsumata no yasu (uo o tsuku mono).

tried [traid] *a.* kokoromita ; tashikana. *see* : **try**.

triennial [traiéniəl] *a.* sannen tsuzuku ; sannengoto no. *n.* san-nengoto no gyōji. ~**ly** *ad.*

trifle [tráifl] *n.* toru ni tarinai koto. *a* ~, chitto ; isasaka. *v.*

moteasobu; kudaranai koto o suru; rōhi suru.

trifling [tráifliŋ] *a.* wazukana; tsumaranai.

trifoliate [traifóuliit] *a.* mitsuba no aru.

trig [trig] *a.* kogireina; ikina.

trigger [trígə] *n.* (jū ya hō no) hikigane.

trigonometric [trigənəmétrik] ~**al** *a.* (*math.*) sankakuhō no.

trigonometry [trìgənɔ́mitri] *n.* (*math.*) sankakuhō.

trilateral [trailǽtərəl] *a.* sampen no aru. *n.* sankakkei.

trill [tril] *n.* furuegoe. *v.* furuegoe de iu; (utau toki) koe o furuwaseru. **trilogy** [trílədʒi] *n.* sandammono; sambugeki; sambukyoku.

trim [trim] *a.* kogireina. *n.* guai; arisama. *v.* kichinto suru; teire o suru. ~**mer** *n.* seiton suru hito. ~**ming** *n.* kazari; teire. ~**ness** *n.*

Trinitarian [trìnitéəriən] *n.* Sammi-ittaisetsu o shinzuru hito.

trinity [tríniti] *n.* sammi-ittai (*the T*~); sammi-ittaisetsu.

trinket [tríŋkit] *n.* kazarimono; tsumaranai mono.

trio [trí:ou] *n.* sanjūsō; mitsugumi ensō.

trip [trip] *n.* karui ashidori; ensoku (ichinichi gurai no). *v.* karuku aruku; tsumazuku; fumihazusaseru. *catch (a person)* ~**ping**, ageashi o toru. ~**per** [trípə] *n.* tohosha. ~**ping** *n.* karui ashidori.

tripartite [traipá:tait] *a.* sambu ni wakareta; sambu de dekita.

tripe [traip] *n.* ushi no ibukuro.

triple [trípl] *a.* sambai (sambu, sanjū) no. *n.* mitsuzoroi. (*base.*) sanruida. *v.* sambai ni suru (naru). ~ *time n.* (*mus.*) sambyōshi.

triplet [tríplit] *n.* sambukutsui; mitsugumi; sanningumi.

triplicate [tríplikit] *a.* sambai no; mitōri no. *v.* [-keit] 3 (san)-tsū (onaji mono o tsukuru).

tripod [tráipəd] *n.* sankyakudai.

trisect [traisékt] *v.* mittsu ni wakeru.

trisyllable [traisíləbl / tri-] *n.* 3-onsetsu go.

trite [trait] *a.* arifureta; tsukai furushita.

triturate [trítjureit] *v.* kosuru; komakai kona ni suru. *n.* nan demo kosutte kona ni suru mono.

triumph [tráiəmf] *n.* shōri; gaisen. *v.* shōri o eru. ~**al** [traiʌ́mfəl] *a.* gaisen no. ~**ant** [traiʌ́mfənt] *a.* shōri o eta. ~**antly**

[traiʌmfəntli] *ad.* kachihokotte.

triumvir [traiʌmvə(:)] *n.* (*pl.* **-viri** [-virai]) (kodai Rōma) sannin gumi shiseikan no hitori.

triumvirate [traiʌmvirit] *n.* santōseiji.

triune [tráiju:n] *a.* sammi ittai no.

trivet [trívit] *n.* gotoku ; sankyakudai.

trivial [tríviəl] *a.* tsumaranu ; sasaina.

triviality [trìviǽliti] *n.* sasai ; kudaranai mono (koto).

triweekly [traiwí:kli] *ad.*, *a.* sanshū ni ikkai (no) ; isshū sankai
trod [trɔd] *v. see :* **tread.**   ⌊(no).

trodden [trɔ́dn] *v. see :* **tread.**

Trojan [tróudʒən] *a.* Toroi no ; Toroijin no. *n.* Toroijin. *T*~
horse (Girisha monogatari) *Troy*-zeme no mokuba.

troll [troul] *n.* (Hokuō Shinwa) dōkutsu no kyojin ; itazura-zuki no kobito. (*mus.*) rinshō no shōka. *v.* rinshō suru ; ugo-ku ito de tsuri o suru.

trolley [trɔ́li] *n.* kassha de denki o tsutaeru shigai densha. ~**bus** *n.* tororii-basu. ~ *car n.* shinai densha.

trombone [trɔ́mboun] *n.* torombōn.

troop [tru:p] *n.* ōzei ; ichidan ; (*pl.* **-s**) guntai. *v.* atsumaru ; su-sumu. ~**er** *n.* kihei ; kibajunsa.

trope [tróup] *n.* hiyuteki ni mochiita go ; ku.

trophy [tróufi] *n.* shōri no kinenhin.

tropic [trɔ́pik] *n.* kaikisen. (*pl.*) nettaichihō. *the* ~ *of Cancer,*
kita kaikisen. *the* ~ *of Capricorn,* minami kaikisen. ~**al** *a.*
nettai no. *n.* nettai no jūmin. ~ *fruits n.* nettai kajitsu.

trot [trɔt] *v.* daku o fumu. *n.* daku (*horse-training*).

troth [trouθ] *n.* (*arch.*)shinjitsu ; chūjitsu ; kon'yaku. *plight one's*
~, kon'yaku suru ; shinjitsu o chikau.   ⌈*food*).

trotter [trɔ́tə] *n.* daku o fumu uma ; buta, hitsuji no ashi (*for*

troubadour [trú:bəduə] *n.* 11 seiki kara 13 seiki made Furansu
ya Itaria ni seiryoku o shimeta jojōshijin.

trouble [trʌ́bl] *n.* momegoto ; shimpai. *v.* sawagaseru. ~**d** *a.*
komatta ; fuanna. ~**some** *a.* urusai.

troublous [trʌ́bləs] *a.* midareta ; sawagashii.   ⌈no tani.

trough [trɔf] *n.* kaibaoke ; tani. ~ *between waves,* nami to nami

trounce [trauns] *v.* utsu ; korasu ; uchimakasu (shiai nado de).

troupe [tru:p] *n.* (haiyū nado no) ichidan ; ichiza.

trousers [tráuzəz] *n.* (*pl.*) zubon.

trousseau [tru:sóu] *n.* yomeiriishō.

trout [traut] *n.* (*fish*) masu.

trow [trou] *v.* (*arch.*) shinzuru.

trowel [tráuəl] *n.* kote (sakan ga tsukau) ; ishokugote.

troy weight [trói wéit] *n.* toroi-kō (toroi-bakari).

truancy [trú:ənsi] *n.* taiman ; michikusa ; zuruyasumi.

truant [trú:ənt] *a.* namakeru ; zurukeru. *n.* namakemono. *play*
 ~, (gakkō nado o) saboru.

truce [tru:s] *n.* kyūsen ; tatakai no chūshi.

truck [trʌk] *n.* butsubutsukōkan ; niguruma. *v.* kōkan suru.

truckle [trʌkl] *v.* hetsurau. ~ *bed*, hikui *bed* ; shiyōnin no *bed*.

truculent [trʌkjulənt] *a.* yabanna ; zankokuna.

trudge [trʌdʒ] *v.* tobo-tobo aruku. *n.* tsukareta ayumi.

true [tru:] *a.* makoto no ; junsuina ; jijitsu ni au. *v.* tadashiku
 jijitsu ni awaseru. ~**-blue** [⊥blu:] *a.*, *n.* shugi nado ni chū-
 ⌐jitsuna hito.
truism [trú:izəm] *n.* jimei no ri.

truly [trú:li] *ad.* masani ; tadashiku ; chūjitsuni.

trump [trʌmp] *v.* damasu ; kirifuda de kiru. ~ *up*, hanashi nado o tsukuru. *n.* torampu no kirifuda ; okunote.

trumpery [trʌmpəri] *a.*, *n.* mikakedaoshi no (mono).

trumpet [trʌmpit] *n.* torampetto ; rappa.

truncate [trʌŋkeit] *v.* atama o kiru. *a.* kiritsumeta.

truncheon [trʌntʃən] *n.* (keikan no) keibō.

trundle [trʌndl] *v.* korogasu (-ru) ; kaiten suru (saseru).

trunk [trʌŋk] *n.* ki no miki ; ~ *line*, kansen ; honsen (tetsudō
 ⌐nado no). kaban.
truss [trʌs] *n.* taba. *v.* tabaneru.

trust [trʌst] *n.* shinnin ; kakushin. *v.* shinnin suru. ~**ee** [trʌstí:]
 n. hokannin. ~**ful** *a.* shinzuru. ~**worthy** [-wə:ði] *a.* shinjirareru. ~**y** *a.* shinzubeki. *n.* shinrai dekiru hito. ⌐shin.
truth [tru:θ] *n.* shinjitsu ; seijitsu. ~**ful** *a.* shinjitsuna ; tada-
 try [trai] *v.* tried ; trying. kokoromiru ; tamesu. *n.* kokoromi.
 ~**ing** *a.* tsurai ; kurushii ; muzukashii. ~**out** [⊥áut] *n.* gemmitsuni shiraberu. ~**-on** [⊥ɔn / ⊥⊥] *n.* shiken shite miru koto.

tryst [trist] *n.* kaigō no yakusoku ; sono basho. *v.* kaigō o ya-
Tsar [tsa:], **Czar**, (mae no Roshia Kōtei). ⌐kusoku suru.

tub [tʌb] *n.* oke ; tarai.

tubby [tʌ́bi] *a.* okejō no ; zunguri shita.

tube [tju:b] *n.* kuda ; chūbu.

tuber [tjú:bə] *n.* kyūkon (yuri no yōna).

tubercle [tjú:bə(:)kl] *n.* chiisana kobu ; kessetsu.

tuberculin [tju:bə́:kjulin] *n.* tsuberukurin chūshaeki.

tuberculosis [tju:bə́:kjulousis] *n.* kekkakubyō.

tuberose [tjú:bərous] *n.* (*flower*) gekkakō ; natsuzuisen.

tubing [tjú:biŋ] *n.* kuda no sonaetsuke.

tubular [tju:bjulə] *a.* kudajō no ; kuda no aru.

T.U.C., TUC Beikoku Rōdō Kumiaikaigi (*Trades Union Congress*).

tuck [tʌk] *n.* nuiage ; nuihida. *v.* age o tsukeru.

Tuesday [tjú:zdi] *n.* Kayōbi.

tuft [tʌft] *n.* fusa ; shigemi ; mori. *v.* fusa o tsukeru. ~**y** *a.* fusa o nasu ; fusa-busa shita.

tug [tʌg] *v.* hiku ; honeoru ; arasou. *n.* hiki. ~ *of war*, tsunahiki. ~**boat** [-ʹbout] *n.* hikifune.

tuition [tju:iʃən] *n.* kyōju ; jugyōryō.

tulip [tjú:lip] *n.* chūrippu. ~**tree** [-tri:] *n.* yurinoki.

tulle [tju:l/tu:l] *n.* amiginu.

tumble [tʌmbl] *v.* korobu (-asu) ; taoreru. *n.* korobi ; tenraku.

tumbler [tʌmblə] *n.* karuwazashi.

tumbrel [tʌmbrəl], **tumbril** [tʌmbril] *n.* nirin no dan'yakusha.

tumid [tjú:mid] *a.* hareta. ~**ity** [tju:míditi] *n.* haremono ; kotumo(u)r [tjú:mə] *n.* dekimono.

tummy [tʌ́mi] *n.* onaka ; pompon (*infant language*). chō.

tumult [tjú:mʌlt] *n.* sawagi ; sōdō.

tumultuous [tjumʌ́ltjuəs] *a.* sōzōshii ; yakamashii.

tun [tʌn] *n.* ōkii taru.

tuna [túːnə] *n.* (*Am.*) (*fish*) maguro.

tunable [tjú:nəbl] *a.* chōshi o awaseru.

tundra [tʌ́ndrə] *n.* koke no hara ; tōdotai.

tune [tju:n] *n.* fushi ; chōshi. *v.* chōshi o awaseru. ~**ful** *a.* chōshi no yoi. *sing a different* (*another*) ~, chigatta hanashi ya taido o toru. *to the* ~ *of* £ ʃ, 5 pondo to iu tagaku no. ~ *in*, rajio o awaseru. ~ *up*, gakki no chōshi o awaseru.

tungsten [tʌ́ŋgstən] *n.* tangusuten.

tunic [tjúːnik] *n.* (kodai Rōma) hiza made no shitagi

tuning fork [tjúːniŋ fɔːk] *n.* onsa.

tunnel [tʌ́nəl] *n.* tonneru. *v.* tonneru o horu.

tunny [tʌ́ni] *n.* maguro.

turban [tɔ́ːbən] *n.* atama ni maku kire (kaikyōkoku no hitotachi no). ⌐kawa.

turbid [tɔ́ːbid] *a.* nigotta ; dorodarake no. *a* ~ *river*, nigotta

turbine [tɔ́ːbain] *n.* tābin ; *a steam* ~, jōki tābin.

turbojet [tɔ́ːboudʒét] *n.* funshasuishinshiki hatsudōki. ⌐ki.

turbulence [tɔ́ːbjuləns] *n.* sawagashisa ; muchakucha ; uzuma-

turbulent [tɔ́ːbjulənt] *a.* sawagashii ; muchakuchana ; rambōna : ~ *water*, uzumaku nagare.

turf [tɔːf] *n.* shibafu. *the* ~, keibajō. *v.* shibafu o shiku. ~man [‐mən] *n.* keibazuki no hito. ~y *a.* shibafu o shiita.

turgid [tɔ́ːdʒid] *a.* harete fukureagatta. ~ity [tɔːdʒíditi] ~ness *n.* hareagari ; ōgesa.

Turk [tɔːk] *n.* Torukojin.

turkey [tɔ́ːki] *n.* (*bird*) shichimenchō. ~ *cock*, shichimenchō no osu. ~ *hen*, shichimenchō no mesu. ~ *poult*, shichimenchō no hina. *T*~ [tɔ́ːki] *n.* Toruko. ⌐buro. *n.* Torukogo.

Turkish [tɔ́ːkiʃ] *a.* Toruko no ; Torukojin no. ~ *bath*, toruko-

turmeric [tɔ́ːmərik] *n.* (*bot*.) ukon ; kyōō ; sono ne.

turmoil [tɔ́ːmɔil] *n.* sawagi ; sōdō.

turn [tɔːn] *v.* mawaru ; tenzuru ; tsukuridasu ; orikaesu ; muku ; ...ni naru. ~ *about*, furi muku. ~ *against*, ...ni somuku. ~ *away*, somukeru. ~ *down*, kyozetsu suru. ~ *in*, ni iru ; toko ni tsuku. ~ *off*, kaiko suru. ~ *on*, (hinette) dasu. ~ *out*, oidasu ; ...ni naru ; ...to wakaru. ~ *over*, hikkurikaesu. ~ *round*, furikaeru. ~ *to*, ...ni yoru. ~ *upon*, no ikan ni yoru. *n.* kaiten ; magari ; heikō. *by*~*s*, jumban ni. *in one's* ~, tachi-kawatte. *in* ~, junji ni. *take* ~*s*, kōtai suru. ~buckle *n.* shimekanagu. ~coat *n.* uragirimono. ~cock *n.* kyūsuisen-gakari. ~down *a.* orikaeshita. ⌐jō.

turner [tɔ́ːnə] *n.* sembankō. ~y *n.* hikimonozaiku ; sembankō-

turning [tɔ́ːniŋ] *n.* kaiten ; tenkō. ~point *n.* tenkōten.

turnip [tɔːnip] *n.* (*vegetable*) kabura. ⌐tsudō no taihisen.

turnout [tɔ́ːnáut] *n.* hito-de ; shussekisha ; sanshutsudaka ; te-

turnover [tɔ́:nòuvə] *n.* tempuku ; orikaeshi ; ikki no sōuriage
turnpike [tɔ́:npaik] *n.* yūryōdōro. ⌐daka.
turnstile [tɔ́:nstail] *n.* kaitenshiki kido.
turntable [tɔ́:nteibl] *n.* kaitendai ; tenshadai.
turpentine [tɔ́:pəntain] *n.* terepin'yu ; terepin.
turpitude [tɔ́:pitju:d] *n.* hiretsu ; haitoku. ⌐ta aoiro).
turquoise [tɔ́:kwɔiz] *n.* torukodama (sorairo no ; midorigakat-
turret [tʌ́rit] *n.* chiisana tō ; (sono sumi ni hō ga sonaete aru).
turtle [tɔ́:tl] *n.* umigame. ~dove [-dʌv] *n.* yamabato.
tusk [tʌsk] *n.* kiba. ~er *n.* kiba no aru dōbutsu.
tussah [tʌ́sə] *n.* yamamayu.
tussle [tʌ́sl] *n.* kumiuchi ; tōsō. *v.* kumiuchi suru.
tussock [tʌ́sək] *n.* kusamura. ~y *a.* kusamura no ōi.
tussore, tussah [tʌ́sə:] *n.*
tut [tʌt] *inter.* shi !, che !
tutelage [tjú:tilidʒ] *n.* hogo ; kōken.
tutelary [tjú:tiləri] *a.* hogo no ; kōken no.
tutor [tjú:tə] *n.* hogosha ; kōkennin. *v.* kateikyōshi o suru
tutorial [tju:tɔ́:riəl] *a.* hogosha no ; kōkennin no.
tuxedo [təksí:dou] *n.* takishiido.
TV terebijon (*television*). ⌐thority).
TVA Teneshi Keikoku Kaihatsukyoku (*Tennessee Valley Au-*
twaddle [twɔ́dl] *n.* tawagoto ; mudaguchi. *v.* mudaguchi o kiku. ⌐ni.
twain [twein] *n., a.* (*arch.*) (2) ni=futatsu (no). *in* ~, mapputatsu
twang [twæŋ] *n.* yumizuru no oto ; hana no oto. *v.* būn to naru (narasu) ; hana ni kakatte hatsuon suru.
tweak [twi:k] *n.* hineru. *v.* hinette (*twist*) ; gui to hiku (*jerk*).
tweed [twi:d] *n.* tsuwiido (sukotchi-ori).
tweezers [twí:zəz] *n.* kenuki. ⌐ni ; jūnibun no ichi.
twelfth [twelfθ] *n.* dai-jūni no ; jūnibun no ichi no. *n.* dai-jū-
twelve [twelv] *n., a.* jūni (no).
twentieth [twéntiiθ] *n., a.* dai-nijū (no) ; nijūbun no ichi (no).
twenty [twénti] *n., a.* (20) nijū (no). ⌐ta.
twice [twais] *ad.* nido ; futatabi. ~**told** *a.* ikudo mo hanashi-
twiddle [twídl] *v.* ijiru ; hinekurimawasu. ~ *one's thumb* =
twirl one's thumb, temochibusata ni oyayubi o kurukuru ma-

wasu.

twig [twig] *n.* koeda. *v.* (*brit sl.*) mitomeru ; chūmoku suru.

twilight [twáilait] *n.* usuakari (tasogare ; shinonome).

twill [twil] *n.* ayaori ; ayarasha.

twin [twin] *a.* futago no ; tsui no. *n.*, *v.* futago (o umu).

twine [twain] *n.* yoriito. *v.* yoru ; makitsuku.

twinge [twindʒ] *n.* hageshiku zukitto itamu : *a* ～ *of rheumatism,* ryūmachisu no hageshii itami. *a* ～ *of remorse,* kōkai no kashaku. 			⌈ru.)

twinkle [twíŋkl] *n.*, *v.* pikari, pikari (to mabataki shite hika-
twinkling [twíŋkliŋ] *n.* kirameki ; mei-metsu suru hikari.

twirl [twə:l] *n.* kaiten. *v.* kurukuru mawasu.

twist [twist] *v.* nejiru(-eru) ; yojiru(-eru). *n.* hitonejiri ; nejipan.

twit [twit] *v.* reishō suru ; hinan suru.

twitch [twitʃ] *v.*, *n.* gui to hiku (koto).

twitter [twítə] *n.* saezuri. *v.* saezuru. 			⌈iru.)

'twixt [twikst] *prep.* =betwixt. (*arch.*) shi (*poem*) nado ni mochi-

two [tu:] *n.*, *a.* ni, futatsu (2) no. (*base.*) ～-bagger [-bǽgə] ni-
ruida. ～-edged *a.* moroba no. ～-fold *a.*, *ad.* nibai no (ni).
～-step *n.* isshu no butō.

twopence [tʌ́pəns] *n.* nipensu.

twopenny [tʌ́pəni] *a.* nipensu no ; yasuppoi.

two-ply [tú:plái] *a.* atsusa 2-bai no ; 2-sō no.

-ty [-ti] *suffix* " 10 " no imi : *twenty* ; *ninety.* (*of being*) ...de aru
koto. *safety, sovereignty, etc.* nado no yōni seishitsu, jōtai, jōken
nado o arawasu. toki niwa " -ity " to naru koto mo aru. *arti-
ficiality, complexity, humidity, etc.*

tympanic membrane [timpǽnik mémbrein] *n.* komaku.

tympanist [tímpənist] *n.* ōdaiko, o ōkesutora de narasu hito.

tympanum [tímpənəm] *n.* (*anat.*) komaku ; koshitsu ; chūji.

type [taip] *n.* kata ; katsuji. *v.* daihyō suru.

typewrite [táiprait] *v.* taipuraitā de utsu ; *typewrite* suru.

typewriter [táipraitə] *n.* taipuraitā.

typhoid [táifɔid] *a.* chifusu. ～ *fever,* chō-chifusu.

typhoon [taifú:n] *n.* taifū ; bōfū.

typhus [táifəs] *n.* hasshinchifusu.

typical [típikəl] *a.* daihyōteki ; tenkeiteki.

typify [típifai] *v.* shōchō suru ; daihyō suru.

typist [táipist] *n.* taipisuto ; taipuraitā-gakari.

typographical [tàipəgrǽfikl] *a.* insatsu no. ~ *error*, insatsu no ayamari.

typography [taipógrəfi] *n.* insatsujutsu.

tyrannical [tirǽnikl] *a.* bōgyaku no ; assei no ; sensei-seiji no.

tyrannize [tírənaiz] *v.* bōsei (sensei-seiji) o okonau.

tyrannous [tírənəs] *a.* =tyrannical.

tyranny [tírəni] *n.* bōgyakuseiji ; asseiseiji.

tyrant [táirənt] *n.* bōkun ; senseikunshu.

tyro [táirou] *n.* shoshinsha.

Tzar [tsɑ:] =Czar.

U

U, u [ju:] *n.* (*pl.* U's, Us, [ju:z]) Eigo *alphabet* dai-21-bamme no moji. ⌐ru.

ubiquitous [jubíkwitəs] *a.* uchū itarutokoro ni aru; henzai su-
ubiquity [jubíkwiti] *n.* henzai; dōji ni itaru tokoro ni aru koto; uchū ni henzai suru koto.

U-boat [jú:bout] *n.* (Doitsu no) sensuikan (*Unterseeboot* no
udder [ʌ́də] *n.* chibusa (ushi nado no). ⌐ryaku.)

ugliness [ʌ́glinis] *n.* minikusa; bukiryō.

ugly [ʌ́gli] *a.* minikui; iyana; (*Am.*) ijiwaruna.

U.K. Igilis Rengō Ōkoku. (*United Kingsdom*).

ulcer [ʌ́lsə] *n.* (*med.*) kaiyō; haremono; ōkina odeki.

ulcerate [ʌ́lsəreit] *v. ulcer* (dekimono) ga dekiru.

ulceration [ʌ̀lsəréiʃən] *n.* kaiyō ga dekiru koto.

ulcerous [ʌ́lsərəs] *a.* kaiyō no dekiru.

ult., ulto. sengetsu (*ultimo=last month*).

ulterior [ʌltíəriə] *a.* kanata no; shōrai no; gengai no imi.

ultimate [ʌ́ltimit] *a.* saigo no; kyūkyoku no. *n.* ∼ **weapon,** saigo no buki; (donna baai demo konnichi dewa bōgyo deki-nai buki) (**ICBM** wa sono hitotsu da to iu).

ultimatum [ʌ́ltimeitəm] *n.* saigotsūchō.

ultra [ʌ́ltrə] *a.* kado no; kagekina. *n.* kagekiha. ⌐koi.
ultramarine [ʌ̀ltrəməríːn] *n., a.* konjō (no); umi no iro yori
ultramontane [ʌ̀ltrəmɔ́ntein] *a., n.* Arupusu-nampō no (hito).

ultraviolet [ʌ̀ltrəváiəlit] *a.* shigaisen no.

ululate [jú:ljuleit] *v.* (inu ya ōkami (*wolf*) no hoeru yōni) hoeru
umbel [ʌ́mbəl] *n.* (*bot.*) sankeikajo. ⌐(*bowl*).

umber [ʌ́mbə] *a., n.* kogecha-iro no (enogu *pigment*).

umbrage [ʌ́mbridʒ] *n.* fukaina kage; urami.

umbrella [əmbrélə] *n.* kōmorigasa; amagasa.

umlaut [úmlaut] *n.* umurauto (boin ga, ta no boin no eikyō de kawaru koto).

umpire [ʌ́mpaiə] *n.* chūsainin; shimpan'in. *v.* chūsai suru; shimpan.

UN, U.N. Kokusairengō (*United Nations (Organization*)).

unable [ʌnéibl] *a.* ...dekinai (*not able to do*).　⌐wakaranai.

unaccountable [ʌnəkáuntəbl] *a.* setsumei shigatai; wake no

unaccustomed [ʌnəkʌ́stəmd] *a.* narenai; (mi)narenai; (kiki) narenai.

unacquainted [ʌnəkwéintid] *a.* shiranai; fuannai no.

unadvisable [ʌnədváizəbl] *a.* futokusaku no; susumerarenai.

unadvised [ʌnədváizd] *a.* shiryo no nai; keisotsuna.

unaffected [ʌnəféktid] *a.* kidoranai; sotchokuna.

unalterable [ʌnɔ́:ltərəbl] *a.* kaerarenai; fuhen no.

unanimity [jùːnənímiti] *n.* kanzen dōi; kanzen itchi.

unanimous [juːnǽniməs] *a.* manjō itchi no; iginai. ∼**ly** *ad.* manjō itchi de.

unapproachable [ʌnəpróutʃəbl] *a.* chikazukigatai.

unarmed [ʌnáːmd] *a.* busō shite inai; sude no.

unassuming [ʌnəsjúːmiŋ] *a.* kidoranai; kensonna.

unattached [ʌnətǽtʃt] *a.* hanarete iru; mushozoku no.

unattractive [ʌnətrǽktiv] a. chūi o hikanai.

unavailing [ʌnəvéiliŋ] *a.* tame ni naranai; yaku ni tatanai.

unavoidable [ʌnəvɔ́idəbl] *a.* sakegatai; yamu o enai.

unaware [ʌnəwɛ́ə] *a.* shiranai. *ad.* = **unawares**.

unawares [ʌnəwɛ́əz] *ad.* shiranai de; omoigakenaku; fuini.

unbar [ʌnbáː] *v.* yokogi o toru; hiraku; *bar* o toru.

unbearable [ʌnbɛ́ərəbl] *a.* taerarenai; gaman dekinai; *not bearable*.

unbecoming [ʌnbikʌ́miŋ] *a.* futekitōna; funiaina; *not becoming*.

unbelief [ʌnbilíːf] *n.* fushinjin; fushinkō; *belief* o motanai.

unbeliever [ʌnbilíːvə] *n.* kaigisha; fushinkōsha; *believe* shinai hito.　　　　　　　　　　　　　　　⌐to shinai.

unbelieving [ʌnbilíːviŋ] *a.* shinjinai; utagaibukai; shinjiyō

unbend [ʌnbénd] *v.* massuguni suru; (magatta no o) yurumeru. ∼**ing** *a.* magaranai.

unbiassed [ʌnbáiəst] *a.* henken no nai; kōheina.

unbind [ʌnbáind] *v.* toku; hanatsu; kaihō suru.

unblemished [ʌnblémiʃt] *a.* ketten no nai; ketten (yogore)

unbolt [ʌnbóult] *v.* kannuki (*bolt*) o hazusu.　　⌐no nai.

unborn [ʌnbɔ́:n] *a.* mada umarenai; mirai no.

unbosom [ʌnbúzəm] *v.* kokoro o akasu.

unbridled [ʌnbráidld] *a.* tazuna no nai ; seishi dekinai.

unbroken [ʌnbróukn] *a.* yaburete inai ; kanzenna.

unburden [ʌnbə́:dn] *v.* ni (*load*) o orosu ; uchiakeru.

uncalled [ʌnkɔ́:ld] *a.* yobarenakatta. ～**for** [-fəə] *a.* fuhitsuyō-na ; futekitōna.

uncanny [ʌnkǽni] *a.* kimi no warui ; bukimina.

uncertain [ʌnsə́:tn] *a.* futashikana ; tashikade nai.

uncertainty [ʌnsə́:tnti] *n.* futei ; fukakujitsu.

unchangeable [ʌntʃéindʒəbl] *a.* fuhenna ; kawariyasukunai.

uncharitable [ʌntʃǽritəbl] *a.* kandai de nai ; kibishii.

unchristian [ʌnkrístʃən] *a.* kirisuto-kyōto de nai.

uncivil [ʌnsívil] *a.* busahōna ; kyōyō no nai.

uncivilized [ʌnsívilaizd] *a.* yabanna ; busahōna.

unclasp [ʌnklásp] *v.* tomegane o hazusu ; tsukanda (*clasp*) mono o hanasu.   「kumin.

uncle [ʌŋkl] *n.* oji ; shichiya. *U. Sam.* Beikokuseifu ; Beiko-

unclean [ʌnklí:n] *a.* fuketsuna. ～**ly** *ad.*

uncomely [ʌnkʌ́mli] *a.* bukiryōna ; kimochi yoku uketorenai.

uncomfortable [ʌnkʌ́mf(ə)təbl] *a.* fuyukaina ; igokochi no warui.

uncommon [ʌnkɔ́mən] *a.* mezurashii ; futsū de nai. ～**ly** *ad.*

uncompromising [ʌnkɔ́mprəmaiziŋ] *a.* jōho shinai ; gankona.

unconcern [ʌnkənsə́:n] *n.* mutonjaku ; heiki. ～**ed** *a.* muton-jakuna. ～**edly** *ad.*

unconditional [ʌnkəndíʃənəl] *a.* mujōken no ; zettaitekina.

unconditioned [ʌnkəndíʃənd] *a.* mujōkenni dekiru.

unconformity [ʌnkənfɔ́:miti] *n.* minna no itchi nashi ni.

unconquerable [ʌnkɔ́ŋkərəbl] *a.* katenai.

unconscionable [ʌnkɔ́nʃənəbl] *a.* fujōrina ; tadashikunai. ～**bargain,** futōkeiyaku.

unconscious [ʌnkɔ́nʃəs] *a.* chikaku shinai ; muishiki no. ～**ly** *ad.* ～**ness** *n.* muishiki ; jinjifusei.

unconstitutional [ʌnkənstitjú:ʃənəl] *a.* kempō ni hansuru.

uncontrollable [ʌnkəntróuləbl] *a.* seigyoshigatai ; te ni oenai.

unconventional [ʌnkənvénʃənəl] *a.* shikitari ni tayoranai.

uncork [ʌnkɔ́:k] *v.* koruku o nuku.

uncounted [Ánkáuntid] *a.* hijōni ōi ; kazoetenai.

uncouple [Ánkápl] *v.* renraku o toku ; (kawahimo o) toku ; ⌈hanasu.

uncouth [Ánkú:θ] *a.* bukakkōna ; mita me ni utsukushiku nai.

uncover [Ánkávə] *v.* ōi o toru ; bakuro surn.

unction [Ánkʃən] *n.* aburanuri ; iambutsu ; netsujō.

unctuous [Ánktʃuəs] *a.* yushitsu no ; abura no aru.

uncurl [Ánkɔ́:l] *v.* chijire o naosu.

undaunted [Ándɔ́:ntid] *a.* daitanna.

undeceive [Ándisí:v] *v.* mayoi o toku ; satoraseru.

undecided [Ándisáidid] *a.* mikettei no ; mitei no.

undefined [Ándifáind] *a.* mada hakkiri kimatte inai.

undeniable [Ándináiəbl] *a.* hinin no dekinai ; iya to ienai.

under [Ándə] *prep.* ...no shita ni ;～no shita o ; o ukete ;...chū. *ad.* shita ni. *a.* shita no ; ototta. ⌈toshishita no, etc.

under- [Ándə] *pref.* shita : ～age [Ándəréidʒ] *a.* toshi ga tarinai ;

underbid [Ándəbíd] *v.* (hoka yori mo) shitane o tsukeru.

underbred [Ándəbréd] *a.* sodachi no warui ; hikui sodachi no.

underbrush [Ándəbrʌʃ] *n.* shitabae ; yabu ; ōkina ki no shita no kamboku. ⌈(hikōki no).

undercarriage [Ándəkǽridʒ] *n.* kurumadai ; chakurikusōchi

undercharge [Ándətʃá:dʒ] *v.* tekitōna gaku yori sukunaku seikyū suru.

underclothes [Ándəklouðz] *n.* (*pl.*) shitagi ; hadagi.

undercover [Ándəkávə] *a.* (*Am.*) himitsuni shita ; naisho no.

undercurrent [Ándəkárənt] *n.* teiryū ; ue niwa mienai soko no nagare.

underdone [Ándədán] *a.* namayaki no ; hanjuku no.

underestimate [Ándəéstimeit] *v.* yasuku mitsumoru ; karuku misugiru. *undervalue* suru.

underfoot [Àndəfút] *ad.* ashi no shita ni ; fumitsukete.

undergarment [Ándəgá:mənt] *n.* shitagi ; hadagi.

undergo [Àndəgóu] *v.* ukeru ; gaman suru. ⌈toranai.

undergraduate [Ándəgrǽdjuit] *n.* daigakusei ; mada *degree* o

underground [Ándəgraund] *a.* chika no ; himitsu no. *n.* chikatetsudō ; chikasoshiki. ～railroad [-réilroud] (*Am.*) chika tetsudō ; tōsōsha (*fugitive*) no tōsō (*escape*) o tasukeru himitsu soshiki.

undergrowth [ʌ́ndəgrouθ] *n*. shitabae (*underbrush*); yabu.

underhand [ʌ́ndəhænd] *a*. himitsu no; fuseina; (*base*.) shitatenage no. **~ed** *a*. nai-nai no.

underlay [ʌ̀ndəléi] *v*. shita ni oku (shiku). ⌐o tsukuru.

underlie [ʌ̀ndəlái] *v*. shita ni aru; shita ni yokotawaru; kiso

underline [ʌ́ndəláin] *n.*, *v*. kasen; go no shita ni sen (o hiku).

underling [ʌ́ndəliŋ] *n*. shitayaku; buka.

undermine [ʌ̀ndəmáin] *v*. shita o horu; yokoana o horu.

undermost [ʌ́ndəmoust] *a*. saikai (ichiban shita) no; saitei no.

underneath [ʌ̀ndəníːθ] *prep.*, *ad*. shita ni (e). *ad*. hikuku.

undernourished [ʌ̀ndənʌ́riʃt] *a*. eiyōfuryō no.

underpass [ʌ́ndəpàːs] *n*. (*Am.*) shita no tōri.

underpay [ʌ̀ndəpéi] *v*. fujūbun ni shiharau. ⌐o motte inai.

underprivileged [ʌ̀ndəprívəlidʒd] *a*. ippan no hito no tokken

underrate [ʌ̀ndəréit] *v*. yasuku mitsumoru; mikubiru (*undervalue*).

underscore [ʌ̀ndəskɔ́ː] *v*. shita ni sen o hiku (*underline*).

undershirt [ʌ́ndəʃɔ̀ːt] *n*. hadagi. ⌐shitaago no tsukideta.

undershot [ʌ́ndəʃət] *a*. shita o nagareru mizu de mawaru;

undersign [ʌ̀ndəsáin] *v*. shita ni kimei suru; owari ni shomei suru. **~ed** *n. the ~ed*, shomei shita hito-tachi.

undersized [ʌ̀ndəsáizd] *a*. kogata no; ōkisa no tarinai.

understand [ʌ̀ndəstǽnd] *v*. **understood; -standing.** ryōkai suru; wakaru; rikai suru. *be understood*, ryakushite aru. *make oneself ~*, omoukoto o iu. **~ing** *n*. ryōkai; rikai.

understate [ʌ̀ndəstéit] *v*. hikaeme ni noberu; sukunaku iu.

understood [ʌ̀ndəstúd] *v*. see: **understand.**

understudy [ʌ́ndəstʌ̀di] *v*. rinji daiyaku ga tsutomaru yō keiko suru. *n*. rinji daiyakuhaiyū (*person who can act as a substitute for an actor or actress*). ⌐kuwadateru.

undertake [ʌ̀ndətéik] *v*. **-took, -taken; -taking.** hikiukeru;

undertaker [ʌ̀ndətéikə] *n*. keikaku suru hito.; sōgiya.

undertaking [ʌ̀ndətéikiŋ] *n*. hikiuke; ukeoi; kuwadate.

undertone [ʌ́ndətoun] *n*. teion; kogoe.

undertook [ʌ̀ndətúk] *v*. see: **undertake.**

undertow [ʌ́ndətóu] *n*. hikinami; kaeshinami (kishi ni yoseta nami ga soko o nagarete kaesu nami).

undervalue [ʌ̀ndəvǽlju:] v. hikuku hyōka suru; mikubiru. *underrate*.

underwear [ʌ́ndəwɛ̀ə] n. hadagi.

underwood [ʌ́ndəwʊ̀d] n. shitabae; yabu (*underbrush*).

underworld [ʌ́ndəwɔ̀:ld] n. gekai; jigoku (*Hades*).

underwrite [ʌ̀ndəráit] v. shomei suru; hokengyō o itonamu.

underwriter [ʌ́ndəràitə] n. hokengyōsha; kaijōhokengyōsha.

underwriting [ʌ́ndəráitiŋ] n. hokengyō; kaijōhokengyō.

undeserved [ʌ̀ndizɔ́:vd] a. futō no; ukeru ni atai shinai. ~**ly** [-vidli] ad. shitō de naku.

undesirable [ʌ̀ndizáirəbl] a. nozomashiku nai.

undetermined [ʌ̀nditɔ́:mind] a. miketsu no; mitei no.

undeveloped [ʌ̀ndivéləpt] a. hattatsu shinai; mikaihatsu no (*not yet developed*).

undisciplined [ʌ̀ndísiplind] a. tekitōna kunren o ukete inai.

undiscovered [ʌ̀ndiskʌ́vəd] a. akirakani sarenai; michi no; mada hakken sarete inai.

undisguised [ʌ̀ndisgáizd] a. kakusanai; arinomama no.

undisturbed [ʌ̀ndistɔ́:bd] a. shizukana; odayakana.

undivided [ʌ̀ndiváidid] a. kanzenna; sennen no.

undo [ʌndú:] v. shinaosu; torikesu; hodoku; hiraku.

undoing [ʌndú:iŋ] n. torikeshi. ⌈koto o hōtte oku.

undone [ʌndʌ́n] a. shite nai; shite shimawanai. *leave things* ~,

undoubted [ʌndáutid] a. utagai no nai; shinjitsu to shite uketoru. ~**ly** ad. tashikani. ⌈dres] n. fudangi.

undress [ʌndrés] v. kimono o nugu; hadaka ni suru. n. [ʌ́n-

undue [ʌndjú:] a. fuhōna; hijōna; futōna.

undulant [ʌ́ndjulənt] a. namiutsu; hajō no.

undulate [ʌ́ndjuleit] v. kifuku suru; namiutsu.

undulation [ʌ̀ndjuléiʃən] n. hadō; kifuku; uneri.

undulatory [ʌ́ndjulətəri] a. hadō suru; kifuku no aru.

unduly [ʌndjú:li] ad. futōni; fuseini.

undutiful [ʌndjú:tif(ə)l] a. oyafukō no; gimushin no nai.

undying [ʌndáiiŋ] a. fushi no; fumetsu no. ⌈hakken suru.

unearth [ʌnɔ́:θ] v. horidasu; hakken suru. ~ *the plot*, imbō o

unearthly [ʌnɔ́:θli] a. genseiteki de nai; kimi no warui.

uneasily [ʌní:zili] ad. fuanni; kenen shite.

uneasiness [ʌníːzinis] *n.* fuan ; kenen.

uneasy [ʌníːzi] *a.* fuanna ; konran shita.

uneducated [ʌnédjukeitid] *a.* mukyōikuna.

unemployable [ʌnemplɔ́iəbl] *a.* yatoi nikui.

unemployed [ʌnimplɔ́id] *a.* shitsugyō no. *the* ∼, shitsugyōsha.

unequal [ʌníːkwəl] *a.* onajiku nai ; fuheikin no. *an* ∼ *contest*, ippōtekina shiai.

unequal(l)ed [ʌníːkwəld] *a.* muhi no ; tobikiri jōtō no.

unequivocal [ʌnikwívəkəl] *a.* aimai de nai ; hakkiri shite iru.

unerring [ʌnɔ́ːriŋ] *a.* ayamari no nai ; tashikana.

UNESCO [ju(ː)néskou] yunesuko ; Kokuren Kyōiku Kagaku Bunka kikō (*United Nations Educational, Scientific, and Cultural Organization*).

uneven [ʌníːvən] *a.* heitan de nai ; onaji de nai.

uneventful [ʌnivéntful] *a.* dekigoto no nai.

unexampled [ʌnigzǽmpld] *a.* zenrei no nai ; mizou no.

unexceptionable [ʌniksépʃənəbl] *a.* hi no uchidokoro no nai ; kanzenna.

unexceptional [ʌniksépʃənəl] *a.* tsūjō no ; reigai no nai.

unexpected [ʌnikspéktid] *a.* igaina ; totsuzen no. ∼**ly** *ad.*

unfailing [ʌnféiliŋ] *a.* tsukinai ; taenai ; tashikana ; ayamari nai.

unfair [ʌnféə] *a.* fukōheina ; hampana (*partial*).

unfaithful [ʌnféiθfəl] *a.* fuchūjitsuna ; shin'yō dekinai.

unfamiliar [ʌnfəmíljə] *a.* mezurashii ; yokushiranai ; shitashimi no nai. 　　　　⌐keru.

unfasten [ʌnfáːsn] *v.* yurumeru ; yurumu ; hazusu ; toku ; to-

unfavo(u)rable [ʌnféivərəbl] *a.* tsugō no warui ; furina.

unfeeling [ʌnfíːliŋ] *a.* mukankakuna ; kanji no nai ; reikokuna.

unfeigned [ʌnféind] *a.* itsuwari no nai ; shinjitsu no.

unfinished [ʌnfíniʃt] *a.* mikansei no ; shiage ni sumanai.

unfit [ʌnfít] *a.* futekitōna. *v.* futekitōni suru.

unflagging [ʌnflǽgiŋ] *a.* otoroenai ; tayumanai.

unfledged [ʌnflédʒd] *a.* hanege no haenai ; mijukuna.

unfold [ʌnfóuld / ʌnfould] *v.* hiraku ; hirogeru.

unfortunate [ʌnfɔ́ːtʃnit] *a. n.* fukōna (hito). ∼**ly** *ad.* fukōni.

unfounded [ʌnfáundid] *a.* konkyo no nai.

unfriendly [ʌnfréndli] *a.* yūjō no nai ; fushinsetsuna.

unfurl [ʌnfə́:l] v. hirogeru; ageru. ～ a sail, ho o ageru.

ungainly [ʌngéinli] a. migurushii; bukakkōna. ～iness n. bukakkō; migurushisa.

ungenerous [ʌndʒénərəs] a. doryō no semai; kechina.

ungentlemanly [ʌndʒéntlmənli] a. shinshirashikunai; gehin

ungodly [ʌngɔ́dli] a. fushinjinna; jaakuna (wicked.) [na.

ungovernable [ʌngʌ́vənəbl] a. seigyō shinikui; te ni amaru (uncontrolable).

ungraceful [ʌngréisfəl] a. yūbi de nai; gehinna; migurushii.

ungracious [ʌngréiʃəs] a. fushinsetsuna; buaisōna; fuyukaina.

ungrammatical [ʌngrəmǽtik(ə)l] a. bumpōihan no; hakakuna.

ungrateful [ʌngréitf(u)l] a. on o shiranai; bōon no.

ungrounded [ʌngráundid] a. konkyo no nai.

ungrudging [ʌngrʌ́dʒiŋ] a. oshimanai; kimae no yoi.

ungual [ʌ́ŋgwəl] a. tsume no; hizume no aru.

unguarded [ʌngɑ́:did] a. shubi (mamori) no nai; fuchūina.

unguent [ʌ́ŋgwənt] n. kōyaku; nankō (kirikizu, yakedo nado ni tsukeru).

ungula [ʌ́ŋgjulə] n. tsume; hizume no katachi.

ungulate [ʌ́ɔgjuleit] a. hizume no aru. n. yūteidōbutsu.

unhallowed [ʌnhǽloud] a. shinsei de nai; kegareta.

unhand [ʌnhǽnd] v. te kara hanasu. ～y [ʌnhǽndi] a. mazui; bukiyōna; fubenna. [ad. unwaruku.

unhappy [ʌnhǽpi] a. fukōna; fushiawasena; mijimena. ～ily

unhealthful [ʌnhélθf(u)l] a. kenkō ni yokunai; shintai ni gai

unhealthy [ʌnhélθi] a. fukenkōna; fukenzenna. [no aru.

unheard-of [ʌnhə́:dɔ̀v] a. zenrei no nai; zendai mimon no.

unhesitating [ʌnhéziteitiŋ] a. chūcho shinai; guzu-guzu shinai.

unhinge [ʌnhíndʒ] v. chōtsugai o hazusu; konran saseru.

unhitch [ʌnhítʃ] v. tokihanasu; hanasu.

unholy [ʌnhóuli] a. shinsei de nai; yogorete iru.

unhook [ʌnhúk] v. hokku o hazusu.

unhorse [ʌnhɔ́:s] v. rakuba saseru; uma o hazusu (basha nado kara).

unicameral [ju:nikǽmərəl] a. ichiinsei no (kokkai de).

unicorn [jú:nikɔ:n] n. (densetsu no) ikkakujū.

unification [jùːnifikéiʃən] *n.* tōitsu ; gōitsu.

uniform [júːnifɔːm] *a.* ichiyō no ; kin'itsu no. *n.* seifuku ; gumpuku. *v.* ichiyōni suru. ～**ity** [jùːnifɔ́ːmiti] *n.* ichiyō. ～**ly** *ad.*

unify [júːnifai] *v.* tōitsu suru ; ichiyō ni suru. ⌊ichiyōni.

unilateral [júːnilǽtərəl] *a.* ippō dake no ; tandoku no.

unimpeachable [ʌ̀nimpíːtʃəbl] *a.* mōshibun no nai ; ketten no nai.

unimportant [ʌ̀nimpɔ́ːtənt] *a.* jūyō de nai ; toru ni taranai.

uninvited [ʌ̀ninváitid] *a.* sashidegamashii ; oshikakeru.

union [júːnjən] *n.* **rengō** ; gōdō ; kumiai. *the Union*, Hoku-Bei Gasshūkoku. *U*～ *Jack*, Eikoku Kokki. ～**ism** *n.* rengōshugi. ～**ist** *n.* rengōronsha ; rōdōkumiaiin.

unique [juː(ː)níːk] *a.* muhi no ; tada hitotsu no. ～**ly** *ad.*

unison [júːnizn] *n.* itchi ; waon.

unit [júːnit] *n.* tan'i. ⌜Yuniteriankyō.

Unitarian [juːnitéəriən] *n.* Yuniteriankyō shinja. ～**ism** *n.*

unitary [júːnitəri] *a.* tan'itsu no ; tan'i no.

unite [juː(ː)náit] *v.* rengō suru ; gappei suru.

united [juː(ː)náitid] *a.* rengō (gappei) shita. ～ *Brethren*, itchi kyōdaiha. *U*～ *(British)* rengōōkoku. ～ *Nations*, Kokusai-Rengo. *the* ～ *States*, Hoku-Bei Gasshūkoku. ～**ly** *ad.* rengō shite. ⌜rasu.

unity [júːniti] *n.* tan'itsu ; hitomatome. *live in* ～, nakayoku ku-

universal [juːnivɔ́ːs(ə)l] *a.* uchū no ; fuhen no. ～ *suffrage*, futsūsenkyoken. ～**ly** *ad.* ippanni.

Universalism [jùːnivɔ́ːsəlizm] *n.* zentaikyūsai shinkō no kyōgi. ～**ist**, kono shinkō no shinja.

universality [jùːnivə(ː)sǽliti] *n.* ippansei ; sekaisei.

universe [júːnivɔːs] *n.* uchū ; ban'yū.

university [jùːnivɔ́ːsiti] *n.* sōgōdaigaku. ～ *man*, daigakushusshinsha ; daigakusei.

unjust [ʌndʒʌ́st] *a.* fusei no ; fugi no ; tadashiku nai.

unjustifiable [ʌndʒʌ́stifaiəbl] *a.* ri ni awanai ; iiwake no deki-

unkempt [ʌnkémpt] *a.* kushikezuranai ; midarete iru. ⌊nai.

unkind [ʌnkáind] *a.* fushinsetsuna.

unknown [ʌnnóun] *a.* shirarete inai.

unlace [ʌnléis] *v.* himo o toku ; himo o yurumeru.

unlawful [ʌnlɔ́:f(ə)l] *a.* fuhōna ; hōritsu o fuminijiru. ⌈no.
unlearn [ʌnlɔ́:n] *v.* naratta koto o wasureru. ～ed *a.* mugaku
unless [ʌnlés] *conj.* moshi...shinakereba ; ...de nakattara. *we shall go unless it rains,* ame ga furanai nara ikō.
unlettered [ʌnlétəd] *a.* mugaku no ; muhitsu no.
unlike [ʌnláik] *a.* onaji de nai ; chigau. ～ly *a.* arisō mo nai.
unlimited [ʌnlímitid] *a.* mugen no ; seigen ga toketa.
unload [ʌnlóud] *v.* ni o orosu ; shimpai o nozoku.
unlock [ʌnlɔ́k] *v.* jō o akeru ; hiraku ; setsumei suru.
unlooked-for [ʌnlúktfɔ́:] *a.* yoki shinai ; igaina ; sagasanakatta.
unloose [ʌnlú:s] *v.* yurumeru ; hodoku ; kaihō suru.
unlucky [ʌnlʌ́ki] *a.* engi no warui ; fuunna.
unman [ʌnmǽn] *v.* memeshiku saseru ; yowaku suru (naru).
unmanly [ʌnmǽnli] *a.* otoko rashiku nai ; hiretsuna.
unmannerly [ʌnmǽnəli] *a.* ogyōgi no warui ; busahōna.
unmask [ʌnmá:sk] *v.* kamen o nugu ; shōtai o arawasu.
unmeaning [ʌnmí:niŋ] *a.* imi no nai.
unmentionable [ʌnménʃənəbl] *a.* kuchi ni suru kachi no nai ; iubekarazaru.
unmerciful [ʌnmɔ́:sif(u)l] *a.* mujihina ; zanninna.
unmindful [ʌnmáin(d)f(u)l] *a.* ki ga tsukanai ; fuchūina ; wa-sure yasui.
unmistakable [ʌnmistéikəbl] *a.* machigai no nai ; meihakuna.
unnatural [ʌnnǽtʃər(ə)l] *a.* fushizenna ; hininjōna.
unnecessary [ʌnnésə(ə)ri] *a.* fuhitsuyōna ; muekina.
unnerve [ʌnnɔ́:v] *v.* shinkei o ubau ; yowarasu.
unnoticed [ʌnnóutist] *a.* hitome ni tsukanai ; medatanai.
unnumbered [ʌnnʌ́mbəd] *a.* musū no ; kazoekirenai. ⌈tion).
UNO [jú:nou] Kokusai Rengō Kiko (*United Nations Organiza-*
unobjectionable [ʌnəbdʒékʃənəbl] *a.* koshō no nai ; igi no nai. ⌈shite inai.
unoccupied [ʌnɔ́kjupaid] *a.* hito no inai ; aite iru ; nani mo
unoffending [ʌnəféndiŋ] *a.* ki ni sawaranai ; gai no nai.
unofficial [ʌnəfíʃəl] *a.* ōyake de nai ; hikōshiki no.
unpack [ʌnpǽk] *v.* tsutsumi o toku ; ni o toku.
unpaid [ʌnpéid] *a.* miharai no ; mukyū no ; minō no.
unparalleled [ʌnpǽrələld] *a.* rui no nai ; muni no.

unpleasant [ʌnpléznt] *a.* ki ni iranai ; fuyukaina.

unprecedented [ʌnprésidəntid] *a.* senrei no nai ; kūzenno.

unprejudiced [ʌnprédʒudist] *a.* kōheina ; henken no nai.

unpremeditated [ʌnpriméditeitid] *a.* mae mae kara kangaete inai ; wazato de nai ; jumbi no nai.

unprepared [ʌnpripéəd] *a.* yōi no nai ; jumbi no nai ; fui no.

unprincipled [ʌnprínsəpld] *a.* shugi no nai ; harenchina.

unproductive [ʌnprədʌ́ktiv] *a.* fuseisantekina.

unqualified [ʌnkwɔ́lifaid] *a.* shikaku no nai ; futekitōna.

unquestionable [ʌnkwéstʃənebl] *a.* utagaenai ; tashikana.

unquiet [ʌnkwáiət] *a.* fuon no ; ochitsukanai ; fuanna.

unravel [ʌnrǽvl] *v.* toku ; hodoku (anda mono o).

unready [ʌnrédi] *a.* yōi no nai ; tebayaku ikanai.

unreasonable [ʌnríːzənəbl] *a.* rikutsu ni awanai ; murina.

unreserved [ʌnrizɔ́ːvd] *a.* fukuzō no nai ; buenryona.

unrest [ʌnrést] *n.* fuon ; fuan ; dōyō *(agitation).*

unrighteous [ʌnráitʃəs] *a.* futōna ; fuseina ; fugina.

unrival(l)ed [ʌnráiv(ə)ld] *a.* kyōsōsha no nai ; tekisuru mono

unroll [ʌnróul] *v.* toku (makimono o) ; hiraku. ⌊ga nai.

UNRRA [ʌ́nrə] Kokusai Rengō Kyūsai Fukkō Kaigi *(United Nations Relief and Rehabilitation Administration).*

unruly [ʌnrúːli] *a.* shimatsu ni oenai ; kimamana ; muhōna.

unsaddle [ʌnsǽdl] *v.* kura o hazusu ; rakuba saseru.

unsafe [ʌnséif] *a.* kikenna. ~ly *ad.* ~ness *n.* ~ty.

unsaid [ʌnséd] *v. a.*iwanai de ; kuchi ni dasanai de. *leave…~,* iwazu ni oku.

unsanitary [ʌnsǽnitəri] *a.* kenkō ni warui ; hieiseitekina.

unsatisfactory [ʌ́nsætisfǽktəri] *a.* fumanzokuna ; fujūbunna.

unsatisfied [ʌ́nsǽtisfaid] *a.* akitaranai de ; manzoku shinai de.

unsatisfying [ʌ́nsǽtisfaiiŋ] *a.* fumanzokuna ; fujūbunna ; omowashiku nai.

unsavo(u)ry [ʌnséivəri] *a.* aji no mazui ; kambashiku nai.

unsay [ʌnséi] *v.* mae itta koto o torikesu ; iinaosu.

UNSC [ʌ́nsk] Kokusairengō Anzen Hoshō Rijikai. *(United Nations Security Council).*

unscathed [ʌnskéiðd] *a.* shōgai o ukenai ; kizutsukerarezu ni

unscientific [ʌ́nsaientifík] *a.* hikagakutekina.

unscramble [ʌ́nskrǽmbl] *a.* konran kara tadashii jōtai ni kae-
unscrew [ʌnskrú:] *v.* neji o nuku ; hazusu ; yurumeru. 　⌊ru.
unscrupulous [ʌ́nskrú:pjuləs] *a.* buenryona ; muhōna.
unseal [ʌ́nsí:l] *v.* kaifū suru.
unsearchable [ʌ́nsə́:tʃəbl] *a.* sagashienai ; fukashigina.
unseasonable [ʌ́nsí:znəbl] *a.* kisetsuhazure no ; jiki o mushi
unseat [ʌ́nsí:t] *v.* rakuba saseru ; taishoku saseru. 　⌊shita.
unseemly [ʌ́nsí:mli] *a.* futekitōna ; funiaina.
unseen [ʌ́nsí:n] *a.* me ni mienai ; mienai.
unselfish [ʌnsélfiʃ] *a.* rikoshin no nai ; garigari de nai.
unsettle [ʌnsétl] *v.* midasu ; dōyō saseru ; ochitsukanaku suru
(naru). -d [ʌnsétld] *a.* futei no ; fuon no ; ochitsukanai.
unsex [ʌnséks] *v.* danseika suru.
unsheathe [ʌnʃí:ð] *v.* saya kara nuku ; nukihanatsu.
unship [ʌnʃíp] *v.* fune kara orosu ; rikuage suru.
unsightly [ʌnsáitli] *a.* minikui.
unskil(l)ful [ʌ́nskílf(u)l] *a.* mazui ; bukiyōna.
unsociable [ʌnsóuʃəbl] *a.* kantanni hito ni shitashimanai.
unsophisticated [ʌ́nsəfístikeitid] *a.* hitozure shite inai ; jum-
bokuna.
unsound [ʌ́nsáund] *a.* kenzen de nai ; kakujitsu de nai.
unsparing [ʌnspéəriŋ] *a.* kandaina ; mono oshimi shinai.
unspeakable [ʌnspí:kəbl] *a.* iu ni iwarenai ; nantomo ienai ;
gongodōdan no (*far beyond linguistic power to express*).
unspotted [ʌnspótid] *a.* hanten no nai ; kizu no nai.
unstable [ʌnstéibl] *a.* fuanteina ; ochitsuki no warui.
unsteady [ʌnstédi] *a.* kengo de nai ; fuanteina.
unstop [ʌnstóp] *v.* jama (*stop*) o toriharau (*take off*).
unstrung [ʌnstrʌ́ŋ] *a.* yurunda ; kinchō o yurumeta. (*weakened
the tention*).
unsubstantial [ʌ́nsəbstǽnʃəl] *a.* jittai no nai (*not substantial*) ;
kyōko de nai (*not firm*).
unthinking [ʌ́nθíŋkiŋ] *a.* kangae no nai ; shiryo no nai.
unthought-of [ʌnθɔ́:t-ɔv] *a.* omoigakenai ; igaina.
untidy [ʌntáidi] *a.* darashi nai ; kirei de nai.
untie [ʌntái] *v.* toku ; hodoku (shibatta (*bound*) mono o).
until [ʌntíl] *conj., prep.* made ; …ni itaru made.

untimely [ʌntáimli] *a.* ori no warui ; jiki o enai.

unto [ʌntu] *prep.* (*arch.*) to ; e ; ni ; made.

untold [ʌntóuld] *a.* hanasarenai ; musū no : *untold number*, ienai hodo no tasū. ⌐saikasō kaikyū.

untouchable [ʌntʌtʃəbl] *a.* sawararenai ; te no todokanai. *n.*

untoward [ʌntóuəd] *a.* fukōna ; gōjōna ; iu koto o kikanai.

untrammel(l)ed [ʌntrǽməld] *a.* jamasarezu ni ; jiyūni.

untried [ʌntráid] *a.* shita koto no nai ; keiken no nai.

untrue [ʌntrú:] *a.* shinjitsu de nai ; nise no.

untruth [ʌntrú:θ] *n.* kyogi ; kyogen. ∼**ful** *a.* uso no.

unused [ʌnjú:st] *a.* narenai.

unusual [ʌnjú:ʒuəl] *a.* futsū de nai ; ijōna. ∼**ly** *ad.* hijōni ; ma-

unutterable [ʌnʌtərəbl] *a.* iu ni iwarenu. ⌊reni.

unveil [ʌnvéil] *v.* vēru (*veil*) o torisaru.

unwarrantable [ʌnwɔ́rəntəbl] *a.* hoshō dekinai ; higōhō no.

unwarranted [ʌnwɔ́rəntid] *a.* hoshō sarete nai ; hoshō no nai.

unwary [ʌnwéəri] *a.* fuchūina ; (goeinashi ni) buyōjinna.

unweight [ʌnwéit] *v.* jūshin o utsusu. ; juryō o herasu.

unwell [ʌnwél] *a.* fukai no ; kibun no sugurenai.

unwholesome [ʌnhóulsəm] *a.* kenkō ni yokunai ; fukenzenna.

unwieldy [ʌnwí:ldi] *a.* atsukai nikui ; omoi.

unwilling [ʌnwíliŋ] *a.* iyagaru ; fuhon'i no.

unwind [ʌnwáind] *v.* hodoku (-eru) ; itomaki ni makinaosu

unwise [ʌnwáiz] *a.* orokana. ; rikō de nai. ⌊(*spool*).

unwittingly [ʌnwítiŋli] *ad.* muishikini ; nanige naku.

unwonted [ʌnwóuntid] *a.* narenai ; futsū to chigau.

unworthy [ʌnwɔ́:ði] *a.* kachi no nai ; …suru ni tarinai.

unwritten [ʌnrítn] *a.* kaite nai. ∼ **law,** fubunritsu.

up [ʌp] *ad., prep.* ue no hō e ; ni itaru made. ∼ *and down*, ōfuku shite ; agattari sagattari. *a.* ue no ; nobori no. *n.* nobori ; han'-ei. ∼*s and downs*, eikoseisui.

UP, U.P., U. P. tsūshinsha (*United Press*).

upas [jú:pəs] *n.* doku no aru ki no isshū.

upbraid [ʌpbréid] *v.* shikaru ; hinan suru.

upbringing [ʌpbríŋiŋ] *n.* yōiku ; kyōiku.

upgrade [ʌpgreid] *n.* noborizaka. *v.* (*Am.*) tōkyū o ageru.

upgrowth [ʌpgrouθ] *n.* seichō ; hatsuiku.

upheaval [ʌphí:v(ə)l] *n.* jōshō; moriagari.

upheave [ʌphí:v] *v.* mochiageru; oshiageru; ryūki suru.

uphill [ʌphil] *a.* noborizaka no; hone no oreru. *ad.* [ʌphíl / ʌphil / ʌphíl] saka no ue e.

uphold [ʌphóuld] *v.* ageru; mochiageru; iji suru.

upholster [ʌphóulstə] *v.* kagu o sonaetsukeru. ～**er** *n.* kagu-shō. ～**y** *n.* kagu (no ōi ya kabekake nado).

upkeep [ʌpki:p] *n.* iji-hi.

upland [ʌplənd] *n.* kōchi; takadai; yama no tokoro.

uplift [ʌplíft] *v.* takameru; kaizen suru. *n.* takameru koto; kaizen.

upon [ʌpón] *prep.* ...no ue ni; ...ni motozuite.

upper [ʌpə] *a.* ue no; jōbu no; get (*or have*) *the* ～ *hand of*, ...ni masaru. *the* U～ Hosue jōin. ～**-class** *a.* jōryūshakai no; jōkyū no. ～**most** *a.* saijō no. ～**-case**, (*print*) ōmoji (*capital letters*) no.

uppish [ʌpiʃ] *a.* (*col.*) hitori de ii ki ni natte iru. (*self assertive*).

upright [ʌprait] *a.* massuguna; shōjikina.

uprising [ʌpráiziŋ] *n.* kishō (*rising in the morning*); hanran (*revolt*); noborizaka (*uphill*).

uproar [ʌprɔə] *n.* ōsawagi; sōdō.

uproarious [ʌprɔ́:riəs] *a.* sawagashii.

uproot [ʌprú:t] *v.* nekosogi ni suru.

upset [ʌpsét] *v.* hikkurikaeru (-su); dainashi ni suru. *n.* tempuku. *a.* hikkurikaetta.

upshot [ʌpʃɔt] *n.* kekka; shūkyoku.

upside [ʌpsàid] *n.* jōbu. ～ *down*, sakasama ni. (heya).

upstairs [ʌpstéəz] *ad.* nikaini. *a.* kaijō no. *n.* nikai. (ijō no

upstanding [ʌpstǽndiŋ] *a.* chokuritsu shite; kōei aru; rippa-

upstart [ʌpstɑ:t] *n.* nariagarimono; narikin. na.

up-to-date [ʌptədéit] *a.* genzai made no; saikin no.

uptown [ʌptáun] *a.* yamanote no. *ad.* yamanote ni(e); (*Am.*) jūtaku chitai ni. (keiki no) uwamuki.

upturn [ʌptɔ́:n] *v.* ue ni mukeru; hikkurikaeru. *n.* neagari;

upward [ʌpwəd] *a.* uwamuki no; jōshō suru. *ad.* ue ni; ue

uranium [juréiniəm] *n.* (*chem.*) uranium; uran. no hō e.

Uranus [júrənəs] *n.* (*astr.*) Tennōsei.

urban [ɔ́:bən] *a.* toshi no; tokai ni aru.

urbane [ə:béin] *a.* teineina; inginna; jōhinna.

urbanity [ə:bǽniti] *n.* teinei; ingin; jōhin.

urbanize [ə́:bənaiz] *v.* machi ya hito o tokaifū ni suru.

urchin [ə́:tʃin] *n.* itazurakko; wampakushōnen.

urea [juríːə] *n.* (*chem.*) nyōso.

urge [ə:dʒ] *v.* isogaseru; unagasu.

urgency [ə́:dʒənsi] *n.* kinkyū; saisoku.   ⌈*ad.* kyūni; asette.

urgent [ə́:dʒənt] *a.* kinkyū no; isogi no; saisoku suru. **~ly**

urinal [júərinəl] *n.* shōbenjo; benki.

urinary [júərinəri] *a.* nyō no. *n.* shōbenjo.

urinate [júərineit] *v.* shōben suru.

urine [júərin] *n.* shōben; nyō.

urn [ə:n] *n.* kame; tsubo; ikotsuire.   ⌈yūsei.

Ursa [ə́:sə] *n.* mesu on kuma. U ~ Major (Minor) Dai-(Shō-)

ursine [ə́:sain] *a.* kuma no; kuma ni nita.

us [əs] *pron.* (' *we* ' no mokutekikaku) wareware o (ni).

U.S., US Amerika Gasshūkoku (*United States*).

U.S.A. *United States of America; United States Army; Union of South Africa.*

usable [júːzəbl] *a.* yaku ni tatsu; mochiirareru.

usage [júːzidʒ] *n.* shiyō; toriatsukai; mochiikata.

use [ju:s] *n.* shiyō; riyō. *in* ~, shiyō shite. (*of*) *no* ~, mueki de. *of* ~, yūeki no. *out of* ~, sutarete. *v.* [ju:z] mochiiru; atsukau. **~ful** [ju:sf(u)l] *a.* yūyōna. **~less** *a.* yaku ni tatanai.

used [ju:st] *a.* ...ni narete; [ju:zd] tsukaifurushita. *be* ~ *to* ...(*s*) ni narete iru. *get* ~ *to*, ...ni nareru. ~ *up*, tsukai furushita.

usher [ʌ́ʃə] *n.* momban; annainin. *v.* annai suru. ~ *out* (*or*, ~ *forth*) soto made miokuru.

U.S.N. Beikoku Kaigun (*U.S. Navy*).   ⌈*lics*).

U.S.S.R., USSR Sobieto Rempō (*Union of Soviet Socialist Repub-*

usual [júːʒuəl] *a.* itsumo no; rei no. *as* ~, itsumo no tōri. **~ly** *ad.* itsumo.   ⌈ken; yōekiken.

usufruct [júːzjufrʌkt] *n.* tsukau kenri; shiyōken; (*leg*) shūeki-

usurer [júːʒərə] *n.* kōrigashi.

usurious [juːʒúəriəs] *a.* kōri o musaboru; kōrigashi no.

usurp [juːzɔ́:p] *v.* ōryō suru. **~er** *n.* ōryōsha.

usurpation [jùːzəpéiʃən] *n.* ōryō.

usury [júːʒuri] *n.* kōri (de kasu koto).

utensil [ju:ténsil] *n.* kigu ; yōgu (kateiyō no dōgu).

uterine [jú:tərin] *a. (anat.)* shikyū no.

uterus [jú:tərəs] *n. (pl.* **-ri** [rai]) *(anat.)* shikyū.

utilitarian [ju:tilitéəriən] *a.* kōriteki ; kōrishugi no. *n.* kōrironsha. ~**ism** *n.* kōrishugi (setsu).

utility [ju:tíliti] *n.* yūyō ; kōyō.

utilize [jú:tilaiz] *v.* riyō suru ; yaku ni tateru.

utmost [Átmoust] *n., a.* kyokugen (no) ; kyokudo (no) ; kyokutan(na). *to the* ~, oyobukagiri.

Utopia [ju:tóupiə] *n.* Risōkyō.

Utopian [ju:tóupiən] *a.* Risōkyō no. *n.* Risōkyō no jūmin.

utter [Átə] *a.* mattaku no. *v.* koe ni dasu. ~**ly** *ad.* mattaku. ~**most** [Átəmoust] (=*utmost*) *a.* kyokudo no ; saidaigen no.

utterance [Átərəns] *n.* hatsugen ; hassei.

uvula [jú:vjulə] *n. (anat.)* ken'yōsui.

uvular [jú:vjulə] *a.* ken'yōsui no.

uxorious [əksɔ́:rjəs] *a.* nyōbōkōkō no ; sainoro no.

V

V, v [vi:] *n.* (*pl.* V's, Vs, [vi:z]) Eigo *alphabet* no dai-22-bamme no moji. ⌈tai Frank.

v [vi:] *v.* tai (versus (*L*)=*againt*) John *v.* (*versus*) *Frank*, John

vacancy [véikənsi] *n.* kūkyo; karappo; ketsuin.

vacant [véikənt] *a.* kūkyo no; haitte inai. ⌈inai.

vacate [vəkéit / véikeit] *v.* kara ni suru; (itte shimatte ato ni)

vacation [vəkéiʃən] *n.* yasumi; nagai kyūka; tachinoki. *take a* ~, kyūka o toru.

vaccinate [væksineit] *v.* shutō (yobōchūsha) o suru.

vaccination [væksinéiʃən] *n.* yobōchūsha (shutō nado).

vaccine [væksi(:)n] *n.* yobōeki; wakuchin; yobōchūshaeki.

vacillate [væsileit] *v.* mayou; dōyō suru.

vacillation [væsiléiʃən] *n.* kimayoi; dōyō.

vacuity [vækjú(:)iti] *n.* kūkyo; karappo.

vacuous [vækjuəs] *a.* kūkyo no; bon'yari shita. ⌈*n.* mahōbin.

vacuum [vækjuəm] *n.* (*pl.* **-ums**; **-ua**) shinkū. ~**bottle** [-bɔtl]

vademecum [véidimí:kəm] *n.* hikkeisho; shūchin hikkei (*book for ready reference*; *anything a person carries about with him as such.*)

vagabond [vægəbɔnd] *n.* furōsha. *n.* furō no (*vagrant*)

vagary [vəgéəri / véigəri] *n.* monozuki; kimagure.

vagrancy [véigrənsi] *n.* hōrō.

vagrant [véigrənt] *n.* furōsha. *a.* furō no; sasurai aruku.

vague [veig] *a.* bon'yari shita; aimaina. ~**ly** *ad.* bakuzen to.

vain [vein] *a.* munashii; jiman suru; miebō no. *in* ~, munashiku. ⌈yoi. ~**ly** *ad.*

vainglorious [veinglɔ́:riəs] *a.* jiman suru; kyoeishin no tsu-

vainglory [veinglɔ́:ri] *n.* jiman; unubore; kyoei.

vale [veil] *n.* (*poet.*) tani; mizo.

valediction [vælidíkʃən] *n.* kokubetsu; kokubetsu no kotoba.

raledictorian [vælidiktɔ́:riən] *n.* (*Am.*) (sotsugyōshiki ni) kokubetsu no ji o noberu gakusei.

valedictory [vælidíktəri] *a.* kokubetsu no. *n.* kokubetsu no ji.

valence, ~cy [véilənsi(i)] *n.* (*chem.*) genshika.

valentine [vǽləntain] *n.* Sei-Varentain-matsuri [ni-gatsu, jū-yokka] (2 gt. 14 k.); erande ita koibito ni kono hi okuru te-gami.

valerian [vəlíəriən] *n.* (*herb*) kanokosō (kono kusa no ne kara totta), shinkei o shizumeru kusuri.

valet [vǽlit] *n.* jūsha; kerai. *v.* jūsha o tsutomeru.

valetudinarian [vælitju:dinéəriən] *a.* byōshin no; kyojakuna. *n.* byōjakusha.

valiant [vǽljənt] *a.* yūkanna. ∼**ly** *ad.* yūkanni.

valid [vǽlid] *a.* kakujitsuna; yūkōna. ∼**ly** *ad.* yūkōni.

validate [vǽlideit] *v.* yūkō ni suru.

validity [vəlíditi] *n.* seitō; kakujitsusei.

valise [vəlí:s] *n.* ryokōkaban.

valley [vǽli] *n.* tanima.

valo(u)r [vǽlə] *n.* yūki.

valorization [vælərizéiʃən] *n.* bukka anteisaku.

valuable [vǽljuəbl] *a.* kōkana; kichōna. *n.* kichōhin.

valuation [væljuéiʃən] *n.* hyōka; sateikakaku o kimeru koto.

value [vǽlju(:)] *n.* kachi; neuchi; sonchō. *v.* hyōka suru; son-chō suru.

valued [vǽlju(:)d] *a.* taisetsuna.

valve [vælv] *n.* ben; barubu; shinkūkan.

valvular [vǽlvjulə] *a.* ben no; ben no tsuita.

vamp [væmp] *n.* kutsu no kawa. *v.* atarashii kawa o tsukeru tsukurou.

vampire [vǽmpaiə] *n.* kyūketsuki; yōfu; hito no chi o suu oni.

van [væn] *n.* (ōi no aru) ōniguruma; massaki; zen'ei (*vanguard*).

vanadium [vənéidiəm] *n.* (*chem.*) banajiumu.

Vandal [vǽndl] *n.* Vandarujin; yabanjin.

vandalism [vǽndəlizm] *n.* bungei hakaishugi; bankō.

vane [vein] *n.* kazami; tsubasa.

vanguard [vǽngɔ:d] *n.* sempō; zen'ei; sossensha.

vanilla [vənílə] *n.* banira; banira no kōmiryō.

vanish [vǽniʃ] *v.* kieuseru; mienaku naru.

vanity [vǽniti] *n.* kyoeishin; unbore; mie.

vanquish [vǽŋkwiʃ] *v.* uchikatsu; seifuku suru.

vantage [vǽntidʒ] *n.* yūetsu; rieki. *coign of* ∼, yūrina chiten.

vanward [vǽnwəd] *a.* sentō e no; sentō no.

vapid [vǽpid] *a.* ki no nuketa; kakki no nai.

vapo(u)r [véipə] *n.* yuge; jōki; suijōki. *v.* jōhatsu suru.

vaporize [véipəraiz] *v.* jōhatsu saseru (suru); kika suru.

vaquero [vækéərou] *n.* ushikai (Amerika seinan chihō ya Mekishiko no *cowboy*).   ⌈mono.

variable [véəriəbl] *a.* kawariyasui; kimaranai. *n.* kawariyasui

variance [véəriəns] *n.* chigai; fuwa; yukichigai.

variant [véəriənt] *a.* kawaru; kotonaru; samazama no.

variation [veəriéiʃən] *n.* henka.

varicolo(u)red [veərikʌ́ləd] *a.* toridori no iro no.

varied [véərid] *a.* henka shita; toridori no.

variegated [véəriəgeitid] *a.* zasshoku no; henka ni tomu.

variety [vəráiiti] *n.* henka; shurui; samazama.

various [véəriəs] *a.* shuju no; henka no aru.

varnish [váːniʃ] *n.* wanisu; nisu. *v.* wanisu o nuru.

varsity [váːsiti] *n.* =**university.**

vary [véəri] *v.* aratamaru; kawaru; henka saseru.

vase [vɑːz] *n.* bin; kabin.

vassal [vǽsəl] *n.* kashin; kerai. ∼**age** *n.* kerai no mibun.

vast [vɑːst] *a.* hiroi; obitadashii; bōdaina.

vat [væt] *n.* ōdaru; ōoke.

Vatican [vǽtikən] *n.* Rōma-Hōōchō.

vaudeville [vóudvil] *n.* uta to odori no karui geki.

vault [vɔːlt] *n.* marutenjō; anagura; kichōhinshitsu. *v.* tobi-
vaunt [vɔːnt] *v.* jiman suru. *n.* jiman.   ⌊noru; tobu.

V-Day [víː dei] *n.* (*Am.*) Dainiji-Sekaitaisen Senshōkinembi.

veal [viːl] *n.* koushi no niku.

vedette [vidét] =∼**boat.** *n.* shōkaitei. kihei sekkō.

veer [viə] *v.* hōkō o kaeru. *n.* hōkōhenkan.   ⌈yasairui no.

vegetable [védʒitəbl] *n.* shokubutsu; yasai. *a.* shokubutsu no;

vegetarian [vedʒitéəriən] *n.* saishokushugisha. *a.* saishoku no.

vegetate [védʒiteit] *v.* seichō suru (shokubutsu no yōni).

vegetation [vedʒitéiʃən] *n.* shokubutsu; (shokubutsu no) seichō.

vegetative [védʒitətiv] *a.* seichō suru; shokubutsusei no.

vehemence [víːiməns] *n.* gekiretsu; hageshisa.

vehement [víːimənt] *a.* hageshii; nesshinna. ∼**ly** *ad.* hageshiku.

vehicle [víːikl] *n.* norimono; kuruma; shudan.

veil [veil] *n.* veiru ; tobari. *v.* ōu ; kakusu.

vein [vein] *n.* (*anat.*) jōmyaku ; kekkan.

veld, veldt [velt] *n.* (Minami-Afurika no) kusahara ; sōgen.

vellum [vélǝm] *n.* jōtō no kawagami (hitsuji no kawa ni nise-
ta mono).

velocipede [vilósipi:d] *n.* (*Am.*) kodomoyō sanrinsha.

velocity [velósiti] *n.* hayasa ; sokudo.

velvet [vélvit] *n.* birōdo. ~**een** [-lí:n] *n.* tōten ; betchin. ~**y** *a.* birōdo no yōna.

venal [ví:nǝl] *n.* baishū shi yasui ; kinsen zuku no. ~**ity** [vi:-
nǽliti] *n.* kinsenzuku ; kane shidai.

vend [vend] *v.* uru. ~**er**, ~**or** *n.* urite.

vendetta [vendétǝ] *n.* kinshin fukushū ; adauchi.

veneer [vǝníǝ] *n.* beniyaita. *v.* beniyaita o kabuseru.

venerable [vénǝrǝbl] *a.* sonkei subeki.

venerate [vénǝreit] *v.* tōtobu ; sonkei suru.

veneration [venǝréiʃǝn] *n.* songen ; agame tattobu koto.

venereal [vǝníǝriǝl] *a.* seikō no ; karyūbyō no.

Venetian [vǝní:ʃǝn] *a.* Itaria, Venisu no. ~ *blind*, ita sudare.
~ *n.* Venisujin.

vengeance [véndʒǝns] *n.* fukushū.

vengeful [véndʒf(u)l] *a.* fukushūshin no aru ; shūnembukai.

venial [ví:niǝl] *a.* yurusubeki ; (tsumi ga) karui.

venison [vénzn] *n.* shika no niku.

venom [vénǝm] *n.* doku ; akui. ~**ous** *a.* doku no aru.

venous [ví:nǝs] *a.* jōmyaku no.

vent [vent] *n.* ana ; deguchi. *give* ~ *to*, o hassuru ; o morasu. *take* ~, shirewataru. *v.* anakara dasu.

ventilate [véntileit] *v.* kaze o tōsu.

ventilation [ventiléiʃǝn] *n.* tsūfū ; (kūki o kaeru) kazatōshi.

ventilator [véntileitǝ] *n.* tsūfūki ; sōfūki.

ventral [véntrǝl] *a.* hara no.

ventricle [véntrikl] *n.* (*anat.*) shinshitsu (shinzō no).

ventriloquism [ventrílǝkwizǝm] *n.* fukuwa (jutsu).

ventriloquist [ventrílǝkwist] *n.* fukuwajutsusha.

venture [véntʃǝ] *n.* bōken ; tōki ; kiken o okasu ; bōken suru.

venturesome [véntʃǝsǝm] *a.* bōkentekina ; daitanna.

venue [vénju:] *n.* (*leg.*) hanzaichi ; saiban kankatsuchi.

Venus [ví:nǝs] *n.* (*Rom. myth.*) ai to bi no megami ; (*astr.*) Kinsei.

veracious [vəréiʃəs] *a.* shinjitsu no ; seijitsuna.

veracity [vərǽsiti] *n.* shinjitsu ; seijitsu.

veranda [vərǽndə] *n.* engawa, Veranda.

verb [vəːb] *n.* (*gram.*) dōshi.

verbal [və́ːbl] *a.* kotoba no ; kōtō no. *n.* henkei dōshi.

verbatim [vəːbáːtim / -béi-] (*L.*) *a.*, *ad.* chikugoteki (ni) (*word by word*).

verbena [vəːbíːnə] *n.* (*bot.*) kumakazura-zoku ; bijozakura.

verbose [və́ːbous] *a.* kotoba no ōi ; kudoi.

verbosity [vəːbɔ́siti] *n.* tagen ; jōchō.

verdancy [və́ːdənsi] *n.* mijuku ; midori iro ; ubu.

verdant [və́ːdənt] *a.* midori no ; aoao to shita ; mijukuna.

verdict [və́ːdikt] *n.* hanketsu ; hyōketsu.

verdigris [və́ːdigris] *n.* rokushō.

verdure [və́ːdjə] *n.* shinryoku.

verge [vəːdʒ] *n.* fuchi ; kiwa ; kyōkai. *be on the ~ af*, ...ni hin- ⌐suru. *v.* chikazuku.

verger [və́ːdʒə] *n.* kenri no hyōshō o motsu hito ; teraotoko ; ⌐dōmori.

verification [vèrifikéiʃən] *n.* tashikame ; kenshō.

verify [vérifai] *v.* tashikameru ; kakujitsu ni suru.

verily [vérili] *ad.* shinni ; jitsuni.

verisimilitude [vèrisimílitju:d] *n.* shinjitsurashisa.

veritable [véritəbl] *a.* shinjitsu no ; hontō no.

verity [vériti] *n.* shinjitsu. *eternal ~*, eikyū fuhen no shinri.

vermicelli [vəːmisélli] *n.* seiyōudon. ⌐chūyōtokki ; mōchō.

vermiform [və́ːmifɔ:m] *a.* zenchūjō no. *~ appendix*, (*anat.*)

vermifuge [və́ːmifju:dʒ] *n.* kuchūzai ; mushikudashi.

vermilion [vəːmíljən] *n.* shu ; shuiro (*brilliant red*).

vermin [və́ːmin] *n.* gaichū ; narazumono (*scoundrel*).

vermouth [və́ːmu:θ] *n.* berumotto-sake.

vernacular [vəːnǽkjulə] *n.* bokokugo. *a.* jikoku no ; chihō no. *~ paper*, jikokugo no shimbun.

vernal [və́ːnəl] *a.* haru no. ⌐zū no kiku.

versatile [və́ːsətail] *a.* tahōmen no sainō aru ; kawariyasui ; yū-

versatility [və̀ːsətíliti] *n.* tagei ; kawariyasui koto ; utsurigi.

verse [vəːs] *n.* uta no ku ; uta ; shi. *~d* [-t] *a.* seitsūshita.

versification [və̀ːsifikéiʃən] *n.* shisaku ; sakushihō ; utatsukuri.

versify [vɔ́:sifai] *v.* shi o tsukuru.

version [vɔ́:ʃən] *n.* hon'yaku; setsumei.

versus [vɔ́:səs] *prep.* (*L.*) tai *see* : **V.**

vertebra [vɔ́:tibrə] *n.* (*pl.* **-rae** [-ri:]; **-s**) sekitsui.

vertebral [vɔ́:tibrəl] *a.* sekitsui no.

vertebrate [vɔ́:tibreit] *a.* sekitsui no aru. *n.* sekitsuidōbutsu.

vertex [vɔ́:teks] *n.* (*pl.* **-tices** [-tisi:z]; **-es**) chōten.

vertical [vɔ́:tikəl] *a.* tate no. *n.* suichokusen.

vertigo [vɔ́:tigou] *n.* memai.

very [véri] *a.* shin no; mattaku no. *ad.* hanahada.

vesicle [vésikl] *n.* (*med.*) mizubōsō (suihōshin).

vesper [véspə] *n.* (*pl.*) yūbe no inori. (*V*~) Yoi no Myōjō. *a.* yūbe no. ~**tine** [-tain] *a.* yūgata no.

vessel [vésl] *n.* yōki; ireru utsuwa; fune.

vest [vest] *n.* chokki; hadagi. *v.* fuku o kiseru (kiru); kenri. nado o ataeru; ~*ed rights*, ataerareta kenri.

Vesta [véstə] *n.* (*Rom. myth.*) kamado no megami.

vestal [véstl] *a.* kamado no megami *Vesta* no; junketsu no. *n. Vesta*-megami ni tsukaeta otome (shojo).

vestibule [véstibju:l] *n.* genkan.

vestige [véstidʒ] *n.* keiseki; atokata.

vestry [véstri] *n.* (*church* no) hōfukushitsu. ~**man** [-mən] *n.*

vesture [véstʃə] *n.* ifuku; kimono. ⌊kyōkaiiin.

veteran [vétərən] *a.* rōkō no. *n.* rōkōsha.

veterinarian [vètərinéəriən] *n.* jūi; kemono (*animals*) no isha.

veterinary [vétərineri] *n. a.* jūi (no).

veto [ví:tou] *n.*, *v.* hinin; hantai (suru); kyohiken.

vex [veks] *v.* komaraseru; jirasu. ~*ed question*, giron no yoku deta mondai (*much discussed question.*).

vexation [vekséiʃən] *n.* shintsū; mushakusha.

vexatious [vekséiʃəs] *a.* urusai; yakkaina. ~**ly** *ad.* urusaku.

via [váiə] *prep.* ...o hete; *by way of*, o keiyu shite; *Via Siberia*, Shiberia keiyu.

viaduct [váiədʌkt] *n.* rikukyō; rikujō no hashi; kōkakyō.

vial [váiəl] *n.* garasubin, (kusuribin nado).

viands [váiəndz] *n. pl.* shokuryōhin, (*articles of food*).

vibrant [váibrənt] *a.* shindō suru.

vibrate [váibreit] *v.* shindō suru ; yuriugokasu.

vibratile [váibrətail] *a.* shindō dekiru ; shindō suru (-seino).

vibration [vaibréiʃən] *n.* shindō.

vicar [víkə] *n.* kyōku no bokushi. ～age [-idʒ] *n.* bokushikan.

vicarious [vaikéəriəs] *a.* dairi no (*deputy*).

vice [vais] *n.* ketten ; futoku ; akutoku.

vice- [vais-] *prefix* …no kawari. ～-admiral [-ǽdmirəl] kaigun chūjō. ～-consul [-kɔ́nsəl] fukuryōji. ～-gerent [-gérent / dʒí-] dairinin. ～-minister [-mínistə] *n.* jikan. ～-president [prézidənt] fukudaitōryō. ～ regal, fukuō no.

viceroy [váisrɔi] *n.* fukuō ; sōtoku.

vice versa [váisivə́:sə] *ad.* (L.) soshite mata sono hantai mo. *Frank blames Fred and v. v.*, Frank wa Fred o hinan shi, mata sono hantai mo. (*Fred wa Frank o*…)

vicinage [vísinidʒ] *n.* kinjo.

vicinity [visíniti] *n.* sekkin ; fukin.

vicious [víʃəs] *a.* ketten no aru ; akutoku no.

vicissitude [visísitju:d] *n.* hensen ; seisui ; henka. *The ～ of life may suddenly make a rich man very poor*, jisei no hensen wa fūsha o tachimachi hijōni mazushiku suru koto mo aru.

victim [víktim] *n.* gisei ; higaisha ; risaisha.

victor [víktə] *n.* shōrisha.

Victorian [viktɔ́:riən] *a.* Victoria jidai no.

victorious [viktɔ́:riəs] *a.* katta ; senshō no.

victory [víktəri] *n.* shōri.

victual [vítl] *n.* shokumotsu. *v.* …ni shokumotsu o kyōkyū suru. ～er *n.* shokuryō kyōkyūgyōsha.

videlicet [vidí:liset] *ad.* sunawachi (*viz.*).

video [vídiou] *a.* (*television*) eizō densōyō no.

vie [vai] *v.* kisou ; arasou ; kyōsō suru.

Vienna [viénə] *n.* Wiin.

Viennese [viení:z] *a.* Wiinjin no. *n.* Wiinjin.

view [vju:] *n.* kansatsu ; iken ; chōbō (nagame). *in ～ of*, o kangaete. *on ～*, chinretsu shite. *with a ～ to*, no tame ni. *v.* miru ; kansatsusuru. ～less *a.* me ni mienai. ～point *n.* kenchi.

vigil [vídʒil] *n.* tetsuya ; tsuya : *all night the mother kept ～ over the sick child*, tetsuya de okāsan wa sono byōki no ko o kambyō shita.

vigilance [vídʒiləns] *n.* nezu no ban ; keikai.

vigilant [vídʒilənt] *a.* nezu ni ki o tsukeru (ban o suru).

vignette [vinjét] *n.* karakusamoyō (hon no *title page* nado ni).

vigo(u)r [vígə] *n.* seiryoku ; genki. ∼**ous** [rəs] *a.* kyōsōna ; genki no yoi.

vile [vail] *a.* iyashii ; imawashii : ∼ *weather*, warui tenki. *a* ∼ *smell*, iyana nioi. ∼ *language*, gebita kotoba.

vilify [vílifai] *v.* akkō suru ; nonoshiru.

villa [vílə] *n.* bessō.

village [vílidʒ] *n.* mura. ∼**r** *n* sommin ; murabito.

villain [vílən] *n.* akkan. ∼**ous** *a.* akutō rashii. ∼**y** *n.* akuji ;

villein [vílin] *n.* nōdo ; chūsei no nōmin.   ⌈zaiaku.

villus [víləs] *n.* (*pl.* -**li** [lai]) jūmō ; nagai yawarakai ke.

vindicate [víndikeit] *v.* yōgo suru ; bengo suru ; shōmei suru.

vindication [vindikéiʃən] *n.* yōgo ; bengo ; shōmei.

vindictive [vindíktiv] *a.* fukushūshin no aru.

vine [vain] *n.* tsurukusa ; budō no ki.

vinegar [vínigə] *n.* su ; shokuyō no su. ∼**y** *a.* su no yōna.

vineyard [vínjəd] *n.* budōen.

vinous [váinəs] *a.* budōshu no ; budōshu ni nita.

vintage [víntidʒ] *n.* budōshūkaku (-ki).

vintner [víntnə] *n.* budōshushō (*whole saler of wine*).

vinyl [váinil] *n.* biniiru ; viniiru.

viol [váiəl] *n.* vaiolin ni nita furui gakki.

viola [vaióulə] *n.* biora ; viora.

violate [váiəleit] *v.* okasu ; somuku.

violation [vaiəléiʃən] *n.* ihan ; bōkō.

violence [váiələns] *n.* mōretsu ; hageshisa ; bōryoku.

violent [váiələnt] *a.* hageshii ; rambōna.

violet [váiəlit] *n.* sumire (iro).   ⌈nist).

violin [vaiəlín] *n.* vaiorin. ∼**ist** [váiəlinist] *n.* teikinka (vaiori-

violoncello [vaiələntʃélou] *n.* sero ; chero.

Vip, V.I.P. jūyōjimbutsu. (*very important person*).

viper [váipə] *n.* dokuhebi ; mamushi ; warumono.

virago [viréigou] *n.* gamigami-onna.   ⌈shojo no ; kiyoi.

virgin [vɔ́:dʒin] *n.* shojo ; otome. *the V* ∼, Seibo Mariya *a.*

virginity [və:dʒíniti] *n.* shojo de aru koto ; junketsu.
viridescent [viridésnt] *a.* tanryokushoku (awai midoriiro) no.
virile [vírəl] *a.* dansei no ; otokorashii.
virility [viríliti] *n.* otoko no seishokuryoku ; yūki ; chikara.
virtu [və:tjú:] *n.* kottōhin no yosa ; sono aikōheki.
virtual [və́:tʃəl] *a.* jissaijō no. ∼**ly** *ad.* jissai. ⌐yotte.
virtue [və́:tju:] *n.* bitoku ; teisō ; biten. *by (or in)* ∼ *of*, …ni
virtuosity [və̀:tʃuɔ́siti] *n.* bijutsuhin kanshikigan ; ongaku no ensō gijutsu. ⌐shu.
virtuoso [və:tjuóusou] *n.* bijutsuhin-kanteika ; ongaku no mei-
virtuous [və́:tjuəs] *a.* yūtoku no ; zenryōna ; tadashii.
virulence [vírjuləns] *n.* yūdoku ; dokusei.
virulent [vírjulənt] *a.* yūdoku no ; akusei no.
virus [váiərəs] *n.* byōdoku ; gaidoku.
visa [víːzə] *n.* (*Fr.*) biza ; ryokōmenjō nado no uragaki. *v.* ura-
visage [vízidʒ] *n.* kao ; kaotsuki. ⌐gaki suru.
vis-a-vis [víːzɑːvíː] *ad.* mukaiatte ; kao tsuki awasete. *prep.* no
viscera [vísərə] *n.* (*pl.*) naizō. ⌐mukai ni.
visceral [vísərəl] *a.* naizō no.
viscid [vísid] *a.* nebaru ; nenchakusei no (koi *syrup* no yōni).
viscose [vískous] *n.* bisukōsu (*cellulose* no genryō).
viscosity [viskɔ́siti] *n.* nenchakuryoku (nebakkosa).
viscount [váikaunt] *n.* shishaku. ∼**ess** *n.* shishakufujin.
viscous [vískəs] *a.* nenchaku suru ; nebaritsuku.
vise [vais], **vice** *n.* manriki ; (*Brit.*) *vice ;* (*Am.*) *vise.* neji de
shimete oite saiku suru.
vise [víːzei] *n.* =**visa.**
visibility [vizəbíliti] *n.* me ni mieru koto.
visible [vízəbl] *a.* me ni mieru ; miyasui.
visibly [vízəbli] *ad.* akirakani.
vision [víʒən] *n.* shikaku ; maboroshi.
visionary [víʒənəri] *a.* kūsō ni fukeru. *n.* kūsōka.
visit [vízit] *v.* mimau ; hōmon suru. *n.* mimai ; taizai ; kembu-
visitant [vízitənt] *n.* hōmonsha ; wataridori. ⌐tsu.
visitation [vizitéiʃən] *n.* junshi ; rinken.
visiting [vízitiŋ] *a.* hōmon no. ∼**card** *n.* meishi.
visitor [vízitə] *n.* raihōsha ; kembutsunin ; hōmonsha.

visor, vizor [váizə] *n.* mempō; kabuto (*helmet*) no mae no bubun (*front part*). (*Am.*) bōshi no hisashi.

vista [vístə] *n.* mitōshi; semai (*narrow*) sukima (*opening*) kara

visual [víʒuəl] *a.* me ni mieru. ⌊no mitōshi (*view through*).

visualize [víʒuəlaiz] *v.* mieruyōni suru.

vital [váitl] *a.* seishi ni kakawaru; jūyōna. ∼**ly** *ad.*

vitality [vaitǽliti] *n.* seikatsuryoku; seimeiryoku. ⌈*lungs*).

vitals [váitlz] *n.* (*pl.*) kyūsho (*necessary organ as heart*; *brains*;

vitamin [váitəmin] *n.* bitamin; vitamin. ⌈*the legal force*).

vitiate [víʃieit] *v.* sokonau; hōritsujō no kenri o ushinau (*destroy*

vitreous [vítriəs] *a.* garasu no; garasushitsu no.

vitrify [vítrifai] *v.* garasu ni suru.

vitriol [vítriəl] *n.* ryūsan.

vituperate [vaitjú:pəreit / vi-˪] *v.* shikaritsukeru.

vituperation [vaitjù:pəréiʃən / vi-˪] *n.* shisseki; akuba (*abuse*).

vituperative [vaitjú:pərətiv] *a.* nonoshiru.

vivacious [vaivéiʃəs] *a.* yōkina; kaikatsuna (*lively*).

vivacity [vaivǽsiti] *n.* yōki; kaikatsu (*liveliness*).

vivarium [vaivéəriəm] *n.* shizen-dōbutsuen.

viva voce [váivə vóusi] kōtō de.

vivid [vívid] *a.* kibi-kibi shita; azayakana. ∼**ly** *ad.*

vivify [vívifai] *v.* ikiiki saseru. ⌈mareru.

viviparous [vaivípərəs] *a.* taisei no (oyato onaji katachi de u-

vivisect [vivisékt / ví-] *v.* ikitamama o kaibō suru.

vivisection [vivisékʃən] *n.* seitaikaibō.

vixen [víksn] *n.* me-gitsune (kitsune no mesu).

viz [viz] sunawachi. *see*: **videricet** [vidí:liset].

vizier [víziə] *n.* (kaikyōkoku no) daijin.

V-mail [ví:meil] *n.* shukusha-firumu yūbin.

vocabulary [vəkǽbjuleri] *n.* goi; yōgoshū.

vocal [vóukəl] *a.* koe no; hassei no; onsei no. ∼ **cords**, seitai. ∼**ist** *n.* seigakuka. ∼**ize** *v.* koe ni hassuru; yūsei ni suru.

vocation [voukéiʃən] *n.* shokugyo. ∼**al** *a.* shokugyōjō no.

vocative [vókətiv] *a.* (*gram.*) yobikake no. *n.* kokaku (∼*case*).

vociferate [vo(u)sífəreit] *v.* sakebu; wameku.

vociferation [vo(u)sifəréiʃən] *n.* sakebi; donari; wameki.

vociferous [vo(u)sífərəs] *a.* sakebu; yakamashii.

vogue [voug] *n.* ryūkō; ninki. *be in* ~, hayatte iru.

voice [vɔis] *n.* koe; onsei; (*gram.*) iikata (-tai). *active* ~, nō-dōtai. *passive* ~, judōtai. *v.* iu. ~**d** [-t] *a.* yūsei no. ~**less** *a.* musei no.

void [vɔid] *a.* kū no; nai; kakete iru. *n.* kūsho. *v.* kara ni suru.

vol., volume. yōseki; kan.

volatile [vɔ́lətail] *a.* kihatsusei no. *gasoline is* ~, g. wa kihatsu-sei de aru. ~ *oil*, kihatsuyu.

volatility [vɔ̀lətíliti] *n.* kihatsusei; keihaku.

volcanic [vɔlkǽnik] *a.* kazan no; kazansayō ni yoru.

volcano [vɔlkéinou] *n.* kazan.

volition [vɔlíʃən] *n.* ishi; sentaku.

volley [vɔ́li] *n.* isseishageki. *by* ~, issei ni. *v.* isseishageki suru.

volleyball [vɔ́libɔːl] *n.* bareibōru.

volplane [vɔ́lplein] *n.* kūchūkassō. *v.* kūchūkassō suru.

volt [voult] *n.* (*elec.*) boruto. ~**meter** *n.* den'atsukei.

voltage [vóultidʒ] *n.* den'atsu.

voltaic [vɔltéiik] *a.* Volta-hōhō ni yoru; denryū no.

volubility [vɔ̀ljubíliti] *n.* nōben; oshaberi.

voluble [vɔ́ljubl] *a.* ryūchōna. ~**bly** *ad.* tōto to.

volume [vɔ́ljum] *n.* maki, (kan) (*book*); satsu; taiseki (*quantity*).

voluminous [vɔljúːminəs] *a.* (*volume*) kansū no ōi; moridakusan no.

voluntary [vɔ́ləntəri] *a.* jihatsu no; shigan no; jiyū no. *n.* ji-hatsuteki kōi. ~**ily** *ad.* jihatsutekini.

volunteer [vɔ̀ləntiə] *n.* yūshisha; shiganhei. *a.* shigan no. *v.* mizukara susunde suru; shigan suru.

voluptuary [vəlʌ́ptʃuəri] *n.* asobihōkeru mono.

voluptuous [vəlʌ́ptʃuəs] *a.* nikuyoku no.

vomit [vɔ́mit] *v.* ōto suru; haku. *n.* hedo; haita obutsu.

voodoo [vúːduː] *n.* kokujin no aida ni aru meishin.

voracious [vouréiʃəs] *a.* unto taberu; don'yokuna. ~**ly** *ad.*

voracity [vo(u)rǽsiti] *n.* taishoku; bōshoku.

vortex [vɔ́ːteks] *n.* (*pl.* **-tices** [-tisiːz]; **-es**) uzumaki; sempū.

votary [vóutəri] *n.* shinja; nesshinka. ⌊(tsumujikaze).

vote [vout] *n.* tōhyō. *v.* tōhyō suru; kaketsu suru. ~**r** [vóutə] *n.* tōhyōsha; senkyonin.

voting [vóutiŋ] *n.* tōhyō ; senkyo.

votive [vóutiv] *a.* kigan no ; kigan no tame hōnō shita.

vouch [vautʃ] *v.* shōmei suru ; hoshō suru. ⁓**er** [váutʃə] *n.* shō-nin ; shōkobukken ; shōko no shina.

vouchsafe [vautʃséif] *v.* ataeru ; tamawaru.

vow [vau] *n.* chikai. *v.* kami ni chikau ; seiyaku suru.

vowel [váuəl] *n.*, *a.* (*phon.*) boin (boon) no. (*cf. consonant*).

voyage [vɔ́iidʒ] *n.* kōkai ; ryokō. *v.* kōkai suru. ⁓**r** [-ə] *n.* ryo-kōsha ; kōkaisha.

voyageur [vwɔjɔzǽːr] *n.* Canada no mujinkyō o ryokō suru (aruttari, *canoe* ni nottari shite) Furansujin.

vs versus (soshō, kyōgi nado de) tai. *See :* V. versus. *tai*....

Vulcan [válkən] *n.* (*Rom. myth.*) hi to kaji no kami.

vulcanite [válkənait] *n.* ebonaito ; kataku shita gomu.

vulcanize [válkənaiz] *v.* iō o kuwaete netsu de shori shi, ya-warakai gomu to suru.

vulgar [válgə] *a.* zokuna ; gehinna. ⁓**ian** [-gɛ́əriən] *n.* zokubu-tsu. ⁓**ism** [válgərism] *n.* yahi. ⁓**ity** [vʌlgǽrti] *n.* zokuaku. ⁓**ize** *v.* gehin ni suru.

vulnerability [vʌlnərəbíliti] *n.* kizutsuki yasui koto.

vulnerable [válnərəbl] *a.* kizutsukerare yasui.

vulpine [válpain] *a.* kitsune no yōna ; zurui.

vulture [válṭʃə] *n.* hagetaka ; don'yokukan.

W

W, w [dʌblju:] (*pl.* W's, Ws, [bʌblju:z]). Eigo *alphabet* dai-23-bamme no moji.

w. *watt, west* no ryaku.

wabble, wobble. [wɔbl] *v.* guragura suru; yureru. *n.* guratsuki. ⌐n. tsumemono.

wad [wɔd] *n.* chiisana yawarakai katamari. *v.* tsumeru. ~**ding**

waddle [wɔdl] *v., n.* aruku (koto); yota-yota aruku (koto).

wade [weid] *v.* (suichū nado o) aruku; aruite wataru. ~**r** *n.* sagi, shigi nado no tori.

wafer [wéifə] *n.* kashi no isshu; oburāto.

waffle [wɔfl] *n.* waffuru (isshu no kashi).

waft [wɑːft] *v.* fukiokuru; tadayou (kūchū ya suijō o).

wag [wæg] *v.* furu (inu ga shippo o); yuriugokasu. *n.* hyōkimmono. ~**gery** [wǽgəri] *n.* kokkei; itazura; jōdan. ~**gish** *a.* kokkeina. ~**tail** *n.* (*bird*) sekirei.

wage [weidʒ] *n.* chingin; hōshū (futsū *pl.*). *v.* okonau; yaru. ~**-earner** [⌐ɔ́:nə] *n.* chinginrōdōsha. ~**worker** [⌐wɔ́:kə] *n.* chingin de hataraku hito.

wager [wéidʒə] *n.* kake; kaketa mono. *v.* kakeru. ~**of battle**, *n.* (*the use of personal combat to decide which party in dispute is right*), daihyō senshu no tatakai de kimeru shōbu.

waggle [wǽgl] *v.* furiugokasu.

wag(g)on [wǽgən] *n.* nibasha. **milk** ~, gyūnyū umpansha. *station* ~, isshu no jidōsha.

waif [weif] *n.* hōrōsha; furōsha; suterareta mono.

wail [weil] *v.* kanashinde naku. *n.* gōkyū (*cry*).

wainscot [wéinskət] *n.* (heya no) kabeita; koshiita; tokuni ita no bubun (*lower part*). ⌐(*Brit.*) otoko no chokki.

waist [weist] *n.* koshi. ~**band** [⌐bænd] *n.* koshiobi. ~**coat**

wait [weit] *v.* matsu. ~ *on* (*or upon*), haberu; kyūji suru. *n.* matsu koto. *lay* (*or lie in*) ~ *for*, o machibuseru. ~**er** *n.* kyūjinin. ~**ress** [⌐ris] *n.* kyūjionna.

waiting [wéitiŋ] *n.* matsu koto. ~**-room** *n.* machiaishitsu.

waive [weiv] v. (*right*, *claim*) nado o suteru; hōki suru.

wake [weik] v. me ga sameru; me o samasu. ~ *at seven every morning*, maiasa 7 ji ni me ga sameru. okosu. *to* ~ *him up*, kare o okosu. n. nezu no ban; tsuya. fune no tōtta ato. *in the* ~ *of*, ni tsuzuite. ~**ful** a. nemurarenu; yudan no nai.

waken [wéikn] v. me o samasu; me o samasaseru.

wale [weil] n. muchiato; mimizubare. v. kizuato o tsukeru.

walk [wɔːk] v. aruku. n. ayumi. *take a* ~, sampo suru. ~**er** n. hokōsha. ~**out** [↙áut] n. sutoraiki.

walkie-talkie [wɔ́ːkitɔ́ːki] n. (*Am.*) keitaiyō musendenwaki.

walking [wɔ́ːkiŋ] n. hokō. ~ *dress*, gaishutsugi. ~ *stick*, tsue. ~ *tour*, ensoku; toho ryokō.

wall [wɔːl] n. kabe; hei. *drive* (*or push*) *to the* ~, kyūchi ni otoshiireru; komaraseru. *go to the* ~, makeru. v. jōheki o megurasu. ~**flower** [↙fláuə] n. (*flow.*) nioiaraseitō. ~**-painting** [↙pèintiŋ] hekiga. ~**paper** [↙pèibə] n. kabegami.

wallet [wɔ́lit] n. satsuire; dōguire.

wallow [wɔ́lou] v. korobimawaru; fukeru. *the pigs* ~ *in the mud*, buta ga doro no naka ni koroge-mawaru. ~ *in money*, ⌞unaru hodo kane ga aru.

walnut [wɔ́ːlnʌt] n. kurumi.

walrus [wɔ́ːlrəs] n. (*zoo.*) seiuchi.

waltz [wɔːlts] n. warutsu. (*music with dance*) ⌜kau kaigara.

wampum [wɔ́mpəm] n. Hoku-Bei dojin ga kahei to shite tsuwan [wɔn] a. iro aozameta; chikara no nai.

wand [wɔnd] n. bō; mahō no tsue.

wander [wɔ́ndə] v. samayou. ~**er** n. samayou hito.

wane [wein] n. suibi; gentai: *be on the* ~, katamuite iru.

want [wɔnt] n. ketsubō; hoshigari. v. ketsubō suru; hoshigaru.

wanting [wɔ́ntiŋ] a. fusoku suru; nakunatte iru. *prep.* ...o nozoite; ...ga nakute wa.

wanton [wɔ́ntən] a. tajōna; fuzakeru. n. uwakimono.

war [wɔː] n. sensō. v. tatakau. *at* ~, kōsenchū de. ~**correspondent**, jūgun kisha. ~**cry** n. toki no koe. ~**fare** [↙fɛə] n. sensō. ~**like** [↙laik] n. kōsenteki no. ~**plane** [↙plein] n. gun'yōki. ~**ship** [↙ʃip] n. gunkan. ~**time** n. senji. ~**monger** [↙mʌŋgə] n. sensō de mōkeru shōnin. ~**hoop** [↙huːp] n. Amerika Indian no *warcry*.

warble [wɔ́ːbl] v. saezuru. ~**r** n. naku tori.

ward [wɔ:d] n. mihari ; kōken. v. hogo suru. ～ off, sakeru. ～-
en [wɔ́:dn] n. tengoku. ～er n. bannin. ～robe n. ishōtodana.
～room n. (gunkan no) shikanshitsu. ⌈kō.

ware [wεə] n. shinamono ; (pl.) shōhin. ～house [-haus] n. sō-
warily [wέərili] ad. yōjin shite. ～iness n. yōjin ; chūi.

warm [wɔ:m] a. atatakana. v. atatameru ; atatamaru. ～ly ad.
atatakaku. ～-blooded [-blʌ́did] a. atatakai. nekketsu no. ～-
hearted [-hɑ́:tid] a. dōjō no aru ; shinsetsuna.

warmth [wɔ:mθ] n. ondan ; atatakasa ; ondo.

warn [wɔ:n] v. keikoku suru. ～ing n. keikoku. ⌈gamu.

warp [wɔ:p] n. tateito ; yugami. v. soraseru ; higamaseru ; yu-

warrant [wɔ́rənt] n. seitōna riyū ; konkyo. v. hoshō suru. ～-
ee [wɔ̀rəntí:] n. hihoshōnin. ～or n. hoshōnin. ～y [-i] n. hoshō ; kyoka.

warren [wɔ́rin] n. yōtojō ; usagi ga katte aru tokoro.

warring [wɔ́:riŋ] a. aiarasou ; tekitai suru.

warrior [wɔ́riə] n. yūshi ; senshi ; sensō o suru hito.

Warsaw [wɔ́:sɔ:] n. Warusō (Poland kyōwakoku no shufu).

wart [wɔ:t] n. ibo. ～y a. ibo no yōna. ～hog n. Afurika ni iru
yasei no ibobuta. (wild hog)

wary [wέəri] a. yōjimbukai ; shinchōna.

was [wɔz] datta ; atta. " be " no kako. 1 (ichi) ninshō, 3 (san)
ninshō, tansū ga shugo no toki).

wash [wɔʃ] v. arau ; sentaku suru. n. arai ; sentaku. ～ one's hand
of, ...to kankei o tatsu. ～able a. arai no kiku. ～ing n. sentaku. ～ out, iro ga nukeru. ～y a. usui ; mizuppoi. ～room
n. sentakushitsu.

Washington [wɔ́ʃiŋtən] n. Washinton, (USA no shufu).

wasp [wɔsp] n. hachi. ～ish a. hachi no yōna.

wassail [wɔ́seil] n. iwaizake ; shukuen.

wastage [wéistidʒ] n. shōmō ; haibutsu.

waste [weist] a. arehateta ; yokeina. v. muda ni suru ; rōhi suru. n. arenohara. ～-paper n. hogugami. ～-basket (Am.) n.
kuzukago. ～ful a. mudana. ～-pipe n. haisuikan. got o ～, su-
terareru. lay ～, hidoku itande iru ; kowarete iru.

wastrel [wéistrəl] n. furōji ; yakuzamono.

watch [wɔtʃ] n. kaichūdokei ; kanshu ; yōjin. keep the ～, tōcho-
ku suru. keep ～, mihari suru. off ～, hiban de. on the ～, ban

o shite. *on* ⁓, tōban de. *v.* miharu; ban o suru. ⁓**ful** *a.* yōjin suru. ⁓**man** *n.* bannin. ⁓**maker** [⁻méikə] *n.* tokeishi. ⁓**word** *n.* aikotoba.

water [wɔ́:tə] *n.* mizu. (*pl.*) kawa; umi. *v.* mizu o kakeru; namida ga deru. ⁓**bird** *n.* mizutori. ⁓**closet** [⁻klɔ̀zit] *n.* (suisen) benjo. ⁓**colo(u)r** [⁻kÀlə] *n.* suisai enogu. ⁓**course** *n.* suiryū. ⁓**fall** *n.* taki. ⁓**fowl** *n.* mizudori. ⁓**ing place,** mizunomiba. ⁓**lily** *n.* suiren. ⁓**line** *n.* kissuisen. ⁓**mark** *n.* suiryōhyō. ⁓**melon** *n.* suika. ⁓**power** [⁻pàuə] *n.* suiryoku. ⁓**proof** *a.* bōsui no. ⁓**shed** *n.* bunsuikai. ⁓**spout** *n.* tatsumaki. ⁓**supply** [⁻səplài] *n.* kyūsui. ⁓**tight** *a.* bōsui no. ⁓**works** *n.* kyūsui-shisetsu. ⁓**y** *a.* mizu no.

watt [wɔt] *n.* watto (denryoku no jitsuyō tan'i).

wattle [wɔ́tl] *n.* (koeda de anda) tsue; kui. tareniku. *v.* amu; kakine nado o *wattle* de tsukuru.

wave [weiv] *n.* nami. *v.* hadō suru; namidataseru.

wavelet [wéivlit] *n.* sazanami.

waver [wéivə] *v.* yuragu; tamerau.

wavy [wéivi] *a.* namidatsu; unetta; namiutsu. ⌐ta.

wax [wæks] *n.* rō; mitsurō. *v.* rō o nuru. ⁓**en** *a.* rō de tsukut

way [wei] *n.* michi; hōkō; yarikata. *all the* ⁓, zutto. *by the* ⁓, tsui de ni; sore wa sōto. *by* ⁓ *of,* …o tōtte. *fight one's* ⁓, funtō shite susumu. *gather* ⁓, sokuryoku o masu. *give* ⁓, michi o yuzuru. *go a long* ⁓, ōini yakudatsu. *have one's* ⁓, omō tōri ni suru. *in a* ⁓, yaya. *in the (or one's)* ⁓, tochū ni; jama ni natte. *lose* ⁓, hayasa ga niburu. *make one's* ⁓, michi o kirihiraku. *make* ⁓, yuzuru. *no — (or* ⁓*s),* sukoshi mo. *on the* ⁓, tochū ni. *out of the* ⁓, michi o hazurete. *work one's* ⁓, jojoni susumu. ⁓ *in,* irikuchi. ⁓ *out,* deguchi. ⁓**farer** [wéifèrə] *n.* tabibito. ⁓**lay** [-léi] *v.* machibuse suru. ⁓**side** [-sáid] *n.* robō. ⁓**ward** [wéiwəd] *a.* wagamamana.

W.C. suisen benjo (*water closet*).

we [wi:] *pron.* warera wa(ga); bokura (watashi-tachi) wa(ga).

weak [wi:k] *a.* yowai; byōshinna. ⁓ **side** *n.* jakuten. ⁓**en** *v.* yowameru. ⁓**ling** *n.* byōshinna hito. ⁓**ly** *a.* yowai. ⁓**ness** *n.* kyojaku.

weal [wi:l] *n.* annei; kōfuku. mimizubare. ⌐*n.* kyojaku.

wealth [welθ] *n.* tomi; fūki. ⁓**y** *a.* hōfuna; tonda.

wean [wi:n] *v.* chibanare saseru.

weapon [wépən] *n.* buki.

wear [wɛə]*v.* **wore, worn; wearing.** kiru (kimono o); motsu (kireji ga). *this coat has worn well,* yoku motta. taeru. **~** *away,* dandan ni heru. **~** *down,* yowaru. **~** *off,* suriherasu. **~** *on,* sorosoro (toki ga) tatsu. *it became hotter as the days wore on,* hi ga tatsu ni tsure atsuku natta. **~** *out,* tsukai sonjiru. *n.* cha-kuyō. **~** *and tear,* surikire. **~ily** *ad.* tsukarete. **~iness** *n.* tsukare. **~isome** [wíərisʌm] *a.* akiaki suru.

weary [wíəri] *a.* tsukarete (iru); taikutsuna. *v.* tsukaresaseru; tsukarere.

weasel [wí:zl] *n.* (*zoo.*) itachi.

weather [wéðə] *n.* tenki. *a.* kazakami no. *v.* fūu ni sarasu (tae-ru). **~board** *n.* shitamiita; kabeita. **~bound** *a.* fūu ni sama-tagerareta. **~cock** *n.* kazami. **~forecast** *n.* tenkiyohō. **~glass** *n.* seiukei. **~proof** *a.* fūu ni taeru. **~wise** *a.* yoku tenki o ateru.

weave [wi:v] *v.* **wove** *or* (*rare*) **weaved, woven** *or commercial* **wove; wearing.** (hata o) oru. **~r** *n.* (hata no) orite.

web [web] *n.* orimono; kumo no su. **~-footed** [⌐fútid] *a.* mizukaki no aru.

wed [wed] *v.* kekkon suru. **~lock** *n.* kekkon-seikatsu.

wedding [wédiŋ] *n.* kekkonshiki. **~ ring** *n.* kekkon-yubiwa.

wedge [wedʒ] *n.* kusabi. *v.* kusabi de waru.

Wednesday [wénzdi] *n.* Suiyōbi.

wee [wi:] *a.* chiisai. *a little* **~,** hon no choppiri.

weed [wi:d] *n.* zassō. *v.* zassō o nozoku. **~y** *a.* zassō no ōi.

weeds [wi:dz] *n.* (*pl.*) mofuku (mibōjin no).

week [wi:k] *n.* shū; isshūkan. **~end** [⌐end] *n.* shūmatsu. **~day** [⌐dei] *n.* shūjitsu (Nichiyō igai no hi).

weekly [wí:kli] *a.* isshūkan no; isshū ikkai no. *n.* shūkanshim-bun (zasshi).

weep [wi:p] *v.* naku; kanashimu.

weevil [wí:vl] *n.* kokuzōmushi.

weft [weft] *n.* yokoito (orimono no).

weigh [wei] *v.* hakari ni kakeru; mekata o hakaru; mekata ga ...aru; kurushimeru. **~** *down,* katsu. omo ni o owasu. **~** *in,* shiaizen ni taijū o hakaru.

weight [weit] *n.* omosa; mekata; (*fig.*) sekinin. *v.* omoku suru. **~y** *a.* omoi; (*fig.*) jūyōna.

weir [wiə] *n.* seki; damu; yama.

weird [wiəd] *a.* kimi no warui ; sugoi.

welcome [wélkəm] *n., a.* kangei (sareru) ; *be* ~ *to*, jiyūni shite yoi : *you are* ~, (yoku irasshai mashita) ; dō itashimashite. *n.* kangei : *give a warm* ~, kokoro o komete mukaeru. *v.* kangei suru. *you will always have a* ~ *here*, itsu demo dōzo oide kudasai.

weld [weld] *n., v.* yōsetsu (suru).

welfare [wélfɛə] *n.* annei ; kōfuku.

welkin [wélkin] *n.* (*poet.*) ōzora ; aozora.   [gensen ; suigen.

well [wel] *n.* ido ; izumi. *v.* wakideru. ~**spring** [wélspriŋ] *n.*

well [wel] *ad.* yoku ; jūbunni. *as* ~, mo mata. *as* ~ *as*, mo dōyō ni. ~ *off*, kurashimuki ga yoi. *a.* tsugō no yoi ; jōbu de aru. *inter.* mā ; sā. ~ *then*, sore dewa. ~**-being** *n.* annei. ~**born** *a.* umare no yoi. ~**-bred** *a.* sodachi no yoi. ~**-known** *a.* yūmeina. ~**-nigh** [-nai] *ad.* hotondo. ~**-timed** *a.* jiki ni kanatta. ~**-to-do** [-tədúː] *a.* yūfukuna. ~**-disposed** [-dispóuzed] *a.* shinsetsuna ; kidate no yoi. ~**-favo(u)red** [-féivəd] *a.* kaodachi no yoi. ~**-fixed** *a.* ii kurashi o shite iru. ~**-conducted** [kəndΛktid] *a.* gyōgi no yoi. ~**-chosen** [-tʃóuzn] *a.* seisensareta. ~**-defined** [difáind] *a.* hakkiri teigisareta. ~**-founded** [-fáundid] *a.* riyū no hakkiri shita. ~**-groomed** [-grúːmd] *a.* teire no yoku todoita. ~**-heeled** *a.* (*Am.*) kanemochi no. ~**-informed** [-infɔ́ːmd] *a.* hiroku shitte iru. ~**-knit** [-nit] *a.* gatchiri shita. ~**-preserved** [-prizɔ́ːvd] *a.* toshi no wari ni wakai. ~**-read** [-réd] *a.* hiroku yonde iru. ~**-spoken** [-spoukn] *a.* yoku hanasareta.

Welsh [welʃ] *a.* Eikoku Wēruzu (*Wales*) no. *n.* Wēruzujin.

welt [welt] *n.* heri ; fuchidori.

welter [wéltə] *v.* korogemawaru ; uneru. *n.* konran ; ōsawagi.

welterweight [wéltəweit] *n.* werutākyū no kentōka.

wen [wen] *n.* (*med.*) kobu.

wench [wentʃ] *n.* shōjo ; wakai musume ; jochū.

wend [wend] *v.* **wended** *or* **went ; wending.** *arch.* yuku ; "*went*" wa kono go no furui *past* no katachi.

went [went] *v. see :* **go** & **wend.**

wept [wept] *v. see :* **weep.**

were [wəː] "*be*" no fukusū kako (*plural, past*). *as it* ~, iwaba.

west [west] *n.* nishi. (*W*~) seiyō. (*Am.*) (*W*~) seibu. *a.* nishi no. *W*~ *Indies*, Nishi-Indo. ~**erly**, ~**ern** *a.* nishi no. *n.* sei-

bugeki. ～ward *a.* seihō no. *ad.* nishi e.
westernize [wéstənaiz] *v.* seiyōfū ni suru.
wet [wet] *a.* nurete iru ; ame no. *n.* shikki. *v.* nurasu.
wether [wéðə] *n.* kyosei-shita ohitsuji. ⌈Unions).
WFTU Sekai Rōdō Kumiai Remmei (*World Federation of Trade*
whack [(h)wæk] *v.* pokat to tataku. *n.* ōda ; naguru oto.
whale [(h)weil] *n.* kujira. *v.* kujira o toraeru. ～**bone** *n.* kujira
no hone. ～**r** *n.* hogeisen ; kujira tori no fune.
whang [(h)wæŋ] *v.* don to utsu.
wharf [(h)wɔːf] *n.* hatoba. ～**age** [-idʒ] *n.* hatoba shiyōryōkin.
what [(h)wɔt] *pron.* nan no? nani o? dono kurai? *that which*
(*relat. pron.*). *and* ～ *not*, sonota iroiro. *not but* ～, tokoro no
koto (mono) igai nai. ～ *by* …～ *by*, …shitari …shitari shite.
～ *for*? naze? ～ *though*, datte nan da? *what's* ～, koto no shinjitsu wa (da). ～**ever**, ～**soever** *pron.*, *a.* donna de arō tomo.
wheat [(h)wiːt] *n.* komugi. ～**en** *a.* komugi no ; komugisei no.
wheedle [(h)wíːdl] *v.* koshiguruma ni noseru.
wheel [(h)wiːl] *n.* wa ; sharin ; jitensha. *v.* gururi to muki o
kaesaseru. ～**barrow** [-bærou] *n.* teoshiguruma. ～**wright**
[-rait] *n.* kurumadaiku.
wheeze [(h)wiːz] *v.*, *n.* zeizei iu (nodo ga). **wheezy** *a.* zeizei iu.
whelm [(h)welm] *v.* mizu de ōu ; attō suru.
whelp [(h)welp] *n.* koinu ; norakurakozō. *v.* (ko o) umu.
when [(h)wen] *ad.* itsu? *conj.* …suru toki (ni). ～**ever** *ad. conj.*
itsu demo …suru toki ni wa.
whence [(h)wens] *ad.* doko kara ; dōshite.
where [(h)wɛə] *ad.* doko e? doko ni? ; …suru tokoro no ; suru
basho. ～**about(s)** [(h)wɛəráuts] *ad.* dono hen ni. *n.* yukue.
～**as** *conj.* de aru kara. ～**at** *ad.* sore ni taishite. ～**by** *ad.* sore
ni yotte. ～**fore** *ad.* da kara ; sono yue ni. *n.* riyū. ～**on** *ad.*
nan no ue ni. ～**soever** *ad.* doko demo. ～**to** *ad.* nan ni. ～**upon**
ad. soreyue ni. ～**with** *ad.* sore o motte. ～**withal** [-wiðɔl]
n. hitsuyōna mono (kane).
wherever [(h)wɛərévə] *ad.* doko e de arō to.
wherry [(h)wéri] *n.* watashibune.
whet [(h)wet] *v.* togu. ～**stone** [-stoun] *n.* toishi.
whether [(h)wéðə] *conj.* (de aru ka) dō ka ; izure ni shite mo.
～ *or no*, iya demo ō demo.

whey [(h)wei] *n.* nyūshō (gyūnyū no suibun).

which [(h)wit∫] *pron.* (*rel.*, *int.*) dore? dochira? suru tokoro no. *a.* dochira no. **~ever** *pron.*, *a.* dochira de atte mo.

whiff [(h)wif] *v.* (kemuri nado o) hitofuki fuku. *n.* hitofuki.

whiffle [(h)wifl] *v.* karuku fuku. guratsuku ; guratsukaseru. **~tree** *n.* (*Am.*) hikizuna o tsuketa bō. *see* : **whippletree**.

Whig [(h)wig] *n.* (*Brit.*) Minkentō-in ; (*Am.*) Dokuritsutō-in.

while [(h)wail] *n.* aida ; zanji. *after a* **~**, shibaraku shite. *all this* **~**, kono (nagai) aidajū. *in a little* **~**, jiki ni. *worth* **~**, honeorigai no aru. *v.* burabura sugosu. *conj.*, *ad.* aida ; to tomo ni ; shikaru ni ippō dewa.

whilst [(h)wailst] *conj.*, *ad.* (*Brit.*) = **while**.

whim [(h)wim] *n.* kimagure.⌐kun itte naku (sono koe).

whimper [(h)wimpə] *v.*, *n.* shikushiku naku (sono koe) ; kun-

whimsey, -sy [(h)wimzi] *n.* kimagure.

whimsical [(h)wimzikl] *a.* kimagurena.⌐goe o dasu.

whine [(h)wain] *n.* nakigoe (chiisai kodomo nado no) *v.* naki-

whinny [(h)wini] *n.* uma no inanaki. *v.* inanaku.

whip [(h)wip] *v.* muchi-utsu ; mawasu (koma o). **~** *off*, nugisuteru. **~** *out*, kyūni nuku (*sword*) ; hikidasu. *n.* muchi. **~cord** [⌐kɔːd] *n.* muchi-nawa. **~lash** [⌐læ∫] *n.* muchi no himo. **~ing boy** *n.* (*scapegoat.*) hito no tsumi o shou hito, mata wa mono. **~stitch** [⌐stit∫] *n.* kire no haji o "matsurinui" suru koto. **~stock** [⌐stɔk] *n.* muchi no e (*handle*).

whippletree [(h)wipltriː] *n.* sharin no yokogi ; uma no hikizuna o shibaritsukete aru yokogi.

whippoorwill [(h)wipəwil] *n.* yotaka no tagui ; nakigoe ga "*wipuawil*" to kikoeru kara.⌐*v.* hyū to tobu.

whir, whirr [(h)wəː] *n.* hyūhyū iu oto ; bunbun mawaru oto.

whirl [(h)wəːl] *v.* guruguru mawaru. **~***up*, maiagaru. *n.* kaiten ; sempū. **~pool** [⌐puːl] *n.* uzumaki. **~wind** *n.* sempū.

whirligig [(h)wəːligig] *n.* koma ; kaiten mokuba.

whisk [(h)wisk] *n.* kobōki ; keiran awadateki ; hitoharai. *v.* satto kakureru ; harai nokeru.

whiskers [(h)wiskəz] *n.* (*pl.*) hōhige ; neko no hige.

whiskey [(h)wiski] *n.* wisukii.⌐suru).

whisper [(h)wispə] *n.*, *v.* sasayaki (-u) ; kosokoso-banashi (o

whist [(h)wist] *v.* isshu no torampu asobi ; *inter.* shi ! shizukani !

whistle [(h)wísl] *n.*, *v.* kuchibue ; yobiko (o fuku).

whit [(h)wit] *n.* sukoshi. *not a* ~, sukoshi mo...nai.

white [(h)wait] *a.* shiroi ; gimpaku no ; keppakuna. *n.* shiroi iro ; hakujin. *v.* shiroku suru. ~ **ant,** *n.* shiroari (*termite*). ~ **lie** *n.* tsumi no nai uso. **the** ~ **House,** Hakuakan ; daitōryō kantei. ~**plague** *n.* haikekkaku. ~**slave** *n.* hakujin shūgyōfu.

whither [(h)wíðə] *ad.*, *conj.* (*to which place*) soko e ; doko e.

whiting [(h)wáitiŋ] *n.* hakua ; mizushikkui.

whitish [(h)wáitiʃ] *a.* yaya shiroi ; shiroppoi.

whitlow [(h)wítlou] *n.* (*med.*) hyōsō.

Whitsunday [(h)wítsʌndi] *n.* Seireikōtansai.

whittle [(h)wítl] *v.* kiru ; sakugen suru ; kezuru.

whiz(z) [(h)wiz] *n.* hyū (oto) (*onomatopoeia*). *v.* hyū to naru.

who [hu:] *pron.* dare ? (...suru) tokoro no hito ; soshite sono-hito wa. ~'s who? dare ga dare ka? jimmeiroku. ~dunit [hù:dánit] *n.* suiri shōsetsu. ~ever [hu:évə], ~soever [-souévə] *pron.* dare de arō to (...suru) mono wa.

whole [houl] *a.* zentai no ; kanzenna ; buji de. *n.* zentai. *as a* ~, zentai kara mite. *on the* ~, gaishite. ~sale *a.* oroshiuri no. ~some *a.* kenkō ni yoi.

wholly [hóuli] *ad.* mattaku.

whom [hu:m] *pron.* "*who*" no mokutekikaku ; dare ni (o)?

whoop [h(w)u:p] *v.* sakebu. *n.* sakebi. ~ing cough, hyakuni-chizeki.

whore [hɔ:] *n.* imbaifu.

whose [hu:z] *pron.* "*who*" mata wa "*which*" no shoyūkaku. "dare no? ", "dore no? ".

why [(h)wai] *ad.*, *conj.* naze ni. ~ *not?* naze ikenai? *inter.* sore da kara (iwanu koto ja nai) ; naruhodo.

wick [wik] *n.* (rōsoku ; rampu nado no) shin.

wicked [wíkid] *a.* warui ; fuseina ; rokudenashi no.

wicker [wíkə] *n.* yanagi no koeda. *a.* eda o ande tsukutta. ~work *n.* yanagizaiku.

wicket [wíkit] *n.* kugurido ; suimon.

wide [waid] *a.* hiroi ; hazureta : *the shot went* ~, mato kara tō-ku hazureta. *ad.* hiroku. ~ *awake*, me o ōkiku hiraite ; hak-kiri me ga samete.

widen [wáidn] *v.* hiroku suru (naru).

widow [wídou] *n.* yamome ; mibōjin. **~er** [wídouə] *n.* otoko yamome. **widow's mite** [-mait] *n.* mazushii hito ga yorokonde suru kenkin ; hinja no ittō.

width [widθ] *n.* hirosa ; haba.

wield [wi:ld] *v.* furuu ; tsukau. *~ a sword (pen, authority, power etc.),* ken (pen, ken'i, seiryoku nado) o furuu (tsukau). **~able** *a.* furui uru. **~er** *n.* furuu hito. **~y** *a.* tsukai yasui ; toriatsukai yasui.

wiener [wíːnə] *n.* (*Am.*) gyū ya buta no chiisai chōzume. **~wurst** [-wə́ːst] *n.* Doitsu shiki chōzume.

wife [waif] *n.* (*pl.* **-ves**) tsuma. **~ly** *a.* tsuma rashii. **~hood** *n.* tsuma no mibun.

wig [wig] *n.* katsura. **~ged** [wigd] *a.* katsura o kabutta. **~like** [-laik] *a.* *wig* no yōna. **~eon** [wídʒən] =**widgeon** *n.* (*bird*) hidorigamo. **~gle** *v.* achirakochira to koashi de chokochoko ugokimawaru. **~gler** *n.* *wiggle* suru hito.

wight [wait] *n.* hito (*arch., or jocul.*) ; *Isle of Wight = Isle of Man.*

wigwam [wígwæm] *n.* Hoku-Bei dojin no koya.

wild [waild] *a.* yasei no ; arai ; yabanna. *n.* areno. *ad.* rambōni ; muchakuchani. **~cat** [wáildkæt] *a.* muteppōna. *n.* yamaneko. **~ strike,** yamanekosōgi. **~fire** *n.* taika ; isshu no hitsukegusuri (shōizai). *spread like wildfire,* tachimachi hirogaru. **~ing** *n.* yasei shokubutsu. **~ish** *a.* yaya sobōna. **~ly** *ad.* yasei de ; kyōbō ni. **~ness** *n.* yasei ; yaban.

wilderness [wíldənis] *n.* areno ; hateshi no nai hirogari.

wile [wail] *n.* takurami ; tekuda. *v.* hito o azamuku.

wilful [wílful] *a.* wagamamana ; koi no.

will [wil] *n.* ishi. *have one's ~,* omou tōri ni suru. yuigon : *v.* ketsui suru ; nozomu. *aux. v.* shi tai ; shi tai to omou. **~ful** *a.* =**wilful**. **~-o'-the-wisp** *n.* onibi. (*aux. v.* no yōhō wa furoku ni). ⌐konde (itashi masu).

willing [wíliŋ] *a.* yorokobu ; yorokonde...suru. **~ly** *ad.* yorokonde (itashi masu).

willow [wílou] *n.* (*bot.*) yanagi. **~y** *a.* shinayakana ; jōhinna.

willy-nilly [wílinili] *ad.* iya demo ō demo.

wilt [wilt] *v.* shibomu ; shibomaseru ; chikara o ushinau.

wily [wáili] *a.* zurui. ⌐togeru.

win [win] *v.* **won; winning.** katte toru ; te ni ireru ; nozomi o

wince [wins] *v., n.* hirumu(i) ; tajirogu(i) (*flinch*).

winch [wintʃ] *n.* makiageki ; winchi.

wind [waind] *v.* **wound** ; **winding** maku ; uneru. ∼ *into a person's favor,* umaku toriiru. ∼ *off,* makimodosu ; tatamu. ∼**up** [wáindʌp] *n.* (*base.*) pitchā ga tōkyū suru jumbi dōsa.

wind [wind] *n.* kaze ; iki. *v.* kagitsukeru ; iki o kiraseru. *get* ∼ *of,* o kagitsukeru. *in the* ∼, (hisokani) okonawarete. *take* ∼, seken ni shirewataru. ∼**cone** *n.* fukinagashi. ∼ **instrument** *n.* kangakki. ∼**fall** *n.* kobore-saiwai. ∼**flower** *n.* anemone. ∼**lass** [⌐ləs] *n.* makiageki. ∼**mill** *n.* kazaguruma. ∼**pipe** *n.* kikan. ∼**shield** *n.* (jidōsha no) kazeyokegarasu.

winding [wáindiŋ] *a.* uneru ; kuneru. ∼ **sheet** *n.* shitai ni kabuseru koromo. ⌐madoshikii.

window [wíndou] *n.* mado. ∼**pane** *n.* madogarasu. ∼**sill** *n.*

windward [wíndwəd] *n., a.* kazakami (no). *ad.* kazakami.

windy [wíndi] *a.* kaze no fuku ; kaze no ataru.

wine [wain] *n.* budōshu. *in* ∼, sake ni yotte. ∼**bibber** [⌐bibə] *n.* ōzakenomi. ∼ **celler** [-sélə] *n.* sakagura. ∼**-colo(u)red** [⌐kʌləd] *n.* komurasaki no akairo. ∼ **gallon** [-gǽlən] *n.* (*Brit.*) 277. 42 *cu. inches.* (*Am.*) 231 *cu. inches.* ∼**glass** *n.* chiisai sakazuki. ∼**ry** [wáinəri] *n.* budōshujōzōkōba. ∼**sap** [wáinsæp] *n.* (*Am.*) fuyuringo no isshu. ∼**skin** *n.* yagi ya buta nado no kanzenna kawa de tsukutta sakebukuro. ∼**y** [wáini] *a. wine* ni kansuru ; *wine* no.

wing [wiŋ] *n.* tsubasa ; hane : *under the* ∼ *of,* no hogo no moto ni. *v.* tsubasa o tsukeru. ∼**ed** [wíŋgd] *a.* tsubasa o tsukete.

wink [wiŋk] *n.* mekubase. *in a* ∼, matataku ma ni. ∼ **meku-winner** [wínə] *n.* shōrisha. ⌐base suru.

winning [wíniŋ] *a.* kokoro o toraeru ; aikyō no aru. *n.* shōri ; (*pl.*) shōhin. ∼ **post** *n.* kesshōten.

winnow [wínou] *v.* tsubu (*grain*) to kara (*chaff*) o fukiwakeru.

winsome [wínsəm] *a.* aikyō no aru. ⌐*n.* sono kikai.

winter [wíntə] *n.* fuyu. *v.* fuyu o sugosu. ∼**ize** *v.* fuyu e no setsubi o hodokosu. ∼**kill** *v.* samusa no tame shinu. ∼**green** *n.* (*Am.*) Kita Amerika no shokubutsu.

wintry [wíntri] *a.* fuyu no ; tsumetai ; reitanna.

wipe [waip] *n.* nugui ; hitofuki. *v.* nuguu.

wire [waiə] *n.* harigane ; densen ; dempō. *v.* dempō o utsu. ∼

guage [⌐géidʒ] *wire* no futosa o hakaru *metre*. ⁓**puller** *n*. aya-tsuriningyō.

wireless [wáiəlis] *n*. musendenshin ; musendenwa. *v*. musen-denshin o utsu. *a*. musen no. ⁓**station** *n*. musendenshinkyo-ku. ⁓**telegraphy** *n*. musendenshin. ⁓**telephone** *n*. musen-denwa. ⁓**photo** [⌐fòutou] *n*. densō shashin. ⁓**puller** [⌐pulə] *n* kage de ito (*string*) o hiku hito.

wiring [wáiəriŋ] *n*. kasen ; fusen.

wiry [wái(ə)ri] *a*. harigane no yōna.

wisdom [wízdəm] *n*. chie ; fumbetsu. ⁓ *tooth*, chieba.

wise [waiz] *a*. kemmeina. *n*. kenjin. *in any* ⁓ (*anyway*), dōshi-te mo. *in no* ⁓, kesshite …nai. ⁓**acre** *n*. rikōburu hito. ⁓**ly** *ad*. kashikoku.

wish [wiʃ] *n*. negai. *have no* ⁓ *to*, …suru ki ga nai. *v*. negau ; hoshigaru. *I* ⁓, shitai ; …yoi ga. ⁓**ful** *a*. nozonde iru.

wisp [wisp] *n*. chiisana taba (yakusō nado no).

wistaria [wistéəriə] *n*. (*bot*.) fuji.

wistful [wístful] *a*. hoshisōna (metsuki ; kaotsuki).

wit [wit] *n*. (*pl*.) chinō ; kichi ; kiten. *at one's* ⁓*'s end*, tohō ni kurete. *lose one's* ⁓*s*, ki ga kuruu. *v*. shiru. *to* ⁓, sunawachi. ⁓**less** *a*. chie no nai ; orokana.

witch [witʃ] *n*. onna-mahōtsukai. *v*. majutsu o kakeru. ⁓**craft** *n*. mahō. ⁓**doctor** *n*. (Afurika de) majinaishi. ⁓**hunt** *n*. (*Am*.) jibun no seijiteki rieki no tame ni hito o hakugai suru koto. ⁓**ery** [wítʃəri] *n*. mahō ; maryoku. ⁓**ing** *n*. mahō o kakeru koto.

with [wið] *prep*. to tomo ni ; motte ; no aru ; o tazusaete.

withal [wiðɔ́:l] *ad*. sono ue ; katsu mata. *prep*. …de.

withdraw [wiðdrɔ́:] *v*. hikkomeru ; torikesu ; shirizoku. ⁓**al** *n*. tekkai.

withe [wiθ / waið] *n*., *v*. yanagi no eda (de shibaru).

wither [wíðə] *v*. shibomu ; kareru ; otoroesaseru. ⁓**s** [wíðəz] *n*. (*pl*.) kubi no ushiro no ichiban takai tokoro no bubun.

withhold [wiðhóuld] *v*. sei suru ; hikaeru ; sashihikaeru.

within [wiðín] *prep*. uchi ni ; inai ni. ⁓ *oneself*, shinchū de. *ad*. uchi ni ; ie no uchi ni. *n*. naibu.

without [wiðáut] *prep*. soto ni ; sezu ni ; nakute. ⁓ *a home*, uchi no nai. *conj.* de nakereba. *ad.* okugai ni. *n.* gaibu.

withstand [wiðstǽnd] *v.* fusegu ; kobamu.

witness [wítnis] *n.* shōko ; shōnin. *in ~ of*, no shōko to shite. *v.* shōsuru ; mokugeki suru : *he ~ed the accident*, kare wa manoatari sono sainan o mitan da.

witticism [wítisizm] *n.* share ; hiniku (tsūrei keibetsuteki).

wittingly [wítiŋli] *ad.* koi ni ; wazato.

witty [wíti] *a.* umai kirikaeshi o suru ; ki no kiita ; atama no ii.

wives [waivz] *n.* **wife** no *pl.*

wizard [wízəd] *n.* mahōtsukai (otoko). **~ry** [wízədri] *n.* mahō.

wizen [wízn] *v.* kareru ; shibomu. **~ed** [-d] *a.* karete ; shibon-wo [wou] *inter.* dōdō ! tomare ! (uma ni iu *to a horse*). ⌐de.

wobble [wóbl] *v.* yoro-yoro suru. *n.* guratsuki ; yoromeki.

woe [wou] *n.* kanashimi ; fukō. *~ is me*, ā kanashii kana. *~ be to*, ni wazawai are ! *~ worth the day !* kyō wa ikanaru akunichi **woke** [wouk] *v. see:* **wake.** ⌐zo !

wold [would] *n.* arechi ; gen'ya ; harappa.

wolf [wulf] *n.* (*pl.* **-ves** [wulvz]) ōkami. *a ~ in sheep's clothing,* gizensha. *cry ~,* uso o itte hito o odokasu. **~ish** *a.* ōkami no yōna.

woman [wúmən] *n.* (*pl.* **women** [wímin]) onna. **~hood** *n.* joseikatagi. **~ish** *a.* memeshii. **~kind** [-kaind] *n.* fujin. **~ly** *a.* onna rashii. **~like** *a.* onna rashii. *~ of the world,* seken o shitte iru fujin. **~-suffragist** [-sʌ́frədʒist] *n.* fujin sanseiken-**womb** [wu:m] *n.* shikyū. ⌐ronja.

won [wʌn] *v. see :* **win.**

wonder [wʌ́ndə] *n.* odoroki ; fushigi. *and no ~,* sore mo dōri de aru. *in ~,* odoroite. *it is no ~ that,* ...mo muri wa nai. *v.* odoroku ; ayashimu. *I ~,* ...ka shira? **~ful** *a.* odoroku beki. **~fully** *ad.* **~ment** *n.* odoroki. ⌐do.

wondrous [wʌ́ndrəs] (*poet.*) *a.* odoroku beki. *ad.* odoroku ho-**wont** [wount / wʌnt] *a.* shūkan de (aru). *n.* narawashi. *v.* narasu. **~ed** *a.* nareta ; tsune no.

woo [wu:] *v.* kyūai suru. **~er** *n.* kyūaisha.

wood [wud] *n.* ki ; zaimoku. mori ; shinrin. *v.* jumoku de ōu. **~bine** [wúdbàin] *n.* suikazura. **~chuck** *n.* risu. **~cock** *n.* yamashigi. **~craft** *n.* shinrin no chishiki. **~cut** *n.* mokuhan.

~**cutter** *n.* kikori. ~**ed** [wúdid] *a.* jumoku no shigette iru. ~**en** *a.* mokusei no. ~ **engraving** [ingréiviŋ] *n.* mokuhanjutsu. ~**land** *n.* shinrin. ~**man** *n.* kikori; somabito. ~**pecker** *n.* kitsutsuki. ~**sman** *n.* shinrintsū; shinrinseikatsusha. ~**work** *n.* mokuseihin. ~**y** *a.* mori no ōi.

woof [wu:f] *n.* yokoito; orimono. ⌈peten ni kakeru.

wool [wul] *n.* yōmō; keito. *pull the* ~ *over one's eyes,* hito o **wool(l)en** [wúlən] *a.* yōmō no; keori no. *n.* keorimono.

wool(l)y [wúli] *a.* yōmō no; yōmō no yōna.

word [wə:d] *n.* kotoba; go. *give one's* ~, yakusoku suru. *hard* ~*s,* akkō; hinan. *in a* ~, mijikaku ieba. *in other* ~*s,* kangen sureba. *in* ~, kuchisaki de. *man of his* ~, yakusoku no katai hito. *send* ~, dengon suru. *upon one's* ~, tashikani. ~ *for* ~, chikugoteki ni. ~**ing** *n.* kotoba-zukai. ~**age** [wə́:didʒ] *n.* ⌈*word* no atsumari. ~**y** *a.* kotoba no. ~**book,** tangoshū. ~**element,** (*gram.*) tango kōsei no yōso. ~ **order,** (*gram.*) bun o **wore** [wɔ:] *v. see:* **wear.** ⌊tsukuru toki no gojun.

work [wə:k] *v.* **worked** *or* (*arch.*) **wrought; working.** *n.* shigoto; seisaku. ~**s,** (*pl.*) (*sing.* no koto mo aru): kikai no bubun; tadashii kōi. *at* ~, shigoto o shite. *make short* ~ *of,* subayaku shigoto kara nukeru. *out of* ~, shoku ga nai. *v.* hataraku; yaku ni tatsu. ~ *off,* dandan herasu. ~ *on,* kikime ga aru. ~ *oneself into favo(u)r,* dandan hito ni toriiru. ~ *one's way,* honeotte susumu. ~ *out,* tsukaraseru; yaritogeru. ~ *up,* gekkō saseru; neriageru. ~**aday** [-ədei] *a.* shigotobi no. ~**day** *n.* shigotobi. ~**er** *n.* hatarakite. ~**house** *n.* (*Am.*) kankain; (*Brit.*) kyūhin'in. ~**ing** *a.* hataraku. ~**man** *n.* shokunin; rōdōsha. ~**manship** *n.* shigoto no tegiwa; dekibae.

world [wə:ld] *n.* sekai; yo no naka; seken. *as the* ~ *goes,* seken dewa. *begin the* ~, seken ni deru. *come into the* ~, kono yo ni umare deru. *for all the* ~, dō iu koto ga arō to. *for the* ~, danjite. *in the* ~, ittai zentai. *man of the* ~, yonareta hito. ~**ling** *n.* zokujin. ~**ly** *a.* seken no; zokukai no. ~**liness** *n.* zokuseken. ~**power** *n.* sekaiteki kyōkoku. ~**-wide** *a.* seken ni shirewatatta.

worm [wə:m] *n.* mushi (chijō o hau); kono yōna hito. *v.* hau yōni susumu; shiranu ma ni irikomaseru. ~**wood** *n.* (*bot.*)

nigayomogi; kurushimi. ~y a. mushi no iru; mushi no yōna.
worn [wɔːn] v. see : **wear**. ~-**out** [-aut] a. tsukarehateta ; yabu-
worrisome [wʌrisəm] a. mendōna ; wazurawashii. ⌐resōna.
worry [wʌri] v. kurushimaseru ; shimpai suru. n. shimpai.
worse [wɔːs] a., ad. **bad** (**worse**, **worst**) no hikakkyū : sarani
warui (ku) ; nao warui (ku). to make matters ~, sono ue komatta koto niwa. ad. ⌐chōna. ~(**p**)**er** n. sūhaisha.
worship [wɔ́ːʃip] n., v. sūhai (suru) ; reihai (suru). ~**ful** a. ki-
worst [wɔːst] a. mottomo warui. saiaku. at the ~, saiaku no
baai demo. be prepared for the ~, man'ichi no kakugo o suru.
get the ~ of it, makeru. put to the ~, makasu. ad. mottomo wa-
worsted [wústid] n. keito no isshu. ⌐ruku. v. makasu.
wort [wɔːt] n. mugimoyashi (malt) kara dekita eki (biiru no
moto).
worth [wɔːθ] n. neuchi. a. neuchi ga aru. be ~ while to, no kachi ga aru. ~**less** a. kachi no nai. ~-**while** a. yarigai no aru ;
jikan o tsubusu kachi ga aru. ⌐butsu.
worthy [wɔ́ːði] a. neuchi no aru ; fusawashii. n. rippana jin-
would [wud] aux. v. " will " no past. ...suru de arō ; ...suru tsumori ; ...suru narawashi datta. ~-**be** [-bi(ː)] a. hitoriyogari no.
wound [wuːnd] n. kizu. v. fushō saseru. ~**ed** [-id] a. kizu tsuita.
wound [waund] v. see : **wind**.
wove [wouv] v. see : **weave**.
woven [wóuvn] v. see : **weave**.
wrack [ræk] n. nansen ; hametsu ; hama ni uchiagerareta kaisō.
wraith [reiθ] n. shinu zengo ni atta hito no yūrei.
wrangle [ræŋgl] n., v. kenka kōron (suru). ~**r** [-ə] n. kenka, kōron suru hito.
wrap [ræp] n. hizakake, katakake, kubimaki, nado. v. maku ;
tsutsumu. ~**per** [-pə] n. tsutsumigami ; furoshiki. ~**pings**
[-piŋz] n. kamitsutsumi. ⌐y [-i] a. unto okotta.
wrath [rɔːθ] n. hageshii ikari. ~**ful** [-f(u)l] a. hageshiku okotta.
wreak [riːk] v. urami o harasu ; fukushū suru.
wreath [riːθ] n. hanawa ; hana no kammuri.
wreathe [riːð] v. wa ni suru ; maku ; nejiru. the smoke ~ed upward, kemuri ga wa ni natte agatta.
wreck [rek] n. (fune, kuruma nado no) nampa ; hametsu. v.

nampa (hakai) suru. **~age** [-idʒ] *n.* hahen. **~er** [-kə] *n.* hakai
wren [ren] *n.* misosazai. ⌞suru hito.
wrench [rentʃ] *v.* gui to nejiru. *n.* hageshii nejiriage ; nejima-
wrest [rest] *v.* gui to nejiru ; nejitoru. ⌞washi.
wrestle [résl] *v.* sumō o toru ; arasou. **~r** [-ə] *n.* sumōtori ;
wrestling [réslin] *n.* resuringu ; kakutō. ⌞surā.
wretch [retʃ] *n.* fukōna hito ; awarena hito. **~ed** [-id] *a.* awarena ; hisanna.
wriggle [rígl] *v.* notautsu ; uneraseru ; kunerasu.
wright [rait] *n.* shokkō ; kōjin. *wheel ~ ; ship ~,* no yōni.
wring [rin] *v.* **wrung ; wringing.** shiboru ; nayamasu. *n.* naji-
ru koto ; shiboru koto.
wrinkle [rínkl] *n.* shiwa. *v.* shiwa o yoseru ; shiwa ga yoru.
wrist [rist] *n.* tekubi. **~band** [-bænd] *n.* sode kuchi. **~let** [-lit]
n. udewa. **~watch** [-wɔtʃ] *n.* udedokei.
writ [rit] *n.* (*leg.*) reijō. kakimono. *Holy ~,* seisho (*Bible*) *v.*
write no mukashi no *p. & p.p.*
write [rait] *v.* **wrote, written ; writing.** kaku. **~ out** *v.* seisho
suru. **~r** [-ə] *n.* chosha ; kakite.
writhe [raið] *v.* (mi o) nejiru ; mimodae suru.
writing [ráitin] *n.* kaku koto ; tenarai. (*pl.*) chosaku. **type-~**
n. taipu shita tatō koto.
written [rítn] *v. see.* : **write** *a.* kaita. **~examination** [-igzæmi-
néiʃən] *n.* hikki shiken. **~ law** [-lɔ:] seibun-hō.
wrong [rɔn] *a.* fusei no. *it is ~ to tell lies,* uso o tsuku koto
wa ikenai ; machigatta. *the ~ answer,* machigatta kotae ; futekitōna. *the ~ clothes for the occation,* (baai ni) futekitōna fukusō
Is there something (anything) *~ with you?* kimi nani ka mazui
koto ga aru kai? *go ~,* umaku ikanai. *in the ~,* machigatte.
~ful [-f(u)l] *a.* fuseina. **~doer** [-dùə] *n.* warui koto o suru
hito. **~headed** [-hédid] *a.* atama ga chotto okashii.
wrote [rout] *v. see* : **write.**
wroth [rɔ:θ] *a.* ōini okotte (iru).
wrought [rɔ:t] *v. see* : **work** *a.* kitaeta. **~ iron** [-aiən] *n.* tantetsu.
wrung [rʌn] *v. see* : **wring.**
wry [rai] *a.* nejireta ; yuganda. *make a ~ face,* kao o shikameru.
wt. jūryō (*weight*).

X

X, x [eks] *n.* (*pl.* X's, Xs [éksiz]). Eigo *alphabet* no dai-24-bamme no moji. Gr. L. otōtte kita ga, kigen wa yappari Semitic. Konnichi Eigo dewa [ks], [gz], [kʃ], [gȝ], [z], [ʃ] no 6 tōri no on ni tsukawareru.

X.D., x.d. haitōochi (*exdividence*).

xebec [zíːbek] *n.* Chichūkai de kaizoku (*pirate*) nado ga shiyō suru sambon-masuto no hansen.

xenon [zénɔn] *n.* kisenon (*chemical element*).

xenophobia [zènɔfóubiɔ] *n.* gaikokujingirai.

Xmas. *Christmas.* ⌐ru.

X ray [éks réi] *n.* (*pl.*) X (ekkus)-sen. *v.* X-sen de chiryō su-

xylography [zailógrɔfi] *n.* mokuhanjutsu.

xylophone [záiləfoun] *n.* mokkin.

Y

Y, y [wai] *n.* (*pl.* Y's, Ys [waiz]) Eigo *alphabet* no dai-25-bamme no moji. Gr. dewa boin [y] de atta ga, Eigo dewa boin no mae de [j], shiin no ato de [i].

yacht [jɔt] *n.* yotto. *v.* yotto o hashiraseru.

yah [jɑ:] *ad.* (*Am. sl.*) yes.

yak [jæk] *n.* (*zoo.*) yaku; rigyū (Chibetto, Chūō Ajia no).

ɟam [jæm] *n.* (*bot.*) yama (no) imo. (*Am.*) kansho (*sweet potatoes*).

yank [jæŋk] *v.* (*Am. sl.*) gui to hipparu.

Yankee [jǽŋki] *n.* Beikokujin. ∼**ism** [-i:zm] *n.* Yankiikatagi.

yap [jæp] *v.* kamitsuku yōni hoeru (*snarl at*); gamigami iu.

yard [jɑ:d] *n.* kakotta niwa; yādo; (nagasa no tan'i; 91.4cm) hogeta. ∼**stick** [-stik] *n.* yādo-jaku.

yarn [jɑ:n] *n.* ito; keito; monogatari. spin a ∼, nagamonoga-tari o suru.

yarrow [jǽrou] *n.* (*bot.*) seiyō-nokogirisō.

yaw [jɔ:] *v.* (fune) shinro kara soreru.

yawl [jɔ:l] *n.* kobune; kansai-bōto.

yawn [jɔ:n] *n.* akubi. *v.* akubi suru. ∼**ing** *a.* akubi o shite iru.

ye [ji:] *pron.* nanjira.

yea [jei] *ad.* shikari; hai (*yes*). *n.* kōtei; sansei.

year [jiə] *n.* toshi; ichinenkan. ∼ *after* ∼ (or, ∼ *by* ∼), nen-nen. ∼ *in*, ∼ *out*, shijū; akete mo kurete mo. ∼**book** *n.* nen-kan. ∼**ling** *n.* (uma nado no) issai. *a.* issai no. ∼**long** *a.* ichi-nenkan no. ∼**ly** *a.* nennen no. *ad.* nennen.

yearn [jə:n] *v.* shitau; akogareru. ∼**ing** *n.* shibo; akogare. *a.* shibo no; akogare no. ∼**ly** *ad.* akogarete.

yeast [ji:st] *n.* iisuto; kōji; kōbo. ∼**y** [-i] iisuto no yōna.

yell [jel] *n.* sakebi; kansei. *v.* sakebu.

yellow [jélou] *a.* kiiroi; okubyōna; ninkitori no. *n.* kiiro; kimi. ∼ **fever** *n.* kōnetsubyō. the ∼ **press** *n.* kōshoku-shim-bun. ∼**back** *n.* sammon shōsetsu. ∼**ish** *a.* kiiroppoi.

yelp [jelp] *n.* (inu no) hoegoe. *v.* kyan-kyan naku.

yeoman [jóumən] *n.* jiyūmin; jisakunō. ∼**ry** *n.* jisakunōen.

yes [jes] *ad.* shikari; hai. *n.* sansei.

yesterday [jéstədi] *n.*, *ad.* kinō. *the day before* ~, ototoi.

yesternight [jestənáit] *n.*, *ad.* (*poet.*) sakuya.

yet [jet] *ad.* mada ; ima made. *and* ~, soredemo ; toni kaku. *as* ~, mada. *not* ~, mada...nai. *conj.* keredomo ; demo.

yew [ju:] *n.* (*bot.*) ichiinoki.

Yiddish [jídiʃ] *n.* Idiishu-go (O-Bei no Yudayajin ga tsukau).

yield [ji:ld] *v.* shōzuru ; sansuru ; makeru ; kōsan suru. *n.* seisandaka ; shūkaku. ~**ing** *a.* ukeireru ; yawarakai.

Y.M.C.A., YMCA Kirisutokyō Seinenkai (*Young Men's Christian Association*).

yoke [jouk] *n.* kubiki ; sokubaku. *v.* kubiki o tsukeru ; sokubaku suru.

yokel [jóukəl] *n.* inakamono ; yajin.

yolk [jouk] *n.* tamago no kimi.

yonder [jóndə], (*arch.*) **yon** [jɔn] *a.* achira no ; mukō no. *ad.* muko ni.

yore [jɔ:] *n.* mukashi. *of* ~, mukashi ; mukashi no.

you [ju:] *pron.* (*sing. & pl.*) anata ; anata-gata.

young [jʌŋ] *a.* wakai. *n.* kodomo. *with* ~, ninshin shite. ~**ling** *n.* wakamono. *a.* wakai. ~**ster** [-stə] *n.* shōnen.

your [juə] *pron.* anata no ; anata-gata no. ~**s** [-z] *pron.* anata no mono. ~**self** [-sélf] *pron.* anata jishin ; jibun de.

youth [ju:θ] *n.* wakasa ; shōnenjidai ; seinen. ~**ful** [-ful] *a.* wakakai.

yowl [jaul] *n.* tōboe ; unarigoe. *v.* tōboe suru ; unaru.

yucca [jʌkə] *n.* (*bot.*) itoran no rui.   (jin) no.

Yugoslavia [ju:gouslá:viə] *n.* Yūgōsurabia. *a.* Yūgōsurabia

yule [ju:l], **yuletide** [jú:taid] *n.* Kurisumasu (no kisetsu).

Y.W.C.A., YWCA Kiristokyō Joshiseinenkai (*Young Women's Christian Association*).

Z

Z, z *Brit.* [zed], *Am.* [zi:] *n.* (*pl.* Z's, Zs). Eigo *alphabet* no dai-26-bamme, saigo no moji. Gr. kara no go ni ōku mochiirarete iru.

zany [zéini] *n.* dōkemono.

zeal [zi:l] *n.* nesshin; netchū. ~**lot** [zélət] *n.* netchūsha. ~**otry** *n.* nekkyō. ~**lous** [zéləs] *a.* nesshinna. ~**ously** *ad.* neszebra [zí:brə] *n.* (*zoo.*) shimauma. [shinni.

zebra [zí:brə] *n.* (*zoo.*) shimauma.

zebu [zí:bu:] *n.* (*zoo.*) kobuushi; hōgyū.

zenana [zená:nə] *n.* (Indo no) fujin no ima.

Zend-Avesta [zéndəvéstə] *n.* Zoroasutākyō no seiten.

zenith [zí:niθ] *n.* tenchō; zetchō; chōjō.

zephyr [zéfə] *n.* (Z~) nishikaze. (*poet.*) soyokaze (*gentle wind*).

Zeppelin [zépəlin] *n.* Tsepperin hikōsen.

zero [zíərou] *n.* zero; kaimu; donzoko. *a.* nani mo nai. ~**hour** [-auə] *n.* yotei no kōdō kaishi no jikan.

zest [zəst] *n.* fūmi (*relish*). *v.* fūmi o soeru.

Zeus [zju:s] *n.* Zeusu no kami. [*Gr. myth.*]. [ta ni suru.

zigzag [zígzæg] *a.* giza-giza ni natta. *ad.* z-jigata ni. *v.* z-jiga-

zinc [ziŋk] *n.* (*met.*) aen; totan. *v.* totambari ni suru.

Zion [záiən] *n.* Shion-zan. (Yerusaremu no oka). ~**ism** [záiənizəm] *n.* Paresuch(t)ina fukki undō.

zip [zip] *n.* pyū-pyū. (tama no tobu oto).

zipper [zípə] *n.* Zippā; chakku.

zippy [zípi] *a.* kibikibi shita; kappatsuna.

zircon [zɔ́:kɔn] *n.* (*met.*) jirukon.

zither [zíθə] *n.* (hiza ni nosete hiku chūko jidai) no gengakki.

zodiac [zóudiæk] *n.* kōdōtai. ~**al** [zo(u)dáiəkl] *a.* jūtai no.

zone [zoun] *n.* chitai; (Kantai, Ontai, Nettai nado no) tai.

zoo [zu:] *n.* dōbutsuen (*zoological garden*).

zoogeography [zo(u)ədʒiógrəfi] *n.* dōbutsu chirigaku.

zoography [zo(u)ógrəfi] *n.* dōbutsu bumpugaku; dōbutsu seitaigaku.

zoological [zo(u)əlɔ́dʒikl] *a.* dōbutsugaku no. ~ **garden** (s)

[ˌz-gáːdn] *n.* dōbutsuen.

zoology[zo(u)ɔ́lədʒi] *n.* dōbutsugaku. **~ist** *n.* dōbutsugakusha.

zoom [zuːm] *n.* (hikōki no) kyūkakudo jōshō. *v.* kyū-jōshō suru; ninkitori o suru.

zoophagous [zouɔ́fəgəs] *a.* (*zoo.*) nikushoku no.

zoophilous [zouɔ́filəs] *a.* (*bot.*) (shokubutsu no tane ga) dōbutsu ni yotte dempasareru.

zoophyte[zó(u)ɔfait]*n.* (*zoo.*) shokuchūrui (sango; hitode nado).

zooplasty [zó(u)ɔplǽsti] *n.* (*med.*) dōbutsusoshiki; ishokujutsu.

Zoroastrian [zɔ́ro(u)ǽstriən] *n., a.* Zoroastākyō (no).

Zouave [zuːáːv] *n.* Zuābu-hei (*France* rikugun no hei no isshu).

Zulu [zúːluː] *n., a.* Zūrū-jin (-go); Minami Afurika *Natal* no ichi shuzoku.

zyme [zaim] *n.* kōso. (*enzyme*).

zymosis [zaimóusis] *n.* hakkō (sayō).

zymotic [zaimɔ́tik] *a.* hakkō no; densembyō no.

zymurgy [zaimɔ́ːdʒi] *n.* (*chem.*) jōzōgaku (hakkō (*fermentation*) no katei (*process*) o kenkyū suru gakumon).

Appendix

(For Japanese Readers)

The Usage of Shall and Will

Shall, Will no Imi

Shall wa " owe "—shakkin ga aru; kari ga aru; " ought to "—
...suru no ga tōzen da, to iu imi.

Will wa " will "—suru tsumori, " wish "—shi tai, to iu imi de
aru.

Kono imi de motte *shall*, *will* wa jodōshi to shite tsugi no
yōni tsukawarete iru.

Kōteibun no imi.

1. *I shall go*...watashi wa ikaneba naranai; Iki (masu) mashō.
2. *I will go*... watashi wa iki tai; iku tsumori.
3. *You shall go*... anata wa ikaneba naranai. (suki da, kirai da
wa iu koto ga dekinai.)
4. *You will go*... anata wa iku tsumori da. Hoka no hito no
kangae o katte ni iu no da kara, ate ni naranai, *reliabliity* ga nai.
5. *He shall go*... 3 no baai to onaji de kare (*he*) ga ikaneba
naranai koto o *you* ni iu node, baai ni yotte wa *you* ni *he* o ika-
sero to iu imi ni mo naru.
6. *He will go*... dai 4 no baai to onaji de *he* no kangae o iu
no de ate ni naranai. Jijitsu e no *reliability* ga nai.

Shimple Future. Kayō ni 1, 4, 6 wa yowai, sekinin no nai
iikata de aru, aite no sashizu o motomeru katachi de aru. Kono wa
wa, aite no sashizu o motomeru katachi de aru kara Eigo dewa, kore wa **Tanjun Mirai** (*Simple
Future*) to itte iru.

Gimombun no Imi

7. *Shall I go?*... watashi wa ikaneba naranai ka? to iu tazune-
kata wa, aite no sashizu o motomeru katachi de aru.
8. *Will I go?*... watashi wa iki tai desu ka? Kore wa muimi
de aru. Jibun no hoshii koto o hito ni kiku no de aru kara.
Tadashi, " *Will you go?* " to kikareta no ni " *Will I go?* to
ossharu no ka? mochiron *I will go* desu yo," to iu imi dewa
naritatsu.
9. *Shall you go?*... anata wa ikaneba naranai ka, to iu imi de
teinei ni naru. Iki masu ka? no imi ni tsukau.

10. *Will you go?* anata wa iku ki ga aru ka? to kiku no da kara futsū "iki mashō" to sasou imi ni naru. Nippongo no "ikanai?" ni ataru. Hito o sasou iikata de aru.

11. *Shall he go?* Kare o ikase mashō (yarimashō) ka? to iu imi de, *you* ni taishi sashizu (*command*) o motomeru imi de aru. Shitagatte "*Yes, he shall* (Ikasete kudasai.)" to iu henji ni naru de arō.

12. *Will he go? he* ga iku ki ga aru ka dō ka wa *he* dake shika shiranai no ni, sore o *you* ni tazuneru no wa kentō chigai de aru.

Tanshiku-kei

Shall, Will no tanshikukei (*contraction*): *Shall* mo *Will* mo, I, *you, he, they* nado to issho ni natta toki hanashi-kotoba dewa gokei ga tanshiku sareru:

I shall (will)=I'll. *You will (shall)*=you'll. *He shall (will)*=he'll. etc.

Negative Contraction (uchikeshi no tanshikukei): *shall not*=shan't; will not=won't. I shan't go=I shall not go. I won't go=I will not go.

Ijō ga kore made Nippon no gakkō de oshierarete iru "**Shall Will no Tsukaikata**" de aru ga, *Thorndike-Barnhart: Comprehensive Desk Dictionary*, niwa tsugi no yōna koto ga kaite aru. Tsugi wa hobo sono yōten de aru:

Eigo no *shall, will* no yōhō wa aru bumpōgakusha-tachi de, sono tsukaikata o ittei shiyō to honeotte iru hito mo aru ga ikkō ittei shita koto ga nai. Keishiki-baranai, hanashi-kotoba-shiki yōhō wa:

Tanjun Mirai (*Simple Future*)

Hanashi ya keishikibaranai kakimono niwa *U. S. A.* ya, Eigo o hanasu Sekai no kakuchi ni oite wa *will* o subete no **person** (*I, you, he* etc.) ni tsukau. Kono *will* no tsukaikata wa insatsubutsu ni mo kōsei o yakamashiku shinai kagiri dondon tsukawareru.

Kyōchō Mirai (*Emphatic Future*)

Mirai ni taisuru tsuyoi ketsui no hyōgen, aruiwa, aru tokuni tsuyoi hyōgen dewa, keishikibaranai tsukaikata wa, kotoba ga de no baai wa *shall* demo *will* demo dochira demo ii. Tada tsuyoku *I shall' go* aruiwa *I will' go* no yōni iu. Shikashi, *shall* ga tsuka-

wareru keikō ga ippan no yōni omowareru ga sukizuki da to
ieyō.

Gimombun no tanshiku-kei wa *won't* ga yoku tsukawareru.
Should to Would. (*shall, will* no kakokei) *Should* to *would* to
wa bunrei o agete sono tsukaikata no setumei ni todomaru.
(Kore wa Thorndike niwa yoranai)

1. *If I were a millionaire I should build a hospital* (Moshi watashi
ga hyakuman-chōja dattara byōin o taterun da ga nā.)
Kore wa genzai no jijitsu de nai koto o katei shite iu baai.

2. *I should work hard in school time.* Watashi wa gakkōjidai
shikkari benkyō subeiki na no da yo. (=**ought to** no yowai
katachi)

3. *I would work hard in spite of the heat.* Atsusa ga nan da,
shikkari hatarakō to kesshin shita no da.

4. Tsugi no *should* wa ninshō ni kankei naku onaji yōni
mochiiru.
If I should be late... (yoshi okurete mo...)
 ,, you should ,, ,, (,,   ,,   ,,)
 ,, he should ,, ,, (,,   ,,   ,,)
...it does not matter. (nāni okuretatte kamaya shinai yo.)

5. *I know that I shall die.* (Watashi wa w. ga shinu (darō)tte
koto o shitte i masu) I knew that I **should** die. (know ga *knew*
ni natta node *shall* ga *should* ni natta dake.—W. wa... shinutte (ningen shinutte) koto o shitte ita.

6. *I know that you will die.* Anata wa shinurutte koto o
shitte iru yo. *I knew that you would die.* Anata wa shinurutte
koto o shitte ita.

7. *The old man would often recount his adventure.* Rōjin wa tabitabi sono bōkendan o (yoku) hanasu no ga okimari datta.
(would repeat—shūkanteki kōi, okonai.)

8. *A simple child—What should it know of death?*—(*Wordsworth*)
Akambo—dō shite **shi** nante koto ga wakarō ka? (Omoi
mo yoranu koto da—shiru hazu ga nai—hango.)

9. *He put the gold under his pillow* **lest** *someone* **should** *steal.*
Kare wa sono kane o makura no shita ni ireta, dare ka ga
nusunja naranai to omotte. (...*lest*...*should* no katachi.)

10. *Would you like me to go with you?* (*if I should be willing*)—
Watashi ga yorokonde iku (yaru) to shitara; watashi ga anata

to issho ni iku no ga osuki deshō ka shira? a) Kore wa goku-teineina iikata. b) Hontō wa *Should you...*? to naru no ga bumpōjō wa tadashii ga koko nimo *shall* no kawari ni *will* ga tsukawarete iru.

11. *Should I give you a little more? Would you give me a little more?* Mae no (10) no baai kara suiryō dekiru teineina ii kata no katachi.

12. *Those who saw the Winter Exhibition of the Royal Academy would notice a portrait of Dr. Adam.* Kono *would* wa "ōkata ki ga tsuitarō" gurai no imi.

Should, would ni deattara daitai konna mono ni atehamete imi o wakaru yōni shite hoshii mono de aru.